SUBARU

SUBARU CARS
1985-92 REPAIR MANUAL

CHILTON'S

Senior Vice President	Ronald A. Hoxter
Publisher	Kerry A. Freeman, S.A.E.
Editor-In-Chief	Dean F. Morgantini, S.A.E.
Director of Manufacturing	Mike D'Imperio
Production Manager	W. Calvin Settle, Jr., S.A.E.
Senior Editor	Richard J. Rivele, S.A.E.
Project Manager	Martin J. Gunther
Editor	James R. Marotta / Peter M. Conti

CHILTON BOOK COMPANY

*ONE OF THE DIVERSIFIED PUBLISHING COMPANIES,
A PART OF CAPITAL CITIES/ABC, INC.*

Manufactured in USA
© 1992 Chilton Book Company
Chilton Way, Radnor, PA 19089
ISBN 0–8019–8259–6
Library of Congress Catalog Card No. 91–058868
1234567890 1098765432

Contents

Contents

SAFETY NOTICE

Proper service and repair procedures are vital to the safe, reliable operation of all motor vehicles, as well as the personal safety of those performing repairs. This manual outlines procedures for servicing and repairing vehicles using safe, effective methods. The procedures contain many NOTES, CAUTIONS and WARNINGS which should be followed along with standard safety procedures to eliminate the possibility of personal injury or improper service which could damage the vehicle or compromise its safety.

It is important to note that the repair procedures and techniques, tools and parts for servicing motor vehicles, as well as the skill and experience of the individual performing the work vary widely. It is not possible to anticipate all of the conceivable ways or conditions under which vehicles may be serviced, or to provide cautions as to all of the possible hazards that may result. Standard and accepted safety precautions and equipment should be used when handling toxic or flammable fluids, and safety goggles or other protection should be used during cutting, grinding, chiseling, prying, or any other process that can cause material removal or projectiles.

Some procedures require the use of tools specially designed for a specific purpose. Before substituting another tool or procedure, you must be completely satisfied that neither your personal safety, nor the performance of the vehicle will be endangered.

Although information in this manual is based on industry sources and is complete as possible at the time of publication, the possibility exists that some car manufacturers made later changes which could not be included here. While striving for total accuracy, Chilton Book Company cannot assume responsibility for any errors, changes or omissions that may occur in the compilation of this data.

PART NUMBERS

Part numbers listed in this reference are not recommendations by Chilton for any product by brand name. They are references that can be used with interchange manuals and aftermarket supplier catalogs to locate each brand supplier's discrete part number.

SPECIAL TOOLS

Special tools are recommended by the vehicle manufacturer to perform their specific job. Use has been kept to a minimum, but where absolutely necessary, they are referred to in the text by the part number of the tool manufacturer. These tools can be purchased, under the appropriate part number, from your Subaru dealer or regional distributor, or an equivalent tool can be purchased locally from a tool supplier or parts outlet. Before substituting any tool for the one recommended, read the SAFETY NOTICE at the top of this page.

ACKNOWLEDGMENTS

The Chilton Book Company expresses appreciation to Subaru of America, Inc., Cherry Hill, NJ for their generous assistance.

1

GENERAL INFORMATION AND MAINTENANCE

HOW TO USE THIS BOOK

Chilton's Total Care Care for the Subaru is intended to help you learn more about the inner working of your vehicle and save you money in it's upkeep and operation.

The first two Sections will be the most used, since they contain maintenance and tune-up information and procedures. Studies have shown that by properly tuning and maintaining your vehicle, you can get at least 10% better gas mileage than with an out-of-tune vehicle. The other Sections deal with the more complex systems of your vehicle. Operating systems from engine through brakes are covered to the extent that the average do-it-yourselfer becomes mechanically involved. As you progress from simple to more complex tasks, you will save money, gain personal satisfaction and help you avoid expensive problems.

A secondary purpose of this book is a reference for owners who want to understand their vehicle and/or their mechanics better. In this case, no tools at all are required.

When you are ready to start a task, and before you any bolts, read through the entire procedure in the book. This will give you the overall view of what tools and supplies will be required. There is nothing more frustrating than having to walk to the bus stop on Monday morning because you were short one bolt on Sunday afternoon. So read ahead and plan ahead. Each operation should be approached logically and all procedures thoroughly understood before attempting any work.

All Sections contain diagnostics, adjustments, maintenance, removal, installation, repair and/or overhaul procedures. When repair is not considered practical, we tell you how to remove the part and then how to install the new or rebuilt replacement. In this way, you at least save the labor costs. Backyard repair of such components as alternators and starters is just not practical.

At this time a few basic mechanic's rules should be mentioned: First, whenever the left-side of the vehicle or engine is referred to, it is meant to specify the driver's side of the vehicle. Conversely, the right-side of the vehicle means the passenger's side.

Next, most screws and bolts are removed by turning them counterclockwise and/or tightened by turning them clockwise. If a screw or bolt becomes frozen, do not try to force it to turn. The

best technique is to use one of the brands of penetrating oil to help the bolt turn. It will also help if you lightly tap the end of the bolt with a hammer to loosen it.

Lastly, safety is always the most important rule. Constantly be aware of the dangers involved in working on a vehicle and take the proper precautions. (See the section in this Section, Servicing Your Vehicle Safely, and the SAFETY NOTICE on the acknowledgment page).

When working on your vehicle pay attention to the instructions provided. By working in an organized manner you will avoid the 3 common mistakes in mechanical work:

1. Incorrect order of assembly, disassembly or adjustment. When taking something apart or putting it together, doing things in the wrong order usually costs extra time, however, it CAN break something. Read the entire procedure before beginning the disassembly. Do everything in the order in which the instructions say you should do it, even if you can't immediately see a reason for it. When you're taking something apart that is very intricate (for example, a carburetor), you might want to draw a picture of how it looks when assembled at one point, in order to make sure you get everything back in its proper position. (We will supply exploded views whenever possible). When making adjustments, especially tune-up adjustments, do them in order. Often, one adjustment affects another and you cannot expect satisfactory results unless each adjustment is made only when it cannot be changed by any other.

2. Overtorquing (or undertorquing). While it is more common for overtorquing to cause damage, undertorquing can cause a fastener to vibrate loose causing serious damage. Especially, when dealing with aluminum parts, pay attention to torque specifications and utilize a torque wrench in assembly. If a torque figure is not available, remember that if you are using the right tool to do the job, you will probably not have to strain yourself to get a fastener tight enough. The pitch of most threads is so slight that the tension you put on the wrench will be multiplied many, many times in actual force on what you are tightening. A good example of how critical torque is can be seen in the case of spark plug installation, especially where you are putting the plug into an aluminum cylinder head. Too little torque can fail to crush the gasket,

causing leakage of combustion gases and consequent overheating of the plug and engine parts. Too much torque can damage the threads or distort the plug, which changes the spark gap.

➡ **There are many commercial products available for ensuring that fasteners won't come loose, even if they are not torqued just right (a very common brand is Loctite®). If you're worried about getting something together tight enough to hold but loose enough to avoid mechanical damage during assembly, one of these products might offer substantial insurance. Read the label on the package and make sure the product is compatible with the materials, fluids and etc. involved before choosing one.**

3. Crossthreading occurs when a part such as a bolt is screwed into a nut or casting at the wrong angle and forced. Crossthreading is more likely to occur if access is difficult. It helps to clean and lubricate the fasteners, then start threading with the part to be installed going straight in. Start the bolt, spark plug or etc. with your fingers. If you encounter resistance, unscrew the part and start over again at a different angle until it can be inserted and turned several turns without much effort. Keep in mind that many parts, especially spark plugs, use tapered threads so that gentle turning will automatically bring the part you're threading to the proper angle if you don't force it or resist a change in angle. Don't put a wrench on the part until it's been turned a couple of turns by hand. If you suddenly encounter resistance, and the part has not been seated fully, don't force it. Pull it back out and make sure it's clean and threading properly.

➡ **Always take your time and be patient, once you have some experience working on your vehicle, it will become an enjoyable hobby.**

TOOLS AND EQUIPMENT

Naturally, without the proper tools and equipment, it is impossible to properly service your vehicle. It would be impossible to catalog each tool that you would need to perform each or any operation in this book. It would also be unwise for the amateur to rush out and buy an expensive set of tools on the theory that he may need one or more of them at sometime.

The best approach is to proceed slowly, gathering a quality set of tools that will be used most frequently. Don't be misled by the low cost of bargain tools. It is far better to spend a little more for better quality. Forged wrenches, 6- or 12-point sockets and fine tooth ratchets are by far preferable to their less expensive counterparts. As any good mechanic can tell you, there are few worse experiences than trying to work on a vehicle with bad tools. Your monetary savings will be far outweighed by frustration and mangled knuckles.

Begin accumulating tools that are used most frequently; those associated with routine maintenance and tune-up.

In addition to the normal assortment of screwdrivers and pliers you should have the following tools for routine maintenance jobs:

1. SAE (or Metric) or SAE/Metric wrenches—sockets and combination open end/box end wrenches in sizes from 1/8–3/4 in. (6–19mm) and a spark plug socket (13/16 in. or 5/8 in. depending on plug type).

➡ If possible, buy various length socket drive extensions. One convenience is that the metric sockets available in the U.S. will all fit the ratchet handles and extensions you may already have (1/4 in., 3/8 in. and 1/2 in. drive).

2. Jackstands, for support
3. Oil filter wrench
4. Oil drain pan and funnel
5. Grease gun, for chassis lubrication
6. Hydrometer, for checking the battery
7. Many rags for wiping up the inevitable mess.

In addition to the above items there are several others that are not absolutely necessary but handy to have around. These include oil dry, a transmission funnel and an usual supply of lubricants, antifreeze and fluids, although these can be purchased as needed. This is a basic list for routine maintenance but only your personal needs and desires can accurately determine your list of tools. If you are serious about maintaining your own vehicle, then a floor jack is as necessary as a spark plug socket. The greatly

increased utility, strength and safety of a hydraulic floor jack makes it pay for itself many times over throughout the years.

The second list of tools is for tune-ups. While the tools involved here are slightly more sophisticated, they need not be outrageously expensive. There are several inexpensive tach/dwell meters on the market that are every bit as good for the average mechanic as an expensive professional model. Just be sure that the

tachometer reads to at least 1,200–1,500 rpm on the scale and that it works on 4- or 6-cylinder engines. A basic list of tune-up equipment could include:

1. Tach/dwell meter.
2. Spark plug wrench.
3. Timing light.
4. Spark plug gauge/adjusting tools.

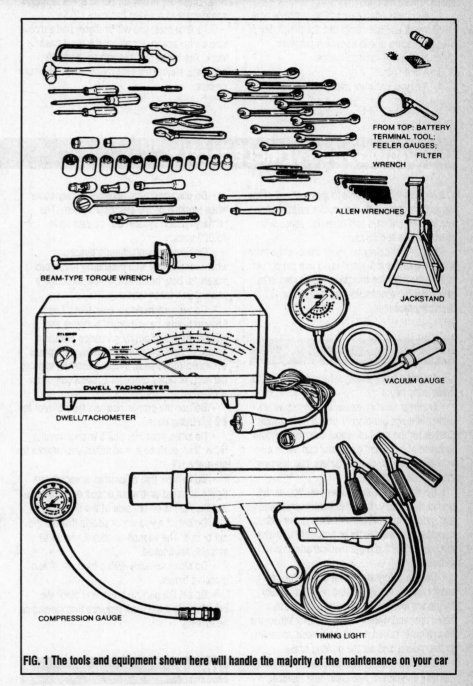

FROM TOP: BATTERY TERMINAL TOOL; FEELER GAUGES; FILTER WRENCH

ALLEN WRENCHES

BEAM-TYPE TORQUE WRENCH

JACKSTAND

DWELL/TACHOMETER

VACUUM GAUGE

COMPRESSION GAUGE

TIMING LIGHT

FIG. 1 The tools and equipment shown here will handle the majority of the maintenance on your car

In addition to these basic tools, there are several other tools and gauges you may find useful. These include:

1. A compression gauge. The screw-in type is slower to use but eliminates the possibility of a faulty reading due to escaping pressure.
2. A manifold vacuum gauge.
3. A test light.
4. A digital volt/ohm meter.

5. An induction meter. This is used for determining whether or not there is current in a wire. These are handy for use if a wire is broken somewhere in a wiring harness.

As a final note, you will probably find a torque wrench necessary for all but the most basic work. The beam type models are perfectly adequate, although the newer click type are more precise.

➡ **Special tools are occasionally necessary to perform a specific job or are recommended to make a job easier. Their use has been kept to a minimum. When a special tool is indicated, it will be referred to by manufacturer's part number. Special tools are available from your Subaru dealer.**

SERVICING YOUR VEHICLE SAFELY

It is virtually impossible to anticipate all of the hazards involved with automotive maintenance and service but care and common sense will prevent most accidents.

The rules of safety for mechanics range from don't smoke around gasoline, to use the proper tool for the job. The trick to avoid injuries is to develop safe work habits and take every possible precaution.

Do's

• Do keep a fire extinguisher and first aid kit within easy reach.
• Do wear safety glasses or goggles when cutting, drilling, grinding or prying. If you wear glasses for the sake of vision, then they should be made of hardened glass that can serve also as safety glasses, or wear safety goggles over your regular glasses.
• Do shield your eyes whenever you work around the battery. Batteries contain sulphuric acid. In case of contact with the eyes or skin, flush the area with water or a mixture of water and baking soda and get medical attention immediately.
• Do use safety stands for any under-car service. Jacks are for raising vehicles. Safety stands are for making sure the vehicle stays raised until you want it to come down. Whenever the vehicle is raised, block the wheels remaining on the ground and set the parking brake.
• Do use adequate ventilation when working with any chemicals. Asbestos dust resulting from brake lining wear can cause cancer.

• Do disconnect the negative battery cable when working on the electrical system. The primary ignition system can contain up to 40,000 volts.
• Do follow manufacturer's directions whenever working with potentially hazardous materials. Both brake fluid and antifreeze are poisonous if taken internally.
• Do properly maintain your tools. Loose hammerheads, mushroomed punches and chisels, frayed or poorly grounded electrical cords, excessively worn screwdrivers, spread wrenches (open end), cracked sockets, slipping ratchets, or faulty droplight sockets can cause accidents.
• Do use the proper size and type of tool for the job being done.
• Do when possible, pull a wrench handle rather than push on it, and adjust your stance to prevent a fall.
• Do be sure that adjustable wrenches are tightly adjusted on the nut or bolt and pulled so that the face is on the side of the fixed jaw.
• Do select a wrench or socket that fits the nut or bolt. The wrench or socket should sit straight, not cocked.
• Do strike squarely with a hammer. Avoid glancing blows.
• Do set the parking brake and block the drive wheels if the work requires that the engine be running.

Don'ts

• Don't run an engine in a garage or anywhere else without proper ventilation — EVER! Carbon monoxide is poisonous. It is absorbed by the body 400 times faster than

oxygen. It takes a long time to leave the human body and can you build up a deadly supply of it in your own system by simply breathing in a little every day. You may not realize you are slowly poisoning yourself. Always use power vents, windows, fans or open the garage doors.
• Don't work around moving parts while wearing a necktie or other loose clothing. Short sleeves are much safer than long, loose sleeves. Hard-toed shoes with neoprene soles protect your toes and give a better grip on slippery surfaces. Jewelry such as watches, fancy belt buckles, beads or body adornment of any kind is not safe when working around a car. Long hair should be hidden under a hat or tied back.
• Don't use pockets for toolboxes. A fall or bump can drive a screwdriver deep into your body. Even a wiping cloth hanging from the back pocket can wrap around a spinning shaft or fan.
• Don't smoke when working around the battery. When the battery is being charged, it gives off explosive hydrogen gas.
• Don't use gasoline to wash your hands. There are excellent soaps available. Gasoline may contain lead. Lead can enter the body through a cut, accumulating in the body and causing serious illness. Gasoline also removes all the natural oils from the skin so that bone dry hands will suck up oil and grease.
• Don't service the air conditioning system unless you are equipped with the necessary tools and training. The refrigerant, R-12, is extremely cold and when exposed to the air, will instantly freeze any surface it comes in contact with, including your eyes. Although the refrigerant is normally non-toxic, R-12 becomes a deadly poisonous gas in the presence of an open flame. One good whiff of the vapors from burning refrigerant can be fatal.

HISTORY

Subaru vehicles are built by Fuji Heavy Industries of Japan. The first Subaru automobile, a minicar, was introduced in 1958. The little car was highly successful in Japan because of its low price and operating cost.

In 1968 the Subaru 360 was introduced into the United States, but the car proved to be too small and was replaced by the larger FF-1 series.

The FF-1, or Star as it was known, was a 1.1 liter engine car. Models included a two door and four door sedan, and a station wagon. All models, as they do today, featured a horizontally opposed (flat) water cooled engine, and independent suspension at all four wheels.

Engine size has increased over the years, from 1100 cc to 3300 cc. A four wheel drive unit, a five speed manual transmission, and an automatic transmission were all introduced in 1975. The four wheel drive, which engages the rear wheels when required, first appeared in station wagon models.

From the one model of the late sixties, to the restyled models of the 90's Subaru (which is the Japanese name for the six star constellation we call Pleiades) has increased its sales in the U.S. market until it is now ranked in the upper Top Ten of all imported cars.

SERIAL NUMBER IDENTIFICATION

Vehicle

▶ SEE FIG. 2

The vehicle identification number (VIN) is stamped on a tab at the top left-side of the dashboard; visible through the windshield. There is also a vehicle identification plate in the engine compartment on the bulkhead.

The serial number consists of a series of model identification numbers followed by a six digit production number.

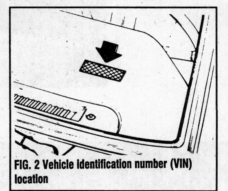

FIG. 2 Vehicle Identification number (VIN) location

Engine

▶ SEE FIG. 4

The engine number is stamped on a plate attached to the front, right-hand side of the crankcase, near the distributor. The serial number consists of an engine code number which is followed by a six digit production number.

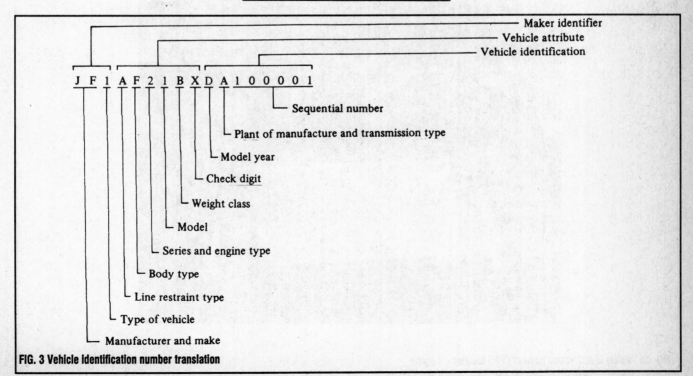

```
                                          Maker identifier
                                          Vehicle attribute
                                          Vehicle identification

J F 1   A F 2 1 B X D A 1 0 0 0 0 1
                          Sequential number
                      Plant of manufacture and transmission type
                    Model year
                  Check digit
                Weight class
              Model
            Series and engine type
          Body type
        Line restraint type
      Type of vehicle
    Manufacturer and make
```

FIG. 3 Vehicle Identification number translation

MFD BY FUJI HEAVY IND. LTD., JAPAN
MFD IN

GVWR: 4110LB(1864KG)
GAWR:FRONT-2095LB 950KG)
REAR -2015LB 914KG)
THIS VEHICLE CONFORMS TO ALL APPLICABLE
FEDERAL MOTOR VEHICLE SAFETY, BUMPER, AND
THEFT PREVENTION STANDARDS IN EFFECT ON
THE DATE OF MANUFACTURE SHOWN ABOVE.

VIN

PASSENGER CAR

FUJI HEAVY INDUSTRIES LTD.

富士重工業株式会社

FIG. 1a Vehicle identification number (VIN) location — Legacy

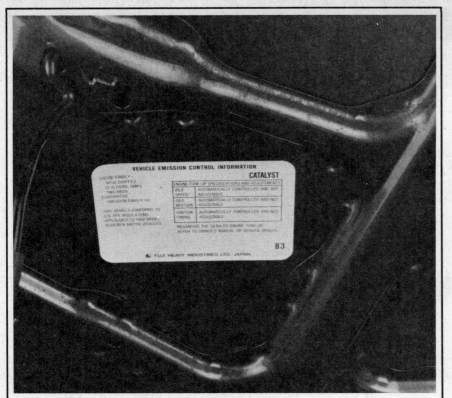

FIG. 2a Vehicle emission control information location—Legacy

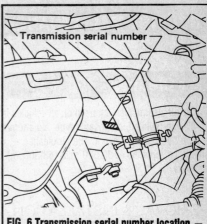

FIG. 6 Transmission serial number location — automatic transmission

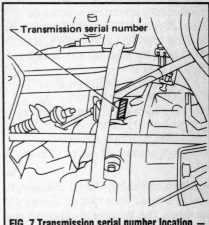

FIG. 7 Transmission serial number location — 4WD manual transmission

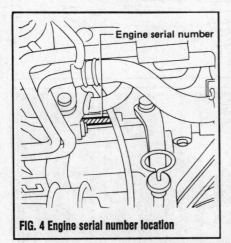

FIG. 4 Engine serial number location

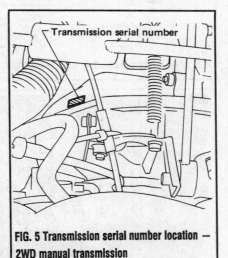

FIG. 5 Transmission serial number location — 2WD manual transmission

PART NUMBER	722011010
GEAR RATIO	3.700
● FUJI HEAVY INDUSTRIES LTD.	J1

FIG. 8 Drive axle identification tag

Transmission and Transaxle

▶ SEE FIGS. 5–7

The transmission number label is attached to the upper surface of the main case on manual transmissions/transaxles and to the converter housing on automatic transmissions.

Drive Axle

▶ SEE FIG. 8

The drive axle identification number is stamped on a tag, located on the rear of the differential. The information includes a part number and gear ratio information.

ROUTINE MAINTENANCE

Air Cleaner

The air cleaner element used on all vehicles is an oil-impregnated, disposable type. No attempt should be made to clean it. The air cleaner should be replaced at 30,000 mile (48,300km) intervals.

REMOVAL & INSTALLATION

◆ SEE FIGS. 9–11

1. Remove the wing nut on the top of the air cleaner housing (carbureted) or loosen the clamps (SPFI and MPFI) and lift off the top of the air cleaner base. Set it aside carefully, as on some models the emission control system hoses are fastened to it.
2. Lift out the old element and discard it.
3. Clean the air filter base with a rag.
4. Place the new element in the base and install the top of the base.
5. Tighten the wing nuts securely (carbureted) or secure the clamps (SPFI and MPFI).

➡ **When checking the air cleaner, it is also a good idea to look at he PCV air filter. The filter is located on the rim of the air filter base. If it is dirty, replace it.**

Fuel Filter

The fuel filter should be replaced and all fuel system hoses and connection should be inspected at 30,000 mile (48,300km) intervals. When the vehicle is operated in extremely cold or hot conditions, contamination of the filter may occur and the filter should be replaced more often.

REMOVAL & INSTALLATION

Carbureted Engines

◆ SEE FIGS. 12–13

1. Locate the fuel filter on a bracket under the center of the vehicle.
2. Disconnect the negative battery terminal from the battery. Raise and support the vehicle on jackstands.

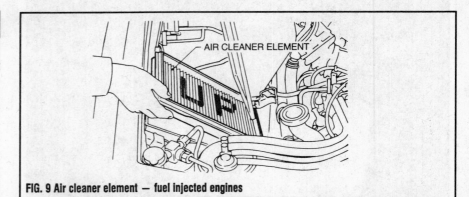

FIG. 9 Air cleaner element — fuel injected engines

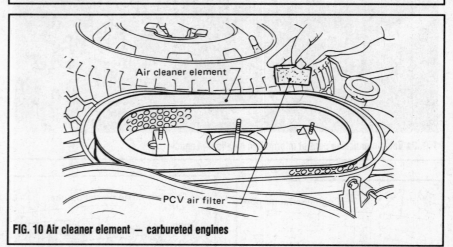

FIG. 10 Air cleaner element — carbureted engines

FIG. 11a Replacing the air cleaner element — Legacy AND SVX

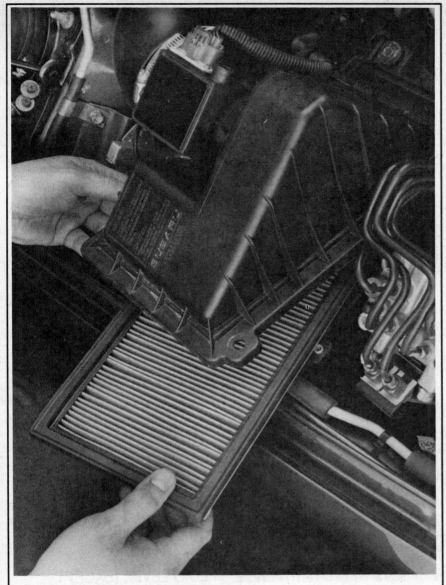

FIG. 11 Air cleaner element — Legacy AND SVX

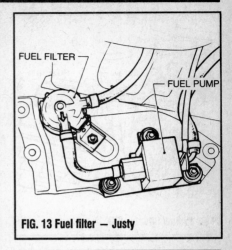

FIG. 13 Fuel filter — Justy

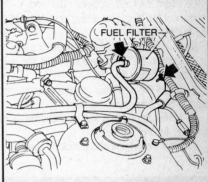

FIG. 14 Fuel filter — fuel injected engine

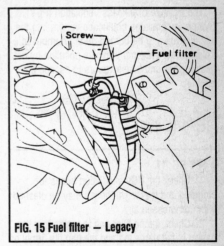

FIG. 15 Fuel filter — Legacy

3. Place a catch pan under fuel filter, to catch the excess fuel.

4. Disconnect the fuel pump electrical connector. Disconnect the hose clamps and the fuel hoses from the fuel filter.

5. As required, remove the bolts from the fuel pump bracket, pull the fuel filter from the bracket and remove it from the vehicle.

6. Install the new filter into the bracket and tighten the bolts as required.

7. Install the hoses on the filter and tighten the clamps.

8. Lower the vehicle and connect the negative battery cable.

9. Start the engine and check for leaks.

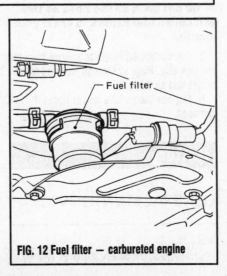

FIG. 12 Fuel filter — carbureted engine

Fuel Injected Models

◆ SEE FIGS. 14–16

1. Locate the fuel filter in the engine compartment on the left fender.

2. Reduce the fuel pressure as follows:

a. Disconnect the electrical wiring connector from the fuel pump.

b. Crank the engine for more than five seconds. If the engine starts, let the engine run until it stops.

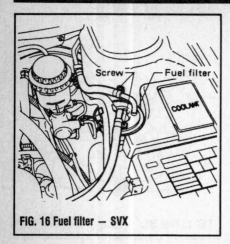

FIG. 16 Fuel filter — SVX

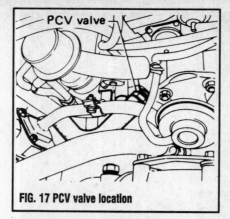

FIG. 17 PCV valve location

c. Turn the ignition switch OFF and reconnect the electrical wiring connector of the fuel pump.

3. Disconnect the negative battery cable.

4. Loosen the hose clamp screws and pull the filter from the bracket.

5. Install the new filter into the bracket and tighten the hose clamp screws.

6. Lower the vehicle and connect the negative battery cable.

7. Start the engine and check for leaks.

PCV Valve

The Positive Crankcase Ventilation (PCV) System recirculates crankcase vapors into the intake stream to be burned during combustion. This system prevents prevents pollution by not allowing the crankcase vapors to escape the engine.

SERVICING

♦ SEE FIG. 17

1. Check the PCV ventilation hoses for clogging and leaks. The hoses may be cleaned with compressed air.

2. Check the oil filler cap to insure that the gasket is not damaged and the cap fits firmly on the filler cap end.

3. Disconnect the hose from the PCV valve.

4. Start the engine and place your finger over the top of the pcv valve. Lightly increase the throttle.

5. The valve and system are operating properly when a vacuum is felt. If no vacuum is felt, replace the PCV valve and check the hoses for obstructions.

6. The PCV valve can be checked while off the vehicle by shaking. If a distinct rattling is noticed, the PCV valve is functioning properly.

Evaporative Emission Canister

The evaporative emission canister is part of a system that prevents fuel vapors contained in the fuel tank and carburetor bowl from being discharged into the air. The gas fumes are absorbed by activated charcoal located in the canister.

SERVICING

♦ SEE FIG. 18

1. Inspect the canister for holes or damage caused by debris.

2. Inspect the hoses to the canister for holes, cracks or other damage.

3. Disconnect the vacuum hose from the canister. Blow air through the hose to ensure that air does not leak.

4. Disconnect the purge hose from the canister. Blow air through the hose to ensure that air does not leak.

➡ **Do not suck on the hose as this will cause fuel vapors to enter your mouth.**

5. Disconnect the evaporation hose from the fuel tank side. Blow air through the hose to ensure that air flows.

6. Replace the canister and/or hoses if damaged.

Battery

GENERAL MAINTENANCE

♦ SEE FIG. 20

Once a year, the battery terminals and the

cable clamps should be cleaned. Remove the side terminal bolts and the cables, negative cable first. Clean the cable clamps and the battery terminals with a wire brush until all corrosion, grease, etc. is removed and the metal is shiny. It is especially important to clean the inside of the clamp thoroughly, since a small deposit of foreign material or oxidation there will prevent a sound electrical connection and inhibit either starting or charging. Special tools are available for cleaning the side terminal clamps and terminals.

Before installing the cables, loosen the battery holddown clamp, remove the battery and check the battery tray. Clear it of any debris and check it for soundness. Rust should be wire brushed away and the metal given a coat of anti-rust paint. Replace the battery and tighten the holddown clamp securely but be careful not to overtighten, this will crack the battery case.

➡ **Batteries can be cleaned using a solution of baking soda and water. Surface coatings on battery cases can actually conduct electricity which will cause a slight voltage drain, so make sure the battery case is clean.**

After the clamps and terminals are clean, reinstall the cables, negative cable last. Give the clamps and terminals a thin external coat of nonmetallic grease after installation, to retard corrosion.

Check the cables at the same time that the terminals are cleaned. If the cable insulation is cracked, broken or the ends are frayed, the cable should be replaced with a new one of the same length and gauge.

FLUID LEVEL (EXCEPT MAINTENANCE FREE BATTERIES)

Check the battery electrolyte level at least once a month, or more often in hot weather or during periods of extended car operation. The level can be checked through the case on translucent polypropylene batteries. The cell caps must be removed on other models. The electrolyte level in each cell should be kept filled to the split ring inside, or the line marked on the outside of the case.

If the level is low, add only distilled water, or colorless, odorless drinking water, through the opening until the level is correct. Each cell is completely separate from the others, so each must be checked and filled individually.

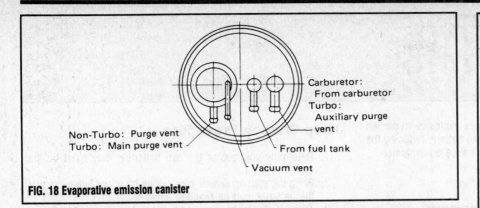

Carburetor:
From carburetor
Turbo:
Auxiliary purge vent

Non-Turbo: Purge vent
Turbo: Main purge vent

From fuel tank

Vacuum vent

FIG. 18 Evaporative emission canister

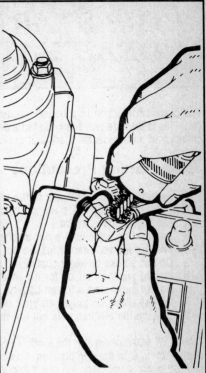

FIG. 20 Cleaning the battery terminals with a wire brush

FIG. 18a Checking the evaporative emission canister—Legacy

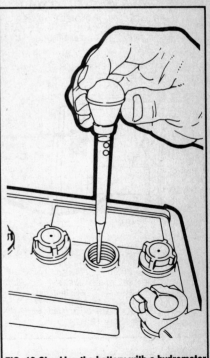

FIG. 19 Checking the battery with a hydrometer

If water is added in freezing weather, the car should be driven several miles to allow the water to mix with the electrolyte. Otherwise, the battery could freeze.

SPECIFIC GRAVITY (EXCEPT MAINTENANCE FREE BATTERIES)

▶ SEE FIG. 19

At least once a year, check the specific gravity of the battery. It should be between 1.20 and 1.26 at room temperature.

The specific gravity can be checked with the use of an hydrometer, an inexpensive instrument available from many sources, including auto parts stores. The hydrometer has a squeeze bulb at one end and a nozzle at the other. Battery electrolyte is sucked into the hydrometer until the float is lifted from its seat. The specific gravity is then read by noting the position of the float. Generally, if after charging, the specific gravity between any two cells varies more than 50 points (0.050), the battery is bad and should be replaced.

It is not possible to check the specific gravity in this manner on sealed (maintenance free) batteries. Instead, the indicator built into the top of the case must be relied on to display any

JUMP STARTING A DEAD BATTERY

The chemical reaction in a battery produces explosive hydrogen gas. This is the safe way to jump start a dead battery, reducing the chances of an accidental spark that could cause an explosion.

Jump Starting Precautions

1. Be sure both batteries are of the same voltage.
2. Be sure both batteries are of the same polarity (have the same grounded terminal).
3. Be sure the vehicles are not touching.
4. Be sure the vent cap holes are not obstructed.
5. Do not smoke or allow sparks around the battery.
6. In cold weather, check for frozen electrolyte in the battery. Do not jump start a frozen battery.
7. Do not allow electrolyte on your skin or clothing.
8. Be sure the electrolyte is not frozen.

CAUTION: Make certin that the ignition key, in the vehicle with the dead battery, is in the OFF position. Connecting cables to vehicles with on-board computers will result in computer destruction if the key is not in the OFF position.

Jump Starting Procedure

1. Determine voltages of the two batteries; they must be the same.
2. Bring the starting vehicle close (they must not touch) so that the batteries can be reached easily.
3. Turn off all accessories and both engines. Put both vehicles in Neutral or Park and set the handbrake.
4. Cover the cell caps with a rag—do not cover terminals.
5. If the terminals on the run-down battery are heavily corroded, clean them.
6. Identify the positive and negative posts on both batteries and connect the cables in the order shown.
7. Start the engine of the starting vehicle and run it at fast idle. Try to start the car with the dead battery. Crank it for no more than 10 seconds at a time and let it cool for 20 seconds in between tries.
8. If it doesn't start in 3 tries, there is something else wrong.
9. Disconnect the cables in the reverse order.
10. Replace the cell covers and dispose of the rags.

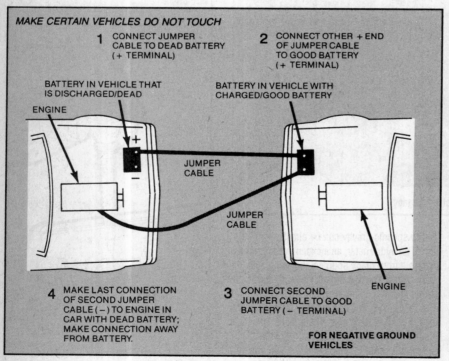

MAKE CERTAIN VEHICLES DO NOT TOUCH

1 CONNECT JUMPER CABLE TO DEAD BATTERY (+ TERMINAL)

2 CONNECT OTHER + END OF JUMPER CABLE TO GOOD BATTERY (+ TERMINAL)

BATTERY IN VEHICLE THAT IS DISCHARGED/DEAD

BATTERY IN VEHICLE WITH CHARGED/GOOD BATTERY

ENGINE

JUMPER CABLE

JUMPER CABLE

4 MAKE LAST CONNECTION OF SECOND JUMPER CABLE (−) TO ENGINE IN CAR WITH DEAD BATTERY; MAKE CONNECTION AWAY FROM BATTERY.

3 CONNECT SECOND JUMPER CABLE TO GOOD BATTERY (− TERMINAL)

ENGINE

FOR NEGATIVE GROUND VEHICLES

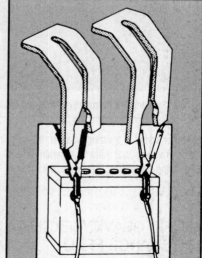

Side terminal batteries occasionally pose a problem when connecting jumper cables. There frequently isn't enough room to clamp the cables without touching sheet metal. Side terminal adaptors are available to alleviate this problem and should be removed after use

signs of battery deterioration. If the indicator is dark, the battery can be assumed to be OK. If the indicator is light, the specific gravity is low, and the battery should be charged or replaced.

:::: WARNING

Keep flame or sparks away from the battery. It gives off explosive hydrogen gas. Battery electrolyte contains sulphuric acid. If you should splash any on your skin or in your eyes, flush the affected area with plenty of clear water. If it lands in your eyes, get medical help immediately.

REPLACEMENT

When it becomes necessary to replace the battery, select a battery with a rating equal to or greater than the battery originally installed. Deterioration, embrittlement and just plain aging of the battery cables, starter motor, and associated wires makes the battery's job harder in successive years. The slow increase in electrical resistance over time makes it prudent to install a new battery with a greater capacity than the old. Details on battery removal and installation are covered in Section 3.

Belts

INSPECTION

Belts should be inspected at 30,000 mile (48,300km) intervals and replaced at 60,000 mile (96,500km) intervals or at the first sign of deterioration.

Inspect belts for signs of glazing or cracking. A glazed belt will be perfectly smooth from slippage, while a good belt will have a slight texture of fabric visible. Cracks usually start at the inner edge of the belt and run outward.

Proper drive belt tension adjustment is important, inadequate tension will result in slippage and wear, while excessive tension will damage the water pump and alternator bearings and cause the belt to fray and crack.

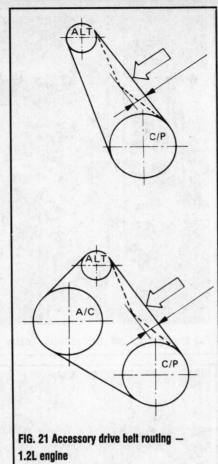

FIG. 21 Accessory drive belt routing — 1.2L engine

TENSION ADJUSTMENT

◆ SEE FIG. 21–24

The procedure for removing and installing an accessory drive belt is the same as for tension adjustment.

Front Side Belt

EXCEPT LEGACY AND SVX
◆ SEE FIG. 25
1. Loosen the alternator mounting bolts.
2. Move the alternator to increase or decrease the belt tension.
3. Tighten the alternator mounting bolts.

LEGACY AND SVX
◆ SEE FIG. 27
1. On SVX, remove the drive belt cover.
2. Loosen the locknut and adjust the slider bolt to obtain the correct belt tension.
3. Tighten the locknut.
4. On SVX, install the drive belt cover.

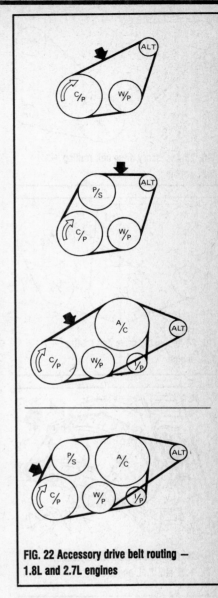

FIG. 22 Accessory drive belt routing — 1.8L and 2.7L engines

Rear Side Belt

The front side belt must be removed in order to remove the rear side belt.

EXCEPT LEGACY AND SVX
◆ SEE FIG. 26
1. Loosen the bolt and special nut securing the idler pulley.
2. Adjust the idler pulley to obtain the correct belt tension.
3. Tighten the bolt and special nut.

LEGACY AND SVX
◆ SEE FIG. 28
1. Loosen the lock bolt on the slider bolt.
2. Adjust the slider pulley to obtain the correct belt tension.
3. Tighten the lock bolt.

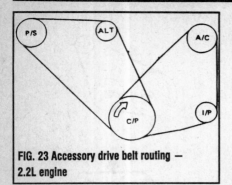

FIG. 23 Accessory drive belt routing —
2.2L engine

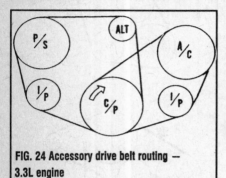

FIG. 24 Accessory drive belt routing —
3.3L engine

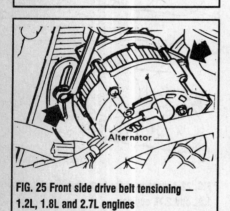

FIG. 25 Front side drive belt tensioning —
1.2L, 1.8L and 2.7L engines

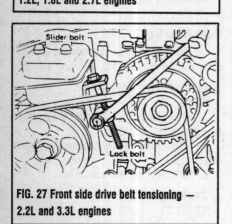

FIG. 27 Front side drive belt tensioning —
2.2L and 3.3L engines

FIG. 26a Right side belt cover removal — Legacy

FIG. 26b Left side belt cover removal — Legacy

FIG. 27a Loosening the lockbolt—Legacy

FIG. 27b Adjusting the slider bolt—Legacy

FIG. 27c Checking belt tension—Legacy

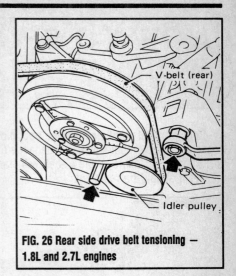

FIG. 26 Rear side drive belt tensioning —
1.8L and 2.7L engines

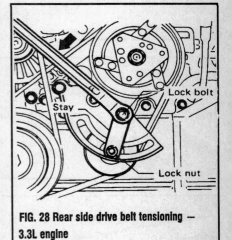

FIG. 28 Rear side drive belt tensioning —
3.3L engine

HOW TO SPOT WORN V-BELTS

V–Belts are vital to efficient engine operation—they drive the fan, water pump and other accessories. They require little maintenance (occasional tightening) but they will not last forever. Slipping or failure of the V–belt will lead to overheating. If your V–belt looks like any of these, it should be replaced.

Cracking or Weathering

This belt has deep cracks, which cause it to flex. Too much flexing leads to heat build–up and premature failure. These cracks can be caused by using the belt on a pulley that is too small. Notched belts are available for small diameter pulleys.

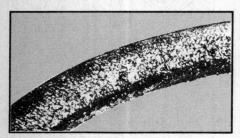

Softening (Grease and Oil)

Oil and grease on a belt can cause the belt's rubber compounds to soften and separate from the reinforcing cords that hold the belt together. The belt will first slip, then finally fail altogether.

Glazing

Glazing is caused by a belt that is slipping. A slipping belt can cause a run-down battery, erratic power steering, overheating or poor accessory performance. The more the belt slips, the more glazing will be built up on the surface of the belt. The more the belt is glazed, the more it will slip. If the glazing is light, tighten the belt.

Worn Cover

The cover of this belt is worn off and is peeling away. The reinforcing cords will begin to wear and the belt will shortly break. When the belt cover wears in spots or has a rough jagged appearance, check the pulley grooves for roughness.

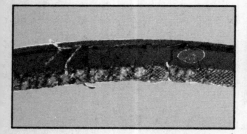

Separation

This belt is on the verge of breaking and leaving you stranded. The layers of the belt are separating and the reinforcing cords are exposed. It's just a matter of time before it breaks completely.

HOW TO SPOT BAD HOSES

Both the upper and lower radiator hoses are called upon to perform difficult jobs in an inhospitable environment. They are subject to nearly 18 psi at under hood temperatures often over 280°F, and must circulate nearly 7500 gallons of coolant an hour — 3 good reasons to have good hoses.

Swollen Hose

A good test for any hose is to feel it for soft or spongy spots. Frequently these will appear as swollen areas of the hose. The most likely cause is oil soaking. This hose could burst at any time, when hot or under pressure.

Cracked Hose

Cracked hoses can usually be seen but feel the hoses to be sure they have not hardened; a prime cause of cracking. This hose has cracked down to the reinforcing cords and could split at any of the cracks.

Frayed Hose End (Due to Weak Clamp)

Weakened clamps frequently are the cause of hose and cooling system failure. The connection between the pipe and hose has deteriorated enough to allow coolant to escape when the engine is hot.

Debris In Cooling System

Debris, rust and scale in the cooling system can cause the inside of a hose to weaken. This can usually be felt on the outside of the hose as soft or thinner areas.

Hoses

Engine coolant hoses should be inspected at 30,000 mile (48,300km) intervals for signs of deterioration and leakage. This service should be performed in conjunction with a complete cooling system service.

REMOVAL & INSTALLATION

1. Place a large pan under the radiator petcock and drain the radiator.
2. Loosen the appropriate clamp for the hose which is to be removed and remove the hose.
3. Put the new hose into place and tighten the clamp. If the clamp is worn or broken replace it.

➡ **Make sure that you have closed the petcock before refilling the radiator.**

4. Refill the radiator, start the engine and check for leaks.

Air Conditioning

SAFETY WARNINGS

Because of the importance of the necessary safety precautions that must be exercised when working with air conditioning systems and R-12 refrigerant, a recap of the safety precautions are outlined.

• Avoid contact with a charged refrigeration system, even when working on another part of the air conditioning system or vehicle. If a heavy tool comes into contact with a section of copper tubing or a heat exchanger, it can easily cause the relatively soft material to rupture.

• When it is necessary to apply force to a fitting which contains refrigerant, as when checking that all system couplings are securely tightened, use a wrench on both parts of the fitting involved, if possible. This will avoid putting torque on the refrigerant tubing. It is advisable, when possible, to use tube or line wrenches when tightening these flare nut fittings.

• DO NOT attempt to discharge the system by merely loosening a fitting or removing the service valve caps and cracking these valves. Precise control is possible only when using the service gauges. Place a rag under the open end of the center charging hose while discharging the system to catch any drops of liquid that

might escape. Wear protective gloves when connecting or disconnecting service gauge hoses.

• Discharge the system only in a well ventilated area, as high concentrations of the gas can exclude oxygen and act as an anesthetic. When leak testing or soldering, this is particularly important, as toxic gas is formed when R-12 contacts any flame.

• Never start a system without first verifying that both service valves are back-seated (if equipped) and that all fittings throughout the system are snugly connected.

• Avoid applying heat to any refrigerant line or storage vessel. Charging may be aided by using water heated to less than 125° to warm the refrigerant container. Never allow a refrigerant storage container to sit out in the sun or near any other heat source, such as a radiator.

• Always wear goggles when working on a system to protect the eyes. If refrigerant contacts the eyes, it is advisable in all cases to see a physician as soon as possible.

• Frostbite from liquid refrigerant should be treated by first gradually warming the area with cool water and then gently applying petroleum jelly. A physician should be consulted.

• Always keep the refrigerant drum fittings capped when not in use. Avoid any sudden shock to the drum, which might occur from dropping it or from banging a heavy tool against it. Never carry a drum in the passenger compartment of a vehicle.

• Always completely discharge the system before painting the vehicle (if the paint is to be baked on), or before welding anywhere near the refrigerant lines.

SYSTEM INSPECTION

The air conditioning system should be checked periodically for worn hoses, loose connections, low refrigerant, leaks, dirt and bugs. If any of these conditions exist, they must be corrected or they will reduce the efficiency of your air conditioning system.

Keep The Condenser Clear

Periodically inspect the front of the condenser for bent fins or foreign material (dirt, bugs, leaves, etc.) If any cooling fins are bent, straighten them carefully with needle-nosed pliers. You can remove any debris with a stiff bristle brush or hose.

Operate The A/C System Periodically

A lot of A/C problems can be avoided by simply running the air conditioner at least once a week, regardless of the season. Let the system run for at least 5 minutes a week (even in the winter), and you'll keep the internal parts lubricated as well as preventing the hoses from hardening.

REFRIGERANT LEVEL CHECK

The first order of business is to find the sight glass. It will either be in the head of the receiver/drier, or in one of the metal lines leading from the top of the receiver/drier. Once you've found it, wipe it clean and proceed as follows:

1. Start the engine and hold engine speed at 1500 rpm.
2. Set the mode switch to A/C position.
3. Set the blower to maximum speed.
4. Set the temperature control lever to COLD position.
5. Open all the windows.
6. Check the sight glass after about 5 minutes.

The bubbles seen through the sight glass are influenced by the ambient temperature. Since the bubbles are hard to see in temperatures below 68°F (20°C), it is possible that a slightly larger amount of refrigerant would be filled, if supplied according to the sight glass. Be sure to recheck the amount when the temperature exceeds 68°F (20°C). The bubbles will show up easier when the temperature is higher.

When the screen in the receiver drier is clogged, the bubbles will appear even if the amount of refrigerant is normal. In this case the outlet side pipe of the receiver drier becomes considerable cold.

GAUGE SETS

Most of the service work performed in air conditioning requires the use of two gauges, one for the high (head) pressure side of the system, the other for the low (suction).

The low side gauge records both pressure and vacuum. Vacuum readings are calibrated from 0 to no less than 60 psi, while the high side gauge measures pressure from 0 to at least 600 psi. Both gauges are threaded into a manifold that contains two hand shut off valves. Proper

Amount of refrigerant / Check item	Almost no refrigerant	Insufficient	Suitable	Too much refrigerant
Temperature of high pressure and low pressure pipes.	Almost no difference between high pressure and low pressure side temperature.	High pressure side is warm and low pressure side is fairly cold.	High pressure side is hot and low pressure side is cold.	High pressure side is abnormally hot.
State in sight glass.	Bubbles flow continuously. Bubbles will disappear and something like mist will flow when refrigerant is nearly gone. *Fig. 25* B4-463	The bubbles are seen at intervals of 1 — 2 seconds. *Fig. 26* B4-464	Almost transparent. Bubbles may appear when engine speed is raised and lowered. No clear difference exists between these two conditions. *Fig. 27* B4-465	No bubbles can be seen.
Pressure of system.	High pressure side is abnormally low.	Both pressure on high and low pressure sides are slightly low.	Both pressures on high and low pressure sides are normal.	Both pressures on high and low pressure sides are abnormally high.
Repair.	Stop compressor and conduct an overall check.	Check for gas leakage, repair as required, replenish and charge system.		Discharge refrigerant from service valve of low pressure side.

manipulation of these valves and the use of the attached test hoses allow the user to perform the following services:

1. Test high and low side pressures.
2. Remove air, moisture, and contaminated refrigerant.
3. Purge the system of refrigerant.
4. Charge the system with refrigerant.

The manifold valves are designed so they have no direct effect on gauge readings, but serve only to provide for, or cut off, flow of refrigerant through the manifold. During all testing and hook-up operations, the valves are kept in a closed position to avoid disturbing the refrigeration system. The valves are opened only to purge the system of refrigerant or to charge it. When purging the system, the center hose is uncapped at the lower end, and both valves are cracked open slightly. This allows refrigerant pressure to force the entire contents of the system out through the center hose. During charging, the valve on the high side of the manifold is closed, and the valve on the low side

is cracked open. Under these conditions, the low pressure in the evaporator will draw refrigerant from the relatively warm refrigerant storage container into the system.

DISCHARGING THE SYSTEM

❋ CAUTION

Perform in a well ventilated area. The compressed refrigerant used in the air conditioning system expands and evaporates into the atmosphere at a temperature of –21.7°F (–29.8°C) or less. This will freeze any surface (including your eyes) that it contacts. In addition, the refrigerant decomposes into a poisonous gas in the presence of flame.

➡ **R-12 refrigerant is a chlorofluorocarbon which, when released into the atmosphere, can contribute to the depletion of the ozone layer. Ozone filters out harmful radiation from the sun. If possible, an approved R-12 Recovery/Recycling machine that meets SAE standards should be employed when discharging the system. Follow the operating instructions provided with the approved equipment exactly to properly discharge the system.**

1. Operate the air conditioner for at least 10 minutes.
2. Attach the gauges, shut off the air conditioner and the engine.
3. Connect the center hose of the gauge to an approved Recovery/Recycling machine. The refrigerant will be discharged there and this precaution will control its uncontrolled exposure.

4. Open the low side hand valve on the gauge slightly.

5. Open the high side hand valve slightly.

➡ **Too rapid a purging process will be identified by the appearance of an oily foam. If this occurs, close the hand valves a little more until this condition stops.**

6. Close both hand valves on the gauge set when the pressures read 0 and all the refrigerant has left the system.

➡ **The system should always be discharged before attempting to remove any hoses or component parts of the air conditioning system.**

EVACUATING THE SYSTEM

1. Connect the high and low pressure charging hoses of the manifold gauge to their respective service valve of the system and ensure that all refrigerant has been discharged from the system.

2. When all pressure has been released from the system, connect the center charging hose to a vacuum pump.

3. Close both valves of the manifold gauge fully. Then start the vacuum pump.

4. Open the low pressure valve and suck the old refrigerant from the system.

5. When the low pressure gauge reading has reached to approximately 19.69 in. Hg, slowly open the high pressure valve.

6. When the pressure inside the system has dropped to 27.95 in. Hg, fully close both valves of the manifold gauge and stop the vacuum pump.

7. Let the system stand for 5–10 minutes in this state and confirm that the reading does not rise.

➡ **If the pressure in the system rises or the specified negative pressure can not be obtained, there is a leak in the system. Immediately charge the system to prevent the entrance of moisture and repair the leak in the system.**

CHARGING THE SYSTEM

⁖ CAUTION

Never attempt to charge the system by opening the high pressure gauge

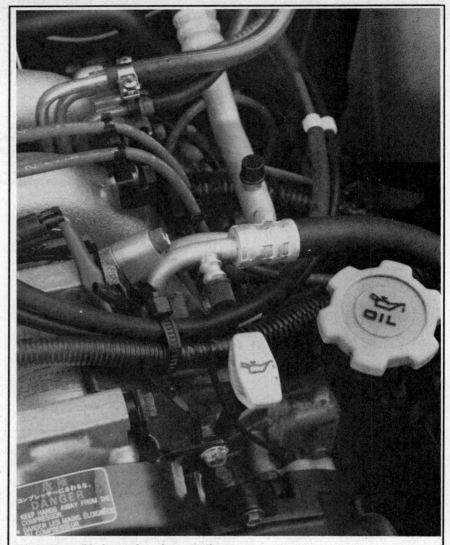

FIG. 29 Air conditioning service valve ports — Legacy

control while the compressor is operating. The compressor accumulating pressure can burst the refrigerant container, causing severe personal injury.

Refrigerant enters the suction side of the system as a vapor while the compressor is running. Before proceeding, the system should be in a partial vacuum after adequate evacuation. Both hand valves on the gauge manifold should be closed.

1. Attach both test hoses to their respective service valve ports. Mid-position manually operated service valves, if present.

2. Install the dispensing valve (closed position) on the refrigerant container. (Single and multiple refrigerant manifolds are available to accommodate one to four 15 oz. cans.)

3. Attach the center charging hose to the refrigerant container valve.

4. Open dispensing valve on the refrigerant valve.

5. Loosen the center charging hose coupler where it connects to the gauge manifold to allow the escaping refrigerant to purge the hose of contaminants.

6. Tighten the center charging hose connector.

7. Purge the low pressure test hose at the gauge manifold.

8. Start the engine, roll down the windows and adjust the air conditioner to maximum cooling. The engine should be at normal operating temperature before proceeding. The heated environment helps the liquid vaporize more efficiently.

FIG. 29a Removing the air conditioning service valve port caps—Legacy

➡ **Placing the refrigerant can in a container of warm water (no hotter than 125°F [52°C]) will speed the charging process. Slight agitation of the can is helpful too, but be careful not to turn the can upside down.**

9. Crack open the low side hand valve on the manifold. Manipulate the valve so that the refrigerant that enters the system does not cause the low side pressure to exceed 40 psi. Too sudden a surge may permit the entrance of unwanted liquid to the compressor. Since liquids cannot be compressed, the compressor will suffer damage if compelled to attempt it.

10. Charge the system with the proper amount of refrigerant by weighing the charged refrigerant with a scale. Overcharging will cause discharge pressure to rise.

- Hitachi: 1.63–1.74 lbs.
- Panasonic: 1.76–1.87 lbs.
- Diesel Kiki: 1.8–2.0 lbs.
- Calsonic: 1.8–2.0 lbs.

11. When the system is fully charged, close the low pressure valve and disconnect hoses from the service ports.

LEAK TESTING

There are several methods of detecting leaks in an air conditioning system; among them, the two most popular are (1) halide leak detection or the open flame method and (2) electronic leak detector.

The Halide Leak Detection tool is a torch like device which produces a yellow-green color when refrigerant is introduced into the flame at the burner. A purple or violet color indicates the presence of large amounts of refrigerant at the burner.

An Electronic Refrigerant Leak Detector tool is a small portable electronic device with an extended probe. With the unit activated, the probe is passed along those components of the system which contain refrigerant. If a leak is detected, the unit will sound an alarm signal or activate a display signal depending on the manufacturer's design. It is advisable to follow the manufacturer's instructions as the design and function of the detection may vary significantly.

⁑ CAUTION

Caution should be taken to operate either type of detector in well ventilated areas, so as to reduce the chance of personal injury, which may result from contact with poisonous gases produced when R-12 is exposed to flame or electric spark.

Windshield Wipers

▸ SEE FIG. 30

For maximum effectiveness and longest element life, the windshield and wiper blades should be kept clean. Dirt, tree sap, road tar and so on will cause streaking, smearing and blade deterioration if left on the glass. It is advisable to wash the windshield carefully with a commercial glass cleaner at least once a month. Wipe off the rubber blades with the wet rag afterwards. Do not attempt to move the wipers by hand. Damage to the motor and drive mechanism will result.

If the blades are found to be cracked, broken or torn, they should be replaced immediately. Replacement intervals will vary with usage, although ozone deterioration usually limits blade life to about one year. If the wiper pattern is smeared or streaked, or if the blade chatters across the glass, the elements should be replaced. It is easiest and most sensible to replace the elements in pairs.

There are basically three different types of refills, which differ in their method of replacement. One type has two release buttons, approximately 1/3 of the way up from the ends of the blade frame. Pushing the buttons down releases a lock and allows the rubber filler to be removed from the frame. The new filler slides back into the frame and locks in place.

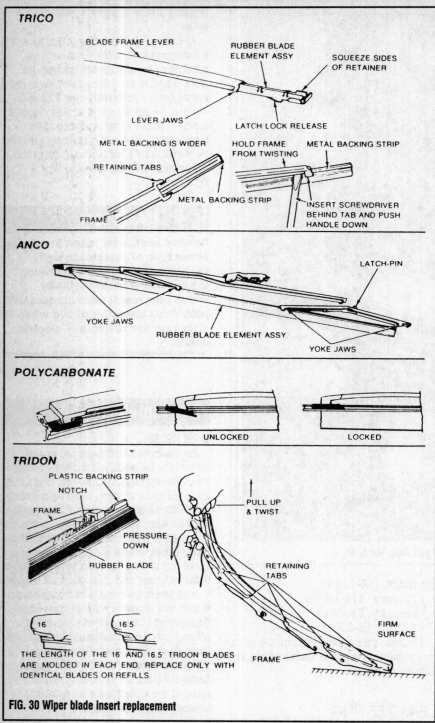

FIG. 30 Wiper blade insert replacement

refill is pushed into place and locked. The metal blade holder and frame will scratch the glass if allowed to touch it.

Tires and Wheels

Tire rotation is recommended every 6,000 miles (9,600km) or so, and a tire pressure check should be performed at regular intervals to obtain maximum tire wear.

TIRE ROTATION

▶ SEE FIG. 31

The pattern of tire rotation you use depends on whether or not your car has a usable spare. Radial tires should not be cross-switched (from one side of the car to the other). They last longer if their direction of rotation is not changed. Snow tires sometimes have directional arrows molded into the side of the carcass. The arrow shows the direction of rotation. They will wear very rapidly if the rotation is reversed. Studded tires will lose their studs if their rotational direction is reversed.

➡ **Mark the wheel position or direction of rotation on radial tires or studded snow tires before removing them.**

TIRE DESIGN

For maximum satisfaction, tires should be used in sets of five. Mixing of different types (radial, bias-belted, fiberglass belted) should be avoided. Conventional bias tires are constructed so that the cords run bead to bead at an angle. Alternate plies run at an opposite angle. This type of construction gives rigidity to both tread and side wall. Bias belted tires are similar in construction to conventional bias ply tires. Belts run at an angle and also at a 90° angle to the bead, as in radial tires. Tread life is improved considerably over the conventional bias tire. The radial tire differs in construction, but instead of the carcass running at an angle of 90° to each other they run at an angle of 90° to the bead. This gives the tread a great deal of rigidity and the side wall a great deal of flexibility (which accounts for the characteristic bulge associated with radial tires).

The second type of refill has two metal tabs which are unlocked by squeezing them together. The rubber filler can then be withdrawn from the frame jaws. A new refill is installed by inserting the refill into the front frame jaws and sliding it rearward to engage the remaining frame jaws. There are usually four jaws. Be certain when installing that the refill is engaged in all of them. At the end of its travel, the tabs will lock into place on the front jaws of the wiper blade frame.

The third type is a refill made from polycarbonate. The refill has a simple locking device at one end which flexes downward out of the groove into which the jaws of the holder fit, allowing easy release. By sliding the new refill through all the jaws and pushing through the slight resistance when it reaches the end of its travel, the refill will lock into position.

Regardless of the type of refill used, make sure that all of the frame jaws are engaged as the

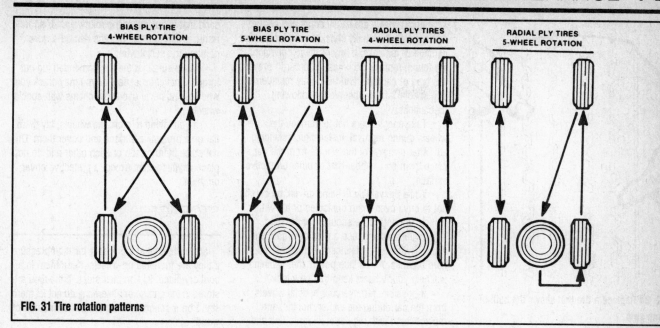

FIG. 31 Tire rotation patterns

INFLATION PRESSURE

Tire inflation is the most ignored item of auto maintenance. Gasoline mileage can drop as much as 0.8% for every 1 pound per square inch (psi) of under inflation.

Two items should be a permanent fixture in every glove compartment: a tire pressure gauge and a tread depth gauge. Check the tire air pressure (including the spare) regularly with a pocket type gauge. Kicking the tires won't tell you a thing, and the gauge on the service station air hose is notoriously inaccurate.

The tire pressures recommended for your car are usually found on the left door or in the owner's manual. Ideally, inflation pressure should be checked when the tires are cool. When the air becomes heated it expands and the pressure increases. Every 10° rise (or drop) in temperature means a difference of 1 psi, which also explains why the tire appears to lose air on a very cold night. When it is impossible to check the tires cold, allow for pressure build-up due to heat. If the hot pressure exceeds the cold pressure by more than 15 psi, reduce your speed, load or both. Otherwise internal heat is created in the tire. When the heat approaches the temperature at which the tire was cured, during manufacture, the tread can separate from the body.

☼ CAUTION

Never counteract excessive pressure build-up by bleeding off air pressure (letting some air out). This will only further raise the tire operating temperature.

Before starting a long trip with lots of luggage, you can add about 2-4 psi to the tires to make them run cooler, but never exceed the maximum inflation pressure on the side of the tire.

TREAD DEPTH

◆ SEE FIG. 32–34

All tires made since 1968, have 7 built-in tread wear indicator bars that show up as $1/2$ in. (13mm) wide smooth bands across the tire when $1/16$ in. (1.6mm) of tread remains. The appearance of tread wear indicators means that the tires should be replaced. In fact, many states have laws prohibiting the use of tires with less than $1/16$ in. (1.6mm) tread.

You can check your own tread depth with an inexpensive gauge or by using a Lincoln head penny. Slip the Lincoln penny into several tread grooves. If you can see the top of Lincoln's head in 2 adjacent grooves, the tires have less than $1/16$ in. (1.6mm) tread left and should be replaced. You can measure snow tires in the same manner by using the tails side of the Lincoln penny. If you can see the top of the Lincoln memorial, it's time to replace the snow tires.

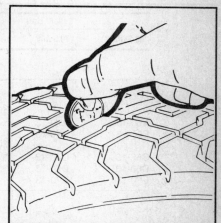

FIG. 32 Using a penny to determine tread depth

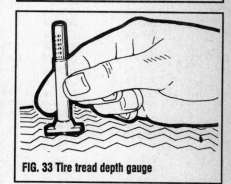

FIG. 33 Tire tread depth gauge

CARE OF SPECIAL WHEELS

If you have invested money in mag, aluminum alloy or sport wheels, special precautions should be taken to make sure your investment is not wasted, and that your special wheels look good for the lifetime of the car.

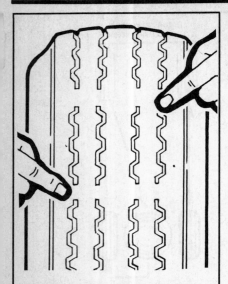

FIG. 34 Replace a tire that shows the built-in bump strip

Special wheels are easily scratched and/or damaged. Occasionally check the rim for cracks, damage or air leaks. If any of these conditions are found, replace the wheel. In order to prevent this type of damage, and the costly replacement of a special wheel, observe the following precautions:

• Take special care not to damage the wheels during removal, installation, balancing etc. After removal of the wheels from the car, place them on a rubber mat or other protective surface.

• While the vehicle is being driven, be careful not to drive over sharp obstacles or allow the wheels to contact the shoulder of the road.

• When washing, use a mild detergent and water. Avoid using cleansers with abrasives, or hard brushes. And a little polish after washing will help your wheels keep that new look.

• If possible, remove your special wheels from the car during the winter months, and replace them with regular steel rims. Salt and sand that is applied to the roadways for snow removal during these months can do severe damage to special wheels.

• Make sure that the recommended lug nut torque is never exceeded, or you may crack your wheels. And never use snow chains with special wheels.

• If you intend to store the wheels, lay them flat on a protective surface and cover them. Do not stack them on top of each other and do not place anything else, except a protective cover, on them.

STORAGE

Store the tires at the proper inflation pressure if they are mounted on wheels. Keep them in a cool dry place, laid on their sides. If the tires are stored in the garage or basement, do not let them stand on a concrete floor. Set them on strips of wood.

"Letter" sizes			Inch Sizes	Metric-inch Sizes		
"60 Series"	"70 Series"	"78 Series"	1965–77	"60 Series"	"70 Series"	"80 Series"
			5.50-12, 5.60-12	165/60-12	165/70-12	155-12
		Y78-12	6.00-12			
		W78-13	5.20-13	165/60-13	145/70-13	135-13
		Y78-13	5.60-13	175/60-13	155/70-13	145-13
			6.15-13	185/60-13	165/70-13	155-13, P155/80-13
A60-13	A70-13	A78-13	6.40-13	195/60-13	175/70-13	165-13
B60-13	B70-13	B78-13	6.70-13	205/60-13	185/70-13	175-13
			6.90-13			
C60-13	C70-13	C78-13	7.00-13	215/60-13	195/70-13	185-13
D60-13	D70-13	D78-13	7.25-13			
E60-13	E70-13	E78-13	7.75-13			195-13
			5.20-14	165/60-14	145/70-14	135-14
			5.60-14	175/60-14	155/70-14	145-14
			5.90-14			
A60-14	A70-14	A78-14	6.15-14	185/60-14	165/70-14	155-14
	B70-14	B78-14	6.45-14	195/60-14	175/70-14	165-14
	C70-14	C78-14	6.95-14	205/60-14	185/70-14	175-14
D60-14	D70-14	D78-14				
E60-14	E70-14	E78-14	7.35-14	215/60-14	195/70-14	185-14
F60-14	F70-14	F78-14, F83-14	7.75-14	225/60-14	200/70-14	195-14
G60-14	G70-14	G77-14, G78-14	8.25-14	235/60-14	205/70-14	205-14
H60-14	H70-14	H78-14	8.55-14	245/60-14	215/70-14	215-14
J60-14	J70-14	J78-14	8.85-14	255/60-14	225/70-14	225-14
L60-14	L70-14		9.15-14	265/60-14	235/70-14	
	A70-15	A78-15	5.60-15	185/60-15	165/70-15	155-15
B60-15	B70-15	B78-15	6.35-15	195/60-15	175/70-15	165-15
C60-15	C70-15	C78-15	6.85-15	205/60-15	185/70-15	175-15
	D70-15	D78-15				
E60-15	E70-15	E78-15	7.35-15	215/60-15	195/70-15	185-15
F60-15	F70-15	F78-15	7.75-15	225/60-15	205/70-15	195-15
G60-15	G70-15	G78-15	8.15-15/8.25-15	235/60-15	215/70-15	205-15
H60-15	H70-15	H78-15	8.45-15/8.55-15	245/60-15	225/70-15	215-15
J60-15	J70-15	J78-15	8.85-15/8.90-15	255/60-15	235/70-15	225-15
	K70-15		9.00-15	265/60-15	245/70-15	230-15
L60-15	L70-15	L78-15, L84-15	9.15-15			235-15
	M70-15	M78-15				255-15
		N78-15				

Note: Every size tire is not listed and many size comparisons are approximate, based on load ratings. Wider tires than those supplied new with the vehicle, should always be checked for clearance.

BUYING NEW TIRES

When buying new tires, give some though to the following points, especially if you are considering a switch to larger tires or a different profile series:

1. All four tires must be of the same construction type. This rule cannot be violated. Radial, bias, and bias-belted tires must not be mixed.

2. The wheels should be the correct width for the tire. Tire dealers have charts of tire and rim compatibility. A mismatch will cause sloppy handling and rapid tire wear. The tread width should match the rim width (inside bead to inside bead) within an inch. For radial tires, the rim width should be 80% or less of the tire (not tread) width.

3. The height (mounted diameter) of the new tires can change speedometer accuracy, engine speed at a given road speed, fuel mileage, acceleration, and ground clearance. Tire manufacturers furnish full measurement specifications.

4. The spare tire should be usable, at least for short distance and low speed operation, with the new tires.

5. There shouldn't be any body interference when loaded, on bumps, or in turns.

FLUIDS AND LUBRICANTS

Fuel and Engine Oil Recommendations

The SAE (Society of Automotive Engineers) grade number indicates the viscosity of the engine oil, and thus its ability to lubricate at a given temperature. The lower the SAE grade number, the lighter the oil. The lower the viscosity, the easier it is to crank the engine in cold weather.

Oil viscosities should be chosen from those oils recommended for the lowest anticipated temperatures during the oil change interval.

Multi-viscosity oils (10W-30, 20W-50, etc.) offer the important advantage of being adaptable to temperature extremes. They allow easy starting at low temperatures, yet give good protection at high speeds and engine temperatures. This is a decided advantage in changeable climates or in long distance touring.

SAE viscosity No. and Applicable Temperature					
(°F)	−30	0	30	60	90
(°C)	−34	−18	0	16	32

10W-30, 10W-40

5W-30

→ **SAE 5W-30 is not recommended for sustained high speed driving.**

The API (American Petroleum Institute) designation indicates the classification of engine oil for use under given operating conditions. Only oils designated for use Service SF or SG should be used. Oils of the SF or SG type perform a variety of functions inside the engine in addition to the basic function as a lubricant. Through a balanced system of metallic detergents and polymeric dispersants, the oil prevents the formation of high and low temperature deposits, and also keeps sludge and dirt particles in suspension. Acids, particularly sulfuric acid, as well as other by-products of combustion, are neutralized. Both the SAE grade number and the API designation can be found on the top of the oil can.

❊ WARNING

Non-detergent or straight mineral oils must never be used.

Fuel

Your Subaru is designed to operate on unleaded regular fuel. In all cases, the minimum octane rating of the fuels used must be at least 87 for models except the SVX and 91 for the SVX.

Use of a fuel too low in octane (a measurement of anti-knock quality) will result in spark knock. Since many factors affect operating efficiency, such as altitude, terrain, air temperature and humidity, knocking may result even though the recommended fuel is being used. If persistent knocking occurs, it may be necessary to switch to a slightly higher grade of gasoline. Continuous or heavy knocking may result in engine damage.

→ **Your engine's fuel requirement can change with time, mainly due to carbon buildup, which changes the compression ratio. If your engine pings, knocks, or runs on, switch to a higher grade of fuel, if possible, and check the ignition timing. If your engine requires unleaded fuel, sometimes changing brands will cure the problem. If it is necessary to retard timing from specifications, don't change it more than a few degrees. Retarded timing will reduce power output and fuel mileage, and will increase engine temperature.**

Engine

OIL LEVEL CHECK

▶ SEE FIG. 37–38

The engine oil level should be checked at regular intervals. For example, whenever the car is refueled. Wait a few minutes after the engine is stopped before checking the oil level or an inaccurate reading will result. Also, the vehicle should be parked on a level surface.

❊ CAUTION

If the low oil pressure warning light comes on while the engine is running, stop the engine immediately and check the oil level.

Remove the dipstick, which is located on the right (passenger) side of the crankcase, and wipe it with a clean cloth. Insert it again and withdraw it. The oil level should be at the F (FULL) upper mark or between the F mark and

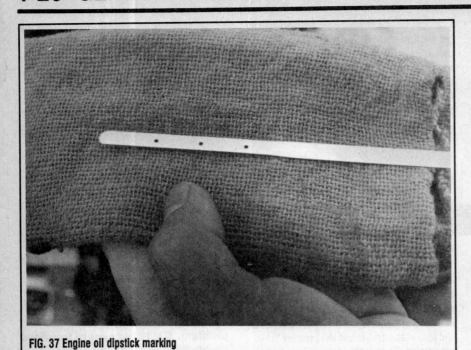

FIG. 37 Engine oil dipstick marking

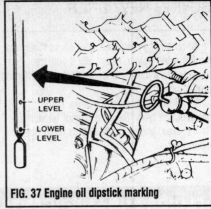

FIG. 37 Engine oil dipstick marking

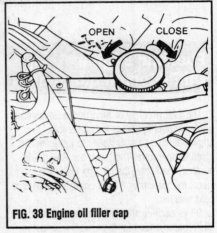

FIG. 38 Engine oil filler cap

FIG. 37a Engine oil dipstick location—Legacy

the lower mark (ADD) on the dipstick. Do not run the engine if the oil level falls below the lower mark.

Add oil as necessary. Use only oil which carries the API designation SF or SG. Always use oil with the proper viscosity rating (SAE number) for your particular driving conditions. Do not overfill. The oil level should never rise above the F mark.

OIL AND FILTER CHANGE

▶ SEE FIG. 39—41

The engine oil should be changed every 3000 miles (4,800km). When the vehicle is operated in severe conditions (dusty conditions, stop-and-go driving or short distance conditions) more frequent changing is recommended.

Use a good quality motor oil of a known brand which meets the API classification SF/SG. The viscosity of the oil to be used should be

determined by the driving conditions most frequently encountered.

All Subaru models are equipped with a spin-off oil filter. On all models, except the Justy, the filter is mounted at the left front of the engine (driver's side). On the Justy, the oil filter is mounted on the side of the engine facing the passengers compartment. It is accessible from either above or below the car's engine compartment.

1. Run the engine for a short period of time. This will make the oil flow more freely and it will carry off more contaminants. Stop the engine.

2. Raise and support the vehicle safely.

3. Remove the oil filler cap from the oil filler tube which is located on the right side of the engine (except on the 1.6L where it is on the left side).

4. Place a drain pan of adequate capacity below the drain plug which is located either at the front of the engine on the Justy, or on the driver's side of the oil pan (all other models). A large, flat pan makes a good container to catch oil.

FIG. 37b Adding engine oil—Legacy

FIG. 40 Engine oil filter

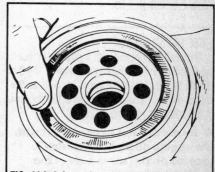

FIG. 41 Lubricate the gasket on a new oil filter with clean engine oil. A dry gasket may not make a good seal and allow the filter to leak

5. Use a wrench of the proper size to loosen the oil pan drain plug. Remove the drain plug while maintaining a slight upward force on it, to keep the oil from running out around it. Allow all of the oil to drain into the container.

6. Remove the container from under the drain hole and wipe any excess oil from around the drain area.

7. Install the drain plug and tighten to 29–33 ft. lbs. (39–44 Nm).

8. Since the oil filter is mounted horizontally, place a pan underneath it to catch the oil that will run out as soon as the filter is loosened.

9. Using a band wrench, turn the filter counterclockwise to remove it.

10. Wipe off the oil filter case and mounting boss with a clean cloth.

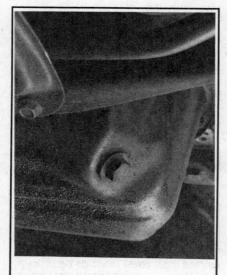

FIG. 39 Engine oil drain plug

11. Install a new filter and gasket, after lubricating the gasket with clean engine oil. Hand-tighten the filter after the rubber gasket contacts the mounting boss. See instructions printed on or packed with the filter as tightening recommendations vary.

➡ **Do not use the band wrench to tighten the oil filter. Tighten it by hand. Over tightening the filter will cause leaks.**

12. Add clean, fresh oil of the proper grade and viscosity through the oil filler tube on the top of the engine. Be sure that the oil level is near the upper F (FULL) mark on the dipstick.

13. Start the engine and allow it to idle until the oil light goes out. Stop the engine, wait a few minutes, and check the oil level. Add oil as necessary, but do not overfill.

14. Remember to replace the oil filler cap. Check for leaks.

Manual Transaxle

In manual transmission models the transmission and drive axle share a common supply of lubricant. On all models, the lubricant level should be checked at regular intervals and changed at 30,000 mile (48,300km) intervals. When the vehicle is frequently operated under severe conditions, the lubricant should be changed at 15,000 mile (24,000km) intervals.

FLUID RECOMMENDATIONS

When changing the fluid, use API GL-5 hypoid gear oil in one of the following viscosities:
- SAE 90 — above 30°F (–1°C)
- SAE 85W — below 30°F (–1°C)
- SAE 80W — below 0°F (–18°C)

LEVEL CHECK

♦ SEE FIG. 42 and 42a

The level is checked with a dipstick in much the same manner as the engine oil level. The fluid should be checked at the same intervals as the engine oil. The dipstick is located at the right rear of the transaxle housing.

➡ **Be careful not to confuse it with the engine oil dipstick, which is located on the same side of the engine.**

Check the transmission oil level with the car parked on a level surface and the engine stopped. The engine should be stopped for at least three minutes before the transaxle oil level is checked.

Pull the dipstick out and wipe it with a clean cloth. Insert the dipstick again and then remove it. The oil level should be between the upper F (FULL) and lower L (LOW) marks. If it is below L, replenish it through the dipstick opening with GL-5 hypoid gear oil, of proper weight. Add a little oil at a time. The distance between the marks on the dipstick is less than a pint. Do not overfill.

DRAIN AND REFILL

1. Raise and support the vehicle safely.
2. Place a container of adequate capacity beneath the drain plug which is located underneath the car, on the bottom of the transaxle housing.

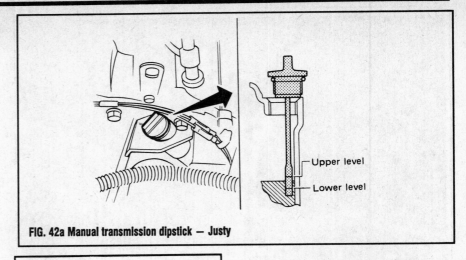

FIG. 42a Manual transmission dipstick — Justy

FIG. 42 Manual transmission dipstick — except Justy

3. Use the proper size wrench, loosen the drain plug slowly while maintaining a slight upward pressure. This will keep the oil from leaking out around the plug. The drain plug is located at the bottom center of the transmission case.
4. Allow all of the lubricant to drain from the transaxle, then install the drain plug and gasket (if so equipped). Tighten the drain plug to 30–35 ft. lbs. (41–47 Nm).
5. Remove the transaxle dipstick and fill the transaxle to the correct capacity. Do not overfill.
6. Use the dipstick to check the level. It should come up to the F (FULL) mark.

Automatic Transaxle

The lubricant supply in the automatic transmission is separate from that in the drive axle. The fluid level should be checked at regular intervals and should be changed every 30,000 miles (48,300km). If the vehicle is frequently operated under severe conditions the lubricant should be changed at 15,000 mile (24,000km) intervals.

FLUID RECOMMENDATION

Dexron®II automatic transmission fluid is recommended by Subaru for use in their automatic transmissions.

LEVEL CHECK

♦ SEE FIG. 43

To check the automatic transmission fluid, drive the car several miles to bring the transmission up to normal operating temperature. Park the car on a level surface, place the gear selector in P position and leave the engine idling.

Open the hood and locate the automatic transmission dipstick on the left side of the engine, near the fire wall. Remove the dipstick, wipe it with a clean rag and reinsert it all the way. Remove it and note the reading.

➡ **While checking the fluid level, smell the oil on the dipstick. If the fluid has a burnt smell, serious transmission problems are indicated.**

As long as the reading is between the upper level and lower level marks the fluid level is correct. If the level is at or below the lower mark, additional fluid is necessary. Add automatic transmission fluid with the Dexron® designation only.

Fluid should be added through the neck of the dipstick hole using a funnel. With the engine still idling, add fluid in small quantities at a time and recheck the level after each addition. Stop when the fluid level is close to the upper level mark. Avoid overfilling, do not fill above the upper mark.

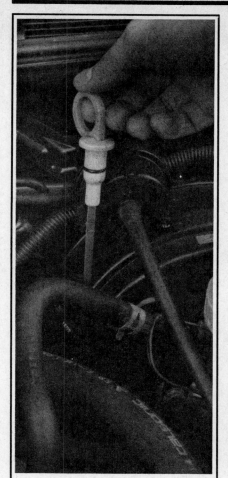

FIG. 43 Automatic transmission dipstick

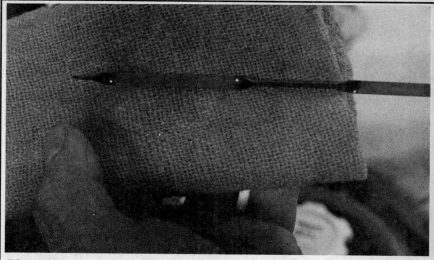

FIG. 43a Automatic transmission dipstick markings

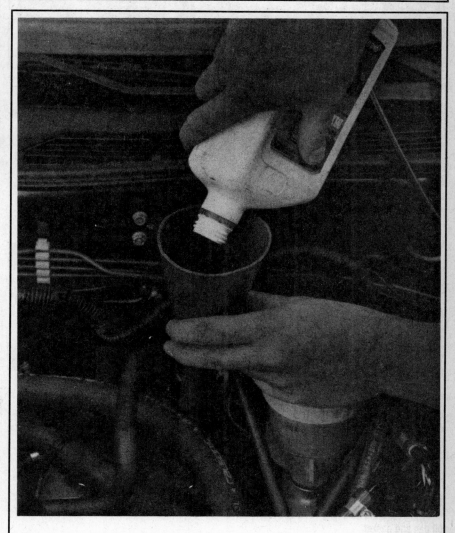

FIG. 43b Adding automatic transmission fluid

DRAIN AND REFILL

♦ SEE FIG. 44

1. Raise and support the vehicle safely.

2. Place a container of adequate capacity beneath the drain plug located at the bottom, center of the transmission case.

3. Remove the drain plug and allow the fluid to drain. The drain plug is located on the bottom left side of the transmission case.

4. After draining, replace the drain plug and gasket. Tighten the plug to 17–20 ft. lbs. (23–26 Nm). Do not overtighten.

5. Remove the transmission dipstick and fill the transmission through the dipstick hole with the proper amount of automatic transmission fluid.

6. Check the fluid level.

FIG. 44 Automatic transmission oil pan showing the drain plug location

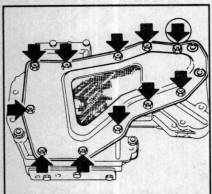

FIG. 45 Automatic transmission oil strainer

PAN AND STRAINER SERVICE

♦ SEE FIG. 45

Normal maintenance does not require removal of the transmission oil pan, or changing or cleaning of the oil strainer. However, if a leak is detected at the transmission oil pan gasket it must be replaced. Some models do not incorporate an oil strainer.

1. Raise and support the vehicle safely.

2. Remove the drain plug and drain the transmission fluid into a suitable container.

3. Remove the mounting bolts and lower the oil pan and gasket.

4. If you wish to remove the oil strainer, simply unbolt it from the valve body. It can be

cleaned in a nonflammable solvent and dried with compressed air or allowed to air dry.

5. Install the oil strainer and tighten the bolts to 26–35 inch lbs. (4–5 Nm).

6. Using a new gasket, install the oil pan and bolts. Tighten the bolts to 30–39 inch lbs. (3.5–4.5 Nm).

7. Lower the vehicle and fill the transmission with fluid. Start the engine and check the transmission fluid level.

Transfer Case

Lubricant to the transfer case is supplied through the transmission. If the level of fluid in the transmission is full, so is the transfer case.

Drive Axle (Front)

The lubricant should be checked at regular intervals and changed at 60,000 mile (96,500km) intervals. When the vehicle is frequently operated under severe conditions, the lubricant should be changed at 30,000 mile (48,300km) intervals.

➡ This section pertains to automatic transmission equipped vehicles only.

FLUID RECOMMENDATIONS

Use gear oil with API classification GL-5 for open differentials and GLS for limited slip differential. Viscosity should be:

- SAE 90 — above 30°F (–1°C)
- SAE 85W — above 30°F (–1°C)
- SAE 80W — below 0°F (–18°C)

LEVEL CHECK

♦ SEE FIG. 46

The lubricant level in the drive axle is checked in the same manner as the engine oil, with the engine off and the vehicle parked on a level surface. The dipstick is located at the right rear of the engine, near the starter motor.

If the lubricant level is not at the upper mark on the dipstick additional gear oil is necessary and should be added through the dipstick filler tube. Use the proper weight oil with API classification of GL-5 or GLS. Do not overfill.

DRAIN AND REFILL

♦ SEE FIG. 47–48

1. Raise and support the vehicle safely.

2. Place a container of adequate capacity beneath the drain plug, located on the lower left side of the differential case, near the left axle shaft.

3. Remove the drain plug and allow the fluid to drain.

4. After draining, replace the drain plug and gasket. Tighten the plug to 17–20 ft. lbs. (23–26 Nm). Do not overtighten.

5. Remove the differential dipstick and fill the differential to the upper mark on the dipstick.

Rear Drive Axle 4WD Only

The lubricant should be checked at regular intervals and changed at 60,000 mile (96,500km) intervals. When the vehicle is frequently operated under severe conditions, the lubricant should be changed at 30,000 mile (48,300km) intervals.

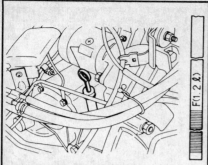

FIG. 46 Front differential dipstick — automatic transmission only

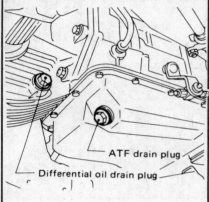

FIG. 47 Front differential drain plug — 3 speed automatic transmission

FIG. 48 Front differential drain plug — 3 speed automatic transmission

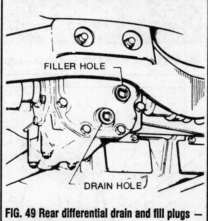

FIG. 49 Rear differential drain and fill plugs — 4WD vehicles except Justy

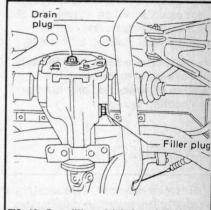

FIG. 49a Rear differential drain and fill plugs — 4WD Justy

FLUID RECOMMENDATIONS

Use gear oil with API classification GL-5 for open differentials and GLS for limited slip differential. Viscosity should be:

- SAE 90 — above 30°F (–1°C)
- SAE 85W — above 30°F (–1°C)
- SAE 80W — below 0°F (–18°C)

LEVEL CHECK

◆ SEE FIG. 49 and 49a

Unlike the procedures outlined above, the lubricant level in the rear differential must be checked from underneath the vehicle.

1. Park the car on a level surface, turn off the engine and engage the parking brake.
2. Crawl under the car from the rear until the differential housing can be reached easily.
3. Remove the filler hole (upper) plug from the back of the differential case.
4. The lubricant should be at the level of the filler hole. If not, add the proper weight gear oil with API classification of GL-5 or GLS.

5. Install the filler plug and tighten to 33 ft. lbs. (44 Nm).

DRAIN AND REFILL

◆ SEE FIG. 49 and 49a

1. Park the car on a level surface, turn off the engine and engage the parking brake.
2. Crawl under the car from the rear until the differential housing can be reached easily.
3. Place a container of adequate capacity beneath the drain plug.
4. Remove the filler hole (upper) plug from the back of the differential case.

5. Remove the drain hole (lower) plug from the back of the differential case and drain all lubricant from the differential.
6. Install the drain hole plug and tighten to 33 ft. lbs. (44 Nm).
7. Fill the differential with the proper grade of lubricant until the level of the lubricant is at the filler hole.
8. Install the filler hole plug and tighten to 33 ft. lbs. (44 Nm).

Cooling System

A complete cooling system check should be performed and the antifreeze replaced at 30,000 mile (48,300km) intervals.

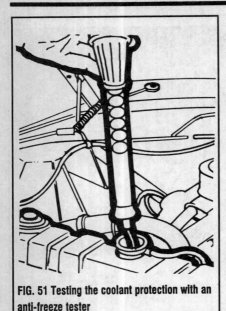

FIG. 51 Testing the coolant protection with an anti-freeze tester

FLUID RECOMMENDATION

A 50/50 mixture of an anti-corrosive ethylene glycol coolant and water is recommended. Since the Subaru crankcase is aluminum, the antifreeze should contain an anti-rust agent.

➡ **Inexpensive antifreeze testers are available to measure the degree of protection provided by the cooling system.**

LEVEL CHECK

The coolant level should be checked at regular intervals or if the temperature gauge registers HOT (H). The coolant level should not fall below the FULL mark on the side of the reserve tank.

DRAIN AND REFILL

◆ SEE FIG. 50, 52–54
1. Pull out the end of the drain tube to the underside of the body from between the undercover and skirt.
2. Place a container of adequate capacity beneath the drain plug and open the plug.
3. Loosen the radiator cap to drain the coolant.
4. Remove and drain the coolant from the reserve tank.
5. On all models except Justy, remove the drain plugs on the side of the engine near the oil filter and drain the coolant from the engine block.

FIG. 51a Engine coolant overflow bottle — Legacy

FIG. 50 Radiator drain plug and tube location.

6. Install and securely tighten the engine drain plugs. Tighten the radiator drain plug.

➡ **Some vehicles are equipped with an air vent plug on the radiator. This plug must be removed while filling the system to allow trapped air to escape the system.**

7. Slowly pour a 50/50 mixture of antifreeze and water into the radiator until it is filled. Install the radiator cap.

8. Fill the coolant recovery tank to the FULL mark.
9. Start the engine and allow it to reach operating temperature.
10. Stop the engine and allow it to cool.
11. Open the radiator cap and fill the radiator with antifreeze. Wait until the engine cools further, then fill the recovery tank to the FULL mark.
12. Start the engine and allow it to reach operating temperature. Check the level in the recovery tank and add antifreeze as necessary.

FLUSHING AND CLEANING THE SYSTEM

◆ SEE FIG. 50, 52–54
The cooling system should be drained, thoroughly flushed and refilled at least every 30,000 miles (48,300km). This operation should be done with the engine cold.
1. Pull out the end of the drain tube to the underside of the body from between the undercover and skirt.
2. Place a container of adequate capacity beneath the drain plug and open the plug.

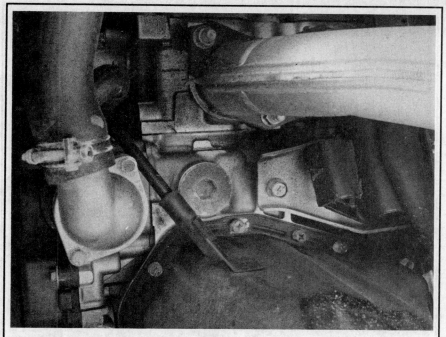

FIG. 52 Engine drain plugs — Legacy and SVX

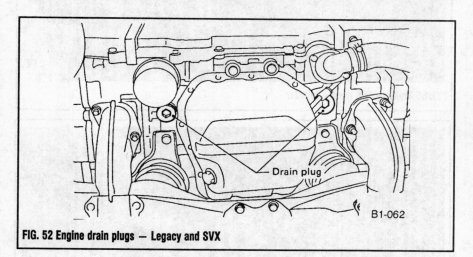

Drain plug

B1-062

FIG. 52 Engine drain plugs — Legacy and SVX

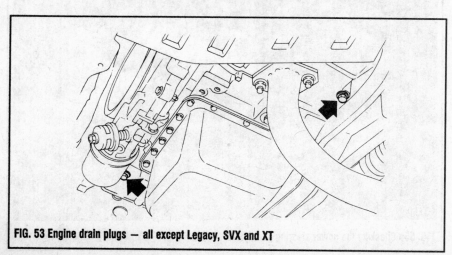

FIG. 53 Engine drain plugs — all except Legacy, SVX and XT

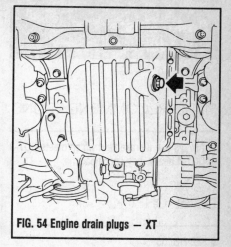

FIG. 54 Engine drain plugs — XT

3. Loosen the radiator cap to drain the coolant.

4. Remove and drain the coolant from the reserve tank.

5. On all models except Justy, remove the drain plugs on the side of the engine near the oil filter and drain the coolant from the engine block.

6. Install and securely tighten the engine drain plugs. Tighten the radiator drain plug.

7. Slowly pour water into the radiator until the system is full. Repeat the draining and filling process several times, until the liquid is nearly colorless.

➡ **Some vehicles are equipped with an air vent plug on the radiator. This plug must be removed while filling the system to allow trapped air to escape the system.**

8. After the last draining, slowly pour a 50/50 mixture of antifreeze and water into the radiator until it is filled. Install the radiator cap.

9. Fill the coolant recovery tank to the FULL mark.

10. Start the engine and allow it to reach operating temperature.

11. Stop the engine and allow it to cool.

12. Open the radiator cap and fill the radiator with antifreeze. Wait until the engine cools further, then fill the recovery tank to the FULL mark.

13. Start the engine and allow it to reach operating temperature. Check the level in the recovery tank and add antifreeze as necessary.

Brake Master Cylinder

FLUID RECOMMENDATIONS

Always use a brake fluid which meets DOT-3 or DOT-4 heavy duty specifications.

LEVEL CHECK

♦ SEE FIG. 55

The brake fluid level should be check at regular intervals. Drain the brake fluid and replace it at 30,000 mile (48,300km) intervals. When the vehicle is frequently used in humid conditions or mountainous areas, change the brake fluid at 15,000 mile (24,000km) intervals.

The brake master cylinder reservoir(s) are made of translucent plastic so that the fluid level may be checked without removing the caps. Check the brake fluid level at regular intervals. If the brake system warning light comes on, stop the car and immediately check the brake fluid level.

If the fluid level in either of the master cylinder reservoir(s) falls below the bottom (MIN) line molded on the side of the reservoir, add brake fluid to bring the level up to the top (MAX) line. Clean the top of the reservoir off before removing the cap to prevent dirt from entering the master cylinder. Pour the fluid slowly to prevent air bubbles from forming. Brake fluid is a good paint remover, so don't spill any on the car's paint.

❊ CAUTION

Do not use a lower grade of brake fluid than specified. Never mix different types of brake fluid. Doing either of the above could cause a brake system failure.

Power Steering Pump

Power steering pump fluid level should be checked at 15,000 mile (24,000km) intervals.

FIG. 55 Brake system master cylinder

FIG. 55a Checking the power steering pump fluid

FLUID RECOMMENDATION

Dexron®II ATF is the recommended fluid for the power steering pump.

LEVEL CHECK

1. Drive the vehicle several miles to raise the power steering system up to normal operating temperature.
2. Park the vehicle on a level surface and stop the engine.
3. Remove the level gauge, wipe it clean, then replace it fully.
4. Remove it again and read the level at the HOT side of the gauge. If the fluid reading is at the lower level or below, add the recommended power steering fluid until it reaches the upper mark.
5. When the fluid level has to be checked without warming up the power steering system, read the level at the COLD side of the gauge and add fluid accordingly.

Steering Gear

FLUID RECOMMENDATION

Subaru recommends only genuine Subaru Valiant Grease M2, Part No. 003608001.

LEVEL CHECK

The steering box does not require greasing unless it has been disassembled.

Windshield Washer

FLUID RECOMMENDATION

Use a commercial solvent and water solution, one part solvent to two parts water for summer. Use the solvent undiluted in winter.

FIG. 55b Windshield washer reservoir

LEVEL CHECK

Check the level of the windshield washer solution in the translucent reservoir tank at the same time the oil is being checked.

Chassis Greasing

Under normal conditions regular chassis greasing is unnecessary, because there are no chassis grease fittings used on Subaru models. The only time greasing is required is as part of chassis component repair or replacement, or if component dust boots and seals have become damaged. If its boot or seal is damaged or leaking, the component will have to be removed, repacked with grease, and a new boot or seal installed.

Because there are no recommended chassis greasing intervals, the chassis suspension and drive train components should be inspected regularly. If a visual inspection turns up a damaged component, dust boot, or seal, consult the appropriate Section for the correct repair or replacement procedure.

Pedals and Linkage

The clutch, brake, and accelerator linkages should be lubricated at the recommended intervals found in the owners manual, with multipurpose chassis grease.

1. Working inside the car, apply a small amount of grease to the pedal pivots and linkage.

2. Working under the hood, grease all pivoting and sliding parts of the accelerator and brake linkages.

Body Lubrication

♦ SEE FIG. 56

Body lubrication should be performed at regularly scheduled intervals.

Apply multipurpose chassis grease to the following areas:
- Hood hinges, lock, and striker
- Door hinges, latch, and striker
- Trunk hinges and striker

➡ **Use grease sparingly on the door and trunk strikers, as they may come into contact with clothing.**

Use powdered graphite to lubricate the following items:
- Door key lock cylinders
- Trunk key lock cylinders

➡ **Do not use oil or grease to lubricate the insides of lock cylinders.**

Use silicone lubricant to preserve the rubber weather stripping around the doors and trunk.

Wheel Bearings

REMOVAL, PACKING AND INSTALLATION

Rear Wheel Bearing

Refer to Section 7 for front wheel bearing and 4-Wheel Drive wheel bearing service.

DRUM BRAKES

♦ SEE FIG. 57 AND 58

1. Raise and support the vehicle safely.
2. Remove the rear wheels and tires.
3. Pry the brake drum cap off using a suitable tool.
4. Flatten the lock washer and loosen the axle nut, then remove the lock washer, lock plate and brake drum. Remove the brake drum taking care not to drop the outer bearing.

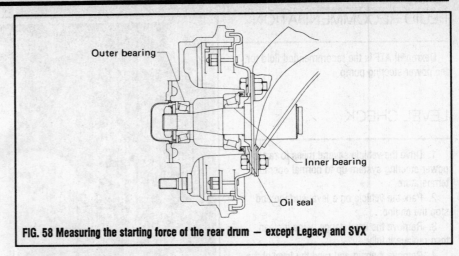

FIG. 58 Measuring the starting force of the rear drum — except Legacy and SVX

Outer bearing

Inner bearing

Oil seal

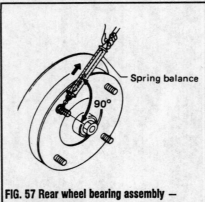

FIG. 57 Rear wheel bearing assembly — except Legacy and SVX

Spring balance

90°

5. Check the condition of the bearing grease. If either the grease appears to be white or if only a small amount of grease remains, remove the bearing from the housing, clean it and pack it with fresh grease.

6. To remove the inner bearing, remove the grease seal using a seal puller or equivalent.

7. Clean the bearings with solvent and let air dry on a shop rag.

➡ **Do not use compressed air to dry the bearings as damage will result.**

8. Place a ball of grease in the palm of your hand and roll the bearing through the grease. Force the grease through the bearing cage into the rollers. Continue to roll the bearing, adding grease to your hand, until the bearing is completely filled with grease.

9. Install the rear bearing and using a soft faced hammer, install the grease seal. Ensure that the seal is fully seated.

10. Install the drum, outer bearing, lock plate, lock washer and axle nut in this order on to the spindle. Always use a new lockplate and lock washer.

11. Tighten the locknut to 36 ft. lbs. (49 Nm) and rotate the drum in both directions to seat the bearings..

12. Loosen the locknut 1/8 turn. Tighten the locknut to obtain a starting force of 2–3 lbs. (8–14 N) on all models except Justy; 3–4 lbs. (14–20 N) on Justy. Ensure that there is no free-play in the bearing.

13. Install the brake drum cap, wheel and tire. Tighten lug nuts to 58–72 ft. lbs. (78–98 Nm).

14. Lower the vehicle and test drive.

DISC BRAKES

1. Raise and support the vehicle safely.
2. While holding the rear wheel by hand, try to move it in and out (toward you and away from you) to check bearing free-play.
3. Remove the rear wheel and tire.
4. If bearing free-play exists, attach a dial gauge to the hub and measure the axial free-play.
5. If free-play is greater than 0.0020 in. (0.05mm), disassemble the rear hub and check the bearings.
6. Pry the rotor cap off with a suitable tool.
7. Unlock the axle nut and remove the nut and washer.
8. Remove the rear disc brake assembly from the backing plate and suspend it out of the way using a wire.
9. Remove the disc rotor from the hub, then remove the hub.
10. Inspect the hub bearings for damage and replace the hub assembly as necessary.
11. Install the hub and using a new washer and locknut, tighten to 123–152 ft. lbs. (167–206 Nm). and lock into place. Install the rotor cap.
12. Install the disc rotor and rear disc brake assembly.
13. Install the rear wheel and tire. Tighten the lug nuts to 58–72 ft. lbs. (78–98 Nm).
14. Lower the vehicle and test drive.

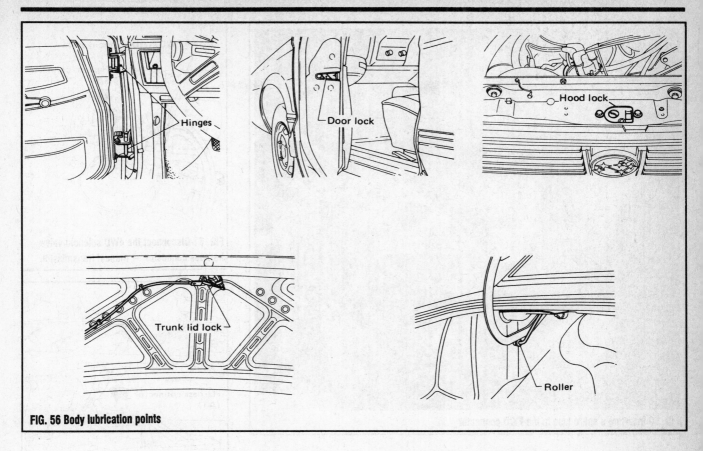

FIG. 56 Body lubrication points

TRAILER TOWING

Subaru's are not recommended as trailer towing vehicles. Factory trailer towing packages are not available, and aftermarket towing hitches should not be installed on your Subaru.

TOWING

2-Door, 3-Door 4-Door, Wagon and XT

▶ SEE FIG. 59 and 60

If the following conditions cannot be met, transport the vehicle using a flat-bed truck.

1. On manual transmission equipped vehicles, turn the differential lock switch to the OFF position and make sure that the differential lock indicator light is not illuminated.

2. If the engine cannot be started to switch the differential lock switch, raise the front wheels

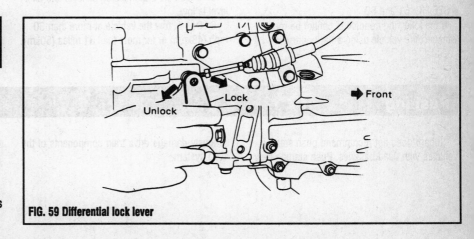

FIG. 59 Differential lock lever

FIG. 60 Inserting a spare fuse in the FWD connector

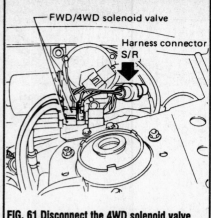

FIG. 61 Disconnect the 4WD solenoid valve harness connector — manual transmission

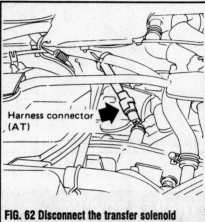

FIG. 62 Disconnect the transfer solenoid harness connector — automatic transmission

and move the lock lever on the right side of the transmission towards the rear.

3. On automatic transmission equipped vehicles, set the car in front wheel drive mode by inserting a spare fuse in the FWD connector inside the engine compartment.

4. Place the vehicle in neutral.

5. Check the transmission oil level and oil if level is low.

6. Do not tow the vehicle at more than 30 mph (48kp/h) or for more than 31 miles (50km).

Loyale

▶ SEE FIG. 61 and 62

If the following conditions cannot be met, transport the vehicle using a flat-bed truck.

1. On manual transmission and 3-speed automatic transmission equipped vehicles, turn the differential lock switch to the OFF position and make sure that the differential lock indicator light is not illuminated.

2. On 4-speed automatic transmission equipped vehicles, set the car in front wheel drive mode by inserting a spare fuse in the FWD connector inside the engine compartment.

3. Disconnect the harness connector for the 4WD solenoid valve (manual transmission) or the transfer solenoid (automatic transmission) inside the engine compartment.

4. Place the vehicle in neutral.

5. Check the transmission oil level and oil if level is low.

6. Do not tow the vehicle at more than 30 mph (48kp/h) or for more than 31 miles (50km).

Legacy and SVX

Do not tow these vehicles with either the front or rear wheels on the ground. Damage to the viscous coupling may result. Transport the vehicle using a flat-bed truck.

Pushing

Subaru does not recommend push starting vehicles with dead batteries. Push starting may seriously damage drive train components of the 4WD system

JACKING

Scissors Type Jack

◆ SEE FIG. 63 and 64

All Subaru models come with a scissors type jack for tire changing. The jack on all models is stored in the engine compartment, rather than in the trunk.

Jacking points are located on both sides of the car, just behind the front wheel well and just forward of the rear wheel well. Do not place the jack underneath the floor pan sheet metal or bumpers.

There are certain safety precautions which should be observed when jacking the vehicle:

1. Always jack the car on a level surface.
2. Set the parking brake if the rear wheels are to be raised (parking brake works on the front wheels). This will keep the car from rolling off the jack.
3. If the front wheels are to be raised, block the rear wheels.
4. Block the wheel diagonally opposite the one which is being raised.
5. If the car is being raised in order to work underneath it, support it with jackstands. Do not place the jackstands against the sheet metal panels beneath the car. The panels will become distorted.

✸ CAUTION

Do not work beneath a vehicle supported only by a tire changing jack.

6. Do not use a bumper jack to raise the vehicle. The bumpers are not designed for this purpose.

Floor Jack

◆ SEE FIG. 66 and 67

When jacking up the front of the car using a floor jack always use the front crossmember as the contact point, never a suspension or steering part and never the engine oil pan. Always block the rear of the back wheels, and always use a block of wood between the saddle of the jack and the crossmember.

When jacking up the rear of the car using a floor jack, place blocks in front of the front wheels and always place the jack in contact with

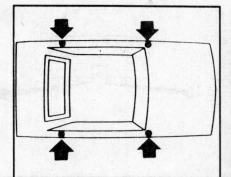

FIG. 63 Jacking points for scissors type jack

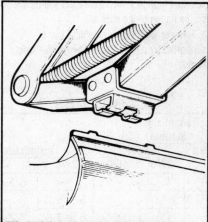

FIG. 64 Scissors type jack locating tabs

FIG. 66 Lifting the vehicle with a floor jack — front

FIG. 66a Supporting the vehicle safely with jackstands

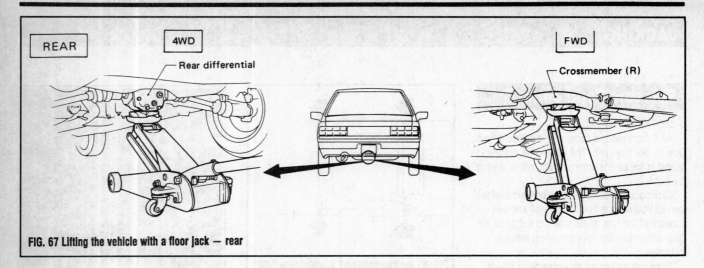

FIG. 67 Lifting the vehicle with a floor jack — rear

the center of the rear crossmember. On four wheel drive models contact the bottom of the rear differential carrier.

Always jack slowly until the car is high enough to place the safety stands in their proper positions. The safety stands should be placed in the same location points as shown for the scissors type jack. Make sure the stands are set on the flange of the side sill.

• Never work under a vehicle that is supported by a jack alone. Always use safety stands.

• Never use cinder blocks or stacks of wood, even if you are only going to be under the vehicle for a few minutes.

• Drive-on trestles or ramps are also handy and a safe way to both raise and support the vehicle.

CAPACITIES

Year	Model	Engine Crankcase	Transmission Manual 4-Speed	Transmission Manual 5-Speed 2WD	Transmission Manual 5-Speed 4WD	Automatic 2WD	Automatic 4WD	Rear Drive Axle	Front Drive Axle	Gasoline Tank (gals.)	Cooling System
1985	Brat	4.2	3.0	—	—	—	6.3–6.8	1.7	1.3	14.5	5.8
	2 Door	4.2⑭	2.6⑯	2.6	—	5.9–6.3	—	1.7	1.3	13.2⑮	5.8⑰
	4 Door	4.2	2.7	2.7	3.5①	6.3–6.8	7.2–7.6	.8	1.3	15.9	5.8
	Wagon	4.2	—	2.7	3.5	6.3–6.8	7.2–7.6①	.8	1.3	15.9	5.8
	XT	4.2	—	2.7	3.5	6.3–6.8	7.2–7.6	.8	1.3	15.9	6.1
1986	Brat	4.2	3.0	—	—	—	—	1.7	1.3	14.5	5.8
	2 Door	4.2⑭	2.6	2.6	3.0	5.9–6.3	—	1.7	1.3	13.2⑮	5.8⑰
	4 Door	4.2	—	2.7②	3.5	6.3–6.8	7.2–7.6	.8	1.3	15.9	5.8
	Wagon	4.2	—	2.7②	3.5	6.3–6.8	7.2–7.6	.8	1.3	15.9	5.8
	3 Door	4.2	—	2.7	3.5	6.3–6.8	7.2–7.6	.8	1.3	15.9	5.8
	XT	4.2	—	2.7	3.5	6.3–6.8	7.2–7.6	.8	1.3	15.9	6.1
1987	Brat	4.2	3.0	—	—	—	—	1.7	1.3	14.5	5.8
	2 Door	4.2⑭	2.7⑯	2.7	—	5.9–6.3	—	1.7	1.3	13.2⑮	5.8⑰
	4 Door	4.2	—	2.7②	3.5	6.3–6.8	7.2–7.6	.8	1.3	15.9	5.8④
	Wagon	4.2	—	2.7②	3.5	6.3–6.8	7.2–7.6	.8	1.3	15.9	5.8④
	3 Door	4.2	—	2.7②	3.5③	6.3–6.8	7.2–7.6	.8	1.3	15.9	5.8
	XT	4.2	—	2.6②	3.5③	9.0	9.0	.8	1.5	15.9	5.8
	Justy	3.0	—	2.1	—	—	—	—	—	9.2	4.5
1988	Brat	4.2	3.0	—	—	—	—	1.7	1.3	14.5	5.8
	2 Door	4.2⑭	2.7⑯	2.7	—	5.9–6.3	—	1.7	1.3	13.2⑮	5.8⑰
	4 Door	4.2	—	2.7	3.5③	6.5–6.7	6.8–7.0⑤	1.7	2.5	15.9	5.8④
	Wagon	4.2	—	2.7	3.5	6.5–6.7	6.8–7.0⑤	1.7	2.5	15.9	5.8④
	3 Door	4.2	—	2.7	3.5③	6.5–6.7	6.8–7.0	1.7	2.5	15.9	5.8

CAPACITIES

Year	Model	Engine Crankcase	Transmission Manual 4-Speed	5-Speed 2WD	4WD	Automatic 2WD	4WD	Rear Drive Axle	Front Drive Axle	Gasoline Tank (gals.)	Cooling System
1988	XT	4.2	—	2.7	3.5	9.8	—	.8	1.5	15.9	5.8
	XT-6	5.3	—	—	—	9.8	10.0	.8	1.5	15.9	7.4
	Justy	3.0	—	2.4	3.5	—	—	.8	—	9.2	4.5
1989	Brat	4.2	3.0	—	—	—	—	1.7	1.3	14.5	5.8
	2 Door	4.2⑭	2.7⑯	2.7	—	5.9–6.3	—	1.7	1.3	13.2⑮	5.8⑰
	4 Door	4.2	—	2.7	3.5③	6.5–6.7	6.8–7.0⑤	.8	1.3⑥	15.9	5.8④
	Wagon	4.2	—	2.7	3.5③	6.5–6.7	6.8–7.0⑤	.8	1.3⑥	15.9	5.8④
	XT	4.2	—	2.7	3.5	9.8	—	.8	1.5	15.9	5.8
	XT-6	5.3	—	—	3.7	9.8	10.0	.8	1.5	15.9	7.4
	Justy	3.0	—	2.4	3.5	3.3–3.6	—	.8	—	9.2	4.9⑦
1990	XT	4.2	—	2.7	3.5	9.8	10.0	.8	1.5	15.9	5.8
	XT-6	5.3	—	—	3.7	9.8	10.0	.8	1.5	15.9	7.4
	Loyale 4 Door	4.2	—	2.7	3.5	6.5–6.7	6.9–7.1⑤	.8	1.3⑧	15.9	5.8⑨
	Loyale Wagon	4.2	—	2.7	3.5	6.5–6.7	6.9–7.1⑤	.8	1.3⑧	15.9	5.8⑨
	Loyale 3 Door	4.2	—	2.7	2.7⑩	6.5–6.7	6.5–6.7⑤⑪	.8	1.3⑧	15.9	5.8⑨
	Legacy 4 Door	4.2	—	2.7	3.5	6.5–6.7	6.9–7.1⑤	.8	1.3⑧	15.9	5.8⑨
	Legacy Wagon	4.2	—	2.7	3.5	6.5–6.7	6.9–7.1⑤	.8	1.3⑧	15.9	5.8⑨
	Justy	3.0	—	2.5	3.6	3.5	4.4	.8	—	9.2	4.9⑨
1991	XT	4.2	—	2.7	3.5	9.8	10.0	.8	1.5	15.9	5.8
	XT-6	5.3	—	—	3.7	9.8	10.0	.8	1.5	15.9	7.4
	Loyale 4 Door	4.2	—	2.7	3.5	6.5–6.7	6.9–7.1⑤	.8	1.3⑧	15.9	5.8⑨
	Loyale Wagon	4.2	—	2.7	3.5	6.5–6.7	6.9–7.1⑤	.8	1.3⑧	15.9	5.8⑨
	Legacy 4 Door	4.8	—	3.5	3.7	8.8	8.8⑫	.8	1.5	15.9	6.2⑬
	Legacy Wagon	4.8	—	3.5	3.7	8.8	8.8⑫	.8	1.5	15.9	6.2⑬
	Justy	3.0	—	2.5	3.6	3.5	4.4	.8	—	9.2	4.9⑦
1992	Loyale 4 Door	4.2	—	2.7	3.5	6.0	6.4	.8	1.3	15.9	5.8
	Loyale Wagon	4.2	—	2.7	3.5	6.0	6.4	.8	1.3	15.9	5.8
	Legacy 4 Door	4.8	—	3.5	3.7	8.8	8.8⑫	.8	1.3	15.9	6.2⑬
	Legacy Wagon	4.8	—	3.5	3.7	8.8	8.8⑫	.8	1.3	15.9	6.2⑬
	Justy	3.0	—	2.5	3.6	3.5	4.4	.8	—	9.2	4.9⑦
	SVX	6.3	—	—	—	10.0	10.0	.8	1.3	18.2	7.4

① Turbo
② 3.5 w/Turbo
③ 3.7 w/Turbo
④ 6.3 GL10 Turbo
⑤ 10.0 w/Turbo
⑥ 3.0 GL10 Turbo
   2.5 w/4WD
⑦ 5.2 W/EVCT
⑧ 1.5 w/Turbo
⑨ 6.3 w/Turbo
⑩ 3.5 w/RS
⑪ 6.9–7.1 w/RS
⑫ 9.4 w/Turbo
⑬ 7.4 w/Turbo
⑭ 3.7 w/1.6L engine
⑮ 11.9 w/4WD
⑯ 3.0 w/4WD
⑰ 5.6 w/1.6L

SCHEDULE OF INSPECTION AND MAINTENANCE SERVICES

Continue periodic maintenance beyond 96,000 km (60,000 miles) or 60 months by returning to the first column of the maintenance schedule and adding 96,000 km (60,000 miles) or 60 months to the column headings.

Symbols used:
R: Replace
I: Inspect, and then adjust, correct or replace if necessary.
P: Perform
  (I) or (P): Recommended service for safe vehicle operation
 *: This maintenance operation is required for all states except California.
  However, we do recommend that this operation be performed on California vehicles as well.

MAINTENANCE ITEM	MAINTENANCE INTERVAL (Number of months or km (miles), whichever occurs first)									REMARKS
	Months	3	7.5	15	22.5	30	37.5	45	52.5	60	
	x1,000 km	4.8	12	24	36	48	60	72	84	96	
	x1,000 miles	3	7.5	15	22.5	30	37.5	45	52.5	60	
1	Drive belt(s) [Except camshaft] (Inspect drive belt tension)					I				R	
2	Timing belt (Camshaft drive belt)					I*				R	
3	Engine oil	R	R	R	R	R	R	R	R	R	See NOTE 1)
4	Engine oil filter	R	R	R	R	R	R	R	R	R	
5	Replace engine coolant and inspect cooling system, hoses and connections					P				P	
6	Replace fuel filter and inspect fuel system hoses and connections					(P)				P	See NOTE 2), 6) & 7)
7	Air filter elements					R				R	
8	Spark plug									R	
9	Differential (Front & Rear) Lubricants (Gear oil)					I					See NOTE 3)
10	Automatic transmission fluid					I					See NOTE 4)
11	Brake fluid					R				R	See NOTE 5)
12	Disc brake pad and disc, Front and rear axle boots and axle shaft joints		I			I		I		I	See NOTE 6)
13	Brake linings and drums (Parking brake)					I				I	See NOTE 6)
14	Inspect brake line and check operation of parking and service brake system		P			P		P		P	See NOTE 6)
15	Steering and suspension		I			I		I		I	See NOTE 6)
16	Front and rear wheel bearing lubricant									(I)	
17	Supplemental restraint system	Inspect every 10 years.									

1) When the vehicle is used under severe driving conditions such as those mentioned below** the engine oil should be changed more often.

2) When the vehicle is used in extremely cold or hot weather areas, contamination of the filter may occur and filter replacement should be performed more often.

3) When the vehicle is frequently operated under severe conditions, replacement should be performed every 48,000 km (30,000 miles).

4) When the vehicle is frequently operated under severe conditions, replacement should be performed every 24,000 km (15,000 miles).

5) When the vehicle is used in high humidity areas or in mountainous areas, change the brake fluid every 24,000 km (15,000 miles) or 15 months, whichever occurs first.

6) When the vehicle is used under severe driving conditions such as those mentioned below** inspection should be performed every 12,000 km (7,500 miles) or 7.5 months, whichever occurs first.

Continue periodic maintenance beyond 96,000 km (60,000 miles) or 60 months by returning to the first column of the maintenance schedule and adding 96,000 km (60,000 miles) or 60 months to the column headings.

Symbols used:
R: Replace
I: Inspect, and then adjust, correct or replace if neces sary.
P: Perform
  (I) or (P): Recommended service for safe vehicle operation
*: This maintenance operation is required for all states except California. However, we do recommend that this operation be performed on California vehicles as well.

	MAINTENANCE ITEM	MAINTENANCE INTERVAL (Number of months or km (miles), whichever occurs first)									REMARKS
		Months	3	7.5	15	22.5	30	37.5	45	52.5	60	
		x1,000 km	4.8	12	24	36	48	60	72	84	96	
		x1,000 miles	3	7.5	15	22.5	30	37.5	45	52.5	60	
1	Drive belt(s) [Except camshaft] (Inspect drive belt tension)						I				R	
2	Camshaft drive belt						I*				R	
3	Engine oil		R	R	R	R	R	R	R	R	R	See NOTE 1)
4	Engine oil filter		R	R	R	R	R	R	R	R	R	
5	Replace engine coolant and inspect cooling system, hoses and connections						P				P	
6	Replace fuel filter and inspect fuel system hoses and connections						(P)				P	See NOTE 2), 6) & 7)
7	Air filter elements						R				R	
8	Spark plug						R				R	
9	Transmission/Differential (Front & Rear) Lubricants (Gear oil)						I					See NOTE 3)
10	Automatic transmission fluid						I					See NOTE 4)
11	Brake fluid						R				R	See NOTE 5)
12	Disc brake pad and disc, Front and rear axle boots and axle shaft joints				I		I		I		I	See NOTE 6)
13	Brake linings and drums (Parking brake)						I				I	See NOTE 6)
14	Inspect brake line and check operation of parking and service brake system				P		P		P		P	See NOTE 6)
15	Clutch and hill-holder system				I		I		I		I	
16	Steering and suspension				I		I		I		I	See NOTE 6)
17	Front and rear wheel bearing lubricant										(I)	

1) When the vehicle is used under severe driving conditions such as those mentioned below**, the engine oil should be changed more often.

2) When the vehicle is used in extremely cold or hot weather areas, contamination of the filter may occur and filter replacement should be performed more often.

3) When the vehicle is frequently operated under severe conditions, replacement should be performed every 48,000 km (30,000 miles).

4) When the vehicle is frequently operated under severe conditions, replacement should be performed every 24,000 km (15,000 miles).

5) When the vehicle is used in high humidity areas or in mountainous areas, change the brake fluid every 24,000 km (15,000 miles) or 15 months, whichever occurs first.

6) When the vehicle is used under severe driving conditions such as those mentioned below*, inspection should be performed every 12,000 km (7,500 miles) or 7.5 months, whichever occurs first.

7) This inspection is not required to maintain emission warranty eligibility and it does not affect the manufacturer's obligations under EPA's in-use compliance program. ** Examples of severe driving conditions:

  (1) Repeated short distance driving. (item 3, 12 and 13 only)
  (2) Driving on rough and/or muddy roads. (Item 12, 13 and 16 only)
  (3) Driving in dusty conditions.
  (4) Driving in extremely cold weather. (Item 3 and 16 only)
  (5) Driving in areas where roads salts or other corrosive materials are used. (Item 6, 12, 13, 14 and 16 only)
  (6) Living in coastal areas. (Item 6, 12, 13, 14 and 16 only)

Troubleshooting Basic Air Conditioning Problems

Problem	Cause	Solution
There's little or no air coming from the vents (and you're sure it's on)	• The A/C fuse is blown • Broken or loose wires or connections • The on/off switch is defective	• Check and/or replace fuse • Check and/or repair connections • Replace switch
The air coming from the vents is not cool enough	• Windows and air vent wings open • The compressor belt is slipping • Heater is on • Condenser is clogged with debris • Refrigerant has escaped through a leak in the system • Receiver/drier is plugged	• Close windows and vent wings • Tighten or replace compressor belt • Shut heater off • Clean the condenser • Check system • Service system
The air has an odor	• Vacuum system is disrupted • Odor producing substances on the evaporator case • Condensation has collected in the bottom of the evaporator housing	• Have the system checked/repaired • Clean the evaporator case • Clean the evaporator housing drains
System is noisy or vibrating	• Compressor belt or mountings loose • Air in the system	• Tighten or replace belt; tighten mounting bolts • Have the system serviced

Sight glass condition
  Constant bubbles, foam or oil streaks
  Clear sight glass, but no cold air
  Clear sight glass, but air is cold
  Clouded with milky fluid
	• Undercharged system
	• No refrigerant at all
	• System is OK
	• Receiver drier is leaking dessicant
		• Charge the system
		• Check and charge the system
		• Have system checked

Large difference in temperature of lines	• System undercharged	• Charge and leak test the system
Compressor noise	• Broken valves • Overcharged • Incorrect oil level • Piston slap • Broken rings • Drive belt pulley bolts are loose	• Replace the valve plate • Discharge, evacuate and install the correct charge • Isolate the compressor and check the oil level. Correct as necessary. • Replace the compressor • Replace the compressor • Tighten with the correct torque specification

Troubleshooting Basic Air Conditioning Problems (cont.)

Problem	Cause	Solution
Excessive vibration	• Incorrect belt tension • Clutch loose • Overcharged • Pulley is misaligned	• Adjust the belt tension • Tighten the clutch • Discharge, evacuate and install the correct charge • Align the pulley
Condensation dripping in the passenger compartment	• Drain hose plugged or improperly positioned • Insulation removed or improperly installed	• Clean the drain hose and check for proper installation • Replace the insulation on the expansion valve and hoses
Frozen evaporator coil	• Faulty thermostat • Thermostat capillary tube improperly installed • Thermostat not adjusted properly	• Replace the thermostat • Install the capillary tube correctly • Adjust the thermostat
Low side low—high side low	• System refrigerant is low • Expansion valve is restricted	• Evacuate, leak test and charge the system • Replace the expansion valve
Low side high—high side low	• Internal leak in the compressor—worn	• Remove the compressor cylinder head and inspect the compressor. Replace the valve plate assembly if necessary. If the compressor pistons, rings or
Low side high—high side low (cont.)		cylinders are excessively worn or scored replace the compressor
	• Cylinder head gasket is leaking • Expansion valve is defective • Drive belt slipping	• Install a replacement cylinder head gasket • Replace the expansion valve • Adjust the belt tension
Low side high—high side high	• Condenser fins obstructed • Air in the system • Expansion valve is defective • Loose or worn fan belts	• Clean the condenser fins • Evacuate, leak test and charge the system • Replace the expansion valve • Adjust or replace the belts as necessary
Low side low—high side high	• Expansion valve is defective • Restriction in the refrigerant hose	• Replace the expansion valve • Check the hose for kinks—replace if necessary
Low side low—high side high	• Restriction in the receiver/drier • Restriction in the condenser	• Replace the receiver/drier • Replace the condenser
Low side and high normal (inadequate cooling)	• Air in the system • Moisture in the system	• Evacuate, leak test and charge the system • Evacuate, leak test and charge the system

Troubleshooting Basic Wheel Problems

Problem	Cause	Solution
The car's front end vibrates at high speed	• The wheels are out of balance • Wheels are out of alignment	• Have wheels balanced • Have wheel alignment checked/adjusted
Car pulls to either side	• Wheels are out of alignment • Unequal tire pressure • Different size tires or wheels	• Have wheel alignment checked/adjusted • Check/adjust tire pressure • Change tires or wheels to same size
The car's wheel(s) wobbles	• Loose wheel lug nuts • Wheels out of balance • Damaged wheel • Wheels are out of alignment • Worn or damaged ball joint • Excessive play in the steering linkage (usually due to worn parts) • Defective shock absorber	• Tighten wheel lug nuts • Have tires balanced • Raise car and spin the wheel. If the wheel is bent, it should be replaced • Have wheel alignment checked/adjusted • Check ball joints • Check steering linkage • Check shock absorbers
Tires wear unevenly or prematurely	• Incorrect wheel size • Wheels are out of balance • Wheels are out of alignment	• Check if wheel and tire size are compatible • Have wheels balanced • Have wheel alignment checked/adjusted

Troubleshooting Basic Tire Problems

Problem	Cause	Solution
The car's front end vibrates at high speeds and the steering wheel shakes	• Wheels out of balance • Front end needs aligning	• Have wheels balanced • Have front end alignment checked
The car pulls to one side while cruising	• Unequal tire pressure (car will usually pull to the low side) • Mismatched tires • Front end needs aligning	• Check/adjust tire pressure • Be sure tires are of the same type and size • Have front end alignment checked
Abnormal, excessive or uneven tire wear See "How to Read Tire Wear"	• Infrequent tire rotation • Improper tire pressure • Sudden stops/starts or high speed on curves	• Rotate tires more frequently to equalize wear • Check/adjust pressure • Correct driving habits
Tire squeals	• Improper tire pressure • Front end needs aligning	• Check/adjust tire pressure • Have front end alignment checked

2

ENGINE PERFORMANCE AND TUNE-UP

GASOLINE ENGINE TUNE-UP SPECIFICATIONS

Year	Model	Engine ID/VIN	Engine Displacement Liters (cc)	Spark Plugs Gap (in.)	Ignition Timing (deg.) MT	Ignition Timing (deg.) AT	Fuel Pump (psi)	Idle Speed (rpm) MT	Idle Speed (rpm) AT	Valve Clearance In.	Valve Clearance Ex.
1985	Brat	5	1.8 (1781)	0.039–0.043	8B	8B	2.6–3.3	800	800	.009–.011	.013–.015
	2DR	2	1.6 (1595)	0.039–0.043	8B	—	1.4–2.1	650	—	.009–.011	.013–.015
	2DR GL	4②	1.8 (1781)	0.039–0.043	8B	8B	2.6–3.3	700	800	.009–.011	.013–.015
	4DR DL④	4②	1.8 (1781)	0.039–0.043	6B	—	2.6–3.3	650	—	Hyd.	Hyd.
	4DR/Wagon	4②	1.8 (1781)	0.039–0.043	8B	8B	2.6–3.3	700	700	Hyd.	Hyd.
	4DR/Wagon GL-10	4②	1.8 (1781)	0.039–0.043	6B	6B	61–71	700	800	Hyd.	Hyd.
	4DR/Wagon Turbo	4②	1.8 (1781)	0.039–0.043	25B	25B	61–71	700	800	Hyd.	Hyd.
	XT	4②	1.8 (1781)	0.039–0.043	6B	6B	61–71	700	800	Hyd.	Hyd.
	XT Turbo	4②	1.8 (1781)	0.039–0.043	25B	25B	61–71	700	800	Hyd.	Hyd.
1986	Brat	5	1.8 (1781)	0.039–0.043	8B	—	2.6–3.3	700	—	.009–.011	.013–.015
	2DR	2	1.6 (1595)	0.039–0.043	8B	—	1.4–2.1	650	—	.009–.011	.013–.015
	2DR GL	2	1.6 (1595)	0.039–0.043	8B	—	1.4–2.1	700	—	.009–.011	.013–.015
	2DR GL	4②	1.8 (1781)	0.039–0.043	8B	8B	2.6–3.3	700	800	.009–.011	.013–.015
	3DR/4DR/Wagon	4②	1.8 (1781)	0.039–0.043	8B	8B	2.6–3.3	700	800	Hyd.	Hyd.
	3DR/4DR/Wagon⑤	4②	1.8 (1781)	0.039–0.043	—	20B	28–43	—	700	Hyd.	Hyd.
	4DR/Wagon Turbo	4②	1.8 (1781)	0.039–0.043	25B	25B	61–71	700	800	Hyd.	Hyd.
	XT	4②	1.8 (1781)	0.039–0.043	6B	6B	61–71	700	800	Hyd.	Hyd.
	XT Turbo	4②	1.8 (1781)	0.039–0.043	25B	25B	61–71	700	800	Hyd.	Hyd.
1987	Brat	5	1.8 (1781)	0.039–0.043	8B	—	2.6–3.3	700	—	.009–.011	.013–.015
	2DR	2	1.6 (1595)	0.039–0.043	8B	—	1.4–2.1	650	—	.009–.011	.013–.015
	2DR GL	2	1.6 (1595)	0.039–0.043	8B	—	1.4–2.1	700	—	.009–.011	.013–.015
	2DR GL	4②	1.8 (1781)	0.039–0.043	8B	8B	2.6–3.3	700	800	.009–.011	.013–.015
	3DR/4DR/Wagon	4②	1.8 (1781)	0.039–0.043	8B	8B	2.6–3.3	700	800	Hyd.	Hyd.
	3DR/4DR/Wagon⑤	4②	1.8 (1781)	0.039–0.043	20B	20B	28–43	700	700	Hyd.	Hyd.
	3DR/4DR Wagon Turbo	4②	1.8 (1781)	0.039–0.043	20B	20B	61–71	700	800	Hyd.	Hyd.
	XT	4②	1.8 (1781)	0.039–0.043	20B	20B	61–71	700	800	Hyd.	Hyd.
	XT Turbo	4②	1.8 (1781)	0.039–0.043	20B	20B	61–71	700	800	Hyd.	Hyd.
	Justy	7⑧	1.2 (1189)	0.039–0.043	5B	—	1.3–2.0	800	—	.006	.010
1988	2DR GL	4②	1.8 (1781)	0.039–0.043	8B	8B	2.6–3.3	700	800	.009–.011	.013–.015
	3DR/4DR/Wagon⑤	4②	1.8 (1781)	0.039–0.043	20B	20B	28–43	700	700	Hyd.	Hyd.
	3DR/4DR Wagon Turbo	4②	1.8 (1781)	0.039–0.043	20B	20B	61–71	700	800	Hyd.	Hyd.
	XT	4②	1.8 (1781)	0.039–0.043	20B	20B	61–71	700	800	Hyd.	Hyd.
	XT-6	4②	2.7 (2672)	0.039–0.043	20B	20B	61–71	700	800	Hyd.	Hyd.
	Justy	7⑧	1.2 (1189)	0.039–0.043	5B	—	1.3–2.0	800	—	.006	.010
1989	2DR GL	4②	1.8 (1781)	0.039–0.043	8B	8B	2.6–3.3	700	800	.009–.011	.013–.015
	3DR/4DR/Wagon⑤	4②	1.8 (1781)	0.039–0.043	20B	20B	28–43	700	700	Hyd.	Hyd.
	3DR/4DR Wagon Turbo	4②	1.8 (1781)	0.039–0.043	20B	20B	61–71	700	800	Hyd.	Hyd.
	XT	4②	1.8 (1781)	0.039–0.043	20B	20B	61–71	700	800	Hyd.	Hyd.
	XT-6	4②	2.7 (2672)	0.039–0.043	20B	20B	61–71	750	750	Hyd.	Hyd.
	Justy	7⑧	1.2 (1189)	0.039–0.043	5B	5B	1.3–2.0	800	800	.006	.010
1990	XT	4②	1.8 (1781)	0.039–0.043	20B	20B	61–71	700	800	Hyd.	Hyd.
	XT-6	4②	2.7 (2672)	0.039–0.043	20B	20B	61–71	750	750	Hyd.	Hyd.
	Justy	7⑧	1.2 (1189)	0.039–0.043	5B	5B	1.3–2.0	800	800	.006	.010

GASOLINE ENGINE TUNE-UP SPECIFICATIONS

Year	Model	Engine ID/VIN	Engine Displacement Liters (cc)	Spark Plugs Gap (in.)	Ignition Timing (deg.) MT	AT	Fuel Pump (psi)	Idle Speed (rpm) MT	AT	Valve Clearance In.	Ex.
1990	Justy GL	7⑧	1.2 (1189)	0.039–0.043	5B	5B	43	700	700	.006	.010
	Loyale	4②	1.8 (1781)	0.039–0.043	20B	20B	28–43	700	700	Hyd.	Hyd.
	Loyale Turbo	4②	1.8 (1781)	0.039–0.043	20B	20B	61–71	700	800	Hyd.	Hyd.
	Legacy	6	2.2 (2212)	0.039–0.043	20B	20B	36	700	700	Hyd.	Hyd.
1991	XT	4②	1.8 (1781)	0.039–0.043	20B	20B	61–71	700	800	Hyd.	Hyd.
	XT-6	4②	2.7 (2672)	0.039–0.043	20B	20B	61–71	750	750	Hyd.	Hyd.
	Justy	7⑧	1.2 (1189)	0.039–0.043	5B	5B	1.3–2.0	800	800	.006	.010
	Justy GL	7⑧	1.2 (1189)	0.039–0.043	5B	5B	43	700	700	.006	.010
	Loyale	4②	1.8 (1781)	0.039–0.043	20B	20B	28–43	700	700	Hyd.	Hyd.
	Legacy	6	2.2 (2212)	0.039–0.043	20B	20B	36	700	700	Hyd.	Hyd.
	Legacy Turbo	6	2.2 (2212)	0.039–0.043	15B	15B	36	700	700	Hyd.	Hyd.
1992	Justy	7⑧	1.2 (1189)	0.039–0.043	5B	5B	1.3–2.0	800	800	.006	.010
	Justy GL	7⑧	1.2 (1189)	0.039–0.043	5B	5B	43	700	700	.006	.010
	Loyale	4②	1.8 (1781)	0.039–0.043	20B	20B	28–43	700	700	Hyd.	Hyd.
	Legacy	6	2.2 (2212)	0.039–0.043	20B	20B	36	700	700	Hyd.	Hyd.
	Legacy Turbo	6	2.2 (2212)	0.039–0.043	15B	15B	36	700	700	Hyd.	Hyd.
	SVX	3	3.3 (3318)	0.039–0.043	—	20B	43	—	610	Hyd.	Hyd.

NOTE: The lowest cylinder pressure should be within 75% of the highest cylinder pressure reading. For example, if the highest cylinder is 134 psi, the lowest should be 101. Engine should be at normal operating temperature with throttle valve in the wide open position.

The underhood specifications sticker often reflects tune-up specification changes in production. Sticker figures must be used if they disagree with those in this chart.

① Code 8: with 4WD
② Code 5: with 4WD
  Code 7: with pneumatic suspension
③ Code 9: with pneumatic suspension
④ 4-speed
⑤ SPFI

TUNE-UP PROCEDURES

In order to extract the full measure of performance, economy and pleasure from your Subaru it is essential that it be properly tuned at regular intervals. A regular tune-up will keep your car's engine running smoothly and will prevent the minor annoying breakdowns and poor performance associated with an untuned engine.

A complete tune-up should be performed at least once every two years for vehicles which see normal or light service. A vehicle which is heavily used should be tuned every year.

If the specifications on the tune-up sticker in the engine compartment of your Subaru disagree with the Tune-up Specifications in this Section, the figures on the sticker must be used. The sticker often reflects changes made during the production run.

A complete tune-up consists of more than just checking spark plugs, ignition points, and condenser. A list of items to inspect and service,

if necessary, while performing the tune-up follows. All of the listed services, adjustments and repairs are covered in various Sections of this book. Check and service if required:

- Spark Plugs
- Spark Plug Wires
- Distributor Breaker Points
- Distributor Cap, Rotor and Condenser
- Operating Parts of the Distributor
- Distributor Vacuum Control
- Ignition Control System (Electronic)
- Ignition Timing
- Battery
- Belts
- Cooling System
- Engine Oil and Oil Filter
- Air Cleaner and PCV Valve
- Emission Control Devices
- Fuel Filter
- Carburetor Choke
- Carburetor Idle Speed and Mixture
- Vacuum Fittings, Hoses and Connections
- Hot Air System
- Engine Compression
- Intake Manifold Vacuum
- Cylinder Head and Intake Manifold Bolts
- Valve Clearances

Spark Plugs

Spark plugs ignite the air and fuel mixture in the cylinder as the piston reaches the top of the compression stroke. The controlled explosion that results forces the piston down, turning the crankshaft and the rest of the drive train.

The average life of a spark plug is 30,000 miles (48,300km). This is, however, dependent on a number of factors: the mechanical condition of the engine; the type of fuel; the driving conditions; and the driver.

When you remove the spark plugs, check their condition. They are a good indicator of the condition of the engine. It is a good idea to remove the spark plugs every 6,000 miles (9,656km) to keep an eye on the mechanical state of the engine.

Check the electrodes and inner and outer porcelain of the plugs, noting the type of deposits and the degree of electrode erosion:

• Normal — Brown to grayish-tan deposits and slight electrode wear indicate correct spark plug heat range.

• Carbon fouled — Dry fluffy carbon deposits on the insulator and electrode are mostly caused by slow speed driving in city, weak ignition, too rich fuel mixture or a dirty air cleaner. If the same conditions exists after repair, it is advisable to replace with plugs having a hotter heat range.

• Oil fouled — Wet black deposits show excessive oil entrance into combustion chamber through worm rings and pistons or excessive clearance between valve guides and stems. If same condition remains after repair, it is advisable to replace with plugs having a hotter heat range.

• Overheating — White or light gray insulator with black or gray grown spots and bluish burnt electrodes indicate engine overheating. Moreover, the appearance results from incorrect ignition timing, loose spark plugs, wrong selection of fuel or incorrect heat range plug. If the same conditions exists after repair, it is advisable to replace with plugs having a colder heat range.

The gap between the center electrode and the side or ground electrode can be expected to increase not more than 0.001 in. (0.025mm) every 1,000 miles (1,609km) under normal conditions.

When a spark plug installed in an engine is functioning properly, the plugs can be taken out, cleaned, regapped, and reinstalled in the engine without doing the engine any harm. When, and if, a plug fouls and begins to misfire, you will have to investigate, correct the cause of the fouling, and either clean or replace the plug.

Spark plugs suitable for use in your Subaru's engine are offered in different heat ranges. The amount of heat which the plug absorbs is determined by the length of the lower insulator. The longer the insulator, the hotter the plug will operate. The shorter the insulator, the cooler it will operate.

A spark plug that absorbs (or retains) little heat and remains to cool will accumulate deposits of lead, oil, and carbon, because it is not hot enough to burn them off. This leads to fouling and consequent misfiring. A spark plug that absorbs too much heat will have no deposits, but the electrodes will burn away quickly and, in some cases, preignition may result.

Preignition occurs when the spark plug tips get so hot that they ignite the fuel/air mixture before the actual spark fires. This premature ignition will usually cause a pinging sound under conditions of low speed and heavy load. In severe cases, the heat may become high enough to start the fuel/air mixture burning throughout the combustion chamber rather than just to the front of the plug. In this case, the resultant explosion will be strong enough to damage pistons, rings, and valves.

In most cases the factory recommended heat range is correct. It is chosen to perform well under a wide range of operating conditions. However, if most of your driving is long distance, high speed travel, you may want to install a spark plug one step colder than standard. If most of your driving is of the short trip variety, when the engine may not always reach operating temperature, a hotter plug may help burn off the deposits normally accumulated under those conditions.

REMOVAL

1. Label and remove the spark plug wires.

2. Remove the wire from the end of the spark plug by grasping the wire by the rubber boot. If the boot sticks to the plug, remove it by twisting and pulling at the same time. Do not pull the wire itself or you will damage the core.

3. Use a appropriately sized spark plug socket to loosen all of the plugs about two turns.

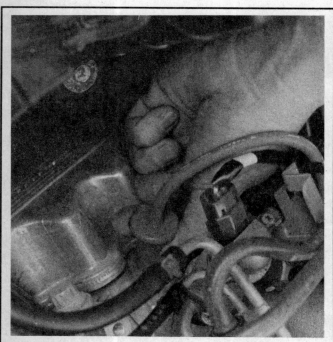

FIG. a Twist the spark plug boot to loosen it from the spark plug

FIG. b Remove the spark plug boot by pulling on the boot only. Do not pull on the wire

FIG. c Remove the spark plug using the proper size spark plug socket

FIG. d Check the sprak plug for signs of abnormal deposits or wear

➡ **The cylinder head is cast from aluminum. Remove the spark plugs when the engine is cold to prevent damage to the threads.**

4. If compressed air is available, apply it to the area around the spark plug holes. Otherwise, use a rag or a brush to clean the area. Be careful not to allow any foreign material to drop into the spark plug holes.

5. Remove the plugs by carefully unscrewing them from the engine.

INSPECTION

♦ SEE FIGS. 1 and 2

Check the plugs for deposits and wear. If they are not going to be replaced, clean the plugs thoroughly. Remember that any kind of deposit will decrease the efficiency of the plug.

Plugs can be cleaned on a spark plug cleaning machine, which can sometimes be found in service stations, or you can do an acceptable job of cleaning with a stiff brush. After cleaning the plugs, the electrodes must be filed flat using an ignition points file. The electrodes must be perfectly flat with sharp edges. Rounded edges reduced the spark plug voltage by as much as 50%.

Check spark plug gap before installation. The ground electrode must be parallel to the center

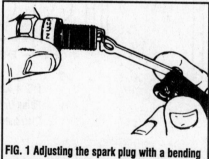

FIG. 1 Adjusting the spark plug with a bending tool

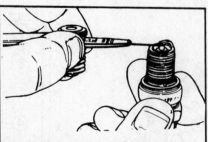

FIG. 2 Checking the spark plug gap with a wire tool

electrode and the specified size wire gauge should pass through the gap with a slight drag. Always check the gap on new plugs, too. They are not always correctly set at the factory.

Do not use a flat feeler gauge when measuring

the gap, as the reading may be inaccurate. Wire gapping tools usually have a bending tool attached. Use that to adjust the side electrode until the proper distance is obtained. Absolutely never bend the center electrode. Also, be careful not to bend the side electrode too far or too often. It may weaken and break off within the engine, requiring removal of the cylinder head to retrieve it.

INSTALLATION

1. Lubricate the threads of the spark plugs with a drop of oil. Install the plugs and tighten them hand tight. Take care not to cross-thread them.

2. Tighten the spark plugs with the socket to 13–17 ft. lbs. (18–24 Nm). Do not apply the same amount of force you would use for a bolt. Just snug them in.

3. Install the wires on their respective plugs. Make sure the wires are firmly connected. You will be able to feel them click into place.

Spark Plug Wires

At every tune-up, visually inspect the spark plug cables for burns, cuts, or breaks in the insulation. Check the boots and the nipples on the distributor cap and coil. Replace any damaged wiring.

Every 30,000 miles (48,300km) or so, the resistance of the wires should be checked with an ohmmeter. Wires with excessive resistance will cause misfiring, and may make the engine difficult to start in damp weather.

To check resistance, remove the distributor cap, leaving the wires attached. Connect one lead of an ohmmeter to an electrode within the cap. Connect the other lead to the corresponding spark plug terminal (remove it from the plug for this test). Replace any wire which shows excessive resistance.

It should be remembered that resistance is also a function of length; the longer the wire the greater the resistance. The following is a guide to the resistance of spark plug wires:

- Up to 15 in. (381mm): 3000–10,000Ω
- 15–25 in. (381–635mm): 4000–15,000Ω
- 25–35 in. (635–889mm): 6000–20,000Ω
- Over 35 in. (889mm): 6000–25,000Ω

If the spark plug wires are found to be defective, replace the wires one at a time. Install the boot firmly over the spark plug. Route the wire over the same path as the original. Insert the nipple firmly into the tower on the cap or the coil.

➡ **A little smear of dielectric grease inside the boots of the spark plug wires will prevent corrosion, and aid in boot removal the next time the plugs are serviced.**

FIRING ORDERS

➡ **To avoid confusion, remove and tag the wires on at a time, for replacement.**

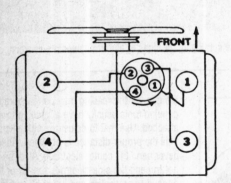

FIG. 3 1.6L and 1.8L Engines
Firing Order: 1–3–2–4
Distributor Rotation: Counterclockwise

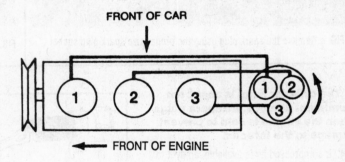

FIG. 4 1.2L Engine
Firing Order: 1–3–2
Distributor Rotation: Counterclockwise

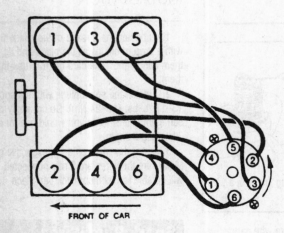

FIG. 5 2.7L Engine
Firing Order: 1–6–3–2–5–4
Distributor Rotation: Counterclockwise

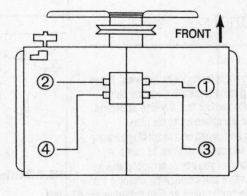

FIG. 6 2.2L Engine
Firing Order: 1–3–2–4
Distributorless Ignition System

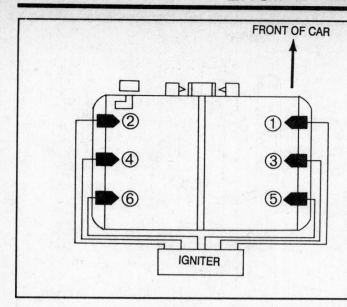

FRONT OF CAR

IGNITER

FIG. 7 3.3L Engine
Firing Order: 1–6–3–2–5–4
Distributorless Ignition System

ELECTRONIC IGNITION

1.8L Carbureted Engine

The Nippondenso Model 100291 and Hitachi Model D4R84 distributors are used on all carbureted 1.8L engines. Production changes have been made from year to year, but the basic design of the distributors has stayed the same. The Hitachi distributor is used on 1985–86 models only.

The Nippondenso and Hitachi electronic ignitions differ from a points type ignition only in the manner the spark is triggered. The secondary side of the ignition system is the same as a points type system.

Located in the distributor, is a four spoke rotor (reluctor) which rests on the distributor shaft where the breaker points are normally found. A pickup coil, consisting of a magnet, coil and wiring, rests on the breaker plate next to the reluctor.

When a reluctor spoke is not aligned with the pickup coil, it generates large lines of flux between itself, the magnet and the pickup coil. This large flux variation results in a high generated voltage in the pickup coil. When a reluctor spoke lines up with the pickup coil, the flux variation is low, thus allowing current to flow to the pickup coil. The ignition primary current is then cut off by the electronic unit, allowing the field in the ignition coil to collapse. The collapse of the ignition coil induces a high secondary

voltage in the conventional manner. The high voltage then flows through the distributor to the spark plug, as usual.

The systems also use a transistorized ignition unit mounted above the ignition coil on the fender well.

Nippondenso Model 100291 Overhaul

DISASSEMBLY

♦ SEE FIGS. 8–12
1. Disconnect the negative battery cable.
2. Remove the distributor from the engine
3. Remove the cap by detaching the spring clip.
4. Remove the rotor.
5. Remove the vacuum controller by removing the snapring and screw.
6. Remove the screw plate which secures the breaker plate in position.
7. Remove the igniter by loosening the screws.
8. Remove the breaker plate.
9. Remove the dust cover. Be careful not to break torque of the cover.

10. Remove the governor spring with needle nose pliers. Remove the snapring, then remove the flyweight. Be careful not to deform the governor spring.
11. Remove the cap from the top of the governor shaft and remove the screw. Pull out the governor shaft and signal rotor.
12. Remove the roll pin from the spiral gear using a punch.
13. Slide the governor shaft from the housing.

INSPECTION

14. Inspect the cap for breather hole clogging, electrode cracks or damage, center carbon wear and spring action. Check the rotor for cracks and damage.
15. Check that the vacuum canister plunger actuates when vacuum is applied using a hang vacuum pump.
16. Using an ohmmeter, check the signal generator. Connect the ohmmeter leads to the wiring harness. Resistance should be 130–190Ω. Move a screwdriver close to and away from the coil iron core. The tester needle should deflect. If the signal generator fails any test, replace it.

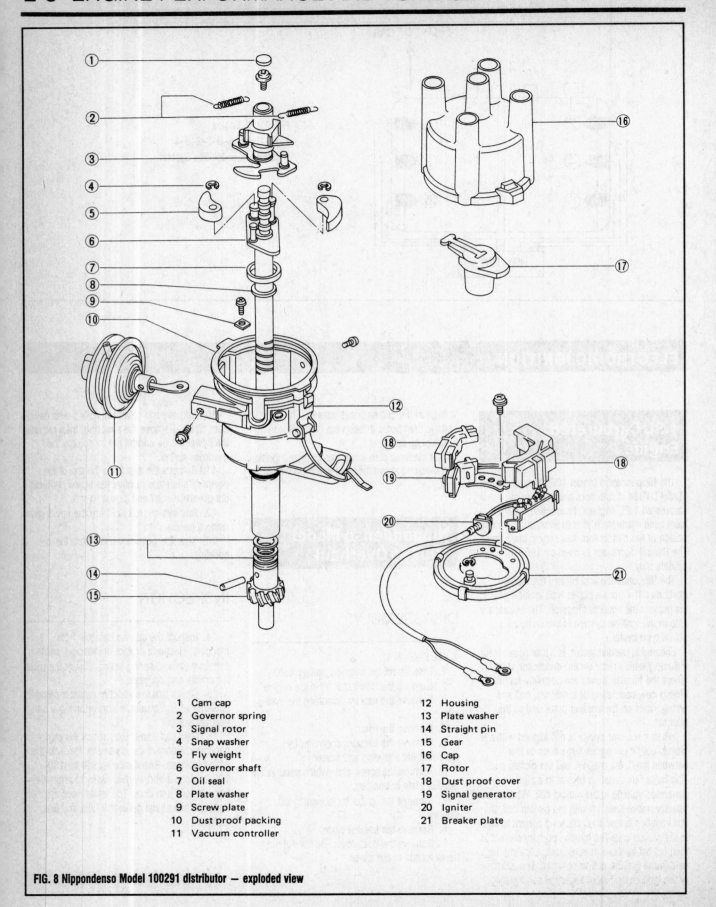

1	Cam cap	12	Housing
2	Governor spring	13	Plate washer
3	Signal rotor	14	Straight pin
4	Snap washer	15	Gear
5	Fly weight	16	Cap
6	Governor shaft	17	Rotor
7	Oil seal	18	Dust proof cover
8	Plate washer	19	Signal generator
9	Screw plate	20	Igniter
10	Dust proof packing	21	Breaker plate
11	Vacuum controller		

FIG. 8 Nippondenso Model 100291 distributor — exploded view

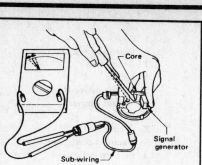

FIG. 9 Testing the signal generator — Nippondenso distributor

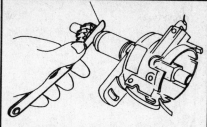

FIG. 10 Checking gear to housing clearance — Nippondenso distributor

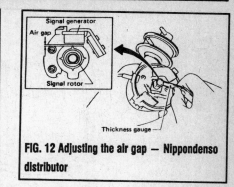

FIG. 12 Adjusting the air gap — Nippondenso distributor

ASSEMBLY

17. Assembly is the reverse of disassembly. Lubricate and install the governor shaft and spiral gear. Select washers that will give a gear-to-housing clearance of 0.0059–0.0197in. (0.15–0.50mm). Install the roll pin and stake it in place.

18. Install the signal rotor by aligning the matchmark scribed on the notch with that of the spiral gear.

19. Install the breaker plate, evenly fitting the set springs into the housing.

20. Adjust the air gap between the signal generator and the signal rotor to 0.008–0.016 in. (0.2–0.4mm).

21. Install the vacuum controller, dust cover, rotor and cap.

22. Install the distributor into the engine, start the engine and check the timing.

Hitachi Model D4R84 Overhaul

DISASSEMBLY

▶ SEE FIGS. 13–16

1. Disconnect the negative battery cable.
2. Remove the distributor from the engine
3. Remove the cap by detaching the spring clip or removing the attaching screws.
4. Remove the rotor and remove the carbon point from the cap.
5. Remove the vacuum controller by removing the screws.
6. Remove the harness by disconnecting the control unit terminals.
7. Pry the reluctor off the shaft using small pry bars.

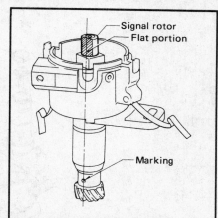

FIG. 11 Installing the signal rotor — Nippondenso distributor

8. Remove the retaining screws and remove the breaker plate.

9. Remove the screws attaching the control unit to the breaker plate. Remove the control unit.

10. Remove the screws attaching the stator and separate the magnet from the stator.

11. Remove the O-ring and toll pin from the spiral gear. Remove the spiral gear from the distributor shaft.

12. Remove the distributor shaft from the housing.

13. Remove the governor springs from the shaft.

14. Remove the the governor weights from the shaft.

INSPECTION

15. Measure the length of the carbon point in the cap. Standard length is 0.39–0.47 in. (10–12mm). If not within specification, replace the carbon point.

16. Measure the insulation resistance of the cap and rotor head. If not more than 50MΩ, replace the cap and rotor.

17. Replace the reluctor if damaged and the stator if bent or scratched.

18. Replace the breaker plate if it binds or does not move smoothly.

19. With the shaft held stationary, manually turn the reluctor counterclockwise. It is working properly if it returns to the original position when released. If not, replace.

20. Apply a vacuum to the vacuum controller using a hand vacuum pump. If it does not hold vacuum, replace it.

ASSEMBLY

21. Assembly is the reverse of disassembly. Apply a coat of grease to the shaft bearing and sliding surface for the breaker plate.

22. Install the governor and weights and springs. Attach the springs to the hook pins.

23. Position the cutout section of the rotor shaft and roll pin holes in line.

24. Using a new roll pin, install the spiral gear so that its alignment mark is aligned with the mark on the housing when the cutout section of the rotor shaft faces the No. 1 cylinder mark on the cap.

25. Align the breaker plate with the retaining screw hole during installation.

26. Press the roll pin into place in parallel with the cutout section of the reluctor.

27. Connect the harness to the control unit.

28. After properly assembling the parts, measure the air gap between the reluctor and stator with a feeler gauge. The air gap should be 0.012–0.020 in. (0.3–0.5mm). If not within specification, adjust the stator to gain specified clearance.

1.8L and 2.7L Fuel Injected Engines

The Hitachi Model D4P84 and D4P86 distributors are used on all SPFI and MPFI equipped 1.8L engines. The Hitachi Model D6P86 distributor is used on all MPFI equipped

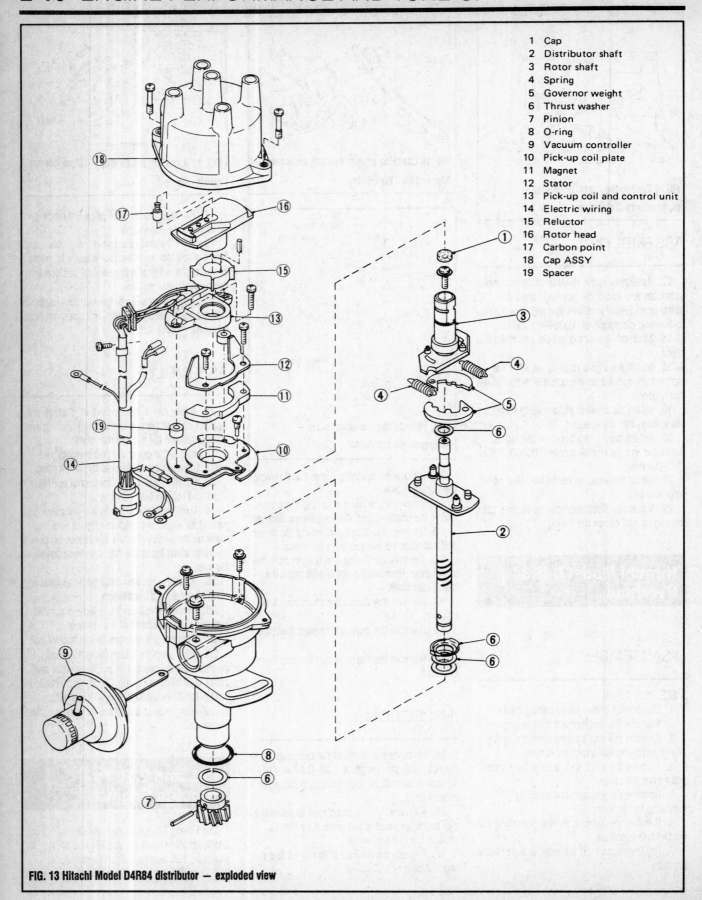

1 Cap
2 Distributor shaft
3 Rotor shaft
4 Spring
5 Governor weight
6 Thrust washer
7 Pinion
8 O-ring
9 Vacuum controller
10 Pick-up coil plate
11 Magnet
12 Stator
13 Pick-up coil and control unit
14 Electric wiring
15 Reluctor
16 Rotor head
17 Carbon point
18 Cap ASSY
19 Spacer

FIG. 13 Hitachi Model D4R84 distributor — exploded view

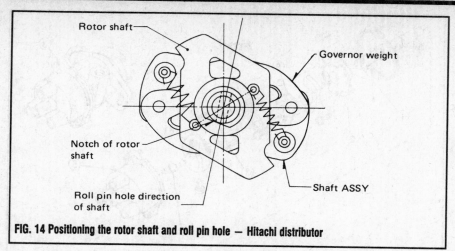

FIG. 14 Positioning the rotor shaft and roll pin hole — Hitachi distributor

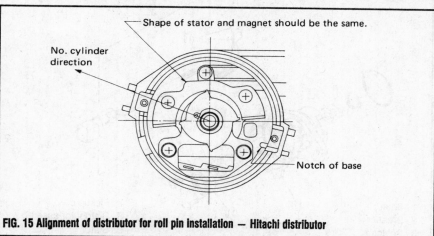

FIG. 15 Alignment of distributor for roll pin installation — Hitachi distributor

2.7L engines. The distributors are equipped with a photoelectric crank angle sensor which transmits a crank angle signal and a cylinder identification signal to the fuel injection control unit.

A signal processing unit, which is built into the distributor housing, consists of and LED and a photodiode. The rotor plate, located between the LED and the photodiode, is secured to the rotor shaft.

The rotor plate has four slit along its periphery through which 90° signals (in terms of distributor angle) are transmitted for cylinder detection. In addition, there are 360 slits through which 1° signals (in terms of distributor angle are transmitted for crank angle detection. Directly above the rotor plate is the LED and below it is the photodiode.

When the ignition switch is turned on, the LED emits light to the photodiode. The rotor plate turns as the engine starts. The light emitted from the LED is then repeatedly interrupted and transmitted through the slits by rotation of the rotor plate. The on-off light signals (for cylinder detection and crank angle detection) are then converted into output signals which are

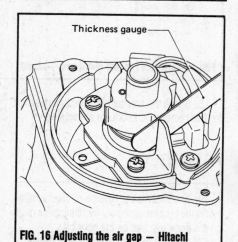

FIG. 16 Adjusting the air gap — Hitachi distributor

transmitted to the fuel injection control unit.

The fuel injection control unit determines optimum ignition timing in response to these output signals and engine operating conditions and transmits an ignition signal to the ignition coil. This type of distributor is not equipped with a centrifugal or vacuum advance mechanism.

The ignition coil, located on the left strut tower in the engine compartment, is equipped with a power transistor igniter. The power transistor amplifies the ignition signal transmitted from the fuel injection control unit. The amplified signal is used to make and break the current flowing through the primary winding of the ignition coil.

Diagnosis

Fault diagnosis of the electronic ignition system is carried out via the fuel injection control unit. See Electronic Engine Controls in Section 4 for further information.

Testing

CARBON POINT

Measure the length of the carbon point in the distributor cap. Standard length should be 0.49–0.47 in. (10–12mm). If not within specification, replace the carbon point.

CAP AND ROTOR

Measure the insulation resistance of the cap and rotor. Resistance should be 50MΩ or more. If not, replace the cap and rotor.

➡ **Subaru does not recommend disassembly of the Model D4P84 or D6P84 distributors. If component replacement is necessary, the distributor should be replaced as an assembly.**

1.2L Carbureted and Fuel Injected Engines

The ignition system is equipped with a newly designed electronic advance angle igniter. The igniter has no mechanical frictional parts. It features vibration proofing, a high level of ignition timing accuracy and minimal quality changes with operation.

The ignition system consists basically of a magnetic pickup, built into the distributor, a control unit, an ignition coil and other related components. The magnetic pickup consists of a reluctor, which rotates in relation to the crankshaft, and a pickup coil. The power transistor, which controls current flow of the coil primary circuit, is housed in the control unit.

The magnetic pickup detects the crankshaft angle and sends a corresponding signal to the operation circuit of the control unit. This determines the optimum length of current flow to the primary circuit of the ignition coil and ignition timing (equivalent to governor advance angle). Current to the primary circuit of the ignition coil is made and broken by the power transistor of the control unit used as a switching control.

Distributor Overhaul

DISASSEMBLY

◆ SEE FIGS. 17–21

1. Disconnect the negative battery cable.
2. Remove the distributor from the engine.
3. Remove the screws attaching the cap to the housing and remove the cap.
4. Remove the screws attaching the rotor, as required and remove the rotor.
5. Remove the rubber packing.
6. Remove the harness from the holder on the distributor. Disconnect the ground strap as necessary.
7. On the carbureted model, place two standard screwdrivers under the reluctor and pry upward to remove.
8. On the carbureted model, remove the screws which secure the breaker assembly and remove the assembly. On the MPFI model, remove the screws which secure the generator assembly and remove the assembly including the harness.

➡ **Do not disassemble the breaker or generator assemblies.**

INSPECTION

9. Check the carbon point for free movement in the cap.
10. Measure the carbon point length with calipers. Minimum length is 0.39 in. (10mm). Replace if not within specification.
11. Check all terminals for corrosion or damage. Clean as necessary.
12. Check the rotor head for deformity or corrosion. Replace as necessary.
13. Check the reluctor for deformity, damage and free play. Replace as necessary.
14. Check the stator for damage or bending. Replace as necessary.

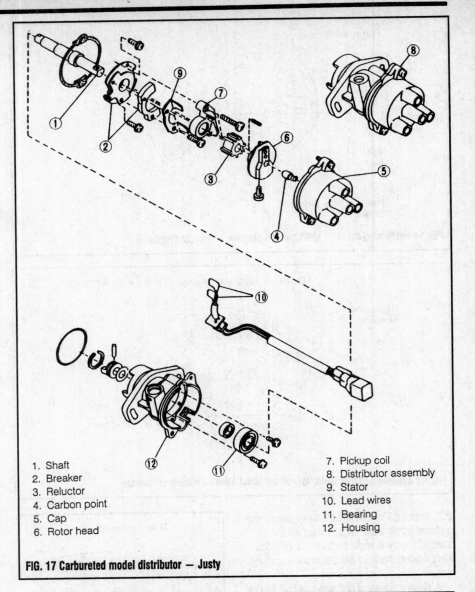

1. Shaft
2. Breaker
3. Reluctor
4. Carbon point
5. Cap
6. Rotor head
7. Pickup coil
8. Distributor assembly
9. Stator
10. Lead wires
11. Bearing
12. Housing

FIG. 17 Carbureted model distributor — Justy

15. Check the breaker plate frictional section for free movement. Lubricate as required.

ASSEMBLY

16. Assembly is the reverse of disassembly. Install the breaker assembly by aligning the mark on the plate with that on the housing.
17. Connect the lead wires to their proper locations.
18. Adjust the air gap between the reluctor and the stator to 0.008–0.016 in. (0.2–0.4mm). Loosen the stator screw to adjust the gap.

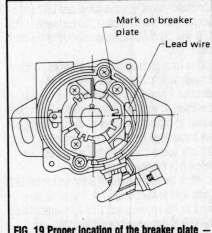

Mark on breaker plate

Lead wire

FIG. 19 Proper location of the breaker plate — carbureted distributor

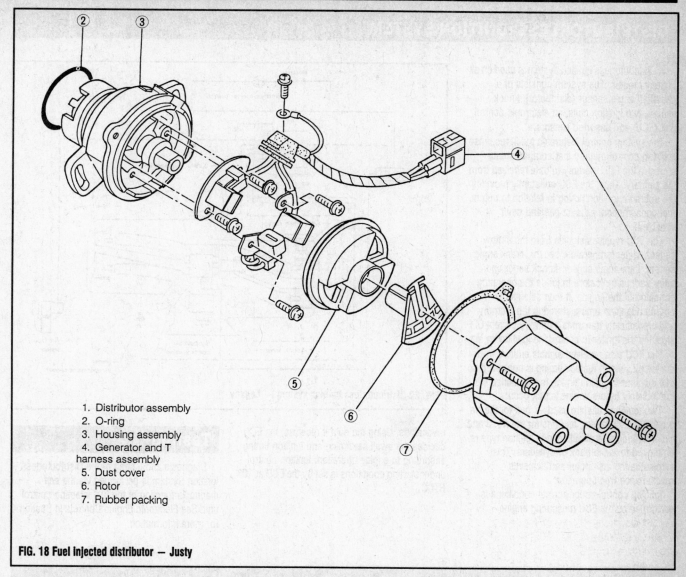

1. Distributor assembly
2. O-ring
3. Housing assembly
4. Generator and T harness assembly
5. Dust cover
6. Rotor
7. Rubber packing

FIG. 18 Fuel injected distributor — Justy

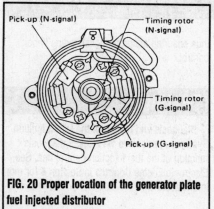

FIG. 20 Proper location of the generator plate fuel injected distributor

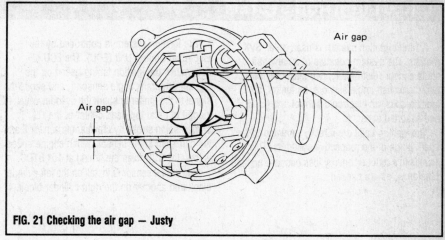

FIG. 21 Checking the air gap — Justy

DISTRIBUTORLESS IGNITION SYSTEM

A Distributorless Ignition system is used on all Legacy models. The system consists of a camshaft angle sensor (distributor), knock sensor, two ignition coils, an electronic control unit (ECU) and assorted sensors.

The system control features a quick response learning control method that compares data stored in the ECU memory to data received from the sensors. Thus, the ECU constantly provides the optimum ignition timing in relation to output, fuel consumption, exhaust gas and other variables.

The ECU receives signals from the airflow sensor, water temperature sensor, crank angle sensor, cam angle sensor, knock senor and other various indicators to judge the operating condition of the engine. It then selects the optimum ignition timing stored in the memory and immediately transmits a primary current OFF signal to the igniter to control the ignition timing.

The ECU also receives signals emitted from the knock sensor. Ignition timing is controlled so that advanced ignition timing is maintained immediately before engine knock occurs.

Two ignition coils are used — one for the No. 1 and No. 2 cylinders, and one for the No. 3 and No. 4 cylinders. A simultaneous ignition type is employed for each bank of cylinders. This eliminates the distributor and achieves maintenance free operation.

Ignition control under normal conditions is performed by the ECU measuring engine

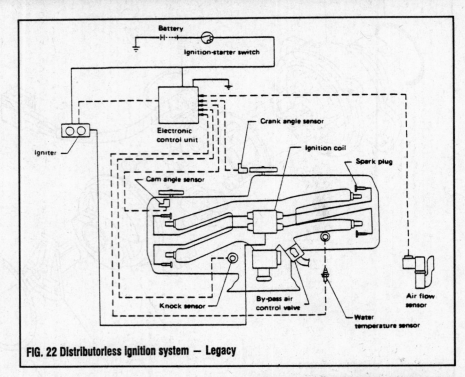

FIG. 22 Distributorless ignition system — Legacy

revolutions. Using the data it receives, the ECU decides the swell set timing and ignition timing according to engine operation. Ignition control under starting conditions is set by the ECU at 10° BTDC.

Testing

Diagnosis and testing of the Distributorless Ignition System is performed via the self diagnosis function of the fuel injection control unit. See Electronic Engine Controls in Section 4 for more information.

DIRECT IGNITION SYSTEM

A Direct Ignition system is used on all SVX models. The system consists of a camshaft angle sensor (distributor), two knock sensors, two crankshaft angle sensors, an igniter, six ignition coils, an electronic control unit (ECU) and assorted sensors.

The ignition coils are directly mounted to the spark plugs of the respective cylinders. This results in a reduced energy loss because no high tension wires are needed.

The ignition system is controlled by the Electronic Control Unit (ECU). The ECU determines the ignition timing based on the signal from crank angle sensor 1, and sends the signal to the igniter to spark the cylinder which is judged to be at top dead center of the compression stroke by crank angle sensor 2 and the camshaft angle sensor. When engine speed is low, the ECU fixes the timing at 10° BTDC.

One knock sensor is install on the left cylinder block and another on the right cylinder block,

thus ensuring accurate digital engine knock control.

Testing

Diagnosis and testing of the Direct Ignition System is performed via the self diagnosis function of the fuel injection control unit. See Electronic Engine Controls in Section 4 for more information.

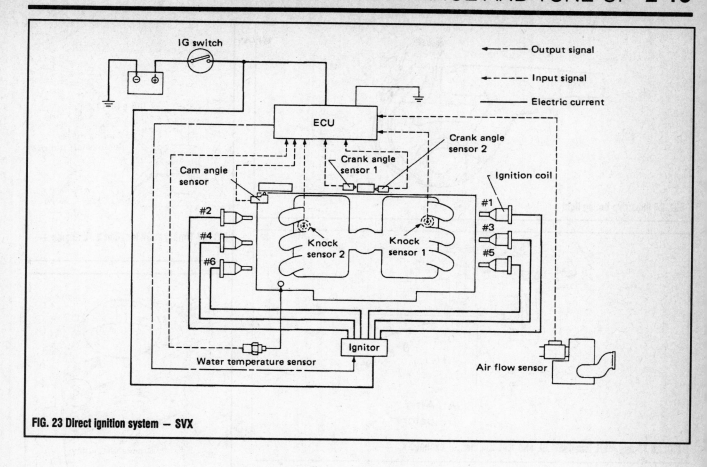

FIG. 23 Direct ignition system — SVX

IGNITION TIMING

Ignition timing is the measurement, in degrees of crankshaft rotation, of the point at which the spark plugs fire in the cylinders. It is measured in degrees before or after Top Dead Center (TDC) of the compression stroke.

Because it takes a fraction of a second for the spark plug to ignite the mixture in the cylinder, the spark plug must fire a little before the piston reaches TDC. Otherwise, the mixture will not be completely ignited as the piston passes TDC and the full power of the explosion will not be used by the engine.

The timing measurement is given in degrees of crankshaft rotation before the piston reaches TDC (BTDC). If the setting for the ignition timing is 8° BTDC, the spark plug must fire 8° before each piston reaches TDC. This only holds true, however, when the engine is at idle speed.

As the engine speed increases, the pistons go faster. The spark plugs have to ignite the fuel even sooner if it is to be completely ignited when the piston reaches TDC. To do this, the distributor has two means to advance the timing of the spark as the engine speed increases: a set of centrifugal weights within the distributor, and a vacuum diaphragm, mounted on the side of the distributor.

If the ignition is set too far advanced (BTDC), the ignition and expansion of the fuel in the cylinder will occur too soon and tend to force the piston down while it is still traveling up. This causes engine ping. If the ignition spark is set too far retarded, after TDC (ATDC), the piston will have already passed TDC and started on its way down when the fuel is ignited. This will cause the piston to be forced down for only a portion of its travel. This results in poor engine performance and lack of power.

Timing marks consist of a scale of degrees on the flywheel and a pointer on the flywheel cover hole. The scale corresponds to the position of the flywheel and a pointer on the flywheel cover hole. The pointer corresponds to the position of the piston in the number 1 cylinder. A stroboscopic (dynamic) timing light is used, which is hooked into the circuit of the No. 1 cylinder spark plug. Every time the spark plug fires, the timing light flashes. By aiming the timing light at the timing marks, the exact position of the piston within the cylinder can be read, since the stroboscopic flash makes the mark appear to be standing still. Proper timing is indicated when the pointer is aligned with the correct number on the scale.

There are three basic types of timing light available. The first is a simple neon bulb with two wire connections (one for the spark plug and one for the plug wire, connecting the light in series). This type of light is quite dim, and must be held closely to the marks to be seen, but it is inexpensive. The second type of light operates from the car battery. Two alligator clips connect to the battery terminals, while a third wire connects to the spark plug with an adapter. This type of light is more expensive, but the xenon bulb provides a nice bright flash which can even be seen in sunlight. The third type replaces the battery source with 110 volt house current. Some timing lights have other functions built into them, such as dwell meters, tachometers, or remote starting switches. These are convenient, in that they reduce the tangle of wires under the

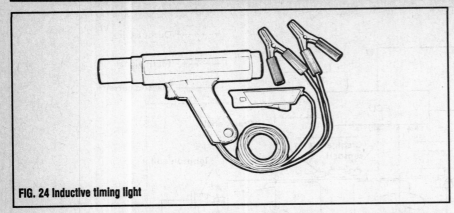

FIG. 24 Inductive timing light

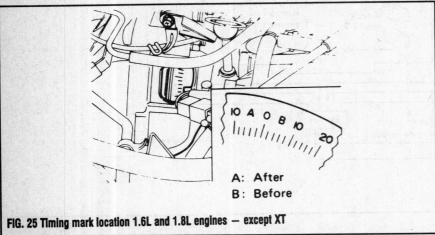

A: After
B: Before

FIG. 25 Timing mark location 1.6L and 1.8L engines — except XT

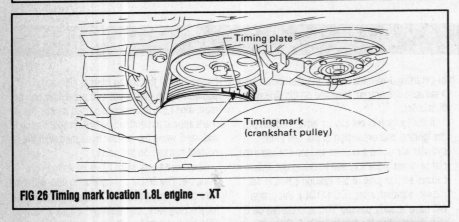

FIG 26 Timing mark location 1.8L engine — XT

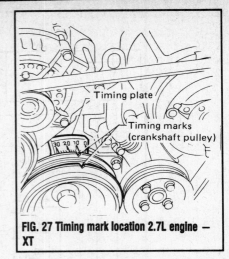

FIG. 27 Timing mark location 2.7L engine — XT

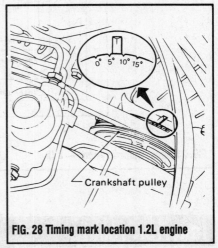

FIG. 28 Timing mark location 1.2L engine

hood, but may duplicate the functions of tools you already have.

If your Subaru has electronic ignition, you should use a timing light with an inductive pickup. This pickup simply clamps onto the No. 1 plug wire, eliminating the adapter. It is not susceptible to crossfiring or false triggering, which may occur with a conventional light, due to the greater voltages produced by electronic ignition.

Timing Mark Location

◆ SEE FIGS. 25–29

On 1.6L engines and 1.8L engines (except XT), the ignition timing marks are located on the edge of the flywheel, at the rear of the engine. The marks mounted on the flywheel are visible through a port in the flywheel housing located just behind the dipstick. A plastic cover protects the port through which the flywheel-mounted marks are visible.

The ignition timing marks on the 1.8L and 2.7L XT engines, are located on the right front side of the engine, near the crankshaft pulley.

The ignition timing marks on the 1.2L engine, are located on the front of the engine, near the crankshaft pulley.

The ignition timing marks on the 2.2L engine, are located on the front of the engine, near the crankshaft pulley.

The ignition timing on the 3.3L engine can only be determined using a Subaru Select Monitor test tool. The ignition timing is set by the fuel injection control unit and cannot be adjusted.

IGNITION TIMING ADJUSTMENT

➡ **An inductive timing light is highly recommended, as it is not susceptible to cross-firing or false triggering.**

Except 2.2L and 3.3L Engine

1. After cleaning the timing marks, connect a timing light and a tachometer to the engine following the manufacturer's instruction.

2. On carbureted models, disconnect and plug the distributor vacuum advance line.

3. On fuel injected models, ensure that the idle switch is **ON**. See Electronic Engine Controls in Section 4 for more information. Connect the test mode connector (green) located in the front part of the trunk on XT and under the left side of the dash on all other models.

➡ **When the test mode connector is connected, the Check Engine light will illuminate. The ignition timing must not be adjusted and cannot be check while the idle switch is OFF or the test mode connector is disconnected.**

4. Start the engine and allow it to reach normal operating temperature. Check and adjust the idle speed to specification.

5. Aim the timing light at the timing marks. The correct timing mark should align with the timing mark indicator.

6. If necessary to adjust the ignition timing, loosen the distributor hold-down bolt, then rotate the distributor to adjust the timing to specification.

➡ **Do not fully remove the distributor hold-down bolt when adjusting the timing.**

7. After adjustment, tighten the distributor hold-down bolt and recheck the ignition timing.

8. Recheck the idle speed and correct as necessary. Turn the engine **OFF**.

9. Disconnect the test mode connector on fuel injected engines. Reconnect the vacuum advance line on carbureted engines.

10. Remove the timing light and tachometer.

2.2L Engine

1. After cleaning the timing marks, connect a timing light and a tachometer to the engine following the manufacturer's instruction.

2. Start the engine and allow it to reach normal operating temperature. Check and adjust the idle speed to specification.

3. Aim the timing light at the timing marks. The correct timing mark should align with the timing mark indicator.

➡ **To increase stability on automatic transmission models, ignition timing while the engine is idling is controlled by the ECU. Ignition timing can vary up to 8° from specification.**

4. If the ignition timing is not correct, a component in the ignition control system is not functioning properly. Perform a fault diagnosis of the ignition control system.

5. Remove the timing light and tachometer.

3.3L Engine

1. Start the engine and allow it to reach operating temperature.

2. Connect a Subaru Select Monitor and measure the ignition timing (function mode 07).

3. If the ignition timing is not correct, a component in the ignition control system is not functioning properly. Perform a fault diagnosis of the ignition control system.

4. Disconnect the monitor and turn the engine **OFF**.

VALVE LASH

Valve lash adjustment determines how far the valves enter the cylinder and how long they stay open and closed.

If the valve clearance is too large, part of the lift of the camshaft will be used in removing the excessive clearance. Consequently, the valve will not be opening as far or for as long as it should. This condition has two effects: the valve train components will emit a tapping sound as they take up the excessive clearance and the engine will perform poorly because the valves are not open fully to allow the proper amount of gases to flow into and out of the engine.

If the valve clearance is too small, the intake valves and the exhaust valves will open too far, stay open too long and will not fully seat on the cylinder head when they close. When a valve seats itself on the cylinder head, it does two things: it seals the combustion chamber so that none of the gases in the cylinder escape, and it cools itself by transferring some of the heat it

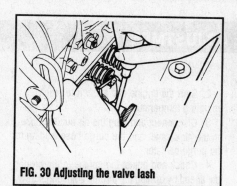

FIG. 30 Adjusting the valve lash

absorbs from the combustion in the cylinder to the cylinder head and into the cooling system. If the valve clearance is too small, the engine will run poorly because of the gases escaping from the combustion chamber. It may also run too lean. The valves will also become overheated and will warp, since they cannot transfer heat unless they are touching the valve seat in the cylinder head.

∷ WARNING

While all valve adjustments must be made as accurately as possible, it is better to have the valve adjustment slightly loose than slightly tight, as a burned valve may result from overly tight adjustments.

VALVE LASH ADJUSTMENT

The valve lash should be checked and adjusted every 15,000 miles (24,000km). It is not necessary to adjust the valve lash on hydraulic lifter equipped vehicles.

➡ **Before adjusting the valve clearance, check the cylinder head torque.**

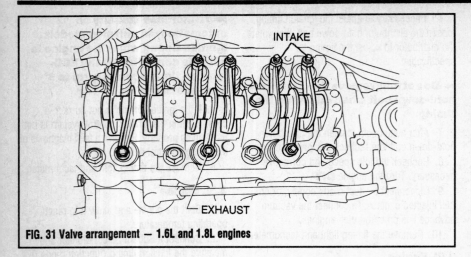

FIG. 31 Valve arrangement — 1.6L and 1.8L engines

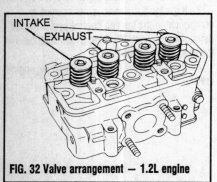

FIG. 32 Valve arrangement — 1.2L engine

1. With the engine cold, rotate the engine so that the No. 1 piston is at top dead center (TDC) of its compression stroke. The No. 1 piston is at top dead center when the distributor rotor is pointing to the No. 1 terminal (as though the distributor cap were in place) and the 0 mark on the flywheel or front pulley is opposite the pointer on the housing or front cover.

2. Check the clearance of both the intake and exhaust valves of the No. 1 cylinder by inserting a feeler gauge between each valve stem and rocker arm.

3. If the clearance is not within specifications, loosen the locknut with the proper size wrench and turn the adjusting stud either in or out until the valve clearance is correct.

➡ **Proper valve clearance is obtained when the feeler gauge slides between the valve stem and the rocker arm with a small amount of resistance.**

4. Tighten the locknut and recheck the valve stem-to-rocker clearance.

5. The rest of the valves are adjusted in the same way. Bring each piston to TDC of its compression stroke, then check and adjust the valves for that cylinder. The proper valve adjustment sequence is 1–3–2–4 for the 1.6L and 1.8L engines; 1–3–2 for the 1.2L engine.

6. When the valve adjustment is complete, install the distributor cap and the valve covers with new gaskets.

7. After adjusting the valve clearance, tighten the rocker arm locknuts to 12–17 ft. lbs. (17–23Nm) for the 1.2L engine and 10–13 ft. lbs. (14–18Nm) for the 1.6L and 1.8L engines.

8. Rotate the crankshaft several times, then recheck the valve clearance.

9. Install the valve covers using new gaskets. Tighten the valve covers to 5–6 ft. lbs. (6–7Nm) on the 1.2L engine and 2–3 ft. lbs. (3–4Nm) on the 1.6L and 1.8L engines.

IDLE SPEED AND MIXTURE ADJUSTMENTS

Idle Speed

ADJUSTMENT

Carburetor

➡ **Inspection of engine idle speed should be carried out after inspection of intake and exhaust valve clearances (except hydraulic lifter equipped engines).**

1. Position gear selector lever in the **N** position on vehicles equipped with M/T, and in the **P** position on vehicles equipped with A/T. Connect a tachometer in accordance with the manufacturer's instructions.

2. Start the engine and allow it to reach operating temperature.

3. Disconnect and plug the air suction hose on the air cleaner and the purge hose leading to the purge canister.

4. Check and adjust the engine to the proper idle speed by turning the throttle adjusting screw.

5. Remove the tachometer.

Electronic Feedback Carburetor (EFC)

➡ SEE FIG. 33

➡ **Before checking or adjusting the idle speed, check ignition timing and adjust, if necessary.**

1. Position gear selector lever in the **N** position on vehicles equipped with M/T, and in the **P** position on vehicles equipped with A/T.

2. Connect the Test Mode connector and the Read Memory connector located under the left side of the dash.

3. Start the engine and allow it to reach normal operating temperature. Then, run engine at 2500 rpm for 1 minute.

4. Disconnect and plug the purge hose to the intake manifold, then connect a tachometer to the engine.

5. Turn all accessories **OFF** and adjust idle to specification.

6. Turn the headlights **ON** and check that the engine idle speed rises slightly. If not, diagnose and correct the problem in the idle-up system. Turn the headlights **OFF**.

7. If equipped with air conditioning, turn the air conditioning **ON**. Check that the engine idle speed rises slightly. If not, diagnose and correct

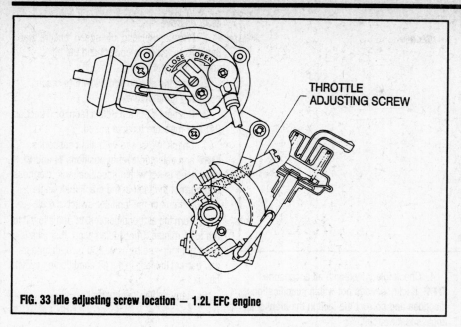

FIG. 33 Idle adjusting screw location — 1.2L EFC engine

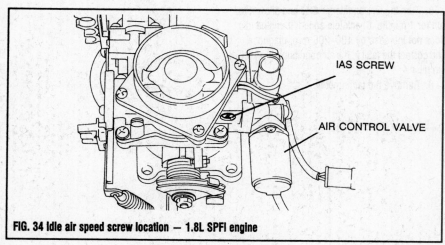

FIG. 34 Idle air speed screw location — 1.8L SPFI engine

the problem in the fast idle control device (FICD) system. Turn the air conditioning **OFF**.

8. Disconnect the test mode and read memory connectors. Remove the tachometer.

Single Point Fuel Injection (SPFI)

▶ SEE FIG. 34

1. Position gear selector lever in the **N** position on vehicles equipped with M/T, and in the **P** position on vehicles equipped with A/T.

2. Connect a tachometer according to the manufacturers instructions. Start the engine and allow it to reach operating temperature.

3. Check and adjust the ignition timing to specification.

4. Increase engine speed to 2500 rpm for 1 minute to heat the oxygen sensor.

5. Disconnect and plug the purge hose leading to the throttle body.

6. Disconnect the air control valve electrical connector from the throttle body.

7. Adjust the idle speed to 500–600 rpm by turning the idle air speed screw.

8. Reconnect the air control valve electrical connector and check that the engine idle increases to specification.

9. If engine idle does not increase to within 100 rpm of specification, the connector is faulty or the harness is broken. Repair as necessary.

10. Remove the tachometer, connect the purge hose and the air control valve electrical connector.

Multi-Point Fuel Injection

1.2L ENGINE

▶ SEE FIG. 35

1. Position gear selector lever in the **N** position on vehicles equipped with M/T, and in the **P** position on vehicles equipped with A/T.

2. Connect the test mode and read memory connectors located under the left side of the dash.

3. Connect a tachometer according to the manufacturers specification. Start the engine and allow it to reach operating temperature.

4. With all accessories **OFF**, adjust the idle to specification using the idle adjusting screw on the throttle body.

5. If equipped with air conditioning, turn the air conditioning **ON**. Check that the engine idle speed rises slightly. If not, diagnose and correct the problem in the fast idle control device (FICD) system. Turn the air conditioning **OFF**.

6. Disconnect the test mode and read memory connectors. Remove the tachometer.

1.8L ENGINE

▶ SEE FIG. 36

1. Position gear selector lever in the **N** position on vehicles equipped with M/T, and in the **P** position on vehicles equipped with A/T.

2. Connect a tachometer according to the manufacturers instructions. Start the engine and allow it to reach operating temperature.

3. Check and adjust the ignition timing to specification.

4. Increase engine speed to 2500 rpm for 1 minute to heat the oxygen sensor.

5. Disconnect and plug the purge hose leading to the throttle body.

6. Adjust the idle speed to specification by turning the idle adjusting screw.

7. Connect the purge hose leading to the throttle body.

8. Remove the tachometer.

2.2L ENGINE

1. Prior to checking idle speed, ensure that the ignition timing is correct and the check engine light is **OFF**.

2. Start the engine and allow it to reach operating temperature.

3. Attach an inductive type tachometer according to the manufacturers instructions.

➡ **The distributorless ignition system used in this vehicle provides spark simultaneously to cylinders 1 and 2. It must be noted that some tachometers may register twice the actual engine speed.**

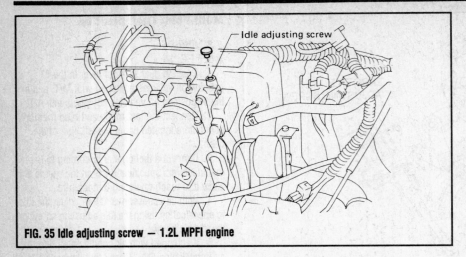

FIG. 35 Idle adjusting screw — 1.2L MPFI engine

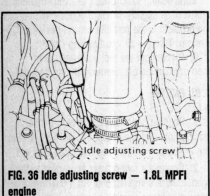

FIG. 36 Idle adjusting screw — 1.8L MPFI engine

4. Check idle speed with all accessories **OFF**. If idle speed is not within specifications, diagnose and correct the fault in the crankshaft angle sensor circuit.

5. Turn the air conditioner **ON** and allow it to run for 1 minute. Check idle speed. If engine idle does not increase by 100–200 rpm, diagnose and correct the fault in the air conditioning switch circuit.

6. Remove the tachometer.

3.3L ENGINE

1. Prior to checking idle speed, ensure that the ignition timing is correct and the check engine light is **OFF**.

2. Start the engine and allow it to reach operating temperature.

3. Connect a Subaru Select Monitor (Function 04) and measure the idle speed.

4. Check idle speed with all accessories **OFF** and selector lever in positions **N** and **D**. If idle speed is not within specifications, diagnose and correct the fault in the crankshaft angle sensor circuit or the inhibitor switch circuit.

5. Turn the air conditioner **ON** and allow it to run for 1 minute. Check idle speed. If engine idle does not increase by 100–200 rpm, diagnose and correct the fault in the air conditioning switch circuit.

6. Remove the Select Monitor.

3

ENGINE AND ENGINE OVERHAUL

ENGINE ELECTRICAL

Ignition Coil

TESTING

Except 2.2L and 3.3L Engine

1. Run the engine until it reaches operating temperature (coil must be hot). Disconnect the high tension wire from the coil tower.
2. Measure the primary resistance between the negative and positive terminals with a digital volt/ohm meter.
3. Measure secondary resistance between the coil tower and the positive terminal with a digital volt/ohm meter.
4. Measure the insulation resistance between the high tension coil tower and the coil case.
5. If any measurement is not within specification, replace the coil.

2.2L Engine

▶ SEE FIG. 1

1. Run the engine until it reaches operating temperature (coil must be hot). Label and disconnect the high tension wires from the coil pack.
2. Measure the primary resistance between high tension towers 1/2 and 3/4 with a digital volt/ohm meter.
3. Measure secondary resistance between coil electrical connector terminals 1/2 and 2/3 with a digital volt/ohm meter.
4. Measure the insulation resistance between the high tension coil tower and the coil case.
5. If any measurement is not within specification, replace the coil.

3.3L Engine

▶ SEE FIG. 2

1. Disconnect the ignition coil harness connector.
2. Remove the ignition coil.
3. Using a digital volt/ohm meter, measure the primary resistance between the connector terminals.

➡ **Since diodes are built into the coil secondary side, secondary resistance can not be measured in the conventional manner. Check secondary coil resistance using the following method.**

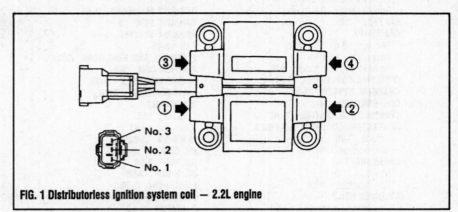

FIG. 1 Distributorless ignition system coil — 2.2L engine

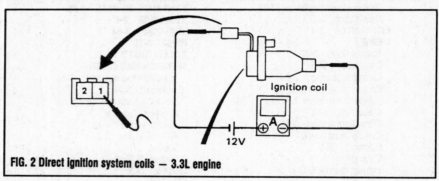

FIG. 2 Direct ignition system coils — 3.3L engine

4. Connect a 12 volt power supply and a digital ammeter in series between the primary and secondary terminals of the ignition coil. Measure the secondary coil resistance.
5. If coil resistance is not within specification, replace the coil.
6. Perform these tests on each ignition coil.
7. Reinstall the coil and connect all electrical connectors.

REMOVAL & INSTALLATION

Except 3.3L Engine

1. Disconnect the negative battery cable.
2. On the 2.2L engine, remove the intake manifold cover.
3. Label and disconnect the wires from the ignition coil.
4. Remove the ignition coil from the mounting bracket.
5. Installation is the reverse of removal.
6. Ensure that the coil wires are connected to their proper positions. Failure to do so could damage the coil.

3.3L Engine

1. Disconnect the positive and negative battery cables. Remove the battery.
2. Remove the air cleaner case.
3. Disconnect the ignition coil harness connector.
4. Loosen the bolts attaching the coil to the cylinder head completely.
5. Grip the bolt head with pliers and pull to remove the coil.
6. Installation is the reverse of removal.
7. Tighten the coil attaching bolts to 13–15 ft. lbs. (17–20 Nm).
8. Ensure that the coil wires are connected to their proper positions. Failure to do so could damage the coil.

Distributor

REMOVAL

1. Remove the air cleaner assembly, taking note of the hose locations.

2. Disconnect the distributor wiring connector.

3. If equipped, note the positions of the vacuum line(s) on the distributor diaphragm, disconnect the lines at the diaphragm. Unsnap the two distributor cap retaining clamps and remove the cap. Position the cap and ignition wires to one side.

➡ **If it is necessary to remove the ignition wires from the cap to get enough room to remove the distributor, make sure to label each wire and the cap for easy and accurate reinstallation.**

4. Use chalk or paint to carefully mark the position of the distributor rotor in relationship to the distributor housing and mark the position of the distributor housing in relationship to the engine block. When this is done, you should have a line on the distributor housing directly in line with the tip of the rotor and another line on the engine block directly in line with the mark on the distributor housing. This is very important because the distributor must be reinstalled in the exact same position from which it was removed, if correct ignition timing is to be maintained.

5. Remove the distributor hold down bolt.

6. Remove the distributor from the engine taking care not to damage or lose the O-ring.

➡ **Do not disturb the engine while the distributor is removed. If you crank or rotate the engine while the distributor is removed you will have to retime the engine.**

INSTALLATION ENGINE NOT ROTATED

7. If the engine was not disturbed while the distributor was removed, position the distributor in the block (make sure the O-ring is in place). Have the rotor aligned with the mark previously scribed on the distributor body and the marks on the distributor body and engine in alignment.

8. Tighten the hold-down bolt finger tight.

9. Reinstall the distributor rotor, cap and wires, if removed. Reconnect the distributor wiring harness. Install the air cleaner.

10. Check the ignition timing and adjust as necessary. Tighten the distributor hold-down bolt

INSTALLATION ENGINE ROTATED

If the engine has been cranked, disassembled, or the timing otherwise lost, proceed as follows:
▶ SEE FIG. 3

1. Remove the plastic dust cover from the timing port on the flywheel housing.

2. Remove the No. 1 spark plug. (No. 1 spark plug is the front plug on the right side of the engine). Use a wrench on the crankshaft pulley bolt (on manual transmission cars place transmission in neutral) and slowly rotate the engine until the TDC 0 mark on the flywheel aligns with the pointer. While turning the engine place your finger over the No. 1 spark plug hole, when you feel air escaping past your finger the piston is on the compression stroke and when the marks align the piston is at TDC (top dead center).

3. An alternate method can be used if Step 2 is impractical. Remove the bolts that hold the right (passenger's) side valve cover and remove the cover to expose the valves on No. 1 cylinder. Rotate the engine so that the valves in No. 1 cylinder are closed and the TDC 0 mark on the flywheel lines up with the pointer.

4. Align the small depression on the distributor drive pinion with the mark on the distributor body. This will align the rotor with the No. 1 spark plug terminal on the distributor cap. Make sure the O-ring is located in the proper position.

5. Align the matchmarks you have made on the distributor body with those on the engine block and install the distributor in the engine. Make sure the drive is engaged.

6. Install the hold down bolt finger tight. Start the engine and adjust the ignition timing to specification.

The Charging System

When the ignition switch is turned on current from the battery passes through the ignition switch to the voltage regulator. The current then passes through a series of resistors, points and coils and sends a small amount of current to the alternator post which is connected to the brushes. The brushes contact slip rings on the rotor and pass a small amount of current into the windings of the rotor. The current passing through the rotor coils creates a magnetic field within the alternator.

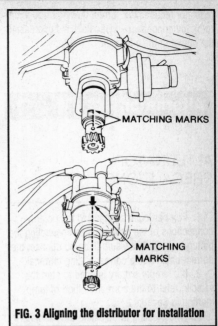

FIG. 3 Aligning the distributor for installation

When the engine is started the rotor is turned by the fan belt. As the rotor turns, a magnetic current is induced in the stationary windings, or stator, located in the alternator housing. The current induced is alternating current (AC) and must be changed to direct current (DC); diodes are used for this purpose.

A technical explanation of how a diode works is not important. It is important to know that a diode is a form of electrical check valve, allowing the current to flow one way but not the other. A negative diode will pass current in a negative direction, and a positive in a positive direction. The positive diodes make up the positive rectifier and the negative diodes make up the negative rectifier.

The stationary windings, or stator, are wound into three sets of windings or phases. Each phase winding is connected to a positive and a negative diode. When the phase winding is passing positive current, the current will flow through the positive diode to the output terminal of the alternator. When the phase winding is passing negative current, the negative diode allows the returning current from the grounded circuit, to pass into the windings to complete the circuit.

The direct current flowing from the alternator output terminal to the battery is used to provide current for the electrical system and to recharge the battery. As electrical demand increases the voltage regulator senses the need and directs more current to pass through the rotor, increasing the magnetic field. This produces greater induction voltage which increases the output of the alternator. When the requirements of the electrical system decrease, the voltage regulator reduces the current flowing through the rotor, lowering the magnetic field and decreasing the output of the alternator.

Alternator

ALTERNATOR PRECAUTIONS

1. Pay particular attention to the polarity connections of the battery when connecting the battery cables. Make sure that you connect the correct cable to the corresponding terminal.

2. If a jumper battery is used to start the vehicle, refer to the correct method of jump starting in Section 1.

3. When testing or adjusting the alternator, install a condenser between the alternator output terminal and the ground. This is to prevent the diode from becoming damaged by a spark which occurs due to testing equipment with a defective connection.

4. Do not operate the alternator with the output terminals disconnected. The diode would be damaged by the high voltage generated.

5. When recharging the battery by a quick charge or any other charging apparatus, disconnect the alternator output terminal before hooking up the charging leads.

6. When installing a battery, always connect the positive terminal first.

7. Never disconnect the battery while the engine is running.

8. Never electric weld around the car without disconnecting the alternator.

9. Never apply any voltage in excess of battery voltage during testing.

10. Never jump a battery for starting purposes with more than the battery voltage.

REMOVAL & INSTALLATION

1. Disconnect the negative battery cable.

2. Label and disconnect the alternator electrical wiring harness.

3. On vehicles equipped with a belt tensioner, loosen the belt tension device and remove the accessory drive belt. On all others, remove the alternator adjusting bolt, move the alternator toward the engine and remove the drive belt.

4. Remove the remaining mounting nuts and bolts while carefully supporting the alternator.

5. Remove the alternator from the engine compartment.

FIG. 3a Unplug the alternator wiring harness

FIG. 3b Use a wrench to remove the alternator-to-battery connection

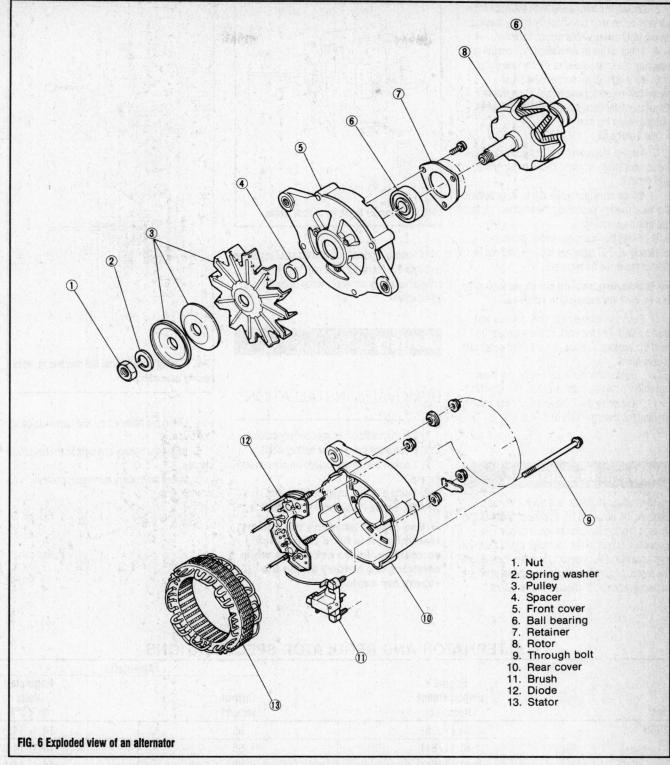

FIG. 6 Exploded view of an alternator

1. Nut
2. Spring washer
3. Pulley
4. Spacer
5. Front cover
6. Ball bearing
7. Retainer
8. Rotor
9. Through bolt
10. Rear cover
11. Brush
12. Diode
13. Stator

➡ **Now is a good time to inspect the drive belt for wear, replace if necessary.**

To Install:

6. Install the alternator on the engine and insert all bolts loosely.

7. Install the accessory drive belt and tension to specification. Tighten all bolts securely.

8. Connect the alternator electrical wiring harness.

9. Connect the negative battery cable. Start the engine and check the alternator for proper operation.

BRUSH REPLACEMENT

◆ SEE FIG. 4–6

1. Remove the alternator from the engine.
2. Remove the through bolts from the alternator.

3. Detach the front cover with the rotor from the rear cover with the stator by lightly tapping on the front cover with a plastic hammer.

4. Separate the brush assembly from the rear cover by removing the nuts on the rear cover.

5. As required, disconnect the brush assembly, diode assembly and IC regulator simultaneously from the stator coil lead wires using a soldering iron.

To Install:

6. Inspect the movement of the brush. If the movement is not smooth, check brush holder and clean it.

7. Check brush for wear. If it is worn beyond the wear marks, located on the brushes, replace the brush assembly.

8. Install the brush assembly, diode assembly and IC regulator into the rear cover. Solder the wires as required.

➡ **Soldering should be done quickly as to not damage the diodes.**

9. Push the brushes into their holders and insert a wire into the back of the alternator to hold the brushes in place. An unfolded paper clip works good.

10. Tighten the diode assembly and brush assembly retaining nuts to 2–3 ft. lbs. (3–4Nm).

11. Assemble the front and rear case halves. Tighten the through bolts to 2–4 ft. lbs. (3–5Nm).

Voltage Regulator

The voltage regulator is a device which controls the output of the alternator. Without this voltage limiting function of the regulator, the excessive output of the alternator could burn out components of the electrical system. In addition, the regulator compensates for seasonal changes in temperature as it affects voltage output.

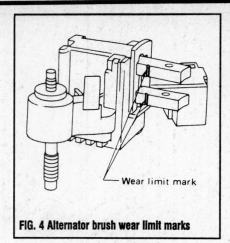

FIG. 4 Alternator brush wear limit marks

All Subaru models have a solid state regulator built into the alternator. The regulator is non-adjustable and is serviced, when necessary, by replacement.

Battery

REMOVAL & INSTALLATION

1. Disconnect the negative battery cable. Then disconnect the positive battery cable.

2. Loosen the battery holddown clamps and remove.

3. Using a battery strap or lifting tool, carefully remove the battery from the vehicle.

➡ **Use care in handling the battery, remember, it is filled with a highly corrosive acid. Do not smoke while servicing the battery as the the vapors are explosive.**

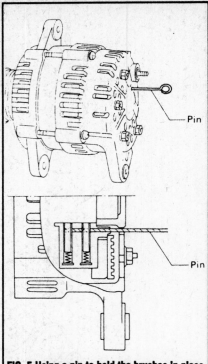

FIG. 5 Using a pin to hold the brushes in place during assembly

4. Clean the battery tray and terminals of all corrosion.

5. Install the battery and tighten the holddown clamps.

6. Install the battery terminals; positive terminal first.

ALTERNATOR AND REGULATOR SPECIFICATIONS

Year	Engine Displacement Liters (cc)	Alternator Output (amps)	Regulated Volts @ 75°F
1985	1.6L (1595)	55	14.1–14.8
	1.8L (1781)	55	14.1–14.8
	1.8L (1781)	60	14.1–14.8
	1.8L (1781)	65	14.1–14.8
1986	1.6L (1595)	55	14.1–14.8
	1.8L (1781)	55	14.1–14.8
	1.8L (1781)	60	14.1–14.8
	1.8L (1781)	65	14.1–14.8

ALTERNATOR AND REGULATOR SPECIFICATIONS

Year	Engine Displacement Liters (cc)	Alternator Output (amps)	Regulated Volts @ 75°F
1987	1.2L (1189)	45	14.2–14.8
	1.6L (1595)	55	14.1–14.8
	1.8L (1781)	55	14.1–14.8
	1.8L (1781)	60	14.1–14.8
	1.8L (1781)	65	14.1–14.8
1988	1.2L (1189)	45	14.2–14.8
	1.6L (1595)	55	14.1–14.8
	1.8L (1781)	55	14.1–14.8
	1.8L (1781)	60	14.1–14.8
	1.8L (1781)	65	14.1–14.8
	2.7L (2672)	90	14.2–14.8
1989	1.2L (1189)	55	14.2–14.8
	1.6L (1595)	55	14.1–14.8
	1.8L (1781)	55	14.1–14.8
	1.8L (1781)	60	14.1–14.8
	1.8L (1781)	65	14.1–14.8
	2.7L (2672)	90	14.2–14.8
1990	1.2L (1189)	55	14.2–14.8
	1.8L (1781)	60	14.1–14.8
	1.8L (1781)	65	14.1–14.8
	2.2L (2212)	85	14.1–14.7
	2.7L (2672)	90	14.2–14.8
1991	1.2L (1189)	55	14.2–14.8
	1.8L (1781)	60	14.1–14.8
	1.8L (1781)	65	14.1–14.8
	2.2L (2212)	85	14.1–14.7
	2.7L (2672)	90	14.2–14.8
1992	1.2L (1189)	55	14.2–14.8
	1.8L (1781)	60	14.1–14.8
	2.2L (2212)	85	14.1–14.7
	3.3L (3318)	95	14.2–14.8

Starter

The magnetic switch starter, used on all engines except the 1.6L, uses a permanent magnetic field system instead of field coils inside the yoke. A spring steel retaining ring is used to retain the magnet, and keep it from springing out when an unexpectedly strong shock is applied to the yoke circumference. When the starter is engaged, current flows through the pull-in and holding coils. This causes the plunger to be pulled in, applying pressure to the shifter lever, which pushes the pinion out. Current flows through the armature and starts it to turn the pinion at a moderate speed, meshing it with the ring gear. When the main switch contacts are closed, full current flows through the armature, fully meshing the pinion with the ring gear, starting the vehicle.

On all engines except the 1.2L and 1.6L, the starter is fitted with a gear reduction mechanism. The gear reduction mechanism may drive the over-running clutch shaft through its own pinion or an idler gear and pinion, depending on the required reduction. The purpose of this system is to increase the torque produced by the starter for its weight.

REMOVAL & INSTALLATION

1. Remove the spare tire from the engine compartment.
2. Disconnect the negative battery cable.

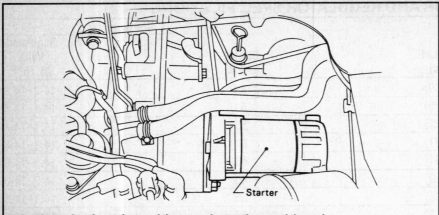

FIG. 7 Starter location at the top of the transaxle near the rear of the engine

FIG. 7a Starter location — Legacy

3. Label and disconnect the wiring harness at the starter, which is located on top of the transaxle at the rear of the engine.

4. Remove the starter attaching bolts (nuts) and pull the starter out.

To Install:

5. Install the starter and tighten the attaching bolts to 34–40 ft. lbs. (46–54Nm). Tighten the nuts to 22–27 ft. lbs. (30–36Nm).

6. Connect the wiring harness.

7. Connect the negative battery cable.

8. Install the spare tire.

MAGNETIC SWITCH REPLACEMENT

On all engines except the 1.2L and 1.6L, the magnetic switch is an integral part of the starter housing. The starter must be completely disassembled to gain access to the switch.

1.2L and 1.6L Engines

♦ SEE FIG. 8

1. With the starter removed from the vehicle, loosen the magnetic switch nut to remove the connecting wire.

2. Remove the magnetic switch by removing the attaching bolts.

3. Separate the torsion spring from the switch.

To Install:

4. Check conductivity between terminal **S** and the switch body. If none, replace the switch.

5. Check conductivity between terminal **M** (the large post) and terminal **S**. If none, replace the switch.

6. With the plunger pushed inward, check conductivity between terminals **M** and **B**. If none, replace the switch.

7. Assemble the switch with the torsion spring and install on the starter.

8. Install and tighten the switch attaching bolts to 5–6 ft. lbs. (6–8Nm).

9. Install the connecting wire and the nut securely.

STARTER OVERHAUL

1.2L Engine

DISASSEMBLY

♦ SEE FIG. 9

1. Position the assembly in a suitable holding fixture. Remove the nut and disconnect the motor wire from the magnetic switch terminal.

2. Remove the two through bolts and separate the torsion spring from the magnetic switch.

3. Remove the dust cover from the rear cover, then remove the E-ring from the shaft.

4. Remove the two starter housing bolts and screws, then separate the housing from the assembly.

5. Remove the brush holder by pushing pushing it down toward the spring, then pulling it up.

6. Holding the gear case firmly, remove the yoke assembly from the gear case.

7. Shift the pinion stopper toward the pinion, and remove the pinion stopper clip with a suitable tool. Then, separate the pinion from the armature.

INSPECTION

8. Using an ohmmeter, make sure that there is no continuity between the commutator and the armature coil core. If there is continuity, replace the armature.

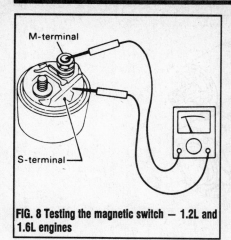

FIG. 8 Testing the magnetic switch — 1.2L and 1.6L engines

9. Using an ohmmeter, check for continuity between the commutator segments. If there is no continuity between any of the segments, replace the armature.

10. If the commutator is dirty, burnt or the runout exceeds 0.0020 in. (0.05mm), use sandpaper # 500–600 to clean the surface. Make sure that the undercut depth between the segments is 0.020–0.031 in. (0.50–0.79mm), clean and free of foreign material. If not, use a scraping tool to scrape out the insulating material.

11. Using an ohmmeter, make sure that there is continuity between the lead wire and the brush lead of the field coil. If there is no continuity, replace the field frame.

12. Using an ohmmeter, make sure that there is no continuity between the field coil and the field frame. If there is continuity, replace the field frame.

13. If the brush length is less than 0.43 in. (11mm) replace the brush and dress with emery cloth.

14. Check the gear teeth for wear or damage, if damaged, replace them. Turn the pinion clockwise and make sure that it rotates freely, try to turn the pinion counterclockwise and make sure that it locks. If the pinion does not respond correctly, replace it.

15. Using an ohmmeter, check for continuity between the grounded terminal and the insulated terminal, then between the grounded terminal and the housing. If there is no continuity in either case, replace the magnetic switch assembly.

16. Check the magnet inside the yoke, if it is defective, replace the yoke assembly.

ASSEMBLY

17. Lubricate the gear case, bearings, rear cover, shift lever operating surfaces, pinion sliding surfaces, and plunger sliding surfaces on the magnetic switch with high temperature grease.

18. Install the the pinion and pinion stopper on the armature.

FIG. 7b Rear starter bolt location — Legacy

FIG. 7c Top starter bolt location — Legacy

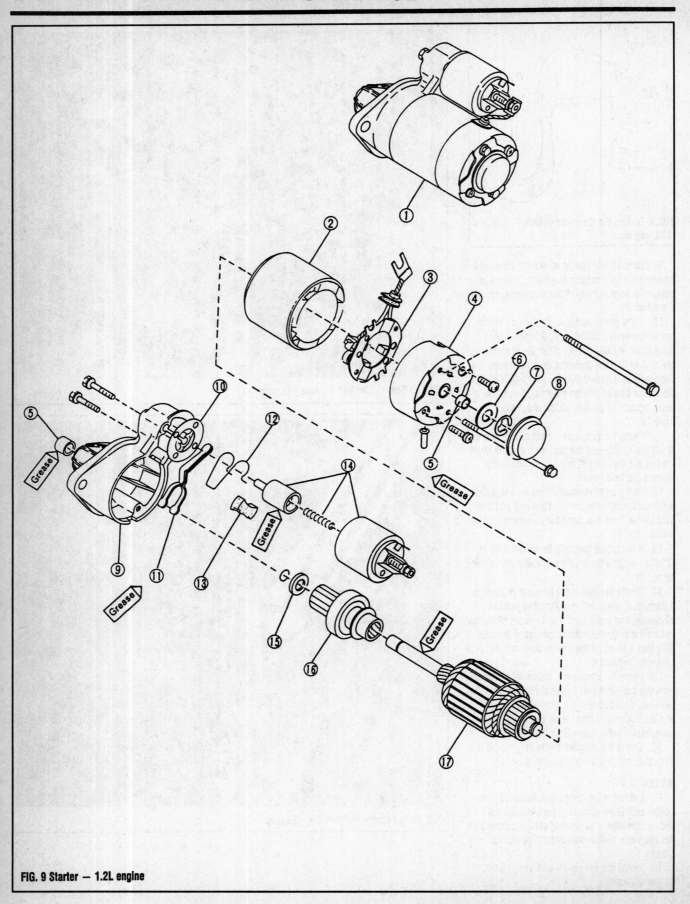

FIG. 9 Starter — 1.2L engine

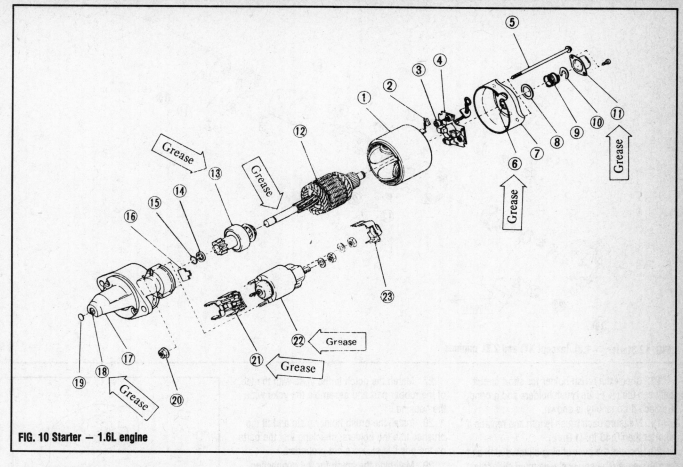

FIG. 10 Starter — 1.6L engine

19. Install the yoke assembly into the gear case.

20. Install the brush holder assembly.

21. Assemble the starter housing. Install the starter housing bolts and screws. Tighten the bolts to 5–6 ft. lbs. (6–7Nm) and the screws to 1–2 ft. lbs. (2–3Nm).

22. Install the dust cover and E-ring.

23. Install the magnetic switch and tighten the through bolts to 4–6 ft. lbs. (6–8Nm).

24. Install the motor wire connector and tighten the nut securely.

1.6L Engine

DISASSEMBLY

♦ SEE FIG. 10 and 11

1. Remove the attaching nut and disconnect the terminal **M** connector. Then, remove the magnetic switch.

2. Remove the end frame cap, lock plate, spring, and rubber seal.

3. Remove the two through bolts and then pull the end frame toward the rear to remove it. Remove the brushes from their holders by first pushing the holder spring aside.

4. Remove the brush holder plate. Then, pull the yoke off the main housing (which surrounds the stator coils). Remove the plate and seal from the rear of the yoke.

5. Unscrew and remove the solenoid lever set bolt. Then, pull the armature, overrunning clutch, and lever out of the yoke.

6. Using a length of pipe the same diameter as the armature shaft, tap the pinion stop collar down toward the starter drive so that it is off the snapring. Use a pair of snapring pliers to remove the snapring from the armature shaft. Slide off the pinion stop collar.

7. Remove the starter drive from the threaded spline, taking care not to damage the spline.

INSPECTION

8. Clean all disassembled parts. Do not use solvent for cleaning the overrunning clutch, armature, magnetic switch or field coil.

9. Measure the clearance between armature shaft and bushing in the housing and between the armature shaft and bushing in the end frame. Clearance should be 0.008 in. (0.2mm) or less.

10. Inspect the surface of the commutator and correct with emery cloth (500 grit) when it is rough. Replace the armature if the outer diameter of the commutator becomes less than 1.209 in. (30.7mm).

11. Check the runout of the commutator. Correct if it exceeds 0.016 in. (0.4mm).

12. Measure the depth of the top surface of each tooth to the commutator surface. If less than 0.008 in. (0.2mm), replace the commutator.

13. Test the armature coil for shorts using a growler test tool. Replace the armature as necessary.

14. Test the armature for continuity between the two segments side by side. If the tester shows no continuity, the circuit is open. Replace the armature.

15. Check the insulation between the field coil (+) terminal and the yoke. If the tester shows continuity, remove the pole cores one by one, locate the grounded part, and replace.

16. Check the field coil for continuity and replace if open.

17. Check the resistance between the connecting lead wire and the colder parts of the brush lead wires. The resistance should be almost zero.

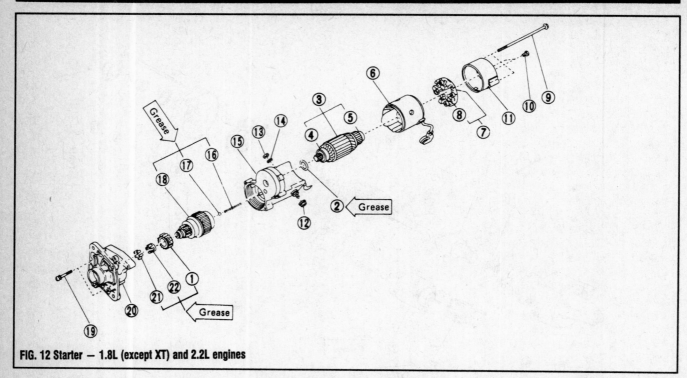

FIG. 12 Starter — 1.8L (except XT) and 2.2L engines

18. Check the brush holder for short circuit between the (+) side brush holders and ground. Replace if continuity is shown.

19. Measure each brush length and replace if shorter than 0.43 in. (11mm).

20. Inspect the overrunning clutch pinion and screw sleeve. The screw sleeve must slide freely along the armature shaft splines. If damage is found or resistance is felt, replace as required.

21. Inspect the pinion teeth and replace the pinion if teeth are damaged. Also inspect the flywheel for damaged teeth.

ASSEMBLY

22. Lubricate the commutator shaft, overrunning clutch, drive lever, housing bushing, end frame bushing, magnetic switch and end frame cap.

23. Position the overrunning clutch and pinion stop collar on the armature shaft. Push the snap ring over the end of the armature shaft. Work it down until it slips in to the snapring groove.

24. Supporting the stop collar as shown (the armature must hang below, unsupported) press the end of the armature shaft downward until the collar rests against the ring and the ring is in the groove of the collar.

25. Install the armature in the housing, position the drive lever and spring, and insert lever set bolt through the lever hole. Tighten the bolt securely.

26. Install the plate and rubber part.

27. Match the notch in the yoke with the tab of the rubber part and assemble the yoke with the housing.

28. Install the brush holder plate and fit the brushes into the holders, checking that the parts on the positive side are not grounded.

29. Matching the notch for the connecting lead wire, position the end frame on the yoke. Install the through bolts, plain washers and spring washers. Tighten the bolts securely.

30. Install the rubber seal, spring, lock plate and end frame cap and secure them with the screws and spring washers.

31. Turn the pinion in its rotating direction (left) and make sure that it rotates smoothly.

32. After engaging the plunger head of the magnetic switch to the drive lever, install the switch on the housing and connect the lead wire to the **M** terminal.

1.8L (except XT) and 2.2L Engines

DISASSEMBLY
◆ SEE FIG. 12

1. Disconnect the lead wire from the magnetic switch.

2. Remove the two through bolts from the end frame.

3. Separate the housing and magnetic switch.

4. Remove the screws securing the end frame to the brush holder.

5. Separate the yoke from the end frame.

6. Remove the brush by lifting up the positive side brush spring using needle nose pliers.

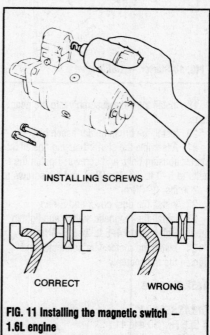

INSTALLING SCREWS

CORRECT   WRONG

FIG. 11 Installing the magnetic switch — 1.6L engine

➡ **Take care not to damage the brush and commutator.**

7. Separate the armature from the yoke.

8. Remove the screws securing the magnetic switch to the housing and separate the housing from the switch.

9. Remove the clutch from the housing. Take out the steel ball and idler gear.

10. Remove the retainer and roller from the housing. Remove the coil spring from the magnetic switch.

INSPECTION

11. Check the insulation between the commutator and armature core using a volt/ohm meter. Insulation should be 0.1M ohm or larger.

12. Check the commutator for out of roundness. Correct or replace the commutator if 0.0020 in. (0.05mm) or more out of round.

13. If commutator surface is rough, polish with a fine grain emery paper (300 grit). If burnt excessively, correct by cutting with a lathe. Do not cut more than 0.04 in. (1mm).

14. The outside diameter of the commutator should be 1.14 in. (29mm) or larger. Replace the commutator if found to be smaller.

15. Inspect the bearing by rotating. No binding should exist and no abnormal noise should be heard.

16. Test the field coil for open circuit using a volt/ohm meter. Continuity should exist.

17. Check the carbon brush length. If more than 1/3 of the original length has been worn away, replace the brush.

18. Test the insulation of the brush holder. Resistance should be 0.1M ohm or more.

19. Check that the pinion can be rotated in the normal direction. Check pinion teeth for wear or damage. If found, also check the flywheel.

ASSEMBLY

20. Grease the ball, rollers and gears with high temperature grease. If you have removed the armature be sure to reinstall the felt washer.

21. Install the coil spring on the magnetic switch. Install the retainer and roller on the housing.

22. Install the steel ball and idler gear. Install the clutch on the housing.

23. Join the housing to the switch and install the screws securing the magnetic switch to the housing.

24. Join the armature and the yoke.

25. Install the brushes using needle nose pliers.

26. Join the yoke and the end frame.

27. Install the screws securing the end frame to the brush holder.

28. Join the housing and magnetic switch.

29. Install the two through bolts from into end frame.

30. Connect the lead wire from the magnetic switch.

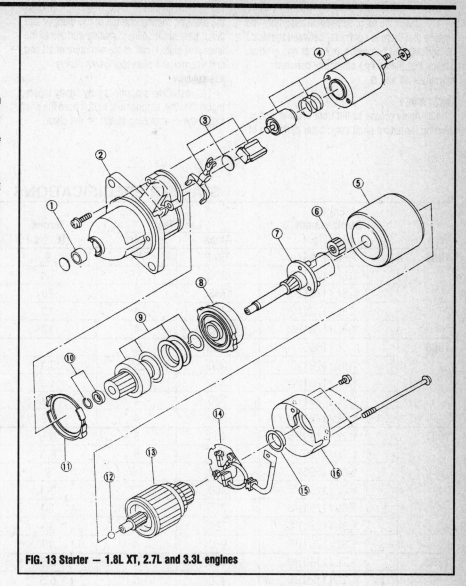

FIG. 13 Starter — 1.8L XT, 2.7L and 3.3L engines

1.8L XT, 2.7L and 3.3L Engines

DISASSEMBLY

▶ SEE FIG. 13

1. Loosen the nut which holds terminal **M** of the magnetic switch and disconnect the connector.

2. Remove the bolts which hold the switch assembly and remove the assembly, plunger and spring from the starter as a unit. Take care not to loose the pinion gap washer.

3. Remove the shaft assembly and overrunning clutch as a unit. Note the direction of the lever.

4. Remove the overrunning clutch from the shaft. Remove the stopper ring by lightly tapping. Remove the ring, stopper and clutch from the shaft.

INSPECTION

5. Check the commutator runout. Runout should not exceed 0.0039 in. (0.10mm).

6. Check the armature for ground. Touch one probe to the commutator segment and the other to the shaft. There should be no continuity.

7. Inspect the teeth of the pinion for wear or damage. Replace if damaged. Also check the flywheel.

8. Ensure that the pinion rotates clockwise smoothly but does not operate in the opposite direction.

9. Inspect the brushes for wear. If the brushes are worn past the service limit marked on the brush, replace them.

10. Ensure that the brush moves smoothly inside the holder.

11. Check the resistance of the brush holder. There should be no continuity between the holder and its plate.

12. Check the magnetic switch assembly and ensure that there is continuity between terminals **S** and **M**, and between terminal **S** and ground. Check that there is no continuity between terminals **M** and **B**.

ASSEMBLY

13. Apply grease to the front bracket sleeve bearing, armature shaft gear, outer periphery of the plunger, mating surface of the plunger and lever, gear shaft splines, mating surface of the lever and clutch, ball at the armature shaft end, and internal and planetary gears during assembly.

14. Install the stopper ring by lightly tapping. Install the ring, stopper and clutch from the shaft. Install the overrunning clutch on the shaft.

15. Install the shaft assembly and overrunning clutch as a unit. Install the lever in the same direction as noted during disassembly.

16. Install the switch assembly, plunger and spring on the starter as a unit. Ensure that the pinion gap washer is installed. Install the bolts which hold the assembly to the housing.

17. Install the connector on terminal **M** of the magnetic switch and tighten the nut securely.

STARTER SPECIFICATIONS

Year	Engine Displacement Liters (cc)	Lock Test		Torque (ft. lbs.)	No-Load Test		
		Amps	Volts		Amps	Volts	RPM
1985	1.6L (1595)	600	7.7	9	50	9.5	5000
	1.8L (1781) ①	300	2.5	5.1	90	11.5	3000
	1.8L (1781) ②	735	5	20	90	11	4000
	1.8L (1781) ③	780	4	13	90	11	3000
	1.8L (1781) ④	980	4	19	90	11	2900
1986	1.6L (1595)	600	7.7	9	50	9.5	5000
	1.8L (1781) ①	300	2.5	5.1	90	11.5	3000
	1.8L (1781) ②	735	5	20	90	11	4000
	1.8L (1781) ③	780	4	13	90	11	3000
	1.8L (1781) ④	980	4	19	90	11	2900
1987	1.2L (1189) ⑤	400	5	6.5	45	11.5	5500
	1.2L (1189) ⑥	400	5	6.5	90	11.5	6600
	1.6L (1595)	600	7.7	9	50	9.5	5000
	1.8L (1781) ①	300	2.5	5.1	90	11.5	3000
	1.8L (1781) ②	735	5	20	90	11	4000
	1.8L (1781) ③	780	4	13	90	11	3000
	1.8L (1781) ④	980	4	19	90	11	2900
1988	1.2L (1189) ⑤	400	5	6.5	45	11.5	5500
	1.2L (1189) ⑥	400	5	6.5	90	11.5	6600
	1.6L (1595)	600	7.7	9	50	9.5	5000
	1.8L (1781) ①	300	2.5	5.1	90	11.5	3000
	1.8L (1781) ②	735	5	20	90	11	4000
	1.8L (1781) ③	780	4	13	90	11	3000
	1.8L (1781) ④	980	4	19	90	11	2900
	2.7L (2672) ③	780	4	13	90	11	3000
	2.7L (2672) ④	980	4	19	90	11	2900
1989	1.2L (1189) ⑤	400	5	6.5	45	11.5	5500
	1.2L (1189) ⑥	400	5	6.5	90	11.5	6600
	1.6L (1595)	600	7.7	9	50	9.5	5000
	1.8L (1781) ①	300	2.5	5.1	90	11.5	3000
	1.8L (1781) ②	735	5	20	90	11	4000
	1.8L (1781) ③	780	4	13	90	11	3000
	1.8L (1781) ④	980	4	19	90	11	2900
	2.7L (2672) ③	780	4	13	90	11	3000
	2.7L (2672) ④	980	4	19	90	11	2900

STARTER SPECIFICATIONS

Year	Engine Displacement Liters (cc)	Lock Test		Torque (ft. lbs.)	No-Load Test		
		Amps	Volts		Amps	Volts	RPM
1990	1.2L (1189) ⑤	400	5	6.5	45	11.5	5500
	1.2L (1189) ⑥	400	5	6.5	90	11.5	6600
	1.8L (1781) ①	300	2.5	5.1	90	11.5	3000
	1.8L (1781) ②	735	5	20	90	11	4000
	1.8L (1781) ③	780	4	13	90	11	3000
	1.8L (1781) ④	980	4	19	90	11	2900
	2.2L (2212) ⑤	800	5	20	90	11	3000
	2.2L (2212) ⑥	735	5	20	90	11	3350
	2.7L (2672) ③	780	4	13	90	11	3000
	2.7L (2672) ④	980	4	19	90	11	2900
1991	1.2L (1189) ⑤	400	5	6.5	45	11.5	5500
	1.2L (1189) ⑥	400	5	6.5	90	11.5	6600
	1.8L (1781) ①	300	2.5	5.1	90	11.5	3000
	1.8L (1781) ②	735	5	20	90	11	4000
	1.8L (1781) ③	780	4	13	90	11	3000
	1.8L (1781) ④	980	4	19	90	11	2900
	2.2L (2212) ⑤	800	5	20	90	11	3000
	2.2L (2212) ⑥	735	5	20	90	11	3350
	2.7L (2672) ③	780	4	13	90	11	3000
	2.7L (2672) ④	980	4	19	90	11	2900
1992	1.2L (1189) ⑤	400	5	6.5	45	11.5	5500
	1.2L (1189) ⑥	400	5	6.5	90	11.5	6600
	1.8L (1781) ①	300	2.5	5.1	90	11.5	3000
	1.8L (1781) ②	735	5	20	90	11	4000
	2.2L (2212) ⑤	800	5	20	90	11	3000
	2.2L (2212) ⑥	735	5	20	90	11	3350
	3.3L (3318)	980	4	17	90	11	3000

① Manual transmission (except XT)
② Automatic transmission (except XT)
③ Manual transmission (XT)
④ Automatic transmission (XT)
⑤ Manual transmission
⑥ Automatic transmission

ENGINE MECHANICAL

Description

The Subaru Quadrozontal four cylinder engine is a unique design. The cylinders are horizontally opposed (flat) which gives the engine very compact dimensions, as well as make it run smoother than an inline four. Unlike other well known flat fours, the Subaru engine is water cooled. Water cooling provides two benefits: the engine is quieter because the water acts as sound insulation and the water cooling makes it easier to provide heat for the passenger compartment.

The engine block is made of aluminum alloy. The split crankcase design incorporates dry cylinder liners that are cast into the block. The engine also adopts the OHC (Overhead Camshaft) system, hydraulic lash adjuster, fuel injection system, and on some models a turbocharger. The engine offers easier maintenance servicing, reliability, low fuel consumption, low noise and powerful performance.

The pistons are made of aluminum which features a small expansion rate. Its top land is provided with valve relief and its skirt section has an elliptical, tapered tapered design to provide heat and wear resistance. Three piston rings are used for each piston, two compression rings and one oil ring. The cylinder liner is a cast dry type.

The cylinder head is also aluminum alloy, with good cooling and high combustion efficiency which, when combined with the bathtub shaped combustion chambers means better performance.

The camshaft case holds the camshaft, and is an aluminum die casting. The oil relief valve for the hydraulic lash adjuster is built into the cam case. The oil filler duct is mounted on the right hand camshaft case, and the distributor on the left hand camshaft case. The valve rockers ride directly on the cam lobes, eliminating the need for push rods and lifters.

The crankshaft is made from special wrought iron which provides sturdiness. All corners of the journals are processed with "deep roll" treatment.

The horizontally opposed engine configuration provides greater strength against bending and torsional stress while reducing the total length of the crankshaft.

Some engines in the Subaru lineup are fitted with turbochargers. The turbocharger is essentially a tiny, ultra high speed air pump. Its compressor is a tiny pinwheel whose finely machined vanes grab air and accelerate it, and then collect the air in a housing to force it into the engine under as much as 7.0 psi pressure. The engine, instead of gasping for air (actually drawing it in) as is usually the case, is pressure fed air and fuel in much greater quantities than is normally supplied.

At the other end of a metal shaft lies the turbine which drives the turbocharger. Utilizing expansion of the hot exhaust coming out of the engine, the turbine actually converts some of what would usually be wasted heat into the power which spins the turbocharger and helps the engine to breathe.

A precision, full floating sleeve type bearing supports the shaft in the middle. Engine oil is supplied to this bearing by the engine's oil pump through a special supply tube. This oil not only lubricates the bearing, but carries heat from the turbocharger shaft. Because of this extra heat, and that generated by the increased power, this is the only Subaru engine to have an external oil cooler.

Pressure charging can raise the temperature of compressed fuel/air mixture to the point where detonation can occur in the cylinders. Several modifications keep detonation from occurring. One is the use of a reduced (7.7 vs 8.7) compression ratio. Another is the addition of a double acting diaphragm on the distributor. When there is positive pressure in the intake manifold, this diaphragm actually retards distributor timing beyond its normal setting. An electronic knock sensor mounted on the cylinder head detects the particular frequency of detonation and may still further retard spark electronically to compensate for unanticipated variations in fuel quality, engine temperature, etc.

In order to protect the engine from excessive stress, which can occur at high rpm where the turbocharger begins to do its maximum work, a waste gate bypasses exhaust gas that would otherwise drive the turbocharger's turbine. Should this device fail, a pressure relief valve in the intake would protect the engine. The waste gate, by forcing more exhaust through the turbine at lower rpms, also helps guarantee good turbocharger performance, and engine torque, over a wide range of rpms.

Engine Overhaul Tips

Most engine overhaul procedures are fairly standard. In addition to specific parts replacement procedures and complete specifications for your individual engine, this Section also is a guide to accepted rebuilding procedures. Examples of standard rebuilding practice are shown and should be used along with specific details concerning your particular engine.

In most instances it is more profitable for the do-it-yourself mechanic to remove, clean and inspect the component, buy the necessary parts and deliver these to a shop for actual machine work. Competent and accurate machine shop services will ensure maximum performance, reliability and engine life.

On the other hand much of the rebuilding work (crankshaft, block, bearings, pistons, rods and other components) is well within the scope of the do-it-yourself mechanic.

Tools

The tools required for an engine overhaul or parts replacement will depend on the depth of your involvement. With a few exceptions, they will be the tools found in a mechanics tool kit. More in-depth work will require any or all of the following:

- a dial indicator (reading in thousandths) mounted on a universal base.
- micrometers and telescope gauges.
- jaw and screw type pullers.
- scraper
- valve spring compressor.
- ring groove cleaner.

- piston ring expander and compressor.
- ridge reamer.
- cylinder hone or glaze breaker.
- Plastigage®.
- engine stand.

Use of most of these tools is illustrated in this Section. Many can be rented for a one time use from a local parts jobber or tool supply house specializing in automotive work.

Occasionally, the use of special tools is called for. See the information on Special Tools and the Safety Notice in the front of this book before substituting another tool.

Inspection Techniques

Procedures and specifications are given in this Section for inspecting, cleaning and assessing the wear limits of most components. Other procedures such as Magnaflux and Zyglo can be used to locate materials flaws and stress cracks. Magnaflux is a magnetic process applicable only to ferrous materials. The Zyglo process coats the material with a fluorescent dye and can be used on any material. Checks for suspected surface cracks can be more readily made using spot check dye. The dye is sprayed onto the suspected area, wiped off and the area sprayed with a developer. Cracks will show up brightly.

Precautions

Aluminum has become very popular for use in engines, due to its low weight. Observe the following precautions when handling aluminum parts.

1. Never hot tank aluminum parts (the caustic hot tank solution will eat the aluminum).

2. Remove all aluminum parts (identification tag, etc.) from engine parts prior to hot tanking.

3. Always coat threads lightly with engine oil or anti-seize to compounds before installation, to prevent seizure.

4. Never over torque bolts or spark plugs, especially in aluminum threads.

Stripped threads in any component can be repaired using any of several commercial repair kits Heli-Coil®, Microdot®, Keenserts®, etc.).

When assembling the engine, any parts that will be in friction contact must be prelubed to provide lubrication at initial start up. Any product specifically formulated for this purpose can be used, but engine oil is not recommended as a prelube.

When semi-permanent (locked, but removable) installation of bolts or nuts is desired, installation should be cleaned or coated

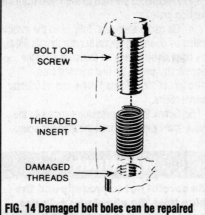

FIG. 14 Damaged bolt holes can be repaired with thread repair inserts

with Loctite® or other similar, commercial non-hardening sealant.

Repairing Damaged Threads

◆ SEE FIG. 14-18

Several methods of repairing damaged threads are available. Heli-Coil® (shown here), Keenserts® and Microdot® are among the most widely used. All involve basically the same principle, drilling out stripped threads, tapping the hole and installing a pre-wound insert, making welding, plugging and oversize fasteners unnecessary.

Two types of thread repair inserts are usually supplied, a standard type for most Inch Course, Inch Fine, Metric Coarse and Metric Fine thread sizes and a spark plug type for to fit most spark plug port sizes. Consult the individual manufacturer's catalog to determine exact applications. Typical thread repair kits will contain a selection of pre-wound threaded inserts, a tap (corresponding to the outside diameter threads of the insert) and an installation tool. Spark plug inserts usually differ because they require a tap equipped with pilot threads and a combined reamer/tap section. Most manufacturers also supply blister-packed thread repair inserts separately in addition to a master kit containing a variety of taps and inserts plus installation tools.

Before effecting a repair to a threaded hole, remove any snapped, broken or damaged bolts or studs. Penetrating oil can be used to free frozen threads. The offending item can be removed with locking pliers or with a screw or stud extractor. After the hole has been cleared, the thread can be repaired as follows:

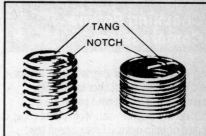

FIG. 15 Standard thread repair insert (left) and spark plug thread insert (right)

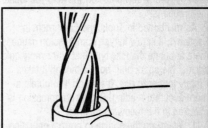

FIG. 16 Drill out the damaged threads with specified drill bit. Drill completely through the hole or to the bottom of a blind hole

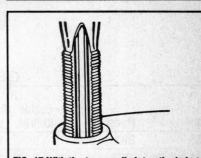

FIG. 17 With the tap supplied, tap the hole to receive the thread insert. Keep the tap well oiled and back it out frequently to avoid clogging the threads

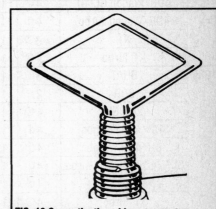

FIG. 18 Screw the thread insert onto the installation tool until the tang engages the slot. Screw the insert into the tapped hole until it is slightly below the top surface. After installation, break off the tang using a hammer and punch

Checking Engine Compression

A noticeable lack of engine power, excessive oil consumption and/or poor fuel mileage measured over an extended period are all indicators of internal wear. Worn piston rings, scored or worn cylinder bores, blown head gaskets, sticking or burnt valves and worn valve seats are all possible culprits here. A check of each cylinder's compression will help you locate the problems.

As mentioned in Tools and Equipment in Section 1, a screw in type compression gauge is more accurate than the type that you simply hold against the spark plug hole, although it takes slightly longer to use. It's worth it to obtain a more accurate reading. Engine compression is checked in the following manner:

1. Warm up the engine to normal operating temperature.

2. Tag the plug wires and remove all spark plugs.

3. Disconnect the high tension lead from the ignition coil.

4. On carbureted cars, fully open the throttle either by operating the carburetor throttle linkage by hand or by having an assistant floor the accelerator pedal. On fuel injected cars, disconnect the cold start valve and all injector connections.

5. Screw the compression gauge into the No.1 spark plug hole until the fitting is snug.

❄ WARNING

Be careful not to crossthread the plug hole. On aluminum cylinder heads use extra care, as the threads in these heads are easily ruined.

6. Ask an assistant to depress the accelerator pedal fully on both carbureted and fuel injected cars. Then while you read the compression gauge, ask the assistant to crank the engine two or three times in short bursts using the ignition switch.

7. Read the compression gauge at the end of each series of cranks, and record the highest of these readings. Repeat this procedure for each of the engines cylinders. Compare the highest reading of each cylinder to the other cylinders. The difference between each cylinder should not be more than 12–14 pounds.

8. If a cylinder is usually low, pour a tablespoon of clean engine oil into the cylinder through the spark plug hole and repeat the compression test. If the compression comes up after adding the oil, it appears that the cylinder's piston rings or bore are damaged or worn. If the compression remains low, the valves may not be seating properly, (a valve job is needed), or the head gasket may be blown near that cylinder. If the compression in any two adjacent cylinders is low, and if the addition of oil doesn't help the compression, there is leakage past the head gasket. Oil and coolant water in the combustion chamber can result from this problem. There may be evidence of water droplets on the engine dipstick when a head gasket has blown.

GENERAL ENGINE SPECIFICATIONS

Year	Model	Engine ID/VIN	Engine Displacement Liters (cc)	Fuel System Type	Net Horsepower @ rpm	Net Torque @ rpm (ft. lbs.)	Bore × Stroke (in.)	Compression Ratio	Oil Pressure @ rpm
1985	BRAT	5	1.8 (1781)	2 bbl	73 @ 4800	94 @ 2400	3.62 × 2.64	8.7:1	57 @ 2500
	2DR	2	1.6 (1595)	2 bbl	69 @ 4800	86 @ 2400	3.62 × 2.36	9.0:1	57 @ 2500
	2DR GL	4②	1.8 (1781)	2 bbl	73 @ 4800	94 @ 2400	3.62 × 2.64	8.7:1	57 @ 2500
	4DR DL④	4②	1.8 (1781)	2 bbl	82 @ 4800	101 @ 2800	3.62 × 2.64	9.5:1	43 @ 5000
	4DR/Wagon	4②	1.8 (1781)	2 bbl	82 @ 4800	101 @ 2800	3.62 × 2.64	9.0:1	43 @ 5000
	4DR/Wagon GL-10	4②	1.8 (1781)	MPFI	94 @ 5200	101 @ 2800	3.62 × 2.64	9.0:1	43 @ 5000
	4DR/Wagon Turbo	4②	1.8 (1781)	MPFI	111 @ 4800	134 @ 2800	3.62 × 2.64	7.7:1	43 @ 5000
	XT	4②	1.8 (1781)	MPFI	94 @ 5200	101 @ 2800	3.62 × 2.64	9.0:1	43 @ 5000
	XT Turbo	4②	1.8 (1781)	MPFI	111 @ 4800	134 @ 2800	3.62 × 2.64	7.7:1	43 @ 5000
1986	BRAT	5	1.8 (1781)	2 bbl	73 @ 4800	94 @ 2400	3.62 × 2.64	8.7:1	57 @ 2500
	2DR	2	1.6 (1595)	2 bbl	69 @ 4800	86 @ 2400	3.62 × 2.36	9.0:1	57 @ 2500
	2DR GL	4②	1.8 (1781)	2 bbl	73 @ 4800	94 @ 2400	3.62 × 2.64	8.7:1	57 @ 2500
	3DR/4DR/Wagon	4②	1.8 (1781)	2 bbl	82 @ 4800	101 @ 2800	3.62 × 2.64	9.5:1	43 @ 5000
	3DR/4DR/Wagon	4②	1.8 (1781)	SPFI	90 @ 5600	101 @ 2800	3.62 × 2.64	9.5:1	43 @ 5000
	3DR/4DR/Wagon Turbo	4②	1.8 (1781)	MPFI	111 @ 4800	134 @ 2800	3.62 × 2.64	7.7:1	43 @ 5000
	XT	4②	1.8 (1781)	MPFI	94 @ 5200	101 @ 2800	3.62 × 2.64	9.0:1	43 @ 5000
	XT Turbo	4②	1.8 (1781)	MPFI	111 @ 4800	134 @ 2800	3.62 × 2.64	7.7:1	43 @ 5000
1987	BRAT	5	1.8 (1781)	2 bbl	73 @ 4800	94 @ 2400	3.62 × 2.64	8.7:1	57 @ 2500
	2DR	2	1.6 (1595)	2 bbl	69 @ 4800	86 @ 2400	3.62 × 2.36	9.0:1	57 @ 2500
	2DR GL	4②	1.8 (1781)	2 bbl	73 @ 4800	94 @ 2400	3.62 × 2.64	8.7:1	57 @ 2500
	3DR/4DR/Wagon	4②	1.8 (1781)	2 bbl	84 @ 5200	101 @ 3200	3.62 × 2.64	9.5:1	43 @ 5000

GENERAL ENGINE SPECIFICATIONS

Year	Model	Engine ID/VIN	Engine Displacement Liters (cc)	Fuel System Type	Net Horsepower @ rpm	Net Torque @ rpm (ft. lbs.)	Bore × Stroke (in.)	Compression Ratio	Oil Pressure @ rpm
1987	4DR ⑤	4②	1.8 (1781)	SPFI	84 @ 5200	101 @ 3200	3.62 × 2.64	9.5:1	43 @ 5000
	3DR/4DR/Wagon	4②	1.8 (1781)	SPFI	90 @ 5200	101 @ 2800	3.62 × 2.64	9.5:1	43 @ 5000
	3DR/4DR/Wagon Turbo	4②	1.8 (1781)	MPFI	115 @ 5200	134 @ 2800	3.62 × 2.64	7.7:1	43 @ 5000
	XT	4②	1.8 (1781)	MPFI	97 @ 5200	103 @ 3200	3.62 × 2.64	9.5:1	43 @ 5000
	XT Turbo	4②	1.8 (1781)	MPFI	115 @ 5200	134 @ 2800	3.62 × 2.64	7.7:1	43 @ 5000
	Justy	7①	1.2 (1189)	2 bbl	66 @ 5200	70 @ 3600	3.07 × 3.27	9.0:1	47 @ 3000
1988	2DR	2	1.6 (1595)	2 bbl	69 @ 4800	86 @ 2400	3.62 × 2.36	9.0:1	57 @ 2500
	4DR ⑤	4②	1.8 (1781)	SPFI	84 @ 5200	101 @ 3200	3.62 × 2.64	9.5:1	43 @ 5000
	3DR/4DR/Wagon	4②	1.8 (1781)	SPFI	90 @ 5200	101 @ 2800	3.62 × 2.64	9.5:1	43 @ 5000
	3DR/4DR/Wagon Turbo	4②	1.8 (1781)	MPFI	115 @ 5200	134 @ 2800	3.62 × 2.64	7.7:1	43 @ 5000
	XT	4②	1.8 (1781)	MPFI	97 @ 5200	103 @ 3200	3.62 × 2.64	9.5:1	43 @ 5000
	XT-6	8③	2.7 (2672)	MPFI	145 @ 5200	156 @ 4000	3.62 × 2.64	7.7:1	43 @ 5000
	Justy	7①	1.2 (1189)	2 bbl	66 @ 5200	70 @ 3600	3.07 × 3.27	9.1:1	47 @ 3000
1989	2DR	2	1.6 (1595)	2 bbl	69 @ 4800	86 @ 2400	3.62 × 2.36	9.0:1	57 @ 2500
	4DR ⑤	4②	1.8 (1781)	SPFI	84 @ 5200	101 @ 3200	3.62 × 2.64	9.5:1	43 @ 5000
	3DR/4DR/Wagon	4②	1.8 (1781)	SPFI	90 @ 5200	101 @ 2800	3.62 × 2.64	9.5:1	43 @ 5000
	3DR/4DR/Wagon Turbo	4②	1.8 (1781)	MPFI	115 @ 5200	134 @ 2800	3.62 × 2.64	7.7:1	43 @ 5000
	XT	4②	1.8 (1781)	MPFI	97 @ 5200	103 @ 3200	3.62 × 2.64	9.5:1	43 @ 5000
	XT-6	8③	2.7 (2672)	MPFI	145 @ 5200	156 @ 4000	3.62 × 2.64	7.7:1	43 @ 5000
	Justy	7①	1.2 (1189)	2 bbl	66 @ 5200	70 @ 3600	3.07 × 3.27	9.1:1	47 @ 3000
1990	XT	4②	1.8 (1781)	MPFI	97 @ 5200	103 @ 3200	3.62 × 2.64	9.5:1	43 @ 5000
	XT-6	8③	2.7 (2672)	MPFI	145 @ 5200	156 @ 4000	3.62 × 2.64	7.7:1	43 @ 5000
	Justy	7①	1.2 (1189)	2 bbl	66 @ 5200	70 @ 3600	3.07 × 3.27	9.1:1	47 @ 3000
	Justy	7①	1.2 (1189)	MPFI	73 @ 5600	71 @ 3600	3.07 × 3.27	9.1:1	47 @ 3000
	Loyale	4②	1.8 (1781)	SPFI	90 @ 5200	101 @ 2800	3.62 × 2.64	9.5:1	43 @ 5000
	Loyale Turbo	4②	1.8 (1781)	MPFI	115 @ 5200	134 @ 2800	3.62 × 2.64	7.7:1	43 @ 5000
	Legacy	6	2.2 (2212)	MPFI	130 @ 5600	137 @ 2400	3.82 × 2.95	9.5:1	43 @ 5000
1991	XT	4②	1.8 (1781)	MPFI	97 @ 5200	103 @ 3200	3.62 × 2.64	9.5:1	43 @ 5000
	XT-6	8③	2.7 (2672)	MPFI	145 @ 5200	156 @ 4000	3.62 × 2.64	7.7:1	43 @ 5000
	Justy	7①	1.2 (1189)	2 bbl	66 @ 5200	70 @ 3600	3.07 × 3.27	9.1:1	47 @ 3000
	Justy	7①	1.2 (1189)	MPFI	73 @ 5600	71 @ 3600	3.07 × 3.27	9.1:1	47 @ 3000
	Loyale	4②	1.8 (1781)	SPFI	90 @ 5200	101 @ 2800	3.62 × 2.64	9.5:1	43 @ 5000
	Legacy	6	2.2 (2212)	MPFI	130 @ 5600	137 @ 2400	3.82 × 2.95	9.5:1	43 @ 5000
	Legacy Turbo	6	2.2 (2212)	MPFI	160 @ 5600	181 @ 2800	3.82 × 2.95	8.0:1	43 @ 5000
1992	Justy	7①	1.2 (1189)	2 bbl	66 @ 5200	70 @ 3600	3.07 × 3.27	9.1:1	47 @ 3000
	Justy	7①	1.2 (1189)	MPFI	73 @ 5600	71 @ 3600	3.07 × 3.27	9.1:1	47 @ 3000
	Loyale	4②	1.8 (1781)	SPFI	90 @ 5200	101 @ 2800	3.62 × 2.64	9.5:1	43 @ 5000
	Legacy	6	2.2 (2212)	MPFI	130 @ 5600	137 @ 2400	3.82 × 2.95	9.5:1	43 @ 5000
	SVX	3	3.3 (3318)	MPFI	230 @ 5400	228 @ 4400	3.82 × 2.95	10.1:1	43 @ 5000

NOTE: Horsepower and torque are SAE net figures. They are measured at the rear of the transmission with all accessories installed and operating. Since the figures vary when a given engine is installed in different models, some are representative rather than exact.
① Code 8: with 4WD
② Code 5: with 4WD
   Code 7: with pneumatic suspension
③ Code 9: with pneumatic suspension
④ 4-speed
⑤ 2WD

VALVE SPECIFICATIONS

Year	Engine ID/VIN	Engine Displacement Liters (cc)	Seat Angle (deg.)	Face Angle (deg.)	Spring Test Pressure (lbs. @ in.)	Spring Installed Height (in.)	Stem-to-Guide Clearance (in.)		Stem Diameter (in.)	
							Intake	Exhaust	Intake	Exhaust
1985	2	4-1.6 (1595)	45	45	33–38 ⑤	1.555	0.0014–0.0026	0.0016–0.0028	0.3130–0.3136	0.3128–0.3134
	4/5/7	4-1.8 (1781)	45	45	112–129 ② ③	1.240	0.0014–0.0026	0.0016–0.0028	0.2736–0.2742	0.2734–0.2740
1986	2	4-1.6 (1595)	45	45	33–38 ⑤	1.555	0.0014–0.0026	0.0016–0.0028	0.3130–0.3136	0.3128–0.3134
	4/5/7	4-1.8 (1781)	45	45	100–115	1.240	0.0014–0.0026	0.0016–0.0028	0.2736–0.2742	0.2734–0.2740
1987	7/8	3-1.2 (1189)	45	45	112–129	1.248	0.0008–0.0020	0.0016–0.0028	0.2742–0.2748	0.2734–0.2740
	2	4-1.6 (1595)	45	45	33–38 ⑤	1.555	0.0014–0.0026	0.0016–0.0028	0.3130–0.3136	0.3128–0.3134
	4/5/7	4-1.8 (1781)	45	45	112–129 ③	1.240	0.0014–0.0026	0.0016–0.0028	0.2736–0.2742	0.2734–0.2740
1988	7/8	3-1.2 (1189)	45	45	112–129	1.248	0.0008–0.0020	0.0016–0.0028	0.2742–0.2748	0.2734–0.2740
	2	4-1.6 (1595)	45	45	33–38 ⑤	1.555	0.0014–0.0026	0.0016–0.0028	0.3130–0.3136	0.3128–0.3134
	4/5/7	4-1.8 (1781)	45	45	112–129 ③	1.240	0.0014–0.0026	0.0016–0.0028	0.2736–0.2742	0.2734–0.2740
	8/9	6-2.7 (2672)	45	45	100–115 ③	1.240	0.0014–0.0026	0.0016–0.0028	0.2736–0.2741	0.2734–0.2740
1989	7/8	3-1.2 (1189)	45	45	112–129	1.248	0.0008–0.0020	0.0016–0.0028	0.2742–0.2748	0.2734–0.2740
	2	4-1.6 (1595)	45	45	33–38 ⑤	1.555	0.0014–0.0026	0.0016–0.0028	0.3130–0.3136	0.3128–0.3134
	4/7	4-1.8 (1781)	45	45	112–129 ③	1.240	0.0014–0.0026	0.0016–0.0028	0.2736–0.2742	0.2734–0.2740
	8/9	6-2.7 (2672)	45	45	100–115 ③	1.240	0.0014–0.0026	0.0016–0.0028	0.2736–0.2741	0.2734–0.2740
1990	7/8	3-1.2 (1189)	45	45	112–129	1.248	0.0008–0.0020	0.0016–0.0028	0.2742–0.2748	0.2734–0.2740
	4/7	4-1.8 (1781)	45	45	112–129 ③	1.240	0.0014–0.0026	0.0016–0.0028	0.2736–0.2742	0.2734–0.2740
	6	4-2.2 (2212)	45	45	92–106	1.150	0.0014–0.0024	0.0016–0.0026	0.2343–0.2348	0.2341–0.2346
	8/9	6-2.7 (2672)	45	45	100–115 ③	1.240	0.0014–0.0026	0.0016–0.0028	0.2736–0.2741	0.2734–0.2740
1991	7/8	3-1.2 (1189)	45	45	112–129	1.248	0.0008–0.0020	0.0016–0.0028	0.2742–0.2748	0.2734–0.2740
	4/7	4-1.8 (1781)	45	45	112–129 ③	1.240	0.0014–0.0026	0.0016–0.0028	0.2736–0.2742	0.2734–0.2740
	6	4-2.2 (2212)	45	45	92–106	1.150	0.0014–0.0024	0.0016–0.0026	0.2343–0.2348	0.2341–0.2346
	8/9	6-2.7 (2762)	45	45	100–115 ③	1.240	0.0014–0.0026	0.0016–0.0028	0.2736–0.2741	0.2734–0.2740

VALVE SPECIFICATIONS

Year	Engine ID/VIN	Engine Displacement Liters (cc)	Seat Angle (deg.)	Face Angle (deg.)	Spring Test Pressure (lbs. @ in.)	Spring Installed Height (in.)	Stem-to-Guide Clearance (in.)		Stem Diameter (in.)	
							Intake	Exhaust	Intake	Exhaust
1992	7/8	3-1.2 (1189)	45	45	112–129	1.248	0.0008–0.0020	0.0016–0.0028	0.2742–0.2748	0.2734–0.2740
	4/7	4-1.8 (1781)	45	45	112–129 ③	1.240	0.0014–0.0026	0.0016–0.0028	0.2736–0.2742	0.2734–0.2740
	6	4-2.2 (2212)	45	45	92–106	1.150	0.0014–0.0024	0.0016–0.0026	0.2343–0.2348	0.2341–0.2346
	3	6-3.3 (3318)	45	45	70–80 ④	0.831	0.0012–0.0022	0.0016–0.0026	0.2344–0.2350	0.2341–0.2346

① XT
② GL with manual transmission: 102–118 lbs.
③ Outer/Inner: 45–52 @ 1.122 in.
④ Outer/Inner: 33–38 @ 0.772 in.
⑤ Outer/Inner: 19–22 @ 1.476 in.

CAMSHAFT SPECIFICATIONS

All measurements given in inches.

Year	Engine ID/VIN	Engine Displacement Liters (cc)	Journal Diameter 1	2	3	4	5	Elevation In.	Ex.	Bearing Clearance	Camshaft End Play
1985	2	4-1.6L (1595)	1.0220–1.0226	1.0220–1.0226	1.4157 1.4163	—	—	1.2693–1.2732	1.2693–1.2732	0.0010–0.0023	0.0008–0.0035
	4/5/7	4-1.8L (1781)	1.4946–1.4953	1.9080–1.9087	1.4946–1.4953	1.5340–② 1.5346	—	③ ④	③ ④	0.0008–0.0021	0.0012–0.0102
	4/5/7	4-1.8L (1781) ①	1.4946–1.4953	1.9080–1.9087	1.8883–1.8890	1.5340–② 1.5346	—	1.5650–1.5689	1.5650–1.5689	0.0008–0.0021	0.0012–0.0102
1986	2	4-1.6L (1595)	1.0220–1.0226	1.0220–1.0226	1.4157 1.4163	—	—	1.2693–1.2732	1.2693–1.2732	0.0010–0.0023	0.0008–0.0035
	4/5/7	4-1.8L (1781)	1.4946–1.4953	1.9080–1.9087	1.4946–1.4953	1.5340–② 1.5346	—	④	④	0.0008–0.0021	0.0012–0.0102
	4/5/7	4-1.8L (1781) ①	1.4946–1.4953	1.9080–1.9087	1.8883–1.8890	1.5340–② 1.5346	—	1.5650–1.5689	1.5650–1.5689	0.0008–0.0021	0.0012–0.0102
1987	7/8	3-1.2L (1189)	—	—	—	—	—	1.4520–1.4528	1.4520–1.4528	—	0.0012–0.0150
	2	4-1.6L (1595)	1.0220–1.0226	1.0220–1.0226	1.4157 1.4163	—	—	1.2693–1.2732	1.2693–1.2732	0.0010–0.0023	0.0008–0.0035
	4/5/7	4-1.8L (1781)	1.8883–1.8890	1.9080–1.9087	1.8889–1.8890	1.5340–② 1.5346	—	1.5650–1.5689	1.5650–1.5689	0.0008–0.0021	0.0012–0.0102
	4/5/7	4-1.8L (1781) ①	1.4946–1.4953	1.9080–1.9087	1.8883–1.8890	1.5340–② 1.5346	—	1.5650–1.5689	1.5650–1.5689	0.0008–0.0021	0.0012–0.0102
1988	7/8	3-1.2L (1189)	—	—	—	—	—	1.4520–1.4528	1.4520–1.4528	—	0.0012–0.0150
	2	4-1.6L (1595)	1.0220–1.0226	1.0220–1.0226	1.4157 1.4163	—	—	1.2693–1.2732	1.2693–1.2732	0.0010–0.0023	0.0008–0.0035
	4/7	4-1.8L (1781)	1.8883–1.8890	1.9080–1.9087	1.8889–1.8890	1.5340–② 1.5346	—	1.5650–1.5689	1.5650–1.5689	0.0008–0.0021	0.0012–0.0102
	4/7	4-1.8L (1781) ①	1.4946–1.4953	1.9080–1.9087	1.8883–1.8890	1.5340–② 1.5346	—	1.5650–1.5689	1.5650–1.5689	0.0008–0.0021	0.0012–0.0102
	8/9	6-2.7L (2672)	1.4946–1.4953	1.9080–1.9087	1.8883–1.8890	1.9474–1.8693	1.5340–② 1.5346	1.5606–1.5646	1.5606–1.5646	0.0008–0.0021	0.0012–0.0102

CAMSHAFT SPECIFICATIONS

All measurements given in inches.

Year	Engine ID/VIN	Engine Displacement Liters (cc)	Journal Diameter					Elevation		Bearing Clearance	Camshaft End Play
			1	2	3	4	5	In.	Ex.		
1989	7/8	3-1.2L (1189)	—	—	—	—	—	1.4520– 1.4528	1.4520– 1.4528	—	0.0012– 0.0150
	2	4-1.6L (1595)	1.0220– 1.0226	1.0220– 1.0226	1.4157 1.4163	—	—	1.2693– 1.2732	1.2693– 1.2732	0.0010– 0.0023	0.0008– 0.0035
	4/7	4-1.8L (1781)	1.8883– 1.8890	1.9080– 1.9087	1.8889– 1.8890	1.5340–② 1.5346	—	1.5650– 1.5689	1.5650– 1.5689	0.0008– 0.0021	0.0012– 0.0102
	4/7	4-1.8L (1781) ①	1.4946– 1.4953	1.9080– 1.9087	1.8883– 1.8890	1.5340–② 1.5346	—	1.5650– 1.5689	1.5650– 1.5689	0.0008– 0.0021	0.0012– 0.0102
	8/9	6-2.7L (2672)	1.4946– 1.4953	1.9080– 1.9087	1.8883– 1.8890	1.9474– 1.8693	1.5340–② 1.5346	1.5606– 1.5646	1.5606– 1.5646	0.0008– 0.0021	0.0012– 0.0102
1990	7/8	3-1.2L (1189)	—	—	—	—	—	1.4520– 1.4528	1.4520– 1.4528	—	0.0012– 0.0150
	4/7	4-1.8L (1781)	1.8883– 1.8890	1.9080– 1.9087	1.8889– 1.8890	1.5340–② 1.5346	—	1.5650– 1.5689	1.5650– 1.5689	0.0008– 0.0021	0.0012– 0.0102
	4/7	4-1.8L (1781) ①	1.4946– 1.4953	1.9080– 1.9087	1.8883– 1.8890	1.5340–② 1.5346	—	1.5650– 1.5689	1.5650– 1.5689	0.0008– 0.0021	0.0012– 0.0102
	6	4-2.2L (2212)	1.4963– 1.4970	1.4766– 1.4774	1.2300– 1.2608			1.2752– 1.2791	1.2752– 1.2791	0.0022– 0.0035	0.0012– 0.0102
	8/9	6-2.7L (2672)	1.4946– 1.4953	1.9080– 1.9087	1.8883– 1.8890	1.9474– 1.8693	1.5340–② 1.5346	1.5606– 1.5646	1.5606– 1.5646	0.0008– 0.0021	0.0012– 0.0102
1991	7/8	3-1.2L (1189)	—	—	—	—	—	1.4520– 1.4528	1.4520– 1.4528	—	0.0012– 0.0150
	4/7	4-1.8L (1781)	1.8883– 1.8890	1.9080– 1.9087	1.8889– 1.8890	1.5340–② 1.5346	—	1.5650– 1.5689	1.5650– 1.5689	0.0008– 0.0021	0.0012– 0.0102
	4/7	4-1.8L (1781) ①	1.4946– 1.4953	1.9080– 1.9087	1.8883– 1.8890	1.5340–② 1.5346	—	1.5650– 1.5689	1.5650– 1.5689	0.0008– 0.0021	0.0012– 0.0102
	6	4-2.2L (2212)	1.4963– 1.4970	1.4766– 1.4774	1.2300– 1.2608	—	—	1.2752– 1.2791	1.2752– 1.2791	0.0022– 0.0035	0.0012– 0.0102
	8/9	6-2.7L (2672)	1.4946– 1.4953	1.9080– 1.9087	1.8883– 1.8890	1.9474– 1.8693	1.5340–② 1.5346	1.5606– 1.5646	1.5606– 1.5646	0.0008– 0.0021	0.0012– 0.0102
1992	7/8	3-1.2L (1189)	—	—	—	—	—	1.4520– 1.4528	1.4520– 1.4528	—	0.0012– 0.0150
	4/7	4-1.8L (1781)	1.8883– 1.8890	1.9080– 1.9087	1.8889– 1.8890	1.5340–② 1.5346	—	1.5650– 1.5689	1.5650– 1.5689	0.0008– 0.0021	0.0012– 0.0102
	6	4-2.2L (2212)	1.4963– 1.4970	1.4766– 1.4774	1.2300– 1.2608	—	—	1.2752– 1.2791	1.2752– 1.2791	0.0022– 0.0035	0.0012– 0.0102
	3	6-3.3L (3318)	1.2577– 1.2584	1.1002– 1.1009	1.1002– 1.1009	1.1002– 1.1009	—	1.5374– 1.5413	1.5689– 1.5728	0.0015– 0.0028	⑤

① XT
② Distributor journal left-hand camshaft only
③ 1985 DL 4-speed manual transmission
   1.5394–1.5433
④ Carbureted and MPFI Turbo 1.5606–1.5646
   SPFI and MPFI 1.5650–1.5689
⑤ Exhaust 0.0008–0.0031
   Intake 0.0012–0.0035

CRANKSHAFT AND CONNECTING ROD SPECIFICATIONS

All measurements are given in inches.

| Year | Engine ID/VIN | Engine Displacement Liters (cc) | Crankshaft | | | | Connecting Rod | | |
			Main Brg. Journal Dia.	Main Brg. Oil Clearance	Shaft End-play	Thrust on No.	Journal Diameter	Oil Clearance	Side Clearance
1985	2	4-1.6 (1595)	2.1636–2.1642	⑥	0.0004–0.0037	2	1.7715–1.7720	0.0008–0.0028	0.0028–0.0130
	4/5/7	4-1.8 (1781)	①	②	0.0004–0.0037	2	1.7715–1.7720	0.0004–0.0021	0.0028–0.0130
1986	2	4-1.6 (1595)	2.1636–2.1642	⑥	0.0004–0.0037	2	1.7715–1.7720	0.0008–0.0028	0.0028–0.0130
	4/5/7	4-1.8 (1781)	①	②	0.0004–0.0037	2	1.7715–1.7720	0.0004–0.0021	0.0028–0.0130
1987	7/8	3-1.2 (1189)	1.6250–1.6290	0.0006–0.0018	0.0031–0.0070	4	0.6531–1.6535	0.0008–0.0021	0.0028–0.0118
	2	4-1.6 (1595)	2.1636–2.1642	⑥	0.0004–0.0037	2	1.7715–1.7720	0.0008–0.0028	0.0028–0.0130
	4/5/7	4-1.8 (1781)	①	②	0.0004–0.0037	2	1.7715–1.7720	0.0004–0.0021	0.0028–0.0130
1988	7/8	3-1.2 (1189)	1.6250–1.6290	0.0006–0.0018	0.0031–0.0070	4	0.6531–1.6535	0.0008–0.0021	0.0028–0.0118
	2	4-1.6 (1595)	2.1636–2.1642	⑥	0.0004–0.0037	2	1.7715–1.7720	0.0008–0.0028	0.0028–0.0130
	4/5/7	4-1.8 (1781)	①	②	0.0004–0.0037	2	1.7715–1.7720	0.0004–0.0021	0.0028–0.0130
	8/9	6-2.7 (2672)	①	②	0.0004–0.0037	3	1.7715–1.6535	0.0004–0.0021	0.0028–0.0118
1989	7/8	3-1.2 (1189)	1.6250–1.6290	0.0006–0.0018	0.0031–0.0070	4	0.6531–1.6535	0.0008–0.0021	0.0028–0.0118
	2	4-1.6 (1595)	2.1636–2.1642	⑥	0.0004–0.0037	2	1.7715–1.7720	0.0008–0.0028	0.0028–0.0130
	4/7	4-1.8 (1781)	①	②	0.0004–0.0037	2	1.7715–1.7720	0.0004–0.0021	0.0028–0.0130
	8/9	6-2.7 (2672)	①	②	0.0004–0.0037	3	1.7715–1.6535	0.0004–0.0021	0.0028–0.0118
1990	7/8	3-1.2 (1189)	1.6250–1.6290	0.0006–0.0018	0.0031–0.0070	4	0.6531–1.6535	0.0008–0.0021	0.0028–0.0118
	4/7	4-1.8 (1781)	①	②	0.0004–0.0037	2	1.7715–1.7720	0.0004–0.0021	0.0028–0.0130
	6	4-2.2 (2212)	2.3616–2.3622	④	0.0012–0.0045	3	2.0466–2.0472	0.0006–③ 0.0017	0.0028–0.0130
	8/9	6-2.7 (2672)	①	②	0.0004–0.0037	3	1.7715–1.6535	0.0004–0.0021	0.0028–0.0118
1991	7/8	3-1.2 (1189)	1.6250–1.6290	0.0006–0.0018	0.0031–0.0070	4	0.6531–1.6535	0.0008–0.0021	0.0028–0.0118
	4/7	4-1.8 (1781)	①	②	0.0004–0.0037	2	1.7715–1.7720	0.0004–0.0021	0.0028–0.0130
	6	4-2.2 (2212)	2.3616–2.3622	④	0.0012–0.0045	3	2.0466–2.0472	0.0006–③ 0.0017	0.0028–0.0130
	8/9	6-2.7 (2672)	①	②	0.0004–0.0037	3	1.7715–1.6535	0.0004–0.0021	0.0028–0.0118
1992	7/8	3-1.2 (1189)	1.6250–1.6290	0.0006–0.0018	0.0031–0.0070	4	0.6531–1.6535	0.0008–0.0021	0.0028–0.0118

CRANKSHAFT AND CONNECTING ROD SPECIFICATIONS

All measurements are given in inches.

| Year | Engine ID/VIN | Engine Displacement Liters (cc) | Crankshaft | | | | Connecting Rod | | |
			Main Brg. Journal Dia.	Main Brg. Oil Clearance	Shaft End-play	Thrust on No.	Journal Diameter	Oil Clearance	Side Clearance
1992	4/7	4-1.8 (1781)	①	②	0.0004–0.0037	2	1.7715–1.7720	0.0004–0.0021	0.0028–0.0130
	6	4-2.2 (2212)	2.3616–2.3622	④	0.0012–0.0045	3	2.0466–2.0472	0.0006–③ 0.0017	0.0028–0.0130
	3	6-3.3 (3318)	2.3619–2.3625	⑤	0.0012–0.0045	5	2.0466–2.0472	0.0008–0.0018	0.0028–0.0130

① Front: 2.1637–2.1642
  Center: 2.1635–2.1642
  Rear: 2.1636–2.1642
② Front and Rear: 0.0001–0.0014
  Center: 0.0003–0.0011
③ Turbo: 0.0010–0.0021

④ No. 1, 5: 0.0787–0.0792
  No. 2, 3, 4: 0.0787–0.0793
⑤ No. 1, 3, 7: 0.0002–0.0014
  No. 2, 4, 6: 0.0005–0.0015
  No. 5: 0.0005–0.0013
⑥ Front and Rear: 0.0004–0.0014
  Center: 0.0004–0.0012

PISTON AND RING SPECIFICATIONS

All measurements are given in inches.

| Year | Engine ID/VIN | Engine Displacement Liters (cc) | Piston Clearance | Ring Gap | | | Ring Side Clearance | | |
				Top Compression	Bottom Compression	Oil Control	Top Compression	Bottom Compression	Oil Control
1985	2	4-1.6L (1595)	0.0004–0.0016	0.0079–0.0138	0.0079–0.0138	0.0120–0.0350	0.0016–0.0031	0.0012–0.0028	0
	4/5/7	4-1.8L (1781)	0.0004–0.0016	0.0079–0.0138	0.0079–0.0138	0.0120–0.0350	0.0016–0.0031	0.0012–0.0028	0
	4/5/7	4-1.8L (1781) ①	0.0006–0.0014	0.0079–0.0138	0.0079–0.0138	0.0120–0.0350	0.0016–0.0031	0.0012–0.0028	0
1986	2	4-1.6L (1595)	0.0004–0.0016	0.0079–0.0138	0.0079–0.0138	0.0120–0.0350	0.0016–0.0031	0.0012–0.0028	0
	4/5/7	4-1.8L (1781)	0.0004–0.0016	0.0079–0.0138	0.0079–0.0138	0.0120–0.0350	0.0016–0.0031	0.0012–0.0028	0
	4/5/7	4-1.8L (1781) ①	0.0006–0.0014	0.0079–0.0138	0.0079–0.0138	0.0120–0.0350	0.0016–0.0031	0.0012–0.0028	0
1987	7/8	3-1.2L (1189)	0.0015–0.0024	0.0079–0.0138	0.0079–0.0138	0.0120–0.0350	0.0014–0.0030	0.0010–0.0026	0
	2	4-1.6L (1595)	0.0004–0.0016	0.0079–0.0138	0.0079–0.0138	0.0120–0.0350	0.0016–0.0031	0.0012–0.0028	0
	4/5/7	4-1.8L (1781)	0.0004–0.0016	0.0079–0.0138	0.0079–0.0138	0.0120–0.0350	0.0016–0.0031	0.0012–0.0028	0
	4/5/7	4-1.8L (1781) ①	0.0006–0.0014	0.0079–0.0138	0.0079–0.0138	0.0120–0.0350	0.0016–0.0031	0.0012–0.0028	0
1988	7/8	3-1.2L (1189)	0.0015–0.0024	0.0079–0.0138	0.0079–0.0138	0.0120–0.0350	0.0014–0.0030	0.0010–0.0026	0
	2	4-1.6L (1595)	0.0004–0.0016	0.0079–0.0138	0.0079–0.0138	0.0120–0.0350	0.0016–0.0031	0.0012–0.0028	0
	4/5/7	4-1.8L (1781)	0.0004–② 0.0016	0.0079–0.0138	0.0079–0.0138	0.0120–0.0350	0.0016–0.0031	0.0012–0.0028	0
	4/5/7	4-1.8L (1781) ①	0.0006–0.0014	0.0079–0.0138	0.0079–0.0138	0.0120–0.0350	0.0016–0.0031	0.0012–0.0028	0
	8/9	6-2.7L (2672)	0.0006–0.0014	0.0079–0.0138	0.0079–0.0138	0.0120–0.0350	0.0016–0.0031	0.0012–0.0028	0

PISTON AND RING SPECIFICATIONS
All measurements are given in inches.

Year	Engine ID/VIN	Engine Displacement Liters (cc)	Piston Clearance	Ring Gap			Ring Side Clearance		
				Top Compression	Bottom Compression	Oil Control	Top Compression	Bottom Compression	Oil Control
1989	7/8	3-1.2L (1189)	0.0015–0.0028	0.0079–0.0138	0.0079–0.0138	0.0120–0.0350	0.0014–0.0030	0.0010–0.0026	0
	2	4-1.6L (1595)	0.0004–0.0016	0.0079–0.0138	0.0079–0.0138	0.0120–0.0350	0.0016–0.0031	0.0012–0.0028	0
	4/7	4-1.8L (1781)	0.0004–② 0.0016	0.0079–0.0138	0.0079–0.0138	0.0120–0.0350	0.0016–0.0031	0.0012–0.0028	0
	4/7	4-1.8L (1781) ①	0.0006–0.0014	0.0079–0.0138	0.0079–0.0138	0.0120–0.0350	0.0016–0.0031	0.0012–0.0028	0
	8/9	6-2.7L (2672)	0.0006–0.0014	0.0079–0.0138	0.0079–0.0138	0.0120–0.0350	0.0016–0.0031	0.0012–0.0028	0
1990	7/8	3-1.2L (1189)	0.0015–0.0028	0.0079–0.0138	0.0079–0.0138	0.0120–0.0350	0.0014–0.0030	0.0010–0.0026	0
	4/7	4-1.8L (1781)	0.0006–② 0.0014	0.0079–0.0138	0.0079–0.0138	0.0120–0.0350	0.0016–0.0031	0.0012–0.0028	0
	4/7	4-1.8L (1781) ①	0.0006–0.0014	0.0079–0.0138	0.0079–0.0138	0.0120–0.0350	0.0016–0.0031	0.0012–0.0028	0
	6	4-2.2L (2212)	0.0004–0.0012	0.0079–③ 0.0138	0.0146–0.0205	0.0079–0.0276	0.0016–0.0031	0.0012–0.0028	0
	8/9	6-2.7L (2672)	0.0006–0.0014	0.0079–0.0138	0.0079–0.0138	0.0120–0.0350	0.0016–0.0031	0.0012–0.0028	0
1991	7/8	3-1.2L (1189)	0.0015–0.0028	0.0079–0.0138	0.0079–0.0138	0.0120–0.0350	0.0014–0.0030	0.0010–0.0026	0
	4/7	4-1.8L (1781)	0.0006–② 0.0014	0.0079–0.0138	0.0079–0.0138	0.0120–0.0350	0.0016–0.0031	0.0012–0.0028	0
	4/7	4-1.8L (1781) ①	0.0006–0.0014	0.0079–0.0138	0.0079–0.0138	0.0120–0.0350	0.0016–0.0031	0.0012–0.0028	0
	6	4-2.2L (2212)	0.0004–0.0012	0.0079–③ 0.0138	0.0146–0.0205	0.0079–0.0276	0.0016–0.0031	0.0012–0.0028	0
	8/9	6-2.7L (2672)	0.0006–0.0014	0.0079–0.0138	0.0079–0.0138	0.0120–0.0350	0.0016–0.0031	0.0012–0.0028	0
1992	7/8	3-1.2L (1189)	0.0015–0.0028	0.0079–0.0138	0.0079–0.0138	0.0120–0.0350	0.0014–0.0030	0.0010–0.0026	0
	4/7	4-1.8L (1781)	0.0006–② 0.0014	0.0079–0.0138	0.0079–0.0138	0.0120–0.0350	0.0016–0.0031	0.0012–0.0028	0
	6	4-2.2L (2212)	0.0004–0.0012	0.0079–③ 0.0138	0.0146–0.0205	0.0079–0.0276	0.0016–0.0031	0.0012–0.0028	0
	3	6-3.3L (3318)	0.0004–0.0012	0.0079–0.0118	0.0146–0.0205	0.0079–0.0236	0.0016–0.0035	0.0012–0.0028	0

① XT
② Turbo 0.0004–0.0012
③ Turbo 0.0079–0.0098

TORQUE SPECIFICATIONS

All readings in ft. lbs.

Year	Engine ID/VIN	Engine Displacement Liters (cc)	Cylinder Head Bolts	Main Bearing Bolts	Rod Bearing Bolts	Crankshaft Damper Bolts	Flywheel Bolts	Manifold Intake	Manifold Exhaust	Spark Plugs	Lug Nut
1985	2	1.6L (1595)	②	⑥	29–31	66–79	30–33	13–16	19–22	13–17	58–72
	4/5/7	1.8L (1781)	②	⑥	29–31	66–79	51–55	13–16	19–22	13–17	58–72
1986	2	1.6L (1595)	②	⑥	29–31	66–79	30–33	13–16	19–22	13–17	58–72
	4/5/7	1.8L (1781)	②	⑥	29–31	66–79	51–55	13–16	19–22	13–17	58–72
1987	7/8	1.2L (1189)	①	30–35	29–33	58–72	65–71	14–22	14–22	13–17	58–72
	2	1.6L (1595)	②	⑥	29–31	66–79	30–33	13–16	19–22	13–17	58–72
	4/5/7	1.8L (1781)	②	⑥	29–31	66–79	51–55	13–16	19–22	13–17	58–72
1988	7/8	1.2L (1189)	①	30–35	29–33	58–72	65–71	14–22	14–22	13–17	58–72
	2	1.6L (1595)	②	⑥	29–31	66–79	30–33	13–16	19–22	13–17	58–72
	4/5/7	1.8L (1781)	②	⑥	29–31	66–79	51–55	13–16	19–22	13–17	58–72
	8/9	2.7L (2672)	④	⑥	29–31	66–79	51–55	13–16	19–22	13–17	58–72
1989	7/8	1.2L (1189)	①	30–35	29–33	58–72	65–71	14–22	14–22	13–17	58–72
	2	1.6L (1595)	②	⑥	29–31	66–79	30–33	13–16	19–22	13–17	58–72
	4/7	1.8L (1781)	②	⑥	29–31	66–79	51–55	13–16	19–22	13–17	58–72
	8/9	2.7L (2672)	④	⑥	29–31	66–79	51–55	13–16	19–22	13–17	58–72
1990	7/8	1.2L (1189)	①	30–35	29–33	58–72	65–71	14–22	14–22	13–17	58–72
	4/7	1.8L (1781)	②	⑥	29–31	66–79	51–55	13–16	19–22	13–17	58–72
	6	2.2L (2212)	③	⑥	32–34	69–76	51–55	21–25	19–26	13–17	58–72
	8/9	2.7L (2672)	④	⑥	29–31	66–79	51–55	13–16	19–22	13–17	58–72
1991	7/8	1.2L (1189)	①	30–35	29–33	58–72	65–71	14–22	14–22	13–17	58–72
	4/7	1.8L (1781)	②	⑥	29–31	66–79	51–55	13–16	19–22	13–17	58–72
	6	2.2L (2212)	③	⑥	32–34	69–76	51–55	21–25	19–26	13–17	58–72
	8/9	2.7L (2672)	④	⑥	29–31	66–79	51–55	13–16	19–22	13–17	58–72
1992	7/8	1.2L (1189)	①	30–35	29–33	58–72	65–71	14–22	14–22	13–17	58–72
	4/7	1.8L (1781)	②	⑥	29–31	66–79	51–55	13–16	19–22	13–17	58–72
	6	2.2L (2212)	③	⑥	32–34	69–76	51–55	21–25	19–26	13–17	58–72
	3	3.3L (3318)	⑤	⑥	32–34	108–123	51–55	17–20	22–29	13–17	58–72

① Tighten all bolts in sequence to 29 ft. lbs. (39Nm).
Tighten all bolts in sequence to 54 ft. lbs. (73Nm).
Loosen all bolts 90° or more in the reverse order of the tighening sequence.
Tighten all bolts in sequence to 51–57 ft. lbs. (70–77Nm).

② Tighten all bolts in sequence to 22 ft. lbs. (29Nm).
Tighten all bolts in sequence to 43 ft. lbs. (59Nm).
Tighten all bolts in sequence to 47 ft. lbs. (64Nm).

③ Tighten all bolts in sequence to 22 ft. lbs. (29Nm).
Tighten all bolts in sequence to 51 ft. lbs. (69Nm).
Loosen all bolts by 180°, then loosen an additional 180°.
Tighten bolts 1 and 2 to 25 ft. lbs. (24Nm) for non-turbo engines and 27 ft. lbs. (37Nm) for turbo engines.

Tighten bolts 3, 4, 5 and 6 to 11 ft. lbs. (15Nm) for non-turbo engines and 14 ft. lbs. (20Nm) for turbo engines.
Tighten all bolts in sequence by 80–90°.
Tighten all bolts in sequence an additional 80–90°.

④ Tighten all bolts in sequence to 29 ft. lbs. (39Nm).
Tighten all bolts in sequence to 47 ft. lbs. (64Nm).
Loosen all bolts at least 90° in the reverse order of the tightening sequence.
Tighten all bolts in sequence to 44–50 ft. lbs. (60–68Nm).

⑤ Tighten all bolts in sequence to 22 ft. lbs. (29Nm).
Tighten all bolts in sequence to 51 ft. lbs. (69Nm).
Loosen all bolts by 180°, then loosen an additional 180°.
Tighten all bolts in sequence to 20 ft. lbs. (27Nm).

Tighten bolts 1, 2, 3 and 4 in the sequence shown by 80–90°.
Tighten bolts 5, 6, 7 and 8 in the sequence shown to 33 ft. lbs. (44Nm).
Tighten all bolts in sequence an additional 80–90°.

⑥ Engine is of the split case design and does not use main bearing caps. Tighten the case half bolts as follows: 3–4 ft. lbs. (6mm); 17–20 ft. lbs. (8mm); 29–35 ft. lbs. (10mm).

Engine

REMOVAL & INSTALLATION

> **※ CAUTION**
>
> **When draining the coolant, keep in mind that cats and dogs are attracted by the ethylene glycol antifreeze, and are quite likely to drink any that is left in an uncovered container or in puddles on the ground. This will prove fatal in sufficient quantity. Always drain the coolant into a sealable container. Coolant should be reused unless it is contaminated or several years old.   The EPA warns that prolonged contact with used engine oil may cause a number of skin disorders, including cancer! You should make every effort to minimize your exposure to used engine oil. Protective gloves should be worn when changing the oil. Wash your hands and any other exposed skin areas as soon as possible after exposure to used engine oil. Soap and water, or waterless hand cleaner should be used.**

Constantly be aware of the dangers involved when working on an automobile and take the proper precautions. Use a safe chain hoist or floor crane of the proper capacity. Work on level ground. Make sure the engine sling is secured properly before lifting the engine. When working underneath a raised car always support it on jackstands. Be careful not to spill brake fluid or engine coolant on painted surfaces of the car body. Cover the front fenders if possible. Remember safety is always the most important rule.

1.2L Engine

1. Disconnect the negative battery terminal from the battery.
2. Raise and support the front of the vehicle on jackstands.
3. Raise and support the hood with the stay so that it opens wider than usual.
4. Position a drain pan under the radiator, remove the drain plug and the radiator cap, then drain the cooling system.

5. Remove the bumper and the grille.
6. Disconnect the electrical connectors and the hoses from the radiator and remove the radiator.
7. Disconnect the hood release cable and remove the radiator upper member.
8. Label, then disconnect the hoses and cables from the air cleaner, the carburetor, the heater unit the brake booster, the clutch, the accelerator cable from the carburetor, the speedometer cable from the transmission and the electrical wiring harness from the distributor.
9. Disconnect the pitching stopper from the bracket.
10. Remove the engine splash covers and the exhaust pipes.
11. Disconnect the gearshift rod and stay from the transmission.
12. Remove the transverse link. Using a rod, remove the spring pin and separate the front axle shaft.
13. Remove the engine/transmission mounting brackets.
14. Using an engine hoist and a cable, attach it to the engine and lift it slightly.
15. Remove the center member and crossmember from the vehicle.
16. Lift the engine/transmission assembly carefully and remove it from the vehicle.
17. Remove the engine from the transmission, then secure the engine to a workstand.

To Install:

18. Attach the engine to the transmission and attach them to an engine hoist and a cable.
19. Lower the engine/transmission slowly and carefully into the vehicle.
20. With the engine/transmission assembly slightly raised, install the center member and crossmember to the vehicle.
21. Completely lower the engine/transmission and install the mounting brackets.
22. Install the front axle shaft, spring pin and transverse link.
23. Install the gearshift rod and stay into the transmission.
24. Install the exhaust pipes and the engine splash cover.
25. Install the pitching stopper.
26. Install all removed hoses.
27. Install the hood release cable.
28. Install the radiator and connect the hoses and electrical connectors.
29. Install the grille and bumper.
30. Make sure that the drain has been placed in the radiator, and fill the radiator with coolant.
31. Lower the vehicle, install the battery and close the hood.

1.6L and 1.8L Carbureted Engines

➡ **On all models, the engine is removed separately from the transaxle.**

1. Open the hood as far as possible and secure it with the stay. Disconnect the negative battery terminal from the battery.
2. Remove the ground cable-to-intake manifold bolt and disconnect the cable. It is unnecessary to remove the cable fully: leave it routed along the side of the body.
3. Remove the spare tire from the engine compartment.
4. Remove the emission control system hoses from the air cleaner. Remove the air cleaner brackets and the wing nut, then lift the air cleaner assembly off the carburetor.
5. Position a drain pan (to catch the gasoline) under the fuel line union. At the union, remove the hose clamp, then pull the hose(s) to disconnect them.
6. Position a drain pan under the engine, remove the drain plug and drain the oil from the crankcase.
7. To drain the engine coolant, perform the following procedures:
   a. Position a clean container, large enough to hold the contents of the cooling system, under the radiator drain plug.
   b. Open the drain plug on the radiator; turn it so that it's slot faces downward.
   c. Disconnect both the hoses from the radiator.
   d. Disconnect the heater hoses from the pipe on the side of the engine.
   e. If equipped with an automatic transmission, disconnect the oil cooler lines from the radiator.
8. Disconnect the following electrical wiring connectors:
   a. Alternator multi-connector
   b. Oil pressure sender connector
   c. Engine cooling fan connectors
   d. Temperature sender connector
   e. Primary distributor lead
   f. Secondary ignition leads (ignition side)
   g. Starter wiring harness
   h. Anti-dieseling solenoid lead
   i. Automatic choke lead
   j. EGR vacuum solenoid
   k. EGR coolant temperature switch
   l. If equipped with an automatic transmission, disconnect the neutral safety switch harness and downshift solenoid harness.
9. Loosen the radiator-to-chassis bolts, remove the ground lead from the upper side of the radiator and the radiator.

➡ **On 4WD models, remove the engine fan from the pulley.**

10. To remove the crankshaft damper, perform the following procedures:

a. Remove the front nut from the damper.

b. Remove the nut on the body bracket and withdraw the damper.

c. Pull the damper rearward, away from the engine lifting hook; be careful not to lose any of the damper parts.

11. Remove the starter-to-engine bolts and the starter from the vehicle.

12. Disconnect the following cables, hoses and linkages, by performing the following procedure:

a. Loosen the screw on the carburetor throttle lever. Remove the outer end of the accelerator cable and withdraw it.

b. Remove the vacuum hose and the purge hose from the vapor canister.

c. If equipped with a manual transmission, remove the clutch return spring from the release lever/intake manifold and the clutch cable from the lever.

d. If equipped with an automatic transmission, disconnect the vacuum hose from the transmission.

e. Disconnect the vacuum hose from the power brake unit (if equipped).

13. On 4WD models, remove the skid plate-to-chassis bolts and the plate.

14. To remove the Y-shaped exhaust pipe, perform the following procedures:

a. Remove the exhaust pipe-to-cylinder head nuts.

b. Remove the exhaust pipe-to-pre-muffler nuts/bolts.

c. While supporting the exhaust pipe by hand, remove the exhaust pipe-to-transmission bracket bolts, then lower the exhaust pipe.

15. If equipped with an automatic transmission, remove the torque converter bolts by performing the following procedures:

a. Remove the timing hole cover from the torque converter housing.

b. Through the timing hole, remove the torque converter-to-drive plate bolts.

➡ **Be careful that the bolts DO NOT fall into the torque converter housing.**

16. Connect a chain hoist and a cable to the engine, with hooks at the front and rear engine hangers. Adjust the hoist so that the weight of the engine is supported but DO NOT raise the engine.

17. Using a floor jack, position it under the transaxle to support it's weight when the engine is removed.

18. Remove the engine-to-transmission nuts (four each on top and bottom).

19. Remove the front engine mount-to-crossmember nuts.

20. Using the hoist, raise the engine slightly — about 1 in. (25mm). Keeping it level, move the engine forward, off the transaxle input shaft.

⁑⁑⁑ **CAUTION**

DO NOT raise the engine more than 1 in. (25mm) prior to removing it from the input shaft or damage may occur to the driveshaft double offset joints. If equipped with a manual transmission, be sure that the input shaft does not interfere with the clutch spring assembly; if equipped with an automatic transmissions, leave the torque converter on the transaxle input shaft.

---

21. Hoist the engine carefully until it is completely out of the vehicle, then secure it onto a workstand.

To Install:

22. To install the engine, use new gaskets and observe the following torque specifications. Torque the transmission-to-engine bolts to 34–40 ft. lbs., the torque converter-to-drive plate bolts to 17–20 ft. lbs., the engine mount-to-crossmember bolts to 14–24 ft. lbs., the crankshaft damper nut to 7–10 ft. lbs., the exhaust pipe-to-engine bolt to 19–22 ft. lbs., the exhaust pipe-to-pre-muffler nuts to 31–38 ft. lbs. and the radiator-to-chassis bolts to 6–10 ft. lbs. Adjust the clutch and accelerator linkage. Refill the crankcase and cooling system.

➡ **Use care not to damage the input shaft splines or the clutch spring when lowering the engine in place.**

23. When installing the crankshaft damper, perform the following adjustments:

a. Tighten the body bracket nut.

b. Turn the front nut until the clearance between the front washer and rubber cushion is 0.

c. Insert the bushing and tighten the front nut.

1.8L OHC, SPFI, MPFI and Turbocharged Engines

1. Open the hood and prop it, securely. Remove the spare tire and the spare tire bracket.

2. If equipped with Turbo or MPFI, perform the following procedures to reduce the fuel pressure:

a. From under the vehicle, disconnect the fuel pump electrical harness connector.

b. Crank the engine for at least 5 seconds. If the engine starts, allow it to run until it stalls.

c. Reconnect the fuel pump connector.

3. Remove the negative battery terminal from the battery.

4. Disconnect the air temperature sensor plug from the engine compartment.

5. Label and disconnect the fuel system hoses and the evaporative emissions system hoses.

6. Label and disconnect the vacuum hoses from the cruise control, the Master-Vac®, the air intake shutter and the heater air intake door.

7. Disconnect the electrical wiring connectors from the the alternator, the EGI, the thermoswitch, the electric fan, the A/C condenser and the ignition coil, then disconnect the main engine harness.

8. Label and disconnect the spark plug wires, the engine ground strap and the fusible link assembly.

9. Disconnect the accelerator linkage. Remove the windshield washer reservoir and position it behind the right strut tower.

10. To remove the power steering pump, perform the following procedures:

a. Loosen the alternator pivot and mounting bolts, then shift the alternator to loosen the drive belt and remove the belt.

b. Remove the pulley from the power steering pump.

c. Remove the power steering pump-to-engine bolts and clamp.

d. Remove the engine oil filler pipe brace.

e. Remove the power steering pump and secure it to the bulkhead without disturbing the pressure lines.

11. Loosen the air intake duct hose clamps and remove the duct; seal the openings to keep dirt out of the air intake passages. Remove the upper cover.

12. Remove the air intake-to-flow meter line and cover the openings.

13. Remove the horizontal damper and clip.

14. To remove the center section of the exhaust pipe, perform the following procedures:

a. Disconnect the temperature sensor connector.

b. If equipped, disconnect the exhaust pipe-to-turbocharger bolts.

c. Remove the rear cover.

d. Remove the center exhaust section-to-transmission bolt.

e. Remove the hanger bolts, then carefully remove the exhaust pipe (clearance is tight) to avoid damage.

f. Slightly loosen the attaching bolts, then remove the torque converter cover.

15. If equipped, disconnect the turbocharger oil supply and drain lines. Remove the turbo-to-exhaust bolts, the turbo assembly, the lower cover and the gasket.

16. Disconnect the electrical connector from the O_2 sensor. Remove the torque converter-to-drive plate bolts.

17. Using a chain hoist, connect it to the crankshaft damper bracket and support the engine. Remove the upper engine-to-transmission bolts; leave the starter in place.

18. Drain the engine coolant, using a hose to lead coolant to a clean container. Disconnect the upper/lower radiator hoses, the oil cooler lines, the ground wire and the radiator.

19. Disconnect the oil cooler lines from the engine and drain the oil into a clean container. Disconnect the heater hoses from the side of the engine.

20. Remove the front engine mount, then the lower engine-to-transmission nuts.

21. Position a floor jack under the transmission, then raise the engine/transmission slightly. Pull the engine forward until the transmission shaft clears the clutch, then carefully raise the engine out of the engine compartment.

22. To install, use new gaskets and observe the following points:

a. After installing all major mounting nuts and bolts finger tight, tighten the upper transmission-to-engine bolts just snug, then, remove the engine/transmission support. Tighten the lower transmission-to-engine bolts, then tighten the engine-to-mount nuts.

b. When torquing the turbocharger (if equipped) and the exhaust system bolts, be sure to go back and forth, tighten the bolts evenly.

23. To complete the installation, reverse the removal process. Observe the following torques:

• Transmission-to-engine bolts to 14–17 ft. lbs.

• Torque converter-to-drive plate bolts to 17–20 ft. lbs.

• Turbocharger-to-exhaust system bolts to 31–38 ft. lbs.

• Exhaust system-to-transmission bolt to 18–25 ft. lbs.

• Exhaust system hanger bolts to 7–13 ft. lbs.

• Rear exhaust pipe joint nuts to 7–13 ft. lbs.

• Power steering pump pulley bolts to 25–30 ft. lbs.

• Power steering pump mounting bolts to 18–25 ft. lbs.

24. Adjust the crankshaft damper by tightening the nuts on the body side of the damper until the clearance is 0.08 in. (2mm); torque the locknuts to 6.5–9.4 ft. lbs. Adjust the accelerator pedal so there is 0.4–1.2 in. (10–30mm) between the pin and stop. Adjust the cable for an end play of 0–0.08 in. (0–2mm) on the actuator side. Replenish all of the fluids. Run the engine to normal operating temperatures and check for leaks in oil cooler and lines.

2.2L Engine

1. Raise and support the vehicle safely.
2. Release the fuel system pressure.
3. Disconnect the battery cables and remove the battery.
4. Drain the coolant.
5. On non-turbo engines, remove the manifold cover.
6. Remove the cooling system, radiator and fan assembly, and reservoir tank.
7. On air conditioning equipped models, discharge the air conditioning system and remove the high pressure hoses.
8. Remove the air intake system. Remove the air intake duct from non-turbo engines and the resonator chamber from turbo engines.
9. Remove the air cleaner upper cover and element.
10. On turbo engines, remove the turbocharger cooling duct and air inlet and outlet ducts.
11. Remove the evaporative canister and bracket.
12. Label and disconnect all electrical connectors, cables and vacuum hoses.
13. Remove the power steering pump.
14. On turbocharged engines, remove the turbocharger unit from the center exhaust pipe.
15. Remove the exhaust system from the engine.
16. On turbocharged engines, remove the clutch damper with bracket.
17. Remove the nut which holds the power side of the starter.
18. Remove the nuts which hold the lower side of the transmission to the engine.
19. Remove the nuts which hold the front cushion rubber to the crossmember.
20. Remove the starter.
21. On turbocharged engines, separate the clutch release fork from the release bearing.
22. On automatic transmission equipped models, separate the torque converter from the drive plate.

23. Remove the pitching stopper and bracket.
24. Disconnect the fuel delivery hose, return hose and evaporation hose.
25. Support the engine with a lifting device and the transmission with a floor jack.
26. Remove the bolt which holds the upper side of the transmission to the engine.
27. Remove the engine.

To Install:

28. Install the clutch release fork and bearing onto the transmission.
29. Install the engine to the transmission and tighten the bolts which holds the right upper side of the transmission to 34–40 ft. lbs. (46–54Nm).
30. Remove the lifting device from the engine and remove the floor jack.
30. Install the pitching stopper and tighten the body side bolt to 35–49 ft. lbs. (47–67Nm) and the bracket side bolt to 33–40 ft. lbs. (44–54Nm).
31. On turbocharged engines, install the clutch operating cylinder and tighten to 25–30 ft. lbs. (34–40Nm).
32. On automatic transmission equipped vehicles, install the torque converter on the drive plate. Tighten the bolts to 17–20 ft. lbs. (23–26Nm).
33. Install the canister and bracket.
34. Install the power steering pump and tighten the bolts to 22–36 ft. lbs. (29–49Nm).
35. Install the starter and tighten the bolts to 22–36 ft. lbs. (29–49Nm).
36. Tighten the nuts which hold the lower side of the transmission to the engine to 34–40 ft. lbs. (46–54Nm).
37. Tighten the nuts which hold the front cushion rubber to the crossmember to 40–61 ft. lbs. (54–83Nm).
38. Install the exhaust system.
39. On turbocharged engines, install the air inlet and outlet ducts.
40. Connect all hoses, electrical connectors and cables previously disconnected.
41. On turbocharged engines, install the turbo cooling duct.
42. Install the air intake system.
43. On vehicles equipped with air conditioning, install the air conditioner high pressure hoses. Tighten to 13–23 ft. lbs. (18–31Nm).
44. Install the cooling system. Tighten bolts to 9–11 ft. lbs. (12–15Nm).
45. Install the manifold cover.
46. Install the battery and connect the battery cables.
47. Fill the radiator with coolant.
48. Check the level of the transmission fluid and add as necessary.
49. Check the level of the engine oil and add as necessary.

50. Start the engine and allow it to reach operating temperature. Check for leaks. Test drive the vehicle.

2.7L Engine

1. Properly relieve the fuel system pressure. Disconnect the negative battery cable. Matchmark and remove the hood.

2. Properly discharge the air conditioning system, if equipped. Drain the engine oil. Drain the cooling system.

3. Disconnect the canister hose and the hose bracket. Disconnect and plug oil. Drain the cooling system.

3. Disconnect the canister hose and the hose bracket. Disconnect and plug the fuel lines.

4. Disconnect the power brake vacuum line booster. If equipped with manual transaxle and 4WD, disconnect the differential lock vacuum hose.

5. Disconnect the engine wiring harness connectors, the oxygen sensor connector, the bypass air valve control connector, the ignition coil and the distributor connector to the crank sensor.

6. Disconnect the alternator connector, the air condition compressor connector, the engine ground connector, the radiator fan motor connector and the thermo-switch electrical connector.

7. Disconnect the accelerator cable. Disconnect the cruise control cable, if equipped. Disconnect and plug the heater hoses.

8. Disconnect the hill holder cable on the clutch release fork side of the assembly, if equipped with manual transaxle.

9. Raise and support the vehicle safely. Disconnect the front exhaust pipe from the engine.

10. Disconnect the front to rear exhaust pipe connection. Disconnect the front exhaust pipe at the transaxle and hanger locations.

11. Lower the vehicle. Disconnect and plug the air conditioning compressor hoses.

12. Remove the radiator fan shroud assembly. If equipped with automatic transaxle, disconnect and plug the fluid lines. Remove the radiator.

13. Remove the timing hole plug. Remove the bolts that retain the torque converter to the driveplate, if equipped with automatic transaxle.

14. Remove the buffer rod mounting bolts. Remove the bolts that support the engine mount to the front crossmember. Remove the bolts that hold the lower side of the engine to the transaxle assembly.

15. Install the proper engine lifting equipment. Properly support the transaxle assembly.

16. Remove the bolts that retain the upper side of the engine to the transaxle

17. Carefully remove the engine from the vehicle. If equipped with manual transaxle, move the engine in the axial direction until the mainshaft is withdrawn from the clutch cover.

To Install:

18. Install the engine taking care to align the mainshaft. Install all bolts and mountings that attach the engine to the transaxle and chassis. Reconnect the torque converter to the engine flywheel (automatic transaxle).

19. Install the radiator, radiator shroud and transaxle fluid cooler lines. Install the air conditioner compressor and lines. Install the exhaust system.

20. Install the hill holder, if equipped. Reconnect all vacuum lines and hoses previously disconnected. Reconnect all electrical connections taking care to clean all connectors and ground locations.

21. Install all fuel lines. Fill the engine with oil, the transaxle with fluid and the cooling system with coolant. Start the engine and allow it to reach operating temperature. Check for leaks. Test drive the vehicle.

3.3L Engine

1. Raise and support the vehicle safely.
2. Release the fuel system pressure.
3. Disconnect the negative battery cable.
4. Remove the under body cover and drain the engine coolant.
5. Remove the radiator and all coolant hoses.
6. Discharge the air conditioning system. Disconnect and plug the air conditioning lines.
7. Remove the air intake system.
8. Disconnect the accelerator cable.
9. Disconnect the cruise control cable.
10. Label and disconnect all wiring harness connectors and cables.
11. Remove the evaporation canister, vacuum hoses and bracket.
12. Remove the exhaust system from the engine.
13. Disconnect the power steering hoses from the gear box.
14. Disconnect the automatic transmission cooler lines.
15. Remove the nuts which hold the lower side of the engine to the transmission and attach the lower side of starter.
16. Remove the nuts which attach the front cushion rubber to the sub-frame.
17. Separate the torque converter from the drive plate.
18. Remove the pitching stopper and bracket.
19. Disconnect the fuel delivery hose, return hose and evaporation hoses.
20. Support the engine with a lifting device and the transmission with a transmission jack.

21. Remove the bolts which hold the upper side of the engine to the transmission.
22. Remove the engine from the vehicle.

To Install:

23. Install the engine to the transmission and tighten the bolts which hold the right upper side of the engine to 34–40 ft. lbs. (46–54Nm).
24. Remove the lifting device and transmission jack.
25. Install the pitching stopper and tighten to 33–40 ft. lbs. (44–54Nm).
26. Install the torque converter to drive plate bolts and tighten to 17–20 ft. lbs. (23–26Nm).
27. Connect all hoses previously disconnected.
28. Install the evaporation canister and bracket.
29. Install the cooling system.
30. Install the nuts which hold the lower side of the engine to the transmission and attach the lower side of the starter. Tighten to 34–40 ft. lbs. (54–83Nm).
31. Install the nuts which hold the front cushion rubber to the sub-frame. Tighten to 40–61 ft. lbs.(54–83Nm).
32. Connect the power steering hoses to the gear box and the automatic transmission cooler lines.
33. Install the exhaust system.
34. Install the engine under cover.
35. Connect all electrical harness connectors.
36. Connect the accelerator cable.
37. Connect the cruise control cable.
38. Connect the high pressure hoses to the air conditioner compressor. Tighten to 13–23 ft. lbs. (18–31Nm).
39. Install the air intake system
40. Connect the negative battery cable.
41. Fill the radiator with coolant.
42. Check the automatic transmission oil level and add as required.
43. Check the power steering fluid level. Add as necessary and bleed all air from the system.
44. Check the engine oil level.
45. Start the engine and allow it to reach operating temperature. Check for leaks. Test drive the vehicle.

Rocker Arm (Valve) Cover

The rocker cover is a light weight and compact aluminum die casting. It adopts a float supporting system with a rubber ring type gasket and an oil seal washer to reduce the noise level.

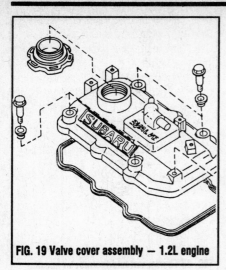

FIG. 19 Valve cover assembly — 1.2L engine

REMOVAL & INSTALLATION

♦ SEE FIGS. 19–22

1. Remove the bolts from the rocker covers.

2. Using a RUBBER hammer, tap the rocker covers to break the seal between the gasket and the valve cover.

3. Remove the rocker cover from the head.

4. Remove the old gasket from the rocker cover and clean the surface of the cylinder head and the rocker cover.

5. Spread Permatex® #2 on the mating surface of the rocker cover (to hold the gasket in place during installation), and install a new gasket.

6. Place the rocker cover on the head, install the bolts and torque to 4 ft. lbs. (5Nm) on all engines except 1.2L and 5 ft. lbs. (6Nm) on 1.2L engine.

Rocker Shafts

REMOVAL & INSTALLATION

➤ The OHC engines DO NOT use a rocker arm shaft, the valve rocker simply floats between the valve stem and the hydraulic lifter, the center of the valve rocker rides against the camshaft.

1.2L Engine

♦ SEE FIG. 23

Subaru recommends removal of the engine for this procedure. This may or may not be necessary depending on the situation.

1. Remove the engine from the vehicle.

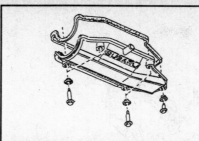

FIG. 20 Valve cover assembly — 1.6L, 1.8L and 2.7L engines

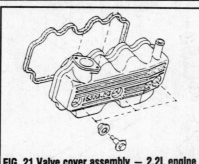

FIG. 21 Valve cover assembly — 2.2L engine

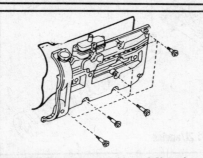

FIG. 22 Valve cover assembly — 3.3L engine

2. Using the Engine Stand tool No. 499815500 or equivalent, attach them to the engine.

3. Remove the suction and the air cleaner hoses from the air cleaner.

4. Loosen the alternator-to-engine bolts, reduce the drive belt tension and remove the drive belt.

5. Using the Crank and Camshaft Pulley Wrench tool No. 499205500 or equivalent, secure the crankshaft pulley and remove the pulley bolt.

6. Remove the timing belt cover. Rotate the crankshaft until the alignment mark on the camshaft sprocket aligns with the pointer on the timing belt housing.

7. Remove the timing belt cover. Loosen the timing belt tensioner bolt ½ turn, move the tensioner to relax the belt tension, remove the timing belt and tighten the bolt.

➤ Before removing the timing belt, be sure to mark it for the direction of rotation.

8. Using the Crank and Camshaft Pulley Wrench tool No. 499205500 or equivalent, secure the camshaft sprocket, then remove the sprocket-to-camshaft bolts and the sprocket.

9. Remove the timing belt housing-to-engine bolts and the housing.

10. Remove the carburetor/throttle body bolts and remove the carburetor/throttle body.

11. Remove the rocker arm cover-to-cylinder head bolts and the cover from the cylinder head.

12. Using the Valve Clearance Adjuster tool No. 498767000 or equivalent, loosen the valve adjuster locknuts and back-off the adjusting screw.

13. Remove the valve rocker arm shaft-to-journal bolt, pull out the rocker arm shaft, then remove the spring washers, the valve rocker arms. Keep the rocker arms and the spring washers in order to make the installation easier.

To Install:

14. Using a putty knife, clean the gasket mounting surfaces. Inspect the rocker arm for wear; the clearance between the rocker arm and the shaft should be 0.0006–0.0022 in. (0.016–0.057mm).

15. To install, use new gaskets, sealant (where necessary) and reverse the removal procedures. Torque the camshaft sprocket-to-camshaft bolts to 8.3–9.0 ft. lbs., the crankshaft pulley-to-crankshaft bolt to 47–54 ft. lbs. Refill the cooling system and the crankcase. Operate the engine until normal operating temperature is reached and check for leaks.

2.2L Engine

♦ SEE FIG. 24

1. Disconnect the PCV hose and remove the rocker cover.

2. Remove the valve rocker assembly by removing bolts 2 through 4 in numerical sequence.

3. Loosen bolt 1 but leave engaged to retain valve rocker assembly.

4. Remove bolts 5 through 8, taking care not to gouge the dowel pin.

5. Remove the valve rocker assembly.

6. Place the valve rocker assembly with the air vent on the rocker arm facing upward into clean engine oil until ready to install. This is done to prevent damaging the hydraulic lash adjuster.

To Install:

7. Install the valve rocker assembly on the cylinder head.

8. Temporarily tighten bolts 1 through 4 equally.

➤ Do not allow the valve rocker assembly to gouge the dowel pins.

9. Tighten bolts 5 through 8 to 9 ft. lbs. (12Nm).

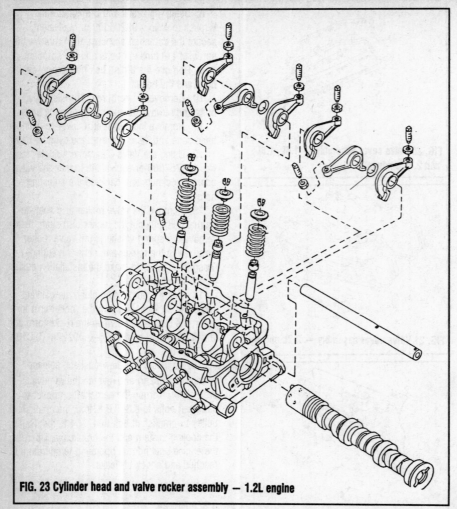

FIG. 23 Cylinder head and valve rocker assembly — 1.2L engine

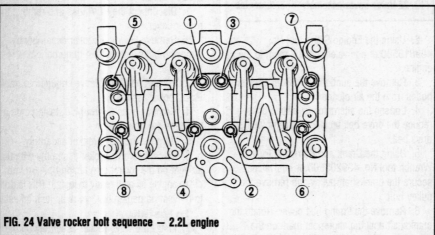

FIG. 24 Valve rocker bolt sequence — 2.2L engine

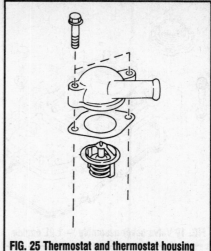

FIG. 25 Thermostat and thermostat housing cover

10. Tighten bolts 1 through 4 to 9 ft. lbs. (12Nm).

11. Install the rocker cover and connect the PCV hose.

Thermostat

REMOVAL & INSTALLATION

◆ SEE FIG. 25

☀ WARNING

Do not perform this operation on a warm engine. Wait until the engine is cold.

1. Position a clean drain pan under the radiator, remove the drain plug and the radiator cap, then drain the cooling system to a level below the thermostat.

☀ CAUTION

When draining the coolant, keep in mind that cats and dogs are attracted by the ethylene glycol antifreeze, and are quite likely to drink any that is left in an uncovered container or in puddles on the ground. This will prove fatal in sufficient quantity. Always drain the coolant into a sealable container. Coolant should be reused unless it is contaminated or several years old.

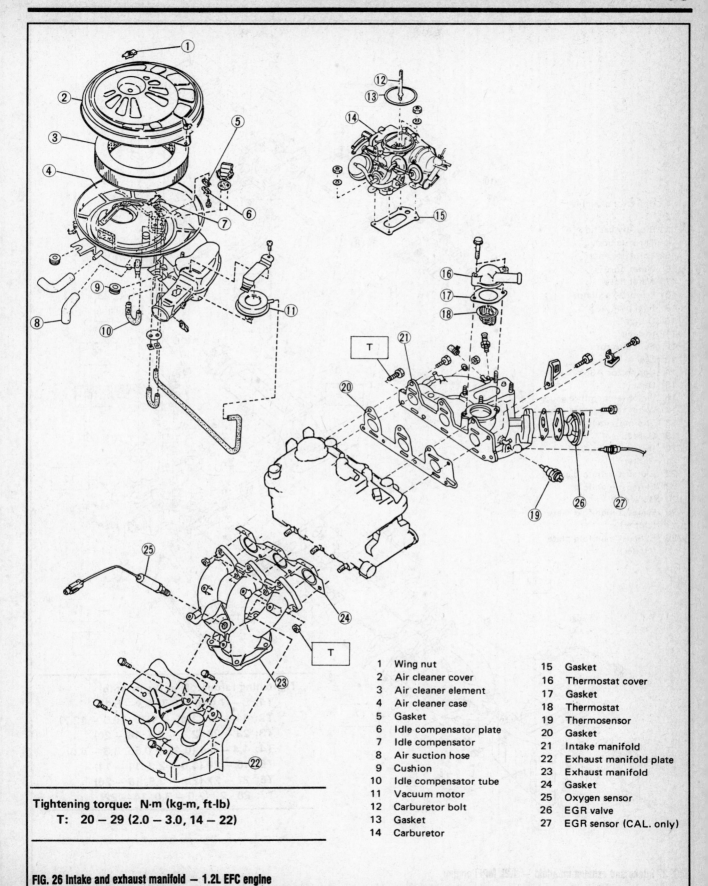

Tightening torque: N·m (kg-m, ft-lb)
T: 20 — 29 (2.0 — 3.0, 14 — 22)

1	Wing nut	15	Gasket
2	Air cleaner cover	16	Thermostat cover
3	Air cleaner element	17	Gasket
4	Air cleaner case	18	Thermostat
5	Gasket	19	Thermosensor
6	Idle compensator plate	20	Gasket
7	Idle compensator	21	Intake manifold
8	Air suction hose	22	Exhaust manifold plate
9	Cushion	23	Exhaust manifold
10	Idle compensator tube	24	Gasket
11	Vacuum motor	25	Oxygen sensor
12	Carburetor bolt	26	EGR valve
13	Gasket	27	EGR sensor (CAL. only)
14	Carburetor		

FIG. 26 Intake and exhaust manifold — 1.2L EFC engine

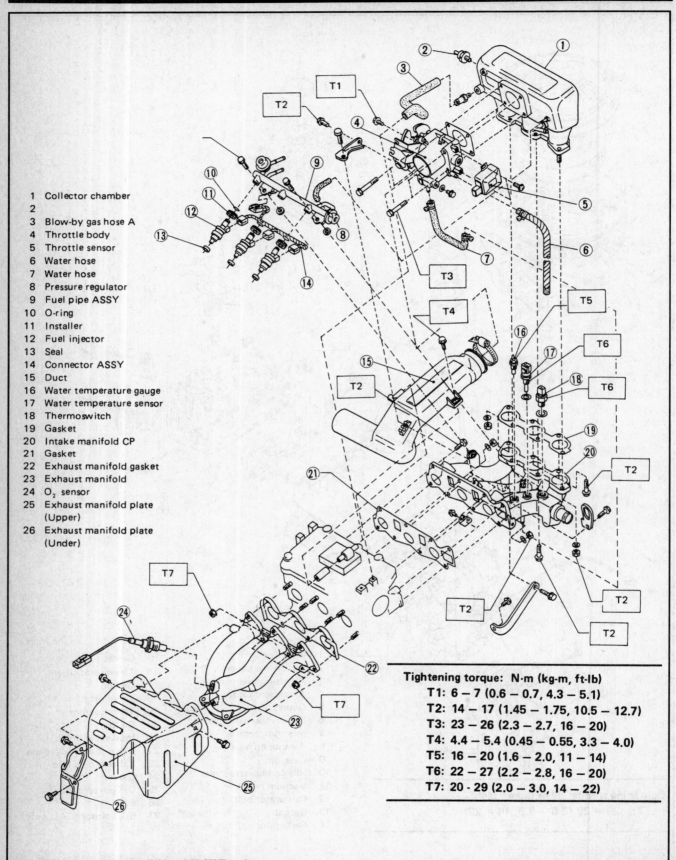

1   Collector chamber
2
3   Blow-by gas hose A
4   Throttle body
5   Throttle sensor
6   Water hose
7   Water hose
8   Pressure regulator
9   Fuel pipe ASSY
10 O-ring
11 Installer
12 Fuel injector
13 Seal
14 Connector ASSY
15 Duct
16 Water temperature gauge
17 Water temperature sensor
18 Thermoswitch
19 Gasket
20 Intake manifold CP
21 Gasket
22 Exhaust manifold gasket
23 Exhaust manifold
24 O₂ sensor
25 Exhaust manifold plate
     (Upper)
26 Exhaust manifold plate
     (Under)

Tightening torque: N·m (kg-m, ft-lb)
T1: 6 — 7 (0.6 — 0.7, 4.3 — 5.1)
T2: 14 — 17 (1.45 — 1.75, 10.5 — 12.7)
T3: 23 — 26 (2.3 — 2.7, 16 — 20)
T4: 4.4 — 5.4 (0.45 — 0.55, 3.3 — 4.0)
T5: 16 — 20 (1.6 — 2.0, 11 — 14)
T6: 22 — 27 (2.2 — 2.8, 16 — 20)
T7: 20 - 29 (2.0 — 3.0, 14 — 22)

FIG. 27 Intake and exhaust manifold — 1.2L MPFI engine

2. Remove the thermostat housing-to-intake manifold bolts, lift the housing and remove the thermostat.

3. Using a putty knife, clean the gasket mounting surfaces. Check and/or replace the thermostat (if necessary).

To Install:

4. Install the thermostat with the jiggle valve facing upward.

5. Using a new gasket and sealant (if necessary), install the thermostat housing.

6. Tighten the housing-to-intake manifold bolts securely.

7. Refill the cooling system.

Intake Manifold

REMOVAL & INSTALLATION

⚠ CAUTION

When draining the coolant, keep in mind that cats and dogs are attracted by the ethylene glycol antifreeze, and are quite likely to drink any that is left in an uncovered container or in puddles on the ground. This will prove fatal in sufficient quantity. Always drain the coolant into a sealable container. Coolant should be reused unless it is contaminated or several years old.

1.2L Engine

ELECTRONIC FEEDBACK CARBURETOR (EFC)

♦ SEE FIG. 26

1. Disconnect the negative battery cable.

2. Drain the coolant. Remove the air cleaner.

3. Disconnect the heater hose and radiator hose from the intake manifold and thermostat cover.

4. Label and disconnect all electrical connectors and ground straps.

5. Remove the accelerator cable from the carburetor.

6. Label and disconnect all vacuum lines.

7. Remove the air suction manifold pipe.

8. Disconnect the fuel lines from the carburetor. Remove the intake manifold along with the carburetor and gasket.

To Install:

9. Clean all gasket mating surfaces thoroughly.

10. Using a new gasket, install the intake manifold and bolts.

11. Tighten the bolts to 14–22 ft. lbs. (20–29Nm). Connect the fuel lines to the carburetor.

12. Install the air suction manifold pipe.

13. Check all vacuum lines for deterioration and replace as necessary. Install all vacuum lines.

14. Install the accelerator cable on the carburetor.

15. Connect all electrical connections and ground straps.

16. Check all coolant hoses for deterioration and replace as necessary. Install the heater hoses, radiator hoses and intake manifold and thermostat cover.

17. Install the air cleaner and fill the coolant system.

18. Connect the negative battery cable.

19. Start the engine, allow it to reach operating temperature and check for vacuum leaks.

MULTI-POINT FUEL INJECTION (MPFI)

♦ SEE FIG. 27

1. Disconnect the negative battery cable.

2. Drain the coolant. Disconnect the PCV hose and remove the air duct.

3. Disconnect the throttle body hose, heater inlet hose and radiator inlet hose from the intake manifold.

4. Label and disconnect all electrical connectors and ground straps.

5. Remove the accelerator cable from the throttle body.

6. Label and disconnect all vacuum lines.

7. Relieve the fuel system pressure and remove the throttle body from the collector chamber.

8. Remove the intake manifold along with the gasket.

To Install:

9. Clean all gasket mating surfaces thoroughly. Using a straight edge and a feeler gauge, inspect the intake manifold for flatness. Distortion should not exceed 0.020 in. (0.5mm).

10. Using a new gasket, install the intake manifold and bolts.

11. Tighten the bolts to 14–22 ft. lbs. (20–29Nm).

12. Install the throttle body on the collector chamber and tighten the nuts to 17–20 ft. lbs. (23–26Nm).

13. Check all vacuum lines for deterioration and replace as necessary. Install all vacuum lines.

14. Install the accelerator cable on the throttle body.

15. Connect all electrical connections and ground straps.

16. Check all coolant hoses for deterioration and replace as necessary. Install the throttle body hose, heater inlet hose and radiator inlet hose from the intake manifold.

17. Connect the PCV hose and install the air duct. Fill the cooling system.

18. Connect the negative battery cable.

19. Start the engine, allow it to reach operating temperature and check for vacuum leaks.

1.6L and 1.8L Carbureted Engines 1.8L SPFI Engine

♦ SEE FIG. 28 and 28a

1. Disconnect the negative battery cable.

2. Drain the cooling system and remove the radiator hose.

3. Remove all distributor high tension wires and remove the distributor as required.

4. Label and disconnect all applicable vacuum hoses.

5. Remove the alternator as required to gain clearance.

6. Remove the silencers and silencer hoses. Remove the air cleaner assembly.

7. Remove the air suction valves and hoses.

8. Remove the EGR cover and EGR pipe.

9. Remove the PCV valve and blow-by hoses.

10. Remove the air bleed from the thermostat case.

11. Label and disconnect all applicable electrical harnesses.

12. Disconnect the fuel lines and accelerator cable.

13. Remove the intake manifold bolts and carefully lift the intake manifold off the engine.

To Install:

14. Clean the gasket mating surfaces thoroughly. Using a straight edge and a feeler gauge, inspect the intake manifold for flatness. Distortion should not exceed 0.020 in. (0.5mm).

15. Install the intake manifold using new gaskets and tighten the bolts to 13–16 ft. lbs. (18–22Nm).

16. Inspect all electrical connectors for damage and replace as necessary. Connect all electrical connectors.

17. Install the air bleed on the thermostat.

18. Install the PCV valve and hoses. Install the EGR cover and pipe, and tighten bolts to 23–27 ft. lbs. (31–37Nm). Install the air suction valve and hoses.

19. Install the silencers and hoses. Install the alternator if removed.

20. Inspect all vacuum lines for damage and replace as necessary. Install all vacuum lines.

21. Install the distributor if removed. Connect all distributor high tension wires.

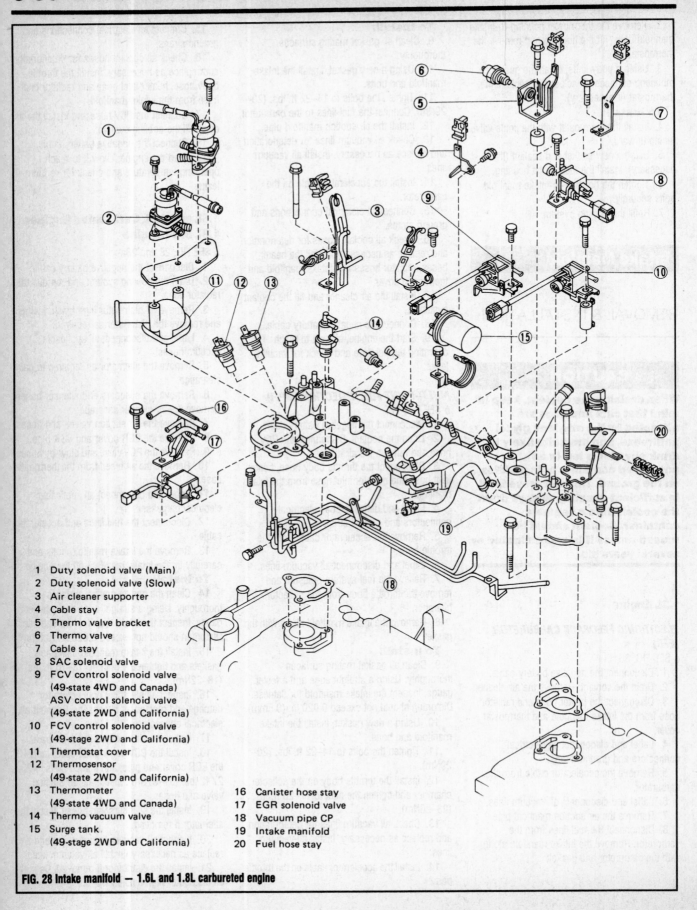

1 Duty solenoid valve (Main)
2 Duty solenoid valve (Slow)
3 Air cleaner supporter
4 Cable stay
5 Thermo valve bracket
6 Thermo valve
7 Cable stay
8 SAC solenoid valve
9 FCV control solenoid valve
   (49-state 4WD and Canada)
   ASV control solenoid valve
   (49-state 2WD and California)
10 FCV control solenoid valve
   (49-stage 2WD and California)
11 Thermostat cover
12 Thermosensor
   (49-state 2WD and California)
13 Thermometer
   (49-state 4WD and Canada)
14 Thermo vacuum valve
15 Surge tank
   (49-stage 2WD and California)

16 Canister hose stay
17 EGR solenoid valve
18 Vacuum pipe CP
19 Intake manifold
20 Fuel hose stay

FIG. 28 Intake manifold — 1.6L and 1.8L carbureted engine

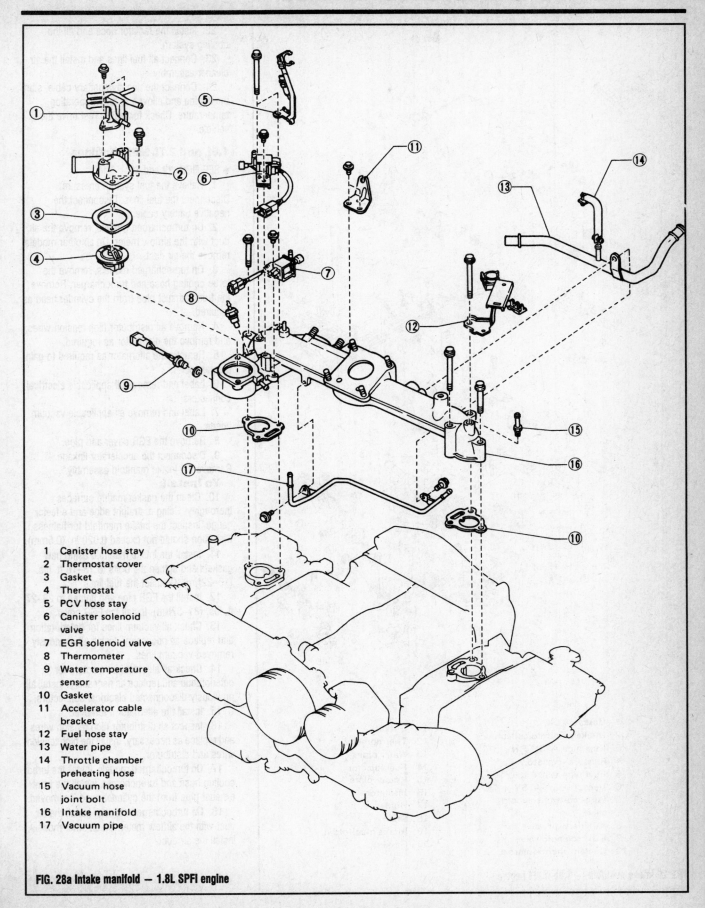

1 Canister hose stay
2 Thermostat cover
3 Gasket
4 Thermostat
5 PCV hose stay
6 Canister solenoid
    valve
7 EGR solenoid valve
8 Thermometer
9 Water temperature
    sensor
10 Gasket
11 Accelerator cable
    bracket
12 Fuel hose stay
13 Water pipe
14 Throttle chamber
    preheating hose
15 Vacuum hose
    joint bolt
16 Intake manifold
17 Vacuum pipe

FIG. 28a Intake manifold — 1.8L SPFI engine

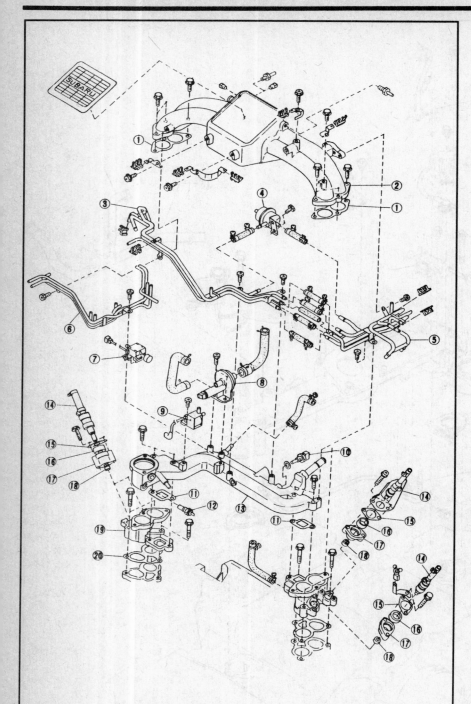

1 Gasket
2 Intake manifold collector
3 Fuel pipe ASSY RH
4 Pressure regulator
5 Fuel pipe ASSY LH
6 Vacuum pipe ASSY
7 Purge control solenoid
   valve
8 Auxiliary air valve
9 EGR solenoid valve
10 Coolant thermosensor

11 Gasket
12 Thermometer
13 Water pipe
14 Fuel injector
15 Holder plate
16 Insulator
17 Holder
18 Seal
19 Intake manifold
20 Gasket

FIG. 29 Intake manifold — 1.8L MPFI engine

22. Install the radiator hose and fill the cooling system.

23. Connect all fuel lines and install the air cleaner assembly.

24. Connect the negative battery cable, start the engine and allow it to reach operating temperature. Check for leaks. Test drive the vehicle.

1.8L and 2.7L MPFI Engines

◆ SEE FIGS. 29 and 30

1. Relieve the fuel system pressure. Disconnect the fuel lines. Disconnect the negative battery cable.

2. On turbocharged models, remove the air duct with the airflow meter. On all other models, remove the air duct.

3. On turbocharged models, remove the turbo cooling hose and turbocharger. Remove the front exhaust pipe from the cylinder head as required.

4. Remove all distributor high tension wires and remove the distributor as required.

5. Remove the alternator as required to gain clearance.

6. Label and remove all applicable electrical connectors.

7. Label and remove all applicable vacuum hoses.

8. Remove the EGR cover and pipe.

9. Disconnect the accelerator linkage. Remove the intake manifold assembly.

To Install:

10. Clean the gasket mating surfaces thoroughly. Using a straight edge and a feeler gauge, inspect the intake manifold for flatness. Distortion should not exceed 0.020 in. (0.5mm).

11. Install the intake manifold using new gaskets and tighten the bolts to 13–16 ft. lbs. (18–22Nm). Connect the fuel lines.

12. Install the EGR pipe and tighten to 23–27 ft. lbs. (31–37Nm). Install the EGR cover.

13. Check all vacuum lines for deterioration and replace as necessary. Install all previously removed vacuum lines.

14. Check all electrical connectors for deterioration and replace as necessary. Install all previously disconnected electrical connectors.

15. Install the alternator if removed.

16. Inspect all distributor high tension wires and replace as necessary. Install the high tension wires and distributor.

17. On turbocharged models, install the turbo cooling hose and turbocharger. Install the front exhaust pipe from the cylinder head if removed.

18. On turbocharged models, install the air duct with the airflow meter. On all other models, install the air duct.

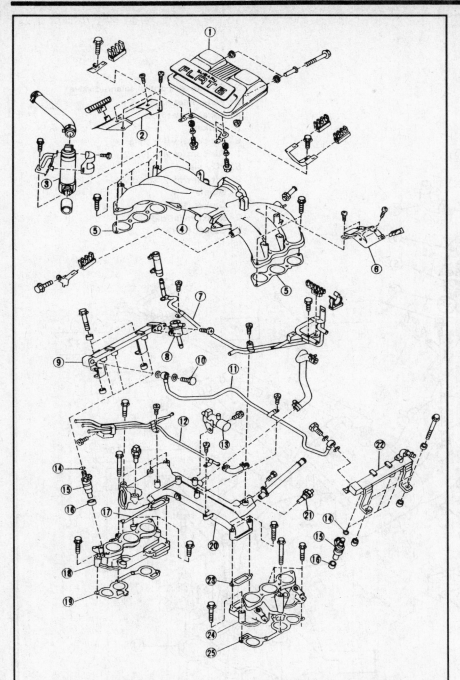

1	Intake manifold cover	13	Purge control solenoid valve
2	Fuel pipe cover RH	14	O-ring
3	By-pass air control valve	15	Fuel injector
4	Intake manifold collector	16	Insulator
5	Gasket	17	Gasket
6	Fuel pipe cover LH	18	Intake manifold RH
7	Fuel pipe ASSY	19	Gasket
8	Pressure regulator	20	Water pipe
9	Fuel pipe RH	21	Coolant thermosensor
10	Union bolt	22	Fuel pipe LH
11	Fuel pipe	23	Gasket
12	Fuel pipe ASSY	24	Intake manifold LH
		25	Gasket

FIG. 30 Intake manifold — 2.7L MPFI engine

19. Connect the negative battery cable. Start the engine and allow it to reach operating temperature. Check for leaks and test drive the vehicle.

2.2L and 3.3L Engines

▶ SEE FIG. 31 and 32

1. Release the fuel system pressure. Disconnect the negative battery cable and remove the engine cover.

2. Drain the cooling system and remove the water pipes as required.

3. Remove power steering pump, alternator and bracket as necessary to gain clearance.

4. Label and disconnect all electrical connectors leading to the intake manifold.

5. Label and disconnect all vacuum hoses leading to the intake manifold. Disconnect the PCV and blow-by hoses.

6. Label and disconnect the ignition high tension wires at the spark plugs and lay them aside.

7. Disconnect the air intake duct.

8. On turbocharged models, disconnect the turbo from the intake manifold and remove as required.

9. Disconnect the fuel supply lines and accelerator linkage.

10. Remove the intake manifold assembly.

To Install:

11. Clean the gasket mating surfaces thoroughly. Using a straight edge and a feeler gauge, inspect the intake manifold for flatness. Distortion should not exceed 0.020 in. (0.5mm).

12. Install the intake manifold and tighten the bolts to specification. On the 2.2L engine tighten the short bolts to 21–25 ft. lbs. (28–34Nm); the long bolts to 4–5 ft. lbs. (6–7Nm). On the 3.3L engine tighten all bolts to 17–20 ft. lbs. (23–26Nm).

13. Install the fuel lines and accelerator linkage.

14. Install the turbocharger assembly.

15. Install the air intake duct.

16. Check the ignition high tension wires for damage and install on the spark plugs.

17. Check all vacuum lines for deterioration and replace as necessary. Install the vacuum lines.

18. Check all electrical connectors for damage and replace as necessary. Install the electrical connectors.

19. Install the PCV valve and blow-by hose.

20. Install the power steering pump and alternator if removed.

21. Install the water pipes and fill the cooling system.

22. Install the engine cover.

23. Start the engine and allow it to reach operating temperature. Check for leaks and test drive the vehicle.

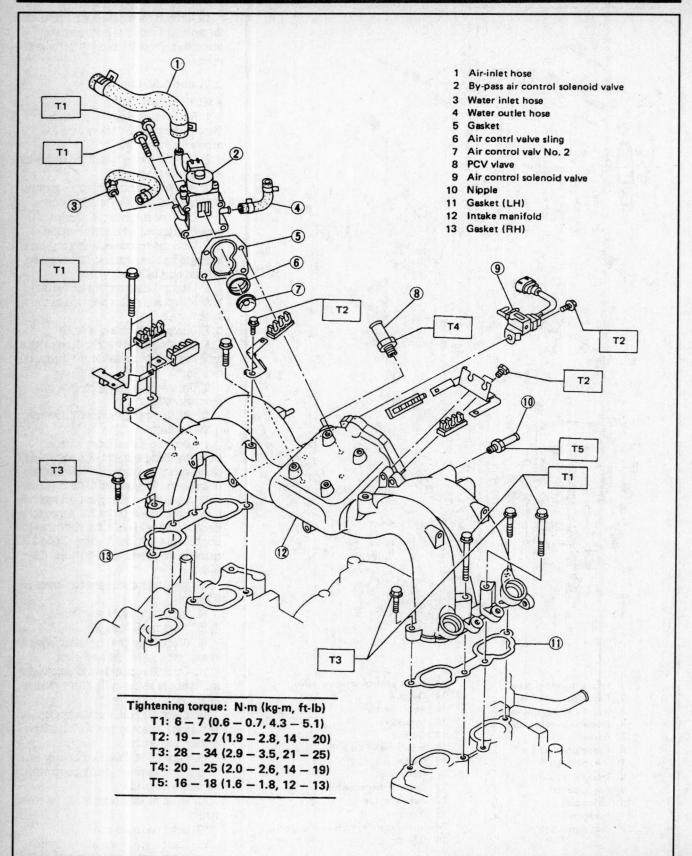

1   Air-inlet hose
2   By-pass air control solenoid valve
3   Water inlet hose
4   Water outlet hose
5   Gasket
6   Air contrl valve sling
7   Air control valv No. 2
8   PCV vlave
9   Air control solenoid valve
10 Nipple
11 Gasket (LH)
12 Intake manifold
13 Gasket (RH)

Tightening torque: N·m (kg-m, ft-lb)
T1: 6 — 7 (0.6 — 0.7, 4.3 — 5.1)
T2: 19 — 27 (1.9 — 2.8, 14 — 20)
T3: 28 — 34 (2.9 — 3.5, 21 — 25)
T4: 20 — 25 (2.0 — 2.6, 14 — 19)
T5: 16 — 18 (1.6 — 1.8, 12 — 13)

FIG. 31 Intake manifold — 2.2L engine

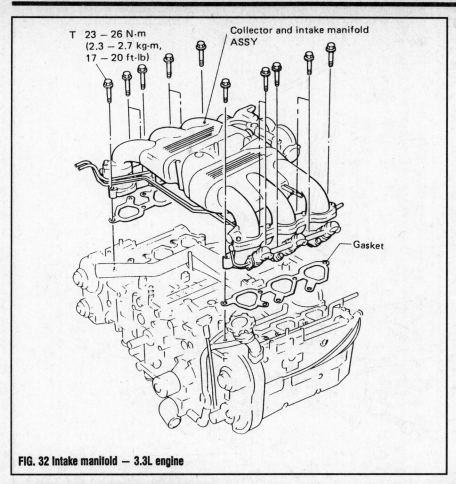

FIG. 32 Intake manifold — 3.3L engine

T 23 — 26 N·m
(2.3 — 2.7 kg-m,
17 — 20 ft-lb)

Collector and intake manifold
ASSY

Gasket

Exhaust Manifolds

REMOVAL & INSTALLATION

1.2L Engine

◆ SEE FIGS. 25 and 26

1. Raise and support the vehicle safely.

2. Remove the exhaust manifold cover-to-exhaust manifold bolts and the cover from the manifold.

3. Disconnect the electrical connector from the oxygen sensor.

4. Remove the exhaust manifold-to-front exhaust pipe nuts/bolts, then separate the pipe from the manifold and discard the gasket.

5. Remove the exhaust manifold-to-cylinder head nuts and the manifold from the vehicle; discard the gasket.

To Install:

6. Clean the gasket mounting surfaces thoroughly.

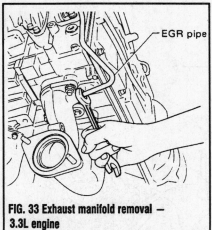

FIG. 33 Exhaust manifold removal —
3.3L engine

EGR pipe

7. Using a new gasket, install the exhaust manifold. Tighten the exhaust manifold-to-cylinder head nuts to 14–22 ft. lbs. (20–29Nm) and the exhaust pipe-to-exhaust manifold nuts/bolts to 17–31 ft. lbs. (23–42Nm).

8. Connect the electrical connector for the oxygen sensor.

9. Install the exhaust manifold cover.

10. Lower the vehicle, start the engine and check for exhaust leaks.

1.6L, 1.8L, 2.2L and 2.7L Engines

On these engines the front exhaust pipe bolts directly to the under side of the cylinder head. No exhaust manifold is used. See Exhaust System in this section for service information.

3.3L Engine

◆ SEE FIG. 33

1. Raise and support the vehicle safely.

2. Disconnect the oxygen sensor harness.

3. Remove the front under cover.

4. Remove the exhaust manifold covers.

5. Remove the front exhaust pipes.

6. Disconnect the EGR pipe from the right exhaust manifold.

7. Remove the exhaust manifolds.

To Install:

8. Clean all gasket mating surfaces thoroughly.

9. Install the exhaust manifolds using new gaskets. Tighten the exhaust manifold-to-cylinder head nuts to 25–33 ft. lbs. (34–44Nm) and the exhaust manifold-to-front exhaust pipe nuts to 22–29 ft. lbs. (29–39Nm).

10. Install the exhaust manifold covers and tighten the bolts to 13–15 ft. lbs. (17–20Nm).

11. Install the front under cover.

12. Connect the oxygen sensor harness.

13. Lower the vehicle. Start the engine and check for leaks.

Turbocharger

REMOVAL & INSTALLATION

◆ SEE FIG. 34

❊ WARNING

Do not allow dirt to enter either the inlet or outlet openings of the turbocharger, or the unit may be destroyed at startup.

1. Loosen clamps and remove the air intake duct from the airflow meter (throttle body) and the turbocharger.

2. Disconnect the vacuum lines from the waste gate valve controller.

3. Remove the cooling and oil lines from the turbocharger.

4. Remove the mounting bolts from the turbocharger exhaust outlet. Separate the pipe from the turbocharger.

4. Remove the turbocharger.

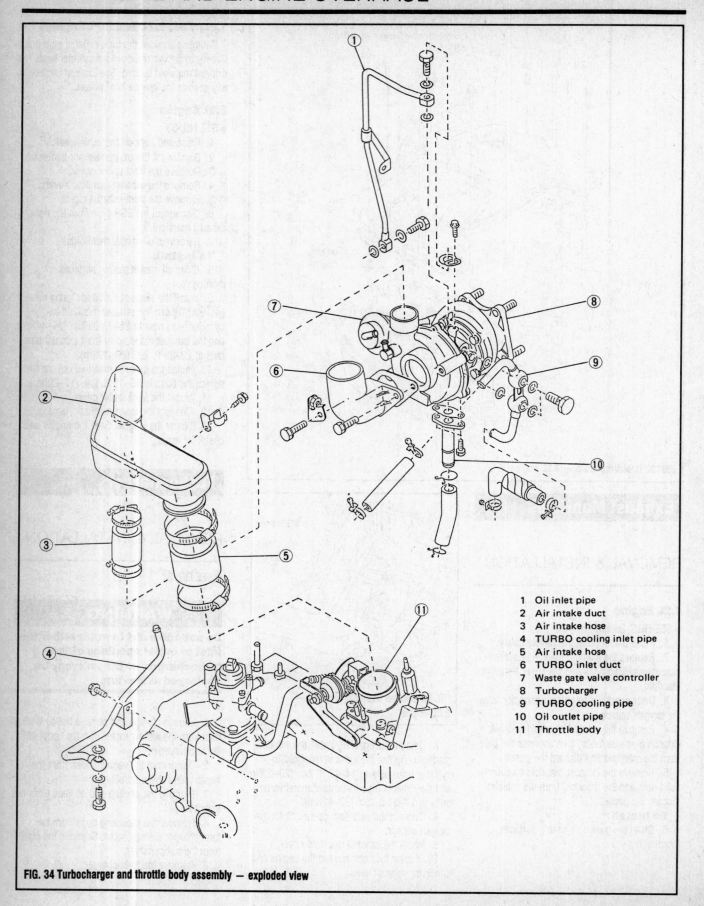

1 Oil inlet pipe
2 Air intake duct
3 Air intake hose
4 TURBO cooling inlet pipe
5 Air intake hose
6 TURBO inlet duct
7 Waste gate valve controller
8 Turbocharger
9 TURBO cooling pipe
10 Oil outlet pipe
11 Throttle body

FIG. 34 Turbocharger and throttle body assembly — exploded view

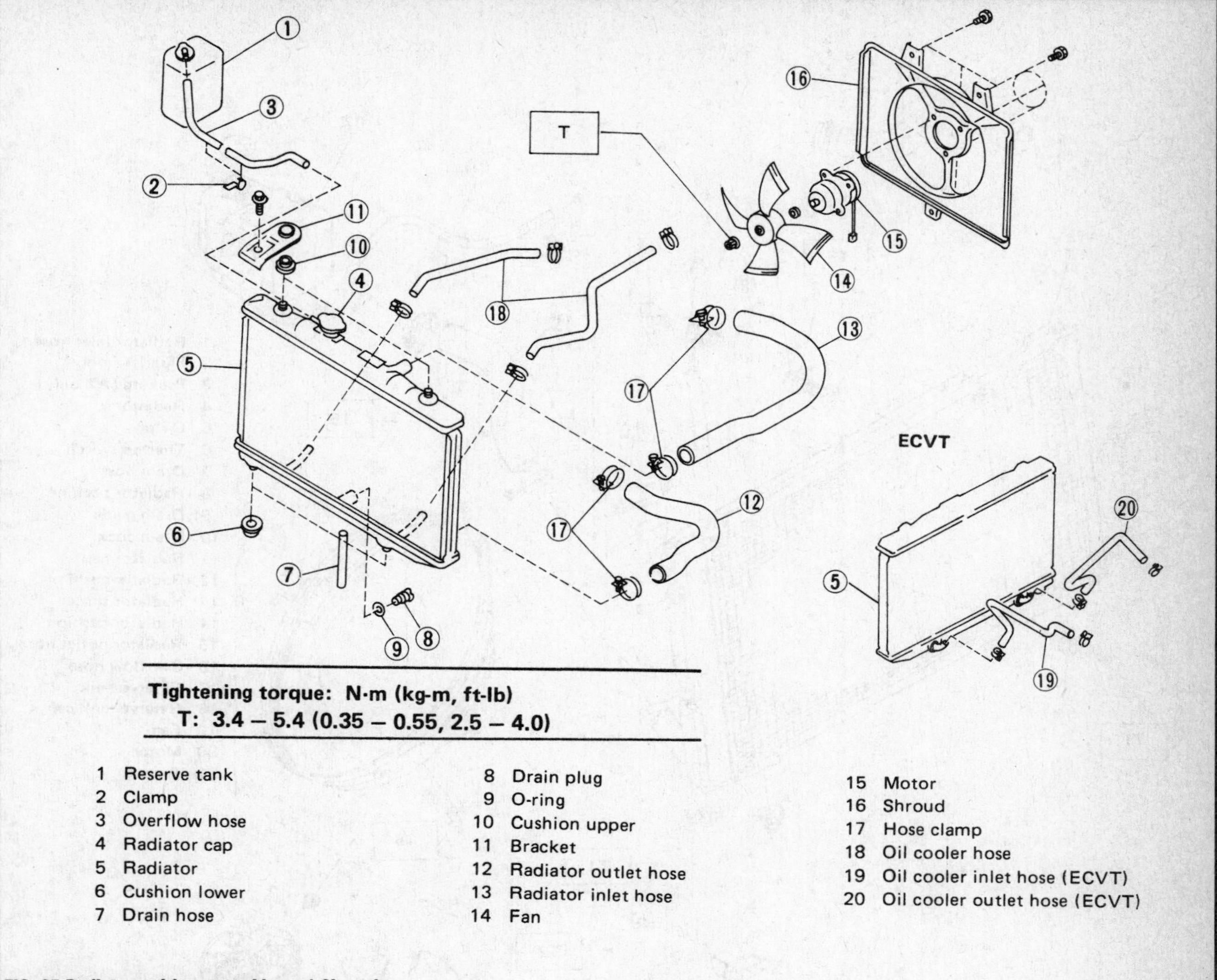

Tightening torque: N·m (kg-m, ft-lb)
T: 3.4 — 5.4 (0.35 — 0.55, 2.5 — 4.0)

1	Reserve tank	8	Drain plug
2	Clamp	9	O-ring
3	Overflow hose	10	Cushion upper
4	Radiator cap	11	Bracket
5	Radiator	12	Radiator outlet hose
6	Cushion lower	13	Radiator inlet hose
7	Drain hose	14	Fan

15	Motor
16	Shroud
17	Hose clamp
18	Oil cooler hose
19	Oil cooler inlet hose (ECVT)
20	Oil cooler outlet hose (ECVT)

FIG. 35 Radiator and fan assembly — 1.2L engine

To Install:

5. Using a new gasket, install the turbocharger on the exhaust manifold. Tighten the turbocharger mounting bolts to 18–25 ft. lbs. (25–34Nm) alternately and evenly.

6. Install the oil and cooling lines. Tighten the oil line banjo bolt to 11–13 ft. lbs. (15–18Nm) and the cooling line banjo bolt to 16–18 ft. lbs. (21–24Nm).

7. Connect the vacuum line to the waste gate valve controller.

8. Install the air intake duct assembly.

➡ **Do not run engine at a high RPM during the first few minutes of operation after servicing. This may damage the turbocharger as the oiling pressurized oil may not reach the turbocharger immediately.**

9. Start the engine and allow it to reach operating temperature. Check for leaks. Test drive the vehicle.

Radiator

REMOVAL & INSTALLATION

◆ SEE FIG. 35–39

1. Disconnect the negative battery cable. Remove the under cover as required and drain the cooling system. Drain the cooling system.

❄ CAUTION

When draining the coolant, keep in mind that cats and dogs are attracted by the ethylene glycol antifreeze, and are quite likely to drink any that is left in an uncovered container or in puddles on the ground. This will prove fatal in sufficient quantity. Always drain the coolant into a sealable container. Coolant should be reused unless it is contaminated or several years old.

2. Loosen the hose clamps and remove the inlet (upper) and outlet (lower) hoses from the radiator. Disconnect inlet and outlet oil cooler lines (automatic transmission).

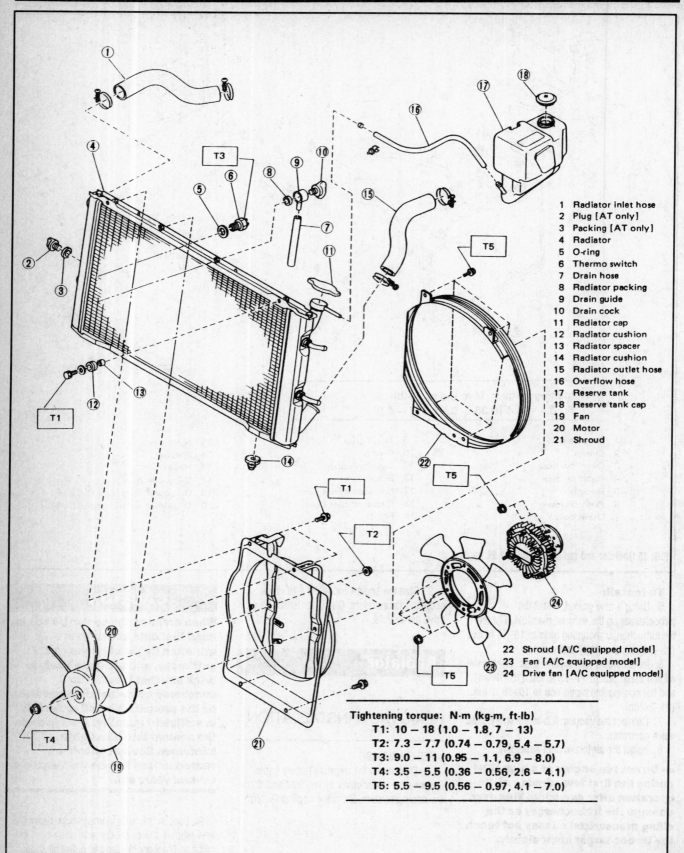

1   Radiator inlet hose
2   Plug [AT only]
3   Packing [AT only]
4   Radiator
5   O-ring
6   Thermo switch
7   Drain hose
8   Radiator packing
9   Drain guide
10 Drain cock
11 Radiator cap
12 Radiator cushion
13 Radiator spacer
14 Radiator cushion
15 Radiator outlet hose
16 Overflow hose
17 Reserve tank
18 Reserve tank cap
19 Fan
20 Motor
21 Shroud

22 Shroud [A/C equipped model]
23 Fan [A/C equipped model]
24 Drive fan [A/C equipped model]

Tightening torque: N·m (kg-m, ft-lb)
T1: 10 — 18 (1.0 — 1.8, 7 — 13)
T2: 7.3 — 7.7 (0.74 — 0.79, 5.4 — 5.7)
T3: 9.0 — 11 (0.95 — 1.1, 6.9 — 8.0)
T4: 3.5 — 5.5 (0.36 — 0.56, 2.6 — 4.1)
T5: 5.5 — 9.5 (0.56 — 0.97, 4.1 — 7.0)

FIG. 36 Radiator and fan assembly — 1.6L and 1.8L engine

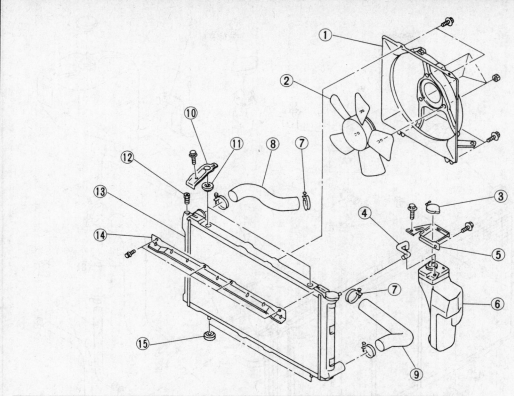

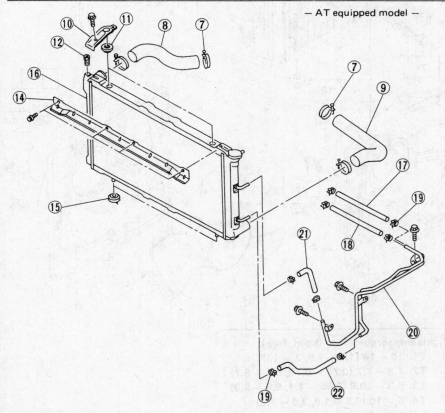

1 Shroud
2 Fan and motor
3 Reservoir tank cap
4 Overflow hose
5 Reservoir tank bracket
6 Reservoir tank
7 Hose clamp
8 Radiator inlet hose
9 Radiator outlet hose
10 Radiator bracket
11 Upper cushion
12 Air vent plug
13 Radiator
14 Radiator cover
15 Lower cushion
— AT equipped model —
16 Radiator
17 ATF inlet hose A
18 ATF outlet hose A
19 Hose clip
20 ATF pipe
21 ATF inlet hose B
22 ATF outlet hose B

FIG. 37 Radiator and fan assembly — 2.2L engine

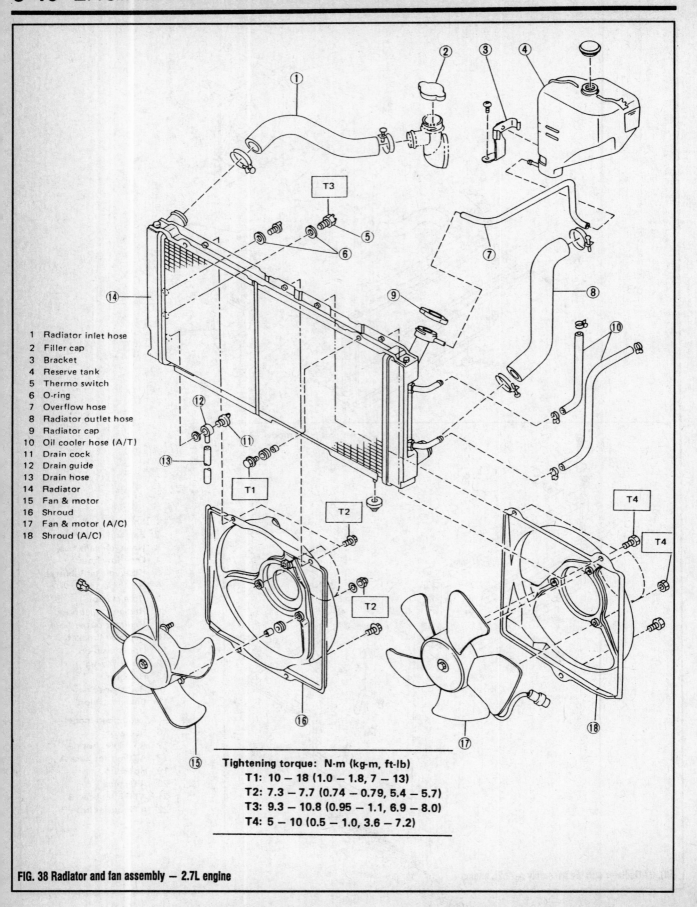

1 Radiator inlet hose
2 Filler cap
3 Bracket
4 Reserve tank
5 Thermo switch
6 O-ring
7 Overflow hose
8 Radiator outlet hose
9 Radiator cap
10 Oil cooler hose (A/T)
11 Drain cock
12 Drain guide
13 Drain hose
14 Radiator
15 Fan & motor
16 Shroud
17 Fan & motor (A/C)
18 Shroud (A/C)

Tightening torque: N·m (kg-m, ft-lb)
T1: 10 — 18 (1.0 — 1.8, 7 — 13)
T2: 7.3 — 7.7 (0.74 — 0.79, 5.4 — 5.7)
T3: 9.3 — 10.8 (0.95 — 1.1, 6.9 — 8.0)
T4: 5 — 10 (0.5 — 1.0, 3.6 — 7.2)

FIG. 38 Radiator and fan assembly — 2.7L engine

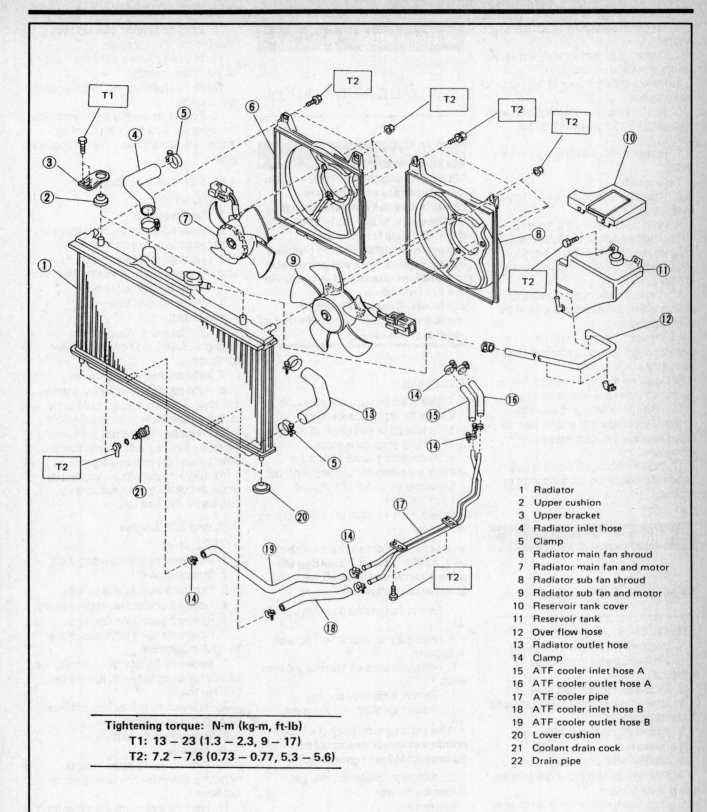

T1	T2

1 Radiator
2 Upper cushion
3 Upper bracket
4 Radiator inlet hose
5 Clamp
6 Radiator main fan shroud
7 Radiator main fan and motor
8 Radiator sub fan shroud
9 Radiator sub fan and motor
10 Reservoir tank cover
11 Reservoir tank
12 Over flow hose
13 Radiator outlet hose
14 Clamp
15 ATF cooler inlet hose A
16 ATF cooler outlet hose A
17 ATF cooler pipe
18 ATF cooler inlet hose B
19 ATF cooler outlet hose B
20 Lower cushion
21 Coolant drain cock
22 Drain pipe

Tightening torque: N·m (kg-m, ft-lb)
T1: 13 – 23 (1.3 – 2.3, 9 – 17)
T2: 7.2 – 7.6 (0.73 – 0.77, 5.3 – 5.6)

FIG. 39 Radiator and fan assembly — 3.3L engine

3. Remove the overflow hose and tank as required.

4. Disconnect the thermoswitch, and electric fan motor electrical connectors.

5. Remove the V-belt cover as required to gain clearance.

6. Remove the radiator attaching bolts and lift the radiator from the vehicle with the fan attached.

7. Remove the fan assembly to service the radiator.

To Install:

8. Inspect the radiator cushions and replace as necessary.

9. Install the fan assembly if removed.

10. Install the radiator and tighten the attaching bolts to 9–17 ft. lbs. (13–23Nm).

11. Install the V-belt cover, overflow hose and tank.

12. Inspect the electrical connectors for damage and replace as necessary. Install the electrical connectors.

13. Inspect the radiator hoses for deterioration and replace as necessary. Install the radiator hoses.

14. Install the transmission cooler lines on automatic transmission equipped vehicles.

15. Install the under cover if removed.

16. Fill the radiator with coolant. Start the engine and allow it to reach operating temperature.

17. Stop the engine and allow it to cool. Remove the radiator cap and add coolant as required.

Engine Fan

REMOVAL & INSTALLATION

♦ SEE FIG. 35–39

1. Disconnect the negative battery cable.

2. Disconnect the fan motor electrical connector.

3. Remove the reservoir tank as required.

4. Remove the nuts and/or bolts attaching the fan to the radiator.

5. Remove the radiator fan assembly.

To Install:

6. Install the radiator fan assembly.

7. Install the attaching nuts and/or bolts and tighten to specification.

8. Inspect the fan motor electrical connector for damage and replace as necessary. Connect the fan motor electrical connector.

9. Connect the negative battery cable.

Water Pump

REMOVAL & INSTALLATION

☼ CAUTION

When draining the coolant, keep in mind that cats and dogs are attracted by the ethylene glycol antifreeze, and are quite likely to drink any that is left in an uncovered container or in puddles on the ground. This will prove fatal in sufficient quantity. Always drain the coolant into a sealable container. Coolant should be reused unless it is contaminated or several years old.

1.2L Engine

1. Disconnect the negative battery cable.

2. Drain the engine oil and coolant.

3. Remove the oil level gauge, oil level gauge guide and level gauge guide sealing.

4. Disconnect the connector from the alternator and remove the alternator and V-belt.

5. Remove the crankshaft pulley and camshaft belt cover.

6. Remove the camshaft belt tensioner spring and tensioner.

➡ **Prior to removing the camshaft belt, scribe a mark indicating the drive direction of the belt for installation reference.**

7. Remove the camshaft drive plate and drive belt.

8. Remove the camshaft drive pulley and driven pulley.

9. Remove the camshaft belt cover and cover mount.

10. Remove the flywheel housing.

11. Remove the oil pan and pan gasket.

➡ **The water pump is part of the crankcase cover and must be disassembled for rebuilding.**

12. Remove the crankcase cover and disassemble the water pump.

To Install:

13. Clean all gasket mating surfaces thoroughly. Use new gaskets during installation.

14. Install the crankcase cover. Install the oil pan and gasket. Install the flywheel housing.

15. Install the camshaft drive belt pulleys, drive belt and drive belt covers.

16. Install the alternator and V-belt. Install the oil level gauge assembly.

17. Fill the engine with oil and the radiator with coolant.

18. Connect the negative battery cable. Start the engine and allow it to reach operating temperature. Check for leaks and test drive the vehicle.

1.6L, 1.8L and 2.7L Engines

♦ SEE FIG. 40

1. Drain the coolant.

2. Disconnect the radiator outlet hose and water bypass hose from the water pump.

3. Loosen the pulley nuts. Loosen the alternator assembly and remove the drive belt.

4. Remove the front belt cover.

5. Remove the water pump.

To Install:

6. Clean the gasket mating surfaces thoroughly. Always use new gaskets during installation.

7. Install the water pump and pulley.

8. Install the alternator, drive belt and drive belt cover. Adjust the drive belt to the proper tension. Tighten the water pump pulley bolts.

9. Inspect the coolant hoses and replace as necessary. Install the radiator outlet hose and water bypass hose on the water pump.

10. Fill the radiator with coolant. Start the engine and allow it to reach operating temperature. Check for leaks.

2.2L and 3.3L Engine

♦ SEE FIG. 41–43

1. Disconnect the negative battery cable.

2. Drain the coolant.

3. Disconnect the radiator outlet hose.

4. Remove the radiator fan motor assembly.

5. Remove the accessory drive belts.

6. Remove the timing belt, tensioner and camshaft angle sensor.

7. Remove the left side camshaft pulley and left side rear timing belt cover. Remove the tensioner bracket.

8. Disconnect the radiator hose and heater hose from the water pump.

9. Remove the water pump.

To Install:

10. Clean the gasket mating surfaces thoroughly. Always use new gaskets during installation.

11. Install the water pump and tighten the bolts, in sequence, to 7–10 ft. lbs. (10–14Nm). After tightening the bolts once, retighten to the same specification again.

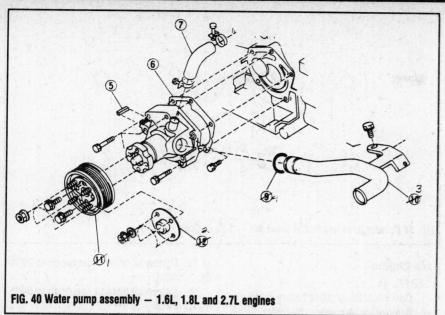

FIG. 40 Water pump assembly — 1.6L, 1.8L and 2.7L engines

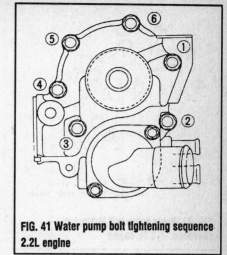

FIG. 41 Water pump bolt tightening sequence 2.2L engine

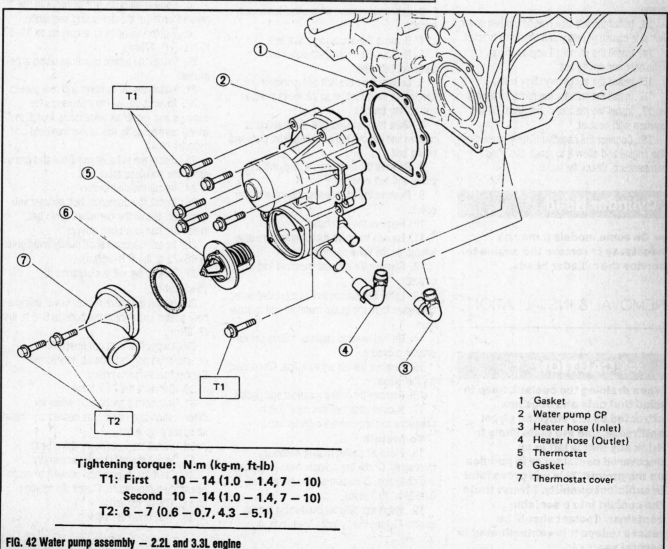

1 Gasket
2 Water pump CP
3 Heater hose (Inlet)
4 Heater hose (Outlet)
5 Thermostat
6 Gasket
7 Thermostat cover

Tightening torque: N.m (kg-m, ft-lb)
T1: First   10 — 14 (1.0 — 1.4, 7 — 10)
     Second   10 — 14 (1.0 — 1.4, 7 — 10)
T2: 6 — 7 (0.6 — 0.7, 4.3 — 5.1)

FIG. 42 Water pump assembly — 2.2L and 3.3L engine

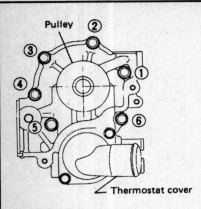

FIG. 43 Water pump bolt tightening sequence — 3.3L engine

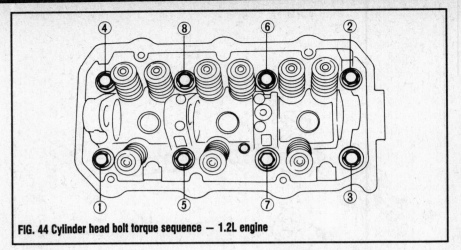

FIG. 44 Cylinder head bolt torque sequence — 1.2L engine

12. Inspect the radiator hoses for deterioration and replace as necessary. Install the radiator hose and heater hose on the water pump.

13. Install the left side rear timing belt cover, left side camshaft pulley and tensioner bracket.

14. Install the camshaft angle sensor, tensioner and timing belt.

15. Install the accessory drive belts.

16. Install the radiator ran motor assembly.

17. Install the radiator outlet hose. Fill the system with coolant.

18. Connect the negative battery cable. Start the engine and allow it to reach operating temperature. Check for leaks.

Cylinder Head

➡ On some models it may be necessary to remove the engine to service the cylinder heads.

REMOVAL & INSTALLATION

❊❊❊ CAUTION

When draining the coolant, keep in mind that cats and dogs are attracted by the ethylene glycol antifreeze, and are quite likely to drink any that is left in an uncovered container or in puddles on the ground. This will prove fatal in sufficient quantity. Always drain the coolant into a sealable container. Coolant should be reused unless it is contaminated or several years old.

1.2L Engine

➡ SEE FIG. 44

1. Disconnect the negative battery cable.
2. Remove the air cleaner assembly
3. Label and remove all applicable vacuum hoses.
4. Remove the accessory drive belt.
5. Remove the crankshaft pulley and camshaft belt cover.
6. Loosen the camshaft belt tensioner bolt 1/2 turn, move the tensioner to the loose position and tighten the bolt.
7. Mark the camshaft belt for direction of rotation and remove the camshaft drive plate and timing belt.
8. Remove the tensioner, spring, driven pulley and belt cover.
9. Remove the PCV hoses and valve rocker cover.
10. Remove the distributor.
11. Loosen the valve rocker nuts to release tension on the valve springs.
12. Remove the exhaust manifold and gasket.
13. Label and disconnect all electrical wiring harnesses from the intake manifold and cylinder head.
14. On fuel injected engines, relieve the fuel system pressure.
15. Remove the air suction pipe. Disconnect the fuel pipes.
16. Remove the intake manifold and gasket.
17. Loosen each cylinder head bolt in sequence and remove the cylinder head.

To Install:

18. Clean all gasket mating surfaces thoroughly. Check the cylinder head for cracks and distortion. Distortion should not exceed 0.0020 in. (0.05mm).
19. Install the cylinder head using a new gasket. Tighten the cylinder head bolts as follows:

a. Tighten all bolts in sequence to 29 ft. lbs. (39Nm).

b. Tighten all bolts in sequence to 54 ft. lbs. (73Nm).

c. Loosen all bolts 90° or more in the reverse order of the tightening sequence.

d. Tighten all bolts in sequence to 51–57 ft. lbs. (70–77Nm).

20. Install the intake manifold using a new gasket.

21. Install the air suction and fuel pipes.

22. Inspect the wiring harnesses for damage and repair as necessary. Install the wiring harnesses to the intake manifold and cylinder head.

23. Install the exhaust manifold and gasket using the stainless steel nuts.

24. Install the distributor.

25. Install the camshaft belt pulleys and tensioner. Install the camshaft drive belt. Install the camshaft belt covers.

26. Install the crankshaft pulley and tighten to 58–72 ft. lbs.(78–98Nm).

27. Adjust the valve clearance to specification.

28. Install the valve rocker cover using a new gasket and tighten the bolts to 5–6 ft. lbs. (7–8Nm).

29. Inspect all vacuum hoses for deterioration and replace as necessary. Connect all vacuum hoses.

30. Connect the PCV hose.

31. Inspect all spark plug wires for deterioration and replace as necessary. Install all spark plug wires.

32. Install the accessory drive belt.

33. Install the air cleaner assembly.

34. Start the engine and allow it to reach operating temperature. Check the ignition timing. Check for leaks.

35. Test drive the vehicle.

1.6L, 1.8L and 2.7L engines

♦ SEE FIG. 45–47 and 50–51

1. Disconnect the negative battery cable.

2. Remove the timing belt, belt cover and related components.

3. On turbocharged engines, remove the turbo cooling pipe together with the union screws and gaskets from the cylinder head.

4. Remove the camshaft cases, lash adjusters and related components.

5. On turbocharged engines, remove the EGR pipe.

6. Remove the accessory drive belts, alternator and air conditioner compressor if not already removed. Remove the bolt attaching the alternator bracket to the cylinder head.

7. On fuel injected engines, relieve the fuel system pressure.

8. Remove the bolts attaching the intake manifold to the cylinder head and remove the intake manifold.

9. Remove the bolt attaching the water bypass pipe bracket to the cylinder head.

10. Remove the spark plugs.

➡ On 2.7L engines, there are two types of cylinder head bolts used. Take note of cylinder head bolt arrangement as the bolts must be placed in their proper locations. Bolts number 1, 2, 9 and 13 measure 4.665 in. (118.5mm). All other bolts measure 5.217 in. (132.5mm).

11. On the 1.6L and 2.7L engines, loosen the cylinder head bolts in the proper sequence. Remove the cylinder heads and gaskets from the cylinder block.

To Install:

12. Clean all gasket mating surfaces thoroughly. Inspect the cylinder head for warpage. Warpage should not exceed 0.0020 in. (0.05mm).

13. Install the cylinder heads using new gaskets.

14. On the 1.6L and 1.8L engines, tighten the cylinder head bolts as follows:

a. Tighten all bolts in sequence to 22 ft. lbs. (29Nm).

b. Tighten all bolts in sequence to 43 ft. lbs. (59Nm).

c. Tighten all bolts in sequence to 47 ft. lbs. (64Nm).

15. On the 2.7L engine, tighten the cylinder head bolts as follows:

a. Tighten all bolts in sequence to 29 ft. lbs. (39Nm).

b. Tighten all bolts in sequence to 47 ft. lbs. (64Nm).

c. Loosen all bolts at least 90° in reverse order of the tightening sequence.

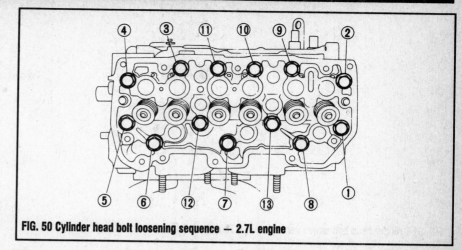

FIG. 50 Cylinder head bolt loosening sequence — 2.7L engine

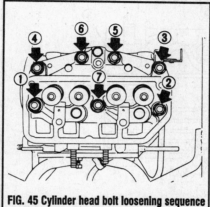

FIG. 45 Cylinder head bolt loosening sequence 1.6L engine

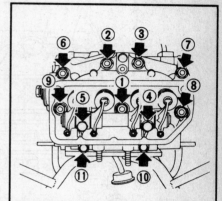

FIG. 46 Cylinder head bolt torque sequence — 1.6L engine

d. Tighten all bolts in sequence to 44–50 ft. lbs. (60–68Nm).

16. Install the spark plugs. Install the water bypass pipe bracket.

17. Install the intake manifold and tighten the bolts to 13–16 ft. lbs. (18–22Nm).

18. Install the alternator and bracket, air conditioner compressor and accessory drive belt.

19. On turbocharged engines, install the EGR pipe. Tighten the bolts to 23–27 ft. lbs. (31–37Nm).

20. Install the camshaft cases, lash adjusters and related components.

21. On turbocharged engines, install the turbo cooling pipe. 16–18 ft. lbs. (21–24Nm).

22. Install the timing belt, belt cover and related components.

23. Connect the negative battery cable.

24. Adjust the valve lash, as required. Start the engine and allow it to reach operating temperature. Adjust the ignition timing.

25. Check for leaks and test drive the vehicle.

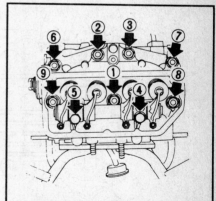

FIG. 47 Cylinder head bolt torque sequence — 1.8L engine

➡ **Depending on the type of cylinder heads used, retightening of the bolts may be necessary after the vehicle has be running.**

2.2L Engine

♦ SEE FIG. 48–49 and 54

1. Disconnect the negative battery cable.

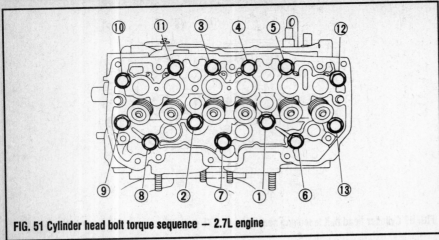

FIG. 51 Cylinder head bolt torque sequence — 2.7L engine

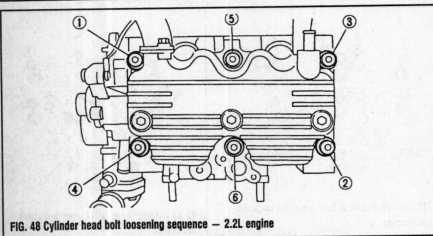

FIG. 48 Cylinder head bolt loosening sequence — 2.2L engine

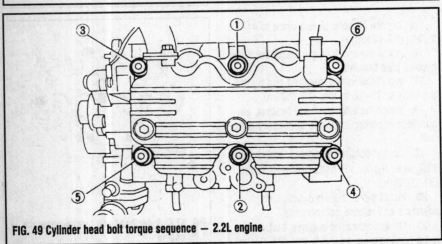

FIG. 49 Cylinder head bolt torque sequence — 2.2L engine

12. Remove the oil level gauge guide attaching bolt on the left cylinder head.

13. Remove the cylinder head bolts in the proper sequence. Leave bolts 1 and 3 installed loosely to prevent the cylinder head from falling.

14. While tapping the cylinder head with a plastic hammer, separate it from the cylinder block.

15. Remove bolts 1 and 3. Remove the cylinder head and gasket.

To Install:

16. Clean all gasket mating surfaces thoroughly. Inspect the cylinder head for warpage. Warpage should not exceed 0.0020 in. (0.05mm).

17. Install the cylinder heads on the block using new gaskets.

18. Tighten the cylinder head bolts, after lubricating them with oil, to the following specifications:

a. Tighten all bolts in sequence to 22 ft. lbs. (29Nm).

b. Tighten all bolts in sequence to 51 ft. lbs. (69Nm).

c. Loosen all bolts by 180°, then loosen an additional 180°.

d. Tighten bolts 1 and 2 to 25 ft. lbs. (24Nm) for non-turbo engines and 27 ft. lbs. (37Nm) for turbo engines.

e. Tighten bolts 3, 4, 5 and 6 to 11 ft. lbs. (15Nm) for non-turbo engines and 14 ft. lbs. (20Nm) for turbo engines.

f. Tighten all bolts in sequence by 80–90°.

g. Tighten all bolts in sequence an additional 80–90°.

➡ **Do not exceed 180° total tightening.**

19. Install the oil level gauge guide attaching bolt on the left cylinder head.

20. Install the timing belt, camshaft sprocket and related components.

21. Install the water pipe.

22. Install the intake manifold and tighten bolts to 21–25 ft. lbs. (28–34Nm). Connect the fuel delivery pipes.

23. Connect the blow-by hose. Install the knock sensor.

24. Connect the oil pressure switch connector.

25. Install the crank and cam angle sensors.

26. Install the connector bracket attaching bolt.

27. Connect the spark plug wires. Connect the PCV hose.

28. Install the valve rocker cover and tighten bolts to 4 ft. lbs. (9Nm).

29. Install the alternator, power steering pump and accessory drive belt.

2. Remove the V-belt, power steering pump, alternator and bracket.

3. Remove the valve rocker cover.

4. Disconnect the PCV hose and spark plug wires.

5. Remove the connector bracket attaching bolt.

6. Remove the crank angle sensor and cam angle sensor.

7. Disconnect the oil pressure switch. Remove the knock sensor.

8. Disconnect the blow-by hose.

9. Relieve the fuel system pressure and disconnect the fuel pipes.

10. Remove the intake manifold and gasket. Remove the water pipe.

11. Remove the timing belt, camshaft sprocket and related components.

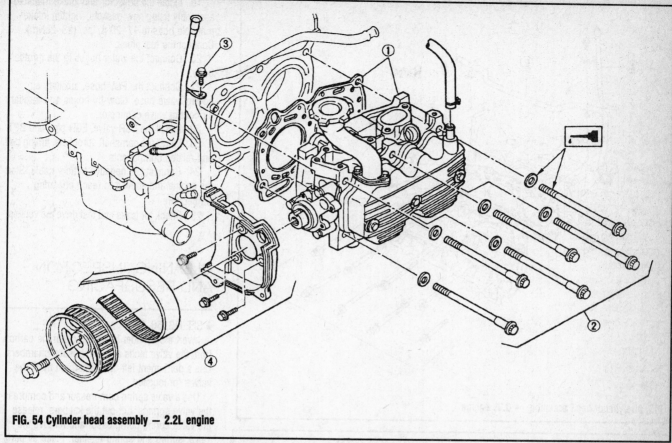

FIG. 54 Cylinder head assembly — 2.2L engine

30. Connect the negative battery cable. Start the engine and allow it to reach operating temperature. Check for leaks and test drive the vehicle.

3.3L Engine

▶ SEE FIG. 52–53 and 55

1. Disconnect the negative battery cable.
2. Remove the timing belt, camshaft sprockets and related components.
3. Remove the EGR valve, EGR pipe and BPT.
4. Disconnect the auxiliary air control valve connector.
5. Disconnect the blow-by hoses and auxiliary air valve hose.
6. Disconnect the PCV hose.
7. Disconnect the water hoses from the throttle body.
8. Relieve the fuel system pressure. Remove the collector and intake manifold assembly with the gaskets.
9. Remove the exhaust manifold and gasket.
10. Remove the cylinder head covers, camshafts and related components.
11. Remove the oil level guide and heater pipe.

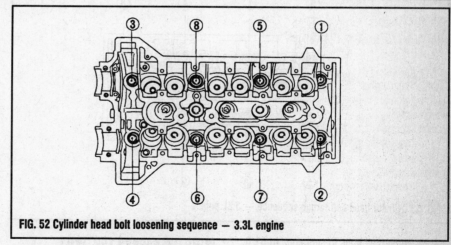

FIG. 52 Cylinder head bolt loosening sequence — 3.3L engine

12. Remove the cylinder head bolts in the proper sequence. Leave bolts 5 and 8 loosely installed to prevent the cylinder head from falling.
13. While tapping the cylinder head with a plastic hammer, separate it from the cylinder block. Remove bolts 5 and 8 to remove the cylinder head and gasket.

To Install:

14. Clean all gasket mating surfaces thoroughly. Inspect the cylinder head for warpage. Warpage should not exceed 0.0020 in. (0.05mm).
15. Install the cylinder head, using new gaskets, on the cylinder block.
16. Tighten the cylinder head bolts, after lubricating them with oil, to the following specifications:

  a. Tighten all bolts in sequence to 22 ft. lbs. (29Nm).

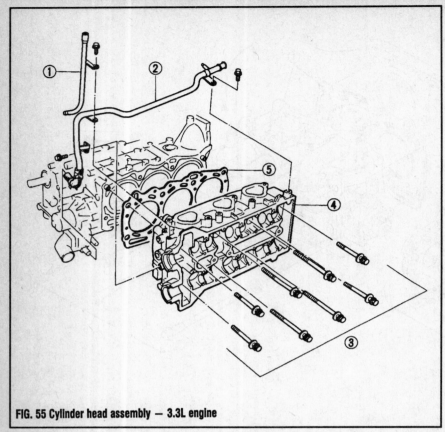

FIG. 55 Cylinder head assembly — 3.3L engine

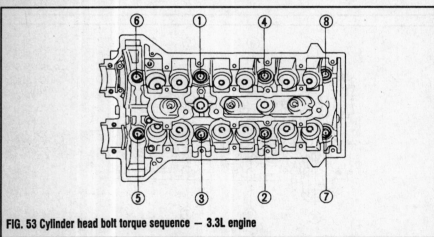

FIG. 53 Cylinder head bolt torque sequence — 3.3L engine

b. Tighten all bolts in sequence to 51 ft. lbs. (69Nm).

c. Loosen all bolts by 180°, then loosen an additional 180°.

d. Tighten all bolts in sequence to 20 ft. lbs. (27Nm).

e. Tighten bolts 1, 2, 3 and 4 in the sequence shown by 80–90°.

f. Tighten bolts 5, 6, 7 and 8 in the sequence shown to 33 ft. lbs. (44Nm).

g. Tighten all bolts in sequence an additional 80–90°.

➡ **Do not exceed 180° total tightening.**

16. Install the heater pipe and oil level gauge.

17. Install the camshafts, cylinder head covers and related components. Tighten the cylinder head cover bolts to 3–4 ft. lbs. (4–5Nm).

18. Install the exhaust manifold using a new gasket. Tighten the bolts to 25–33 ft. lbs. (29–39Nm).

19. Install the collector and intake manifold assembly using new gaskets. Tighten intake manifold bolts to 17–20 ft. lbs. (23–26Nm). Connect the fuel pipes.

20. Connect the water hoses to the throttle body.

21. Connect the PCV hose, auxiliary air control valve hose, blow-by hoses and auxiliary air control valve connector.

22. Install the EGR valve, EGR pipe and BPT.

23. Install the camshaft sprockets, timing belt and related components.

24. Connect the negative battery cable. Start the engine and allow it to reach operating temperature.

25. Check for leaks and test drive the vehicle.

CLEANING, INSPECTION AND RESURFACING

♦ SEE FIG. 56–57

Invert the cylinder head and clean the carbon from the valve faces and combustion chambers. Use a permanent felt-tip marker and mark the valves for location.

Use a valve spring compressor and compress the valve springs. Lift out the keepers, release the valve spring compressor and remove the valve, spring and spring retainer. Place all parts removed in order so that they can be reinstalled on the same cylinder.

Remove the valves from the cylinder head. Chip away any remaining carbon from the valve heads, combustion chambers and ports. Use a rotary wire brush on an electric drill. Be sure that the deposits are actually removed, rather than burned. Clean the valve faces with a wire wheel taking care not to remove the location numbering. Clean the cylinder head and component parts in an engine cleaning solvent.

Check the cylinder head for warpage by placing a straightedge across the gasket surface. Using feeler gauges, determine the clearance at the center of the straight edge. Measure across the diagonals, along the longitudinal centerline and across the cylinder head at several points. Should the warpage exceed 0.0020 in. (0.05mm) the cylinder head must be resurfaced. Be sure to observe the following grinding limits:

- 1.2L Engine: 0.008 in. (0.2mm)
- 1.6L, 1.8L and 2.7L Engines: 0.012 in. (0.3mm)
- 2.2L Engine: 0.004 in. (0.1mm)
- 3.3L Engine: 0.012 in. (0.3mm)

Clean the valve stems with lacquer thinner. Clean the valve guides using solvent and an expanding wire type valve guide cleaning brush.

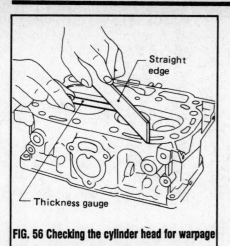

FIG. 56 Checking the cylinder head for warpage

FIG. 57 Removing the valve spring assembly with a compressor

Insert the valve into the guide it was removed from. With the valve slightly off of the valve seat, rock the valve face and stem back and forth. Excessive wobble means a worn guide, valve stem or both.

Measure the valve stems with a micrometer and compare the reading with the specifications to determine whether valve stem or guide wear is responsible for any excessive clearance. Replace or repair as necessary.

Valves

REMOVAL

1. Remove the valve system and related components.
2. Remove the cylinder head.
3. Using a valve spring compressor, compress the valve spring and remove the valve spring key retainer.
4. Remove each valve spring assembly.

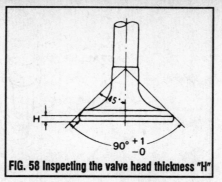

FIG. 58 Inspecting the valve head thickness "H"

➡ **Mark each valve assembly for location, as the valves must be installed on their original seats.**

5. Remove the valve oil seal using pliers.

➡ **Take care not to damage the lips of the valve oil seals.**

6. Remove the valves.

INSPECTION

♦ SEE FIG. 58

1. Inspect the cylinder head in the valve seat area for signs of damage or cracking.
2. Check the seat of the valve for any sign of poor contact or damage and repair as necessary.
3. Check the head and stem of each valve for burn, wear and deformation and replace valve as necessary.
4. Check the valve head thickness "H". If smaller than minimum specification, replace the valve. Valve head minimum thickness specifications are as follows:

- 1.2L Engine — 0.020 in. (0.5mm) intake; 0.020 in. (0.5mm) exhaust.
- 1.6L Engine — 0.020 in. (0.5mm) intake; 0.031 in. (0.8mm) exhaust.
- 1.8L Engine — 0.031 in. (0.8mm) intake; 0.051 in. (1.3mm) exhaust.
- 2.2L Engine — 0.031 in. (0.8mm) intake; 0.031 in. (0.8mm) exhaust.
- 2.7L Engine — 0.031 in. (0.8mm) intake; 0.031 in. (0.8mm) exhaust.
- 3.3L Engine — 0.024 in. (0.6mm) intake; 0.031 in. (0.8mm) exhaust.

5. Check the valve springs for damage, free length and tension. Replace the valve spring if not to specification.

REFACING

Using a valve grinder, resurface the valves according to specifications. The valve head

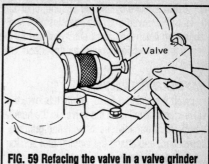

FIG. 59 Refacing the valve in a valve grinder

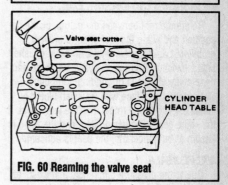

FIG. 60 Reaming the valve seat

thickness should be greater than the minimum specification after refacing. The valve stem top should also be squared and resurfaced, by placing the stem in the V-block of the grinder, and turning it while pressing lightly against the grinding wheel.

REAMING THE VALVE SEAT

Select a reamer of the correct seat angle, slightly larger than the diameter of the valve seat, and assemble it with a pilot of the correct size. Install the pilot into the valve guide, and using steady pressure, turn the reamer clockwise.

✸ WARNING

Do not turn the reamer counterclockwise.

Remove only as much material as necessary to clean the seat. Check the concentricity of the seat. Coat the valve face with Prussian blue dye, install and rotate it on the valve seat. Using the dye marked area as a centering guide, center and narrow the valve seat to specifications with correction cutters.

After making correction cuts, recheck the position of the valve seat on the valve face using Prussian blue dye.

POWER RESURFACING

Select a pilot of the correct size, and a coarse stone of the correct seat angle. Lubricate the pilot if necessary, and install the tool in the valve guide. Move the stone on and off the seat at approximately two cycles per second, until all flaws are removed from the seat. Install a fine stone, and finish the seat. Center and narrow the seat using correction stones, as described above.

HAND LAPPING VALVES

Invert the cylinder head, lightly lubricate the valve stems, and install the valves in the head as numbered. Coat valve seats with fine grinding compound, and attach the lapping tool suction cup to a valve head.

➡ **Moisten the suction cup.**

Rotate the tool between the palms, changing position and lifting the tool often to prevent grooving. Lap the valve until a smooth, polished seat is evident. Remove the valve and tool, and rinse away all traces of grinding compound.

Coat the valve face with Prussian blue dye, install the valve, and rotate it on the valve seat. If the entire seat becomes coated, and the valve is known to be concentric, the seat is concentric.

VALVE SEALS

Due to the pressure differential that exists at the ends of the intake valve guides (atmospheric pressure above, manifold vacuum below), oil is drawn through the valve guides into the intake port. This has been alleviated somewhat since the addition of positive crankcase ventilation, which lowers the pressure above the guides. To reduce blow-by, Subaru employs valve stem seals which must be pressed (or tapped) into position over the valve stem and guide boss. Recently, Teflon guide seals have become popular. Consult a parts supplier or machinist concerning availability and suggested usages.

➡ **When installing seals, ensure that a small amount of oil is able to pass the seal to lubricate the valve guides. Otherwise, excessive wear may result.**

Factory seals should be inspected and replaced if the seal lip is damaged or the spring is out of place. Also, whenever the seating surfaces of valve and seat are reconditioned or the guide is replaced, the seal should be replaced.

INSTALLATION

1. Lubricate the valve stems, and install the valves in the cylinder head as numbered.
2. Lubricate and position the seals (if used) and the valve springs.
3. Install the spring retainers, compress the springs, and insert the keys.

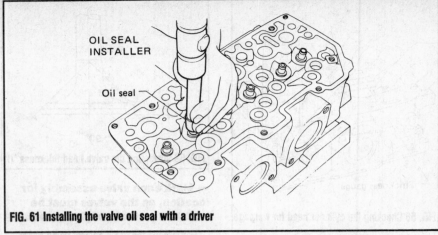
FIG. 61 Installing the valve oil seal with a driver

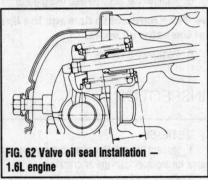
FIG. 62 Valve oil seal installation — 1.6L engine

4. Tap the head of the valve lightly with a wooden hammer to seat the keys.
5. Install the cylinder head.
6. Install the valve system and related components.
7. Adjust the rocker arm clearance as required.

Valve Stem Seals

REPLACEMENT

◆ SEE FIG. 61–62

Replace the oil seal if the lip is damaged or the spring is out of place. Also replace the oil seal when the surfaces of the valves and valve seats are refaced or the valve guides are replaced.

The following procedure may be performed with the cylinder head on the cylinder block by using a chuck and a compressed air source to fill the cylinder with air. This will hold the valve closed and prevent it from dropping into the cylinder.

1. Remove the cylinder head.
2. Using a spring compressor, remove the valve and valve spring assembly.

3. Using pliers, remove the valve stem oil seal.
4. Install the new oil seal with an oil seal driver.
5. On the 1.6L engine, install the seal so that it is positioned 0.913 in. (23.2mm) above the spring perch.
6. On the 1.2L, 1.8L and 2.7L engines, do not confuse the intake and exhaust oil seals. The intake seal measures 0.512 in. (13mm) and the exhaust seal measures 0.425 in. (10.8mm).
7. On the 2.2L and 3.3L engines, do not confuse the intake and exhaust oil seals. The intake seal is black and the exhaust seal is brown.
8. Install the valve and valve spring assembly.
9. Install the cylinder head.

Valve Springs

REMOVAL

◆ SEE FIG. 57

The following procedure may be performed with the cylinder head on the cylinder block by using a chuck and a compressed air source to fill the cylinder with air. This will hold the valve closed and prevent it from dropping into the cylinder.

1. Remove the valve system and related components.
2. Remove the cylinder head.
3. Using a valve spring compressor, compress the valve spring and remove the valve spring key retainer.
4. Remove each valve spring assembly.

INSPECTION

1. Place the spring on a flat surface next to a square. Measure the height of the spring, and rotate it against the edge of the square to measure distortion.

2. If spring distortion exceeds specification, replace the spring.

3. Check the spring installed and compressed tension using a spring pressure tester. If not within specification, spring pressure may be adjusted with shims.

4. Check the spring free length. If not within specification, replace the spring.

INSTALLATION

1. Lubricate the valve stems, and install the valves in the cylinder head as numbered.

2. Lubricate and position the seals (if used) and the valve springs.

3. Install the spring retainers, compress the springs, and insert the keys.

4. Tap the head of the valve lightly with a wooden hammer to seat the keys.

5. Install the cylinder head.

6. Install the valve system and related components.

7. Adjust the rocker arm clearance as required.

Valve Seats

REMOVAL & INSTALLATION

The valve seats in your Subaru engine cannot be replaced. The intake and the exhaust valve seats should be inspected for wear and defects. If the valve seat is found to be damaged, the contact surface can be corrected with a valve seat cutter or reamer.

The valve seats should be corrected when the valve guides are replaced. If valve seat wear exceeds specifications, the heads will have to be replaced.

Valve seat wear limit is measured in the direction of the valve axis.

Valve Guides

The valve guides are pressed in and should be replaced if the stem-to-guide clearance exceeds specification. Replacement should be done by an equipped machine shop.

Valve guides that are not excessively worn or distorted may, in some cases, be knurled rather than replaced. Knurling is a process in which metal is displaced and raised, thereby reducing clearance. Knurling also provides excellent oil control. The possibility of knurling rather than replacing valve guides should be discussed with a machinist.

REMOVAL & INSTALLATION

♦ SEE FIG. 63

1. Remove the cylinder head.

2. Remove the valve springs, keepers, retainers and oil seals.

3. Mount a dial indicator at a 90° angle to the valve stem. With the valve lifted off the seat, wiggle the valve and measure the valve-to-stem clearance.

4. If not within specification, remove the valve and measure the valve stem diameter. If valve stem diameter is not within specification, replace the valve.

5. If the valve stem diameter is within specification, the valve guide is worn and must be replaced.

6. Drive the valve guide out using a valve guide remover.

7. Ream the cylinder head to provide the necessary interference fit for the new valve guide. Check with the manufacturer for specifications.

8. Install the new valve guide using a valve guide installation tool. The valve guide should project as follows:

• 1.2L Engine — 0.807 in. (20.5mm) intake; 0.807 in. (20.5mm) exhaust.

• 1.6L Engine — 0.708 in. (18mm) intake; 0.905 in. (23mm) exhaust.

• 1.8L Engine — 0.709 in. (18mm) intake; 0.709 in. (18mm) exhaust.

• 2.2L Engine — 0.699 in. (17.8mm) intake; 0.699 in. (17.8mm) exhaust.

• 2.7L Engine — 0.690 in. (17.5mm) intake; 0.690 in. (17.5mm) exhaust.

• 3.3L Engine — 0.335 in. (8.5mm) intake; 0.335 in. (8.5mm) exhaust.

9. Ream the inside of the valve guide to provide the required oil clearance for the valve.

10. Install the valve, oil seal, spring, retainer and keeper.

11. Reassemble the cylinder head and install.

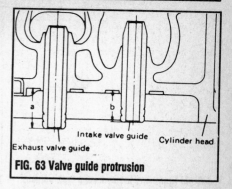

FIG. 63 Valve guide protrusion

Hydraulic Lash Adjuster

REMOVAL & INSTALLATION

♦ SEE FIG. 64

1.6L Engine

❈❈❈ CAUTION

The EPA warns that prolonged contact with used engine oil may cause a number of skin disorders, including cancer! You should make every effort to minimize your exposure to used engine oil. Protective gloves should be worn when changing the oil. Wash your hands and any other exposed skin areas as soon as possible after exposure to used engine oil. Soap and water, or waterless hand cleaner should be used.

1. Disconnect the blow-by and PCV hoses.

2. Remove the valve rocker cover.

3. Loosen the valve rocker assembly and remove the pushrod.

4. Raise and support the vehicle safely.

5. Remove the nuts which support the front engine mounting and slightly raise the engine using a floor jack.

6. Remove the drain plug and drain the engine oil.

7. Remove the oil pan.

8. Remove the hydraulic lifter. Use of a magnet facilitates removal.

To Install:

9. Install the hydraulic lifter.

10. Install the oil pan and tighten the bolts to 3–4 ft. lbs. (4–5Nm). Install the drain plug.

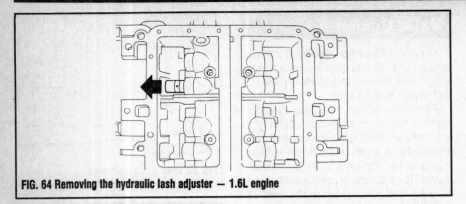

FIG. 64 Removing the hydraulic lash adjuster — 1.6L engine

11. Lower the engine and reconnect the front engine mount.

12. Lower the vehicle.

13. When adjusting the hydraulic lash adjusters, position the engine so that the No. 1 cylinder is at TDC on the compression stroke. Then, adjust the intake and exhaust valves on cylinder No. 1, the exhaust valve on cylinder No. 3 and the intake valve on cylinder No. 4.

14. Adjust the hydraulic lash adjuster as follows:

   a. Raise the bend of the lock washer and loosen the lock nut. Turn the valve rocker screw clockwise 4 turns. This will open the valves.

   b. Leave the valves open for 15 minutes to bleed down the lash adjusters.

   c. Unscrew the valve rocker screw gradually. The rocker arm will stop moving due to the closing of the valve. This is the zero lash point.

   d. Unscrew the valve rocker by 1.5 additional turns.

   e. Tighten the locknut and bend the lock washer.

15. Position the No. 1 cylinder at TDC on the compression stroke to adjust the intake and exhaust valve on cylinder No. 1, exhaust valve on cylinder No. 3, and intake valve on cylinder No. 4.

16. Turn the engine so that the No. 2 cylinder is at TDC on the compression stroke. Then adjust the remaining valves.

17. Install the valve rocker cover. Connect the blow-by and PCV hoses.

1.8L and 2.7L Engines

▶ SEE FIG. 65–66

1. Disconnect the negative battery cable.

2. Remove the distributor.

3. Remove the timing belt, belt cover and related components.

4. Remove the water pipe, oil filler duct and PCV hoses.

5. On turbocharged engines, remove the EGR pipe cover, pipe clamps and EGR pipe.

6. Remove the valve rocker covers.

7. Remove the camshaft cases, camshaft support and camshaft as a unit.

➡ **When removing the camshaft case, the valve rockers may fall. Lay a shop rag under the unit to protect the rockers from damage.**

8. Remove the hydraulic lash adjusters from the cylinder head. Keep them in order as they must be installed into their original positions.

To Install:

9. With the adjuster set in a vertical position, push the adjuster pivot downward by hand. If the pivot is depressed more than 0.020 in. (0.5mm), put the adjuster in a container filled with oil and move the plunger to pump up the adjuster. If the adjuster will not pump up, replace the adjuster.

10. Insert the valve lash adjusters into the cylinder head.

11. Apply grease to the valve rockers and install.

12. Install the camshaft case and tighten the retaining bolts to 13–15 ft. lbs. (17–20Nm).

13. Lubricate the valve system thoroughly. Install the valve rocker covers and tighten to 3–4 ft. lbs. 4–5Nm).

14. Install the PCV hoses, EGR pipe, pipe clamps and EGR pipe. Tighten the pipe to 23–27 ft. lbs. (31–37Nm).

15. Install the oil filler duct and water pipe.

16. Install the timing belt, belt cover and related components.

17. Install the distributor after turning engine to TDC for the No. 1 cylinder.

2.2L Engine

▶ SEE FIG. 67

1. Disconnect the PCV hose and remove the rocker cover.

2. Remove the valve rocker assembly. Remove bolts 2–4 in numerical sequence. Loosen bolt 1 and leave engaged to support rocker assembly. Remove bolts 5–8 in numerical sequence.

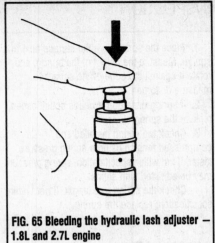

FIG. 65 Bleeding the hydraulic lash adjuster — 1.8L and 2.7L engine

3. Remove the hydraulic lash adjuster from the tip of the rocker arm. If necessary use pliers, but take care not to scratch the adjuster.

To Install:

4. Inspect the adjuster for scratches and replace as necessary. Submerge the lash adjuster in oil and push the check ball in using an appropriately sized rod.

5. With the check ball pushed in, move the plunger up and down at one second intervals until all air bubbles disappear.

6. When all air bubbles are removed, remove the rod and quickly push the plunger in to ensure it is locked. If the plunger does not lock properly, replace the adjuster.

7. Install the valve lash adjusters on the rocker arms.

8. Install the valve rocker assembly on the cylinder head. Temporarily tighten the four outer bolts.

9. Tighten the four inner bolts to 9 ft. lbs. (12Nm). Tighten the four outer bolts to the same specification.

10. Disconnect the PCV hose and remove the rocker cover. Tighten the rocker cover bolts to 4 ft. lbs. (5Nm).

3.3L Engine

1. Remove the timing belt, camshaft sprockets and related parts.

2. Remove the intake and exhaust camshafts.

3. Remove the hydraulic lash adjusters from the tops of the valve springs. Keep the adjusters in order as they must be installed to their original positions.

4. Lubricate the lash adjusters and install on the valve springs.

5. Install the intake and exhaust camshafts.

6. Install the timing belt, camshaft sprockets and related parts.

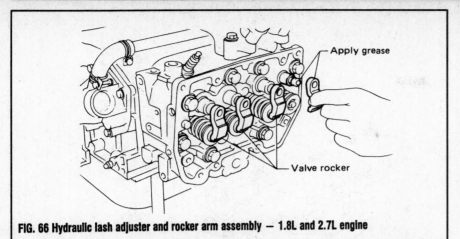

FIG. 66 Hydraulic lash adjuster and rocker arm assembly — 1.8L and 2.7L engine

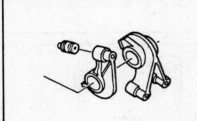

FIG. 67 Hydraulic lash adjuster and rocker arm assembly — 2.2L engine

Oil Pan

REMOVAL & INSTALLATION

✳ CAUTION

The EPA warns that prolonged contact with used engine oil may cause a number of skin disorders, including cancer! You should make every effort to minimize your exposure to used engine oil. Protective gloves should be worn when changing the oil. Wash your hands and any other exposed skin areas as soon as possible after exposure to used engine oil. Soap and water, or waterless hand cleaner should be used.

1. To remove the oil pan, it is not necessary that the engine be removed from the vehicle. Drain the engine oil.

2. Remove the attaching bolts which hold the oil pan to the bottom of the crankcase, and remove the oil pan.

3. Remove the oil pan gasket and clean the mating surfaces of the oil pan and the crankcase.

4. Install the oil pan using a new gasket. Tighten the oil pan bolts to 3–4 ft. lbs. (4–5Nm).

5. Fill the engine with oil.

Oil Pump

REMOVAL & INSTALLATION

✳ CAUTION

The EPA warns that prolonged contact with used engine oil may cause a number of skin disorders, including cancer! You should make every effort to minimize your exposure to used engine oil. Protective gloves should be worn when changing the oil. Wash your hands and any other exposed skin areas as soon as possible after exposure to used engine oil. Soap and water, or waterless hand cleaner should be used.   When draining the coolant, keep in mind that cats and dogs are attracted by the ethylene glycol antifreeze, and are quite likely to drink any that is left in an uncovered container or in puddles on the ground. This will prove fatal in sufficient quantity. Always drain the coolant into a sealable container. Coolant should be reused unless it is contaminated or several years old.

1.2L Engine

◆ SEE FIG. 68

The oil pump is an integral part of the crankcase cover, located at the front of the engine.

1. Raise and support the vehicle safely.
2. Drain the engine oil.
3. Remove the oil level gauge, the oil level gauge guide and the level gauge guide seal.
4. Disconnect the electrical connectors from the alternator. Remove the alternator-to-engine mounting bolts, the drive belt and the alternator from the engine.
5. Remove the crankshaft pulley bolt and the crankshaft pulley.
6. Remove the timing belt cover-to-engine bolts and the cover from the engine.
7. Remove the timing belt tensioner-to-engine bolts, the spring and the tensioner.
8. Using a piece of chalk, mark the rotating direction of the timing belt.
9. Remove the crankshaft drive plate and the timing belt.
10. Remove the camshaft sprocket-to-camshaft bolts and the sprocket from the camshaft.
11. Remove the inner timing belt cover-to-engine bolts and the cover from the engine.
12. From under the engine, remove the flywheel housing cover-to-engine bolts and the cover from the engine.
13. Remove the oil pan-to-engine bolts and the pan from the engine; discard the gasket. Remove the oil strainer-to-engine bolts and the strainer assembly from the engine.
14. Remove the water pump cover-to-crankcase cover bolts and the water pump cover. Use a screwdriver to lock the balance shaft, then remove the water pump impeller.
15. Remove the crankcase cover-to-engine bolts and the cover from the engine.
16. Remove the oil pump cover-to-crankcase cover bolts, the cover, the outer rotor and the inner rotor with the shaft.

To Install:

17. Clean all gasket mating surfaces thoroughly.
18. Inspect the oil pump parts for wear and/or damage; replace the parts if necessary.
19. Pack the oil pump with petroleum jelly and reassemble. By packing the oil pump, a vacuum will be created upon initial fire-up and allow oil pressure to build immediately.
20. Install the crankcase cover and water pump.
21. Install the oil strainer using a new O-ring, and oil pan using a new gasket. Tighten the oil pan bolts to 3–4 ft. lbs. (4–5Nm).
22. Install the flywheel housing cover.

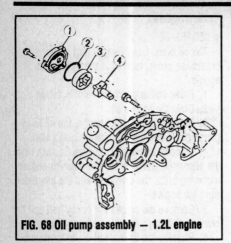

FIG. 68 Oil pump assembly — 1.2L engine

23. Install the camshaft sprockets, crankshaft sprocket, timing belt and related components.

24. Install the crankshaft pulley and bolt.

25. Install the alternator and connect the electrical connectors.

26. Install the oil level gauge, the oil level gauge guide and the level gauge guide seal.

27. Fill the engine with oil. Connect the negative battery cable.

28. Start the engine and allow it to reach operating temperature. Check for adequate oil pressure. Then, check for leaks.

29. Adjust the ignition timing as required.

1.6L Engine

▶ SEE FIG. 69

The oil pump can be removed with the engine in the vehicle. The oil pump is located on the front of the engine and has the oil filter mounted on it. The pump and filter may be removed as an assembly.

1. Unfasten the 4 bolts which secure the pump to the engine.

2. Remove the pump, complete with the gasket and filter.

3. Remove the filter from the pump and disassemble the pump.

To Install:

4. Wash the disassembled oil pump in solvent.

5. Check the outside diameter of the oil pump rotor shaft. If worn or damaged, replace it.

6. Check the gear and rotor. Drive gear outside diameter should be 1.1693–1.1709 in. (29.70–29.74mm). Rotor outside diameter should be 1.5957–1.5968 in. (40.53–40.56mm). If not within specification, replace as necessary.

7. Check the clearance between the pump drive gear and pump rotor. If clearance is greater than 0.008 in. (0.2mm), replace the drive gear and rotor as an assembly.

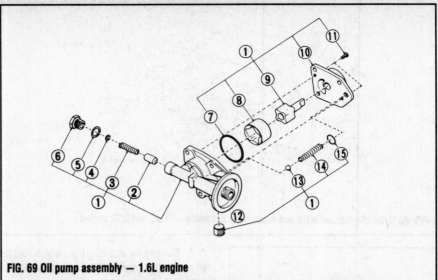

FIG. 69 Oil pump assembly — 1.6L engine

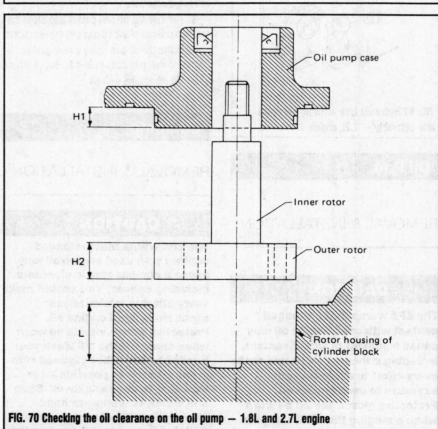

FIG. 70 Checking the oil clearance on the oil pump — 1.8L and 2.7L engine

8. Check the side clearance between the pump case and pump rotor, and between the pump case and drive gear. If clearance is greater than 0.008 in. (0.2mm), replace the necessary components.

9. Lay a straight edge across the pump case and measure the clearance between the pump case and the rotor. If greater than 0.0098 in. (0.25mm), replace the necessary components.

10. Check the relief valve spring. Free length should be 1.854 in. (47.1mm).

11. Check the bypass valve and spring in the same manner.

12. Install the oil filter on the pump boss.

13. Using new gaskets and O-rings, fit the pump to the crankcase and carefully engage the pump drive with the slot in the end of the camshaft. Be sure that the pump mounts flush to the block.

14. Secure the pump with the 4 mounting bolts.

15. Check the engine oil level and add oil, as necessary, to replace any that was lost.

1.8L and 2.7L Engines

♦ SEE FIG. 70

The engine oil pump is located at the front of the engine. The oil filter is attached to the oil pump.

1. Disconnect the negative battery cable.
2. Place an oil pan under the crankcase, remove the drain plug and drain the oil from the crankcase.
3. Remove the left and right front timing belt covers.
4. Loosen the tensioner mounting bolts on the #1 cylinder.
5. Turn the tensioner to fully loosen the belt, then tighten the mounting bolts.
6. Using a piece of chalk, mark the rotating direction of the timing belt, then remove the belt from the vehicle.
7. Remove the oil pump-to-engine bolts and the oil pump along with the oil filter from the cylinder block.
8. Remove the oil pump's outer rotor from the cylinder block.
9. Disassemble the oil pump.

To Install:

10. Wash the disassembled components in solvent.
11. Check the outside diameter of the inner rotor shaft. Shaft diameter should be 1.4035–1.4055 in. (35.65–35.70mm).
12. Check the outside diameter of the outer rotor. Diameter should be 1.9665–1.9685 in. (49.95–50.00mm).
13. Check the clearance between the outer rotor and the cylinder block rotor housing. If clearance is greater than 0.0087 in. (0.22mm), replace the rotor.
14. Measure the height of the case projection H1 plus the oil pump inner and outer rotors H2.
15. Measure the depth of the rotor housing bore L in the cylinder block.
16. Calculate the side clearance C using the following equation: $C = L - (H1 + H2)$. If the side clearance is greater than 0.00071 in. (0.18mm), replace the pump inner and outer rotors with oversized versions.
17. Using new gaskets and O-rings, assemble the oil pump. Tighten the oil pump pulley to 13–15 ft. lbs. (18–21Nm). Tighten the by-pass spring plug to 23–27 ft. lbs.31–37Nm).
18. Install the oil pump on the cylinder block.
19. Install the timing belt and related components.
20. Fill the engine with oil. Connect the negative battery cable.

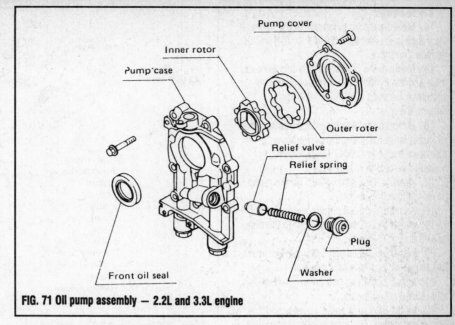
FIG. 71 Oil pump assembly — 2.2L and 3.3L engine

21. Start the engine and allow it to reach operating temperature. Check for adequate oil pressure. Check for leaks.
22. Adjust the ignition timing as required.

2.2L Engine

♦ SEE FIG. 71

1. Drain the engine oil.
2. Drain the coolant.
3. Remove the belt tensioner bracket.
4. Remove the water pump.
5. Remove the oil pump by prying it loose from the front of the engine with two pry bars.

➡ **Take care not to scratch the gasket mating surfaces.**

To Install:

6. Measure the tip clearance of the rotors. If clearance is greater than 0.0071 in. (0.18mm), replace the rotors.
7. Measure the clearance between the outer rotor and the cylinder block rotor housing. If clearance exceeds 0.0079 in. (0.20mm), replace the rotor.
8. Measure the side clearance between the oil pump inner rotor and the pump cover. If clearance exceeds 0.0047 in. (0.12mm), replace the rotor or pump body.
9. Install a new front oil seal on the pump cover using a driver.
10. Assemble the oil pump.
11. Using fluid packing, Three bond 1215 or equivalent, install the oil pump. Tighten the oil pump bolts to 5 ft. lbs. (6Nm).
12. Install the water pump and belt tensioner bracket.
13. Fill the engine with oil and the radiator with coolant.

14. Start the engine and allow it to reach operating temperature. Check for adequate oil pressure. Check for leaks.

3.3L Engine

♦ SEE FIG. 71

1. Disconnect the negative battery cable.
2. Drain the engine oil.
3. Remove the under cover.
4. Remove the bolts which connect the power steering oil cooler pipe assembly to the body.

➡ **Do not remove the pipe assembly.**

5. Remove the radiator fan motor assemblies.
6. Remove the drive belt cover and drive belts.
7. Remove the air conditioner belt idler assembly.
8. Remove the power steering pump bracket.

➡ **Do not remove the power steering pump.**

9. Remove the crank angle sensors and crankshaft pulley.
10. Remove the timing belt covers, timing belt and related components.
11. Remove the crankshaft sprocket, belt idlers, belt tensioner and tensioner bracket.
12. Remove the oil pump by prying it from the engine with two pry bars.

➡ **Take care not to scratch the gasket mating surfaces.**

13. Disassemble the oil pump.

To Install:

14. Measure the tip clearance of the rotors. If clearance is greater than 0.0071 in. (0.18mm), replace the rotors.

15. Measure the clearance between the outer rotor and the cylinder block rotor housing. If clearance exceeds 0.0079 in. (0.20mm), replace the rotor.

16. Measure the side clearance between the oil pump inner rotor and the pump cover. If clearance exceeds 0.0047 in. (0.12mm), replace the rotor or pump body.

17. Install a new front oil seal on the pump cover using a driver.

18. Assemble the oil pump.

19. Install the oil pump and tighten the bolts to 4–5 ft. lbs. (5–6Nm).

20. Install the crankshaft sprocket, belt idlers, belt tensioner and tensioner bracket.

21. Install the timing belt covers, timing belt and related components.

22. Install the crank angle sensors and crankshaft pulley.

23. Install the power steering pump bracket.

24. Install the air conditioner belt idler assembly.

25. Install the drive belt cover and drive belts.

26. Install the radiator fan motor assemblies.

27. Install the bolts which connect the power steering oil cooler pipe assembly to the body.

28. Install the under cover and fill the engine with oil.

29. Connect the negative battery cable.

30. Start the engine and allow it to reach operating temperature. Check for adequate oil pressure and check for leaks.

Oil Cooler

REMOVAL & INSTALLATION

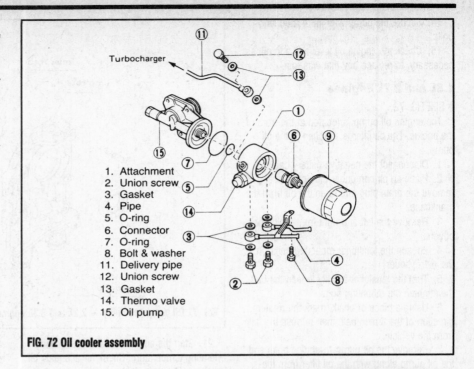

1. Attachment
2. Union screw
3. Gasket
4. Pipe
5. O-ring
6. Connector
7. O-ring
8. Bolt & washer
11. Delivery pipe
12. Union screw
13. Gasket
14. Thermo valve
15. Oil pump

FIG. 72 Oil cooler assembly

1. Put an oil drain pan nearby. Remove the two bolts connecting the oil cooler lines to the bottom of the attachment. Drain oil into the pan.

2. Remove the bolt connecting the bracket for these two oil lines to the block. Pull the oil lines away from the block and drain them into the pan.

3. Remove the three oil cooler mounting bolts and remove it.

4. To install, reverse the above procedure, using new sealing gaskets on the cooler lines. Torque the piping brace-to-block bolt to 20 ft. lbs., and the piping-to-attachment bolts to 25 ft. lbs.

Crankshaft Pulley

REMOVAL & INSTALLATION

1. Disconnect the negative battery cable.
2. Remove the accessory drive belt.
3. Using a puller, remove the crankshaft pulley
4. Install the pulley and tighten the pulley bolt to specification.
5. Install the accessory drive belt. Tension belt to specification.
6. Connect the negative battery cable.

Timing Gear Cover

REMOVAL & INSTALLATION

1.6L Engine

The timing gears on the 1.6L engine are located at the rear of the engine and are covered by the flywheel housing. In order to remove the flywheel housing the engine must be removed from the vehicle.

1. Remove the engine from the vehicle.

2. Separate the engine from the transaxle. If equipped with an automatic transaxle, remove the torque converter with the transaxle.

3. On manual transmission equipped vehicles, remove the clutch assembly from the flywheel and the flywheel from the crankshaft. On automatic transaxle equipped vehicles, remove the converter drive plate from the crankshaft.

4. Remove the flywheel housing-to-engine bolts and work the housing from the two aligning dowels.

5. Using a puller, remove the flywheel housing oil seal.

To Install:

6. Using a driver, install a new flywheel housing oil seal.

7. Clean the gasket mating surface thoroughly and apply a fresh coat of Three Bond® or equivalent.

8. Install the flywheel housing and tighten the bolts to 14–20 ft. lbs. (19–27Nm).

9. On manual transmission equipped vehicles, install the flywheel and tighten the bolts to 30–33 ft. lbs. (41–45Nm). Install the clutch assembly.

10. On automatic transmission equipped vehicles, tighten the drive plate to crankshaft bolts to 36–39 ft. lbs. (49–53Nm).

11. Install the transaxle to the engine and tighten the bolts to 34–40 ft. lbs. (46–54Nm).

12. Install the engine and transaxle assembly in the vehicle.

Timing Belt Cover and Seal

REMOVAL & INSTALLATION

1.2L Engine
♦ SEE FIG. 73

1. Loosen the alternator-to-engine bolts, relax the drive belt tension and remove the drive belt from the front of the engine.

2. Using a socket wrench (through the hole in the right fender) and the Crank/Crankshaft Pulley Wrench tool No. 499205500 or equivalent (to hold the crankshaft pulley), remove the crankshaft pulley-to-crankshaft bolt and the pulley from the crankshaft.

3. Remove the timing belt cover-to-engine bolts and the cover from the engine.

4. Install the timing belt cover and tighten the bolts securely.

5. Install the crankshaft pulley and tighten the bolt to 58–72 ft. lbs. (78–98Nm).

6. Install the accessory drive belt and tighten to the proper tension.

1.8L and 2.7L Engines
♦ SEE FIG. 74 and 77

1. Loosen the water pump pulley nut/bolts and the alternator-to-engine bolts, the remove the drive belt.

2. Disconnect the electrical connector from the oil pressure switch.

3. Remove the oil level gauge guide with the gauge.

4. Remove the timing hole cover from the top of the flywheel housing.

5. Using the Flywheel Stopper tool No. 498277000 or equivalent (MT), or the Drive Plate Stopper tool No. 498407000 or equivalent (AT), insert it through the timing hole (in the flywheel housing) and lock the flywheel.

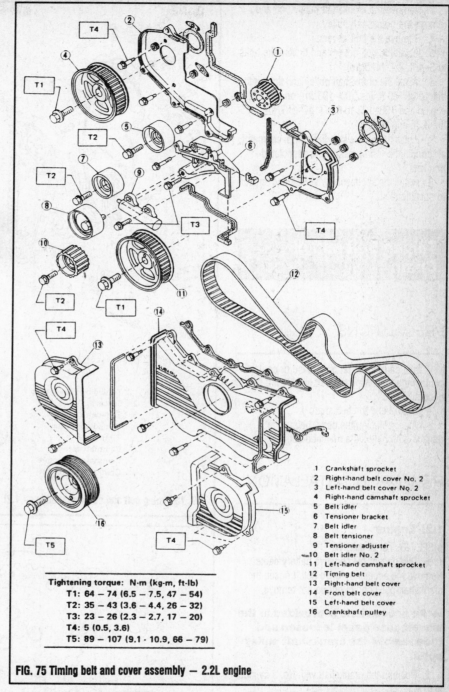

Tightening torque: N·m (kg-m, ft-lb)
T1: 64 – 74 (6.5 – 7.5, 47 – 54)
T2: 35 – 43 (3.6 – 4.4, 26 – 32)
T3: 23 – 26 (2.3 – 2.7, 17 – 20)
T4: 5 (0.5, 3.6)
T5: 89 – 107 (9.1 - 10.9, 66 – 79)

1 Crankshaft sprocket
2 Right-hand belt cover No. 2
3 Left-hand belt cover No. 2
4 Right-hand camshaft sprocket
5 Belt idler
6 Tensioner bracket
7 Belt idler
8 Belt tensioner
9 Tensioner adjuster
10 Belt idler No. 2
11 Left-hand camshaft sprocket
12 Timing belt
13 Right-hand belt cover
14 Front belt cover
15 Left-hand belt cover
16 Crankshaft pulley

FIG. 75 Timing belt and cover assembly — 2.2L engine

6. Remove the crankshaft pulley bolt and using a puller, remove the crankshaft pulley.

7. If equipped with a turbocharger, remove the belt cover plate.

8. Remove the left side, the right side and the front timing belt cover.

To Install:

9. Install the timing belt covers and tighten the bolts to 3–4 ft.lbs. (4–5Nm).

10. Install the crankshaft pulley and tighten the bolt to 66–79 ft. lbs. (89–107Nm).

11. Remove the flywheel stopper tool.

12. Install the oil level guide and gauge.

13. Connect the oil pressure switch electrical connector.

14. Install the water pump pulley and drive belt. Tighten the drive belt to the proper tension.

2.2L and 3.3L Engines
♦ SEE FIG. 75

1. Remove the accessory drive belt.

2. As required, remove the power steering pump, alternator, air conditioner compressor and associated brackets.

3. Remove the crankshaft pulley bolt and remove the crankshaft pulley.

4. Remove the belt covers.

5. Install the belt covers and tighten the bolts to 3–4 ft. lbs. (4–5Nm).

6. Install the crankshaft pulley and tighten the bolt to 69–76 ft. lbs. (93–103Nm) on the 2.2L engine and 108–123 ft. lbs. (147–167Nm) on the 3.3L engine.

7. Install the power steering pump, alternator, air conditioner compressor and associated brackets.

8. Install the accessory drive belt and tension to specification.

Timing Belt and/or Chain

PRECAUTIONS

• Take care not to let oil, grease or coolant contact the belt. Wipe the belt quickly if a spill occurs.

• Do not bend the belt sharply.

• When replacing the belts, be sure to replace both belts as a matched set.

REMOVAL & INSTALLATION

1.2L Engine

♦ SEE FIG. 73, 76 and 78

1. Disconnect the negative battery cable. Remove the accessory drive belt. Loosen the crankshaft pulley bolts but do not remove.

➡ **An access hole is provided in the wheelhouse panel to loosen and then remove the crankshaft pulley bolts.**

2. Position the crankshaft with No. 3 cylinder at TDC.

3. Remove the crankshaft bolts and pulley. Remove the outer front timing belt cover.

4. Loosen the tensioner bolt and position it in the direction that loosens the belt. Tighten the tensioner bolt in that position.

5. Remove the camshaft drive pulley plate. Mark the timing belt, if to be used again, in the direction of rotation for reinstallation. Remove the belt from the sprockets.

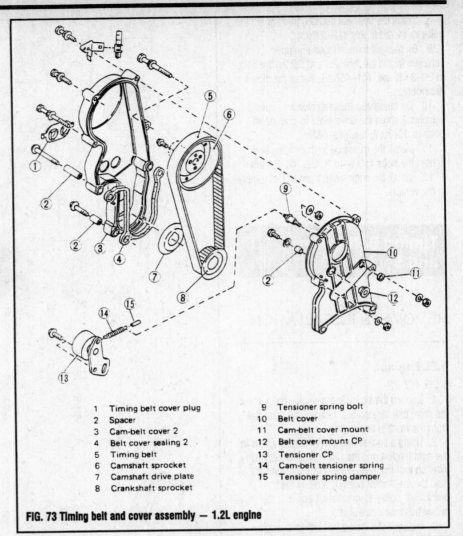

1	Timing belt cover plug	9	Tensioner spring bolt
2	Spacer	10	Belt cover
3	Cam-belt cover 2	11	Cam-belt cover mount
4	Belt cover sealing 2	12	Belt cover mount CP
5	Timing belt	13	Tensioner CP
6	Camshaft sprocket	14	Cam-belt tensioner spring
7	Camshaft drive plate	15	Tensioner spring damper
8	Crankshaft sprocket		

FIG. 73 Timing belt and cover assembly — 1.2L engine

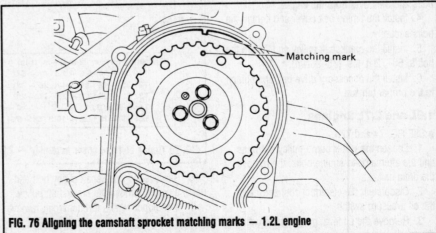

FIG. 76 Aligning the camshaft sprocket matching marks — 1.2L engine

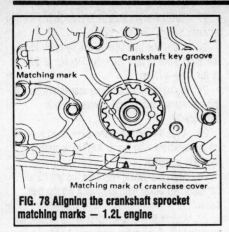

FIG. 78 Aligning the crankshaft sprocket matching marks — 1.2L engine

6. If necessary, remove the tensioner and spring. Remove the camshaft pulley. Remove the inner belt cover and cover mount, only as required.

To Install:

7. When installing the timing belt, rotate and align the matchmark of the camshaft driven pulley 0.120 in. (3mm) diameter hole with the matchmark of the cam belt side cover.

8. Align the matchmark of the camshaft drive pulley and the crankshaft cover. Install the camshaft drive belt.

9. Ensure that each rocker arm can be moved. Loosen the tensioner bolt 1/2 turn.

10. Tighten the tensioner bolt below the adjusting wheel first. Tighten the other bolt. Check to be sure all sprocket and housing matching marks are in agreement.

11. Install the camshaft drive pulley plate.

12. Install the cam belt cover.

13. Install the crankshaft pulley and bolts. Tighten the crankshaft bolts to 58–72 ft. lbs. (78–98Nm).

14. Check and adjust the valve clearance.

15. Install the accessory drive belts and tension to specification.

16. Connect the negative battery cable. Start the engine and allow it to reach operating temperature. Test drive the vehicle and check for leaks.

1.8L Engine

▶ SEE FIG. 74, 79–81

1. Remove the accessory drive belt, water pump pulley and pulley cover.

2. Remove the oil level gauge and guide. Disconnect the oil pressure switch electrical connector.

3. Remove the crankshaft pulley.

4. On turbocharged engines, remove the belt cover plate.

5. Remove the timing belt covers.

6. Loosen the timing belt tensioner mounting bolts 1/2 turn and slacken the timing belt. Tighten the mounting bolts.

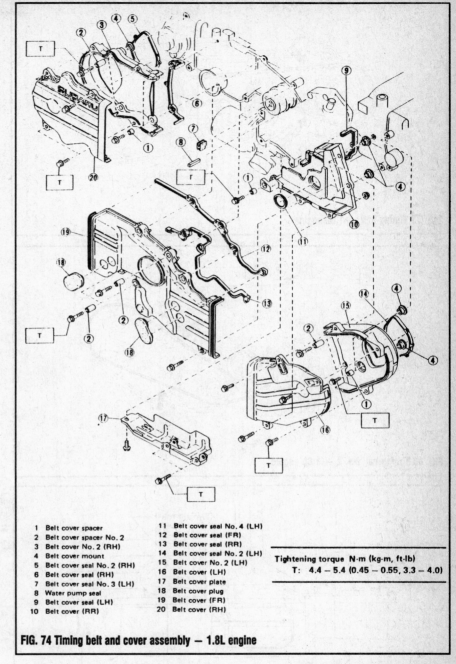

1	Belt cover spacer	11	Belt cover seal No. 4 (LH)
2	Belt cover spacer No. 2	12	Belt cover seal (FR)
3	Belt cover seal No. 2 (RH)	13	Belt cover seal (RR)
4	Belt cover mount	14	Belt cover seal No. 2 (LH)
5	Belt cover seal No. 2 (RH)	15	Belt cover No. 2 (LH)
6	Belt cover seal (RH)	16	Belt cover (LH)
7	Belt cover seal No. 3 (LH)	17	Belt cover plate
8	Water pump seal	18	Belt cover plug
9	Belt cover seal (LH)	19	Belt cover (FR)
10	Belt cover (RR)	20	Belt cover (RH)

Tightening torque N·m (kg-m, ft-lb)
T: 4.4 – 5.4 (0.45 – 0.55, 3.3 – 4.0)

FIG. 74 Timing belt and cover assembly — 1.8L engine

7. Mark the rotating direction of the timing belt, then remove the belt.

8. Perform the same procedure for the No. 2 timing belt. Remove the crankshaft sprockets.

9. Remove both tensioners together with the tensioner springs.

10. Remove the belt idler. Remove the camshaft sprockets.

11. Remove the No. 2 belt covers.

To Install:

12. Inspect the timing belt for breaks, cracks and wear. Replace as required.

13. Check the belt tensioner and idler for smooth rotation. Replace if noisy or excessive play is noticed.

14. Install the left hand belt cover seal No. 3 to the cylinder block.

15. Install the left hand belt cover seal, left hand belt cover seal No. 4, and belt cover mount to the right rear belt cover, then install the assembly on the cylinder block. Tighten to 3–4 ft. lbs. 4–5Nm).

16. Install the left hand belt cover seal No. 2 and belt cover mounts to left hand belt cover No. 2, then install to the cylinder head and camshaft case. Tighten to 3–4 ft. lbs. 4–5Nm).

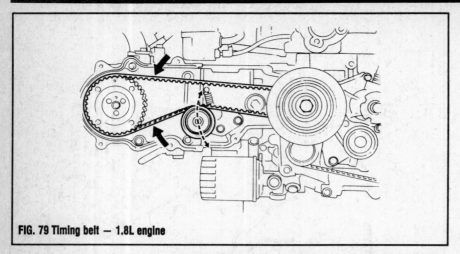

FIG. 79 Timing belt — 1.8L engine

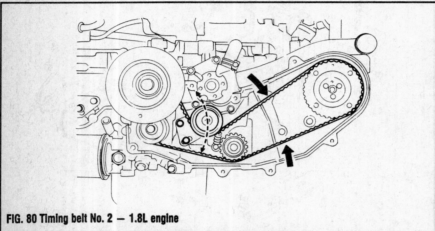

FIG. 80 Timing belt No. 2 — 1.8L engine

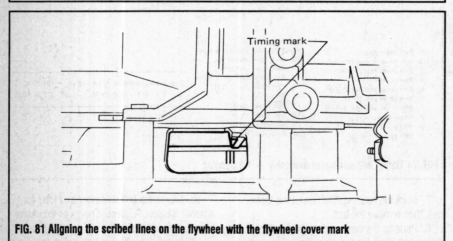

FIG. 81 Aligning the scribed lines on the flywheel with the flywheel cover mark

17. Install the right hand belt cover seal, belt cover seal No. 2 and belt cover mounts to the right hand belt cover No. 2, then install to the cylinder head and camshaft case. Tighten to 3–4 ft. lbs. 4–5Nm).

18. Install the camshaft sprockets to the right and left camshafts. Tighten the bolts gradually in two ro three steps to 6–7 ft. lbs. (9–10Nm).

19. Attach the tensioner spring to the tensioner, then install to the right side of the cylinder block. Tighten the bolts temporarily by hand.

20. Attach the tensioner spring to the bolt, tighten the right side bolt and then loosen 1/2 turn.

21. Push down tensioner until it stops, then temporarily tighten the left bolt.

22. Install the left side tensioner in the same manner.

23. Install the belt idler to the cylinder block using care not to turn the seal. Tighten to 29–35 ft. lbs. (39–47Nm).

24. Install sprockets to the crankshaft. Install the crankshaft pulley and tighten the bolt temporarily.

25. Align the center of the three lines scribed on the flywheel with the timing mark on the flywheel housing.

26. Align the timing mark on the left hand camshaft sprocket with the notch on the belt cover.

27. Attach timing belt No. 2 to the crankshaft sprocket No. 2, oil pump sprocket, belt idler, and camshaft sprocket in that order. Avoid downward slackening of the belt.

28. Loosen tensioner No. 2 lower bolt 1/2 turn to apply tension. Push timing belt by hand to ensure smooth movement of tensioner.

29. Apply 25 ft. lbs. (new belt) or 18 ft. lbs. (used belt) torque to the camshaft sprocket in counterclockwise direction. While applying torque tighten tensioner No. 2 lower bolt temporarily, then tighten upper bolt temporarily.

30. Tighten the lower bolt, then the upper bolt to 13–15 ft. lbs. (17–20Nm) in that order.

31. Check that the flywheel timing mark and left hand camshaft sprocket mark are in their proper positions.

32. Turn the crankshaft one turn clockwise from the position where timing belt No. 2 was installed, and align the center of the three lines on the flywheel with the timing mark on the flywheel housing.

33. Align the timing mark on the right hand camshaft sprocket with the notch in the belt cover.

34. Attach the timing belt to the crankshaft sprocket and camshaft sprocket, avoiding slackening of the belt on the upper side.

35. Loosen the tensioner 1/2 turn to apply tension to the belt. Push the belt by hand to ensure smooth operation.

36. Apply 25 ft. lbs. (new belt) or 18 ft. lbs. (used belt) torque to the camshaft sprocket in counterclockwise direction. While applying torque tighten tensioner left bolt temporarily, then tighten right bolt temporarily.

37. Tighten the left bolt, then the right bolt to 13–15 ft. lbs. (17–20Nm) in that order.

38. Check that the flywheel timing mark and left hand camshaft sprocket mark are in their proper positions.

39. Remove the crankshaft pulley.

40. Install the right front belt cover seals and belt cover plug. Install the belt covers to the cylinder block.

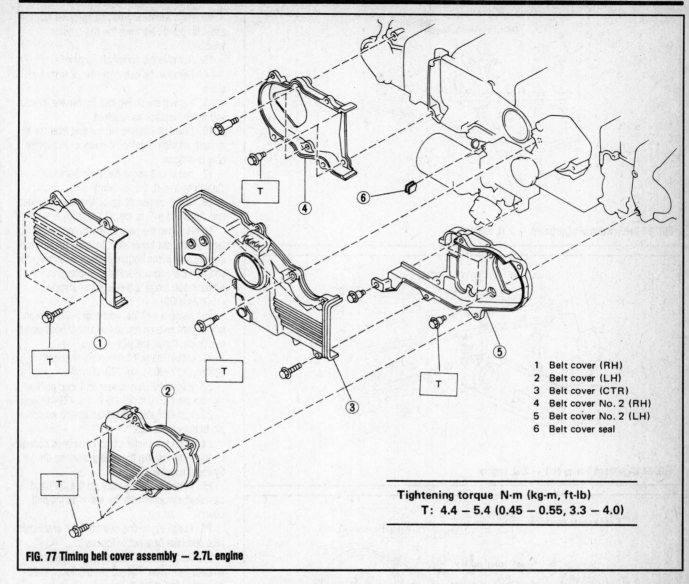

1	Belt cover (RH)
2	Belt cover (LH)
3	Belt cover (CTR)
4	Belt cover No. 2 (RH)
5	Belt cover No. 2 (LH)
6	Belt cover seal

Tightening torque N·m (kg-m, ft-lb)
T: 4.4 — 5.4 (0.45 — 0.55, 3.3 — 4.0)

FIG. 77 Timing belt cover assembly — 2.7L engine

41. On turbocharged engines, install the belt cover plate.

42. Install the crankshaft pulley and tighten to 66–79 ft. lbs. (89–107Nm).

43. Install the water pump pulley and tighten to 6–7 ft. lbs. (9–10Nm). Install the pulley cover, oil level guide and gauge and oil pressure switch connector.

44. Install and properly tension the accessory drive belt.

2.7L Engine

▸ SEE FIG. 77, 81–85

1. Remove the accessory drive belt, water pump pulley and pulley cover.

2. Remove the oil level gauge and guide. Disconnect the oil pressure switch electrical connector.

3. Remove the crankshaft pulley.

4. Remove the timing belt covers.

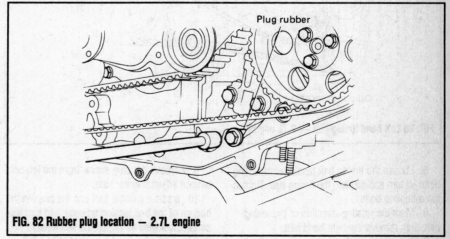

FIG. 82 Rubber plug location — 2.7L engine

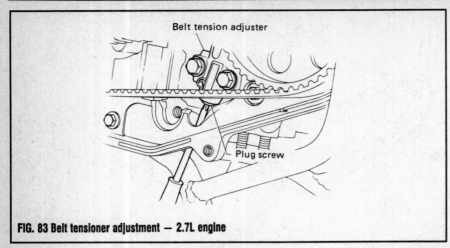

FIG. 83 Belt tensioner adjustment — 2.7L engine

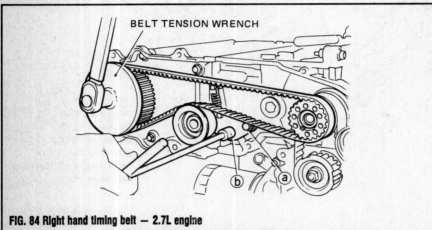

FIG. 84 Right hand timing belt — 2.7L engine

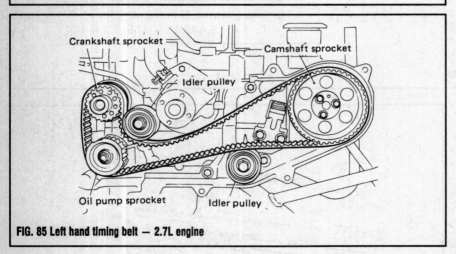

FIG. 85 Left hand timing belt — 2.7L engine

5. Loosen the timing belt tensioner mounting bolts ½ turn and slacken the timing belt. Tighten the mounting bolts.

6. Mark the rotating direction of the timing belt, then remove the right hand belt.

7. Remove the right hand tensioner. Remove the crankshaft sprocket.

8. Remove the idler pulley and rubber plug.

9. Remove the plug screw from the left belt tension adjuster lower side.

10. Insert a suitable tool into the hose in the bottom of the belt tension adjuster and turn the screw clockwise to loosen the belt tension. Install a belt adjuster stopper (13082AA000). Remove the left belt tensioner.

11. Remove the left timing belt after marking the rotating direction.

12. Remove the crankshaft sprocket No. 2 and idler pulley. Remove the belt tension adjuster.

13. Remove the camshaft sprockets.

14. Remove the belt cover No. 2 from both sides.

15. Inspect the timing belt for breaks, cracks and wear. Replace as required.

16. Check the belt tensioner and idler for smooth rotation. Replace if noisy or excessive play is noticed.

17. Install belt cover No. 2 on both sides. Tighten to 3–4 ft. lbs. 4–5Nm).

18. Install camshaft sprockets on both sides and tighten to 8–9 ft. lbs. (11–13Nm).

19. Remove the plug screw from the belt tension adjuster lower side. Insert a suitable tool into the hole in the bottom of the tension adjuster and turn the screw clockwise to compress the rubber boot. Install a belt adjuster stopper (13082AA000).

20. Using a syringe, add engine oil through the air vent hole on top of the rubber boot until it overflows. Install the plug screw.

21. Install the belt tension adjuster and tighten to 17–20 ft. lbs. (23–26Nm).

22. Install the plug rubber and idler pulley. Tighten the pulley to 29–35 ft. lbs. (39–47Nm).

23. Install crankshaft sprocket with no dowel pin to the crankshaft.

24. Align the center of the three lines scribed on the flywheel with the timing mark on the flywheel housing.

25. Align the timing mark on the left hand camshaft sprocket with the notch on the belt cover.

26. Install the timing belt from the crankshaft side and take care not to loosen it.

27. Install the left tensioner and check for smooth operation. Tighten the tensioner to 29–35 ft. lbs. (39–47Nm).

28. Remove the belt adjuster stopper from the belt tension adjuster.

29. Check that the end of the left tensioner arm contacts the top of the belt tension adjuster.

30. Make sure that the flywheel timing mark and left hand camshaft sprocket timing mark are in the proper positions.

31. Turn the crankshaft one turn clockwise from the position where the left timing belt was installed and align the center of the three lines scribed on the flywheel with the timing mark on the flywheel housing.

32. Align the mark on the right hand camshaft sprocket with the notch in the belt cover.

33. Temporarily tighten both belt tensioner bolts while forcing the tensioner against spring pressure (downward).

34. Install the crankshaft sprocket.

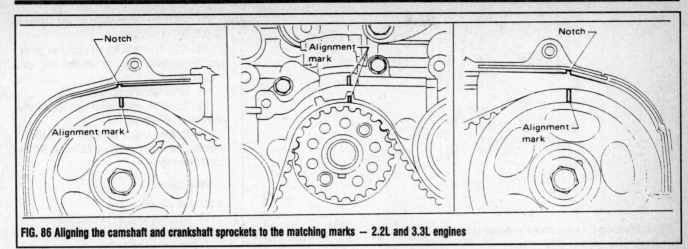

FIG. 86 Aligning the camshaft and crankshaft sprockets to the matching marks — 2.2L and 3.3L engines

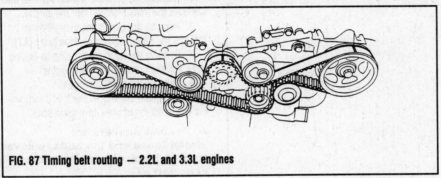

FIG. 87 Timing belt routing — 2.2L and 3.3L engines

35. Install the timing belt from the crankshaft side and take care no to loosen it.

36. Loosen the left tensioner bolt by ½ turn to apply tension to the belt.

37. Apply 33–55 ft. lbs. torque to the camshaft sprocket in a counterclockwise direction and tighten the tensioner bolts temporarily.

38. Tighten the left, then right tensioner bolts to 17–20 ft. lbs. (23–26Nm).

39. Make sure that the flywheel timing mark and left hand camshaft sprocket timing mark are in the proper positions.

40. Install the center belt cover and crankshaft pulley. Tighten pulley bolt to 66–79 ft. lbs. (89–107Nm).

41. Install the oil level gauge guide, water pipe, water pump pulley and belt covers.

42. Install and properly tension the accessory drive belt.

2.2L and 3.3L Engines

◆ SEE FIG. 86–87

The 2.2L and 3.3L OHC engine uses a single cam belt drive system with a serpentine type belt. The left side of the engine uses a hydraulic cam belt tensioner which is continuously self adjusting.

1. Remove the accessory drive belt.

2. Remove the crankshaft pulley bolt and crankshaft pulley.

3. Remove the cam belt covers. Align the camshaft sprockets so each sprocket notch aligns with the cam cover notches. Align the crankshaft sprocket top tooth notch, located at the rear of the tooth, with the notch on the crank angle sensor boss. Mark the 3 alignment points as well as the direction of cam belt rotation.

4. Loosen the tensioner adjusting bolts and remove the bottom 3 idlers, the cam belt and the cam belt tensioner. The cam sprockets can then be removed with a modified camshaft sprocket wrench tool.

5. If the sprockets are removed, note the reference sensor at the rear of the left cam sprocket.

To Install:

6. Install the crankshaft sprocket and all of the idlers except for the lower right. Compress the hydraulic tensioner in a vise slowly and temporarily secure the plunger with a pin. Install the tensioner and the pulley.

7. After the cam belt components are installed, align the crankshaft sprocket notch on the rear sprocket tooth with the crank angle sensor boss. This places the sprocket notch in the 12 o'clock position.

8. Align the camshaft sprockets with the notches in the cam belt cover. As the directional marked belt is installed, align the marks on the belt with the crankshaft sprocket and the left camshaft sprocket. Install the lower right idler.

9. Load the tensioner by pushing it towards the crankshaft with a prybar and tighten the bolts. Remove the tensioner retention pin and the belt tension is automatically set. Rock the crankshaft back and forth 1 time to distribute the belt tension.

10. Verify the correctness of the timing by noting that the notches on the 2 cam pulleys and the notch on the crankshaft pulley all point to the 12 o'clock position when the belt is properly installed.

11. Complete the engine component assembly by installing the cam belt covers, the crankshaft pulley bolt and pulley and the remaining components.

Camshaft Sprocket (OHC Engines)

REMOVAL & INSTALLATION

The procedure for removing and installing the camshaft sprockets is identical to the removal and installation of the timing belts. See Timing Belt Removal and Installation above.

Camshaft and Bearings

On some models it may be necessary to remove the engine from the vehicle to perform this service.

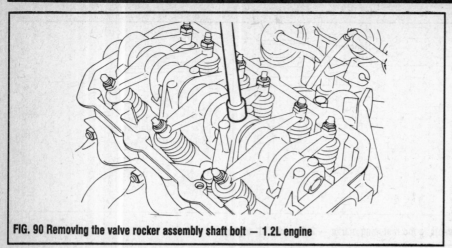

FIG. 90 Removing the valve rocker assembly shaft bolt — 1.2L engine

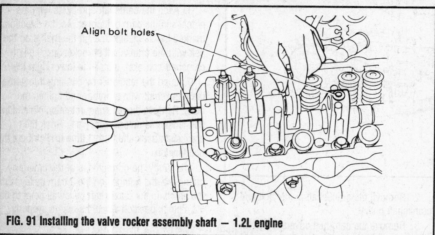

Align bolt holes

FIG. 91 Installing the valve rocker assembly shaft — 1.2L engine

REMOVAL & INSTALLATION

> ⁂ **CAUTION**
>
> When draining the coolant, keep in mind that cats and dogs are attracted by the ethylene glycol antifreeze, and are quite likely to drink any that is left in an uncovered container or in puddles on the ground. This will prove fatal in sufficient quantity. Always drain the coolant into a sealable container. Coolant should be reused unless it is contaminated or several years old.

1.2L Engine

♦ SEE FIG. 90–91

1. Disconnect the negative battery cable.
2. Remove the timing belt. Remove the camshaft driven pulley.
3. Remove the valve rocker cover and slacken the valve rocker adjustment.
4. Remove the bolt from the valve rocker shaft journal and pull the valve rocker shaft out from the cylinder head. Remove the spring washer and valve rockers.
5. Remove the camshaft taking care not to damage the bearings.

To Install:

6. Clean and check the disassembled components for damage and replace as necessary.
7. Measure the rocker arm-to-shaft clearance. If clearance is greater than 0.0022 in. (0.057mm), replace the components as required.
8. Replace the rocker shaft spring if a permanent set is noted.
9. Lubricate and install the camshaft.
10. Measure the thrust clearance of the camshaft with the breaker case installed. If greater than 0.020 in. (0.5mm), grind the breaker surface of the cylinder head until the thrust clearance fall within specification.
11. Install the valve rocker assembly but do not adjust the valve clearance.

12. Install the camshaft pulley and tighten to 8–9 ft. lbs. (11–12Nm).
13. Align the marks for the camshaft pulley and the crankshaft sprocket with their respective matchmarks.
14. Install the timing belt assembly.
15. Adjust the valve rocker clearance. Install the valve rocker cover.
16. Start the engine and allow it to reach operating temperature. Check for leaks. Set the ignition timing.

1.6L Engine

♦ SEE FIG. 88–89

The camshaft turns on journals that are machined directly into the crankcase.

1. Remove the engine from the vehicle, then separate the transmission from the engine.
2. Remove the clutch assembly/flywheel (MT) or the torque converter drive plate (AT).
3. Remove the flywheel housing-to-engine bolts and the housing from the engine.
4. Remove the crankshaft gear.
5. Straighten the lockwashers and remove the camshaft thrust plate-to-engine bolts.

➡ **The lockwashers are straightened and the bolts removed through the access holes in the camshaft gear.**

6. Remove the rocker arm-to-cylinder head covers, the rocker arm-to-cylinder head assemblies, the push rods and valve lifters.

➡ **The push rods and valve lifters must be returned to their original positions during assembly.**

7. Pull the camshaft toward the rear of the engine and remove it from the engine; be careful not to damage the bearing journals and/or the camshaft lobes. Remove the oil seal.

To Install:

8. Clean all gasket mating surfaces thoroughly. Use new gaskets and seals when reassembling the engine.
9. Using a dial indicator and a pair of V-blocks, measure the camshaft runout. If greater than 0.0020 in. (0.05mm), replace the camshaft.
10. Measure the thrust clearance between the camshaft and camshaft plate. If greater than 0.008 in. (0.2mm), remove the camshaft gear and replace the plate.
11. Inspect the journals for damage or wear. Replace the camshaft as required.
12. Measure the camshaft gear runout. If greater than 0.0098 in. (0.25mm), replace the camshaft gear.
13. Measure the backlash between the camshaft and crankshaft gear. If greater than 0.0039 in. (0.10mm), replace the camshaft gear.

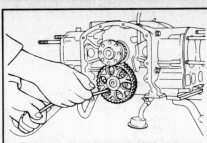

FIG. 88 Tightening the camshaft thrust plate — 1.6L engine

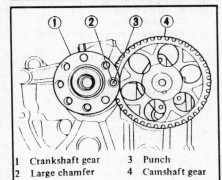

1	Crankshaft gear	3	Punch
2	Large chamfer	4	Camshaft gear

FIG. 89 Aligning the camshaft and crankshaft gears — 1.6L engine

14. Install a new oil seal. Install the camshaft into the engine, taking care not to damage the journals.

15. One of the bolt holes in the crankshaft gear has a larger chamfer than the others. Install the crankshaft gear so that the punch mark in the camshaft gear cam be seen through the this hole. Install the crankshaft gear.

16. Install the rocker arm assemblies, the push rods and valve lifters. Install the rocker arm covers.

17. Install the camshaft thrust plate-to-engine bolts. Install the crankshaft gear. Measure the camshaft endplay, it should be 0.008 in. (0.20mm).

18. Install the transmission on the engine and the engine in the vehicle.

19. Install the flywheel housing on the engine.

20. Install the clutch assembly/flywheel (MT) or the torque converter drive plate (AT).

21. Refill the cooling system and the crankcase. Start the engine, allow it to reach normal operating temperatures and check for leaks.

1.8L and 2.7L Engines

♦ SEE FIG. 92–93

1. Disconnect the negative battery cable.
2. Drain the cooling system.
3. Remove the timing belt, belt covers and related components.
4. Remove the distributor.

5. Remove the water pipe assembly and oil filler duct.

6. On turbocharged engines, remove the EGR pipe cover, pipe clamps and EGR pipe.

7. Remove the valve rocker covers.

8. Remove the camshaft case, camshaft support and camshaft as a complete unit.

➡ **When removing the camshaft case, the valve rockers may come off their mounting. To prevent them from being damaged, place a rag under the head.**

9. Remove the valve lash adjusters from the cylinder head.

➡ **Be sure to keep the adjusters and the rockers in the proper order for reinstallation.**

10. Remove the camshaft support from the camshaft case. Carefully remove the camshaft from its mounting.

11. Remove an oil relief valve, relief valve spring, oil relief pipe and plug to the camshaft case.

To Install:

12. Measure the camshaft runout. If runout exceeds 0.0010 in. (0.025mm), replace the camshaft.

13. Check the camshaft journals for damage or wear. If the surface of the camshaft or valve rocker is damaged or worn, repair by removing the minimum necessary amount, otherwise replace the damaged components.

14. With the valve lash adjuster in a vertical position, push the adjuster pivot quick and hard by hand. If the pivot is depressed more than 0.020 in. (0.5mm), put the adjuster in a container of light oil and move the plunger up and down until the depression is within specification. If the adjuster will not come within specification, replace it.

15. Install an oil seal into the camshaft support, then attach the O-ring.

16. Install an oil relief valve, relief valve spring, oil relief pipe and plug to the camshaft case.

17. Install the woodruff key on the camshaft and press fit the distributor gear. Insert the camshaft into the case and install the camshaft support. Tighten to 4–5 ft. lbs. (6–7Nm).

18. Install the valve lash adjusters into their original positions.

19. Apply grease to the valve rockers and install.

20. Install the O-ring to the camshaft case by setting the camshaft so that the cam pin is at the 12 o'clock position.

➡ **Be sure to coat the camshaft assembly with clean engine oil prior to installation.**

21. Install the camshaft case to the cylinder head, using sealing compound 1207B or equivalent. Torque the retaining bolts 17–20 ft. lbs. (23–27Nm).

22. Install the valve rocker cover assemblies and tighten to 3–4 ft. lbs. (4–5Nm).

23. Install the PCV hoses, and on turbocharged engines install the EGR pipe, clamps and pipe cover. Tighten the EGR pipe to 23–27 ft. lbs. (31–37Nm).

24. Install the oil filler duct and water pipe.

25. Install the timing belt, belt cover and related parts.

26. Fill the radiator with coolant. Start the vehicle and adjust the ignition timing. Test drive the vehicle and check for leaks.

2.2L Engine

♦ SEE FIG. 94

1. Remove the timing belt covers, the timing belt, camshaft sprockets and related components necessary to expose the camshaft.

2. Remove the valve rocker covers. Remove the rocker arm assemblies.

3. To remove the left camshaft, perform the following procedures:

a. Remove the cam angle sensor.

b. Remove the oil dipstick tube attaching bolt.

c. Remove the camshaft support on the left side.

d. Remove the O-ring.

e. Remove the camshaft and oil seal (as necessary) from the left side.

4. To remove the right camshaft, perform the following procedures:

a. Remove the camshaft support on the right side.

b. Remove the O-ring.

c. Remove the camshaft and seal (rear) from the right side. Remove the oil seal from the camshaft support.

To Install:

5. To install the left camshaft, perform the following procedures:

a. Lubricate the camshaft journals, install the oil seal (rear) and install the camshaft into the cylinder head.

b. Install the O-ring into the camshaft support and install the support.

c. Install oil seal into the camshaft support.

d. Install the bolt into the dipstick tube and install the camshaft sensor.

6. To install the right camshaft, perform the following procedures:

a. Lubricate the camshaft journals and install the right camshaft.

b. Install the O-ring into the camshaft support and install the support.

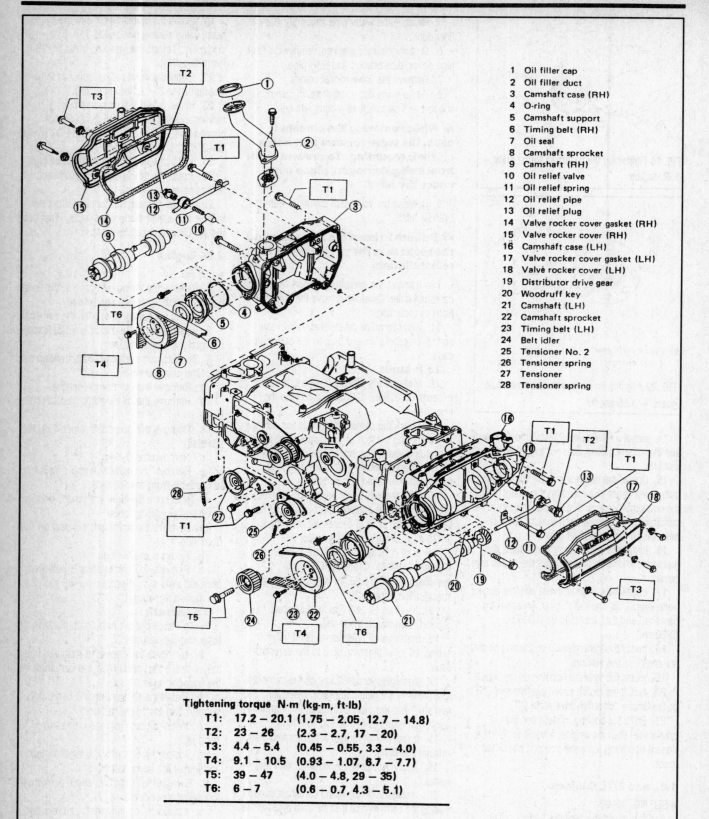

1 Oil filler cap
2 Oil filler duct
3 Camshaft case (RH)
4 O-ring
5 Camshaft support
6 Timing belt (RH)
7 Oil seal
8 Camshaft sprocket
9 Camshaft (RH)
10 Oil relief valve
11 Oil relief spring
12 Oil relief pipe
13 Oil relief plug
14 Valve rocker cover gasket (RH)
15 Valve rocker cover (RH)
16 Camshaft case (LH)
17 Valve rocker cover gasket (LH)
18 Valve rocker cover (LH)
19 Distributor drive gear
20 Woodruff key
21 Camshaft (LH)
22 Camshaft sprocket
23 Timing belt (LH)
24 Belt idler
25 Tensioner No. 2
26 Tensioner spring
27 Tensioner
28 Tensioner spring

Tightening torque N·m (kg-m, ft-lb)	
T1:	17.2 − 20.1 (1.75 − 2.05, 12.7 − 14.8)
T2:	23 − 26 (2.3 − 2.7, 17 − 20)
T3:	4.4 − 5.4 (0.45 − 0.55, 3.3 − 4.0)
T4:	9.1 − 10.5 (0.93 − 1.07, 6.7 − 7.7)
T5:	39 − 47 (4.0 − 4.8, 29 − 35)
T6:	6 − 7 (0.6 − 0.7, 4.3 − 5.1)

FIG. 92 Camshaft case assembly — 1.8L engine

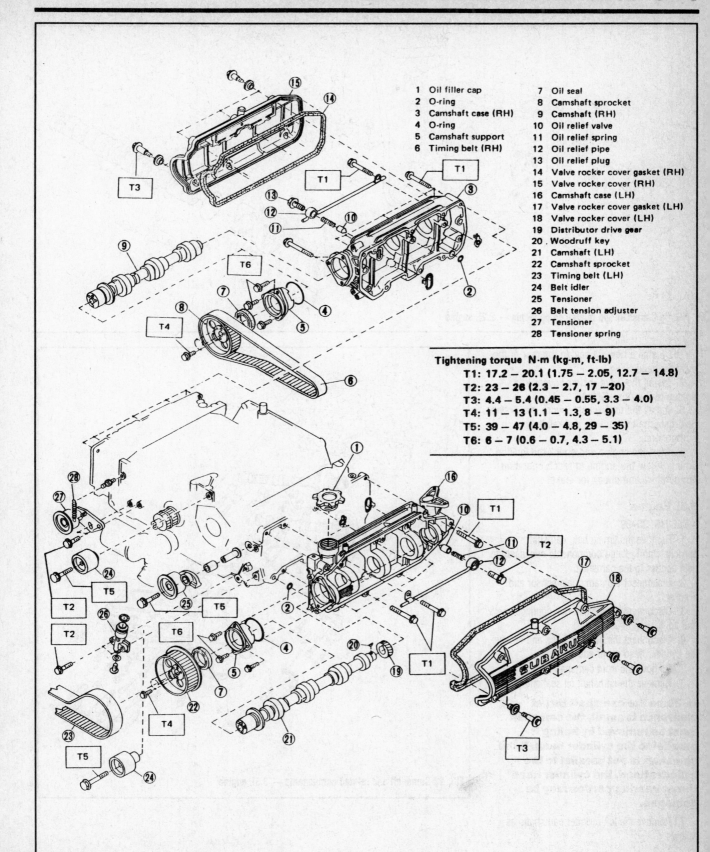

1 Oil filler cap
2 O-ring
3 Camshaft case (RH)
4 O-ring
5 Camshaft support
6 Timing belt (RH)
7 Oil seal
8 Camshaft sprocket
9 Camshaft (RH)
10 Oil relief valve
11 Oil relief spring
12 Oil relief pipe
13 Oil relief plug
14 Valve rocker cover gasket (RH)
15 Valve rocker cover (RH)
16 Camshaft case (LH)
17 Valve rocker cover gasket (LH)
18 Valve rocker cover (LH)
19 Distributor drive gear
20 Woodruff key
21 Camshaft (LH)
22 Camshaft sprocket
23 Timing belt (LH)
24 Belt idler
25 Tensioner
26 Belt tension adjuster
27 Tensioner
28 Tensioner spring

Tightening torque N·m (kg-m, ft-lb)
T1: 17.2 — 20.1 (1.75 — 2.05, 12.7 — 14.8)
T2: 23 — 26 (2.3 — 2.7, 17 — 20)
T3: 4.4 — 5.4 (0.45 — 0.55, 3.3 — 4.0)
T4: 11 — 13 (1.1 — 1.3, 8 — 9)
T5: 39 — 47 (4.0 — 4.8, 29 — 35)
T6: 6 — 7 (0.6 — 0.7, 4.3 — 5.1)

FIG. 93 Camshaft case assembly — 2.7L engine

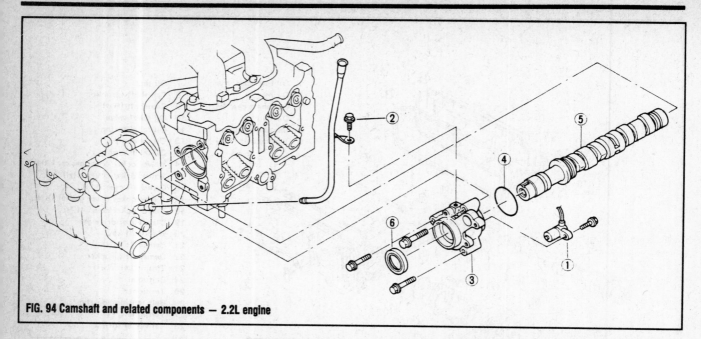

FIG. 94 Camshaft and related components — 2.2L engine

c. Install a new oil seal in the rear of the cylinder head.

7. Install the valve rocker covers and tighten to 4 ft. lbs. (5Nm).

8. Install the timing belt covers, the timing belt, camshaft sprockets and related components.

9. Start the engine and check the ignition timing. Allow the engine to reach operating temperature and check for leaks.

3.3L Engine

♦ SEE FIG. 95–99

1. Remove the timing belt, camshaft sprockets and related components necessary to gain access to the camshaft.

2. Disconnect the cam angle sensor and bracket.

3. Disconnect the ignition coil connectors and coils.

4. Disconnect the blow-by hose and remove the cylinder head cover and gasket.

5. Remove the front camshaft cap.

6. Remove the camshaft oil seal and plug.

➡ **Since the camshaft thrust clearance is small, the camshaft must be removed by holing it parallel to the cylinder head. If the camshaft is not parallel to the cylinder head, the cylinder head thrust bearing portion may be damaged.**

7. Remove the left cylinder camshafts as follows:

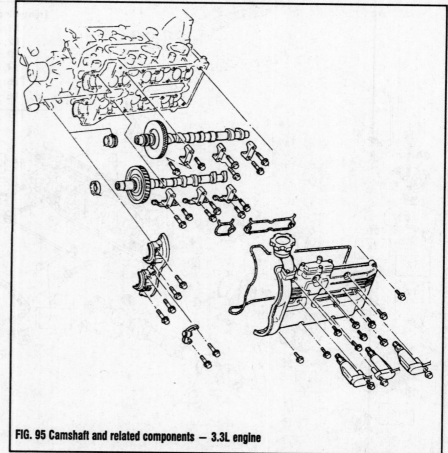

FIG. 95 Camshaft and related components — 3.3L engine

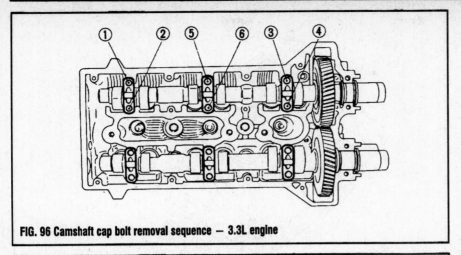

FIG. 96 Camshaft cap bolt removal sequence — 3.3L engine

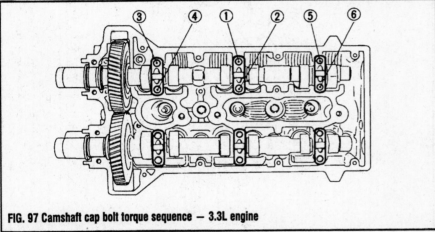

FIG. 97 Camshaft cap bolt torque sequence — 3.3L engine

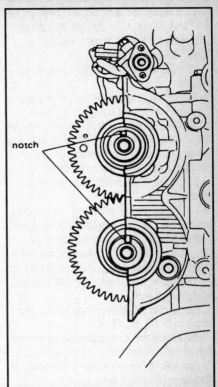

FIG. 98 Aligning the notches on the front of the camshaft — 3.3L engine

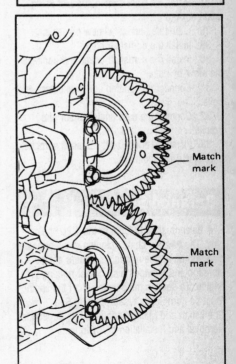

FIG. 99 Aligning the matchmarks on the rear of the camshaft sprocket — 3.3L engine

8. Rotate the intake (upper) and exhaust (lower) camshafts to that the notch at the front of the camshafts faces the 6 o'clock position on the left cylinder head and the 12 o'clock position on the right cylinder head.

9. Inspect the rear of the camshaft and check that the matchmarks on the rear gears are aligned.

10. Install a service bolt to the sub-gear mounting bolt hole of the intake camshaft gear to secure the sub-gear and driven gear.

➡ **When removing the camshafts, ensure that the torsional spring force of the sub-gear has been eliminated.**

11. Loosen the intake camshaft bolt caps in sequence. Make sure that, as the bolts are turned, the clearance between the camshaft journal and the cylinder head journal bearing increases evenly at three places. If not, tighten the bolts and repeat the loosening procedure.

12. Remove the camshaft cap while holding the intake camshaft with one hand, then remove the camshaft. Rotate the exhaust camshaft clockwise to gain required clearance.

13. Arrange the camshaft caps in the order they were removed. They must be installed to their original positions.

14. Perform the same procedure for the exhaust camshaft.

15. Remove the hydraulic lash adjusters. Keep the lash adjusters in the order they were removed. They must be installed into their original positions.

To Install:

16. Inspect the camshafts for scratches, flaking and wear. Measure the camshaft runout. If it exceeds 0.0008 in. (0.02mm), replace it.

17. Measure the thrust clearance of the camshaft with the hydraulic lash adjusters not installed. If thrust clearance exceeds 0.0051 in. (0.13mm) for the intake and 0.0047 in. (0.12mm) for the exhaust, replace the camshaft caps and the cylinder head as an assembly. If necessary replace the camshaft.

18. Measure the camshaft journal oil clearance with the lash adjusters not installed. If clearance exceeds 0.0039 in. (0.10mm), replace the worn components.

19. Measure the camshaft gear backlash with the intake sub-gear not installed. If backlash exceeds 0.0118 in. (0.30mm), replace the camshafts as a set.

20. Lubricate and install the hydraulic lash adjusters.

21. Lubricate and install the camshafts with the notch on the front facing the 6 o'clock position for the left cylinder head camshafts and the 12 o'clock position for the right cylinder head camshafts. Ensure that the marks for both camshafts are facing the same position.

22. Install the camshaft caps and tighten hand tight.

23. Tighten the bolts on the camshaft caps equally, a little at a time, in the correct sequence. Make sure that, as the bolts are turned, the clearance between the camshaft journal and the cylinder head journal bearing decreases evenly at three places. If not, loosen the bolts and repeat the tightening procedure.

24. Tighten the camshaft cap bolts a final torque of 3–4 ft. lbs. (4–5Nm).

25. Ensure that the matchmarks on the rear side of the camshaft gears are aligned. If not, disassemble the camshaft and perform the installation procedure again.

26. Remove the sub-gear securing bolt from the camshaft.

27. Install the front camshaft cover using fluid packing.

28. Lubricate and install new oil seals.

29. Install the camshaft plug.

30. Install the camshaft cover and connect the blow-by hose.

31. Connect the ignition coil connectors and coils.

32. Connect the cam angle sensor and bracket.

33. Install the timing belt, camshaft sprockets and related components.

Balance Shaft

A balance shaft is fitted to the 1.2L engine only. The balance shaft, spinning in the opposite direction of engine rotation, counters engine vibration and provides a smoother running engine. To service the balance shaft the engine must be completely disassembled. See Crankshaft and Main Bearings in this Section for Removal and Installation procedures.

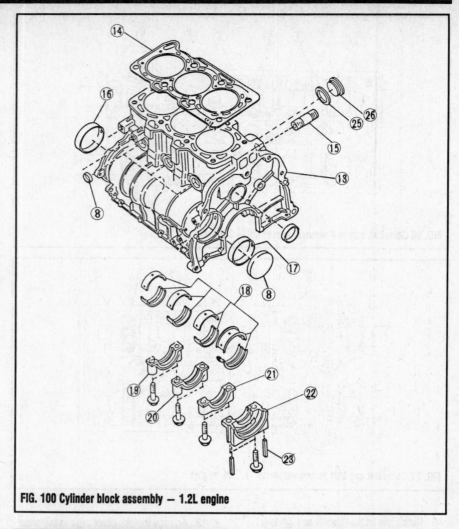

FIG. 100 Cylinder block assembly — 1.2L engine

Piston, Connecting Rods, Crankshaft and Bearings

All engines except the 1.2L are of the split case design. In order to remove any of the internal components, the case halves must be split. In other words, for the piston and connecting rod combination to be removed, the crankshaft must be removed and vise-versa.

REMOVAL

1.2L Engine

♦ SEE FIG. 100–102

1. Remove the engine from the vehicle.
2. Remove the timing belt, belt covers and related components. Remove the cylinder heads.

3. Remove the oil pan and the oil strainer assembly.

4. Stamp the cylinder number on the machined surfaces of the bolt bosses of the connecting rod and cap for identification when reinstalling. If the pistons are to be removed from the connecting rod, mark the cylinder number on the piston with a silver pencil or quick drying paint for proper cylinder identification and cap to rod location.

5. Examine the cylinder bore above the ring travel. If a ridge exists, remove it with a ridge reamer before attempting to remove the piston and rod assembly.

6. Remove the rod bearing cap and bearing.

7. Install a guide hose over the rod bolt threads; this will prevent damage to the bearing journal and rod bolt threads.

8. Using a hammer handle, remove the rod/piston assemblies through the top of the cylinder bore

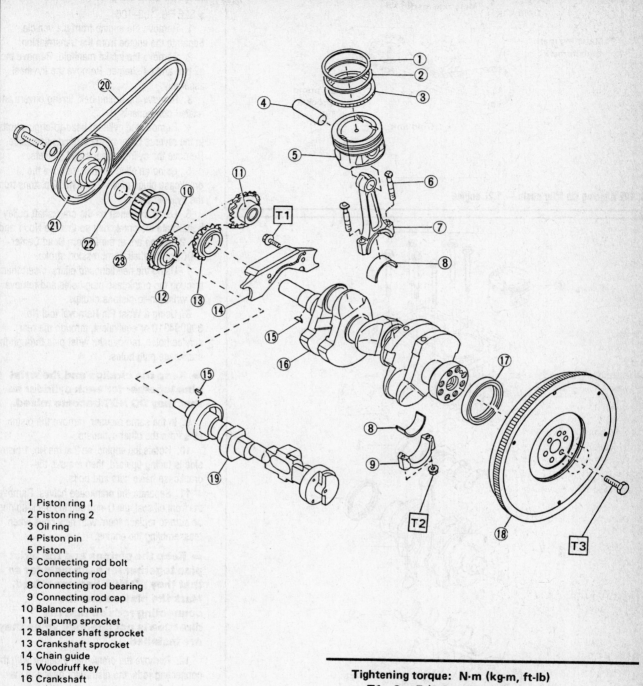

1 Piston ring 1
2 Piston ring 2
3 Oil ring
4 Piston pin
5 Piston
6 Connecting rod bolt
7 Connecting rod
8 Connecting rod bearing
9 Connecting rod cap
10 Balancer chain
11 Oil pump sprocket
12 Balancer shaft sprocket
13 Crankshaft sprocket
14 Chain guide
15 Woodruff key
16 Crankshaft
17 Oil seal
18 Flywheel
19 Balancer shaft
20 V-belt
21 Crankshaft pulley
22 Crankshaft drive plate
23 Camshaft drive pulley

Tightening torque: N·m (kg-m, ft-lb)
T1: 6 — 7 (0.6 — 0.7, 4.3 — 5.1)
T2: 39 — 45 (4.0 — 4.6, 29 — 33)
T3: 88 — 96 (9.0 — 9.8, 65 — 71)

FIG. 101 Crankshaft, rod and piston assembly — 1.2L engine

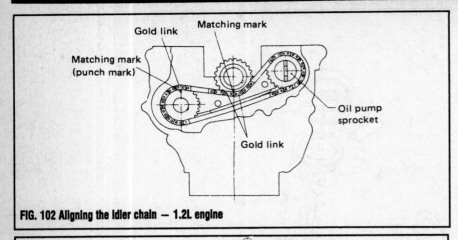

FIG. 102 Aligning the idler chain — 1.2L engine

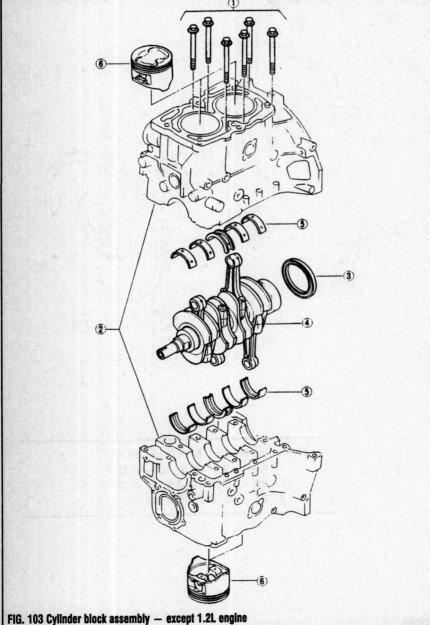

FIG. 103 Cylinder block assembly — except 1.2L engine

Except 1.2L Engine

▶ SEE FIG. 103–106

1. Remove the engine from the vehicle. Separate the engine from the transmission.

2. Remove the intake manifold. Remove the oil pan and oil strainer. Remove the flywheel assembly.

3. Remove the timing belt, timing covers and related components.

4. Remove the cylinder head-to-engine bolts, in the reverse order of the torquing sequence. Remove the cylinder heads and gaskets.

5. Using an allen wrench, remove the crankcase plugs of No. 1 and No. 2 pistons from the cylinder block.

6. Using a wrench on the crankshaft pulley bolt, rotate the crankshaft so that the No. 1 and No. 2 pistons are at the Bottom Dead Center (BDC) of the their compression stroke.

7. Using the needlenosed pliers, insert them through the crankcase plug holes and remove the wrist pin-to-pistons circlips.

8. Using a Wrist Pin Removal tool No. 399094310 or equivalent, through the rear service holes, remove the wrist pins through the crankcase plug holes.

➥ **Keep the circlips and the wrist pins together for each cylinder so that they DO NOT become mixed.**

9. In the same manner, remove the piston pins from the other cylinders.

10. Rotate the engine, so that the No. 1 piston side is facing upward, then remove the crankcase halve nuts and bolts.

11. Separate the crankcase halves. Remove the front oil seal, the O-ring and the back-up ring; be sure to replace them with new ones when reassembling the engine.

➥ **Keep the pistons and the wrist pins together for each cylinder so that they DO NOT become mixed. Mark the pistons and the connecting rods so that the direction is not changed when they are installed.**

12. Remove the crankshaft together with the connecting rods, the distributor gear and the crankshaft gear as an assembly.

13. Remove the ridge from the top of the cylinder (unworn area), using a Ridge Reamer tool, to facilitate the removal of the pistons by performing the following procedures:

   a. Place the piston at the bottom of its bore and cover it with a rag.

   b. Cut the ridge away using a ridge reamer, exercising extreme care to avoid cutting too deeply.

   c. Remove the rag and remove the cuttings that remain on the piston.

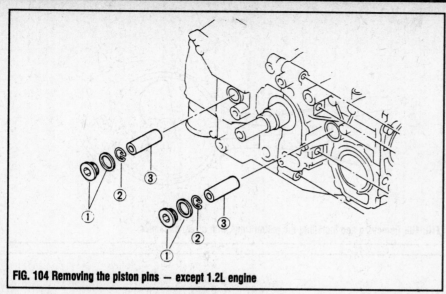

FIG. 104 Removing the piston pins — except 1.2L engine

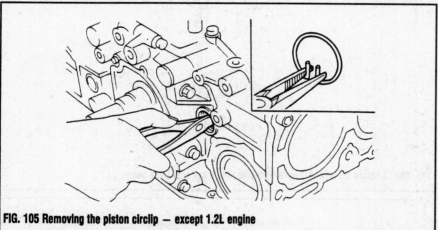

FIG. 105 Removing the piston circlip — except 1.2L engine

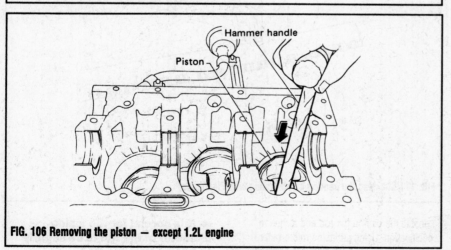

FIG. 106 Removing the piston — except 1.2L engine

14. Using a hammer handle or a wooden bar, force the pistons out through the top of the cylinder block.

CLEANING AND INSPECTION

♦ SEE FIG. 107–114

> **⁂ WARNING**
>
> **Do not hot tank clean any aluminum parts or they will be ruined. Use carburetor solvent for cleaning.**

Pistons

Using a piston ring expanding tool, remove the piston rings from the pistons; any other method (screwdriver blades, pliers, etc.) usually results in the rings being bent, scratched or distorted and/or the piston itself being damaged.

Clean the varnish from the piston skirts and pins with a cleaning solvent. DO NOT WIRE BRUSH ANY PART OF THE PISTON. Clean the ring grooves with a groove cleaner and make sure that the oil ring holes and slots are clean.

Inspect the piston for cracked ring lands, scuffed or damaged skirts, eroded areas at the top of the piston. Replace the pistons that are damaged or show signs of excessive wear. Inspect the piston ring grooves for nicks or burrs that might cause the rings to hang up.

Measure the piston skirt perpendicular to the piston pin axis and note this figure for the piston clearance check. If installing replacement pistons, follow the manufacturers recommendations on where to measure the piston.

Cylinder Bores

Using a telescoping gauge or an inside micrometer, measure the diameter of the cylinder bore, perpendicular (90°) to the piston pin, at 1–2½ in. (25–64mm) below the surface of the cylinder block. The difference between the two measurements is the piston clearance.

If the clearance is within specifications or slightly below (after the cylinders have been bored or honed), finish honing is all that is necessary. If the clearance is excessive, try to obtain a slightly larger piston to bring the clearance within specifications. If this is not possible, obtain the first oversize piston and hone the cylinder or (if necessary) bore the cylinder to size.

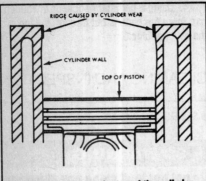

FIG. 107 The ridge at the top of the cylinder wall must be removed prior to removing the piston.

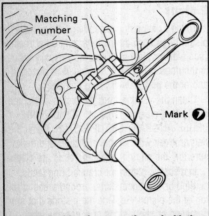

FIG. 110 Position the connecting rod with the mark toward the front of the engine

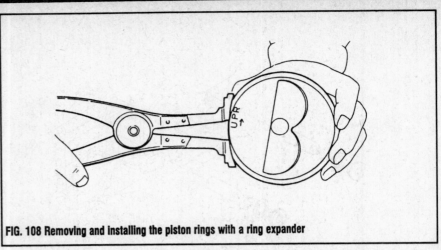

FIG. 108 Removing and installing the piston rings with a ring expander

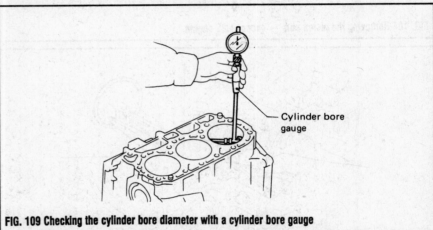

FIG. 109 Checking the cylinder bore diameter with a cylinder bore gauge

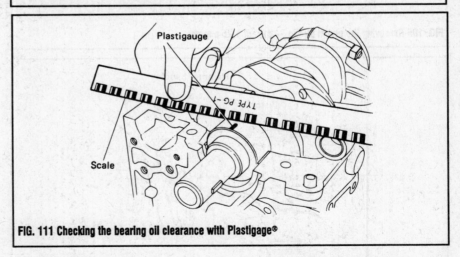

FIG. 111 Checking the bearing oil clearance with Plastigage®

When measuring the cylinder bore, take measurements in several places. If the cylinder bore is tapered or is out-of-round, it is advisable to rebore for the smallest possible oversize piston and rings. After measuring, mark the pistons with a felt-tip pen for reference during assembly.

➡ **Boring of the cylinder block should be performed by a reputable machine shop with the proper equipment. In some cases, clean-up honing can be done with the cylinder block in the vehicle, but most excessive honing and all cylinder boring MUST BE done with the block stripped and removed from the vehicle.**

Connecting Rods

Wash the connecting rods in cleaning solvent and dry with compressed air. Check for twisted or bent rods and inspect for nicks or cracks. Replace the connecting rods that are damaged.

Install the cap on the rod and torque to specification. Using an inside micrometer, measure the inside bore diameter perpendicular (90°) to the axis of rod and once again along the axis of the rod. If the two measurements are not within specification, have the rod resized by a competent machine shop.

➡ **It is normal for the inside diameter of the rod to be slightly larger when measured perpendicular (90°) to the axis of the rod.**

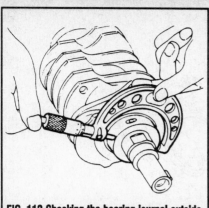

FIG. 112 Checking the bearing journal outside diameter with a micrometer

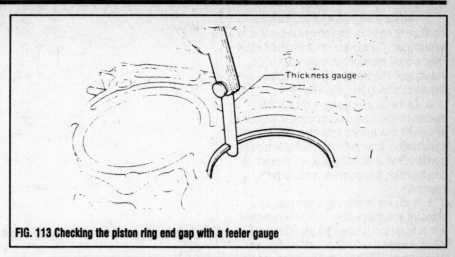

FIG. 113 Checking the piston ring end gap with a feeler gauge

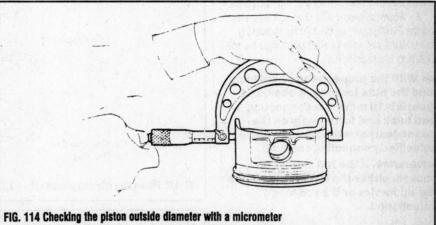

FIG. 114 Checking the piston outside diameter with a micrometer

Crankshaft and Main Bearings

Measure the bearing journals using a micrometer, to determine diameter, journal taper and eccentricity. If crankshaft journals appear defective, or do not meet tolerances, the crankshaft will require grinding.

Assemble the case halves with the bearings installed and torque to specification. Using a telescope gauge and micrometer, measure bearing I.D. parallel to piston axis and at 30° on each side of piston axis. Subtract journal O.D. from bearing I.D. to determine oil clearance.

An alternate method is to measure the oil clearance on each crankshaft bearing by means of Plastigage®.

Wipe off oil, dust, etc. on the surfaces to be measured. Install the bearings in the crankcase and set the crankshaft in position. Cut the Plastigage® to the bearing width and place it on the journal parallel with the crankshaft axis. Be careful not to put it on the oil hole or groove. Bring together the crankcase halves and tighten the bolts and nut to the specified torque.

⁙ WARNING

During the work, the crankshaft must not be turned nor the crankcase inverted.

Remove all the bolts and nut and separate the crankcase. Measure the Plastigage® width with the scale printed on the Plastigage® case. If the measurement is not within the specification, replace the defective bearing with an undersize one, and replace or recondition the crankshaft as necessary.

CHECKING RING END GAP

The piston ring end gap should be checked while the rings are removed from the pistons. Incorrect end gap indicates that the wrong size rings are being used; ring breakage could result if not corrected.

1. Compress the new piston ring into a cylinder (one at a time).

2. Squirt some clean oil into the cylinder so that the ring and the top 2 in. (51mm) of the cylinder wall are coated.

3. Using an inverted piston, push the ring approximately 1 in. (25mm) below the top of the cylinder.

4. Using a feeler gauge, measure the ring gap and compare it to specification. Carefully remove the ring from the cylinder.

5. If the gap is smaller than specification, file the ring ends using an appropriate piston ring file. If greater, the cylinder bore must be honed to the next oversize or the piston rings are incorrect.

CONNECTING ROD BEARING REPLACEMENT

Replacement bearings are available in standard size and undersize (for reground crankshafts). Connecting rod-to-crankshaft bearing clearance is checked using Plastigage® at either the top or the bottom of each crank journal. The Plastigage® has a range of 0.001–0.003 in. (0.0254–0.0762mm).

1. Remove the rod cap with the bearing shell. Completely clean the bearing shell and the crank journal, blow any oil from the oil hole in the crankshaft; place the Plastigage® lengthwise along the bottom center of the lower bearing shell, then install the cap with the shell and torque the bolt or nuts to specification. DO NOT turn the crankshaft with the Plastigage® on the bearing.

2. Remove the bearing cap with the shell. The flattened Plastigage® will be found sticking to either the bearing shell or the crank journal. DO NOT remove it yet.

3. Use the scale printed on the Plastigage® envelope to measure the flattened material at its widest point. The number within the scale which most closely corresponds to the width of the Plastigage® indicates the bearing clearance in thousandths of an inch and milimeters.

4. Check the specifications chart in this Section for the desired clearance. It is advisable to install a new bearing if the clearance exceeds specification; however, if the bearing is in good condition and is not being checked because of bearing noise, bearing replacement is not necessary.

5. If you are installing new bearings, try a standard size, then each undersize in order until one is found that is within the specified limits when checked for clearance with Plastigage®; each undersize shell has its size stamped on it.

6. When the proper size shell is found, clean off the Plastigage®, oil the bearing thoroughly, reinstall the cap with its shell and torque the rod bolt nuts to specifications.

➡ **With the proper bearing selected and the nuts torqued, it should be possible to move the connecting rod back and forth freely on the crank journal as allowed by the specified connecting rod end clearance. If the rod cannot be moved, either the rod bearing is too far undersize or the rod is misaligned.**

INSTALLATION

♦ SEE FIG. 115–117

➡ **During installation, lubricate all moving components with oil. When the engine is first started, oil pressure will take time to build. The oil used to lubricate the engine during the first few seconds of operation must be placed on moving surfaces during installation.**

1.2L Engine

1. Install the crankshaft lower bearings and place the crankshaft into the cylinder block after lubricating it with oil. Install the crankshaft so that the chain connecting the balance shaft and oil pump sprocket is as shown in the illustration.

2. Install the upper bearings in the main caps and install the caps on the engine. Tighten the main bearing cap bolts/nuts to specification.

3. Check the crankshaft end-play. If not within specification, the thrust surface of the crankshaft must be corrected prior to assembly.

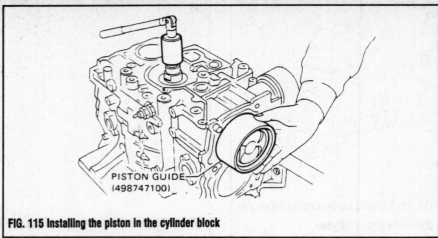
FIG. 115 Installing the piston in the cylinder block

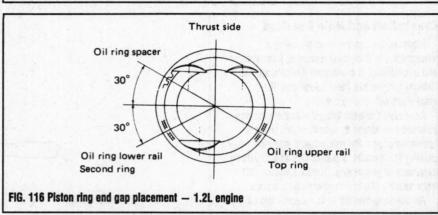
FIG. 116 Piston ring end gap placement — 1.2L engine

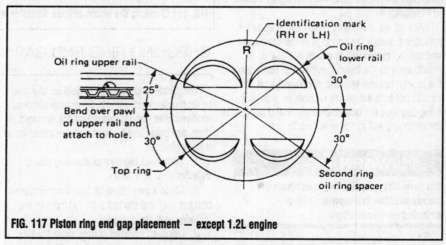
FIG. 117 Piston ring end gap placement — except 1.2L engine

4. Install the rod bearing on the connecting rod. Install the piston rings on the piston using a ring expander.

5. Position the piston rings as shown in the illustration and install the ring compressor. Install rubber boots over the rod bolts.

6. Install the piston into its cylinder with the Fuji Industries mark facing the front of the engine and tap into place using a wooden hammer handle. Remove the rubber boot, install the rod cap so that the protruding ridge faces the front of the engine and tighten the bolt/nut to specification.

7. Install the oil strainer assembly and oil pan.

8. Install the cylinder heads.

9. Install the timing belt, belt covers and related components. Adjust the valve lash.

10. Install the engine in the vehicle.

Except 1.2L engine

1. Install the connecting rods onto the crankshaft and tighten the cap bolts to specification.

2. Install new crankshaft bearings into the cylinder blocks and the crankshaft assembly into the left hand cylinder block.

3. Using Three-bond® 1215 sealant or equivalent, apply it along the mating surface of the cylinder block. Install the right hand cylinder block onto the assembly. Torque the cylinder block bolts to 17–20 ft. lbs. (23–26Nm) for the 8mm bolts and 29–35 ft. lbs. (39–47Nm) for the 10mm bolts.

4. Using a dial indicator, check the crankshaft thrust clearance. If not within specification, the crankshaft thrust surface must be corrected.

5. Using a piston ring expander tool, install new rings onto the pistons. Position the piston rings gaps as shown in the illustration.

6. Using engine oil, lubricate the piston assembly. Turn the crankshaft so that the No. 1 and No. 2 connecting rods are positioned at BDC.

7. Using the Piston Ring Compression tool No. 398744300 or equivalent, compress the piston rings into the piston assembly. Then, using a hammer handle, drive the piston assembly into the cylinder block.

8. Using the Piston Pin Guide tool No. 399284300 or equivalent, install the piston pin and the circlip through the service hole.

9. Repeat this procedure to install the remaining pistons.

10. Apply fluid packing to the piston pin plugs and tighten to 46–56 ft. lbs. (62–76Nm).

11. Install the front and rear oil seals using a driver.

12. Install the oil strainer and oil pan.

13. Install the cylinder heads and torque to specification.

14. Install the timing belt, belt covers and related components.

15. Install the intake manifold and tighten to specification.

16. Join the engine and transaxle. Install the engine in the vehicle.

BREAK-IN PROCEDURE

Start the engine, and allow it to run at low speed for a few minutes, while checking for leaks. Stop the engine, check the oil level, and fill as necessary. Restart the engine, and fill the cooling system to capacity. Check the point dwell angle and adjust the ignition timing and the valves. Run the engine at low to medium speed (800–2,500 rpm) for approximately 1/2 hour, and retorque the cylinder head bolts. Road test the car, and check again for leaks.

Follow the manufacturer's recommended engine break-in procedure and maintenance schedule for new engines.

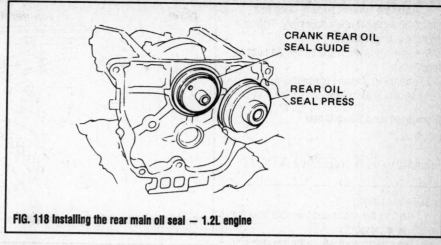

FIG. 118 Installing the rear main oil seal — 1.2L engine

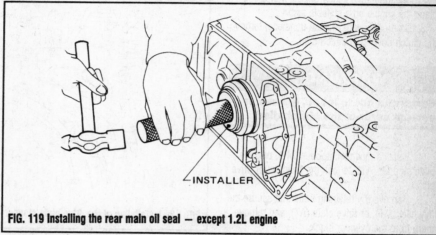

FIG. 119 Installing the rear main oil seal — except 1.2L engine

Rear Main Oil Seal

REPLACEMENT

1.2L Engine

♦ SEE FIG. 118

1. Remove the engine from the vehicle and separate the engine from the transaxle

2. Remove the clutch assembly and the flywheel or torque converter and flexplate from the crankshaft.

3. Using a small pry bar, pry the rear oil seal from the crankcase; be careful not to damage the crankshaft or the crankcase housing.

4. Install the new oil seal and lubricate with engine oil.

5. Using the Crankshaft Rear Oil Seal Guide tool No. 498725600 or equivalent, and the Rear Oil Seal Press tool No. 498725500 or equivalent, drive the new oil seal into the housing until it seats.

6. Install the clutch assembly and flywheel or flexplate and torque converter. Tighten the flywheel/flexplate bolts to specification.

7. Join the engine and transaxle. Install the assembly in the vehicle.

Except 1.2L Engine

♦ SEE FIG. 119

1. Remove the engine from the vehicle. Remove the transmission-to-engine bolts and separate the transmission from the engine.

2. Using the Clutch Disc Guide tool 499747000 or equivalent, remove the clutch assembly/flywheel (MT). If equipped with an AT, remove the torque converter flexplate from the crankshaft.

3. Remove the flywheel housing from the engine. Using a small pry bar, pry the oil seal from the housing.

4. Install the new oil seal and press it into the flywheel housing using the appropriate driver.

5. Install the flywheel housing using new gaskets and sealant where necessary. Tighten the bolts to specification.

6. Install the flywheel and tighten the bolts to specification.

7. Join the engine and transmission. Install the assembly in the vehicle.

Flywheel and Ring Gear

REMOVAL & INSTALLATION

♦ SEE FIG. 120–121

1. Remove the engine and transaxle from the vehicle as an assembly.

2. Separate the engine from the transaxle and place the engine on a suitable stand.

3. On models with manual transaxle, remove the clutch cover and clutch disc.

░░░ WARNING

Be careful not to let oil, grease or coolant contact the clutch disc.

4. Install a flywheel stopper (MT), or drive plate stopper (AT), to lock the flywheel or drive plate.

5. Remove the retaining bolts that secure the flywheel (MT), or drive plate (AT), and remove them from the cylinder block.

To Install:

6. Install the flywheel or driveplate and tighten the retaining bolts as follows : 65–71 ft. lbs. (88–97Nm) on the 1.2L engine; 30–33 ft. lbs. (41–45Nm) on the 1.6L engine and 51–55 ft. lbs. (69–75Nm) on all other engines.

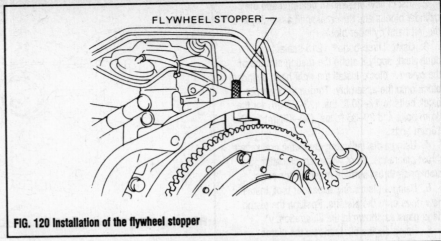

FIG. 120 Installation of the flywheel stopper

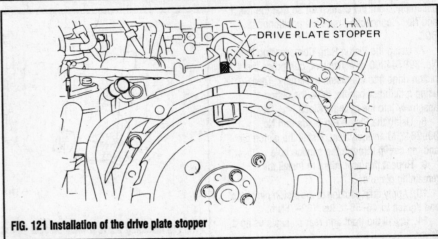

FIG. 121 Installation of the drive plate stopper

7. Install the clutch assembly on manual transaxle vehicles.

8. Join the engine and transaxle assemblies. Install the engine/transaxle assembly in the vehicle.

EXHAUST SYSTEM

♦ SEE FIG. 122–127

General Description

The exhaust system is suspended by hangers and clamps attached to the frame member. Annoying rattles and noise vibrations in the exhaust system are usually caused by misalignment of parts. When aligning the system, leave all bolts and nuts loose until all parts are properly aligned, then tighten from front to rear. Make sure that you are wearing some form of eye protection when removing or installing the exhaust system, to prevent eye injury. Never work on the exhaust system of a vehicle that has been recently used. Exhaust systems reach very high temperatures and can cause severe burns. Always allow the car to cool down before starting any repairs to the exhaust.

The Catalytic Converter is an emission control device added to a gasoline engines exhaust system to reduce hydrocarbon and carbon monoxide pollutants in the exhaust gas stream. The catalyst in the converter is not serviceable.

Periodic maintenance of the exhaust system is not required. However, if the vehicle is raised for other service, it is advisable to check the general condition of the catalytic converter, exhaust pipes and muffler.

Testing for leaks in the exhaust system is not a difficult task. Look for black sooty deposits around joints, on the pipes and on the muffler. The presence of black soot indicates a leak. If a leak is suspected but cannot be found, pour a tiny amount of mineral spirits into the carburetor or throttle body with the engine running. The smoke created by the mineral spirits will be seen escaping from the area of the exhaust leak.

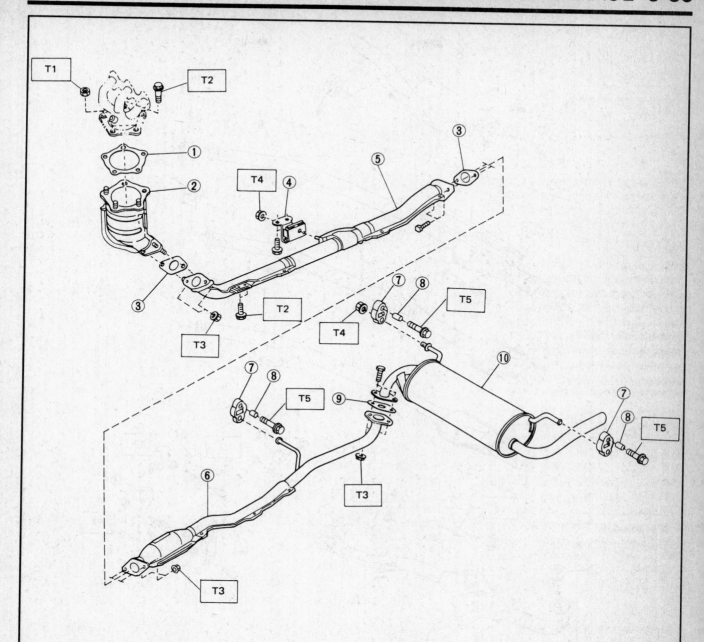

1 Front exhaust gasket
2 Front exhaust pipe
3 Rear exhaust gasket
4 Exhaust pipe cushion
5 Rear exhaust pipe A
6 Rear exhaust pipe B
7 Cushion rubber
8 Spacer
9 Muffler gasket
10 Muffler

Tightening torque: N·m (kg-m, ft-lb)
T1: 16 - 25 (1.6 - 2.6, 12 - 19)
T2: 23 - 42 (2.3 - 4.3, 17 - 31)
T3: 51 - 86 (5.2 - 8.8, 38 - 64)
T4: 13 - 23 (1.3 - 2.3, 9 - 17)
T5: 18 - 31 (1.8 - 3.2, 13 - 23)

FIG. 122 Exhaust system — 1.2L engine

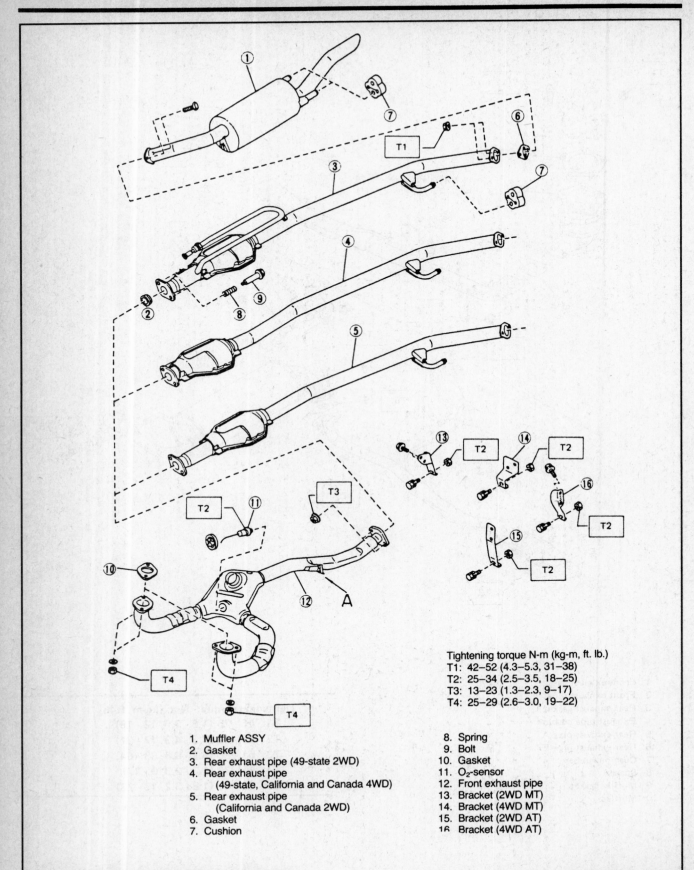

Tightening torque N-m (kg-m, ft. lb.)
T1: 42–52 (4.3–5.3, 31–38)
T2: 25–34 (2.5–3.5, 18–25)
T3: 13–23 (1.3–2.3, 9–17)
T4: 25–29 (2.6–3.0, 19–22)

1. Muffler ASSY
2. Gasket
3. Rear exhaust pipe (49-state 2WD)
4. Rear exhaust pipe
   (49-state, California and Canada 4WD)
5. Rear exhaust pipe
   (California and Canada 2WD)
6. Gasket
7. Cushion

8. Spring
9. Bolt
10. Gasket
11. O₂-sensor
12. Front exhaust pipe
13. Bracket (2WD MT)
14. Bracket (4WD MT)
15. Bracket (2WD AT)
16. Bracket (4WD AT)

FIG. 123 Exhaust system — 1.6L and 1.8L non-turbo engine

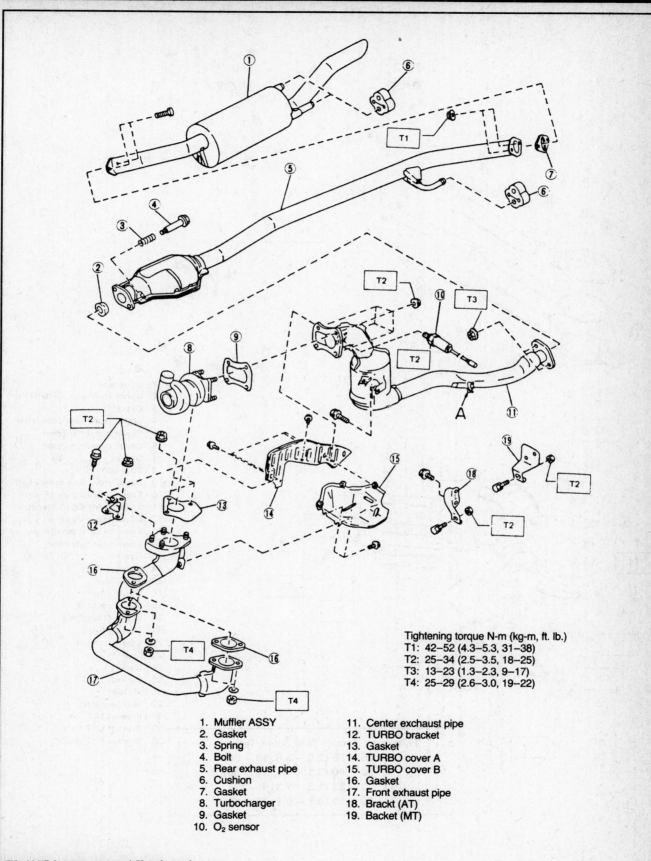

Tightening torque N-m (kg-m, ft. lb.)
T1: 42–52 (4.3–5.3, 31–38)
T2: 25–34 (2.5–3.5, 18–25)
T3: 13–23 (1.3–2.3, 9–17)
T4: 25–29 (2.6–3.0, 19–22)

1. Muffler ASSY
2. Gasket
3. Spring
4. Bolt
5. Rear exhaust pipe
6. Cushion
7. Gasket
8. Turbocharger
9. Gasket
10. O₂ sensor

11. Center exchaust pipe
12. TURBO bracket
13. Gasket
14. TURBO cover A
15. TURBO cover B
16. Gasket
17. Front exhaust pipe
18. Brackt (AT)
19. Backet (MT)

FIG. 124 Exhaust system — 1.8L turbo engine

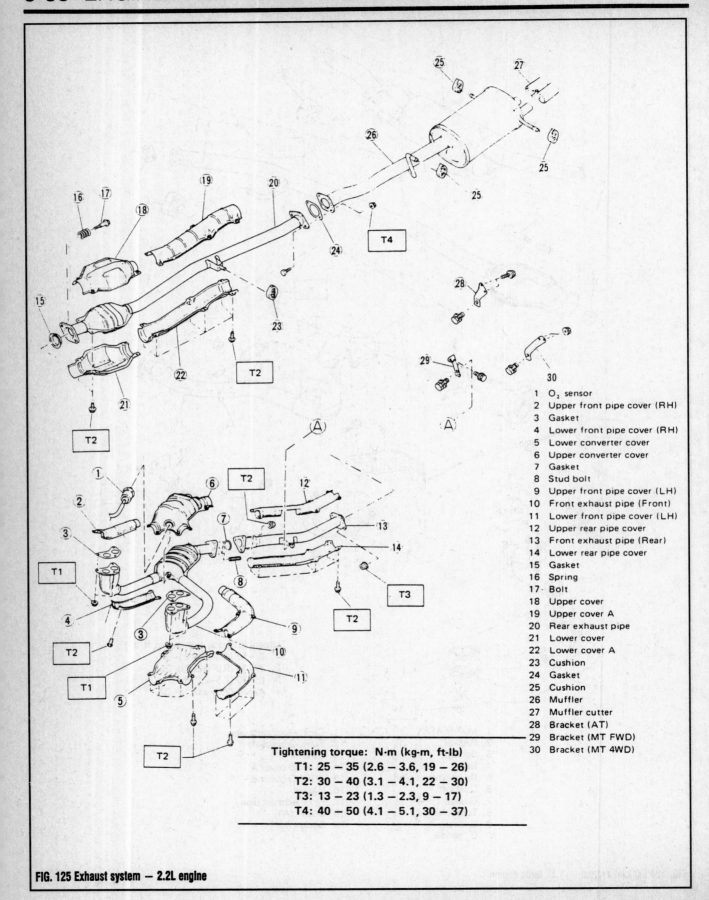

1 O₂ sensor
2 Upper front pipe cover (RH)
3 Gasket
4 Lower front pipe cover (RH)
5 Lower converter cover
6 Upper converter cover
7 Gasket
8 Stud bolt
9 Upper front pipe cover (LH)
10 Front exhaust pipe (Front)
11 Lower front pipe cover (LH)
12 Upper rear pipe cover
13 Front exhaust pipe (Rear)
14 Lower rear pipe cover
15 Gasket
16 Spring
17 Bolt
18 Upper cover
19 Upper cover A
20 Rear exhaust pipe
21 Lower cover
22 Lower cover A
23 Cushion
24 Gasket
25 Cushion
26 Muffler
27 Muffler cutter
28 Bracket (AT)
29 Bracket (MT FWD)
30 Bracket (MT 4WD)

Tightening torque: N·m (kg-m, ft-lb)
T1: 25 – 35 (2.6 – 3.6, 19 – 26)
T2: 30 – 40 (3.1 – 4.1, 22 – 30)
T3: 13 – 23 (1.3 – 2.3, 9 – 17)
T4: 40 – 50 (4.1 – 5.1, 30 – 37)

FIG. 125 Exhaust system — 2.2L engine

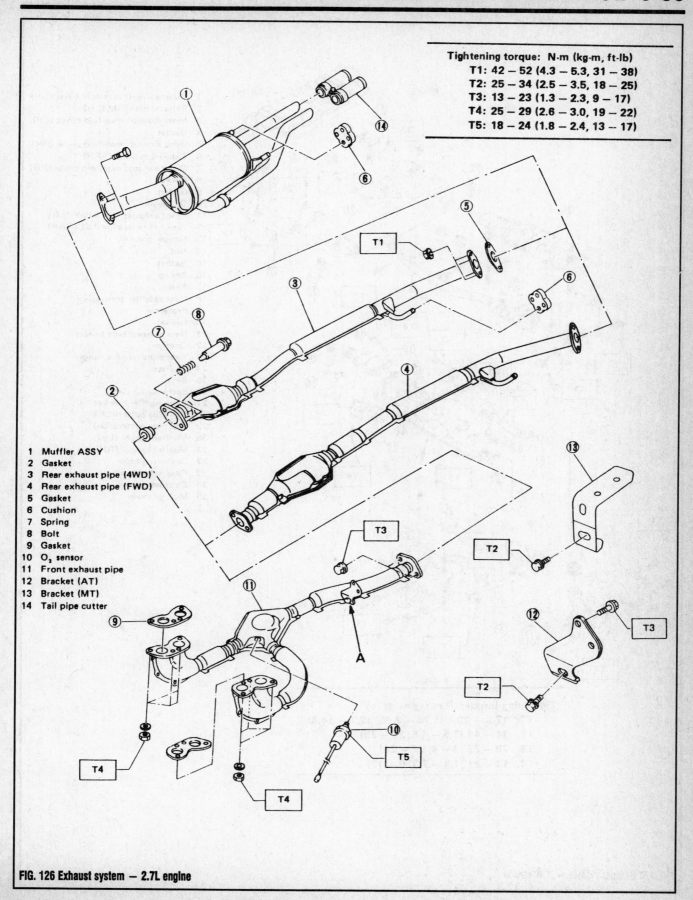

Tightening torque: N·m (kg-m, ft-lb)
T1: 42 — 52 (4.3 — 5.3, 31 — 38)
T2: 25 — 34 (2.5 — 3.5, 18 — 25)
T3: 13 — 23 (1.3 — 2.3, 9 — 17)
T4: 25 — 29 (2.6 — 3.0, 19 — 22)
T5: 18 — 24 (1.8 — 2.4, 13 — 17)

1   Muffler ASSY
2   Gasket
3   Rear exhaust pipe (4WD)
4   Rear exhaust pipe (FWD)
5   Gasket
6   Cushion
7   Spring
8   Bolt
9   Gasket
10 O₂ sensor
11 Front exhaust pipe
12 Bracket (AT)
13 Bracket (MT)
14 Tail pipe cutter

FIG. 126 Exhaust system — 2.7L engine

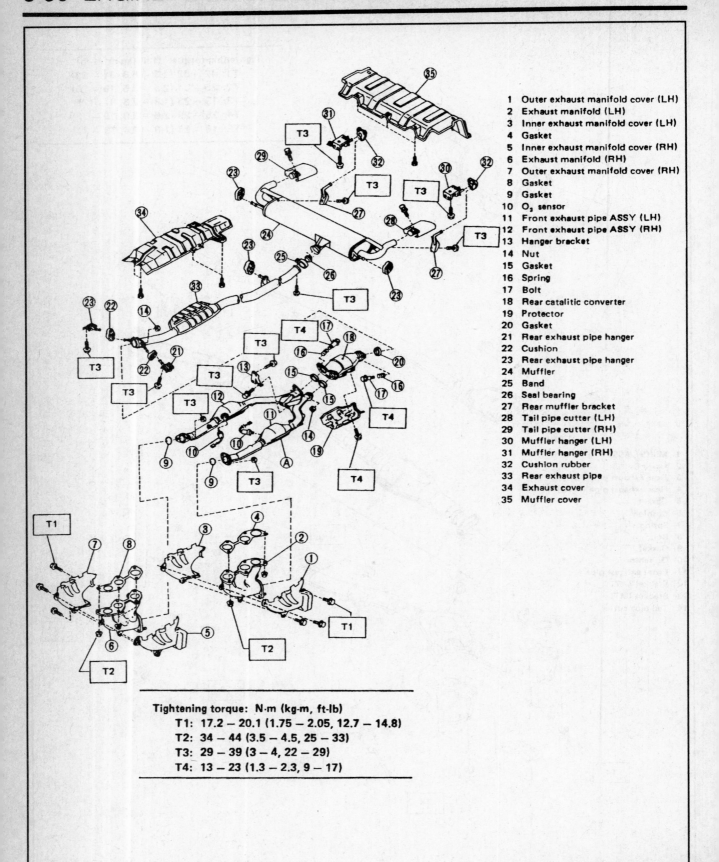

1   Outer exhaust manifold cover (LH)
2   Exhaust manifold (LH)
3   Inner exhaust manifold cover (LH)
4   Gasket
5   Inner exhaust manifold cover (RH)
6   Exhaust manifold (RH)
7   Outer exhaust manifold cover (RH)
8   Gasket
9   Gasket
10 O$_2$ sensor
11 Front exhaust pipe ASSY (LH)
12 Front exhaust pipe ASSY (RH)
13 Hanger bracket
14 Nut
15 Gasket
16 Spring
17 Bolt
18 Rear catalitic converter
19 Protector
20 Gasket
21 Rear exhaust pipe hanger
22 Cushion
23 Rear exhaust pipe hanger
24 Muffler
25 Band
26 Seal bearing
27 Rear muffler bracket
28 Tail pipe cutter (LH)
29 Tail pipe cutter (RH)
30 Muffler hanger (LH)
31 Muffler hanger (RH)
32 Cushion rubber
33 Rear exhaust pipe
34 Exhaust cover
35 Muffler cover

Tightening torque: N·m (kg-m, ft-lb)
      T1: 17.2 — 20.1 (1.75 — 2.05, 12.7 — 14.8)
      T2: 34 — 44 (3.5 — 4.5, 25 — 33)
      T3: 29 — 39 (3 — 4, 22 — 29)
      T4: 13 — 23 (1.3 — 2.3, 9 — 17)

FIG. 127 Exhaust system — 3.3L engine

Front Exhaust Pipe (Non-Turbo)

REMOVAL & INSTALLATION

1. Disconnect the oxygen sensor harness.
2. As required, remove the air duct from the upper shell cover.
3. Loosen (Do not remove) the nuts which hold the front exhaust pipe to the exhaust port of the engine.
4. Disconnect the front and rear exhaust pipes.
5. Disconnect the front exhaust pipe and bracket.
6. While holding the front exhaust pipe with one hand, remove the nuts which hold the front exhaust pipe to the exhaust port. The front exhaust pipe can then be disconnected.

➡ **During Installation, do not tighten any connections more then hand tight until the entire exhaust system has been installed. Be sure to install a new gasket at the exhaust port. Use only nuts specified by the manufacturer. Do not remove the gasket placed between the front and rear exhaust pipes. When the front exhaust pipe needs to be replaced, the gasket must be replaced also.**

7. Install the front exhaust pipe and bracket.
8. Connect the front and rear exhaust pipes.
9. Align exhaust system and tighten all exhaust system nuts and bolts to specification. Work from front to rear.
10. Connect the oxygen sensor harness.
11. Start the engine and allow it to reach operating temperature. Check for leaks.

Front Exhaust Pipe (Turbocharged Models)

REMOVAL & INSTALLATION

1. Remove turbocharger covers, and disconnect the center exhaust pipe. Remove the turbocharger unit.
2. Remove the nuts which hold the turbocharger bracket to the front exhaust pipe.

3. Remove underguard and right undercover.
4. Loosen the engine mount bracket and pitching stopper. Then slightly raise the engine until the bolts protrude beyond the surface of the crossmember.
5. Disconnect the front exhaust pipe from the engines exhaust port, and remove through the clearance between the crossmember and the cylinder head.

☼ WARNING

Be sure to remove the bolts only after the engine has cooled off. Before disassembling parts, spray with penetrating lubricant to loosen rust deposits.

6. Install the gasket onto the stud bolts at the engine's exhaust port with its flat surface facing the engine. If the gasket is tilted, it may catch on a thread and then will not drop down over the bolt.
7. Temporarily tighten the front exhaust pipe to engine's exhaust port with the nuts.
8. Lower the engine. Tighten the engine mount bracket and properly adjust the pitching stopper.
9. Install the underguard and right undercover.
10. Connect the front exhaust pipe to the turbocharger bracket.
11. Properly tighten the front exhaust pipe at the engine's exhaust port.
12. Connect the oxygen sensor connector.
13. Install the turbocharger unit, center the exhaust pipe and turbocharger covers.

Center Exhaust Pipe (Turbo Vehicles Only)

REMOVAL & INSTALLATION

1. Remove turbocharger covers.
2. Disconnect the oxygen sensor connector.
3. Remove the flange nuts which hold the center exhaust pipe to turbocharger unit.

☼ WARNING

Be sure to remove the bolts only after the engine has cooled off. Before disassembling parts, spray with penetrating lubricant to loosen rust deposits.

4. Remove the flange nuts from the transmission side.
5. Disconnect the center and rear exhaust pipes.
6. Disconnect the center exhaust pipe from the bracket located on the lower side of the transmission.
7. Remove the center exhaust pipe from the body.

☼ CAUTION

Do not allow the turbocharger cover mounting bracket to Interfere with the brake pipe cover located in the front toe board. Be sure not to damage the steering universal joint. Do not damage the gasket used on the lower side of the turbocharger unit or turbocharger cover.

To Install:

8. Install the gasket onto the stud bolts on the turbocharger unit. Connect the center exhaust pipe flange and temporarily tighten it with nuts.

☼ CAUTION

Be sure not to damage the gasket used on the lower side of the turbocharger unit and turbocharger cover.

9. Temporarily connect the center exhaust pipe and bracket located on the transmission side.
10. Temporarily connect the center and rear exhaust pipes, and center exhaust pipe to the bracket located on the lower side of the transmission with new nuts.
11. Tighten the nuts and bolts at the turbocharger unit bracket, (on the transmission side) and the bracket (on the lower side of the transaxle), in that order, to specified torque.
12. Install turbocharger covers.

Rear Exhaust Pipe

REMOVAL & INSTALLATION

1. Disconnect the rear exhaust pipe from the front exhaust pipe (Non-Turbo), center exhaust pipe (turbocharged models).

2. Disconnect the rear exhaust pipe from the muffler assembly. To prevent damage to the bumper or rear skirt by the muffler, wrap a cloth around the tail pipe.

3. Remove rear exhaust pipe from the rubber cushion. To help in its, apply a coat of penetrating lubricant to the mating surface of the rubber cushion in advance.

To Install:

4. Temporarily connect the rear exhaust pipe and the muffler assembly.

5. Temporarily connect the rear exhaust pipe and the front exhaust pipe (Non-Turbo), center exhaust pipe (turbocharged models).

6. Insert exhaust pipe bracket into the rubber cushion.

7. Adjust the clearance between the temporarily installed parts and tighten to specified torque.

Muffler Assembly

REMOVAL & INSTALLATION

1. Remove the bolts and self locking nuts which hold the rear exhaust pipe to the muffler assembly.

2. Remove the left and right rubber cushions from the muffler assembly and detach the muffler assembly.

3. Installation is in the reverse order of the removal procedure.

ADJUSTMENTS

1. After installing exhaust system parts, check to make sure clearances between parts and car body are sufficient enough to prevent contact.

2. If any clearance is not, loosen all connections.

3. Adjust when necessary to obtain proper clearances.

4. Tighten all connections securely.

ENGINE MECHANICAL SPECIFICATIONS

Component	U.S.	Metric
1987-92 1.2L engine		
Cylinder head		
Surface warpage limit	0.0020 in.	0.05mm
Surface grinding limit	0.008 in.	0.2mm
Standard height	4.39 in.	111.5mm
Valve seat angle	90°	
Valve seat contact width		
Intake	0.039 in.	1.0mm
Exhaust	0.051 in.	0.8mm
Valve guide		
Inner diameter	0.2756-0.2762 in.	7.000-7.015mm
Protrusion	0.807 in.	20.5mm
Valve		
Overall length		
Intake	4.26 in.	108.2mm
Exhaust	4.28 in.	108.8mm
Head edge thickness limit	0.039 in.	1.0mm
Stem diameter		
Intake	0.2742-0.2748 in.	6.965-6.980mm
Exhaust	0.2734-0.2740 in.	6.945-6.960mm
Stem oil clearance		
Intake	0.0008-0.0020 in.	0.020-0.050mm
Exhaust	0.0016-0.0028 in.	0.040-0.070mm
Valve spring		
Free length	1.8311 in.	46.51mm
Tension @ 1.248 in. height	112.79-129.76 lbs.	51.15-58.85 kg
Valve rocker		
Rocker arm to shaft clearance	0.0006-0.0020 in.	0.016-0.052mm
Crankcase		
Cylinder bore		
Diameter	3.0709-3.0718 in.	78.000-78.024mm
Taper limit	0.0020 in.	0.05mm
Out of roundness limit	0.0020 in.	0.05mm
Cylinder to piston clearance	0.0015-0.0024 in.	0.038-0.062mm
Cylinder overbore limit	0.039 in.	1.0mm
Case warpage	0.0020 in.	0.05mm

ENGINE MECHANICAL SPECIFICATIONS

Component	U.S.	Metric
1987-92 1.2L engine		
Piston and Piston pin		
Piston outer diameter	3.0689-3.0698 in.	77.950-77.974mm
Piston pin bore inner diameter	0.7108-0.7111 in.	18.055-18.062mm
Piston pin outer diameter	0.7103-0.7105 in.	18.041-18.047mm
Piston pin to bore clearance	0.0005-0.0007 in.	0.012-0.018mm
Piston ring		
Ring gap		
Top and second	0.0079-0.0138 in.	0.2-0.35mm
Oil ring	0.012-0.035 in.	0.3-0.9mm
Ring to groove clearance		
Top	0.0014-0.0030 in.	0.035-0.075mm
Second	0.0010-0.0026 in.	0.025-0.065mm
Oil ring	0 in.	0mm
Connecting rod		
Twist per 3.94 in. (100mm)	0.004 in.	0.1mm
Thrust clearance	0.0028-0.0118 in.	0.07-0.30mm
Piston pin to rod clearance	0.0007-0.0016 in.	0.018-0.041mm
Crankshaft		
Bend limit	0.0012 in.	0.03mm
Out of roundness	0.0012 in.	0.03mm
Grinding limit	0.0008 in.	0.02mm
Thrust clearance	0.0031-0.0070 in.	0.08-0.177mm
Main journal diameter	1.6525-1.6529 in.	41.974-41.985mm
Main journal oil clearance	0.0006-0.0018 in.	0.014-0.045mm
Rod journal diameter	1.6531-1.6535 in.	41.989-42.000mm
Rod journal oil clearance	0.0008-0.0021 in.	0.020-0.053mm
Camshaft		
Thrust clearance	0.0012-0.0150 in.	0.03-0.38mm
Balance shaft		
Thrust clearance limit	0.020 in.	0.5mm
1985-89 1.6L engine		
Cylinder head		
Surface warpage limit	0.002 in.	0.05mm
Surface grinding limit	0.020 in.	0.50mm
Standard height	3.528 in.	89.6mm
Valve seat angle	90-150°	
Valve seat contact width		
Intake	0.028-0.051 in.	0.7-1.3mm
Exhaust	0.039-0.071 in.	1.0-1.8mm
Valve guide		
Inner diameter	0.3150-0.3156 in.	8.0-8.015mm
Protrusion		
Intake	0.689-0.728 in.	17.5-18.5mm
Exhaust	0.886-0.925 in.	22.5-23.5mm
Valve		
Overall length		
Intake	4.29 in.	109mm
Exhaust	4.30 in.	109.3mm
Head edge thickness limit		
Intake	0.020 in.	0.5mm
Exhaust	0.031 in.	0.8mm
Stem diameter		
Intake	0.3130-0.3136 in.	7.950-7.956mm
Exhaust	0.3128-0.3134 in.	7.945-7.960mm
Stem oil clearance		
Intake	0.0014-0.0026 in.	0.035-0.065mm
Exhaust	0.0016-0.0028 in.	0.040-0.070mm
Valve spring		
Solid lifter		
Free length		
Outer spring	1.783 in.	45.3mm
Inner spring	1.921 in.	48.8mm

ENGINE MECHANICAL SPECIFICATIONS

Component	U.S.	Metric
1985-89 1.6L engine		
Tension		
Outer @ 1.555 in./39.5mm	32.9-38.1 lbs.	14.9-17.3 kg
Inner @ 1.476 in./37.5mm	19.0-21.0 lbs.	8.6-10.0 kg
Squareness		
Outer	0.079 in.	2.0mm
Inner	0.083 in.	2.1mm
Hydraulic lifter		
Free length		
Outer spring	1.909 in.	48.5mm
Inner spring	2.087 in.	53.0mm
Tension		
Outer @ 1.555 in./39.5mm	51.4-58.9 lbs.	23.3-26.7 kg
Inner @ 1.181 in./30.0mm	26.0-30.6 lbs.	11.8-30.6 kg
Squareness		
Outer	0.083 in.	2.1mm
Inner	0.091 in.	2.3mm
Valve rocker		
Inner diameter of arm	0.7093-0.7100 in.	18.016-18.034mm
Outer diameter of shaft	0.7080-0.7088 in.	17.982-18.003mm
Rocker arm to shaft clearance	0.0005-0.0020 in.	0.013-0.052mm
Valve lifter		
Solid lifter		
Crankcase bore inner diameter	0.8268-0.8276 in.	21.0-21.021mm
Lifter outer diameter	0.8248-0.8256 in.	20.949-20.970mm
Lifter to bore clearance	0.0012-0.0028 in.	0.030-0.072mm
Hydraulic lifter		
Crankcase bore inner diameter	0.8263-0.8283 in.	20.988-21.040mm
Lifter outer diameter	0.8248-0.8255 in.	20.950-20.968mm
Lifter to bore clearance	0.0008-0.0035 in.	0.020-0.090mm
Push rod		
Overall length	8.62-8.64 in.	219-219.4mm
Deflection at center	0.016 in.	0.4mm
Crankcase		
Cylinder bore		
Diameter	3.6214-3.6226 in.	91.985-92.015mm
Taper limit	0.0020 in.	0.015mm
Out of roundness limit	0.0020 in.	0.050mm
Cylinder to piston clearance	0.0004-0.0016 in.	0.010-0.040mm
Cylinder overbore limit	0.0197 in.	0.50mm
Case warpage	0.0020 in.	0.05mm
Protrusion of stud bolt	3.563-3.642 in.	90.5-92.5mm
Piston and Piston pin		
Piston outer diameter	3.6205-3.6216 in.	91.960-91.990mm
Piston pin bore inner diameter	0.8267-0.8271 in.	20.999-21.009mm
Piston pin outer diameter	0.8265-0.8268 in.	20.992-21.000mm
Piston pin to bore clearance	0.0002-0.0004 in.	0.004-0.010mm
Piston ring		
Ring gap		
Top	0.0079-0.0138 in.	0.20-0.35mm
Second	0.0079-0.0138 in.	0.20-0.35mm
Oil ring	0.0079-0.0354 in.	0.20-0.90mm
Ring to groove clearance		
Top	0.0016-0.0031 in.	0.04-0.08mm
Second	0.0012-0.0028 in.	0.03-0.07mm
Oil ring	0 in.	0mm
Connecting rod		
Center to center length	4.3287-4.3327 in.	109.95-110.05mm
Twist per 3.94 in. (100mm)	0.0039 in.	0.10mm
Thrust clearance	0.0028-0.0130 in.	0.070-0.330mm
Piston pin to bushing clearance	0-0.0009 in.	0-0.022mm
Bushing bore diameter	0.8268-0.8274 in.	21.0-21.016mm

ENGINE MECHANICAL SPECIFICATIONS

Component	U.S.	Metric
1985-89 1.6L engine		
Crankshaft		
Bend limit	0.0014 in.	0.035mm
Out of roundness	0.0012 in.	0.03mm
Taper	0.0028 in.	0.07mm
Grinding limit	0.0098 in.	0.25mm
Thrust clearance	0.0004-0.0037 in.	0.01-0.095mm
Main journal diameter		
Front and rear	1.9668-1.9673 in.	49.957-49.970mm
Center	1.9673-1.9678 in.	49.970-49.982mm
Main journal oil clearance	0.0004-0.0014 in.	0.010-0.035mm
Rod journal diameter	1.7715-1.7720 in.	44.995-45.010mm
Rod journal oil clearance	0.0008-0.0028 in.	0.020-0.070mm
Camshaft		
Bend limit	0.0020 in.	0.05mm
Thrust clearance	0.0008-0.0035 in.	0.020-0.090mm
Journal outer diameter		
Front and center	1.0220-1.0226 in.	25.959-25.975mm
Rear	1.4457-1.4163 in.	35.959-35.975mm
Journal to bore clearance	0.0010-0.0023 in.	0.025-0.059mm
Camshaft gear		
Runout	0.0098 in.	0.25mm
Backlash	0.0039 in.	0.10mm
Oil pump		
Drive gear diameter	1.1693-1.1709 in.	29.70-29.74mm
Rotor diameter	1.5957-1.5968 in.	40.53-40.56mm
Drive gear to rotor tip clearance	0.0008-0.0047 in.	0.02-0.12mm
Rotor to case axial clearance	0.0012-0.0051 in.	0.03-0.13mm
Gear to case axial clearance	0.0012-0.0051 in.	0.03-0.13mm
Rotor to case radial clearance	0.0059-0.0083 in.	0.15-0.21mm
Relief valve spring		
Free length	1.854 in.	40.7mm
Tension @ 1.319 in. height	8.56-9.44 lbs/	3.88-4.28 kg
Bypass valve spring		
Free length	1.602 in.	40.7mm
Tension @ 1.224 in. height	0.805-0.893 lbs.	0.365-0.405 kg
1985-92 1.8L engine (except XT)		
Cylinder head		
Surface warpage limit	0.0020 in.	0.05mm
Surface grinding limit	0.012 in.	0.3mm
Standard height	3.567 in.	90.6mm
Valve seat angle	90°	
Valve seat contact width		
Intake	0.047-0.071 in.	1.2-1.8mm
Exhaust	0.059-0.079 in.	1.5-2.0mm
Valve guide		
Inner diameter	0.2756-0.2762 in.	7.000-7.015mm
Protrusion	0.689-0.728 in.	17.5-18.5mm
Valve		
Overall length		
Non-turbo	4.2354 in.	107.58mm
Turbo		
Intake	4.2354 in.	107.58mm
Exhaust	4.256 in.	108.1mm
Head edge thickness limit		
Non-turbo	0.051 in.	1.3mm
Turbo		
Intake	0.051 in.	1.3mm
Exhaust	0.071 in.	1.8mm
Stem diameter		
Intake	0.2736-0.2742 in.	6.950-6.965mm
Exhaust	0.2734-0.2740 in.	6.945-6.960mm

ENGINE MECHANICAL SPECIFICATIONS

Component	U.S.	Metric
1985-92 1.8L engine (except XT)		
Stem oil clearance		
Intake	0.0014-0.0026 in.	0.035-0.065mm
Exhaust	0.0016-0.0028 in.	0.040-0.070mm
Valve spring		
Free length		
Outer spring	2.035 in.	51.7mm
Inner spring	1.980 in.	50.3mm
Tension		
Outer @ 1.643 in./41.5mm	39.9-45.9 lbs.	18.1-20.8 kg
Inner @ 1.516 in./38.5mm	19-8-22.7 lbs.	9.0-10.3 kg
Squareness		
Outer	0.091 in.	2.3mm
Inner	0.087 in.	2.2mm
Valve lash adjuster		
Crankcase bore inner diameter	0.8430-0.8453 in.	21.413-21.470mm
Lifter outer diameter	0.8417-0.8422 in.	21.680-21.393mm
Lifter to bore clearance	0.0008-0.0035 in.	0.020-0.090mm
Crankcase		
Cylinder bore		
Diameter	3.6214-3.6226 in.	91.985-92.015mm
Taper limit	0.0020 in.	0.050mm
Out of roundness limit	0.0020 in.	0.050mm
Cylinder to piston clearance	0.0004-0.0016 in.	0.010-0.040mm
Cylinder overbore limit	0.012 in.	0.3mm
Case warpage	0.0020 in.	0.050mm
Piston and Piston pin		
Piston outer diameter	3.6205-3.6216 in.	91.960-91.990mm
Piston pin bore inner diameter	0.8267-0.8271 in.	20.999-21.009mm
Piston pin outer diameter	0.8265-0.8268 in.	20.994-21.000mm
Piston pin to bore clearance	0.00004-0.00059 in.	0.001-0.015mm
Piston ring		
Ring gap		
Top and second	0.0079-0.0138 in.	0.2-0.35mm
Oil ring	0.012-0.035 in.	0.3-0.9mm
Ring to groove clearance		
Top	0.0016-0.0031 in.	0.040-0.080mm
Second	0.0012-0.0028 in.	0.030-0.070mm
Oil ring	0 in.	0mm
Connecting rod		
Center to center length	4.6043-4.6083 in.	1116.95-117.05mm
Twist per 3.94 in. (100mm)	0.0039 in.	0.10mm
Thrust clearance	0.0028-0.0130 in.	0.070-0.330mm
Piston pin to rod clearance	0-0.0009 in.	0-0.022mm
Rod small bore diameter	0.8268-0.8274 in.	21.000-21.016mm
Crankshaft		
Bend limit	0.0014 in.	0.035mm
Out of roundness	0.0012 in.	0.030mm
Grinding limit	0.0098 in.	0.250mm
Thrust clearance	0.0004-0.0037 in.	0.010-0.095mm
Main journal diameter	2.1637-2.1642 in.	54.957-54.972mm
Main journal oil clearance		
Front and rear	0.0004-0.0014 in.	0.003-0.036mm
Center	0.0003-0.0011 in.	0.008-0.027mm
Rod journal diameter	1.7715-1.7720 in.	44.995-45.010mm
Rod journal oil clearance	0.0004-0.0021 in.	0.010-0.054mm
Camshaft		
Bend limit	0.0010 in.	0.025mm
Thrust clearance	0.0012-0.0102 in.	0.030-0.260mm
Journal outer diameter		
Front and rear	1.4946-1.4953 in.	37.964-37.980mm
Center	1.9080-1.9087 in.	48.464-48.480mm
Distributor	1.5340-1.5346 in.	38.964-38.980mm
Oil clearance	0.0008-0.0021 in.	0.020-0.054mm

ENGINE MECHANICAL SPECIFICATIONS

Component	U.S.	Metric
1985-92 1.8L engine (except XT)		
Camshaft case		
Camshaft journal inner diameter		
Front	1.4961-1.4972 in.	38.000-38.030mm
Center	1.9094-1.9102 in.	48.500-48.518mm
Rear	1.8898-1.8905 in.	48.000-48.018mm
Distributor	1.5354-1.5361 in.	39.000-39.018mm
1985-91 1.8L XT engine		
Cylinder head		
Surface warpage limit	0.0020 in.	0.05mm
Surface grinding limit	0.012 in.	0.3mm
Standard height	3.567 in.	90.6mm
Valve seat angle	90°	
Valve seat contact width		
Intake	0.047-0.071 in.	1.2-1.8mm
Exhaust	0.059-0.079 in.	1.5-2.0mm
Valve guide		
Inner diameter	0.2756-0.2762 in.	7.000-7.015mm
Protrusion	0.689-0.728 in.	17.5-18.5mm
Valve		
Overall length		
Non-turbo	4.2354 in.	107.58mm
Turbo		
Intake	4.2354 in.	107.58mm
Exhaust	4.256 in.	108.1mm
Head edge thickness limit		
Non-turbo	0.051 in.	1.3mm
Turbo		
Intake	0.051 in.	1.3mm
Exhaust	0.071 in.	1.8mm
Stem diameter		
Intake	0.2736-0.2742 in.	6.950-6.965mm
Exhaust	0.2734-0.2740 in.	6.945-6.960mm
Stem oil clearance		
Intake	0.0014-0.0026 in.	0.035-0.065mm
Exhaust	0.0016-0.0028 in.	0.040-0.070mm
Valve spring		
Free length		
Outer spring	1.996 in.	50.7mm
Inner spring	1.980 in.	50.3mm
Tension		
Outer @ 1.643 in./41.5mm	45.6-53.6 lbs.	20.7-24.3 kg
Inner @ 1.516 in./38.5mm	19-8-22.7 lbs.	9.0-10.3 kg
Squareness		
Outer	0.087 in.	2.2mm
Inner	0.087 in.	2.2mm
Valve lash adjuster		
Crankcase bore inner diameter	0.8430-0.8453 in.	21.413-21.470mm
Lifter outer diameter	0.8417-0.8422 in.	21.680-21.393mm
Lifter to bore clearance	0.0008-0.0035 in.	0.020-0.090mm
Crankcase		
Cylinder bore		
Diameter	3.6214-3.6226 in.	91.985-92.015mm
Taper limit	0.0020 in.	0.050mm
Out of roundness limit	0.0020 in.	0.050mm
Cylinder to piston clearance	0.0004-0.0016 in.	0.010-0.040mm
Cylinder overbore limit	0.012 in.	0.3mm
Case warpage	0.0020 in.	0.050mm
Piston and Piston pin		
Piston outer diameter	3.6209-3.6213 in.	91.970-91.980mm
Piston pin bore inner diameter	0.8267-0.8271 in.	20.999-21.009mm
Piston pin outer diameter	0.8265-0.8268 in.	20.994-21.000mm
Piston pin to bore clearance	0.00004-0.00059 in.	0.001-0.015mm

ENGINE MECHANICAL SPECIFICATIONS

Component	U.S.	Metric
1985-91 1.8L XT engine		
Piston ring		
Ring gap		
Top and second	0.0079-0.0138 in.	0.2-0.35mm
Oil ring	0.012-0.035 in.	0.3-0.9mm
Ring to groove clearance		
Top	0.0016-0.0031 in.	0.040-0.080mm
Second	0.0012-0.0028 in.	0.030-0.070mm
Oil ring	0 in.	0mm
Connecting rod		
Center to center length	4.6043-4.6083 in.	1116.95-117.05mm
Twist per 3.94 in. (100mm)	0.0039 in.	0.10mm
Thrust clearance	0.0028-0.0130 in.	0.070-0.330mm
Piston pin to rod clearance	0-0.0009 in.	0-0.022mm
Rod small bore diameter	0.8268-0.8274 in.	21.000-21.016mm
Crankshaft		
Bend limit	0.0014 in.	0.035mm
Out of roundness	0.0012 in.	0.030mm
Grinding limit	0.0098 in.	0.250mm
Thrust clearance	0.0004-0.0037 in.	0.010-0.095mm
Main journal diameter	2.1637-2.1642 in.	54.957-54.972mm
Main journal oil clearance		
Front and rear	0.0001-0.0014 in.	0.003-0.036mm
Center	0.0003-0.0011 in.	0.008-0.027mm
Rod journal diameter	1.7715-1.7720 in.	44.995-45.010mm
Rod journal oil clearance	0.0004-0.0021 in.	0.010-0.054mm
Camshaft		
Bend limit	0.0010 in.	0.025mm
Thrust clearance	0.0012-0.0102 in.	0.030-0.260mm
Journal outer diameter		
Front	1.4946-1.4953 in.	37.964-37.980mm
Center	1.9080-1.9087 in.	48.464-48.480mm
Rear	1.8883-1.8890 in.	47.964-47.980mm
Distributor	1.5340-1.5346 in.	38.964-38.980mm
Oil clearance	0.0008-0.0021 in.	0.020-0.054mm
Camshaft case		
Camshaft journal inner diameter		
Front	1.4961-1.4972 in.	38.000-38.030mm
Center	1.9094-1.9102 in.	48.500-48.518mm
Rear	1.8898-1.8905 in.	48.000-48.018mm
Distributor	1.5354-1.5361 in.	39.000-39.018mm
1988-91 2.7L XT-6 engine		
Cylinder head		
Surface warpage limit	0.0030 in.	0.075mm
Surface grinding limit	0.012 in.	0.3mm
Standard height	3.567 in.	90.6mm
Valve seat angle	90°	
Valve seat contact width		
Intake	0.047-0.071 in.	1.2-1.8mm
Exhaust	0.059-0.079 in.	1.5-2.0mm
Valve guide		
Inner diameter	0.2756-0.2762 in.	7.000-7.015mm
Protrusion	0.67-0.71 in.	17-18mm
Valve		
Overall length	4.2354 in.	107.58mm
Head edge thickness limit	0.051 in.	1.3mm
Stem diameter		
Intake	0.2736-0.2742 in.	6.950-6.965mm
Exhaust	0.2734-0.2740 in.	6.945-6.960mm
Stem oil clearance		
Intake	0.0014-0.0026 in.	0.035-0.065mm
Exhaust	0.0016-0.0028 in.	0.040-0.070mm

ENGINE MECHANICAL SPECIFICATIONS

Component	U.S.	Metric
1988-91 2.7L XT-6 engine		
Valve spring		
Free length		
Outer spring	2.035 in.	51.7mm
Inner spring	1.980 in.	50.3mm
Tension		
Outer @ 1.643 in./41.5mm	39.9-45.9 lbs.	18.1-20.8 kg
Inner @ 1.516 in./38.5mm	19-8-22.7 lbs.	9.0-10.3 kg
Squareness		
Outer	0.091 in.	2.3mm
Inner	0.087 in.	2.2mm
Valve lash adjuster		
Crankcase bore inner diameter	0.8425-0.8441 in.	21.400-21.441mm
Lifter outer diameter	0.8417-0.8422 in.	21.680-21.393mm
Lifter to bore clearance	0.0003-0.0024 in.	0.007-0.061mm
Crankcase		
Cylinder bore		
Diameter	3.6214-3.6226 in.	91.985-92.015mm
Taper limit	0.0020 in.	0.050mm
Out of roundness limit	0.0020 in.	0.050mm
Cylinder to piston clearance	0.0006-0.0014 in.	0.015-0.035mm
Cylinder overbore limit	0.020 in.	0.5mm
Case warpage	0.0030 in.	0.075mm
Piston and Piston pin		
Piston outer diameter	3.6209-3.6213 in.	91.970-91.980mm
Piston pin bore inner diameter	0.8267-0.8271 in.	20.999-21.009mm
Piston pin outer diameter	0.8265-0.8268 in.	20.994-21.000mm
Piston pin to bore clearance	0.00004-0.00059 in.	0.001-0.015mm
Piston ring		
Ring gap		
Top and second	0.0079-0.0138 in.	0.2-0.35mm
Oil ring	0.012-0.035 in.	0.3-0.9mm
Ring to groove clearance		
Top	0.0016-0.0031 in.	0.040-0.080mm
Second	0.0012-0.0028 in.	0.030-0.070mm
Oil ring	0 in.	0mm
Connecting rod		
Center to center length	4.6043-4.6083 in.	1116.95-117.05mm
Twist per 3.94 in. (100mm)	0.0039 in.	0.10mm
Thrust clearance	0.0028-0.0130 in.	0.070-0.330mm
Piston pin to rod clearance	0-0.0009 in.	0-0.022mm
Rod small bore diameter	0.8268-0.8274 in.	21.000-21.016mm
Crankshaft		
Bend limit	0.0014 in.	0.035mm
Out of roundness	0.0012 in.	0.030mm
Grinding limit	0.0098 in.	0.250mm
Thrust clearance	0.0004-0.0037 in.	0.010-0.095mm
Main journal diameter	2.1637-2.1642 in.	54.957-54.972mm
Main journal oil clearance		
Front and rear	0.0001-0.0014 in.	0.003-0.036mm
Center	0.0003-0.0011 in.	0.008-0.027mm
Rod journal diameter	1.7715-1.7720 in.	44.995-45.010mm
Rod journal oil clearance	0.0004-0.0021 in.	0.010-0.054mm
Camshaft		
Bend limit	0.0010 in.	0.025mm
Thrust clearance	0.0012-0.0102 in.	0.030-0.260mm
Journal outer diameter		
Front	1.4946-1.4953 in.	37.964-37.980mm
Center	1.9080-1.9087 in.	48.464-48.480mm
Center II	1.8883-1.8890 in.	47.964-47.980mm
Rear	1.8883-1.8890 in.	47.964-47.980mm
Distributor	1.5340-1.5346 in.	38.964-38.980mm
Oil clearance	0.0008-0.0021 in.	0.020-0.054mm

ENGINE MECHANICAL SPECIFICATIONS

Component	U.S.	Metric
1988-91 2.7L XT-6 engine		
Camshaft case		
Camshaft journal inner diameter		
Front	1.4961-1.4972 in.	38.000-38.030mm
Center	1.9094-1.9102 in.	48.500-48.518mm
Center II	1.8898-1.8907 in.	48.000-48.025mm
Rear	1.8898-1.8905 in.	48.000-48.018mm
Distributor	1.5354-1.5361 in.	39.000-39.018mm
1990-92 2.2L engine		
Cylinder head		
Surface warpage limit	0.0020 in.	0.05mm
Surface grinding limit	0.004 in.	0.1mm
Standard height	3.870 in.	98.3mm
Valve seat angle	90°	
Valve seat contact width		
Intake	0.028 in.	0.7mm
Exhaust	0.039 in.	1.0mm
Valve guide		
Inner diameter	0.2362-0.2367 in.	6.000-6.012mm
Protrusion	0.689-0.709 in.	17.5-18.0mm
Valve		
Overall length		
Intake	3.976 in.	101.0mm
Exhaust	3.984 in.	101.2mm
Head edge thickness limit		
Intake	0.039 in.	1.0mm
Exhaust	0.047 in.	1.2mm
Stem diameter		
Intake	0.2343-0.2348 in.	5.950-5.965mm
Exhaust	0.2341-0.2346 in.	5.945-5.960mm
Stem oil clearance		
Intake	0.0014-0.0024 in.	0.035-0.062mm
Exhaust	0.0016-0.0026 in.	0.040-0.067mm
Valve spring		
Free length	1.8173 in.	46.16mm
Tension @ 1.457 in. height		42.8-49.4 lbs.
19.4-22.4 kg		
Squareness	0.079 in.	2.0mm
Crankcase		
Cylinder bore		
Diameter	3.8151-3.8155 in.	96.905-96.915mm
Taper limit	0.0006 in.	0.015mm
Out of roundness limit	0.0004 in.	0.010mm
Cylinder to piston clearance	0.004-0.0012 in.	0.010-0.030 mm
Cylinder overbore limit	0.020 in.	0.060mm
Case warpage	0.0020 in.	0.05mm
Piston and Piston pin		
Piston outer diameter	3.8144-3.8148 in.	96.885-96.895mm
Piston pin bore inner diameter	0.9055-0.9057 in.	23.000-23.006mm
Piston pin outer diameter	0.9053-0.9055 in.	22.994-23.000mm
Piston pin to bore clearance	0.0002-0.0003 in.	0.004-0.008mm
Piston ring		
Ring gap		
Top	0.0079-0.0138 in.	0.20-0.35mm
Second	0.0146-0.0205 in.	0.37-0.52mm
Oil ring	0.0079-0.0276 in.	0.20-0.70mm
Ring to groove clearance		
Top	0.0016-0.0031 in.	0.040-0.080mm
Second	0.0012-0.0028 in.	0.030-0.070mm
Connecting rod		
Twist per 3.94 in. (100mm)	0.0039 in.	0.070-0.330mm
Thrust clearance	0.0028-0.0130in.	0.070-0.330mm
Piston pin to rod clearance	0-0.0009 in.	0-0.022mm

ENGINE MECHANICAL SPECIFICATIONS

Component	U.S.	Metric
1990-92 2.2L engine		
Crankshaft		
Bend limit	0.0014 in.	0.035mm
Out of roundness	0.0012 in.	0.030mm
Grinding limit	0.0098 in.	0.250mm
Thrust clearance	0.0012-0.0045 in.	0.030-0.115mm
Main journal diameter	2.3616-2.3622 in.	59.984-60.000mm
Main journal oil clearance	0.0004-0.0012 in.	0.010-0.030mm
Rod journal diameter	2.0466-2.0472 in.	51.984-52.000mm
Rod journal oil clearance	0.0006-0.0017 in.	0.0158-0.0438mm
Camshaft		
Bend limit	0.0010 in.	0.025mm
Thrust clearance	0.0012 in.	0.0102mm
Journal outer diameter		
Front	1.2573-1.2579 in.	31.935-31.950mm
Center	1.4738-1.4744 in.	37.435-37.450mm
Rear	1.4935-1.49741 in.	37.935-37.950mm
Oil clearance	0.0022-0.0035 in.	0.055-0.090mm
Camshaft journal inner diameter		
Front	1.2600-1.2608 in.	32.005-32.025mm
Center	1.4766-1.4774 in.	37.505-37.525mm
Rear	1.4963-1.4970 in.	38.005-38.025mm
1992 3.3L engine		
Cylinder head		
Surface warpage limit	0.0020 in.	0.05mm
Surface grinding limit	0.0118 in.	0.3mm
Standard height	5.0200 in.	127.5mm
Valve seat angle	90°	
Valve seat contact width		
Intake	0.039 in.	1.0mm
Exhaust	0.059 in.	1.5mm
Valve guide		
Inner diameter	0.2362-0.2367 in.	6.000-6.012mm
Protrusion	0.335 in.	8.5mm
Valve		
Overall length		
Intake	3.5433 in.	90.0mm
Exhaust	3.5768 in.	90.85mm
Head edge thickness limit		
Intake	0.031 in.	0.8mm
Exhaust	0.039 in.	1.0mm
Stem diameter		
Intake	0.2344-0.2350 in.	5.955-5.970mm
Exhaust	0.2341-0.2346 in.	5.945-5.960mm
Stem oil clearance		
Intake	0.0012-0.0022 in.	0.030-0.057mm
Exhaust	0.0016-0.0026 in.	0.040-0.067mm
Valve spring		
Free length		
Outer spring	1.433 in.	36.4mm
Inner spring	1.374 in.	34.9mm
Tension		
Outer @ 1.14 in. height	28-32 lbs.	12.7-14.5 kg
Inner @ 1.083 in. height	13.2-15 lbs.	6-6.8 kg
Squareness		
Outer spring	0.063 in.	1.6mm
Inner spring	0.059 in.	1.5mm

ENGINE MECHANICAL SPECIFICATIONS

Component	U.S.	Metric
1992 3.3L engine		
Crankcase		
Cylinder bore		
Diameter	3.8151-3.8155 in.	96.905-96.915mm
Taper limit	0.0006 in.	0.015mm
Out of roundness limit	0.0004 in.	0.010mm
Cylinder to piston clearance	0.004-0.0012 in.	0.010-0.030 mm
Cylinder overbore limit	0.020 in.	0.060mm
Case warpage	0.0020 in.	0.05mm
Piston and Piston pin		
Piston outer diameter	3.8144-3.8148 in.	96.885-96.895mm
Piston pin bore inner diameter	0.9055-0.9057 in.	23.000-23.006mm
Piston pin outer diameter	0.9053-0.9055 in.	22.994-23.000mm
Piston pin to bore clearance	0.0002-0.0003 in.	0.004-0.008mm
Piston ring		
Ring gap		
Top	0.0079-0.0138 in.	0.20-0.35mm
Second	0.0146-0.0205 in.	0.37-0.52mm
Oil ring	0.0079-0.0276 in.	0.20-0.70mm
Ring to groove clearance		
Top	0.0016-0.0031 in.	0.040-0.080mm
Second	0.0012-0.0028 in.	0.030-0.070mm
Connecting rod		
Twist per 3.94 in. (100mm)	0.0039 in.	0.070-0.330mm
Thrust clearance	0.0028-0.0130in.	0.070-0.330mm
Piston pin to rod clearance	0-0.0009 in.	0-0.022mm
Crankshaft		
Bend limit	0.0014 in.	0.035mm
Out of roundness	0.0012 in.	0.030mm
Grinding limit	0.0098 in.	0.250mm
Thrust clearance	0.0028-0.0130 in.	0.070-0.330mm
Main journal diameter	2.3616-2.3622 in.	59.984-60.000mm
Main journal oil clearance	0.0004-0.0012 in.	0.010-0.030mm
Rod journal diameter	2.0466-2.0472 in.	51.984-52.000mm
Rod journal oil clearance	0.0008-0.0018 in.	0.020-0.046mm
Camshaft		
Bend limit	0.0008 in.	0.02mm
Thrust clearance		
Intake	0.0012 in.	0.0035mm
Exhaust	0.0008-0.0031 in.	0.02-0.08mm
Journal outer diameter		
Front	1.2577-1.2584 in.	31.946-31.963mm
All others	1.1002-1.1009 in.	27.946-27.963mm
Oil clearance	0.0015-0.0028 in.	0.037-0.072mm

Troubleshooting Basic Charging System Problems

Problem	Cause	Solution
Noisy alternator	• Loose mountings • Loose drive pulley • Worn bearings • Brush noise • Internal circuits shorted (High pitched whine)	• Tighten mounting bolts • Tighten pulley • Replace alternator • Replace alternator • Replace alternator
Squeal when starting engine or accelerating	• Glazed or loose belt	• Replace or adjust belt
Indicator light remains on or ammeter indicates discharge (engine running)	• Broken fan belt • Broken or disconnected wires • Internal alternator problems • Defective voltage regulator	• Install belt • Repair or connect wiring • Replace alternator • Replace voltage regulator
Car light bulbs continually burn out— battery needs water continually	• Alternator/regulator overcharging	• Replace voltage regulator/alternator
Car lights flare on acceleration	• Battery low • Internal alternator/regulator problems	• Charge or replace battery • Replace alternator/regulator
Low voltage output (alternator light flickers continually or ammeter needle wanders)	• Loose or worn belt • Dirty or corroded connections • Internal alternator/regulator problems	• Replace or adjust belt • Clean or replace connections • Replace alternator or regulator

Troubleshooting Basic Starting System Problems

Problem	Cause	Solution
Starter motor rotates engine slowly	• Battery charge low or battery defective • Defective circuit between battery and starter motor • Low load current • High load current	• Charge or replace battery • Clean and tighten, or replace cables • Bench-test starter motor. Inspect for worn brushes and weak brush springs. • Bench-test starter motor. Check engine for friction, drag or coolant in cylinders. Check ring gear-to-pinion gear clearance.
Starter motor will not rotate engine	• Battery charge low or battery defective • Faulty solenoid • Damage drive pinion gear or ring gear • Starter motor engagement weak • Starter motor rotates slowly with high load current • Engine seized	• Charge or replace battery • Check solenoid ground. Repair or replace as necessary. • Replace damaged gear(s) • Bench-test starter motor • Inspect drive yoke pull-down and point gap, check for worn end bushings, check ring gear clearance • Repair engine

Troubleshooting Basic Starting System Problems

Problem	Cause	Solution
Starter motor drive will not engage (solenoid known to be good)	• Defective contact point assembly	• Repair or replace contact point assembly
	• Inadequate contact point assembly ground	• Repair connection at ground screw
	• Defective hold-in coil	• Replace field winding assembly
Starter motor drive will not disengage	• Starter motor loose on flywheel housing	• Tighten mounting bolts
	• Worn drive end busing	• Replace bushing
	• Damaged ring gear teeth	• Replace ring gear or driveplate
	• Drive yoke return spring broken or missing	• Replace spring
Starter motor drive disengages prematurely	• Weak drive assembly thrust spring	• Replace drive mechanism
	• Hold-in coil defective	• Replace field winding assembly
Low load current	• Worn brushes	• Replace brushes
	• Weak brush springs	• Replace springs

Troubleshooting Engine Mechanical Problems

Problem	Cause	Solution
External oil leaks	• Fuel pump gasket broken or improperly seated	• Replace gasket
	• Cylinder head cover RTV sealant broken or improperly seated	• Replace sealant; inspect cylinder head cover sealant flange and cylinder head sealant surface for distortion and cracks
	• Oil filler cap leaking or missing	• Replace cap
External oil leaks	• Oil filter gasket broken or improperly seated	• Replace oil filter
	• Oil pan side gasket broken, improperly seated or opening in RTV sealant	• Replace gasket or repair opening in sealant; inspect oil pan gasket flange for distortion
	• Oil pan front oil seal broken or improperly seated	• Replace seal; inspect timing case cover and oil pan seal flange for distortion
	• Oil pan rear oil seal broken or improperly seated	• Replace seal; inspect oil pan rear oil seal flange; inspect rear main bearing cap for cracks, plugged oil return channels, or distortion in seal groove
	• Timing case cover oil seal broken or improperly seated	• Replace seal
	• Excess oil pressure because of restricted PCV valve	• Replace PCV valve
	• Oil pan drain plug loose or has stripped threads	• Repair as necessary and tighten
	• Rear oil gallery plug loose	• Use appropriate sealant on gallery plug and tighten
	• Rear camshaft plug loose or improperly seated	• Seat camshaft plug or replace and seal, as necessary
	• Distributor base gasket damaged	• Replace gasket

Troubleshooting Engine Mechanical Problems (cont.)

Problem	Cause	Solution
Excessive oil consumption	• Oil level too high • Oil with wrong viscosity being used • PCV valve stuck closed • Valve stem oil deflectors (or seals) are damaged, missing, or incorrect type • Valve stems or valve guides worn • Poorly fitted or missing valve cover baffles • Piston rings broken or missing • Scuffed piston • Incorrect piston ring gap • Piston rings sticking or excessively loose in grooves • Compression rings installed upside down • Cylinder walls worn, scored, or glazed	• Drain oil to specified level • Replace with specified oil • Replace PCV valve • Replace valve stem oil deflectors • Measure stem-to-guide clearance and repair as necessary • Replace valve cover • Replace broken or missing rings • Replace piston • Measure ring gap, repair as necessary • Measure ring side clearance, repair as necessary • Repair as necessary • Repair as necessary
Connecting rod bearing noise	• Insufficient oil supply • Carbon build-up on piston • Bearing clearance excessive or bearing missing • Crankshaft connecting rod journal out-of-round • Misaligned connecting rod or cap • Connecting rod bolts tightened improperly	• Inspect for low oil level and low oil pressure • Remove carbon from piston crown • Measure clearance, repair as necessary • Measure journal dimensions, repair or replace as necessary • Repair as necessary • Tighten bolts with specified torque
Piston noise	• Piston-to-cylinder wall clearance excessive (scuffed piston) • Cylinder walls excessively tapered or out-of-round • Piston ring broken • Loose or seized piston pin • Connecting rods misaligned • Piston ring side clearance excessively loose or tight • Carbon build-up on piston is excessive	• Measure clearance and examine piston • Measure cylinder wall dimensions, rebore cylinder • Replace all rings on piston • Measure piston-to-pin clearance, repair as necessary • Measure rod alignment, straighten or replace • Measure ring side clearance, repair as necessary • Remove carbon from piston
Valve actuating component noise	• Insufficient oil supply • Push rods worn or bent • Rocker arms or pivots worn	• Check for: (a) Low oil level (b) Low oil pressure (c) Plugged push rods (d) Wrong hydraulic tappets (e) Restricted oil gallery (f) Excessive tappet to bore clearance • Replace worn or bent push rods • Replace worn rocker arms or pivots

Troubleshooting Engine Mechanical Problems (cont.)

Problem	Cause	Solution
Valve actuating component noise	• Foreign objects or chips in hydraulic tappets	• Clean tappets
	• Excessive tappet leak-down	• Replace valve tappet
	• Tappet face worn	• Replace tappet; inspect corresponding cam lobe for wear
	• Broken or cocked valve springs	• Properly seat cocked springs; replace broken springs
	• Stem-to-guide clearance excessive	• Measure stem-to-guide clearance, repair as required
	• Valve bent	• Replace valve
	• Loose rocker arms	• Tighten bolts with specified torque
	• Valve seat runout excessive	• Regrind valve seat/valves
	• Missing valve lock	• Install valve lock
	• Push rod rubbing or contacting cylinder head	• Remove cylinder head and remove obstruction in head
	• Excessive engine oil (four-cylinder engine)	• Correct oil level
	• Piston ring gaps not properly staggered	• Repair as necessary
	• Excessive main or connecting rod bearing clearance	• Measure bearing clearance, repair as necessary
No oil pressure	• Low oil level	• Add oil to correct level
	• Oil pressure gauge, warning lamp or sending unit inaccurate	• Replace oil pressure gauge or warning lamp
	• Oil pump malfunction	• Replace oil pump
	• Oil pressure relief valve sticking	• Remove and inspect oil pressure relief valve assembly
	• Oil passages on pressure side of pump obstructed	• Inspect oil passages for obstruction
	• Oil pickup screen or tube obstructed	• Inspect oil pickup for obstruction
	• Loose oil inlet tube	• Tighten or seal inlet tube
Low oil pressure	• Low oil level	• Add oil to correct level
	• Inaccurate gauge, warning lamp or sending unit	• Replace oil pressure gauge or warning lamp
	• Oil excessively thin because of dilution, poor quality, or improper grade	• Drain and refill crankcase with recommended oil
	• Excessive oil temperature	• Correct cause of overheating engine
	• Oil pressure relief spring weak or sticking	• Remove and inspect oil pressure relief valve assembly
	• Oil inlet tube and screen assembly has restriction or air leak	• Remove and inspect oil inlet tube and screen assembly. (Fill inlet tube with lacquer thinner to locate leaks.)
	• Excessive oil pump clearance	• Measure clearances
	• Excessive main, rod, or camshaft bearing clearance	• Measure bearing clearances, repair as necessary
High oil pressure	• Improper oil viscosity	• Drain and refill crankcase with correct viscosity oil
	• Oil pressure gauge or sending unit inaccurate	• Replace oil pressure gauge
	• Oil pressure relief valve sticking closed	• Remove and inspect oil pressure relief valve assembly

Troubleshooting Engine Mechanical Problems (cont.)

Problem	Cause	Solution
Main bearing noise	• Insufficient oil supply	• Inspect for low oil level and low oil pressure
	• Main bearing clearance excessive	• Measure main bearing clearance, repair as necessary
	• Bearing insert missing	• Replace missing insert
	• Crankshaft end play excessive	• Measure end play, repair as necessary
	• Improperly tightened main bearing cap bolts	• Tighten bolts with specified torque
	• Loose flywheel or drive plate	• Tighten flywheel or drive plate attaching bolts
	• Loose or damaged vibration damper	• Repair as necessary

Troubleshooting the Cooling System

Problem	Cause	Solution
High temperature gauge indication— overheating	• Coolant level low	• Replenish coolant
	• Fan belt loose	• Adjust fan belt tension
	• Radiator hose(s) collapsed	• Replace hose(s)
	• Radiator airflow blocked	• Remove restriction (bug screen, fog lamps, etc.)
	• Faulty radiator cap	• Replace radiator cap
	• Ignition timing incorrect	• Adjust ignition timing
	• Idle speed low	• Adjust idle speed
	• Air trapped in cooling system	• Purge air
	• Heavy traffic driving	• Operate at fast idle in neutral intermittently to cool engine
	• Incorrect cooling system component(s) installed	• Install proper component(s)
	• Faulty thermostat	• Replace thermostat
	• Water pump shaft broken or impeller loose	• Replace water pump
	• Radiator tubes clogged	• Flush radiator
	• Cooling system clogged	• Flush system
	• Casting flash in cooling passages	• Repair or replace as necessary. Flash may be visible by removing cooling system components or removing core plugs.
	• Brakes dragging	• Repair brakes
	• Excessive engine friction	• Repair engine
	• Antifreeze concentration over 68%	• Lower antifreeze concentration percentage
	• Missing air seals	• Replace air seals
	• Faulty gauge or sending unit	• Repair or replace faulty component
	• Loss of coolant flow caused by leakage or foaming	• Repair or replace leaking component, replace coolant
	• Viscous fan drive failed	• Replace unit
Low temperature indication— undercooling	• Thermostat stuck open	• Replace thermostat
	• Faulty gauge or sending unit	• Repair or replace faulty component

Troubleshooting the Cooling System (cont.)

Problem	Cause	Solution
Coolant loss—boilover	• Overfilled cooling system	• Reduce coolant level to proper specification
	• Quick shutdown after hard (hot) run	• Allow engine to run at fast idle prior to shutdown
	• Air in system resulting in occasional "burping" of coolant	• Purge system
	• Insufficient antifreeze allowing coolant boiling point to be too low	• Add antifreeze to raise boiling point
	• Antifreeze deteriorated because of age or contamination	• Replace coolant
	• Leaks due to loose hose clamps, loose nuts, bolts, drain plugs, faulty hoses, or defective radiator	• Pressure test system to locate source of leak(s) then repair as necessary
Coolant loss—boilover	• Faulty head gasket	• Replace head gasket
	• Cracked head, manifold, or block	• Replace as necessary
	• Faulty radiator cap	• Replace cap
Coolant entry into crankcase or cylinder(s)	• Faulty head gasket	• Replace head gasket
	• Crack in head, manifold or block	• Replace as necessary
Coolant recovery system inoperative	• Coolant level low	• Replenish coolant to FULL mark
	• Leak in system	• Pressure test to isolate leak and repair as necessary
	• Pressure cap not tight or seal missing, or leaking	• Repair as necessary
	• Pressure cap defective	• Replace cap
	• Overflow tube clogged or leaking	• Repair as necessary
	• Recovery bottle vent restricted	• Remove restriction
Noise	• Fan contacting shroud	• Reposition shroud and inspect engine mounts
	• Loose water pump impeller	• Replace pump
	• Glazed fan belt	• Apply silicone or replace belt
	• Loose fan belt	• Adjust fan belt tension
	• Rough surface on drive pulley	• Replace pulley
	• Water pump bearing worn	• Remove belt to isolate. Replace pump.
	• Belt alignment	• Check pulley alignment. Repair as necessary.
No coolant flow through heater core	• Restricted return inlet in water pump	• Remove restriction
	• Heater hose collapsed or restricted	• Remove restriction or replace hose
	• Restricted heater core	• Remove restriction or replace core
	• Restricted outlet in thermostat housing	• Remove flash or restriction
	• Intake manifold bypass hole in cylinder head restricted	• Remove restriction
	• Faulty heater control valve	• Replace valve
	• Intake manifold coolant passage restricted	• Remove restriction or replace intake manifold

NOTE: *Immediately after shutdown, the engine enters a condition known as heat soak. This is caused by the cooling system being inoperative while engine temperature is still high. If coolant temperature rises above boiling point, expansion and pressure may push some coolant out of the radiator overflow tube. If this does not occur frequently it is considered normal.*

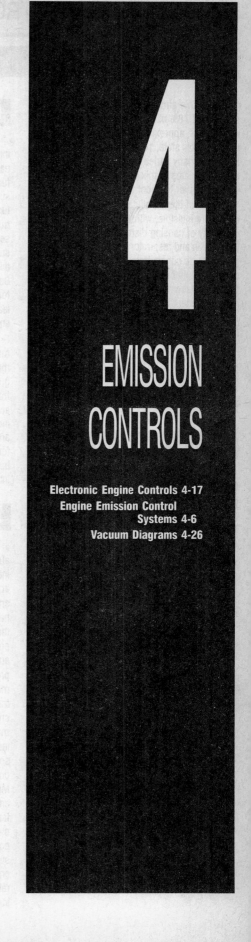

4

EMISSION CONTROLS

AIR POLLUTION

The earth's atmosphere, at or near sea level, consists of 78% nitrogen, 21% oxygen and 1% other gases, approximately. If it were possible to remain in this state, 100% clean air would result. However, many varied causes allow other gases and particulates to mix with the clean air, causing the air to become unclean or polluted.

Certain of these pollutants are visible while others are invisible, with each having the capability of causing distress to the eyes, ears, throat, skin and respiratory system. Should these pollutants be concentrated in a specific area and under the right conditions, death could result due to the displacement or chemical change of the oxygen content in the air. These pollutants can cause much damage to the environment and to the many man made objects that are exposed to the elements.

To better understand the causes of air pollution, the pollutants can be categorized into 3 separate types, natural, industrial and automotive.

Natural Pollutants

Natural pollution has been present on earth before man appeared and is still a factor to be considered when discussing air pollution, although it causes only a small percentage of the present overall pollution problem existing in our country. It is the direct result of decaying organic matter, wind born smoke and particulates from such natural events as plains and forest fires (ignited by heat or lightning), volcanic ash, sand and dust which can spread over a large area of the countryside.

Such a phenomenon of natural pollution has been recent volcanic eruptions, with the resulting plume of smoke, steam and volcanic ash blotting out the sun's rays as it spreads and rises higher into the atmosphere, where the upper air currents catch and carry the smoke and ash, while condensing the steam back into water vapor. As the water vapor, smoke and ash traveled on their journey, the smoke dissipates into the atmosphere while the ash and moisture settle back to earth in a trail hundred of miles long. In many cases, lives are lost and millions of dollars of property damage result, and ironically, man can only stand by and watch it happen.

Industrial Pollution

Industrial pollution is caused primarily by industrial processes, the burning of coal, oil and natural gas, which in turn produces smoke and fumes. Because the burning fuels contain much sulfur, the principal ingredients of smoke and fumes are sulfur dioxide (SO_2) and particulate matter. This type of pollutant occurs most severely during still, damp and cool weather, such as at night. Even in its less severe form, this pollutant is not confined to just cities. Because of air movements, the pollutants move for miles over the surrounding countryside, leaving in its path a barren and unhealthy environment for all living things.

Working with Federal, State and Local mandated rules, regulations and by carefully monitoring the emissions, industries have greatly reduced the amount of pollutant emitted from their industrial sources, striving to obtain an acceptable level. Because of the mandated industrial emission clean up, many land areas and streams in and around the cities that were formerly barren of vegetation and life, have now begun to move back in the direction of nature's intended balance.

Automotive Pollutants

The third major source of air pollution is the automotive emissions. The emissions from the internal combustion engine were not an appreciable problem years ago because of the small number of registered vehicles and the nation's small highway system. However, during the early 1950's, the trend of the American people was to move from the cities to the surrounding suburbs. This caused an immediate problem in the transportation areas because the majority of the suburbs were not afforded mass transit conveniences. This lack of transportation created an attractive market for the automobile manufacturers, which resulted in a dramatic increase in the number of vehicles produced and sold, along with a marked increase in highway construction between cities and the suburbs. Multi-vehicle families emerged with much emphasis placed on the individual vehicle per family member. As the increase in vehicle ownership and usage occurred, so did the pollutant levels in and around the cities, as the suburbanites drove daily to their businesses and employment in the city and its fringe area, returning at the end of the day to their homes in the suburbs.

It was noted that a fog and smoke type haze was being formed and at times, remained in suspension over the cities and did not quickly dissipate. At first this "smog", derived from the words "smoke" and "fog", was thought to result from industrial pollution but it was determined that the automobile emissions were largely to blame. It was discovered that as normal automobile emissions were exposed to sunlight for a period of time, complex chemical reactions would take place.

It was found the smog was a photo chemical layer and was developed when certain oxides of nitrogen (NOx) and unburned hydrocarbons (HC) from the automobile emissions were exposed to sunlight and was more severe when the smog would remain stagnant over an area in which a warm layer of air would settle over the top of a cooler air mass at ground level, trapping and holding the automobile emissions, instead of the emissions being dispersed and diluted through normal air flows. This type of air stagnation was given the name "Temperature Inversion".

Temperature Inversion

In normal weather situations, the surface air is warmed by the heat radiating from the earth's surface and the sun's rays and will rise upward, into the atmosphere, to be cooled through a convection type heat expands with the cooler upper air. As the warm air rises, the surface pollutants are carried upward and dissipated into the atmosphere.

When a temperature inversion occurs, we find the higher air is no longer cooler but warmer than the surface air, causing the cooler surface air to become trapped and unable to move. This warm air blanket can extend from above ground level to a few hundred or even a few thousand feet into the air. As the surface air is trapped, so are the pollutants, causing a severe smog condition. Should this stagnant air mass extend to a few thousand feet high, enough air movement with the inversion takes place to allow the smog layer to rise above ground level but the pollutants still cannot dissipate. This inversion can remain for days over an area, with only the smog level rising or lowering from ground level to a few hundred feet high. Meanwhile, the pollutant levels increases, causing eye irritation, respirator problems, reduced visibility, plant damage and in some cases, cancer type diseases.

This inversion phenomenon was first noted in the Los Angeles, California area. The city lies in a basin type of terrain and during certain weather conditions, a cold air mass is held in the basin while a warmer air mass covers it like a lid.

Because this type of condition was first documented as prevalent in the Los Angeles area, this type of smog was named Los Angeles Smog, although it occurs in other areas where a large concentration of automobiles are used and the air remains stagnant for any length of time.

Internal Combustion Engine Pollutants

Consider the internal combustion engine as a machine in which raw materials must be placed so a finished product comes out. As in any machine operation, a certain amount of wasted material is formed. When we relate this to the internal combustion engine, we find that by

putting in air and fuel, we obtain power from this mixture during the combustion process to drive the vehicle. The by-product or waste of this power is, in part, heat and exhaust gases with which we must concern ourselves.

HEAT TRANSFER

The heat from the combustion process can rise to over 4000°F (2204°C). The dissipation of this heat is controlled by a ram air effect, the use of cooling fans to cause air flow and having a liquid coolant solution surrounding the combustion area and transferring the heat of combustion through the cylinder walls and into the coolant. The coolant is then directed to a thin-finned, multi-tubed radiator, from which the excess heat is transferred to the outside air by 1 or all of the 3 heat transfer methods, conduction, convection or radiation.

The cooling of the combustion area is an important part in the control of exhaust emissions. To understand the behavior of the combustion and transfer of its heat, consider the air/fuel charge. It is ignited and the flame front burns progressively across the combustion chamber until the burning charge reaches the cylinder walls. Some of the fuel in contact with the walls is not hot enough to burn, thereby snuffing out or Quenching the combustion process. This leaves unburned fuel in the combustion chamber. This unburned fuel is then forced out of the cylinder along with the exhaust gases and into the exhaust system.

Many attempts have been made to minimize the amount of unburned fuel in the combustion chambers due to the snuffing out or "Quenching", by increasing the coolant temperature and lessening the contact area of the coolant around the combustion area. Design limitations within the combustion chambers prevent the complete burning of the air/fuel charge, so a certain amount of the unburned fuel is still expelled into the exhaust system, regardless of modifications to the engine.

EXHAUST EMISSIONS

Composition Of The Exhaust Gases

The exhaust gases emitted into the atmosphere are a combination of burned and unburned fuel. To understand the exhaust emission and its composition review some basic chemistry.

When the air/fuel mixture is introduced into the engine, we are mixing air, composed of nitrogen (78%), oxygen (21%) and other gases (1%) with the fuel, which is 100% hydrocarbons (HC), in a semi-controlled ratio. As the combustion process is accomplished, power is produced to move the vehicle while the heat of combustion is transferred to the cooling system. The exhaust gases are then composed of nitrogen, a diatomic gas (N_2), the same as was introduced in the engine, carbon dioxide (CO2), the same gas that is used in beverage carbonation and water vapor (H_2O). The nitrogen (N_2), for the most part passes through the engine unchanged, while the oxygen (O_2) reacts (burns) with the hydrocarbons (HC) and produces the carbon dioxide (CO_2) and the water vapors (H_2O). If this chemical process would be the only

process to take place, the exhaust emissions would be harmless. However, during the combustion process, other pollutants are formed and are considered dangerous. These pollutants are carbon monoxide (CO), hydrocarbons (HC), oxides of nitrogen (NOx) oxides of sulfur (SOx) and engine particulates.

Lead (Pb), is considered 1 of the particulates and is present in the exhaust gases whenever leaded fuels are used. Lead (Pb) does not dissipate easily. Levels can be high along roadways when it is emitted from vehicles and can pose a health threat. Since the increased usage of unleaded gasoline and the phasing out of leaded gasoline for fuel, this pollutant is gradually diminishing. While not considered a major threat lead is still considered a dangerous pollutant.

HYDROCARBONS

Hydrocarbons (HC) are essentially unburned fuel that have not been successfully burned during the combustion process or have escaped into the atmosphere through fuel evaporation. The main sources of incomplete combustion are

rich air/fuel mixtures, low engine temperatures and improper spark timing. The main sources of hydrocarbon emission through fuel evaporation come from the vehicle's fuel tank and carburetor bowl.

To reduce combustion hydrocarbon emission, engine modifications were made to minimize dead space and surface area in the combustion chamber. In addition the air/fuel mixture was made more lean through improved carburetion, fuel injection and by the addition of external controls to aid in further combustion of the hydrocarbons outside the engine. Two such methods were the addition of an air injection system, to inject fresh air into the exhaust manifolds and the installation of a catalytic converter, a unit that is able to burn traces of hydrocarbons without affecting the internal combustion process or fuel economy.

To control hydrocarbon emissions through fuel evaporation, modifications were made to the fuel tank and carburetor bowl to allow storage of the fuel vapors during periods of engine shut-down, and at specific times during engine operation, to purge and burn these same vapors by blending them with the air/fuel mixture.

CARBON MONOXIDE

Carbon monoxide is formed when not enough oxygen is present during the combustion process to convert carbon (C) to carbon dioxide (CO_2). An increase in the carbon monoxide (CO) emission is normally accompanied by an increase in the hydrocarbon (HC) emission because of the lack of oxygen to completely burn all of the fuel mixture.

Carbon monoxide (CO) also increases the rate at which the photo chemical smog is formed by speeding up the conversion of nitric oxide (NO) to nitrogen dioxide (NO_2). To accomplish this, carbon monoxide (CO) combines with oxygen (O_2) and nitrogen dioxide (NO_2) to produce carbon dioxide (CO_2) and nitrogen dioxide (NO_2). ($CO + O_2 + NO = CO_2 + NO_2$).

The dangers of carbon monoxide, which is an odorless, colorless toxic gas are many. When carbon monoxide is inhaled into the lungs and passed into the blood stream, oxygen is replaced by the carbon monoxide in the red blood cells, causing a reduction in the amount of oxygen being supplied to the many parts of the body. This lack of oxygen causes headaches, lack of coordination, reduced mental alertness and should the carbon monoxide concentration be high enough, death could result.

NITROGEN

Normally, nitrogen is an inert gas. When heated to approximately 2500°F (1371°C) through the combustion process, this gas becomes active and causes an increase in the nitric oxide (NOx) emission.

Oxides of nitrogen (NOx) are composed of approximately 97–98% nitric oxide (NO2). Nitric oxide is a colorless gas but when it is passed into the atmosphere, it combines with oxygen and forms nitrogen dioxide (NO2). The nitrogen dioxide then combines with chemically active hydrocarbons (HC) and when in the presence of sunlight, causes the formation of photo chemical smog.

OZONE

To further complicate matters, some of the nitrogen dioxide (NO_2) is broken apart by the sunlight to form nitric oxide and oxygen. (NO_2 + sunlight = NO + O). This single atom of oxygen then combines with diatomic (meaning 2 atoms) oxygen (O_2) to form ozone (O_3). Ozone is 1 of the smells associated with smog. It has a pungent and offensive odor, irritates the eyes and lung tissues, affects the growth of plant life and causes rapid deterioration of rubber products. Ozone can be formed by sunlight as well as electrical discharge into the air.

The most common discharge area on the automobile engine is the secondary ignition electrical system, especially when inferior quality spark plug cables are used. As the surge of high voltage is routed through the secondary cable, the circuit builds up an electrical field around the wire, acting upon the oxygen in the surrounding air to form the ozone. The faint glow along the cable with the engine running that may be visible on a dark night, is called the "corona discharge." It is the result of the electrical field passing from a high along the cable, to a low in the surrounding air, which forms the ozone gas. The combination of corona and ozone has been a major cause of cable deterioration. Recently, different types and better quality insulating materials have lengthened the life of the electrical cables.

Although ozone at ground level can be harmful, ozone is beneficial to the earth's inhabitants. By having a concentrated ozone layer called the 'ozonosphere', between 10 and 20 miles (16–32km) up in the atmosphere much of the ultra violet radiation from the sun's rays are absorbed and screened. If this ozone layer were not present, much of the earth's surface would be burned, dried and unfit for human life.

There is much discussion concerning the ozone layer and its density. A feeling exists that this protective layer of ozone is slowly diminishing and corrective action must be directed to this problem. Much experimenting is presently being conducted to determine if a problem exists and if so, the short and long term effects of the problem and how it can be remedied.

OXIDES OF SULFUR

Oxides of sulfur (SOx) were initially ignored in the exhaust system emissions, since the sulfur content of gasoline as a fuel is less than $\frac{1}{10}$ of 1%. Because of this small amount, it was felt that it contributed very little to the overall pollution problem. However, because of the difficulty in solving the sulfur emissions in industrial pollutions and the introduction of catalytic converter to the automobile exhaust systems, a change was mandated. The automobile exhaust system, when equipped with a catalytic converter, changes the sulfur dioxide (SO_2) into the sulfur trioxide (SO_3).

When this combines with water vapors (H_2O); a sulfuric acid mist (H_2SO_4) is formed and is a very difficult pollutant to handle and is extremely corrosive. This sulfuric acid mist that is formed, is the same mist that rises from the vents of an automobile storage battery when an active chemical reaction takes place within the battery cells.

When a large concentration of vehicles equipped with catalytic converters are operating in an area, this acid mist will rise and be distributed over a large ground area causing land, plant, crop, paints and building damage.

PARTICULATE MATTER

A certain amount of particulate matter is present in the burning of any fuel, with carbon constituting the largest percentage of the particulates. In gasoline, the remaining percentage of particulates is the burned remains of the various other compounds used in its manufacture. When a gasoline engine is in good internal condition, the particulate emissions are low but as the engine wears internally, the particulate emissions increase. By visually inspecting the tail pipe emissions, a determination can be made as to where an engine defect may exist. An engine with light gray smoke emitting from the tail pipe normally indicates an increase in the oil consumption through burning due to internal engine wear. Black smoke would indicate a defective fuel delivery system, causing the engine to operate in a rich mode. Regardless of the color of the smoke, the internal part of the engine or the fuel delivery system should be repaired to a "like new" condition to prevent excess particulate emissions.

Diesel and turbine engines emit a darkened plume of smoke from the exhaust system because of the type of fuel used. Emission control regulations are mandated for this type of emission and more stringent measures are being used to prevent excess emission of the particulate matter. Electronic components are being introduced to control the injection of the fuel at precisely the proper time of piston travel, to achieve the optimum in fuel ignition and fuel usage. Other particulate after-burning components are being tested to achieve a cleaner particular emission.

Good grades of engine lubricating oils should be used, meeting the manufacturers specification. "Cut-rate" oils can contribute to the particulate emission problem because of their low "flash" or ignition temperature point. Such oils burn prematurely during the combustion process causing emissions of particulate matter.

The cooling system is an important factor in the reduction of particulate matter. With the cooling system operating at a temperature specified by the manufacturer, the optimum of combustion will occur. The cooling system must be maintained in the same manner as the engine oiling system, as each system is required to perform properly in order for the engine to operate efficiently for a long time.

Other Automobile Emission Sources

Before emission controls were mandated on the internal combustion engines, other sources of engine pollutants were discovered, along with the exhaust emission. It was determined the engine combustion exhaust produced 60% of the total emission pollutants, fuel evaporation from the fuel tank and carburetor vents produced 20%, with the another 20% being produced through the crankcase as a by-product of the combustion process.

CRANKCASE EMISSIONS

Crankcase emissions are made up of water, acids, unburned fuel, oil fumes and particulates. The emissions are classified as hydrocarbons (HC) and are formed by the small amount of unburned, compressed air/fuel mixture entering the crankcase from the combustion area during the compression and power strokes, between the cylinder walls and piston rings. The head of the compression and combustion help to form the remaining crankcase emissions.

Since the first engines, crankcase emissions were allowed to go into the air through a road draft tube, mounted on the lower side of the engine block. Fresh air came in through an open oil filler cap or breather. The air passed through the crankcase mixing with blow-by gases. The motion of the vehicle and the air blowing past the open end of the road draft tube caused a low pressure area at the end of the tube. Crankcase emissions were simply drawn out of the road draft tube into the air.

To control the crankcase emission, the road draft tube was deleted. A hose and/or tubing was routed from the crankcase to the intake manifold so the blow-by emission could be burned with the air/fuel mixture. However, it was found that intake manifold vacuum, used to draw the crankcase emissions into the manifold, would vary in strength at the wrong time and not allow the proper emission flow. A regulating type valve was needed to control the flow of air through the crankcase.

Testing, showed the removal of the blow-by gases from the crankcase as quickly as possible, was most important to the longevity of the engine. Should large accumulations of blow-by gases remain and condense, dilution of the engine oil would occur to form water, soots, resins, acids and lead salts, resulting in the formation of sludge and varnishes. This condensation of the blow-by gases occur more frequently on vehicles used in numerous starting and stopping conditions, excessive idling and when the engine is not allowed to attain normal operating temperature through short runs. The crankcase purge control or PCV system will be described in detail later in this section.

FUEL EVAPORATIVE EMISSIONS

Gasoline fuel is a major source of pollution, before and after it is burned in the automobile engine. From the time the fuel is refined, stored, pumped and transported, again stored until it is pumped into the fuel tank of the vehicle, the gasoline gives off unburned hydrocarbons (HC) into the atmosphere. Through redesigning of the storage areas and venting systems, the pollution factor has been diminished but not eliminated, from the refinery standpoint. However, the automobile still remained the primary source of vaporized, unburned hydrocarbon (HC) emissions.

Fuel pumped form an underground storage tank is cool but when exposed to a warner ambient temperature, will expand. Before controls were mandated, an owner would fill the fuel tank with fuel from an underground storage tank and park the vehicle for some time in warm area, such as a parking lot. As the fuel would warm, it would expand and should no provisions or area be provided for the expansion, the fuel would spill out the filler neck and onto the ground, causing hydrocarbon (HC) pollution and creating a severe fire hazard. To correct this condition, the vehicle manufacturers added overflow plumbing and/or gasoline tanks with built in expansion areas or domes.

However, this did not control the fuel vapor emission from the fuel tank and the carburetor bowl. It was determined that most of the fuel evaporation occurred when the vehicle was stationary and the engine not operating. Most vehicles carry 5–25 gallons (19–95 liters) of gasoline. Should a large concentration of vehicles be parked in one area, such as a large parking lot, excessive fuel vapor emissions would take place, increasing as the temperature increases.

To prevent the vapor emission from escaping into the atmosphere, the fuel system is designed to trap the fuel vapors while the vehicle is stationary, by sealing the fuel system from the atmosphere. A storage system is used to collect and hold the fuel vapors from the carburetor and the fuel tank when the engine is not operating. When the engine is started, the storage system is then purged of the fuel vapors, which are drawn into the engine and burned with the air/fuel mixture.

The components of the fuel evaporative system will be described in detail later in this section.

EMISSION CONTROLS

Crankcase Ventilation System

OPERATION

▶ SEE FIG. 1–4

A Positive Crankcase Ventilation (PCV) system is used to help reduce emission of blow-by gasses into the atmosphere. The system consists of a sealed oil filler cap, rocker covers with an emission outlet and fresh air inlet, connecting hoses, PCV valve and air cleaner.

At part throttle, blow-by gas in the crankcase flows into the intake manifold through the PCV valve by the strong vacuum of the intake manifold. Under this condition, the fresh air is introduced into the crankcase through the rocker cover fresh air inlet.

At wide open throttle, a part of the blow-by gas flows into the air intake duct through the connecting hose and is drawn to the throttle chamber. The system uses this route because the reduced intake manifold vacuum is not able to draw the increased amount of blow-by gases generated by the wide open throttle condition through the PCV valve.

TESTING

The PCV valve should be checked at regular intervals and replaced as required. If the valve is found to be defective, do not clean, replace it. Connection and system hoses can be cleaned by using compressed air. Check all hoses for clogging, split or hardening condition. Replace as necessary.

1. With the engine running, remove the valve from its mounting. A hissing sound should be heard and vacuum should be felt from the inlet side of the valve.

2. Reinstall the valve. Remove the crankcase inlet air cleaner. Loosely hold a piece of stiff paper over the opening in the rocker cover. Allow one minute for the crankcase pressure to reduce. The paper should then be pulled against the rocker cover with noticeable force. Replace the inlet air cleaner in the rocker cover.

3. With the engine stopped, remove the PCV valve and shake. A clicking sound should be heard indicating that the valve is not stuck.

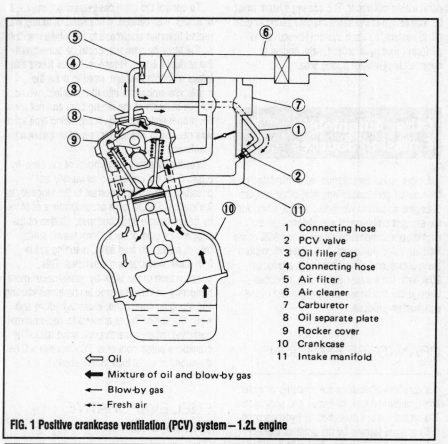

⇐ Oil
◀ Mixture of oil and blow-by gas
← Blow-by gas
◀-- Fresh air

1 Connecting hose
2 PCV valve
3 Oil filler cap
4 Connecting hose
5 Air filter
6 Air cleaner
7 Carburetor
8 Oil separate plate
9 Rocker cover
10 Crankcase
11 Intake manifold

FIG. 1 Positive crankcase ventilation (PCV) system—1.2L engine

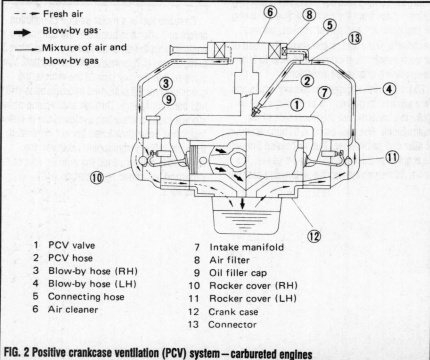

--→ Fresh air
➤ Blow-by gas
→ Mixture of air and blow-by gas

1 PCV valve
2 PCV hose
3 Blow-by hose (RH)
4 Blow-by hose (LH)
5 Connecting hose
6 Air cleaner
7 Intake manifold
8 Air filter
9 Oil filler cap
10 Rocker cover (RH)
11 Rocker cover (LH)
12 Crank case
13 Connector

FIG. 2 Positive crankcase ventilation (PCV) system—carbureted engines

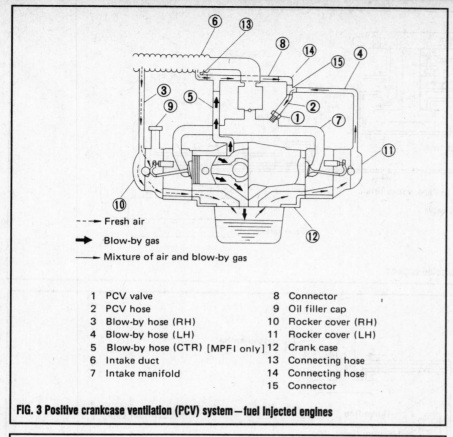

--- ► Fresh air

➡ Blow-by gas

⟶ Mixture of air and blow-by gas

1	PCV valve	8	Connector
2	PCV hose	9	Oil filler cap
3	Blow-by hose (RH)	10	Rocker cover (RH)
4	Blow-by hose (LH)	11	Rocker cover (LH)
5	Blow-by hose (CTR) [MPFI only]	12	Crank case
6	Intake duct	13	Connecting hose
7	Intake manifold	14	Connecting hose
		15	Connector

FIG. 3 Positive crankcase ventilation (PCV) system — fuel Injected engines

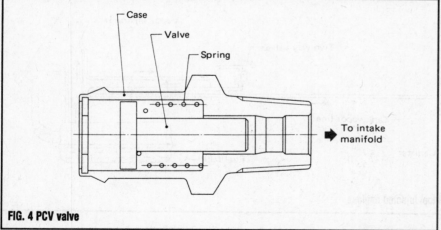

FIG. 4 PCV valve

4. If the valve fails any of the above tests, it should be replaced.

Evaporative Emission Control System

OPERATION

► SEE FIG. 5–8

The evaporative emission control system is employed to prevent evaporated fuel in the fuel tank or carburetor bowl (carbureted engines only) from being discharged into the atmosphere. System components differ slightly according to the model of the vehicle and the type of fuel system, but all systems function in the same manner.

Gasoline vapor from the fuel tank (and carburetor bowl) is introduced into a canister mounted in the engine compartment. This canister is filled with activated charcoal which absorbs the vapors and stores them. This function of the canister is continuous and is performed whether the engine is running or stopped; the function of the float chamber ventilation valve is only performed when the engine is stopped.

In order to clear the charcoal canister of vapors, the system purges the canister while the engine is running. When predetermined engine conditions are met, usually when the engine is at normal operating temperature and running at a speed greater than idle, a purge control valve opens to allow the stored vapors to enter the intake tract. The purge control valve can be vacuum or electrically controlled.

Once the purge control valve is open, the stored vapors in the canister are drawn, along with the incoming air/fuel charge, into the combustion chamber and burned. Fresh air is allowed to enter the canister through a filter in the bottom to fully purge the system.

Most models use a fuel separator, mounted on the fuel tank, to prevent liquid fuel from being transferred to the charcoal canister in the event of severe cornering or abrupt stops. Liquid fuel in the separator is returned to the fuel tank through a hose at the rear of the tank. On the, a fuel cut valve is used to control liquid fuel from entering the vapor pipe. The rising level of the fuel from the tank causes a float to move op and close the cap hole to prevent fuel entering the pipe.

A two-way valve is used on all vehicles to allow the fuel tank to breathe. When a vacuum is created in the fuel tank due to the fuel pump suck fuel, the two-way valve opens to allow a flow of air from the vapor canister to the tank. When pressure is built up in the tank, the valve opens in the opposite direction to allow the pressure to be vented into the charcoal canister. In the event of a two-way valve failure, the fuel cap is fitted with a valve to allow the tank to ingest air. This will prevent a collapse of the tank.

TESTING

There are several things which should be checked if a malfunction of the evaporative emission control system is suspected. These include deterioration of the vacuum lines, deteriorated, disconnected or pinched hoses, improperly routed hoses and/or a defective filler cap.

In the most severe cases of evaporative emissions system failure, the fuel tank may collapse. This condition is caused by a clogged or pinched vent line, a defective vapor separator, or a plugged or incorrect filler cap. The incorrect or faulty components do not allow the fuel tank to breathe and thus create a vacuum in the tank, causing it to collapse.

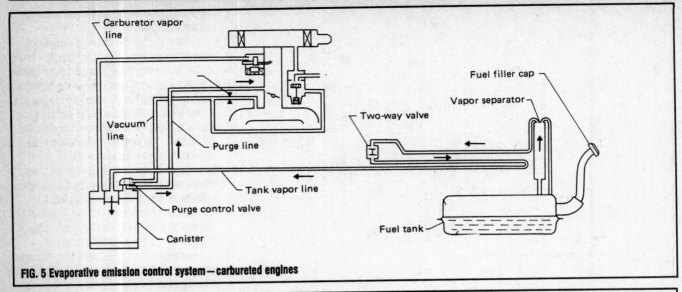

FIG. 5 Evaporative emission control system — carbureted engines

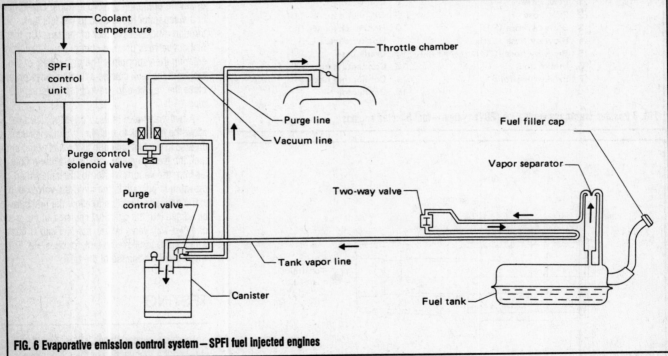

FIG. 6 Evaporative emission control system — SPFI fuel injected engines

Purge Lines and Canister

1. Remove the fuel filler cap.

2. Disconnect the evaporation line at the evaporation pipe.

3. Check for an unobstructed evaporation line on the fuel tank side by blowing air into the hose. A little resistance should be felt due to the two-way valve.

➡ **Take care not to suck on the hose as this causes fuel evaporation vapors to enter your mouth. This may cause serious injury.**

4. Check for an unobstructed evaporation line on the canister side by blowing air into the hose. A little resistance should be felt due to the two-way valve.

5. If an obstruction is found, remove the two-way valve and retest. If the obstruction is still present, clean or replace the line. If not, test the two-way valve and replace as necessary.

6. Check all lines for cracks or deterioration. Replace as necessary.

7. Check the exterior of the canister for damage and replace as necessary.

Two-way Valve

1. Remove the two-way valve.

2. Check for air passage by blowing air into the lower nipple. A little resistance should be felt due to the functioning of the valve.

3. Repeat the test blowing into the upper nipple.

4. Check the valve case for cracks for deterioration.

5. Replace the valve if it fails any of the above tests.

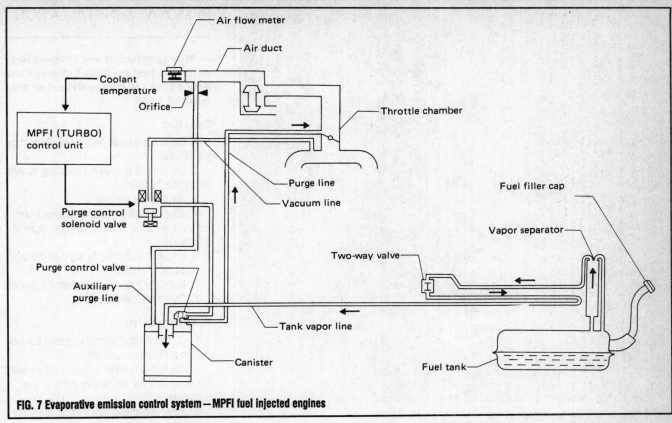

FIG. 7 Evaporative emission control system — MPFI fuel injected engines

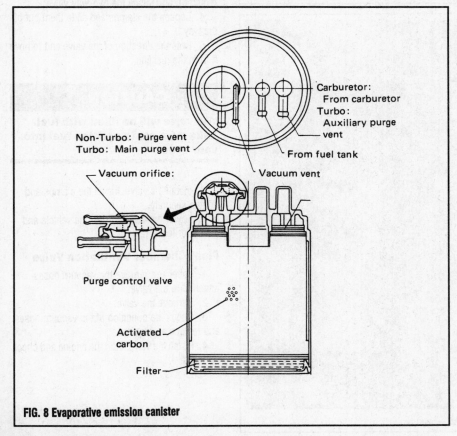

FIG. 8 Evaporative emission canister

Canister Purge Control Valve

The canister purge control valve is part of the fuel system and controlled by the engine control unit. For diagnosis and testing procedures, refer to Electronic Engine Controls in this Section.

Float Chamber Ventilation Valve

This valve is used on carbureted engines only.

1. Check the resistance between the (+) and (−) terminals. Resistance should be 16–20 ohms for the Justy and 32.7–39.9 for all other vehicles. If not, replace the solenoid valve.

2. Check the resistance between the (+) and (−) terminals and the solenoid valve body. Resistance should be 1M ohm or more. If not, replace the solenoid valve.

3. Check the vacuum passage for opening and closing operation while applying electric current to both (+) and (−) terminals. If the vacuum passage fails to open when current is not applied or fails to close when current is applied, replace the solenoid valve.

Fuel Filler Cap

1. To test the filler cap (if it is the safety valve type), clean it and place it against your.

2. Blow into the relief valve housing.

3. If the cap passes pressure with light blowing or if it fails to release with hard blowing, it is defective and must be replaced.

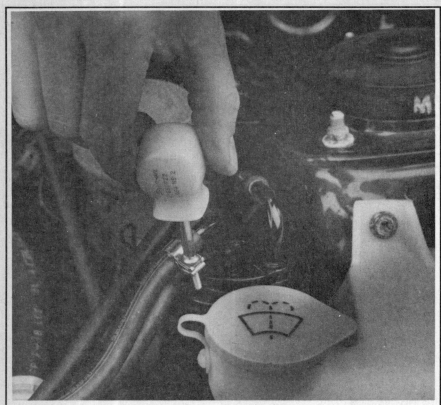

FIG. 8a Removing the evaporative emission canister hoses—Legacy

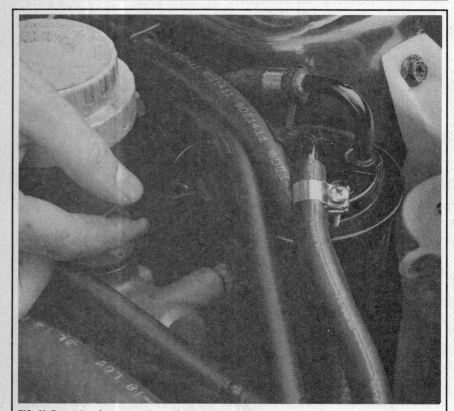

FIG. 8b Removing the evaporative emission canister—Legacy

REMOVAL & INSTALLATION

➡ **When replacing any evaporative emission system hoses, always use hoses that are fuel resistant or are marked EVAP.**

Canister

1. Label and remove the vacuum lines from the canister.
2. Loosen and remove the attaching screws holding the canister.
3. Remove the canister.
4. When installing the canister, check and replace any vacuum hoses that show signs of deterioration.
5. Inspect the canister for signs of damage and replace as required.
6. Install the canister and tighten the screws.
7. Connect the vacuum lines.

Two-Way Valve

1. On fuel injected vehicles, release the fuel system pressure as required.
2. The two-way valve is located on the fuel line either near the fuel tank or in the engine compartment.
3. Raise and support the vehicle safely (as required), and locate the two-way valve.
4. Loosen the clamps and slide them out of the way.
5. Note the direction of the valve and remove it from the fuel line.

❄ CAUTION

The valve will be filled with fuel. Take care not to spill the fuel into your eyes.

6. Install the valve, install the clamps and tighten securely.
7. Lower the vehicle. Start the vehicle and check for leaks.

Float Chamber Ventilation Valve

1. Label and remove the vacuum hoses attached to the valve.
2. Remove the valve.
3. Check the condition of the vacuum hoses and replace as required.
4. Install the valve, start the engine and check for leaks.

Exhaust Gas Recirculation (EGR) System

♦ SEE FIG. 9–14

OPERATION

The function of the Exhaust Gas Recirculation (EGR) system is the reduction of NOx (oxides of nitrogen) by reducing the combustion temperature through recirculating a part of the exhaust gas into the cylinders.

The EGR valve opens in response engine vacuum. A thermo-valve, or on computer controlled engines a solenoid valve, is used to control the amount of vacuum reaching the EGR valve. When engine performance would suffer due to the recirculating gasses, normally during start-up, the valves remained closed to not allow vacuum to reach the EGR valve. When predetermined conditions are met, the valves open to allow the EGR valve to function according engine vacuum.

TESTING

➡ **The EGR system on the SVX is diagnosed and tested via the on board diagnostics.**

EGR Valve and Flow Passages

1. Start the engine and allow it to reach operating temperature.

2. Looking through the opening in the EGR valve body, check if the valve shaft moves when the engine is revved to 3000–3500 rpm under a no load condition. If the shaft moves, goto Step 4.

➡ **During the test in Step 2, the EGR solenoid valve should be removed from SPFI fuel injected engines.**

3. If the shaft does not move, check the EGR valve with a hand vacuum pump. Apply 8 in. Hg of vacuum and see if the shaft moves. If not, remove the valve and clean or replace. If the valve functions properly, check for leaks in the EGR vacuum lines.

4. With the engine idling, connect a hand vacuum pump to the EGR valve. Apply 8 in. Hg of vacuum to the valve. The engine should stall or idle roughly. If not, clean the obstruction from the exhaust gas passages in the cylinder head.

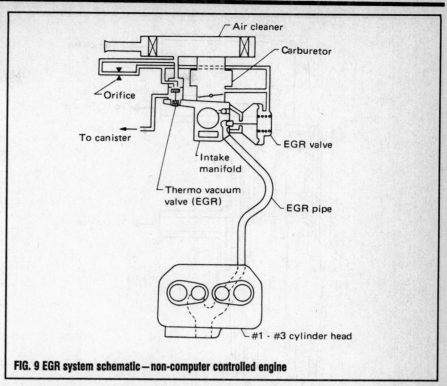

FIG. 9 EGR system schematic—non-computer controlled engine

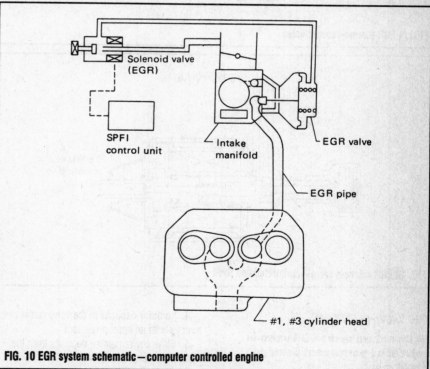

FIG. 10 EGR system schematic—computer controlled engine

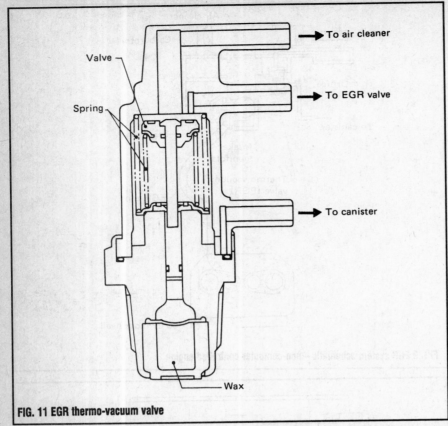

FIG. 11 EGR thermo-vacuum valve

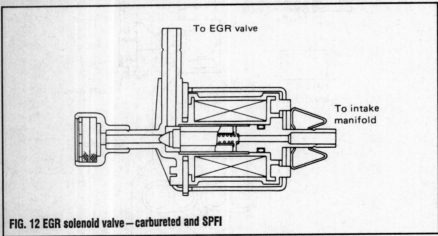

FIG. 12 EGR solenoid valve—carbureted and SPFI

EGR VALVE CLEANING

➡ **Do not wash the EGR valve in solvent as permanent damage could result.**

1. Hold the valve assembly in hand and lightly tap with a plastic hammer to remove the exhaust deposits from the valve seat.
2. With a wire brush, remove the deposits from the mounting surfaces of the valve.
3. Depress the valve and look at the seat area. If valve and seat are not clean, repeat the cleaning procedures above.

4. Look for deposits in the valve outlet and remove with an appropriate tool.
5. Blow any remaining deposits from the valve with compressed air.
6. Check the EGR valve for proper operation using a hand vacuum pump.

EXHAUST GAS PASSAGE CLEANING

1. Inspect the EGR gas inlet to intake manifold for deposits. Remove any deposits present with a hooked awl taking care to minimize the amount of material falling into the intake manifold.

2. Remove all deposits using a vacuum.
3. Remove the EGR pipe and lightly tap with a plastic hammer to loosen deposits. Blow clean using compressed air.

Thermo-Vacuum Valve

This valve is used only on non-computer controlled engines.

1. Drain the cooling system and remove the thermo-vacuum valve.
2. With the valve at 86°F (30°C) or less, air should pass through the first and second port when the third port is plugged. Air should pass through the second and third port when the first port is plugged.
3. Heat the valve to 104°F (40°C) and repeat the tests in Step 2. Air should not pass.
4. If the valve does not function properly, it should be replaced.

Vacuum Solenoid Valve

1. Remove the electrical connector.
2. Check the resistance between the positive and negative terminals of the valve. Resistance should be 32.7–39.9 ohms.
3. Check the resistance between the positive or negative terminals and the body. Resistance should be 1M ohm or more.
4. Check the vacuum passage for opening and closing operation while applying electric current on both the positive and negative terminals. With no electricity applied, the passage between the EGR and intake manifold ports should be open. When the electricity is applied, the passage between the EGR and intake manifold ports should be closed.
5. If the valve does not function properly, it should be replaced.

REMOVAL & INSTALLATION

EGR Valve

1. Detach the vacuum hose from the EGR valve.
2. Remove the two nuts which secure the EGR valve to the intake manifold.
3. Remove the valve and gasket from the manifold.

To Install:

4. Inspect the exhaust gas passages in the intake manifold and clean as necessary. Clean the EGR valve as necessary.
5. Using a new gasket, install the EGR valve.
6. Tighten the EGR valve securing nuts to 17-19 ft. lbs.
7. Check the vacuum hose for deterioration and replace as necessary. Install the hose on the EGR valve.

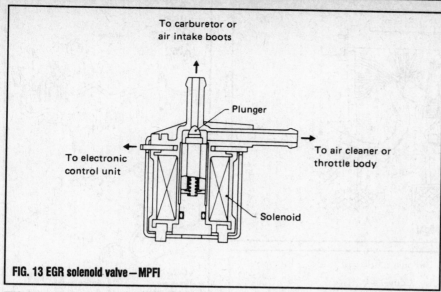

FIG. 13 EGR solenoid valve — MPFI

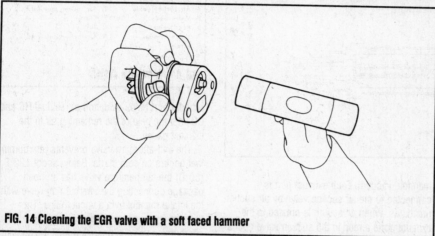

FIG. 14 Cleaning the EGR valve with a soft faced hammer

Thermo-Vacuum Valve

1. Drain the cooling system below the level of the thermo-vacuum valve.
2. Label and remove the vacuum hoses.
3. Remove the thermo-valve using an appropriately sized wrench.

To Install:

4. Install the thermo-vacuum valve after coating the threads with sealant. Tighten the valve securely.
5. Inspect the vacuum hoses for signs of deterioration and replace as necessary.
6. Connect the vacuum hoses.
7. Refill the cooling system.

Vacuum Solenoid Valve

1. Disconnect the vacuum solenoid wiring harness.
2. Label and remove the vacuum hoses.
3. Remove the solenoid valve attaching screws and remove the solenoid valve.

To Install:

4. Inspect the vacuum hoses for signs of deterioration and replace as necessary.
5. Connect the vacuum hoses.
6. Connect the vacuum solenoid wiring harness.

Service Maintenance Reminder Light

▶ SEE FIG. 15

Some models are equipped with an EGR warning light, located in the instrument cluster, that will illuminate at approximately 30,000–50,000 miles. When the EGR light is lit, it is indicating that the EGR system should be checked and possibly that the EGR valve should be replaced.

➡ **It should be noted that turbocharged California specification vehicles do not use the warning light system.**

After the EGR system has been checked and all necessary maintenance performed, reset the warning light as follows:

1. Remove the left cover under the instrument panel. Pull down the warning light connectors from behind the fuse panel.
2. Locate the single pin blue connector that is connected to another single pin blue connector. Near the blue connectors is a single green connector that is not connected to any wire terminal.
3. Unplug the connector from the blue connector and plug it into the green connector. This will reset the warning light.

Oxygen Sensor

▶ SEE FIG. 16

The oxygen sensor is a type of concentration cell that generates an electrical signal to the ratio of oxygen in the exhaust gases. The signal is greater when the engine is running rich (smaller air-fuel ratio) and smaller when the engine is running lean (larger air-fuel ratio). As the mixture changes, the oxygen sensor sends signals to the engine control unit to adjust the fuel mixture as required.

The oxygen sensor is installed on either the exhaust manifold or in the exhaust pipe near the catalytic converter.

TESTING

Oxygen sensor diagnosis and testing is covered in Electronic Engine Controls under the specific type of fuel system used on your vehicle.

REMOVAL & INSTALLATION

1. Disconnect the oxygen sensor electrical connector.
2. Remove the exhaust manifold plate, as required.
3. Apply penetrating solvent to the threaded portion of the oxygen sensor, and leave it for one minute or more.
4. Loosen the sensor by turning it 10-40° with a wrench.
5. Apply penetrating solvent again and leave it for one minute or more.
6. Remove the oxygen sensor.

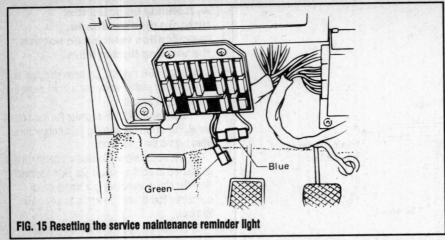

FIG. 15 Resetting the service maintenance reminder light

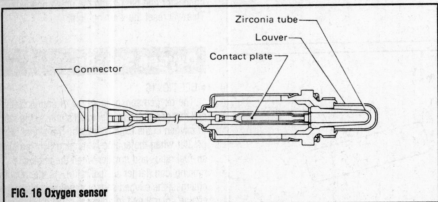

FIG. 16 Oxygen sensor

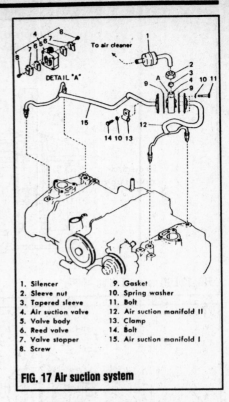

1. Silencer
2. Sleeve nut
3. Tapered sleeve
4. Air suction valve
5. Valve body
6. Reed valve
7. Valve stopper
8. Screw
9. Gasket
10. Spring washer
11. Bolt
12. Air suction manifold II
13. Clamp
14. Bolt
15. Air suction manifold I

FIG. 17 Air suction system

➡ **When removing, do not force the oxygen sensor, especially when the exhaust manifold is cold, otherwise it will damage the exhaust manifold.**

To Install:

7. Apply an anti-seize compound only to the threaded portion of the sensor.

8. Install the sensor into the exhaust manifold and torque it 18-25 ft. lbs.

9. Install the exhaust manifold plate, as required.

10. Connect the oxygen sensor electrical connector.

Air Injection (AI) System

OPERATION

♦ SEE FIG. 17 and 18

The AI system utilizes the vacuum created by exhaust gas pulsation and normal intake manifold vacuum. Each exhaust port is connected to the air suction valve by air suction manifolds. When a vacuum is created in the exhaust ports a reed in the suction valve opens allowing fresh air to be sucked into the exhaust ports. When there is pressure rather than vacuum in the exhaust ports, the reed in the air suction valve closes, preventing the flow of exhaust gases.

The fresh air sucked through the air suction valve is used for oxidation of HC and CO in the exhaust passages and partly for combustion in the cylinders

The system incorporates an electronically controlled solenoid that either deactivates this system entirely, or partially a short time after the engine is started cold. The only way to determine that there is a problem with this system is to remove the solenoid and test it electrically.

These models also incorporate an Air Suction Valve which can be disassembled and serviced. See the procedure below for service.

Various models have an exhaust port liner made from stainless steel plate built into the cylinder head as one unit. The port liner has a built in air layer which decreases heat transfer to the cylinder head while keeping the exhaust port at a higher temperature. The insulation of the exhaust port helps oxidation of residual HC and CO with the help of the remaining air in the exhaust gases.

The anti-afterburn valve prevents afterburning that occurs on cold starts. Below about 122°F (50°C) the temperature valve has an open passage connecting the afterburning valve with the intake manifold via a vacuum line. The vacuum line remains opened and the afterburning valve in operation until the coolant temperature becomes hot enough to shut off the vacuum and override the afterburning system.

TESTING

Air Suction Valve

1. Remove the air suction valve.

2. Blow air through the air inlet to see if air flows smoothly through the outlet while emitting a hissing sound. If air dies not flow smoothly, the read valve is stuck closed. Replace the reed valve.

3. Blow air through the outlet to see if air flows through the inlet. If air flows, the reed valve is broken or stuck open. Replace the reed valve.

4. Check the valve after it has been disassembled, as follows:

　a. Check the inlet and outlet case for cracks or damage.

　b. Check the gasket for cracks or damage.

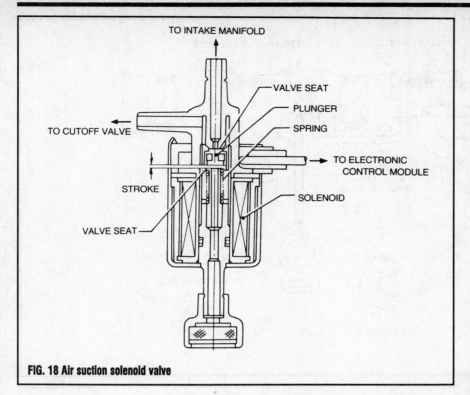

FIG. 18 Air suction solenoid valve

Labels in figure:
TO INTAKE MANIFOLD
TO CUTOFF VALVE
STROKE
VALVE SEAT
VALVE SEAT
PLUNGER
SPRING
TO ELECTRONIC CONTROL MODULE
SOLENOID

c. Clean the reed valve thoroughly.

d. Check for check for waves, cracks or dents in the seat.

e. Check the the reed for cracks or a broken point.

f. Check the valve for a rusty stopper.

OVERHAUL

1. Remove the three screws, and separate the control valve assembly, seat, and reed valve cover.

2. Separate the reed valve assembly by pulling it and its gasket from the inside of the valve cover.

3. Remove the O-ring from the control valve assembly.

4. Now, inspect the valve parts as follows:

a. Apply vacuum to the vacuum inlet. The valve should retract fully. Release the vacuum. The valve should extend fully.

b. Check the O-ring for cracks or other damage.

c. Inspect the reed valve gasket for damage. Then, clean the reed valve in a safe, non-volatile solvent and inspect it for any damage such as waviness, cracks or dents, or rust.

5. Replace all damaged or worn parts.

6. Install the O-ring on the control valve assembly.

7. Join the reed valve assembly making sure the gasket stay inside of the valve cover.

8. Install the three screws, joining the control valve assembly, seat, and reed valve cover.

Air Suction Solenoid

1. Remove the solenoid electrical connector.

2. Check the resistance between the (+) and (–) terminals. Resistance should be 32.7–39.9 ohms.

3. Check the resistance between the (+) or (–) terminals and the solenoid body. Resistance should be 1M ohm or more.

4. Check the vacuum passage for opening and closing operation while applying battery voltage to the (+) and (–) terminals.

5. If the solenoid does not function as specified, replace the solenoid.

REMOVAL & INSTALLATION

Air Suction Valve

1. Remove the air silencer or secondary air cleaner.

2. Remove the four bolts which run through the air suction valve, mounting it between the two air suction manifolds.

3. Pull the suction valve from between the manifolds. Take care not to damage the reeds.

➡ **If the gaskets on the sides of the air suction valve are worn or damaged, replace them.**

4. Using new gaskets install the air suction valve and tighten the bolts securely.

5. Install the air silencer or secondary air cleaner.

Air Suction Manifolds

1. Remove the air silencer or secondary air cleaner and the air suction valve.

2. Remove the clamp which supports the right side suction manifold by loosening the mounting bolt.

3. Loosen the threaded sleeves (two on each manifold) which mount the suction manifolds to the engine. Lift off the manifolds.

4. Remember to lightly oil the threaded sleeves before mounting the suction manifold to the engine.

5. Install the manifolds and tighten the sleeves securely.

6. Install the clamp which supports the right side suction manifold.

7. Install the air silencer or secondary air cleaner and the air suction valve.

Hot Air Control System

The hot air control system is used on carbureted vehicles only. The purpose of the system is to reduce HC emissions and improve engine performance during warmup. This is accomplished by deflecting either cool outside air or warm engine heated air into the carburetor, depending upon engine operating conditions.

The system works automatically be means of a temperature sensor and vacuum motor. The temperature sensor detects the inlet air temperature and controls the flow of vacuum to the vacuum motor. Together they regulate the air control valve, mounted in the air horn.

The possible combinations of inlet (underhood) air temperatures and vacuum readings, and the resulting valve operation, are as follows:

• Under hood temperature below 100°F (38°C) with vacuum below 1.57 in Hg at motor diaphragm — valve closed and cold air admitted.

• Under hood temperature below 100°F (38°C) with vacuum above 6.30 in Hg at motor diaphragm — valve closed and hot air admitted.

• Under hood temperature between 100–127°F (38–53°C) with varying vacuum at motor diaphragm — valve open and hot/cold air mixture admitted.

• Under hood temperature above 127°F (53°C) with no vacuum at motor diaphragm — valve open and cold air admitted.

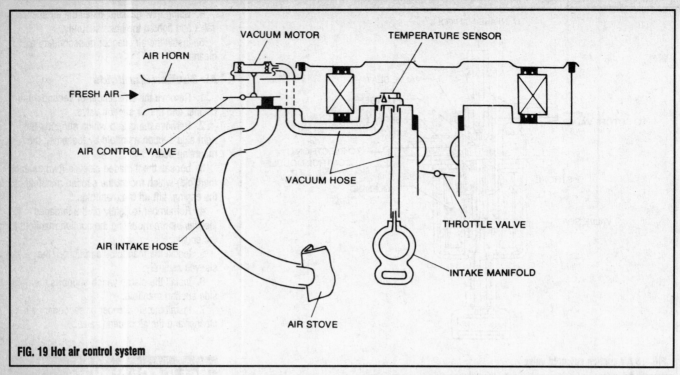

FIG. 19 Hot air control system

TESTING

Air Control Valve

1. If the car is running, turn off engine.
2. Place a mirror at the end of the air cleaner.
3. Inspect the position of the air control valve. The proper position is with the fresh air vent open and the hot air inlet closed.
4. If the position is not as described in Step 3, check the air control valve linkage for sticking.

Vacuum Motor

1. Keep mirror in position and engine off.
2. Remove the vacuum hose from the vacuum motor.
3. Connect a separate piece of the same type of hose to the now vacant vacuum motor. Insert the other end of the new hose into your mouth and draw in a breath, creating a vacuum in the vacuum motor.
4. Check the position of the air control valve. The fresh air vent should be closed and the hot air inlet open.
5. Now, pinch the hose attached to the vacuum motor so that the vacuum is not instantly lost. The valve position described in #4 should be maintained for more than 30 seconds.
6. If the motor does not function properly, it should be replaced.

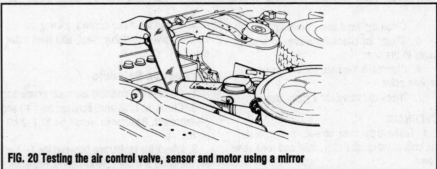

FIG. 20 Testing the air control valve, sensor and motor using a mirror

Temperature Sensor

❄ WARNING

Engine must be cold before starting this test.

1. Keep the mirror in position, as described above.
2. Start the engine and keep it idling.
3. Check the position of the air control valve immediately after starting. The fresh air vent should be closed and the hot air inlet open.
4. Continue to watch the air control valve as the engine warms up. The fresh air vent should gradually open.
5. If the sensor does not function properly, it should be replaced.

REMOVAL & INSTALLATION

Temperature Sensor

1. Remove the air cleaner cover and filter.
2. Using pliers, flatten the clip securing the vacuum hose to the temperature sensor and remove the hose.
3. Now pull the same clip completely away from the sensor. Lift the sensor off the air cleaner.

➡ **The gasket between the sensor and air cleaner is glued to the air cleaner and should be removed. Always install a new clip when the temperature sensor is reinstalled.**

4. Install the sensor and attach a new clip.
5. Install the air cleaner cover and filter.

Vacuum Motor

1. Remove the screws securing the vacuum motor to the air cleaner.

2. Disconnect the vacuum motor valve shaft from the air control valve, and remove the vacuum motor from the air cleaner.

3. Install the vacuum motor valve shaft on the air control valve.

4. Install the vacuum motor on the air cleaner and tighten the screws securely.

ELECTRONIC ENGINE CONTROLS

Electronic Controlled Carburetor (ECC)

An electronically controlled carburetor (ECC) is used on 1985–1988 1.6L and 1.8L engines.

The air/fuel ratio of an engine equipped with a catalytic converter needs to be controlled to a value within a very narrow range to allow the converter purify the exhaust gas. The ECC system is employed to control the air/fuel ratio.

The system includes: an oxygen sensor, and electronic control module (ECM, a duty solenoid and a carburetor. The components provide a feedback system to control the air/fuel ratio during operation by supplying a measured amount of air into the carburetor air bleeders. To avoid feedback during certain driving conditions, vacuum switches, a thermosensor and an engine speed sensing circuit are provided.

ECC COMPONENT FUNCTIONS

Oxygen Sensor

The oxygen sensor is installed on the exhaust manifold and provides information to the Electronic Control Module (ECM) that pertains to the amount of pollutants in the exhaust gases caused by an over rich or lean air/fuel ratio.

Electronic Control Module (ECM)

Upon receiving information from the oxygen sensor (value of the air/fuel mixture) the ECM signals the duty solenoid to allow either more or less air into the carburetor to maintain the correct air/fuel mixture.

Duty Solenoid

The Duty Solenoid(s) is (are) controlled by the ECM. At a given signal, the Duty Solenoid will admit more or less air to the carburetor, maintaining the proper air/fuel ratio.

➡ **On engines equipped with an Hitachi carburetor, two duty solenoids are installed on the exhaust manifold. Models equipped with a C-W carburetor have the duty solenoid mounted on the carburetor.**

Vacuum Switches and Thermosensor

Vacuum switches, thermosensors (and speed sensing circuits) furnish information to the ECM to help determine the air/fuel ratio.

TESTING

Self-Diagnosis Function

The system has a self-diagnosis function. When trouble occurs, the Electronic Control System (ECS) lamp is illuminated and the trouble code is displayed on the oxygen sensor lamp in morse code.

Changeover From Regular Mode To Test Mode

The self-diagnosis function is available in two modes: Regular Mode and Test Mode. It is automatically changed over to the test mode by connecting the test mode connector located under the dash near the steering column.

Electronic Fuel-Controlled Carburetor (EFC)

An electronic fuel-controlled carburetor is used on all 1987–92 1.2L Justy engines.

The EFC system controls the exhaust gas emissions before entering the catalyst by regulation of the air/fuel ratio. This enables the 3-way catalyst to reduce hydrocarbons (HC), carbon monoxide (CO) and oxides of nitrogen.

When there is little oxygen content in the exhaust gas and the output voltage of the oxygen sensor is larger than the "Slice Level" (averaged voltage which has been calculated from pear-ratio becomes lean. The amount of controlled fuel is determined by the duty ratio which is defined as a percent of the opening time of the solenoid valve to 1 pulse cycle.

When the oxygen content in the exhaust gas is large and the output voltage of the oxygen sensor is smaller than the Slice Level, the air/fuel ratio becomes rich.

Outside the feedback control zone or under specific operating conditions, such as cold starting, acceleration and the warning-up of the oxygen sensor, the control unit fixes control signals at a constant flow rate to control the air/fuel, regardless of the output voltage from the oxygen sensor, to maintain good driveability under all operating conditions. The speed of increasing or decreasing the amount of air/fuel vary with the operating conditions of the vehicle, such as idling, acceleration and cruising.

EFC COMPONENT FUNCTIONS

Oxygen Sensor

The oxygen sensor generates electromotive force according to the ratio of the oxygen concentration in the air to that in the exhaust gases. Its characteristic is that the electromotive force is changed, with respect to the optimum air/fuel ratio (14.7:1). The force is larger on the rich side and smaller on the lean side of the mixture.

Control Unit

The EFC control unit is a digital computer which consists of the following 3 functions:

• Deciding whether the air/fuel ratio is in a rich or lean condition, according to the output voltage of the oxygen sensor.

• Sending control signals to enrich the mixture to the carburetor (duty solenoid valve) when a lean mixture exists and signals to make the mixture lean when a rich condition exists.

• Fixing control signals under specific driving conditions.

Duty Solenoid Valve

The duty solenoid valve is incorporated in the carburetor and is controlled by a signal from the control unit. The signal is sent to control the duration ratio of current flow (the duty value). The duty solenoid valve is equipped with a control air bleed and a control fuel jet. When current flows through the valve, the plunger inside moves downward. This opens the port to the control air bleed and closes the port to the control fuel jet. When there is no current, a spring moves the plunger upward. This closes the port to the control air bleed and opens the port to the control fuel jet. These ports are routed to both the slow and main ports on the primary side of the carburetor. The air/fuel ratio varies with the duration of current flow (duty value) through the duty solenoid valve.

Vacuum Sensor and Vacuum Line Charging (VLC) Solenoid Valve

The vacuum sensor provides accurate linear and continuous sensing of changes in the intake manifold vacuum pressure. A solenoid valve is installed in the pressure line between the intake manifold and the pressure sensor. When the solenoid valve is off, the vacuum sensor measures vacuum pressure in the intake manifold. When the solenoid valve is on, the sensor measures air pressure through the filter. These measurements are sent to the control unit, which determines the operating condition of the engine, and the atmospheric pressure in areas where the vehicle is operated.

Thermosensor

The thermosensor is equipped with 2 terminals. One terminal is used for the control unit and the other is for the thermometer. The control unit reads the resistance of the thermosensor, which changes with coolant temperature, to monitor the warm-up condition of the engine (helps to enrich the mixture ratio during the warm-up).

High Altitude Compensator (HAC) System

The high altitude compensator system is a solenoid valve type. The solenoid valve opens when atmospheric pressure detected by the pressure sensor is 26.38 in. Hg or less. Air is sent to the auxiliary air passage, located near the main air bleed of the carburetor, after it is filtrated by a filter and regulated by the orifice. This causes the air/fuel ratio to become leaner in response to the diminished oxygen content at high altitude.

TESTING

Self-Diagnosis Function

The EFC system is complete with a self-diagnosing function. When a malfunction occurs, the **CHECK ENGINE** light is illuminated and the trouble code is displayed on the oxygen sensor monitor lamp. The self-diagnosis function consists of 3 modes: U-Check mode, Read Memory mode and D-Check mode. Two connectors (Read Memory and Test Mode) are used for mode selection.

U-Check Mode

The U-Check mode is used to check the EFC components necessary for start-up and driveability. When a fault occurs, the **CHECK ENGINE** light is illuminated to indicate that inspection is necessary. The diagnosis of other components that do not effect start-up and driveability are excluded from this mode.

Read Memory Mode

This mode is used to read past problems (even when the vehicle monitor lamps are not illuminated). It is used to detect poor contact or loose connections of connector, harness, etc.

D-Check Mode
This mode is used to check the entire system and to detect faulty components.

Clear Memory

This is used to clear the trouble code from the memory after repairs have been made.

GENERAL INFORMATION

The Single Point Fuel Injection system is used on 1986–92 1.8L engines. The system electronically controls the amount of fuel metered from the injector, and supplies the optimum air/fuel mixture under all operating conditions of the engine. Features of the SPFI system are as follows:

• Precise control of of the air/fuel mixture is accomplished by an increased number of input signals transmitting engine operating conditions to the control unit.

• The use of hot wire type air flow meter not only eliminates the need for high altitude compensation, but improves driving performance at high altitudes.

• The air control valve automatically regulates the idle speed to the set value under all engine operating conditions.

• Ignition timing is electrically controlled, thereby allowing the use of complicated spark advances characteristics.

• Wear of the air flow meter and fuel injector is automatically corrected so that they maintain their original performance.

• Troubleshooting can easily be accomplished by the built-in self-diagnosis function.

SPFI SYSTEM COMPONENTS

Air Flow Meter

The SPFI system incorporates a hot wire type air flow meter. This meter converts the amount of air taken into the engine into an electric signal by the use of the heat transfer between the incoming air and a heating resistor (hot wire) located in the air intake. Feature of the air flow meter are as follows:

• High altitude compensation is made automatically

• Quick response

• No moving parts

• Compact

The cold wire detects the temperature of in flowing air, then current flows through the hot wire so that the temperature difference between the hot and cold wires may be kept constant.

Throttle Chamber Assembly

The throttle chamber assembly of the SPFI system consists of an injector, throttle sensor, air control valve and a pressure regulator that are combined into the body. The throttle chamber assembly is a single-bore, down-draft type, that is equipped with an injector in the intake passage of the throttle valve. It consists of 3 systems:

1. Fuel system
2. By-pass air control system
3. Throttle sensor system

FUEL SYSTEM

Fuel is fed from the fuel inlet pipe, then is injected from the injector. Fuel flows around the injector to keep it cool. The pressure regulator controls fuel pressure and returns un-injected fuel to the fuel tank through the fuel return pipe. The fuel injector is operated by a signal from the SPFI control unit, based on engine speed and load.

BY-PASS AIR CONTROL SYSTEM

An air passage, by-passing the throttle valve, is provided to direct the air into the lower portion of the throttle valve. The air control valve is located in the middle of this passage and controls the amount of air during engine starting, idle speed, etc.

The air control valve is controlled by signals from the SPFI control unit and regulates the opening of the by-pass to maintain idle speed at the set value. By the use of the air control valve, the system can provide the following functions:

• Improved engine warm-up performance
• Compensation of idle speed according to altitude
• Compensation of idle speed with the A/C system operating
• Compensation for idle speed fluctuation with wear

THROTTLE SENSOR SYSTEM

A throttle position sensor is incorporated with a potentiometer and an idle switch interlocked with the throttle valve shaft. This sensor sends the SPFI control unit a potentiometer output signal corresponding to the opening of the throttle valve and a idle switch signal that turns **ON** only when the throttle is opened to the idle position. Using these signals, the SPFI control unit precisely controls the air/fuel ratio during acceleration and deceleration as well as idling.

Ignition System

The ignition system consists of a distributor containing a photoelectric crank angle sensor, an ignition coil equipped with a power transistor and the SPFI control unit. The crank-angle signal and reference signal detected by the photoelectric crank-angle sensor are sent to the SPFI control unit. The SPFI control unit determines the optimum ignition timing from these signals and other engine operating parameters, and transmits an ignition signal to the ignition coil igniter. The igniter amplifies this ignition signal and causes the primary current to flow intermittently in the ignition coil.

Air/Fuel Ratio Control System

This system has been designed to stabilize the quality of the hot-wire type air flow meter and fuel injector, to maintain their original performance by correcting their qualitative variation and wear. By learning the feedback control amount of the O_2 sensor, the system controls the SPFI control unit to automatically set a coefficient of correction, thereby, the fuel injector always achieves fuel injection under all operating conditions.

Oxygen Sensor

The oxygen sensor is mounted on the front exhaust pipe, and is used to sense oxygen concentration in the exhaust gas. If the fuel ratio is leaner than the optimum air/fuel mixture (14.7:1), the exhaust gas contains more oxygen. If the fuel ratio is richer than the optimum air/fuel ratio, the exhaust gas hardly contains oxygen. Therefore, examination of the oxygen concentration in the exhaust gas makes it possible to show whether the air/fuel ratio is leaner or richer than the optimum air/fuel mixture.

The oxygen sensor incorporates a zirconia tube (ceramic) which generates voltage if there is a difference in oxygen concentration between the inside and outside of the tube. The inside and outside of the zirconia tube is coated with platinum for the purpose of catalysis and electrode provisions. The hexagon screw on the outside is grounded to the exhaust pipe, and the inside is connected to the SPFI control unit through a harness.

When a rich air/fuel mixture is burnt in the cylinder in the oxygen in the exhaust gases reacts almost completely through the catalytic action of the platinum coating on the surface of the zirconia tube. This results in very large difference in the oxygen concentration between the inside and the outside, and the electromotive force generated is large.

When a lean air/fuel mixture is burnt in the cylinder, oxygen remains in the exhaust gases even after the catalytic action, and this results in a small difference in the oxygen concentration. The electromotive force is very small.

The difference in oxygen concentration changes greatly in the area of the optimum air/fuel ratio, and the change in the electromotive force is also large. By inputting this information to the SPFI control unit, the air/fuel ratio of the supplied mixture can be determined easily. The O_2 sensor does not generate much electromotive force when the temperature is low. The electromotive force stabilizes at temperatures of approximately 572–752°F (300–400°C).

Coolant Thermosensor

The coolant thermosensor is located on the thermocasing of the intake manifold. Its thermistor changes resistance with respect to temperature. A water temperature signal converted into resistance is transmitted to the control unit, to control the amount of fuel injection, ignition timing, purge control solenoid valve, etc.

EGR Gas Temperature Sensor

CALIFORNIA MODELS

The EGR gas temperature sensor is located in the EGR gas passage on the intake manifold. An EGR gas temperature signal converted into resistance is sent to the control unit for EGR system diagnosis.

Kick-Down Control System

On models equipped with automatic transmissions, a throttle sensor is used in place of the previous kick-down switch. It sends a signal to the control unit to set the throttle valve to a specified position. When the throttle valve is in that position, the kick-down control relay turns on.

TESTING

Self-Diagnosis System

The self-diagnosis system detects and indicates faults, in various inputs and outputs of the electronic control unit. The **CHECK ENGINE** light, located on the instrument panel, indicates a fault or trouble, and the LED (light emitting diode) in the control unit indicates a trouble code. A fail-safe function is incorporated into the system to ensure minimal driveability if a failure of a sensor occurs.

Self-Diagnosis Function

The SPFI control unit carries out the computational processing of the input information received from various sensors and produces the output information for operating the fuel injectors, fuel pump, etc. This computational processing reads out all the input/output information to examine matching with the predetermined levels (proper values or ranges). If a predetermined level is not satisfied, or a fault is detected, the warning lamp signals the driver. When this occurs, the self-diagnosis function is performed.

Fail-Safe Function

When a component has been found faulty in the self-diagnosis function, the SPFI control unit generates the faulty signal and carries out the computational processing. When this occurs, the fail-safe function is performed.

Function Of Self-Diagnosis

The self-diagnosis function consists of 4 modes: U-check mode, Read memory mode, D-check mode and Clear code mode. Two connectors (Read memory and Test mode) and 2 lamps (**CHECK ENGINE** and O$_2$ monitor) are used. The connectors are used for mode selection and the lamps monitor the type of problem.

U-CHECK MODE

The U-Check mode diagnosis only the SPFI components necessary for start-up and driveabilty. When a fault occurs, the warning lamp (**CHECK ENGINE**) lights to indicate to the user that inspection is necessary. The diagnosis of other components which do not effect start-up and driveabilty are excluded from this mode.

READ MEMORY CODE

This mode is used to read past problems (even when the vehicle monitor lamps are off). It is most effective in detecting poor contacts or loose connections of the connectors, harness, etc.

D-CHECK MODE

This mode is used to check the entire SPFI system and to detect faulty components.

CLEAR MEMORY MODE

This mode is used to clear the trouble code from the memory after all faults have been corrected.

Multi-Point Fuel Injection (MPFI) System

➡ **This section covers all Multi-Point Fuel Injected models except for the 1990–92 Legacy and 1992 SVX. The Legacy and SVX are covered in separate Sections**

The MPFI system supplies the optimum air/fuel mixture to the engine under all various operating conditions. System fuel, which is pressurized at a constant pressure, is injected into the intake air passage of the cylinder head. The amount of fuel injected is controlled by the intermittent injection system where the electromagnetic injection valve (fuel injector) opens only for a short period of time, depending on the amount of air required for 1 cycle of operation. During system operation, the amount injection is determined by the duration of an electric pulse sent to the fuel injector, which permits precise metering of the fuel.

All the operating conditions of the engine are converted into electric signals, resulting in additional features of the system, such as improved adaptability and easier addition of compensating element. The MPFI system also incorporates the following features:
- Reduced emission of exhaust gases
- Reduction in fuel consumption
- Increased engine output
- Superior acceleration and deceleration
- Superior starting and warm-up performance in cold weather since compensation is made for coolant and intake air temperature
- Good performance with turbocharger, if equipped

MPFI SYSTEM COMPONENTS

Air Flow Meter

The MPFI system incorporates a hot wire type air flow meter. This meter converts the amount of air taken into the engine into an electric signal by using the heat transfer between the incoming air and a heating resistor (hot wire) located in the air intake. Features of the air flow meter are as follows:
- High altitude compensation is made automatically
- Quick response
- There are no moving parts
- Its compact

Throttle Body

When depressing on the gas pedal, the throttle body opens/closes its valve to regulate the amount of air to be taken in to the combustion chamber. Negative pressure (positive pressure at supercharging) is generated according to the opening of the throttle valve, then is applied to the pressure ports for EGR control and canister purge. The pressure is used for controlling the EGR valve and canister purge.

On models equipped with 4 cylinder engines, during idling, the throttle valve is almost fully closed and the air flow through the throttle body is less than the air passing through the system. More than half of the air necessary for idling is supplied to the intake manifold through the idle bypass passage. Turning the idle adjust screw, on the idle bypass passage, can change the air flow to adjust the number of revolutions during idling. To prevent the number of revolutions from decreasing when the A/C is turned **ON**, the fast idle bypass passage is provided with a valve that is operated by the fast idle solenoid.

➡ **Fast engine idle rpm can not be adjusted by turning the fast idle adjusting screw.**

On models equipped with 6 cylinder engines, during idling, the throttle valve is almost fully closed and the air flow through the throttle body is less than the air passing through the system. More than half the air necessary for idling is supplied to the intake manifold through the bypass air control valve. The bypass air control valve properly controls the number of revolutions during idling, so no need for adjustment is necessary.

On all models, a throttle position sensor is incorporated with a potentiometer and an idle switch, interlocked with the throttle valve shaft. The throttle position sensor sends the MPFI control unit a potentiometer output signal corresponding to the opening of the throttle, and an idle switch signal that turns **ON** only when the throttle is opened the idle position. Using these signals, the MPFI control unit controls the air/fuel ratio during acceleration, deceleration and at idle.

By-Pass Air Control Valve

MODELS EQUIPPED WITH 6 CYLINDER ENGINE

The by-pass air control valve is controlled by a signal sent from the MPFI control unit. It controls the flow-rate of air passing through the by-pass passage, allowing the engine to operate at optimum speed under all various conditions. This results in stabilized exhaust gas emission, improved fuel economy and better performance. Features of the by-pass air control valve are as follows:
- The by-pass passage opens partially when the engine is idling. When the engine is under a load (A/C turned **ON**), the by-pass passage opens wider to allow more air to pass through. This maintains the specified engine idling rpm.
- When the engine is cold, the by-pass passage opens widely to allow more air to pass through. This speeds up engine warm-up.
- Variations in engine idling rpm over time are compensated for.
- When the throttle valve closes, a sudden drop in engine rpm is prevented to improve driving performance.

➡ **When battery voltage drops momentarily, the by-pass valve sometimes activates to increase idling speed to 900 rpm. Before the engine reaches normal operating temperature, idling speed between N or P range and sometimes the D range sometimes differs. However, these are not problems.**

Auxiliary Air Valve

MODELS EQUIPPED WITH 4 CYLINDER ENGINE

The auxiliary air valve is used to increase air flow when the engine is started at low temperature, and until the engine reaches normal operating temperature. It consists of a coiled bi-metal, a bi-metal-operated shutter valve and an electric heater element for bi-metal. This passing air flow (during start-up) is increased as the temperature becomes lower. After the engine has been started, the heating is preformed by the heater element to which current is supplied from the fuel pump relay circuit. Thereby, the shutter valve turns gradually to decrease the air flow. After a certain elapsed time, the shutter valve is closed.

Ignition System

The ignition system consists of a battery, an ignition coil, distributor, spark plugs, knock sensor, MPFI control unit and spark plug wires.

The crank angle sensor, built into the distributor, detects the reference crank angle and the positioned crank angle. An electronic signal of both angles is sent to the MPFI control unit which is used in conjunction with the fuel injection system. The MPFI control unit determines spark advance angle and spark timing. The signal from spark timing is determined by the control unit, and is sent to the power transistor where it makes the primary circuit to the ignition coil, where high voltage current is generated in the secondary circuit. The high voltage of the secondary circuit is sent to the spark plug of each cylinder.

Under normal operating conditions, the spark advance angle is calculated from the following 3 factors:
- Engine speed compensation
- Advanced when starting the engine
- Advanced in all driving conditions, except when starting the engine, after engine rpm exceeds specifications

When knocking occurs, a signal is sent from the knock sensor to the MPFI control unit. The MPFI control unit then retards spark timing to prevent engine knocking.

A knock sensor is installed on the cylinder block, and senses knocking signals from each cylinder. The knock sensor is a piezo-electric type which converts knocking vibrations into electric signals. It consists of a piezo-electric element, a weight and a case. If knocking occurs in the engine, the weight in the case moves the piezo-electric element to generate voltage.

Air/Fuel Ratio Control System

This system stabilizes the quality of the hot-wire type air flow meter and the fuel injectors to maintain their original performance by correcting their variation and aging.

By learning the amount of feedback of the oxygen sensor, the system sends signals to the control unit to automatically set a coefficient of correction, thereby, the fuel injector always achieves fuel injection under all conditions.

Oxygen Sensor

The oxygen sensor is installed in the center exhaust pipe and is used to sense oxygen concentration in the exhaust gas. If the fuel ratio is leaner than the optimum ratio (14.7:1), the exhaust gas contains more oxygen. If the fuel ratio is richer than the optimum ratio (14.7:1), the exhaust gas contains little oxygen. Therefore, the oxygen concentration in the exhaust gas makes it possible to determine whether the air/fuel ratio is richer or leaner than the optimum ratio (14.7:1).

The oxygen sensor incorporates a zirconia tube (ceramic) which generates voltage, if there is a difference in oxygen concentration between the inside and outside of the tube. The inside and outside of the zirconia tube is coated with platinum for catalysis and electrode provision. The screw on the outside of the sensor is grounded to the exhaust pipe and its lead is connected to the MPFI control unit through the harness.

When a rich air/fuel mixture is burnt in the cylinder, the oxygen in the exhaust gases reacts almost completely through the catalytic action of the platinum coating on the surface of the zirconia tube. This results in a very large difference in the oxygen concentration between the inside and outside of the tube, and the electromotive force generated is large.

When a lean air/fuel mixture is burnt in the cylinder, oxygen remains in the exhaust gases even after the catalytic action, resulting in a small difference in the oxygen concentration. The electromotive force is very small.

The difference in oxygen concentration changes greatly in the area of the optimum air/fuel ratio, and changes in the electromotive force is also large. By inputting this information into the MPFI control unit, the air/fuel ratio can be determined easily. The oxygen sensor does not generate much electromotive force when the temperature is low. The electromotive force stabilizes at temperatures of approximately 572–752°F (300–400°C). California models use a ceramic heater to improve performance at low temperatures.

Fuel Injector

The fuel injector injects fuel according to the valve opening signal received from the MPFI control unit. The nozzle is attached on the top of the injector. The needle valve is lifted by the solenoid coil through the plunger when the valve opening signal is received.

Since the injection opening varies, the lifted level of the needle valve and the regulated controlled fuel pressure are kept constant, the amount of fuel to be injected can be controlled only by the valve opening signal from the MPFI control unit. At the fuel inlet of the injector, a filter is mounted to prevent dust from entering the system.

Coolant Thermosensor

The coolant thermosensor is installed on the waterpipe which is made of aluminum alloy. Its thermistor changes resistance with respect to temperature. The thermosensor sends the coolant temperature signal to the MPFI control unit, which determines the amount fuel volume to be injected.

Dropping Resistor

The dropping resistor used on some XT models equipped with 4 cylinder engines serves as a voltage control to maintain optimum injector driving current.

Pressure Regulator

The pressure regulator is divided into 2 chambers: the fuel chamber and the spring chamber. Fuel is supplied to the fuel chamber, through the fuel inlet, connected to the injector. A difference in pressure between the fuel chamber and the spring chamber connected with the intake manifold causes the diaphragm to be pushed down, causing fuel to be fed back to the fuel tank through the return line. By the returning of the fuel, as to balance the above pressure difference and the spring force, fuel pressure is kept at a constant pressure of 36.3 psi against the intake manifold pressure.

Pressure Switch

On some sedans and wagons equipped with 4 cylinder turbocharged engines are equipped with 2 positive pressure switches(which are combinations of a pressure withstanding diaphragm and microswitch) are mounted on the body strut mount. One switch operates when the intake manifold pressure reaches 1.97 in. Hg causing the **TURBO** indicator lamp to illuminate, indicating that the turbocharger has begun its supercharging operation. At the same time, it transmits a load signal to the MPFI control unit for canceling the air/fuel ratio feedback control. The other switch operates at a pressure of 18.50 in. Hg for cutting off fuel when an abnormal rise in supercharging pressure occurs, due to a malfunction of the wastegate or other fault, thereby preventing damage to the engine.

Turbocharger

Some models are equipped with a turbocharger. The turbocharger performs supercharging with the use of the wasted energy in the high temperature exhaust gases. The turbocharger provides the following features:

• Less power loss with the use of the exhaust gas energy
• Light in weight and compact in size for better adaptability
• Better matching with the engine load
• Easy and efficient adjustment of the supercharge pressure by the passing through the exhaust gas passage

In the design of this turbocharger system, particular consideration has been given to performance. With the optimum turbocharger design and the suitable tuning of the intake and exhaust systems, it is capable of providing powerful torque even at low speed, quick response and superb operability.

FUNCTION OF THE WASTE GATE VALVE

As engine speed increases with the opening of the throttle valve, the amount of exhaust gas increases. This increases the rotational speed of the turbine (approximately 20,000–120,000 rpm), supercharging pressure and the output. Excessive supercharging pressure may cause knocking and a heavier thermal load on the piston causing engine damage. To prevent this, a waste gate valve and its controller are installed. By sensing the supercharging pressure, the waste gate valve restricts it below a predetermined level.

While the supercharging pressure is lower than the predetermined level, the waste gate valve is closed so that all the exhaust gas is carried through the turbine. When it reaches the predetermined level, the waste gate controller lets the supercharging pressure push the diaphragm, causing the linked waste gate valve to open. With the waste gate valve opened, some of the exhaust gas is allowed to flow into the exhaust gas pipe by bypassing the turbine. This decreases the turbine rotating energy to keep the supercharging pressure constant.

LUBRICATION

The turbocharger is lubricated by the engine oil from the oil pump. Since the turbocharger turbine and the compressor shaft reach a maximum of several hundred thousand revolutions per minute, full-floating type bearings are used to form desirable lubrication films on the inside and outside of the bearing during engine operation. The oil supplied to the turbocharger also cools the heat from the exhaust gas in the turbine so they are not sent to the bearings.

COOLING

The turbocharger is water cooled for higher reliability and durability. The coolant from the coolant drain hose under the engine cylinder head is directed to the coolant passage, through a pipe provided in the turbocharger bearing housing. After cooling the bearing housing, coolant is directed into the thermostat case in the intake manifold through a pipe.

TESTING

Self-Diagnosis System

The self-diagnosis system detects and indicates faults, in various inputs and outputs of the electronic control unit. The **CHECK ENGINE** light, located on the instrument panel, indicates a fault or trouble, and the LED (light emitting diode) in the control unit indicates a trouble code. A fail-safe function is incorporated into the system to ensure minimal driveability if a failure occurs.

The MPFI control unit carries out the computational processing of the input information received from various sensors and produces the output information for operating the fuel injectors, fuel pump, etc. This computational processing reads out all the input/output information to examine matching with the predetermined levels (proper values or ranges). If a predetermined level is not satisfied, or a fault is found, the warning lamp signals the driver.

Function Of Self-Diagnosis

The self-diagnosis function consists of 4 modes: U-check mode, Read memory mode, D-check mode and Clear code mode. Two connectors (Read memory and Test mode) and 2 lamps (**CHECK ENGINE** and O_2 monitor) are used. The connectors are used for mode selection and the lamps monitor the type of problem.

U-CHECK MODE

The U-Check mode diagnostics only the MPFI components necessary for start-up and driveabilty. When a fault occurs, the **CHECK ENGINE** light illuminates to indicate to the user that inspection is necessary. The diagnosis of other components, which do not effect start-up and driveability, are excluded from this mode.

READ MEMORY MODE

This mode is used to read past problems (even when the vehicle monitor lamps are off). It is most effective in detecting poor contacts or loose connections of the connectors, harness, etc.

D-CHECK MODE

This mode is used to check the entire MPFI system and to detect faulty components.

CLEAR MEMORY MODE

This mode is used to clear the trouble code from the memory after all faults have been corrected.

Legacy and SVX Multi-Point Fuel Injection (MPFI) System

General Information

The MPFI system used on the 1990–92 Legacy and the 1992 SVX models supplies the optimum air/fuel mixture to the engine under all various operating conditions. System fuel, which is pressurized at a constant pressure, is injected into the intake air passage of the cylinder head. The amount of fuel is controlled by an intermittent injection system where the electro-magnetic injection valve (fuel injector) opens only for a short period of time, depending on the amount of air required for 1 cycle of operation. When operating, the amount of injection is determined by the duration of an electric pulse (signal) sent to the fuel injector, which permits precise metering of the fuel. All the operating conditions of the are converted into electric signals, which results in improved adaptability, easier addition of compensating element, etc. Characteristics of the MPFI system are as follows:

• Reduced emission of harmful exhaust gases
• Reduced in fuel consumption
• Increased engine output
• Superior acceleration and deceleration
• Superior startability and warm-up performance in cold weather since compensation is made for coolant and intake air temperature

SYSTEM COMPONENTS

Air Control System

Air, which is drawn in and filtered by the air cleaner, is metered and sent to the throttle body through the air intake boot. From the throttle body, the air is controlled by the open/close operation of the throttle valve and is then delivered to the intake manifold. From the intake manifold, it is distributed to the cylinders to mix with the fuel injected by the fuel injectors. Then, the air/fuel mixture is sent into the cylinders. Some of the air is sent to the by-pass air control valve which controls the engine idle speed.

AIR FLOW SENSOR

The MPFI system uses 2 different types of air flow sensors. On vehicles equipped with automatic transmission, a hot film type sensor is used. On vehicles equipped with manual transmission, a hot wire type air flow sensor is used. These air flow sensors convert the amount of air taken into the engine into an electric signal by using the heat transfer between the incoming air and a heating resistor (hot film or hot wire) located in the air intake. Characteristics of these flow sensors are as follows:
- High altitude compensation is made automatically
- Quick response
- There are no moving parts
- Compact

THROTTLE BODY

When depressing the accelerator pedal, the throttle body opens/closes its valve to control the amount of air to be taken into the combustion chamber. During idling, the throttle valve is almost fully closed. More than half the air necessary for idling is supplied to the intake manifold through the by-pass air control valve. The by-pass air control valve controls the number of revolutions during idling, so that no adjustment is necessary.

THROTTLE SENSOR

A throttle position sensor is incorporated with a potentiometer and an idle switch interlocked with the throttle valve shaft. It sends the MPFI control unit an potentiometer output signal, relating to the opening of the throttle valve, and an idle switch signal that turns **ON** only when the throttle is opened to the idle position. Using these signals, the MPFI control unit controls the air/fuel ratio during acceleration and deceleration as well as idling.

BY-PASS AIR CONTROL VALVE

The by-pass air control valve consists of an air cut valve, duty control valve, intake air passage and a coolant passage. The air cut valve contains a bi-metallic substance which responds to coolant temperature, and a duty control valve which is controlled by a signal sent from the ECU. The ECU tells the duty control valve to bring the engine rpm as close to preset idle speed as possible. When the coolant temperature is low, the air-cut valve is fully opened by the action of the bi-metallic substance, so that the air flow required for low coolant temperature is maintained.

Fuel System

Fuel is pressurized by the fuel pump, which is built into the fuel tank, and is delivered to the injectors by the fuel line and the fuel filter. Fuel pressure to the injectors is controlled by as pressure regulator. From the injectors, fuel is injected into the intake manifold where it is mixed with air, and then is sent to the cylinders. Injection timing, and the amount of fuel injected, is controlled by the ECU.

PRESSURE REGULATOR

The pressure regulator is divided into the fuel chamber and the spring chamber by a diagram. Fuel is fed to the fuel chamber through the fuel inlet connected with the injector. A difference in pressure between the fuel chamber and the spring chamber causes the diagram to be pushed down, and the fuel is fed back to the fuel tank through the return line. The returning fuel, as to balance the above pressure difference and the spring force, fuel pressure is kept at a constant pressure of 36.3 psi, against the intake manifold pressure.

FUEL INJECTOR

The fuel injector injects fuel according to the signal received by the ECU. The nozzle is attached on the top of the fuel injector. The needle valve (models equipped with automatic transmission) or ball valve (models equipped with manual transmission) is lifted up by the solenoid coil through the plunger on arrival of the valve opening signal. Since injection opening, lifted level of the valve and the regulator-controlled fuel pressure are kept constant, the amount of fuel to be injected can be controlled only by the valve opening signal from the ECU. Characteristics of the fuel injector are as follows:
- High heat resistance
- Low driving noise
- Easy to service
- Compact

Sensors and Switches

OXYGEN SENSOR

The Oxygen sensor is used to determine the oxygen concentration in the exhaust gas. If the fuel ratio is leaner than optimum air/fuel ratio (14.7:1), the exhaust gas contains more oxygen. If the fuel ratio is richer than the optimum air/fuel ratio (14.7:1), the exhaust gas contains hardly any oxygen. Examination of the oxygen concentration in the exhaust gas makes it possible to determine whether the air/fuel ratio is leaner or richer than the optimum air/fuel ratio (14.7:1).

The oxygen sensor incorporates a zirconia tube (ceramic) which generates voltage, if there is a difference in oxygen concentration between the inside and outside of the tube. The inside and outside zirconia tube is coated with platinum for the purpose of catalysis and electrode provision. The hexagon screw on the outside is grounded to the exhaust pipe, and the inside is connected to the ECU through the harness. A ceramic heater is installed to improve performance at low temperatures.

When a rich air/fuel mixture is burnt in the cylinder, the oxygen in the exhaust gases reacts almost completely through the catalytic action of the platinum coating on the surface of the zirconia tube. This results in a difference in the oxygen concentration between the inside and outside, and a large electromotive force is generated.

When a lean air/fuel mixture is burnt in the cylinder, oxygen remains in the exhaust gases even after the catalytic action, resulting in a small difference in the oxygen concentration, and a small electromotive force is generated.

The difference in oxygen concentration changes greatly in the area of the optimum air/fuel ratio (14.7:1), and a large change in the electromotive force occurs. By the inputting of this information to the MPFI control unit, the air/fuel ratio can be determined easily. The O_2 sensor does not generate much electromotive force when the temperature is low. The electromotive force stabilizes at a temperature of approximately 572–752°F (300–400°C).

WATER TEMPERATURE SENSOR

The water temperature sensor is installed on the water pipe, and is constructed of an aluminum alloy. Its thermistor changes resistance with respect to temperature. A signal, converted into resistance, is sent to the ECU to control the amount of fuel injection, ignition timing, purge control solenoid valve, etc.

KNOCK SENSOR

The knock sensor is installed on the cylinder block, and senses knocking signals from each cylinder. The knock sensor is a piezo-electric type, which converts knocking vibrations into signals. The sensor consists of a piezo-electric element, weight and case. When knocking occurs in the engine, the weight in the case moves, causing the piezo-electric element to generate voltage.

CRANK ANGLE SENSOR

The crank angle sensor is installed on the oil pump, located in the front of the cylinder block, to detect the crank angle position. It is designed so the ECU can accurately read the number of pulses which occur when the protrusions provided at the perimeter of the crank sprocket (rotating together with the crankshaft) cross the crank angle sensor.

The crank sprocket is provided with 6 protrusions. Crank rotation causes these protrusions to cross the crank angle sensor so the magnetic fluxes in the coil change with the change in the air gap between the sensor pickup and the sprocket. The change in the air gap, produces an electromotive force, which is then sent to the ECU.

CAM ANGLE SENSOR

The cam angle sensor is located on the left-hand camshaft support, to detect the combustion cylinder at any time. It is designed so the ECU can read the number of pulses which occur when the protrusions provided on the back of the LH camshaft drive sprocket cross the sensor.

Construction, and operating principle of the cam angle sensor are similar to those of the crank angle sensor. A total of 7 protrusions (1 each at 2 locations, 2 at 1 location and 3 at 1 location) are arranged in 4 equal parts on the sprocket.

SPEED SENSOR

The speed sensor consists of a magnetic rotor which is routed by a speedometer cable and a reed switch. It is built into the combination meter (speedometer). One rotation of the magnetic rotor turns the reed switch **ON/OFF** 4 times to produce a signal. The signal is used as a vehicle speed signal which is sent to the ECU.

ATMOSPHERIC PRESSURE SENSOR

The atmospheric pressure sensor is built into the ECU. It uses an "absolute" pressure sensor design. It purpose is to detect the atmospheric pressure used to compensate for pressure at high altitudes and to maintain driving stability.

The signal from the sensor is also used for "shift control," on vehicles equipped with automatic transmission at high altitudes.

AIR CONDITIONING SWITCH AND RELAY

The A/C switch turns the A/C system on/off. The on/off operation of the switch is sent to the ECU. The A/C cut relay breaks the current flow to the compressor through the use of an output signal from the ECU, for a short period of time, when a full throttle signal (sent from the throttle

sensor) enters the ECU while the compressor is operating. This prevents the degradation of acceleration performance and stabilizes driving performance. The A/C cut relay is installed in the fuse box, located at the left side of the engine compartment.

Control System

The ECU receives signals sent from various sensors and switches to determine engine operating conditions, and emits output signals to provide the optimum control and/or functioning of various systems. The ECU controls the following:

- Fuel injection control
- Ignition system control
- By-pass air control (idle speed control)
- Canister purge control
- Radiator fan control
- Fuel pump control
- A/C cut control
- Self-diagnosis function
- Fail-safe function

FUEL INJECTION CONTROL

The ECU receives signals from various sensors to control the amount of fuel to be injected, and fuel injection timing. Sequential fuel injection control is used over the entire engine operating range, except when starting. The sequential fuel injection system is designed so that fuel is injected at a specific time to provide maximum air intake efficiency for each cylinder. Fuel injection is completed just before the intake valve begins to open.

The amount of fuel injected by the injector valve depends upon the length of time it remains open. Fuel injection timing is determined by a signal sent to the injector by the ECU according to varying engine operations. Feedback control is accomplished by the means of a learning control. As a result, the fuel injection control system is responsive and accurate in design and function.

Correction Coefficients

Correction coefficients are used to correct the basic duration of fuel injection so that the air/fuel ratio meets the requirements of varying engine operations. These correction coefficients are as follows:

1. Air/Fuel Ratio Coefficient: To provide the optimum air/fuel ratio in relation to engine speed and the basic amount of fuel injected.

2. Start Increment Coefficient: Increases the amount of fuel injected only when cranking the engine, which improves starting ability.

3. Water Temperature Coefficient: Used to increase the amount of fuel injected in relation to a signal from the water temperature sensor, for easier starting when the engine is cold. The

lower the water temperature, the greater the increment rate.

4. After-Start Increment Coefficient: Increases the amount of fuel injected for a certain period of time immediately after the engine starts, to stabilize engine operation.

5. Full Increment Coefficient: Increases the amount of fuel injected by a signal from the throttle sensor in relation to a signal from the air flow sensor.

6. Acceleration Increment Coefficient: Compensates for time lags of air flow measurement and/or fuel injection during acceleration, to provide quick response.

Air/Fuel Ratio Feedback Coefficient (Alpha)

This feedback coefficient uses the O_2 sensor's voltage (electromotive force) as a signal to be sent to the ECU. When low voltage is entered, the ECU determines it as a lean mixture, and when high voltage is entered, it determines it as a rich mixture. Therefore, when the air/fuel ratio is richer, the amount of fuel injected is decreased. When the air/fuel ratio leaner, the amount of fuel injected is increased. This means, the air/fuel ratio is compensated so that it comes as close to the optimum air/fuel ratio as possible (14.7:1), on which the 3-way catalyst operates most effectively.

Learning Control System

The air/fuel ratio learning control system constantly memorizes the amount of correction required in relation to the basic amount of fuel to be injected (basic amount of fuel injected is determined after several cycles of fuel injection), so that the correction affected by the feedback control is minimized. Quick response and accurate control of variations in the air/fuel ratio, sensor's and actuators characteristics during operation, as well as in the air/fuel ratio with the time of engine operation, are achieved. Accurate control contributes much stability of exhaust gases and driving performance.

IGNITION CONTROL SYSTEM

The ECU receives signals from the air flow sensor, water temperature sensor, crank angle sensor, cam angle sensor, knock sensor, etc., to determine the operating condition of the engine. It then selects the optimum ignition timing stored in the memory and immediately sends a signal to the igniter to control ignition timing.

When the ECU receives signals from the knock sensor, it ensures that advanced ignition timing is maintained immediately before engine knock occurs. This system features a quick-to-response learning control method by which information stored in the ECU memory is processed in comparison with information from various sensors and switches.

The ECU constantly provides the optimum ignition timing in relation to output, fuel consumption, exhaust gas, etc., according to various engine operating conditions, the octane rating of the fuel used, etc.

The ignition system uses 2 ignition coils. One for the No. 1 and No. 2 cylinders, and 1 for the No. 3 and No. 4 cylinders. Simultaneous ignition occurs for cylinders No. 1 and No. 2 on 1 hand, and No. 3 and No. 4 on the other. This eliminates the distributor and achieves maintenance free operation.

Ignition control under normal engine conditions: Between the 97 degrees signal and the 65 degrees signal, the ECU measures the engine revolutions, and by using this information it decides the dwell set timing and ignition timing according to the engine condition.

Ignition control under starting conditions: Engine revolutions fluctuate at the starting condition, so the ECU cannot control the ignition timing. When such a condition exists, ignition timing is fixed at 10 degrees BTDC by using the 10 degrees signal.

BY-PASS AIR CONTROL (IDLE SPEED CONTROL)

The ECU activates the by-pass air control valve to control the amount of by-pass air flowing through the throttle valve in relation to signals from the crank angle sensor, cam angle sensor, water temperature sensor and the A/C switch, so the proper idle speed specified for each engine load is achieved.

The by-pass air control valve uses a duty solenoid design so that the amount of valve lift is determined by certain operating frequency. For this reason, the by-pass air flow is regulated by controlling the duty ratio. The relationship between the duty ratio, valve lift and by-pass air flow is the duty ratio (high) increases valve lift and by-pass air flow. By-pass air control features the following advantages:

• Compensation for engine speed, under A/C system and electrical loads

• Increases in idle speed during engine warm-up

• A dashpot function during the time the throttle valve is quickly closed

• Prevention of engine speed variations over time

CANISTER PURGE CONTROL

The ECU receives signals from the water temperature sensor, vehicle speed sensor and crank angle sensor to control the purge control

solenoid. Canister purge takes place during vehicle operation, except under certain conditions (during idling, etc.). The purge line is connected to the throttle chamber to purge fuel evaporation gas from the canister according to the amount of intake air.

RADIATOR FAN CONTROL

The ON/OFF control of the radiator fan (models not equipped with A/C) is controlled by the ECU which receives signals sent from the water temperature sensor and the vehicle speed sensor. On models equipped with A/C, the ECU receives signals from the water temperature sensor, vehicle speed sensor and the A/C switch. These signals simultaneously turn ON/OFF the main radiator fan and the A/C auxiliary fan as well as setting them at HI or LO speed.

FUEL PUMP OPERATION

The ECU receives a signal from the crank angle sensor and turns the fuel pump relay ON/OFF to control fuel pump operation. The fuel pump will stop operating if the engine stalls with the ignition switch in the **ON** position.

AIR CONDITIONING CUT CONTROL

When the ECU receives a full-open signal from the throttle sensor while the A/C system is operating, the A/C cut relay turns OFF for certain period of time to stop the compressor. This prevents degradation of output during acceleration and stabilizes driveability.

POWER SUPPLY CONTROL

When the ECU receives an ON signal from the ignition switch, current flows through the ignition relay. This turns the ignition relay ON so that power is supplied to the injectors, air flow sensor, by-pass air control valve, etc. Power to the above components, except the fuel injectors is turned OFF for approximately 5 seconds after the ECU receives an OFF signal from the ignition switch. The fuel injectors stop fuel injection after the ignition switch is turned **OFF** because the injection signal is cut off.

Diagnosis and Testing

SELF-DIAGNOSIS SYSTEM

The self-diagnosis system detects and indicates faults, in various inputs and outputs of

the electronic control unit. The warning lamp (**CHECK ENGINE** light), located on the instrument panel indicates a fault or trouble, and the LED (light emitting diode) in the ECU indicates a trouble code. A fail-safe function is incorporated into the system to ensure minimal driveability if a failure of a sensor occurs.

Function Of Self-Diagnosis

The self-diagnosis function consists of 4 modes: U-check mode, Read memory mode, D-check mode and Clear code mode. Two connectors, Read memory and Test mode, and 2 lamps, **CHECK ENGINE** and Oxygen sensor monitor, are used. The connectors are used for mode selection and the lamps monitor the type of problem.

Fail-Safe Function

When a component has been found faulty in the self-diagnosis function, the ECU generates the faulty signal and carries out the computational processing. When this occurs, the fail-safe function is performed.

U-CHECK MODE

The U-Check mode diagnosis only the MPFI components necessary for start-up and driveabilty. When a fault occurs, the **CHECK ENGINE** light illuminates to indicate to the user that inspection is necessary. The diagnosis of other components which do not effect start-up and driveabilty are excluded from this mode.

READ MEMORY CODE

This mode is used to read past problems (even when the vehicle monitor lamps are off). It is most effective in detecting poor contacts or loose connections of the connectors, harness, etc.

D-CHECK MODE

This mode is used to check the entire MPFI system and to detect faulty components.

CLEAR MEMORY MODE

This mode is used to clear the trouble code from the memory after all faults have been corrected.

VACUUM DIAGRAMS

◆ SEE FIG. 21–31

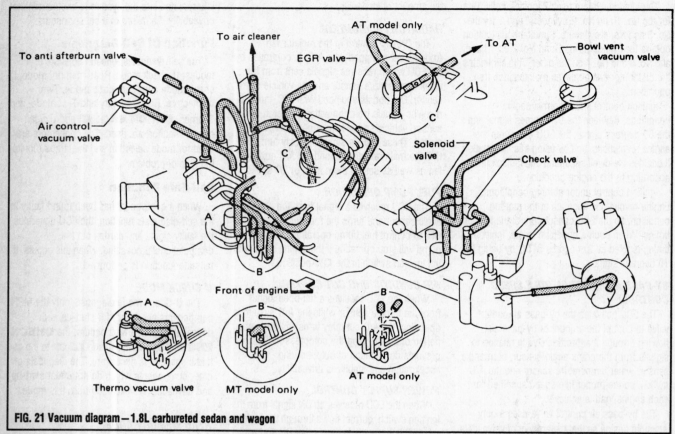

FIG. 21 Vacuum diagram — 1.8L carbureted sedan and wagon

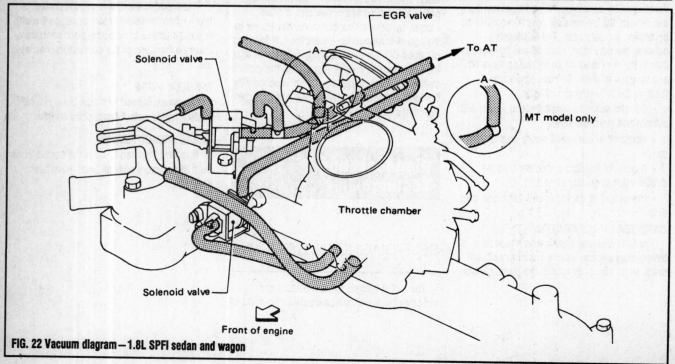

FIG. 22 Vacuum diagram — 1.8L SPFI sedan and wagon

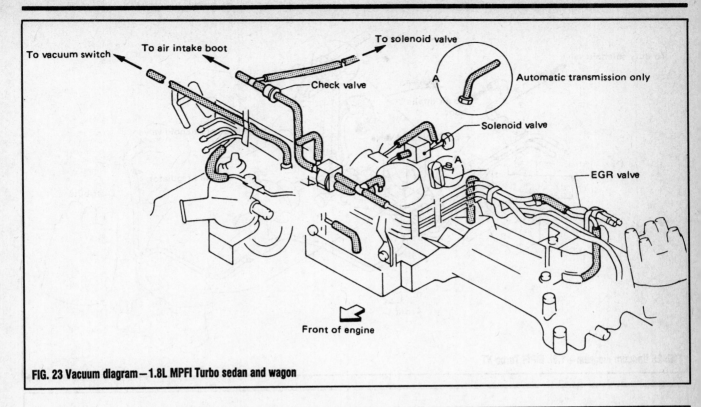

FIG. 23 Vacuum diagram—1.8L MPFI Turbo sedan and wagon

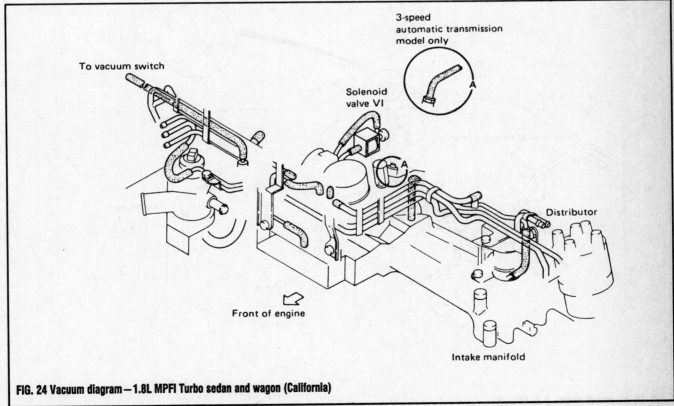

FIG. 24 Vacuum diagram—1.8L MPFI Turbo sedan and wagon (California)

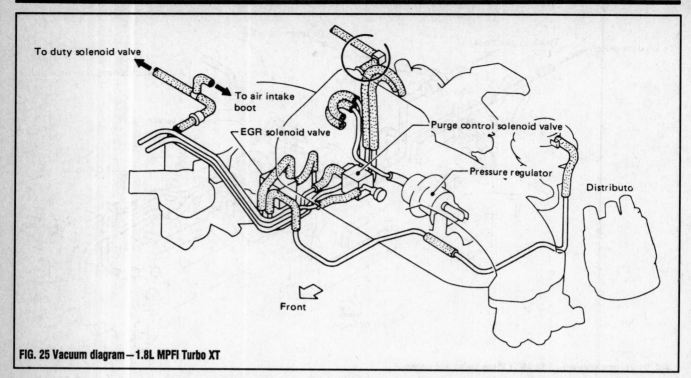

FIG. 25 Vacuum diagram—1.8L MPFI Turbo XT

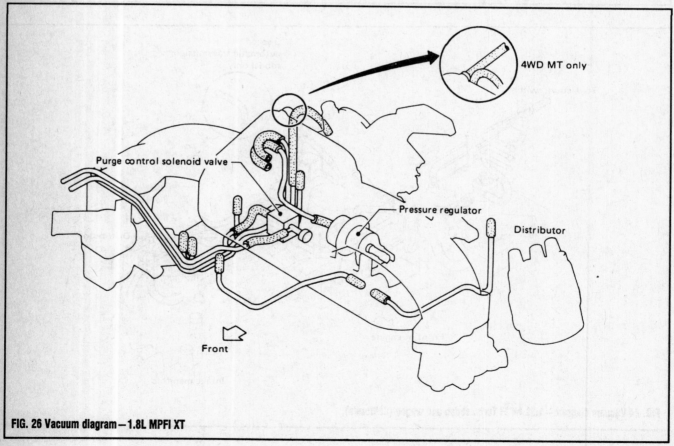

FIG. 26 Vacuum diagram—1.8L MPFI XT

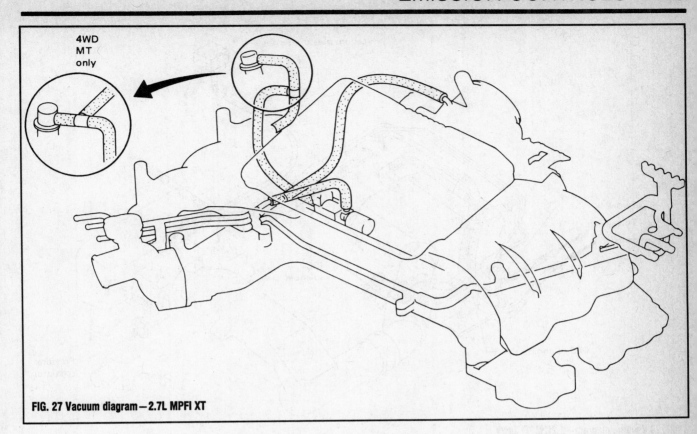

4WD MT only

FIG. 27 Vacuum diagram—2.7L MPFI XT

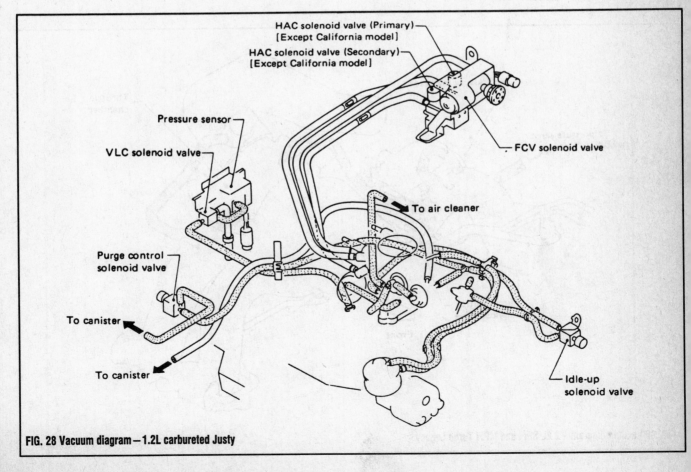

HAC solenoid valve (Primary) [Except California model]

HAC solenoid valve (Secondary) [Except California model]

Pressure sensor

VLC solenoid valve

FCV solenoid valve

To air cleaner

Purge control solenoid valve

To canister

To canister

Idle-up solenoid valve

FIG. 28 Vacuum diagram—1.2L carbureted Justy

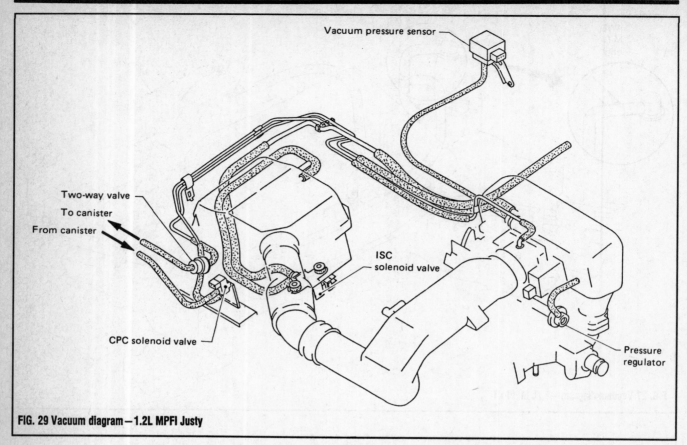

FIG. 29 Vacuum diagram—1.2L MPFI Justy

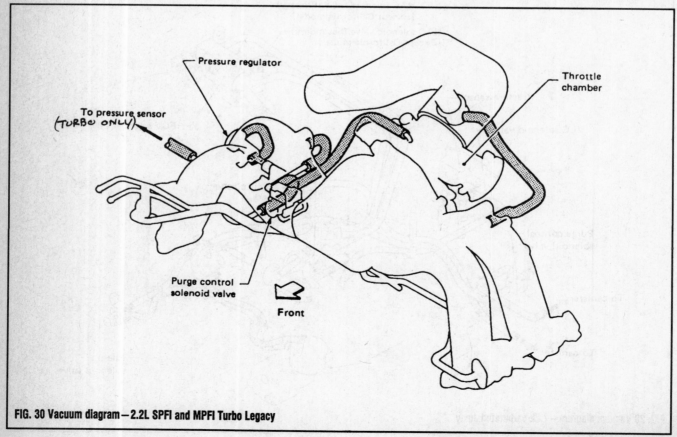

FIG. 30 Vacuum diagram—2.2L SPFI and MPFI Turbo Legacy

5

FUEL

SYSTEM

CARBURETED FUEL SYSTEM

Electric Fuel Pump

REMOVAL & INSTALLATION

1. Remove the fuel delivery hoses from the fuel pump.
2. Disconnect the electrical harness connector from the fuel pump.
3. Loosen the fuel pump bracket-to-chassis nuts or bolts and the pump from the vehicle; be careful not to lose any washers or cushions.
4. Inspect the fuel pump; if found to be defective, replace it.
5. To install, reverse the removal procedures. Be sure the ground wire does not contact the pump body or the unit may vibrate. Start the engine and check for leaks.

PRESSURE TESTING

1. Raise and support the vehicle on jackstands.
2. Using a fuel pressure gauge, connect into the fuel line.
3. Turn the ignition switch On and observe the fuel pressure; it should be 2.6-3.3 psi (carbureted), 61-71 psi (MPFI) or 36-50 psi (SPFI). If the fuel pump does not meet specifications, replace the pump.
4. After testing, disconnect the pressure gauge and reconnect the fuel line.

Carburetor

Three types of carburetor are used on Subaru vehicles. All 1.2L engines use a DFC-328 carburetor; 1.6L engines use a DCP-306 carburetor and 1.8L engines use a DCZ-328 carburetor.

The carburetor supplies the correct mixture of fuel and air to the engine under varying conditions. Despite their complexity in design, carburetors function because of a simple physical principle (the venturi principle). Air is drawn into the engine by the pumping action of the pistons. As the air enters the top of the carburetor it passes through a venturi, which is nothing more than a restriction in the throttle bore. The air speeds up as it passes through the venturi causing a slight drop in pressure. The

pressure drop pulls fuel from the float bowl through a nozzle into the throttle bore, where it mixes with the air and forms a fine mist which is distributed to the cylinders through the intake manifold.

The carburetor uses a progressive linkage between the primary and secondary circuit. For optimum performance plus fuel economy, the secondary circuit of the carburetor is used only at high engine rpm. Normal low speed operation is handled by the primary circuit.

On later models the carburetor is provided with a coasting by-pass system which helps control exhaust emissions during deceleration.

An automatic control choke is used on all carburetors. The automatic choke and a throttle chamber are heated by engine coolant to prevent throttle bore icing, help the engine start and run well in the coldest conditions.

The basic systems of the carburetor are:
1. The float system
2. The primary side
   a. Slow system
   b. Main system
   c. Accelerator pump
   d. Power system
   e. Choke system
   f. Slow float shutoff system

3. Secondary side
   a. Step system
   b. Main system
4. Coasting by-pass system.

➡ If you are planning to clean, rebuild or replace your carburetor be sure you understand what is necessary. Read all instructions, have all parts and tools on hand and keep everything as clean as possible. Remember the gasoline mileage and the performance depend on how well you do the job.

ADJUSTMENTS

Automatic Choke Mechanism

◆ SEE FIG. 1

1. With the carburetor removed from the engine, set the fast idle cam adjusting lever on the fourth highest step of the fast idle cam.
2. Check to be sure that the choke valve is fully closed.
3. Measure the clearance between the lower edge of the primary throttle valve and its bore.

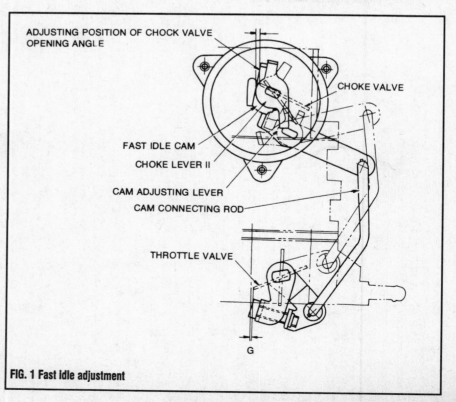

ADJUSTING POSITION OF CHOCK VALVE
OPENING ANGLE

CHOKE VALVE

FAST IDLE CAM

CHOKE LEVER II

CAM ADJUSTING LEVER

CAM CONNECTING ROD

THROTTLE VALVE

G

FIG. 1 Fast idle adjustment

4. Measurement should be as follows:
• DFC-328: 0.0303 in. (0.77mm)
• DCZ-328: 0.0472–0.0587 in. (1.20–1.49mm)
• DCP-306: 0.0386–0.0528 in. (0.98–1.34mm)

5. If not within specification, turn the fast idle adjusting screw.

Vacuum Break Opening Angle

▶ SEE FIG. 4

1. Move the throttle lever while lightly holding the choke valve with your hand to keep it fully closed. Release your hand to make sure the choke valve is fully closed.

2. With the choke valve kept closed, connect a portable vacuum pump to the vacuum break diaphragm and continue to apply vacuum pressure until the diaphragm shaft moves a complete stroke toward the diaphragm.

3. Measure the clearance (R) while lightly holding choke valve with your hand. Clearance should be as follows:
• DFC-328: 0.063 in. (1.6mm)
• DCZ-328: 0.059–0.075 in. (1.5–1.9mm)
• DCP-306: 0.059–0.075 in. (1.5–1.9mm)

4. If not within specification, adjust by bending the pawl at the tip of the lever.

Float and Fuel Level

The float level may be adjusted with the carburetor installed on the engine, by removing the air horn as follows:

▶ SEE FIG. 2 and 5

1. Disconnect the accelerator pump actuating rod from the pump lever.

2. Remove the throttle return spring.

3. Disconnect the choke cable from the choke lever, and remove it from the spring hanger.

4. Remove the spring hanger, the choke bellcrank and the remaining air horn retaining screws.

5. Lift the air horn slightly, disconnect the choke connecting rod, and remove the air horn.

6. Invert the air horn (float up), and measure the distance between the surface of the air horn and the float.

7. Clearance should be as follows:
• DFC-328: 0.437 in. (11.1mm)
• DCZ-328: 0.435–0.492 in. (11.5–12.5mm)
• DCP-306: 0.393 in. (10mm)

8. If not within specification, bend the float arm until the clearance correct.

9. Invert the air horn to its installed position.

10. On the DCZ-328 and DCP-306 carburetors, measure the distance between the float arm and the needle valve seat. On the DFC-328 carburetor, measure the distance between the choke chamber and the bottom of the float.

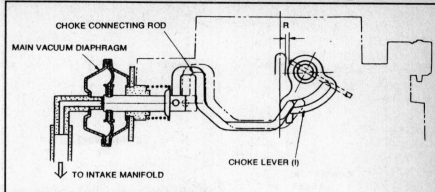

FIG. 4 Vacuum break opening angle adjustment

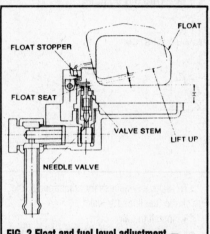

FIG. 2 Float and fuel level adjustment — except DFC-328

11. Clearance should be as follows:
• DCF-328: 1.835 in. (46.6mm)
• DCZ-328: 0.059–0.075 in. (1.5–1.9mm)
• DCP-306: 0.051–0.067 in. (1.3–1.7mm)

12. If not within specification, adjust by bending the float stops.

Primary/Secondary Throttle Linkage

▶ SEE FIG. 3

1. With the carburetor removed from the engine, operate the linkage so that the connecting rod contacts the groove on the end of the secondary actuating lever.

2. Measure the clearance between the lower end of the primary throttle valve and its bore.

3. Clearance should be as follows:
• DFC-328: 0.236 in. (6.0mm)
• DCZ-328: 0.271–0.275 in. (6.89–6.99mm)
• DCP-306: 0.236 in. (6.0mm)

3. If not within specification, adjust the clearance by bending the connecting rod.

4. Check to make sure that the linkage operates smoothly after performing the adjustment.

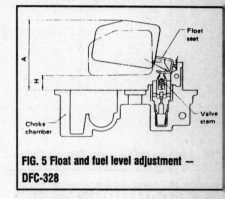

FIG. 5 Float and fuel level adjustment — DFC-328

REMOVAL & INSTALLATION

Except 1.2L Engine

1. Remove the air cleaner.

2. Disconnect the fuel delivery, return and air vent hoses.

3. Disconnect the main diaphragm, distributor advancer, EGR and canister vacuum hoses.

4. Disconnect hoses for duty solenoid valves (California and 49 state 2WD models).

5. Disconnect FCV and secondary main air bleed hoses (High altitude configuration only).

6. Disconnect the harness connector.

7. Disconnect the accelerator cable from the throttle lever.

8. Drain the coolant so as to prevent it from flowing out.

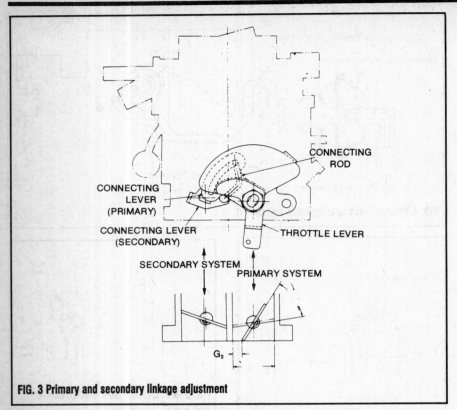

CONNECTING ROD

CONNECTING LEVER (PRIMARY)

CONNECTING LEVER (SECONDARY)

THROTTLE LEVER

SECONDARY SYSTEM

PRIMARY SYSTEM

G_2

FIG. 3 Primary and secondary linkage adjustment

> ## ❄ CAUTION
>
> **When draining the coolant, keep in mind that cats and dogs are attracted by the ethylene glycol antifreeze, and are quite likely to drink any that is left in an uncovered container or in puddles on the ground. This will prove fatal in sufficient quantity. Always drain the coolant into a sealable container. Coolant should be reused unless it is contaminated or several years old.**

9. Remove the carburetor attaching nuts and the carburetor

To Install:

10. Install the carburetor onto the intake manifold securely, using the carburetor attaching nuts.

11. Connect the accelerator cable to the throttle lever.

12. Connect the harness connector.

13. Connect the FCV and secondary main air bleed hoses (if so equipped).

14. Connect the hoses to the duty solenoid.

15. Connect the main diaphragm, distributor advancer, EGR and canister vacuum hoses.

16. Connect the fuel delivery, return and air vent hoses.

17. Make any necessary adjustments and check the fuel lines for leaks.

18. Install the air cleaner.

1.2L Engine

1. Disconnect the negative battery terminal from the battery.

2. Remove the air cleaner by performing the following procedures:

   a. Label and disconnect these hoses from the air cleaner: The Blow-by hose, the ASV hose, the vacuum hose, the air duct and the boot.

   b. Remove the brake booster vacuum-to-air cleaner hose.

   c. Remove the distributor-to-ignition coil from the clamp.

   d. Remove the air cleaner mounting bolts and the wing nut, then remove the air cleaner from the carburetor.

3. Disconnect and remove the accelerator cable, the vacuum hoses, the fuel hose(s) and the electrical connectors.

4. Remove the carburetor-to-intake manifold bolts, the carburetor and the gasket.

   To Install:

5. Using a new gasket, install the carburetor and tighten the attaching nuts.

6. Install the accelerator cable, vacuum hoses, fuel hoses and electrical connections.

7. Install the air cleaner and connect all vacuum hoses.

8. Connect the negative battery cable.

CARBURETOR OVERHAUL

♦ SEE FIG. 6–8

Generally, when a carburetor requires major service, a rebuilt one is purchased on an exchange basis, or a kit may be bought for overhauling the carburetor

The kit contains the necessary parts and some form of instructions for carburetor rebuilding. The instructions may vary between a simple exploded view and detailed step-by-step rebuilding instructions. Unless you are familiar with carburetor overhaul, it is best to purchase a rebuilt carburetor.

There are some general overhaul procedures which should always be observed:

• Efficient carburetion depends greatly on careful cleaning and inspection during overhaul since dirt, gum, water, or varnish in or on the carburetor parts are often responsible for poor performance.

• Overhaul your carburetor in a clean, dust-free area. Carefully disassemble the carburetor, referring often to the exploded views. Keep all similar and look-alike parts segregated during disassembly and cleaning to avoid accidental interchange during assembly. Make a note of all jet sizes.

• When the carburetor is disassembled, wash all parts (except diaphragms, electric choke units, pump plunger, and any other plastic, leather, fiber, or rubber parts) in clean carburetor solvent. Do not leave parts in the solvent any longer than is necessary to sufficiently loosen the deposits. Excessive cleaning may remove the special finish from the float bowl and choke valve bodies, leaving these parts unfit for service. Rinse all parts in clean solvent and blow them dry with compressed air or allow them to air dry. Wipe clean all cork, plastic, leather, and fiber parts with a clean, lint-free cloth.

• Blow out all passages and jets with compressed air and be sure that there are no restrictions or blockages. Never use wire or similar tools to clean jets, fuel passages, or air bleeds. Clean all jets and valves separately to avoid accidental interchange.

• Check all parts for wear or damage. If wear or damage is found, replace the defective parts.

DISASSEMBLY

1. Remove the carburetor from the vehicle and place on a suitable work stand.

2. Remove the throttle return spring.

3. Remove the pump lever shaft screw, pump lever, washer and spring washer.

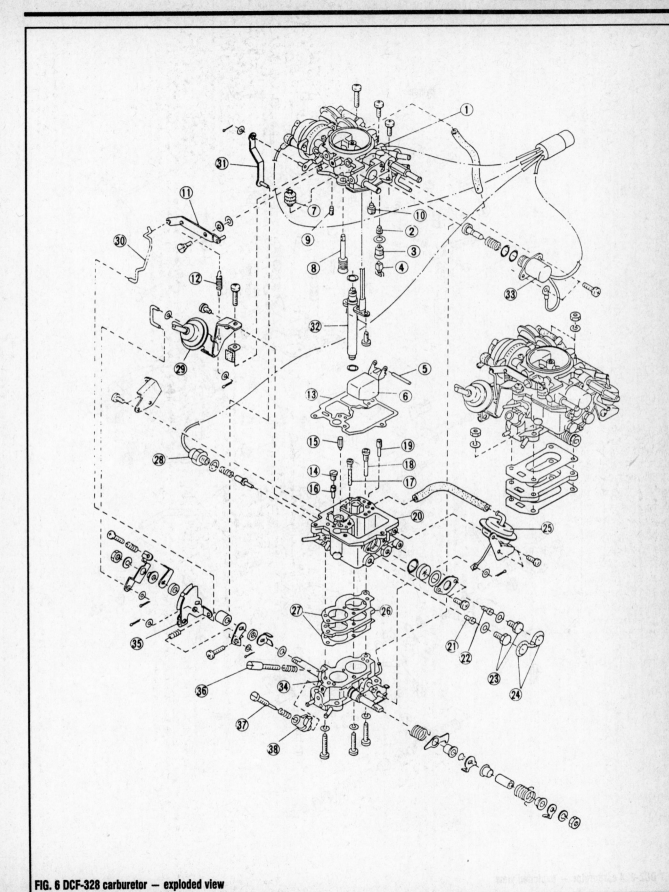

FIG. 6 DCF-328 carburetor — exploded view

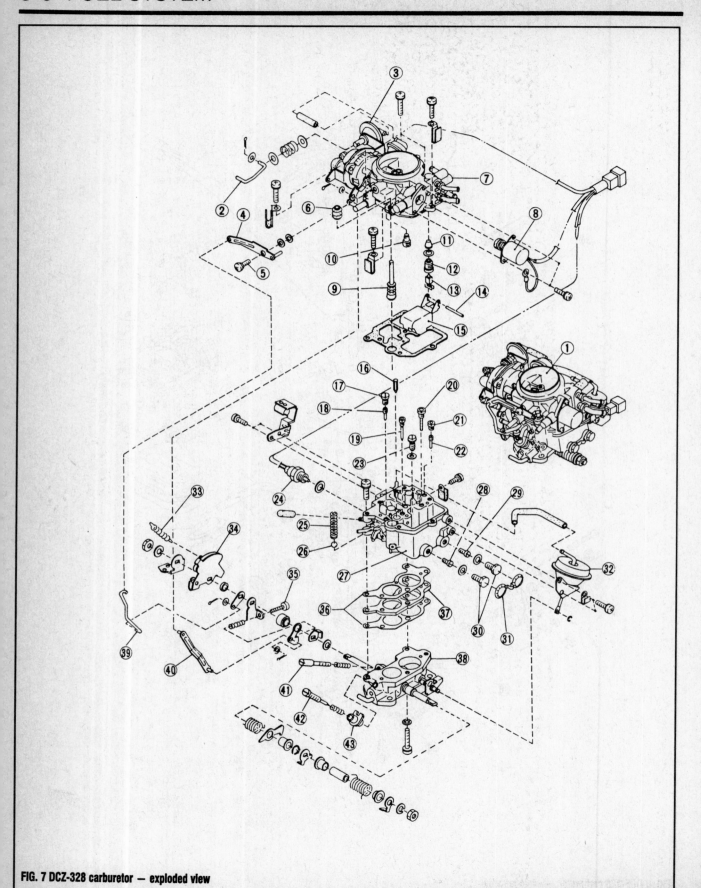

FIG. 7 DCZ-328 carburetor — exploded view

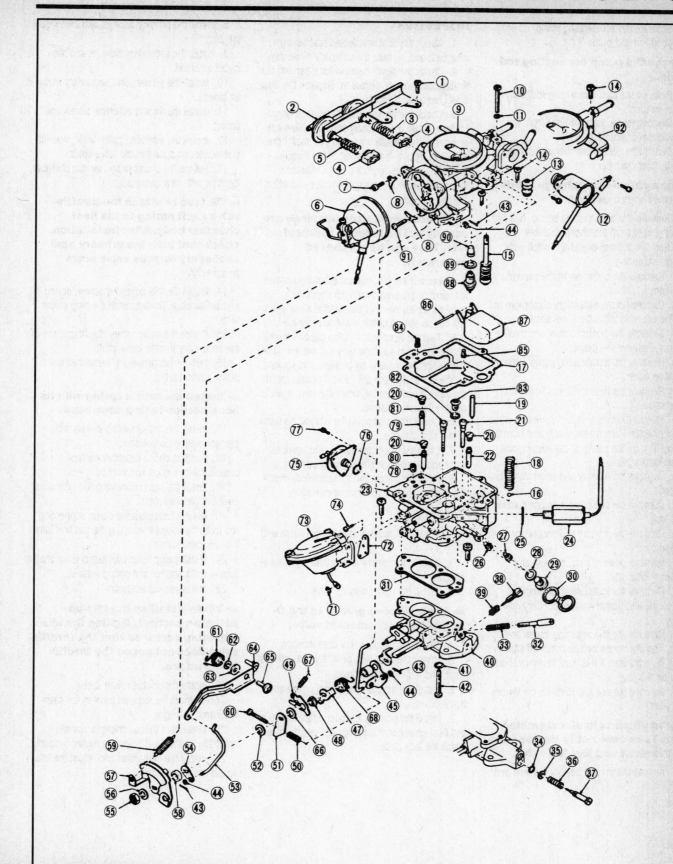

FIG. 8 DCP-306 carburetor — exploded view

4. Separate the accelerating pump connecting rod and pump lever.

➡ **Leave the pump connecting rod as it is.**

5. Remove the cam connecting rod, cotter pin and washer.

6. Disconnect the vacuum hose from the main vacuum diaphragm.

7. Detach the choke chamber and gasket from the float chamber.

➡ **Take care not to damage the duty solenoid valve or float.**

8. Remove the piston return spring, ball and injector weight from the choke chamber

9. Remove the anti-dieseling switch with plunger and spring.

10. Remove the cotter pin of the secondary diaphragm.

11. Disconnect the secondary diaphragm rod from the secondary throttle valve shaft.

12. Separate the float chamber and throttle chamber. Remove the gasket.

13. Remove the accelerating pump piston and pump cover.

14. Remove the float shaft and float with needle valve.

15. Pull out the duty solenoid valve lead wires from connector. Remove the rear holder from the housing. Pry up the pawls of the housing and remove the terminal.

16. Remove the primary and secondary slow air bleed.

17. Remove the switch vent solenoid valve and O-ring.

18. Remove the primary and secondary main air bleeds.

19. Remove primary plug, primary and secondary slow jets.

20. Remove the lockplate, float chamber drain plugs, and primary and secondary main jets.

21. Remove the idle adjusting screw and spring. The idle screw can be removed after turning its protector. It if is hard to remove, drill a hole on the plug.

22. Remove the nut and parts on the throttle valve shaft.

➡ **Keep all parts in disassembled order. Take care not to damage the throttle shaft and throttle valve.**

23. remove the throttle adjusting screw and spring.

INSPECTION

1. Check the float needle and seat for wear. If wear is found, replace the complete assembly.

2. Check the float hinge pin for wear and the float(s) for dents or distortion. Replace the float if fuel has leaked into it.

3. Check the throttle and choke shaft bores for wear or an out-of-round condition. Damage or wear to the throttle arm, shaft, or shaft bore will often require replacement of the throttle body. These parts require a close tolerance. Wear may allow air leakage, which could affect starting and idling.

➡ **Throttle shafts and bushings are usually not included in overhaul kits. They can be purchased separately.**

4. Inspect the idle mixture adjusting needles for burrs or grooves. Any such condition requires replacement of the needle, since you will not be able to obtain a satisfactory idle.

5. Test the accelerator pump check valves. They should pass air one way but not the other. Test for proper seating by blowing and sucking on the valve. Replace the valve if necessary. If the valve is satisfactory, wash the valve again to remove breath moisture.

6. Check the bowl cover for warped surfaces with a straightedge.

7. Closely inspect the valves and seats for wear and damage, replacing as necessary.

8. After the carburetor is assembled, check the choke valve for freedom of operation.

ASSEMBLY

1. Install the switch vent solenoid valve with O-rings.

2. Install the primary and secondary slow air bleeds.

3. Install the duty solenoid valve.

➡ **Apply silicone grease to the O-ring of the duty solenoid valve.**

4. Install the needle valve case washer.

5. Install the float with needle valve and float shaft, and adjust the float level.

6. Install the accelerating pump piston and pump cover.

7. Install the primary and secondary main jets and float chamber drain plugs with washers and install the lock plate.

8. Install the primary slow jet and then install the plug.

9. Install the secondary slow jet and then install air bleed.

10. Install the primary and secondary main air bleeds.

11. Install the throttle adjusting screw and spring.

12. Install the adjusting plate, lever, washer, sleeve, etc. onto the throttle valve shaft.

13. Put the flat chamber and throttle chamber together with new gaskets.

➡ **Be sure to attach the throttle valve shaft spring to the float chamber body. After installation, check that both the primary and secondary throttle valve move properly.**

14. Install the idle adjusting screw, spring and screw case. Do not install the plug at this time.

15. Connect the secondary diaphragm rod to the secondary throttle valve shaft.

16. Install injector weight. Install ball and piston return spring.

➡ **Install the return spring with its hook portion facing downward.**

17. Install the anti-dieseling switch with plunger, spring and washer.

18. Position choke chamber on float chamber with gasket and clamps.

19. Install the cam connecting rod with cotter pins and plain washers.

20. Connect accelerating pump connecting rod to pump lever by inserting the rod end into hole in pump lever.

21. Install pump lever with pump lever shaft screw, plain washer and spring washer.

22. Install idle-up actuator.

➡ **When installing the idle-up actuator, securely tighten the idle adjusting screw so that the throttle valve does not gouge the throttle bore surface.**

23. Install the throttle return spring.

24. Connect the vacuum hose to the main vacuum diaphragm.

25. Make sure that all linkages operate smoothly and all lead wires are routed properly.

26. Install the carburetor and adjust the idle speed and idle mixture.

SINGLE POINT FUEL INJECTION (SPFI) SYSTEM

The SPFI is used on the 1.8L engine only. The system electronically controls the amount of injection from the fuel injector, and supplies the optimum air/fuel mixture under all operating conditions of the engine. Features of the SPFI system are as follows:

• Precise control of of the air/fuel mixture is accomplished by an increased number of input signals transmitting engine operating conditions to the control unit.

• The use of hot wire type air flow meter not only eliminates the need for high altitude compensation, but improves driving performance at high altitudes.

• The air control valve automatically regulates the idle speed to the set value under all engine operating conditions.

• Ignition timing is electrically controlled, thereby allowing the use of complicated spark advances characteristics.

• Wear of the air flow meter and fuel injector is automatically corrected so that they maintain their original performance.

• Troubleshooting can easily be accomplished by the built-in self-diagnosis function.

Relieving The Fuel System Pressure

➡ **This procedure must be performed prior to servicing any component of the fuel injection system which contains fuel.**

1. Disconnect the fuel pump connector at the fuel pump.

2. Crank the engine for 5 seconds or more to relieve the fuel pressure. If the engine starts during this time, allow it to run until it stalls.

3. Connect the fuel pump connector.

➡ **Additional information and testing procedures are located under "Electronic Engine Controls" in Section 6.**

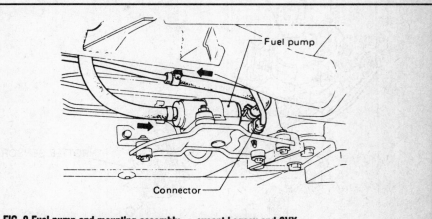

FIG. 9 Fuel pump and mounting assembly — except Legacy and SVX

Electric Fuel Pump

REMOVAL & INSTALLATION

◆ SEE FIG. 9

1. Release the fuel system pressure and disconnect the negative battery cable.

2. Keep the fuel pump harness disconnected after releasing the fuel system pressure.

3. Raise and support the vehicle safely.

4. Clamp the middle portion of the thick hose connecting the pipe and the pump to prevent fuel from flowing out of the tank.

5. Loosen the hose clamp and disconnect the hose.

6. Remove the three pump bracket mounting bolts and remove the pump together with the pump damper.

To Install:

7. If the pump and damper have been removed from the bracket, reinstall and tighten the bolts securely.

8. Install the hose and tighten the clamp screw to 0.7–1.1 ft. lbs. (1.0–1.5 Nm).

9. Install the pump bracket in position to the vehicle body and secure it with the bolts.

➡ **Take care to position the rubber cushion properly.**

10. Connect the pump harness connector.

11. Connect the negative battery cable and test the fuel pump for proper operation.

TESTING

1. Turn the ignition **ON** and listen for the fuel pump to make a growling sound. Turn the ignition **OFF**.

2. Release the fuel system pressure. Disconnect the pump connector and crank the engine for 5 seconds or more. If the engine starts, allow it to run until it stops. Turn the ignition **OFF** and install the fuel pump connector.

3. Disconnect the fuel hose at the fuel pump.

4. Connect a gauge in-line using a T-fitting.

5. Start the engine and measure the fuel pressure.

6. Release the fuel system pressure and remove the gauge.

Throttle Body

REMOVAL & INSTALLATION

◆ SEE FIG. 10

1. Disconnect the negative battery cable.

2. Remove the air intake duct.

3. Remove the air control valve inlet hose.

4. Remove the PCV hoses.

5. Label and disconnect all electrical connectors on the throttle body.

6. Loosen the throttle body attaching screws evenly as to not warp the throttle body.

7. Remove the throttle body.

To Install:

8. Install the throttle body using a new gasket. Tighten to 13–15 ft. lbs. (18–21 Nm).

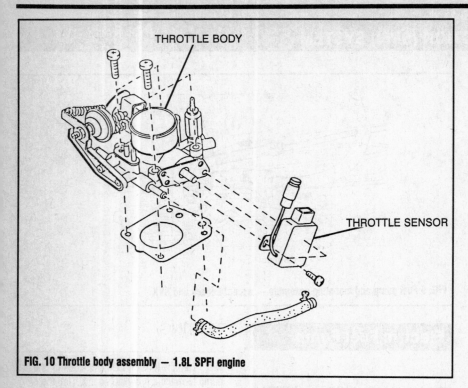

THROTTLE BODY

THROTTLE SENSOR

FIG. 10 Throttle body assembly — 1.8L SPFI engine

9. Connect the electrical connectors.
10. Install the air control valve inlet hose and PCV hoses.
11. Install the air intake duct.
12. Connect the negative battery cable.

Airflow Meter

REMOVAL & INSTALLATION

♦ SEE FIG. 11
1. Disconnect the negative battery cable.
2. Remove the air intake boot by loosening the clamps and sliding the boot from the airflow meter.
3. Disconnect the airflow meter electrical connector.
4. Remove the airflow meter attaching bolts.
5. Remove the airflow meter and discard the gasket.
   To install:
6. Using a new gasket, install the airflow meter. Tighten the bolts carefully as the air cleaner housing is plastic.
7. Install the airflow meter electrical connector.
8. Install the intake air boot and tighten the clamps securely.
9. Connect the negative battery cable.

TESTING

♦ SEE FIG. 12
1. Check for leaks or damage in the connection between the air intake boot and the air flow meter. Repair if necessary.
2. Disconnect the electrical connector from the air flow meter, then remove the air intake boot, and the air flow meter from the air cleaner assembly.
3. Check the exterior of the air flow meter for damage.
4. Check the interior of the air flow meter for foreign particles, water, or oil in the passages, especially in the bypass. If any of the above faults are noted, replace the air flow meter.
5. If none of the above faults are noted, proceed as follows:
   a. Turn the ignition switch to the **OFF** position, then install the air flow meter onto air cleaner assembly.
   b. Disconnect the air flow meter electrical connector, then slide back the rubber boot.

➡ **Conduct the following test by connecting the tester pins to the connector terminals on the side from which the rubber boot was removed.**

c. Using an ohmmeter, measure the resistance between terminal B on the connector and ground. Ohmmeter should read 10 ohms. If ohmmeter reading exceeds 10 ohms, check the harness and internal circuits of the control unit for discontinuity.
d. Turn the ignition switch to the **ON** position.
e. Using a voltmeter, measure voltage across power terminal R and ground. Voltmeter should read 10 volts. If specifications are not as specified, check the power line (battery, fuse, control unit, harness connector, etc).
f. Connect the air flow meter electrical connector. Using a voltmeter, connect the positive lead of the tester to terminal W and the negative lead of the tester to terminal B and measure voltage across the 2 terminals. Voltmeter should read 0.1–0.5 volts. If specifications are not as specified, replace the air flow meter.
g. Remove the upper section of the air cleaner assembly, then blow air in from the air cleaner side and check if voltage across terminals W and B is higher than specification obtained in Step f. If not, replace the air flow meter.

Throttle Position Sensor

REMOVAL & INSTALLATION

♦ SEE FIG. 10
1. Disconnect the negative battery cable.
2. Remove the 2 screws securing the throttle sensor to the throttle body.
3. Disconnect the throttle sensor electrical connector.
4. Remove the throttle sensor by pulling it in the axial direction of the throttle shaft.
5. Remove the throttle sensor O-ring and discard.
   To install:
6. Using a new throttle sensor O-ring, install the throttle sensor and tighten the screw hand tight.
7. Connect the throttle sensor electrical connector.
8. Connect the negative battery cable.
9. Adjust the throttle sensor.

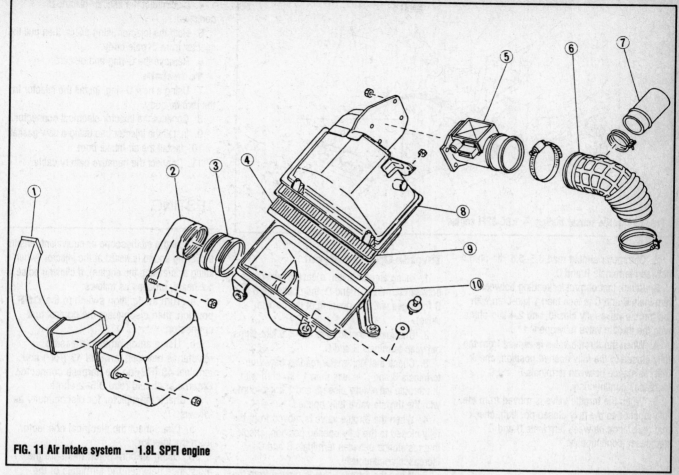

FIG. 11 Air intake system — 1.8L SPFI engine

Adjustment

IDLE CONTACT

1. Using an ohmmeter, check that continuity exists between terminals A and B, when the throttle is fully closed, and that no continuity exists when the throttle is fully opened.

2. Adjust the throttle sensor by turning it until the following specifications are met.

3. Insert a feeler gauge (thickness gauge) of 0.0122 in (0.31mm) between the stopper screw on the throttle chamber and the stopper (this corresponds to the throttle opening of 1.0 degree). Ensure that continuity exists between terminals A and B.

4. Insert a feeler gauge (thickness gauge) of 0.0311 in (0.79mm) between the stopper screw on the throttle chamber and the stopper (this corresponds to a throttle opening of 2.5 degrees). Ensure that continuity exists between terminals A and B.

THROTTLE OPENING SIGNAL

1. Using an ohmmeter, measure resistance between terminals B and D, then between B and C (changes with the opening of the throttle valve).

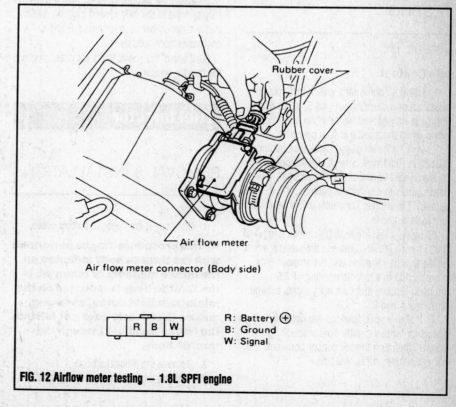

R: Battery ⊕
B: Ground
W: Signal

FIG. 12 Airflow meter testing — 1.8L SPFI engine

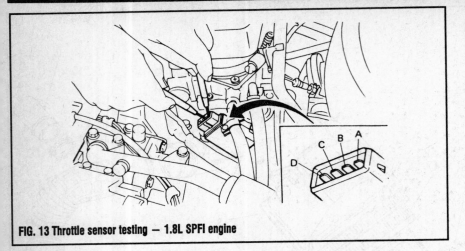

FIG. 13 Throttle sensor testing — 1.8L SPFI engine

2. Ohmmeter should read 3.5–6.5 kilo-ohms between terminals B and D.

3. Check that ohmmeter reading between terminals B and C is less than 1 kilo-ohm with the throttle valve fully closed, and 2.4 kilo-ohms with the throttle valve fully opened.

4. When the throttle valve is moved from the fully closed to the fully opened position, check that resistance between terminals B and C increases continuously.

5. When the throttle valve is moved from the fully opened to the fully closed position, check that resistance between terminals B and C decreases continuously.

TESTING

◆ SEE FIG. 13

Idle Contact

1. Using an ohmmeter, check that continuity exists between terminals A and B, when the throttle is fully closed, and that no continuity exists when the throttle is fully opened.

2. Insert a feeler gauge (thickness gauge) of 0.0122 in (0.31mm) between the stopper screw on the throttle chamber and the stopper (this corresponds to the throttle opening of 1.0 degree). Ensure that continuity exists between terminals A and B.

3. Insert a feeler gauge (thickness gauge) of 0.0311 in (0.79mm) between the stopper screw on the throttle chamber and the stopper (this corresponds to a throttle opening of 2.5 degrees). Ensure that continuity exists between terminals A and B.

4. If above specifications are not as specified, loosen throttle sensor attaching screws, then turn throttle sensor body until the correct adjustment is obtained.

Throttle Opening Signal

1. Using an ohmmeter, measure resistance between terminals B and D, then between B and C (changes with the opening of the throttle valve).

2. Ohmmeter should read 3.5–6.5 kilo-ohms between terminals B and D.

3. Check that ohmmeter reading between terminals B and C is less than 1 kilo-ohm with the throttle valve fully closed, and 2.4 kilo-ohms with the throttle valve fully opened.

4. When the throttle valve is moved from the fully closed to the fully opened position, check that resistance between terminals B and C increases continuously.

5. When the throttle valve is moved from the fully opened to the fully closed position, check that resistance between terminals B and C decreases continuously.

6. If any of the above faults are noted, replace the throttle sensor.

Fuel Injector

REMOVAL & INSTALLATION

◆ SEE FIG. 14

1. Disconnect the negative battery cable.

➡ **This procedure may be performed with the throttle body mounted on the intake manifold or removed. If the throttle body is mounted on the intake manifold during servicing, ensure that debris does not fall into the intake manifold through the throttle body.**

2. Remove the air intake boot.
3. Remove the injector cap and gasket.

4. Disconnect the injector electrical connector.

5. Hold the injector using pliers, then pull the injector from throttle body.

6. Remove the O-ring and discard.

To Install:

7. Using a new O-ring, install the injector in the throttle body.

8. Connect the injector electrical connector.

9. Install the injector cap using a new gasket.

10. Install the air intake boot.

11. Connect the negative battery cable.

TESTING

1. Using a stethoscope or equivalent, ensure a clicking sound is heard at the injector (when idling or cranking the engine). If clicking noise is not heard, proceed as follows:

a. Turn the ignition switch to the **OFF** position, then disconnect the control unit connector.

b. Using an ohmmeter, measure resistance between terminal 43 (RW) and terminal 48 (RB) on the harness connector. Ohmmeter should read 0.5–2 ohms.

2. Check the injector for discontinuity as follows:

a. Disconnect the electrical connector from the injector.

b. Using an ohmmeter, measure the resistance between the terminals of the connector. Ohmmeter should read 0.5–2 ohms.

c. If specifications are not as specified, replace the injector.

3. Check the injector for insulation as follows:

a. Using an ohmmeter, measure resistance between each terminal of the connector on the injector side and ground. Ohmmeter should read 1 mega-ohm.

b. If specifications are not as specified, replace the injector.

4. If specifications obtained in Step 1 are not as specified, but specifications obtained in Steps 2 and 3 are within specifications, check the harness for discontinuity and the connector for poor connection.

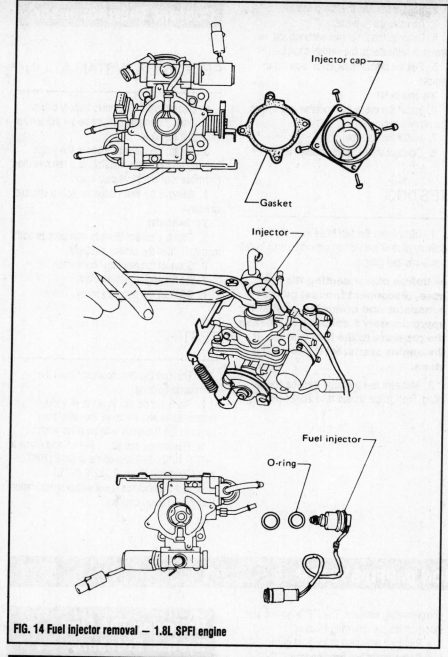

FIG. 14 Fuel injector removal — 1.8L SPFI engine

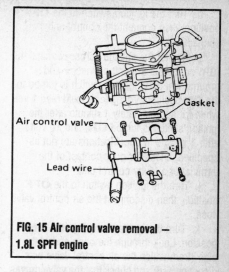

FIG. 15 Air control valve removal — 1.8L SPFI engine

Air Control Valve

REMOVAL & INSTALLATION

♦ SEE FIG. 15

1. Disconnect the negative battery cable.
2. Disconnect the injector lead wire from the clamp.
3. Remove the air control valve, gasket and lead wire from the venturi chamber.
4. Using a new gasket, install the air control valve.
5. Connect the injector lead wire.
6. Connect the negative battery cable.

TESTING

1. Disconnect the electrical connector to the air control valve while the engine is idling. Check the engine rpm drops.
2. Connect air control valve connector, and check to see that engine rpm resumes its original position.

➥ **Disconnecting the connector causes a change in the engine rpm when the engine is cold. However, when the engine is warm, it causes a smaller change or almost no change at all.**

3. If the engine shows no rpm change, proceed as follows:
   a. Stop the engine, then disconnect the the electrical connector from the air control valve.
   b. Turn the ignition switch to the **ON** position.
   c. Using a voltmeter, measure the voltage across power terminal BW on the air control valve connector and ground. Voltmeter should read 10 volts. If voltage obtained is less than specified, check the harness.
   d. Turn the ignition switch to the **OFF** position. Using an ohmmeter, measure the resistance between each terminal of the connector on the air control valve. Ohmmeter should read 7.3–13 ohms at −4–176°F (−20–80°C). If specifications are not as specified, replace the air control valve.
   e. Using an ohmmeter, measure the insulation resistance between each terminal of the connector on the air control valve and ground. Ohmmeter should read 1 mega-ohm. If specifications are not as specified, replace the air control valve.
   f. Connect the air control valve connector, then disconnect control unit electrical connector.
   g. Turn the ignition switch to the **ON** position. Using a voltmeter, measure voltage between terminal 45 (GR) of the control unit connector and ground. Voltmeter should read 10 volts. If specifications are not as specified, check the harness between the air control valve and the control unit.

h. Turn the ignition switch to the **OFF** position, then connect the control unit connector.

i. Monitor the voltage across terminal 45 (GR) on the control unit connector and ground, when the ignition switch is turned to the **ON** position. Voltmeter should read 1 volt when for approximately 1 minute after the ignition switch is turned **ON**, and 10 volts after 1 minute. If specifications are not as specified, check for poor contact of the terminal or a faulty control unit.

j. Turn the ignition switch to the **OFF** position, then disconnect the air control valve hose.

k. Turn the ignition switch to the **ON** position. Look through the open end of the pipe (from which the air control valve was disconnected) and check that the valve moves from the fully closed position to the fully opened position, 1 minute after the ignition switch is turned to the **ON** position.

Fuel Pressure Regulator

REMOVAL & INSTALLATION

1. Disconnect the negative battery cable.

2. Relieve the fuel system pressure.
3. Remove the fuel line.
4. Remove the 2 screws securing the pressure regulator to the venturi chamber.
5. Pull the pressure regulator upward to remove.
   To install:
6. Install the pressure regulator and tighten the screws securely.
7. Install the fuel line.
8. Connect the negative battery cable.

TESTING

1. Disconnect the fuel hose from the fuel delivery pipe of the throttle chamber, then install a suitable fuel gauge.

➡ **Before disconnecting the fuel hose, disconnect the fuel pump connector and crank the engine for approximately 5 seconds to release the pressure in the fuel system. If the engine starts, let it run until it stops.**

2. Measure fuel pressure with the engine idling. Fuel gauge should read 20–24 psi.

Coolant Thermosensor

REMOVAL & INSTALLATION

1. Disconnect the negative battery cable.
2. Drain the engine coolant below the level of the intake manifold.
3. Locate the thermosensor at the water housing on the intake manifold and remove the thermosensor electrical connector.
4. Remove the thermosensor with a suitable wrench.
   To install:
5. Coat the sensor threads with sealant and install. Tighten the sensor securely.
6. Connect the electrical connector.
7. Fill the engine with coolant.
8. Connect the negative battery cable.

TESTING

1. Remove the thermosensor from the thermostat housing.
2. Place the sensor in water of various temperatures and measure the resistance between the terminals with an ohmmeter.
3. Resistance should be 7–11.5 kilo-ohms at 14°F (–10°C), 2–3 kilo-ohms at 68°F (20°C), and 700–1000 ohms at 122°F (50°C).
4. If the resistance is not within specification, replace the thermosensor.

MULTI-POINT FUEL INJECTION (MPFI) SYSTEM

The MPFI system supplies the optimum air/fuel mixture to the engine under all various operating conditions. System fuel, which is pressurized at a constant pressure, is injected into the intake air passage of the cylinder head. The amount of fuel injected is controlled by the intermittent injection system where the electromagnetic injection valve (fuel injector) opens only for a short period of time, depending on the amount of air required for 1 cycle of operation. During system operation, the amount injection is determined by the duration of an electric pulse sent to the fuel injector, which permits precise metering of the fuel.

All the operating conditions of the engine are converted into electric signals, resulting in additional features of the system, such as improved adaptability and easier addition of

compensating element. The MPFI system also incorporates the following features:
  • Reduced emission of exhaust gases
  • Reduction in fuel consumption
  • Increased engine output
  • Superior acceleration and deceleration
  • Superior starting and warm-up performance in cold weather since compensation is made for coolant and intake air temperature
  • Good performance with turbocharger, if equipped

Relieving The Fuel System Pressure

➡ **This procedure must be performed prior to servicing any component of the fuel injection system which contains fuel.**

1. Disconnect the fuel pump connector at the fuel pump.
2. Crank the engine for 5 seconds or more to relieve the fuel pressure. If the engine starts during this time, allow it to run until it stalls.
3. Connect the fuel pump connector.

➡ **Additional Information and testing procedures are located under "Electronic Engine Controls" in Section 4.**

Electric Fuel Pump

REMOVAL & INSTALLATION

◆ SEE FIG. 9 and 16

1. Release the fuel system pressure and disconnect the negative battery cable.
2. Keep the fuel pump harness disconnected after releasing the fuel system pressure.
3. Raise and support the vehicle safely.
4. Clamp the middle portion of the thick hose connecting the pipe and the pump to prevent fuel from flowing out of the tank.
5. Loosen the hose clamp and disconnect the hose.
6. Remove the three pump bracket mounting bolts and remove the pump together with the pump damper.

To Install:

7. If the pump and damper have been removed from the bracket, reinstall and tighten the bolts securely.
8. Install the hose and tighten the clamp screw to 0.7–1.1 ft. lbs. (1.0–1.5 Nm).
9. Install the pump bracket in position to the vehicle body and secure it with the bolts.

➡ **Take care to position the rubber cushion properly.**

10. Connect the pump harness connector.
11. Connect the negative battery cable and test the fuel pump for proper operation.

TESTING

1. Turn the ignition **ON** and listen for the fuel pump to make a growling sound. Turn the ignition **OFF**.
2. Release the fuel system pressure. Disconnect the pump connector and crank the engine for 5 seconds or more. If the engine starts, allow it to run until it stops. Turn the ignition **OFF** and install the fuel pump connector.
3. Disconnect the fuel hose at the fuel pump.
4. Connect a gauge in-line using a T-fitting.
5. Start the engine and measure the fuel pressure.
6. Release the fuel system pressure and remove the gauge.

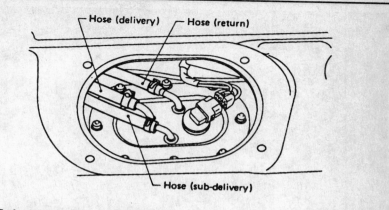

FIG. 16 Fuel pump assembly — Legacy and SVX

FIG. 16a Removing the engine cover—Legacy

Throttle Body

REMOVAL & INSTALLATION

1. Disconnect the negative battery cable.
2. Remove the air intake duct assembly.
3. Remove the engine cover, as required.
4. Drain the cooling system.
5. Remove the water hoses leading to the throttle body.
6. Remove the emissions gas hoses and as required, the auxiliary air hose.
7. Label and disconnect all electrical connectors from the throttle body.
8. Remove the bracket holding the throttle body to the cylinder head.
9. Disconnect the accelerator cable, and cruise control cable if equipped.
10. Remove the bolts attaching the throttle body to the air plenum.
11. Remove the throttle body and discard the gasket.

FIG. 16b Top of engine view showing throttle body and coil pack—Legacy

To Install:

12. Using a new gasket, install the throttle body and tighten the bolts to 17–20 ft. lbs. (23–26 Nm).

13. Install the throttle body bracket and tighten the bolts to 10–13 ft. lbs. (14–17 Nm).

14. Connect the accelerator cable, and cruise control cable if equipped.

15. Connect all electrical connectors to the throttle body.

16. Install the blow-by gas hose.

17. Install the water hoses leading to the throttle body.

18. Fill the cooling system.

19. Install the air intake duct assembly.

20. Connect the negative battery cable.

TESTING

♦ SEE FIG. 17–19

1.8L Engine

1. Insert a feeler gauge between the stopper screw of the throttle body and the stopper, and check for continuity between the following terminals:
   - 1.8L Loyale—terminals A and C
   - 1.8L XT—terminals 4 and 3

2. Check that there is continuity between the terminals when the throttle is fully closed.

3. Check that there is continuity between the terminals when a 0.0217 in. (0.55mm) feeler gauge is inserted between the throttle body screw and the stopper.

4. Check that there is no continuity between the terminals when a 0.0362 in. (0.92mm) feeler gauge is inserted between the throttle body screw and the stopper.

5. If not within specifications, loosen the screws securing the throttle switch and adjust until all specifications are met.

6. Measure the resistance between the sensor signal and ground on the throttle sensor connector terminals as follows:
   - 1.8L Loyale—terminals 1 and 2
   - 1.8L XT—terminals 3 and 2

7. Resistance should be 6–18 kilo-ohms. If not, replace the throttle opening sensor.

8. Measure the resistance between the throttle sensor connector terminals 1 and 3. Resistance should be 5.8–17.8 kilo-ohms when the throttle valve is fully closed and 1.5–5.1 kilo-ohms when the throttle valve is fully open.

9. Ensure that the resistance changes smoothly between the fully closed and fully open positions. If resistance is not within specifications, replace the sensor.

10. Start the engine and allow it to reach normal operating temperature. Check the idle speed.

11. Under a non-loaded state, turn the throttle lever by hand to increase engine rpm until the end of the dash pot comes off the throttle cam.

12. Gradually return the throttle lever, then check engine rpm when the throttle cam contacts the end of the dash pot. Engine rpm should be 2800–3400.

13. If rpm is not as specified, loosen the dash pot lock nut, then turn the dash pot until engine rpm is within specification. Tighten locknut.

14. After adjustment, rev the engine to ensure that the idle speed returns correctly as the throttle is released.

2.7L Engine

1. Disconnect the throttle sensor connector.

2. Insert a feeler gauge between the stopper screw of the throttle body and the stopper, and check for continuity between terminals 4 and 3.

3. Check that there is 5 kilo-ohms resistance maximum between the terminals when a 0.0138 in. (0.35mm) feeler gauge is inserted between the throttle body screw and the stopper.

4. Check that there is 1 mega-ohm resistance minimum between the terminals when a 0.0295 in. (0.75mm) feeler gauge is inserted between the throttle body screw and the stopper.

5. If not within specifications, loosen the screws securing the throttle switch and adjust until all specifications are met.

6. Measure the resistance between terminals 1 and 4. Resistance should be 3–7 kilo-ohms.

7. Measure the resistance between terminals 2 and 4. Resistance should be 2.

8. Ensure that the resistance changes smoothly between the fully closed and fully open positions. If resistance is not within specifications, replace the sensor.

2.2L Engine

1. Turn the ignition switch **ON**.

2. Measure the voltage between the ECU connector terminal and ground. Voltage should be as follows:
   - Terminal 2 and ground: 4.4–4.8 volts with the throttle fully open
   - Terminal 2 and ground: 0.7–1.6 volts with the throttle fully closed
   - Terminal 3 and ground: 5 volts
   - Terminal 1 and ground: 0 volts

3. Ensure voltage smoothly decreases in response to throttle opening. If measurements are not within specification, check and repair the ECU terminals or harness.

4. Disconnect the connector from the throttle sensor. Measure the resistance between throttle sensor terminals 2 and 3. Resistance should be 12 kilo-ohms.

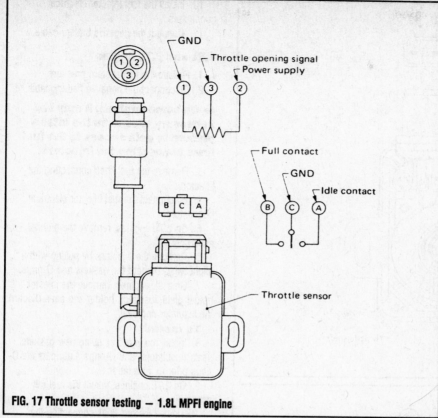

FIG. 17 Throttle sensor testing — 1.8L MPFI engine

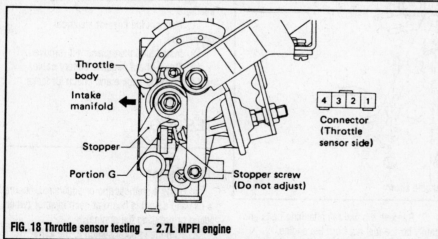

FIG. 18 Throttle sensor testing — 2.7L MPFI engine

5. Measure the resistance between terminals while slowly opening the throttle valve from the closed position. Resistance should be as follows:
- Terminals 2 and 4: 10–12 kilo-ohms with the throttle valve fully closed
- Terminals 2 and 4: 3–5 kilo-ohms with the throttle valve fully open

6. Ensure resistance smoothly increases in response to throttle opening. If measurements are not within specification, replace the throttle sensor.

7. Disconnect connectors from ECU and throttle sensor.

8. Measure resistance between ECU connector and throttle sensor connectors. Resistance should be as follows:
- ECU terminal 1 and throttle sensor terminal 2: 0 ohms
- ECU terminal 2 and throttle sensor terminal 4: 0 ohms
- ECU terminal 3 and throttle sensor terminal 3: 0 ohms

9. Measure resistance between throttle sensor connectors and ground. Resistance should be as follows:
- Terminal 2 and ground: 1 mega-ohm minimum
- Terminal 4 and ground: 1 mega-ohm minimum
- Terminal 3 and ground: 1 mega-ohm minimum

10. If resistance is not within specification, check and repair the harness or connector.

3.3L Engine

1. Turn the ignition switch **OFF**.

2. Disconnect the throttle sensor connector.

3. Measure the resistance between throttle sensor connector terminals 1 and 3. Resistance should be 5 kilo-ohms.

4. Measure the resistance between terminals 2 and 3 while slowly opening the throttle valve from the closed position.

5. Resistance should be 10–12 kilo-ohms when the throttle valve is closed and 3–5 kilo-ohms when the throttle is open. Ensure that the resistance increases in response to throttle valve opening.

6. If the throttle body fails the checks up to this point, replace it.

7. Disconnect the ECU connectors and measure the resistance of the harness connector between the ECU and the throttle sensor. Resistance should be as follows:
- ECU terminal 3 and throttle sensor terminal 2: 0 ohms
- ECU terminal 2 and throttle sensor terminal 1: 0 ohms
- ECU terminal 1 and throttle sensor terminal 3: 0 ohms

8. If measurements are not within specification, check and repair the harness or connector.

9. Measure the resistance of the harness connector between the throttle sensor connector and ground. Resistance should be as follows:
- Terminal 2 and ground: 1 mega-ohm minimum
- Terminal 1 and ground: 1 mega-ohm minimum
- Terminal 3 and ground: 1 mega-ohm minimum

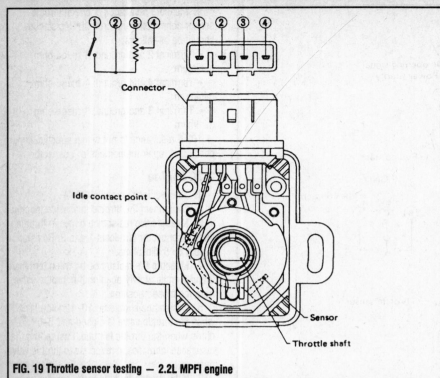

FIG. 19 Throttle sensor testing — 2.2L MPFI engine

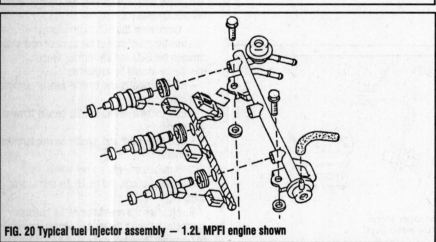

FIG. 20 Typical fuel injector assembly — 1.2L MPFI engine shown

Fuel Injector

♦ SEE FIG. 20

REMOVAL & INSTALLATION

Except 1.8L and 2.7L Engines

1. Relieve the fuel system pressure.
2. Disconnect the negative battery cable.
3. Label and disconnect the fuel injector electrical connectors.
4. Label and remove the hoses attached to the fuel rail.

5. Remove the fuel rail attaching bolts and gently lift the fuel rail from the engine.

➡ **Some fuel injectors may be removed with the fuel rail while others may remain in the engine.**

6. Remove the fuel injectors by pulling with a slight twist. Discard all gaskets and O-rings.

To Install:

7. Install the fuel injectors using new gaskets and O-rings. Lubricate the O-rings prior to installation.
8. Install the fuel rail and tighten the attaching bolts securely.
9. Install all hoses attached to the fuel rail.

10. Install the fuel injector electrical connectors.
11. Connect the negative battery cable.

1.8L and 2.7L Engine

1. Relieve the fuel system pressure.
2. Disconnect the negative battery cable.

➡ **On some engines, it may be necessary to remove the intake plenum to gain access to the fuel lines connecting the injectors.**

3. Remove the fuel lines connecting the injectors.
4. Disconnect the fuel injector electrical connectors.
5. On 2.7L engines, remove the fuel rail assembly.
6. Remove the injectors by pulling with a slight twist. Discard the gaskets and O-rings.
7. On 1.8L engines, remove the injector holder plate, insulator, holder and seal. Discard the insulator and seal.

To Install:

8. Install the injectors using new gaskets, seals (insulators) and O-rings. Lubricate the O-rings prior to installation.
9. On 2.7L engines, install the fuel rail assembly.
10. Install the fuel lines connecting the injectors.
11. Connect the injector electrical connectors.
12. Install the intake plenum if removed.
13. Connect the negative battery cable.
14. Start the engine and check for leaks.

TESTING

1.2L Engine

1. Using a stethoscope or equivalent, ensure a clicking sound is heard at each injector (when idling or cranking the engine).
2. Turn the ignition switch to the **OFF** position, then disconnect the control unit connector.
3. Measure the voltage between fuel injector connector terminal 1 and ground. Resistance should be 9 volts or above. If not, repair fuel injector power circuit.
4. Measure resistance between fuel injector connector terminals. Resistance should be as follows:

- Terminals 1 and 2: 10–18 ohms
- Terminals 1 and 3: 10–18 ohms
- Terminals 1 and 4: 10–18 ohms

5. If resistance is not within specification, repair engine harness. If engine harness is good, replace fuel injector.

6. Connect the fuel injector connector. Turn the ignition **ON**.

7. Measure the resistance between ECU connector terminals and ground. Resistance should be as follows:

- Terminal 12 and ground: 8 volts or more
- Terminal 25 and ground: 8 volts or more
- Terminal 11 and ground: 8 volts or more

8. If not within specification, repair harness connector between ECU and fuel injectors.

9. Turn ignition **OFF** and disconnect the ECU connector.

10. Measure resistance between ECU connector terminal and ground. Resistance should be as follows:

- Terminal 13 and ground: below 10 mega-ohms
- Terminal 26 and ground: below 10 mega-ohms

11. If not within specification, repair harness connector between ECU and ground.

1.8L Engine

1. Using a stethoscope or equivalent, ensure a clicking sound is heard at each injector (when idling or cranking the engine).

2. Turn the ignition switch to the **OFF** position, then disconnect the control unit connector.

3. Using a voltmeter, measure voltage between ground and terminals 49 (W), 50 (W), 51 (WR) (WL on XT models), and 52 (WR) (WL on XT models) on the control unit connector.

4. Voltmeter should read 12 volts at all terminals.

d. If voltmeter reads below 10 volts in any line, the harness from the battery to the control unit through the resistor and injector is broken or shorted.

5. Disconnect each fuel injector electrical connector.

6. Using an ohmmeter, measure resistance between the terminals of each injector. Ohmmeter should read 2–3 ohms at each injector. If ohmmeter reads infinity, the circuit is broken. If ohmmeter reads 0 ohm, the circuit is shorted. Replace injector.

7. Using a voltmeter, measure voltage between the terminals of each injector connector and ground. Voltmeter should read 12 volts. If voltage obtained is less than 10 volts, the harness from the battery to the injector through the resistor is disconnected or shorted.

8. Disconnect the electrical connector from the resistor.

9. Using an ohmmeter, measure the resistance between terminals (W) and (B) of the resistor. Ohmmeter should read 5.8–6.5 ohms. If specifications are not as specified, replace the resistor.

10. Using a voltmeter, measure voltage between terminal 5 (R) of the body harness connector and ground. Voltmeter should read 12 volts.

2.2L Engine

1. Using a stethoscope or equivalent, ensure a clicking sound is heard at each injector (when idling or cranking the engine).

2. Disconnect the fuel injector connector.

3. Measure the voltage between fuel injector connector terminal 2 and ground. Voltage should be 10 volts minimum. If not, repair the harness or connector.

4. Measure the resistance between the injector terminals. Resistance should be 10–12 ohms. If not, replace the fuel injector.

5. Connect the fuel injector connector.

6. Measure the voltage between each fuel injector terminal of the ECU connector and ground. Resistance should be as follows:

- Terminal 11 and ground: 10 volts minimum
- Terminal 12 and ground: 10 volts minimum
- Terminal 13 and ground: 10 volts minimum
- Terminal 26 and ground: 10 volts minimum

7. If not within specification, repair the harness or connector.

8. Disconnect ECU connector.

9. Measure the resistance between ground and ECU connector terminals 24 and 25. Resistance should be 0 ohms, If not, repair the harness or connector.

2.7L Engine

1. Using a stethoscope or equivalent, ensure a clicking sound is heard at each injector (when idling or cranking the engine).

2. Disconnect the control unit connector.

3. Using a voltmeter, measure voltage between ground and terminals 49 (W), 50 (W), 51 (WR), 52 (WR), 53 (WY) and 54 (WY) on the control unit connector.

4. Voltmeter should read 12 volts at all terminals.

5. If voltmeter reads below 10 volts in any line, the harness from the battery to the control unit through the resistor and injector is broken or shorted.

6. Disconnect each fuel injector electrical connector.

7. Using an ohmmeter, measure resistance between the terminals of each injector. Ohmmeter should read 13.8 ohms at each injector. If ohmmeter reads infinity, the circuit is broken. If ohmmeter reads 0 ohm, the circuit is shorted. Replace injector.

8. Using a voltmeter, measure voltage between the terminals of each injector and ground. Voltmeter should read 12 volts at each injector. If voltage obtained is less than 10 volts at any injector, the harness from the battery to the injector is disconnected or shorted.

3.3L Engine

1. Using a stethoscope or equivalent, ensure a clicking sound is heard at each injector (when idling or cranking the engine).

2. Turn the ignition switch **OFF**. Disconnect the fuel injector connector.

3. Measure the voltage between fuel injector connector terminal 2 and ground. Voltage should be 10 volts minimum. If not, repair the harness or connector.

4. Measure the resistance between the injector terminals. Resistance should be 11–12 ohms. If not, replace the fuel injector.

5. Connect the fuel injector connector.

6. Measure the voltage between each fuel injector terminal of the ECU connector and ground. Resistance should be as follows:

- Terminal 1 and ground: 10 volts minimum
- Terminal 11 and ground: 10 volts minimum
- Terminal 12 and ground: 10 volts minimum
- Terminal 13 and ground: 10 volts minimum
- Terminal 26 and ground: 10 volts minimum
- Terminal 12 (connector E59) and ground: 10 volts minimum

7. If not within specification, repair the harness or connector.

8. Disconnect ECU connector.

9. Measure the resistance between ground and ECU connector terminals 24 and 25. Resistance should be 0 ohms, If not, repair the harness or connector.

Pressure Regulator

REMOVAL & INSTALLATION

1. Locate the pressure regulator on the fuel rail near the injectors.

2. Relieve the fuel system pressure.

3. Disconnect the negative battery cable.

4. Remove the vacuum line leading to the regulator.

5. Loosen the fuel line nuts and remove the regulator.

To Install:

6. Install the regulator and tighten the fuel line nuts securely.

7. Install the vacuum line on the regulator.

8. Connect the negative battery cable.

9. Start the engine and check for leaks.

10. Check for correct fuel pressure.

Airflow Meter

REMOVAL & INSTALLATION

1. Disconnect the negative battery cable.

2. Disconnect the connector from the airflow meter.

3. Remove the engine harness from the clip.

4. Loosen the hose clamps securing the air intake boot and remove the air intake boot assembly.

5. Loosen the bolts attaching the air flow meter to the air cleaner assembly and remove the airflow meter.

To Install:

6. Install the airflow meter and tighten the bolts to 3–5 ft. lbs. (4–7 Nm).

7. Install the air intake boot assembly and tighten the attaching clamps to securely.

8. Install the engine harness on the clip and connect the airflow meter connector.

9. Connect the negative battery cable.

TESTING

1.8L and 2.7L Engines

1. Check the exterior of the airflow meter, intake boot and electrical connections for damage. Repair as necessary.

2. Check the interior for foreign matter, water or oil in the passages, especially in the bypass. If any of the above are noted, replace the air flow sensor.

3. Turn the ignition switch to the **OFF** position.

4. Install the air flow meter to the air cleaner.

5. Disconnect the air flow meter electrical connector, then slide back the rubber boot from the connector.

➡ **Conduct the following test by connecting the tester pins to the connector terminals on the side from which the the rubber boot was removed.**

6. Connect an ohmmeter between the body (B) and ground (BR) terminals on the connector. Ohmmeter should read 10 ohms. If reading is higher, check the harness and wiring to the control unit for discontinuity and the ground terminals on the intake manifold for poor contact.

7. Turn the ignition switch to the **ON** position with the engine **OFF**, then connect the air flow meter connector.

8. Measure the voltage across the power terminal and ground. The power terminals are as follows:

- 1.8L Loyale — terminal SA
- 1.8L XT — terminal W
- 2.7L XT — terminal R

9. Voltage should be a minimum of 10 volts. If not, check the condition of the components in the power line (battery, fuse, control unit harness, connectors).

10. Measure the voltage across the signal terminal and ground terminal. The terminals are as follows:

- 1.8L Loyale—terminals SA and BR
- 1.8L XT—terminals W and BR
- 2.7L XT—terminals W and BR

11. Voltage should be 1–2 volts for all models. If not, replace the air flow meter.

12. Remove the airflow meter from the air cleaner side and blow air into the air cleaner side while repeating the checks in Step 10. If the voltage does not increase, replace the airflow meter.

13. Install the air flow meter on the air cleaner. Start and allow the engine to reach normal operating temperature.

14. Operate the vehicle at a speed greater than 15 mph for at least 1 minute (rev engine over 2000 rpm).

15. With engine idling, check voltage across terminal (LgR) on the air flow meter connector and ground. Voltmeter should read 0 volts.

16. Check that 12 volts are present across terminal (LgR) and ground as soon as the ignition switch is turned to the **OFF** position. If not, check the harness from the control unit to the airflow meter for discontinuity.

2.2L ENGINE

1. Turn the ignition switch **ON** but do not start the engine.

2. Measure the voltage between the ECU connector terminals and body ground as follows:

- Terminal 8 and ground: 10–13 volts
- Terminal 9 and ground: 0–0.3 volts
- Terminal 10 and ground: 0 volts

3. Start the engine and repeat the test as follows:

- Terminal 8 and ground: 13–14 volts
- Terminal 9 and ground: 0.8–1.2 volts
- Terminal 10 and ground: 0 volts

4. If readings are not within specification, check for a damaged ECU terminal and repair.

5. Turn the engine **OFF** and disconnect the ECU and airflow sensor connectors.

6. Measure the resistance between the ECU and airflow sensor connectors as follows:

- ECU terminal 8 and airflow terminal 1: 0 ohms
- ECU terminal 9 and airflow terminal 4: 0 ohms
- ECU terminal 10 and airflow terminal 2: 0 ohms

7. If readings are not within specification, check for a damaged harness or connector and repair.

8. Measure the resistance between the airflow sensor connector and ground as follows:

- Terminal 1 and ground: 1 mega-ohm minimum
- Terminal 4 and ground: 1 mega-ohm minimum
- Terminal 2 and ground: 1 mega-ohm minimum
- Terminal 3 and ground: 0 ohms

9. If readings are not within specification, replace the airflow sensor.

3.3L ENGINE

1. Turn the ignition switch **ON** but do not start the engine.

2. Measure the voltage between the ECU connector terminals and body ground as follows:

- Terminal 11 and ground: 10–13 volts
- Terminal 5 and ground: 0–0.3 volts
- Terminal 6 and ground: 0 volts

3. Start the engine and repeat the test as follows:

- Terminal 11 and ground: 13–14 volts
- Terminal 5 and ground: 0.8–1.2 volts
- Terminal 6 and ground: 0 volts

4. If readings are not within specification, check for a damaged ECU terminal and repair.

5. Turn the engine **OFF** and disconnect the ECU and airflow sensor connectors.

6. Measure the resistance between the ECU and airflow sensor connectors as follows:

- ECU terminal 11 and airflow terminal 5: 0 ohms
- ECU terminal 4 and airflow terminal 3: 0 ohms
- ECU terminal 5 and airflow terminal 2: 0 ohms
- ECU terminal 6 and airflow terminal 1: 0 ohms

7. If readings are not within specification, check for a damaged harness or connector and repair.

8. If reading are within specification, replace the airflow sensor.

Air Temperature Sensor

REMOVAL & INSTALLATION

1.2L Engine

1. Disconnect the negative battery cable.
2. Disconnect the air temperature sensor connector.
3. Remove the air temperature sensor from the air cleaner assembly.
   To Install:
4. Install the air temperature sensor and tighten securely.
5. Connect the air temperature sensor connector.
6. Connect the negative battery cable.

TESTING

1.2L Engine

1. Turn the ignition switch **ON** but do not start the engine.
2. Measure the voltage across the ECU connector terminals as follows:
   • Terminals 6 and 1: 0.15–4.85 volts
   • Terminals 6 and 2: 0.15–4.85 volts
3. If readings are not within specification, check for a broken harness or connector and repair.
4. Turn the ignition switch **OFF** and disconnect the air temperature sensor connector.
5. Measure the resistance between the air temperature sensor terminals. Resistance should be 2–3 kilo-ohms at 68°F (20°C) or 270–370 ohms at 176°F (80°C).
6. If readings are not within specification, replace the air temperature sensor.
7. Disconnect the ECU connector.
8. Measure the resistance between the ECU connector terminals and the air temperature sensor connector terminals as follows:
   • ECU terminal 6 and air temperature terminal 2: below 1 ohm
   • ECU terminal 1 and air temperature terminal 1: below 1 ohm
   • ECU terminal 2 and air temperature terminal 1: below 1 ohm
9. If readings are not within specification, check for a broken harness or connector and repair.

10. Measure the resistance between the ECU connector terminal 6 and ground. Resistance should be infinite. If not, check for a broken harness or connector and repair.

Throttle Sensor

REMOVAL & INSTALLATION

1. Disconnect the negative battery cable.
2. Disconnect the throttle sensor connector.
3. Loosen the throttle sensor attaching screws.
4. Remove the throttle sensor.
   To Install:
5. Install the throttle sensor and loosely tighten the screws.
6. Connect the throttle sensor electrical connector.
7. Connect the negative battery cable.
8. Adjust the throttle sensor to the correct specifications and tighten the sensor attaching screws securely.

ADJUSTMENT

1.8L Engine

1. Insert a feeler gauge between the stopper screw of the throttle body and the stopper, and check for continuity between the following terminals:
   • 1.8L Loyale—terminals A and C
   • 1.8L XT—terminals 4 and 3
2. Check that there is continuity between terminals when the throttle is fully closed.
3. Check that there is continuity between the terminals when a 0.0217 in. (0.55mm) feeler gauge is inserted between the throttle body screw and the stopper.
4. Check that there is no continuity between the terminals when a 0.0362 in. (0.92mm) feeler gauge is inserted between the throttle body screw and the stopper.

2.7L Engine

1. Disconnect the throttle sensor connector.
2. Insert a feeler gauge between the stopper screw of the throttle body and the stopper, and check for continuity between terminals 4 and 3.
3. Check that there is 5 kilo-ohms resistance maximum between the terminals when a 0.0138 in. (0.35mm) feeler gauge is inserted between the throttle body screw and the stopper.

4. Check that there is 1 mega-ohm resistance minimum between the terminals when a 0.0295 in. (0.75mm) feeler gauge is inserted between the throttle body screw and the stopper.

2.2L Engine

1. Turn the ignition switch **ON**.
2. Measure the voltage between the ECU connector terminal and ground. Voltage should be as follows:
   • Terminal 2 and ground: 4.4–4.8 volts with the throttle fully open
   • Terminal 2 and ground: 0.7–1.6 volts with the throttle fully closed
   • Terminal 3 and ground: 5 volts
   • Terminal 1 and ground: 0 volts
3. Ensure voltage smoothly decreases in response to throttle opening. If measurements are not within specification, check and repair the ECU terminals or harness.
4. Disconnect the connector from the throttle sensor. Measure the resistance between throttle sensor terminals 2 and 3. Resistance should be 12 kilo-ohms.
5. Measure the resistance between terminals while slowly opening the throttle valve from the closed position. Resistance should be as follows:
   • Terminals 2 and 4: 10–12 kilo-ohms with the throttle valve fully closed
   • Terminals 2 and 4: 3–5 kilo-ohms with the throttle valve fully open
6. Ensure resistance smoothly increases in response to throttle opening. If measurements are not within specification, replace the throttle sensor.

3.3L Engine

1. Turn the ignition switch **OFF**.
2. Disconnect the throttle sensor connector.
3. Measure the resistance between throttle sensor connector terminals 1 and 3. Resistance should be 5 kilo-ohms.
4. Measure the resistance between terminals 2 and 3 while slowly opening the throttle valve from the closed position.
5. Resistance should be 10–12 kilo-ohms when the throttle valve is closed and 3–5 kilo-ohms when the throttle is open. Ensure that the resistance increases in response to throttle valve opening.

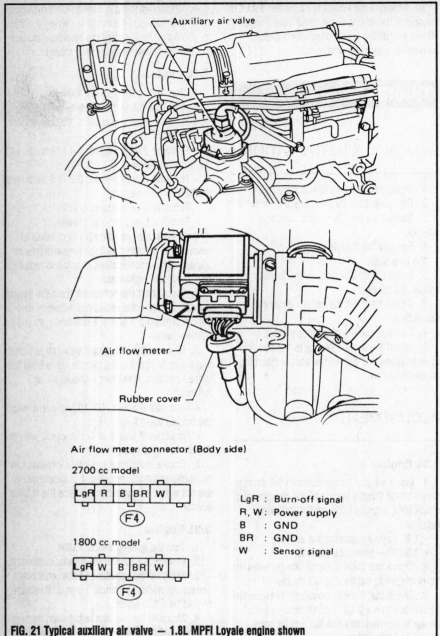

FIG. 21 Typical auxiliary air valve — 1.8L MPFI Loyale engine shown

Auxiliary Air Valve

♦ SEE FIG. 21

REMOVAL & INSTALLATION

1.8L Engine

1. Disconnect the negative battery cable.
2. Disconnect the air valve electrical connector.
3. Disconnect the hose leading to the air valve.
4. Remove the air valve retaining screws, then remove the air valve.
   To Install:
5. Install the air valve and tighten the retaining screws securely.
6. Connect the air valve hose.
7. Connect the air valve electrical connector.
8. Connect the negative battery cable.

TESTING

1.8L Engine

1. Pinch the hose connecting the air intake duct and the auxiliary air valve, then note engine rpm change. With the engine cold, engine idle speed drops as the hose is pinched. With the engine hot, reduction in engine rpm is within 100.
2. When the engine is started, the auxiliary air valve is heated by the built-in heater and its shutter valve gradually closes. This causes engine rpm to lower gradually until the specified idling rpm is reached. If the engine speed does not drop to the idling rpm smoothly, the heater circuit or the heater power supply circuit may be faulty. Proceed as follows:
3. Disconnect the auxiliary air valve electrical connector.
4. Using an ohmmeter, measure the resistance between the 2 terminals on the auxiliary air valve. Ohmmeter should read other than 0 ohms and infinity.
5. If ohmmeter reads 0 or infinity, replace the auxiliary air valve.
6. Disconnect the auxiliary air valve electrical connector.
7. Using a voltmeter, check the voltage on the auxiliary air valve connector.
8. With the engine running, voltmeter should read 12 volts or more. If specifications are not as specified, check the harness and connector for faults.

Bypass Air Control Valve

REMOVAL & INSTALLATION

1. Disconnect the negative battery cable.
2. Disconnect the air valve electrical connector.
3. Disconnect the hose leading to the air valve.
4. Remove the air valve retaining screws, then remove the air valve.
   To Install:
5. Install the air valve and tighten the retaining screws securely.
6. Connect the air valve hose.
7. Connect the air valve electrical connector.
8. Connect the negative battery cable.

TESTING

2.2L Engine

1. Turn the ignition switch **ON**.

2. Measure the voltage between bypass air control solenoid valve connector terminal 2 and ground. Resistance should be 10 volts minimum. If not, repair harness connector or fusible link.

3. Disconnect connector from bypass air control solenoid valve.

4. Measure resistance between solenoid valve terminals. Resistance should be as follows:
   - Terminals 1 and 2: 9 ohms
   - Terminals 2 and 3: 9 ohms

5. If voltage is not within specification, replace the solenoid valve.

6. Turn the ignition switch **ON**.

7. Measure the voltage between ECU connector terminal and ground. Resistance for non-turbo models should be as follows:
   - Terminal 2 and ground (non-turbo): 7 volts
   - Terminal 1 and ground (non-turbo): 6 volts

8. Resistance for turbo models should increase or decrease 1 minute after ignition switch is turned **ON** as follows:
   - Terminal 2 and ground: 0 to 12 volts
   - Terminal 1 and ground: 12 to 0 volts

9. If resistance is not within specification, check harness between ECU and air control valve.

10. Disconnect connectors from ECU and bypass air control solenoid valve.

11. Measure resistance between ECU connector and solenoid valve connector. Resistance should be as follows:
   - ECU terminal 2 and solenoid valve terminal 1: 0 ohms
   - ECU terminal 1 and solenoid valve terminal 3: 0 ohms

12. Measure resistance between solenoid valve connector and ground. Resistance should be as follows:
   - Solenoid valve terminal 1 and ground: 1 mega-ohm minimum
   - Solenoid valve terminal 3 and ground: 1 mega-ohm minimum

13. If not within specification, repair harness or connector.

2.7L Engine

1. Disconnect the bypass air control valve electrical connector.

2. Using an ohmmeter, measure the resistance between terminals (1) and (2) on the bypass air control valve. Ohmmeter should read 9.5–11.5 ohms.

3. Using an ohmmeter, measure resistance between terminals (2) and (3) on the bypass air control valve. Ohmmeter should read 8.5–10.5 ohms.

4. Using an ohmmeter, measure resistance between terminal (2) and the valve body, and terminal (3) and the valve body. Ohmmeter should read infinity in both tests.

5. If not within specifications, replace the bypass air control valve.

3.3L Engine

1. Turn the ignition switch **ON**.

2. Measure the voltage between ECU connector terminal 14 and ground. Voltage should be 10 volts minimum. If not, check harness connector between ECU and main relay.

3. Turn the ignition switch **OFF**.

4. Disconnect connector from ECU and main relay. Measure resistance of harness connector between ECU terminal 14 and main relay terminal 4. Resistance should be 0 ohms. If not, check harness connector between ECU and main relay.

5. Turn the ignition switch **ON**.

6. Measure the voltage between main relay connector and ground. Resistance should be as follows:
   - Terminal 1 and ground: 10 volts minimum
   - Terminal 2 and ground: 10 volts minimum

7. Repair or replace the main relay, connector or harness.

8. Turn the ignition switch **ON**.

9. Measure the voltage between ECU connector and ground. Resistance should be as follows:
   - Terminal 2 and ground: 7 volts minimum
   - Terminal 1 and ground: 7 volts minimum

10. If not within specification, repair harness connector between ECU and solenoid valve.

11. Turn the ignition switch **OFF**.

12. Disconnect the ECU connectors.

13. Separate the throttle body from collector and disconnect connector from bypass air control valve.

14. Measure the resistance of harness connector between ECU and solenoid valve. Resistance should be as follows:
   - ECU terminal 2 and solenoid valve terminal 3: 0 ohms
   - ECU terminal 1 and solenoid valve terminal 1: 0 ohms

15. If not within specification, repair harness connector between ECU and solenoid valve.

Idle Speed Control (ISC) Solenoid

REMOVAL & INSTALLATION

1.2L Engine

1. Disconnect the negative battery cable.
2. Disconnect the vacuum lines from the ISC.
3. Disconnect the ISC electrical connector.
4. Remove the ISC from the throttle body.

To install:

5. Install the ISC on the throttle body and tighten the attaching screws securely.
6. Connect the vacuum lines to the ISC.
7. Connect the ISC electrical connector.
8. Connect the negative battery cable.
9. Start the engine, check and adjust the idle speed as necessary.

TESTING

1.2L Engine

1. Connect the test mode connector.
2. Turn the ignition switch **ON**.
3. Check the ISC valve for operating vibration.
4. Disconnect the test mode connector and turn the ignition switch **OFF**.
5. Disconnect the ISC electrical harness.
6. Measure the resistance between the ISC connector terminals. Resistance should be 20–30 ohms.

Fast Idle Control Device (FICD)

REMOVAL & INSTALLATION

1.2L Engine

1. Disconnect the negative battery cable.
2. Disconnect the vacuum lines from the FICD.
3. Disconnect the FICD electrical connector.
4. Remove the FICD from the throttle body.

To install:

5. Install the FICD on the throttle body and tighten the attaching screws securely.
6. Connect the vacuum lines to the FICD.
7. Connect the FICD electrical connector.
8. Connect the negative battery cable.
9. Start the engine, check and adjust the idle speed as necessary.

FUEL TANK

REMOVAL & INSTALLATION

Justy

1. Release the fuel system pressure.
2. Remove the rear seat and package shelf.
3. Disconnect the rollover valve and separator.
4. Remove the access hole lid and disconnect the wiring harness.
5. Disconnect the filler hose and air vent hose.
6. Raise and support the vehicle safely.
7. Drain the fuel through the delivery pipe.
8. Support the fuel tank with a floor jack.
9. Remove the parking brake cable and fuel filter bracket.
10. Disconnect the fuel hoses leading to the tank.
11. Remove the tank attaching bolts and lower the tank.

To Install:

12. Raise the tank and install the attaching bolts. Tighten to 9–17 ft. lbs. (13–23 Nm).
13. Connect the fuel hoses leading to the tank.
14. Install the parking brake cable and fuel filter bracket.
15. Lower the vehicle.
16. Connect the filler hose and air vent hose.
17. Connect the wiring harness and install the access hole lid.
18. Connect the rollover valve and separator.
19. Install the rear seat and package shelf.

Except Justy

1. Release the fuel system pressure.
2. Remove the muffler and rear differential assembly (4WD). On SVX, remove the rear sub-frame.
3. Remove the fuel filler cap and drain the fuel.
4. Remove the fuel filler pipe protector.
5. Remove the fuel filler hose, air vent and delivery hose.
6. Raise and support the vehicle safely.
7. Support the fuel tank with a floor jack.
8. Loosen the attaching bolts and lower the fuel tank.
9. Disconnect the harness connector.

To Install:

10. Connect the harness connector.
11. Raise the fuel tank and install the attaching bolts. Tighten to 9–17 ft. lbs. (13–23 Nm).
12. Lower the vehicle.
13. Install the fuel filler hose, air vent and delivery hose.
14. Install the fuel filler pipe protector.
15. Install the fuel filler cap.
16. Install the muffler and rear differential assembly (4WD).

SENDING UNIT REPLACEMENT

Justy

1. Release the fuel system pressure.
2. Remove the rear seat.
3. Remove the access hole lid and disconnect the wiring harness.
4. Loosen the sending unit nuts and remove.

To Install:

5. Install the sending unit and tighten the nuts to 16–28 inch lbs. (2–3 Nm) in a star pattern.
6. Connect the wiring harness and install the access hole lid.
7. Install the rear seat.

Except Justy

1. Release the fuel system pressure.
2. Remove the mat from the trunk.
3. Remove the access hole lid and disconnect the wiring harness.
4. Loosen the sending unit nuts and remove.

To Install:

5. Install the sending unit and tighten the nuts to 16–28 inch lbs. (2–3 Nm) in a star pattern.
6. Connect the wiring harness and install the access hole lid.
7. Install the rear seat.

6

CHASSIS ELECTRICAL

UNDERSTANDING AND TROUBLESHOOTING ELECTRICAL SYSTEMS

At the rate which both import and domestic manufacturers are incorporating electronic control systems into their production lines, it won't be long before every new vehicle is equipped with one or more on-board computer. These electronic components (with no moving parts) should theoretically last the life of the vehicle, provided nothing external happens to damage the circuits or memory chips.

While it is true that electronic components should never wear out, in the real world malfunctions do occur. It is also true that any computer-based system is extremely sensitive to electrical voltages and cannot tolerate careless or haphazard testing or service procedures. An inexperienced individual can literally do major damage looking for a minor problem by using the wrong kind of test equipment or connecting test leads or connectors with the ignition switch **ON**. When selecting test equipment, make sure the manufacturers instructions state that the tester is compatible with whatever type of electronic control system is being serviced. Read all instructions carefully and double check all test points before installing probes or making any test connections.

The following section outlines basic diagnosis techniques for dealing with computerized automotive control systems. Along with a general explanation of the various types of test equipment available to aid in servicing modern electronic automotive systems, basic repair techniques for wiring harnesses and connectors is given. Read the basic information before attempting any repairs or testing on any computerized system, to provide the background of information necessary to avoid the most common and obvious mistakes that can cost both time and money. Although the replacement and testing procedures are simple in themselves, the systems are not, and unless one has a thorough understanding of all components and their function within a particular computerized control system, the logical test sequence these systems demand cannot be followed. Minor malfunctions can make a big difference, so it is important to know how each component affects the operation of the overall electronic system to find the ultimate cause of a problem without replacing good components unnecessarily. It is not enough to use the correct test equipment; the test equipment must be used correctly.

Safety Precautions

❋❋❋ CAUTION

Whenever working on or around any computer based microprocessor control system, always observe these general precautions to prevent the possibility of personal injury or damage to electronic components.

• Never install or remove battery cables with the key **ON** or the engine running. Jumper cables should be connected with the key **OFF** to avoid power surges that can damage electronic control units. Engines equipped with computer controlled systems should avoid both giving and getting jump starts due to the possibility of serious damage to components from arcing in the engine compartment when connections are made with the ignition **ON**.

• Always remove the battery cables before charging the battery. Never use a high output charger on an installed battery or attempt to use any type of "hot shot" (24 volt) starting aid.

• Exercise care when inserting test probes into connectors to insure good connections without damaging the connector or spreading the pins. Always probe connectors from the rear (wire) side, NOT the pin side, to avoid accidental shorting of terminals during test procedures.

• Never remove or attach wiring harness connectors with the ignition switch **ON**, especially to an electronic control unit.

• Do not drop any components during service procedures and never apply 12 volts directly to any component (like a solenoid or relay) unless instructed specifically to do so. Some component electrical windings are designed to safely handle only 4 or 5 volts and can be destroyed in seconds if 12 volts are applied directly to the connector.

• Remove the electronic control unit if the vehicle is to be placed in an environment where temperatures exceed approximately 176°F (80°C), such as a paint spray booth or when arc or gas welding near the control unit location in the car.

ORGANIZED TROUBLESHOOTING

When diagnosing a specific problem, organized troubleshooting is a must. The complexity of a modern automobile demands that you approach any problem in a logical, organized manner. There are certain troubleshooting techniques that are standard:

1. Establish when the problem occurs. Does the problem appear only under certain conditions? Were there any noises, odors, or other unusual symptoms?

2. Isolate the problem area. To do this, make some simple tests and observations; then eliminate the systems that are working properly. Check for obvious problems such as broken wires, dirty connections or split or disconnected vacuum hoses. Always check the obvious before assuming something complicated is the cause.

3. Test for problems systematically to determine the cause once the problem area is isolated. Are all the components functioning properly? Is there power going to electrical switches and motors? Is there vacuum at vacuum switches and/or actuators? Is there a mechanical problem such as bent linkage or loose mounting screws? Doing careful, systematic checks will often turn up most causes on the first inspection without wasting time checking components that have little or no relationship to the problem.

4. Test all repairs after the work is done to make sure that the problem is fixed. Some causes can be traced to more than one component, so a careful verification of repair work is important to pick up additional malfunctions that may cause a problem to reappear or a different problem to arise. A blown fuse, for example, is a simple problem that may require more than another fuse to repair. If you don't look for a problem that caused a fuse to blow, for example, a shorted wire may go undetected.

Experience has shown that most problems tend to be the result of a fairly simple and obvious cause, such as loose or corroded connectors or air leaks in the intake system; making careful inspection of components during testing essential to quick and accurate troubleshooting. Special, hand held computerized testers designed specifically for diagnosing the engine control system are available from a variety of after market sources, as well as from the vehicle manufacturer, but care should be taken that any test equipment being used is designed to diagnose that particular computer controlled system accurately without damaging the control unit (ECU) or components being tested.

➡ **Pinpointing the exact cause of trouble in an electrical system can sometimes only be accomplished by the use of special test equipment. The following describes commonly used test equipment and explains how to put it to best use in diagnosis. In addition to the information covered below, the manufacturer's instructions booklet provided with the tester should be read and clearly understood before attempting any test procedures.**

TEST EQUIPMENT

♦ SEE FIGS. 1–17

Jumper Wires

Jumper wires are simple, yet extremely valuable, pieces of test equipment. Jumper wires are merely wires that are used to bypass sections of a circuit. The simplest type of jumper wire is merely a length of multistrand wire with an alligator clip at each end. Jumper wires are usually fabricated from lengths of standard automotive wire and whatever type of connector (alligator clip, spade connector or pin connector) that is required for the particular vehicle being tested. The well equipped tool box will have several different styles of jumper wires in several different lengths. Some jumper wires are made with three or more terminals coming from a common splice for special purpose testing. In cramped, hard-to-reach areas it is advisable to have insulated boots over the jumper wire terminals in order to prevent accidental grounding, sparks, and possible fire, especially when testing fuel system components.

Jumper wires are used primarily to locate open electrical circuits, on either the ground (–) side of the circuit or on the hot (+) side. If an electrical component fails to operate, connect the jumper wire between the component and a good ground. If the component operates only with the jumper installed, the ground circuit is open. If the ground circuit is good, but the component does not operate, the circuit between the power feed and component is open. You can sometimes connect the jumper wire directly from the battery to the hot terminal of the component, but first make sure the component uses 12 volts in operation. Some electrical

components, such as fuel injectors, are designed to operate on about 4 volts and running 12 volts directly to the injector terminals can burn out the wiring. By inserting an inline fuse holder between a set of test leads, a fused jumper wire can be used for bypassing open circuits. Use a 5 amp fuse to provide protection against voltage spikes. When in doubt, use a voltmeter to check the voltage input to the component and measure how much voltage is being applied normally. By moving the jumper wire successively back from the lamp toward the power source, you can isolate the area of the circuit where the open is located. When the component stops functioning, or the power is cut off, the open is in the segment of wire between the jumper and the point previously tested.

✳ CAUTION

Never use jumpers made from wire that is of lighter gauge than used in the circuit under test. If the jumper wire is of too small gauge, it may overheat and possibly melt. Never use jumpers to bypass high resistance loads (such as motors) in a circuit. Bypassing resistances, in effect, creates a short circuit which may, in turn, cause damage and fire. Never use a jumper for anything other than temporary bypassing of components in a circuit.

12 Volt Test Light

The 12 volt test light is used to check circuits and components while electrical current is flowing through them. It is used for voltage and ground tests. Twelve volt test lights come in different styles but all have three main parts; a ground clip, a probe, and a light. The most commonly used 12 volt test lights have pick-type probes. To use a 12 volt test light, connect the ground clip to a good ground and probe wherever necessary with the pick. The pick should be sharp so that it can penetrate wire insulation to make contact with the wire, without making a large hole in the insulation. The wrap-around light is handy in hard to reach areas or where it is difficult to support a wire to push a probe pick into it. To use the wrap around light, hook the wire to probed with the hook and pull the trigger. A small pick will be forced through the wire insulation into the wire core.

✳ CAUTION

Do not use a test light to probe electronic ignition spark plug or coil wires. Never use a pick-type test light to probe wiring on computer controlled systems unless specifically instructed to do so. Any wire insulation that is pierced by the test light probe should be taped and sealed with silicone after testing.

Like the jumper wire, the 12 volt test light is used to isolate opens in circuits. But, whereas the jumper wire is used to bypass the open to operate the load, the 12 volt test light is used to locate the presence of voltage in a circuit. If the test light glows, you know that there is power up to that point; if the 12 volt test light does not glow when its probe is inserted into the wire or connector, you know that there is an open circuit (no power). Move the test light in successive steps back toward the power source until the light in the handle does glow. When it does glow, the open is between the probe and point previously probed.

➡ **The test light does not detect that 12 volts (or any particular amount of voltage) is present; it only detects that some voltage is present. It is advisable before using**

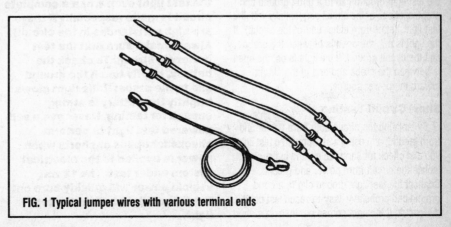

FIG. 1 Typical jumper wires with various terminal ends

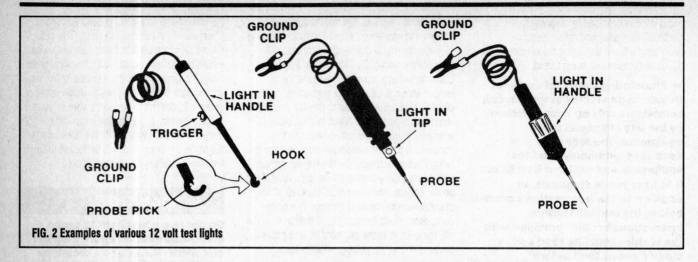

FIG. 2 Examples of various 12 volt test lights

the test light to touch its terminals across the battery posts to make sure the light is operating properly.

Self-Powered Test Light

The self-powered test light usually contains a 1.5 volt pen light battery. One type of self-powered test light is similar in design to the 12 volt test light. This type has both the battery and the light in the handle and pick-type probe tip. The second type has the light toward the open tip, so that the light illuminates the contact point. The self-powered test light is dual purpose piece of test equipment. It can be used to test for either open or short circuits when power is isolated from the circuit (continuity test). A powered test light should not be used on any computer controlled system or component unless specifically instructed to do so. Many engine sensors can be destroyed by even this small amount of voltage applied directly to the terminals.

Open Circuit Testing

To use the self-powered test light to check for open circuits, first isolate the circuit from the vehicle's 12 volt power source by disconnecting the battery or wiring harness connector. Connect the test light ground clip to a good ground and probe sections of the circuit sequentially with the test light. (start from either end of the circuit). If the light is out, the open is between the probe and the circuit ground. If the light is on, the open is between the probe and end of the circuit toward the power source.

Short Circuit Testing

By isolating the circuit both from power and from ground, and using a self-powered test light, you can check for shorts to ground in the circuit. Isolate the circuit from power and ground. Connect the test light ground clip to a good ground and probe any easy-to-reach test point in the circuit. If the light comes on, there is a short

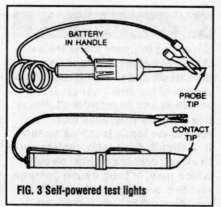

FIG. 3 Self-powered test lights

somewhere in the circuit. To isolate the short, probe a test point at either end of the isolated circuit (the light should be on). Leave the test light probe connected and open connectors, switches, remove parts, etc., sequentially, until the light goes out. When the light goes out, the short is between the last circuit component opened and the previous circuit opened.

➡ **The 1.5 volt battery in the test light does not provide much current. A weak battery may not provide enough power to illuminate the test light even when a complete circuit is made (especially if there are high resistances in the circuit). Always make sure that the test battery is strong. To check the battery, briefly touch the ground clip to the probe; if the light glows brightly the battery is strong enough for testing. Never use a self-powered test light to perform checks for opens or shorts when power is applied to the electrical system under test. The 12 volt vehicle power will quickly burn out the 1.5 volt light bulb in the test light.**

Voltmeter

A voltmeter is used to measure voltage at any point in a circuit, or to measure the voltage drop across any part of a circuit. It can also be used to check continuity in a wire or circuit by indicating current flow from one end to the other. Voltmeters usually have various scales on the meter dial and a selector switch to allow the selection of different voltages. The voltmeter has a positive and a negative lead. To avoid damage to the meter, always connect the negative lead to the negative (–) side of circuit (to ground or nearest the ground side of the circuit) and connect the positive lead to the positive (+) side of the circuit (to the power source or the nearest power source). Note that the negative voltmeter lead will always be black and that the positive voltmeter will always be some color other than black (usually red). Depending on how the voltmeter is connected into the circuit, it has several uses.

A voltmeter can be connected either in parallel or in series with a circuit and it has a very high resistance to current flow. When connected in parallel, only a small amount of current will flow through the voltmeter current path; the rest will flow through the normal circuit current path and the circuit will work normally. When the voltmeter is connected in series with a circuit, only a small amount of current can flow through the circuit. The circuit will not work properly, but the voltmeter reading will show if the circuit is complete or not.

Available Voltage Measurement

Set the voltmeter selector switch to the 20V position and connect the meter negative lead to the negative post of the battery. Connect the positive meter lead to the positive post of the battery and turn the ignition switch ON to provide a load. Read the voltage on the meter or digital display. A well charged battery should register over 12 volts. If the meter reads below 11.5

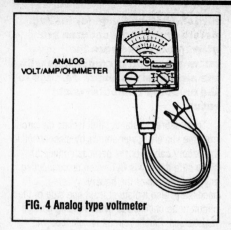

ANALOG
VOLT/AMP/OHMMETER

FIG. 4 Analog type voltmeter

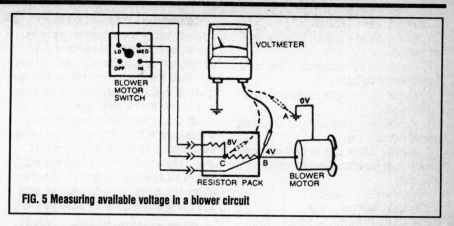

VOLTMETER

BLOWER
MOTOR
SWITCH

0V

RESISTOR PACK

BLOWER
MOTOR

FIG. 5 Measuring available voltage in a blower circuit

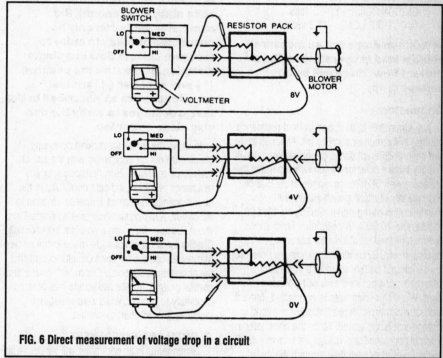

BLOWER
SWITCH

RESISTOR PACK

BLOWER
MOTOR

VOLTMETER

8V

4V

0V

FIG. 6 Direct measurement of voltage drop in a circuit

volts, the battery power may be insufficient to operate the electrical system properly. This test determines voltage available from the battery and should be the first step in any electrical trouble diagnosis procedure. Many electrical problems, especially on computer controlled systems, can be caused by a low state of charge in the battery. Excessive corrosion at the battery cable terminals can cause a poor contact that will prevent proper charging and full battery current flow.

Normal battery voltage is 12 volts when fully charged. When the battery is supplying current to one or more circuits it is said to be "under load". When everything is off the electrical system is under a "no-load" condition. A fully charged battery may show about 12.5 volts at no load; will drop to 12 volts under medium load; and will drop even lower under heavy load. If the battery is partially discharged the voltage decrease under heavy load may be excessive, even though the battery shows 12 volts or more at no load. When allowed to discharge further, the battery's available voltage under load will decrease more severely. For this reason, it is important that the battery be fully charged during all testing procedures to avoid errors in diagnosis and incorrect test results.

Voltage Drop

When current flows through a resistance, the voltage beyond the resistance is reduced (the larger the current, the greater the reduction in voltage). When no current is flowing, there is no voltage drop because there is no current flow. All points in the circuit which are connected to the power source are at the same voltage as the power source. The total voltage drop always equals the total source voltage. In a long circuit with many connectors, a series of small, unwanted voltage drops due to corrosion at the connectors can add up to a total loss of voltage which impairs the operation of the normal loads in the circuit.

INDIRECT COMPUTATION OF VOLTAGE DROPS

1. Set the voltmeter selector switch to the 20 volt position.
2. Connect the meter negative lead to a good ground.
3. Probe all resistances in the circuit with the positive meter lead.
4. Operate the circuit in all modes and observe the voltage readings.

DIRECT MEASUREMENT OF VOLTAGE DROPS

1. Set the voltmeter switch to the 20 volt position.
2. Connect the voltmeter negative lead to the ground side of the resistance load to be measured.
3. Connect the positive lead to the positive side of the resistance or load to be measured.

4. Read the voltage drop directly on the 20 volt scale.

Too high a voltage indicates too high a resistance. If, for example, a blower motor runs too slowly, you can determine if there is too high a resistance in the resistor pack. By taking voltage drop readings in all parts of the circuit, you can isolate the problem. Too low a voltage drop indicates too low a resistance. If, for example, a blower motor runs too fast in the MED and/or LOW position, the problem can be isolated in the resistor pack by taking voltage drop readings in all parts of the circuit to locate a possibly shorted resistor. The maximum allowable voltage drop under load is critical, especially if there is more than one high resistance problem in a circuit because all voltage drops are cumulative. A small drop is normal due to the resistance of the conductors.

HIGH RESISTANCE TESTING

1. Set the voltmeter selector switch to the 4 volt position.

2. Connect the voltmeter positive lead to the positive post of the battery.

3. Turn on the headlights and heater blower to provide a load.

4. Probe various points in the circuit with the negative voltmeter lead.

5. Read the voltage drop on the 4 volt scale. Some average maximum allowable voltage drops are:

    FUSE PANEL — 7 volts
    IGNITION SWITCH — 5 volts
    HEADLIGHT SWITCH — 7 volts
    IGNITION COIL (+) — 5 volts
    ANY OTHER LOAD — 1.3 volts

➡ **Voltage drops are all measured while a load is operating; without current flow, there will be no voltage drop.**

Ohmmeter

The ohmmeter is designed to read resistance (ohms) in a circuit or component. Although there are several different styles of ohmmeters, all will usually have a selector switch which permits the measurement of different ranges of resistance (usually the selector switch allows the multiplication of the meter reading by 10, 100, 1,000, and 10,000). A calibration knob allows the meter to be set at zero for accurate measurement. Since all ohmmeters are powered by an internal battery (usually 9 volts), the ohmmeter can be used as a self-powered test light. When the ohmmeter is connected, current from the ohmmeter flows through the circuit or component being tested. Since the ohmmeter's internal resistance and voltage are known values, the amount of current flow through the meter depends on the resistance of the circuit or component being tested.

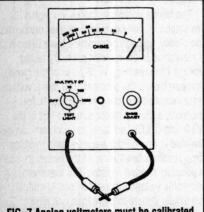

FIG. 7 Analog voltmeters must be calibrated before use by touching the probes together and turning the adjusting knobs

The ohmmeter can be used to perform continuity test for opens or shorts (either by observation of the meter needle or as a self-powered test light), and to read actual resistance in a circuit. It should be noted that the ohmmeter is used to check the resistance of a component or wire while there is no voltage applied to the circuit. Current flow from an outside voltage source (such as the vehicle battery) can damage the ohmmeter, so the circuit or component should be isolated from the vehicle electrical system before any testing is done. Since the ohmmeter uses its own voltage source, either lead can be connected to any test point.

➡ **When checking diodes or other solid state components, the ohmmeter leads can only be connected one way in order to measure current flow in a single direction. Make sure the positive (+) and negative (–) terminal connections are as described in the test procedures to verify the one-way diode operation.**

In using the meter for making continuity checks, do not be concerned with the actual resistance readings. Zero resistance, or any resistance readings, indicate continuity in the circuit. Infinite resistance indicates an open in the circuit. A high resistance reading where there should be none indicates a problem in the circuit. Checks for short circuits are made in the same manner as checks for open circuits except that the circuit must be isolated from both power and normal ground. Infinite resistance indicates no continuity to ground, while zero resistance indicates a dead short to ground.

RESISTANCE MEASUREMENT

The batteries in an ohmmeter will weaken with age and temperature, so the ohmmeter must be calibrated or "zeroed" before taking measurements. To zero the meter, place the selector switch in its lowest range and touch the two ohmmeter leads together. Turn the calibration knob until the meter needle is exactly on zero.

➡ **All analog (needle) type ohmmeters must be zeroed before use, but some digital ohmmeter models are automatically calibrated when the switch is turned on. Self-calibrating digital ohmmeters do not have an adjusting knob, but its a good idea to check for a zero readout before use by touching the leads together. All computer controlled systems require the use of a digital ohmmeter with at least 10**

megohms impedance for testing. Before any test procedures are attempted, make sure the ohmmeter used is compatible with the electrical system or damage to the on-board computer could result.

To measure resistance, first isolate the circuit from the vehicle power source by disconnecting the battery cables or the harness connector. Make sure the key is OFF when disconnecting any components or the battery. Where necessary, also isolate at least one side of the circuit to be checked to avoid reading parallel resistances. Parallel circuit resistances will always give a lower reading than the actual resistance of either of the branches. When measuring the resistance of parallel circuits, the total resistance will always be lower than the smallest resistance in the circuit. Connect the meter leads to both sides of the circuit (wire or component) and read the actual measured ohms on the meter scale. Make sure the selector switch is set to the proper ohm scale for the circuit being tested to avoid misreading the ohmmeter test value.

✳ WARNING

Never use an ohmmeter with power applied to the circuit. Like the self-powered test light, the ohmmeter is designed to operate on its own power supply. The normal 12 volt automotive electrical system current could damage the meter!

Ammeters

An ammeter measures the amount of current flowing through a circuit in units called amperes or amps. Amperes are units of electron flow which indicate how fast the electrons are flowing through the circuit. Since Ohms Law dictates that current flow in a circuit is equal to the circuit voltage divided by the total circuit resistance, increasing voltage also increases the current level (amps). Likewise, any decrease in resistance will increase the amount of amps in a circuit. At normal operating voltage, most circuits have a characteristic amount of amperes, called "current draw" which can be measured using an ammeter. By referring to a specified current draw rating, measuring the amperes, and comparing the two values, one can determine what is happening within the circuit to aid in diagnosis. An open circuit, for example, will not allow any current to flow so the

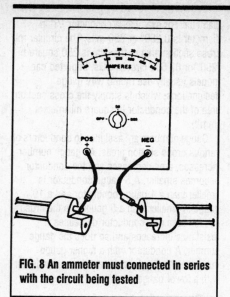

FIG. 8 An ammeter must connected in series with the circuit being tested

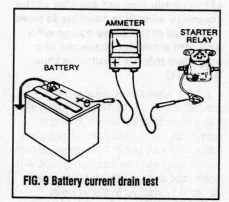

FIG. 9 Battery current drain test

ammeter reading will be zero. More current flows through a heavily loaded circuit or when the charging system is operating.

An ammeter is always connected in series with the circuit being tested. All of the current that normally flows through the circuit must also flow through the ammeter; if there is any other path for the current to follow, the ammeter reading will not be accurate. The ammeter itself has very little resistance to current flow and therefore will not affect the circuit, but it will measure current draw only when the circuit is closed and electricity is flowing. Excessive current draw can blow fuses and drain the battery, while a reduced current draw can cause motors to run slowly, lights to dim and other components to not operate properly. The ammeter can help diagnose these conditions by locating the cause of the high or low reading.

Multimeters

Different combinations of test meters can be built into a single unit designed for specific tests. Some of the more common combination test devices are known as Volt/Amp testers, Tach/

Dwell meters, or Digital Multimeters. The Volt/Amp tester is used for charging system, starting system or battery tests and consists of a voltmeter, an ammeter and a variable resistance carbon pile. The voltmeter will usually have at least two ranges for use with 6, 12 and 24 volt systems. The ammeter also has more than one range for testing various levels of battery loads and starter current draw and the carbon pile can be adjusted to offer different amounts of resistance. The Volt/Amp tester has heavy leads to carry large amounts of current and many later models have an inductive ammeter pickup that clamps around the wire to simplify test connections. On some models, the ammeter also has a zero-center scale to allow testing of charging and starting systems without switching leads or polarity. A digital multimeter is a voltmeter, ammeter and ohmmeter combined in an instrument which gives a digital readout. These are often used when testing solid state circuits because of their high input impedance (usually 10 megohms or more).

The tach/dwell meter combines a tachometer and a dwell (cam angle) meter and is a specialized kind of voltmeter. The tachometer scale is marked to show engine speed in rpm and the dwell scale is marked to show degrees of distributor shaft rotation. In most electronic ignition systems, dwell is determined by the control unit, but the dwell meter can also be used to check the duty cycle (operation) of some electronic engine control systems. Some tach/dwell meters are powered by an internal battery, while others take their power from the car battery in use. The battery powered testers usually require calibration much like an ohmmeter before testing.

Special Test Equipment

A variety of diagnostic tools are available to help troubleshoot and repair computerized engine control systems. The most sophisticated of these devices are the console type engine analyzers that usually occupy a garage service bay, but there are several types of after market electronic testers available that will allow quick circuit tests of the engine control system by plugging directly into a special connector located in the engine compartment or under the dashboard. Several tool and equipment manufacturers offer simple, hand held testers that measure various circuit voltage levels on command to check all system components for proper operation. Although these testers usually cost about $300-500, consider that the average computer control unit (or ECM) can cost just as much and the money saved by not replacing perfectly good sensors or components in an attempt to correct a problem could justify the

purchase price of a special diagnostic tester the first time it's used.

These computerized testers can allow quick and easy test measurements while the engine is operating or while the car is being driven. In addition, the on-board computer memory can be read to access any stored trouble codes; in effect allowing the computer to tell you where it hurts and aid trouble diagnosis by pinpointing exactly which circuit or component is malfunctioning. In the same manner, repairs can be tested to make sure the problem has been corrected. The biggest advantage these special testers have is their relatively easy hookups that minimize or eliminate the chances of making the wrong connections and getting false voltage readings or damaging the computer accidentally.

➡ **It should be remembered that these testers check voltage levels in circuits; they don't detect mechanical problems or failed components if the circuit voltage falls within the preprogrammed**

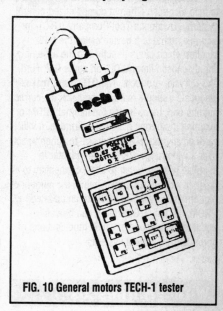

FIG. 10 General motors TECH-1 tester

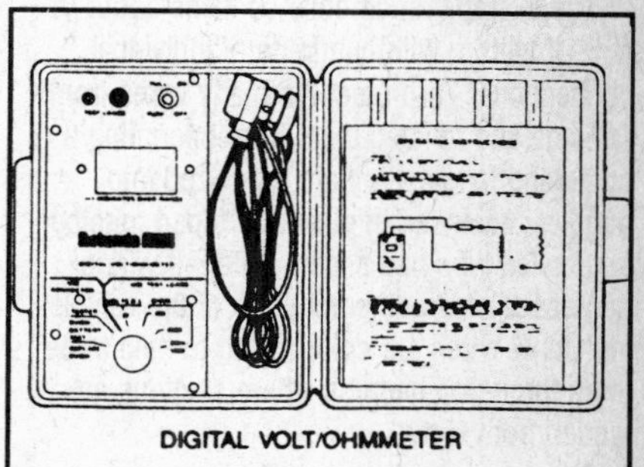

DIGITAL VOLT/OHMMETER

FIG. 11 Digital volt-ohm meter used to test Ford vehicles

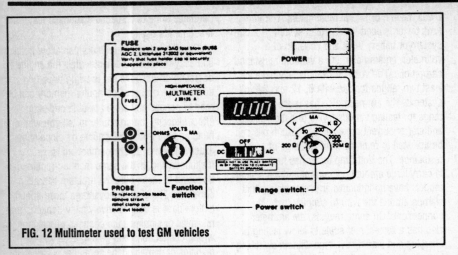

FIG. 12 Multimeter used to test GM vehicles

limits stored in the tester PROM unit. Also, most of the hand held testes are designed to work only on one or two systems made by a specific manufacturer.

A variety of after market testers are available to help diagnose different computerized control systems. Owatonna Tool Company (OTC), for example, markets a device called the OTC Monitor which plugs directly into the assembly line diagnostic link (ALDL) on some GM, Ford and Chrysler products. The OTC tester makes diagnosis a simple matter of pressing the correct buttons and, by changing the internal PROM or inserting a different diagnosis cartridge, it will work on any model from full size to subcompact, over a wide range of years. An adapter is supplied with the tester to allow connection to all types of ALDL links, regardless of the number of pin terminals used. By inserting an updated PROM into the OTC tester, it can be easily updated to diagnose any new modifications of computerized control systems.

Wiring Harnesses

The average automobile contains about 1/2 mile of wiring, with hundreds of individual connections. To protect the many wires from damage and to keep them from becoming a confusing tangle, they are organized into bundles, enclosed in plastic or taped together and called wire harnesses. Different wiring harnesses serve different parts of the vehicle. Individual wires are color coded to help trace them through a harness where sections are hidden from view.

A loose or corroded connection or a replacement wire that is too small for the circuit will add extra resistance and an additional voltage drop to the circuit. A ten percent voltage drop can result in slow or erratic motor operation, for example, even though the circuit is complete. Automotive wiring or circuit conductors can be in any one of three forms:

1. Single strand wire
2. Multistrand wire
3. Printed circuitry

Single strand wire has a solid metal core and is usually used inside such components as alternators, motors, relays and other devices. Multistrand wire has a core made of many small strands of wire twisted together into a single conductor. Most of the wiring in an automotive electrical system is made up of multistrand wire, either as a single conductor or grouped together in a harness. All wiring is color coded on the insulator, either as a solid color or as a colored wire with an identification stripe. A printed circuit is a thin film of copper or other conductor that is printed on an insulator backing. Occasionally, a printed circuit is sandwiched between two sheets of plastic for more protection and flexibility. A complete printed circuit, consisting of conductors, insulating material and connectors for lamps or other components is called a printed circuit board. Printed circuitry is used in place of individual wires or harnesses in places where space is limited, such as behind instrument panels.

Wire Gauge

Since computer controlled automotive electrical systems are very sensitive to changes in resistance, the selection of properly sized wires is critical when systems are repaired. The wire gauge number is an expression of the cross section area of the conductor. The most common system for expressing wire size is the American Wire Gauge (AWG) system.

Wire cross section area is measured in circular mils. A mil is 1/1000" (0.001"); a circular mil is the area of a circle one mil in diameter. For example, a conductor 1/4" in diameter is 0.250" or 250 mils. The circular mil cross section area of the wire is 250 squared (250")or 62,500 circular mils. Imported car models usually use metric wire gauge designations, which is simply the cross section area of the conductor in square millimeters (mm").

Gauge numbers are assigned to conductors of various cross section areas. As gauge number increases, area decreases and the conductor becomes smaller. A 5 gauge conductor is smaller than a 1 gauge conductor and a 10 gauge is smaller than a 5 gauge. As the cross section area of a conductor decreases, resistance increases and so does the gauge number. A conductor with a higher gauge number will carry less current than a conductor with a lower gauge number.

➡ **Gauge wire size refers to the size of the conductor, not the size of the complete wire. It is possible to have two wires of the same gauge with different diameters because one may have thicker insulation than the other.**

A 2 volt automotive electrical systems generally use 10, 12, 14, 16 and 18 gauge wire. Main power distribution circuits and larger accessories usually use 10 and 12 gauge wire. Battery cables are usually 4 or 6 gauge, although 1 and 2 gauge wires are occasionally used. Wire length must also be considered when making repairs to a circuit. As conductor length increases, so does resistance. An 18 gauge wire, for example, can carry a 10 amp load for 10 feet without excessive voltage drop; however if a 15 foot wire is required for the same 10 amp load, it must be a 16 gauge wire.

An electrical schematic shows the electrical current paths when a circuit is operating properly. It is essential to understand how a circuit works before trying to figure out why it doesn't. Schematics break the entire electrical system down into individual circuits and show only one particular circuit. In a schematic, no attempt is made to represent wiring and components as they physically appear on the vehicle; switches and other components are shown as simply as possible. Face views of harness connectors show the cavity or terminal locations in all multi-pin connectors to help locate test points.

If you need to backprobe a connector while it is on the component, the order of the terminals must be mentally reversed. The wire color code can help in this situation, as well as a keyway, lock tab or other reference mark.

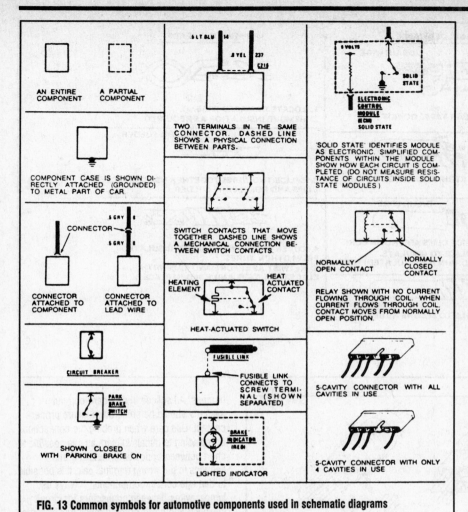

FIG. 13 Common symbols for automotive components used in schematic diagrams

Soldering Techniques

Successful soldering requires that the metals to be joined be heated to a temperature that will melt the solder—usually 360-460°F (182-238°C). Contrary to popular belief, the purpose of the soldering iron is not to melt the solder itself, but to heat the parts being soldered to a temperature high enough to melt the solder when it is touched to the work. Melting flux-cored solder on the soldering iron will usually destroy the effectiveness of the flux.

➡ Soldering tips are made of copper for good heat conductivity, but must be "tinned" regularly for quick transference of heat to the project and to prevent the solder from sticking to the iron. To "tin" the iron, simply heat it and touch the flux-cored solder to the tip; the solder will flow over the hot tip. Wipe the excess off with a clean rag, but be careful as the iron will be hot.

After some use, the tip may become pitted. If so, simply dress the tip smooth with a smooth file and "tin" the tip again. An old saying holds that "metals well cleaned are half soldered." Flux-cored solder will remove oxides but rust, bits of insulation and oil or grease must be removed with a wire brush or emery cloth. For maximum strength in soldered parts, the joint must start off clean and tight. Weak joints will result in gaps too wide for the solder to bridge.

If a separate soldering flux is used, it should be brushed or swabbed on only those areas that are to be soldered. Most solders contain a core of flux and separate fluxing is unnecessary. Hold the work to be soldered firmly. It is best to solder on a wooden board, because a metal vise will only rob the piece to be soldered of heat and make it difficult to melt the solder. Hold the soldering tip with the broadest face against the work to be soldered. Apply solder under the tip close to the work, using enough solder to give a heavy film between the iron and the piece being soldered, while moving slowly and making sure the solder melts properly. Keep the work level or the solder will run to the lowest part and favor the thicker parts, because these require more heat to melt the solder. If the soldering tip overheats (the solder coating on the face of the tip burns up), it should be retinned. Once the soldering is completed, let the soldered joint stand until cool. Tape and seal all soldered wire splices after the repair has cooled.

Wire Harness and Connectors

The on-board computer (ECM) wire harness electrically connects the control unit to the various solenoids, switches and sensors used

WIRING REPAIR

Soldering is a quick, efficient method of joining metals permanently. Everyone who has the occasion to make wiring repairs should know how to solder. Electrical connections that are soldered are far less likely to come apart and will conduct electricity much better than connections that are only "pig-tailed" together. The most popular (and preferred) method of soldering is with an electrical soldering gun. Soldering irons are available in many sizes and wattage ratings. Irons with higher wattage ratings deliver higher temperatures and recover lost heat faster. A small soldering iron rated for no more than 50 watts is recommended, especially on electrical systems where excess heat can damage the components being soldered.

There are three ingredients necessary for successful soldering; proper flux, good solder and sufficient heat. A soldering flux is necessary to clean the metal of tarnish, prepare it for soldering and to enable the solder to spread into tiny crevices. When soldering, always use a resin flux or resin core solder which is non-corrosive and will not attract moisture once the job is finished. Other types of flux (acid core) will leave a residue that will attract moisture and cause the wires to corrode. Tin is a unique metal with a low melting point. In a molten state, it dissolves and alloys easily with many metals. Solder is made by mixing tin with lead. The most common proportions are 40/60, 50/50 and 60/40, with the percentage of tin listed first. Low priced solders usually contain less tin, making them very difficult for a beginner to use because more heat is required to melt the solder. A common solder is 40/60 which is well suited for all-around general use, but 60/40 melts easier, has more tin for a better joint and is preferred for electrical work.

TWISTED/SHIELDED CABLE

OUTER JACKET — DRAIN WIRE

MYLAR →

1. REMOVE OUTER JACKET.
2. UNWRAP ALUMINUM/MYLAR TAPE. DO NOT REMOVE MYLAR.

3. UNTWIST CONDUCTORS. STRIP INSULATION AS NECESSARY.

DRAIN WIRE

4. SPLICE WIRES USING SPLICE CLIPS AND ROSIN CORE SOLDER. WRAP EACH SPLICE TO INSULATE.
5. WRAP WITH MYLAR AND DRAIN (UNINSULATED) WIRE.

6. TAPE OVER WHOLE BUNDLE TO SECURE AS BEFORE

TWISTED LEADS

1. LOCATE DAMAGED WIRE.
2. REMOVE INSULATION AS REQUIRED

SPLICE & SOLDER

3. SPLICE TWO WIRES TOGETHER USING SPLICE CLIPS AND ROSIN CORE SOLDER.

4. COVER SPLICE WITH TAPE TO INSULATE FROM OTHER WIRES.
5. RETWIST AS BEFORE AND TAPE WITH ELECTRICAL TAPE AND HOLD IN PLACE.

FIG. 14 Typical wire repair methods

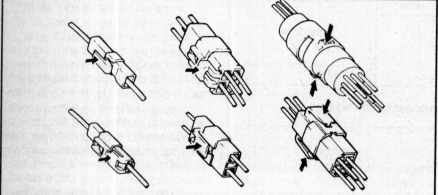

FIG. 15 Various types of locking connectors. Depress the locks to at the arrows to separate the connector

by the control system. Most connectors in the engine compartment or otherwise exposed to the elements are protected against moisture and dirt which could create oxidation and deposits on the terminals. This protection is important because of the very low voltage and current levels used by the computer and sensors. All connectors have a lock which secures the male and female terminals together, with a secondary lock holding the seal and terminal into the connector. Both terminal locks must be released when disconnecting ECM connectors.

These special connectors are weather-proof and all repairs require the use of a special terminal and the tool required to service it. This tool is used to remove the pin and sleeve terminals. If removal is attempted with an ordinary pick, there is a good chance that the terminal will be bent or deformed. Unlike standard blade type terminals, these terminals cannot be straightened once they are bent. Make certain that the connectors are properly seated and all of the sealing rings in place when connecting leads. On some models, a hinge-type flap provides a backup or secondary locking feature for the terminals. Most secondary locks are used to improve the connector reliability by retaining the terminals if the small terminal lock tangs are not positioned properly.

Molded-on connectors require complete replacement of the connection. This means splicing a new connector assembly into the harness. All splices in on-board computer systems should be soldered to insure proper contact. Use care when probing the connections or replacing terminals in them as it is possible to short between opposite terminals. If this happens to the wrong terminal pair, it is possible to damage certain components. Always use jumper wires between connectors for circuit checking and never probe through weatherproof seals.

Open circuits are often difficult to locate by sight because corrosion or terminal misalignment are hidden by the connectors. Merely wiggling a connector on a sensor or in the wiring harness may correct the open circuit condition. This should always be considered when an open circuit or a failed sensor is indicated. Intermittent problems may also be caused by oxidized or loose connections. When using a circuit tester for diagnosis, always probe connections from the wire side. Be careful not to damage sealed connectors with test probes.

All wiring harnesses should be replaced with identical parts, using the same gauge wire and connectors. When signal wires are spliced into a harness, use wire with high temperature insulation only. With the low voltage and current levels found in the system, it is important that the best possible connection at all wire splices be made by soldering the splices together. It is seldom necessary to replace a complete harness. If replacement is necessary, pay close attention to insure proper harness routing. Secure the harness with suitable plastic wire

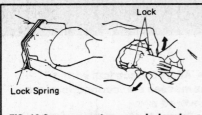

FIG. 16 Some connectors use a lock spring instead of molded lock tabs

clamps to prevent vibrations from causing the harness to wear in spots or contact any hot components.

➡ **Weatherproof connectors cannot be replaced with standard connectors. Instructions are provided with replacement connector and terminal packages. Some wire harnesses have mounting indicators (usually pieces of colored tape) to mark where the harness is to be secured.**

In making wiring repairs, it's important that you always replace damaged wires with wires that are the same gauge as the wire being replaced. The heavier the wire, the smaller the gauge number. Wires are color-coded to aid in identification and whenever possible the same color coded wire should be used for replacement. A wire stripping and crimping tool is necessary to install solderless terminal connectors. Test all crimps by pulling on the wires; it should not be possible to pull the wires out of a good crimp.

Wires which are open, exposed or otherwise damaged are repaired by simple splicing. Where possible, if the wiring harness is accessible and the damaged place in the wire can be located, it is best to open the harness and check for all possible damage. In an inaccessible harness, the wire must be bypassed with a new insert, usually taped to the outside of the old harness.

When replacing fusible links, be sure to use fusible link wire, NOT ordinary automotive wire. Make sure the fusible segment is of the same gauge and construction as the one being replaced and double the stripped end when crimping the terminal connector for a good contact. The melted (open) fusible link segment of the wiring harness should be cut off as close to the harness as possible, then a new segment spliced in as described. In the case of a

damaged fusible link that feeds two harness wires, the harness connections should be replaced with two fusible link wires so that each circuit will have its own separate protection.

➡ **Most of the problems caused in the wiring harness are due to bad ground connections. Always check all vehicle ground connections for corrosion or looseness before performing any power feed checks to eliminate the chance of a bad ground affecting the circuit.**

Repairing Hard Shell Connectors

Unlike molded connectors, the terminal contacts in hard shell connectors can be replaced. Weatherproof hard-shell connectors with the leads molded into the shell have non-replaceable terminal ends. Replacement usually involves the use of a special terminal removal tool that depress the locking tangs (barbs) on the connector terminal and allow the connector to be removed from the rear of the shell. The connector shell should be replaced if it shows any evidence of burning, melting, cracks, or breaks. Replace individual terminals that are burnt, corroded, distorted or loose.

➡ **The insulation crimp must be tight to prevent the insulation from sliding back on the wire when the wire is pulled. The insulation must be visibly compressed under the crimp tabs, and the ends of the crimp should be turned in for a firm grip on the insulation.**

The wire crimp must be made with all wire strands inside the crimp. The terminal must be fully compressed on the wire strands with the ends of the crimp tabs turned in to make a firm grip on the wire. Check all connections with an ohmmeter to insure a good contact. There should be no measurable resistance between the wire and the terminal when connected.

Mechanical Test Equipment

Vacuum Gauge

Most gauges are graduated in inches of mercury (in.Hg), although a device called a

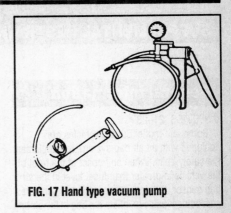

FIG. 17 Hand type vacuum pump

manometer reads vacuum in inches of water (in. H2O). The normal vacuum reading usually varies between 18 and 22 in.Hg at sea level. To test engine vacuum, the vacuum gauge must be connected to a source of manifold vacuum. Many engines have a plug in the intake manifold which can be removed and replaced with an adapter fitting. Connect the vacuum gauge to the fitting with a suitable rubber hose or, if no manifold plug is available, connect the vacuum gauge to any device using manifold vacuum, such as EGR valves, etc. The vacuum gauge can be used to determine if enough vacuum is reaching a component to allow its actuation.

Hand Vacuum Pump

Small, hand-held vacuum pumps come in a variety of designs. Most have a built-in vacuum gauge and allow the component to be tested without removing it from the vehicle. Operate the pump lever or plunger to apply the correct amount of vacuum required for the test specified in the diagnosis routines. The level of vacuum in inches of Mercury (in.Hg) is indicated on the pump gauge. For some testing, an additional vacuum gauge may be necessary.

Intake manifold vacuum is used to operate various systems and devices on late model vehicles. To correctly diagnose and solve problems in vacuum control systems, a vacuum source is necessary for testing. In some cases, vacuum can be taken from the intake manifold when the engine is running, but vacuum is normally provided by a hand vacuum pump. These hand vacuum pumps have a built-in vacuum gauge that allow testing while the device is still attached to the component. For some tests, an additional vacuum gauge may be necessary.

SUPPLEMENTAL RESTRAINT SYSTEM (AIR BAG)

General Information

▶ SEE FIGS. 21–23

Some late model Subaru vehicles are equipped with an air bag system, to supplement the safety belts. When an impact at the front of the vehicle is greater than a set level in the air bag sensor, the sensor senses it and generates an electrical pulse to inflate the bag in the air bag module, preventing the drivers body from contacting the steering wheel.

The SRS air bag consists of an control unit, left and right front sensors, 2 safety sensors built into the control unit and an air bag module containing an air bag and inflator. The left and right front sensors and the 2 safety sensors are connected in parallel respectively, and the front sensors and safety sensors are connected in series, so that the air bag will inflate if at least 1 front sensor and one safety sensor sense an impact at the same time.

The components of the SRS system are not owner serviceable and no attempts should be made to repair the system, however, when working on any of the electrical systems inside of the vehicle, the air bag system must be disarmed. This can be accomplished by following the disarming procedure given in this section.

➡ All SRS electrical wiring harnesses and connections are covered with yellow outer insulation.

SYSTEM OPERATION

The SRS is designed to deploy the air bag when the safing sensor and any of the 4 sensors (front crash zone sensor, center crash zone sensor, left crash zone sensor or tunnel sensor) simultaneously make contact, with the ignition switch in the **ON** position. Air bag deployment

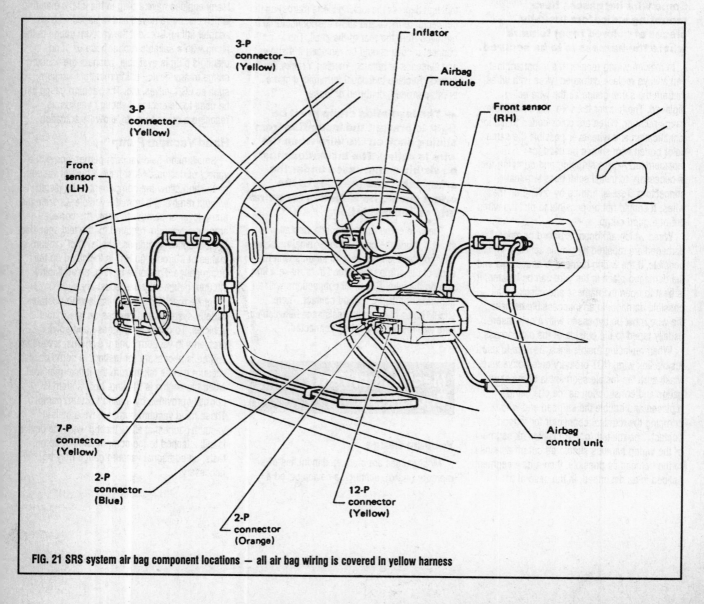

FIG. 21 SRS system air bag component locations — all air bag wiring is covered in yellow harness

will occur in a frontal or near frontal impact of moderate to severe force.

The diagnostic unit monitors the SRS system and stores data, should any faults be detected in the system. When the engine is started or the ignition switch is in the **ON** or **START** position, the SRS warning light should illuminate for approximately 7 seconds and then turn off. This indicates that the system is operational.

SYSTEM COMPONENTS

Air Bag Module

The air bag module, located in the center of the steering wheel, contains a folded air bag and an inflator unit.

Spiral Cable

The spiral cable, located in the steering column, ensures an uninterrupted electrical circuit to the air bag module, while allowing rotation of the steering wheel. This cable is sometimes referred to as a clock spring.

Warning Lamp

The warning lamp, located in the instrument panel, indicates operational status of the SRS.

SRS Control Unit

The SRS control unit, monitors the SRS system and stores data, should any faults be detected in the system.

Air Bag Connector

The SRS system connectors use a double lock mechanism and a coupling error detection system. If the connector is not properly connected, the air bag warning light will illuminate on the instrument cluster.

The proper method for using these connectors is to press the release tab on the connector until the green lever pops up, this will unlock the connector. Then pull the connector apart while pushing the lever down. To reconnect the connectors, push the halves together until a click is heard then push the green lever down until another click is heard.

SERVICE PRECAUTIONS

✳✳✳ CAUTION

To avoid deployment when servicing the SIR system or components in the immediate area, do not use electrical test equipment such as battery or A.C. powered voltmeter, ohmmeter, etc. or any type of tester other than specified on the air bag system. Do not use a non-powered probe tester. To avoid personal injury all precautions must be strictly adhered to.

• Do not disassemble any air bag system components.

• Always carry an inflator module with the trim cover pointed away.

• Always place an inflator module on the workbench with the pad side facing upward, away from loose objects.

• After deployment, the air bag surface may contain sodium hydroxide dust. Always wear gloves and safety glasses when handling the assembly. Wash hands with mild soap and water afterwards.

• When servicing any SRS parts, discard the old bolts and replace with new ones.

• The SRS must be inspected 10 years after the vehicle's manufacture date shown on the certification label located on the left front door latch post.

• Always inspect the air bag sensors and steering wheel pad, when the vehicle has been involved in a collision (even in cases of minor collision) where the air bag did not deploy.

• Always use a fine needle test lead for testing, to prevent damaging the connector terminals.

• Never disconnect any electrical connection with the ignition switch **ON** unless instructed to do so in a test.

• Before disconnecting the negative battery cable, make a record of the contents memorized by each memory system like the clock, audio, etc., when service or repairs are completed make certain to reset these memory systems.

• Always wear a grounded wrist static strap when servicing any control module or component labeled with a Electrostatic Discharge (ESD) sensitive device symbol.

• Avoid touching module connector pins.

• Leave new components and modules in the shipping package until ready to install them.

• Always touch a vehicle ground after sliding across a vehicle seat or walking across vinyl or carpeted floors to avoid static charge damage.

• All sensors are specifically calibrated to a particular series.

The sensors, mounting brackets and wiring harness must never be modified from original design.

• Never strike or jar a sensor, or deployment could happen.

• The inflator module must be deployed before it is scrapped.

• Any visible damage to sensors requires component replacement.

• Never bake dry paint on vehicle or subject the vehicle to temperatures exceeding 200°F (93°C), without disabling the air bag system and removing the inflator module, crash zone sensors, SRS diagnosis unit and the spiral cable.

• Do not interchange sensors between models or years.

• Do not install used air bag system parts from another vehicle.

• Never allow welding cables to lay on, near or across any vehicle electrical wiring.

• When ever any SRS parts are removed, always use new retaining bolts.

• Caution labels are important when servicing the air bag system in the field. If they are dirty or damaged, replace them with new ones.

DISARMING THE SYSTEM

➡ **Be sure to properly disconnect and connect the air bag connector.**

1. Turn the ignition switch to the **OFF** position.
2. Disconnect the negative battery cable.

✳✳✳ CAUTION

Wait at least 10 minutes after disconnecting the battery cable before doing any further work. The SRS system is designed to retain enough voltage to deploy the air bag for a short time, even after the battery has been disconnected. Serious injury may result from unintended air bag deployment, if work is done on the SRS system immediately after the battery cable is disconnected.

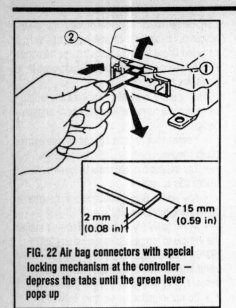

FIG. 22 Air bag connectors with special locking mechanism at the controller — depress the tabs until the green lever pops up

3. Remove the lower lid from the steering column and disconnect the connector between the air bag module and spiral cable.

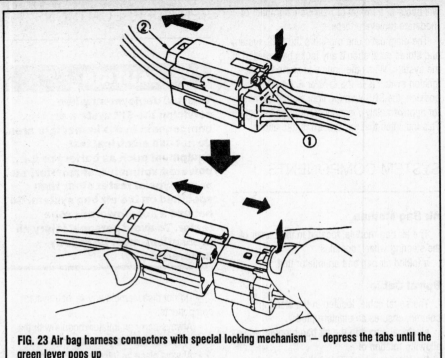

FIG. 23 Air bag harness connectors with special locking mechanism — depress the tabs until the green lever pops up

ENABLING THE SYSTEM

1. Reconnect the connector between the air bag module and spiral cable. Then install the

lower steering column lid.
2. Reconnect the negative battery cable.
3. Turn the ignition switch to the **ON** position and observe the SRS warning light. The SRS warning light should illuminate for approximately

7 seconds, turn OFF and remain OFF for at least 45 seconds.

4. If the SRS warning light function as indicated in Step 3, the SRS system is functioning properly.

HEATING AND AIR CONDITIONING

Heater Blower Motor

◆ SEE FIGS. 18–19

REMOVAL & INSTALLATION

Justy

1. Disconnect the negative battery cable.
2. Remove the coupler that connects the instrument panel harness to the blower motor.
3. Remove the coupler that connects the resistor to the instrument panel harness.
4. Detach the blower assembly. Remove the screws retaining the blower motor to the blower assembly.
5. Remove the motor assembly. Remove the nut retaining the fan to the motor assembly.

To install:
6. Install the motor assembly and tighten the nuts to specification.
7. Install the couplers that connect the resistor to the instrument panel and the instrument panel to the blower motor.
8. Connect the negative battery cable.

XT Coupe, Legacy and SVX

➡ **Depending upon working clearance the air conditioning system may have to be discharged in order to service the blower motor. If this is the case, be sure to observe all the required safety precautions when discharging and recharging the air conditioning system.**

1. Disconnect the negative battery cable.
2. Remove the lower instrument panel cover on the passenger side of the vehicle.
3. Remove the glove box assembly, as required for working clearance.
4. Remove the heater duct, if not equipped with air conditioning.
5. If equipped with air conditioning, separate the evaporator from the blower assembly.
6. Disconnect the blower motor harness and the resistor electrical harness connector.
7. Remove the blower motor retaining bolts. Remove the blower motor assembly from its mounting.

To install:
8. Install the blower motor retaining bolts and tighten to 4–7 ft. lbs. Connect the blower motor harness and the resistor electrical harness connector.

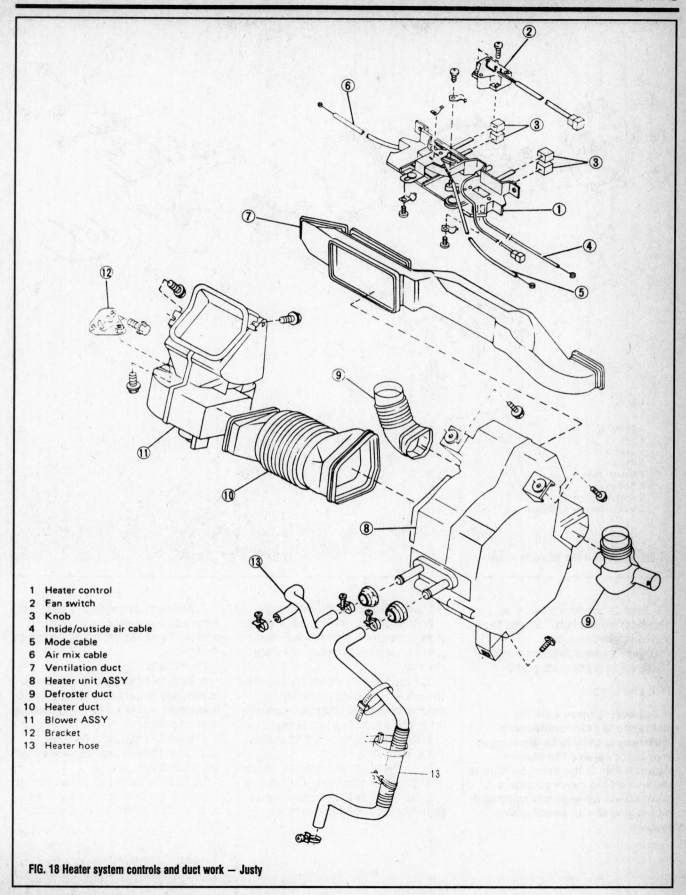

1 Heater control
2 Fan switch
3 Knob
4 Inside/outside air cable
5 Mode cable
6 Air mix cable
7 Ventilation duct
8 Heater unit ASSY
9 Defroster duct
10 Heater duct
11 Blower ASSY
12 Bracket
13 Heater hose

FIG. 18 Heater system controls and duct work — Justy

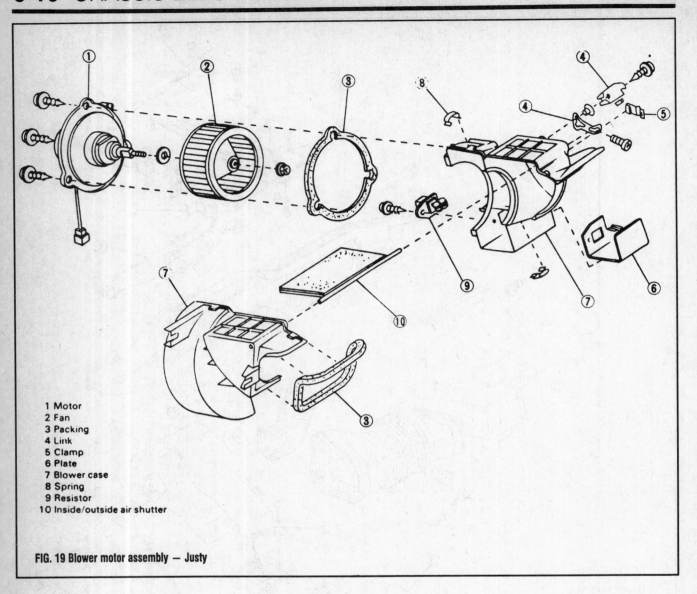

1 Motor
2 Fan
3 Packing
4 Link
5 Clamp
6 Plate
7 Blower case
8 Spring
9 Resistor
10 Inside/outside air shutter

FIG. 19 Blower motor assembly — Justy

9. Install the evaporator to the blower assembly as required. Install the heater duct as required. Install the glove box.

10. Install the lower instrument panel cover and connect the negative battery cable.

STD. and Loyale

➡ **Depending upon working clearance the air conditioning system may have to be discharged in order to service the blower motor. If this is the case, be sure to observe all the required safety precautions when discharging and recharging the air conditioning system.**

1. Disconnect the negative battery cable.

2. Remove the lower instrument panel cover on the passenger side of the vehicle. Remove the glove box assembly, as required for working clearance.

3. If equipped with a vacuum actuator, set the control lever to the **CIRC** position and disconnect the vacuum hose from the assembly. Remove the actuator from its mounting.

4. Remove the heater duct, if not equipped with air conditioning.

5. If equipped with air conditioning, separate the evaporator from the blower assembly.

6. Disconnect the blower motor harness and the resistor electrical harness connector.

7. Remove the blower motor retaining bolts. Remove the blower motor assembly from its mounting. As required, separate the fan from the blower motor.

To Install:

8. Install the blower motor and tighten the retaining bolts to specification. Connect the blower motor harness and the resistor electrical harness connector.

9. Install the evaporator to the blower assembly as required. Install the heater duct as required. Install the glove box.

10. Install the vacuum actuator and connect the vacuum line. Install the lower instrument panel cover and connect the negative battery cable.

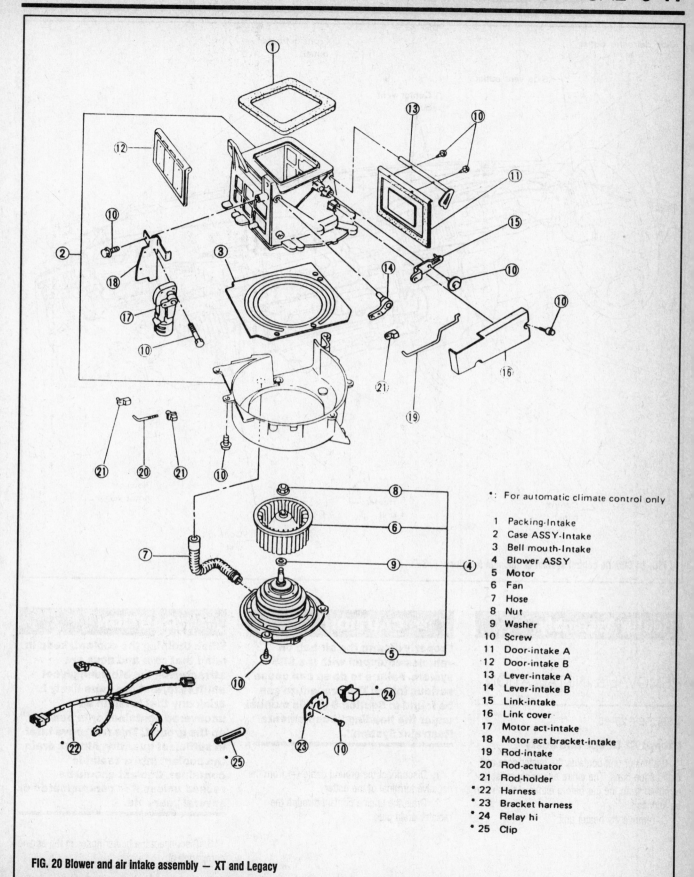

*: For automatic climate control only

1 Packing-Intake
2 Case ASSY-Intake
3 Bell mouth-Intake
4 Blower ASSY
5 Motor
6 Fan
7 Hose
8 Nut
9 Washer
10 Screw
11 Door-intake A
12 Door-intake B
13 Lever-intake A
14 Lever-intake B
15 Link-intake
16 Link cover
17 Motor act-intake
18 Motor act bracket-intake
19 Rod-intake
20 Rod-actuator
21 Rod-holder
22 Harness
23 Bracket harness
24 Relay hi
25 Clip

FIG. 20 Blower and air intake assembly — XT and Legacy

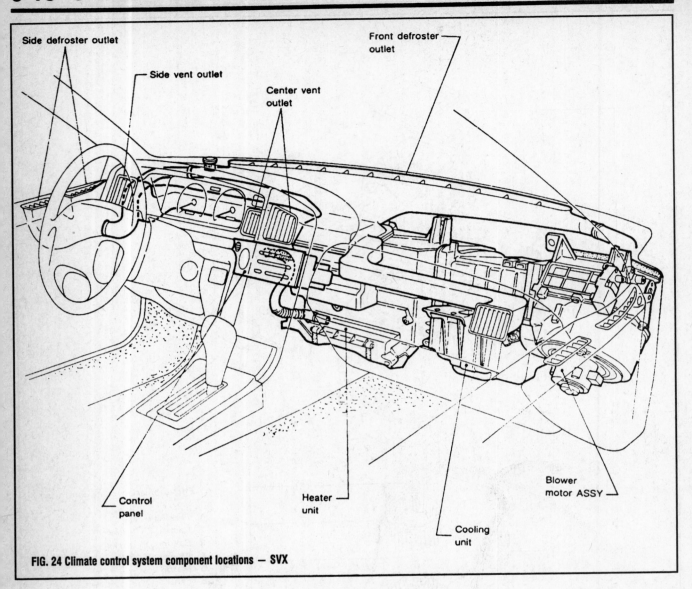

FIG. 24 Climate control system component locations — SVX

Heater Assembly

REMOVAL & INSTALLATION

▶ SEE FIGS. 25–26

Except XT Coupe and Justy

The heater unit contains the heater core and distribution flaps. The entire assembly must be removed from the car before either of these can be serviced.

To remove the heater unit:

✳ CAUTION

Properly disarm the air bag on vehicles equipped with the SRS system. Failure to do so can cause serious injury. The procedure can be found in Section 6 of this manual under the heading "Supplemental Restraint System".

1. Disconnect the ground cable (–) from the negative terminal of the battery.
2. Drain the engine coolant through the radiator drain plug.

✳ CAUTION

When draining the coolant, keep in mind that cats and dogs are attracted by the ethylene glycol antifreeze, and are quite likely to drink any that is left in an uncovered container or in puddles on the ground. This will prove fatal in sufficient quantity. Always drain the coolant into a sealable container. Coolant should be reused unless it is contaminated or several years old.

3. Disconnect the heater hoses in the engine compartment.

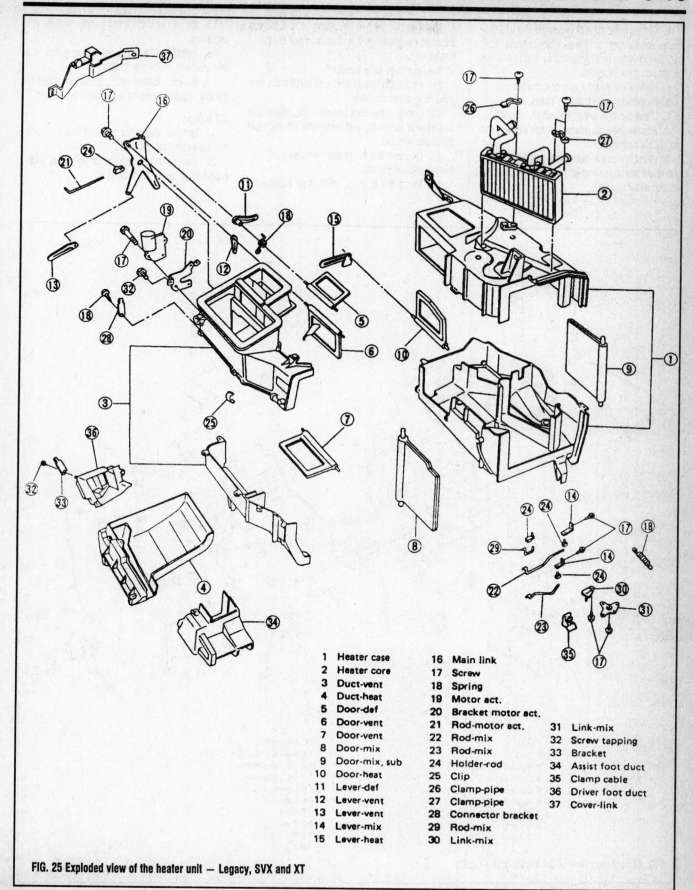

1	Heater case	16	Main link
2	Heater core	17	Screw
3	Duct-vent	18	Spring
4	Duct-heat	19	Motor act.
5	Door-def	20	Bracket motor act.
6	Door-vent	21	Rod-motor act.
7	Door-vent	22	Rod-mix
8	Door-mix	23	Rod-mix
9	Door-mix, sub	24	Holder-rod
10	Door-heat	25	Clip
11	Lever-def	26	Clamp-pipe
12	Lever-vent	27	Clamp-pipe
13	Lever-vent	28	Connector bracket
14	Lever-mix	29	Rod-mix
15	Lever-heat	30	Link-mix

31	Link-mix
32	Screw tapping
33	Bracket
34	Assist foot duct
35	Clamp cable
36	Driver foot duct
37	Cover-link

FIG. 25 Exploded view of the heater unit — Legacy, SVX and XT

4. Remove the rubber grommet the heater hoses run through on the kick panel inside the car. The location is slightly above and to the right of the accelerator pedal.

5. Remove the radio box or console.

6. Remove the instrument panel.

7. If the car has a luggage shelf, remove it.

8. Disconnect the heater control cables and fan motor harness.

9. Disconnect the duct between the heater unit and blower assembly. Remove the right and left defroster nozzles.

10. Remove the two mounting bolts at the top sides of the heater unit. Lift up and out on the heater unit.

To Install the unit:

11. Install the heater unit and tighten the two mounting bolts securely.

12. Connect the duct between the heater unit and blower assembly and install the left and right defroster nozzles.

13. Connect the fan motor harness and heater control cables.

14. Install the luggage shelf, if so equipped.

15. Install the instrument panel, console and radio box.

16. Install the heater hose rubber grommets and connect the heater hoses.

17. Fill the radiator with coolant, connect the battery, start the engine and check for leaks.

XT Coupe

1. Remove heater hoses (inlet and outlet) in engine compartment.

2. Drain as much coolant as possible, and plug heater pipes with cloth.

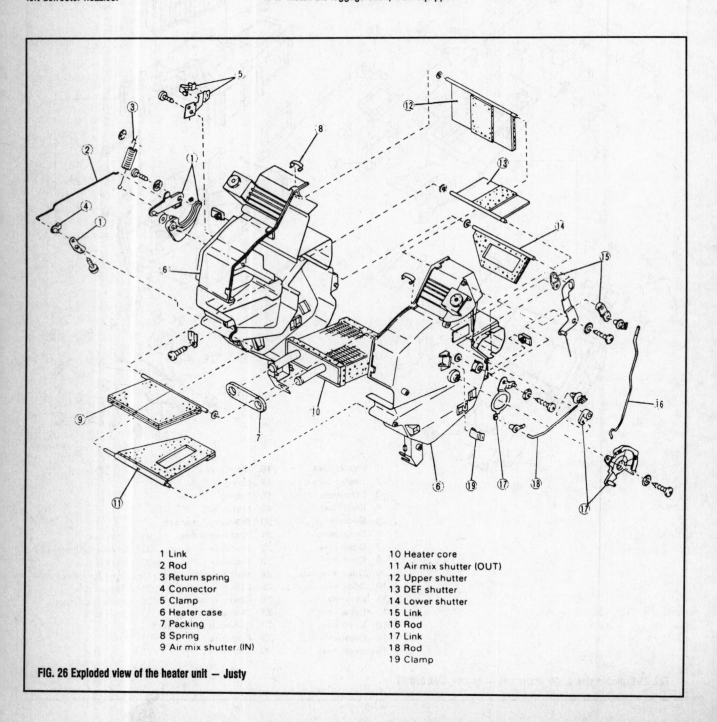

1 Link
2 Rod
3 Return spring
4 Connector
5 Clamp
6 Heater case
7 Packing
8 Spring
9 Air mix shutter (IN)
10 Heater core
11 Air mix shutter (OUT)
12 Upper shutter
13 DEF shutter
14 Lower shutter
15 Link
16 Rod
17 Link
18 Rod
19 Clamp

FIG. 26 Exploded view of the heater unit — Justy

3. Remove the instrument panel.

4. Disconnect connector of harness coming from motor and temperature control cable.

5. Remove the heater unit.

6. Torque the heater unit mounting bolts to 4.0–6.9 ft. lbs. (5.4–9.3 Nm)

Justy

1. Disconnect the negative battery terminal from the battery.

2. Place a catch pan under the radiator, remove the drain plug and drain the cooling system to a level below the heater unit.

3. From the engine compartment, remove the inlet/outlet hoses from the heater unit.

4. From under the instrument panel, pull the right/left defroster ducts from the defroster nozzles, then, pull the ducts from the heater unit.

5. Disconnect the fan switch-to-blower motor electrical wiring connector(s).

6. From behind the right side of the center instrument panel, disconnect the air mix control cable from the heater unit. From behind the left side of the center instrument panel, disconnect the mode control cable from the heater unit.

7. Remove the heater unit-to-center instrument panel bolts.

8. Remove the glove box (pocket)-to-instrument panel screws and the glove box.

9. From the blower assembly, disconnect the inside/outside air control cable.

10. Remove the instrument panel assembly.

11. Remove the heater unit-to-chassis bolts and the blower assembly-to-chassis bolts, then the heater unit; be careful not to spill the residual coolant in the heater core.

To install:

➡ When removing the heater unit assembly through body hole, be careful not to damage the heater pipe.

12. To install the mode cable, perform the following procedures:

a. Place the mode lever in the VENT position.

b. Turn the mode lever downward so that the link boss (which connects the cable ring) is positioned farthest from the clamp (flush mounted) to heat case.

c. Position the mode cable ring in the link boss, pull it fully toward the clamp and clamp it securely; make sure that the mode link does not move from its lowest position.

d. Push the cable ring into the link boss, then ensure proper connection.

13. To install the inside/outside air cable, perform the following procedures:

a. Manually set the inside/outside air shutter to allow the inside blower air inlet to Open.

b. On the control panel, position the inside/outside air control lever on CIRC. Position the inside/outside air cable ring in the blower link boss, pull it fully toward the clamp flush-mounted to the heater case and clamp it securely; make sure that the blower link does not move away from its position.

c. Push the cable connecting ring into the link boss, to ensure that it is properly connected.

14. To install the air mix cable, perform the following procedures:

a. On the control panel, position the temperature control lever to the HOT position.

b. Turn the air mix link downward so that the air mix link boss is positioned farthest from the clamp (flush-mounted) to the heater case.

c. Position the air mix cable ring in the link boss, pull it fully toward the clamp and clamp it; be sure that the link does not move away from its lowest position.

d. Push the cable connecting ring into the link boss to ensure proper connection.

15. Install the remaining components. Refill the cooling system. Start the engine, allow it to reach normal operating temperatures and check for leaks.

Heater Core

REMOVAL & INSTALLATION

All Models Except Justy

➡ The heater unit must be removed from the car to service the heater core. Depending upon working clearance the air conditioning system may have to be discharged in order to service the blower motor. If this is the case, be sure to observe all the required safety precautions when discharging and recharging the air conditioning system.

1. Disconnect the negative battery cable. Drain the cooling system.

2. Disconnect the heater hoses from the heater core assembly.

3. Remove the instrument panel assembly.

4. Disconnect the electrical harness connector from the blower motor assembly. Disconnect the temperature control cable.

5. Remove the heater unit retaining bolts. Remove the heater unit from the vehicle.

6. Remove the heater core retaining connectors. Remove the heater core from its mounting.

To Install:

7. Pressure test the heater core prior to installation. Install the heater core in the heater unit, and the heater unit in the vehicle.

8. Reconnect all electrical connections. Install the heater hoses.

9. Fill the cooling system with coolant. Connect the negative battery cable. Start the engine and bring to operating temperature. Check for leaks.

Justy

1. Disconnect the negative battery cable. Drain the cooling system.

2. Disconnect the heater hoses from the heater core assembly.

3. Pull off the right and left defroster ducts from the defroster nozzles. Pull the ducts from the heater unit.

4. Disconnect the electrical wires from the fan switch and the blower motor.

5. Disconnect the air mix cable from the heater unit. Disconnect the mode cable from the heater unit.

6. Remove the bolts that retain the heater unit to the instrument panel.

7. As required, for working clearance remove the glove box door assembly.

8. Disconnect the inside/outside air control cable from the blower assembly.

9. Remove the instrument panel assembly.

10. Remove the heater unit retaining bolts. Remove the heater unit from the vehicle.

11. Remove the heater core cushion. Loosen the heater core holder and than remove it. Pull the heater core from its mounting and remove it from the heater case.

To Install:

12. Pressure test the new heater core prior to installation.

13. Install the heater core in the heater cushion, then install the heater core/unit assembly in the vehicle.

14. Install the instrument panel, control cables and glove box door. Connect the heater mode and control cables to the heater box. Connect all electrical connections previously disconnected.

15. Install the defroster nozzles and the heater hoses. Fill the cooling system with coolant.

16. Connect the negative battery cable, start the engine and check for leaks.

Air Conditioning Compressor

♦ SEE FIGS. 27–33

REMOVAL & INSTALLATION

➡ **There are many different types of**

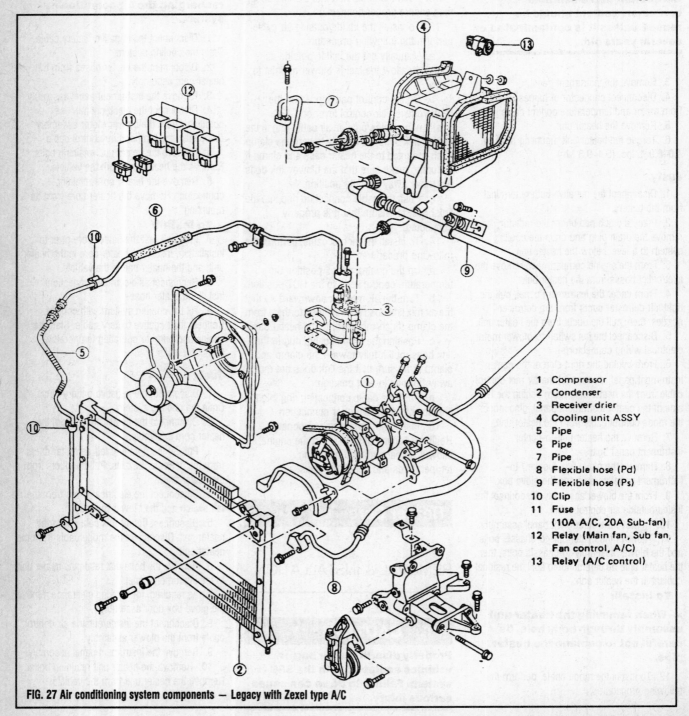

1	Compressor
2	Condenser
3	Receiver drier
4	Cooling unit ASSY
5	Pipe
6	Pipe
7	Pipe
8	Flexible hose (Pd)
9	Flexible hose (Ps)
10	Clip
11	Fuse (10A A/C, 20A Sub-fan)
12	Relay (Main fan, Sub fan, Fan control, A/C)
13	Relay (A/C control)

FIG. 27 Air conditioning system components — Legacy with Zexel type A/C

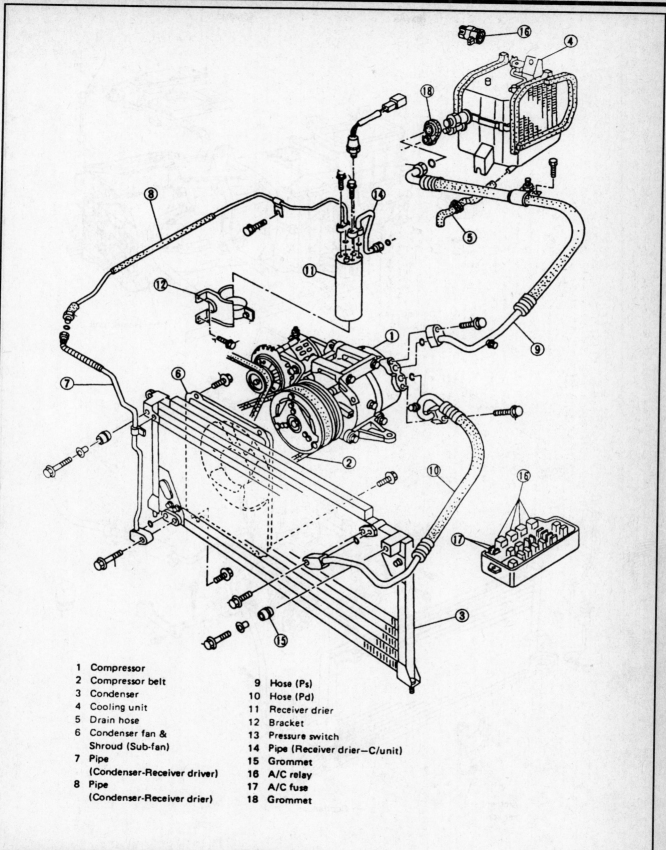

1	Compressor		
2	Compressor belt	9	Hose (Ps)
3	Condenser	10	Hose (Pd)
4	Cooling unit	11	Receiver drier
5	Drain hose	12	Bracket
6	Condenser fan &	13	Pressure switch
	Shroud (Sub-fan)	14	Pipe (Receiver drier—C/unit)
7	Pipe	15	Grommet
	(Condenser-Receiver driver)	16	A/C relay
8	Pipe	17	A/C fuse
	(Condenser-Receiver drier)	18	Grommet

FIG. 28 Air conditioning system components — Legacy with Calsonic A/C

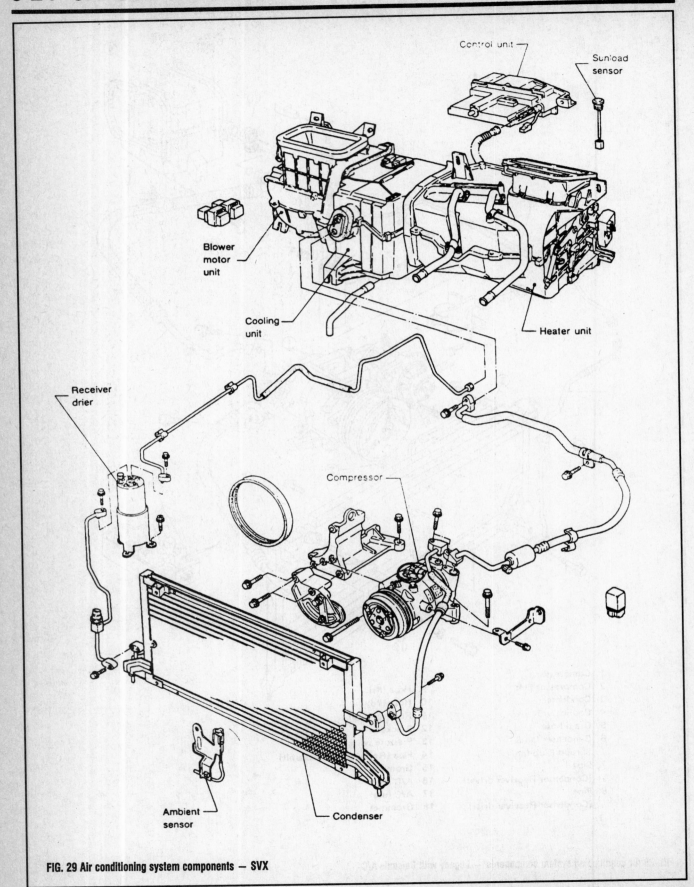

FIG. 29 Air conditioning system components — SVX

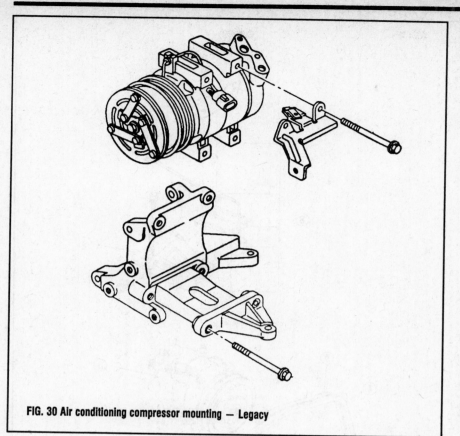

FIG. 30 Air conditioning compressor mounting — Legacy

air conditioning compressors used on each of the models covered in this manual, the removal and installation procedure that is given is a general procedure. Some differences is the mounting brackets will exist. Refer to the illustrations for specific vehicles.

1. Disconnect the negative battery cable.
2. Properly discharge the air conditioning system.
3. Disconnect both of the refrigerant lines from the compressor and plug the openings. Be sure not to lose the O-rings when disconnecting the lines.
4. Remove the bolts from the alternator and compressor belt cover and remove the cover.
5. Remove the alternator drive belt.
6. Loosen the lock bolt on the idler pulley and remove the compressor belt.
7. Disconnect the alternator harness connector from the alternator.
8. Disconnect the compressor wire connector from the harness connector.
9. On some models, remove the compressor-to-lower bracket mounting bolts and remove the lower bracket. Remove the compressor-to-upper bracket mounting bolts and remove the compressor from the engine.

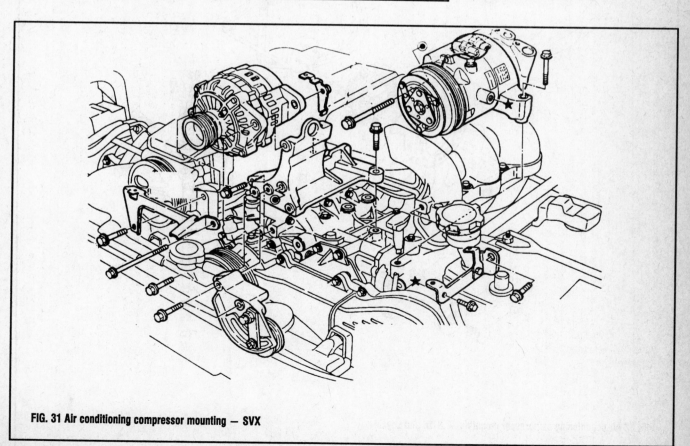

FIG. 31 Air conditioning compressor mounting — SVX

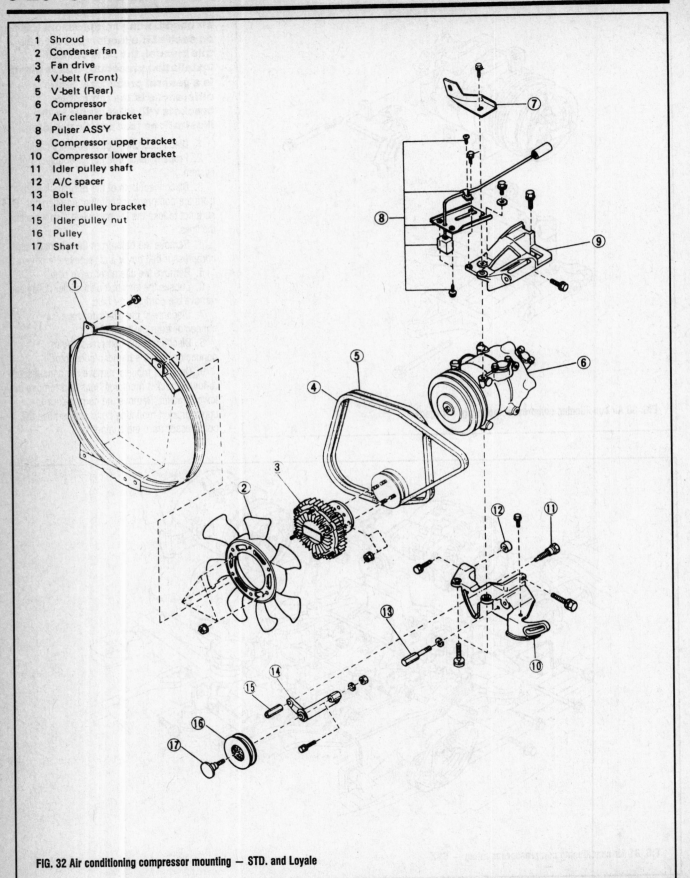

1 Shroud
2 Condenser fan
3 Fan drive
4 V-belt (Front)
5 V-belt (Rear)
6 Compressor
7 Air cleaner bracket
8 Pulser ASSY
9 Compressor upper bracket
10 Compressor lower bracket
11 Idler pulley shaft
12 A/C spacer
13 Bolt
14 Idler pulley bracket
15 Idler pulley nut
16 Pulley
17 Shaft

FIG. 32 Air conditioning compressor mounting — STD. and Loyale

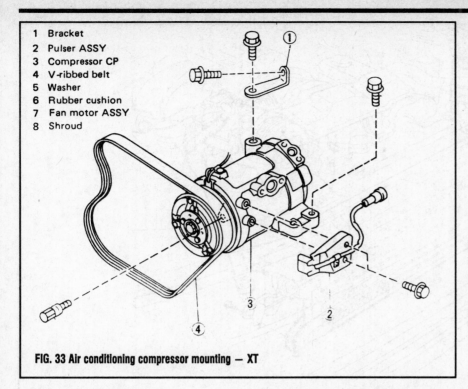

1 Bracket
2 Pulser ASSY
3 Compressor CP
4 V-ribbed belt
5 Washer
6 Rubber cushion
7 Fan motor ASSY
8 Shroud

FIG. 33 Air conditioning compressor mounting — XT

3. Remove the front grille.
4. If equipped with and air guide, remove it.
5. On SVX, remove the belt cover and upper radiator bracket.
6. Disconnect and plug the refrigerant lines from the condenser. On SVX, remove the radiator and condenser fans.
7. Remove the upper condenser mounting bolts, on some models the condenser can now be pulled out of the vehicle.
8. On SVX, raise and support the front of the vehicle and remove the under cover, remove the lower condenser mounting bolts. Lower the vehicle. Remove the condenser by pushing the radiator back to the engine and pulling it out.

To Install:
9. Install the condenser in position and install the retaining bolts. Tighten the retaining bolts to 7 ft. lbs. (10 Nm). On SVX, raise the vehicle and install the lower bolts and the under cover.
10. Apply a light coat of refrigerant oil to the O-rings and connect the refrigerant lines to the condenser. Tighten the lines to 14 ft. lbs. (20 Nm).
11. Install the upper radiator bracket, radiator and condenser fans, and belt cover on SVX.
12. Install the front grille.
13. Connect the negative battery cable and properly fill the refrigerant system.

10. On other models, remove the compressor-to-bracket bolts and remove the compressor from the engine.

To Install:
11. Install the compressor in position on the engine. Tighten the compressor mounting bolts to: 14–22 ft. lbs. (20–30 Nm) on STD. and Loyale models, 25–33 ft. lbs. (34–44 Nm) on XT models, 17–31 ft. lbs. (23–42 Nm) on Legacy models and 23–29 ft. lbs. (31–39 Nm) on SVX.
12. Reconnect the electrical leads to the compressor and alternator.
13. Install the compressor and alternator belts. Adjust to the proper tension.
14. Apply a coating of compressor oil to the O-rings on the refrigerant lines and connect the lines to the compressor. Tighten the lines to 7–14 ft. lbs. (10–20 Nm).
15. Install the drive belt cover, if equipped.

16. Connect the negative battery cable. Properly evacuate and charge the air conditioning system.

Condenser

REMOVAL & INSTALLATION

◆ SEE FIGS. 34–35

➡ **On the SVX, the vehicle will have to be raised to remove the 2 lower condenser mounting bolts.**

1. Disconnect the negative battery cable.
2. Properly discharge the air conditioning system.

Evaporator Core

REMOVAL & INSTALLATION

◆ SEE FIGS. 36–40

Except Legacy and SVX
1. Open the hood and remove the spare tire (if necessary).
2. Disconnect the negative battery terminal.
3. Refer to Section 1 for refrigerant discharge procedure and discharge the refrigerant.
4. Disconnect the evaporator discharge pipe, suction pipe and grommets.
5. Remove the evaporator core under cover.
6. Remove the pocket assembly.
7. Disconnect the harness connector from the evaporator.
8. Remove the two retaining bands and remove the evaporator.
9. Reverse the removal procedure to install the unit. Tighten the discharge pipe to 7–14 ft. lbs. (10–20 Nm), the nut on the suction side to 14–22 ft. lbs. (20–29 Nm).

FIG. 34 Condenser mounting — STD. and Loyale

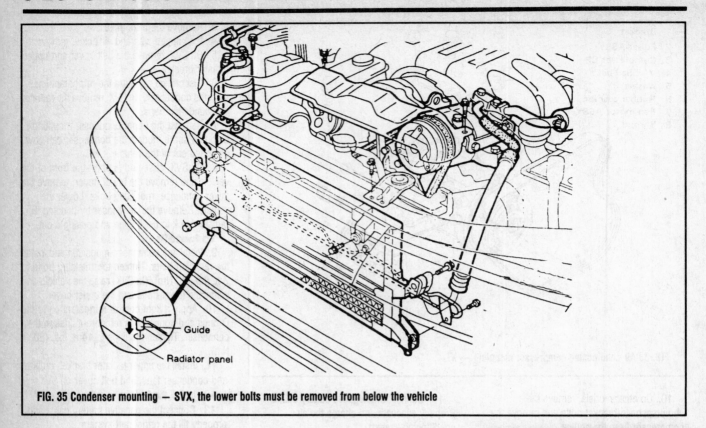

Guide

Radiator panel

FIG. 35 Condenser mounting — SVX, the lower bolts must be removed from below the vehicle

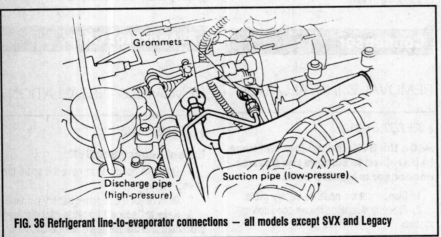

Grommets

Discharge pipe (high-pressure)

Suction pipe (low-pressure)

FIG. 36 Refrigerant line-to-evaporator connections — all models except SVX and Legacy

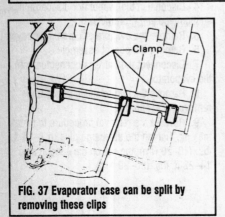

Clamp

FIG. 37 Evaporator case can be split by removing these clips

➡ **When installing the evaporator into the car body, make sure that the wiring harness and vacuum hose do not get caught between the body parts.**

10. Properly recharge the refrigerant system.

Legacy and SVX

1. Disconnect the negative battery cable.

✱✱✱ CAUTION

Properly disarm the air bag on vehicles equipped with the SRS system. Failure to do so can cause serious injury. The procedure can be found in Section 6 of this manual under the heading "Supplemental Restraint System".

2. On models equipped with an air bag, properly disarm the air bag.

3. Properly discharge the refrigerant system. Disconnect and plug the discharge and suction pipes in the engine compartment. Remove the grommets.

4. Remove the glove box assembly and remove the bolts retaining the glove box support bracket.

5. Disconnect the electrical leads from the evaporator case.

6. Disconnect the drain hose from the case.

7. Remove the evaporator case mounting bolts and remove the evaporator case from the vehicle.

8. The evaporator case can be separated in order to remove the evaporator from the unit, as well as the expansion valve. To separate the case, use a small prybar and remove the clips that retain the case halves.

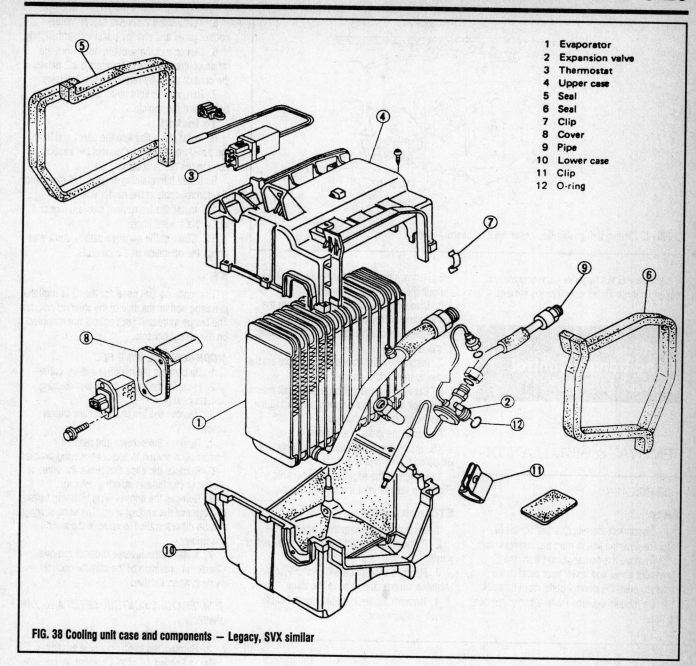

1 Evaporator
2 Expansion valve
3 Thermostat
4 Upper case
5 Seal
6 Seal
7 Clip
8 Cover
9 Pipe
10 Lower case
11 Clip
12 O-ring

FIG. 38 Cooling unit case and components — Legacy, SVX similar

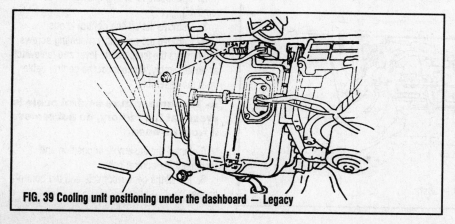

FIG. 39 Cooling unit positioning under the dashboard — Legacy

To Install:

9. Position the evaporator case assembly into the vehicle and install the mounting bolts. Tighten the bolts to 7 ft. lbs. (10 Nm).

10. Reconnect the electrical leads and the drain tube.

11. Install the glove box assembly support and the glove box.

12. Connect the suction and discharge lines in the engine compartment. Coat the O-rings lightly with refrigerant oil and tighten the connections. Tighten the nut on the discharge side to 18 ft. lbs. (25 Nm) and the nut on the suction side to 7 ft. lbs. (10 Nm).

FIG. 40 Cooling unit positioning under the dashboard — SVX

13. Connect the negative battery cable and properly charge the air conditioning system.

Heating and Air Conditioning Control Panel

REMOVAL & INSTALLATION

♦ SEE FIGS. 41–46

Justy

1. Disconnect the negative battery cable.
2. Remove the knobs from the control levers.
3. Remove the center pocket from the instrument panel and insert your hand in the pocket to push the control panel from its back.
4. On models equipped with a radio, remove the radio.

5. Remove the center panel attaching screws and pull the control panel forward.
6. Disconnect the control cables from the control panel. Disconnect the fan switch connector. Remove the panel from the vehicle.

To Install:

7. Install the panel in position and connect the cables to the control levers.
8. Connect the fan switch lead. Install the panel back into the center panel and install the center panel retaining screws.
9. Install the radio, if equipped.
10. Install the center pocket and install the knobs on the control levers.
11. Connect the negative battery cable and check the operation of the control panel.

STD. and Loyale

1. Disconnect the negative battery cable.
2. Remove the control knobs from the control panel.
3. Remove the instrument cluster visor retaining screws and remove the visor.
4. Remove the temperature control cable from the heater unit.

5. Remove the 2 screws that retain the control panel and pull the panel forward slightly.
6. Disconnect the vacuum hose from the mode control panel and separate the 2 halves of the control panel by removing the 3 screws.
7. Remove the light bulbs and remove the panel from the vehicle.

To Install:

8. Install the bulbs into the panel and install the panel into position. Connect the vacuum hose to the mode control.
9. Install the retaining screws and reconnect the control cable at the heater unit.
10. Install the instrument cluster visor and install the control knobs.
11. Connect the negative battery cable and check the operation of the controls.

XT

The mode control panel for the XT is mounted in a wing pod on the side of the steering column. The temperature and fan controls are mounted on the center console.

MODE CONTROL WING POD

1. Disconnect the negative battery cable.
2. Remove the upper and lower steering column covers.
3. Remove the lower instrument cluster cover.
4. Remove the screws that retain the combination switch to the control wing bracket.
5. Remove the clips that retain the wires to the lower cluster and steering column.
6. Remove the control wing retaining bolts and remove the control wing. The control wing can be disassembled to remove the switch assembly.
7. Install in the reverse order of removal. Check the operation of the climate control system when finished.

TEMPERATURE CONTROL LEVER AND FAN SWITCH

1. Disconnect the negative battery cable.
2. Remove the center console assembly (refer to Section 10 of this manual for console removal).
3. Remove the switch control knobs.
4. Remove the assembly mounting screws and remove the temperature lever and fan switch as an assembly, disconnect the control cable from the assembly.

➡ **The temperature control cable is preset at the factory, do not remove it from its base.**

5. Install the assembly in position and reconnect the control cable.
6. Install the center console and the control knobs.

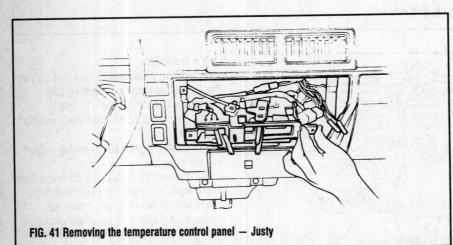

FIG. 41 Removing the temperature control panel — Justy

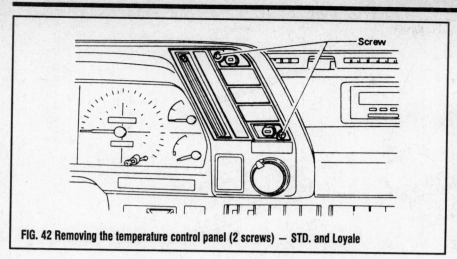

FIG. 42 Removing the temperature control panel (2 screws) — STD. and Loyale

7. Connect the negative battery cable. Check the operation of the system.

Legacy

1. Disconnect the negative battery cable.

> ❄ **CAUTION**
>
> **Properly disarm the air bag on vehicles equipped with the SRS system. Failure to do so can cause serious injury. The procedure can be found in Section 6 of this manual under the heading "Supplemental Restraint System".**

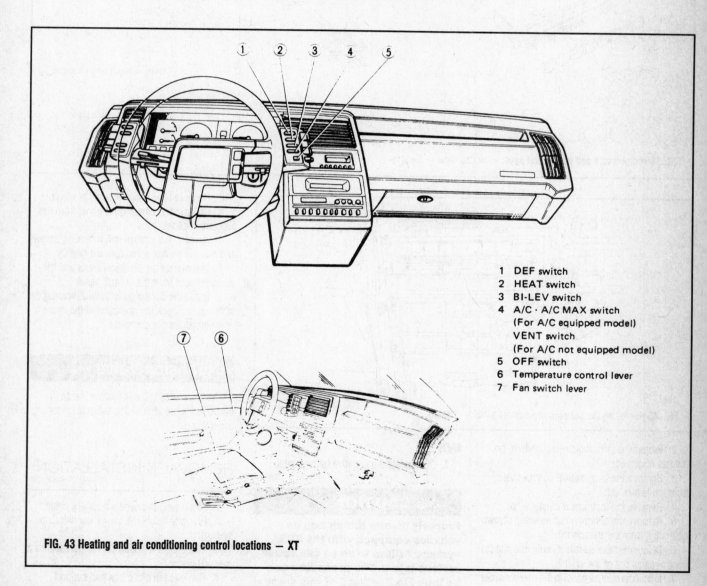

1 DEF switch
2 HEAT switch
3 BI-LEV switch
4 A/C · A/C MAX switch
   (For A/C equipped model)
   VENT switch
   (For A/C not equipped model)
5 OFF switch
6 Temperature control lever
7 Fan switch lever

FIG. 43 Heating and air conditioning control locations — XT

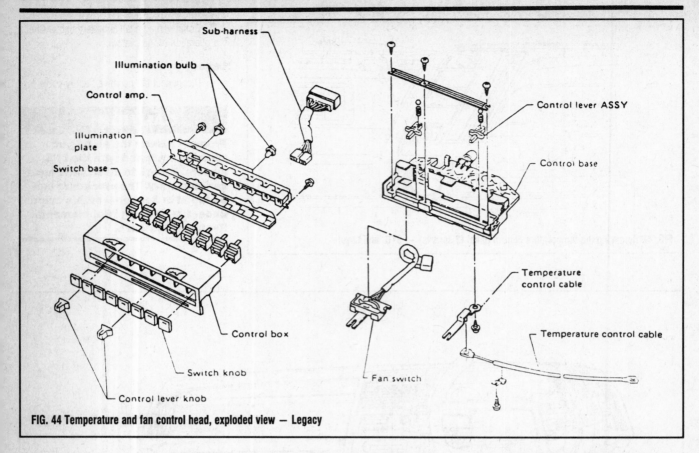

FIG. 44 Temperature and fan control head, exploded view — Legacy

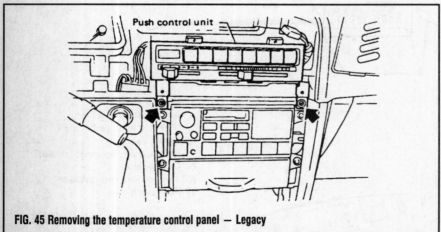

FIG. 45 Removing the temperature control panel — Legacy

2. Properly disarm the air bag system, on models equipped.

3. Remove the temperature control cable from the heater unit.

4. Remove the instrument cluster visor.

5. Remove the control panel retaining screws and pull it from the dashboard.

6. Disconnect the electrical leads and pull the control panel out of the vehicle.

7. Install the control panel in the reverse order of removal. Check the operation of the system after installation is complete.

SVX

1. Disconnect the negative battery cable.

> ### ✳ CAUTION
>
> **Properly disarm the air bag on vehicles equipped with the SRS system. Failure to do so can cause serious injury. The procedure can be found in Section 6 of this manual under the heading "Supplemental Restraint System".**

2. Remove the instrument cluster cover.

3. Remove the center grille panel from the instrument panel.

4. Remove the control unit mounting screws and pull the control panel forward slightly.

5. Disconnect the electrical leads and the aspirator duct from the control panel.

6. Install the control panel in the reverse order of removal. Check the operation of the system when installation is complete.

Expansion Valve

The expansion valve is located inside the evaporator case attached to the evaporator assembly.

REMOVAL & INSTALLATION

1. Disconnect the negative battery cable.

2. Properly discharge the air conditioning system.

3. Disconnect and plug the refrigerant lines at the evaporator.

4. Remove the glove box and support brackets.

5. Loosen and remove the evaporator bands.

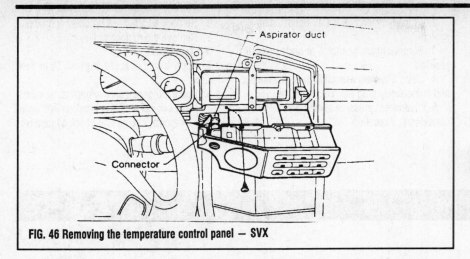

FIG. 46 Removing the temperature control panel — SVX

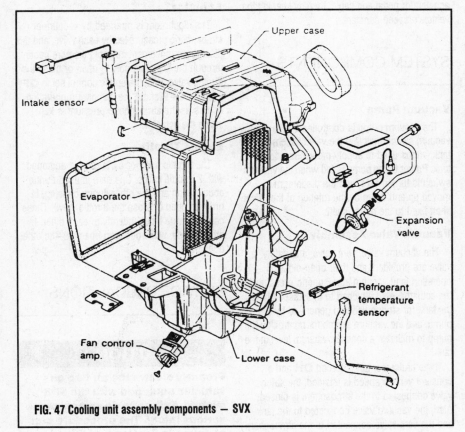

FIG. 47 Cooling unit assembly components — SVX

6. Disconnect the air conditioner thermo-switch wire connector.

7. Remove the evaporator securing bolts and nuts.

8. Disconnect the drain hose and remove the evaporator assembly.

9. Remove the evaporator case attaching clips and screws.

10. Separate the case halves and remove the evaporator.

11. Separate the expansion valve from the evaporator.

To Install:

12. Connect the expansion valve to the evaporator assembly.

13. Install the evaporator assembly into the case halves.

14. Secure evaporator case assembly together.

15. Install the evaporator assembly and connect drain hose.

16. Connect the thermo-switch wire connector.

17. Install the evaporator housing securing bands.

18. Install the glove box assembly.

19. Reconnect the refrigerant lines at the evaporator. Tighten the suction hose-to-the evaporator to 7 ft. lbs. (10 Nm) and the receiver pip-to-evaporator to 18 ft. lbs. (25 Nm).

20. Connect the negative battery cable.

21. Charge, evacuate and leak test the air conditioning system.

Receiver/Drier

REMOVAL & INSTALLATION

1. Disconnect the negative battery cable.

2. Properly discharge the air conditioning system.

3. Disconnect the receiver/drier pressure switch wire connector.

4. Disconnect and plug the receiver/drier refrigerant lines.

5. Remove the receiver/drier bracket attaching bolts.

6. Remove the receiver/drier assembly.

7. Install the receiver/drier in position and tighten the mounting bolts to 7 ft. lbs. (10 Nm).

8. Reconnect the electrical leads and connect the refrigerant pipes to the receiver, tighten them except on SVX and Legacy, to 12 ft. lbs. (17 Nm). On SVX and Legacy tighten the line retaining bolts to 7 ft. lbs. (10 Nm).

9. Properly recharge the refrigerant system. Connect the negative battery cable and check the operation of the system.

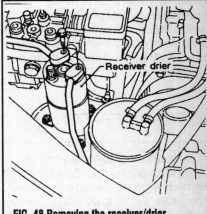

FIG. 48 Removing the receiver/drier

Refrigerant Lines

REMOVAL & INSTALLATION

1. Disconnect the negative battery cable.

2. Properly discharge the air conditioning system.

3. Remove chassis, engine or body parts, if required.

4. Using a backup wrench loosen, disconnect and immediately plug the refrigerant line.

5. Disconnect pressure switch wire connectors, if required.

6. Remove all attaching brackets and bolts.

7. Remove the refrigerant lines.

To Install:

8. Apply a light coat of refrigerant oil to new O-rings.

9. Route refrigerant lines in original locations.

10. Use original securing brackets and bolts.

11. Evacuate, charge and check system for leaks.

CRUISE CONTROL

GENERAL INFORMATION

♦ SEE FIG. 49

The cruise control automatically controls the vehicle speed and allows the vehicle to run at a constant speed without depressing the accelerator pedal. In operation, when the driver sets a desired speed with the cruise control switch, the built-in micro-computer compares the speed set in the memory with the actual running speed detected by feedback signals from the speedometer. This feedback system operates the throttle of the carburetor or throttle body to correct the speed difference, thereby keeping the vehicle at a constant speed. The major components are the main switch, cruise switch, control unit, vacuum pump and valve assembly, actuator, clutch switch and stop and brake switch.

➡ **The use of the speed control is not recommended when driving conditions do not permit maintaining a constant speed, such as in heavy traffic or on roads that are winding, icy, snow covered or slippery.**

SYSTEM OPERATION

Cruise control unit compares the actual vehicle speed detected by feedback signals from the speed sensor incorporated in the speedometer with the speed set in the memory memorized when the set switch was turned **ON**. A signal is then transmitted according to the difference between the 2 speeds.

This signal is transmitted to the solenoid valves of the valve assembly located in the engine compartment. The movement of the actuator operates the throttle valve through the accelerator pedal and cable, thereby keeping the vehicle's speed constant.

SYSTEM COMPONENTS

Vacuum Pump

The vacuum pump is controlled by the vacuum switch built into the valve assembly tank, and is used to supply the vacuum to the tank. Power to the pump is fed when the vacuum switch is turned **ON**, and the diaphragm is moved up and down by the rotation of the offset shaft fixed to the motor shaft.

Vacuum Valve Assembly

The vacuum valve, vent valve, and safety valve are provided, and their open-close operation lead vacuum/atmospheric pressure to the actuator. Also attached to this assembly is the tank for storing vacuum generated by the pump, and the vacuum switch for controlling the pump to maintain a constant vacuum level in the tank.

If the cruise control is turned **ON** and a constant vehicle speed is attained, the safety valve connected to the atmosphere is closed. Also, the vacuum valve connected to the tank and the vent valve connected to the atmosphere operate to lead the atmosphere/vacuum to the actuator. When the cruise control is canceled, the vacuum valve closes to shut off the tank vacuum, and the safety valve opens to allow atmospheric pressure to enter the actuator.

The vacuum in the tank is consumed by the operation of the vacuum valve. If the vacuum in the tank reaches 12.6 in. Hg (42.7 kPa) the vacuum switch is turned **ON**, and the pump feeds the vacuum into the tank. When the vacuum in the tank reaches 14.96 in. Hg (50.7kPa) the vacuum switch turns **OFF** to stop the pump.

Actuator

The diaphragm is operated by vacuum or atmospheric pressure led by each valve, and this diaphragm movement actuates the wire cable through the link assembly to open or close the throttle valve. With the cruise control set to **OFF** (system **OFF** state), no diaphragm operation occurs as the atmospheric pressure is kept inside the actuator.

Engine Throttle

The throttle body or carburetor is equipped with 2 throttle cams. One cam is used during acceleration and the other during cruising, in order to open or close the throttle valve. These cams operate independently of each other. In other words, while one cam operates, the other does not.

SERVICE PRECAUTIONS

❊❊❊ CAUTION

Properly disarm the air bag on vehicles equipped with the SRS system. Failure to do so can cause serious injury. The procedure can be found in Section 6 of this manual under the heading "Supplemental Restraint System".

• Never disconnect any electrical connection with the ignition switch **ON** unless instructed to do so in a test.

• Always wear a grounded wrist static strap when servicing any control module or component labeled with a Electrostatic Discharge (ESD) sensitive device symbol.

• Avoid touching module connector pins.

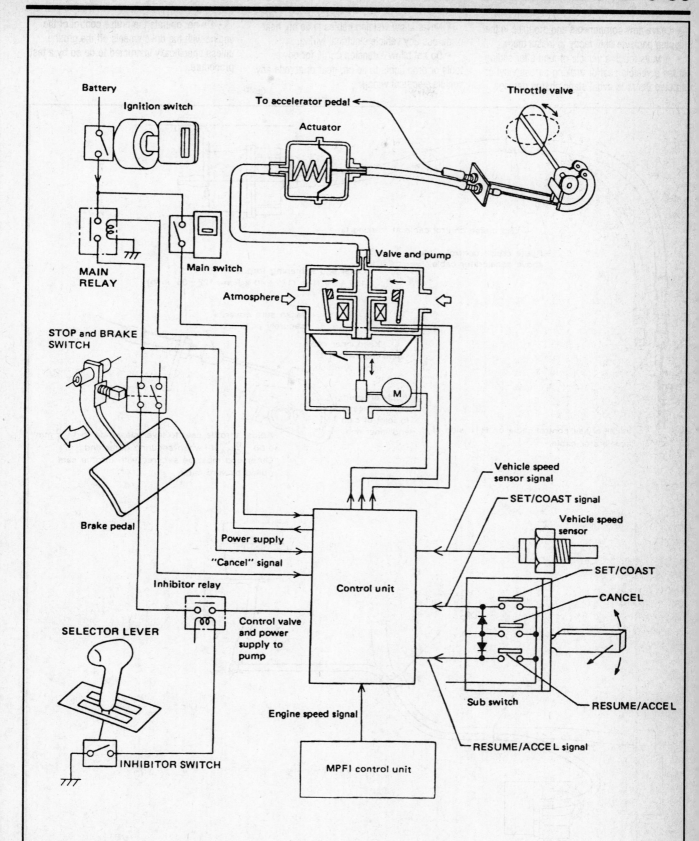

FIG. 49 Cruise control system component diagram

- Leave new components and modules in the shipping package until ready to install them.
- Always touch a vehicle ground after sliding across a vehicle seat or walking across vinyl or carpeted floors to avoid static charge damage.

- Never allow welding cables to lie on, near or across any vehicle electrical wiring.
- Do not allow extension cords for power tools or drop lights to lie on, near or across any vehicle electrical wiring.

- Do not operate the cruise control or the engine with the drive wheels off the ground unless specifically instructed to do so by a test procedure.

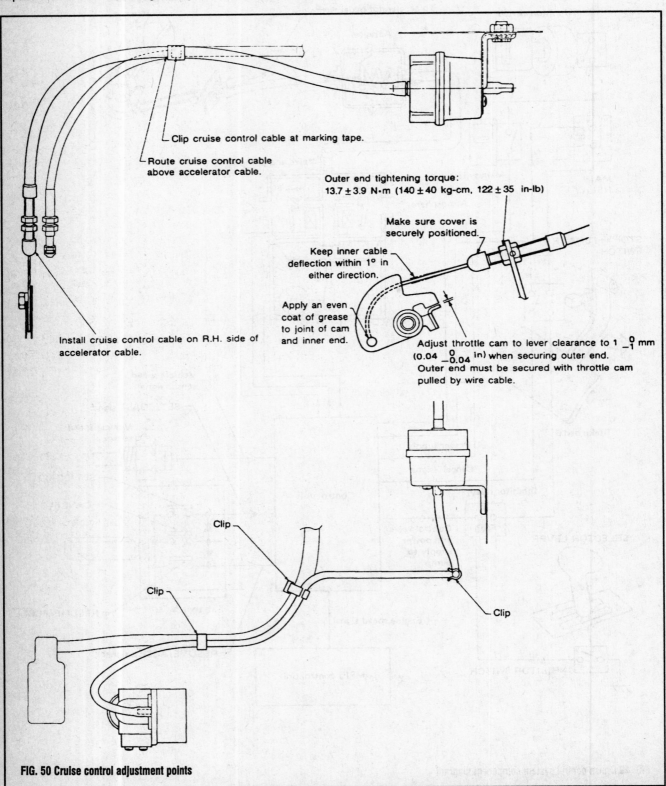

Clip cruise control cable at marking tape.

Route cruise control cable above accelerator cable.

Install cruise control cable on R.H. side of accelerator cable.

Outer end tightening torque:
13.7 ± 3.9 N·m (140 ± 40 kg-cm, 122 ± 35 in-lb)

Make sure cover is securely positioned.

Keep inner cable deflection within 1° in either direction.

Apply an even coat of grease to joint of cam and inner end.

Adjust throttle cam to lever clearance to $1 \, _{-1}^{\, 0}$ mm $(0.04 \, _{-0.04}^{\quad 0}$ in) when securing outer end. Outer end must be secured with throttle cam pulled by wire cable.

Clip

Clip

Clip

FIG. 50 Cruise control adjustment points

Control Cable

ADJUSTMENT

▶ SEE FIG. 50

Except XT

The actuator wire cable sagging can be adjusted by changing the position of the actuator-to-pedal bracket mounting bolt. Adjust the bracket so that the control cable play is 0.04–0.08 in. (1–2mm). Be sure to adjust the accelerator when the pedal is held in the fully returned position. Be careful not to apply excessive load to the wire cable when adjusting or installing; otherwise the actuator may be deformed or damaged.

XT

When securing the cable outer end, adjust the clearance between the throttle cam and the lever to 0–0.08 in. (0–2mm) using the adjusting nut. Ensure that there is no free play between the throttle cam and the cable.

➡ **Do not bend the control cable too sharply; otherwise, it will not operate smoothly. When installing the cam to the inner end of the control cable, do not bend or crush the inner cable.**

Vacuum Pump and Valve

REMOVAL & INSTALLATION

▶ SEE FIG. 51

STD. and XT

✲✲✲ CAUTION

Be careful, the exhaust system and turbocharger temperatures are high while the engine is operating. Serious burns could result from contact.

1. Ensure that the ignition is **OFF**.
2. Removing the air cleaner and air flow meter:
   a. Loosen the hose clamp.
   b. Remove the boot from the air cleaner cover.
   c. Release the clips on the air cleaner cover.
   d. Place the air cleaner cover together with the air flow meter on the engine.

➡ **Always keep air cleaner, vacuum hose, etc. free from dirt and dust.**

3. Disconnect the wiring harness connector and hose connector of the vacuum pump assembly.
4. Remove the vacuum pump assembly and the valve assembly as a unit. Tighten the mounting nuts to 65 inch lbs. (7.4 Nm).
5. To install, reverse the removal procedure. Check the operation of the system.

Legacy and SVX

1. Disconnect the negative battery cable.
2. Disconnect the wiring harness connector and hose. Be sure to always disconnect the hose at the body pipe side.
3. Remove the attaching nuts, disconnect he ABS sensor connector clip from the bracket and remove the vacuum pump assembly.
4. Installation is the reverse order of the removal procedure. Be sure to connect the hose and wiring connector during installation. Tighten the mounting nuts to 65 inch lbs. (7.4 Nm).

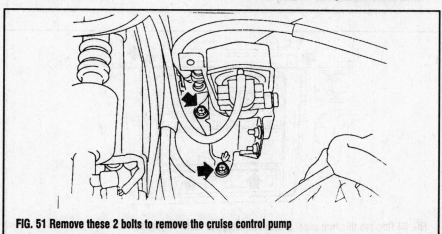

FIG. 51 Remove these 2 bolts to remove the cruise control pump

Actuator Assembly

REMOVAL & INSTALLATION

▶ SEE FIG. 52

Legacy and SVX

1. Disconnect the negative battery cable.
2. Remove the intake manifold cover. Remove the nut which secures the control cable end to throttle cam, and remove control cable end.

FIG. 52 Remove these 3 bolts to remove the cruise control actuator

3. Remove the attaching bolts and actuator assembly.

4. Remove the clip bands from the control cable. Disconnect the vacuum pipe and vacuum hose.

5. Installation is the reverse order of the removal procedure. Be sure to connect the hose and wiring connector during installation. Tighten the mounting nuts to 65 inch lbs. (7.4 Nm).

RADIO

Never operate the radio without a speaker. Damage to the output transistors will result. If the speaker must be replaced, use a speaker of correct impedance (ohms) or else the output transistors will require replacement in short order. Never operate the radio with the speaker leads shorted together.

The radio is mounted in the center portion of the dash board, with speakers mounted in various locations through out the vehicle. Most models contain 2 to 4 speakers, 2 mounted in the front of the vehicle (usually in the door panels or in the lower portion of the dash board) and 2 mounted in the rear of the vehicle. The SVX is equipped with 6 speakers, 2 tweeters mounted in the top of the dash board, 2 full range speakers mounted in the front doors and 2 larger speakers mounted in the rear shelf. The SVX can also be equipped with a compact disc player mounted below the radio.

Radio

REMOVAL & INSTALLATION

♦ SEE FIGS. 53–57

Except SVX

1. Disconnect the negative battery cable.

※※ CAUTION

Properly disarm the air bag on vehicles equipped with the SRS system. Failure to do so can cause serious injury. The procedure can be found in Section 6 of this manual under the heading "Supplemental Restraint System".

2. Remove the clock on XT models. On Justy, remove the radio trim panel and the center panel. On Loyale and STD. models, remove the trim panel that surrounds the radio. On Legacy,

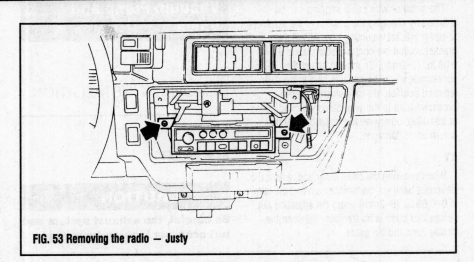

FIG. 53 Removing the radio — Justy

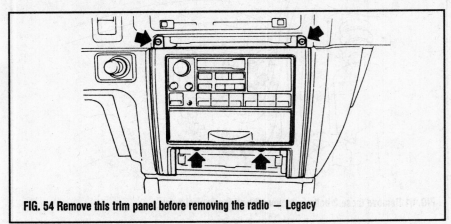

FIG. 54 Remove this trim panel before removing the radio — Legacy

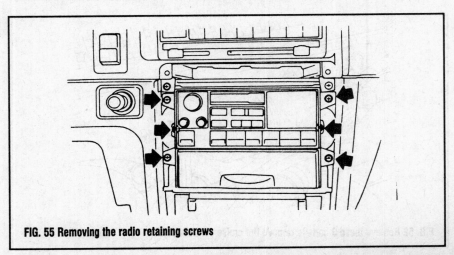

FIG. 55 Removing the radio retaining screws

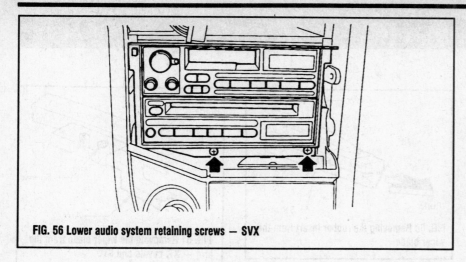

FIG. 56 Lower audio system retaining screws — SVX

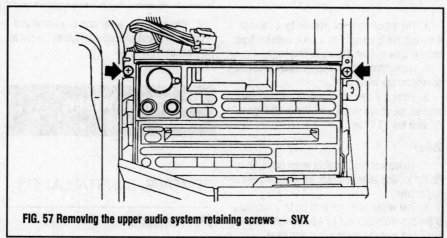

FIG. 57 Removing the upper audio system retaining screws — SVX

remove the cup holder, the ashtray and the center panel.

3. Remove the radio attaching screws and pull the radio body forward.

4. Disconnect the electrical connectors and the antenna cable.

5. Remove the radio from the vehicle.

6. Install the radio in position in the dash board and connect the electrical leads.

7. Install the trim pieces that were removed.

8. Check the operation of the radio.

SVX

1. Disconnect the negative battery cable.

> **※※ CAUTION**
>
> **Properly disarm the air bag on vehicles equipped with the SRS system. Failure to do so can cause serious injury. The procedure can be found in Section 6 of this manual under the heading "Supplemental Restraint System".**

2. Place the steering wheel in its lowest position.

3. Remove the lower instrument cluster trim panel.

4. Remove the instrument cluster visor retaining screws and remove the visor. Disconnect the clock when removing the visor.

5. Remove the center ventilation grille from above the radio housing.

6. Remove the ventilation control panel. Open the radio housing cover and carefully pry its back panel off with a small prybar.

7. Remove the center trim panel. Remove the left console panel and disconnect the antenna wires (2). Remove the ashtray.

8. Remove the radio mounting screws, close the radio cover door and remove the radio body. Disconnect the leads from the rear of the radio.

➡ **If the vehicle is equipped with a CD player it is removed with the radio body.**

To install:

9. Install the radio in position and connect the electrical leads. Open the radio cover and install the retaining screws.

10. Connect the antenna wires and install the left side panel on the console. Install the ashtray and center panel.

11. Install the inner panel to the radio cover. Install the climate control panel and the center ventilation grille.

12. Install the instrument cluster visor, make sure to connect the clock. Install the lower instrument cluster trim panel.

13. Connect the negative battery cable. Check the operation of the audio system.

Stereo Speakers

REMOVAL & INSTALLATION

To remove any of the speakers in the vehicle; locate the speaker to be removed, carefully remove its covering grille and remove the speaker retaining screws. Lift the speaker from the opening and disconnect the electrical leads. When installing the replacement speaker, always use a speaker of the same impedance as the one removed. Failure to use the correct speaker will cause damage to the radio.

➡ **The removal of some door speakers requires the removal of the door panel. For door panel removal procedures, refer to Section 10 of this manual.**

WINDSHIELD WIPERS

Blade and Arm Replacement

REMOVAL & INSTALLATION

♦ SEE FIGS. 58–61

Front

EXCEPT XT, LOYALE AND STD.

1. To replace the complete wiper blade, lift up on the locking lever and slide the blade off of the wiper arm.

2. The wiper arms are held on by a cap nut. If the cap nut is covered by a boot, slide the boot back and away from the wiper arm base.

3. Loosen the nut and apply upward pressure to remove the wiper arm.

4. Place the new wiper arm in position and reverse the above procedure. Tighten the nut to 13 ft. lbs. (18 Nm).

XT, LOYALE AND STD.

1. To replace the rubber part of the wiper blade, lift up on the lever and slide the rubber off of the blade.

2. To remove the blade assembly, remove the 2 small screws that retain the blade to the arm and remove the blade.

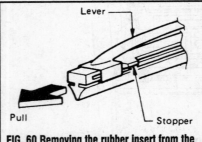

FIG. 60 Removing the rubber insert from the wiper blade

3. The wiper arms are held on by a cap nut. If the cap nut is covered by a boot, slide the boot back and away from the wiper arm base.

4. Loosen the nut and apply upward pressure to remove the wiper arm.

5. Place the new wiper arm in position and reverse the above procedure. Tighten the nut to 65 inch lbs. (7.4 Nm).

Rear

1. To replace the complete wiper blade, lift up on the locking lever and slide the blade off of the wiper arm.

2. The wiper arms are held on by a cap nut. If the cap nut is covered by a boot, slide the boot back and away from the wiper arm base.

3. Loosen the nut and apply upward pressure to remove the wiper arm.

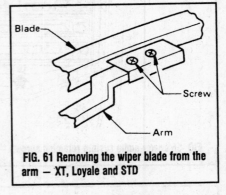

FIG. 61 Removing the wiper blade from the arm — XT, Loyale and STD

4. Place the new wiper arm in position and reverse the above procedure. Tighten the nut to 65 inch lbs. (7.4 Nm).

Windshield Wiper Motor

REMOVAL & INSTALLATION

♦ SEE FIGS. 62–65

Except Justy

1. Disconnect the negative battery cable.

2. Remove the wiper blades from the wiper arms by pulling the retaining lever up and sliding the blade away from the arm.

3. Slide the covering boot up the wiper arm.

4. Remove the wiper arms to linkage nuts and the arms.

5. Disconnect the electrical wiring connectors from the wiper motor.

6. Remove the cowl to body screws and the cowl from the vehicle.

7. Find or fabricate a ring which has the same diameter as the outer diameter of the plastic joint that retains the linkage to the wiper motor. Force the ring down over the joint to force the 4 plastic retaining jaws inward, then disconnect and remove the linkage.

8. Remove the wiper motor to firewall bolts and the motor.

To Install:

9. Install the wiper motor and tighten the attaching bolts. Tighten the bolts to 65 inch lbs. (7.4 Nm).

10. Install the wiper linkage. Install the cowl. Connect the wiper electrical wiring harness.

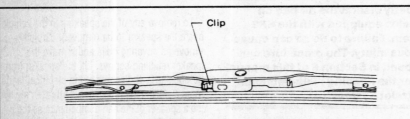

FIG. 58 Removing the wiper blade from the arm — except XT, Loyale and STD

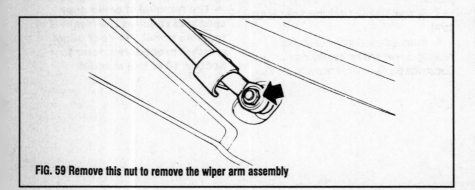

FIG. 59 Remove this nut to remove the wiper arm assembly

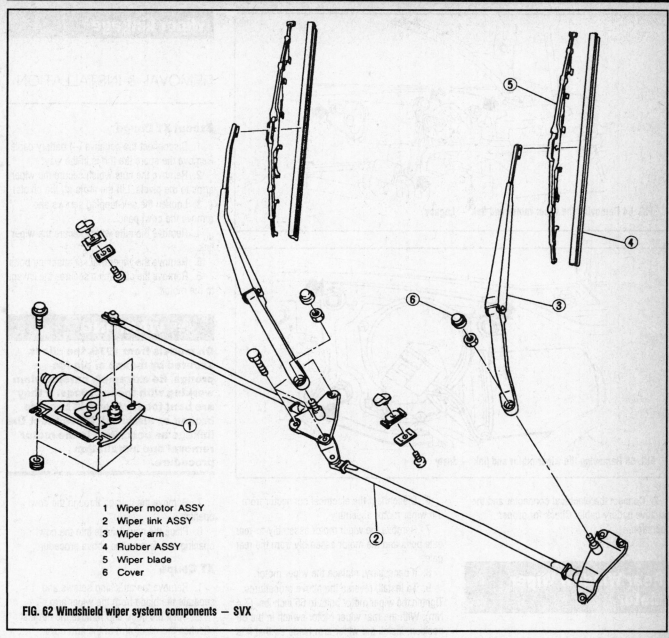

1 Wiper motor ASSY
2 Wiper link ASSY
3 Wiper arm
4 Rubber ASSY
5 Wiper blade
6 Cover

FIG. 62 Windshield wiper system components — SVX

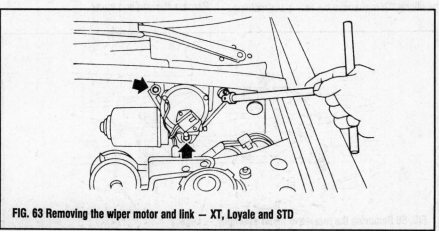

FIG. 63 Removing the wiper motor and link — XT, Loyale and STD

11. Connect the negative battery cable and install the wiper arms after the ignition switch has been on for a few seconds to put the linkage in the parked position.

Justy

1. Disconnect the negative battery cable.
2. At the wiper motor, disconnect the electrical connector.
3. Remove the wiper motor to cowl bolts.
4. Separate the wiper link from the motor.
5. If necessary, replace the wiper motor.

To Install:

6. Install the wiper motor and tighten the cowl bolts. Install the wiper link on the motor. Tighten the bolts to 65 inch lbs. (7.4 Nm).

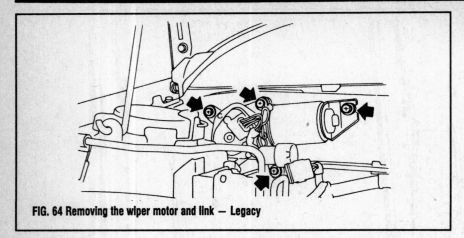

FIG. 64 Removing the wiper motor and link — Legacy

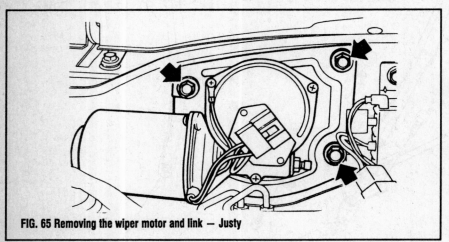

FIG. 65 Removing the wiper motor and link — Justy

7. Connect the electrical connector and the negative battery cable. Check for proper operation.

Rear Window Wiper Motor

REMOVAL & INSTALLATION

1. At the rear window, pull the wiper blade outward from the arm and press down on the clip, then remove the blade from the arm.

2. Remove the wiper arm cover.

3. Loosen the wiper arm-to-wiper assembly nut, then remove the nut and the arm from the assembly.

4. Remove the wiper assembly-to-rear gate cap, nut and cushion.

5. From inside of the rear gate, remove the wiper motor assembly trim panel.

6. Disconnect the electrical connector from the wiper motor assembly.

7. Remove the wiper motor assembly-to-rear gate bolts and the motor assembly from the rear gate.

8. If necessary, replace the wiper motor.

9. To install, reverse the above procedures. Tighten the wiper motor bolts to 65 inch lbs. (7.4 Nm). With the rear wiper motor switch in the off position, install the wiper arm blade so that it is positioned 25mm above the rear glass molding.

Wiper Linkage

REMOVAL & INSTALLATION

Except XT Coupe

1. Disconnect the negative (–) battery cable. Remove the spare tire if it is in the way.

2. Remove the nuts which secure the wiper arms to the pivots. Lift the arms off the pivots.

3. Loosen the self-tapping screws and remove the cowl panel.

4. Remove the nuts which secure the wiper link.

5. Remove the wiper bracket attaching bolts.

6. Remove the clip which secures the linkage to the motor.

❈ WARNING

On models from 1976, the clip is secured by means of plastic prongs. Be extremely careful when working with these prongs. If they are bent too far they will become broken or distorted. Disconnect the linkage as described in the motor removal and installation procedure.

7. Remove the linkage through the cowl opening.

8. Place the new linkage into the cowl opening and reverse the above procedure.

XT Coupe

1. Remove the attaching screws and separate the blade from the wiper arm.

2. Open the hood and remove the nut that attaches the wiper arm to the arm cover. Remove the arm and cover.

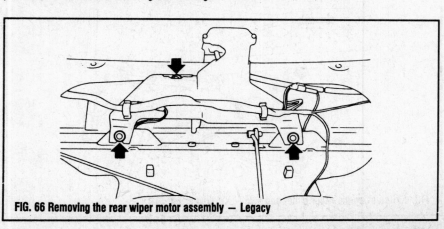

FIG. 66 Removing the rear wiper motor assembly — Legacy

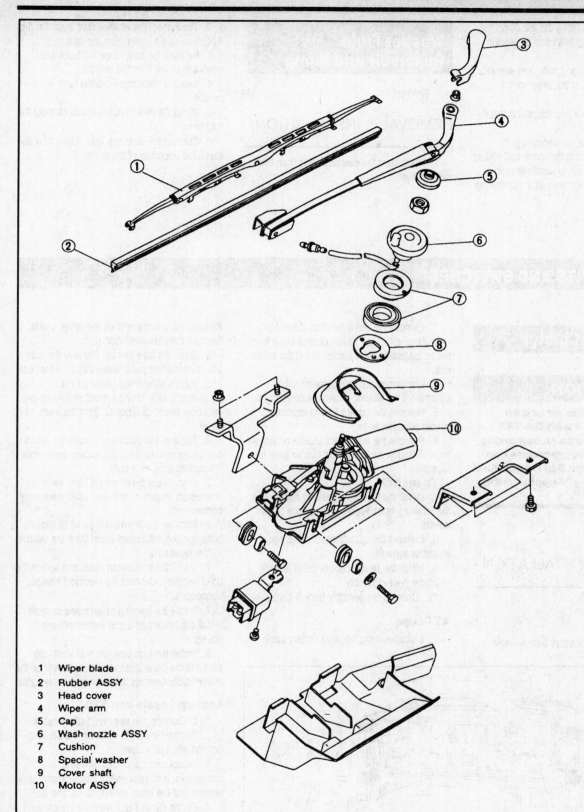

1　Wiper blade
2　Rubber ASSY
3　Head cover
4　Wiper arm
5　Cap
6　Wash nozzle ASSY
7　Cushion
8　Special washer
9　Cover shaft
10　Motor ASSY

FIG. 65a Rear wiper and washer components — SVX

3. Detach the plugs fitting the molding.

4. Remove the fixing bolts and detach the wiper motor assembly.

5. Remove the bolts and nuts, and separate the wheel assembly from the wiper motor assembly.

6. Reverse the above procedure and install the new linkage.

7. Adjust the linkage, as necessary, by loosening the flange bolt at the motor and sliding the linkage back and forth to obtain proper sweep. Tighten the flange bolt, after completing the adjustment.

Washer Fluid Reservoir and Pump

REMOVAL & INSTALLATION

1. Disconnect the electrical lead from the washer pump.

2. Disconnect the washer fluid lines. On the SVX, remove the cover from the tank.

3. Remove the tank mounting bolts and remove the tank from the vehicle.

4. Remove the pump from the tank, if needed.

5. Install the tank in position and connect the fluid lines.

6. Connect the electrical lead, fill the tank and check the operation of the pump.

INSTRUMENTS AND SWITCHES

Instrument Cluster

✳✳✳ CAUTION

Properly disarm the air bag on vehicles equipped with the SRS system. Failure to do so can cause serious injury. The procedure can be found in Section 6 of this manual under the heading "Supplemental Restraint System".

REMOVAL & INSTALLATION

◆ SEE FIGS. 67–74

Justy

1. Disconnect the negative battery cable.

2. Remove the defroster duct assembly.

3. Disconnect the heater control cable from the inside/outside air selector rod at the heater unit.

4. Disconnect the speedometer cable. Disconnect the electrical harness connectors.

5. Remove the covers for the instrument cluster retaining bolts.

6. Remove the instrument cluster retaining bolts. Remove the instrument cluster from its mounting.

To Install:

7. Install the instrument cluster and tighten the retaining bolts securely. Install the screw covers.

8. Connect the speedometer cable and electrical harness.

9. Install the heater control cable and the defroster duct assembly.

10. Connect the negative battery cable.

XT Coupe

1. Disconnect the negative battery cable.

Remove the lower cover on the driver's side. Remove the side ventilation duct.

2. Open the fuse box lid. Remove the fuse box to instrument panel screws and the fuse box.

3. Remove the lower cover on the passenger's side. Using a medium prybar, pry the upper cover, at 3 points, from the instrument panel.

4. Remove the console. Remove the steering column assembly, the combination meter and the control wing as a unit.

5. Disconnect the electrical harness connectors from the radio and other necessary components.

6. Remove the instrument panel to chassis bolts and the instrument panel from the vehicle.

To Install:

7. Install the instrument panel and tighten the bolts securely. Connect the electrical harness connectors.

8. Install the steering column and console. Install the lower and upper instrument panel covers.

9. Install the fuse box, the side ventilation duct and the lower instrument panel cover on the drivers side. Connect the negative battery cable.

Legacy, Loyale and STD.

1. Disconnect the negative battery cable.

2. Remove the bolts securing the steering column and pull it down.

3. Disconnect the electrical wiring connectors, then remove the cluster visor screws and the visor, except on GL and GLF.

4. On the GL and GLF, remove the center ventilator control lever by pulling it. Remove the 3 screws accessible through the ventilator grille to the right of the cluster and the 1 screw accessible through the grille on the left. Remove the visor.

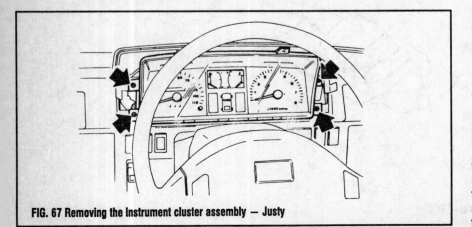

FIG. 67 Removing the instrument cluster assembly — Justy

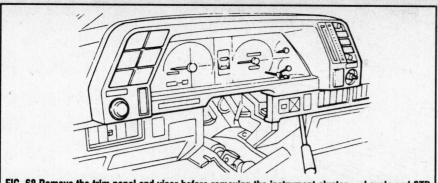

FIG. 68 Remove the trim panel and visor before removing the instrument cluster — Loyale and STD

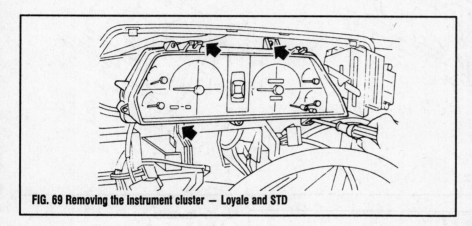

FIG. 69 Removing the Instrument cluster — Loyale and STD

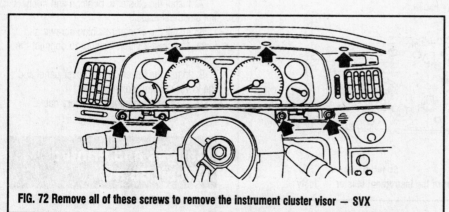

FIG. 72 Remove all of these screws to remove the instrument cluster visor — SVX

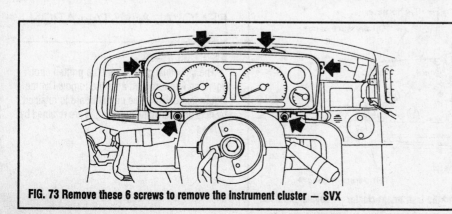

FIG. 73 Remove these 6 screws to remove the instrument cluster — SVX

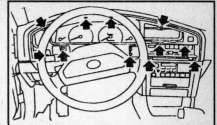

FIG. 70 Remove all of these screws to remove the instrument cluster visor — Legacy

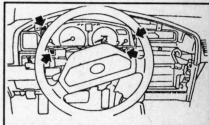

FIG. 71 Remove these 4 screws to remove the Instrument cluster — Legacy

5. On the station wagon 4WD GL, remove the turn signal light switch.

6. Remove the cluster retaining screws, then pull the cluster out far enough to disconnect the speedometer cable and electrical connectors from behind, then remove the cluster assembly from the vehicle.

To Install:

7. Install the instrument cluster. Connect all electrical connectors and the speedometer cable. Tighten the attaching screws securely.

8. Install the ventilator control lever on GL and GLF models. Install the turn signal light switch on 4WD GL models.

9. Install the cluster visor screws and the visor. Lift the steering column and tighten the bolts to specification. Connect the negative battery cable.

SVX

1. Disconnect the negative battery cable. Properly disarm the air bag.

2. Move the steering wheel to its lowest tilt position. Remove the lower steering column cover.

3. Remove the lower cluster cover and the screws that retain the cluster visor.

4. Disconnect the clock while pulling the visor away from the cluster.

5. Remove the screws that retain the cluster and tilt the cluster forward. Disconnect the electrical leads.

6. Remove the cluster from the vehicle.

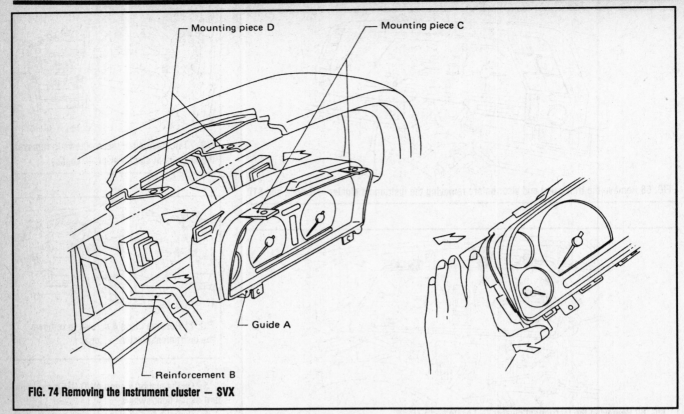

FIG. 74 Removing the instrument cluster — SVX

Mounting piece D

Mounting piece C

Guide A

Reinforcement B

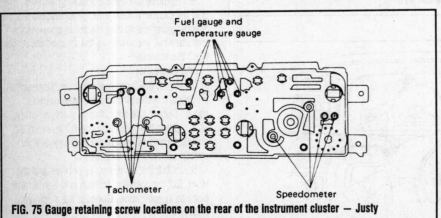

Fuel gauge and
Temperature gauge

Tachometer

Speedometer

FIG. 75 Gauge retaining screw locations on the rear of the instrument cluster — Justy

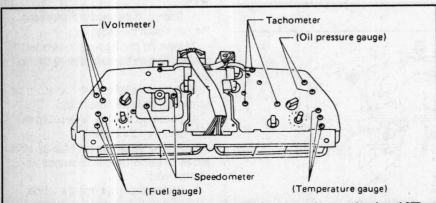

(Voltmeter)

Tachometer

(Oil pressure gauge)

Speedometer

(Fuel gauge)

(Temperature gauge)

FIG. 77 Gauge retaining screw locations on the rear of the instrument cluster — Loyale and STD

To Install:

7. Install the cluster in position and connect the electrical leads.

8. Install the cluster retaining screws and install the cluster visor. Be sure to connect the clock.

9. Install the lower cluster cover panel and the lower steering column cover.

10. Connect the negative battery cable.

Gauges and Printed Circuit Board

REMOVAL & INSTALLATION

◆ SEE FIGS. 75–79

The individual gauges and the printed circuit board can be removed after the removal of the instrument cluster. The circuit board is retained by nuts and the individual gauges are retained by screws.

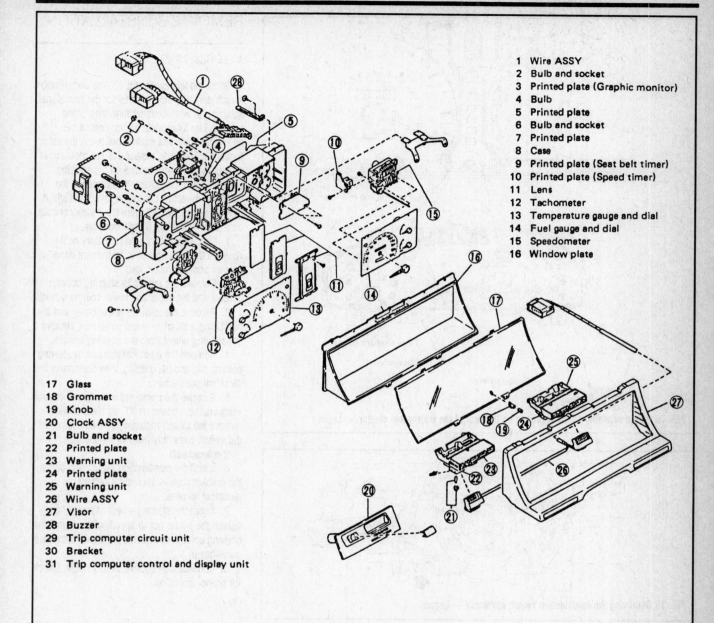

1 Wire ASSY
2 Bulb and socket
3 Printed plate (Graphic monitor)
4 Bulb
5 Printed plate
6 Bulb and socket
7 Printed plate
8 Case
9 Printed plate (Seat belt timer)
10 Printed plate (Speed timer)
11 Lens
12 Tachometer
13 Temperature gauge and dial
14 Fuel gauge and dial
15 Speedometer
16 Window plate

17 Glass
18 Grommet
19 Knob
20 Clock ASSY
21 Bulb and socket
22 Printed plate
23 Warning unit
24 Printed plate
25 Warning unit
26 Wire ASSY
27 Visor
28 Buzzer
29 Trip computer circuit unit
30 Bracket
31 Trip computer control and display unit

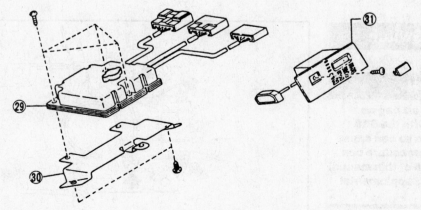

FIG. 76 Exploded view of the instrument cluster — XT

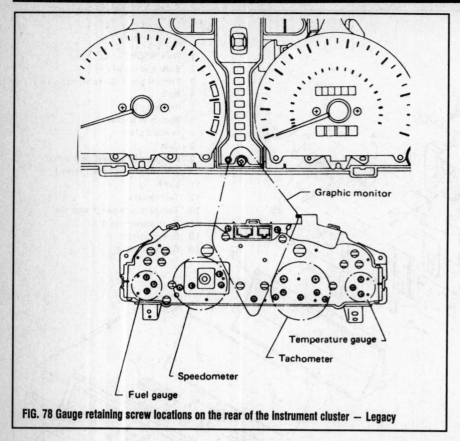

FIG. 78 Gauge retaining screw locations on the rear of the instrument cluster — Legacy

- Graphic monitor
- Temperature gauge
- Tachometer
- Speedometer
- Fuel gauge

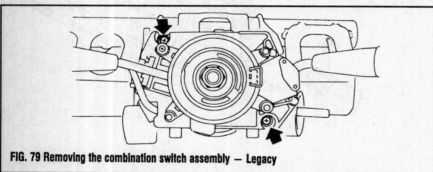

FIG. 79 Removing the combination switch assembly — Legacy

Combination Switch

✳ CAUTION

Properly disarm the air bag on vehicles equipped with the SRS system. Failure to do so can cause serious injury. The procedure can be found in Section 6 of this manual under the heading "Supplemental Restraint System".

REMOVAL & INSTALLATION

♦ SEE FIGS. 79–80

On all models except the XT, the combination switch contains the switches for the turn signal, lighting and wiper/washer functions of the vehicle. The XT models do not control the headlights from this switch, but retain the other functions. The stalk assemblies are mounted to a main switch body located on the steering column. Once the assembly is removed the individual switches can be removed. On all models except the SVX there are 2 stalk controls, on the SVX there are 3 stalk controls.

1. Disconnect the negative battery cable. Remove the lower cover to instrument panel screws and the lower cover.

2. Remove the covers to steering column screws and the upper and lower column covers.

3. Remove the steering wheel cover and the nut. Using a steering wheel puller tool, remove the steering wheel from the steering column.

4. Remove the electrical harness to steering column clip and band fitting, then disconnect the electrical connectors.

5. Remove the combination switch to control wing bracket screws on XT, on other models remove the switch mounting screws. Remove the switch assembly from its mounting.

To Install:

6. Install the combination switch and tighten the bracket screws securely. Connect the electrical harness.

7. Install the steering wheel assembly and tighten the center nut to specification. Install the steering column covers and the lower instrument panel cover.

8. Connect the negative battery cable. Check for proper operation.

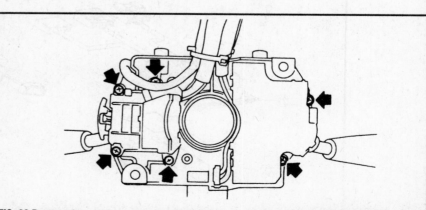

FIG. 80 Remove these screws to remove the switch assemblies from the combination switch body — Legacy

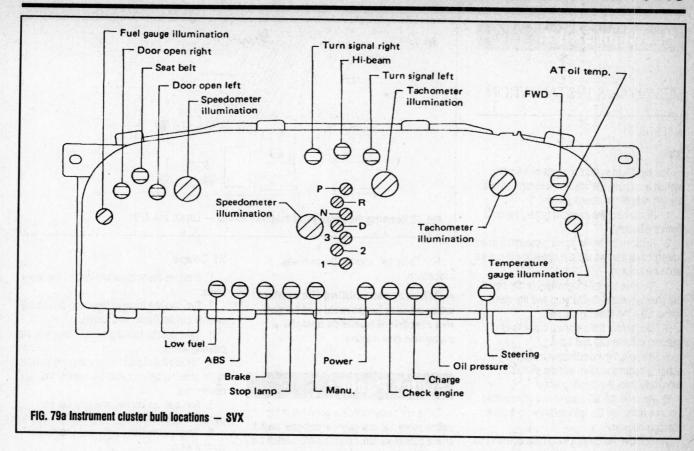

FIG. 79a Instrument cluster bulb locations — SVX

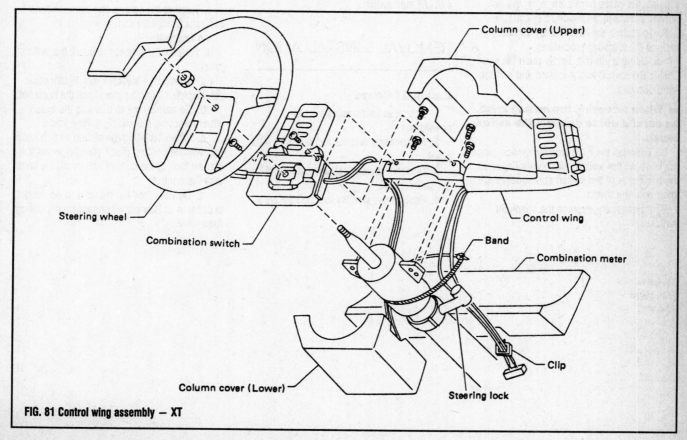

FIG. 81 Control wing assembly — XT

Headlight Switch

REMOVAL & INSTALLATION

♦ SEE FIG. 81

XT

The headlight switch is a part of a lighting switch assembly, installed on a control wing at the left side of the steering wheel.

1. Disconnect the negative battery terminal from the battery.

2. Remove the lower steering column (upper/lower) cover screws and the upper/lower covers from the column.

3. Remove the steering wheel center cover, the steering wheel-to-shaft nut and the steering wheel from the steering column.

4. Disconnect the electrical harness-to-steering column clip and band.

5. Remove the combination switch-to-steering column screws and the switch assembly from the steering wheel.

6. Remove the left control wing-to-steering column bolts and the left control wing from the steering column.

7. Remove the control wing case screws and separate the cases from each other; this will provide access to the headlight switch.

8. To replace the headlight switch knob, perform the following procedures:

a. Using a pin rod, lightly push the pawl (inside the switch knob) inward and pull the knob outward.

➡ **When removing the switch knob, be careful not to damage the switch brush.**

b. To install the knob onto the switch, place the knob on the switch, place your finger on the back side of the switch and squeeze the knob onto the switch.

9. If necessary, replace the headlight switch.

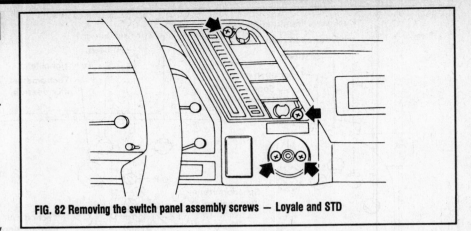

FIG. 82 Removing the switch panel assembly screws — Loyale and STD

10. To install, reverse the removal procedure.

➡ **When reassembling the control wing cases; be careful not to get the electrical harness caught between the cases.**

Switch Panel

There are many switches provided in the switch panel, i.e. rear window defogger switch, cruise control switch, height control switch and 4WD AT auto switch.

REMOVAL & INSTALLATION

Except XT Coupe

1. Detach all knobs using a small screwdriver.

2. Remove two screws, and pull out switch panel.

3. Disconnect electrical connectors and take out switch panel.

4. Reverse the process to install the panel.

XT Coupe

1. Remove the screws and detach the lower cover.

2. Remove the fixing screws and detach the column covers (upper and lower).

3. Take out the steering wheel cover and the steering wheel.

4. Detach the clip and band fitting the harness to the steering column, and disconnect the connectors.

5. Remove the screws and take out the combination switch.

6. Remove the fixing bolts and detach the control wing.

7. Remove the screws and separate case A and case B from the control wing.

To Install:

8. Reverse the process to install the switch panel.

a. To remove switch knob, lightly push pawl inside it using a pin and pull the knob out.

b. Be careful not to damage the brush when removing the sliding switch knob.

c. When installing the sliding switch knob and volume control, place your finger on the rear surface of the control and mesh the knob with the control.

d. Do not allow the harness to be caught in cases A or B or pulled unnecessarily during Assembly.

LIGHTING

Headlights

REMOVAL & INSTALLATION

▶ SEE FIGS. 82a–88

Except XT

1. Disconnect the negative battery cable.
2. Remove the front grille retaining screws and remove the grille.

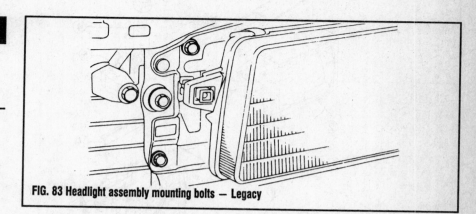

FIG. 83 Headlight assembly mounting bolts — Legacy

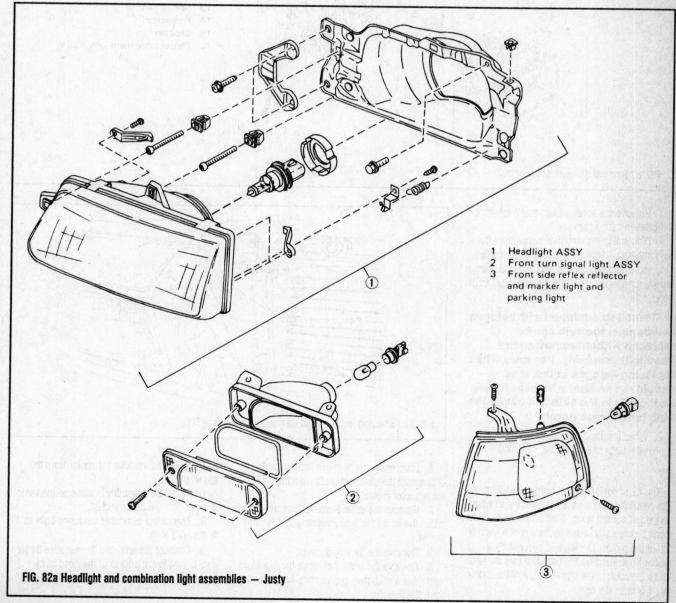

1 Headlight ASSY
2 Front turn signal light ASSY
3 Front side reflex reflector and marker light and parking light

FIG. 82a Headlight and combination light assemblies — Justy

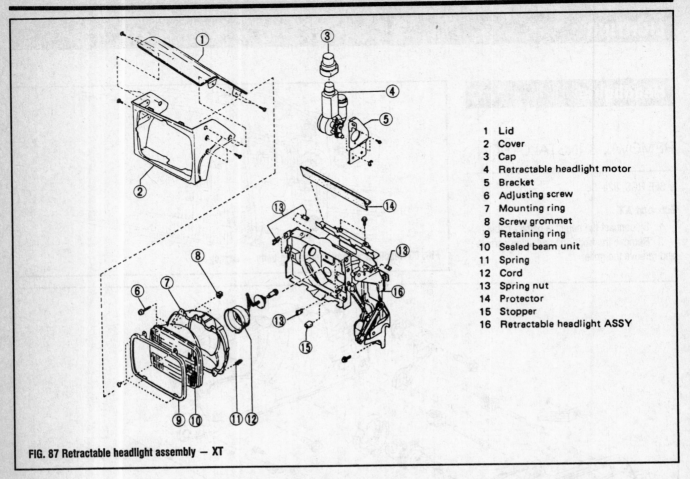

FIG. 87 Retractable headlight assembly — XT

1   Lid
2   Cover
3   Cap
4   Retractable headlight motor
5   Bracket
6   Adjusting screw
7   Mounting ring
8   Screw grommet
9   Retaining ring
10 Sealed beam unit
11 Spring
12 Cord
13 Spring nut
14 Protector
15 Stopper
16 Retractable headlight ASSY

3. Remove the screws that secure the front combination light assembly.

4. Disconnect the electrical connectors from the combination light and headlight assemblies.

5. Remove the headlight assembly retaining screws (or nuts) and remove the assembly from the vehicle.

➡ **On models equipped with halogen headlamps, the bulb can be replaced without removing the headlight assembly. Use care when replacing halogen bulbs, they should not be held with bare hands as the oils in the skin will cause the bulb to fail prematurely.**

6. When installing the assembly, be sure to tighten the bolts to 61 inch lbs. (6.9 Nm).

XT

The XT is equipped with pop-up headlamps. The headlamp motors are actuated by a switch on the left control wing. If the light fails to raise, it can be manually raised by means of a knob on top of the motor. The knob is covered by a rubber boot. Remove the boot and turn the knob in the direction of the arrow on top of the motor, this will raise the light.

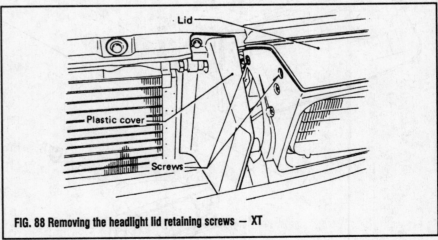

FIG. 88 Removing the headlight lid retaining screws — XT

1. Disconnect the negative battery cable. Disconnect the electrical leads from the light and the retractor motor.

2. Remove the grille. Remove the screws that retain the lid on the light assembly and remove the lid.

3. Remove the headlight cover.

4. Remove the bolts that retain the headlight assembly and motor, and remove the assembly from the vehicle.

5. If needed, remove the motor from the assembly.

6. Install the assembly in place on the vehicle and reinstall the cover and lid.

7. Torque the assembly mounting bolts to 17 ft. lbs. (23 Nm).

8. Connect the lead and the negative battery cable. Test the operation of the headlights.

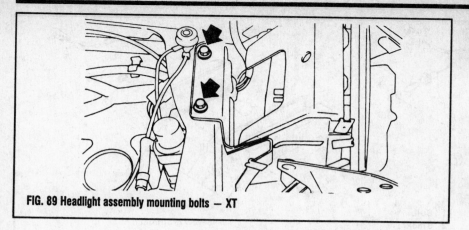

FIG. 89 Headlight assembly mounting bolts — XT

Signal and Marker Lights

REMOVAL & INSTALLATION

♦ SEE FIGS. 84–86

Front Turn Signal and Parking Lights

1. Disconnect the negative battery cable.

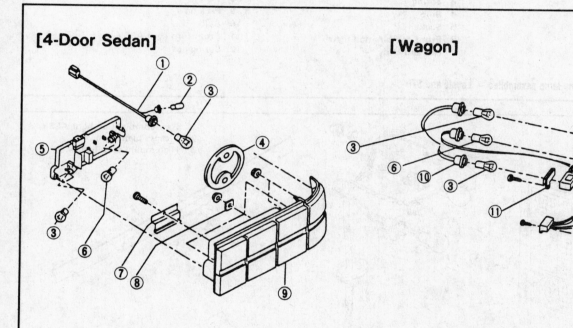

[4-Door Sedan]

[Wagon]

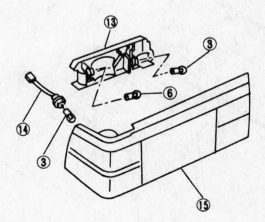

[3-Door]

1	Socket
2	Bulb
3	Bulb
4	Packing
5	Socket CP
6	Bulb
7	Shade
8	Packing
9	Lens and body
10	Socket
11	Cover
12	Lens and body
13	Socket CP
14	Socket
15	Lens and body

FIG. 85 Rear combination lamp assemblies — Loyale and STD

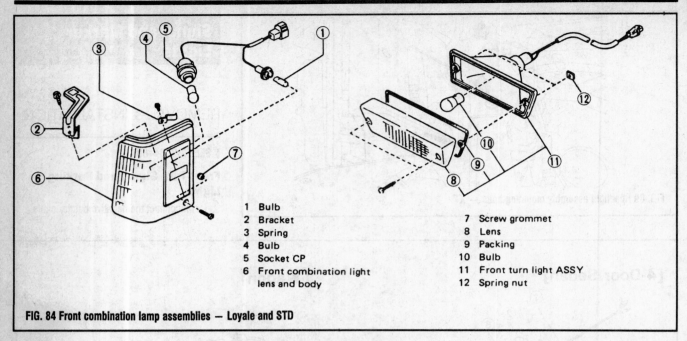

1 Bulb
2 Bracket
3 Spring
4 Bulb
5 Socket CP
6 Front combination light
  lens and body

7 Screw grommet
8 Lens
9 Packing
10 Bulb
11 Front turn light ASSY
12 Spring nut

FIG. 84 Front combination lamp assemblies — Loyale and STD

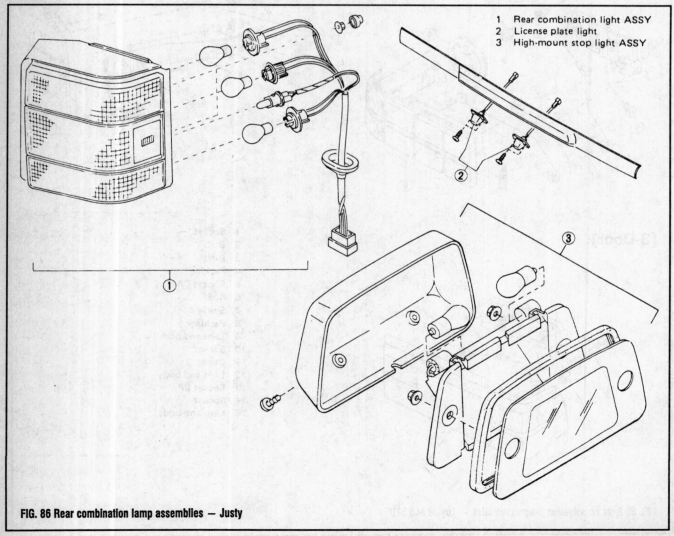

1 Rear combination light ASSY
2 License plate light
3 High-mount stop light ASSY

FIG. 86 Rear combination lamp assemblies — Justy

2. Remove the two screws which secure the lens cover and gasket to the vehicle.

3. Grasp the bulb firmly and pull it from the electrical connector.

4. Replace the old bulb, install the lens cover and connect the battery cable.

Side Marker Lights

1. Disconnect the negative battery cable.

2. Remove the two screws which secure the lens cover and gasket to the vehicle.

3. Pull the lens cover, with the electrical wire, away from the vehicle.

4. Remove the lens cover from the bulb receptacle.

5. Grasp the bulb firmly and pull it from the electrical connector.

6. Replace the old bulb, install the lens cover and connect the battery cable.

Rear Turn Signal, Brake and Parking Lights

1. Disconnect the negative battery cable.

2. Working from inside the trunk, remove the protective covering from the tail light panel.

3. Unsnap the panel covering the bulb to be replaced.

4. Remove the old bulb from the electrical connector and insert a new bulb.

5. Reinstall the electrical panel, replace the protective covering and close the trunk.

TRAILER WIRING

Wiring the car for towing is fairly easy. There are a number of good wiring kits available and these should be used, rather than trying to design your own. All trailers will need brake lights and turn signals as well as tail lights and side marker lights. Most states require extra marker lights for overly wide trailers. Also, most states have recently required back-up lights for trailers, and most trailer manufacturers have been building trailers with back-up lights for several years.

Additionally, some Class I, most Class II and just about all Class III trailers will have electric brakes.

Add to this number an accessories wire, to operate trailer internal equipment or to charge the trailer's battery, and you can have as many as seven wires in the harness.

Determine the equipment on your trailer and buy the wiring kit necessary. The kit will contain all the wires needed, plus a plug adapter set which included the female plug, mounted on the bumper or hitch, and the male plug, wired into, or plugged into the trailer harness.

When installing the kit, follow the manufacturer's instructions. The color coding of the wires is standard throughout the industry.

One point to note some domestic vehicles, and most imported vehicles, have separate turn signals. On most domestic vehicles, the brake lights and rear turn signals operate with the same bulb. For those vehicles with separate turn signals, you can purchase an isolation unit so that the brake lights won't blink whenever the turn signals are operated, or, you can go to your local electronics supply house and buy four diodes to wire in series with the brake and turn signal bulbs. Diodes will isolate the brake and turn signals. The choice is yours. The isolation units are simple and quick to install, but far more expensive than the diodes. The diodes, however, require more work to install properly, since they require the cutting of each bulb's wire and soldering in place of the diode.

One final point, the best kits are those with a spring loaded cover on the vehicle mounted socket. This cover prevents dirt and moisture from corroding the terminals. Never let the vehicle socket hang loosely; always mount it securely to the bumper or hitch.

CIRCUIT PROTECTION

Fusible Link

LOCATION

All Models – Except Justy

The fusible link is located next to the battery positive terminal. All current except for the starter motor flows through it. If excessive current flows through the fusible link the fusible metal melts, thus breaking the circuit and protecting the electrical equipment from damage.

REMOVAL & INSTALLATION

1. Disconnect the negative battery cable.

2. Cut the damaged fuse link from the wiring harness and discard it. If the fuse link is one of three circuits feed by a single feed wire, cut it out of harness at each splice end and discard.

3. Identify and obtain proper fuse link and butt connectors for attaching the fuse link to the harness.

4. Strip away approximately 1/2 in. (13mm) of insulation from the two wiring ends. Attach the replacement fuse link to stripped wire ends with two proper size butt connectors.

5. Solder the connectors and wires and insulate with electrical tape.

Circuit Breaker

Circuit breakers provide the same protection as fuses. Unlike fuses most circuit breakers only have to be reset, and not replaced. Circuit breakers are used only in models equipped with power windows, and are located underneath the front seat.

REMOVAL & INSTALLATION

1. Remove the malfunctioning fuse or circuit breaker by pulling it out of its cavity.

2. Replace the blown fuse or circuit breaker with one of proper amp rating for the circuit, by pushing straight in until the fuse or circuit breaker seats itself fully into the cavity.

Fuses and Flashers

The fuse box is located underneath the instrument panel, on the left side. The amperage for each fuse is stamped on the fuse box cover.

If equipped with 4WD, a fuse holder is located near the ignition coil. For servicing purposes, to change 4WD to FWD, insert a 15A fuse into the FWD fuse holder. The FWD pilot lamp (on the instrument panel) will turn On to indicate the vehicle is set in the FWD mode.

On the Justy model, a main fuse is located in the engine compartment, next to the brake master cylinder; all current (except for the starter) will flow through this fuse. When replacing the main fuse(s), be aware of the amperage rating; a 30A (pink) or a 60A (yellow).

Modules and Computers

Legacy

- **Air Suspension Control Module** — is located under the driver's seat.
- **Anti-lock Brake Control Module** — is located under front passenger seat.
- **Automatic Shoulder Belt Control Module (sedan)** — is located in left side of trunk, near left trunk lid hinge mount.
- **Automatic Shoulder Belt Control Module (wagon)** — is located on left rear shock tower, just below rear speaker.
- **Automatic Transaxle Control Module** — is located under left dash, immediately to left of steering column.
- **Check Connector (Black)** — is located behind left side of center console, under dashboard.
- **Cruise Control Module** — is located under right dash, to right of glove box.
- **Daytime Running Light Control Module (Canada)** — is located under right dash, above right kick panel.
- **Diagnosis Connector** — is located behind left side of center console, under dashboard.

- **ECU** — is located under left dash, to left of steering column.
- **Fuse Box** — is located under left side of instrument panel.
- **Illumination Control Unit** — is located behind center dashboard, to left of glovebox.
- **MPFI Control Module** — is located behind left dash, above fuse box.
- **Shift Lock Control Module** — is located under left center dash, behind left side of center console.
- **Sunroof Control Module** — is located in roof, at rear of sunroof.
- **Test Mode Connector (green)** — is located is located below right side of steering column.
- **Turn Signal/Flasher Module** — is located behind center dashboard, to left of glove box.
- **Wastegate Valve and Controller (1991)** — is located at exhaust side of turbocharger.

Loyale

- **Automatic Transaxle Control Module (4 speed)** — is located in left quarter panel.
- **MPFI Module** — is located under left dash, directly below the steering column.
- **Power Window Control Module** — is located under the front passenger seat.

Justy

- **Automatic Seat Belt Module** — is located behind right front kick panel.
- **Check Connector (under dash)** — is located under left side dashboard.
- **Check Connectors (ECVT)** — are located in ECVT module harness at the control module.
- **Check Connectors (underhood)** — are located in wire harness at left front shock tower.
- **Daytime Running Lamp Control Module (Canada)** — is located behind right front kick panel.
- **ECVT Module** — is located under left dash, above hood release.
- **EFC Control Module** — See Fuel Control Module
- **Front Wiper Intermittent Control Module** — is located behind the fusebox.

- **Fuel Control Module (EFC or MPFI)** — is located under left dash, near hood release.
- **Illumination Control Module** — is located on brake pedal bracket.
- **MPFI Control Module** — See Fuel Control Module
- **Read Memory Connector** — is located under left dashboard.
- **SELECT Diagnostic Connector** — is located in wire harness, just below ignition coil on firewall.
- **Shift Lock Module** — is located on brake pedal bracket.

XT

- **Automatic Seat Belt Control Module** — is located in right quarter panel, behind right door.
- **Automatic Transaxle Control Module** — is located in left quarter panel, behind left door.
- **Check Connectors (underhood, 17-pin and 11-pin)** — are located in wire harness at left side of firewall.
- **Cruise Control Module** — is located in right side dash, above glove box light assembly.
- **Illumination Control Module** — is located on top of steering column, under upper column cover.
- **Intermittent Wiper Module** — is located in center console, just ahead of shifter assembly.
- **Mode Control Module** — is located under left center dash, behind center console.
- **MPFI Control Module** — is located in front of trunk, mounted to underside of rear window shelf.
- **Pneumatic Suspension Control Module** — is located under the driver's seat.
- **Power Window Control Module** — is located under front passenger seat.
- **Read Memory Connector** — is located in wiring harness at front of trunk, under rear window shelf. The connectors are black.
- **Test Mode Connectors** — are located in front of trunk, under rear window shelf. The 2 connectors are green.

SVX

For all SVX module, relay and computer locations, refer to the wiring diagrams at the end of this section.

Troubleshooting Basic Turn Signal and Flasher Problems

Most problems in the turn signals or flasher system can be reduced to defective flashers or bulbs, which are easily replaced. Occasionally, problems in the turn signals are traced to the switch in the steering column, which will require professional service.

F = Front   R = Rear   ● = Lights off   ○ = Lights on

Problem		Solution
Turn signals light, but do not flash		• Replace the flasher
No turn signals light on either side		• Check the fuse. Replace if defective. • Check the flasher by substitution • Check for open circuit, short circuit or poor ground
Both turn signals on one side don't work		• Check for bad bulbs • Check for bad ground in both housings
One turn signal light on one side doesn't work		• Check and/or replace bulb • Check for corrosion in socket. Clean contacts. • Check for poor ground at socket
Turn signal flashes too fast or too slow		• Check any bulb on the side flashing too fast. A heavy-duty bulb is probably installed in place of a regular bulb. • Check the bulb flashing too slow. A standard bulb was probably installed in place of a heavy-duty bulb. • Check for loose connections or corrosion at the bulb socket
Indicator lights don't work in either direction		• Check if the turn signals are working • Check the dash indicator lights • Check the flasher by substitution

Troubleshooting Basic Turn Signal and Flasher Problems

Most problems in the turn signals or flasher system can be reduced to defective flashers or bulbs, which are easily replaced. Occasionally, problems in the turn signals are traced to the switch in the steering column, which will require professional service.

F = Front   R = Rear   ● = Lights off   o = Lights on

Problem		Solution
One indicator light doesn't light		• On systems with 1 dash indicator: See if the lights work on the same side. Often the filaments have been reversed in systems combining stoplights with taillights and turn signals. Check the flasher by substitution • On systems with 2 indicators: Check the bulbs on the same side Check the indicator light bulb Check the flasher by substitution

Troubleshooting Basic Lighting Problems

Problem	Cause	Solution
Lights		
One or more lights don't work, but others do	• Defective bulb(s) • Blown fuse(s) • Dirty fuse clips or light sockets • Poor ground circuit	• Replace bulb(s) • Replace fuse(s) • Clean connections • Run ground wire from light socket housing to car frame
Lights burn out quickly	• Incorrect voltage regulator setting or defective regulator • Poor battery/alternator connections	• Replace voltage regulator • Check battery/alternator connections
Lights go dim	• Low/discharged battery • Alternator not charging • Corroded sockets or connections • Low voltage output	• Check battery • Check drive belt tension; repair or replace alternator • Clean bulb and socket contacts and connections • Replace voltage regulator
Lights flicker	• Loose connection • Poor ground • Circuit breaker operating (short circuit)	• Tighten all connections • Run ground wire from light housing to car frame • Check connections and look for bare wires
Lights "flare"—Some flare is normal on acceleration—if excessive, see "Lights Burn Out Quickly"	• High voltage setting	• Replace voltage regulator
Lights glare—approaching drivers are blinded	• Lights adjusted too high • Rear springs or shocks sagging • Rear tires soft	• Have headlights aimed • Check rear springs/shocks • Check/correct rear tire pressure

Troubleshooting Basic Lighting Problems

Problem	Cause	Solution
Turn Signals		
Turn signals don't work in either direction	• Blown fuse • Defective flasher • Loose connection	• Replace fuse • Replace flasher • Check/tighten all connections
Right (or left) turn signal only won't work	• Bulb burned out • Right (or left) indicator bulb burned out • Short circuit	• Replace bulb • Check/replace indicator bulb • Check/repair wiring
Flasher rate too slow or too fast	• Incorrect wattage bulb • Incorrect flasher	• Flasher bulb • Replace flasher (use a variable load flasher if you pull a trailer)
Indicator lights do not flash (burn steadily)	• Burned out bulb • Defective flasher	• Replace bulb • Replace flasher
Indicator lights do not light at all	• Burned out indicator bulb • Defective flasher	• Replace indicator bulb • Replace flasher

Troubleshooting Basic Windshield Wiper Problems

Problem	Cause	Solution
Electric Wipers		
Wipers do not operate— Wiper motor heats up or hums	• Internal motor defect • Bent or damaged linkage • Arms improperly installed on linking pivots	• Replace motor • Repair or replace linkage • Position linkage in park and reinstall wiper arms
Electric Wipers		
Wipers do not operate— No current to motor	• Fuse or circuit breaker blown • Loose, open or broken wiring • Defective switch • Defective or corroded terminals • No ground circuit for motor or switch	• Replace fuse or circuit breaker • Repair wiring and connections • Replace switch • Replace or clean terminals • Repair ground circuits
Wipers do not operate— Motor runs	• Linkage disconnected or broken	• Connect wiper linkage or replace broken linkage
Vacuum Wipers		
Wipers do not operate	• Control switch or cable inoperative • Loss of engine vacuum to wiper motor (broken hoses, low engine vacuum, defective vacuum/fuel pump) • Linkage broken or disconnected • Defective wiper motor	• Repair or replace switch or cable • Check vacuum lines, engine vacuum and fuel pump • Repair linkage • Replace wiper motor
Wipers stop on engine acceleration	• Leaking vacuum hoses • Dry windshield • Oversize wiper blades • Defective vacuum/fuel pump	• Repair or replace hoses • Wet windshield with washers • Replace with proper size wiper blades • Replace pump

Troubleshooting Basic Dash Gauge Problems

Problem	Cause	Solution
Coolant Temperature Gauge		
Gauge reads erratically or not at all	• Loose or dirty connections • Defective sending unit	• Clean/tighten connections • Bi-metal gauge: remove the wire from the sending unit. Ground the wire for an instant. If the gauge registers, replace the sending unit.
	• Defective gauge	• Magnetic gauge: disconnect the wire at the sending unit. With ignition ON gauge should register COLD. Ground the wire; gauge should register HOT.
Ammeter Gauge—Turn Headlights ON (do not start engine). Note reaction		
Ammeter shows charge Ammeter shows discharge Ammeter does not move	• Connections reversed on gauge • Ammeter is OK • Loose connections or faulty wiring • Defective gauge	• Reinstall connections • Nothing • Check/correct wiring • Replace gauge
Oil Pressure Gauge		
Gauge does not register or is inaccurate	• On mechanical gauge, Bourdon tube may be bent or kinked	• Check tube for kinks or bends preventing oil from reaching the gauge
	• Low oil pressure	• Remove sending unit. Idle the engine briefly. If no oil flows from sending unit hole, problem is in engine.
	• Defective gauge	• Remove the wire from the sending unit and ground it for an instant with the ignition ON. A good gauge will go to the top of the scale.
	• Defective wiring	• Check the wiring to the gauge. If it's OK and the gauge doesn't register when grounded, replace the gauge.
	• Defective sending unit	• If the wiring is OK and the gauge functions when grounded, replace the sending unit
All Gauges		
All gauges do not operate	• Blown fuse • Defective instrument regulator	• Replace fuse • Replace instrument voltage regulator
All gauges read low or erratically	• Defective or dirty instrument voltage regulator	• Clean contacts or replace
All gauges pegged	• Loss of ground between instrument voltage regulator and car • Defective instrument regulator	• Check ground • Replace regulator

Troubleshooting Basic Dash Gauge Problems

Problem	Cause	Solution
Warning Lights		
Light(s) do not come on when ignition is ON, but engine is not started	· Defective bulb · Defective wire · Defective sending unit	· Replace bulb · Check wire from light to sending unit · Disconnect the wire from the sending unit and ground it. Replace the sending unit if the light comes on with the ignition ON.
Light comes on with engine running	· Problem in individual system · Defective sending unit	· Check system · Check sending unit (see above)

Troubleshooting the Heater

Problem	Cause	Solution
Blower motor will not turn at any speed	· Blown fuse · Loose connection · Defective ground · Faulty switch · Faulty motor · Faulty resistor	· Replace fuse · Inspect and tighten · Clean and tighten · Replace switch · Replace motor · Replace resistor
Blower motor turns at one speed only	· Faulty switch · Faulty resistor	· Replace switch · Replace resistor
Blower motor turns but does not circulate air	· Intake blocked · Fan not secured to the motor shaft	· Clean intake · Tighten security
Heater will not heat	· Coolant does not reach proper temperature · Heater core blocked internally · Heater core air-bound · Blend-air door not in proper position	· Check and replace thermostat if necessary · Flush or replace core if necessary · Purge air from core · Adjust cable
Heater will not defrost	· Control cable adjustment incorrect · Defroster hose damaged	· Adjust control cable · Replace defroster hose

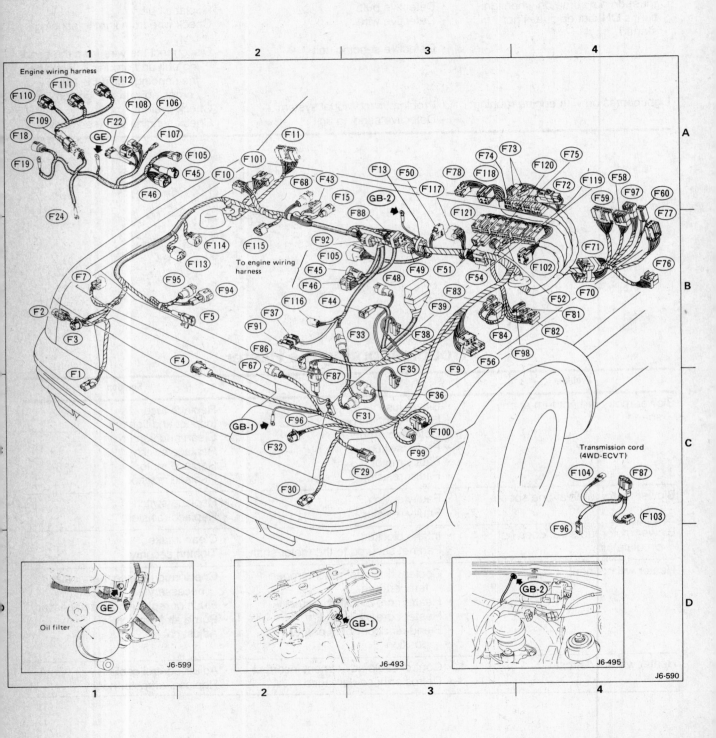

Front wiring harness and ground points — 1990–92 Justy MPFI model

Connector			Connecting to		
No.	Pole	Color	Area	No.	Name
F1	2		C–1		Front turn signal light (RH)
F2	2		B–1		Parking light (RH)
F3	3	Black	B–1		Headlight (RH)
F4	2		B–2		Horn
F5	1	Gray	B–2		O$_2$ Sensor
F7	2		B–1		Solenoid (CPC)
F9	6	Pink	B–3		Check connector
F10	4	Black	A–2		Front wiper motor
F11	20	Black	A–2	i35	Instrument panel wiring harness
F13	2		B–3		For A/C (OP)
F15	1		A–2		For A/C (OP)
F18	2		A–1		Alternator
F19	1		A–1		
F22	2		A–1		Water temperature sensor
F24	1		A–1		Oil pressure switch
F29	2		C–3		Parking light (LH)
F30	2		C–2		Front turn signal light (LH)
F31	2		C–3		Back-up light switch (MT)
F32	3	Black	C–2		Headlight (LH)
F33	4		B–2		Transmission cord ↔ Front wiring harness (MT)
F35	2		C–3		Rear washer pump
F36	2	Black	C–3		4WD indicator light switch (MT)
F37	1	Black	B–2		Starter (MT)
F38	2		B–3		Front washer pump
F39	3		B–3		Main fuse box
F43	2	Black	A–2		For A/C (OP)
F44	1		B–3		Battery
F45	2	Gray	B–3		Engine wiring harness ↔ Front wiring harness
F46	12	Black	B–3		
F48	2	Black	B–3		Brake fluid level sensor
F49	2	Black	B–3		Condenser (For ignition coil)
F50	2	Black	B–3		Ignition coil
F51	2 x 2	Green	B–3		Test mode
F52	1 x 2	Black	B–3		Read memory
F54	9	Yellow	B–3		Serial communication
F56	11	Black	B–3		Check connector
F58	6	Blue	A–4	i2	Instrument panel wiring harness
F59	20	Black	A–4	i1	
F60	3		A–4	i3	
F67	2		B–2		Radiator fan motor
F68	4	Black	A–2		4WD/FWD solenoid valve (MT)
F70	4	Brown	B–4		Diode (For ignition relay & horn)
F71	4	Brown	B–4		Diode (For front & rear washer)
F72	2 x 2		A–4		Memory back-up (ECVT)
F73	1 x 2		A–4		Check mode (ECVT)
F74	18		A–3		ECVT unit
F75	12		A–4		
F76	12	Black	B–4		Shift lock unit (ECVT)
F77	6	Black	B–4	i40	Instrument panel wiring harness (ECVT)
F78	4		A–3		Fuel pump relay
F81	2	Black	B–4		Stop light switch
F82	2	Blue	B–4		Clutch switch
F83	2		B–3		Accelerator switch (ECVT)
F84	2	Blue	B–3		Throttle position switch (ECVT)
F86	2	Black	B–2		Electro-magnetic clutch coil (ECVT)
F87	2		C–2		Transmission cord ↔ Front wiring harness (ECVT FWD)
	6	Black	C–4		Transmission cord ↔ Front wiring harness (ECVT 4WD)

Connector			Connecting to		
No.	Pole	Color	Area	No.	Name
F88	6	Brown	B–3		Fro A/C (OP)
F91	1	Black	B–2		Starter (ECVT)
F92	6	Brown	B–3		For A/C (OP)
F94	2		B–2		For A/C (OP)
F95	2		B–2		For A/C (OP)
F96	1	Brown	C–2		Line pressure solenoid
F97	4	Blue	A–4	i55	Instrument panel harness
F98	2		B–4		Interlock switch (Clutch switch) (MT)
F99	2	White	C–3		DRL resistor
F100	5	Brown	C–3		DRL relay (Canada only)
F101	10	White	A–2		DRL unit
F102	4	Blue	B–4		Starter interlock relay (MT)
F103	2	White	C–4		4WD switch (ECVT)
F104	2		C–4		4WD solenoid (ECVT)
F105	6	Black	B–3		Engine wiring harness ↔ Front wiring harness
F106	2		A–1		Radiator fan switch
F107	1		A–1		Thermometer
F108	3		A–1		Throttle sensor
F109	4	Gray	A–1		Engine wiring harness No. 2 ↔ Engine wiring harness
F110	2	Gray	A–1		Injector No. 1
F111	2	Gray	A–1		Injector No. 2
F112	2	Gray	A–1		Injector No. 3
F113	2		B–2		Air temperature sensor
F114	2		B–2		ISC VSV
F115	3	Black	B–2		Pressure sensor
F116	4	Gray	B–2		Crank angle & Cylinder distinction sensor
F117	4	Gray	B–3		Igniter
F118	6	Brown	A–3		Main relay
F119	26		B–4		MPFI unit
F120	22		B–3		
F121	16		B–3		

Front wiring harness and ground point connector identification — 1990–92 Justy MPFI model

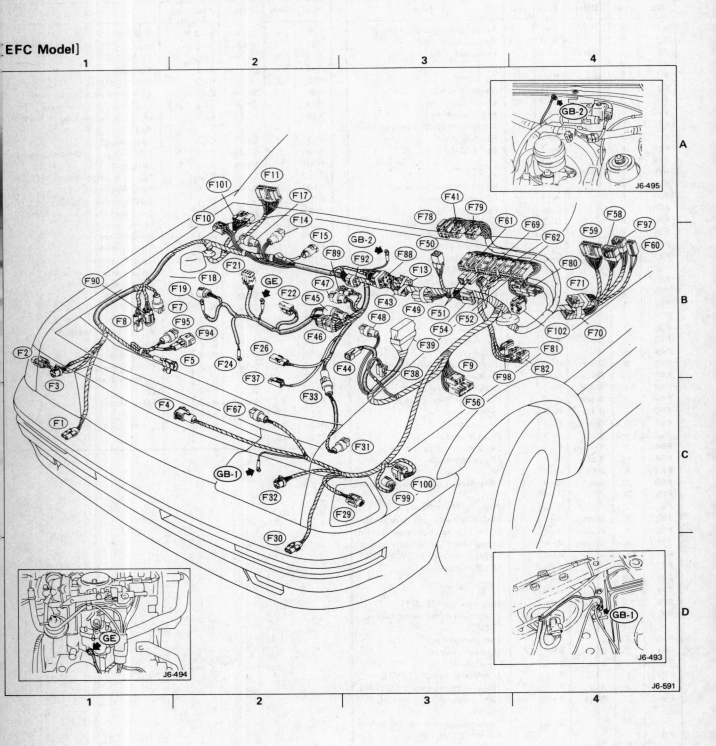

Front wiring harness and ground points — 1990–92 Justy EFC model

Connector				Connecting to	
No.	Pole	Color	Area	No.	Name
F1	2		C—1		Front turn signal light (RH)
F2	2		B—1		Parking light (RH)
F3	3	Black	B—1		Headlight (RH)
F4	2		C—2		Horn
F5	1		B—1		O₂ Sensor
F7	2		B—1		Solenoid (CPC)
F8	2	Green	B—1		Solenoid (VLC)
F9	6	Pink	B—3		Check connector
F10	4	Black	A—2		Front wiper motor
F11	20	Black	A—2	i35	Instrument panel wiring harness
F13	2		B—3		For A/C (OP)
F14	4	Black	B—2		Solenoid (HAC)
F15	1		B—2		For A/C (OP)
F17	2	Black	B—2		Solenoid (FCV)
F18	2	Gray	B—2		} Alternator
F19	1		B—2		
F21	6	Gray	B—2		Carburetor (C.F.C, Duty, Choke)
F22	2	Black	B—2		Water temperature sensor & Thermometer
F24	1		B—2		Oil pressure switch
F26	2	Green	B—2		Distributor
F29	2		C—3		Parking light (LH)
F30	2		D—2		Front turn signal light (LH)
F31	2		C—3		Back-up light switch
F32	3	Black	C—2		Headlight (LH)
F33	4		C—2		Transmission cord ↔ Front wiring harness
F37	1		B—2		Starter
F38	2		B—3		Front washer pump
F39	3		B—3		Main fuse box
F41	4		B—3		Radiator fan relay
F43	1		B—3		For A/C (OP)
F44	1		B—3		Battery
F45	2	Gray	B—2		} Engine wiring harness ↔ Front wiring harness
F46	16	Black	B—2		
F47	2	Black	B—2		Idle up solenoid
F48	2	Black	B—3		Brake fluid level sensor
F49	2	Black	B—3		Condenser (For ignition coil)
F50	4	Black	B—3		Ignition coil
F51	2 x 2	Green	B—3		Test mode
F52	1 x 2	Black	B—3		Read memory
F54	9	Yellow	B—3		Serial communication
F56	11	Black	C—3		Check connector
F58	6	Blue	B—4	i2	
F59	20	Black	B—4	i1	} Instrument panel wiring harness
F60	3		B—4	i3	
F61	14		B—3		EFC unit
F62	22		B—4		EFC unit
F67	2		C—2		Radiator fan motor
F69	16		B—3		EFC unit
F70	4	Brown	B—4		Diode (For ignition relay & horn)
F71	4	Brown	B—4		Diode (For front washer motor)
F78	6	Brown	B—3		Fuel pump relay
F79	4		B—3		Ignition relay
F80	2 x 2	Black	B—4		Sealed earth connector
F81	2	Black	B—4		Stop light switch
F82	2	Blue	B—4		Clutch switch

Connector				Connecting to	
No.	Pole	Color	Area	No.	Name
F88	6	Brown	B—3		For A/C (OP)
F89	2		B—3		Solenoid (EGR)
F90	3	Green	B—1		Pressure sensor
F92	4	Blue	B—3		For A/C (OP)
F94	2	Blue	B—2		For A/C (OP)
F95	2		B—1		For A/C (OP)
F97	4	Blue	B—4	i55	Instrument panel harness
F98	2		B—3		Interlock switch (Clutch switch)
F99	2	White	C—3		DRL resistor
F100	5	Brown	C—3		DRL relay } (Canada only)
F101	10	White	A—2		DRL unit
F102	4	Blue	B—4		Starter interlock relay

Front wiring harness and ground point connector identification — 1990–92 Justy EFC model

Electrical Fuel Control System (EFC)

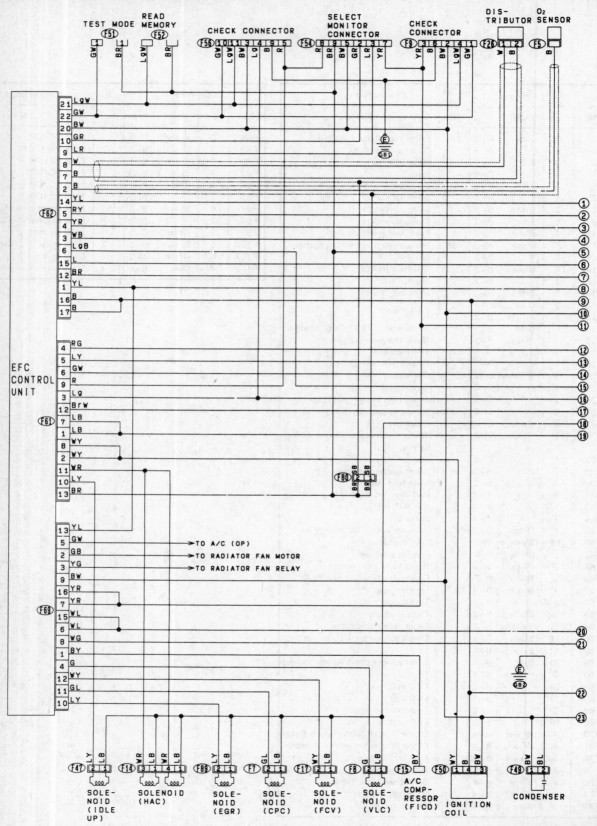

Electrical fuel control system (EFC) — 1990–92 Justy

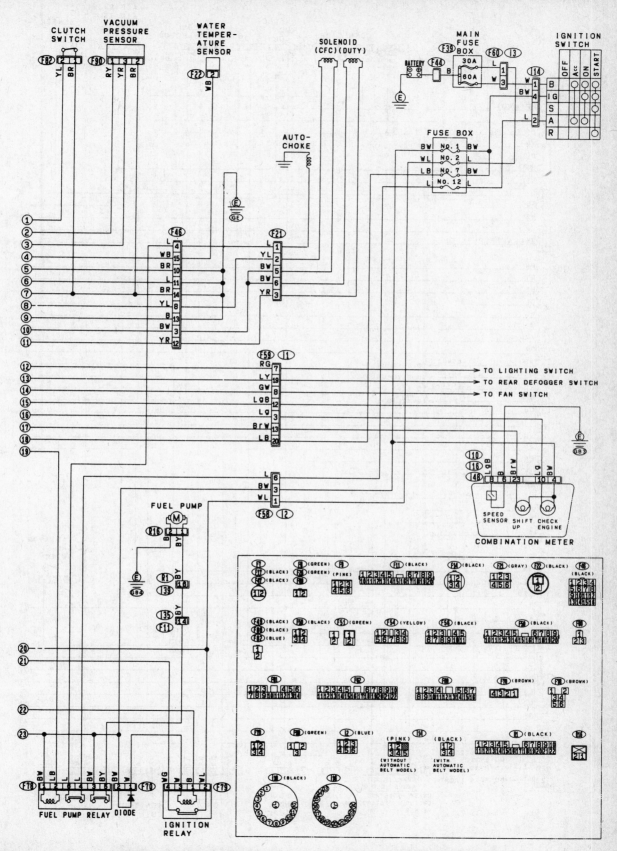

Electrical fuel control system – 1990–92 Justy (EFC) continued

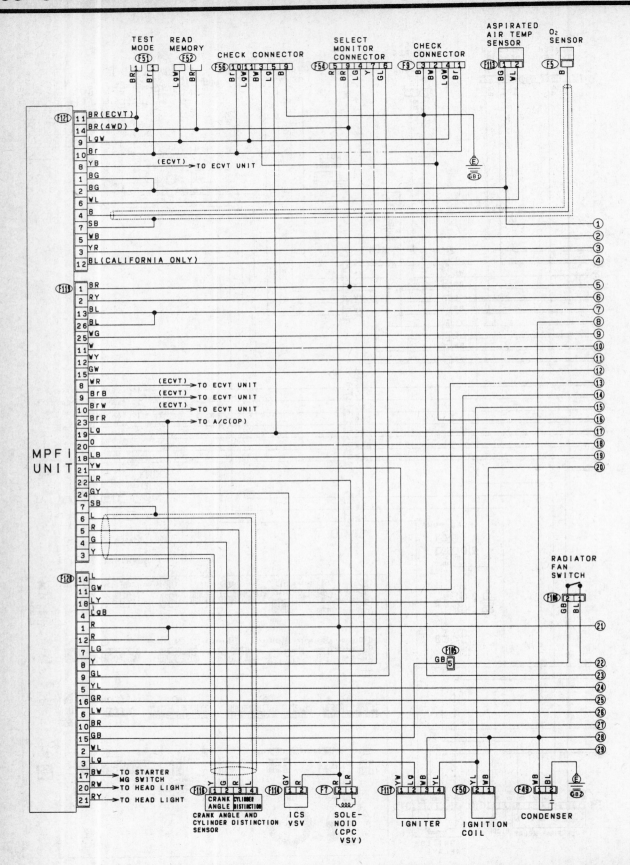

Multi-point fuel injection system (MPFI) — 1990–92 Justy

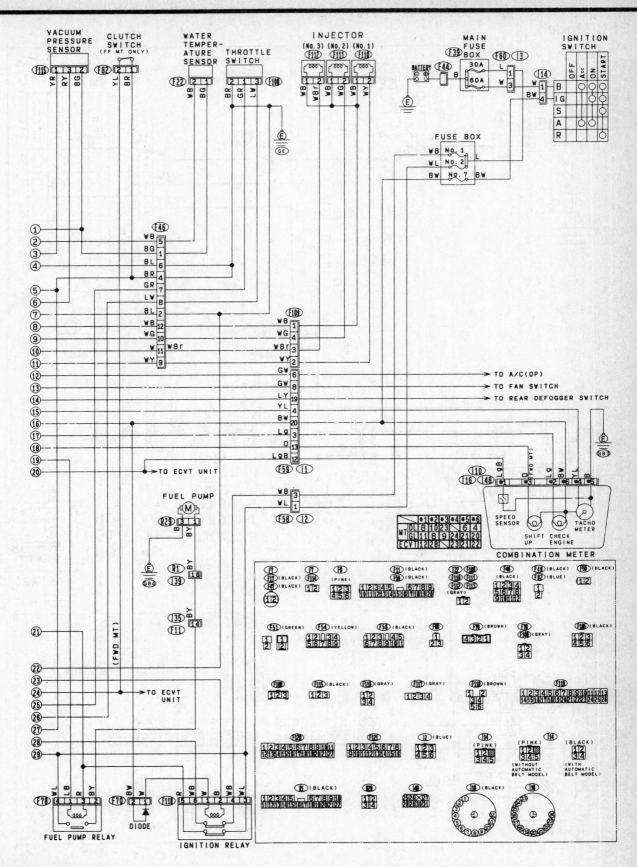

Multi-point fuel injection system (MPFI) — 1990–92 Justy continued

(EFC Model)

Starting and ignition system — EFC 1990–92 Justy

(MPFI Model)

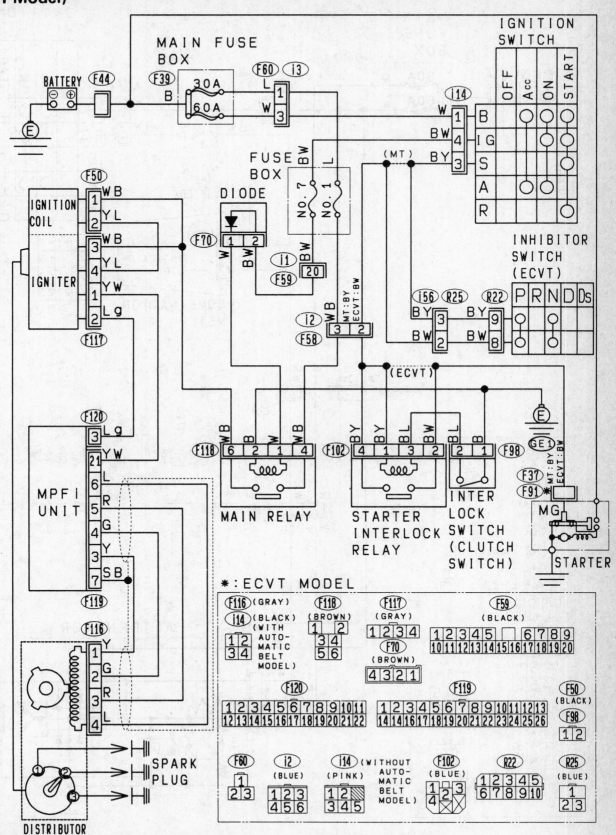

Starting and ignition system — MPFI 1990–92 Justy

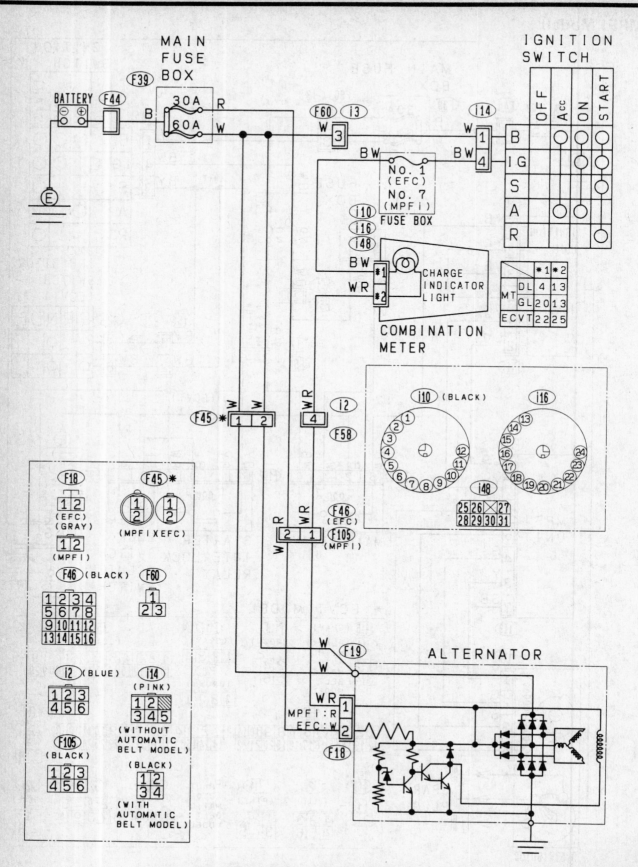

Charging system — 1990–92 Justy

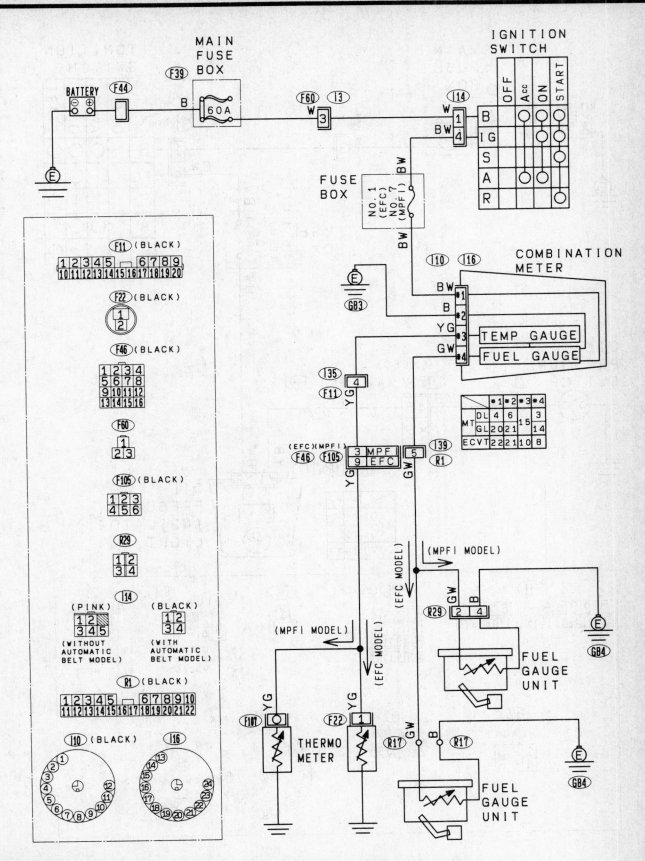

Fuel and temperature gauge — 1990–92 Justy

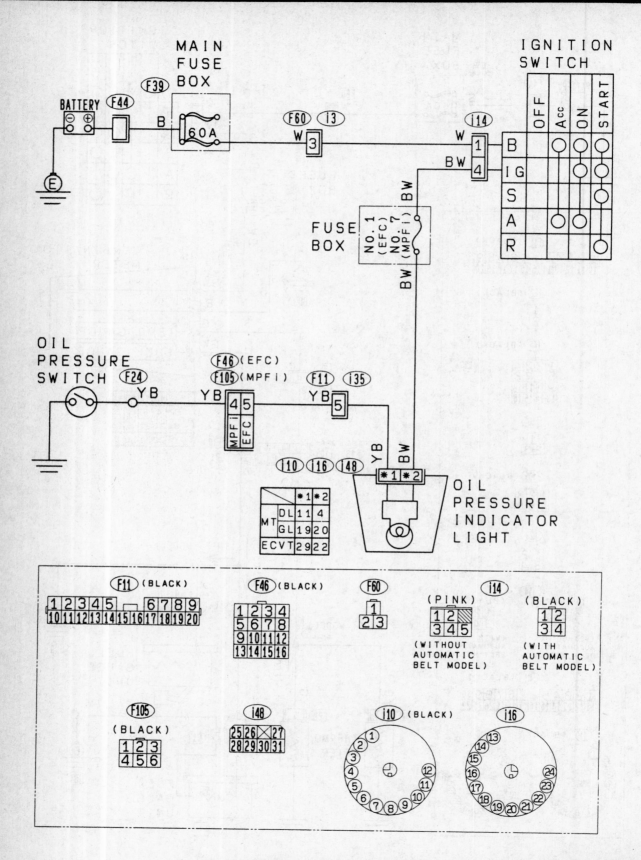

Oil pressure light — 1990–92 Justy

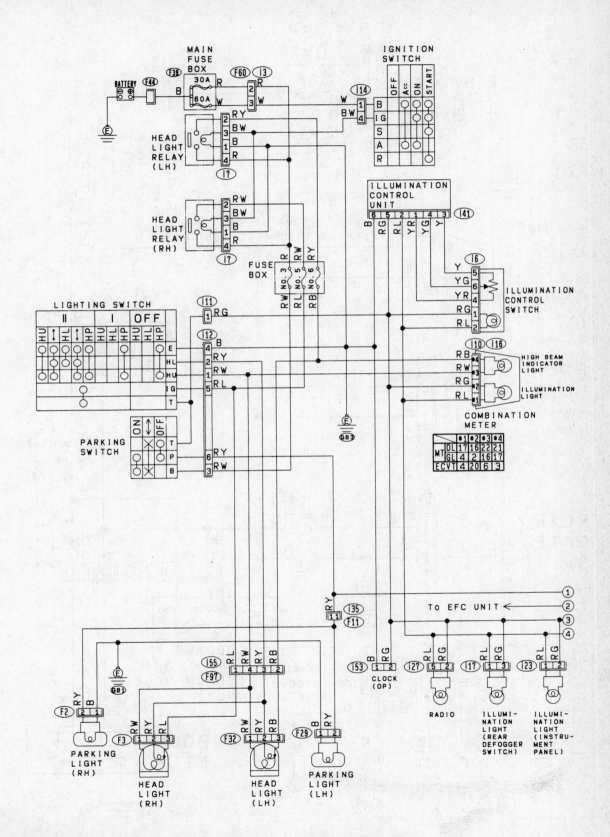

Lighting system — 1990–92 Justy

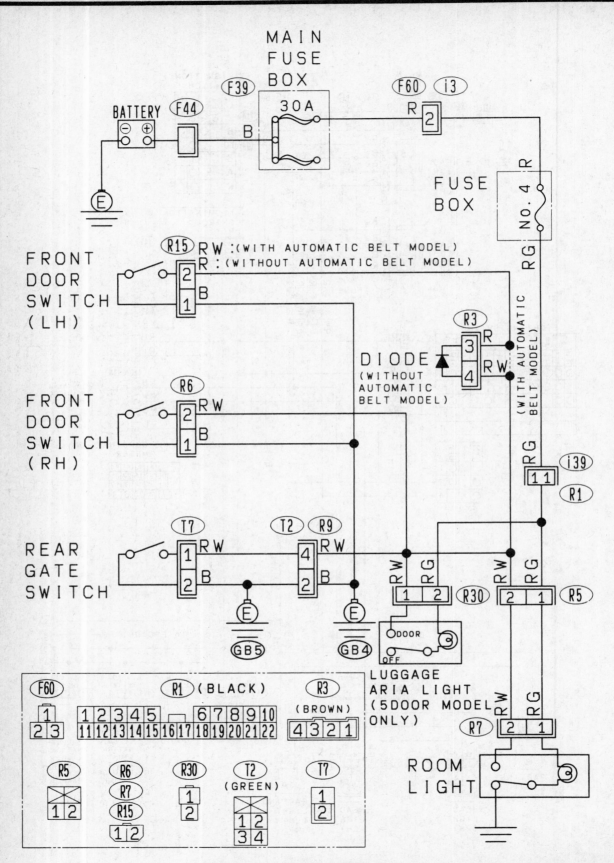

Room light — 1990–92 Justy

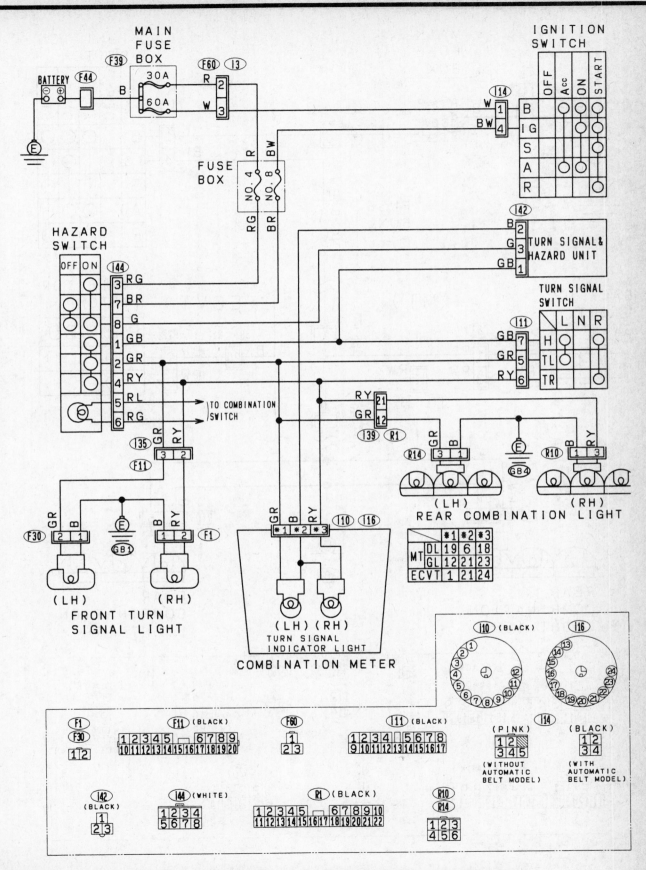

Turn signal and hazard warning system — 1990–92 Justy

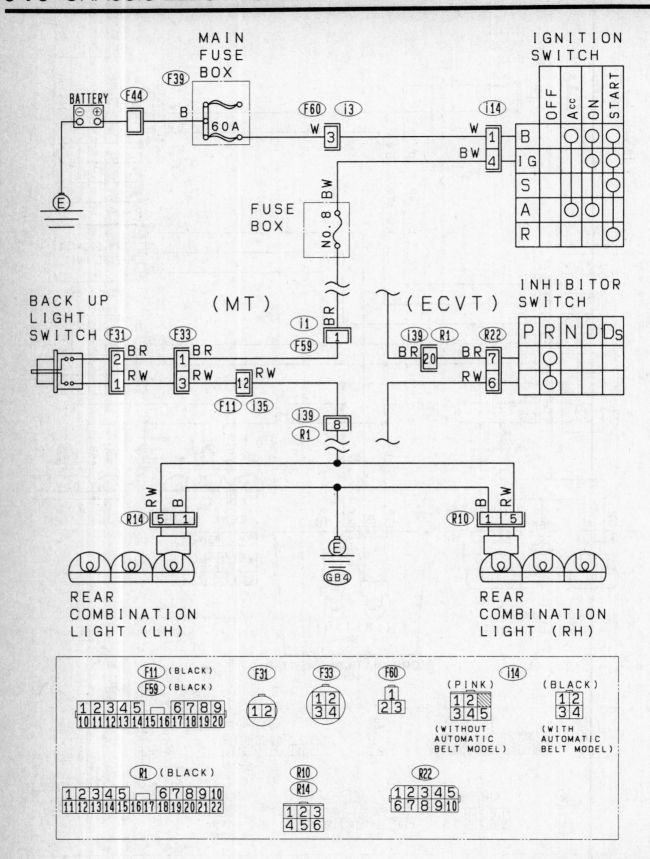

Backup light system — 1990–92 Justy

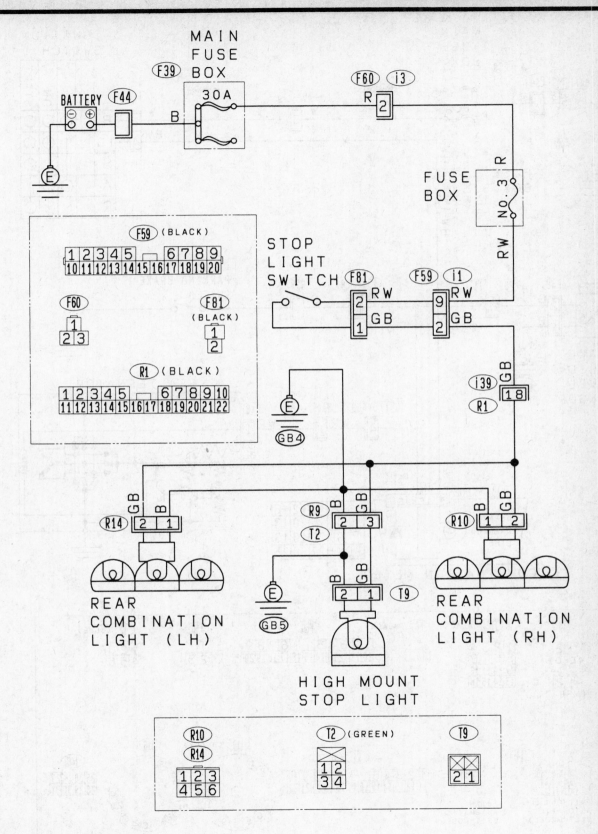

Stop light system — 1990–92 Justy

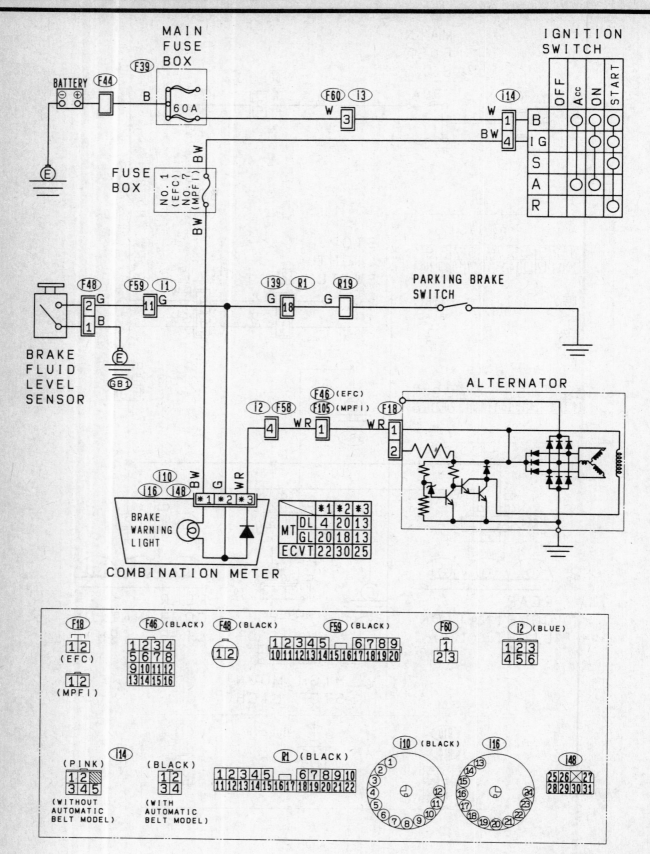

Parking brake and brake fluid level warning system — 1990–92 Justy

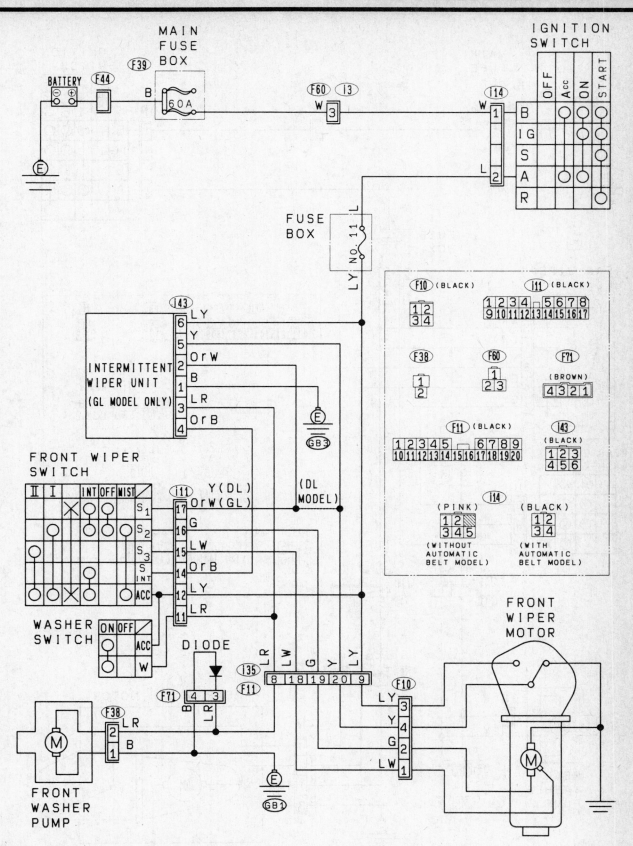

Front wiper and washer — 1990–92 Justy

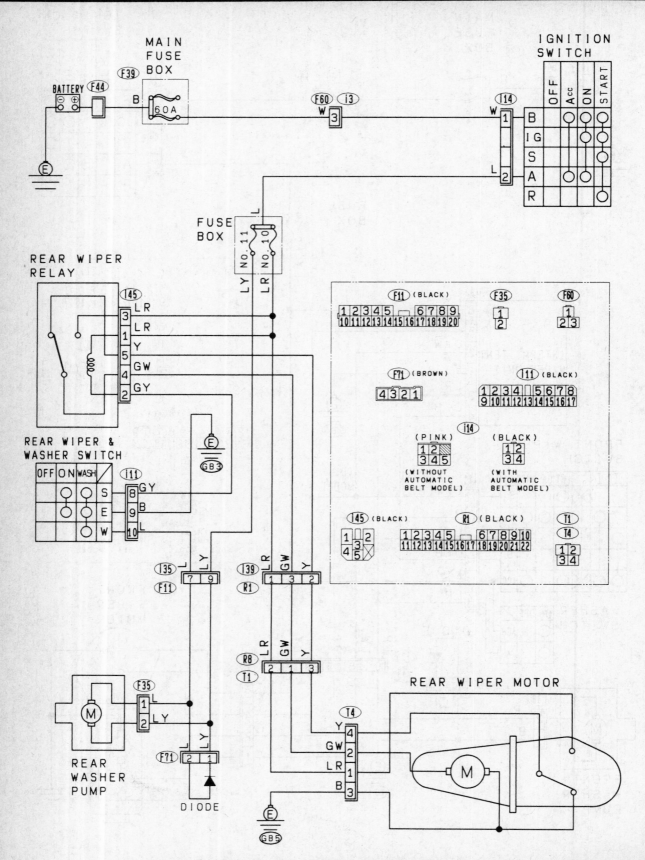

Rear wiper and washer — 1990–92 Justy

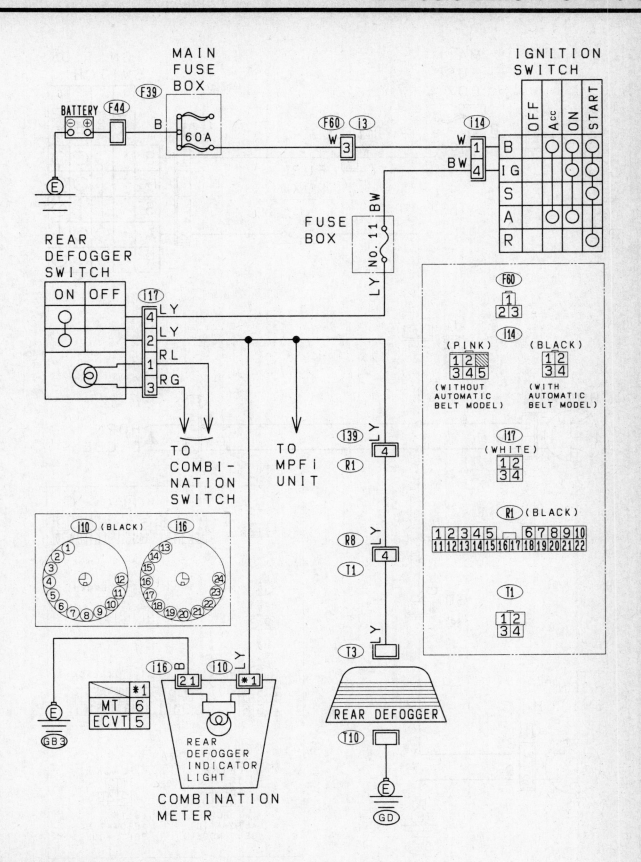

Rear window defogger — 1990–92 Justy

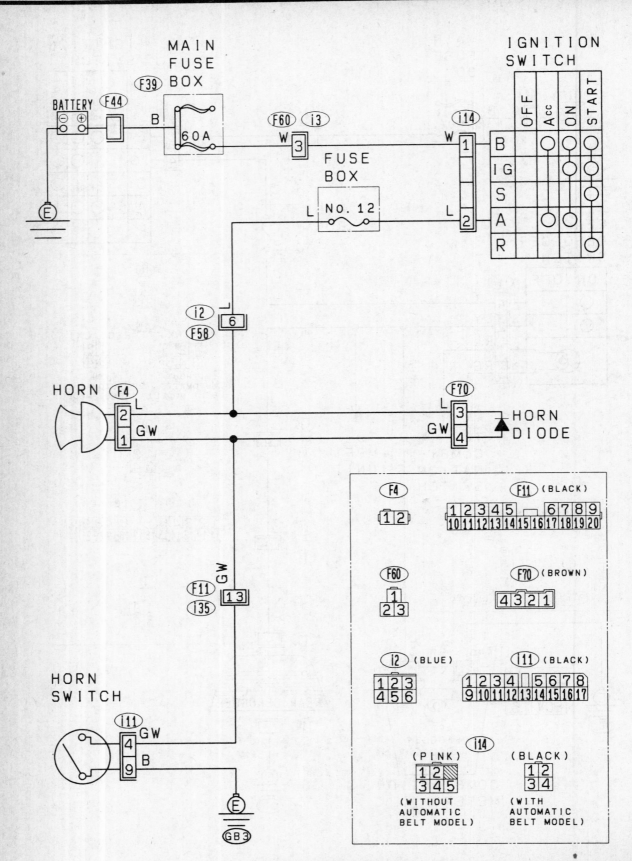

Horn — 1990–92 Justy

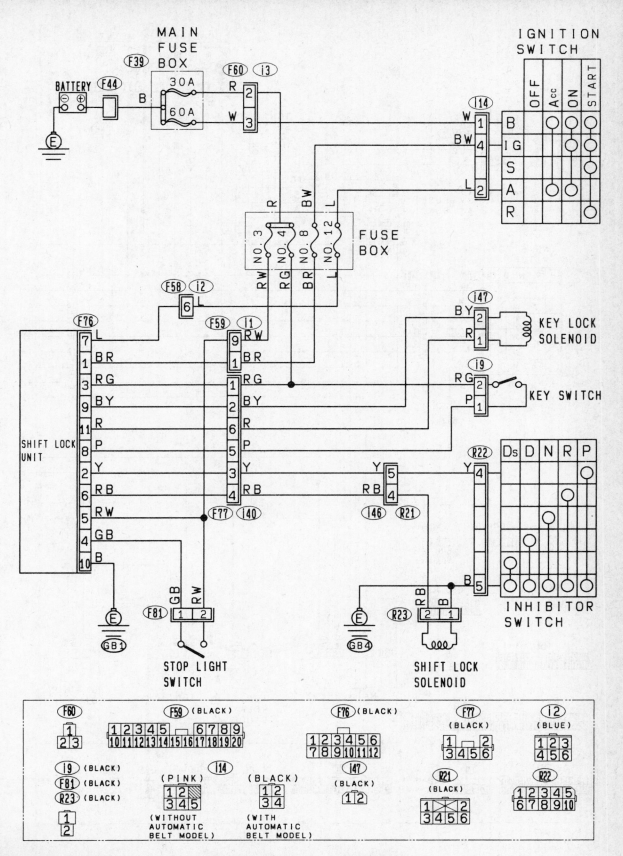

Shift lock system — 1990–92 Justy

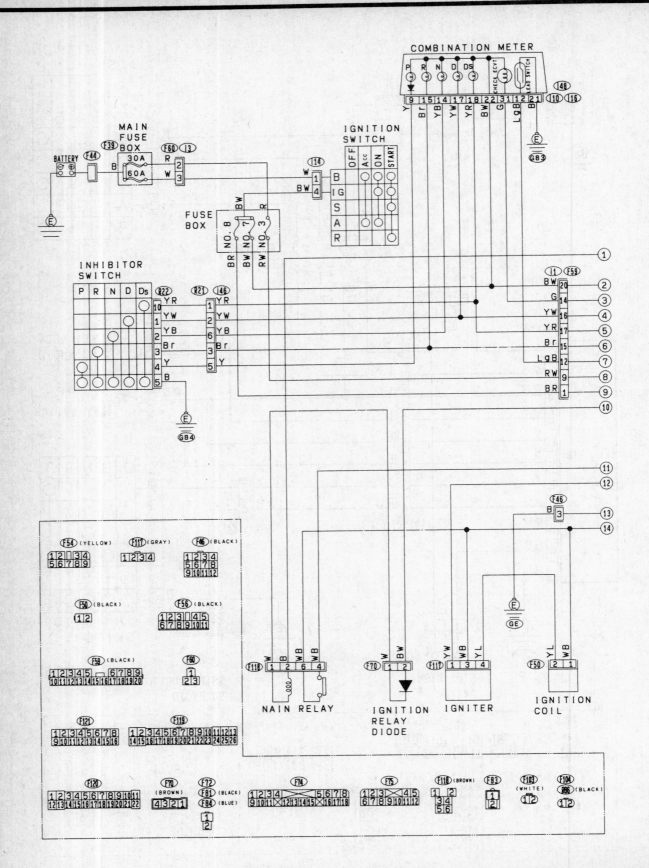

ECVT system — 1990–92 Justy

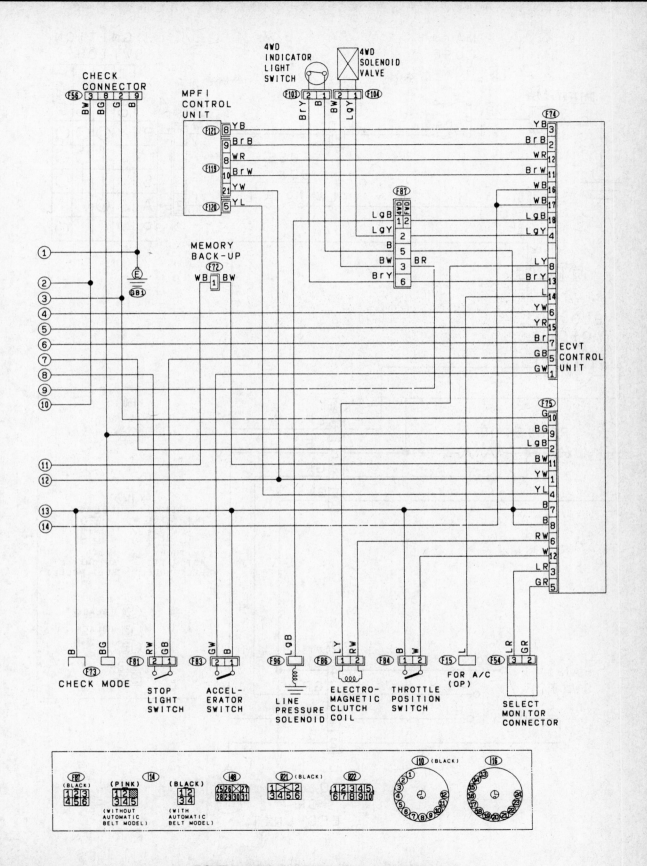

ECVT system — 1990–92 Justy continued

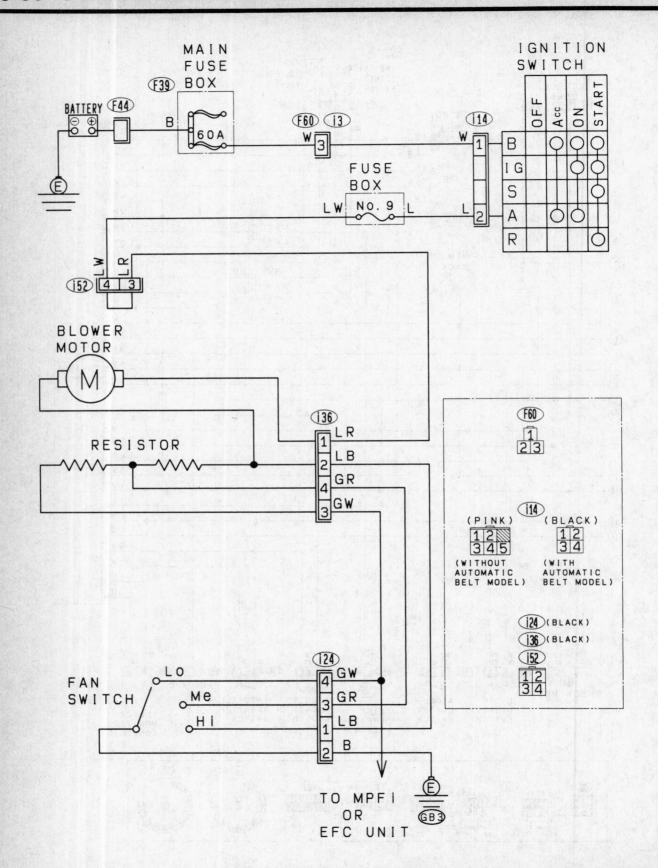

Heater fan motor — 1990–92 Justy

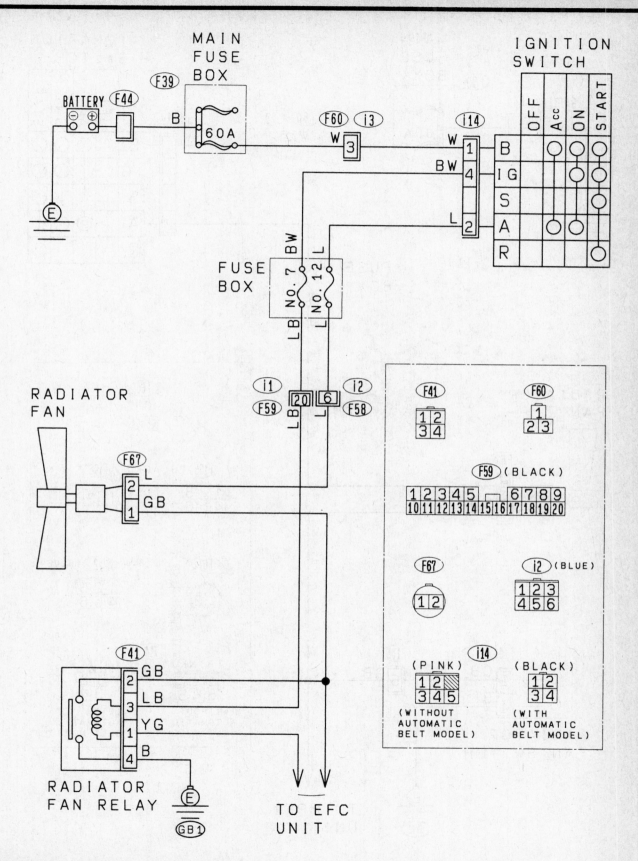

Radiator fan motor — 1990–92 Justy EFC model

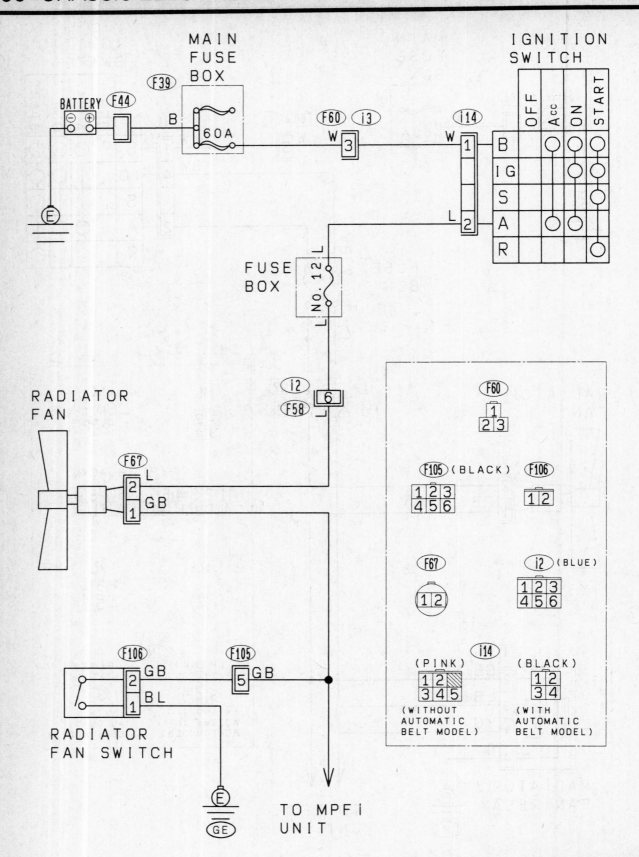

Radiator fan motor — 1990–92 Justy MPFI model

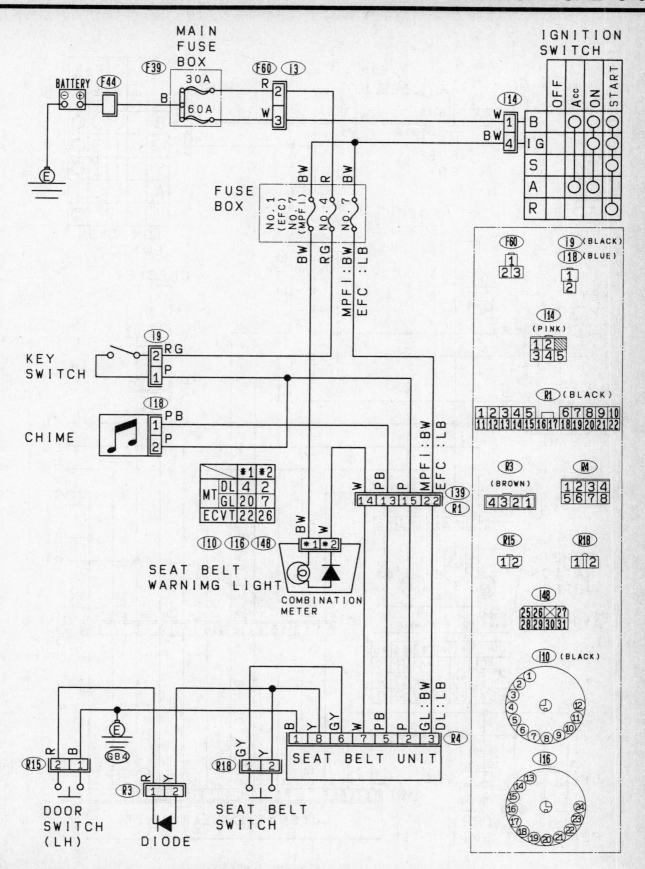

Seat belt and key warning system — 1990–92 Justy

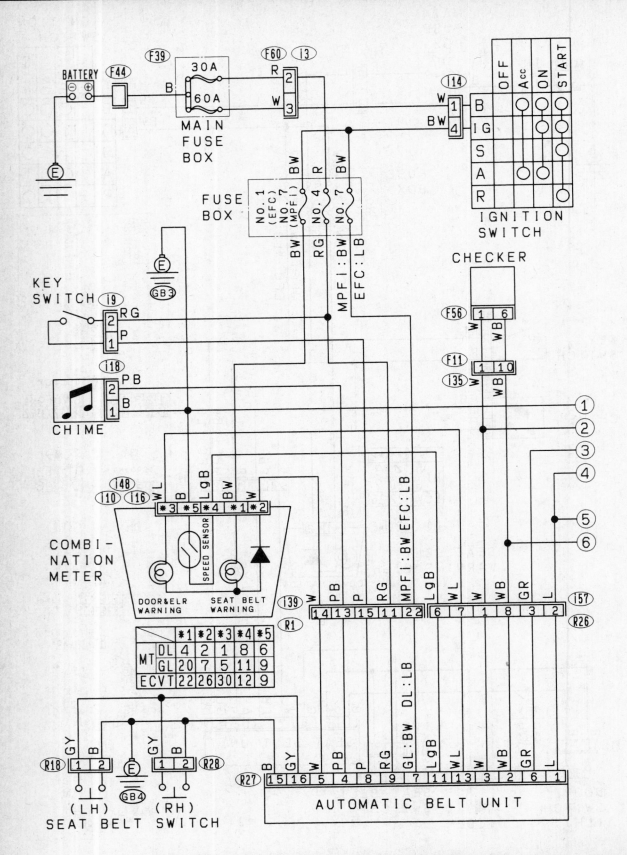

Automatic belt and key warning system — 1990–92 Justy

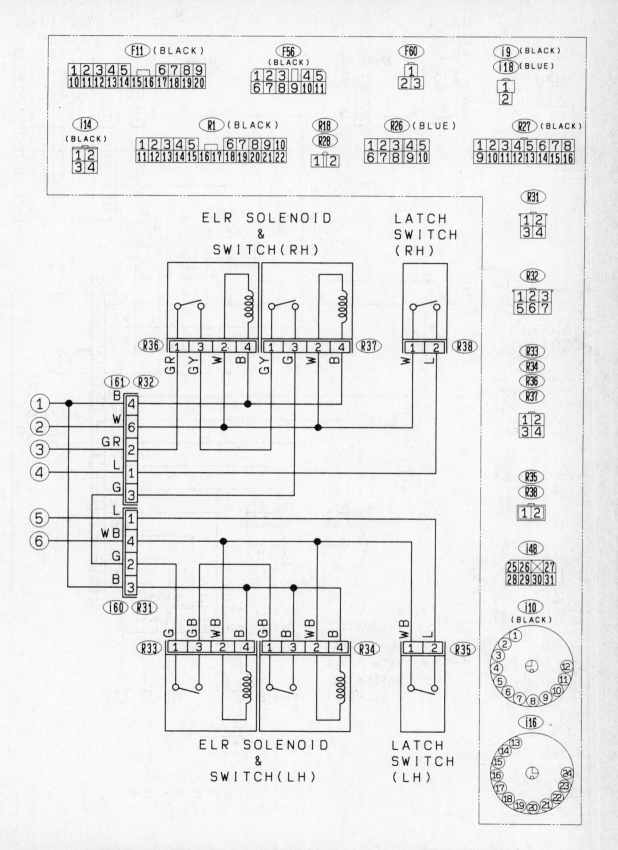

Automatic belt and key warning system — 1990–92 Justy continued

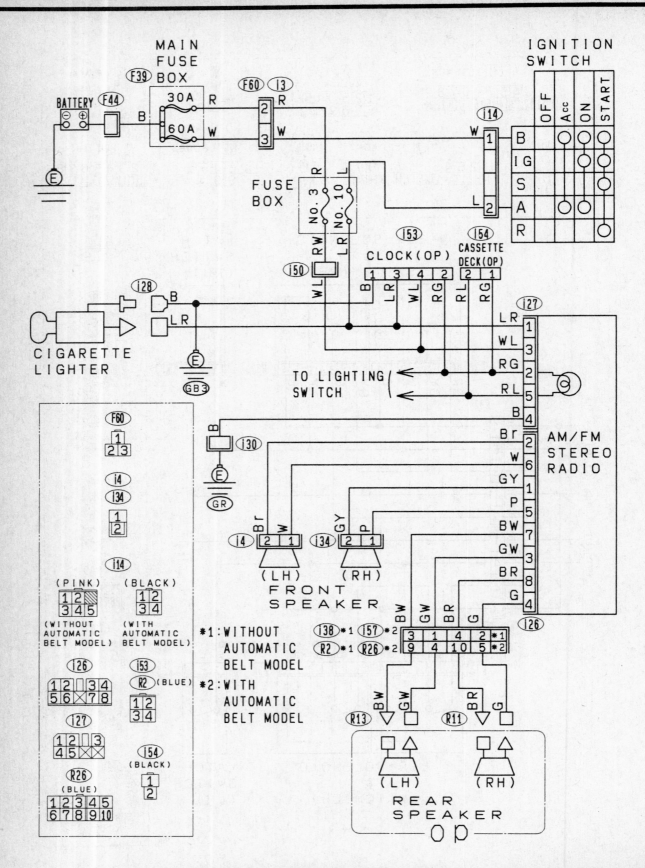

Radio and cigarette lighter — 1990–92 Justy

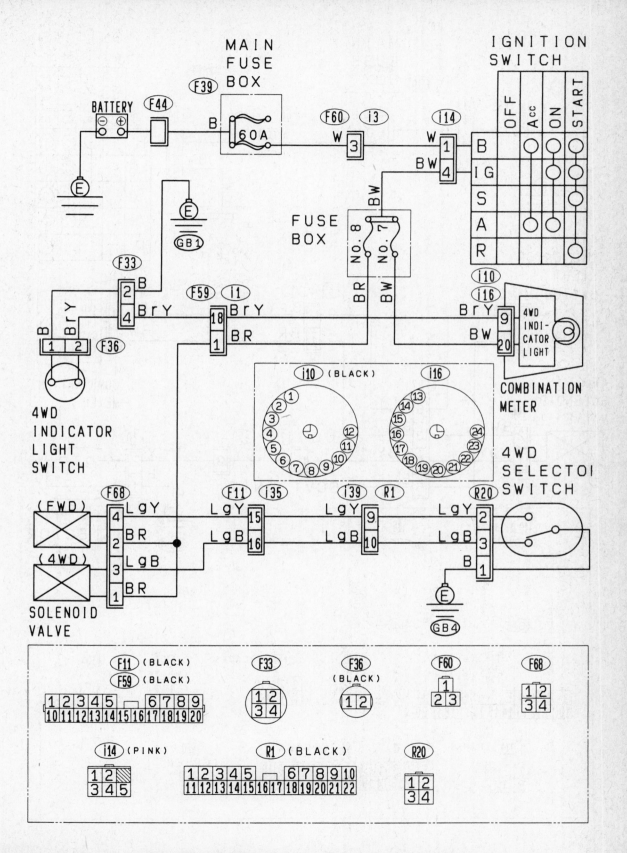

4WD manual transmission system — 1990–92 Justy

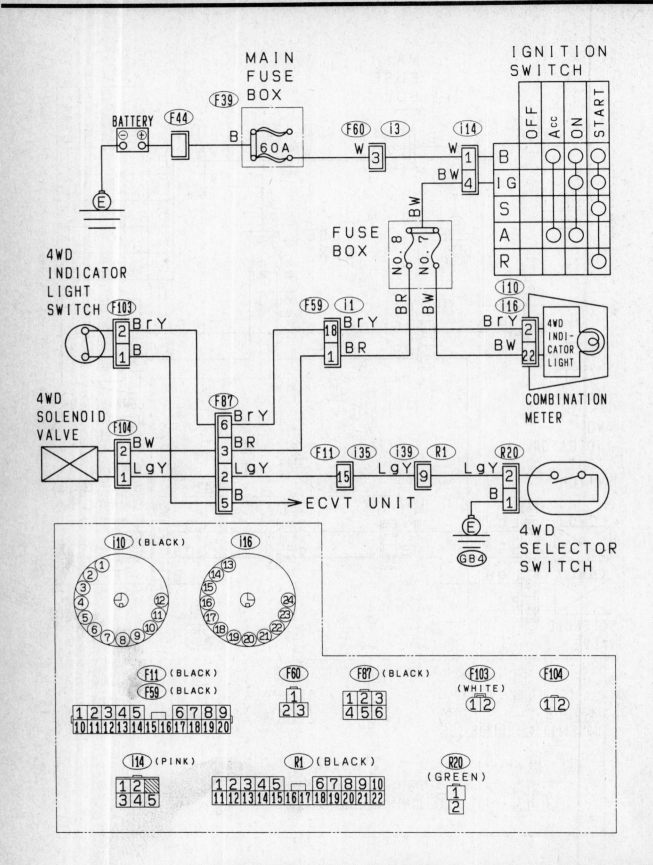

4WD ECVT system — 1990–92 Justy

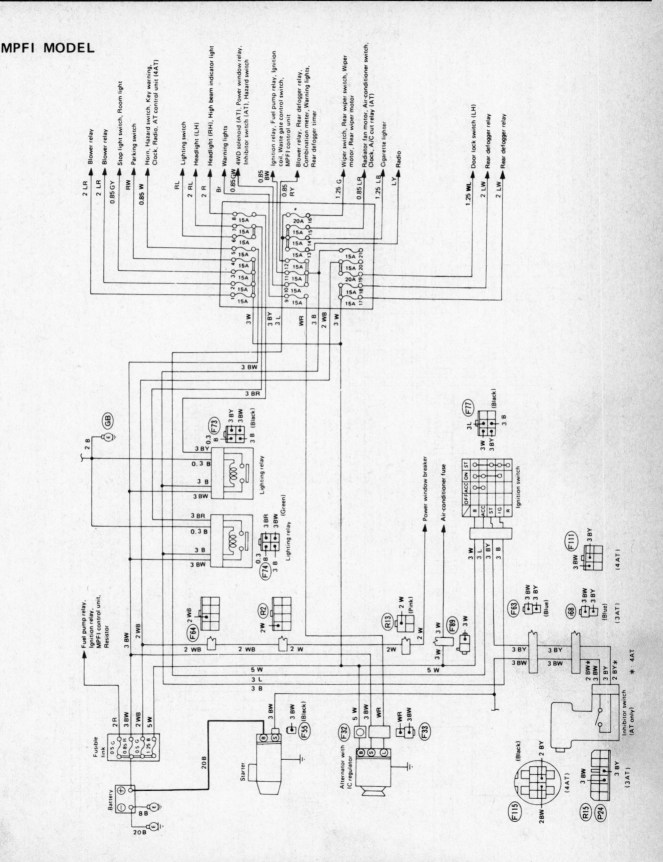

MPFI MODEL

Power supply routing — 1990–92 Loyale MPFI

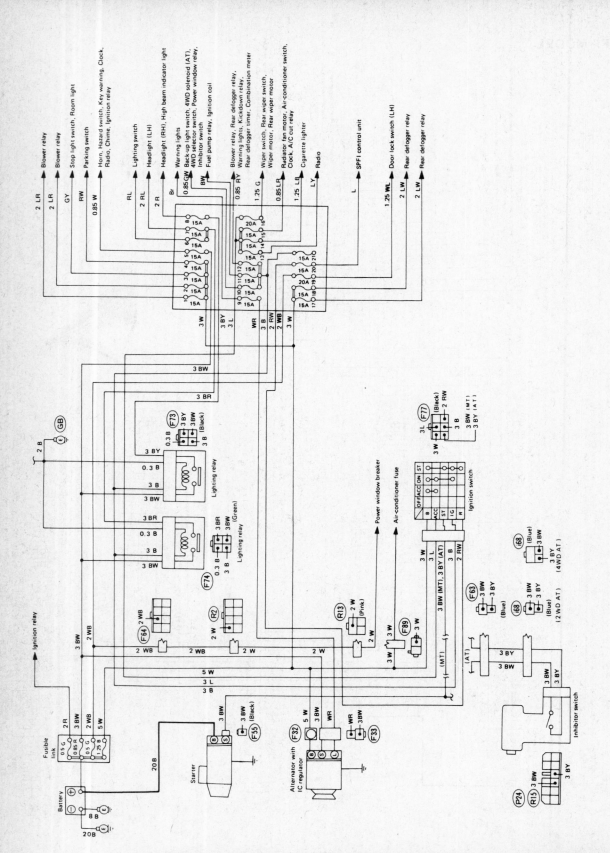

Power supply routing — 1990–92 Loyale SPFI

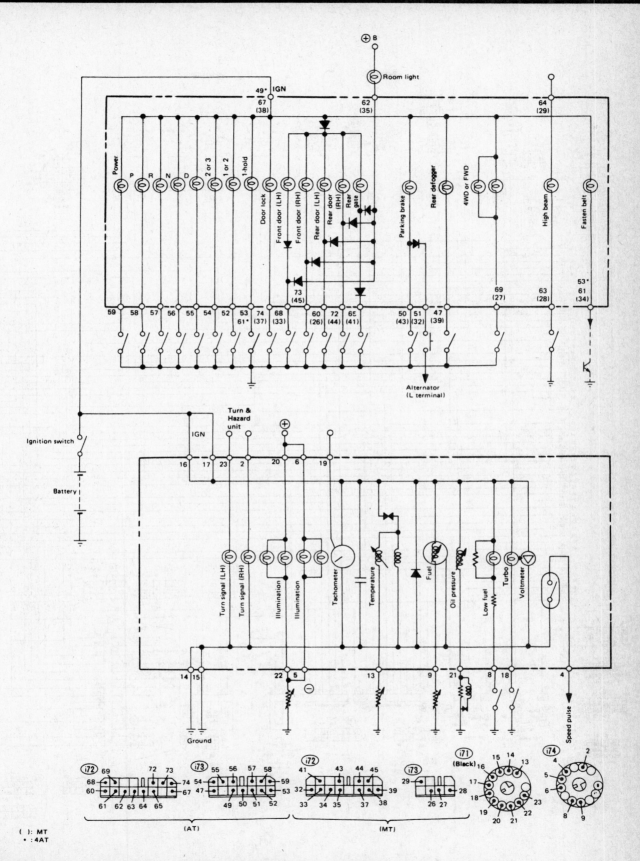

Instrument panel wiring — 1990–92 Loyale

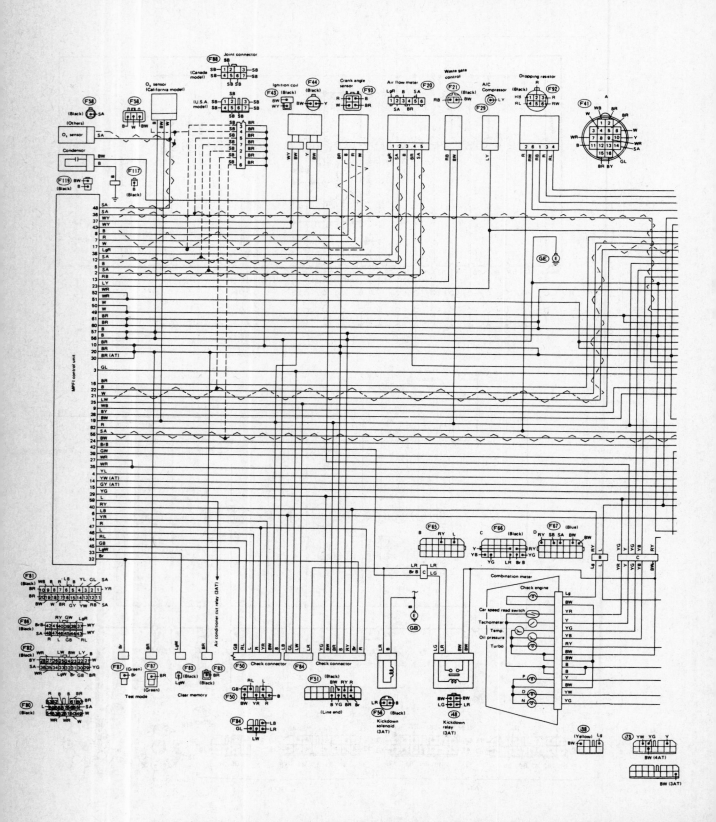

Engine electrical system — 1990–92 Loyale SPFI

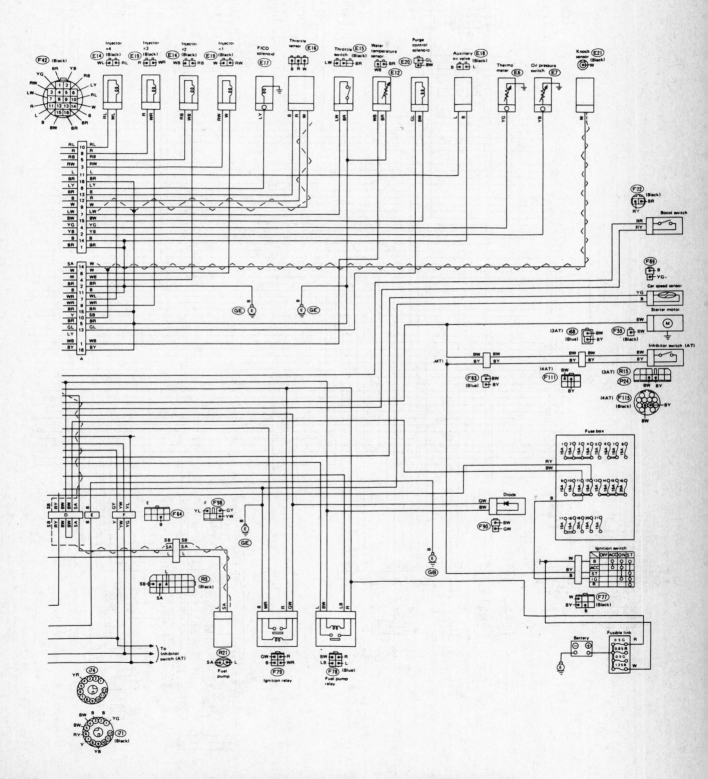

Engine electrical system — 1990–92 Loyale SPFI

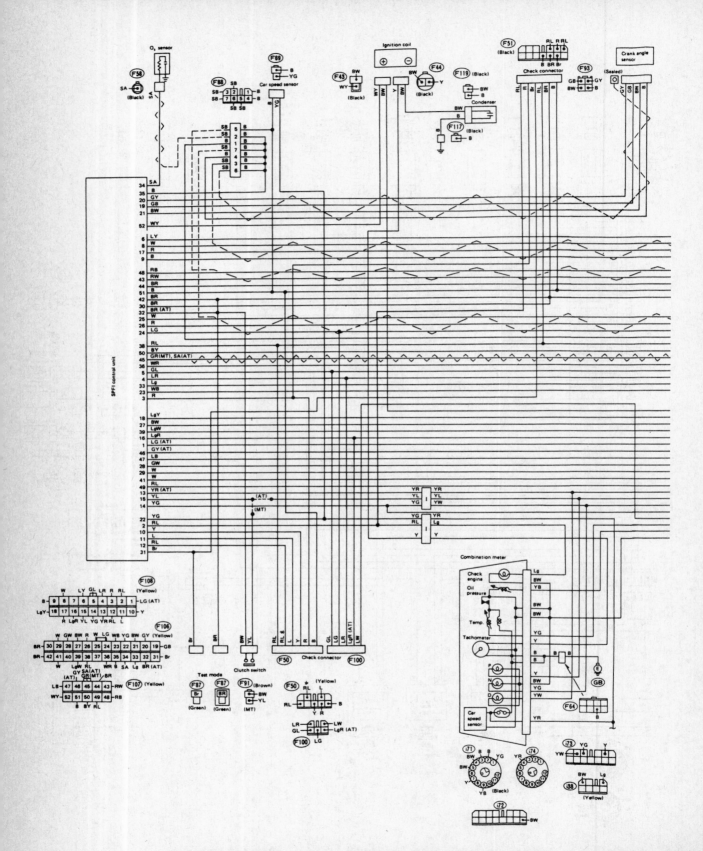

Engine electrical system — 1990–92 Loyale MPFI

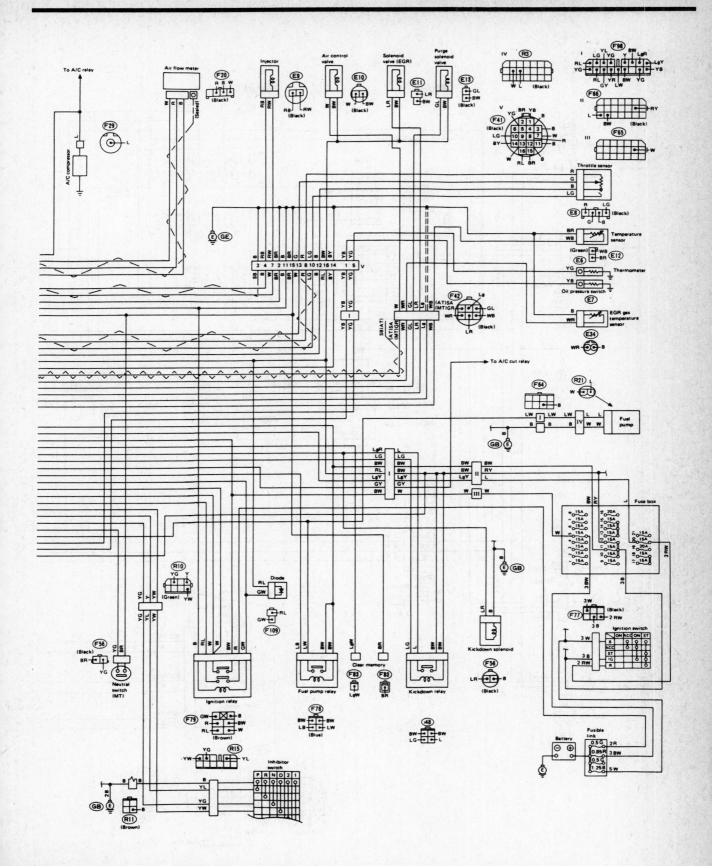

Engine electrical system — 1990–92 Loyale MPFI continued

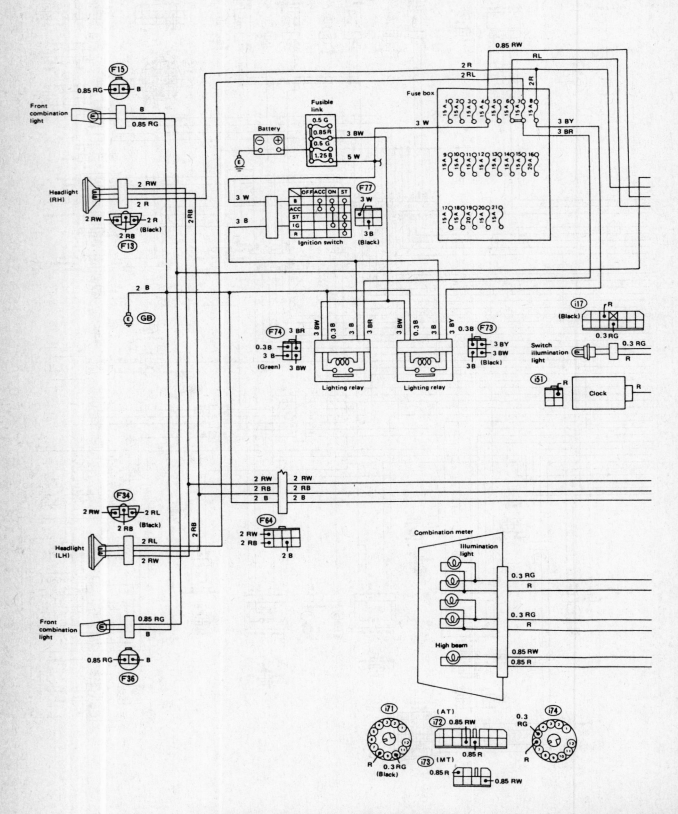

Lighting system wiring — 1990–92 Loyale

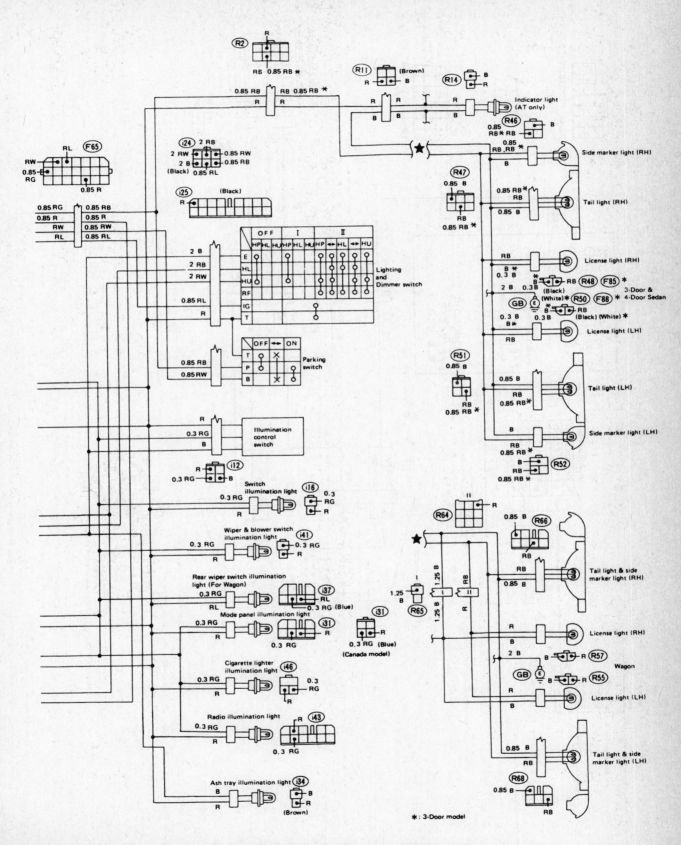

Lighting system wiring — 1990–92 Loyale

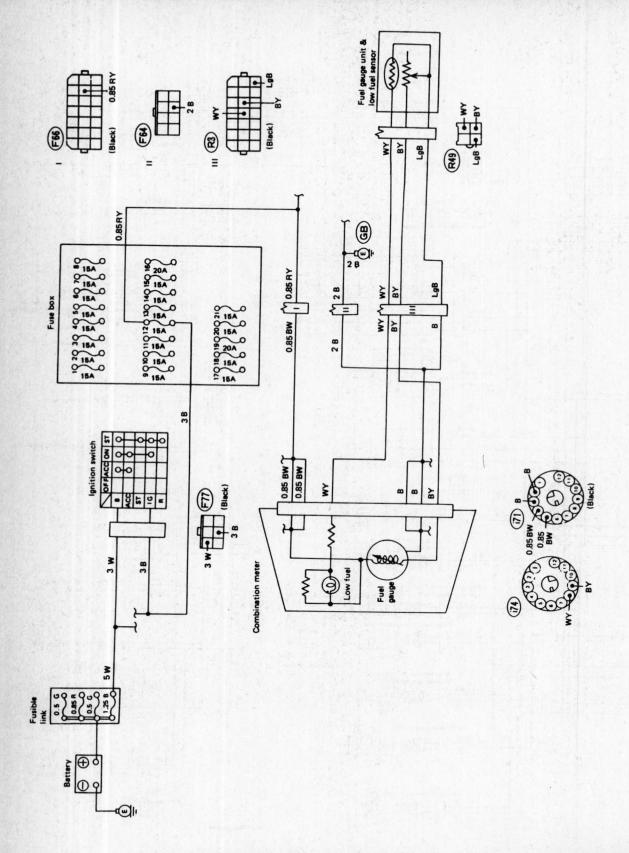

Fuel gauge wiring — 1990–92 Loyale

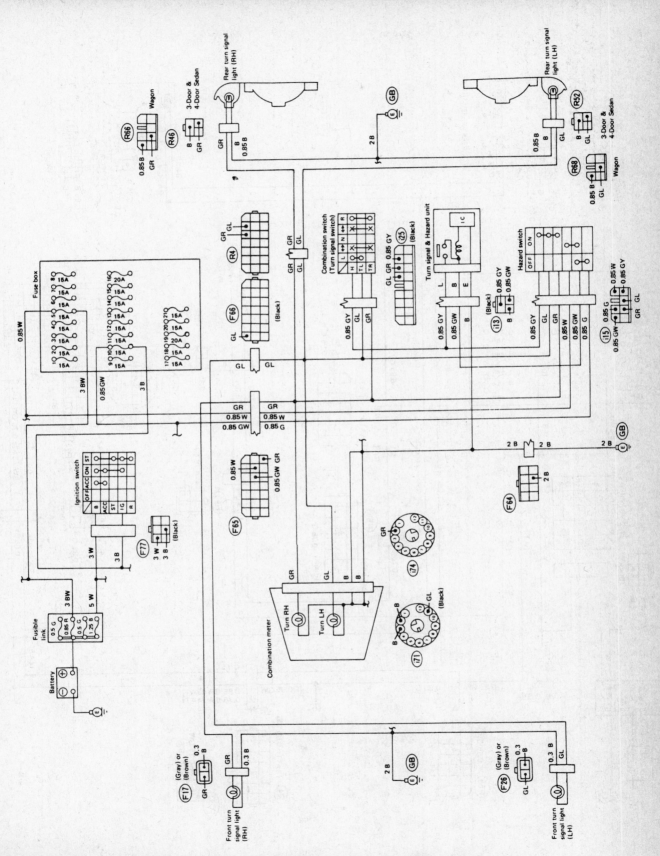

Turn signal and hazard warning light — 1990–92 Loyale

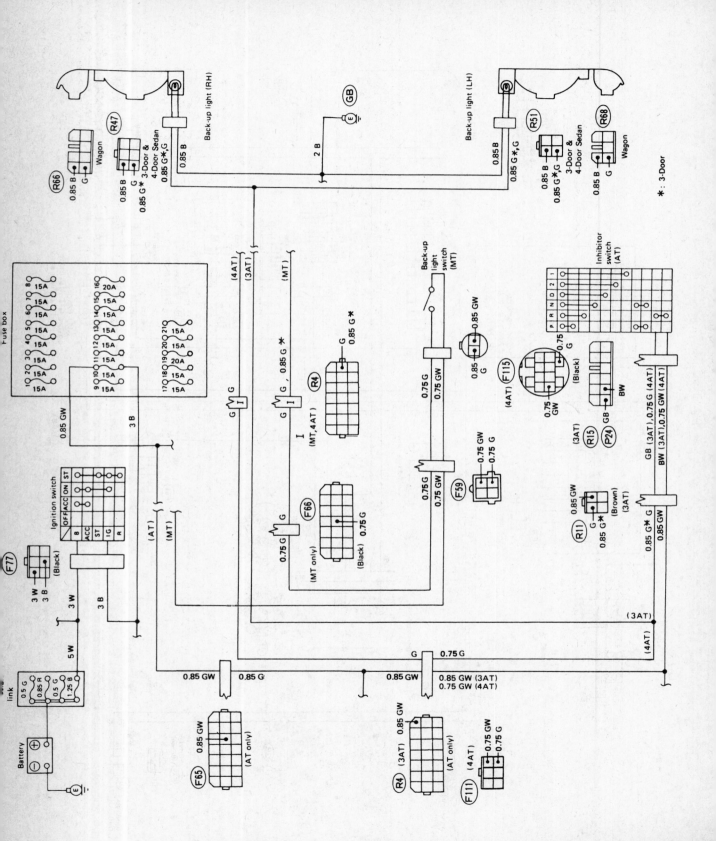

Backup light wiring — 1990–92 Loyale

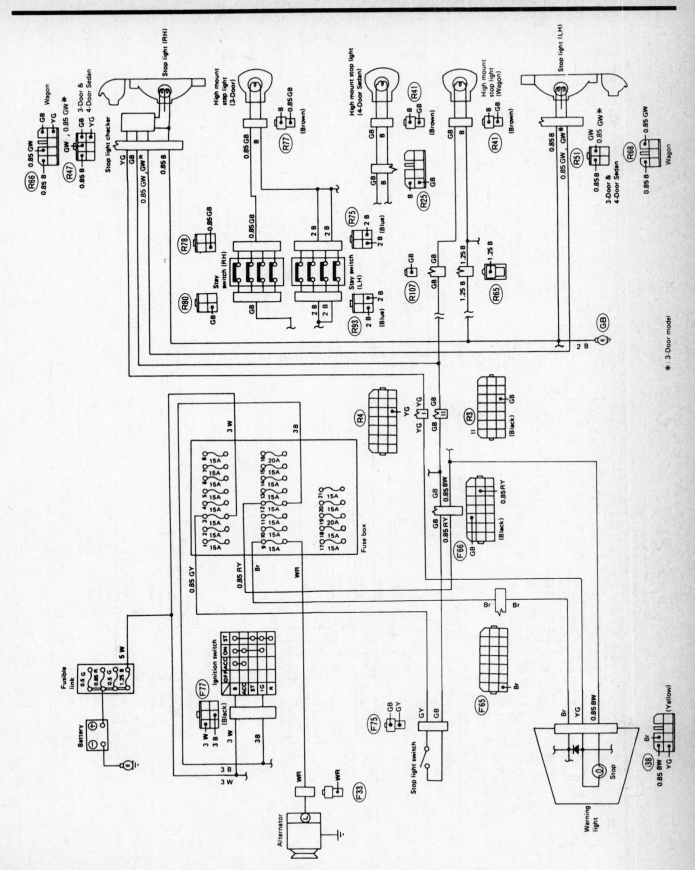

Stop light wiring — 1990–92 Loyale

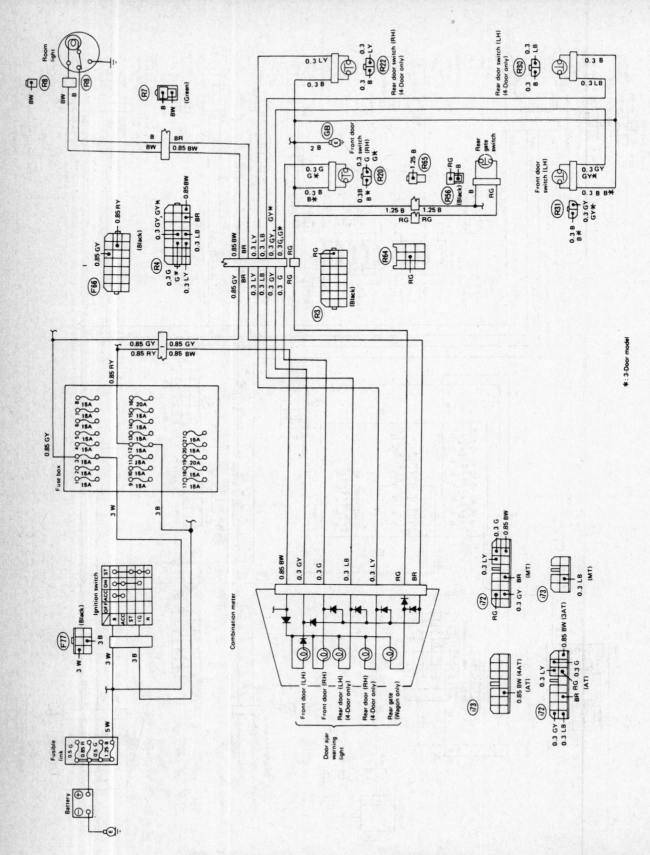

Room light and door switch — 1990–92 Loyale

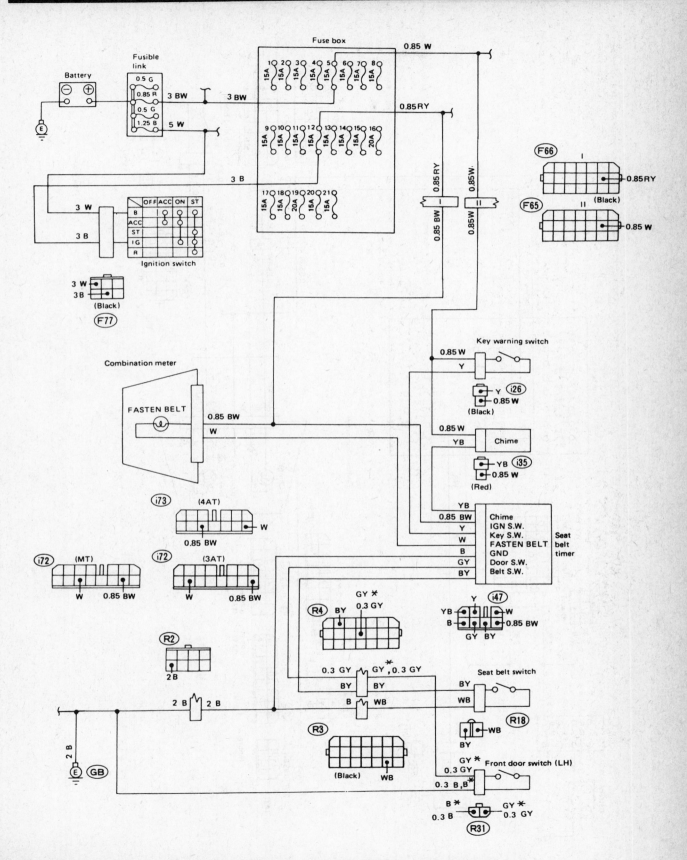

Seat belt and key warning system — 1990–92 Loyale

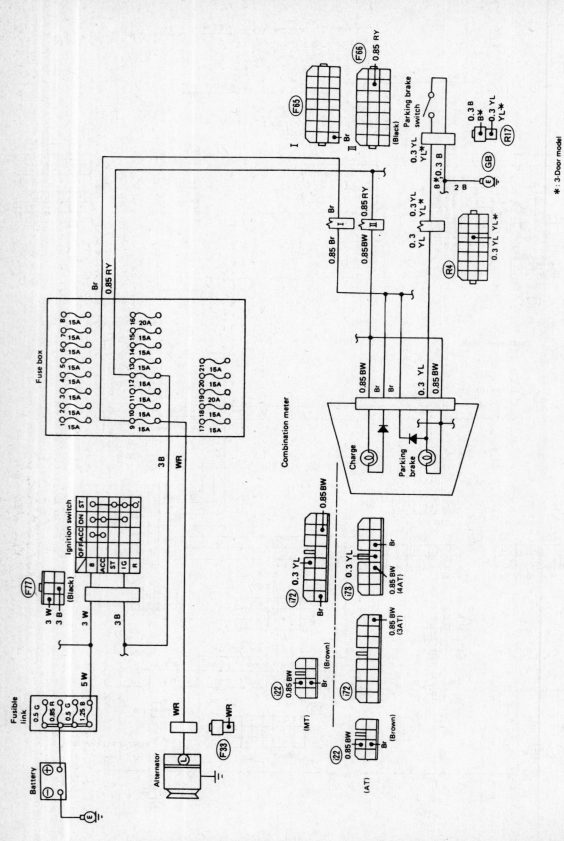

Park brake warning system — 1990–92 Loyale

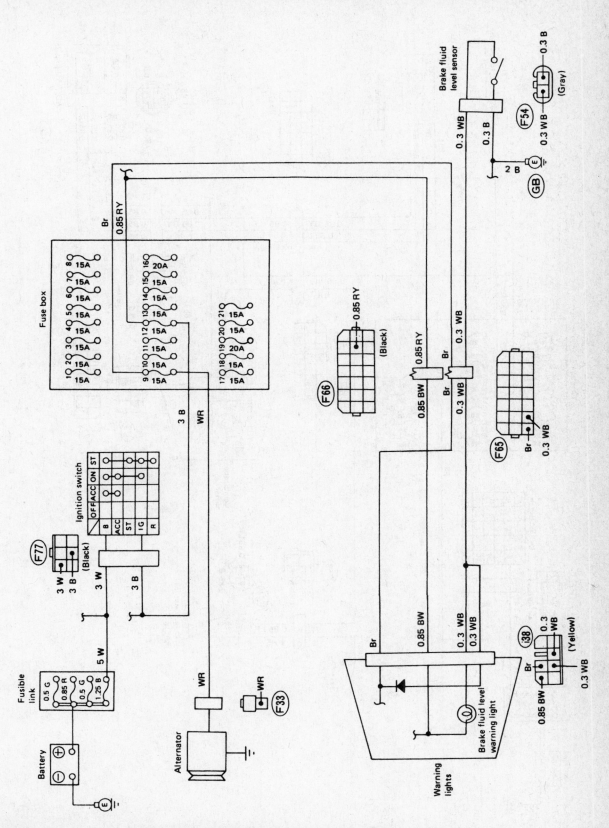

Brake fluid level warning system — 1990–92 Loyale

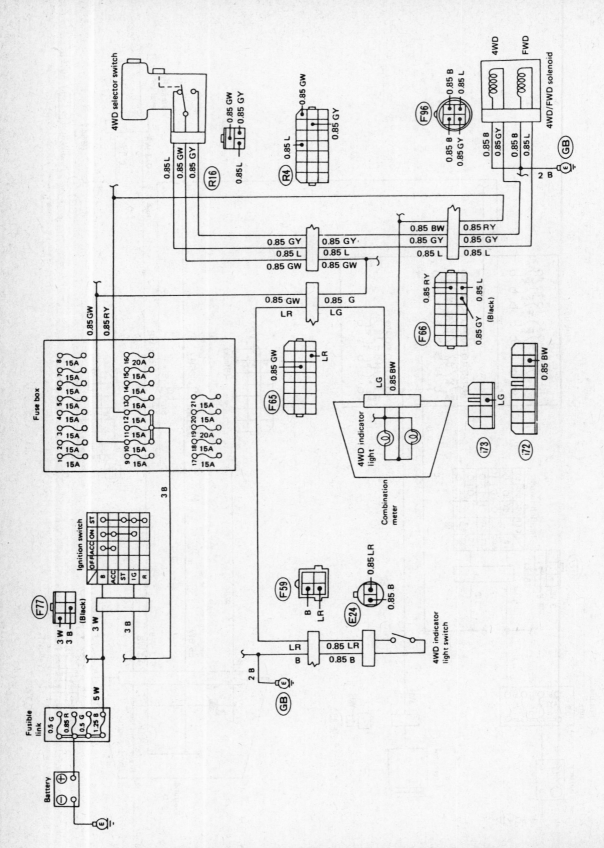

4WD manual transmission control system — 1990–92 Loyale

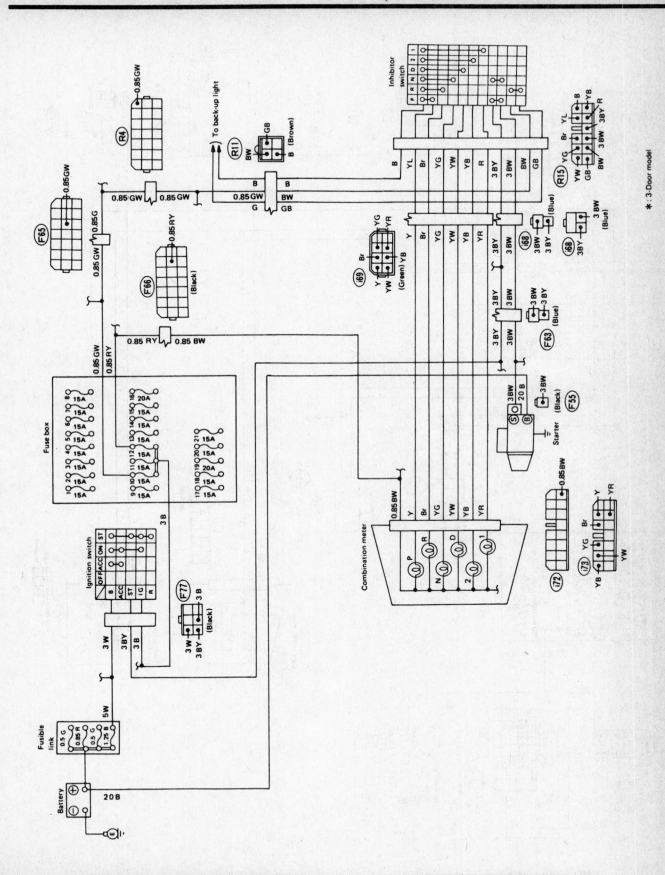

Automatic transmission shift indicator system — 1990-92 Loyale 3 speed model

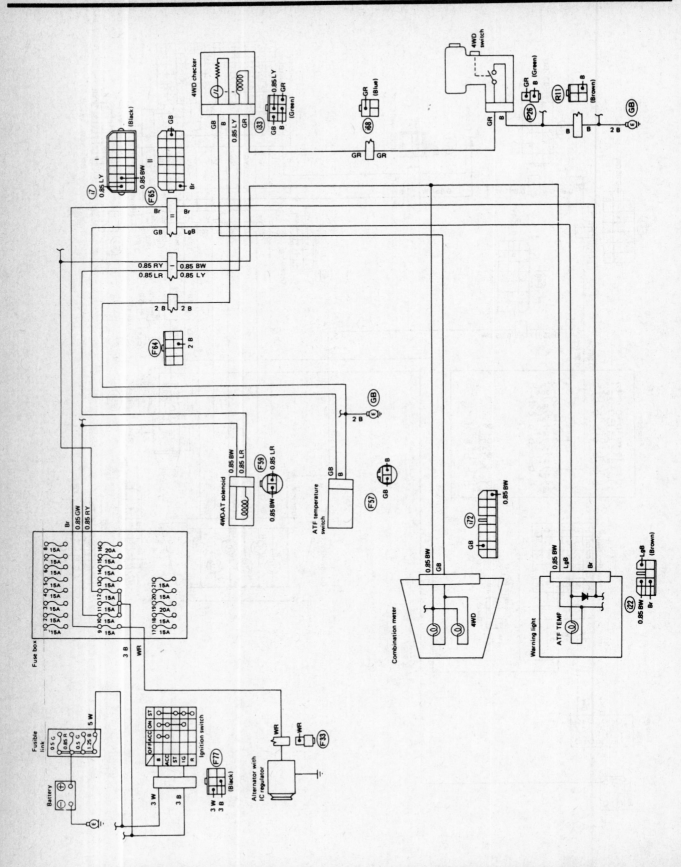

4WD automatic transmission control system — 1990– 92 Loyale 3 speed model

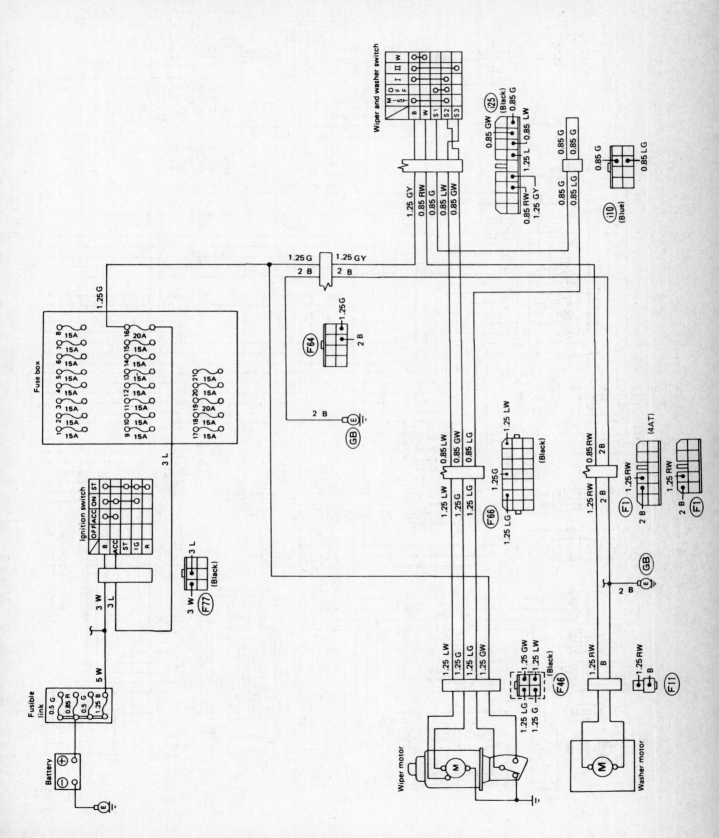

Windshield wiper and washer — 1990–92 Loyale

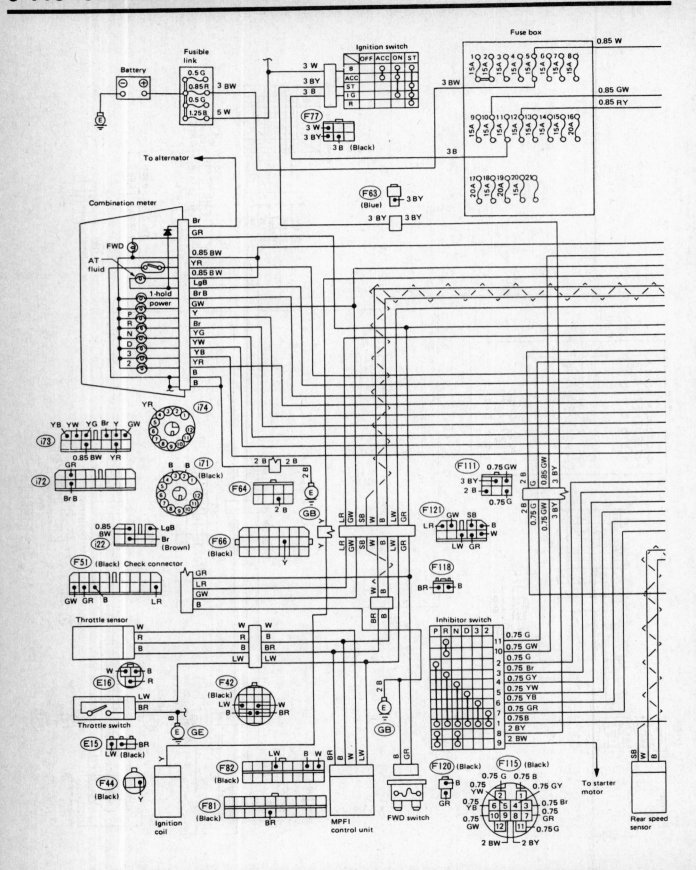

4WD automatic transmission control system — 1990–92 Loyale 4 speed model

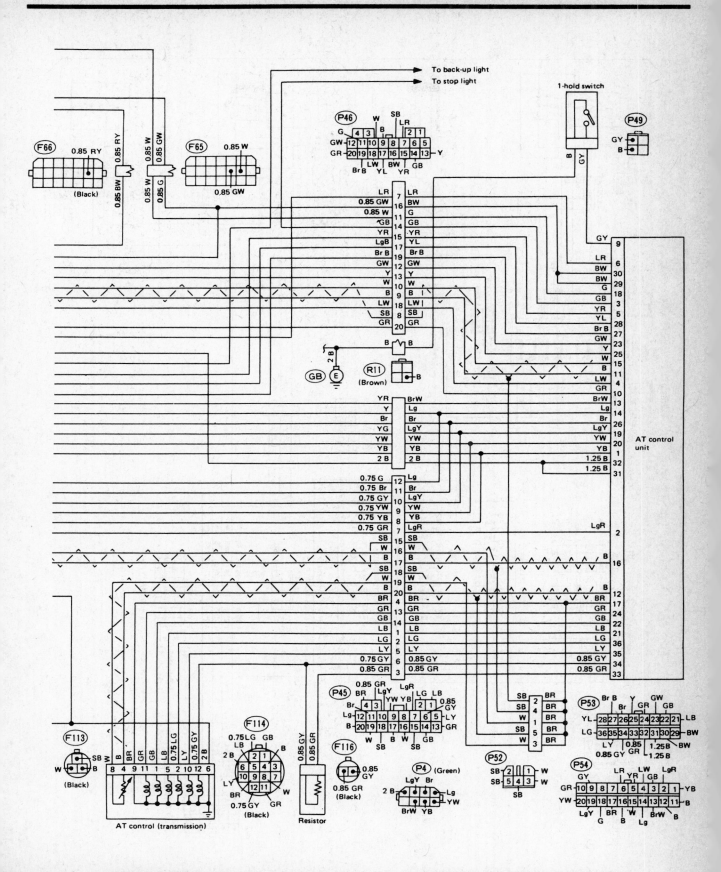

4WD automatic transmission control system — 1990–92 Loyale 4 speed model

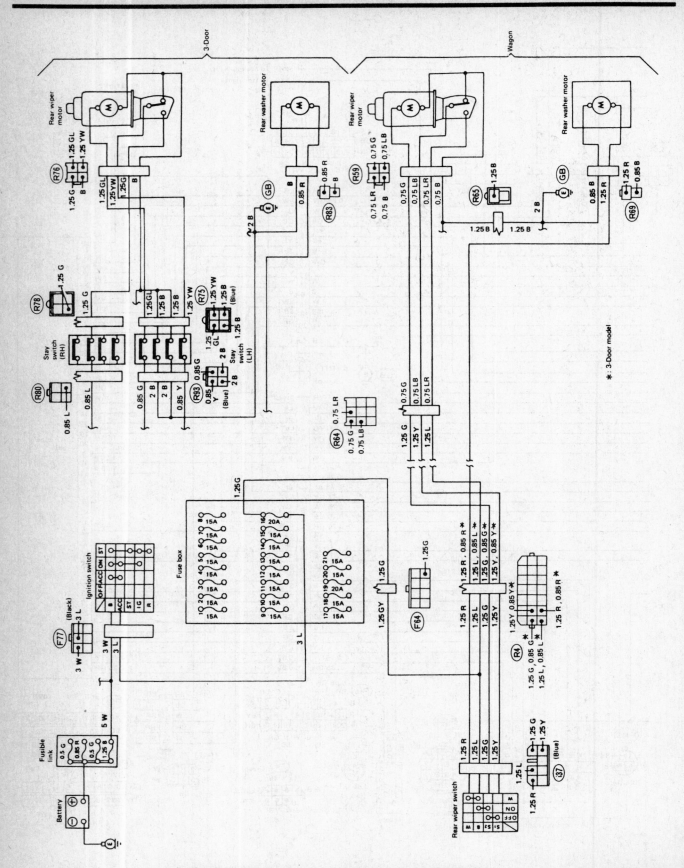

Rear window wiper and washer — 1990–92 Loyale

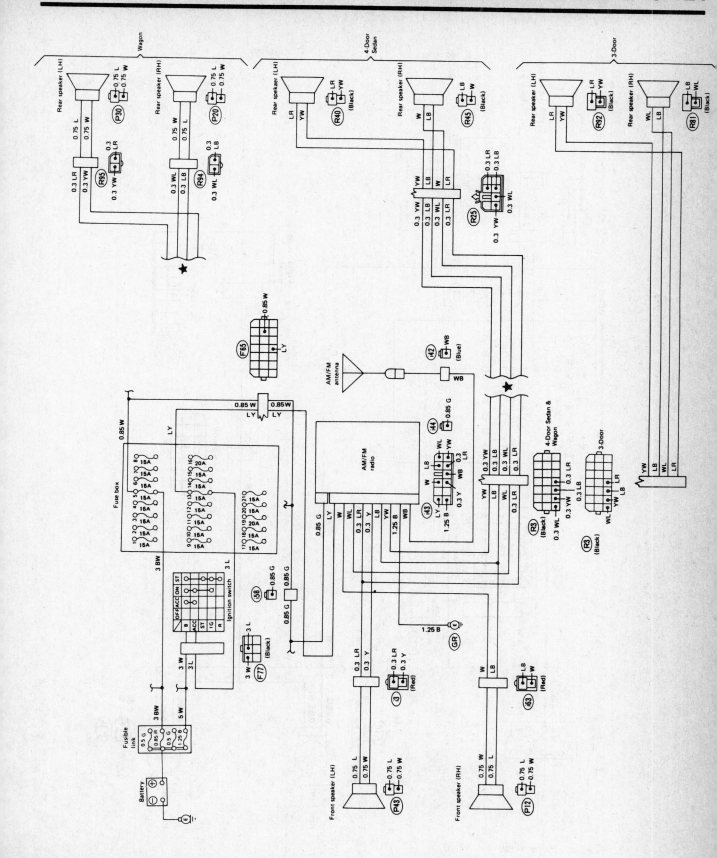

Radio wiring — 1990–92 Loyale

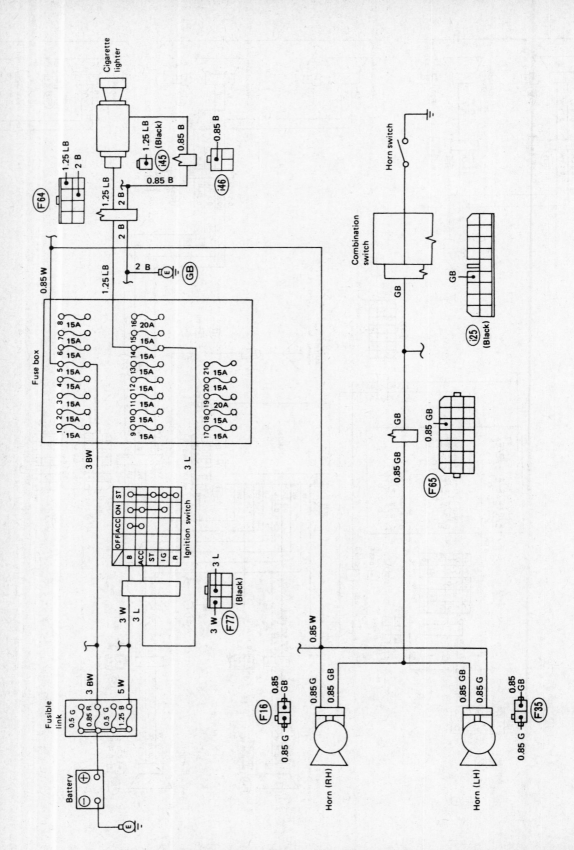

Horn and cigarette lighter — 1990–92 Loyale

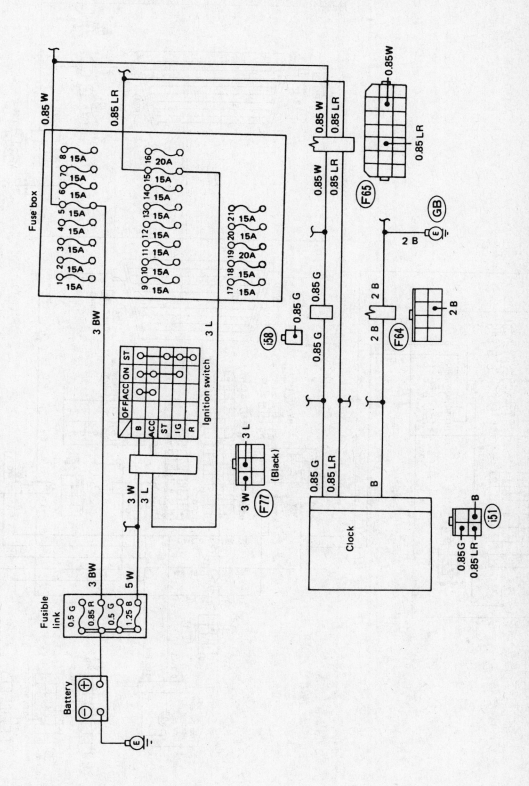

Clock wiring — 1990–92 Loyale

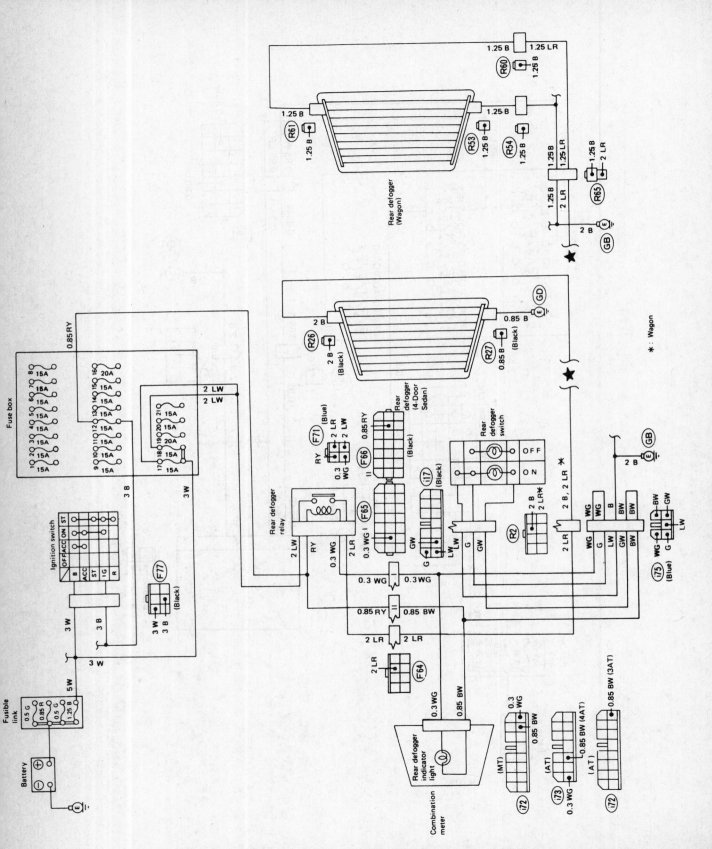

Rear window defogger — 1990–92 Loyale except 3 door

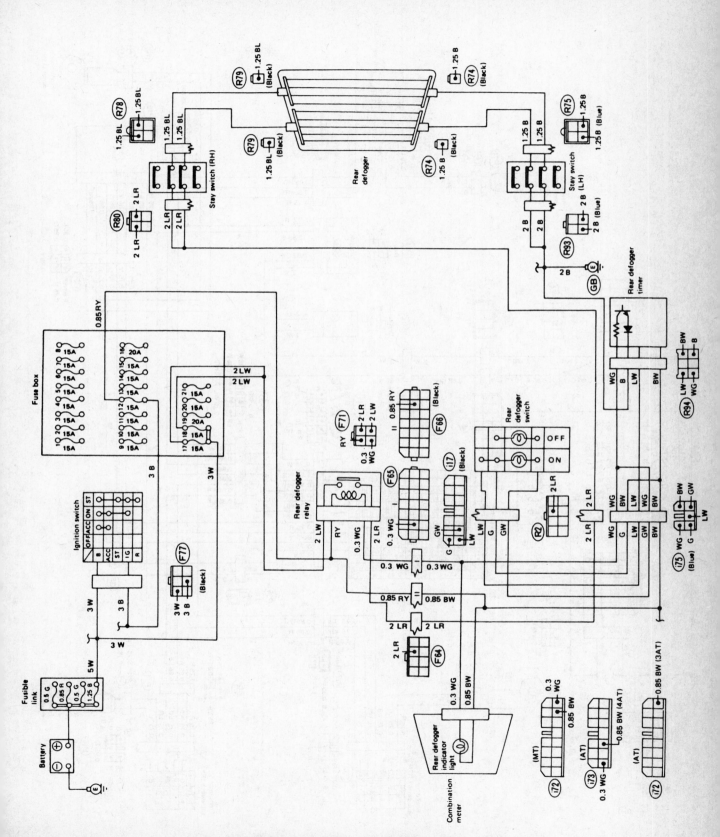

Rear window defogger — 1990–92 Loyale 3 door

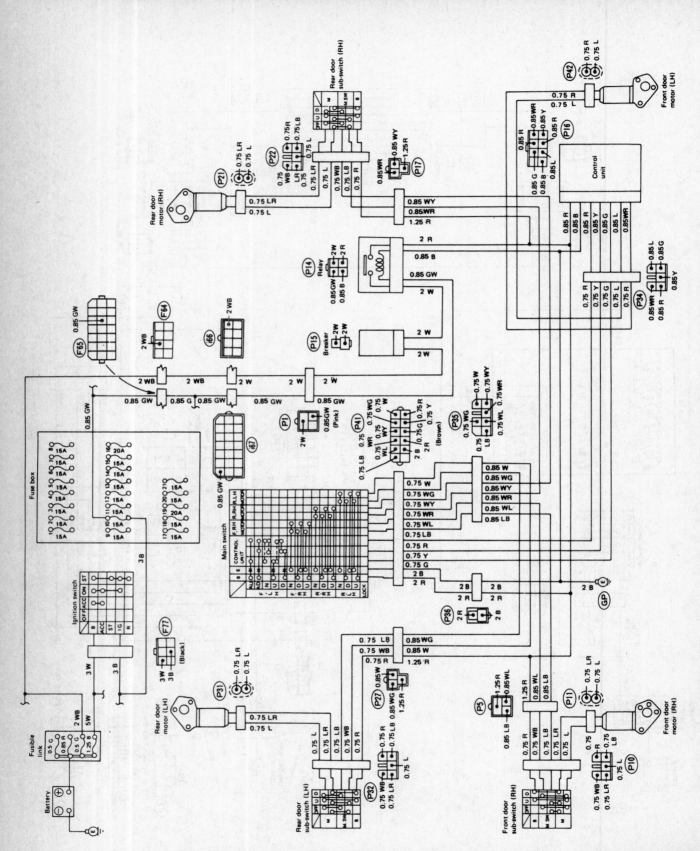

Power window — 1990–92 Loyale sedan and wagon

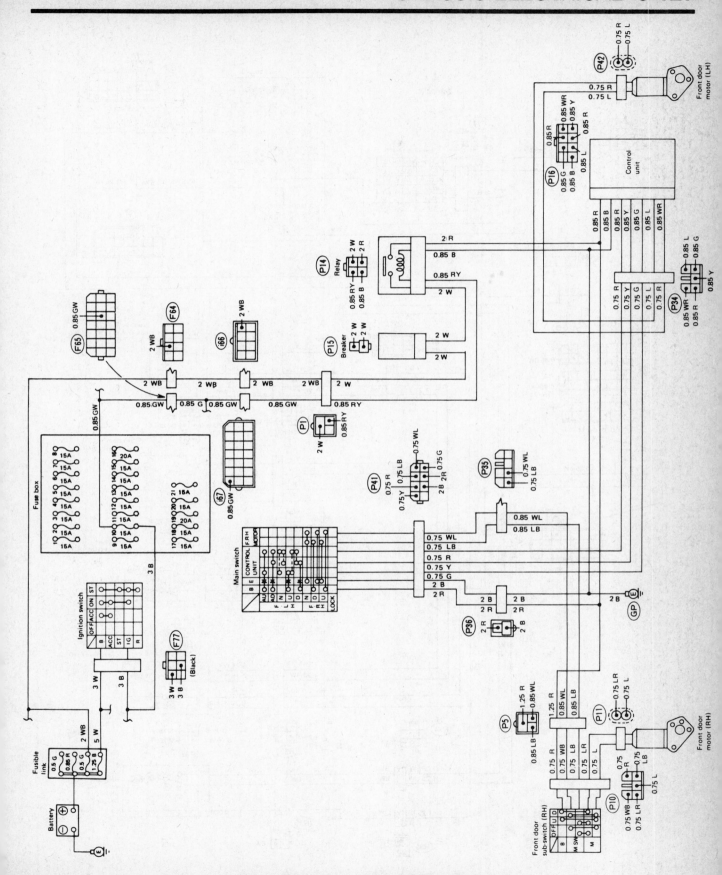

Power window — 1990–92 Loyale 3 door

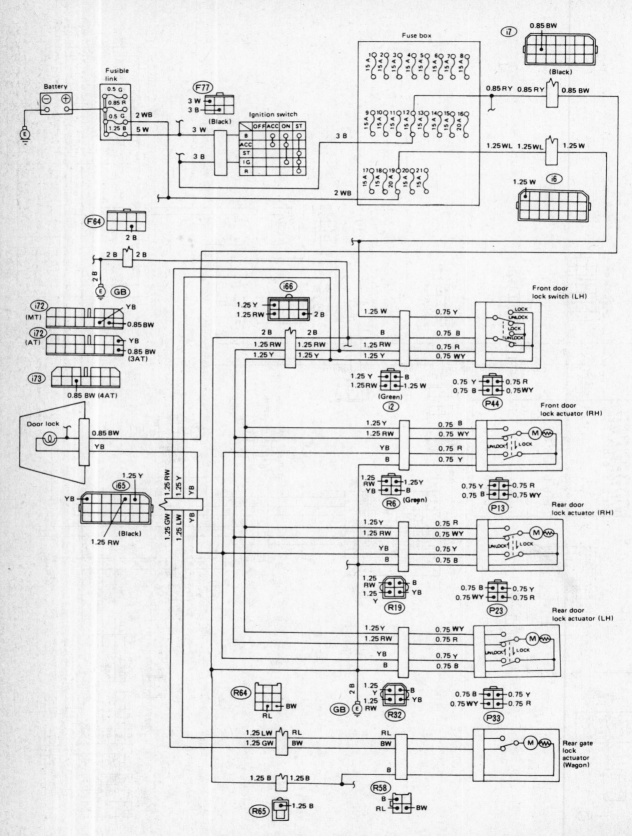

Door lock system — 1990–92 Loyale

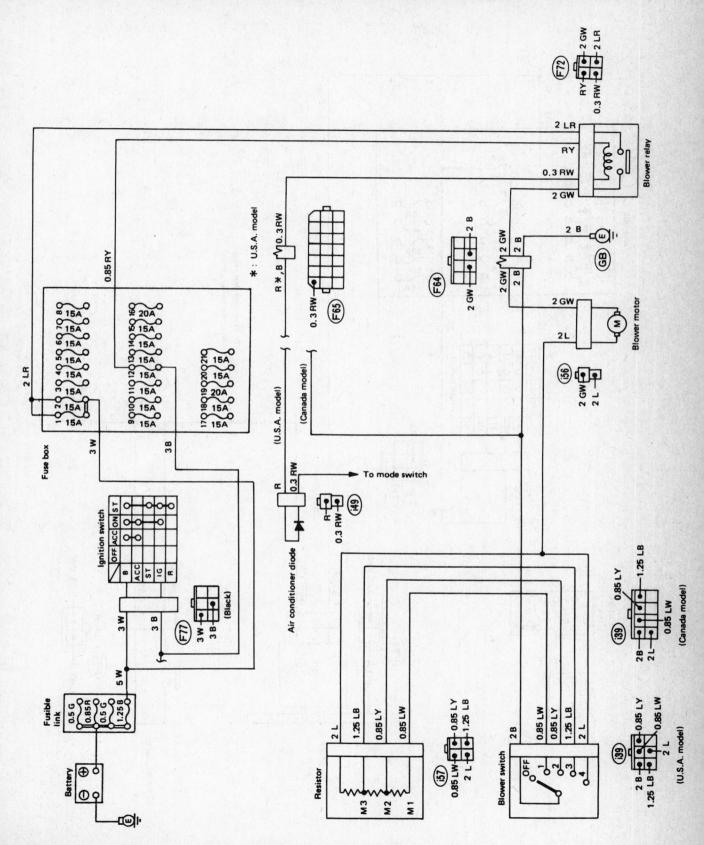

Blower motor — 1990–92 Loyale

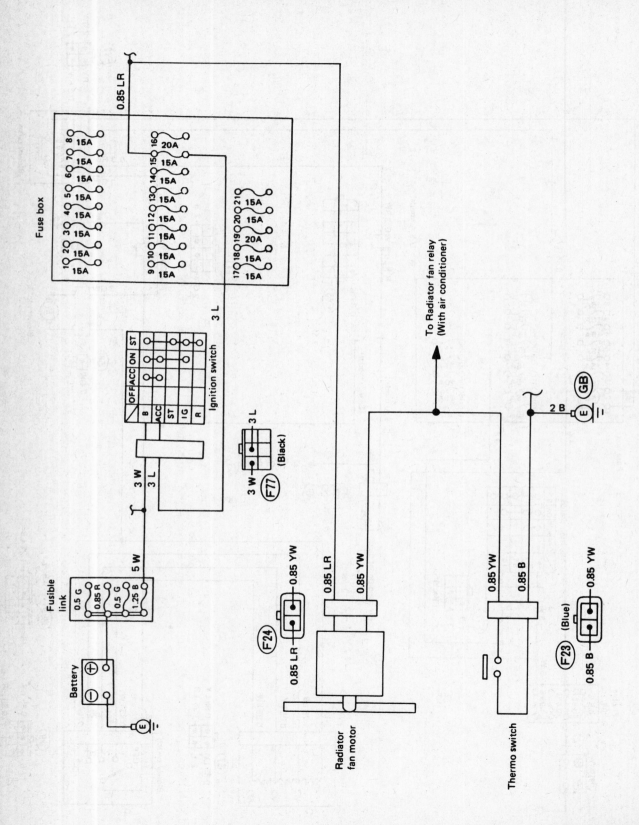

Radiator fan motor — 1990–92 Loyale

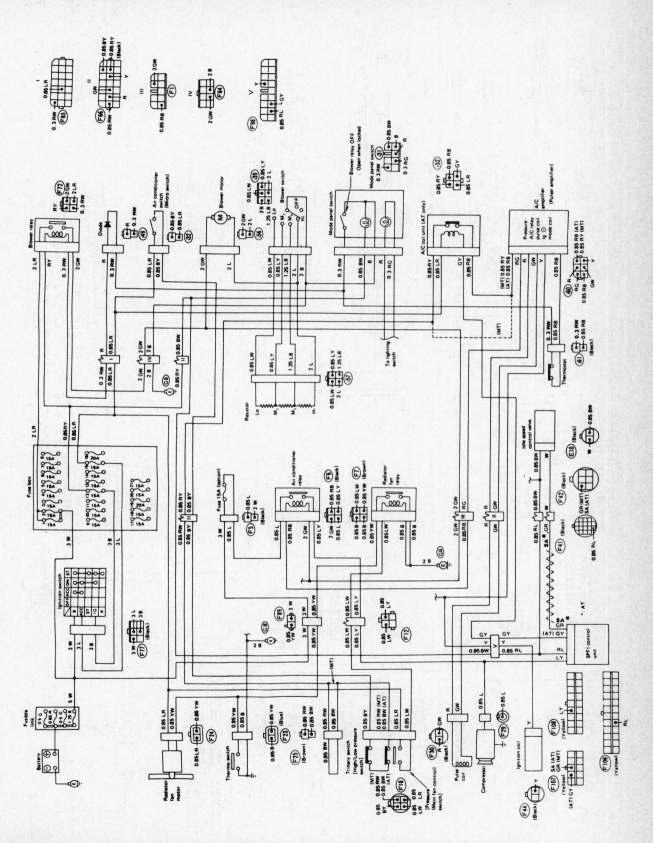

Hitachi air conditioning system (USA) — 1990–92 Loyale

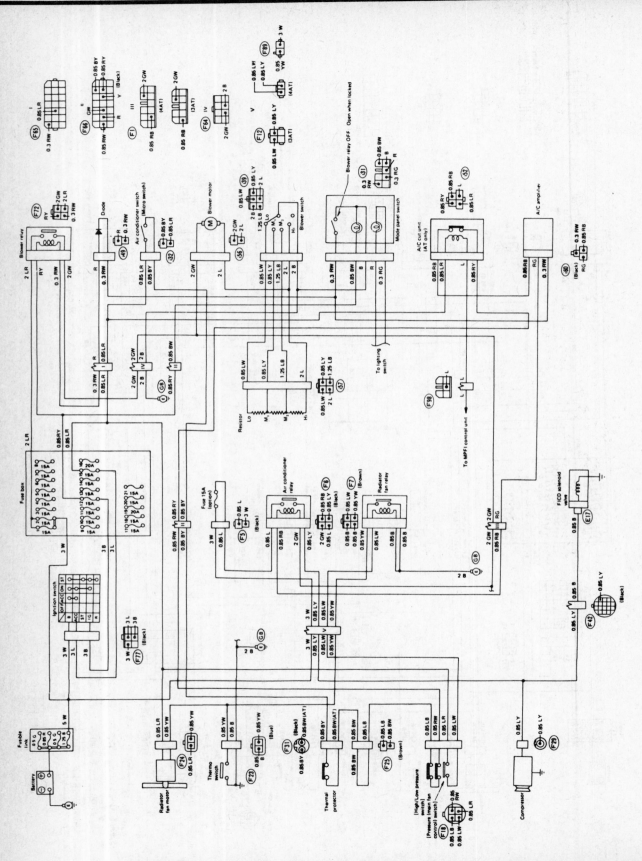

Panasonic air conditioning system (USA) — 1990–92 Loyale

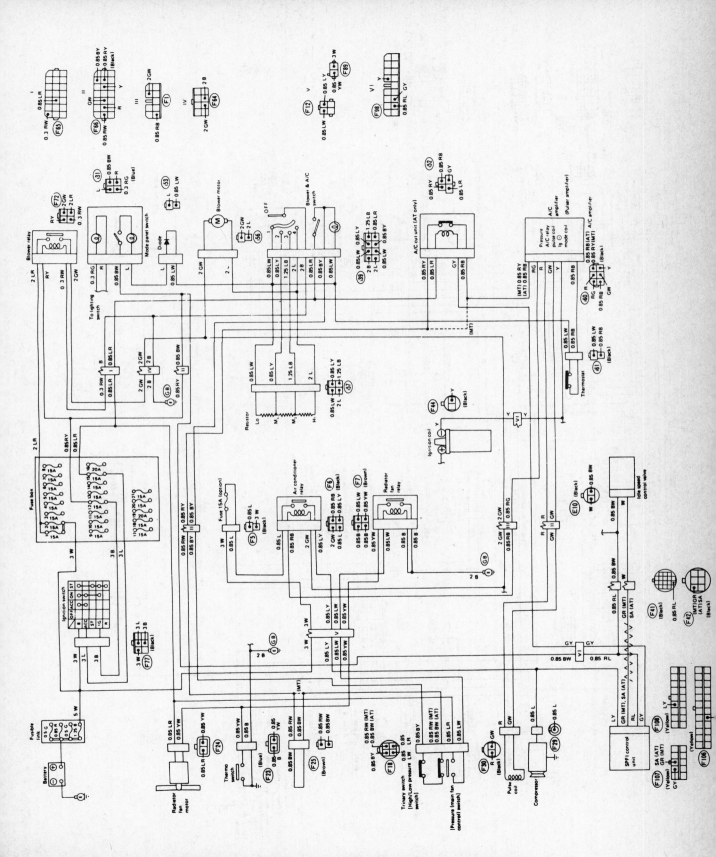

Hitachi air conditioning system (Canada) — 1990–92 Loyale

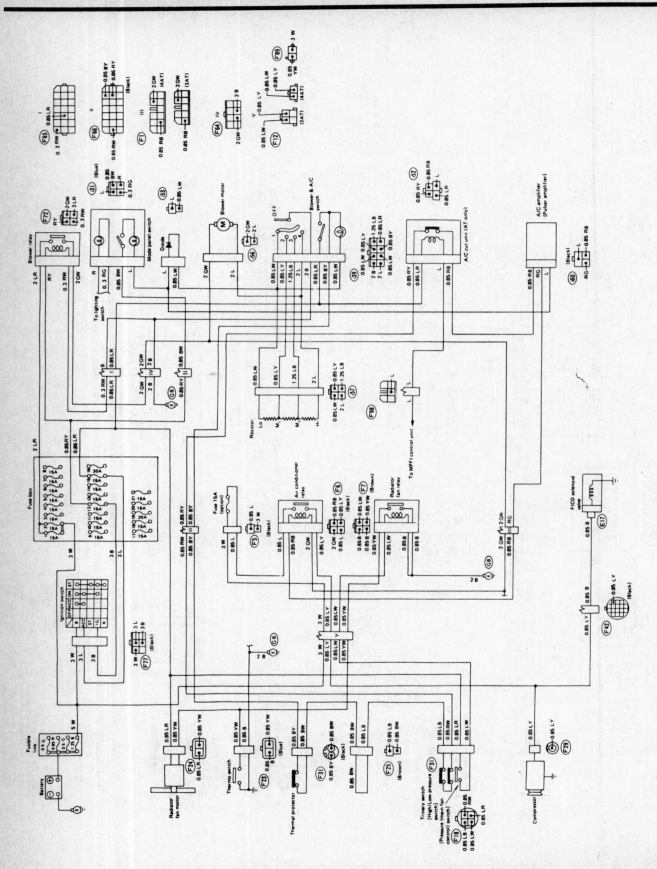

Panasonic air conditioning system (Canada) — 1990–92 Loyale

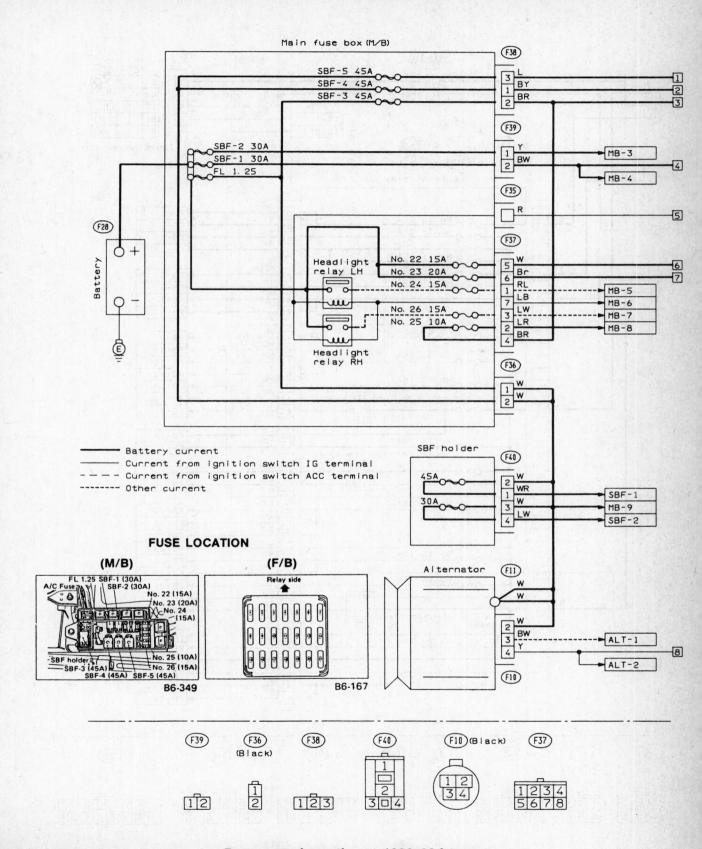

Power supply routing — 1990–92 Legacy

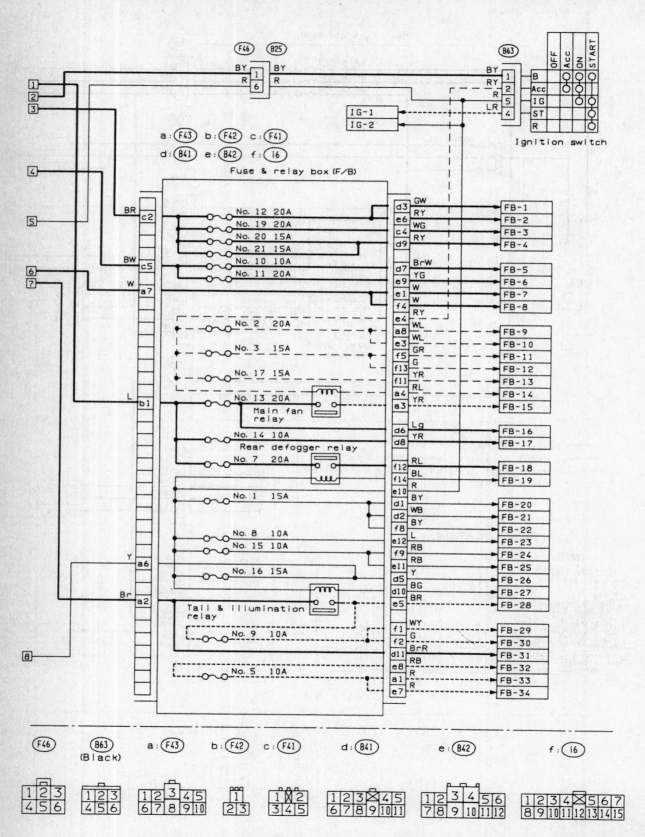

Power supply routing — 1990–92 Legacy continued

No.	Load
MB-3	Ignition relay: Fig. 27, 28 Fuel pump relay: Fig. 28 Injectors: Fig. 28
MB-4	P/W circuit breaker: Fig. 49 Automatic shoulder belt control unit: Fig. 59 Sunroof relay: Fig. 54
MB-5	Headlight LH: Fig. 30, 31
MB-6	Diode (Lighting): Fig. 30, 31 Lighting switch: Fig. 30 Daytime running light control unit: Fig. 31
MB-7	Head light RH: Fig. 30, 31 Combination meter: Fig. 30, 31
MB-8	Radio: Fig. 55 Height control unit: Fig. 58 Spot light: Fig. 54 F/B light: Fig. 33, 34 Room light (Wagon): Fig. 33, 34 Step lights: Fig. 33 Luggage room light: Fig. 33, 34 Trunk room light: Fig. 37
MB-9	A/C relay holder: Fig. 41
SBF-1	Hydraulic unit: Fig. 61
SBF-2	A/S compressor: Fig. 58
ALT-1	Combination meter: Fig. 26, 35, 45 Daytime running light control unit: Fig. 31
ALT-2	Diode (MPFI): Fig. 28
IG-1	Inhibitor switch: Fig. 27, 28, 31 Starter interlock relay: Fig. 27, 31 MPFI control unit: Fig. 28
IG-2	Daytime running light control unit: Fig. 31 Daytime running light relay: Fig. 31 Daytime running light high-beam relay: Fig. 31
FB-1	Stop and Brake switch: Fig. 35, 39, 40, 50, 61 Stop light switch: Fig. 35, 39, 40, 61
FB-2	Shift lock control unit: Fig. 40 Horn relay: Fig. 53 Condenser (Horn): Fig. 53
FB-3	Hydraulic unit: Fig. 61
FB-4	Blower motor relay: Fig. 41, 56
FB-5	A/S compressor relay: Fig. 58 A/S charge solenoid: Fig. 58 A/S discharge solenoid: Fig. 58 A/S solenoids: Fig. 58

No.	Load
FB-6	Front door lock switch LH: Fig. 51, 52
FB-7	Shift lock control unit: Fig. 40 Key warning switch: Fig. 40, 59, 61 Power antenna: Fig. 55 Automatic shoulder belt control unit: Fig. 59
FB-8	Hazard switch: Fig. 36
FB-9	Front washer motor: Fig. 42
FB-10	Front wiper motor: Fig. 42 Front wiper switch: Fig. 42 Rear washer motor: Fig. 43 Rear wiper relay: Fig. 43 Rear wiper motor: Fig. 43 Shift lock control unit: Fig. 40
FB-11	Cigarette lighter: Fig. 53
FB-12	Remote controlled rearview mirror switch: Fig. 57
FB-13	Radio: Fig. 55
FB-14	Diode (A/C): Fig. 41 A/C pressure switch: Fig. 41 MPFI control unit: Fig. 29
FB-15	A/C short connector: Fig. 29, 41 Main fan motor: Fig. 29, 41
FB-16	A/C Main fan relay: Fig. 41
FB-17	AT control unit: Fig. 39 MPFI control unit: Fig. 28
FB-18	Rear defogger switch: Fig. 44 Condenser (Rear defogger): Fig. 44 Rear defogger (Heat wire): Fig. 44
FB-19	Rear defogger switch: Fig. 44
FB-20	Inhibitor switch: Fig. 38 Back-up light switch: Fig. 38
FB-21	Shift lock control unit: Fig. 40
FB-22	Hazard switch: Fig. 36
FB-23	ABS-G sensor: Fig. 61 ABS control unit: Fig. 61 Main relay: Fig. 53 Cruise control main switch: Fig. 53

Power supply routing — 1990–92 Legacy continued

No.	Load
FB-24	Combination meter: Fig. 24, 28, 33, 34, 35, 39, 45, 46, 48, 54, 58, 59, 60, 61 Automatic shoulder belt control unit: Fig. 59 Height control switch: Fig. 58 Mode control panel: Fig. 56 Seat belt timer: 60
FB-25	P/W relay: Fig. 49 Check connector: Fig. 39, 58 Evaporation thermo switch: Fig. 41 Blower motor relay: Fig. 41, 56 Height control unit: Fig. 58 Sunroof relay: Fig. 54 Vanity mirror light: Fig. 54 FRESH/RECIRC actuator: Fig. 56
FB-26	AT control unit: Fig. 39 Fuel pump relay: Fig. 28 MPFI control unit: Fig. 28
FB-27	Lighting switch: Fig. 32
FB-28	Parking switch: Fig. 32
FB-29	Illumination lights: Fig. 32 Combination meter: Fig. 32
FB-30	Illumination control unit: Fig. 32 Illumination lights: Fig. 32
FB-31	Parking switch: Fig. 32
FB-32	Parking switch: Fig. 32
FB-33	Side marker lights: Fig. 32
FB-34	Rear combination lights (Tail light): Fig. 32 License plate lights: Fig. 32

Power supply routing — 1990–92 Legacy continued

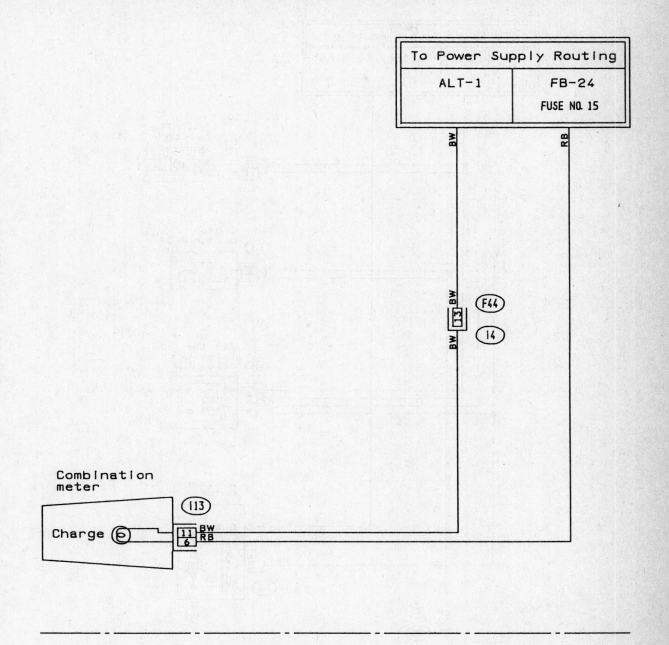

```
┌─────────────────────────────────┐
│   To Power Supply Routing       │
├──────────────┬──────────────────┤
│   ALT-1      │   FB-24          │
│              │   FUSE NO. 15    │
└──────────────┴──────────────────┘
```

BW · RB

BW · i3 · (F44) · BW · (i4)

Combination
meter

Charge (C) · (i13) · 11 6 · BW RB

(i13)   (F44)

```
┌─┬─┬─┬─┬─┬─┬─┬─┬─┬──┬──┬──┐
│1│2│3│4│5│6│7│8│9│10│11│12│
└─┴─┴─┴─┴─┴─┴─┴─┴─┴──┴──┴──┘
```

```
┌─┬─┬─┬─┬──┬──┬──┬──┐
│1│2│3│4│ │5│6│7│8│
├─┼──┼──┼──┼──┼──┼──┼──┤
│9│10│11│12│13│14│15│16│17│
└─┴──┴──┴──┴──┴──┴──┴──┘
```

Charging system — 1990–92 Legacy

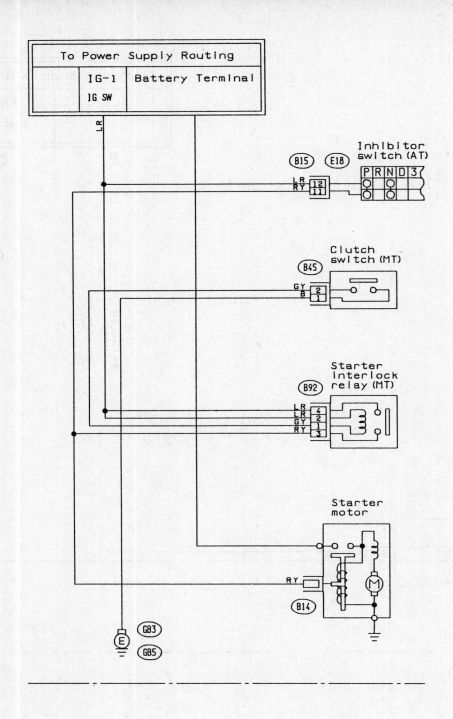

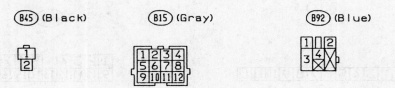

Starting system — 1990–92 Legacy

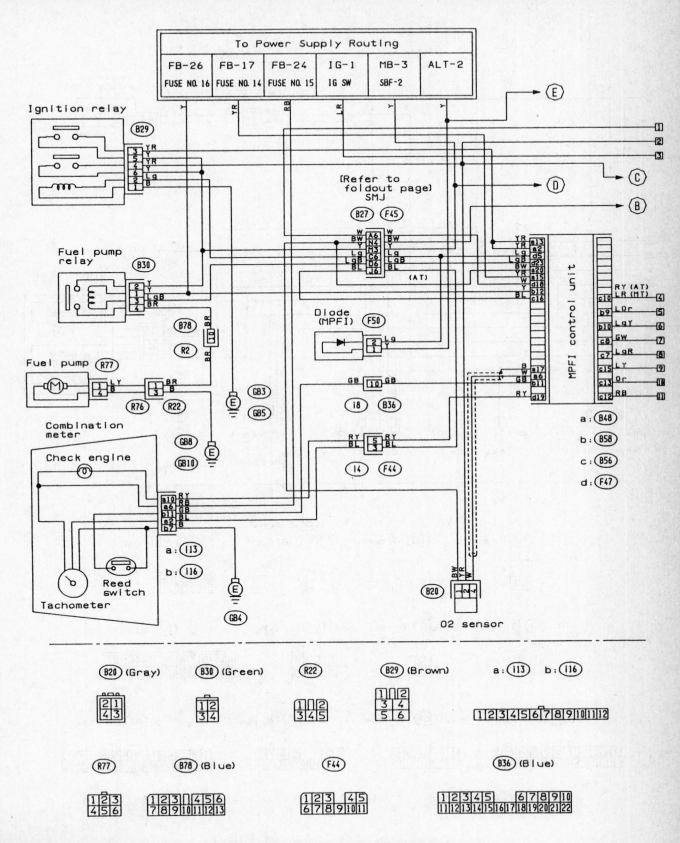

Engine electrical — 1990–92 Legacy MPFI

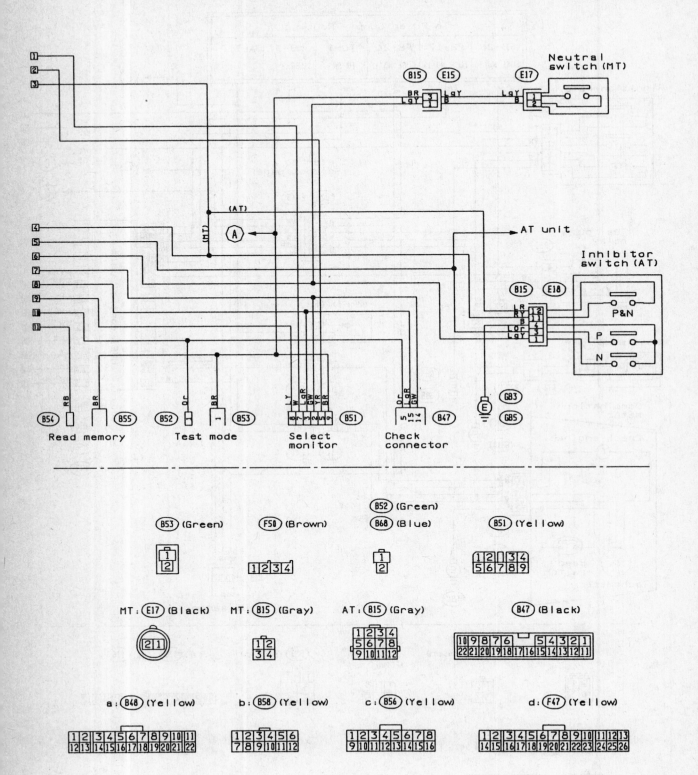

Engine electrical — 1990–92 Legacy MPFI continued

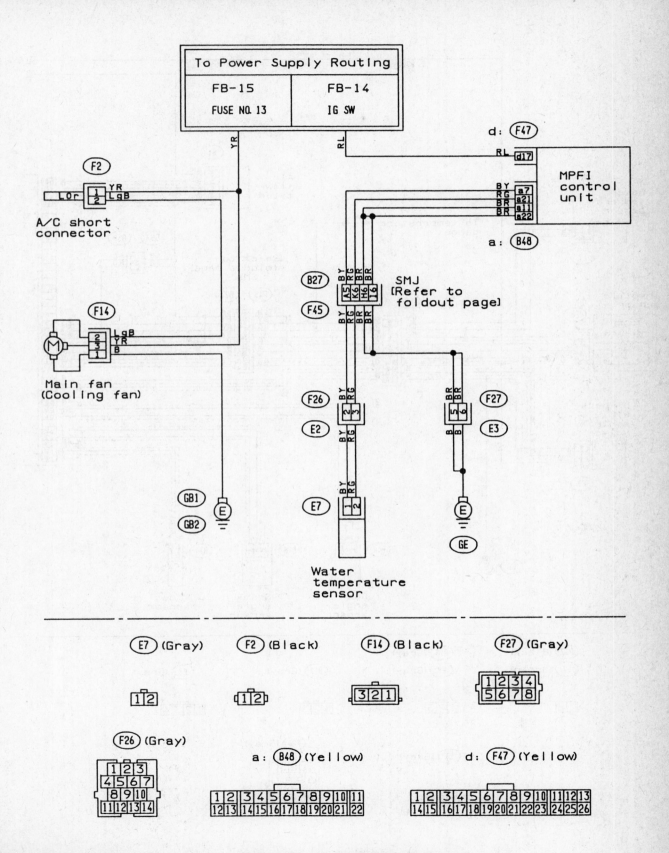

Cooling fan — 1990-92 Legacy

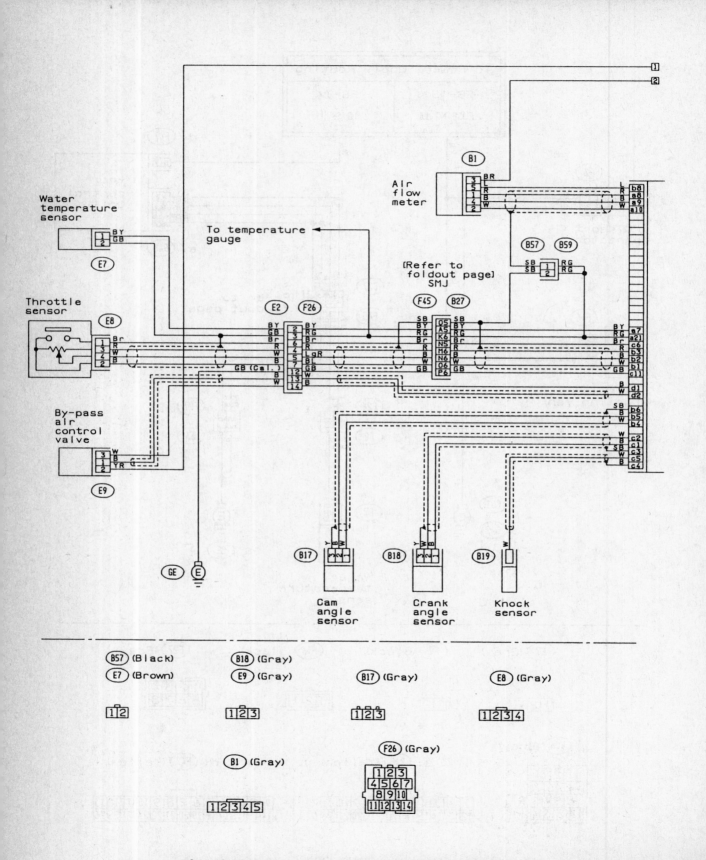

Engine electrical — 1990–92 Legacy MPFI continued

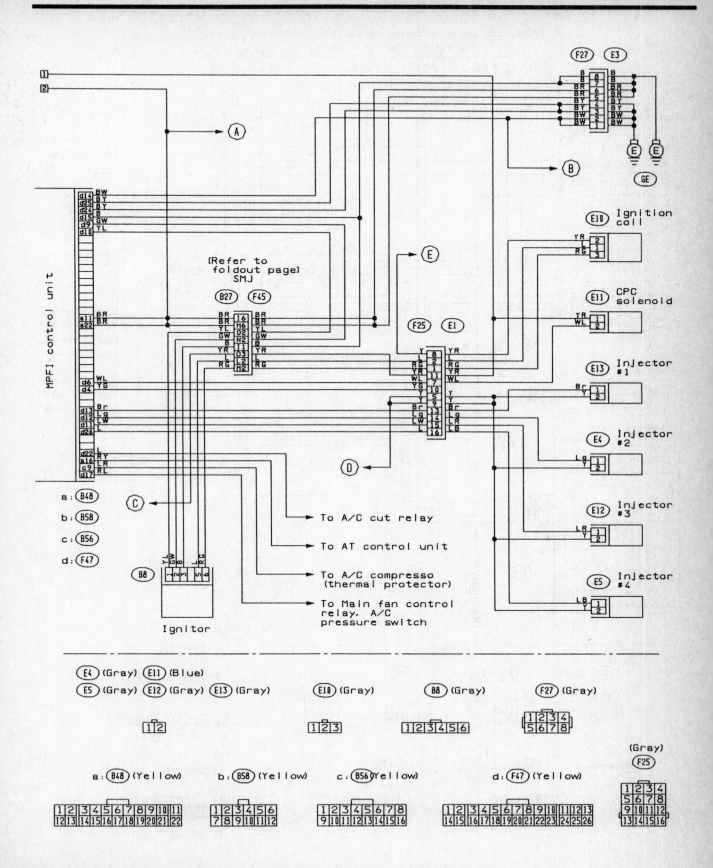

Engine electrical — 1990–92 Legacy MPFI continued

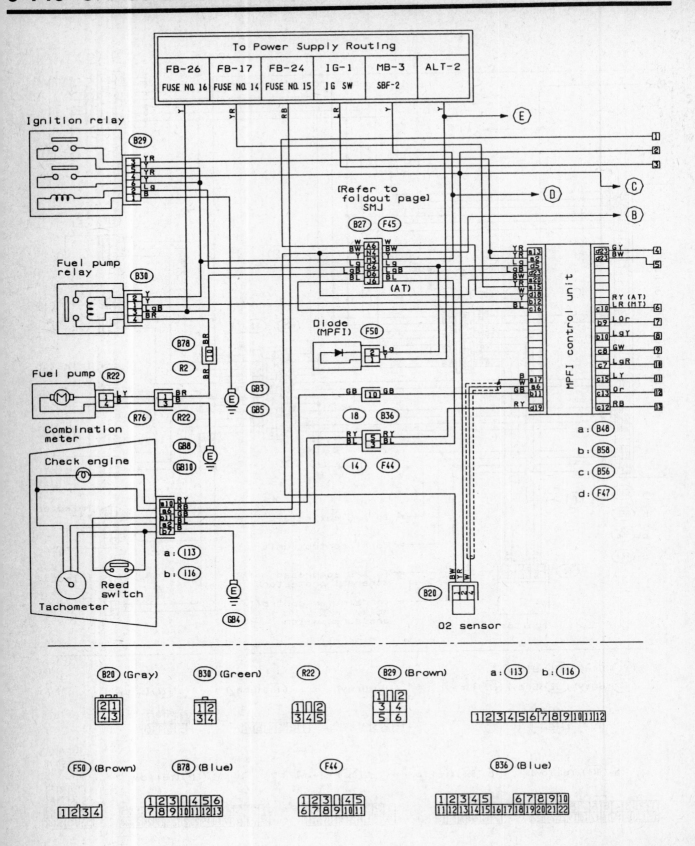

Engine electrical — 1990–92 Legacy Turbo

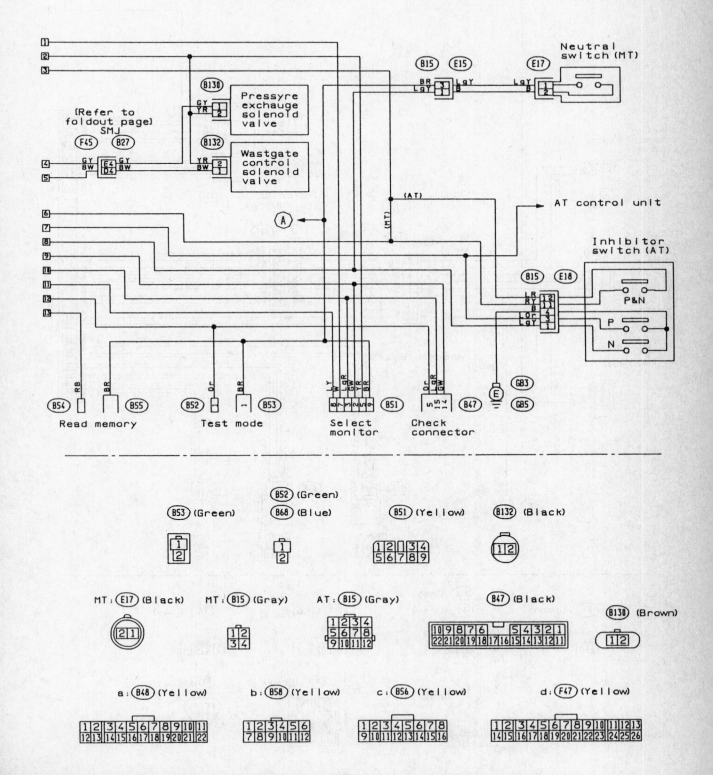

Engine electrical — 1990-92 Legacy Turbo continued

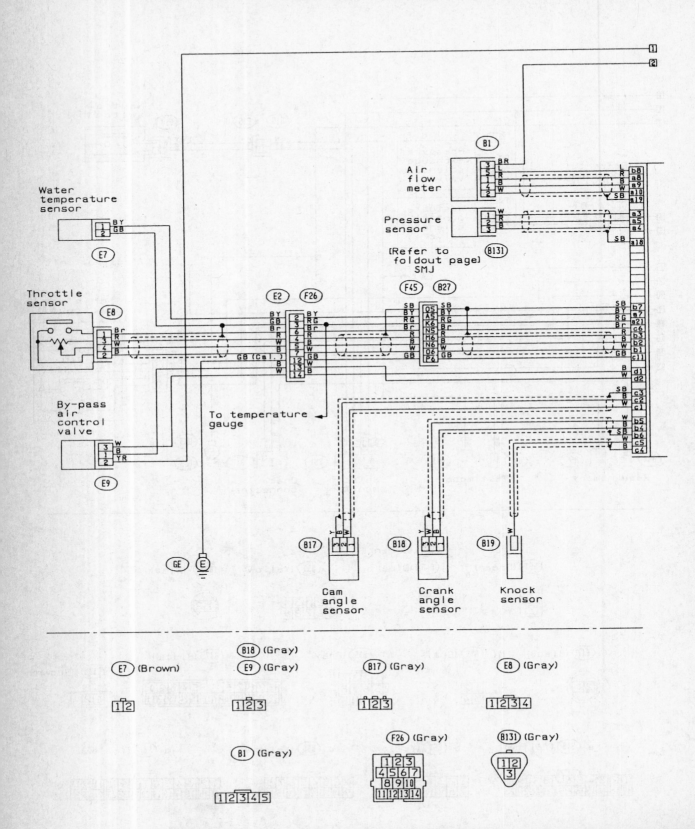

Engine electrical — 1990–92 Legacy Turbo continued

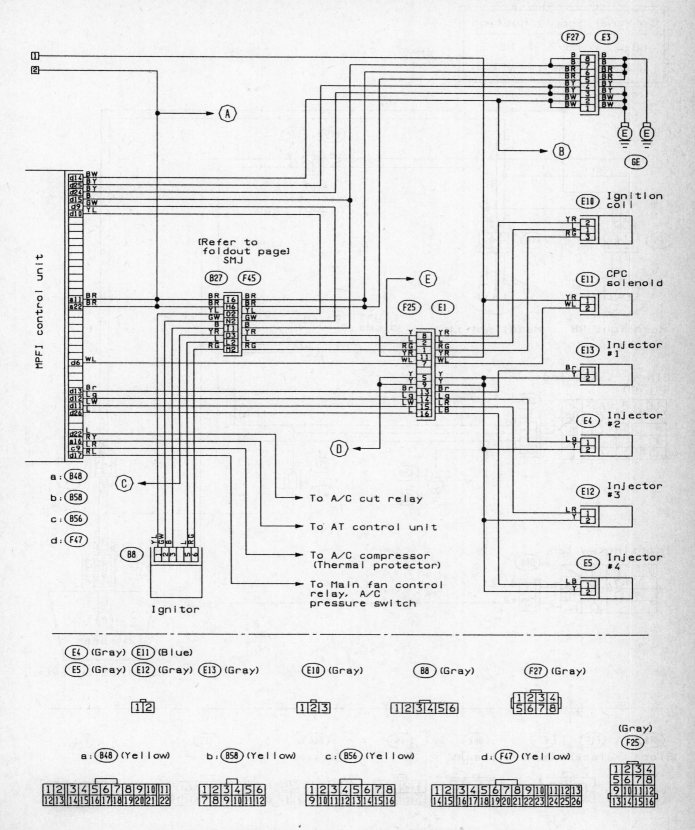

Engine electrical — 1990–92 Legacy Turbo continued

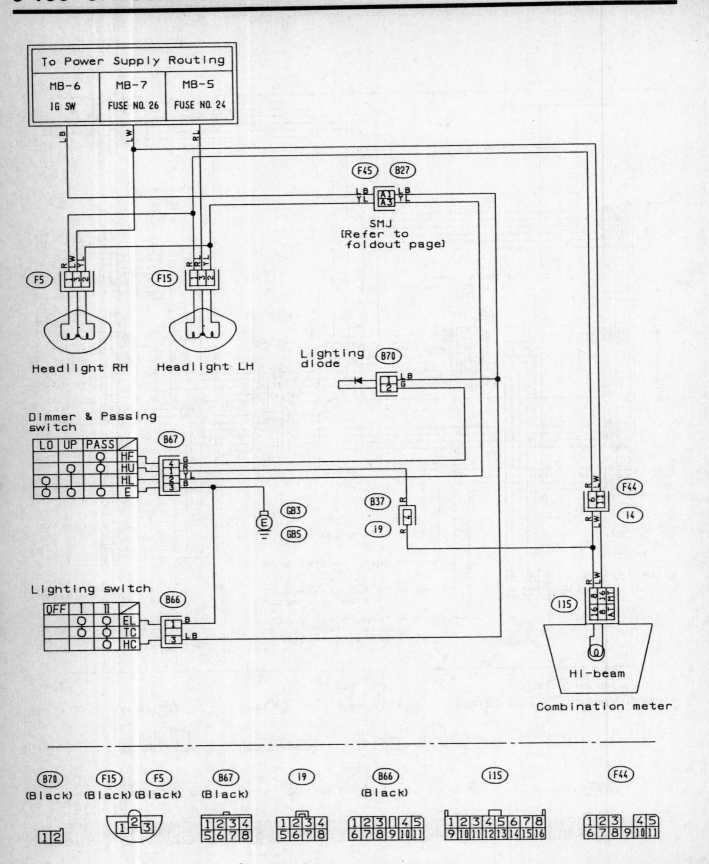

Headlights — 1990–92 Legacy USA

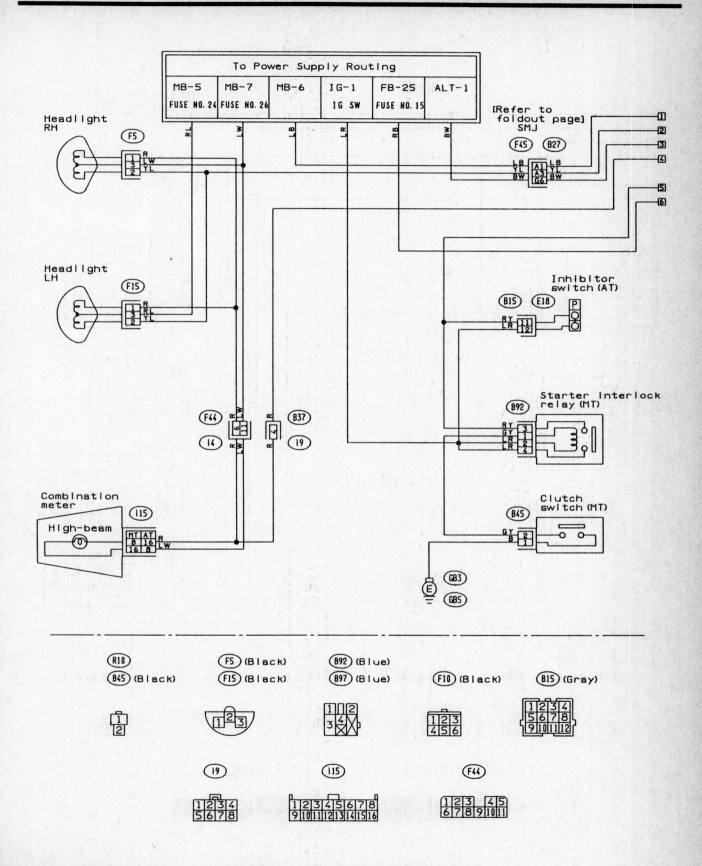

Headlights — 1990-92 Legacy Canada

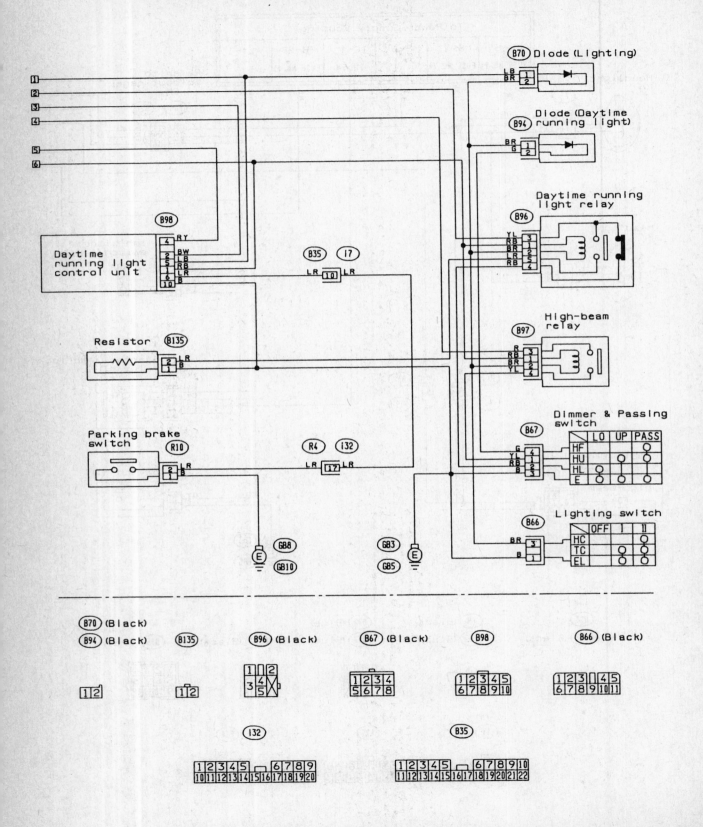

Headlights — 1990–92 Legacy Canada continued

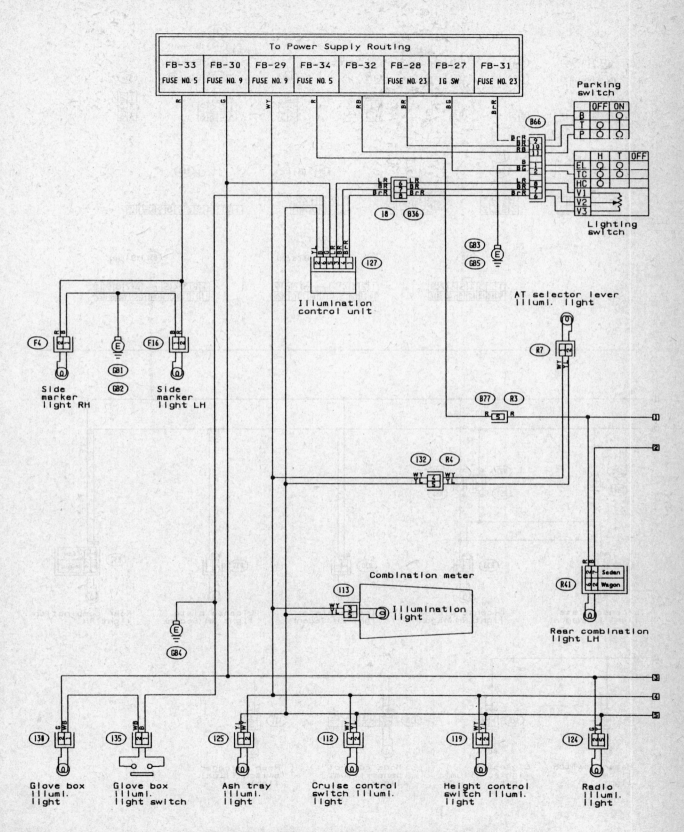

Illumination and tail lights — 1990–92 Legacy

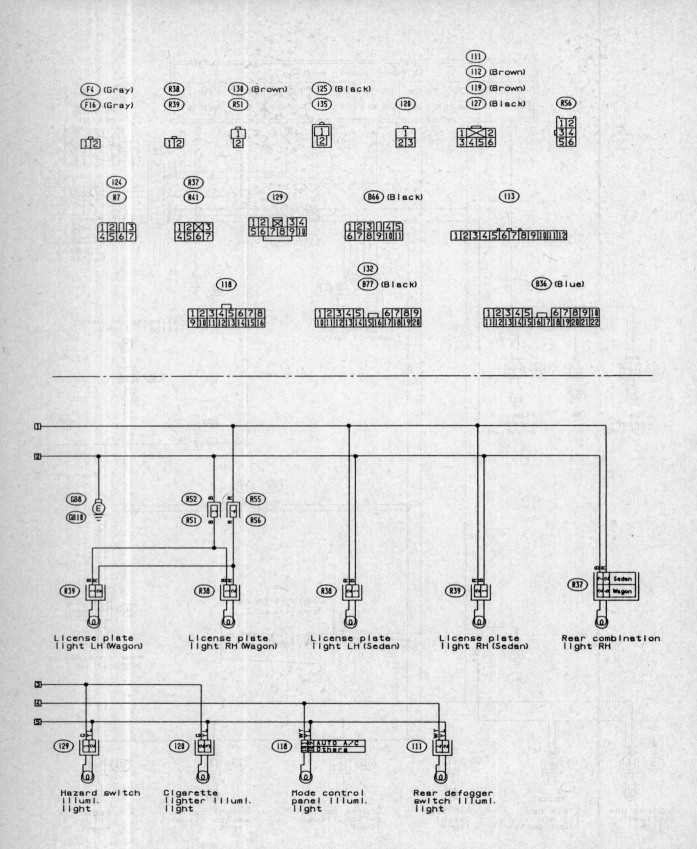

Illumination and tail lights — 1990–92 Legacy continued

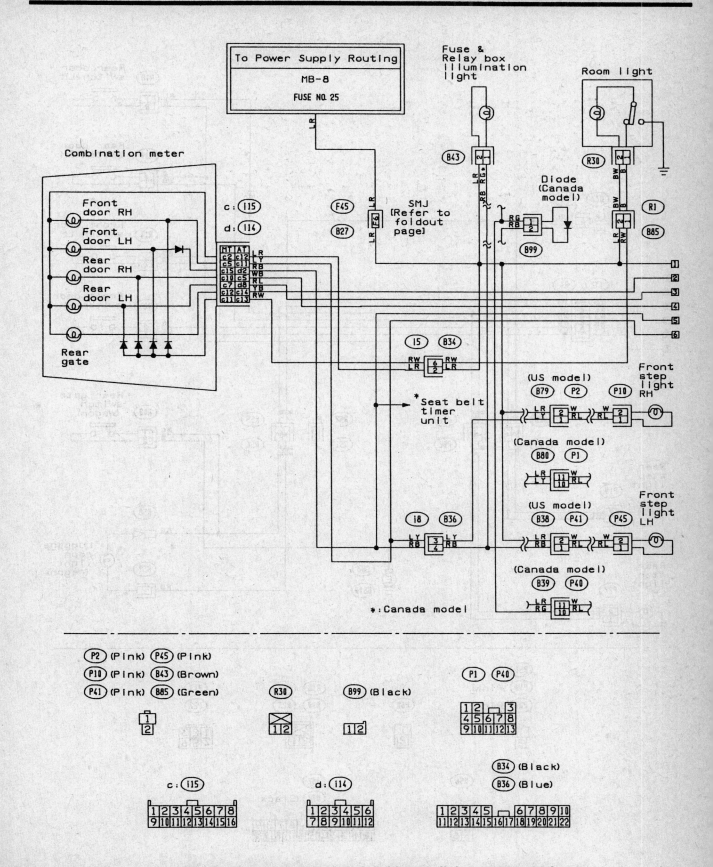

Room light and door switch, with step light — 1990– 92 Legacy

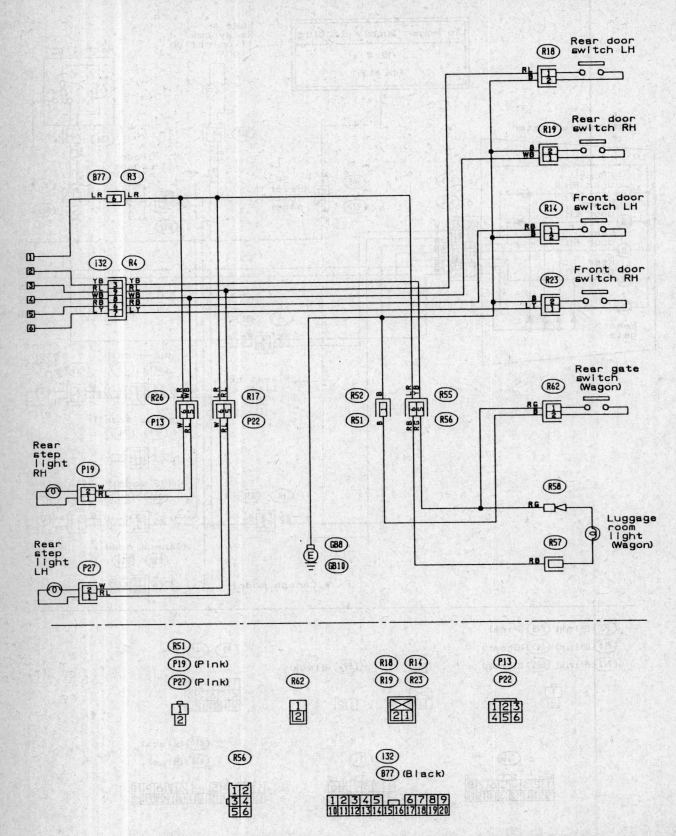

Room light and door switch, with step light — 1990–92 Legacy continued

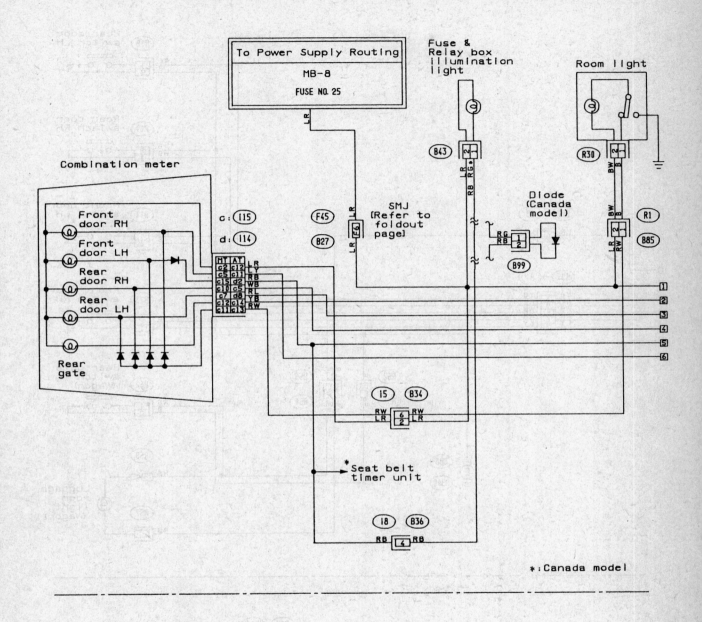

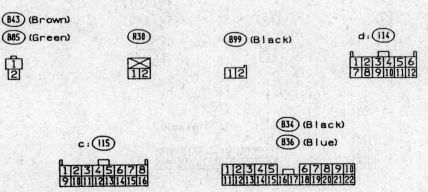

Room light and door switch, without step light — 1990–92 Legacy

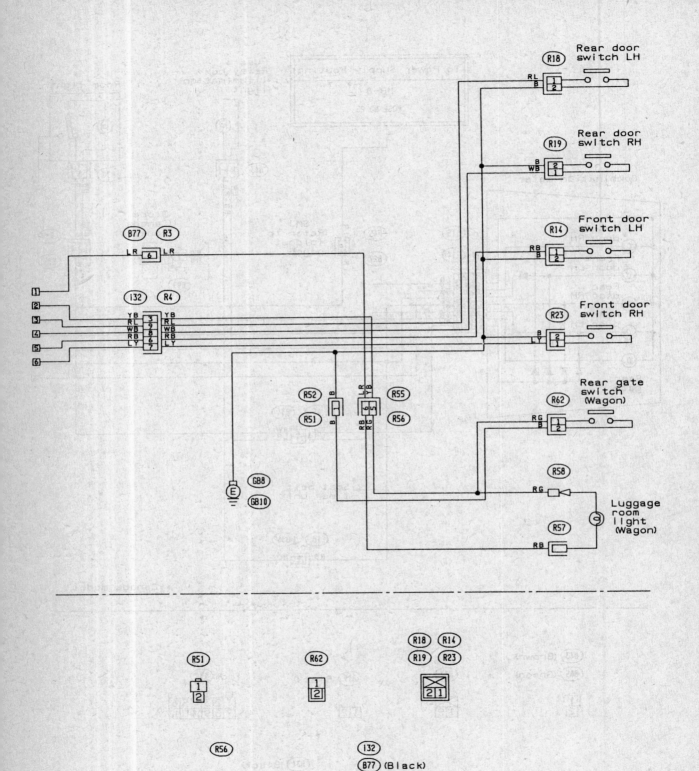

Room light and door switch, without step light — 1990–92 Legacy continued

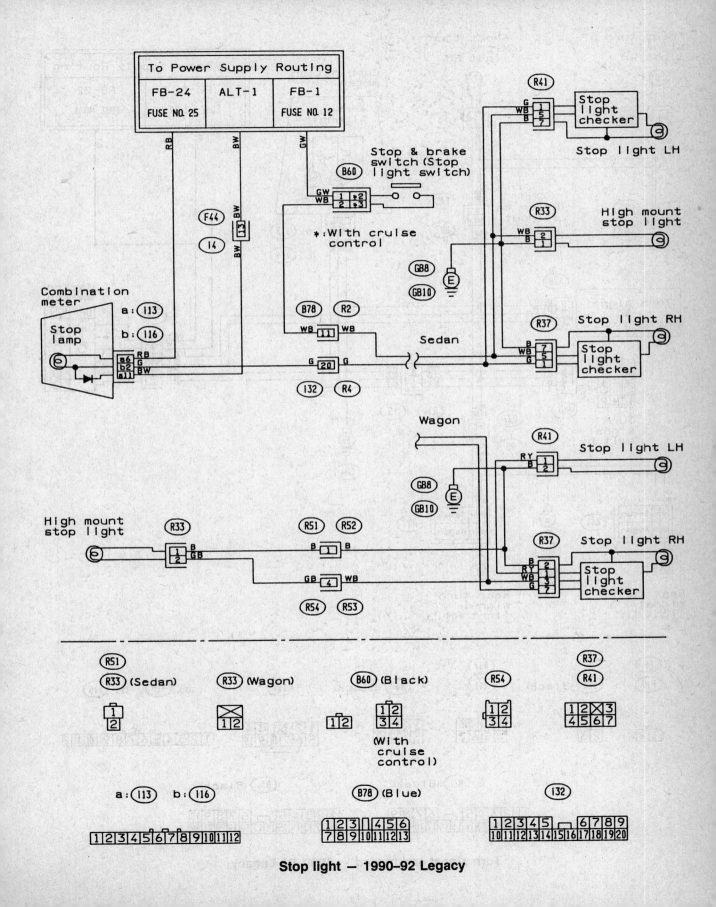

Stop light — 1990–92 Legacy

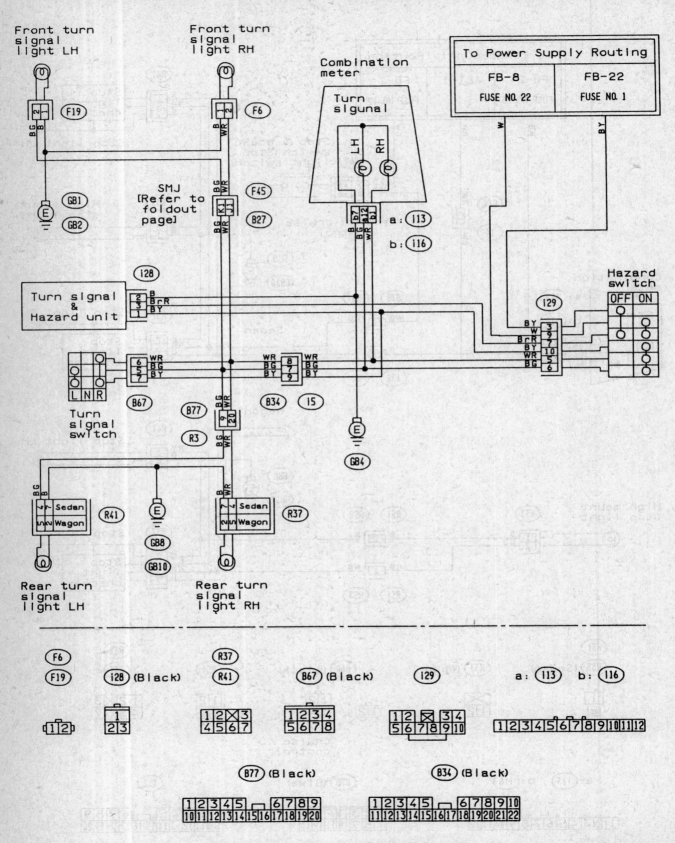

Turn signal and hazard — 1990–92 Legacy

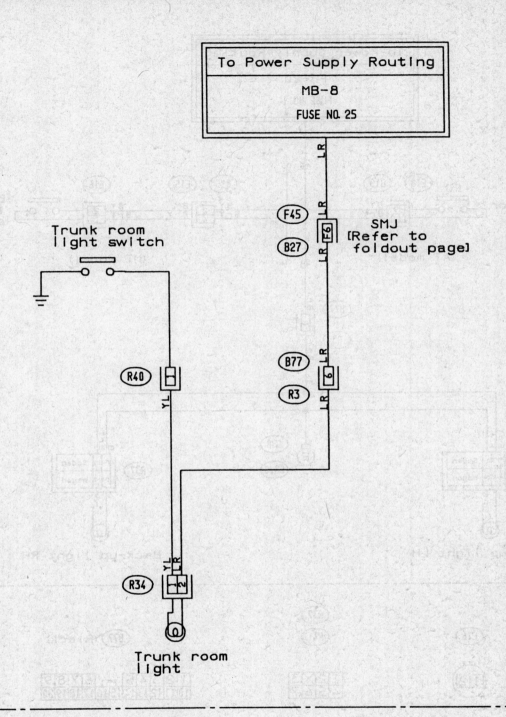

Trunk room light — 1990–92 Legacy

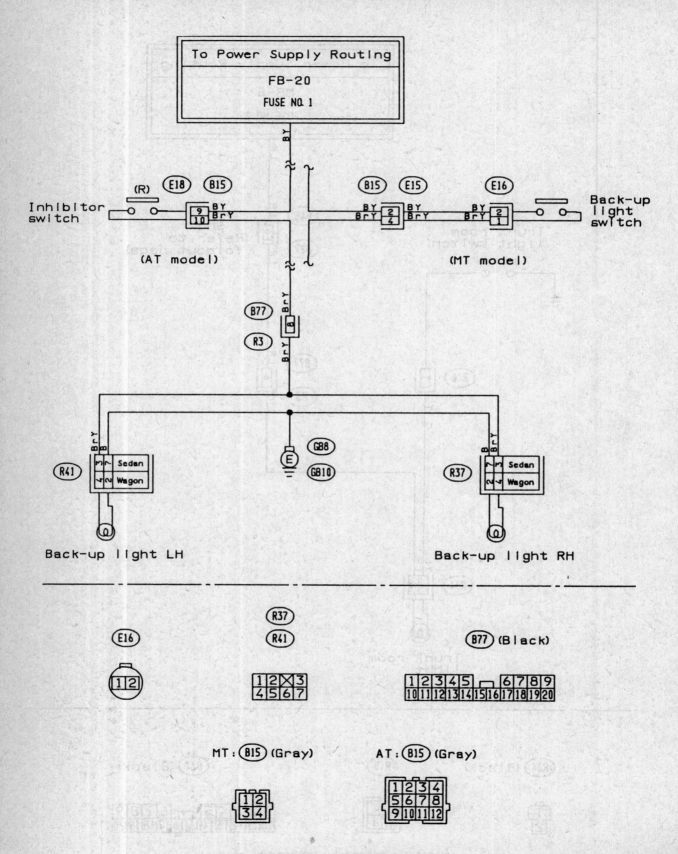

Backup light — 1990–92 Legacy

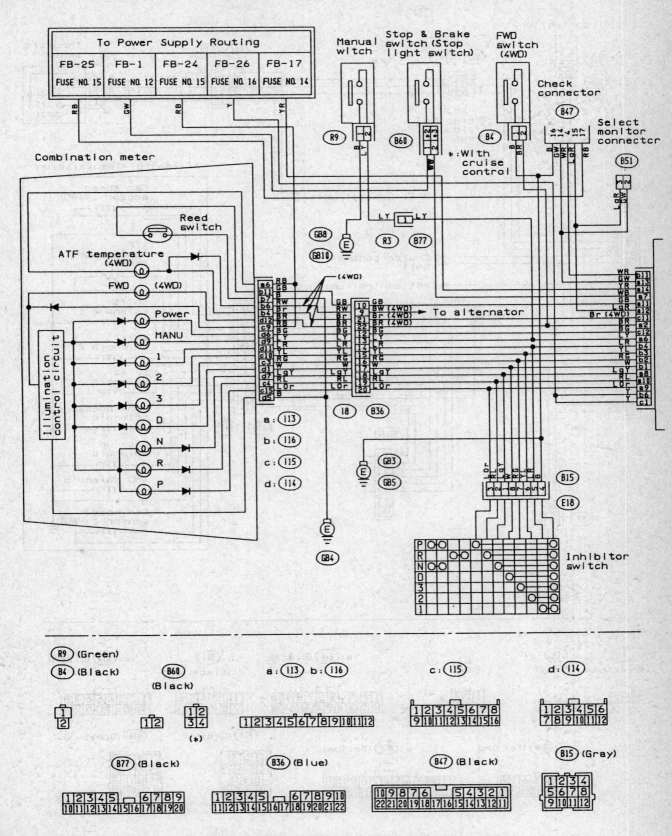

Automatic transmission control — 1990–92 Legacy

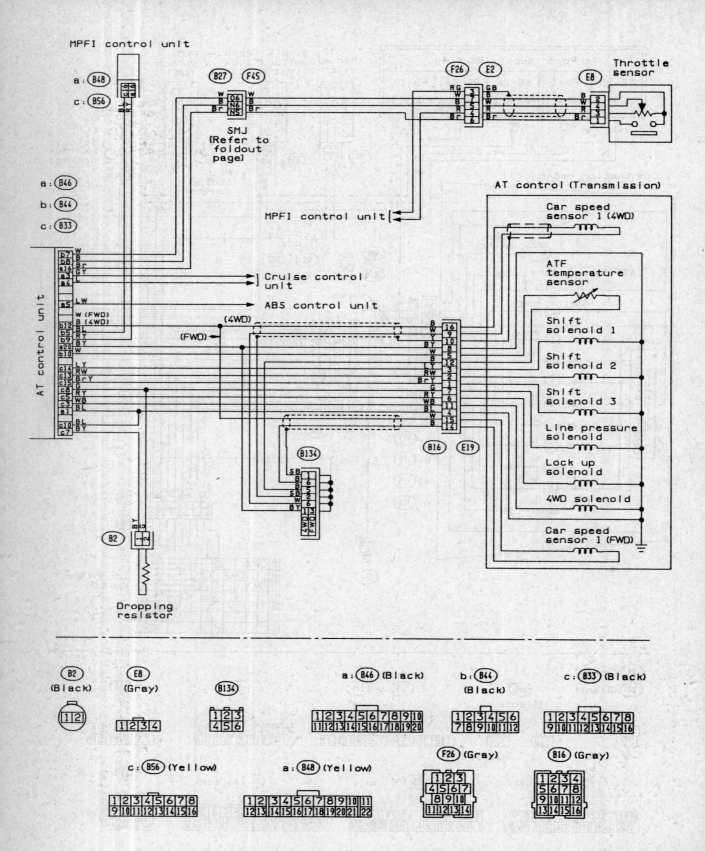

Automatic transmission control — 1990–92 Legacy continued

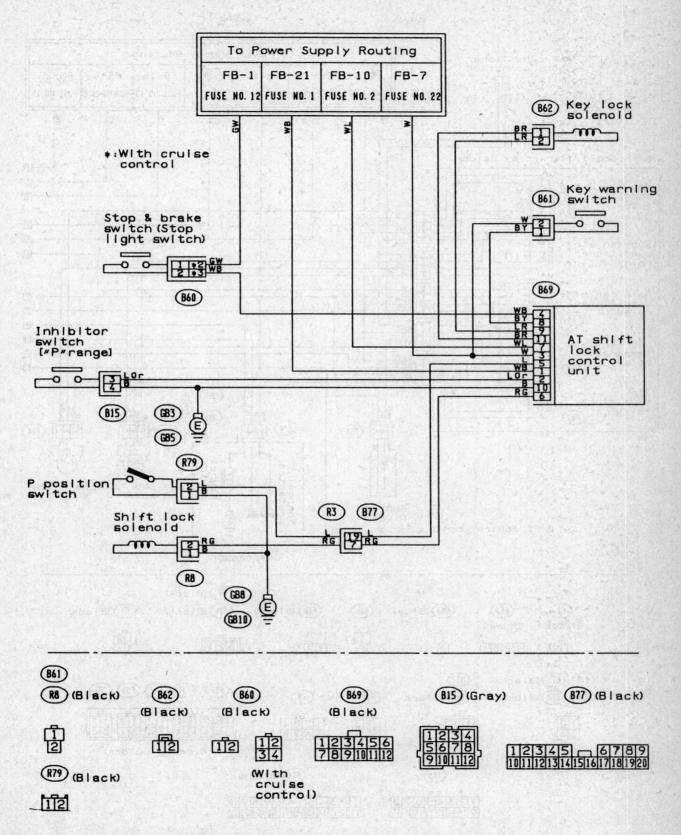

Automatic transmission shift lock — 1990–92 Legacy

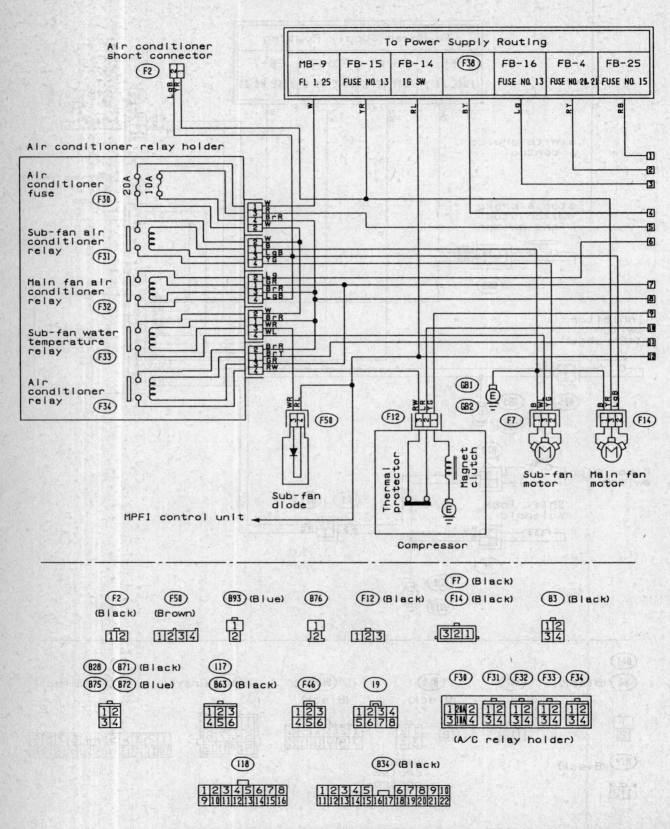

Manual air conditioner — 1990–92 Legacy

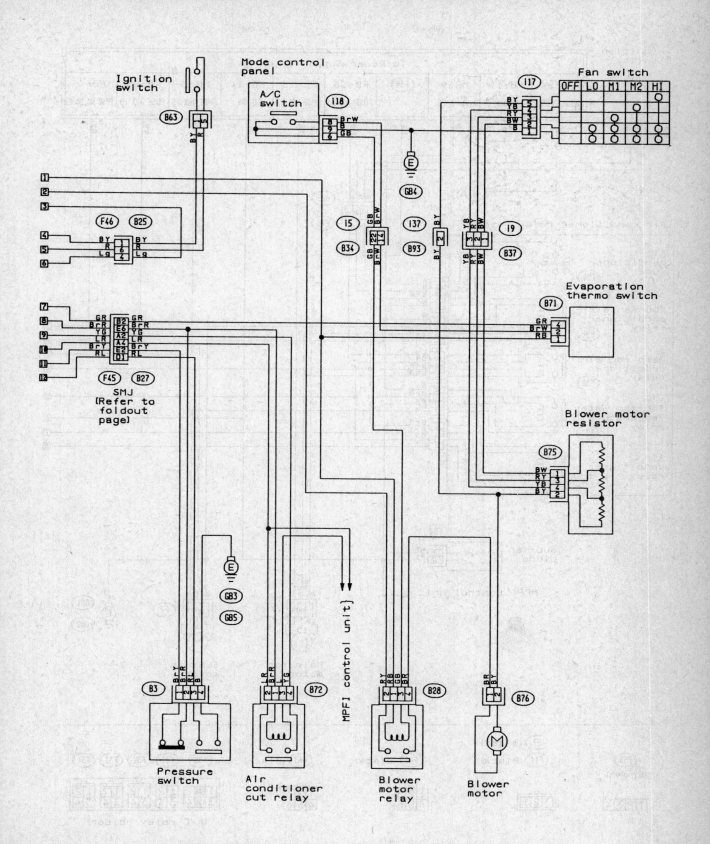

Manual air conditioner — 1990–92 Legacy continued

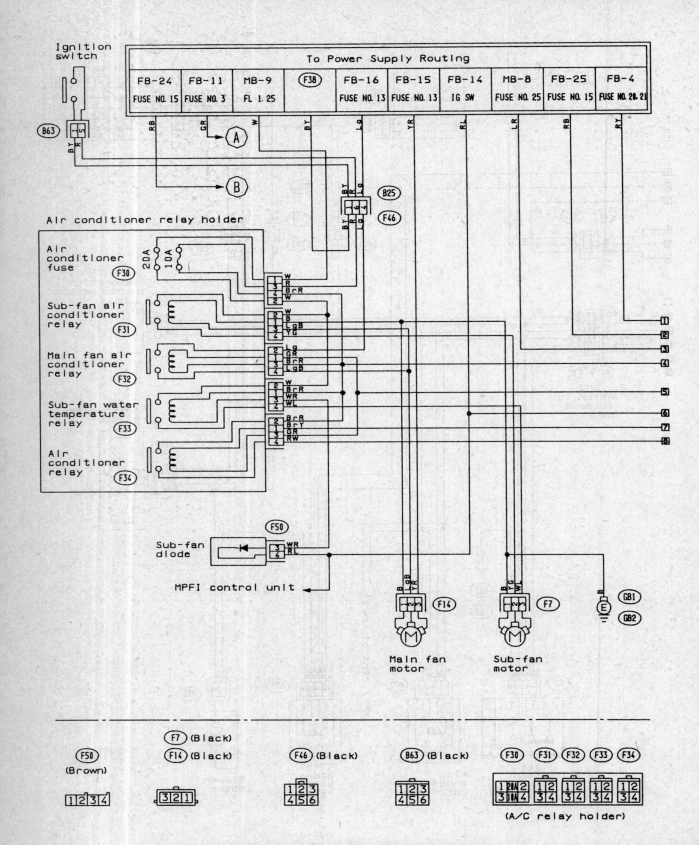

Automatic air conditioner — 1990-92 Legacy

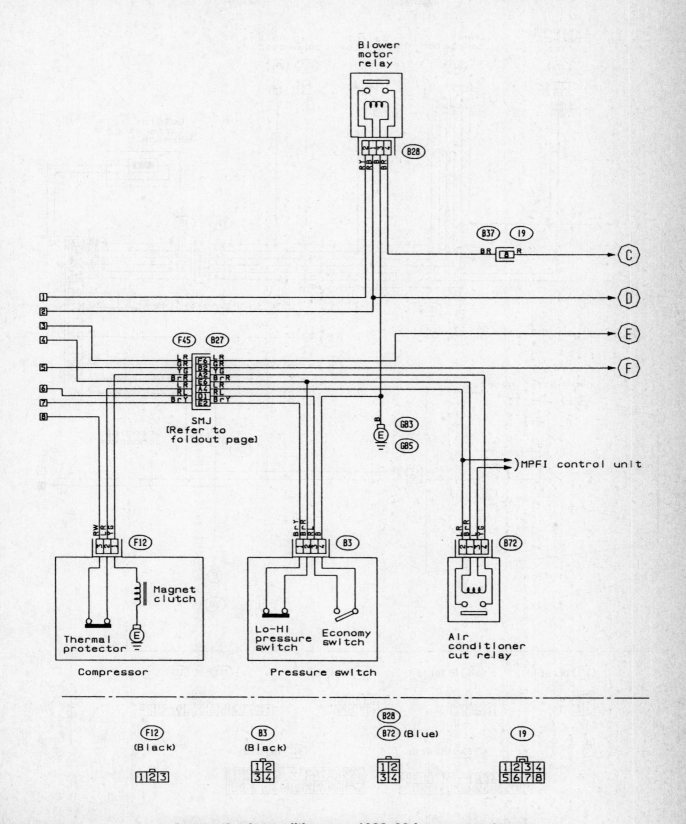

Automatic air conditioner — 1990–92 Legacy continued

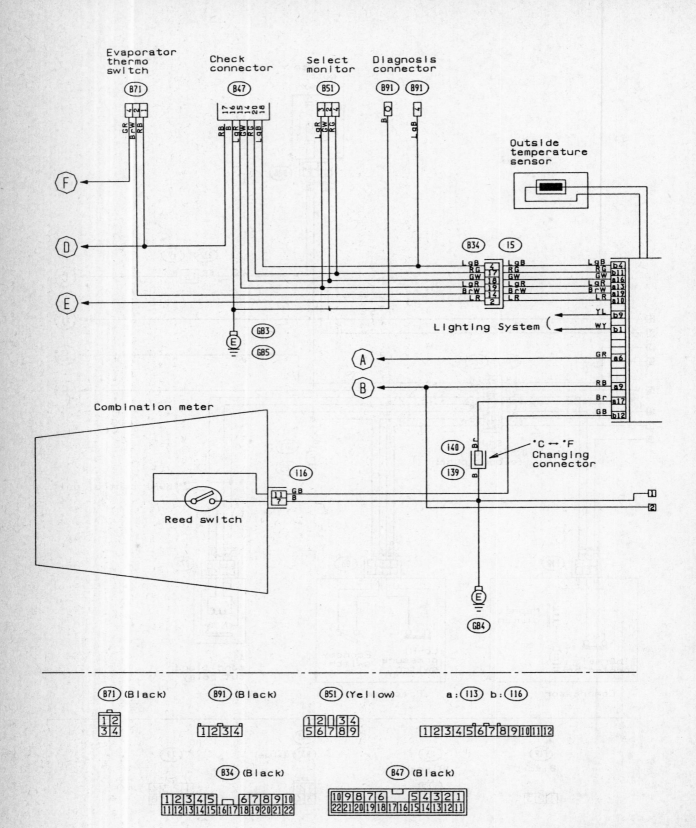

Automatic air conditioner — 1990–92 Legacy continued

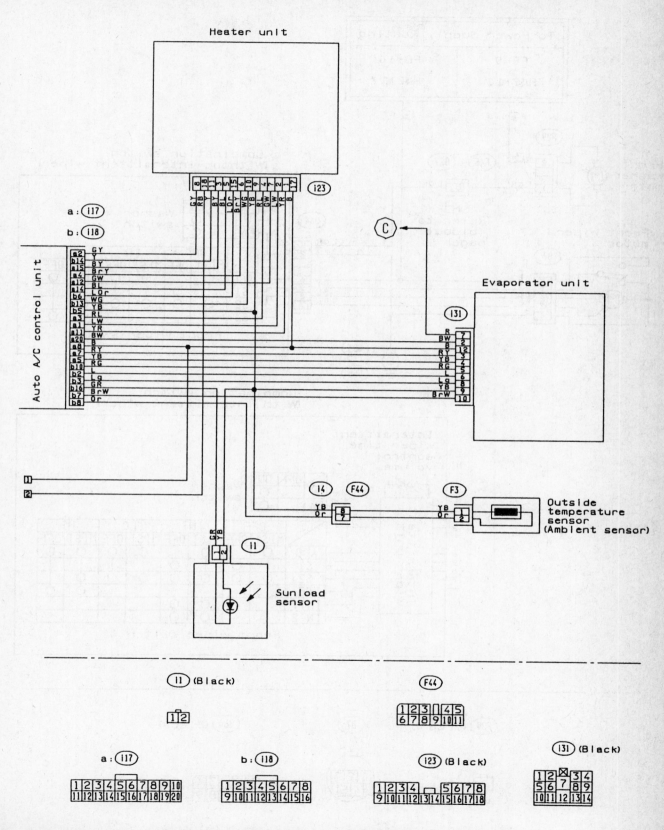

Automatic air conditioner — 1990–92 Legacy continued

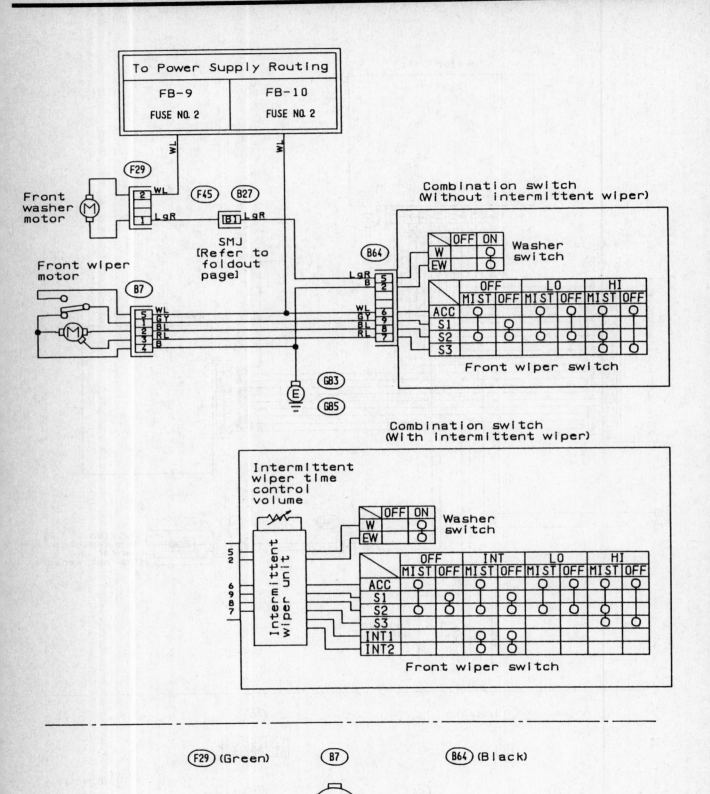

Windshield wiper and washer — 1990–92 Legacy

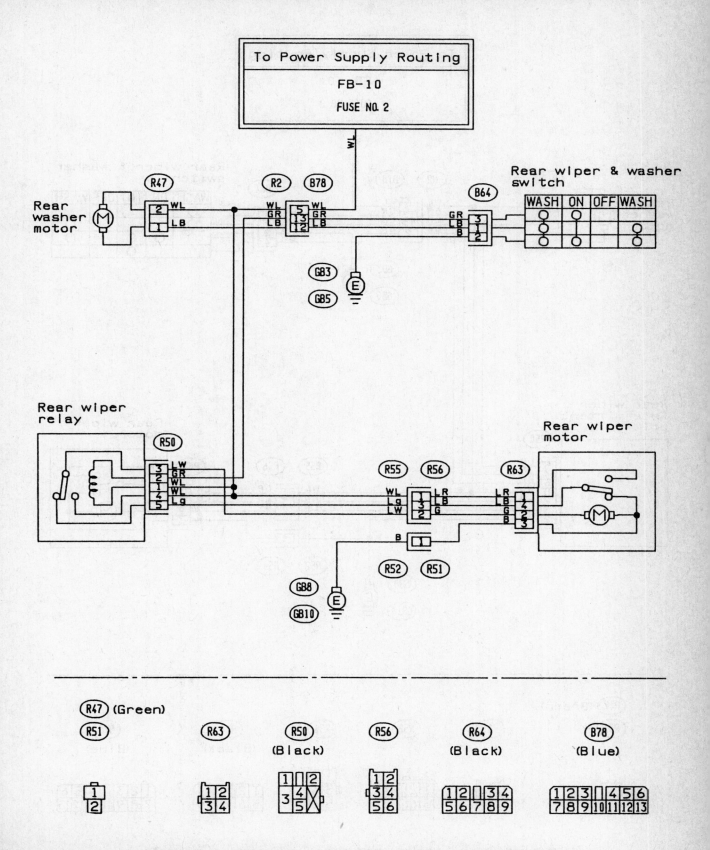

Rear wiper and washer — 1990–92 Legacy without intermittent wiper

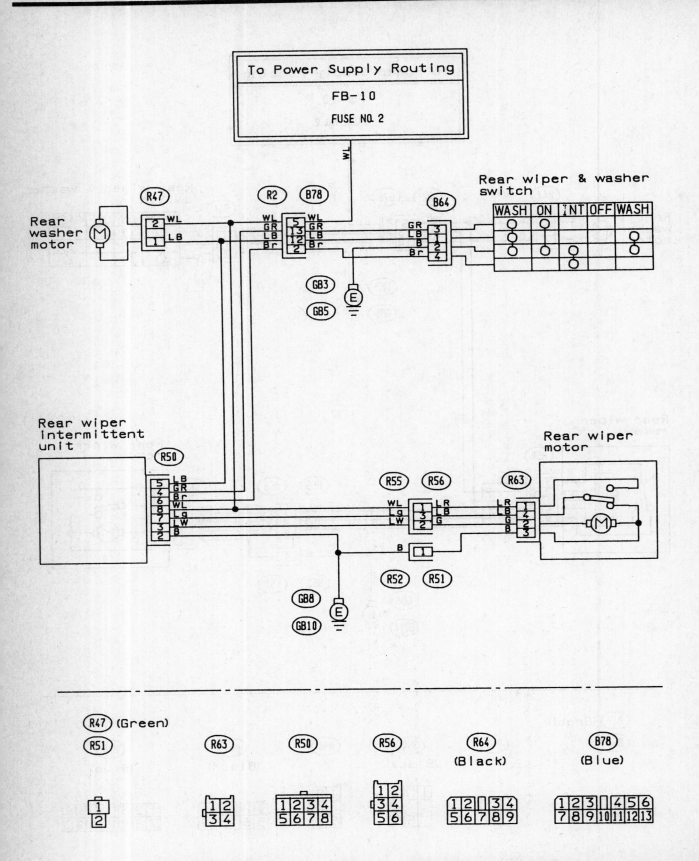

Rear wiper and washer — 1990–92 Legacy with intermittent wiper

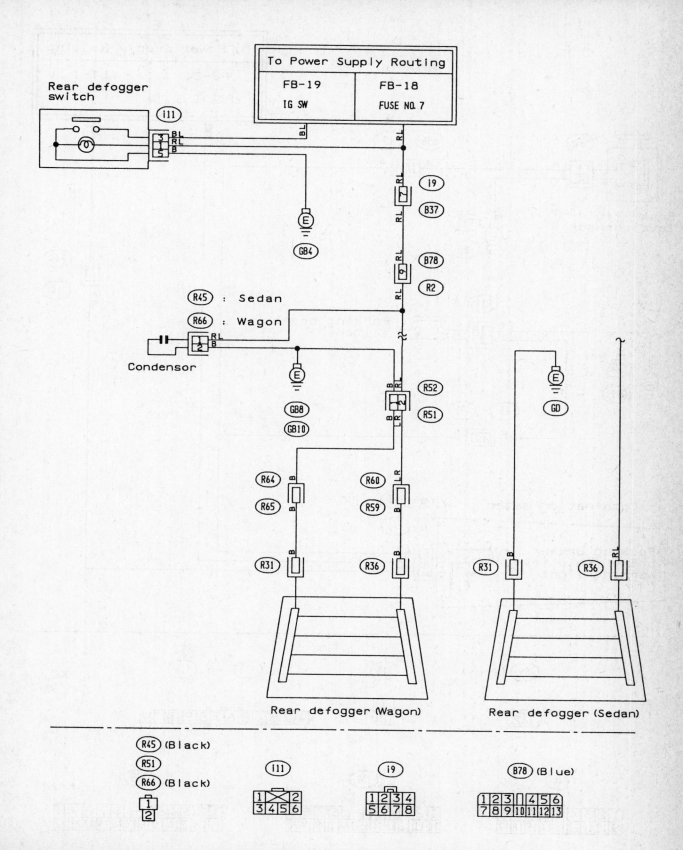

Rear window defogger — 1990–92 Legacy

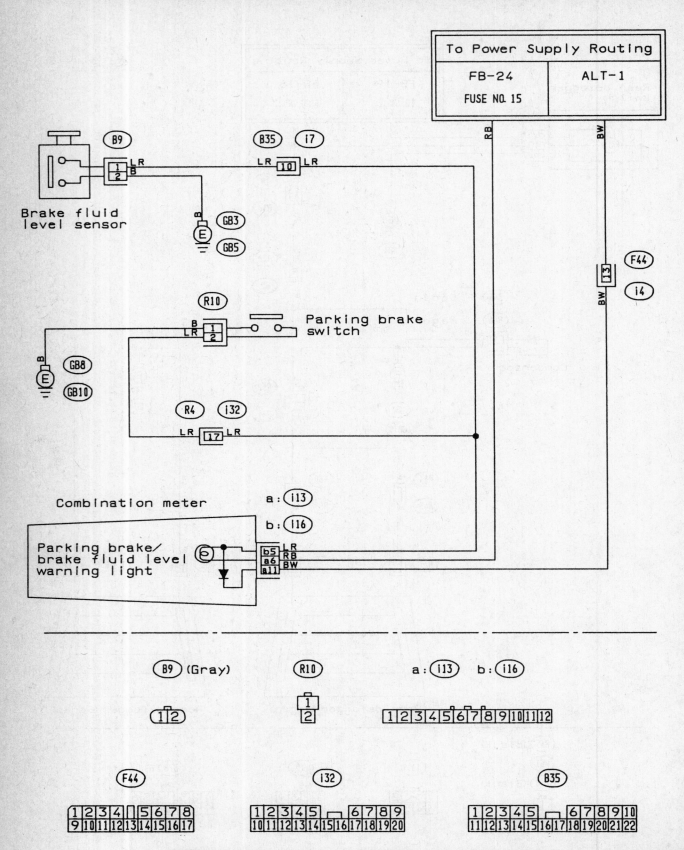

Parking brake and brake fluid level warning — 1990–92 Legacy

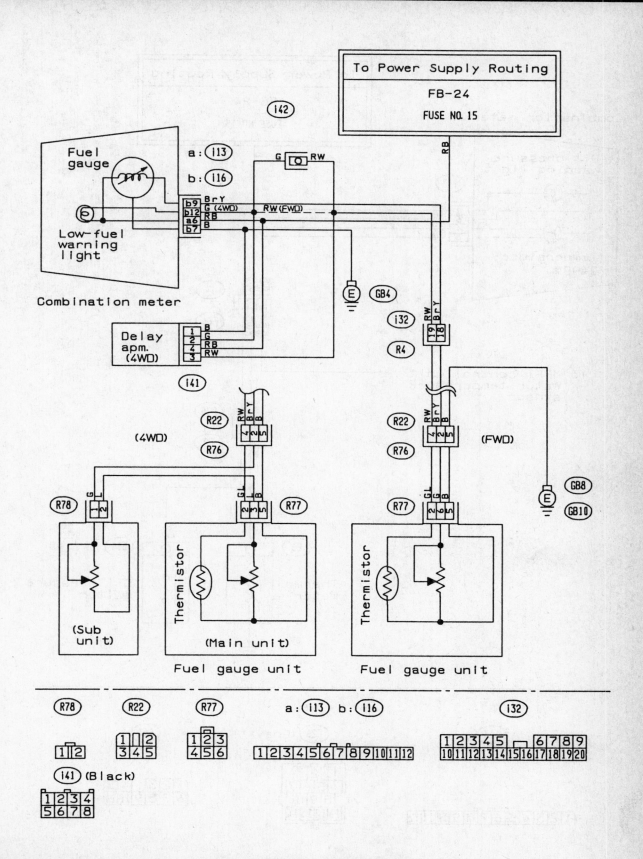

Fuel gauge — 1990–92 Legacy

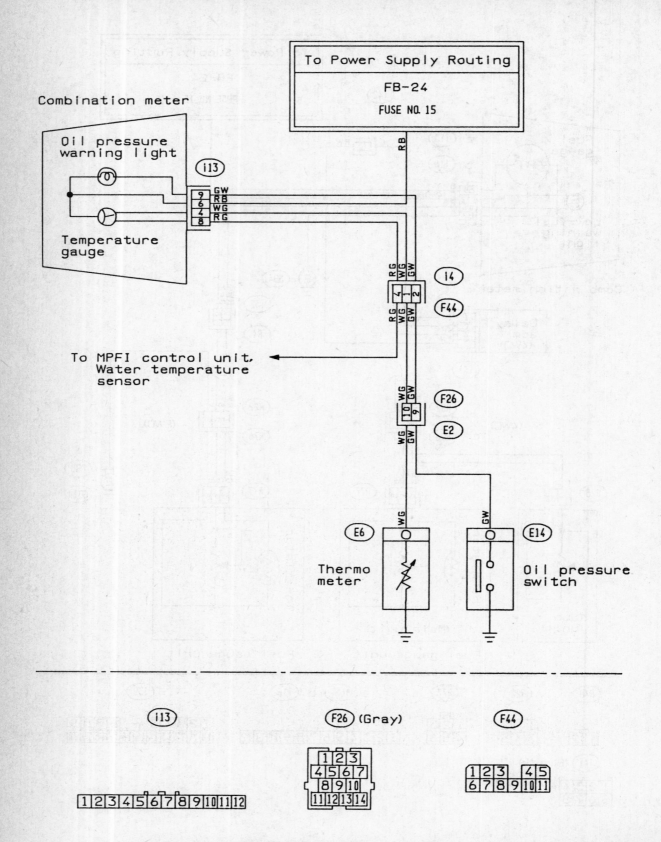

Oil pressure and temperature gauges — 1990–92 Legacy

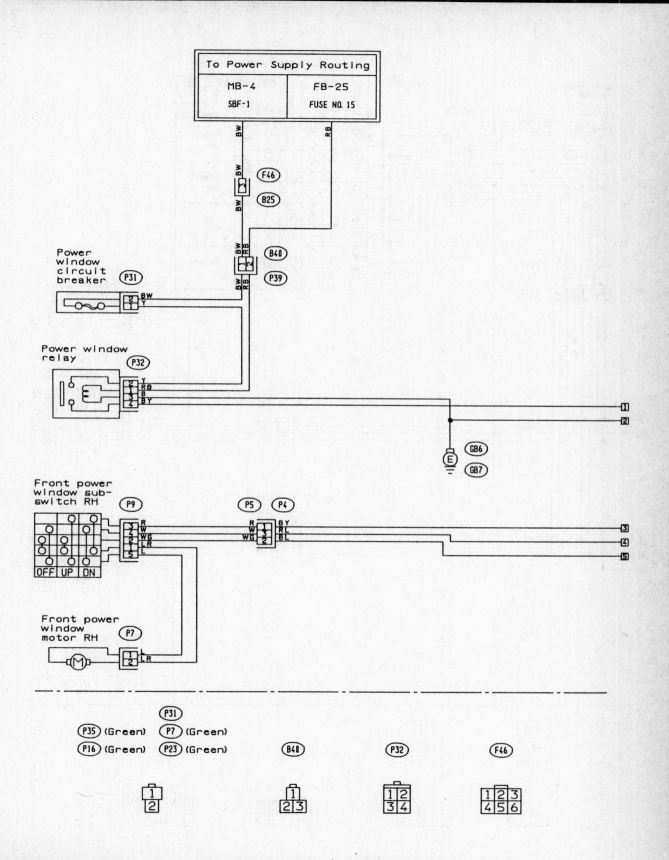

Power window — 1990-92 Legacy

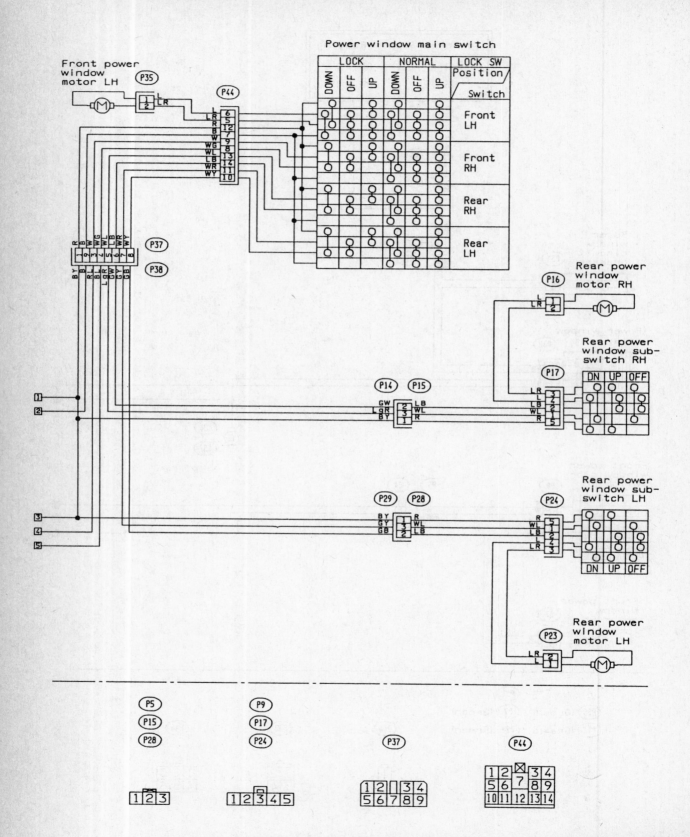

Power window — 1990–92 Legacy continued

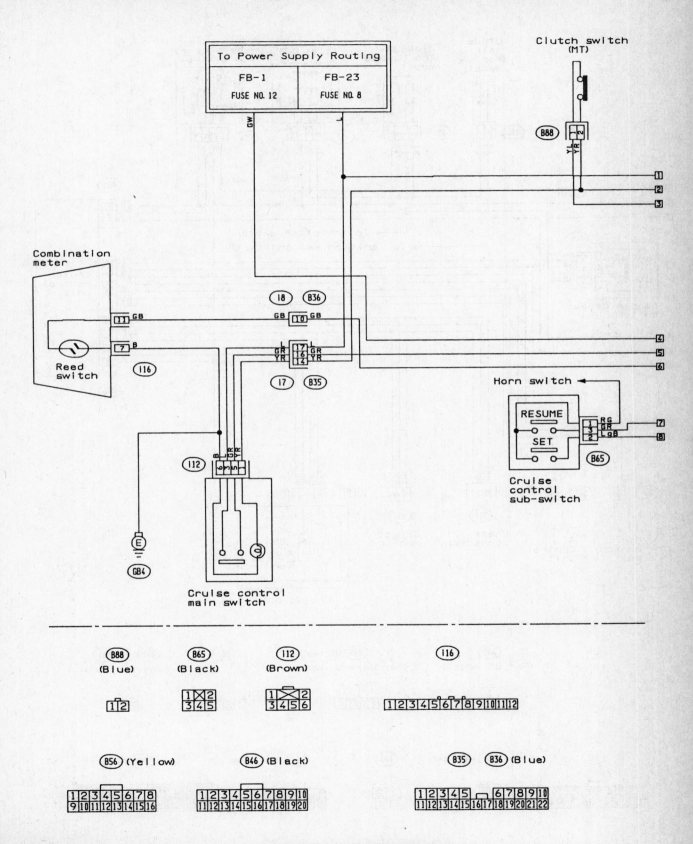

Cruise control — 1990–92 Legacy

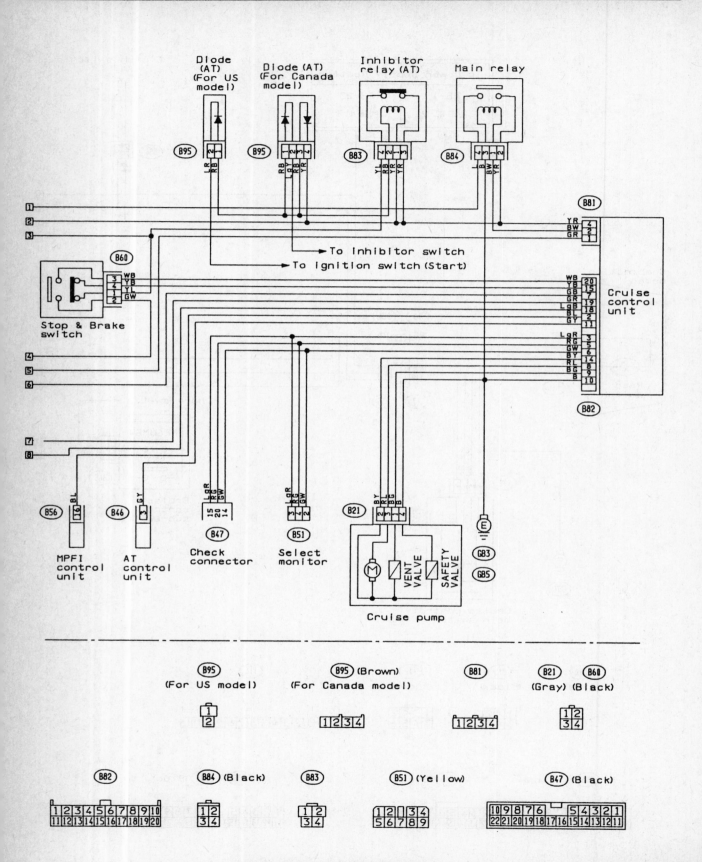

Cruise control — 1990–92 Legacy

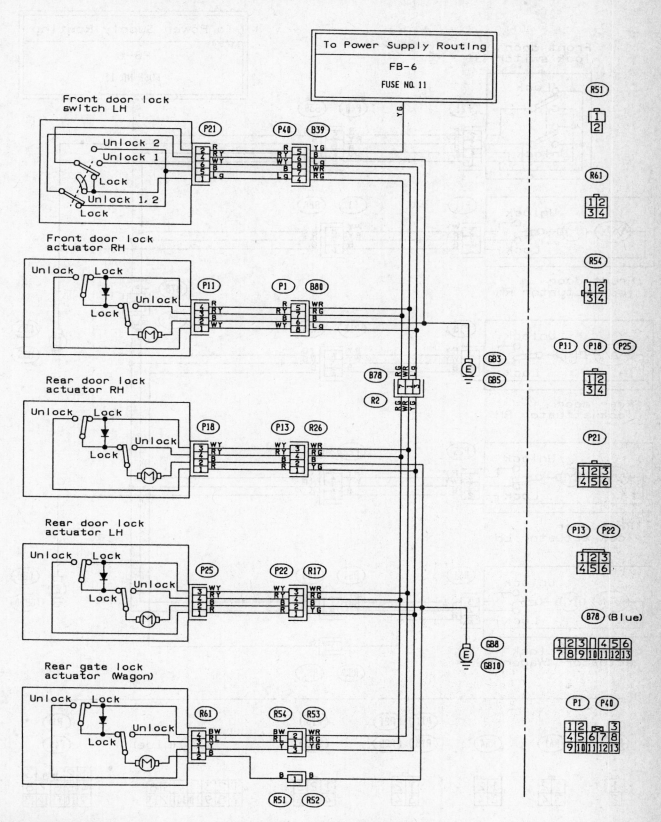

Door lock — 1990–92 Legacy USA

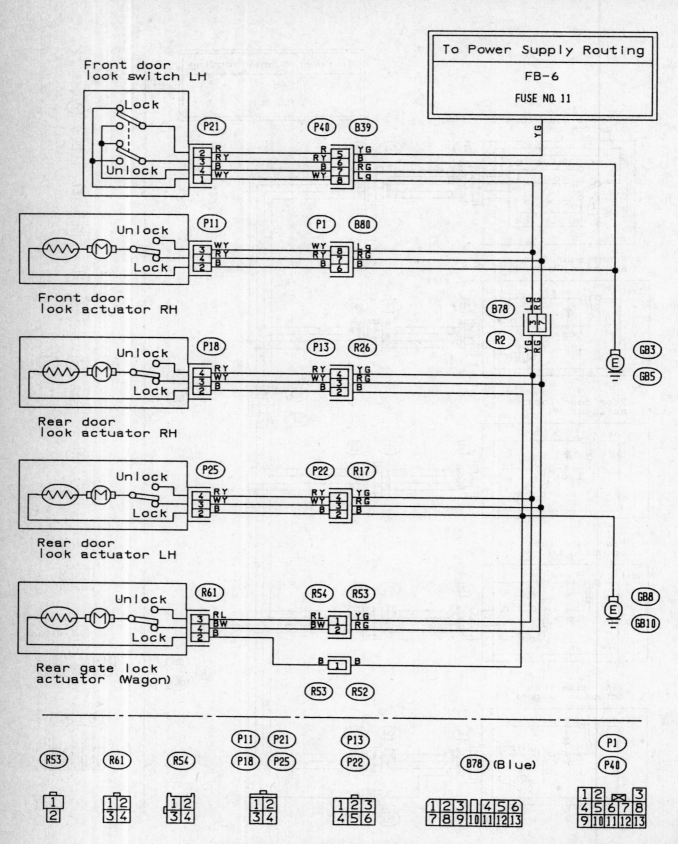

Door lock – 1990–92 Legacy Canada

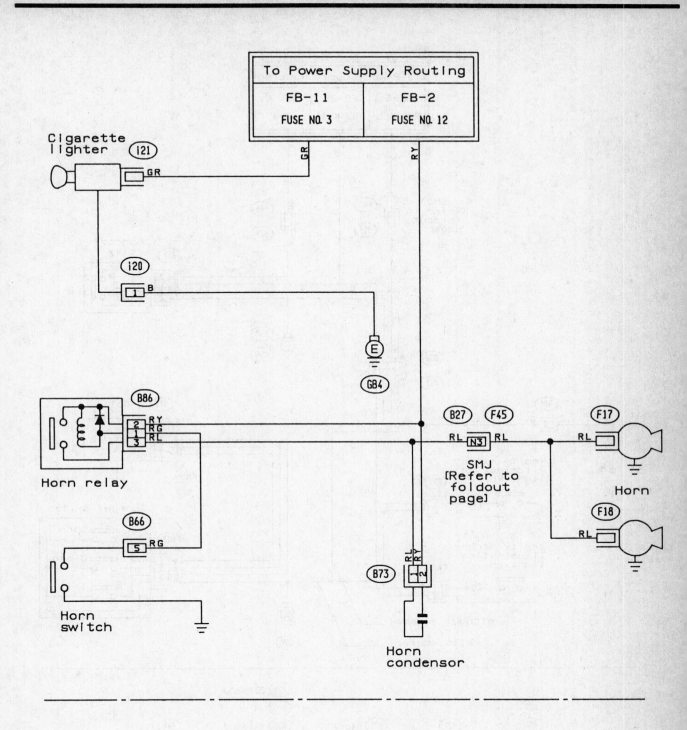

Horn and cigarette lighter — 1990–92 Legacy

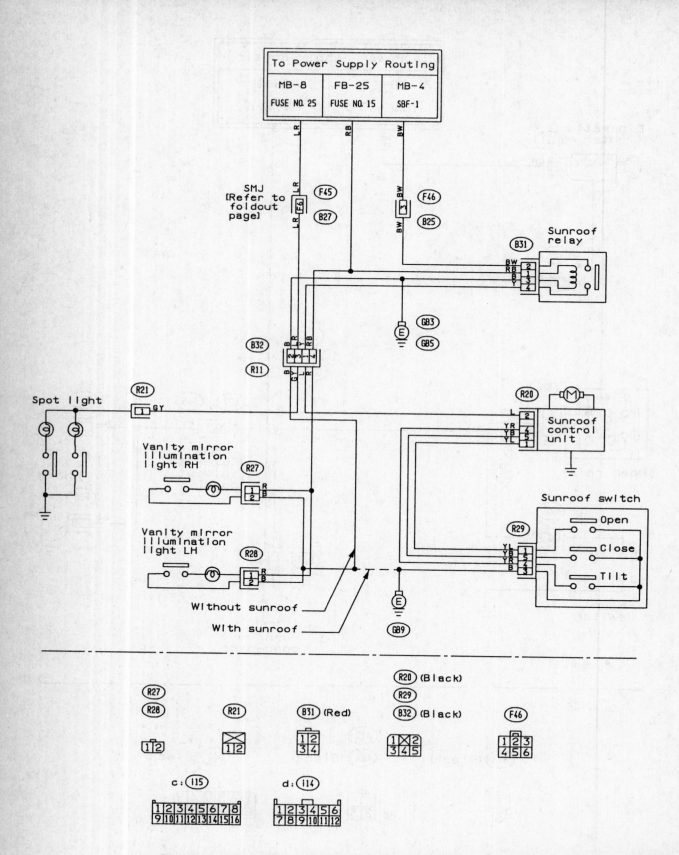

Sunroof, spot light and vanity mirror — 1990–92 Legacy

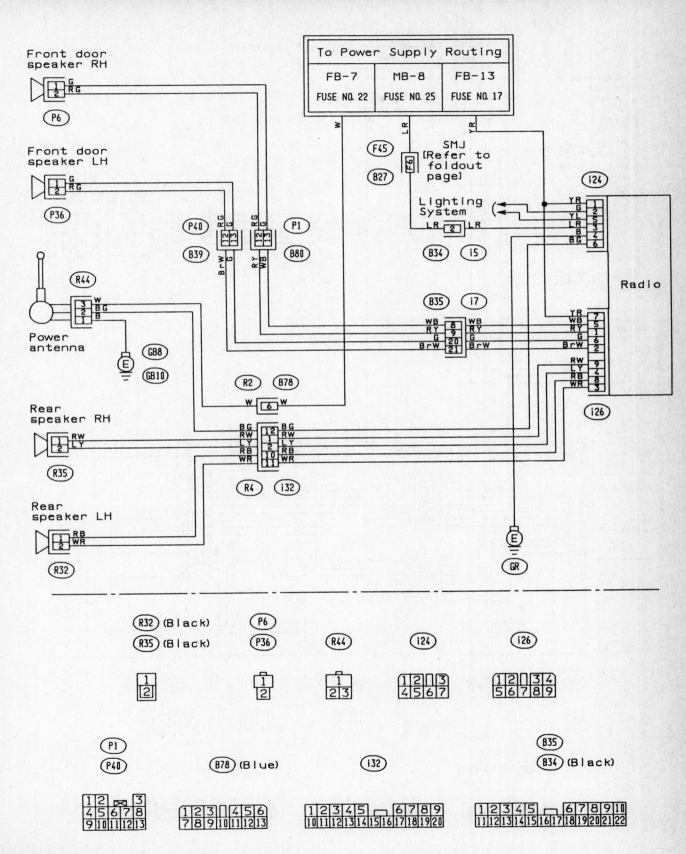

Radio and power antenna — 1990–92 Legacy

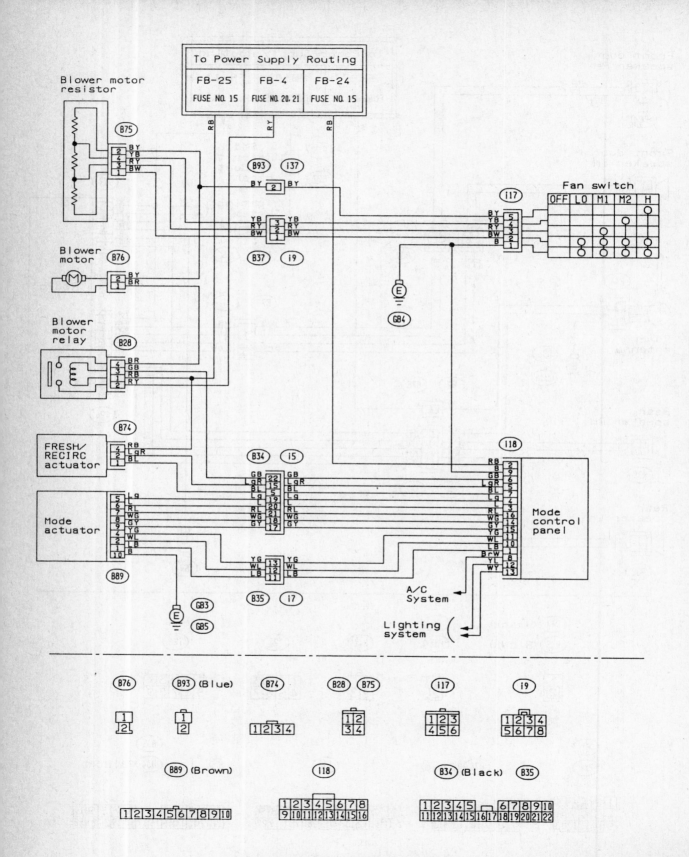

Mode selector — 1990–92 Legacy

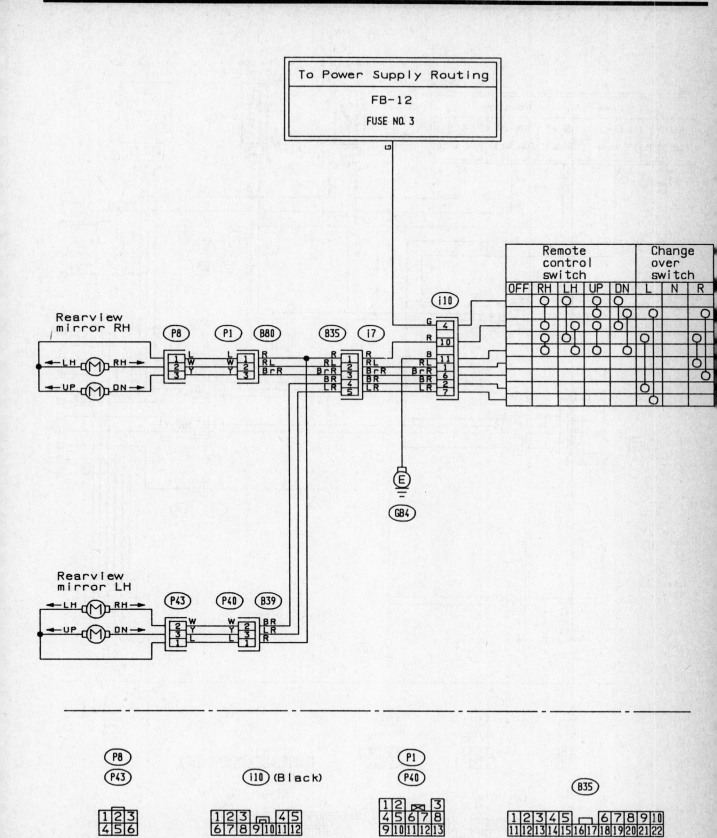

Remote controlled rearview mirror — 1990–92 Legacy

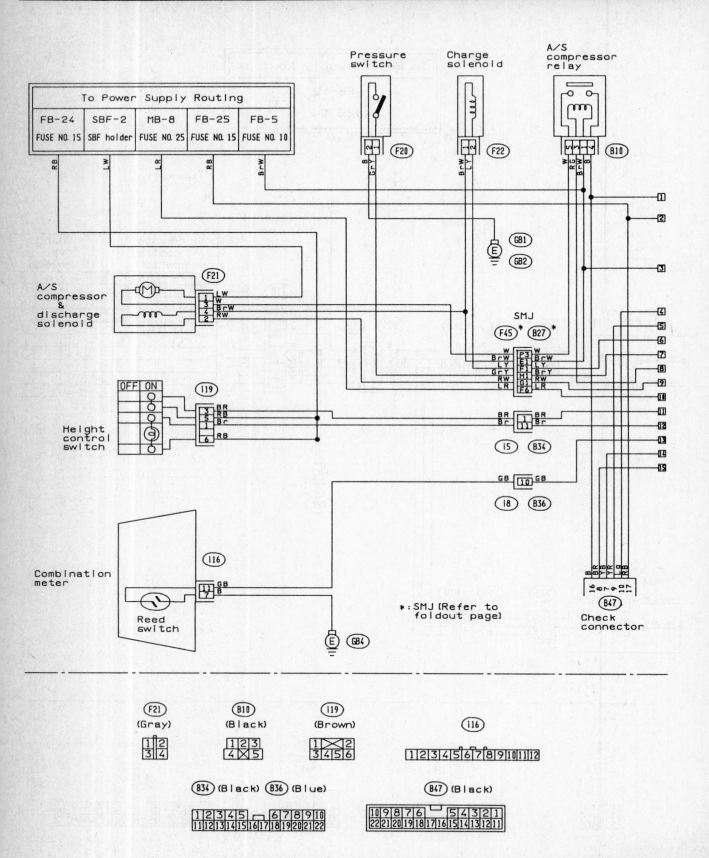

Pneumatic air suspension — 1990–92 Legacy

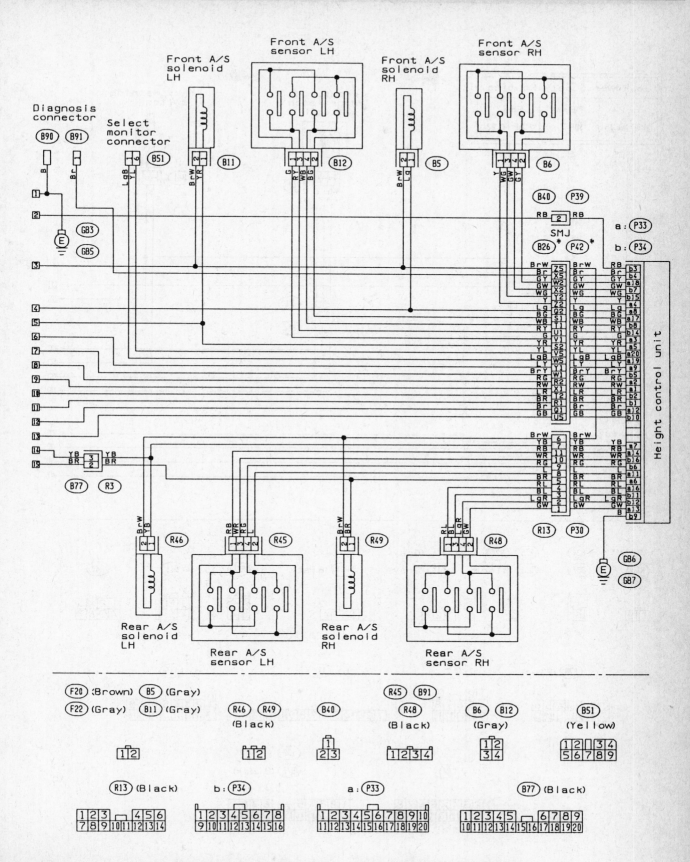

Pneumatic air suspension — 1990–92 Legacy continued

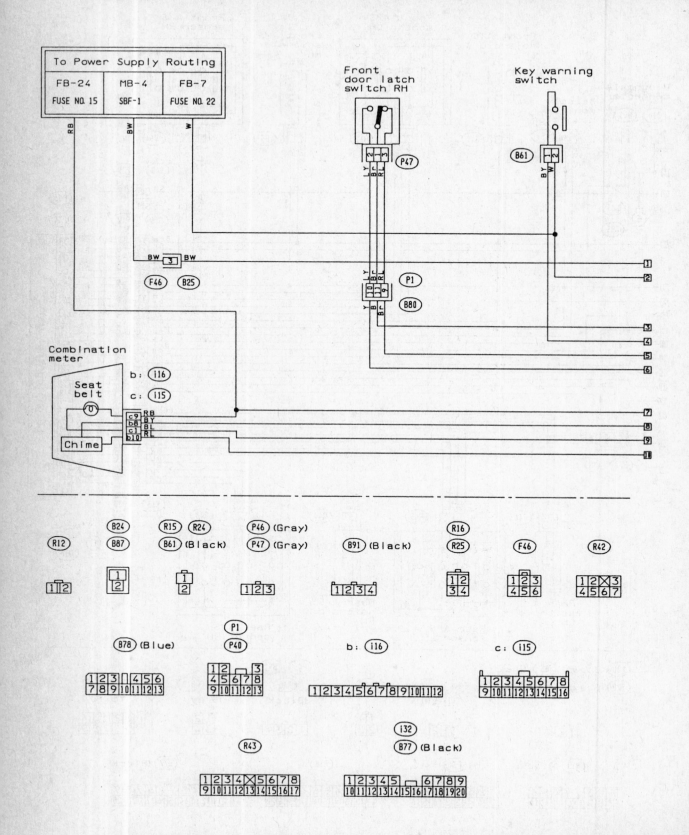

Automatic seat belt and key warning chime — 1990– 92 Legacy USA

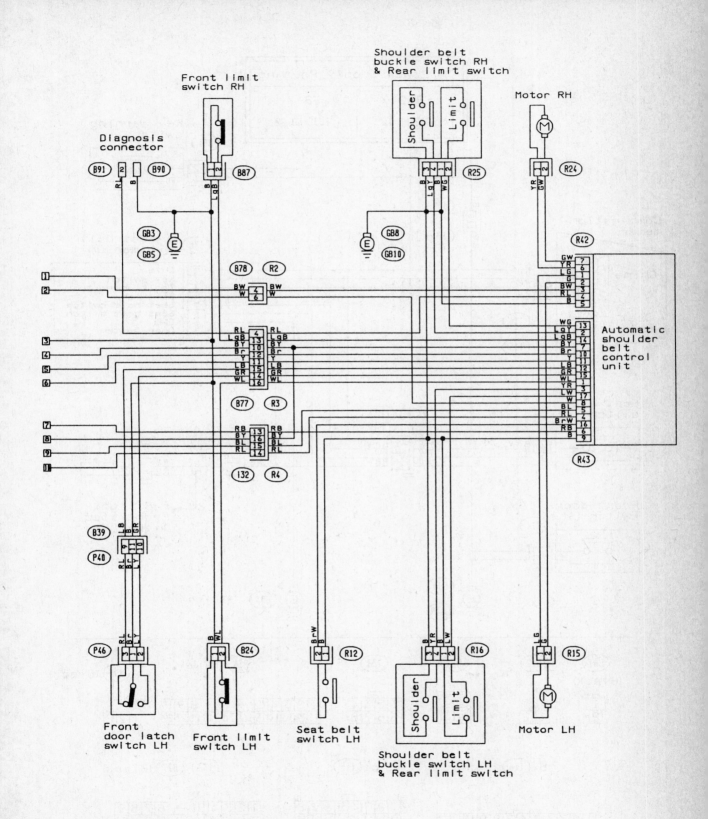

Automatic seat belt and key warning chime — 1990–92 Legacy USA continued

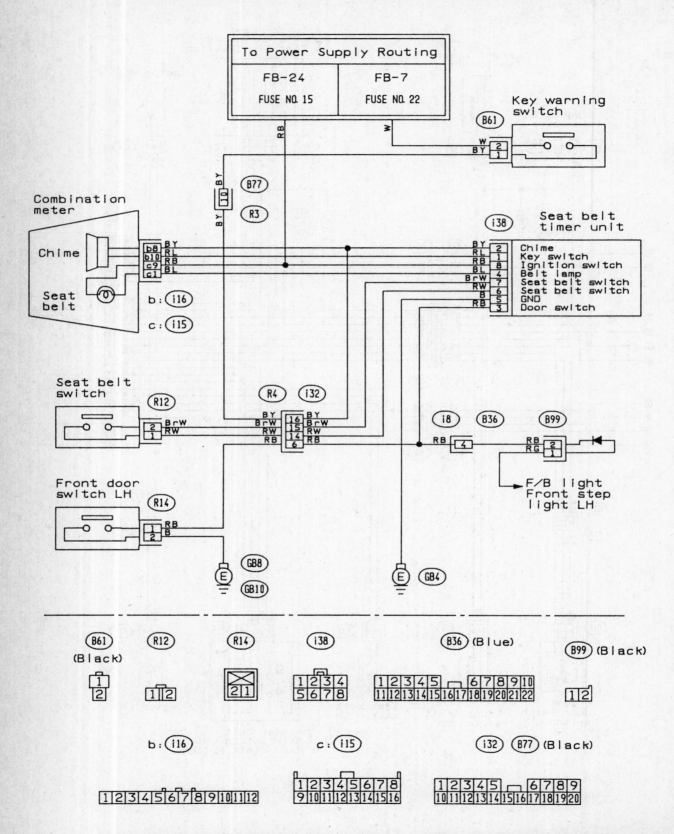

Automatic seat belt and key warning chime — 1990–92 Legacy Canada

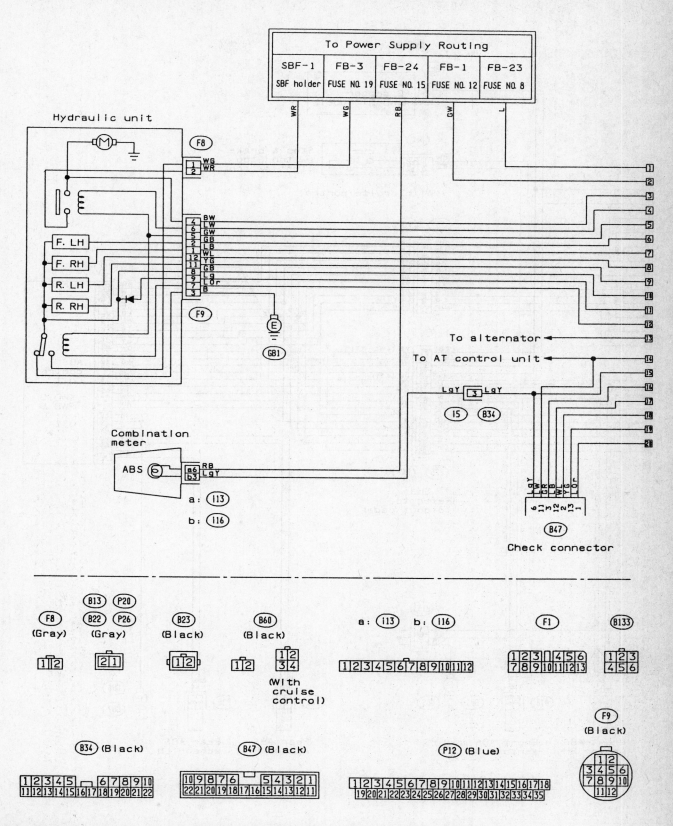

Anti-lock brake system (ABS) — 1990–92 Legacy

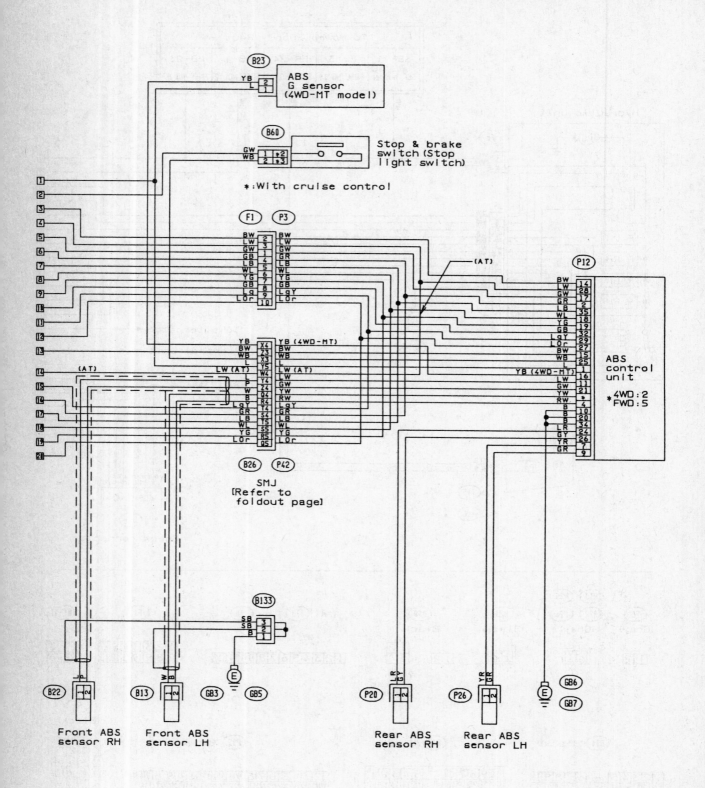

Anti-lock brake system (ABS) — 1990-92 Legacy continued

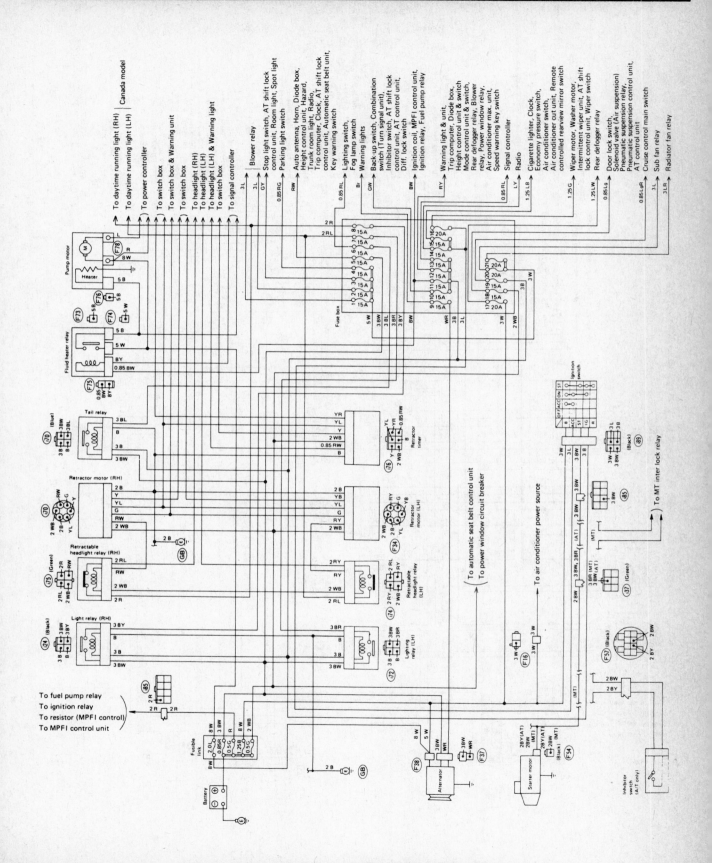

Power supply routing — 1989-91 XT 2700cc engine

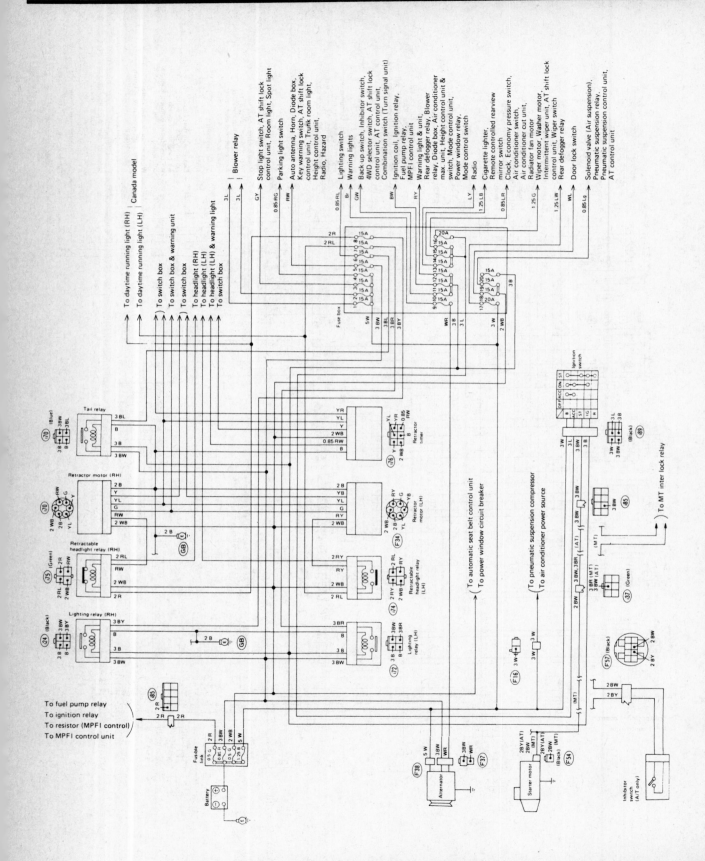

Power supply routing — 1989-91 XT 1800cc engine

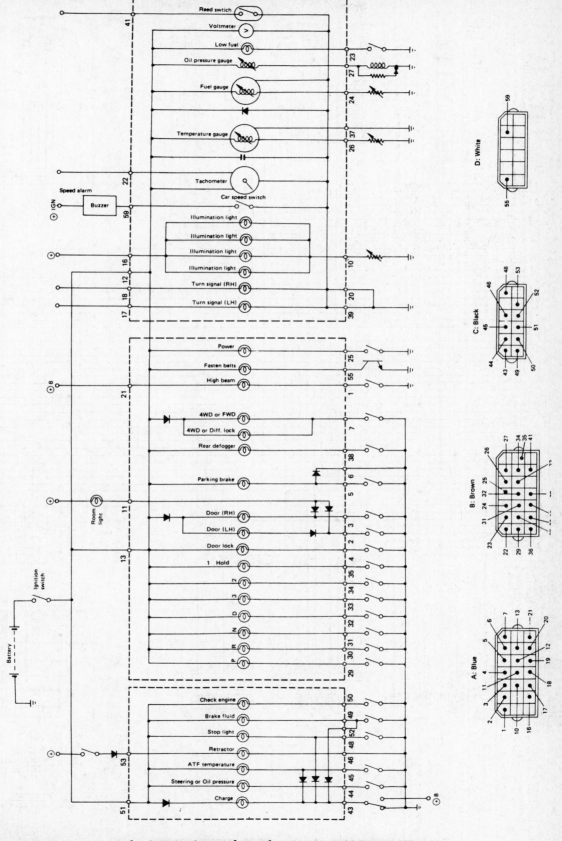

Instrument panel, analog type — 1989–91 XT

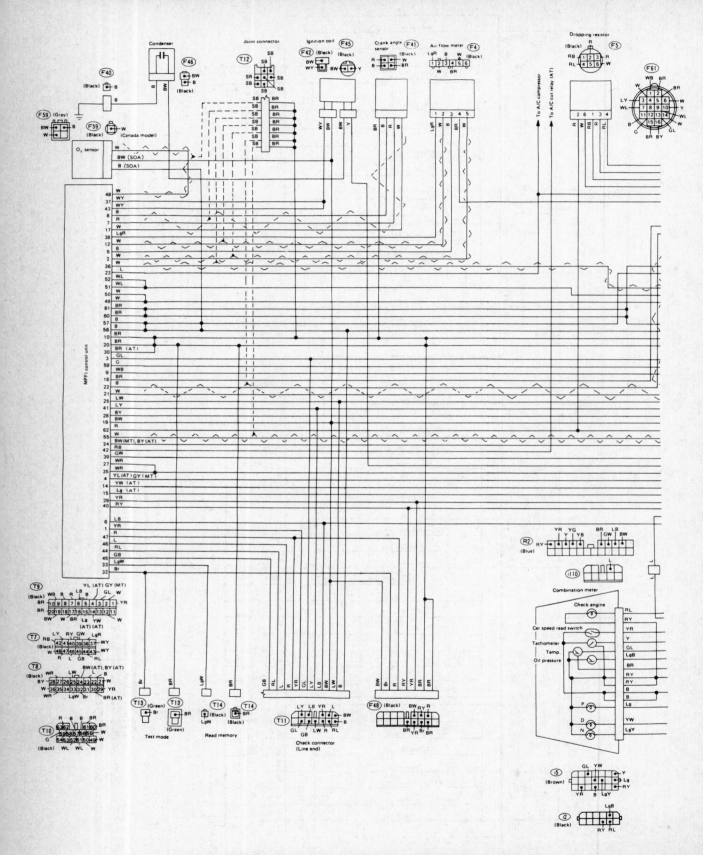

Engine electrical system — 1989–91 XT 1800cc engine

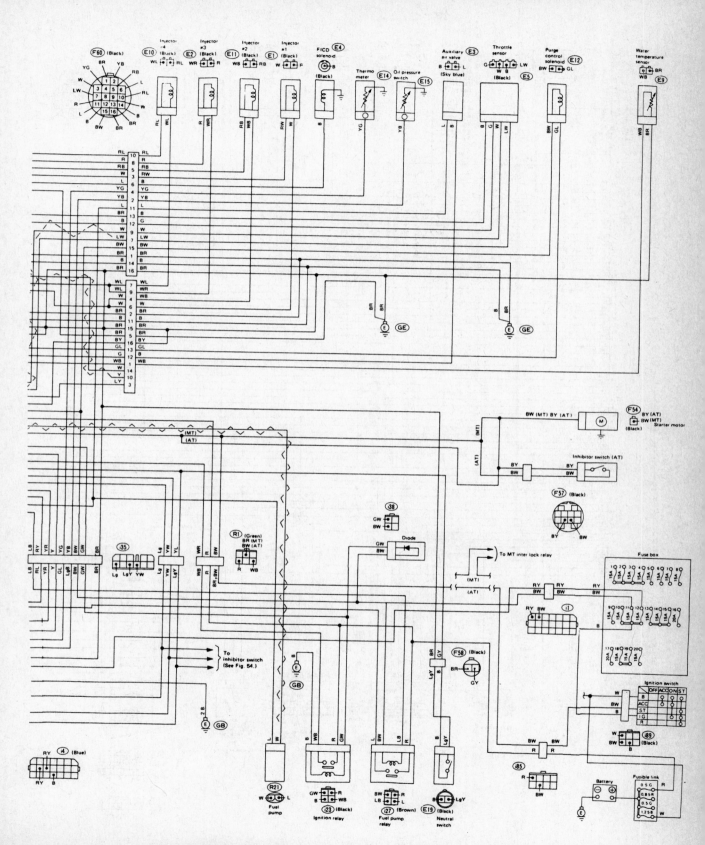

Engine electrical system — 1989–91 XT 1800cc engine continued

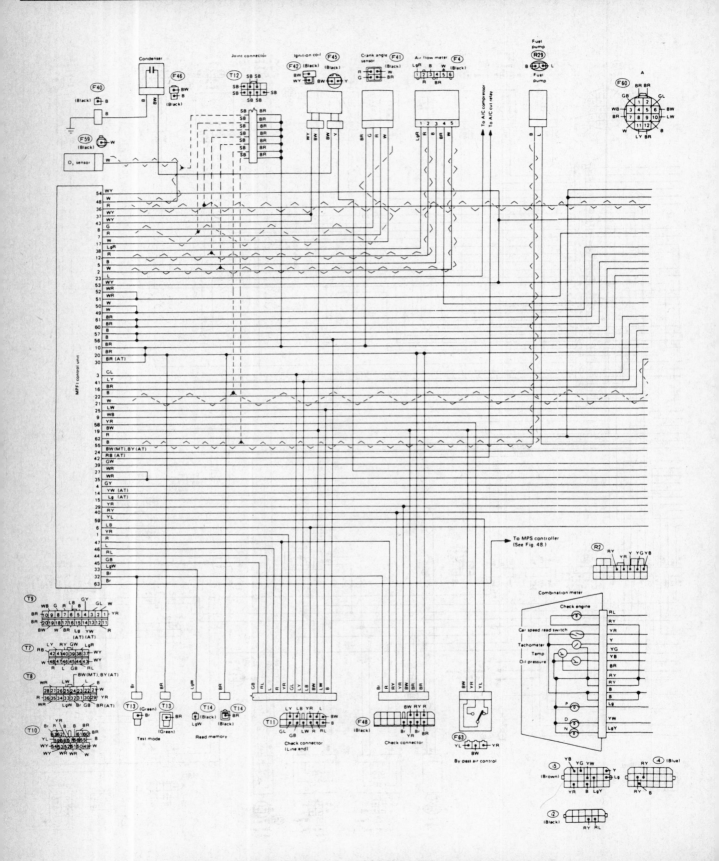

Engine electrical system — 1989–91 XT 2700cc engine

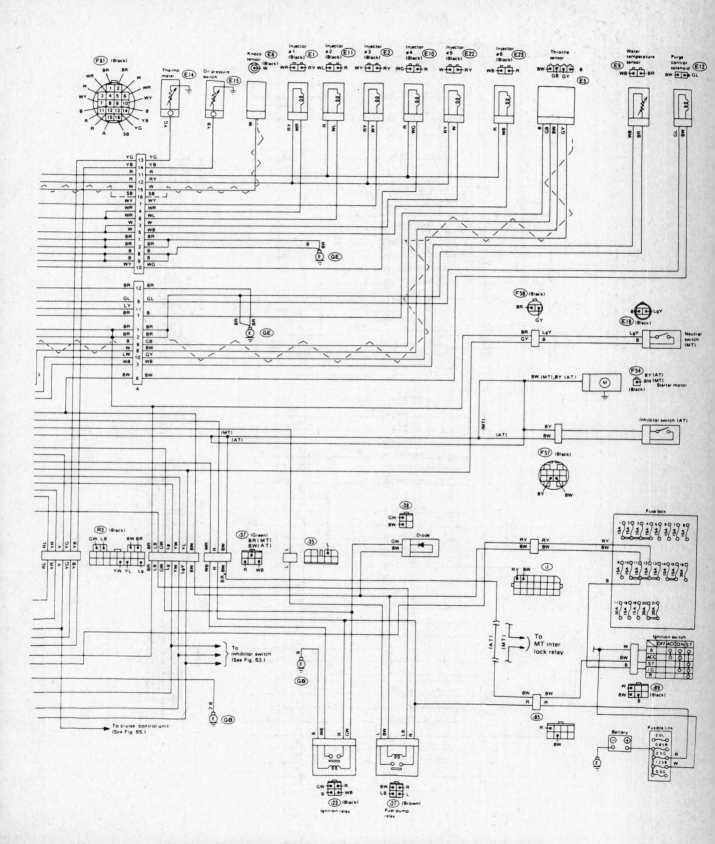

Engine electrical system — 1989–91 XT 2700cc engine continued

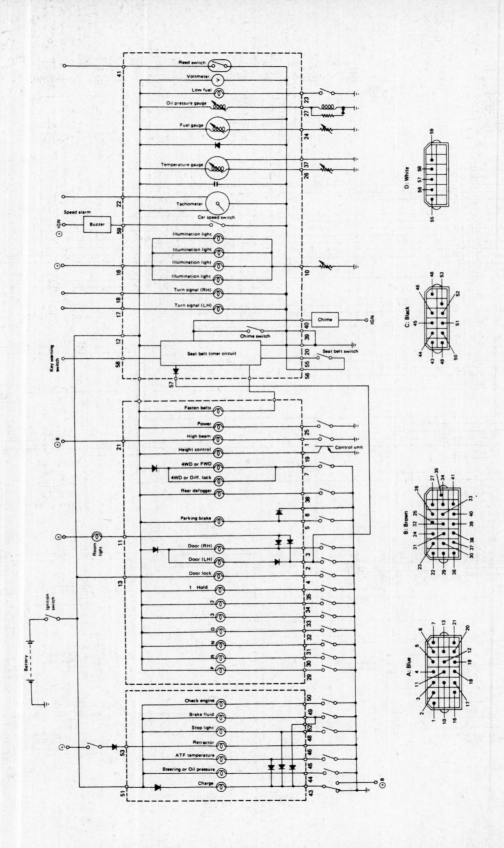

Instrument panel (Canada), analog type — 1989–91 XT

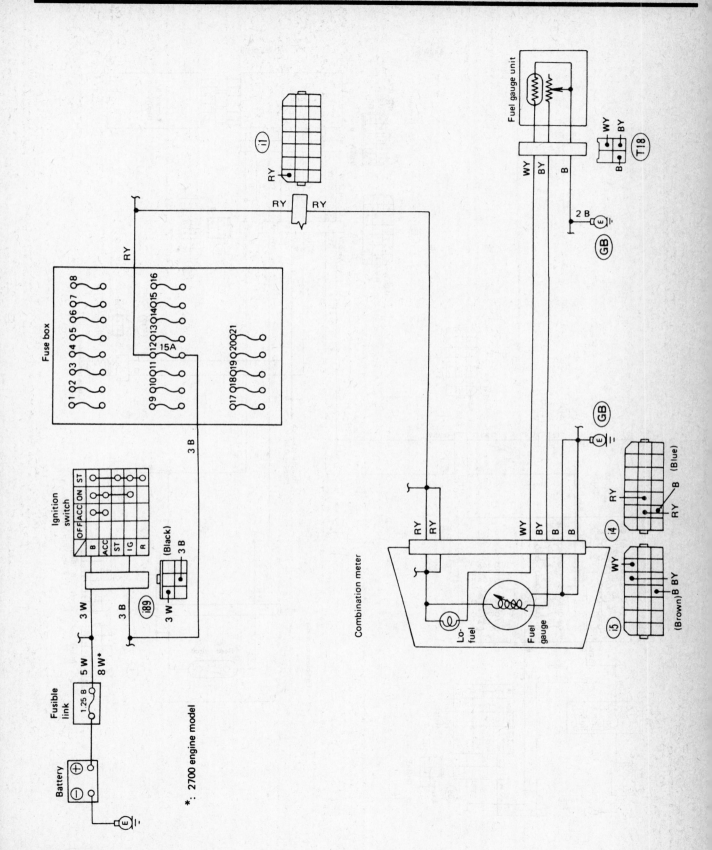

Fuel gauge — 1989–91 XT

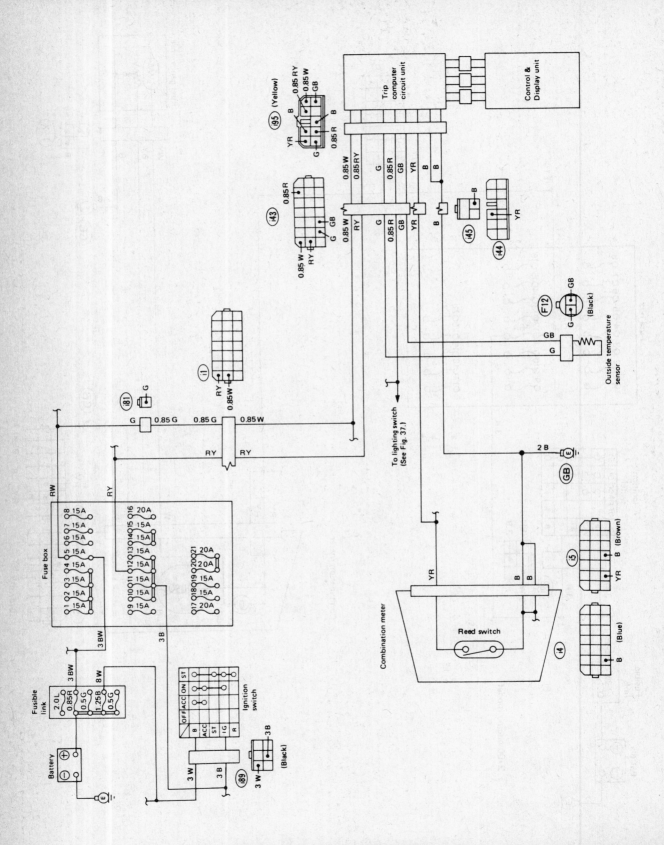

Trip computer — 1989–91 XT 2700cc engine

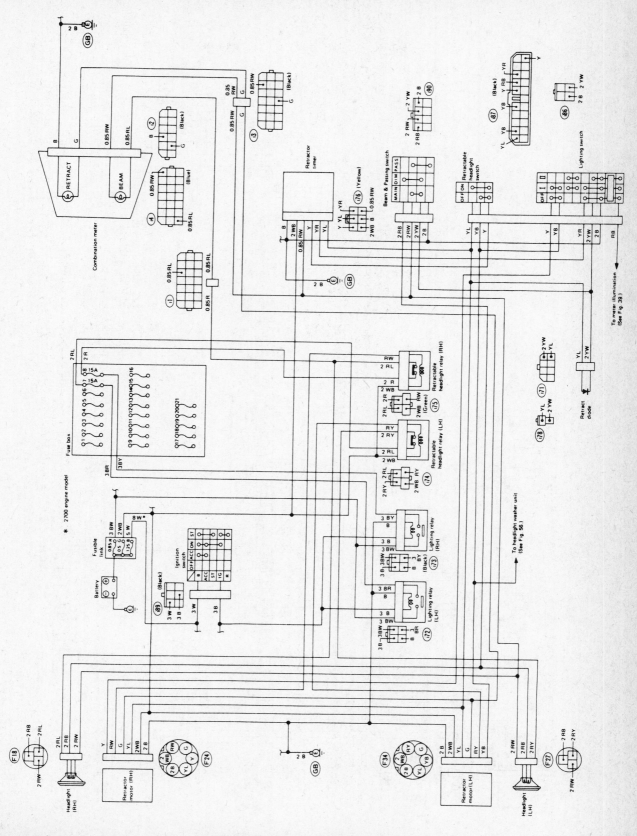

Lighting system — 1989–91 XT (USA)

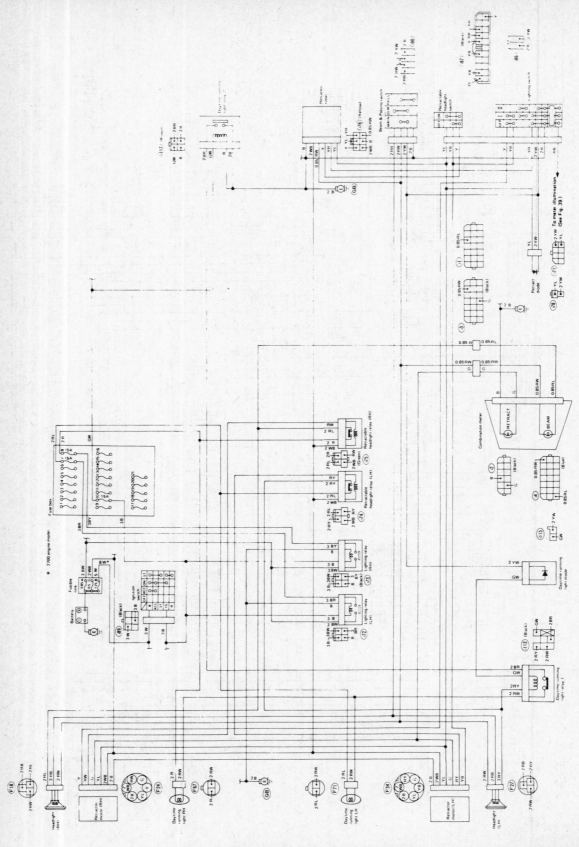

Lighting system — 1989–91 XT (Canada)

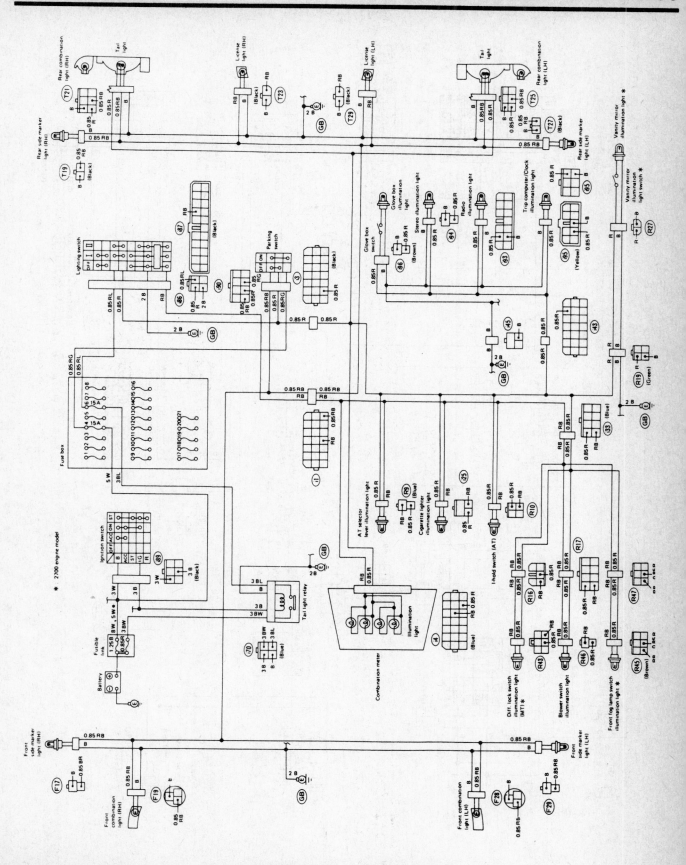

Lighting system — 1989–91 XT 4WD

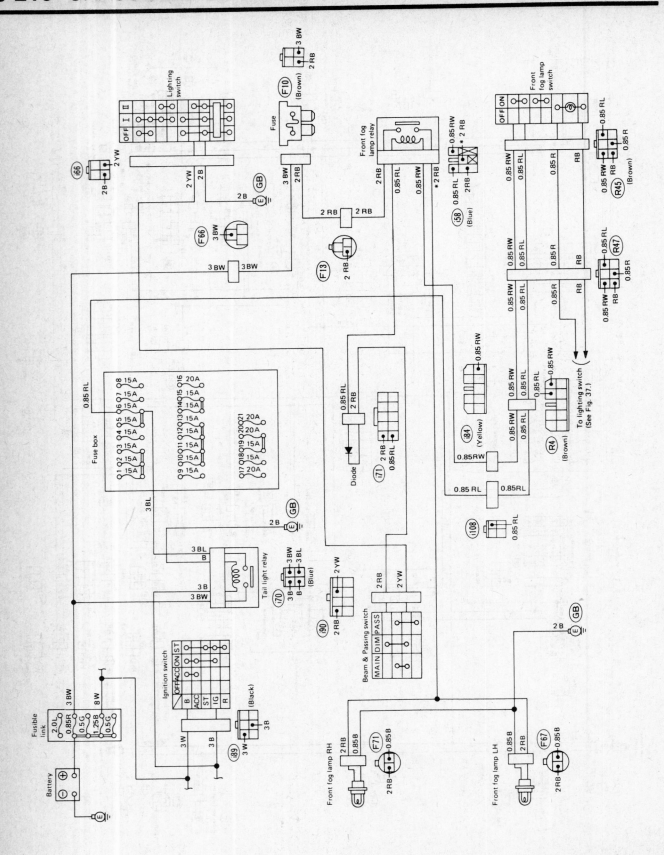

Fog light — 1989-91 XT

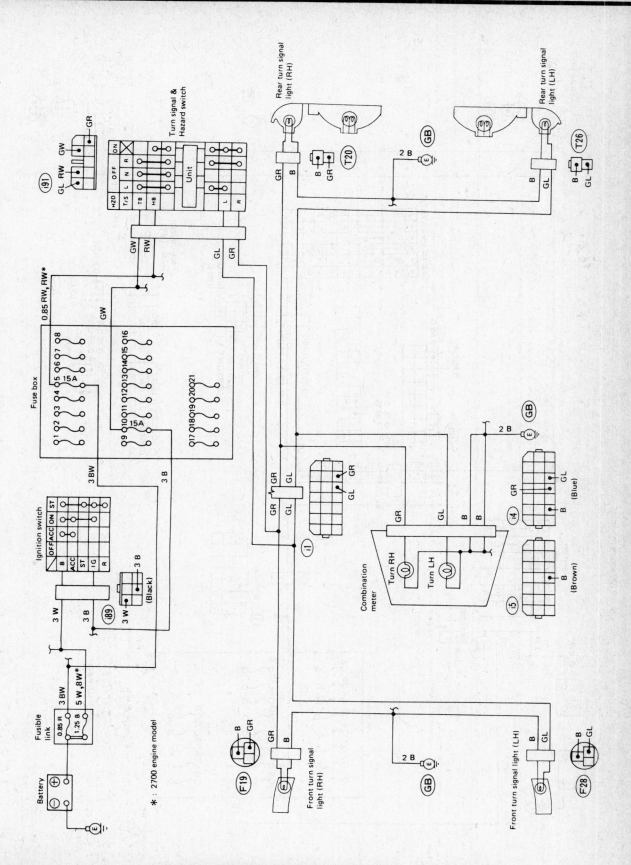

Turn signal and hazard warning light — 1989–91 XT

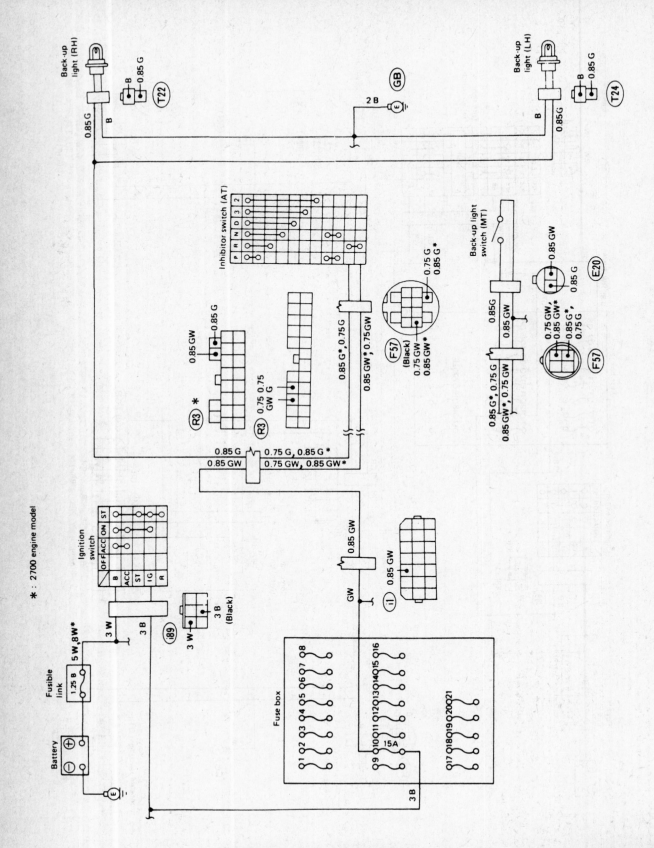

Backup light — 1989-91 XT

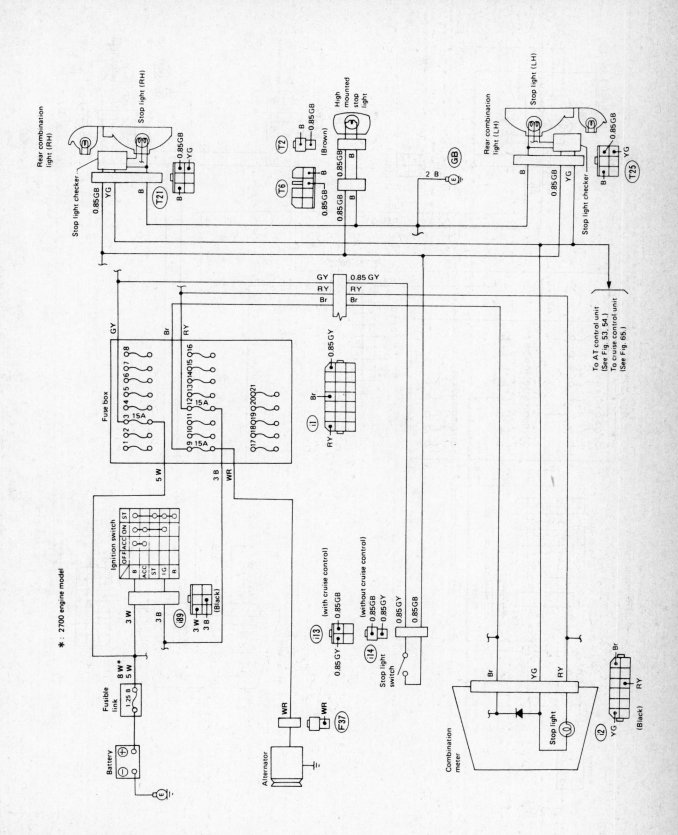

Stop light — 1989–91 XT

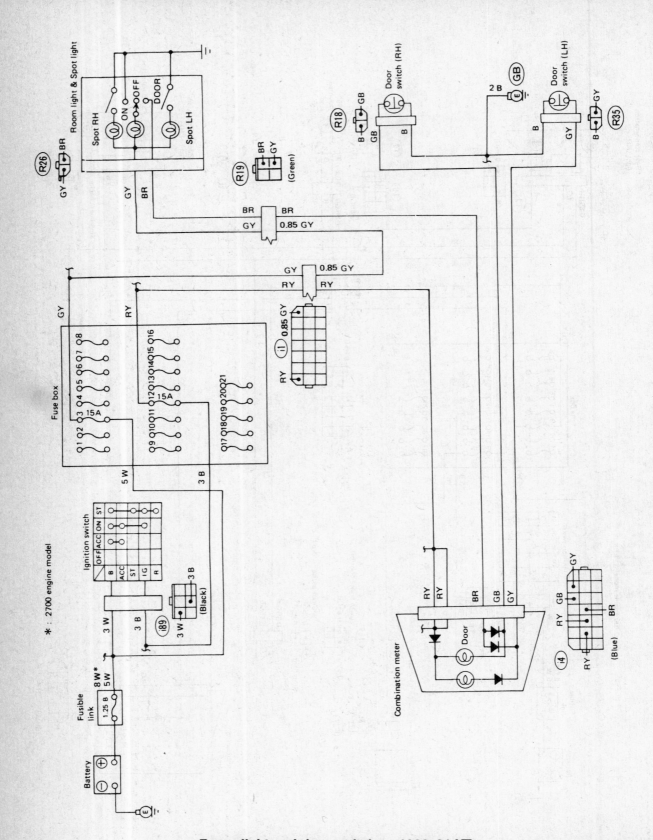

Room light and door switch — 1989–91 XT

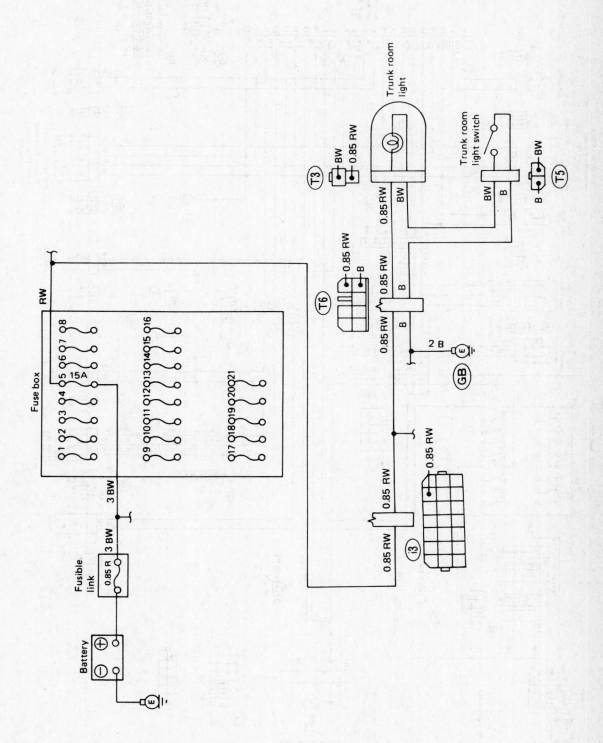

Trunk room light — 1989–91 XT

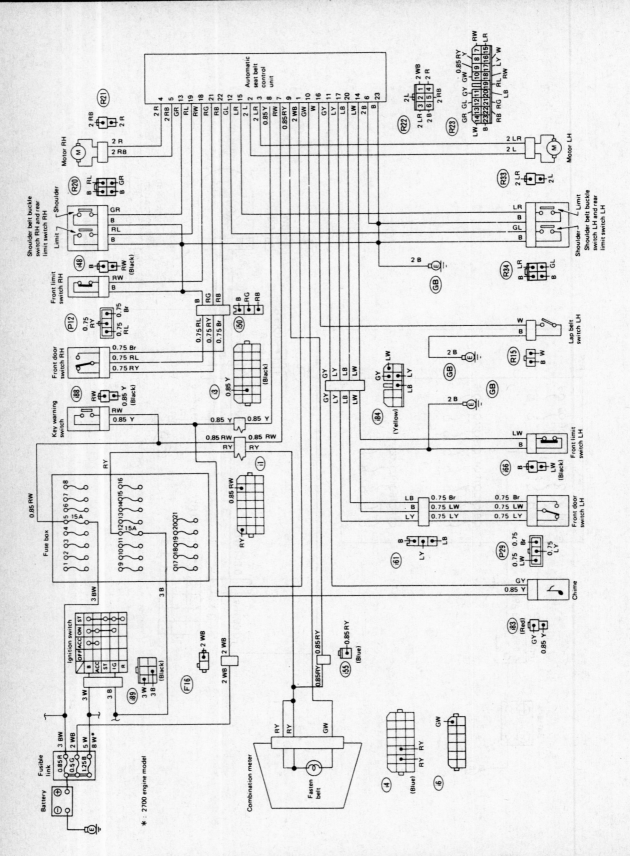

Seat belt and key warning system, automatic seat belt — 1989–91 XT

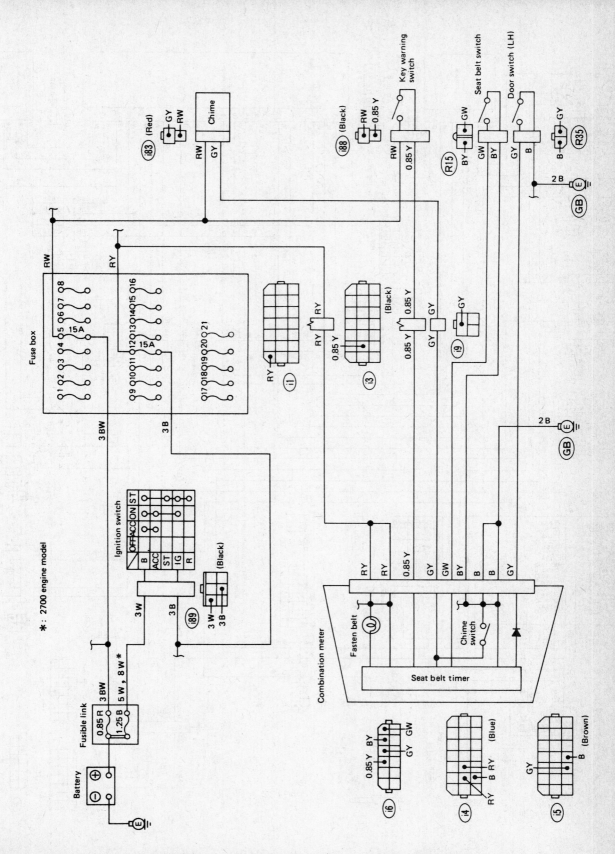

Seat belt and key warning system — 1989–91 XT Canada

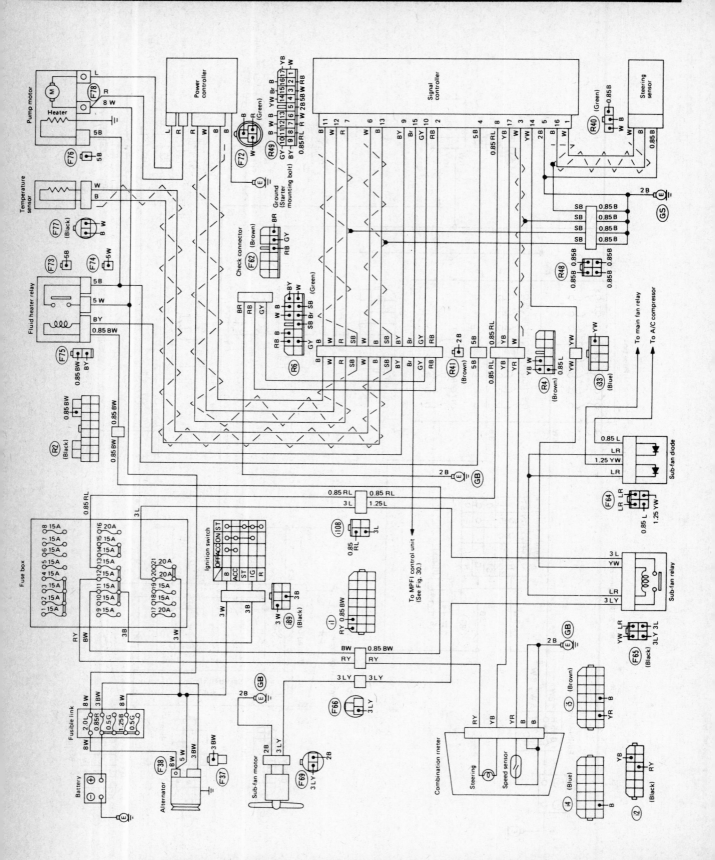

Electronic controlled motor drive power steering arm — 1989–91 XT

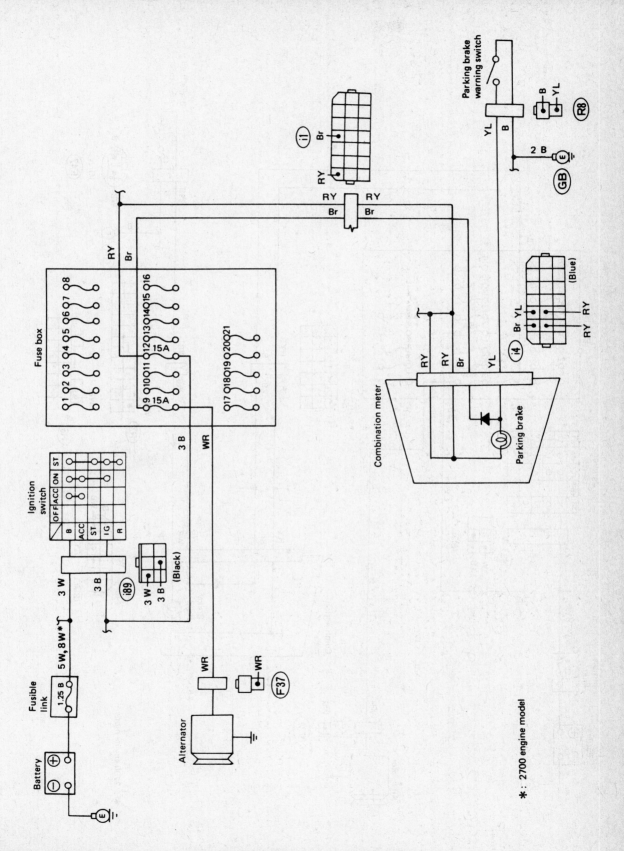

Parking brake system — 1989–91 XT

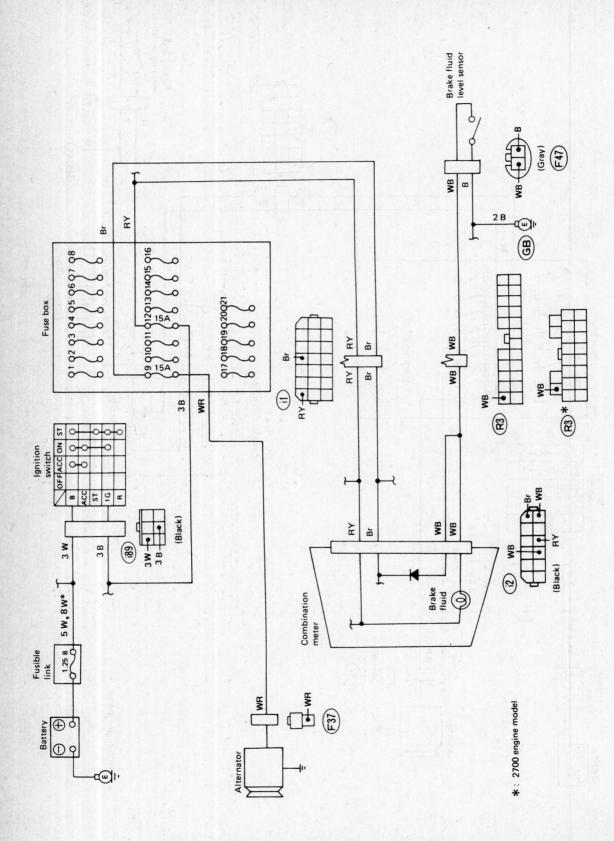

Brake fluid level warning system — 1989–91 XT

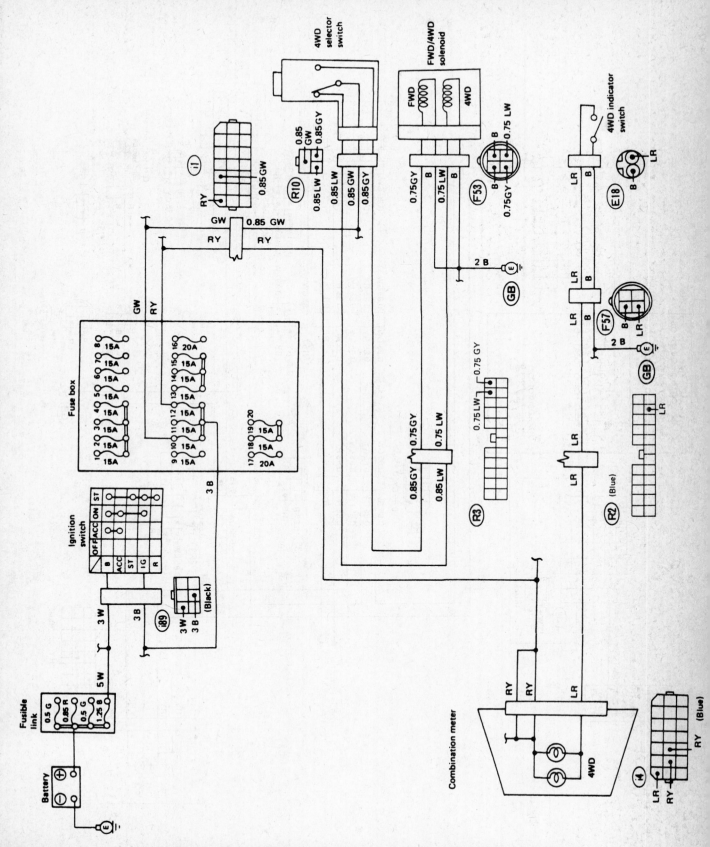

4WD manual transmission system — 1989–91 XT selective 4WD

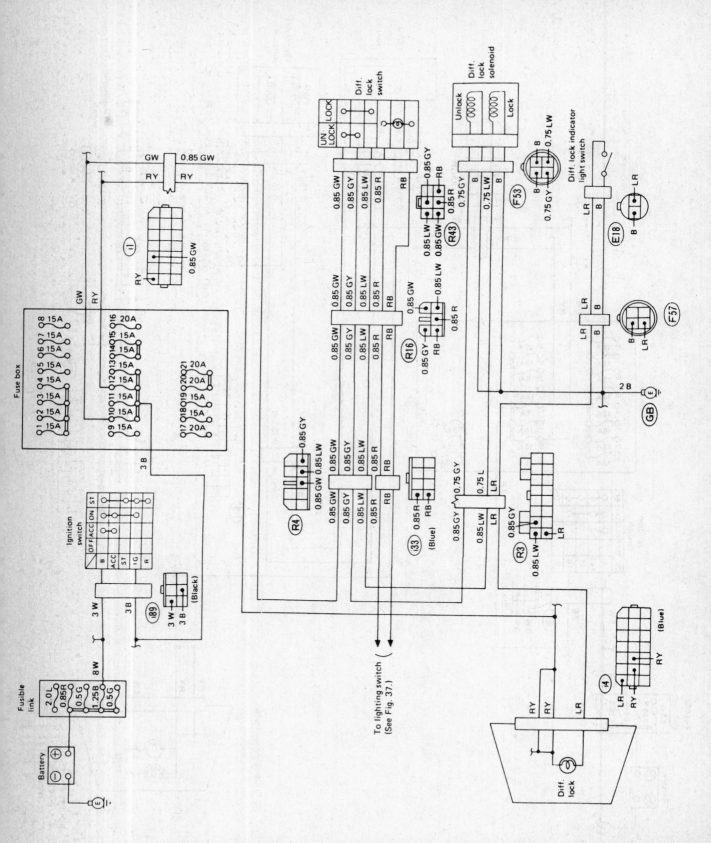

4WD manual transmission system — 1989–91 XT full- time 4WD

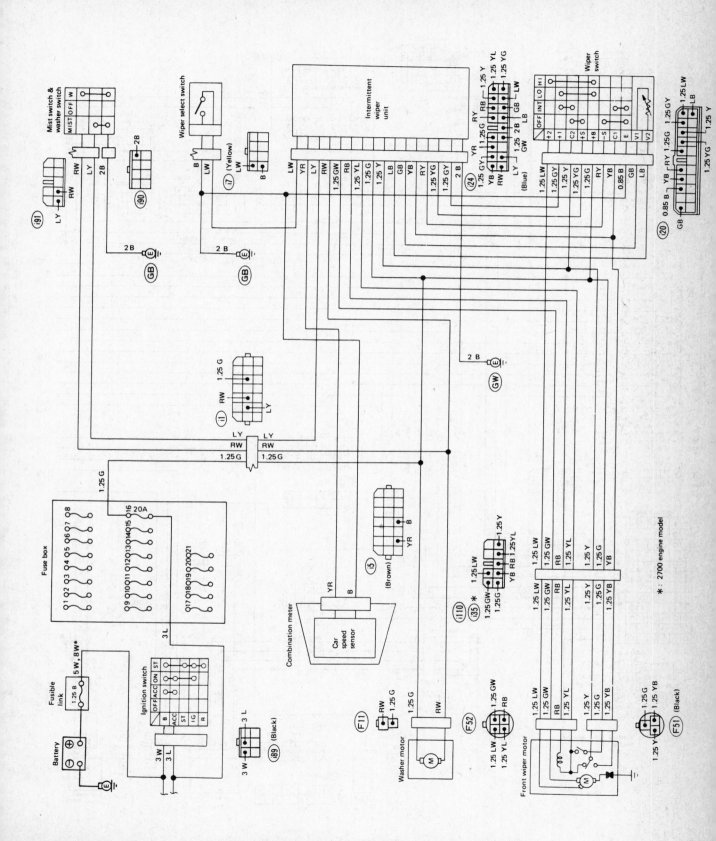

Windshield wiper and washer — 1989–91 XT

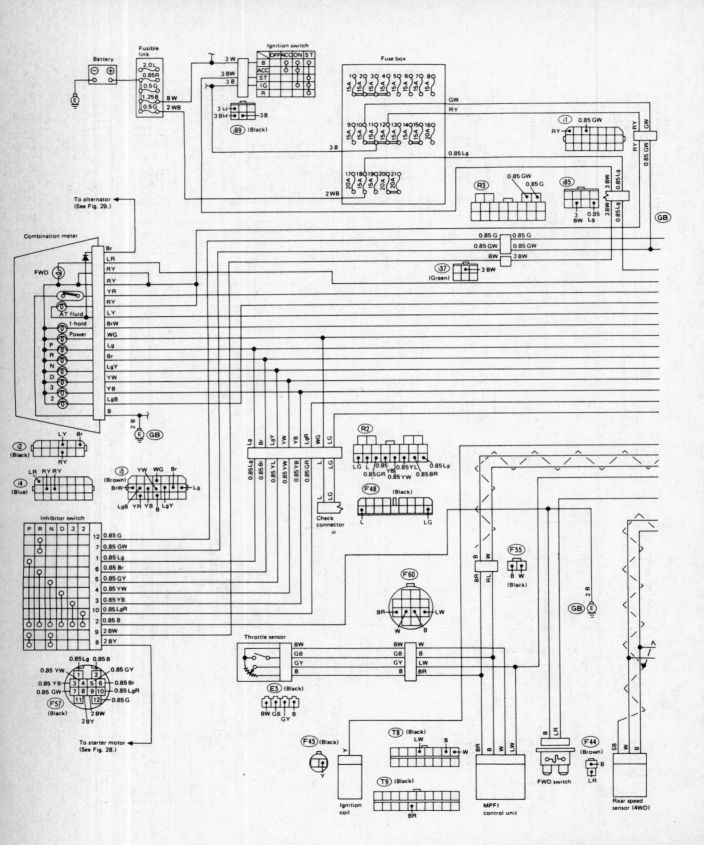

Automatic transmission control system — 1989–91 XT 2700cc engine

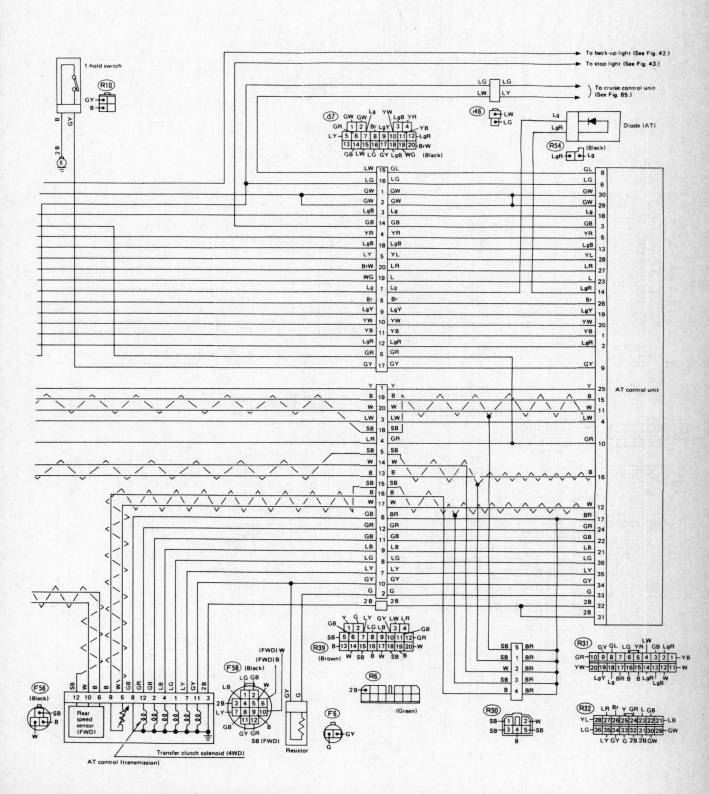

Automatic transmission control system — 1989–91 XT 2700cc engine

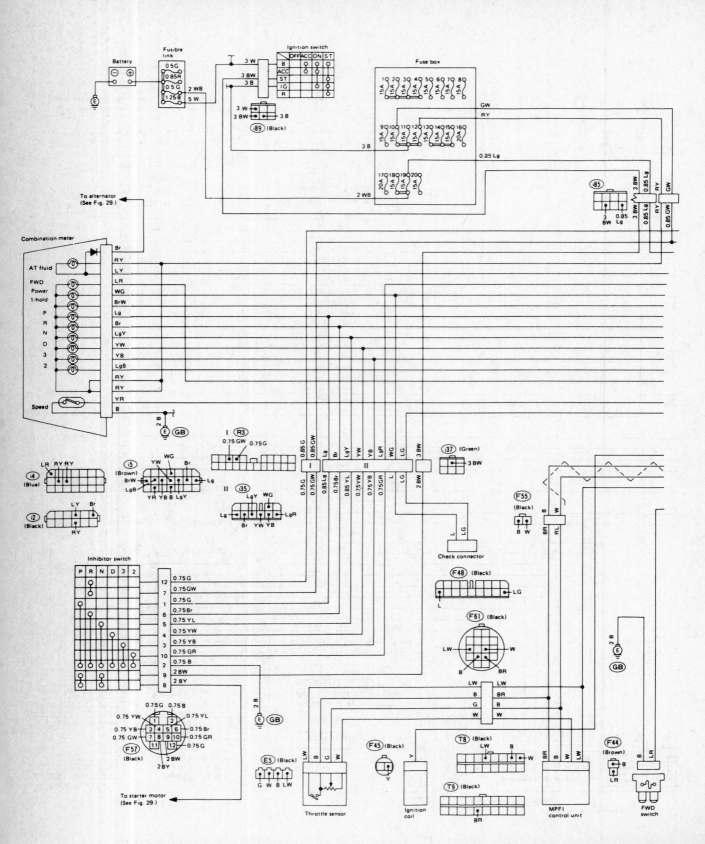

Automatic transmission control system — 1989–91 XT 1800cc engine

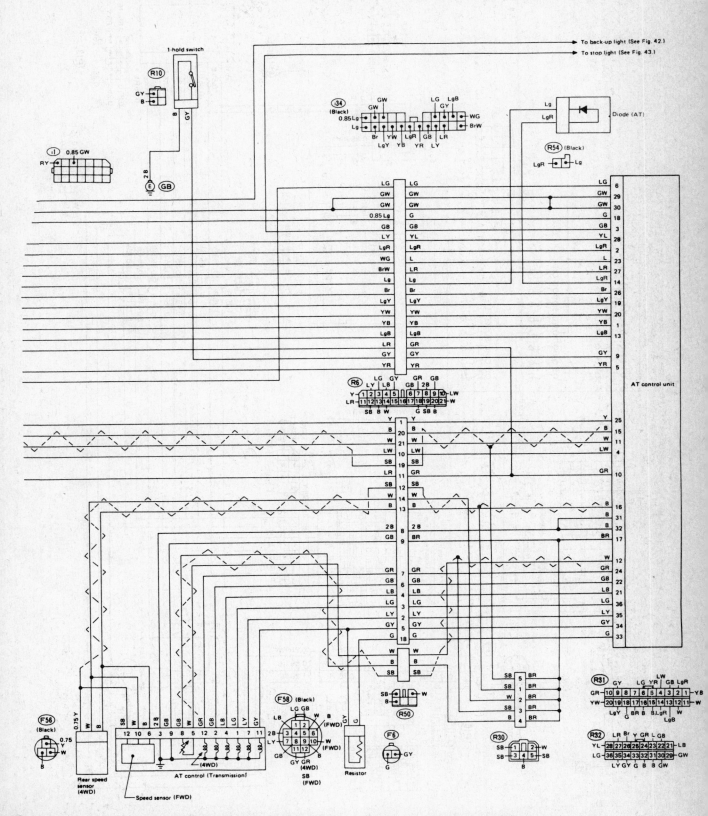

Automatic transmission control system — 1989–91 XT 1800cc engine

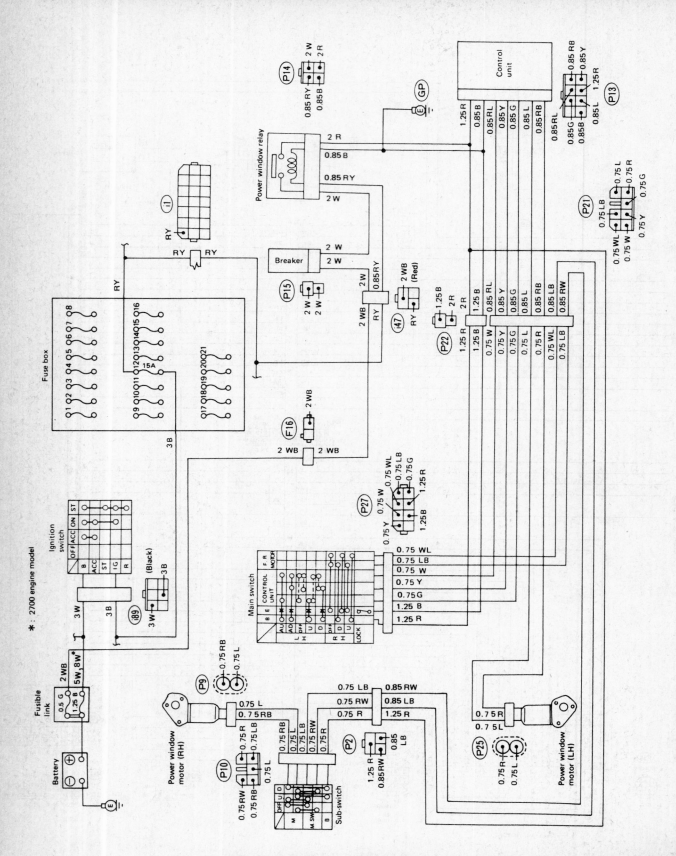

Power window — 1989–91 XT

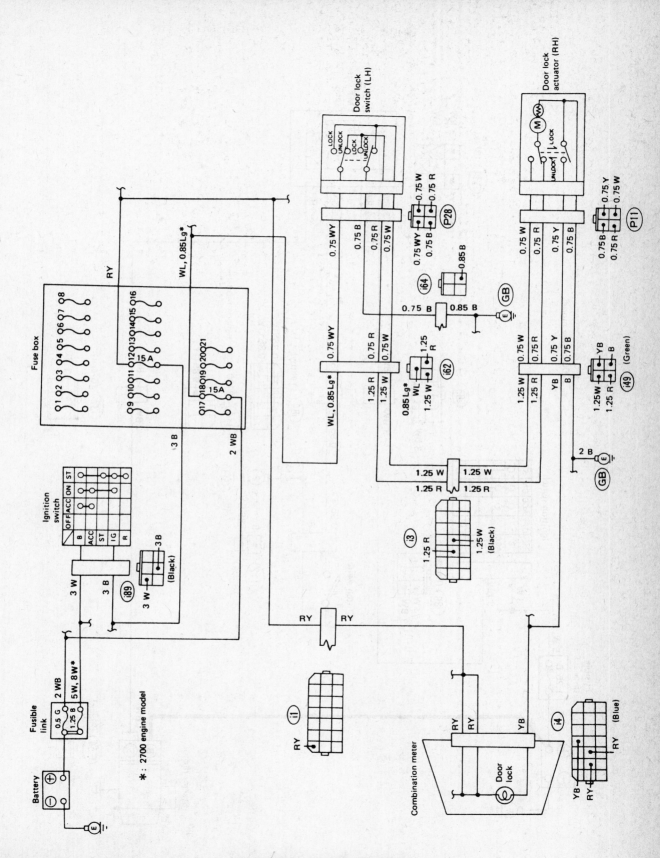

Door lock — 1989–91 XT

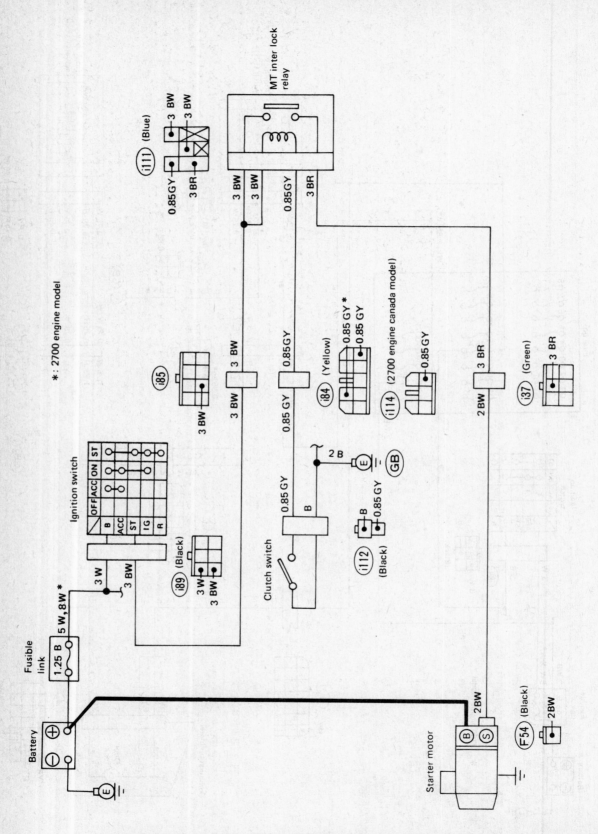

Starting system — 1989–91 XT manual transmission

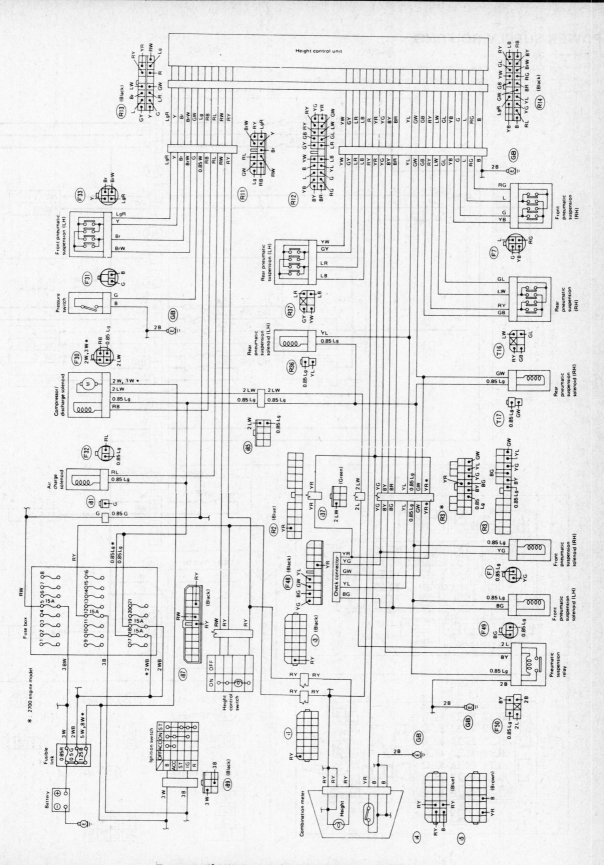

Pneumatic suspension system — 1989–91 XT

1. POWER SUPPLY ROUTING

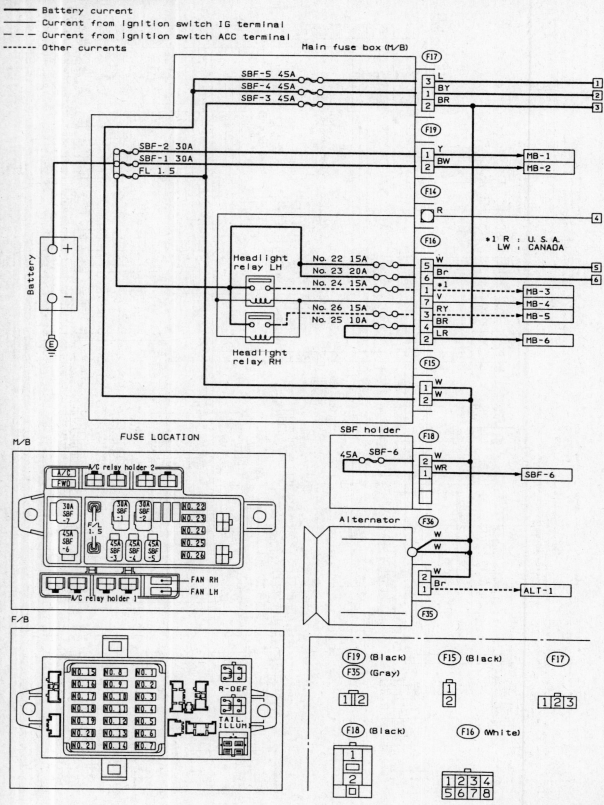

Power supply routing — 1992 SVX

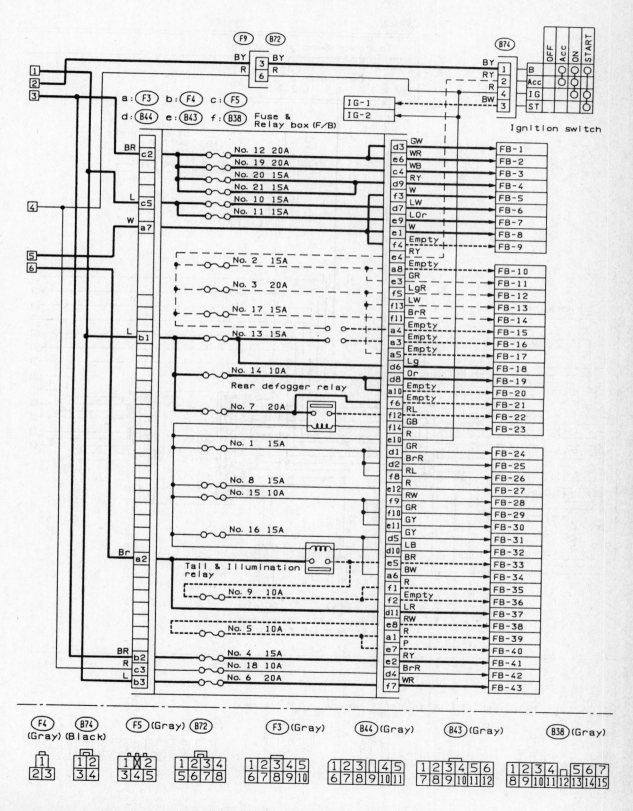

Power supply routing — 1992 SVX continued

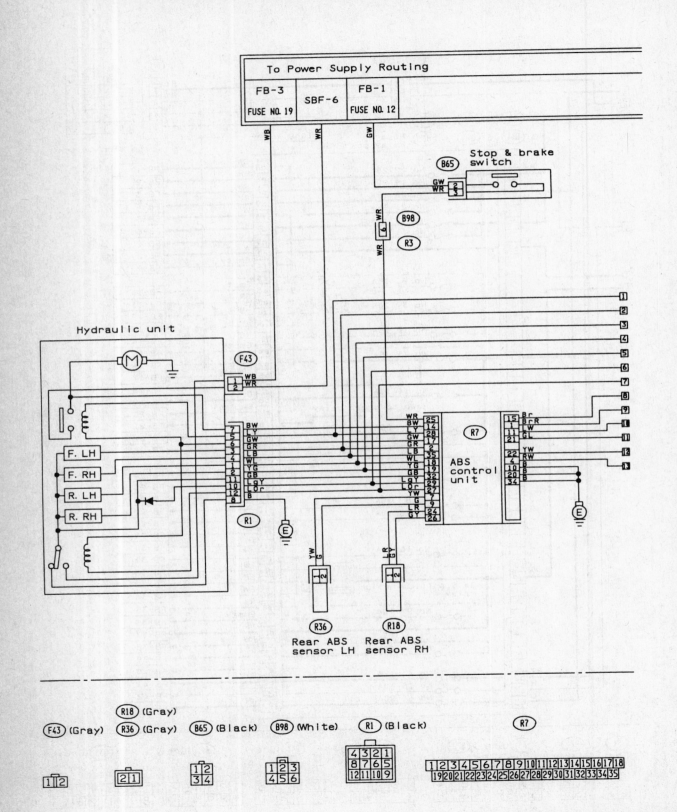

Anti-lock brake system (ABS) — 1992 SVX

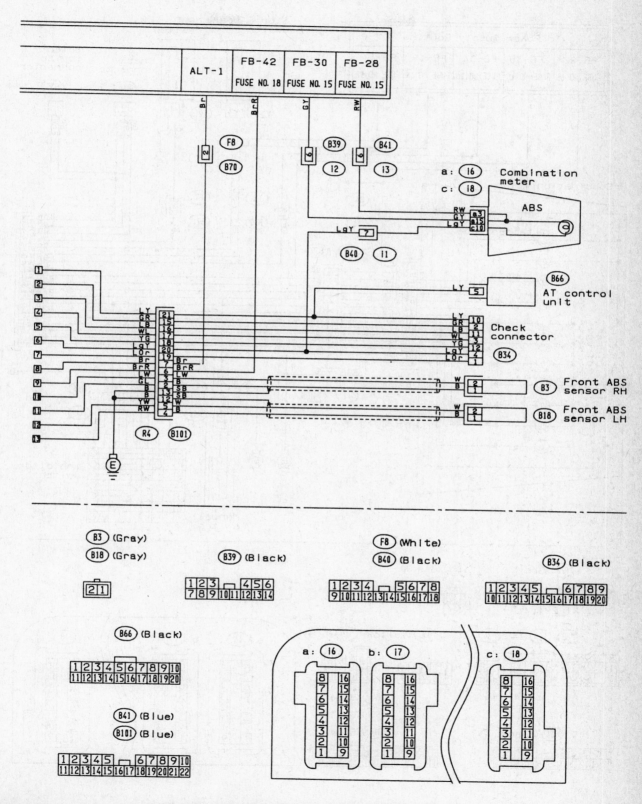

Anti-lock brake system (ABS) — 1992 SVX continued

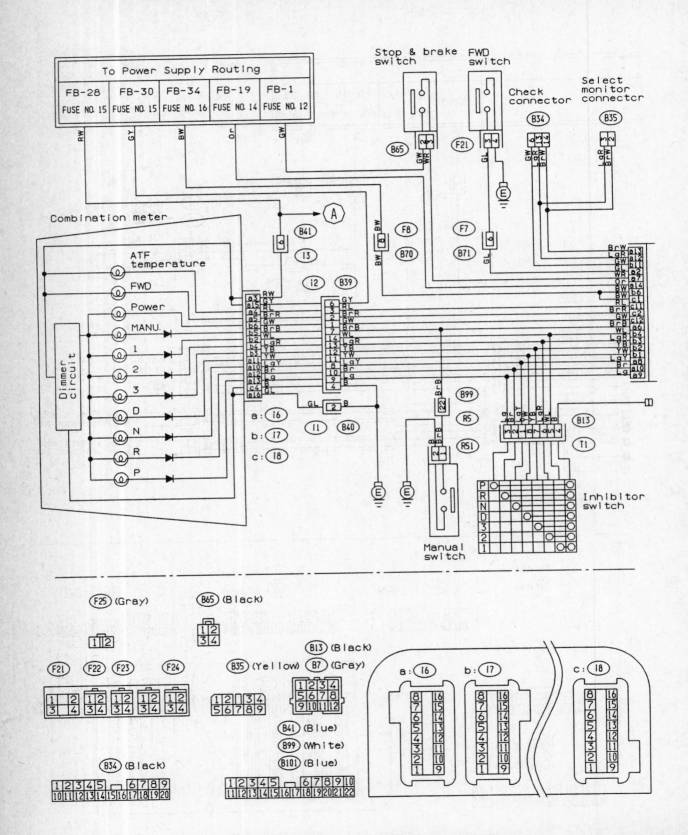

Automatic transmission control system — 1992 SVX

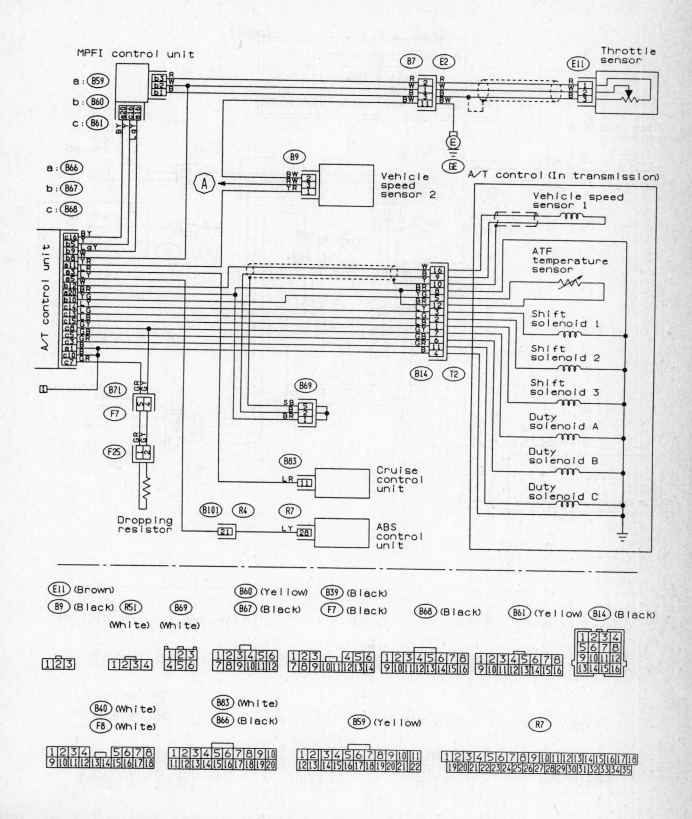

Automatic transmission control system — 1992 SVX continued

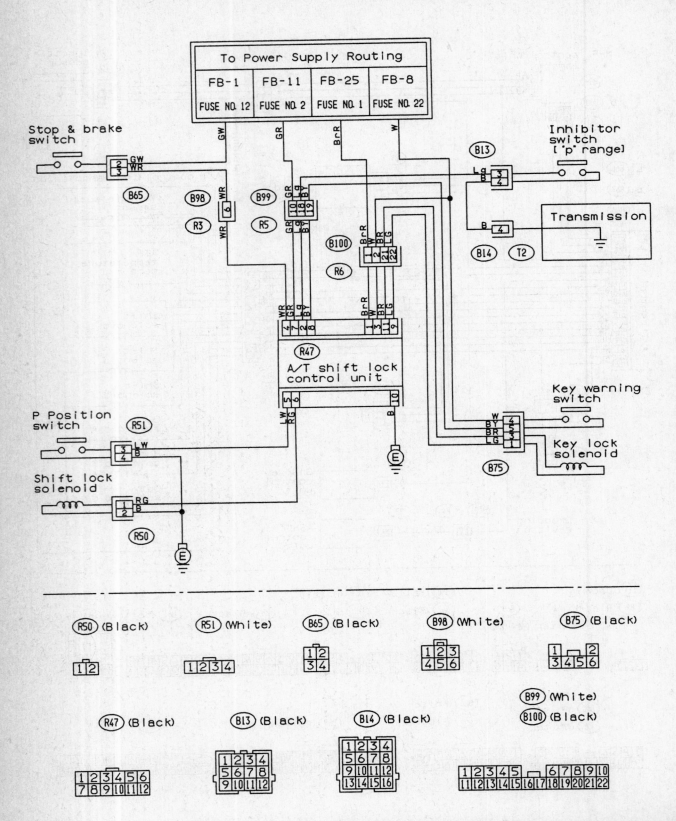

Automatic transmission shift lock system — 1992 SVX

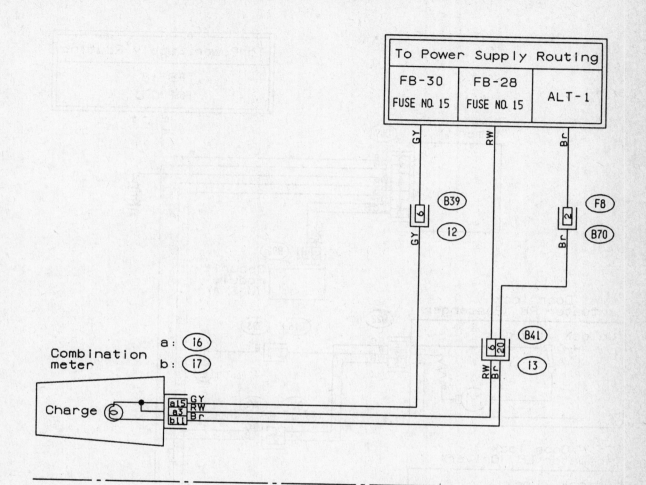

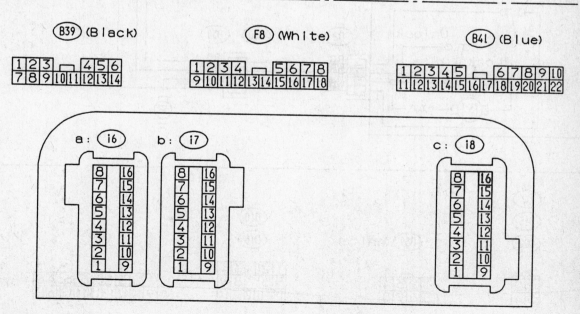

Charging system — 1992 SVX

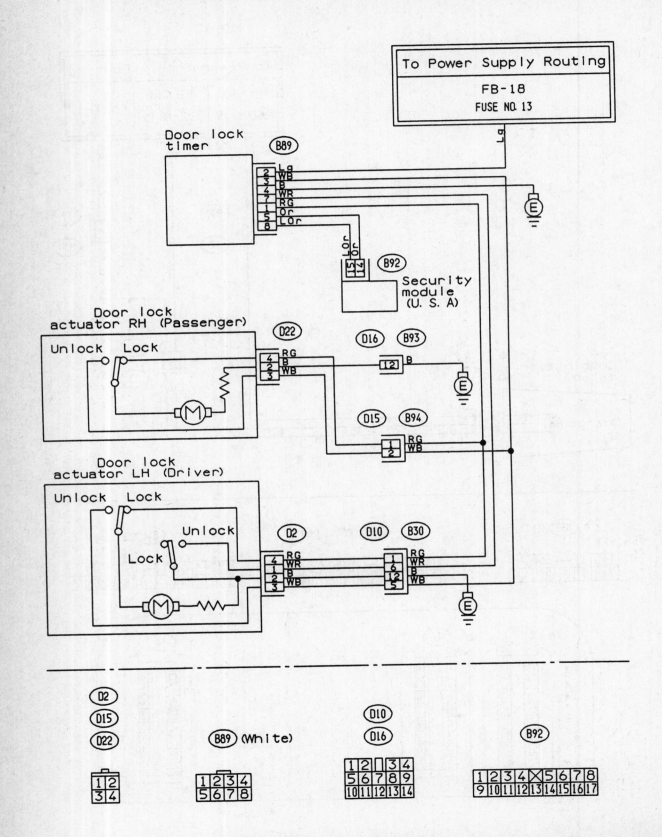

Door lock system — 1992 SVX USA

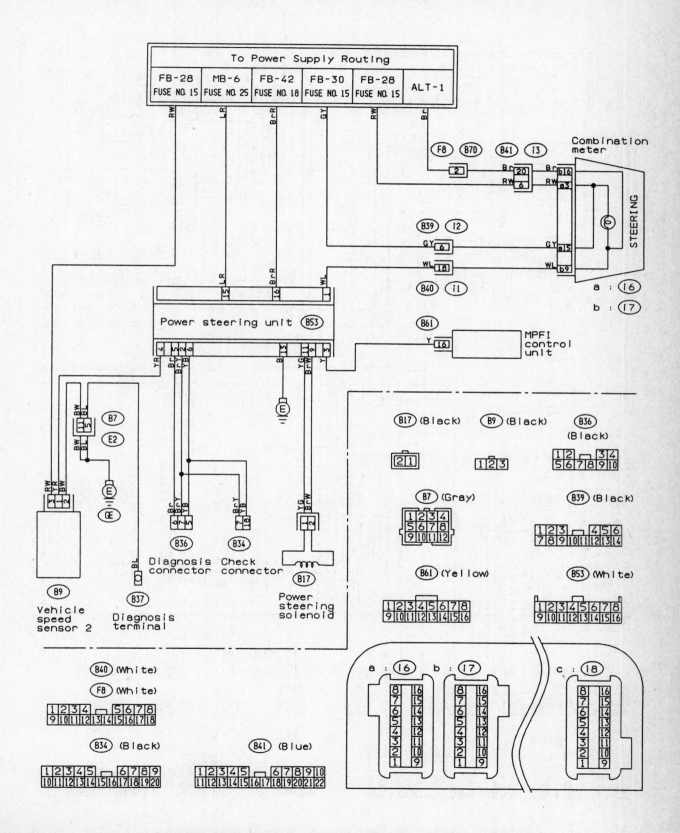

Electronically controlled power steering system – 1992 SVX

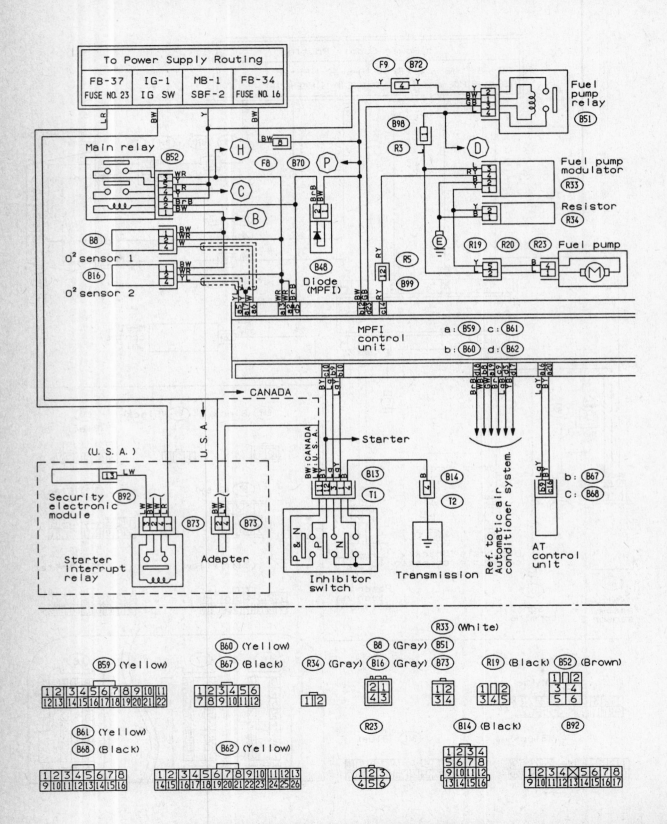

Engine electrical system — 1992 SVX MPFI

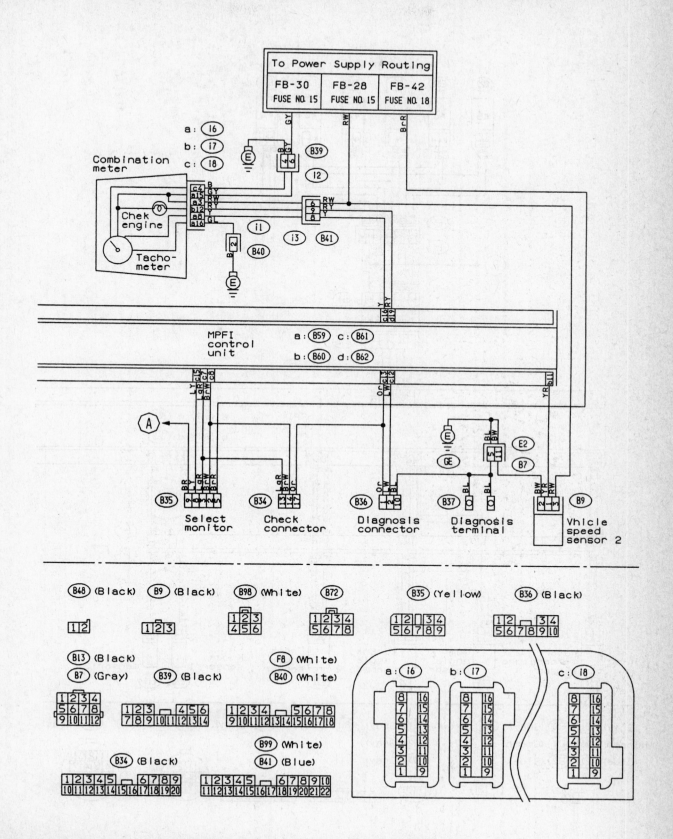

Engine electrical system — 1992 SVX MPFI continued

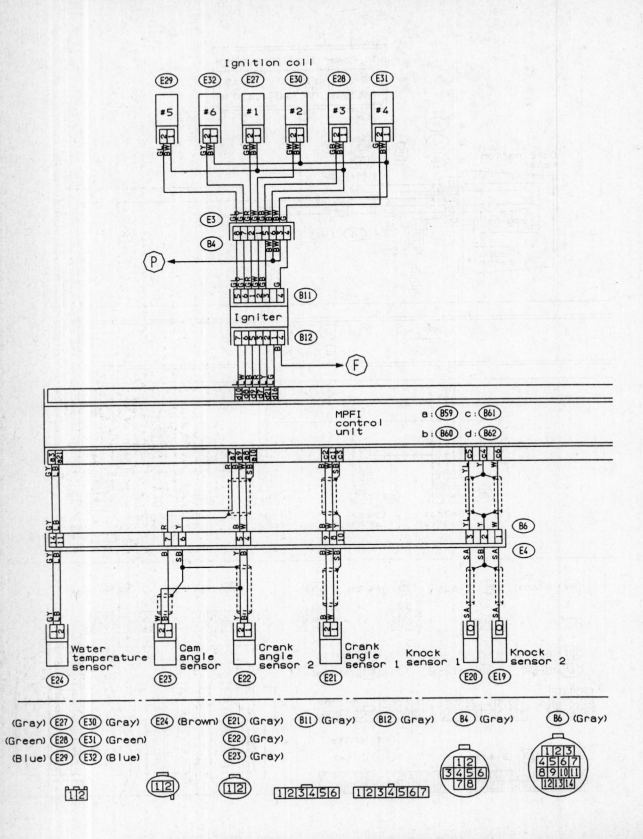

Engine electrical system — 1992 SVX MPFI continued

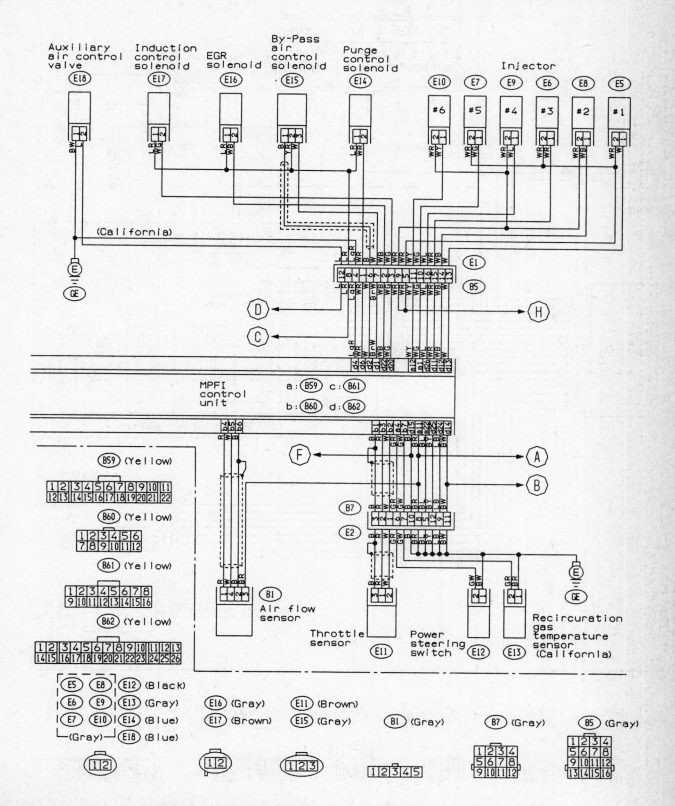

Engine electrical system — 1992 SVX MPFI continued

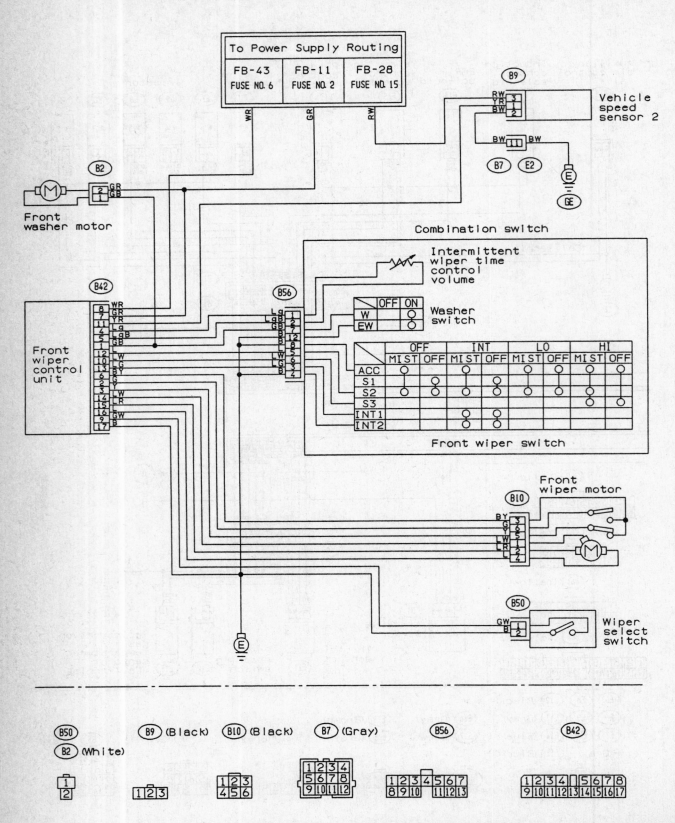

Front wiper and washer system — 1992 SVX

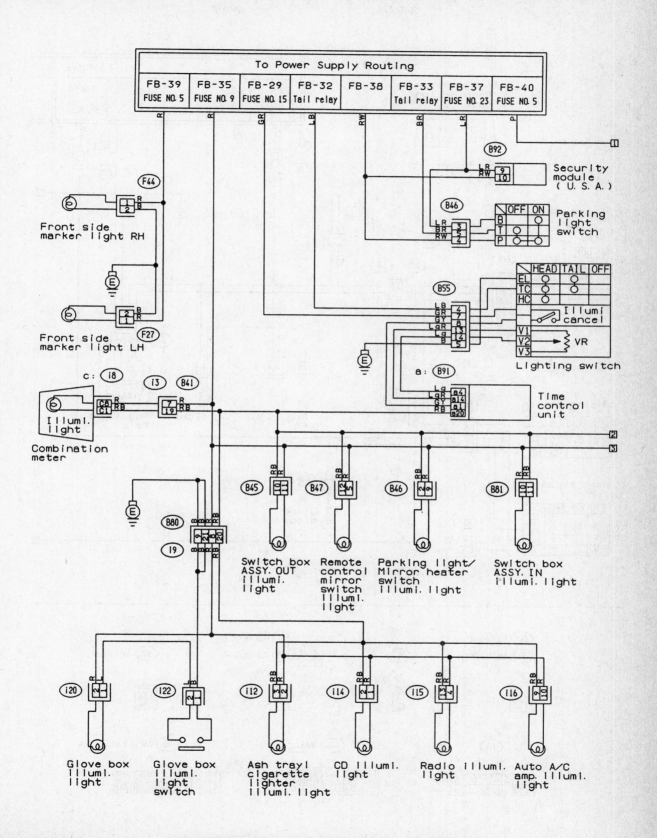

Illumination and tail light system — 1992 SVX

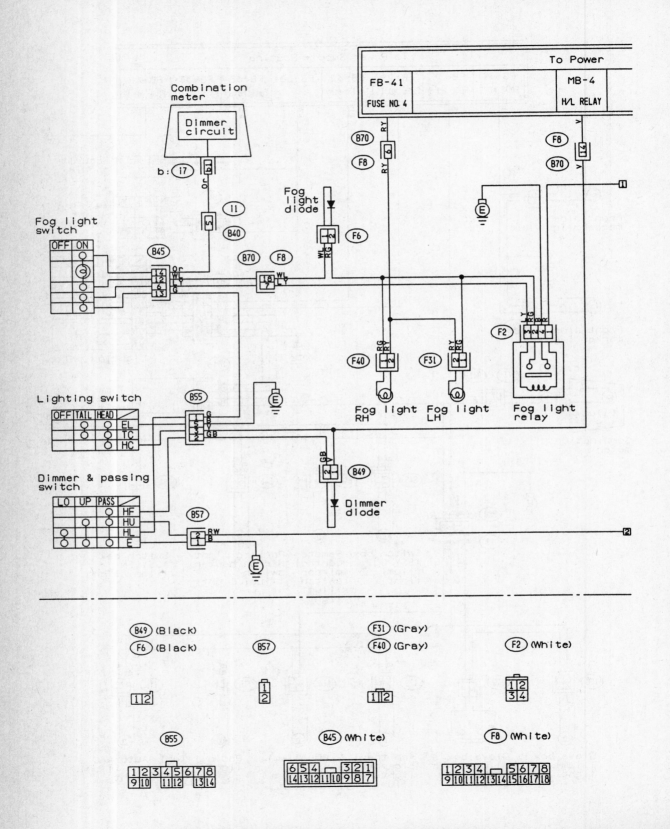

Headlight and fog light system — 1992 SVX USA

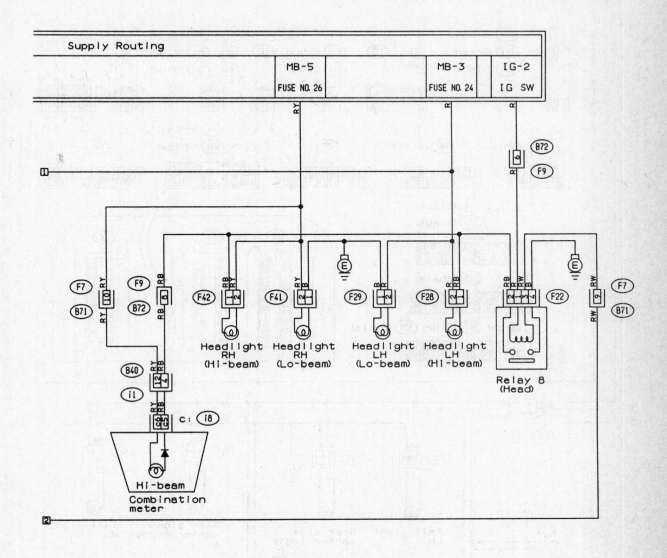

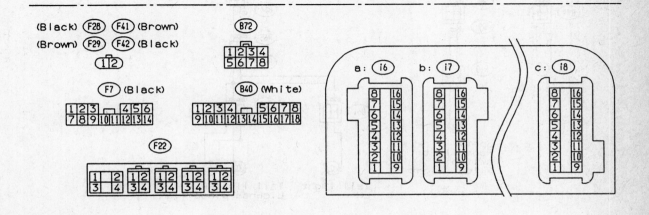

Headlight and fog light system — 1992 SVX USA continued

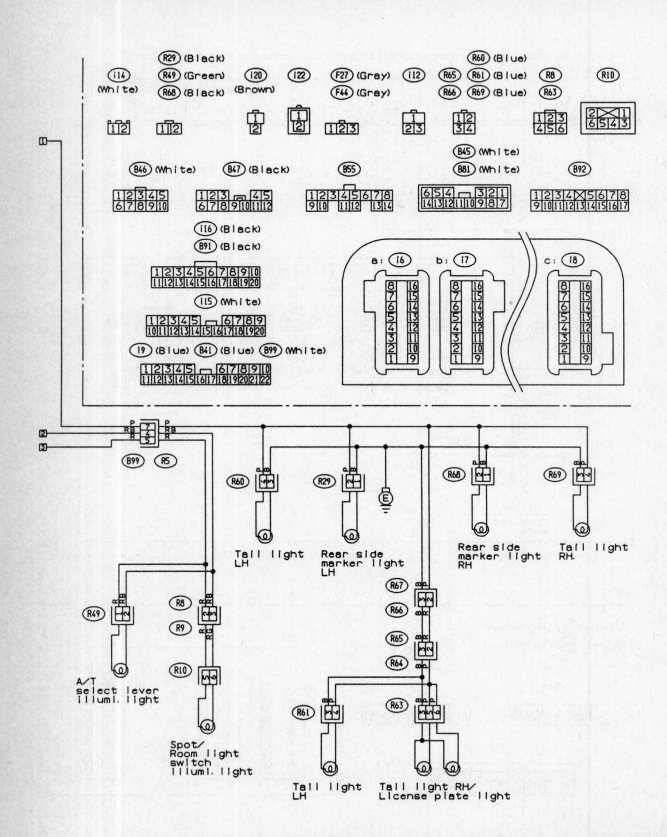

Illumination and tail light system — 1992 SVX continued

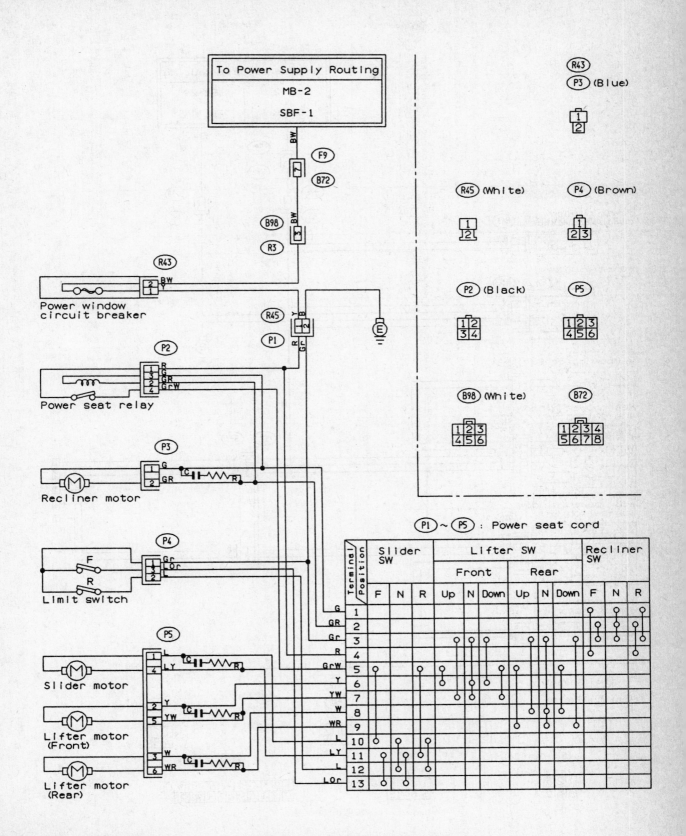

Power seat system — 1992 SVX

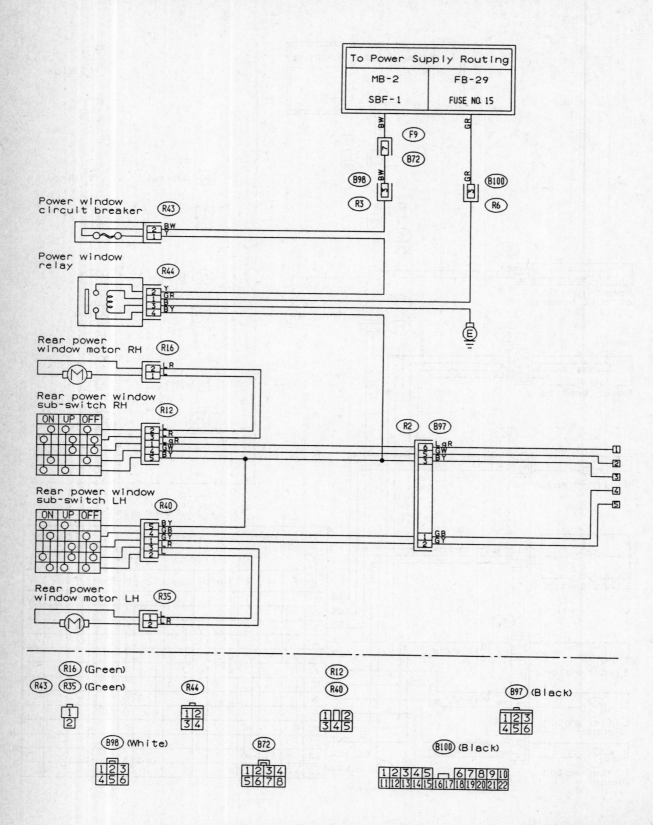

Power window system — 1992 SVX

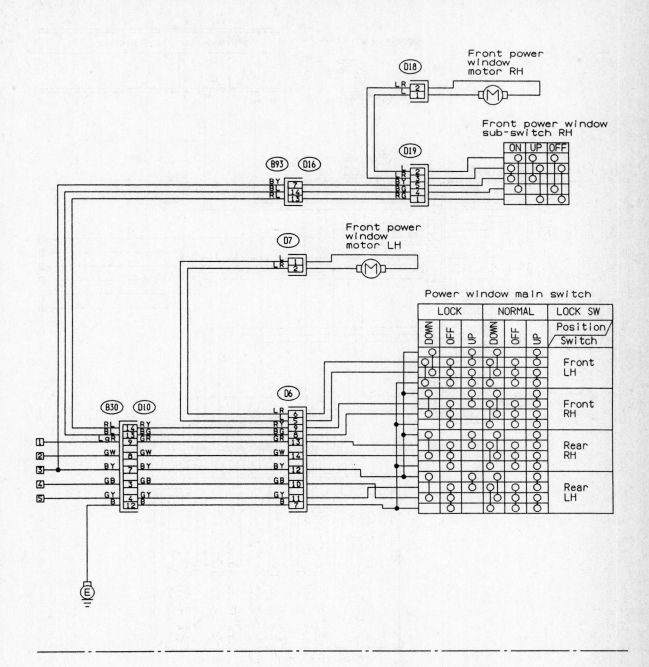

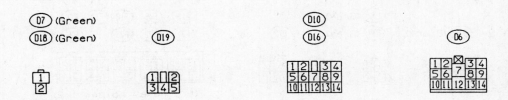

Power window system — 1992 SVX continued

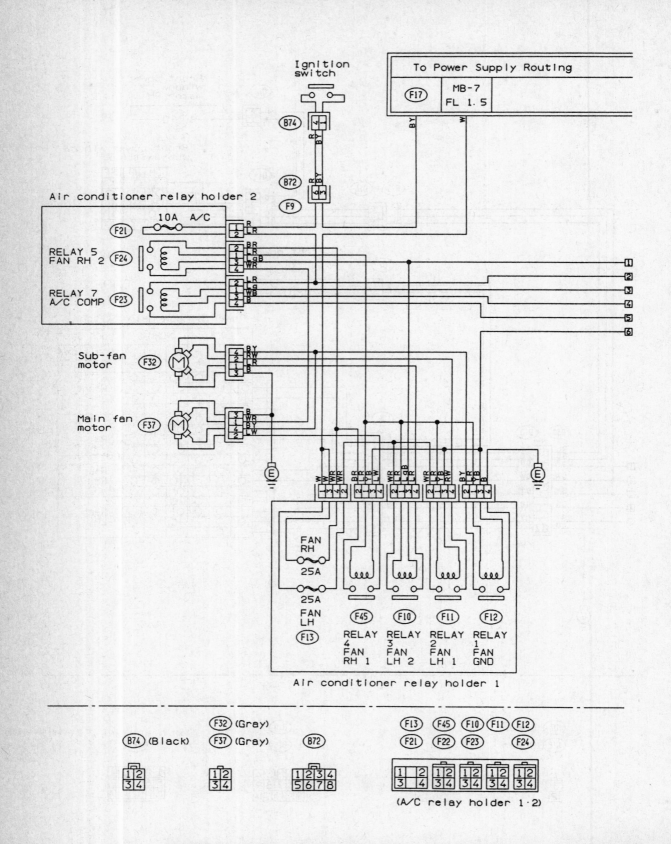

Radiator fan and air conditioner system — 1992 SVX

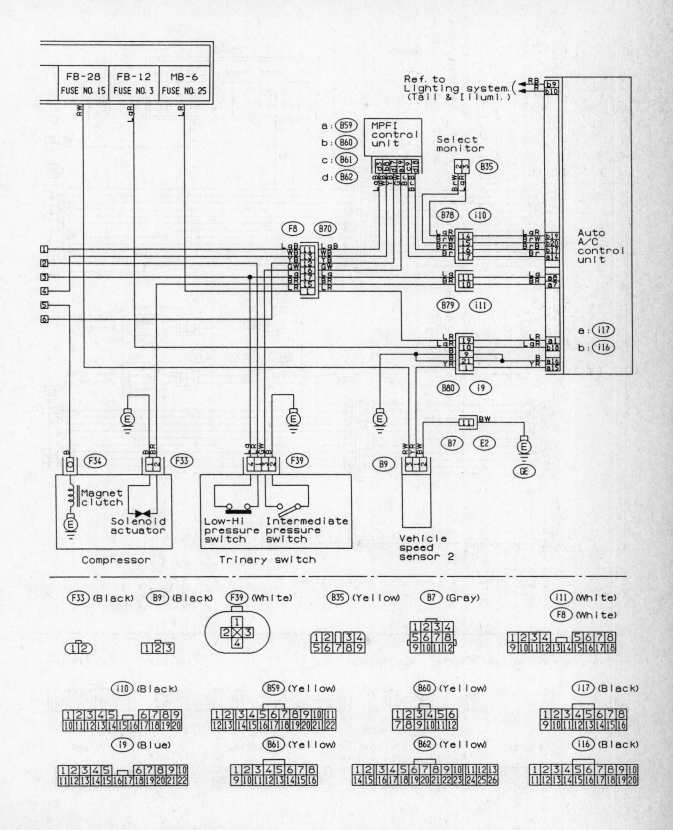

Radiator fan and air conditioner system — 1992 SVX continued

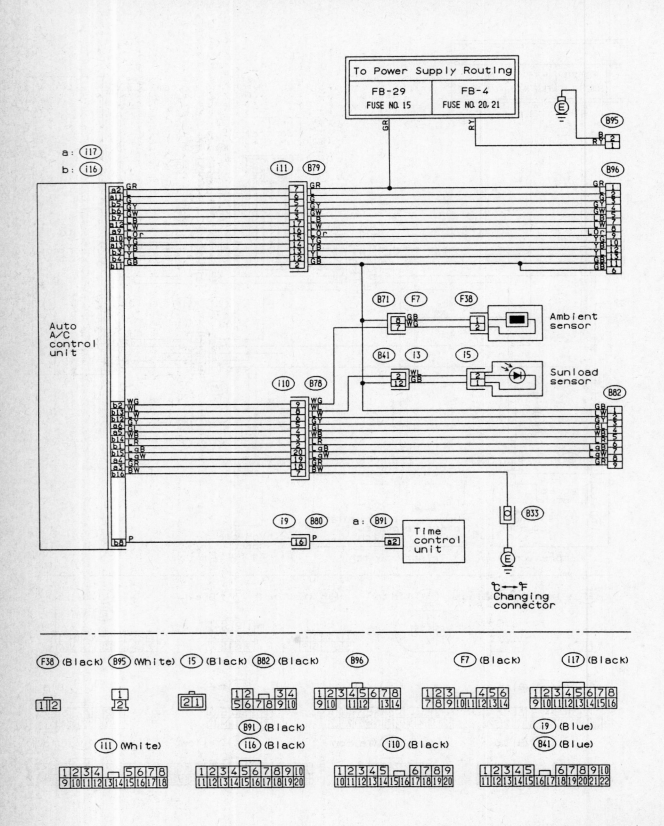

Radiator fan and air conditioner system — 1992 SVX continued

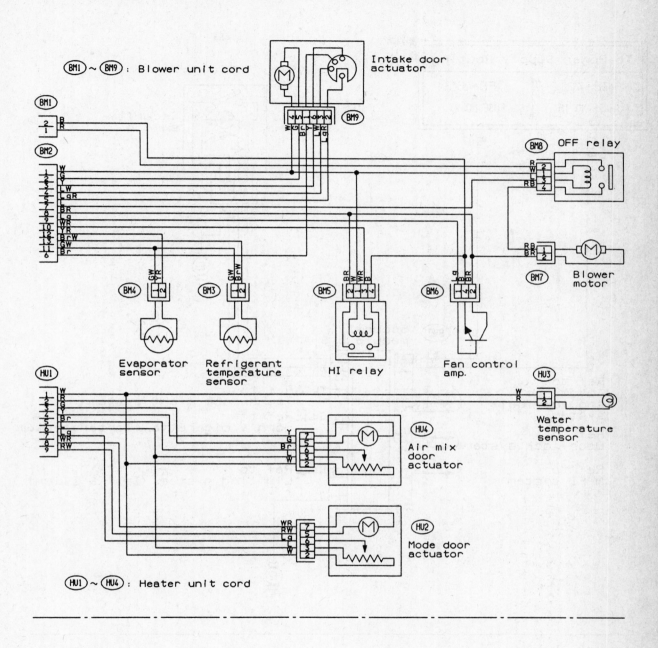

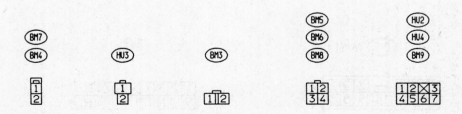

Radiator fan and air conditioner system — 1992 SVX continued

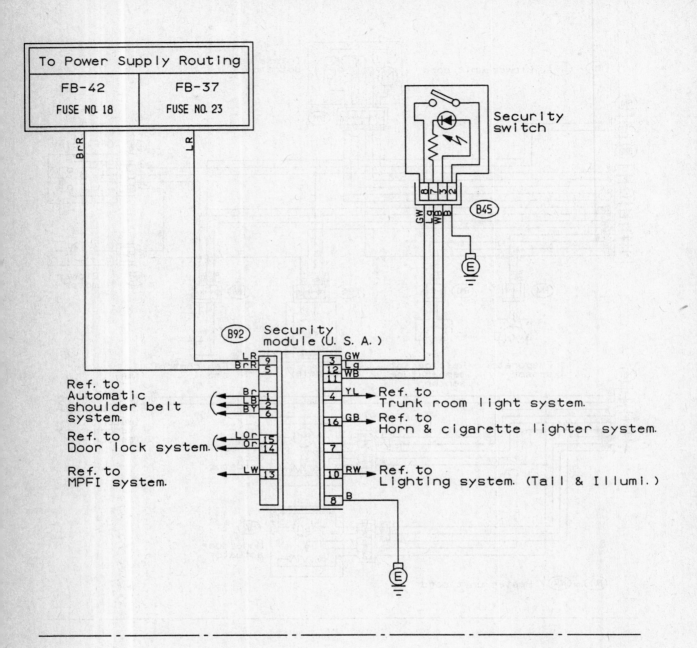

Security system — 1992 SVX

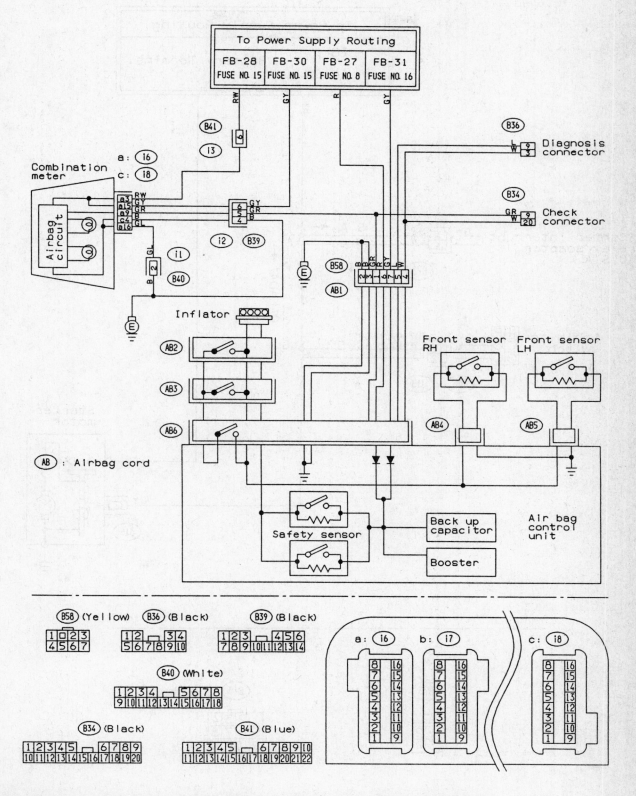

Supplemental restraint system (SRS) — 1992 SVX

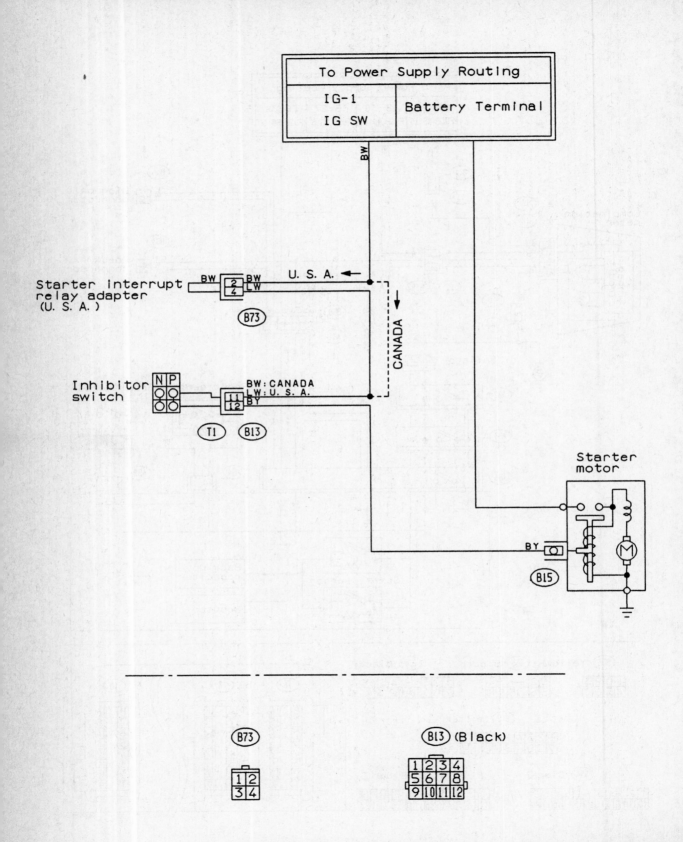

Starting system — 1992 SVX

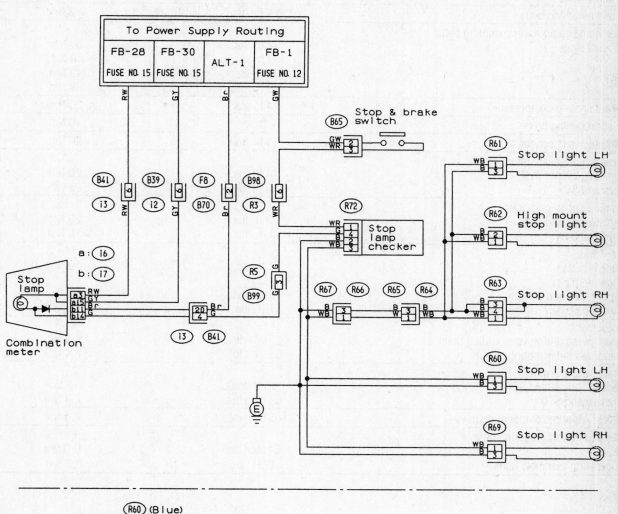

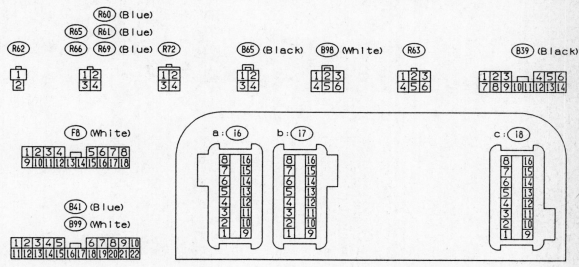

Stop light system — 1992 SVX

TORQUE SPECIFICATIONS

Component	English	Metric
Blower motor bolts	7 ft. lbs.	10 Nm
Heater unit mounting bolts	6.9 ft. lbs.	9.3 Nm
Air conditioning compressor mounting bolts		
STD. and Loyale	22 ft. lbs.	30 Nm
XT	33 ft. lbs.	44 Nm
Legacy	31 ft. lbs.	42 Nm
SVX	29 ft. lbs.	39 Nm
Refrigerant lines-to-compressor	14 ft. lbs.	20 Nm
Condenser retaining bolts	7 ft. lbs.	10 Nm
Refrigerant lines to condenser	14 ft. lbs.	20 Nm
Discharge pipe-to-evaporator		
Except Legacy and SVX	14 ft. lbs.	20 Nm
Legacy and SVX	18 ft. lbs.	25 Nm
Suction pipe nut-to-evaporator		
Except Legacy and SVX	22 ft. lbs.	29 Nm
Legacy and SVX	7 ft. lbs.	10 Nm
Receiver/Drier		
Mounting bolts	7 ft. lbs.	10 Nm
Refrigerant pipes		
Except SVX and Legacy	12 ft. lbs.	17 Nm
SVX and Legacy	7 ft. lbs.	10 Nm
Cruise control		
Vacuum pump and valve mounting bolts	65 inch lbs.	7.4 Nm
Actuator assembly mounting nuts	65 inch lbs.	7.4 Nm
Windshield wiper arm nut		
Except XT, Loyale and STD.	13 ft. lbs.	18 Nm
XT, Loyale and STD.	65 inch lbs.	7.4 Nm
Windshield wiper motor mounting nuts	65 inch lbs.	7.4 Nm
Headlamp assembly mounting nuts		
except XT	61 inch lbs.	6.9 Nm
XT-headlamp assembly bolts	17 ft. lbs.	23 Nm

7

DRIVE TRAIN

UNDERSTANDING THE MANUAL TRANSAXLE

Because of the way an internal combustion engine breathes, it can produce torque, or twisting force, only within a narrow speed range. Most modern, overhead valve engines must turn at about 2,500 rpm to produce their peak torque. By 4,500 rpm they are producing so little torque that continued increases in engine speed produce no power increases.

The torque peak on overhead camshaft engines is, generally, much higher, but much narrower.

The manual transaxle and clutch are employed to vary the relationship between engine speed and the speed of the wheels so that adequate engine power can be produced under all circumstances. The clutch allows engine torque to be applied to the transaxle input shaft gradually, due to mechanical slippage. The car can, consequently, be started smoothly from a full stop.

The transaxle changes the ratio between the rotating speeds of the engine and the wheels by the use of gears. 4-speed or 5-speed transaxles are most common. The lower gears allow full engine power to be applied to the wheels during acceleration at low speeds.

The clutch drive plate is a thin disc, the center of which is splined to the transaxle input shaft. Both sides of the disc are covered with a layer of material which is similar to brake lining and which is capable of allowing slippage without roughness or excessive noise.

The clutch cover is bolted to the engine flywheel and incorporates a diaphragm spring which provides the pressure to engage the clutch. The cover also houses the pressure plate. The driven disc is sandwiched between the pressure plate and the smooth surface of the flywheel when the clutch pedal is released, thus forcing it to turn at the same speed as the engine crankshaft.

The transaxle contains a mainshaft which passes all the way through the transaxle, from the clutch to the halfshafts. This shaft is separated at one point, so that front and rear portions can turn at different speeds.

Power is transmitted by a countershaft in the lower gears and reverse. The gears of the countershaft mesh with gears on the mainshaft, allowing power to be carried from one to the other. All the countershaft gears are integral with that shaft, while several of the mainshaft gears can either rotate independently of the shaft or be locked to it. Shifting from one gear to the next causes one of the gears to be freed from rotating with the shaft and locks another to it. Gears are locked and unlocked by internal dog clutches which slide between the center of the gear and the shaft. The forward gears usually employ synchronizers; friction members which smoothly bring gear and shaft to the same speed before the toothed dog clutches are engaged.

The clutch is operating properly if:

1. It will stall the engine when released with the vehicle held stationary.
2. The shift lever can be moved freely between 1st and reverse gears when the vehicle is stationary and the clutch disengaged.

A clutch pedal free-play adjustment is incorporated in the linkage. If there is about 25-50mm of motion before the pedal begins to release the clutch, it is adjusted properly. Inadequate free-play wears all parts of the clutch releasing mechanisms and may cause slippage. Excessive free-play may cause inadequate release and hard shifting of gears.

Some clutches use a hydraulic system in place of mechanical linkage. If the clutch fails to release, fill the clutch master cylinder with fluid to the proper level and pump the clutch pedal to fill the system with fluid. Bleed the system in the same way as a brake system. If leaks are located, tighten loose connections or overhaul the master or slave cylinder as necessary.

Front wheel drive cars do not have conventional rear axles or drive shafts. Instead, power is transmitted from the engine to a transaxle, or a combination of transmission and drive axle, in one unit. Both the transaxle and drive axle accomplish the same function as their counterparts in a front engine/rear drive axle design. The difference is in the location of the components.

In place of a conventional driveshaft, a front wheel drive design uses two driveshafts, sometimes called halfshafts, which couple the drive axle portion of the transaxle to the wheels. Universal joints or constant velocity joints are used just as they would in a rear wheel drive design.

MANUAL TRANSAXLE

Identification

Each of the Subaru transaxles can be identified by locating the number on the transaxle housing. For application of the individual transaxles, refer to the procedures in this section.

Adjustments

LINKAGE

Standard Transaxle (Including 4WD)

There are no adjustments that can be made on the shift linkage for standard transmissions or for the rear drive system. If you experience looseness or too much play in shifting it is a sign of worn parts, which should be replaced.

Back-up Light Switch

REMOVAL & INSTALLATION

This switch is mounted on the transmission lever shaft and is bolted to the transmission.

1. Disconnect the negative battery cable.
2. Disconnect the electrical connector and remove the old switch.

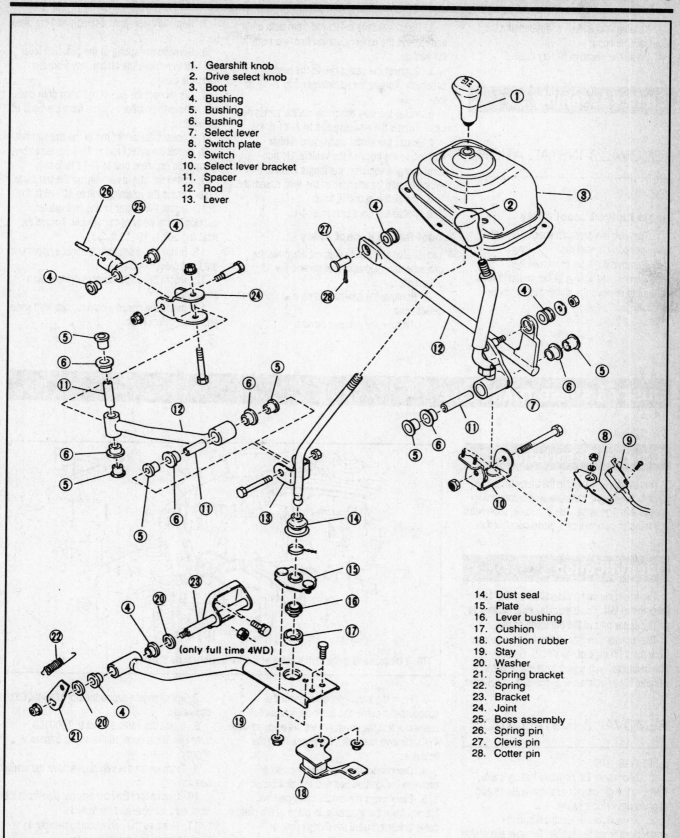

1. Gearshift knob
2. Drive select knob
3. Boot
4. Bushing
5. Bushing
6. Bushing
7. Select lever
8. Switch plate
9. Switch
10. Select lever bracket
11. Spacer
12. Rod
13. Lever

14. Dust seal
15. Plate
16. Lever bushing
17. Cushion
18. Cushion rubber
19. Stay
20. Washer
21. Spring bracket
22. Spring
23. Bracket
24. Joint
25. Boss assembly
26. Spring pin
27. Clevis pin
28. Cotter pin

(only full time 4WD)

FIG. 1 Exploded view of the dual range shifter assembly

3. Install a new switch and reconnect the electrical connector.

4. Install the negative battery cable.

Shifter Assembly

REMOVAL & INSTALLATION

▶ SEE FIG. 1

Single Range Except Justy

1. Remove the gearshift knob. Raise and safely support the vehicle.

2. Remove the front crossmember.

3. Remove the spring of the gearshift lever and bolt to remove the shifter stay from the transaxle case.

4. Disconnect the select rod from both ends and remove the rubber cushion from the body of the vehicle.

5. Connect the select rod to the boss assembly. Torque the retaining bolt to 7–11 ft. lbs.

6. Install the stay assembly on the transaxle case. Torque the retaining bolt to 7–11 ft. lbs.

7. Install the shifter spring and rubber cushion to the body of the vehicle. On non-turbocharged vehicles, the longer hook end of spring should be attached at the joint assembly.

8. Install the gearshift knob.

9. Install the front crossmember.

Dual Range Except Justy

1. Raise and safely support. Remove the crossmember, exhaust system and the driveshaft.

2. Remove the gearshift knob and the drive select knob.

3. Remove the console covers.

4. Remove the switch assembly and the plate boot.

5. Remove the spring of the gearshift lever and bolt to remove the shifter stay from the transaxle case.

6. Disconnect the select rod from both ends and remove the rubber cushion from the body of the vehicle.

7. Connect the select rod to the transfer rail.

8. Install the select rod at the joint assembly. Torque the retaining bolt to 7–11 ft. lbs.

9. Install the stay assembly on the transaxle case. Torque the retaining bolt to 10–16 ft. lbs.

10. Install the shifter spring and rubber cushion to the body of the vehicle. Torque the retaining bolt to 10–16 ft. lbs.

11. Install the driveshaft, exhaust system and the front crossmember.

12. Install the shifter boot and the switch assembly.

13. Install the console covers, gearshift knob and drive select knob.

JUSTY 5-SPEED TRANSAXLE

General Description

This transaxle is used in the Justy from 1987–92. It is a 5-speed transaxle with 5 forward speeds and 1 reverse. The transaxle, differential and transfer case are of 1 piece construction.

Identification

The transaxle can be identified by the 11th letter in the VIN. The transaxle serial number is on the upper part of the transaxle case.

The transaxle can be determined as follows from the 11th digit of the VIN; B—Gumma Manufacturer — 5-speed front wheel drive, G—Gumma Manufacturer — 5-speed 4 wheel drive.

REMOVAL & INSTALLATION

▶ SEE FIGS. 2–8

1. Disconnect the negative battery cable. Remove the air cleaner assembly. Raise and support the vehicle safely.

2. Disconnect the electrical wiring connectors from the starter. Remove the starter to transaxle bolts and the starter from the vehicle.

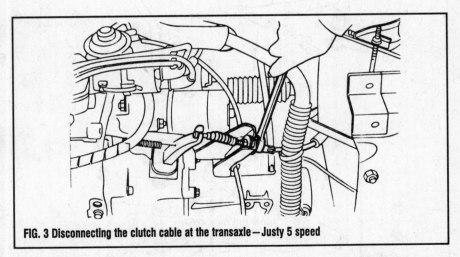

FIG. 3 Disconnecting the clutch cable at the transaxle—Justy 5 speed

3. From the transaxle, disconnect the speedometer cable, the back-up light switch connector and the ground cable. If equipped with 4WD, remove the activation hoses from the actuator.

4. Disconnect the electrical connector between the ignition coil and the distributor.

5. Disconnect the clutch cable and the bracket from the transaxle. In place of the clutch cable bracket, install the lifting hook, or equivalent.

6. Removing the pitching stopper and brackets between the transaxle and chassis.

7. Install engine supporter tool 921540000 or equivalent.

8. Install the vertical hoist to T000100 transaxle lifting hook and raise the transaxle slightly.

9. From under the vehicle, remove the under covers.

10. Disconnect the rear exhaust pipe from the front exhaust pipe and the vehicle.

11. Remove the center crossmember to engine/transaxle assembly bolts.

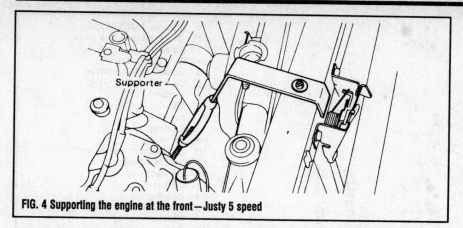

FIG. 4 Supporting the engine at the front—Justy 5 speed

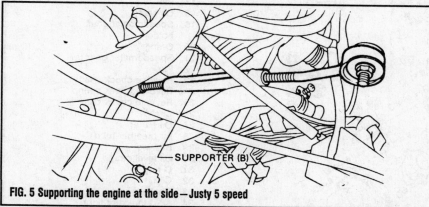

FIG. 5 Supporting the engine at the side—Justy 5 speed

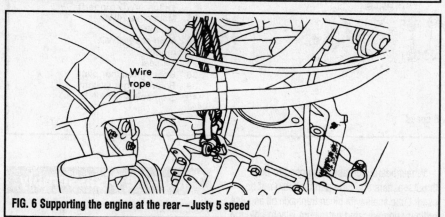

FIG. 6 Supporting the engine at the rear—Justy 5 speed

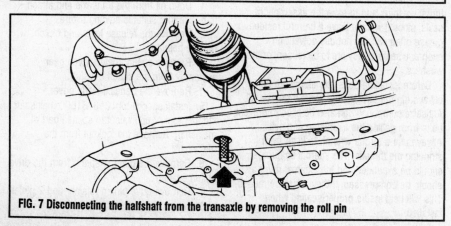

FIG. 7 Disconnecting the halfshaft from the transaxle by removing the roll pin

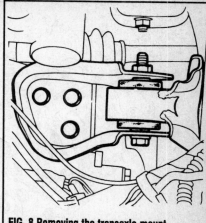

FIG. 8 Removing the transaxle mount— Justy 5 speed

12. Using a pin punch and a hammer, drive out the axle shaft to driveshaft spring pin. Discard the spring pin and separate the axle shaft.

13. Remove the transaxle mounting bracket.

14. Disconnect the gearshift rod and stay from the transaxle.

15. Properly support the engine assembly. Remove the transaxle to engine bolts.

16. Using the vertical hoist, lift the transaxle from the vehicle.

To Install:

17. Install the transaxle assembly in the vehicle and install the transaxle-to-engine bolts. Install the gearshift rods on the transaxle.

18. Join the axle shaft and the differential. Install a new axle shaft spring pin. Install the center crossmember and tighten bolts to 27–49 ft. lbs. (37–67 Nm).

19. Install the rear exhaust pipe, engine under covers, pitching stopper and brackets, clutch cable, electrical connectors, speedometer cable, 4WD activation hoses, starter wires and starter-to-transaxle bolts.

20. Lower the vehicle, connect the negative battery cable, check the transaxle fluid and test drive the vehicle.

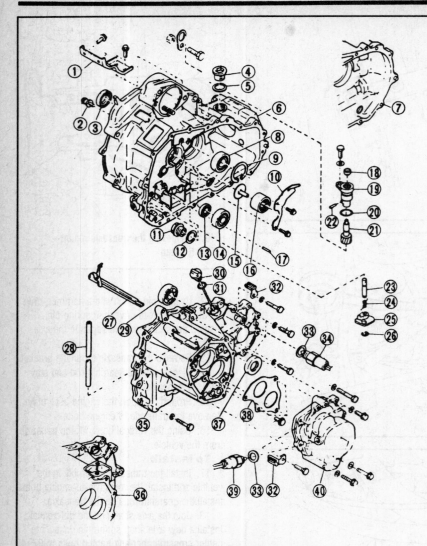

1. Stiffener (4WD models)
2. Clutch release fork pivot
3. Oil seal
4. Plug (4WD models)
5. Gasket (4WD models)
6. Clutch housing (4WD models)
7. Clutch housing (FWD models)
8. Bearing
9. Snapring
10. Drive pinion rear retainer
11. Oil drain plug
12. Gasket
13. Oil seal
14. Bearing
15. Drive pinion oil guide
16. Needle bearing
17. Pin
18. Oil seal
19. Speedometer shaft holder
20. O-ring
21. Speedometer gear unit
22. Pin
23. Reverse check shaft
24. Reverse check spring
25. Reverse check cam
26. Circlip
27. Oil garter
28. Air breather tube
29. Bearing
30. Oil level gauge
31. O-ring
32. Clip
33. Gasket
34. 4WD indicator light switch (4WD models)
35. Main case (4WD models)
36. Main case (FWD models)
37. Oil seal
38. Bearing retainer plate
39. Back-up light switch
40. Side cover

FIG. 2 Exploded view of the transaxle case—Justy 5 speed

Bench Overhaul

BEFORE DISASSEMBLY

Cleanliness is an important factor in the overhaul of the manual transaxle. Before opening up this unit, the entire outside of the transaxle assembly should be cleaned, preferable with a high pressure washer such as a car wash spray unit. Dirt entering the transaxle internal parts will negate all the time and effort spent on the overhaul. During inspection and reassembly all parts should be thoroughly cleaned with solvent then dried with compressed air. Wiping cloths and rags should not be used to dry parts.

Wheel bearing grease, long used to hold thrust washers and lube parts, should not be used. Lube seals with clean transaxle oil and use ordinary unmedicated petroleum jelly to hold the thrust washers and to ease the assembly of seals, since it will not leave a harmful residue as grease often will. Do not use solvent on neoprene seals, if they are to be reused, or thrust washers.

Before installing bolts into aluminum parts, always dip the threads into clean transaxle oil. Antiseize compound can also be used to prevent bolts from galling the aluminum and seizing. Always use a torque wrench to keep from stripping the threads. The internal snaprings should be expanded and the external rings should be compressed, if they are to be reused. This will help insure proper seating when installed.

Transaxle Disassembly

◆ SEE FIGS. 9–14

1. Drain oil from the transaxle and attach transaxle to a suitable holding fixture.
2. Remove the release lever and clutch release bearing.
3. Remove speedometer driven gear assembly from the clutch housing.
4. Remove the transaxle side cover.
5. Install special tool 398781600 mainshaft stopper tool or equivalent to splined part of mainshaft. Remove the locknut from the mainshaft.
6. Remove the outer snapring from the drive pinion bearing.
7. Remove drive pinion retainer and 2 pinion cotters.

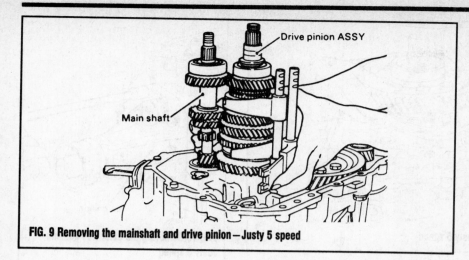

FIG. 9 Removing the mainshaft and drive pinion—Justy 5 speed

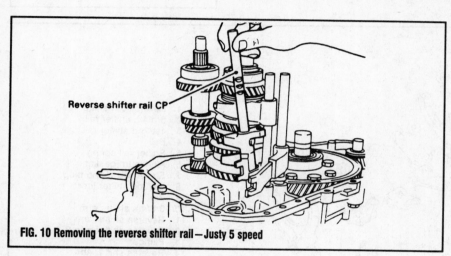

FIG. 10 Removing the reverse shifter rail—Justy 5 speed

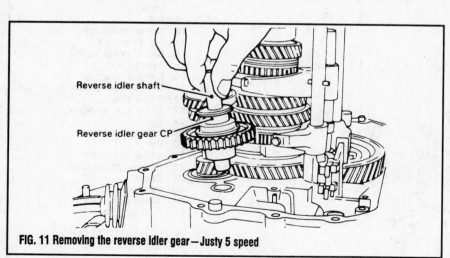

FIG. 11 Removing the reverse idler gear—Justy 5 speed

8. Remove pin from reverse shifter rail.

9. Remove the 5th gear hub and sleeve with 5th gear shifter fork assembly.

10. Remove synchronizer ring and 5th gear from drive pinion.

11. Remove lock washer and 5th gear from mainshaft.

12. Remove bearing retainer plate.

13. Remove the outer snapring from the drive pinion bearing.

14. Remove shifter rail spring plug, gasket and remove fork spring and ball from plug mounting hole in 3 locations.

15. Remove the main case from the clutch housing.

16. Remove the thrust clearance adjusting washers from the differential side bearings.

17. Remove the gear shifter arm assembly from the clutch housing.

18. Remove the reverse idler shaft and gear assembly.

19. Remove the reverse shifter rail.

20. Remove mainshaft assembly and drive pinion assembly with related parts.

21. Remove the differential assembly.

22. Remove pin from selector arm in the clutch housing. Remove shift connecting rod from the clutch housing.

23. Remove the clip from the reverse check shaft, reverse check cam and reverse check spring. Remove the reverse check shaft from the clutch housing.

24. Remove the drive pinion retainer from the clutch housing.

25. On 4WD vehicles perform the following procedures:

   a. Remove extension retaining bolts and separate extension and gasket from the clutch housing.

   b. Remove bearing case assembly and height adjusting shim(s) from the clutch housing assembly.

   c. Remove transfer side cover, transfer lever, transfer cover/diaphragm and cover at clutch housing.

   d. Remove transfer shaft assembly from the main case.

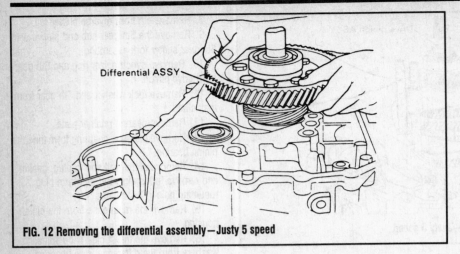

FIG. 12 Removing the differential assembly—Justy 5 speed

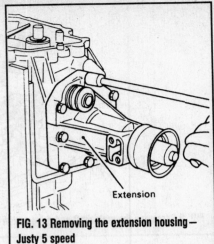

FIG. 13 Removing the extension housing—Justy 5 speed

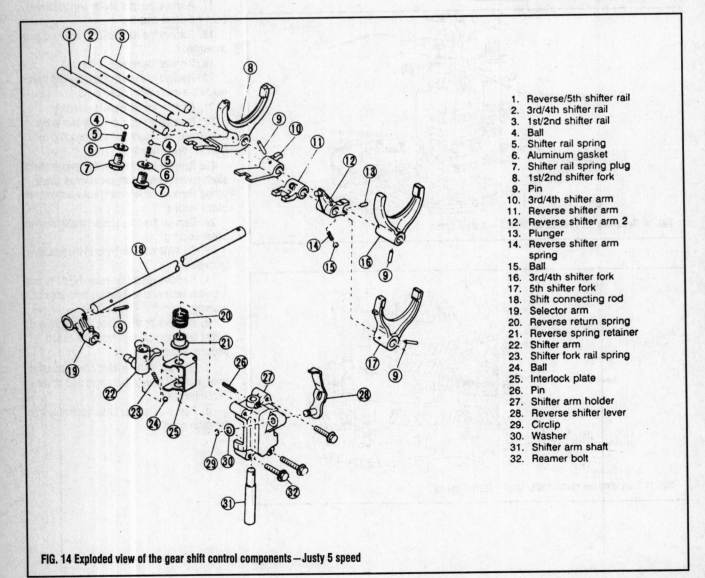

1. Reverse/5th shifter rail
2. 3rd/4th shifter rail
3. 1st/2nd shifter rail
4. Ball
5. Shifter rail spring
6. Aluminum gasket
7. Shifter rail spring plug
8. 1st/2nd shifter fork
9. Pin
10. 3rd/4th shifter arm
11. Reverse shifter arm
12. Reverse shifter arm 2
13. Plunger
14. Reverse shifter arm spring
15. Ball
16. 3rd/4th shifter fork
17. 5th shifter fork
18. Shift connecting rod
19. Selector arm
20. Reverse return spring
21. Reverse spring retainer
22. Shifter arm
23. Shifter fork rail spring
24. Ball
25. Interlock plate
26. Pin
27. Shifter arm holder
28. Reverse shifter lever
29. Circlip
30. Washer
31. Shifter arm shaft
32. Reamer bolt

FIG. 14 Exploded view of the gear shift control components—Justy 5 speed

Unit Disassembly and Assembly

GEAR SHIFTER ARM ASSEMBLY

Disassembly

1. Remove pin holding shifter arm to shifter arm shaft.
2. Remove the shifter arm shaft from shifter arm holder, interlock plate, shifter arm, fork rail spring, check ball, reverse spring retainer and reverse return spring in order.
3. Remove clip on top shifter arm holder and washer from reverse shifter lever complete assembly.

Inspection

1. Check shifter arm and related parts for excessive wear or damage.
2. Check reverse return spring for tension.
3. Check shifter arm shaft for excessive wear or damage.

Assembly

1. Install reverse shifter lever assembly to shifter arm holder.
2. Measure clearance between clip and lever. Select adjusting washer so clearance is between 0.002–0.008 in. (0.2–0.5mm).
3. Install interlock plate, shifter arm, check ball, spring, reverse spring retainer and reverse return spring into shifter arm holder.
4. Install shifter arm shaft with retaining pin.

DRIVE PINION ASSEMBLY

Disassembly

♦ SEE FIG. 15

1. Using suitable press remove drive pinion bearing, 5th gear thrust plate, 5th gear bushing as an assembly.
2. Remove washer (replace upon installation), 4th gear, synchronizer ring, 3rd/4th hub assembly and spacer key.

3. Remove gear thrust spacer, synchronizer ring, 3rd gear, gear thrust spacer, 2nd gear, synchronizer ring, gear thrust spacer, reverse gear assembly, synchronizer ring and 1st gear in order.

Inspection

1. Check all bearings for wear and or damage.
2. Check bearing inner and outer races for wear.
3. Check that bearings turn smoothly and do not make abnormal noise when turned.
4. Check that thrust spacer surfaces are not scored or worn.
5. Check gears for broken tooth surfaces, damage or excessive wear.
6. Check side or thrust clearance of all forward drive gears.
7. Check clearance between synchronizer ring and cone. Press ring against cone and measure clearance between inter facial surfaces of ring and cone. The standard valve is 0.047 in. (1.2mm). The service wear limit is 0.020 in. (0.05mm).

Assembly

1. Install new washer onto drive pinion.
2. Install synchronizer hub so that portion that has no splines will be positioned away from the oil hole on drive pinion.

➡ **This portion with no spline tooth serves as gear thrust spacer key installing position for securing spacer.**

3. Install gear thrust spacer with notched end toward 4th gear side. Align splines and insert key in the notched groove.
4. Install 4th gear washer, face oil groove surface of washer toward 4th gear.
5. Install bearing assembly with stamped mark toward spline shaft.
6. Install 5th gear thrust plate and press on 5th gear bushing using suitable tools.

MAINSHAFT ASSEMBLY

Disassembly

The mainshaft assembly is serviced only be pressing off the mainshaft bearing using suitable press and tools.

Inspection

Check the ball bearings for wear and or damage. Check that the bearings turn smoothly and do not make abnormal noise when turned.

Assembly

The mainshaft assembly is serviced only by pressing on the mainshaft bearing using suitable press and tools.

DIFFERENTIAL

Disassembly

♦ SEE FIG. 16

1. Remove the final gear.
2. Remove the differential side gear adjusting washer from the final gear side.
3. Remove pin from differential assembly.
4. Remove pinion shaft, pinions, side gears and adjusting washer.
5. Remove bearing from the differential case. Remove the speedometer gear plate and gear assembly.

Inspection

1. Check all gears and pinion shaft tooth surfaces for damage, excessive wear or cracks.
2. Check bearings for wear or damage.
3. Check differential case for wear or cracks.
4. Check plastic speedometer gear and gear plate for cracks.

Assembly

1. Install bearing onto final gear.
2. Install speedometer gear and plate into differential case. Install bearing.
3. Install pinion, washer, side gear, pinion shaft and pin on differential case side.
4. Install washer and side gear on final gear side.
5. Install differential case to final gear torque final gear retaining bolts to 42–49 ft. lbs.
6. Measure backlash. The standard valve for backlash is 0.0020–0.0059 in. (0.05–0.15mm). Install the correct washer(s) with the chamfered side of the inside diameter toward the differential side gear.
7. After correct backlash is set check that the final drive gear assembly turns smoothly.

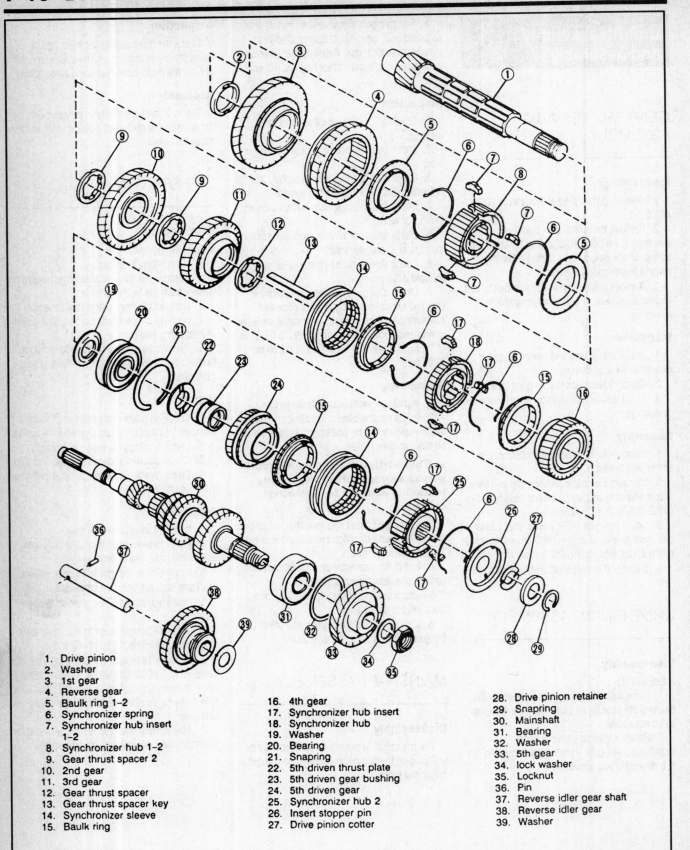

1. Drive pinion
2. Washer
3. 1st gear
4. Reverse gear
5. Baulk ring 1–2
6. Synchronizer spring
7. Synchronizer hub insert 1–2
8. Synchronizer hub 1–2
9. Gear thrust spacer 2
10. 2nd gear
11. 3rd gear
12. Gear thrust spacer
13. Gear thrust spacer key
14. Synchronizer sleeve
15. Baulk ring

16. 4th gear
17. Synchronizer hub insert
18. Synchronizer hub
19. Washer
20. Bearing
21. Snapring
22. 5th driven thrust plate
23. 5th driven gear bushing
24. 5th driven gear
25. Synchronizer hub 2
26. Insert stopper pin
27. Drive pinion cotter

28. Drive pinion retainer
29. Snapring
30. Mainshaft
31. Bearing
32. Washer
33. 5th gear
34. lock washer
35. Locknut
36. Pin
37. Reverse idler gear shaft
38. Reverse idler gear
39. Washer

FIG. 15 Exploded view of the gear component parts — Justy 5 speed

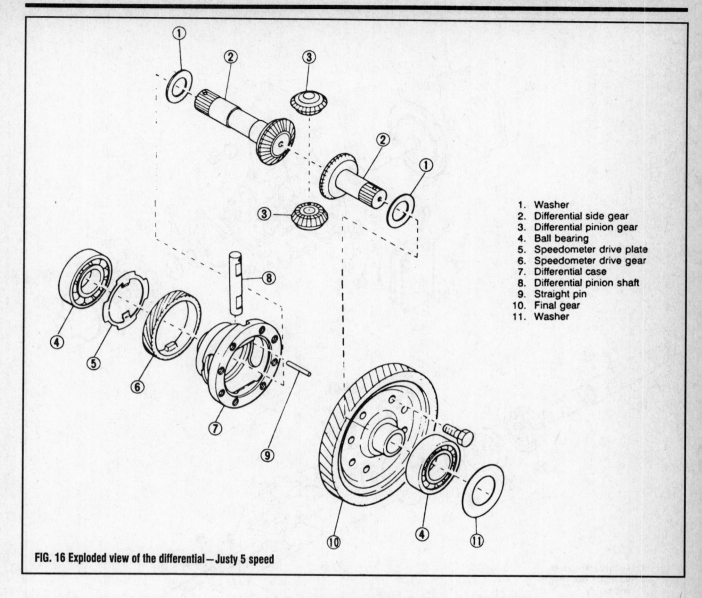

1. Washer
2. Differential side gear
3. Differential pinion gear
4. Ball bearing
5. Speedometer drive plate
6. Speedometer drive gear
7. Differential case
8. Differential pinion shaft
9. Straight pin
10. Final gear
11. Washer

FIG. 16 Exploded view of the differential—Justy 5 speed

TRANSFER SHAFT

Disassembly

▶ SEE FIG. 17–18

1. Remove the snapring.
2. Remove the locknut and washer.
3. Remove the hypoid drive gear, transfer shaft collar and bearing.
4. Remove washer, transfer gear and synchronizer hub.
5. Remove the key from the transfer shaft.

Inspection

1. Check all bearings for wear and or damage.
2. Check bearing inner and outer races for wear.
3. Check that bearings turn smoothly and do not make abnormal noise when turned.
4. Check that bushing sliding surfaces are not damaged or worn.
5. Check gears for broken tooth surfaces, damage or excessive wear.

Assembly

1. Install hypoid drive and driven gear as a set.
2. Install transfer gear collar on hypoid drive gear and press on with key to transfer shaft.
3. Install bearing.
4. Install the synchronizer hub onto transfer shaft.
5. Install transfer gear and washer.
6. Press fit outer snapring. The outer snapring thickness is 0.0988 in. (2.51mm).
7. Install lock washer and torque locknut to 54–62 ft. lbs.

BEARING CASE

Disassembly

1. Remove the locknut and lock washer.
2. Remove the hypoid driven gear.
3. Remove the front bearing cone.
4. Remove the rear bearing cone from the hypoid driven gear.
5. Remove bearing races from the bearing case.

Inspection

1. Check all bearings and cones for wear and or damage.
2. Check bearing inner and outer races for wear.
3. Check that bearings turn smoothly and do not make abnormal noise when turned.

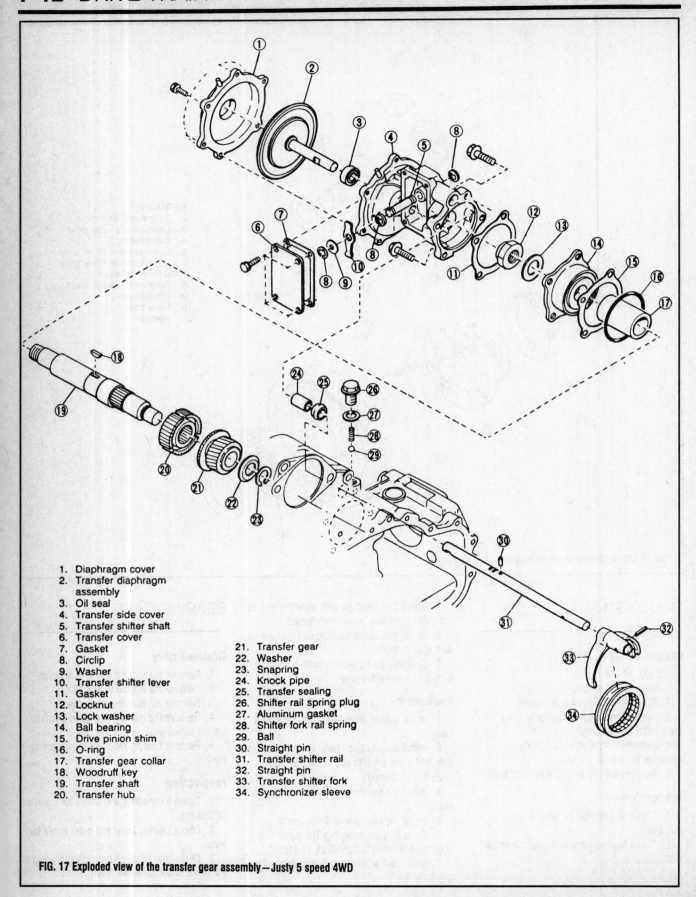

1. Diaphragm cover
2. Transfer diaphragm assembly
3. Oil seal
4. Transfer side cover
5. Transfer shifter shaft
6. Transfer cover
7. Gasket
8. Circlip
9. Washer
10. Transfer shifter lever
11. Gasket
12. Locknut
13. Lock washer
14. Ball bearing
15. Drive pinion shim
16. O-ring
17. Transfer gear collar
18. Woodruff key
19. Transfer shaft
20. Transfer hub

21. Transfer gear
22. Washer
23. Snapring
24. Knock pipe
25. Transfer sealing
26. Shifter rail spring plug
27. Aluminum gasket
28. Shifter fork rail spring
29. Ball
30. Straight pin
31. Transfer shifter rail
32. Straight pin
33. Transfer shifter fork
34. Synchronizer sleeve

FIG. 17 Exploded view of the transfer gear assembly—Justy 5 speed 4WD

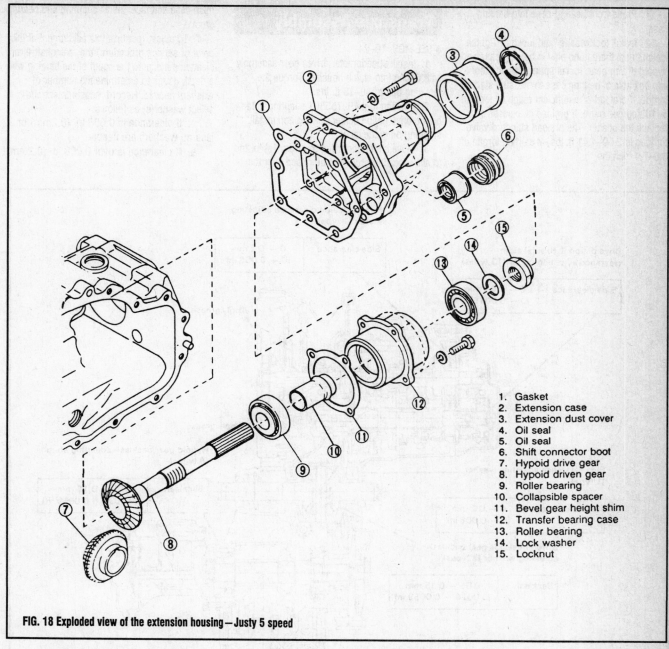

FIG. 18 Exploded view of the extension housing—Justy 5 speed

1. Gasket
2. Extension case
3. Extension dust cover
4. Oil seal
5. Oil seal
6. Shift connector boot
7. Hypoid drive gear
8. Hypoid driven gear
9. Roller bearing
10. Collapsible spacer
11. Bevel gear height shim
12. Transfer bearing case
13. Roller bearing
14. Lock washer
15. Locknut

4. Check gears for broken tooth surfaces, damage or excessive wear.

Assembly

➡ **The hypoid gear height is adjusted by the selection of a bevel gear height adjusting shim(s).**

1. Install front and rear bearing races into bearing case.

2. Install the rear bearing cone onto the bevel gear dummy shaft tool 498505402 and insert into bearing case.

3. With front bearing cone and lock washer installed on tool 498505402, tighten locknut finger tight.

4. Again tighten locknut in 2 or 3 steps but do not tighten locknut all the way. The dummy shaft should be able to be turned by hand.

5. A load measurement should be taken at this point of the service procedure. Turn bearing case several times and install spring balance tool in bolt hole in bearing case. The load measurement should be taken at the time the bearing starts moving. The standard valve for load is 2.09–4.41 ft. lbs. at starting torque of 3.5–7.4 inch lbs.

6. Install tool 4985055700 bevel gear gauge assembly through transfer shaft hole in clutch housing.

7. Install bearing case with dummy shaft assembled into clutch housing and tighten at several locations.

8. Measure space between gauge and dummy shaft top. The bevel gear height shim thickness is obtained by subtracting gauge readings from 0.04 in. (1mm). Remove dummy shaft and bevel gear gauge assembly and disassemble dummy shaft.

9. Install hypoid driven gear in place of the dummy shaft. Press rear bearing cone onto hypoid driven gear.

10. Install hypoid driven gear, with collapsible spacer into bearing case.

11. Press front bearing cone into bearing case.

12. Install lock washer and locknut. Tighten locknut until there is no play in bearing case and hypoid driven gear. Install spring balance tool into bolt hole of bearing case to measure starting torque. If preload is insufficient retighten locknut 5–10 degrees more. If preload is excessive replace the spacer. The preload standard valve for load is 2.09–4.41 ft. lbs. at starting torque of 3.5–7.4 inch lbs.

Transaxle Assembly

◆ SEE FIGS. 19–24

1. Install speedometer driven gear assembly with O-ring into clutch housing. Torque the retaining bolt to 10–13 ft. lbs.

2. Position tool 499755501 snapring guide on the drive pinion center bearing and install snapring on guide taper.

3. Move shift connecting rod from 1st to 2nd to allow bearing groove to be raised over the main case end face. Install snapring into bearing groove.

4. To adjust (perform this adjustment at this point of service procedure) the mainshaft thrust clearance measure the depth of the bearing with a depth gauge to determine the number of washers needed. Record measurement and select washer(s) as follows:

a. If clearance is 0.008 in. (0.2mm) or less no washers are needed.

b. If clearance is over 0.008 in. (0.2mm)

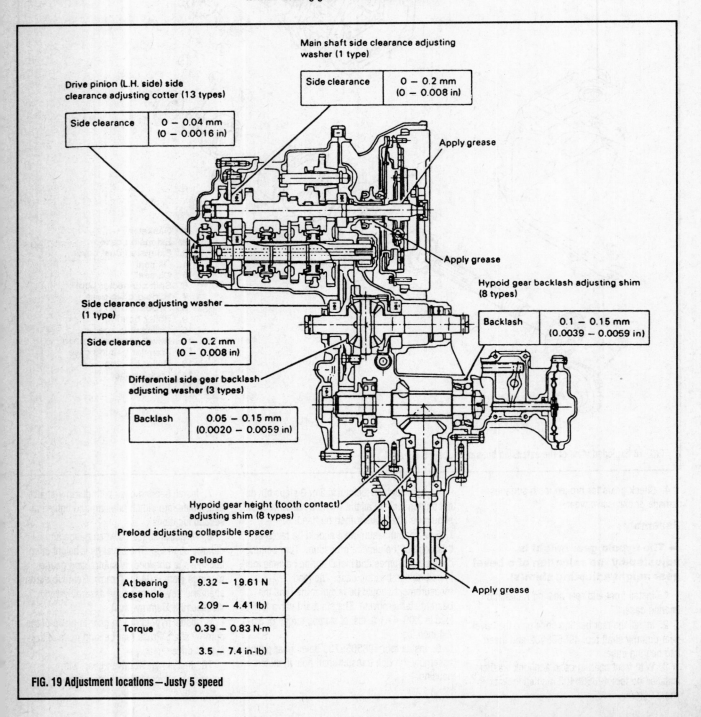

Main shaft side clearance adjusting washer (1 type)

Side clearance	0 – 0.2 mm (0 – 0.008 in)

Drive pinion (L.H. side) side clearance adjusting cotter (13 types)

Side clearance	0 – 0.04 mm (0 – 0.0016 in)

Apply grease

Apply grease

Hypoid gear backlash adjusting shim (8 types)

Backlash	0.1 – 0.15 mm (0.0039 – 0.0059 in)

Side clearance adjusting washer (1 type)

Side clearance	0 – 0.2 mm (0 – 0.008 in)

Differential side gear backlash adjusting washer (3 types)

Backlash	0.05 – 0.15 mm (0.0020 – 0.0059 in)

Hypoid gear height (tooth contact) adjusting shim (8 types)

Preload adjusting collapsible spacer

	Preload
At bearing case hole	9.32 – 19.61 N
	2.09 – 4.41 lb)
Torque	0.39 – 0.83 N·m
	3.5 – 7.4 in-lb)

Apply grease

FIG. 19 Adjustment locations—Justy 5 speed

Gear Position	Side clearance of gear in. (mm)
1st	0.0043–0.0142 (0.11–0.36)
2nd	0.0043–0.0169 (0.11–0.43)
3rd	0.0043–0.0169 (0.11–0.43)
4th	0.0020–0.0118 (0.05–0.30)
5th	0.0039–0.0098 (0.10–0.25)

FIG. 20 Thrust clearance specifications – Justy 5 speed

Part No.	Thickness in. (mm)
803027041	0.0394 (1.000)
803027042	0.0413 (1.050)
803027043	0.0433 (1.100)

FIG. 21 Differential gear backlash washer selection chart – Justy 5 speed

Part No.	Thickness in. (mm)
441375401	0.0929 (2.36)
441375402	0.0945 (2.40)
441375403	0.0961 (2.44)
441375404	0.0976 (2.48)
441375405	0.0992 (2.52)
441375406	0.1008 (2.56)
441375407	0.1024 (2.60)
441375408	0.1039 (2.64)
441375409	0.1055 (2.68)
441375501	0.1071 (2.72)
441375502	0.1087 (2.76)
441375503	0.1102 (2.80)
441375504	0.1118 (2.84)

FIG. 22 Drive pinion cotter selection chart – Justy 5 speed

Part No.	Thickness in. (mm)
33189KA000	0.0059 (0.150)
33189KA010	0.0069 (0.175)
33189KA020	0.0079 (0.200)
33189KA030	0.0089 (0.225)
33189KA040	0.0098 (0.250)
33189KA050	0.0108 (0.275)
33189KA060	0.0118 (0.300)
33189KA070	0.0197 (0.500)

FIG. 23 Bevel gear height shim selection chart – Justy 5 speed

Part No.	Thickness in. (mm)
841968601	0.0059 (0.150)
841968602	0.0079 (0.200)
841968603	0.0098 (0.250)
841968604	0.0118 (0.300)
841968605	0.0197 (0.500)
841968606	0.0069 (0.175)
841968607	0.0089 (0.225)
841968608	0.0108 (0.275)

FIG. 24 Hypoid gear backlash pinion shim selection chart – Justy 5 speed

8. Stake the locknut in 2 different locations. Install 5th gear synchronizer ring onto bushing on drive pinion assembly.

9. Install 5th shifter fork in synchronizer sleeve groove. Align 5th shifter fork hole with reverse shifter rail and install hub assembly onto the drive pinion.

10. Align holes in fork and rail and install spring pin.

11. Adjust drive pinion thrust clearance at this point of the service procedure as follows:

   a. Measure clearance between washer and drive pinion cotter.

   b. Select a cotter to obtain clearance measuring from 0–0.0016 in. (0–0.4mm).

   c. Install selected cotter and drive pinion retainer. Install outer snapring.

12. Install transaxle side cover to main case and torque the retaining bolts to 17–20 ft. lbs.

13. Install reverse light switch assembly with new gasket to case.

14. Install correct (oil seal marked L) differential gear oil seal into the main case.

15. Install bearing of transfer shaft in case on 4WD vehicles.

16. Install transaxle oil garter onto main case.

17. Install 4WD switch assembly, if equipped.

18. Install differential assembly into clutch housing.

19. Install drive pinion and mainshaft assembly with 1st/2nd fork and 3rd/4th fork assemblies.

20. Install plunger into reverse shifter arm of shifter rail. Install reverse shifter rail complete assembly into housing.

21. Position reverse idler shaft with spring pin attached together with reverse idler gear into housing. The spring pin height is 0.20–0.24 in. (5–6mm).

22. Install reverse shifter lever of shifter arm with reverse idler gear. Install shifter arm and interlock plate on each rail. Install shifter arm assembly to clutch housing and torque the retaining bolts to 6.7–7.8 ft. lbs. (9.1–10.6 Nm).

23. At this point of the service procedure adjust the thrust clearance of the differential assembly as follows:

   a. Install bearing height gauge tool 499575400 on main case and measure depth of outer race of bearing. This measurement is recorded with symbol H2.

   b. Measure depth of bearing in main case assembly. This measurement is recorded with symbol H1.

   c. Make calculations using the equations to select washer(s) so that clearance may be adjusted to 0–0.008 in. (0–0.2mm).

   d. The equation C (thrust clearance) = H1 - (20.5mm - H2) the dimensions are in millimeters. The equation C (thrust clearance) = H1 - (0.807 in. -H2) the dimensions are in inches (mm).

   e. If clearance is 0.008 in. (0.2mm) or less no washers are needed.

   f. If clearance is over 0.008 in. (0.2mm) and less than 0.016 in. (0.4mm) use 1 washer (part number 803061020).

   g. If clearance is more than 0.016 in. (0.4mm) use 2 washers (part number 803061020).

24. Install washer(s) selected from adjustment procedure on the main case side.

25. Install main case assembly onto clutch housing. Torque retaining bolts in sequence (work from center to ends) to 17–20 ft. lbs. (23–26 Nm).

26. Install shifter fork rail spring and gasket into main case at rail end. Torque shifter rail plug to 13.4–15.6 ft. lbs. (18.1–21.1 Nm).

27. Install bearing to the front of the mainshaft.

and less than 0.016in. (0.4mm) use 1 washer (part number 803046020).

   c. If clearance is more than 0.016 in. (0.4mm) use 2 washers (part number 803046020).

5. Install thrust clearance adjusting washer to mainshaft bearing and install bearing retainer plate to main case. Torque the retaining bolts to 17–20 ft. lbs.

6. Install tool 398781600 mainshaft stopper and align it with the housing groove.

7. Install 5th gear and locknut. Torque the locknut to 54–62 ft. lbs.

28. Install correct differential gear oil seal (marked R) into clutch housing.

29. Install bearing at right of differential then install snapring.

30. Press main case dowel and extension dowel into place.

31. Install clutch release fork pivot and torque to 11–18 ft. lbs. (15–25 Nm).

32. Install drive pinion oil guide, needle bearing and drive pinion RH bearing retainer at the right side of drive pinion by tightening bolts to 6.7–7.8 ft. lbs. (9.1–10.6 Nm).

33. Install knock ball to reverse check location. Ball must be point staked at 2 locations on its circumference.

34. Install reverse check shaft with pin into clutch housing.

35. Install reverse check spring and reverse check cam onto shaft with retaining clip.

36. Install shift connecting rod in housing and fasten selector arm with pin.

37. On 4WD vehicles the transfer shaft assembly and bearing case assembly must be installed.

38. At this point of the service procedure selection of a bevel gear backlash adjusting shim(s) must be performed as follows on 4WD vehicles:

   a. Install transfer shaft assembly in the clutch housing.

   b. With bevel gear height shim (selected through height adjustment) attached to bearing case assembly install bearing case to clutch housing and torque retaining bolts to 20–24 ft. lbs. (26–28 Nm).

   c. Insert dial indicator through backlash adjusting hole and set it on hypoid driven gear.

   d. Pull transfer shaft assembly until gear backlash becomes zero. Measure clearance between clutch housing end face and bearing flange.

   e. Remove the bearing case assembly and transfer shaft assembly.

   f. Attach a selected shim to transfer shaft and install to clutch housing. Hold transfer shaft assembly in position and measure backlash.

   g. The standard valve specification for backlash is 0.0039–0.0059 in. (0.1–0.15mm). If the backlash is not obtained vary transfer shaft assembly shim.

39. Install transfer shaft assembly into main case with drive pinion shim and O-ring. Torque the retaining bolts to 13–16 ft. lbs.

40. Apply a thin even coat of red lead or equivalent to hypoid driven gear teeth surface. Tighten bolts 20–24 ft. lbs. to fasten bearing case assembly together with bevel gear height shim.

41. Check backlash again at this point of the service procedure. The standard valve specification for backlash is 0.0039–0.0059 in. (0.10–0.15mm).

42. Check hypoid gear tooth contact. Readjust if proper backlash or contact tooth pattern is not obtained.

43. Install oil seal into extension case. Install extension complete assembly to clutch housing tighten bolts 17–20 ft. lbs.

44. Install oil seal and knock pipe into transfer side case. Install transfer shifter shaft into the side cover. The knock pipe installed height is 0.39–0.43 in. (10–11mm) and the transfer shifter shaft installed height is 0.3760–0.3917 in. (9.55–9.95mm).

45. Align knock pipe with transfer rail hole in clutch housing. Install transfer side cover, adjusting shim(s), shaft assembly bearing and torque retaining bolts 13–16 ft. lbs.

46. Install shifter fork to shifter rail with pin. Install the shifter fork and rail with synchronizer sleeve into side cover from main case side.

47. Install diaphragm assembly from side cover side.

48. Install shifter lever with washer to transfer shifter shaft with retaining clip.

49. Install diaphragm cover to side cover with retaining bolts.

50. Install transfer cover to clutch housing and torque retaining bolts to 6.7–7.8 ft. lbs.

51. Install backlash measuring hole plug in clutch housing and torque plug to 30–35 ft. lbs.

52. Install check ball and spring in clutch housing and tighten plug to 13.4–15.6 ft. lbs.

5-SPEED FWD TRANSAXLE

General Information

The Subaru front wheel drive transaxle has 5 forward speeds and 1 reverse gear. This transaxle has only single range capability. This transaxle is used in front wheel drive only applications.

Identification

The transaxle can be identified by the 11th letter in the vehicle identification number located on the bulkhead panel of the engine compartment.

The transaxle serial number label is mounted on the the upper surface of the main case.

The manual transaxle 11th letter code is as follows: B-Gumma manufacturer — 5-speed manual transaxle

Metric Fasteners

Metric tools will be required to service this transaxle. Due to the large number of alloy parts used in this transaxle, torque specifications should be strictly observed. Before installing capscrews into aluminum parts, dip the bolts into clean transmission fluid as this will prevent the screws from galling the aluminum threads, thus causing damage.

Metric fastener dimensions are very close to the dimensions of the familiar inch system fasteners. For this reason replacement fasteners must have the same measurement and strength as the original fastener.

Do not attempt to interchange metric fasteners for inch system fasteners. Mismatched or incorrect fasteners can cause damage to the unit and possible personal injury. Care should be taken to reuse fasteners in their original locations.

REMOVAL & INSTALLATION

Legacy

◆ SEE FIGS. 25–28

1. Disconnect the negative battery cable. If equipped with a turbocharger, remove the manifold cover.

2. Remove the air intake duct. If equipped with a turbocharger, discharge the air conditioning and disconnect the air conditioner pressure hose. Remove the resonator chamber, air inlet and outlet ducts.

FIG. 25 Removing the halfshaft roll pin — Legacy FWD 5 speed transaxle

3. Disconnect all cables and harness connectors attached to the transaxle. Remove the starter.

4. Remove the pitching stopper rod and bracket. On turbocharged models, remove the clutch operating cylinder assembly and free the release fork. Remove the transaxle oil level gauge.

5. Remove the connector holder bracket. Remove the turbocharger cooling ducts and disconnect the center exhaust pipe from the turbocharger.

6. Remove the upper transaxle attaching bolts. Remove the driveshaft, gearshift system, front stabilizer and halfshafts.

7. Remove the nuts holding the lower side fo the engine to the transaxle. Install a transaxle jack. Remove the rear cushion rubber mounting nuts and rear crossmember. Remove the transaxle.

8. On turbocharged models, remove the release bearing from the clutch cover.

To Install:

9. Install the transaxle and temporarily tighten bolts. Install the clutch release assembly on Turbo models.

10. Install the rear cushion and crossmember. Tighten cushion bolts to 20–35 ft. lbs. (27–47 Nm); crossmember front bolts to 87–116 ft. lbs. (118–157 Nm), rear 40–61 ft. lbs. (54–83 Nm). Tighten the transaxle to engine bolts to 34–40 ft. lbs. (46–54 Nm).

11. After tightening all bolts check that the release fork is in the proper position. Install the halfshafts, and temporarily install the transverse link and stabilizer.

12. Install the gear shift system and driveshaft. Lower the vehicle and tighten the transverse link to 43–51 ft. lbs. (59–69 Nm); stabilizer to 14–2 ft. lbs. (20–29 Nm).

13. Install the connector holder bracket, pitching stopper, tubrocharger cooling duct, clutch operating cylinder, air conditioner hoses, resonator, air inlet and outlet.

14. Install the starter assembly. Connect all previously disconnected harnesses and connectors.

15. Connect the negative battery cable, check the transaxle fluid level and test drive the vehicle.

Loyale, STD. and XT

♦ SEE FIGS. 30–31

1. Disconnect the negative battery cable. Remove the air cleaner assembly.

2. Remove the clutch cable and the hill holder cable. Remove the speedometer cable.

3. Remove the oxygen sensor electrical connector and the neutral switch connector.

4. Disconnect the electrical connections at the back up light.

5. Disconnect the starter electrical connections. Remove the starter retaining bolts. Remove the starter from the transaxle case.

6. Remove the air intake boot. Disconnect the pitching stopper rod from its mounting bracket. Remove the right side engine to transaxle mounting bolt.

7. Install engine support bracket 927160000 and engine support tool 927150000 or their equivalents. Remove the buffer rod from the engine and body side bracket.

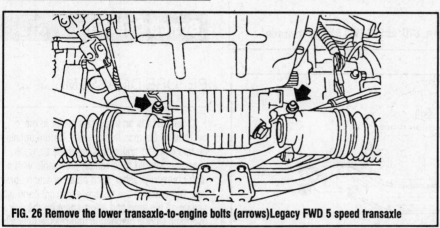

FIG. 26 Remove the lower transaxle-to-engine bolts (arrows)Legacy FWD 5 speed transaxle

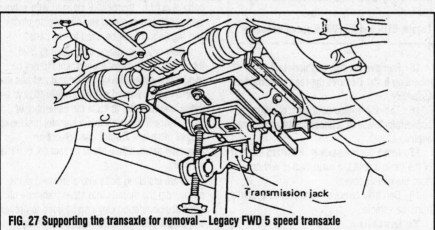

Transmission jack

FIG. 27 Supporting the transaxle for removal — Legacy FWD 5 speed transaxle

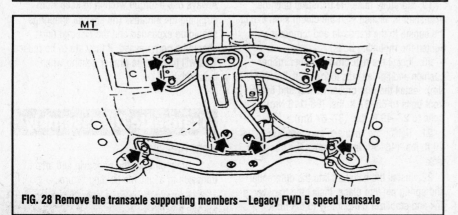

MT

FIG. 28 Remove the transaxle supporting members — Legacy FWD 5 speed transaxle

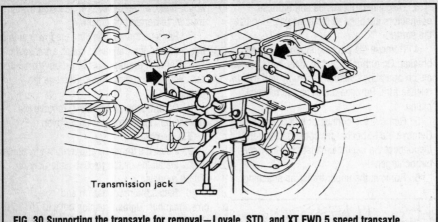

FIG. 30 Supporting the transaxle for removal—Loyale, STD. and XT FWD 5 speed transaxle

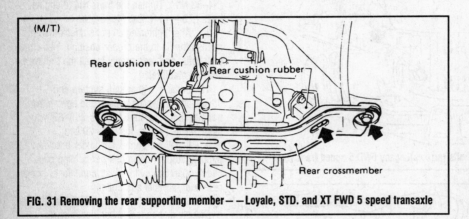

FIG. 31 Removing the rear supporting member——Loyale, STD. and XT FWD 5 speed transaxle

➡ **Before attaching the special engine support tools, connect the adjuster to the buffer rod assembly on the right side of the engine.**

8. Raise and support the vehicle safely.

9. Disconnect the exhaust pipes at the exhaust manifold flange. Remove the exhaust system up to the rear exhaust pipe assembly.

10. Remove the complete gear shift assembly.

11. Loosen the upper bolt and nut from the plate that secures the transverse link to the stabilizer. Remove the lower bolt and separate the link from the stabilizer.

12. Remove the right brake cable bracket from the transverse link. Remove the bolt retaining the link to the crossmember on each side.

13. Lower the transverse link. Using tool 398791700 or equivalent, remove the spring pin and separate the axle shaft from the driveshaft on each side of the assembly by pushing the rear of the tire outward.

14. Remove the engine to transaxle mounting bolts. Position the proper transaxle jack under the transaxle assembly.

15. Remove the rear cushion rubber mounting bolts. Remove the rear crossmember assembly.

16. Turn the engine support tool adjuster counterclockwise in order to slightly raise the engine.

17. Move the transaxle jack toward the rear of the vehicle until the mainshaft is withdrawn from the clutch cover.

18. Carefully remove the transaxle assembly from the vehicle.

To install:

19. Carefully raise the transaxle until the mainshaft is aligned with the clutch side. Install the engine to the transaxle and temporarily tighten the mounting bolts.

20. Install the rear crossmember rubber cushion and tighten nuts to 20–35 ft. lbs. (27–47 Nm). Install the rear crossmember and tighten front bolts to 65–87 ft. lbs. (88–118 Nm); rear bolts to 27–49 ft. lbs. (37–67 Nm).

21. Tighten the engine to transaxle nuts to 34–40 ft. lbs. (46–54 Nm). Remove the transaxle jack.

22. Install the halfshaft into the differential and spring pin into place. Install the transverse link and stabilizer temporarily to the front

crossmember. Install the brake cable bracket. Lower the vehicle and tighten transverse link bolt to 43–51 ft. lbs. (59–69 Nm); stabilizer bolts to 14–22 ft. lbs. (20–29 Nm).

23. Install the gearshift system. Install the starter, pitching stopper, timing hole plug, air intake boot and speedometer cable. Reconnect all electrical and vacuum connectors.

24. Connect the clutch cable and hill holder. Install the front exhaust pipe.

25. Connect the negative battery cable, check the transaxle fluid level and test drive the vehicle.

Bench Overhaul

BEFORE DISASSEMBLY

Cleanliness is an important factor in the overhaul of the manual transaxle. Before opening up this unit, the entire outside of the transaxle assembly should be cleaned, preferable with a high pressure washer such as a car wash spray unit. Dirt entering the transaxle internal parts will negate all the time and effort spent on the overhaul. During inspection and reassembly all parts should be thoroughly cleaned with solvent then dried with compressed air. Wiping cloths and rags should not be used to dry parts.

Wheel bearing grease, long used to hold thrust washers and lube parts, should not be used. Lube seals with clean transaxle oil and use ordinary unmedicated petroleum jelly to hold the thrust washers and to ease the assembly of seals, since it will not leave a harmful residue as grease often will. Do not use solvent on neoprene seals, if they are to be reused, or thrust washers.

Before installing bolts into aluminum parts, always dip the threads into clean transaxle oil. Antiseize compound can also be used to prevent bolts from galling the aluminum and seizing. Always use a torque wrench to keep from stripping the threads. The internal snaprings should be expanded and the external rings should be compressed, if they are to be reused. This will help insure proper seating when installed.

Transaxle Disassembly

◆ SEE FIGS. 32–33

1. Drain oil from the transaxle and attach transaxle to a suitable holding fixture.

2. Remove the release lever and clutch release bearing.

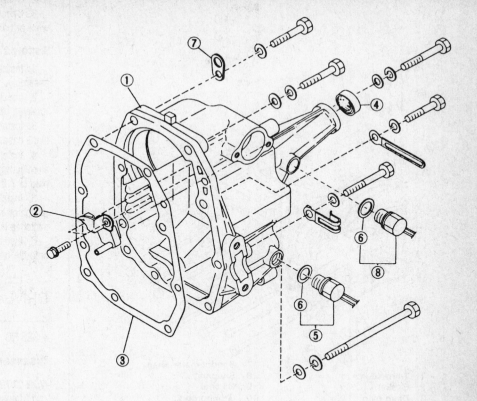

FWD Non-TURBO

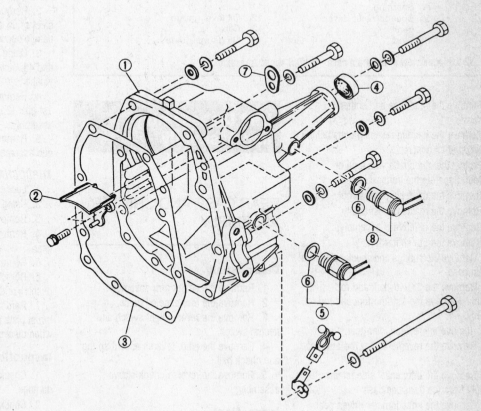

FWD TURBO

1. Rear case
2. Oil sguide
3. Case gasket
4. Oil seal
5. Back-up light switch
6. Gasket
7. Hanger
8. Neutral switch

FIG. 33 Exploded view of the rear case—FWD 5 speed transaxle

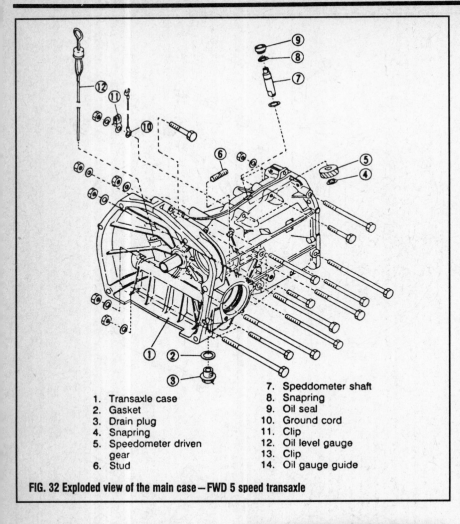

FIG. 32 Exploded view of the main case—FWD 5 speed transaxle

1. Transaxle case
2. Gasket
3. Drain plug
4. Snapring
5. Speedometer driven gear
6. Stud
7. Speddometer shaft
8. Snapring
9. Oil seal
10. Ground cord
11. Clip
12. Oil level gauge
13. Clip
14. Oil gauge guide

3. Remove the rear case and shifter assembly.

4. Remove the bearing retaining bolts behind drive pinion shaft assembly.

5. Protect the stubshafts with tape or equivalent. Separate the transaxle case.

6. Remove the drive pinion assembly.

7. Remove the mainshaft assembly.

8. Remove the differential assembly.

9. Remove the 5th shifter fork.

10. Remove the springs and check balls from the main case.

11. Remove the 3rd/4th fork and rod assembly. Remove the 1st/2nd fork and rod assembly.

12. Remove the reverse idler gear.

13. Remove the reverse shifter rod arm and rod.

14. Remove the differential side retainer assembly from the transaxle case.

15. Remove the speedometer driven gear and speedometer shaft assembly.

Unit Disassembly and Assembly

REAR CASE AND SHIFTER ASSEMBLY

Disassembly

1. Remove the shifter arm assembly.
2. Remove the rear case oil guide.
3. Remove the reverse light switch and neutral switch.
4. Remove the plug, reverse accent spring and check ball.
5. Remove the reverse check sleeve assembly.

Inspection

1. Check shifter arm for excessive wear or damage.

2. Check oil guide for cracks or damage.
3. Check reverse check sleeve for excessive wear or being deformed.

Assembly

1. Install oil seal into bore of rear case assembly.

2. Install oil guide to rear of case and torque retaining bolts to 5 ft. lbs.

3. Install the reverse check sleeve assembly in the case. Torque the retaining bolts to 7 ft. lbs.

4. Install check ball, reverse accent spring, aluminum gasket and plug in order. Tighten the plug to 7 ft. lbs.

5. Install the neutral switch and reverse light switch on rear case. Tightening torque for switches is 13 ft. lbs.

6. Install the shifter arm complete assembly onto the rear case.

DRIVE PINION SHAFT

♦ SEE FIG. 34

Disassembly

NON-TURBOCHARGED ENGINE

1. Loosen the locknut using suitable tools.

2. Remove insert stopper plate, insert guide, sleeve/hub assembly, balk ring, 5th gear and needle bearing.

3. Using a suitable press remove bearing, 3rd and 4th gears, 5th bearing race, 5th gear thrust washer.

4. Remove 2nd gear and bearing. Remove 1st gear, 2nd bearing inner race and gear/hub assembly.

5. Remove 1st bearing inner race and gear/hub assembly.

TURBOCHARGED ENGINE

1. Loosen the locknut using suitable tools.

2. Using a suitable press remove 5th gear.

3. Remove 5th driven gear and woodruff key.

4. Remove the bearing, 3rd gear and 4th gear.

5. Remove the 2nd gear assembly.

6. Remove 1st gear assembly, 2nd gear gear bushing and gear/hub assembly.

7. Remove 1st gear bushing, 1st gear driven thrust plate and bearing (always replace bearing when disassembled).

Inspection

1. Check all bearings for wear and or damage.

2. Check bearing inner and outer races for wear.

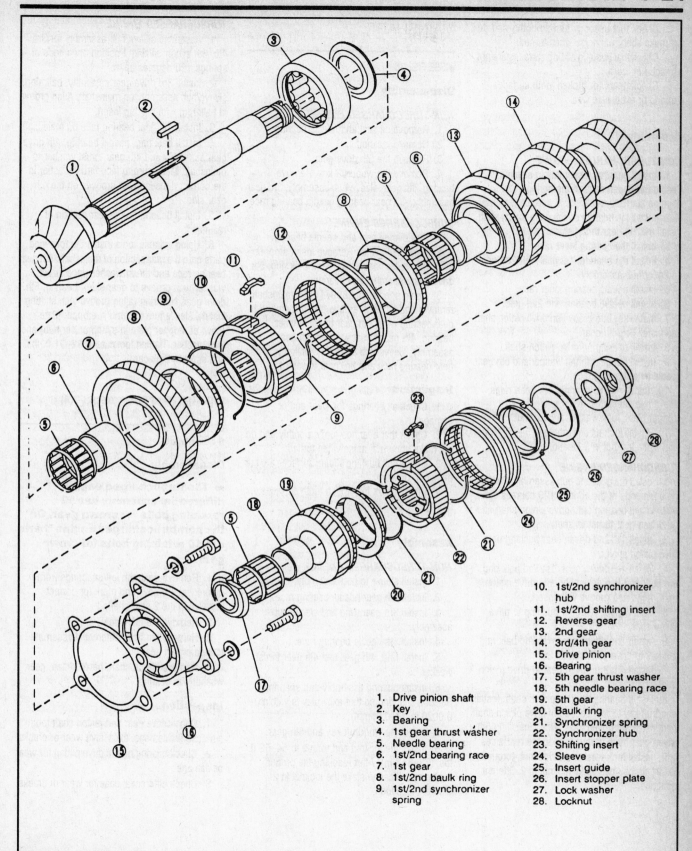

1. Drive pinion shaft
2. Key
3. Bearing
4. 1st gear thrust washer
5. Needle bearing
6. 1st/2nd bearing race
7. 1st gear
8. 1st/2nd baulk ring
9. 1st/2nd synchronizer
   spring
10. 1st/2nd synchronizer
    hub
11. 1st/2nd shifting insert
12. Reverse gear
13. 2nd gear
14. 3rd/4th gear
15. Drive pinion
16. Bearing
17. 5th gear thrust washer
18. 5th needle bearing race
19. 5th gear
20. Baulk ring
21. Synchronizer spring
22. Synchronizer hub
23. Shifting insert
24. Sleeve
25. Insert guide
26. Insert stopper plate
27. Lock washer
28. Locknut

FIG. 34 Exploded view of the drive pinion shaft—FWD 5 speed transaxle

3. Check that bearings turn smoothly and do not make abnormal noise when turned.

4. Check that bushing sliding surfaces are not damaged or worn.

5. Check gears for broken tooth surfaces, damage or excessive wear.

Assembly

NON-TURBOCHARGED ENGINE

1. Install gear/hub assembly in sleeve. Position the open ends of the springs 120 degrees apart.

2. Install the bearing on the drive pinion shaft. Install the 1st gear thrust shaft.

3. Install the bearing inner race.

4. Install the bearing, 1st gear, 1st/2nd ring and gear/hub assembly.

5. Install needle bearing inner race.

6. Install needle bearing and 2nd gear.

7. Install key into groove on drive pinion shaft and install 3rd/4th gear.

8. Install bearing on drive pinion shaft.

9. Install 5th gear thrust washer and 5th gear needle inner bearing race.

10. Install needle bearing, 5th gear, rings, sleeve/hub assembly, insert guide, insert stopper plate, lock washer and locknut.

11. Install locknut and torque to 54–62 ft. lbs. then stake locknut in 2 locations.

TURBOCHARGED ENGINE

1. Install the gear and hub assembly. Position the open ends of the springs 120 degrees apart.

2. Install bearing onto drive pinion shaft and 1st driven gear thrust washer.

3. Install 1st/2nd driven gear bushing onto drive pinion shaft.

4. Install 1st driven gear, 1st/2nd balk ring and gear and hub assembly onto drive pinion shaft. Align ring groove with insert.

5. Install 1st/driven gear bushing to drive pinion shaft.

6. Install 2nd driven gear, 1st/2nd balk ring and key to drive pinion shaft.

7. Install 4th/3rd driven gear to drive pinion shaft.

8. Install bearing to drive pinion shaft. Install woodruff key to rear section of drive pinion shaft then install 5th driven gear. When installing 5th driven gear have groove face to the rear side.

9. Install lock washer and locknut, torque to 82–91 ft. lbs. then stake locknut in 2 different locations.

MAINSHAFT

♦ SEE FIG. 35

Disassembly

NON-TURBOCHARGED ENGINE

1. Remove oil seal and needle bearing.
2. Remove locknut.
3. Remove the 5th drive gear.
4. Remove the woodruff key. Remove bearing, 4th gear, sleeve/hub assembly, 3rd gear assembly, 4th gear bearing needle bearing race.

TURBOCHARGED ENGINE

1. Remove oil seal and needle bearing.
2. Remove locknut. Remove insert stopper plate, sleeve/hub assembly, No.2 balk ring, 5th drive gear assembly and bearing.
3. Using special tool 899714110 mainshaft remover and a press remove the following: 5th gear bearing race, 5th gear thrust washer, bearing, 4th gear thrust washer, 4th gear assembly, sleeve/hub assembly, balk ring, 4th gear bearing race and 3rd gear assembly.

Inspection

1. Check all bearings for wear and or damage.

2. Check that bearings turn smoothly and do not make abnormal noise when turned.

3. Check that bushing sliding surfaces are not damaged or worn.

4. Check gears for broken tooth surfaces, damage or excessive wear.

Assembly

NON-TURBOCHARGED ENGINE

1. Install sleeve to hub assembly.

2. Install 5th gear needle bearing race.

3. Install 3rd gear, ring and sleeve/hub assembly.

4. Install 5th needle bearing race.

5. Install ring, 4th gear and 4th gear thrust washer.

6. Install bearing assembly and snapring. Select a snapring so that axial play is within 0–0.0020 in. (0–0.05mm).

7. Install the woodruff key and 5th gear.

8. Install the locknut and torque to 54–62 ft. lbs. (73–84 Nm). After reaching the proper torque specification stake the locknut in 2 different locations.

TURBOCHARGED ENGINE

1. Assemble sleeve/hub assembly for 3rd/4th, 5th synchronizing. Position open ends of springs 120 degrees apart.

2. Install 3rd drive gear assembly, balk ring, sleeve/hub assembly on mainshaft. Align groove in balk ring with shifting insert.

3. Install 4th gear bearing race on mainshaft.

4. Install balk ring, needle bearing, 4th drive gear assembly and 4th gear thrust washer to mainshaft. Make sure to face thrust washer in the correct direction with grooves on the 4th gear side.

5. Install bearing on the rear section of mainshaft.

6. Using suitable tools install the following parts onto the rear section of mainshaft: 5th gear bearing race and thrust washer (face thrust washer with groove to gear side), bearing, 5th drive gear, balk ring (align groove with shifting insert), sleeve/hub assembly, stopper plate (pawl of stopper plate in synchronizer hub) and lock washer. Tighten locknuts to 82–91 ft. lbs. and stake in 2 places.

DIFFERENTIAL ASSEMBLY

♦ SEE FIG. 36

Disassembly

➡ **The turbocharged engine differential assembly has 12 retaining bolts for crown gear. On the non-turbocharged engine there are 10 retaining bolts for crown gear.**

1. Remove right and left snaprings from differential. Remove and mark for correct installation the 2 stub shafts.

2. Remove the drive gear.

3. Remove pin from differential assembly toward crown gear.

4. Remove pinion shaft, bevel pinion, gear, washer and bearing.

Inspection

1. Check drive gear and pinion shaft tooth surfaces for damage, excessive wear or cracks.

2. Check bearing on the drive pinion for wear or damage.

3. Check differential case for wear or cracks.

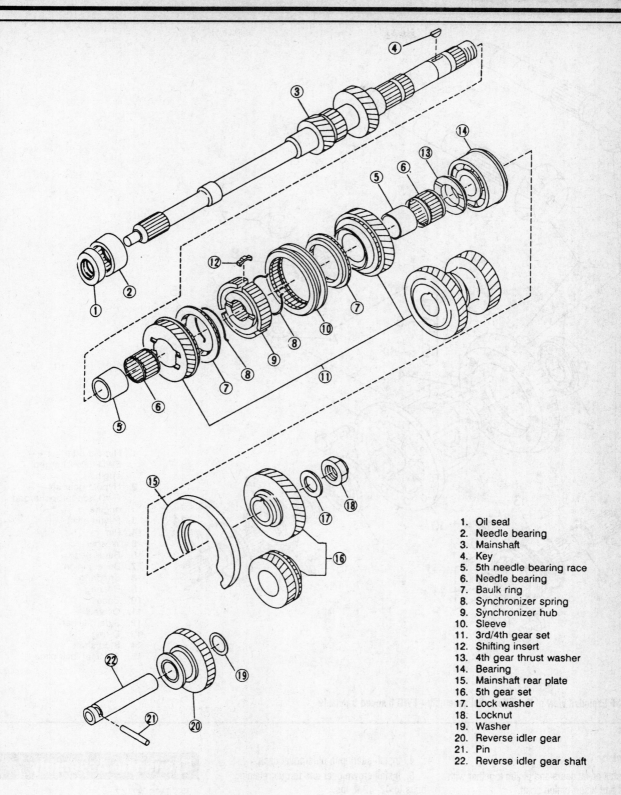

FIG. 35 Exploded view of the mainshaft assembly—FWD 5 speed transaxle

1. Oil seal
2. Needle bearing
3. Mainshaft
4. Key
5. 5th needle bearing race
6. Needle bearing
7. Baulk ring
8. Synchronizer spring
9. Synchronizer hub
10. Sleeve
11. 3rd/4th gear set
12. Shifting insert
13. 4th gear thrust washer
14. Bearing
15. Mainshaft rear plate
16. 5th gear set
17. Lock washer
18. Locknut
19. Washer
20. Reverse idler gear
21. Pin
22. Reverse idler gear shaft

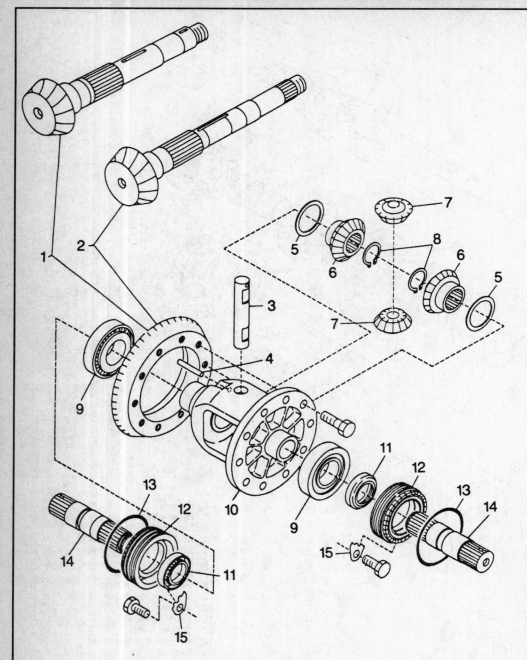

1. Hypoid gear set — — FWD turbocharged engine
2. Hypoid gear set — — FWD non-turbocharged engine
3. Pinion shaft
4. Pin
5. Washer
6. Bevel gear
7. Bevel pinion
8. Snapring
9. Bearing
10. Case
11. Oil seal
12. Side retainer
13. O-ring
14. Stub shaft
15. Retainer lock plate

FIG. 36 Exploded view of the differential assembly—FWD 5 speed transaxle

Assembly

1. Install bevel gears and pinion together with washers and insert pinion shaft.

2. Measure the backlash between bevel gear and pinion. The standard specification is 0.0051–0.0071 in. (0.013–0.18mm).

3. Align pinion shaft and differential case and install pin into holes from the crown gear side. Lock pin after installing.

4. Install bearing in differential case.

5. Install crown gear and torque retaining bolts to 42–49 ft. lbs.

6. Install stub shafts in differential case with snaprings. Make sure clearance between shafts and the case is 0–0.008 in. (0–0.2mm). If not within specifications replace snapring.

Transaxle Assembly

♦ SEE FIGS. 37–47

1. Install interlock plungers in correct holes on the inner wall of the transaxle case.

2. Install reverse idler gear assembly and lock in place with pin.

3. Install reverse fork rod and reverse fork rod arm with snapring.

Part No.	Thickness in. (mm)
803135011	0.0364–0.0374 (0.925–0.950)
803135012	0.0374–0.0384 (0.950–0.975)
803135013	0.0384–0.0394 (0.975–1.000)
803135014	0.0394–0.0404 (1.000–1.025)
803135015	0.0404–0.0413 (1.025–1.050)

FIG. 37 Differential washer selection chart—FWD 5 speed transaxle non-turbocharged engine

Part Number	Thickness in. (mm)
803038021	0.0364–0.0374 (0.925–0.950)
803038022	0.0384–0.0394 (0.975–1.000)
803038023	0.0404–0.0413 (1.025–1.050)

FIG. 38 Differential washer selection chart—FWD 5 speed transaxle turbocharged engine

Part Number	Thickness in. (mm)
805028011	0.0413 (1.05)
805208012	0.0472 (1.20)

FIG. 39 Differential assembly snapring selection chart—FWD 5 speed transaxle turbocharged engine

Part Number	Thickness in. (mm)
805026010	0.0413 (1.05)
031526000	0.0472 (1.20)

FIG. 40 Differential assembly snapring selection chart—FWD 5 speed transaxle non-turbocharged engine

Part No.	Thickness in. (mm)
441967111	0.0059 (0.15)
441967112	0.0069 (0.175)
441967113	0.0079 (0.20)
441967114	0.0089 (0.225)
441967115	0.0098 (0.25)
441967116	0.0108 (0.275)
441967117	0.0118 (0.30)
441967118	0.0197 (0.50)

FIG. 41 Drive pinion adjustment shim selection chart—FWD 5 speed transaxle non-turbocharged engine

Part No.	Thickness in. (mm)
32295 AA030	0.0059 (0.150)
32295 AA040	0.0069 (0.175)
32295 AA050	0.0079 (0.200)
32295 AA060	0.0089 (0.225)
32295 AA070	0.0098 (0.250)
32295 AA080	0.0108 (0.275)
32295 AA090	0.0118 (0.300)
32295 AA100	0.0197 (0.500)

FIG. 42 Drive pinion adjustment shim selection chart—FWD 5 speed transaxle turbocharged engine

Part No.	Thickness in. (mm)
803015081	0.024–0.031 (0.6–0.8)
803015082	0.039–0.047 (1.0–1.2)
803015083	0.055–0.063 (1.4–1.6)
803015084	0.071–0.079 (1.8–2.0)
803015085	0.087–0.094 (2.2–2.4)

FIG. 43 Reverse idler gear shaft washer selection—FWD 5 speed transaxle non-turbocharged engine

Part No.	Thickness in. (mm)
803020151	0.016 (0.4)
803020152	0.043 (1.1)
803020153	0.059 (1.5)
803020154	0.075 (1.9)
803020155	0.091 (2.3)

FIG. 44 Reverse idler gear shaft washer selection—FWD 5 speed transaxle turbocharged engine

Part No.	Thickness in. (mm)
805022010	0.0965 (2.45)
805022011	0.0976 (2.48)
805022012	0.0988 (2.51)
805022013	0.1000 (2.54)
805022014	0.1012 (2.57)
805022015	0.1024 (2.60)
805022016	0.1035 (2.63)
805022017	0.1047 (2.66)
805022018	0.1059 (2.69)
805022019	0.1122 (2.85)
805022030	0.0953 (2.42)
805022031	0.0941 (2.39)

FIG. 45 Mainshaft snapring selection chart—FWD 5 speed transaxle non-turbocharged engine

4. Install check ball, spring and gasket in reverse shifter rod hole. Torque ball plug to 14 ft. lbs.

5. Position reverse shifter rod toward reverse side. Adjust so clearance between reverse idler gear assembly position and case wall is 0.059–0.118 in. (1.5–3.0mm) on non-turbocharged engines and 0.236–0.295 in. (6.0–7.5mm) on turbocharged engines using a reverse shifter lever assembly.

6. After installing a suitable reverse shifter lever assembly, shift into the neutral position. Adjust so clearance between reverse idler gear assembly and transaxle case wall is 0–0.020 in. (0–0.5mm), using washer(s).

7. Install rod and fork assembly.

8. Install checking balls, springs and gaskets into 3rd/4th gear and 1st/2nd gear rod holes and install plugs. Torque retaining plugs to 14 ft. lbs.

9. Adjust the drive pinion shim as follows:

a. The upper figure on the drive pinion is the match number for combining it with the crown gear. The lower figure is for the shim adjustment. If no lower figure is shown, the valve is zero. The figure on the crown gear is the matched number for the drive pinion.

b. Place the drive pinion shaft in case without shims and torque to 20–24 ft. lbs.

Part No.	Stamp	Thickness in. (mm)
441347001	T81-1	0.1772–0.1823 (4.50–4.63)
441347002	T81-2	0.1720–0.1772 (4.37–4.50)

FIG. 46 Mainshaft rear plate selection chart—FWD 5 speed transaxle non-turbocharged engine

Part No.	Identification	Thickness in. (mm)
32294AA040	1	0.1575–0.1626 (4.0–4.13)
32294AA050	2	0.1524–0.1575 (3.87–4.0)

FIG. 47 Mainshaft rear plate selection chart—FWD 5 speed transaxle turbocharged engine

c. Install special tool 499917500 gauge assembly so that the scale reads 0.5 when the plate and the scale end are on the same level.

d. Position the gauge by inserting the knock pin of the gauge into the hole in the transaxle case.

e. Slide the drive pinion gauge scale and read the valve at the point where it matches with the end face of the drive pinion.

f. The thickness of the shim shall be determined by adding the valve indicated on the drive pinion to the valve indicated on the gauge. Add if the figure on the drive pinion is prefixed by (+) sign and subtract if the figure is prefixed by a (-) sign. Do not use more than 3 shims.

10. Install the differential assembly in the transaxle case.

11. Install mainshaft assembly into the transaxle case.

12. Install drive pinion with the correct amount of shims into the transaxle case.

13. Select suitable 1st/2nd, 3rd/4th and 5th shifter fork complete assemblies. Measure rod end clearances A and B. If any clearance is not within specifications, replace rod or fork as required. On non-turbocharged engines the figure A = 0.012–0.063 in. (0.3–1.6mm) in clearance. The figure B = 0.012–0.063 in. (0.3–1.6mm) in clearance. On turbocharged engines the figure A = 0.020–0.059 in. (0.5–1.5mm) in clearance. The figure B = 0.024–0.055 in. (0.6–1.4mm) in clearance.

14. Install both halves of the transaxle case together and torque the bolts in sequence.

SELECTIVE (4WD/FWD) 5-SPEED TRANSAXLE

General Information

On this transaxle, a selector switch in the shift lever allows the driver to choose 4WD or front wheel drive. The switch can be operated at any time, regardless of the shifter position.

Identification

This transaxle is used in the STD., Loyale and XT.

The transaxle can be identified by the 11th letter in the vehicle identification number located on the bulkhead panel of the engine compartment.

The transaxle serial number label is mounted on the the upper surface of the main case.

The manual transaxle 11th letter code is as follows:

D: Gumma manufacturer — 4WD 5-speed manual transaxle

E: Gumma manufacturer — 4WD dual-range (sedan and Wagon only)

Removal and Installation

1. Disconnect the negative battery cable. Remove the air cleaner assembly.

2. Remove the clutch cable and the hill holder cable. Remove the speedometer cable.

3. Remove the oxygen sensor electrical connector and the neutral switch connector.

4. If equipped with 4WD, remove the disconnect the electrical connections at the back up light and differential lock indicator switch assembly. Disconnect the differential lock vacuum hose.

5. Disconnect the starter electrical connections. Remove the starter retaining bolts. Remove the starter from the transaxle case.

6. Remove the air intake boot. Disconnect the pitching stopper rod from its mounting bracket. Remove the right side engine to transaxle mounting bolt.

7. Install engine support bracket 927160000 and engine support tool 927150000 or their equivalents. Remove the buffer rod from the engine and body side bracket.

➡ **Before attaching the special engine support tools, connect the adjuster to the buffer rod assembly on the right side of the engine.**

8. Raise and support the vehicle safely.

9. Disconnect the exhaust pipes at the exhaust manifold flange. Remove the exhaust system up to the rear exhaust pipe assembly.

10. If equipped with 4WD, matchmark and remove the driveshaft. Remove the complete gear shift assembly.

11. Loosen the upper bolt and nut from the plate that secures the transverse link to the stabilizer. Remove the lower bolt and separate the link from the stabilizer.

12. Remove the right brake cable bracket from the transverse link. Remove the bolt retaining the link to the crossmember on each side.

13. Lower the transverse link. Using tool 398791700 or equivalent, remove the spring pin and separate the axle shaft from the driveshaft on each side of the assembly by pushing the rear of the tire outward.

14. Remove the engine to transaxle mounting bolts. Position the proper transaxle jack under the transaxle assembly.

15. Remove the rear cushion rubber mounting bolts. Remove the rear crossmember assembly.

16. Turn the engine support tool adjuster counterclockwise in order to slightly raise the engine.

17. Move the transaxle jack toward the rear of the vehicle until the mainshaft is withdrawn from the clutch cover.

18. Carefully remove the transaxle assembly from the vehicle.

To Install:

19. Carefully raise the transaxle until the mainshaft is aligned with the clutch side. Install the engine to the transaxle and temporarily tight the mounting bolts.

20. Install the rear crossmember rubber cushion and tighten nuts to 20–35 ft. lbs. (27–47 Nm). Install the rear crossmember and tighten front bolts to 65–87 ft. lbs. (88–118 Nm); rear bolts to 27–49 ft. lbs. (37–67 Nm).

21. Tighten the engine to transaxle nuts to 34–40 ft. lbs. (46–54 Nm). Remove the transaxle jack.

22. Install the halfshaft into the differential and spring pin into place. Install the transverse link and stabilizer temporarily to the front crossmember. Install the brake cable bracket. Lower the vehicle and tighten transverse link bolt to 43–51 ft. lbs. (59–69 Nm); stabilizer bolts to 14–22 ft. lbs. (20–29 Nm).

23. Install the gearshift system. Install the driveshaft (4WD vehicles). Install the starter, pitching stopper, timing hole plug, air intake boot and speedometer cable. Reconnect all electrical and vacuum connectors.

24. Connect the clutch cable and hill holder. Install the front exhaust pipe.

25. Connect the negative battery cable, check the transaxle fluid level and test drive the vehicle.

Bench Overhaul

BEFORE DISASSEMBLY

Cleanliness is an important factor in the overhaul of the manual transaxle. Before opening up this unit, the entire outside of the transaxle assembly should be cleaned, preferable with a high pressure washer such as a car wash spray unit. Dirt entering the transaxle internal parts will negate all the time and effort spent on the overhaul. During inspection and reassembly all parts should be thoroughly cleaned with solvent then dried with compressed air. Wiping cloths and rags should not be used to dry parts.

Wheel bearing grease, long used to hold thrust washers and lube parts, should not be used. Lube seals with clean transaxle oil and use ordinary unmedicated petroleum jelly to hold the thrust washers and to ease the assembly of seals, since it will not leave a harmful residue as grease often will. Do not use solvent on neoprene seals, if they are to be reused, or thrust washers.

Before installing bolts into aluminum parts, always dip the threads into clean transaxle oil. Antiseize compound can also be used to prevent bolts from galling the aluminum and seizing. Always use a torque wrench to keep from stripping the threads. The internal snaprings should be expanded and the external rings should be compressed, if they are to be reused. This will help insure proper seating when installed.

Transaxle Disassembly

◆ SEE FIGS. 48–49

1. Drain oil from the transaxle and attach transaxle to a suitable holding fixture.

2. Remove the release lever and clutch release bearing.

3. Remove high-low shifter rod assembly on dual range applications.

4. Remove the clutch actuator and cable assembly on single range applications.

5. Remove the transfer cover retaining bolts and cover.

6. Remove plug from the transfer case and remove gasket, spring and ball from inside the case on dual range applications.

7. Set transfer shifter rod in LOW position. Remove the clip from the transfer shifter rod complete assembly on dual range applications.

8. Set transfer shifter rod in HIGH position and remove rod holding the shifter fork. Remove the transfer shifter rod complete assembly on dual range applications.

9. Remove the pins and clips from the interlock rod. Remove the interlock rod by rotating rod 90 degrees and pulling it out on dual range applications.

10. Remove the transfer shifter fork complete assembly on dual range applications. The

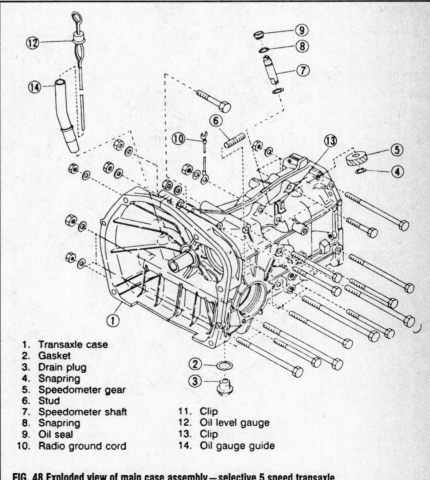

1. Transaxle case
2. Gasket
3. Drain plug
4. Snapring
5. Speedometer gear
6. Stud
7. Speedometer shaft
8. Snapring
9. Oil seal
10. Radio ground cord
11. Clip
12. Oil level gauge
13. Clip
14. Oil gauge guide

FIG. 48 Exploded view of main case assembly — selective 5 speed transaxle

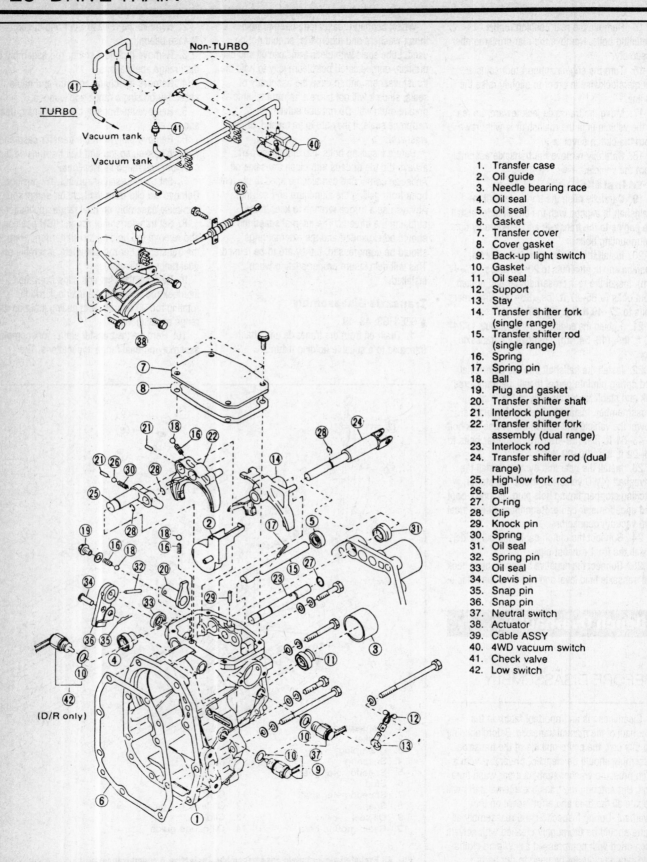

Non-TURBO

TURBO

Vacuum tank

Vacuum tank

(D/R only)

1. Transfer case
2. Oil guide
3. Needle bearing race
4. Oil seal
5. Oil seal
6. Gasket
7. Transfer cover
8. Cover gasket
9. Back-up light switch
10. Gasket
11. Oil seal
12. Support
13. Stay
14. Transfer shifter fork (single range)
15. Transfer shifter rod (single range)
16. Spring
17. Spring pin
18. Ball
19. Plug and gasket
20. Transfer shifter shaft
21. Interlock plunger
22. Transfer shifter fork assembly (dual range)
23. Interlock rod
24. Transfer shifter rod (dual range)
25. High-low fork rod
26. Ball
27. O-ring
28. Clip
29. Knock pin
30. Spring
31. Oil seal
32. Spring pin
33. Oil seal
34. Clevis pin
35. Snap pin
36. Snap pin
37. Neutral switch
38. Actuator
39. Cable ASSY
40. 4WD vacuum switch
41. Check valve
42. Low switch

FIG. 49 Exploded view of transfer case and control system — selective 5 speed transaxle

transfer shifter fork complete assembly has a spring and ball in it. Be careful not to damage the O-ring in the rod.

11. Remove the high-low fork rod on dual range applications. Be careful not to drop ball, spring and interlock plunger that are built in the fork rod.

12. Remove pin in transfer shifter fork assembly on single range applications. Remove the transfer shifter rod and transfer shifter fork on single range applications. Also remove ball and ball spring from the transfer case.

➡ **When removing the fork, move the reverse checking sleeve toward outside by slightly loosening it.**

13. Remove extension and transfer gear assembly.

14. Remove the shifter shaft from the right side of the transfer case on single range applications.

15. Remove the transfer case plug with gasket and then remove reverse accent spring and ball.

16. Remove the reverse check sleeve assembly.

17. Remove the shifter fork assembly screw from the selector arm.

18. Remove the transfer case and shifter assembly.

19. Remove the bearing retaining bolts behind the drive pinion shaft assembly.

20. Remove the input shaft holder mounting bolts on dual range applications.

21. Remove the high-low shifter lever assembly on dual range applications.

22. Remove the mainshaft rear plate.

23. Protect the stubshafts with tape or equivalent.

24. Separate the transaxle case by removing 17 retaining bolts.

25. Remove drive pinion shaft assembly.

26. Remove the high-low fork and shaft assembly on dual range applications.

27. Remove mainshaft and input shaft assembly from the case on dual range applications.

28. Separate mainshaft assembly from the input shaft assembly on dual range applications.

29. Remove mainshaft assembly from transaxle case on single range applications.

30. Remove the differential assembly from the transaxle case.

31. Remove 5th shifter fork. Remove the 3 checking ball plugs from the case.

32. Remove 1st/2nd shifter fork and rod assembly. Remove 3rd/4th shift fork and rod assembly.

➡ **When removing shifter rods, keep all other rods in the neutral position.**

33. Remove the reverse idler gear shaft and gear assembly.

34. Remove the outer snapring and pull out the reverse shifter rod arm from the reverse fork rod. Remove ball, spring, and interlock plunger from rod.

35. Remove the reverse shifter lever.

36. Remove the differential side retainer assembly from the case.

37. Remove the speedometer assembly.

38. Remove the snapring from the high-low countershaft on dual range applications.

39. Remove the pin from the high-low countershaft on dual range applications.

40. Remove the high-low countergear on dual range applications. Be careful not to drop needle bearings and collar contained in the countergear.

Unit Disassembly and Assembly

EXTENSION AND TRANSFER GEAR ASSEMBLY

Disassembly
◆ SEE FIG. 50

1. Remove the 4WD switch assembly.

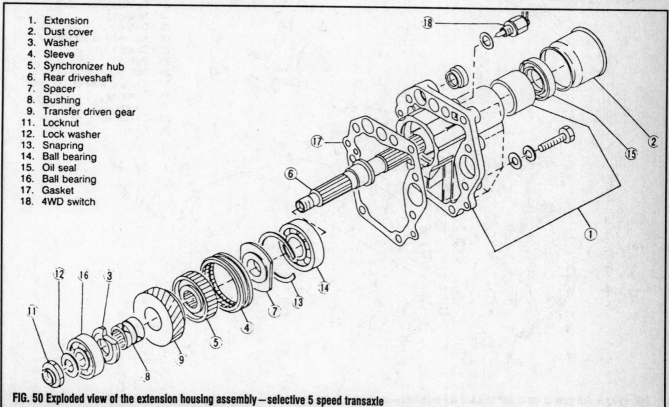

1. Extension
2. Dust cover
3. Washer
4. Sleeve
5. Synchronizer hub
6. Rear driveshaft
7. Spacer
8. Bushing
9. Transfer driven gear
11. Locknut
12. Lock washer
13. Snapring
14. Ball bearing
15. Oil seal
16. Ball bearing
17. Gasket
18. 4WD switch

FIG. 50 Exploded view of the extension housing assembly — selective 5 speed transaxle

2. Remove the snapring from the extension and transfer gear assembly.

3. Remove the shaft from the extension and transfer gear assembly.

4. Position sleeve coupling in the drive range and remove the locknut.

5. Remove the bearing, 4th gear thrust washer, transfer driven gear and coupling sleeve from the shaft.

6. Using suitable tools remove shaft drive bushing, transfer synchronizer hub, rear drive spacer and bearing.

Inspection

1. Check all bearings for wear and or damage.

2. Check bearing inner and outer races for wear.

3. Check that bearings turn smoothly and do not make abnormal noise when turned.

4. Check that bushing sliding surfaces are not damaged or worn.

5. Check gears for broken tooth surfaces, damage or excessive wear.

Assembly

1. Install oil seal on rear of the extension assembly using suitable tool.

2. Install transfer rear oil seal on the extension assembly.

3. Install 4WD switch on the extension assembly with aluminum washer torque the retaining bolt to 13 ft. lbs.

4. Install bearing onto the rear shaft using suitable tool.

5. Install rear drive spacer, synchronizer hub and sleeve on the shaft.

6. Install transfer driven gear bushing with retainer on shaft.

7. Install coupling sleeve, transfer driven gear and thrust washer on the shaft.

8. Install bearing and retainer on shaft with suitable tools.

9. Position sleeve coupling in the drive range

and tighten the locknut to 54–62 ft. lbs. Stake the locknut at 4 positions after tightening.

10. Install rear shaft in the extension assembly then install snapring in the groove inside the extension assembly.

TRANSFER CASE AND SHIFTER ASSEMBLY

Disassembly

◆ SEE FIG. 51

1. Remove the shifter arm assembly and selector arm from the transfer case.

2. Remove the oil guide from the transfer case.

3. Remove the reverse light switch assembly and neutral switch assembly if so equipped.

4. Remove the reverse check sleeve assembly from the transfer case.

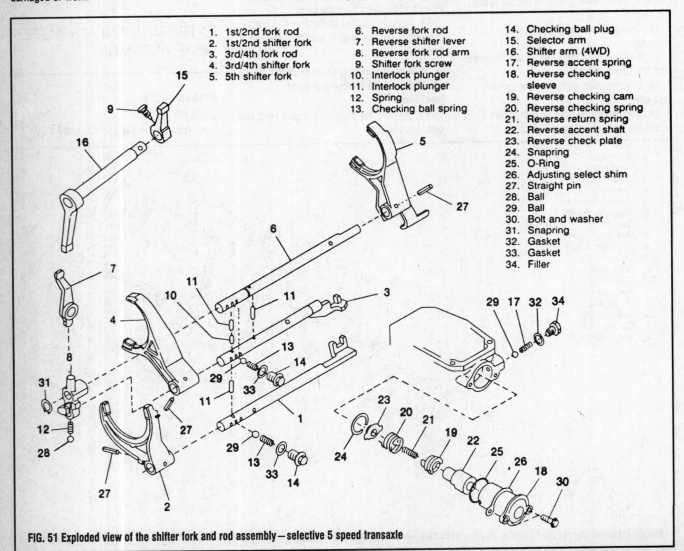

1. 1st/2nd fork rod	6. Reverse fork rod	14. Checking ball plug
2. 1st/2nd shifter fork	7. Reverse shifter lever	15. Selector arm
3. 3rd/4th fork rod	8. Reverse fork rod arm	16. Shifter arm (4WD)
4. 3rd/4th shifter fork	9. Shifter fork screw	17. Reverse accent spring
5. 5th shifter fork	10. Interlock plunger	18. Reverse checking sleeve
	11. Interlock plunger	19. Reverse checking cam
	12. Spring	20. Reverse checking spring
	13. Checking ball spring	21. Reverse return spring
		22. Reverse accent shaft
		23. Reverse check plate
		24. Snapring
		25. O-Ring
		26. Adjusting select shim
		27. Straight pin
		28. Ball
		29. Ball
		30. Bolt and washer
		31. Snapring
		32. Gasket
		33. Gasket
		34. Filler

FIG. 51 Exploded view of the shifter fork and rod assembly—selective 5 speed transaxle

Inspection

1. Check shifter arm for excessive wear or damage.

2. Check selector arm from excessive wear or damage.

3. Replace the gearshift mechanism if bent or defective in any way.

Assembly

1. Install needle bearing race in the bore in the transfer case.

2. Install front oil seal into the bore in transfer case using suitable tools.

3. Install the reverse light switch assembly and neutral switch assembly to transfer case. Torque the switch assemblies with aluminum washer to 13 ft. lbs.

4. Install oil seal into bore in the transfer case.

5. Install oil guide.

6. Install reverse check sleeve assembly onto transfer case and torque the retaining bolts to 7 ft. lbs.

7. Press oil seal in the right boss section of the transfer case.

8. Press oil seal into the bore for transfer shifter rod at rear of the transfer case. Insert transfer shifter shaft into the right side of the transfer case on single range applications.

DRIVE PINION SHAFT ASSEMBLY

Disassembly

▶ SEE FIG. 52

1. Loosen the locknut using suitable tools.

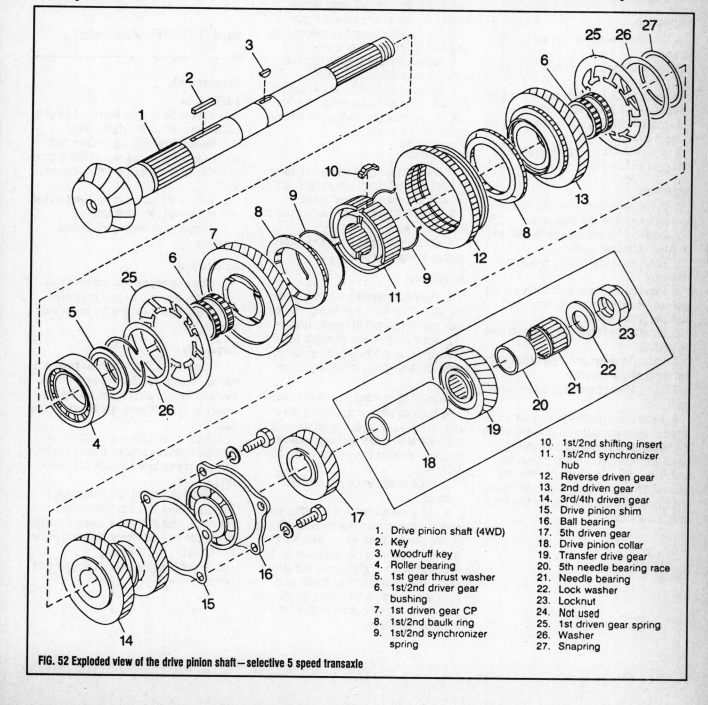

10. 1st/2nd shifting insert
11. 1st/2nd synchronizer hub
12. Reverse driven gear
13. 2nd driven gear
14. 3rd/4th driven gear
15. Drive pinion shim
16. Ball bearing
17. 5th driven gear
18. Drive pinion collar
19. Transfer drive gear
20. 5th needle bearing race
21. Needle bearing
22. Lock washer
23. Locknut
24. Not used
25. 1st driven gear spring
26. Washer
27. Snapring

1. Drive pinion shaft (4WD)
2. Key
3. Woodruff key
4. Roller bearing
5. 1st gear thrust washer
6. 1st/2nd driver gear bushing
7. 1st driven gear CP
8. 1st/2nd baulk ring
9. 1st/2nd synchronizer spring

FIG. 52 Exploded view of the drive pinion shaft—selective 5 speed transaxle

2. Remove the 5th needle bearing race, needle bearing and transfer drive gear.

3. Remove the drive pinion collar.

4. Remove 5th driven gear and woodruff key.

5. Remove the bearing, 3rd driven gear and 4th driven gear.

6. Remove the 2nd driven gear assembly.

7. Remove 1st drive gear assembly, 2nd gear gear bushing (remove key) and gear/hub assembly.

8. Remove 1st gear bushing, 1st gear driven thrust plate and bearing (always replace bearing when disassembled).

Inspection

1. Check all bearings for wear and or damage.

2. Check bearing inner and outer races for wear.

3. Check that bearings turn smoothly and do not make abnormal noise when turned.

4. Check that bushing sliding surfaces are not damaged or worn.

5. Check gears for broken tooth surfaces, damage or excessive wear.

Assembly

1. Install gear and hub assembly. Position open ends of springs 120 degrees apart.

2. Install bearing onto drive pinion shaft and 1st driven gear thrust washer.

3. Install driven gear bushing onto drive pinion shaft.

4. Install 1st drive gear, 1st/2nd balk ring and gear and hub assembly to drive pinion shaft. Align ring groove with insert.

5. Install 1st/2nd driven gear bushing to drive pinion shaft.

6. Install 2nd driven gear, 1st/2nd balk ring and key to drive pinion shaft.

7. Install 4th/3rd driven gear to drive pinion shaft.

8. Install bearing to drive pinion shaft. Install woodruff key to rear section of drive pinion shaft then install 5th driven gear. When installing 5th driven gear have groove face to the rear side.

9. Install drive pinion collar, transfer drive gear and 5th needle bearing race. Install bearing and locknut, torque to 82–91 ft. lbs. then stake locknut in 2 places.

MAINSHAFT ASSEMBLY

Disassembly

♦ SEE FIG. 53

1. Remove oil seal and bearing on single range applications.

2. Remove locknut. Remove insert stopper plate, sleeve/hub assembly, No. 2 balk ring, 5th drive gear assembly and bearing.

3. Using special tool 899714110 mainshaft remover and a press remove the following: 5th gear bearing race, 5th gear thrust washer, bearing, 4th gear thrust washer, 4th gear assembly, sleeve/hub assembly, balk ring, 4th gear bearing race and 3rd gear assembly.

4. Remove the outer snapring from the mainshaft on dual range applications.

5. Remove the following parts on dual range applications: sleeve/hub assembly, high–low balk ring, low input gear, bearing, low input gear spacer, ball and bearing.

Inspection

1. Check all bearing for wear and or damage.

2. Check that bearings turn smoothly and do not make abnormal noise when turned.

3. Check that bushing sliding surfaces are not damaged or worn.

4. Check gears for broken tooth surfaces, damage or excessive wear.

Assembly

1. Assemble sleeve/hub assembly for 3rd/4th, 5th and high-low synchronizing. Position open ends of springs 120 degrees apart.

2. Install 3rd drive gear assembly, balk ring, sleeve/hub assembly for 3rd/4th bearing on mainshaft. Align groove in balk ring with shifting insert.

3. Install 4th gear bearing race on mainshaft.

4. Install balk ring, needle bearing, 4th drive gear assembly and 4th gear thrust washer to mainshaft. Make sure to face thrust washer in the correct direction with grooves on the 4th gear side.

5. Install bearing on the rear section of mainshaft.

6. Using suitable tools install the following parts onto the rear section of mainshaft: 5th gear bearing race and thrust washer (face thrust washer with groove to gear side), bearing, 5th drive gear, balk ring (align groove with shifting insert), sleeve/hub assembly, stopper plate (pawl of stopper plate in synchronizer hub) and lock washer. Tighten locknuts to 82–91 ft. lbs. and stake in 2 places.

7. On dual range applications install the following parts to the front section of the mainshaft: needle bearing, ball, input low gear spacer (face the groove side toward input gear), needle bearing, input low gear, high/low balk ring (align with shifting insert) and sleeve/hub assembly.

8. Install outer snapring to the rod section of the mainshaft. Always use a new snapring. Select an outer snapring so that axial clearance between snapring and hub is within 0.0024–0.0039 in. (0.060–0.100mm). If the input gear is hard to rotate, tap gear end face toward the front.

INPUT SHAFT ASSEMBLY

Disassembly

♦ SEE FIG. 54

1. Remove the oil guide from insert on shaft holder. Remove input shaft holder shim.

2. Remove inner snapring. Position input shaft holder stationary and remove shaft (protect oil seal by wrapping splines of shaft with vinyl tape).

3. Remove the outer snapring. Remove input shaft retainer and cotter (half snapring).

4. Remove inner snapring and bearing assembly.

Inspection

1. Check bearing for wear and or damage.

2. Check snaprings for wear or damage.

3. Check input shaft for nicks, cracks and damage.

Assembly

1. Install inner snapring between input shaft gear and bearing. Select a snapring so that clearance between snapring and bearing is 0–0.0031 in. (0–0.008 mm). Install bearing on the input shaft.

2. Install cotter, retainer and snapring on input shaft. Select a suitable cotter so that the axial play of bearing is 0–0.0031 in. (0–0.08 mm).

3. Install oil seal into input shaft holder.

4. Insert input shaft into holder. Install snapring to input shaft holder. Select a snapring so that clearance between snapring and bearing is 0–0.0031 in (0–0.008 mm).

5. Install O-ring and oil guide on input shaft holder.

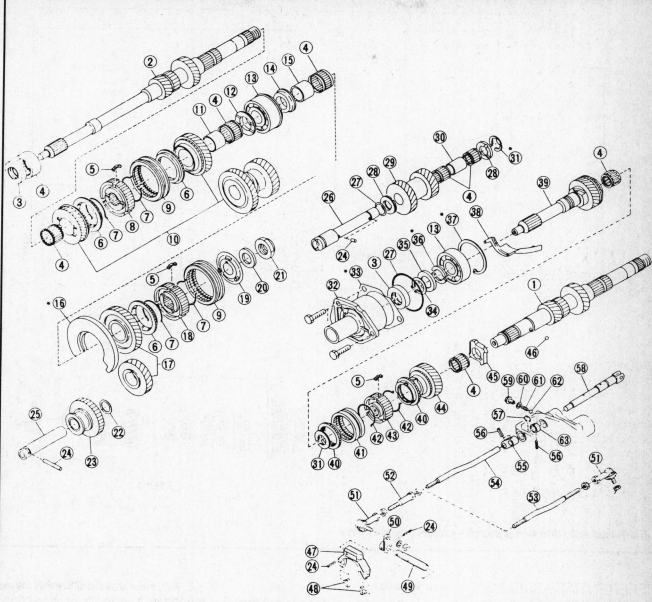

1. Transaxle mainshaft (dual range)
2. Transaxle mainshaft (single range and FWD Turbo)
3. Oil seal
4. Needle bearing
5. Shifting insert
6. Baulk ring
7. Synchronizer spring
8. Synchronizer hub
9. Coupling sleeve
10. 3rd/4th gear set
11. Needle bearing race
12. 4th gear thrust washer
13. Ball bearing
14. 5th gear thrust washer
15. 5th needle bearing race
16. Main shaft rear plate
17. 5th gear set
18. Synchronizer hub
19. Insert stopper plate
20. Lock washer
21. Locknut
22. Washer
23. Reverse idler gear
24. Straight pin
25. Reverse idler gear shaft
26. High-low counter shaft
27. O-Ring
28. High-low counter washer
29. Counter gear
30. Counter gear collar
31. Snapring
32. Input shaft holder
33. Input shaft shim
34. Snapring
35. Input shaft retainer
36. Input shaft cotter
37. Snapring
38. Oil guide
39. Input shaft
40. High-low baulk ring
41. High-low coupling sleeve
42. High-low synchronizer spring
43. High-low synchronizer hub
44. Input low gear
45. Input low gear spacer
46. Ball
47. High-low shifter fork
48. High-low shifter piece
49. High-low shifter shaft
50. High-low shifter lever
51. Ball joint rod
52. Rod adjusting screw
53. High-low shifter rod (Selective 4WD)
54. High-low shifter rod (Full-Time 4WD)
55. High-low rod arm
56. Straight pin
57. Snapring
58. High-low shifter rod
59. Plug
60. Gasket
61. Checking ball spring
62. Ball
63. High-low shifter arm (Full-Time 4WD dual range only)

FIG. 53 Exploded view of the mainshaft and high-low shift linkage—selective 5 speed transaxle

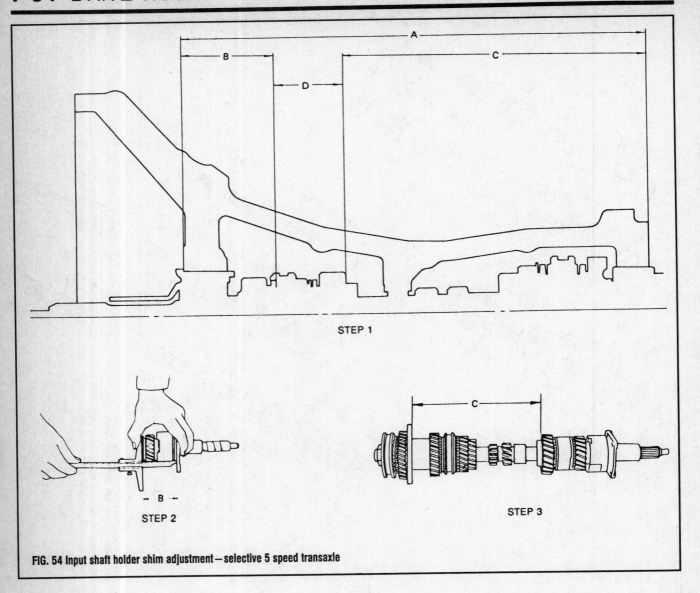

FIG. 54 Input shaft holder shim adjustment — selective 5 speed transaxle

DIFFERENTIAL ASSEMBLY

Disassembly

♦ SEE FIG. 55

1. Remove right and left snaprings from differential. Remove and mark for correct installation the 2 stub shafts.
2. Remove the drive gear.
3. Remove pin from differential assembly.
4. Remove pinion shaft, bevel pinion, gear, washer and bearing.

Inspection

1. Check drive gear and pinion shaft tooth surfaces for damage, excessive wear or cracks.
2. Check bearing on the drive pinion for wear or damage.
3. Check differential case for wear or cracks.

Assembly

1. Install bevel gear and pinion together with washers and insert pinion shaft. Position the chamfered side of the washer toward gear.
2. Measure the backlash between bevel gear and pinion. The standard specification is 0.005–0.0071 in. (0.013–0.18 mm). Be sure the pinion gear tooth contacts adjacent gear teeth during measurement.

3. Align pinion shaft and differential case and install pin into holes from the crown gear side. Lock pin after installing.
4. Install bearing in differential case.
5. Install crown gear and torque retaining bolts to 42–49 ft. lbs.
6. Install stub shafts in differential case with snaprings. Make sure clearance between shafts and the case is 0–0.008 in. (0–0.2mm). If not within specifications replace snapring.

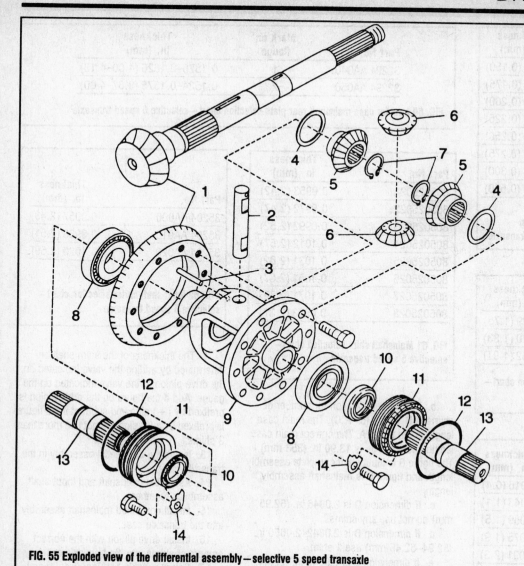

1. Hypoid gear set (Selective 4WD)
2. Pinion shaft
3. Straight pin
4. Washer
5. Differential bevel gear
6. Differential bevel pinion
7. Snapring
8. Roller bearing
9. Differential case
10. Oil seal
11. Differential side retainer
12. O-ring
13. Axle drive shaft
14. Retainer lock plate

FIG. 55 Exploded view of the differential assembly—selective 5 speed transaxle

Transaxle Assembly

♦ SEE FIGS. 55a–62

1. Install 2 interlock plungers in holes on the inner wall of the transaxle case.

2. Install reverse idler gear assembly and lock in place with pin.

3. Install reverse fork rod and reverse fork rod arm with snapring.

4. Install check ball, spring and gasket in reverse shifter rod hole. Torque ball plug to 14 ft. lbs.

5. Position reverse shifter rod toward reverse side. Adjust so clearance between reverse idler gear assembly and case wall is 0.236–0.295 in. (6.0–7.5 mm), using a reverse shifter lever assembly.

6. After installing a suitable reverse shifter lever assembly, shift into the neutral position.

Adjust so clearance between reverse idler gear assembly and transaxle case wall is 0–0.020 in. (0–0.5 mm), using washer(s).

7. Install rod and fork assembly. Install interlock plunger onto 3rd/4th fork rod. Install 3rd/4th fork rod into the 3rd/4th shifter fork and lock with pin. Install interlock plunger on reverse fork side. Install 1st/2nd fork rod into the 1st/2nd shifter fork and lock with pin. Install interlock plunger on 3rd/4th fork side. Install 5th shifter

Part No.	Thickness in. (mm)
803038021	0.0364–0.0374 (0.925–0.950)
803038022	0.0384–0.0394 (0.975–1.000)
803038023	0.0404–0.0413 (1.025–1.050)

FIG. 55a Differential washer selection chart—selective 5 speed transaxle

Part No.	Thickness in. (mm)
805028011	0.0413 (1.05)
805208012	0.0472 (1.20)

FIG. 56 Differential snapring selection chart—selective 5 speed transaxle

Part No.	Thickness in. (mm)
32295 AA030	0.0059 (0.150)
32295 AA040	0.0069 (0.175)
32295 AA050	0.0079 (0.200)
32295 AA060	0.0089 (0.225)
32295 AA070	0.0098 (0.250)
32295 AA080	0.0108 (0.275)
32295 AA090	0.0118 (0.300)
32295 AA100	0.0197 (0.500)

FIG. 57 Drive pinion adjustment shim selection chart—selective 5 speed transaxle

Part No.	Thickness in. (mm)
805162011	0.0689 (1.75)
805162012	0.0720 (1.83)
805162013	0.0752 (1.91)

FIG. 58 Input shaft snapring selection chart—selective 5 speed transaxle

Part No.	Thickness in. (mm)
803020151	0.016 (0.4)
803020152	0.043 (1.1)
803020153	0.059 (1.5)
803020154	0.075 (1.9)
803020155	0.091 (2.3)

FIG. 59 Reverse idler gear shaft washer selection chart—selective 5 speed transaxle

Part No.	Mark on Gauge	Thickness in. (mm)
32294 AA040	1	0.1575–0.1626 (4.00–4.13)
32294 AA050	2	0.1524–0.1575 (3.87–4.00)

FIG. 60 transfer case mainshaft rear plate selection chart—selective 5 speed transaxle

Part No.	Thickness in. (mm)
805025021	0.0953 (2.42)
805025022	0.0972 (2.47)
805025023	0.0992 (2.52)
805025024	0.1012 (2.57)
805025025	0.1031 (2.62)
805025026	0.1051 (2.67)
805025027	0.1071 (2.72)
805025028	0.0933 (2.37)

FIG. 61 Mainshaft shim selection chart—selective 5 speed transaxle

Part No.	Thickness in. (mm)
35204 AA000	0.0957 (2.43)
35204 AA010	0.0988 (2.51)
35204 AA020	0.1020 (2.59)

FIG. 62 input shaft cotter selection chart—selective 5 speed transaxle

fork assembly on the rear of the reverse fork rod and lock with pin.

8. Install checking balls, springs and gaskets into 3rd/4th gear and 1st/2nd gear rod holes and install plugs. Torque retaining plus to 14 ft. lbs.

9. On dual range applications install O-ring and pin on the front of the counter gear shaft.

10. Install the counter gear shaft assembly into the transaxle case. Position the cut out portion of the counter gear shaft to the top of the transaxle case.

11. Adjust the input shaft holder as follows with shims on dual range applications:

a. Place mainshaft assembly and input shaft assembly in case without shims.

b. The proper equation for number of shims is D = A - (B + C). The main case length is the figure A. The correct main case length specification is 13.90 in. (353 mm). The figure B is input shaft complete assembly length and figure C is mainshaft assembly length.

c. If dimension D is 2.0846 in. (52.95 mm) do not use any shims.

d. If dimension D is 2.0842–2.0650 in. (52.94–52.45 mm) use 1 shim.

e. If dimension D is 2.0646 in. (52.44 mm) use 2 shims. This is the maximum amount of shims that can be used. The thickness of shims is 0.0177–0.0217 in. (0.045–0.55 mm).

12. Adjust the drive pinion as follows:

a. The upper figure on the drive pinion is the match number for combining it with the crown gear. The lower figure is for the shim adjustment. If no lower figure is shown, the valve is zero. The figure on the crown gear is the matched number for the drive pinion.

b. Place the drive pinion shaft in case without shims and torque to 20–24 ft. lbs.

c. Install special tool 499917500 gauge assembly so that the scale reads 0.5 when the plate and the scale end are on the same level.

d. Position the gauge by inserting the knock pin of the gauge into the hole in the transaxle case.

e. Slide the drive pinion gauge scale and read the valve at the point where it matches with the end face of the drive pinion.

f. The thickness of the shim shall be determined by adding the valve indicated on the drive pinion to the valve indicated on the gauge. Add if the figure on the drive pinion is prefixed by (+) sign and subtract if the figure is prefixed by a (–) sign. Do not use more than 3 shims.

13. Install the differential assembly in the transaxle case.

14. Assemble mainshaft and input shaft assemblies together.

15. Install combined mainshaft assembly into the transaxle case.

16. Install drive pinion with the correct amount of shims into the transaxle case.

17. Select suitable 1st/2nd, 3rd/4th and 5th shifter fork complete assemblies. Measure rod end clearances A and B. If any clearance is not within specifications, replace rod or fork as required. The figure A = 0.020–0.059 in. (0.5–1.5 mm) in clearance. The figure B = 0.024–0.055 in. (0.6–1.4 mm) in clearance.

18. Install both halves of the transaxle case together and torque the bolts in sequence. Torque all 8 mm bolts in sequence to 17–20 ft. lbs. and all 10 mm bolts in sequence to 27–31 ft. lbs.

19. Install the input shaft holder retaining bolts on dual range applications. Torque retaining bolts to 13–16 ft. lbs.

20. Adjust the differential hypoid gear and set the bearing preload as follows:

a. Position the transaxle case downward and place special tool 399780104 weight on the bearing cup.

b. Screw retainer assembly into case from the bottom. Shift into 5th gear turn the mainshaft several times. Screw in retainer until while turning mainshaft until a light resistance is felt. This is the contact point of hypoid gear and the drive pinion.

c. Remove the weight and screw in retainer without O-ring on the upper side and stop at the point where slight resistance is felt. At this point, the backlash between the hypoid gear and the drive pinion is zero.

d. Install lock plate. Loosen the retainer on the lower side by 1½ notches of the lock plate and turn in the retainer on the upper sides by the same amount.

e. Turn in the retainer on the upper side additionally by ½–1 notch in order to apply preload on bearing.

f. Tighten temporarily both the upper and lower lock plates. Mark both holder and lock plate for later readjustment.

g. Turn mainshaft several times while tapping around retainer lightly.

h. Using a dial indicator gauge check the backlash. The correct specification for backlash is 0.0051–0.0071 in. (0.13–0.18 mm).

i. Check tooth contact of hypoid gear using red lead or equivalent. If incorrect make the necessary corrections.

21. After checking the tooth pattern, remove the lock plate. Loosen retainer and install O-ring tighten retainer into the correct or adjusted position. Tighten lock plate 16–20 ft. lbs. Perform this operation on both upper and lower retainers.

22. Using special tool 498147000 depth gauge measure the amount of bearing protrusion from the transaxle main case surface and select the proper plate. Tap lightly in order to make the clearance zero between the main case surface and the moving flange of the bearing.

23. Install the transfer case and shifter assembly. Torque the retaining bolts to 18 ft. lbs.

24. Install selector arm. Torque the retaining bolts to 14 ft. lbs.

25. Install ball, reverse accent spring, aluminum gasket and plug. Torque plug to 7 ft. lbs.

26. Check for neutral position adjustment. To adjust place adjustment shim between reverse check sleeve assembly and transaxle case.

27. Check reverse plate adjustment. Shift from 5th gear to reverse to check mechanism for proper operation and if arms return to the neutral when released from the reverse position. Replace reverse check plate as necessary.

28. Install extension with transfer case gasket and torque the retaining bolts to 25–30 ft. lbs.

29. Install the high-low fork rod assembly on dual range applications.

30. Install the transfer shifter fork complete assembly on dual range Applications.

31. Install the interlock rod on dual range applications.

32. Install the transfer shifter rod assembly on dual range application.

33. Install clip onto the transfer shifter rod groove on dual range applications.

34. Install check ball, ball spring and gasket in transfer case and tighten plug to 7 ft. lbs. on dual range applications.

35. Install high-low shifter lever on dual range applications.

36. Install the high-low shifter rod assembly. Torque the nut to 14 ft. lbs. and the ball joint assembly to 14 ft. lbs. on dual range applications.

37. Install transfer shifter fork on single range applications.

38. Install spring and ball in transfer case on single range applications.

39. Install transfer shift rod on single range applications.

40. Install the actuator and cable assembly. Torque retaining bolts to 12 ft. lbs. on single range applications.

41. On single range applications adjust actuator and cable assembly as follows:

a. Connect transfer shifter lever to transfer shifter shaft.

b. Apply vacuum pressure to actuator until cable is shortened as much as possible.

c. While applying vacuum, turn turnbuckle in direction that shortens cable until it no longer turns.

d. Back off turnbuckle 180 degrees and torque locknuts to 3.6 ft. lbs.

e. Check that the actuator operates correctly and smoothly.

42. Install transfer cover and tighten retaining bolts to 11–13 ft. lbs.

43. Install retaining spring on release lever and install lever to transaxle.

44. Install release bearing on release lever.

45. Install dust release cover onto the transaxle case.

FULL TIME 4WD TRANSAXLE

General Information

The full time 4WD transaxle is based on the selective 5-speed transaxle, the overall case design and operation are the same.

Identification

This transaxle is used in the 1985-92 STD., Legacy, Loyale and XT.

The transaxle can be identified by the 11th letter in the vehicle identification number located on the bulkhead panel of the engine compartment.

The transaxle serial number label is mounted on the the upper surface of the main case.

The manual transaxle 11th letter code is as follows:

G: Gumma manufacturer — full time 4WD 5-speed

Removal and Installation

The removal and installation of this transaxle is the same as the Selective 5-speed found earlier in this section.

Bench Overhaul

BEFORE DISASSEMBLY

Cleanliness is an important factor in the overhaul of the manual transaxle. Before opening up this unit, the entire outside of the transaxle assembly should be cleaned, preferable with a high pressure washer such as a car wash spray unit. Dirt entering the transaxle internal parts will negate all the time and effort spent on the overhaul. During inspection and reassembly all parts should be thoroughly cleaned with solvent then dried with compressed air. Wiping cloths and rags should not be used to dry parts.

Wheel bearing grease, long used to hold thrust washers and lube parts, should not be used. Lube seals with clean transaxle oil and use ordinary unmedicated petroleum jelly to hold the thrust washers and to ease the assembly of seals, since it will not leave a harmful residue as grease often will. Do not use solvent on neoprene seals, if they are to be reused, or thrust washers.

Before installing bolts into aluminum parts, always dip the threads into clean transaxle oil. Antiseize compound can also be used to prevent bolts from galling the aluminum and seizing. Always use a torque wrench to keep from stripping the threads. The internal snaprings should be expanded and the external rings should be compressed, if they are to be reused. This will help insure proper seating when installed.

Transaxle Disassembly

▶ SEE FIG. 63

1. Drain oil from the transaxle and attach transaxle to a suitable holding fixture.

2. Remove the release lever and clutch release bearing.

3. Remove high-low shifter rod assembly on dual range applications.

4. Remove the clutch actuator and cable assembly on single range applications.

5. Remove the transfer cover retaining bolts and cover.

6. Remove plug from the transfer case on dual range applications.

7. Remove plug from the extension assembly remove the spring and ball.

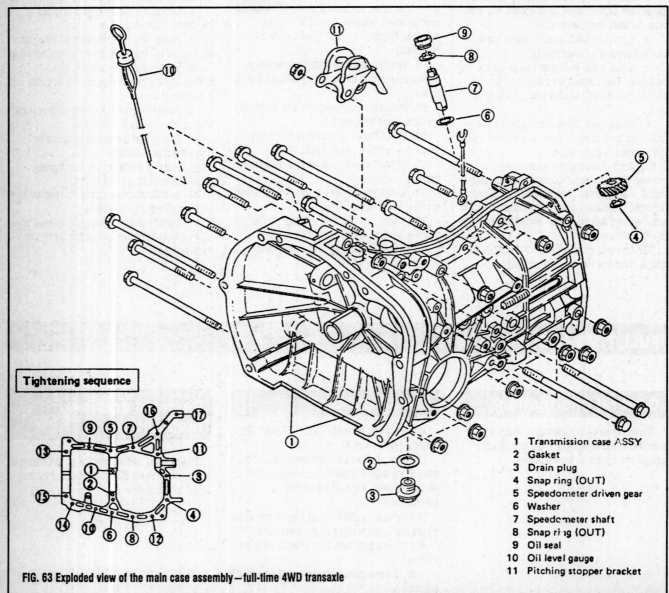

Tightening sequence

1	Transmission case ASSY
2	Gasket
3	Drain plug
4	Snap ring (OUT)
5	Speedometer driven gear
6	Washer
7	Speedometer shaft
8	Snap ring (OUT)
9	Oil seal
10	Oil level gauge
11	Pitching stopper bracket

FIG. 63 Exploded view of the main case assembly—full-time 4WD transaxle

8. Remove the rear cover and bracket assembly.

9. Remove the extension assembly. Remove center differential and extension assembly with high-low shifter arm.

10. Remove plug, reverse accent spring and ball. Remove the reverse check sleeve assembly.

11. Remove the shifter fork screw securing selector arm to shifter arm assembly.

12. Remove transfer case and shifter assembly.

13. Remove bearing retaining bolts.

14. Remove the holder mounting bolts on dual range applications.

15. Remove the high-low shifter lever assembly on dual range applications.

16. Remove the mainshaft rear plate.

17. Protect the stubshafts with tape or equivalent. Separate the transaxle case.

18. Remove the drive pinion assembly.

19. Remove the high-low shifter fork assembly on dual range applications.

20. Remove the mainshaft assembly and input shaft assembly on dual range applications.

21. Remove the differential assembly.

22. Remove the 5th shifter fork.

23. Remove the springs and check balls from the main case.

24. Remove the fork and rod.

25. Remove the reverse idler gear.

26. Remove the reverse shifter rod arm and rod.

27. Remove the reverse shifter lever.

28. Remove the differential side retainer and speedometer driven gear.

29. Remove the snapring from the countershaft on dual range applications.

30. Remove the pin, countershaft, countergear and washers on dual range applications.

Unit Disassembly and Assembly

CENTER DIFFERENTIAL AND EXTENSION ASSEMBLY

Disassembly

▶ SEE FIGS. 64–65

1. Remove the snapring from the transfer shifter rod assembly on dual range applications.

2. Remove the shifter rod assembly.

3. Remove the outer snapring from center differential bearing.

4. Press out center differential. Remove inner snapring and remove the bearing. Always replace the bearing after removal.

5. Separate transfer drive gear and differential case. Remove the shaft, pinions, bevel gear, washer and needle bearings (mark for correct installation).

Inspection

1. Check all bearings for wear and or damage.

2. Check bearing inner and outer races for wear.

3. Check that bearings turn smoothly and do not make abnormal noise when turned.

4. Check gears for broken tooth surfaces, damage or excessive wear.

5. Check differential case for cracks, damage or wear.

Assembly

1. Install bearing to extension assembly with snapring.

2. Select a snapring so that side clearance between the snapring and bearing is 0–0.008 in. (0–0.2mm).

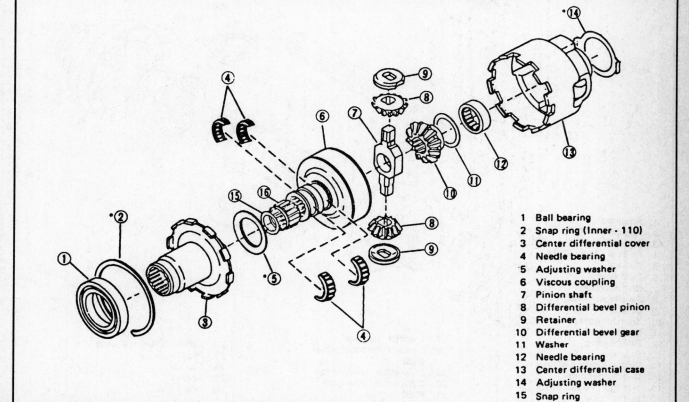

1 Ball bearing
2 Snap ring (Inner - 110)
3 Center differential cover
4 Needle bearing
5 Adjusting washer
6 Viscous coupling
7 Pinion shaft
8 Differential bevel pinion
9 Retainer
10 Differential bevel gear
11 Washer
12 Needle bearing
13 Center differential case
14 Adjusting washer
15 Snap ring
16 Roller bearing

FIG. 65 Exploded view of the center differential assembly—full-time 4WD transaxle

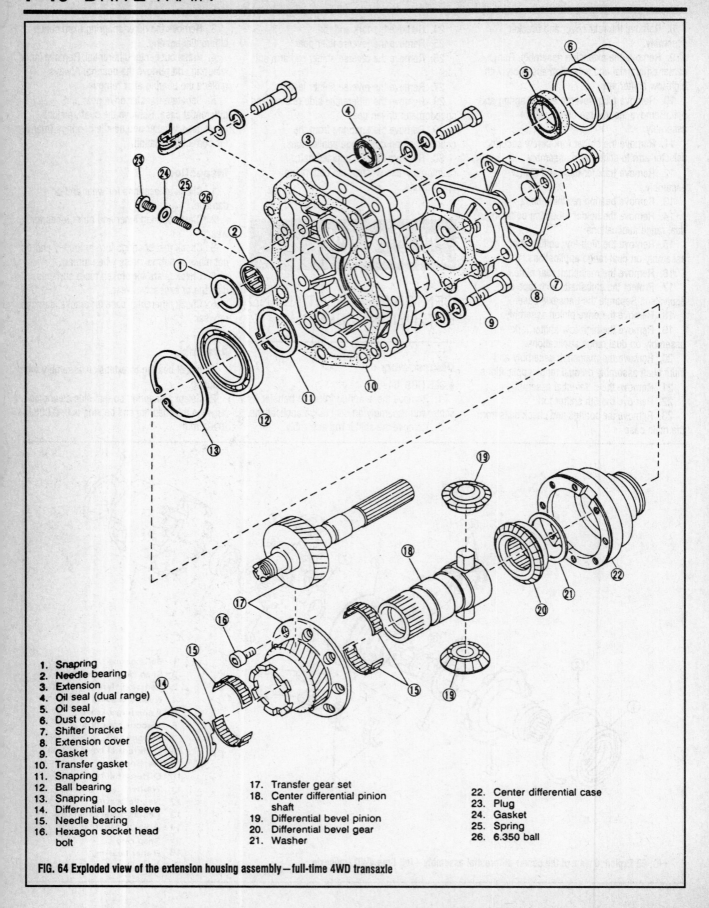

1. Snapring
2. Needle bearing
3. Extension
4. Oil seal (dual range)
5. Oil seal
6. Dust cover
7. Shifter bracket
8. Extension cover
9. Gasket
10. Transfer gasket
11. Snapring
12. Ball bearing
13. Snapring
14. Differential lock sleeve
15. Needle bearing
16. Hexagon socket head bolt

17. Transfer gear set
18. Center differential pinion shaft
19. Differential bevel pinion
20. Differential bevel gear
21. Washer

22. Center differential case
23. Plug
24. Gasket
25. Spring
26. 6.350 ball

FIG. 64 Exploded view of the extension housing assembly—full-time 4WD transaxle

3. Install center differential assembly as follows:

a. Install differential bevel washer and bevel gear in the center differential case.

b. Install differential bevel pinion to center differential pinion shaft and insert the unit into the case.

c. Install bearing halves to the pinion shaft. Install transfer drive gear and torque retaining bolts to 17–19 ft. lbs.

d. Set backlash adjustment with dial indicator gauge. Select a differential bevel washer so that pinion shaft can move 0.0157–0.0236 in. (0.40–0.60mm) in a axial direction.

4. Using suitable press, press center differential in place.

5. Install outer snapring. Select a snapring so that side clearance between snapring and bearing is 0–0.008 in. (0–0.2mm).

6. Install the transfer shifter rod assembly on dual range applications.

TRANSFER CASE AND SHIFTER ASSEMBLY

Disassembly

♦ SEE FIGS. 66–67

1. Remove the shifter arm assembly, selector arm and reverse check sleeve assembly from the transfer case.

2. Remove the oil guide from the transfer case.

3. Remove the reverse light switch, neutral switch, differential lock pilot switch and 4WD low switch dual range applications.

4. Remove the differential lock lever assembly.

5. Remove fork, differential lock shaft and lock sleeve.

6. Place splined end of transfer driven gear in a vise. Remove the lock plates and retaining nuts.

7. Press out transfer driven gear.

8. Remove the snapring press out bearing assembly.

9. Remove the inner snapring and press out needle bearing.

Inspection

1. Check shifter arm for excessive wear or damage.

2. Check selector arm for excessive wear or damage.

3. Check all bearings for wear and or damage.

4. Check bearing inner and outer races for wear.

5. Check that bearings turn smoothly and do not make abnormal noise when turned.

Assembly

1. Install needle bearing race in the bore in the transfer case.

2. Install the bearing assembly with snapring. Select a snapring so that side clearance between snapring and bearing is 0–0.004 in. (0–0.1mm).

3. Install transfer driven gear using suitable press and tools.

4. Install lock washer. Place splined end of transfer driven gear in a vise and tighten lock nut to 54–62 ft. lbs. Stake the locknut in 4 different places.

5. Install differential lock shaft, lock sleeve, fork and rod in order.

6. Install pin into place for differential lock switch. Note the direction of the check ball groove in the rod and position the dog clutch of the differential lock sleeve toward the rear.

7. Install the differential lock lever.

8. Install the differential lock pilot switch, 4WD low switch dual range applications, neutral switch and reverse light switch. Tightening torque for switches is 17–19 ft. lbs.

9. Install the reverse check sleeve assembly in the case.

10. Install the transfer oil guide and torque to 7 ft. lbs.

DRIVE PINION SHAFT ASSEMBLY

Disassembly

♦ SEE FIG. 68

1. Loosen the locknut using suitable tools.

2. Remove the drive pinion from the driven shaft assembly.

3. To remove the drive pinion assembly remove differential bevel gear sleeve, drive pinion spacer (note position for correct installation), 2 washers, thrust bearing, needle bearing, drive pinion collar, needle bearing and thrust bearing.

4. Remove the bearing (note position for correct installation) using a suitable press.

5. To remove the driven gear assembly remove the locknut. Press off 5th gear and remove the woodruff key.

6. Remove bearing and 3rd/4th driven gear using press. Remove the key and the 2nd driven gear assembly. Remove 1st driven gear, 2nd gear bushing, gear and hub using suitable tools.

Inspection

1. Check all bearings for wear and or damage.

2. Check bearing inner and outer races for wear.

3. Check that bearings turn smoothly and do not make abnormal noise when turned.

4. Check that bushing sliding surfaces are not damaged or worn.

5. Check gears for broken tooth surfaces, damage or excessive wear.

Assembly

1. Install gear and hub assembly. Position open ends of springs 120 degrees apart.

2. To install the driven shaft assembly install 1st driven gear, 1st/2nd balk ring and gear/hub assembly onto the driven shaft.

3. Install 2nd driven gear bushing onto the driven shaft.

4. Install 2nd driven gear, 1st/2nd balk ring and install onto the driven shaft. After installing key on the driven shaft install the 3rd/4th driven gear using a suitable press.

5. Install set of roller bearings onto the driven shaft.

6. Position the woodruff key in the groove on the rear of the driven shaft. Install 5th driven gear onto shaft using suitable tools.

7. Install lock washers and locknut. Torque the locknut to 174–188 ft. lbs. Stake the locknut at 2 different positions and check that starting torque of the roller bearing is 0.9–13.0 inch lbs. (0.1–1.5 Nm).

8. To install the drive pinion shaft assembly install bearing in the correct position (knock pin hole in outer race is offset) onto drive pinion. Install washer using suitable tools.

9. Install thrust bearing and needle bearing. Install the driven shaft assembly.

10. Install the drive pinion collar, needle bearing, washer, thrust bearing, washer, drive pinion spacer (install in proper direction) and differential bevel gear sleeve in order.

11. Adjust thrust bearing preload as follows:

a. After installing drive pinion collar, needle bearing, washer, thrust bearing select a spacer and sleeve so that dimension H is zero through a visual check.

b. Install washer, lockwasher and locknut.

c. Measure starting torque while tightening locknut to 81–93 ft. lbs. The starting torque is 2.6–6.9 inch lbs. (0.3–0.8 Nm). Stake the locknut at 4 different locations.

d. If starting torque is not within the specified limit, select new spacer or sleeve and recheck.

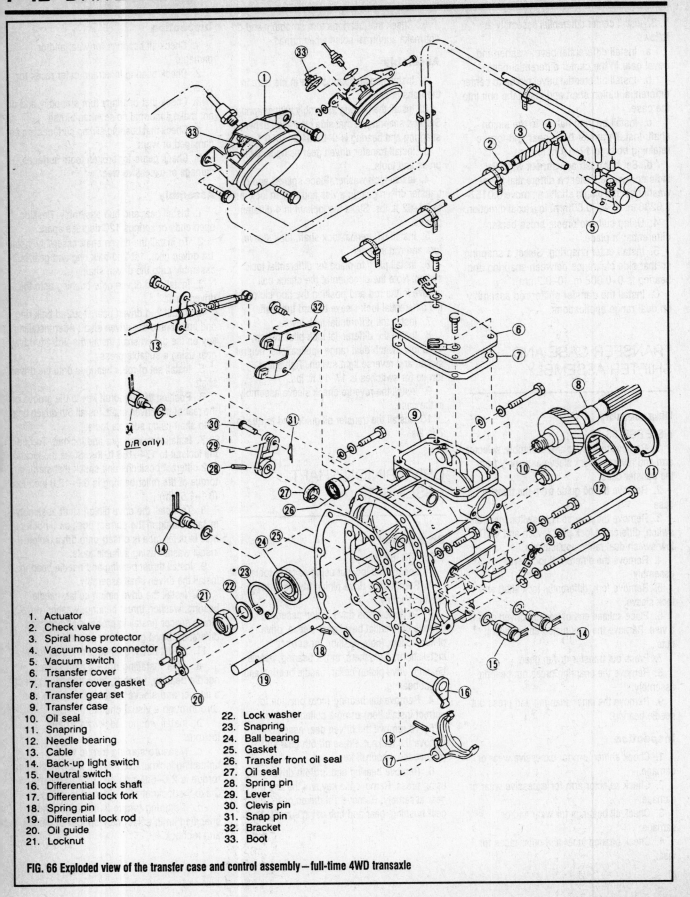

1. Actuator
2. Check valve
3. Spiral hose protector
4. Vacuum hose connector
5. Vacuum switch
6. Trsansfer cover
7. Transfer cover gasket
8. Transfer gear set
9. Transfer case
10. Oil seal
11. Snapring
12. Needle bearing
13. Cable
14. Back-up light switch
15. Neutral switch
16. Differential lock shaft
17. Differential lock fork
18. Spring pin
19. Differential lock rod
20. Oil guide
21. Locknut

22. Lock washer
23. Snapring
24. Ball bearing
25. Gasket
26. Transfer front oil seal
27. Oil seal
28. Spring pin
29. Lever
30. Clevis pin
31. Snap pin
32. Bracket
33. Boot

FIG. 66 Exploded view of the transfer case and control assembly—full-time 4WD transaxle

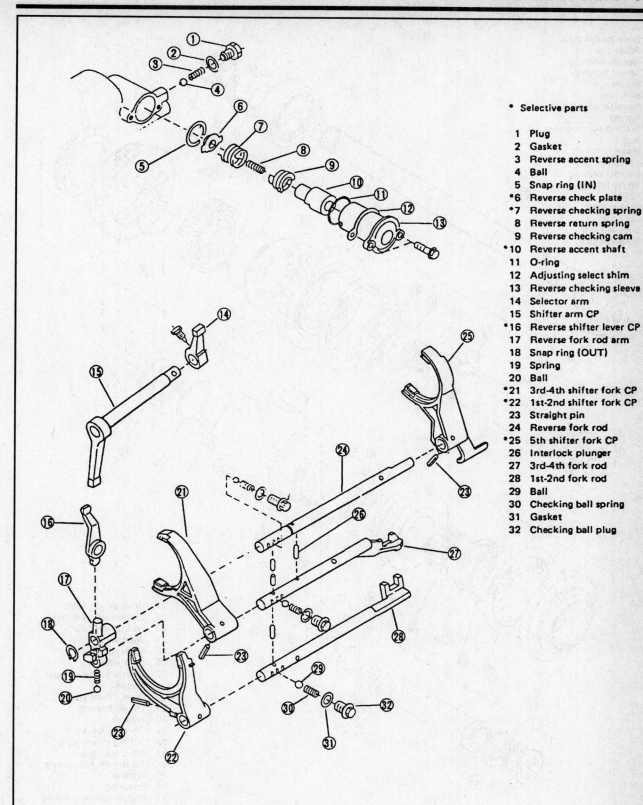

* Selective parts

1   Plug
2   Gasket
3   Reverse accent spring
4   Ball
5   Snap ring (IN)
*6 Reverse check plate
*7 Reverse checking spring
8   Reverse return spring
9   Reverse checking cam
*10 Reverse accent shaft
11 O-ring
12 Adjusting select shim
13 Reverse checking sleeve
14 Selector arm
15 Shifter arm CP
*16 Reverse shifter lever CP
17 Reverse fork rod arm
18 Snap ring (OUT)
19 Spring
20 Ball
*21 3rd-4th shifter fork CP
*22 1st-2nd shifter fork CP
23 Straight pin
24 Reverse fork rod
*25 5th shifter fork CP
26 Interlock plunger
27 3rd-4th fork rod
28 1st-2nd fork rod
29 Ball
30 Checking ball spring
31 Gasket
32 Checking ball plug

FIG. 67 Exploded view of the shifter fork and shifter rod assembly—full-time 4WD transaxle

1. Drive pinion collar
2. Roller bearing
3. Needle bearing
4. Thrust bearing
5. Washer
6. Balk ring
7. Reverse driven gear
8. Spring
9. 1st/2nd synchronizer hub
10. Insert
11. 1st driven gear
12. Needle bearing
13. Woodruff key
14. Key
15. Driven shaft
16. Locknut
17. Lock washer
20. Roller bearing

21. Drive pinion shim
22. 2nd driven gear bush
23. 2nd driven gear
24. Washer
25. Locknut
26. Lock washer
27. Differential bevel gear sleeve
28. Drive pinion spacer
29. Thrust bearing
30. Washer
31. Drive pinion shaft
32. 3rd/4th driven gear
33. 5th driven gear
34. 1st driven gear spring
35. Washer
36. Snapring
37. 2nd driven gear spring

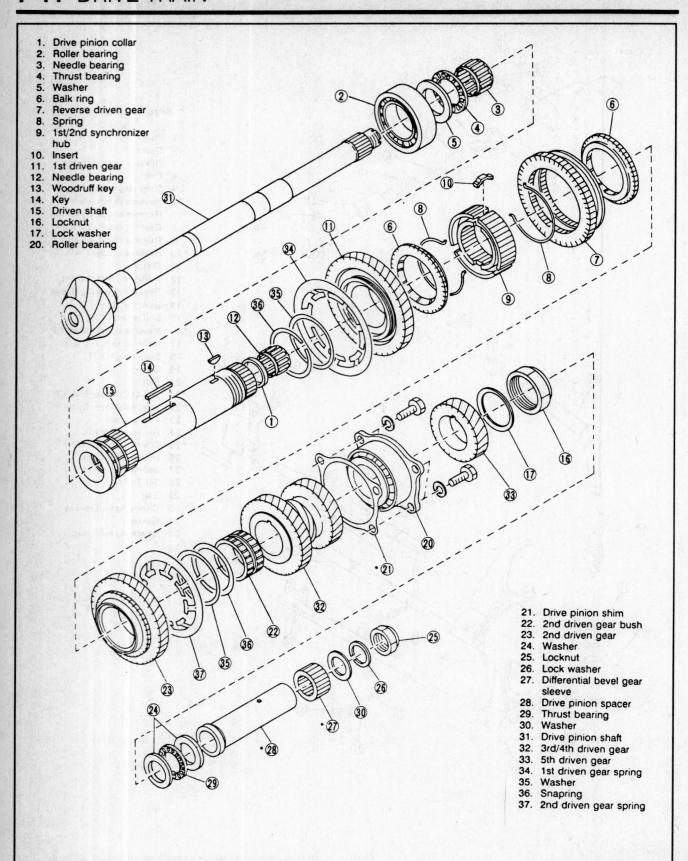

FIG. 68 Exploded view of the drive pinion shaft assembly — full-time 4WD transaxle

MAINSHAFT ASSEMBLY

Disassembly

♦ SEE FIG. 69

1. Remove oil seal and bearing on single range applications.

2. Remove locknut. Remove insert stopper plate, sleeve/hub assembly, No. 2 balk ring, 5th drive gear assembly and bearing.

3. Using special tool 899714110 mainshaft remover and a press remove the following: 5th gear bearing race, 5th gear thrust washer, bearing, 4th gear thrust washer, 4th gear

assembly, sleeve/hub assembly, balk ring, 4th gear bearing race and 3rd gear assembly.

4. Remove the outer snapring from the mainshaft on dual range applications.

5. Remove the following parts on dual range applications: sleeve/hub assembly, high-low balk ring, low input gear, bearing, low input gear spacer, ball and bearing.

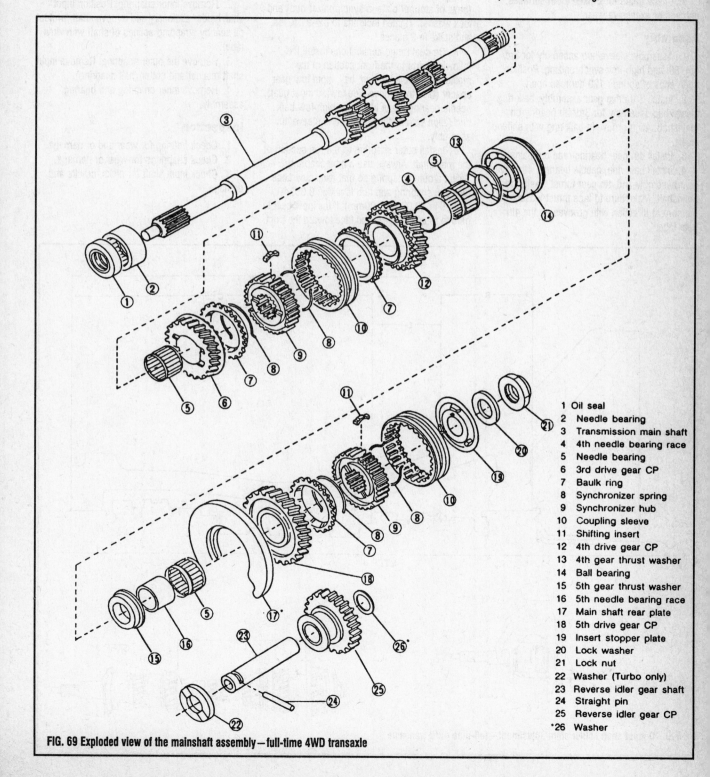

1	Oil seal
2	Needle bearing
3	Transmission main shaft
4	4th needle bearing race
5	Needle bearing
6	3rd drive gear CP
7	Baulk ring
8	Synchronizer spring
9	Synchronizer hub
10	Coupling sleeve
11	Shifting insert
12	4th drive gear CP
13	4th gear thrust washer
14	Ball bearing
15	5th gear thrust washer
16	5th needle bearing race
17	Main shaft rear plate
18	5th drive gear CP
19	Insert stopper plate
20	Lock washer
21	Lock nut
22	Washer (Turbo only)
23	Reverse idler gear shaft
24	Straight pin
25	Reverse idler gear CP
*26	Washer

FIG. 69 Exploded view of the mainshaft assembly—full-time 4WD transaxle

Inspection

1. Check all bearings for wear and or damage.

2. Check that bearings turn smoothly and do not make abnormal noise when turned.

3. Check that bushing sliding surfaces are not damaged or worn.

4. Check gears for broken tooth surfaces, damage or excessive wear.

Assembly

1. Assemble sleeve/hub assembly for 3rd/4th, 5th and high-low synchronizing. Position open ends of springs 120 degrees apart.

2. Install 3rd drive gear assembly, balk ring, sleeve/hub assembly for 3rd/4th bearing on mainshaft. Align groove in balk ring with shifting insert.

3. Install 4th gear bearing race on mainshaft.

4. Install balk ring, needle bearing, 4th drive gear assembly and 4th gear thrust washer to mainshaft. Make sure to face thrust washer in the correct direction with grooves on the 4th gear side.

5. Install bearing on the rear section of mainshaft.

6. Using suitable tools install the following parts onto the rear section of mainshaft: 5th gear bearing race and thrust washer (face thrust washer with groove to gear side), bearing, 5th drive gear, balk ring (align groove with shifting insert), sleeve/hub assembly, stopper plate (pawl of stopper plate in synchronizer hub) and lock washer. Tighten locknuts to 82–91 ft. lbs. and stake in 2 places.

7. On dual range applications install the following parts to the front section of the mainshaft: needle bearing, ball, input low gear spacer (face the groove side toward input gear), needle bearing, input low gear, high-low balk ring (align with shifting insert) and sleeve/hub assembly.

8. Install outer snapring to the rod section of the mainshaft. Always use a new snapring. Select a outer snapring so that axial clearance between snapring and hub is within 0.0024–0.0039 in. (0.060–0.100mm). If the input gear is hard to rotate, tap gear end face toward the front.

INPUT SHAFT ASSEMBLY

Disassembly

◆ SEE FIG. 70

1. Remove the oil guide from insert on shaft holder. Remove input shaft holder shim.

2. Remove inner snapring. Position input shaft holder stationary and remove shaft (protect oil seal by wrapping splines of shaft with vinyl tape).

3. Remove the outer snapring. Remove input shaft retainer and cotter (half snapring).

4. Remove inner snapring and bearing assembly.

Inspection

1. Check bearing for wear and or damage.
2. Check snaprings for wear or damage.
3. Check input shaft for nicks, cracks and damage.

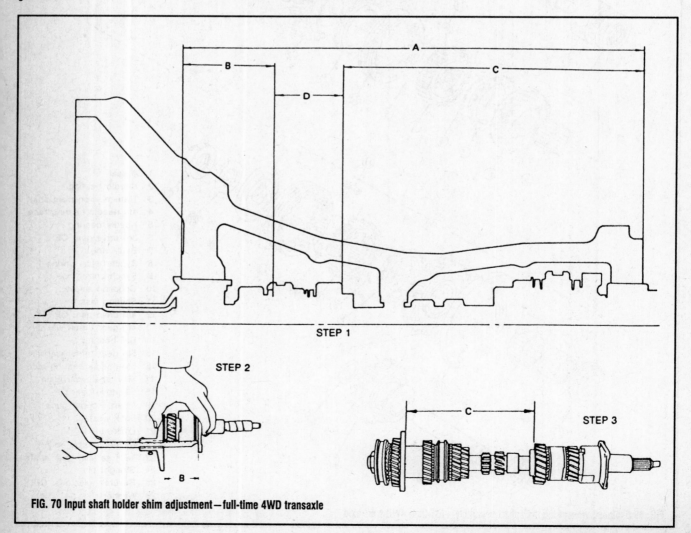

FIG. 70 Input shaft holder shim adjustment —full-time 4WD transaxle

Assembly

1. Install inner snapring between input shaft gear and bearing. Select a snapring so that clearance between snapring and bearing is 0–0.0031 in. (0–0.008mm). Install bearing on the input shaft.

2. Install cotter, retainer and snapring on input shaft. Select a suitable cotter so that the axial play of bearing is 0–0.0031 in. (0–0.08mm).

3. Install oil seal into input shaft holder.

4. Insert input shaft into holder. Install snapring to input shaft holder. Select a snapring so that clearance between snapring and bearing is 0–0.0031 in. (0–0.008mm).

5. Install O-ring and oil guide on input shaft holder.

DIFFERENTIAL ASSEMBLY

Disassembly

▶ SEE FIG. 71

1. Remove right and left snaprings from differential. Remove and mark for correct installation the 2 stub shafts.

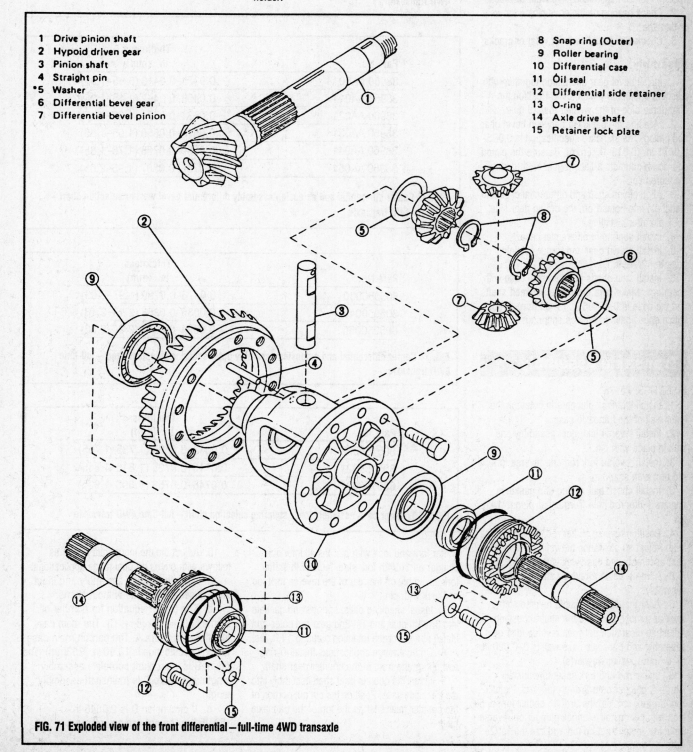

1 Drive pinion shaft
2 Hypoid driven gear
3 Pinion shaft
4 Straight pin
*5 Washer
6 Differential bevel gear
7 Differential bevel pinion
8 Snap ring (Outer)
9 Roller bearing
10 Differential case
11 Oil seal
12 Differential side retainer
13 O-ring
14 Axle drive shaft
15 Retainer lock plate

FIG. 71 Exploded view of the front differential—full-time 4WD transaxle

2. Remove the drive gear.

3. Remove pin from differential assembly toward crown gear.

4. Remove pinion shaft, bevel pinion, gear, washer and bearing.

Inspection

1. Check drive gear and pinion shaft tooth surfaces for damage, excessive wear or cracks.

2. Check bearing on the drive pinion for wear or damage.

3. Check differential case for wear or cracks.

Assembly

1. Install bevel gear and pinion together with washers and insert pinion shaft. Position the chamfered side of the washer toward gear.

2. Measure the backlash between bevel gear and pinion. The standard specification is 0.005–0.0071 in. (0.013–0.18mm). Be sure the pinion gear tooth contacts adjacent gear teeth during measurement.

3. Align pinion shaft and differential case and install pin into holes from the crown gear side. Lock pin after installing.

4. Install bearing in differential case.

5. Install crown gear and torque retaining bolts to 42–49 ft. lbs.

6. Install stub shafts in differential case with snaprings. Make sure clearance between shafts and the case is 0–0.008 in. (0–0.2mm). If not within specifications replace snapring.

Transaxle Assembly

♦ SEE FIGS. 72–75

1. Install interlock plungers in holes on the inner wall of the transaxle case.

2. Install reverse idler gear assembly and lock in place with pin.

3. Install reverse fork rod and reverse fork rod arm with snapring.

3. Install check ball, spring and gasket in reverse shifter rod hole. Torque ball plug to 14 ft. lbs.

4. Position reverse shifter rod toward reverse side. Adjust so clearance between reverse idler gear assembly and case wall is 0.236–0.295 in. (6.0–7.5mm), using a reverse shifter lever assembly.

5. After installing a suitable reverse shifter lever assembly, shift into the neutral position. Adjust so clearance between reverse idler gear assembly and transaxle case wall is 0–0.020 in. (0–0.5mm), using washer(s).

6. Install rod and fork assembly. Install interlock plunger onto 3rd/4th fork rod. Install 3rd/4th fork rod into the 3rd/4th shifter fork and lock with pin. Install interlock plunger on reverse fork side. Install 1st/2nd fork rod into the 1st/2nd

Part No.	Thickness in. (mm)
805180020	0.0677–0.0701 (1.72–1.78)
805180030	0.0736–0.0760 (1.87–1.93)
805180040	0.0866–0.0819 (2.02–2.08)

FIG. 72 Center differential and extension assembly inner snapring selection chart—full-time 4WD transaxle

Part No.	Thickness in. (mm)
38960 AA001	0.0374–0.0413 (0.95–1.05)
38960 AA011	0.0453–0.0492 (1.15–1.25)
38960 AA021	0.0531–0.0571 (1.35–1.45)
38960 AA031	0.0610–0.0650 (1.55–1.65)
38960 AA041	0.0689–0.0728 (1.75–1.85)
38960 AA051	0.0768–0.0807 (1.95–2.05)

FIG. 73 Center differential and extension assembly differential bevel washer selection chart—full-time 4WD transaxle

Part No.	Thickness in. (mm)
805050030	0.0776–0.0799 (1.97–2.03)
805050040	0.0835–0.0858 (2.12–2.18)
805050050	0.0894–0.0917 (2.27–2.33)

FIG. 74 Center differential and extension assembly outer snapring selection chart—full-time 4WD transaxle

Part No.	Thickness in. (mm)
805156020	0.0683–0.0695 (1.735–1.765)
805156021	0.0715–0.0726 (1.815–1.845)
805156022	0.0746–0.0758 (1.895–1.925)

FIG. 75 Transfer case assembly inner snapring selection chart—full-time 4WD transaxle

shifter fork and lock with pin. Install interlock plunger on 3rd/4th fork side. Install 5th shifter fork assembly on the rear of the reverse fork rod and lock with pin.

7. Install checking balls, springs and gaskets into 3rd/4th gear and 1st/2nd gear rod holes and install plugs. Torque retaining plugs to 14 ft. lbs.

8. On dual range applications install O-ring and pin on the front of the counter gear shaft.

9. Install the counter gear shaft assembly into the transaxle case. Position the cut out portion of the counter gear shaft to the top of the transaxle case.

10. Adjust the the input shaft holder as follows with shims on dual range applications:

a. Place mainshaft assembly and input shaft assembly in case without shims.

b. The proper equation for number of shims is $D = A - (B + C)$. The main case length is the figure A. The correct main case length specification is 13.90 in. (353mm). The figure B is input shaft complete assembly length and figure C is mainshaft assembly length.

c. If dimension D is 2.0846 in. (52.95mm) do not use any shims.

d. If dimension D is 2.0842–2.0650 in. (52.94–52.45mm) use 1 shim.

e. If dimension D is 2.0646 in. (52.44mm) use 2 shims. This is the maximum amount of shims that can be used. The thickness of shims is 0.0177–0.0217 in. (0.045–0.55mm).

11. Adjust the drive pinion as follows:

a. The upper figure on the drive pinion is the match number for combining it with the crown gear. The lower figure is for the shim adjustment. If no lower figure is shown, the valve is zero. The figure on the crown gear is the matched number for the drive pinion.

b. Place the drive pinion shaft in case without shims and torque to 20–24 ft. lbs.

c. Install special tool 499917500 gauge assembly so that the scale reads 0.5 when the plate and the scale end are on the same level.

d. Position the gauge by inserting the knock pin of the gauge into the hole in the transaxle case.

e. Slide the drive pinion gauge scale and read the valve at the point where it matches with the end face of the drive pinion.

f. The thickness of the shim shall be determined by adding the valve indicated on the drive pinion to the valve indicated on the gauge. Add if the figure on the drive pinion is prefixed by (+) sign and subtract if the figure is prefixed by a (-) sign. Do not use more than 3 shims.

12. Install the differential assembly in the transaxle case.

13. Assemble mainshaft and input shaft assemblies together on dual range applications.

14. Install combined mainshaft assembly in to the transaxle case.

15. Install drive pinion with the correct amount of shims into the transaxle case.

16. Select suitable 1st/2nd, 3rd/4th and 5th shifter fork complete assemblies. Measure rod end clearances A and B. If any clearance is not within specifications, replace rod or fork as required. The figure A = 0.020–0.059 in. (0.5–1.5mm) in clearance. The figure B = 0.024–0.055 in. (0.6–1.4mm) in clearance.

17. Install both halves of the transaxle case together and torque the bolts in sequence. Torque all 8mm bolts in sequence to 17–20 ft. lbs. and all 10mm bolts in sequence to 27–31 ft. lbs.

18. Tighten bearing attaching bolts at the drive pinion rear.

19. Install the input shaft holder retaining bolts on dual range applications. Torque retaining bolts to 13–16 ft. lbs.

20. Adjust the differential hypoid gear and set the bearing preload as follows:

a. Position the transaxle case downward and place special tool 399780104 weight on the bearing cup.

b. Screw retainer assembly into case from the bottom. Shift into 5th gear turn the mainshaft several times. Screw in retainer until while turning mainshaft until a slight resistance is felt. This is the contact point of hypoid gear and the drive pinion.

c. Remove the weight and screw in retainer without O-ring on the upper side and stop at the point where slight resistance is felt. At this point, the backlash between the hypoid gear and the drive pinion is zero.

d. Install lock plate. Loosen the retainer on the lower side by 1½ notches of the lock plate and turn in the retainer on the upper sides by the same amount.

e. Turn in the retainer on the upper side additionally by ½–1 notch in order to apply preload on bearing.

f. Tighten temporarily both the upper and lower lock plates. Mark both holder and lock plate for later readjustment.

g. Turn mainshaft several times while tapping around retainer lightly.

h. Using a dial indicator gauge check the backlash. The correct specification for backlash is 0.0051–0.0071 in. (0.13–0.18mm).

h. Check tooth contact of hypoid gear using red lead or equivalent. If incorrect make the necessary corrections.

21. After checking the tooth pattern, remove the lock plate. Loosen retainer and install O-ring tighten retainer into the correct or adjusted position. Tighten lock plate 16–20 ft. lbs. Preform this operation on both upper and lower retainers.

22. Using special tool 498147000 depth gauge measure the amount of bearing protrusion from the transaxle main case surface and select the proper mainshaft rear plate. Tap lightly in order to make the the clearance zero between the main case surface and the moving flange of the bearing.

23. Install the transfer case and shifter assembly. Torque the retaining bolts to 18 ft. lbs.

24. Install selector arm. Torque the retaining bolts to 14 ft. lbs.

25. Install ball, reverse accent spring, aluminum gasket and plug. Torque plug to 7 ft. lbs.

26. Check for neutral position adjustment. To adjust place adjustment shim between reverse check sleeve assembly and transaxle case.

27. Check reverse plate adjustment. Shift from 5th gear to reverse to check mechanism for proper operation and if arms returns to the neutral when released from the reverse position. Replace reverse check plate as necessary.

28. Install high-low shifter arm on the transfer shifter rod with spring.

29. Install center differential and extension assembly on transfer case. Torque the extension assembly retaining bolts to 26–30 ft. lbs.

30. Install check ball, ball spring and gasket on transfer case side and tighten plug to 7 ft. lbs. Check that shifter and related parts operate properly.

31. Install check ball, ball spring and gasket in extension assembly and tighten plug to 14–16 ft. lbs.

32. Install extension cover and shifter bracket torque retaining bolts to 22–26 ft. lbs.

33. Install high-low shifter lever on dual range applications.

34. Install the high-low shifter rod assembly on dual range applications. Tightening torque is 14 ft. lbs.

35. Adjust the high-low shifter rod assembly as follows:

a. Move the high-low shifter rod to LO and insert pin in bores in transfer case and shifter rod.

b. Hold front rod ball joint from turning, turn rod adjusting screw counterclockwise as view from the rear of the screw.

c. Back off rod adjusting screw 90 degrees from the point at which the rod is hard to move.

d. Tighten front and rear locknuts while preventing the rod from turning.

e. Remove stopper pin and check transfer shifter rod for proper operation.

36. Install transfer cover and differential lock bracket.

37. Install the actuator and cable assembly. Torque retaining bolts to 11–13 ft. lbs.

38. Adjust actuator cable as follows:

a. Move the differential lock lever to the center differential lock side while turning mainshaft.

b. Apply vacuum pressure to actuator to pull cable forward.

c. Align the bore in the differential lock lever with the hole at the end of cable using the turnbuckle. Secure with a clevis pin and snap pin.

d. Back off turnbuckle 180 degrees in the compression direction and torque locknuts to 3.6 ft. lbs.

e. Check that the actuator operates correctly and smoothly.

39. Install the release lever to transaxle.

Front Halfshafts

REMOVAL & INSTALLATION

◆ SEE FIGS. 76–78

Justy

1. Raise and support the vehicle safely.

Remove the tire and wheel assembly.

2. Remove the disc brake assembly. Remove the dust cover, cotter pin, castle nut, conical spring. Remove the center piece, using the proper tools.

3. Pull the hub and disc assembly from the halfshaft. Remove the disc cover from the housing.

4. Drive out the spring pin connecting the halfshaft to the differential, using the proper tool.

5. Remove the cotter pin and the castle nut from the tie rod end ball joint.

6. Remove the tie rod end ball joint from the knuckle arm, using the proper puller.

7. Remove the bolt that retains the housing to the strut. Carefully push down the housing in order to remove it from the strut.

8. Remove the ball joint of the transverse link from the housing. Remove the housing and the halfshaft assembly as a complete unit.

9. Separate the housing from the halfshaft, using removal tools 922493000 and 921122000 or their equivalents.

To Install:

10. Join the housing and halfshaft using installation tool 927210000.

11. Install housing and axle assembly to strut but do not tighten.

12. Install the dust seal on the spindle. Insert the halfshaft into the differential and install the

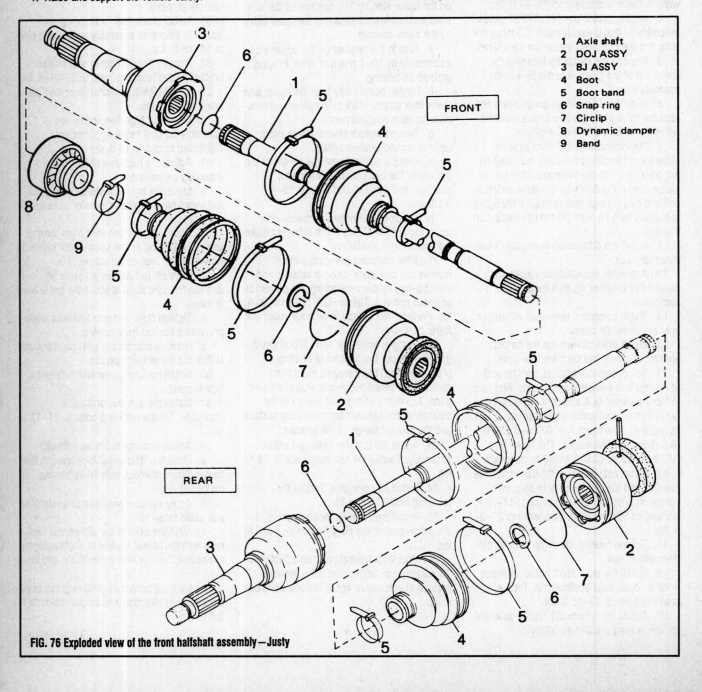

FRONT

1 Axle shaft
2 DOJ ASSY
3 BJ ASSY
4 Boot
5 Boot band
6 Snap ring
7 Circlip
8 Dynamic damper
9 Band

REAR

FIG. 76 Exploded view of the front halfshaft assembly — Justy

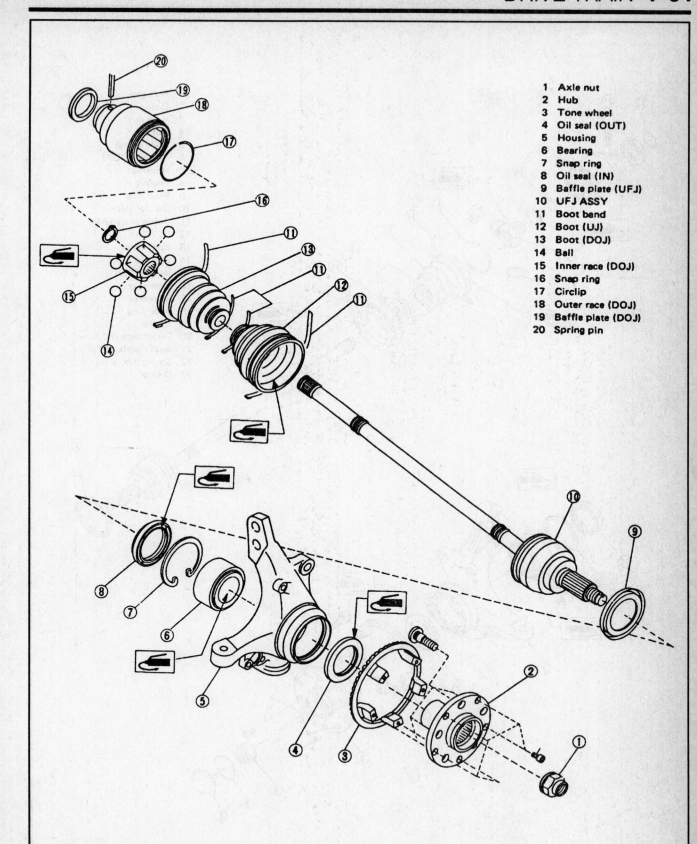

1 Axle nut
2 Hub
3 Tone wheel
4 Oil seal (OUT)
5 Housing
6 Bearing
7 Snap ring
8 Oil seal (IN)
9 Baffle plate (UFJ)
10 UFJ ASSY
11 Boot band
12 Boot (UJ)
13 Boot (DOJ)
14 Ball
15 Inner race (DOJ)
16 Snap ring
17 Circlip
18 Outer race (DOJ)
19 Baffle plate (DOJ)
20 Spring pin

FIG. 77 Exploded view of the front halfshaft assembly with double offset joint

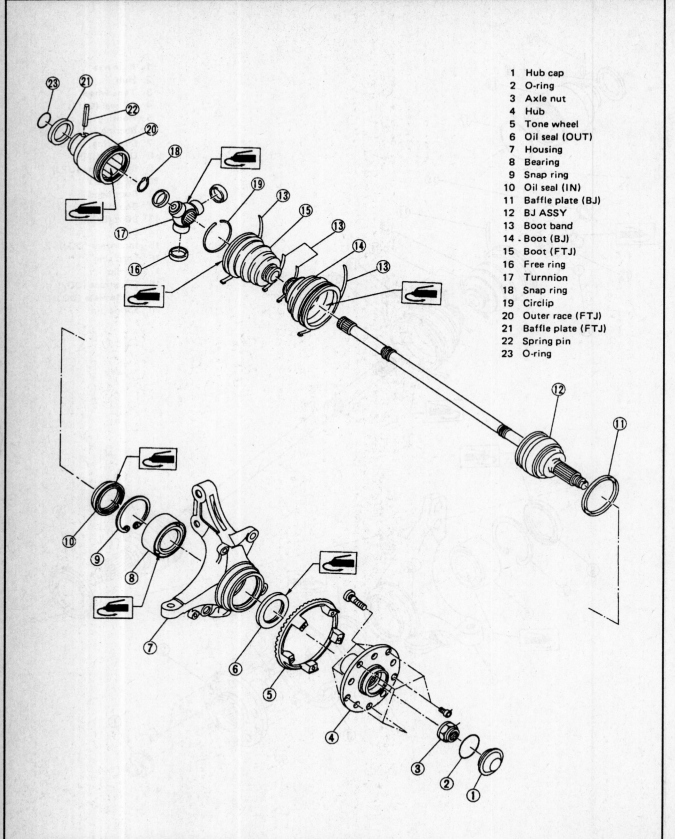

1 Hub cap
2 O-ring
3 Axle nut
4 Hub
5 Tone wheel
6 Oil seal (OUT)
7 Housing
8 Bearing
9 Snap ring
10 Oil seal (IN)
11 Baffle plate (BJ)
12 BJ ASSY
13 Boot band
14 Boot (BJ)
15 Boot (FTJ)
16 Free ring
17 Turnnion
18 Snap ring
19 Circlip
20 Outer race (FTJ)
21 Baffle plate (FTJ)
22 Spring pin
23 O-ring

FIG. 78 Exploded view of the front halfshaft assembly with free-ring tripod joint — SVX

spring pin. Lubricate the splines with grease.

13. Install the tie rod end ball joint and tighten the nut to 18–22 ft. lbs. (25–29 Nm). Tighten the housing-to-strut bolt to 25–33 ft. lbs. (34–44 Nm).

14. Install the disc cover, hub, disc brake assembly and castle nut. Install the caliper assembly.

15. Install the wheel and tire, lower the vehicle and test drive.

Except Justy

1. Release the parking brake. Raise and support the vehicle safely. Remove the tire and wheel assembly.

2. Pull out the parking brake cable outer clip from the caliper. Disconnect the parking brake cable end from the caliper lever.

3. Drive out the double offset joint spring pin, using the proper tools.

4. Loosen the 2 retaining bolts and remove the disc brake assembly from the housing. Remove the 2 bolts that connect the housing and the damper strut.

5. Remove the dust cover, cotter pin. Disconnect the tie rod end ball joint from the housing knuckle arm, using the proper puller tool.

6. Remove the halfshaft from the differential spindle along with the housing assembly.

7. Remove the housing from the halfshaft, using tool 926470000 or equivalent.

To Install:

8. Install the halfshaft into the hub using installer 922431000, or equivalent. Take care not to damage the inner oil seal lip. Tighten the axle nut temporarily.

9. Install the double offset joint on the spindle and drive a new spring pin into place. Install the tie rod and tighten the nut to 61–83 ft. lbs. (83–113 Nm).

10. Install the axle nut and tighten to 137 ft. lbs. (186 Nm).

11. Install the disc brake assembly and parking brake. Install the wheel and tire.

12. Lower the vehicle and test drive.

OVERHAUL

▶ SEE FIGS. 79–85

1. Remove the bands from the boots at both the constant velocity and double offset joints, and slide the boots away from the joints.

2. Pry the circlip out of the double offset joint, and slide the outer race of the joint off the shaft.

3. Remove the balls from the cage, rotate the cage slightly, and slide the cage inward on the axle shaft.

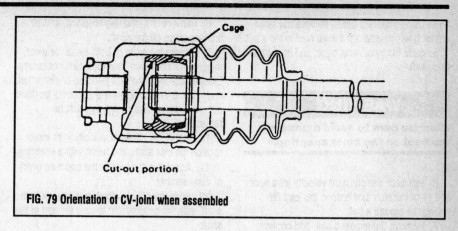

FIG. 79 Orientation of CV-joint when assembled

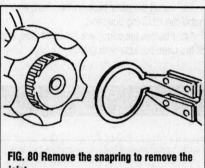

FIG. 80 Remove the snapring to remove the joint

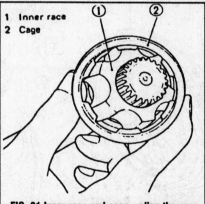

FIG. 81 Inner race and cage—align the cage with the protruded part of the inner race

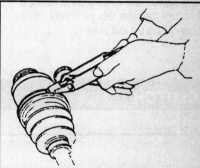

FIG. 84 Install the CV-boot and band—make sure to pull the band snug

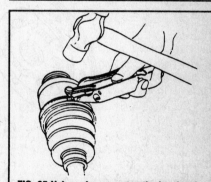

FIG. 85 Using a hammer, tap the band end down until it is snug—use care not to rip the boot

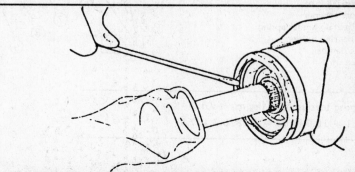

FIG. 83 Pull back on the shaft slightly to make sure that the circlip is seated completely

4. Using snapring pliers, remove the outer snapring which retains the inner race to the shaft.

5. Slide the inner race, cage, and boot off the axle shaft.

❊❊❊ WARNING

Exercise care to avoid damaging the boot on the inner snapring.

6. Pull back the constant velocity joint boot and pivot the stub axle around the joint far enough to expose a ball.

7. Remove the exposed ball, and continue this procedure until all balls are removed, at which time the outer race (stub axle) may be removed from the axle shaft.

8. Remove the retaining snapring, and slide the inner race off the shaft.

9. Inspect the parts of both joints for wear, damage, or corrosion, and replace if necessary. Examine the axle shaft for bending or distortion, and replace if evident. Should the boots be dried out, cracked, or distorted, they must be replaced.

10. Install the constant velocity joint inner race on the axle shaft, and retain with a snapring.

11. Assemble the joint in the opposite order of disassembly.

12. Slide the double offset joint cage onto the shaft, with the counterbore toward the end of the shaft.

13. Install the inner race on the shaft, and install the retaining snapring.

14. Position the cage over the inner race, and fill the cage pockets with grease.

15. Insert the balls into the cage.

16. Fill the well in the outer race with approximately 1 oz. grease, and slide the outer race onto the axle shaft.

17. Install the retaining circlip, and add 1 oz. more grease to the interior of the joint. Fill the boot with approximately 1 oz. grease, and slide it into position over the double offset joint.

18. Fill the constant velocity joint boot with 3 oz. grease, and install the boot over the joint.

19. Band the boots on both joints tightly enough that they cannot be turned by hand.

❊❊❊ WARNING

Use only grease specified for use in constant velocity joints.

CLUTCH

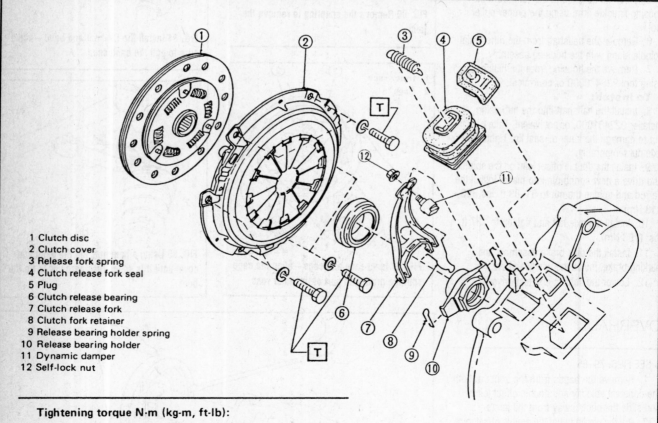

1 Clutch disc
2 Clutch cover
3 Release fork spring
4 Clutch release fork seal
5 Plug
6 Clutch release bearing
7 Clutch release fork
8 Clutch fork retainer
9 Release bearing holder spring
10 Release bearing holder
11 Dynamic damper
12 Self-lock nut

Tightening torque N·m (kg-m, ft-lb):
T: 9.1 — 10.6 (0.93 — 1.08, 6.7 — 7.8)

FIG. 86 Clutch system components—mechanical clutch

Adjustment

♦ SEE FIGS. 86–87

Some models are equipped with an mechanical clutch system, these are adjustable. Other models are equipped with an hydraulic system, there are no adjustments on these.

CABLE ADJUSTMENT

The clutch cable can be adjusted at the cable bracket where the cable is attached to the side of the transmission housing. To adjust the length of the cable, remove the circlip and clamp, slide the cable end in the direction desired and then replace the circlip and clamp into the nearest gutters on the cable end. The cable should not be stretched out straight nor should it have right angle kinks in it. Any curves should be gradual.

PEDAL HEIGHT

Adjust the pedal with the return stop bolt, so that its pad is on the same level as the brake pedal pad.

Check to be sure that the stroke of the pedal is 128-138mm. Check the clutch release fork stroke. It should be 17mm.

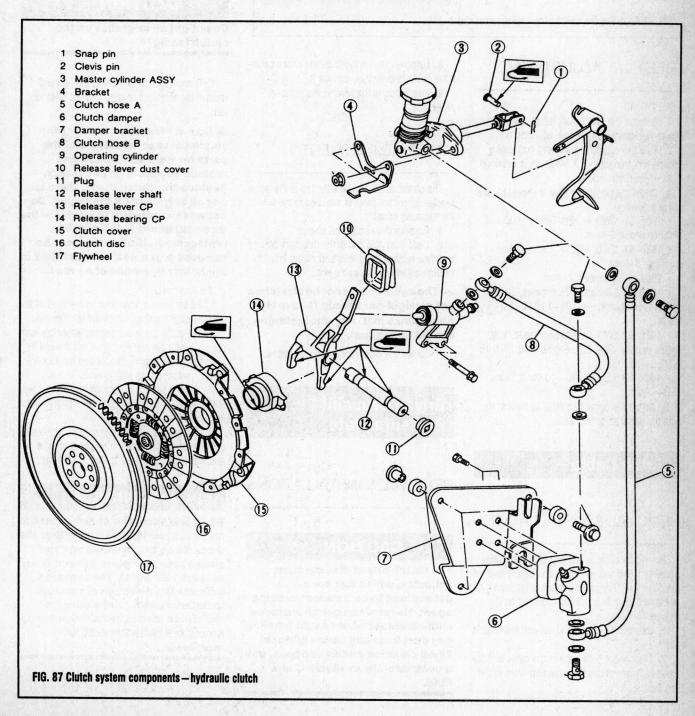

1   Snap pin
2   Clevis pin
3   Master cylinder ASSY
4   Bracket
5   Clutch hose A
6   Clutch damper
7   Damper bracket
8   Clutch hose B
9   Operating cylinder
10 Release lever dust cover
11 Plug
12 Release lever shaft
13 Release lever CP
14 Release bearing CP
15 Clutch cover
16 Clutch disc
17 Flywheel

FIG. 87 Clutch system components — hydraulic clutch

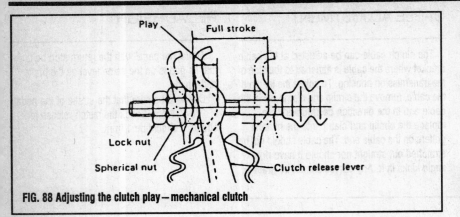

FIG. 88 Adjusting the clutch play—mechanical clutch

FREE PLAY ADJUSTMENT

▶ SEE FIG. 88

1. Remove the clutch fork return spring and loosen the locknut on the fork adjusting nut.

2. Turn the adjusting nut (wing nut) until a release fork free play of 3.5-4.5mm is obtained.

3. Tighten the locknut.

4. Check the pedal free play. It should be one of the following.

• 1985–87 (2WD — Non-Turbo, 1600 and 1800 engines): 3-4mm

• 1985–87 (2WD/4WD — Turbo, 1.8L engines): 3-4mm

• 1987 (1.2L engine): 2-4mm

• 1988–92 1.8L and 2.7L engines, 2WD except turbocharger — 0.08–0.12 in. (2.0–3.0mm).

• 1988–92 2WD/4WD turbocharged, 1.8L engine and the 4WD 2.7L engine — 0.12–0.16 in. (3.0–4.0mm).

• 1988–92 1.2L engine — 0.08–0.16 in. (2.0–4.0mm).

5. Adjust the pedal free play, as necessary, with the pedal adjusting bolt.

Clutch Cable

REMOVAL & INSTALLATION

The clutch cable is connected to the clutch pedal at 1 end and to the clutch release lever at the other end. The cable conduit is retained by a bolt and clamp on a bracket mounted on the flywheel housing.

1. If necessary, raise and support the vehicle safely.

2. Disconnect both ends of the cable and the conduit, then remove the assembly from under the vehicle.

3. Using engine oil, lubricate the clutch cable. If the cable is defective, replace it.

4. Installation is the reverse the removal procedure.

CABLE ADJUSTMENT

The clutch cable can be adjusted at the cable bracket where the cable is attached to the side of the transaxle housing.

1. Remove the circlip and clamp.

2. Slide the cable end in the direction desired and then replace the circlip and clamp into the nearest gutters on the cable end.

➡ **The cable should not be stretched out straight nor should it have right angle kinks in it. Any straightening should be gradual.**

3. Check the clutch for proper operation.

Driven Disc and Pressure Plate

REMOVAL & INSTALLATION

❊❊❊ CAUTION

The clutch driven disc contains asbestos, which has been determined to be a cancer causing agent. Never clean clutch surfaces with compressed air! Avoid inhaling any dust from any clutch surface! When cleaning clutch surfaces, use a commercially available brake fluid.

1. Disconnect the negative battery cable. Remove the transmission as outlined earlier in this section.

2. Gradually unscrew the six bolts (6mm) which hold the pressure plate assembly on the flywheel. Loosen the bolts only one turn at a time, working around the pressure plate. Do not unscrew all the bolts on one side at one time.

3. When all of the bolts have been removed, remove the clutch plate and disc.

❊❊❊ CAUTION

Do not get oil or grease on the clutch facing.

4. Remove the two retaining springs and remove the throwout bearing and the release fork.

➡ **Do not disassemble either the clutch cover or disc. Inspect the parts for wear or damage and replace any parts as necessary. Replace the clutch disc if there is any oil or grease on the facing. Do not wash or attempt to lubricate the throwout bearing. If it requires replacement, the bearing may be removed and a new one installed in the holder by means of a press.**

To Install:

5. Fit the release fork boot on the front of the transmission housing. Install the release fork.

6. Insert the throwout bearing assembly and secure it with the two springs. Coat the inside diameter of the bearing holder and the fork-to-holder contact points with grease.

7. Insert a pilot shaft through the clutch cover and disc, then insert the end of the pilot into the needle bearing.

8. Tighten the pressure plate bolts gradually, one turn at a time, until the proper torque is reached. Tighten to 12.7 ft. lbs. (17.2 Nm).

❊❊❊ WARNING

When installing the clutch pressure plate assembly, make sure that the O marks on the flywheel and the clutch pressure plate assembly are at least 120° apart. These marks indicate the direction of residual unbalance. Also, make sure that the clutch disc is installed properly, noting the FRONT and REAR markings.

9. After installation of the transaxle in the car, perform the adjustments outlined above.

Clutch Master Cylinder, Slave Cylinder and Damper

REMOVAL & INSTALLATION

The clutch master cylinder is located on the firewall near the brake master cylinder. The clutch slave cylinder and damper are located on the top of the transaxle housing. To remove the clutch master cylinder, disconnect and plug the fluid lines. Disconnect the pin retainer at the clutch pedal and remove the mounting bolts. To remove the slave cylinder and damper, disconnect and plug the fluid lines and remove the mounting bolts. Tighten the master cylinder mounting bolts to 15 ft. lbs. (21 Nm). and the slave cylinder, and damper mounting bolts to 30 ft. lbs. (41 Nm). Tighten the fluid hoses to 13 ft. lbs. (18 Nm). Be sure to bleed the system when complete.

SYSTEM BLEEDING

◆ SEE FIGS. 89–90

➡ **To properly bleed the system, it must be bled at the slave cylinder and at the damper. Each of these has an air bleeder on it.**

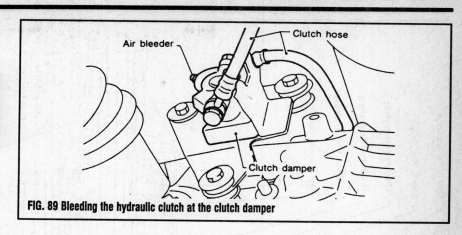
FIG. 89 Bleeding the hydraulic clutch at the clutch damper

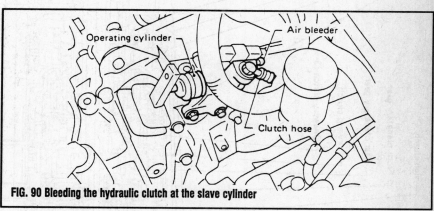
FIG. 90 Bleeding the hydraulic clutch at the slave cylinder

1. Connect a vinyl tube to the air bleeder on the damper and put the other end in a jar with clean clutch fluid.
2. With the help of an assistant depressing the clutch pedal, slowly open the bleeder valve. Close the bleeder valve and release the pedal.

Repeat this process until no air bubbles appear in the jar.
3. Move the tube to the bleeder on the slave cylinder and repeat the process. Check the operation of the clutch after the bleed procedure is complete.

AUTOMATIC TRANSAXLE

➡ **The Justy uses an unique automatic transmission known as the Electronic Constantly Variable Transaxle (ECVT). This transaxle is considerably different from standard transaxles, as such the following description does not apply to the ECVT. A brief description of the ECVT can be found following this section on automatic transaxles.**

Understanding Automatic Transaxles

◆ SEE FIG. 91

The automatic transaxle allows engine torque and power to be transmitted to the drive wheels within a narrow range of engine operating speeds. The transaxle will allow the engine to turn fast enough to produce plenty of power and torque at very low speeds, while keeping it at a sensible rpm at high vehicle speeds. The transaxle performs this job entirely without driver assistance. The transaxle uses a light fluid as the medium for the transaxle of power. This fluid also works in the operation of various hydraulic control circuits and as a lubricant. Because the transaxle fluid performs all of these three functions, trouble within the unit can easily travel from one part to another. For this reason, and because of the complexity and unusual operating principles of the transaxle, a very sound understanding of the basic principles of operation will simplify troubleshooting.

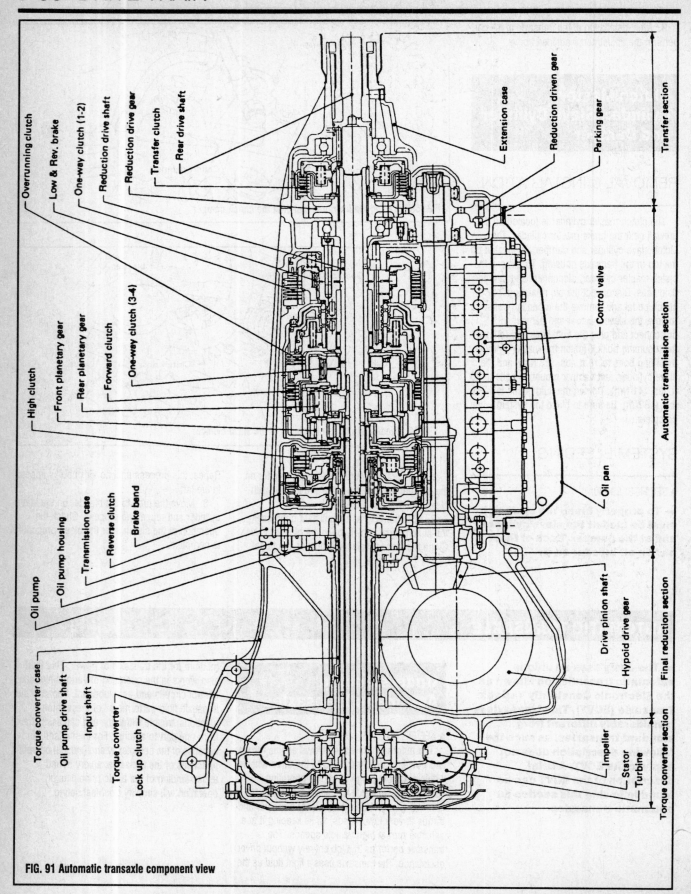

FIG. 91 Automatic transaxle component view

THE TORQUE CONVERTER

The torque converter replaces the conventional clutch. It has three functions:

1. It allows the engine to idle with the vehicle at a standstill, even with the transaxle in gear.

2. It allows the transaxle to shift from range to range smoothly, without requiring that the driver close the throttle during the shift.

3. It multiplies engine torque to an increasing extent as vehicle speed drops and throttle opening is increased. This has the effect of making the transaxle more responsive and reduces the amount of shifting required.

The torque converter is a metal case which is shaped like a sphere that has been flattened on opposite sides. It is bolted to the rear end of the engine's crankshaft. Generally, the entire metal case rotates at engine speed and serves as the engine's flywheel.

The case contains three sets of blades. One set is attached directly to the case. This set forms the torus or pump. Another set is directly connected to the output shaft, and forms the turbine. The third set is mounted on a hub which, in turn, is mounted on a stationary shaft through a one-way clutch. This third set is known as the stator.

A pump, which is driven by the converter hub at engine speed, keeps the torque converter full of transaxle fluid at all times. Fluid flows continuously through the unit to provide cooling.

Under low speed acceleration, the torque converter functions as follows:

The torus is turning faster than the turbine. It picks up fluid at the center of the converter and, through centrifugal force, slings it outward. Since the outer edge of the converter moves faster than the portions at the center, the fluid picks up speed.

The fluid then enters the outer edge of the turbine blades. It then travels back toward the center of the converter case along the turbine blades. In impinging upon the turbine blades, the fluid loses the energy picked up in the torus.

If the fluid were now to immediately be returned directly into the torus, both halves of the converter would have to turn at approximately the same speed at all times, and torque input and output would both be the same.

In flowing through the torus and turbine, the fluid picks up two types of flow, or flow in two separate directions. It flows through the turbine blades, and it spins with the engine. The stator, whose blades are stationary when the vehicle is being accelerated at low speeds, converts one type of flow into another. Instead of allowing the fluid to flow straight back into the torus, the stator's curved blades turn the fluid almost 90° toward the direction of rotation of the engine.

Thus the fluid does not flow as fast toward the torus, but is already spinning when the torus picks it up. This has the effect of allowing the torus to turn much faster than the turbine. This difference in speed may be compared to the difference in speed between the smaller and larger gears in any gear train. The result is that engine power output is higher, and engine torque is multiplied.

As the speed of the turbine increases, the fluid spins faster and faster in the direction of engine rotation. As a result, the ability of the stator to redirect the fluid flow is reduced. Under cruising conditions, the stator is eventually forced to rotate on its one-way clutch in the direction of engine rotation. Under these conditions, the torque converter begins to behave almost like a solid shaft, with the torus and turbine speeds being almost equal.

THE PLANETARY GEARBOX

The ability of the torque converter to multiply engine torque is limited. Also, the unit tends to be more efficient when the turbine is rotating at relatively high speeds. Therefore, a planetary gearbox is used to carry the power output of the turbine to the halfshafts.

Planetary gears function very similarly to conventional transaxle gears. However, their construction is different in that three elements make up one gear system, and, in that all three elements are different from one another. The three elements are: an outer gear that is shaped like a hoop, with teeth cut into the inner surface; a sun gear, mounted on a shaft and located at the very center of the outer gear; and a set of three planet gears, held by pins in a ring-like planet carrier, meshing with both the sun gear and the outer gear. Either the outer gear or the sun gear may be held stationary, providing more than one possible torque multiplication factor for each set of gears. Also, if all three gears are forced to rotate at the same speed, the gearset forms, in effect, a solid shaft.

Most modern automatics use the planetary gears to provide either a single reduction ratio of about 1.8:1, or two reduction gears: a low of about 2.5:1, and an intermediate of about 1.5:1. Bands and clutches are used to hold various portions of the gearsets to the transaxle case or to the shaft on which they are mounted. Shifting is accomplished, then, by changing the portion of each planetary gearset which is held to the transaxle case or to the shaft.

THE SERVOS AND ACCUMULATORS

The servos are hydraulic pistons and cylinders. They resemble the hydraulic actuators used on many familiar machines, such as bulldozers. Hydraulic fluid enters the cylinder, under pressure, and forces the piston to move to engage the band or clutches.

The accumulators are used to cushion the engagement of the servos. The transaxle fluid must pass through the accumulator on the way to the servo. The accumulator housing contains a thin piston which is sprung away from the discharge passage of the accumulator. When fluid passes through the accumulator on the way to the servo, it must move the piston against spring pressure, and this action smooths out the action of the servo.

THE HYDRAULIC CONTROL SYSTEM

The hydraulic pressure used to operate the servos comes from the main transaxle oil pump. This fluid is channeled to the various servos through the shift valves. There is generally a manual shift valve which is operated by the transaxle selector lever and an automatic shift valve for each automatic upshift the transaxle provides: i.e., 2-speed automatics have a low/high shift valve, while 3-4 speeds have a 1-2 valve, a 2-3 valve, a 3-4 valve.

There are two pressures which effect the operation of these valves. One is the governor pressure which is affected by vehicle speed. The other is the modulator pressure which is affected by intake manifold vacuum or throttle position. Governor pressure rises with an increase in vehicle speed, and modulator pressure rises as the throttle is opened wider. By responding to these two pressures, the shift valves cause the upshift points to be delayed with increased throttle opening to make the best use of the engine's power output.

Most transaxles also make use of an auxiliary circuit for downshifting. This circuit may be actuated by the throttle linkage or the vacuum line which actuates the modulator, or by a cable or solenoid. It applies pressure to a special downshift surface on the shift valve or valves.

The transaxle modulator also governs the line pressure, used to actuate the servos. In this way, the clutches and bands will be actuated with a force matching the torque output of the engine.

Electronic Constantly Variable Transaxle (ECVT)

♦ SEE FIGS. 93–94

The ECVT is used in the Justy. This transaxle combines a electronically controlled magnetic clutch with a variable transaxle that is driven by steel belt pulleys to provide high running performance, low fuel consumption and ease of control.

The transaxle is controlled by a microcomputer which constantly monitors engine speed, vehicle speed and throttle position. It uses these signals to control the magnetic clutch. The magnetic clutch controls the width of the drive pulley faces and thus provides the shifting effect.

The power from the transaxle is transmitted through a special steel belt that runs between 2 variable pulleys, as the power is transmitted from the engine through the transaxle, the control computer varies the space between the pulleys depending on engine load, vehicle speed and throttle position. The varying of the pulleys allows the belt to ride in a constantly changing space, this has the effect of a continuous gear change.

The overall driving effect of the ECVT is very smooth. The constant adjustment of the pulleys means that the transaxle works more efficiently to transmit power to the drive wheels.

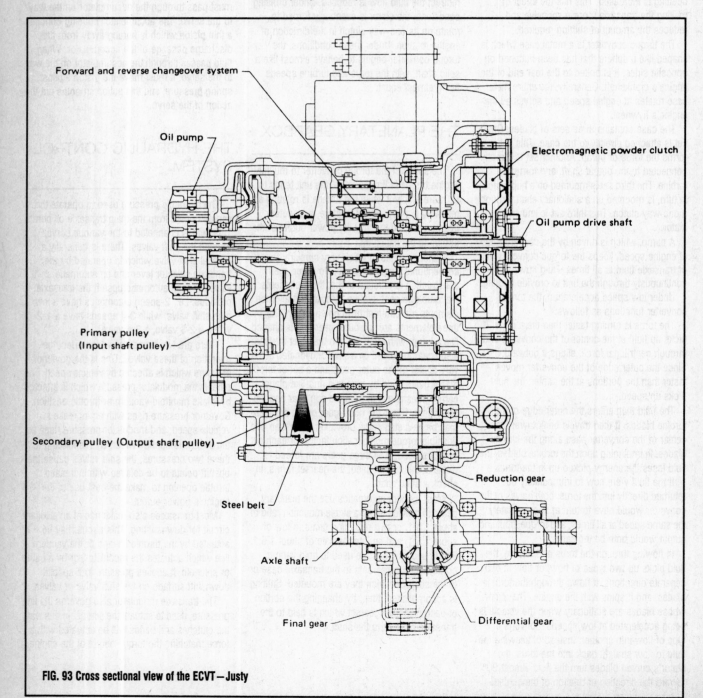

Forward and reverse changeover system

Oil pump

Electromagnetic powder clutch

Oil pump drive shaft

Primary pulley (Input shaft pulley)

Secondary pulley (Output shaft pulley)

Steel belt

Reduction gear

Axle shaft

Final gear

Differential gear

FIG. 93 Cross sectional view of the ECVT—Justy

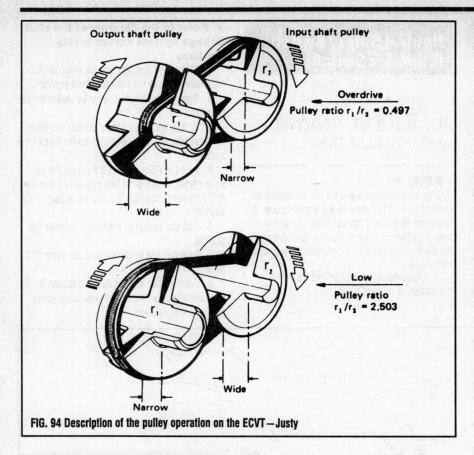

FIG. 94 Description of the pulley operation on the ECVT—Justy

Adjustments

Except Justy ECVT

The linkage adjustment is important for the automatic transmission. Great care should be exercised because improper adjustment will result in damage to the transmission.

To determine if adjustment is necessary, check the shifting operation with the engine off and the parking brake applied. While holding in the release button with your thumb, move the selector lever forward until you can feel that the transmission is in PARK. Then move the lever back and feel for the five remaining positions. If the gear selector indicator points to the proper gear at each stop, and if the selector lever does not jump when the release button is let go, the shift linkage is properly adjusted. If this is not the case adjustment is necessary.

1. Place the gear selector in N position.
2. Loosen the adjusting nuts on the linkage rod.
3. Check that the manual lever on the transmission is in the **N** detent position.
4. Set the gear selector lever so that it clicks in the neutral position.
5. Tighten the adjusting nuts.

BRAKE BAND ADJUSTMENT

Except Justy ECVT

This adjustment can be performed on the outside of the transmission.

1. Park the car on a level surface or support it on jackstands, engine off.
2. Locate the adjusting screw above the pan on the left side of the transmission.
3. Loosen the locknut.
4. On 1985 and later models, torque the adjusting screw to 18 ft. lbs. (25 Nm), then turn it back exactly 3/4 turn.
5. Tighten the lock nut.

Following the above procedure will adjust the transmission brake band to the factory specified setting. However, if any of the following conditions are detected the adjusting screw can be moved 1/4 turn in either direction:

Turn 1/4 turn clockwise if the transmission:
- jolts when shifting from 1st to 2nd
- engine speed abruptly rises from 2nd to 3rd, or,
- shift delays in kickdown from 3rd to 2nd.

Turn 1/4 turn counterclockwise if:
- car slips from 1st to 2nd, or
- there is braking action at shift from 2nd to 3rd.

Oil Pan and Filter

REMOVAL & INSTALLATION

♦ SEE FIG. 92

➡ **Normal maintenance does not require removal of the transmission oil pan, or changing or cleaning of the oil strainer. However, if a leak is detected at the transmission oil pan gasket it must be replaced.**

1. Park the car on a level surface or support it on jackstands, engine off.
2. Remove the drain plug and drain the transmission fluid into a suitable container.
3. Remove the mounting bolts and lower the oil pan and gasket.
4. Reverse the above process to install the pan. Always use a new pan gasket.

If you wish to remove the oil strainer, simply unbolt it from the valve body after step 3 above. It can be cleaned in fresh gasoline and dried with compressed air or allowed to air dry.

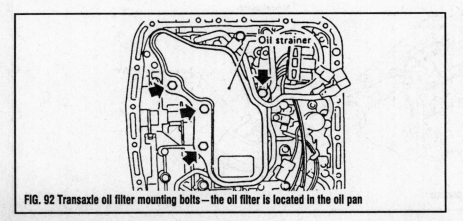

FIG. 92 Transaxle oil filter mounting bolts—the oil filter is located in the oil pan

THROTTLE LINKAGE

The control valve assembly of the automatic transmission is governed by intake manifold vacuum rather than throttle position, therefore, there is no linkage which requires adjustment.

KICKDOWN SOLENOID

The kickdown solenoid is located on the right side of the transmission case. The switch is operated by the upper part of the accelerator lever inside the car, and its position can be varied to give slower or quicker kickdown response. To test its function press the accelerator to the floor with the engine off and the ignition switch on. An audible click should be heard from the solenoid.

Neutral Safety Switch (Inhibitor Switch)

ADJUSTMENT, REMOVAL AND INSTALLATION

◆ SEE FIG. 94a

This switch is mounted on the transmission lever shaft and is bolted to the transmission. It functions to prevent the car from starting in any gear position but Park or Neutral, and to activate the back up lights when in reverse. Adjustment is as follows.

1. Disconnect the linkage rod from the transmission manual lever.

➡ **Refer to the diagram of the shift linkage system earlier in this Section.**

2. Make sure that the manual lever on the transmission is in the neutral detent position.

3. Remove the manual lever by taking off the mounting nut.

4. Remove the two safety switch mounting bolts and the setscrew from the lower face of the switch.

5. Insert a 1.5mm drill bit through the set screw hole. Turn the switch slightly so that the drill bit passes through into the back part of the switch.

6. Bolt the switch in place and remove the drill bit.

7. Reinstall the setscrew and the manual lever.

8. Connect the linkage rod and adjust, if necessary, according to the procedure given earlier in this Section.

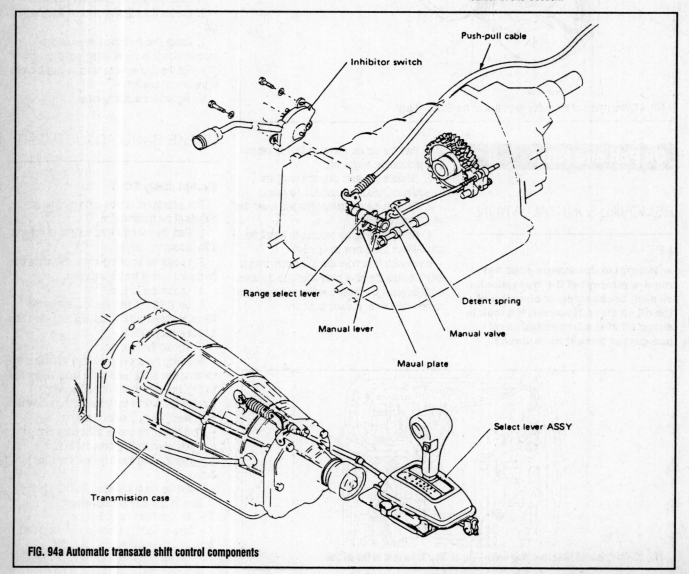

FIG. 94a Automatic transaxle shift control components

To remove the switch, proceed as above but also disconnect the wire harness from the switch after step 4. Installation involves connecting the wire and then following steps 5 through 8.

Transaxle

REMOVAL & INSTALLATION

Justy

WITH ECVT TRANSAXLE

➡ **When removing and installing ECVT transaxle, always remove and install the engine and transaxle as an assembly.**

1. Disconnect the negative battery cable. Drain the coolant by removing drain plug from radiator.

2. Remove the grille. Disconnect hoses and electric wiring from radiator and remove the radiator.

3. Remove front hood release cable and remove radiator upper support member. Disconnect horn and remove the air cleaner assembly.

4. Disconnect the following hoses and cables:
   a. Hoses from carburetor
   b. Hoses from the heater unit
   c. Hose for brake booster
   d. Clutch cable
   e. Accelerator cable
   f. Choke cable from carburetor, if equipped
   g. Speedometer cable
   h. Distributor wiring

5. Disconnect selector cable. Set selector lever at **N** position. Remove clip and detach selector cable from bracket. Remove snap pin, clevis pin and separate selector cable from transaxle.

6. Remove the pitching stopper from the bracket.

7. Disconnect the starter cable, engine wiring harness connectors, ground lead terminals and brush holder harness connector.

8. Remove the hanger from the rear of transaxle.

9. Remove under covers and remove the exhaust system.

10. Remove the driveshaft from transaxle.

11. Remove transverse link.

12. Remove the spring pin retaining the axle shaft by using a suitable tool and separate front axle shaft from the transaxle.

13. Remove engine and transaxle mounting brackets.

14. Raise the engine and remove center member and crossmember.

15. Lift up the engine/transaxle assembly carefully and remove it from the vehicle.

To Install:

16. Position the engine/transaxle assembly in the vehicle. Install engine and transaxle mounting brackets.

17. Install center member and crossmember.

18. Install the axle shaft to transaxle with new spring pin.

19. Install gearshift rod and stay to transaxle.

20. Install the exhaust system. Connect driveshaft to transaxle.

21. Install transverse link and under covers to the vehicle.

22. Reconnect the pitching stopper to bracket.

23. Reconnect the following hoses and cables:
   a. Hoses to carburetor
   b. Hoses to the heater unit
   c. Hose to brake booster
   d. Clutch cable to transaxle
   e. Accelerator cable
   f. Choke cable from carburetor, if equipped
   g. Speedometer cable
   h. Distributor wiring

24. Reconnect the starter cable, engine wiring harness connectors, ground lead terminals and brush holder harness connector. Install the air cleaner assembly.

25. Install radiator upper member and connect hood release cable to lock assembly. Reconnect the horn.

26. Install the radiator and connect hoses and electric wiring. Attach grille to the vehicle.

27. Refill the coolant. Reconnect the battery cable.

28. Check all fluid levels. Road test vehicles for proper operation in all driving ranges.

XT Coupe

1.8L AND 2.7L ENGINES

1. Disconnect the negative battery cable. Remove the air cleaner assembly.

2. Remove the clutch cable and the hill holder cable. Remove the speedometer cable. Remove the torque converter from the drive plate.

3. Remove the oxygen sensor electrical connector and the neutral switch connector.

4. If equipped with 4WD, remove the disconnect the electrical connections at the back up light and differential lock indicator switch assembly. Disconnect the differential lock vacuum hose.

5. Disconnect the starter electrical connections. Remove the starter retaining bolts. Remove the starter from the transaxle case.

6. Remove the air intake boot. Disconnect the pitching stopper rod from its mounting bracket. Remove the right side engine to transaxle mounting bolt.

7. Install engine support bracket 927160000 and engine support tool 927150000 or their equivalents. Remove the buffer rod from the engine and body side bracket.

➡ **Before attaching the special engine support tools, connect the adjuster to the buffer rod assembly on the right side of the engine.**

8. Raise and support the vehicle safely.

9. Disconnect the exhaust pipes at the exhaust manifold flange. Remove the exhaust system up to the rear exhaust pipe assembly.

10. If equipped with 4WD, matchmark and remove the driveshaft. Remove the complete gear shift assembly.

11. Loosen the upper bolt and nut from the plate that secures the transverse link to the stabilizer. Remove the lower bolt and separate the link from the stabilizer.

12. Remove the right brake cable bracket from the transverse link. Remove the bolt retaining the link to the crossmember on each side.

13. Lower the transverse link. Using tool 398791700 or equivalent, remove the spring pin and separate the axle shaft from the driveshaft on each side of the assembly by pushing the rear of the tire outward.

14. Remove the engine to transaxle mounting bolts. Position the proper transaxle jack under the transaxle assembly. Disconnect the transaxle cooler lines.

15. Remove the rear cushion rubber mounting bolts. Remove the rear crossmember assembly.

16. Turn the engine support tool adjuster counterclockwise in order to slightly raise the engine.

17. Move the transaxle jack toward the rear of the vehicle until the mainshaft is withdrawn from the clutch cover.

18. Carefully remove the transaxle assembly from the vehicle.

To Install:

19. Carefully raise the transaxle until the mainshaft is aligned with the clutch side. Install the engine to the transaxle and temporarily tighten the mounting bolts.

20. Install the rear crossmember rubber cushion and tighten nuts to 20–35 ft. lbs. (27–47 Nm). Install the rear crossmember and tighten front bolts to 65–87 ft. lbs. (88–118 Nm); rear bolts to 27–49 ft. lbs. (37–67 Nm).

21. Tighten the engine-to-transaxle nuts to 34–40 ft. lbs. (46–54 Nm). Remove the transaxle jack.

22. Install the halfshaft into the differential and spring pin into place. Install the transverse link and stabilizer temporarily to the front crossmember. Install the brake cable bracket. Lower the vehicle and tighten transverse link bolt to 43–51 ft. lbs. (59–69 Nm); stabilizer bolts to 14–22 ft. lbs. (20–29 Nm).

23. Install the gearshift system. Install the driveshaft (4WD vehicles). Install the starter, pitching stopper, timing hole plug, air intake boot and speedometer cable. Reconnect all electrical and vacuum connectors.

24. Connect the clutch cable and hill holder. Install the front exhaust pipe. Connect the oil cooler lines. Install and tighten the torque converter mounting bolts to 17–20 ft. lbs. (23–26 Nm).

25. Connect the negative battery cable, check the transaxle fluid level and test drive the vehicle.

1800 Sedan/Station Wagon, Loyale and XT Coupe

2WD AND 4WD NON-ELECTRONIC 3 AND 4-SPEED TRANSAXLES

1. Disconnect the negative battery cable.
2. Remove clamp from spare tire supporter and remove the spare tire.

➡ **Use care when removing spare tire assembly from the vehicle.**

3. Remove spare tire supporter and battery clamp.

4. Remove speedometer cable and retaining clip. Before disconnecting speedometer cable, remove front exhaust pipe on 4-speed automatic transaxle.

5. Disconnect the following electrical harness connections on the 3-speed automatic transaxle:
   a. Oxygen sensor connector
   b. ATF temperature switch connector
   c. Kickdown solenoid valve connector
   d. 4WD solenoid valve connector on 4WD equipped vehicles

6. Disconnect the following electrical harness connections on the 4-speed automatic transaxle:
   a. Oxygen sensor connector
   b. Transaxle harness connector
   c. Inhibitor switch connector
   d. Revolution sensor connector on 4WD equipped vehicles

7. Disconnect the diaphragm vacuum hose on 3-speed automatic transaxle and 4WD vacuum hose on 4WD equipped vehicles.

8. Remove clip band which secures air breather hose to pitching stopper.

9. Remove the pitching stopper rod. Remove the starter.

10. Remove timing hole inspection plug and remove the 4 bolts which hold torque converter to driveplate.

11. Support the engine assembly with special engine support tool 926610000 or equivalent.

12. Remove engine-to-transaxle mounting nut and bolt on the right side.

13. Remove the exhaust system.

➡ **Apply a penetrating oil or equivalent to all exhaust retaining nuts in advance to facilitate removal.**

14. On turbocharged vehicles, remove accelerator cable cover and upper and lower turbocharger covers. Remove the center exhaust pipe at turbocharger location and at rear exhaust pipe. Remove any exhaust brackets or hangers that attach to the transaxle, as necessary.

15. On non-turbocharged vehicles, disconnect front exhaust pipe from the engine and from the rear exhaust pipe. Remove any exhaust brackets or hangers that attach to the transaxle as necessary.

16. Drain all transaxle fluid from the oil pan.

17. Remove the driveshaft on 4WD vehicles. Plug the opening at the rear of extension housing to prevent oil from flowing out.

18. Disconnect the linkage rod for a 3-speed or cable for a 4-speed. from the select lever.

19. Remove stabilizer from transverse link by loosening (not removing) nut and bolt on the lower side of plate.

20. Remove parking brake cable bracket from transverse link and bolt holding transverse link to crossmember on each side. Lower the transverse link.

21. Remove spring pin and separate axle shaft from transaxle on each side.

➡ **Use a suitable tool to remove spring pin. Discard old spring pin and always install a new pin.**

22. Disconnect the axle shaft from transaxle on each side. Be sure to remove axle shaft from transaxle by pushing the rear of tire outward.

23. Remove engine-to-transaxle mounting nuts.

24. Disconnect oil cooler hoses and oil supply pipe. Be careful not to damage the oil supply pipe O-ring.

25. Place transaxle jack or equivalent under transaxle. Always support transaxle case with a transaxle jack.

➡ **Do not place jack under oil pan otherwise oil pan may be damaged.**

26. Remove rear cushion rubber mounting nuts and rear crossmember. Move torque converter and transaxle as a unit away from the engine. Remove the transaxle.

To Install:

27. Install transaxle to engine and temporarily tighten engine-to-transaxle mounting nuts.

28. Install rear crossmember to rear cushion rubber mounts. Align rear cushion guide with rear crossmember guide hole and tighten nuts.

29. Install rear crossmember to chassis. Be careful not to damage threads. Torque rear crossmember bolts to 39–49 ft. lbs. (52–67 Nm).

30. Tighten engine to transaxle nuts on the lower side to 34–40 ft. lbs. (46–54 Nm). Remove transaxle jack from the vehicle.

31. Install axle shaft to transaxle and install spring pin into place.

➡ **Always use new spring pin. Be sure to align the halfshaft and shaft from the transaxle at chamfered holes and engage shaft splines correctly.**

32. Install transverse link temporarily to front crossmember by using bolt and self-locking nut. Do not complete final torque at this point.

33. Install stabilizer temporarily to transverse link. Install parking brake cable bracket to transverse link.

34. Connect the linkage rod for a 3-speed or cable for a 4-speed to the select lever. Make sure the lever operates smoothly all across the operating range.

35. Install propeller shaft on 4WD vehicles. Torque propeller shaft to rear differential retaining bolts to 13–20 ft. lbs. (18–20 Nm) and center bearing location retaining bolts to 25–33 ft. lbs. (34–44 Nm).

36. Connect oil cooler hoses and oil supply pipe. Lower vehicle to floor.

37. Tighten transverse link to front crossmember mounting bolts and transverse link to stabilizer mounting bolts with the tires placed on the ground when the vehicle is not loaded. Tightening torque for transverse link to front crossmember (self-locking nuts) 43–51 ft. lbs. and transverse link to stabilizer 14–22 ft. lbs.

38. Tighten engine to transaxle nuts on the upper side to 34–40 ft. lbs.

39. Raise vehicle and safely support. Install exhaust system.

➡ **Before installing exhaust system, connect speedometer cable on 4-speed vehicles.**

40. On turbocharged vehicles, install the center exhaust pipe at turbocharger location and at rear exhaust pipe. Install any exhaust brackets or hangers that attach to the transaxle as necessary. Install upper and lower turbocharger covers and accelerator cable cover.

41. On non-turbocharged vehicles, connect front exhaust pipe to the engine and rear exhaust pipe. Install any exhaust brackets or hangers that attach to the transaxle as necessary.

42. Remove the special engine support tool. Install and tighten torque converter to driveplate mounting bolts to 17–20 ft. lbs.

43. Install timing hole inspection plug.

44. Install starter.

45. Install pitching stopper. Be sure to tighten the bolt for the body side first and then the 1 for engine or transaxle side. Tightening torque for chassis side is 27–49 ft. lbs. and for engine or transaxle side is 33–40 ft. lbs.

46. Reconnect the following electrical harness connections on the 3-speed automatic transaxle:

   a. Oxygen sensor connector
   b. ATF temperature switch connector
   c. Kickdown solenoid valve connector
   d. 4WD solenoid valve connector on 4WD equipped vehicles

47. Reconnect the following electrical harness connections on the 4-speed automatic transaxle:

   a. Oxygen sensor connector
   b. Transaxle harness connector
   c. Inhibitor switch connector
   d. Revolution sensor connector on 4WD equipped vehicles

48. Reconnect the diaphragm vacuum hose on 3-speed automatic transaxle and 4WD vacuum hose on 4WD equipped vehicles.

49. Secure air breather hose to pitching stopper with a clip band.

50. Reconnect the speedometer cable. Manually tighten cable nut all the way and then turn it approximately 30 degrees more with a tool.

51. Connect the battery ground cable. Refill and check transaxle oil level.

52. Install spare tire supporter and battery clamp. Install spare tire.

53. Road test vehicle for proper operation across all operating ranges.

XT Coupe, Legacy and SVX

4-SPEED ELECTRONIC TRANSAXLE

1. Disconnect the negative battery cable.

2. Remove speedometer cable or electronic wiring connector from speed sensor.

3. Disconnect the following electrical harness connections on the automatic transaxle:

   a. Oxygen sensor connector
   b. Transaxle harness connector
   c. Inhibitor switch connector
   d. Revolution sensor connector on 4WD equipped vehicles
   e. Crankshaft and camshaft angle sensor connector on Legacy vehicles
   f. Knock sensor connectors and transaxle ground terminal on Legacy vehicles

4. Remove clip band which secures air breather hose to pitching stopper.

5. Remove the starter and air intake boot.

6. Remove timing hole inspection plug and remove the 4 bolts which hold torque converter to driveplate.

7. Disconnect pitching stopper rod from bracket.

8. Remove engine to transaxle mounting nut and bolt on the right side.

9. Remove the buffer rod from the vehicle. Support the engine assembly with special engine support tool or equivalent.

10. Remove the exhaust system. Remove exhaust brackets or hangers that attach to the transaxle, as necessary.

11. Matchmark and remove the driveshaft on 4WD vehicles. Plug the opening at the rear of extension housing to prevent oil from flowing out.

12. Disconnect the gear shift cable from the transaxle select lever.

13. Remove stabilizer from transverse link.

14. Remove parking brake cable bracket from transverse link and bolt holding transverse link to crossmember on each side. Lower the transverse link.

15. Remove spring pin and separate halfshaft from transaxle on each side.

➡ **Use a suitable tool to remove spring pin. Discard old spring pin and always install a new pin.**

16. Disconnect the halfshaft from transaxle on each side. Be sure to remove axle shaft from transaxle by pushing the rear of tire outward.

17. Remove engine to transaxle mounting nuts.

18. Disconnect oil cooler hoses.

19. Place transaxle jack or equivalent, under transaxle. Always support transaxle case with a transmission jack.

➡ **Do not place jack under oil pan otherwise oil pan may be damaged.**

20. Remove rear cushion rubber mounting nuts and rear crossmember.

21. Move torque converter and transaxle as a unit away from the engine. Remove the transaxle.

To Install:

22. Install transaxle to engine and temporarily tighten engine to transaxle mounting nuts.

23. Install rear crossmember to rear cushion rubber mounts. Align rear cushion guide with rear crossmember guide hole and tighten nuts.

24. Install rear crossmember to chassis; be careful not to damage threads. Torque rear crossmember bolts to 39–49 ft. lbs.

25. Tighten engine to transaxle retaining nuts to 34–40 ft. lbs. Remove transaxle jack from the vehicle.

26. Remove the engine support tool and install buffer rod.

27. Install axle shaft to transaxle and install spring pin into place.

➡ **Always use new spring pin. Be sure to align the axle shaft and shaft from the transaxle at chamfered holes and install shaft splines correctly.**

28. Install transverse link temporarily to front crossmember by using bolt and self locking nut. Do not complete final torque at this point.

29. Install stabilizer temporarily to transverse link. Install parking brake cable bracket to transverse link.

30. Lower vehicle to floor. Tighten transverse link to front crossmember mounting bolts and transverse link to stabilizer mounting bolts with the tires placed on the ground when the vehicle is not loaded. Tightening torque for transverse link to front crossmember (self locking nuts) 43–51 ft. lbs. and transverse link to stabilizer 14–22 ft. lbs.

31. Raise and safely support the vehicle. Reconnect the gear shift cable to the select lever. Make sure the lever operates smoothly all across the operating range.

32. Install propeller shaft on 4WD vehicles. Torque propeller shaft-to- rear differential retaining bolts to 17–24 ft. lbs. and center bearing location retaining bolts to 25–33 ft. lbs.

33. Connect oil cooler hoses.

34. Tighten engine to transaxle bolts to 34–40 ft. lbs.

35. Install starter.

36. Install pitching stopper. Be sure to tighten the bolt for the body side first and then the 1 for engine or transaxle side. Tightening torque for chassis side is 27–49 ft. lbs. and for engine or transaxle side is 33–40 ft. lbs.

37. Install and tighten torque converter-to-driveplate mounting bolts to 17–20 ft. lbs.

38. Install timing hole inspection plug, air intake boot and air breather hose to pitching stopper.

39. Reconnect the following electrical harness connections on the automatic transaxle:

a. Oxygen sensor connector
b. Transaxle harness connector
c. Inhibitor switch connector
d. Revolution sensor connector on 4WD equipped vehicles
e. Crankshaft and camshaft angle sensor connector on Legacy

f. Knock sensor connectors and transaxle ground terminal on Legacy

40. Reconnect the speedometer cable. Manually tighten cable nut all the way and then turn it approximately 30 degrees more with a tool.

41. Install exhaust system and exhaust brackets or hangers that attach to the transaxle, as necessary.

42. Connect the battery ground cable. Refill and check transaxle oil level.

43. Road test vehicle for proper operation across all operating ranges.

Halfshafts

REMOVAL & INSTALLATION

The removal of the front halfshafts for vehicles with automatic transaxle is the same as for those with manual transaxles. Refer to the procedure earlier in this section for halfshaft removal, installation and CV-joint overhaul.

TRANSFER CASE (4WD ONLY)

The transfer case for driving the rear wheels mounts directly to the back of the transaxle case and is part of the transaxle. It provides a direct drive (l:1 gear ratio) coupling to the rear differential. This means that when the 4WD unit is engaged, the transmission provides equal power to the front and rear differentials. When the 4WD unit is not engaged power is transmitted to only the front wheels. In either case shifting of the transmission remains the same. Late models have dual range 4WD.

The drive selector can be shifted at any time, with or without clutching. However, if you shift the drive selector while the car is moving the steering wheel should be in the straight forward position. This minimizes the load on the rear drive system and shifting is made easier.

➡ **You may feel a braking action when turning a sharp corner in four wheel drive. This is a normal phenomenon which arises from the difference in turning radius between the front wheels and the rear wheels, and will not occur when running in front wheel drive.**

DRIVE SELECTOR ADJUSTMENT

There are no adjustments available for the drive selector. If you notice looseness or too much play in shifting it is a sign of worn parts, which must be replaced.

REMOVAL & INSTALLATION

The transfer case must be removed as an assembly with the transaxle. The procedure can be found earlier in this section.

DRIVELINE

Rear Drive System

▶ SEE FIGS. 96–97

The rear drive system of the four wheel drive models contains a differential unit, a driveshaft connected to the output shaft of the transfer case, and an axle shaft running to each rear wheel. The driveshaft is equipped with two maintenance free universal joints and a ball spline at the transfer case connection. To aid in reducing drive train noise and vibration, the differential is mounted to the vehicle body with three or four rubber bushings, one or two at the front and two at the rear of the differential carrier.

Understanding Drive Axles

Power enters the axle from the driveshaft via the companion flange. The flange is mounted on the drive pinion shaft. The drive pinion shaft and gear which carry the power into the differential turn at engine speed. The gear on the end of the pinion shaft drives a large ring gear the axis of rotation of which is 90° away from the of the pinion. The pinion and gear reduce the gear ratio of the axle, and change the direction of rotation to turn the axle shafts which drive both wheels. The axle gear ratio is found by dividing the number of pinion gear teeth into the number of ring gear teeth.

The ring gear drives the differential case. The case provides the two mounting points for the ends of a pinion shaft on which are mounted two pinion gears. The pinion gears drive the two side gears, one of which is located on the inner end of each axle shaft.

By driving the axle shafts through the arrangement, the differential allows the outer drive wheel to turn faster than the inner drive wheel in a turn.

The main drive pinion and the side bearings, which bear the weight of the differential case, are shimmed to provide proper bearing preload, and to position the pinion and ring gears properly.

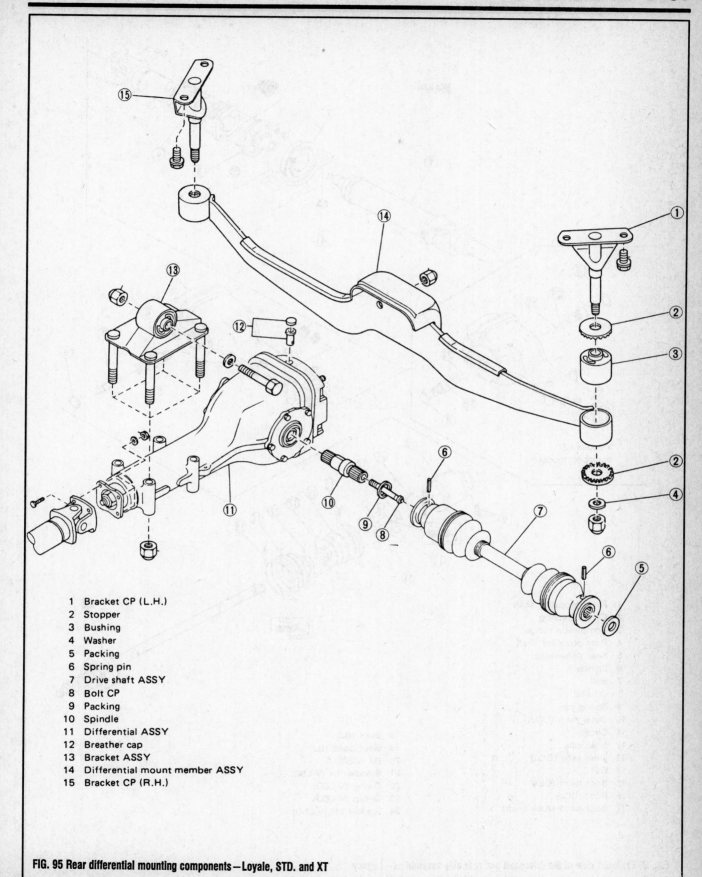

1 Bracket CP (L.H.)
2 Stopper
3 Bushing
4 Washer
5 Packing
6 Spring pin
7 Drive shaft ASSY
8 Bolt CP
9 Packing
10 Spindle
11 Differential ASSY
12 Breather cap
13 Bracket ASSY
14 Differential mount member ASSY
15 Bracket CP (R.H.)

FIG. 95 Rear differential mounting components—Loyale, STD. and XT

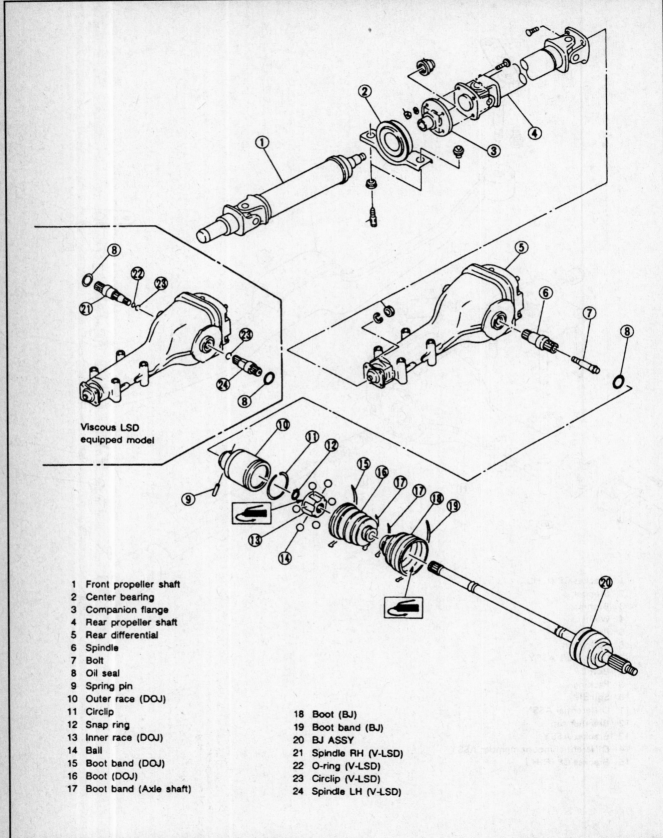

Viscous LSD
equipped model

1   Front propeller shaft
2   Center bearing
3   Companion flange
4   Rear propeller shaft
5   Rear differential
6   Spindle
7   Bolt
8   Oil seal
9   Spring pin
10 Outer race (DOJ)
11 Circlip
12 Snap ring
13 Inner race (DOJ)
14 Ball
15 Boot band (DOJ)
16 Boot (DOJ)
17 Boot band (Axle shaft)

18 Boot (BJ)
19 Boot band (BJ)
20 BJ ASSY
21 Spindle RH (V-LSD)
22 O-ring (V-LSD)
23 Circlip (V-LSD)
24 Spindle LH (V-LSD)

FIG. 96 Exploded view of the driveshaft and rear axle assemblies—Legacy

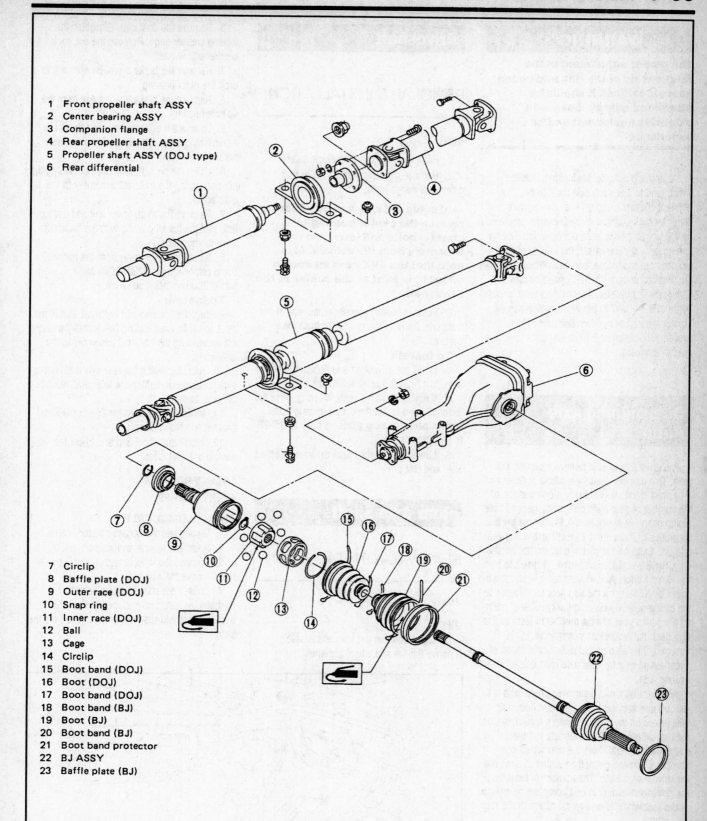

1 Front propeller shaft ASSY
2 Center bearing ASSY
3 Companion flange
4 Rear propeller shaft ASSY
5 Propeller shaft ASSY (DOJ type)
6 Rear differential

7 Circlip
8 Baffle plate (DOJ)
9 Outer race (DOJ)
10 Snap ring
11 Inner race (DOJ)
12 Ball
13 Cage
14 Circlip
15 Boot band (DOJ)
16 Boot (DOJ)
17 Boot band (DOJ)
18 Boot band (BJ)
19 Boot (BJ)
20 Boot band (BJ)
21 Boot band protector
22 BJ ASSY
23 Baffle plate (BJ)

FIG. 97 Exploded view of the driveshaft and rear axle assemblies—SVX

❉❉❉ WARNING

The proper adjustment of the relationship of the ring and pinion gears is critical. It should be attempted only by those with extensive equipment and/or experience.

Limited slip differentials include clutches which tend to link each axle shaft to the differential case. Clutches may be engaged either by spring action or by pressure produced by the torque on the axles during a turn. During turning on a dry pavement, the effects of the clutches are overcome, and each wheel turns at the required speed. When slippage occurs at either wheel, however, the clutches will transmit some of the power to the wheel which has the greater amount of traction. Because of the presence of clutches, limited slip units require a special lubricant.

Determining Axle Ratio

The drive axle is said to have a certain axle ratio. This number (usually a whole number and a decimal fraction) is actually a comparison of the number of gear teeth on the ring gear and the pinion gear. For example, a 4.11 rear means that theoretically, there are 4.11 teeth on the ring gear and one tooth on the pinion gear or, put another way, the driveshaft must turn 4.11 times to turn the wheels once. Actually, on a 4.11 rear, there might be 37 teeth on the ring gear and 9 teeth on the pinion gear. By dividing the number of teeth on the pinion gear into the number of teeth on the ring gear, the numerical axle ratio (4.11) is obtained. This also provides a good method of ascertaining exactly what axle ratio one is dealing with.

Another method of determining gear ratio is to jack up and support the car so that both rear wheels are off the ground. Make a chalk mark on the rear wheel and the driveshaft. Put the transaxle in neutral. Turn the rear wheel one complete turn and count the number of turns that the driveshaft makes. The number of turns that the driveshaft makes in one complete revolution of the rear wheel is an approximation of the rear axle ratio.

Driveshaft

REMOVAL & INSTALLATION

4WD

1. Raise and support the vehicle safely.
2. Remove the driveshaft flange to rear differential flange bolts.

➡ **If equipped with a center bearing, remove the center bearing to chassis bolts and lower the assembly from the vehicle. Also note that the SVX uses an double offset type joint at the center of the driveshaft.**

3. Position a drain pan under the rear of the transaxle. Remove the driveshaft from the vehicle.

To install:

4. Install the driveshaft and tighten the flange bolts to 17–24 ft. lbs. (24–32 Nm).
5. If equipped with a center bearing, raise the assembly and install the center bearing bolts. Tighten center bearing attaching bolts to 25–33 ft. lbs. (34–44 Nm).
6. Lower the vehicle, check the transaxle fluid level and test drive.

Rear Axle Shafts

REMOVAL & INSTALLATION

Justy

2WD

1. Raise and support the vehicle safely. Remove the tire and wheel assembly.

2. Remove the dust cap. Straighten the locking washer edge. Remove the nut, lock washer and washer.
3. Remove the brake drum. Be sure not to drop the outer bearing.
4. Remove the brake line bracket from the spindle housing.
5. Loosen the bolts and remove the brake assembly. Suspend the assembly aside with wire.
6. Using the proper tools, drive out the spring pin connecting the halfshaft assembly to the differential.
7. Remove the strut, lower link and trailing link. Pull the housing along with the halfshaft from its mounting.
8. Separate the housing from the halfshaft, using removal tools 922493000 and 921122000 or their equivalent.

To install:

9. Join the housing and halfshaft. Install the strut, lower link and trailing link. Install the spring pin connecting the halfshaft assembly to the differential.
10. After tightening the rear axle halfshaft-to-axle housing nut, tighten the axle shaft nut 30 degrees further.
11. Install the brake assembly, brake line bracket and brake drum.
12. Install the wheel and tire, lower the vehicle and test drive.

Legacy and SVX

◆ SEE FIG. 98–99

2WD — LEGACY ONLY

1. Disconnect the negative battery cable.
2. Raise the vehicle and support safely.
3. Remove the wheels and unlock the axle nut. Remove the axle nut.
4. Loosen the parking brake adjuster. Remove the disc brake assembly from the backing plate and suspend it with a wire from the strut.

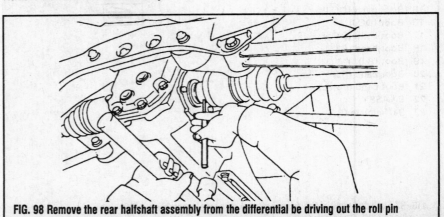

FIG. 98 Remove the rear halfshaft assembly from the differential be driving out the roll pin

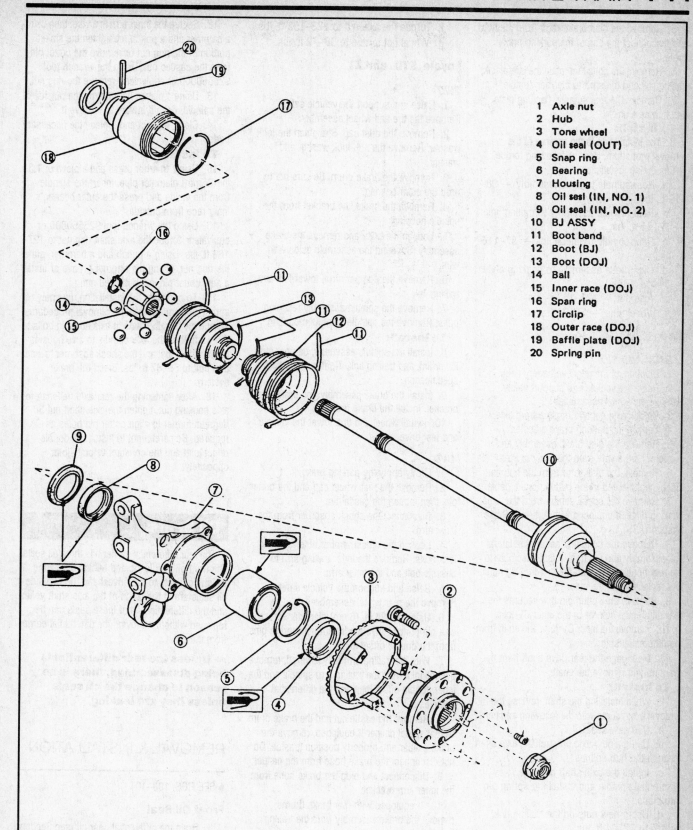

1 Axle nut
2 Hub
3 Tone wheel
4 Oil seal (OUT)
5 Snap ring
6 Bearing
7 Housing
8 Oil seal (IN, NO. 1)
9 Oil seal (IN, NO. 2)
10 BJ ASSY
11 Boot band
12 Boot (BJ)
13 Boot (DOJ)
14 Ball
15 Inner race (DOJ)
16 Span ring
17 Circlip
18 Outer race (DOJ)
19 Baffle plate (DOJ)
20 Spring pin

FIG. 99 Exploded view of the rear halfshaft and hub assemblies—SVX and Legacy

5. Remove the disc brake rotor from the hub and disconnect the end of the parking brake cable.

6. Remove the bolts that retain the lateral link, trailing link and the strut to the rear spindle.

7. Remove the rear spindle, backing plate and hub as a unit.

To Install:

8. The installation is the reverse of the removal procedure. Use the following torque values during installation.

   a. Rear spindle to strut assembly — 98–119 ft. lbs.

   b. Rear spindle assembly to trailing link — 72–94 ft. lbs.

   c. Rear spindle to lateral link — 87–116 ft. lbs.

   d. Disc brake assembly to backing plate — 34–43 ft. lbs.

   e. Axle nut — 123–152 ft. lbs.

   f. Wheel nuts — 58–72 ft. lbs.

4WD

LEGACY AND SVX

1. Disconnect the negative battery cable.

2. Raise the vehicle and support safely. Remove the wheel assemblies.

3. Unlock axle nut and remove from axle.

4. Loosen the parking brake adjuster.

5. Remove the disc brake assembly and suspend it on a wire from the body or strut.

6. Remove the disc rotor from the hub and disconnect the end of the parking brake cable.

7. Remove the speed sensor from the backing plate, if equipped with Anti-lock Brake System (ABS).

8. Remove the bolts that secure the lateral link assembly and the trailing link assembly to the rear housing. Discard the self-locking nuts and replace with new nuts.

9. Remove the spring pin that secures the rear differential spindle to the inner CV-joint.

10. Remove the inner CV-joint and shaft from the differential spindle.

11. Disengage the rear drive shaft from the rear hub and remove the shaft.

To Install:

12. When installing the shaft, reverse the removal procedures with the following additions:

   a. Use new seals.

   b. Using a new axle nut, pull the axle shaft through the hub splines.

   c. Install the axle shaft onto the differential spindle and install the spring pin into place.

   d. Using new nuts on the trailing link, tighten to 72–94 ft. lbs.

   e. Torque disc brake assembly to the rear housing assembly bolts/nuts to 34–43 ft. lbs.

   f. Torque the axle nut to 123–152 ft. lbs.

   g. Wheel nut torque to 58–72 ft. lbs.

Loyale, STD. and XT

2WD

1. Raise and support the vehicle safely. Remove the tire and wheel assembly.

2. Remove the dust cap. Straighten the lock washer. Remove the nut, lock washer and washer.

3. Remove the brake drum. Be sure not to drop the outer bearing.

4. Remove the brake line bracket from the spindle housing.

5. Loosen the bolts and remove the brake assembly. Suspend the assembly aside with wire.

6. Remove the damper strut, lower link and trailing link.

7. Remove the spindle assembly retaining bolts. Remove the spindle from its mounting.

To Install:

8. Install the spindle assembly, damper strut, lower link and trailing link. Tighten all bolts to specification.

9. Install the brake assembly and brake line bracket. Install the brake drum.

10. Install wheel and tire, lower the vehicle and test drive.

4WD

1. Firmly apply the parking brake.

2. Remove the rear wheel cap and the cotter pin, then loosen the castle nut.

3. Disconnect the shock absorber from the inner arm.

4. Loosen the crossmember outer bushing lock bolts. Remove the inner trailing arm to chassis bolt and the inner arm.

5. Raise and support the vehicle safely. Remove the rear wheel assemblies.

6. Using a 0.24 in. (6mm) diameter steel rod or a pin punch, drive the inner/outer spring pins from the double offset joints.

7. With the trailing arm fully lowered, remove the ball joint from the trailing arm spindle and the inner double offset joint and the differential spindle.

8. Remove the castle nut and the brake drum or rear wheel caliper If equipped, remove the brake caliper and properly position it aside. Do not disconnect the brake hose from the caliper.

9. Disconnect and plug the brake hose from the inner arm bracket.

10. If equipped with rear brake drums, remove the brake assembly from the trailing arm.

11. Disconnect the inner arm from the outer arm and remove the inner arm from the vehicle.

12. Secure the inner arm in a vise, then using a hammer and a punch, straighten the staked portion of the ring nut or remove the cotter pin from the castled nut. Using the wrench tool 925550000 or equivalent, remove the ring nut.

13. Using a plastic hammer on the outside of the spindle, drive it inward to remove it.

14. Clean, inspect and replace the necessary parts.

To Install:

15. Using an arbor press and a piece of 1.38 in. (35mm) diameter pipe, insert the spindle from the inside and press the outer bearing's inner race from outside.

16. Using the wrench tool 925550000 or equivalent, torque the axle shaft ring nut to 127–163 ft. lbs. Using a punch and a hammer, stake the ring nut, facing the ring nut groove or install a new cotter pin in the castled nut.

17. To complete the installation, use new spring pins and reverse the removal procedures. Torque the backing plate to axle housing bolts to 34–43 ft. lbs., the axle spindle to axle housing nut to 145 ft. lbs. and the shock absorber to inner arm bolt to 65–87 ft. lbs. Bleed the brake system.

18. After tightening the rear axle halfshaft to axle housing nut, tighten the axle shaft nut 30 degrees further to align cotter pin holes as required. Be careful not to install the double offset joint and the constant velocity joint oppositely.

Oil Seals

The rear differential carrier has three oil seals. The front oil seal is located behind the flange which connects to the driveshaft. The two side oil seals are at the union of the axle shaft yokes and the differential. All of these seals can be replaced without removing the differential carrier from the car.

➡ **Unless the rear differential is being disassembled, there is no reason to change the oil seals unless they are leaking.**

REMOVAL & INSTALLATION

◆ SEE FIGS. 100–101

Front Oil Seal

1. Drain the differential gear oil (see Section 1).

2. Raise the rear wheels and support the car n jack stands.

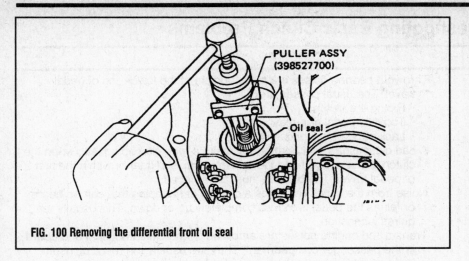

FIG. 100 Removing the differential front oil seal

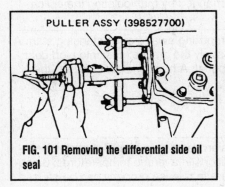

FIG. 101 Removing the differential side oil seal

3. Remove the driveshaft as outlined earlier in this section.

4. Measure the turning resistance of the differential companion flange. To do this, attach either a spring scale or an inch pound torque wrench to one of the mounting holes. Make sure that the flange turns smoothly, and then turn the flange through one complete revolution using the scale or torque wrench. Mark down the reading registered. It will be used during installation.

5. Remove the drive pinion nut while holding the companion flange with a flange or pipe wrench.

6. Remove the companion flange and oil seal with a puller.

7. Using a drift, tap in a new oil seal.

➡ **Apply axle grease between the oil seal lips.**

8. Install the companion flange.

9. Tighten the pinion nut to 123–145 ft. lbs. (167–196 Nm). The proper torque has been reached when the turning resistance of the companion flange is the same as it was when measured in step 4 above.

10. Stake the pinion nut with a punch.

Side Oil Seal

1. Drain the differential oil (see Section 1).

2. Raise the rear wheels and support the car on jack stands.

3. Remove the side yolk retaining bolt and pull the side yolk out of the differential carrier.

4. Extract the oil seal with a puller.

5. Using a drift, tap in a new oil seal.

➡ **Apply axle grease between the oil seal lips.**

6. Install the side yoke and tighten the retaining bolt.

Rear Differential Carrier

REMOVAL & INSTALLATION

1. Drain the differential oil (see Section 1).

2. Raise the rear wheels and support the car on jackstands.

3. Remove the exhaust pipe and muffler as outlined in the Engine Removal section of Section 3.

4. Remove the driveshaft and axle shafts.

5. Support the differential carrier with a jack.

6. Remove the two nuts securing the differential to the rear mounting bracket.

7. Remove the two bolts securing the differential to the front mounting bracket.

8. Lower the jack and remove the differential.

9. To install reverse steps 1 through 8. Observe the following torque specifications:
   • Rear mounting nuts: 53 ft. lbs. (72 Nm)
   • Front mounting bolts: 53 ft. lbs. (72 Nm)

Differential

REMOVAL & INSTALLATION

1. Raise and support the rear of the vehicle.

2. Drain the differential oil into a suitable container by removing the drain plug.

3. Disconnect the driveshaft from the companion flange.

4. Remove the axle shafts, the procedure can be found earlier in this section.

5. Remove the differential carrier retaining bolts from the axle housing.

6. Remove the carrier from the axle housing, you may have to loosen it with a soft mallet.

To Install:

7. Install the carrier in position and install the mounting bolts.

8. Install the axle shafts and connect the driveshaft to the companion flange.

9. Fill the differential with the correct amount of oil, that is until it just starts to come out of the filler plug hole.

10. Lower the vehicle.

Troubleshooting Basic Clutch Problems

Problem	Cause
Excessive clutch noise	Throwout bearing noises are more audible at the lower end of pedal travel. The usual causes are: · Riding the clutch · Too little pedal free-play · Lack of bearing lubrication A bad clutch shaft pilot bearing will make a high pitched squeal, when the clutch is disengaged and the transmission is in gear or within the first 2″ of pedal travel. The bearing must be replaced. Noise from the clutch linkage is a clicking or snapping that can be heard or felt as the pedal is moved completely up or down. This usually requires lubrication. Transmitted engine noises are amplified by the clutch housing and heard in the passenger compartment. They are usually the result of insufficient pedal free-play and can be changed by manipulating the clutch pedal.
Clutch slips (the car does not move as it should when the clutch is engaged)	This is usually most noticeable when pulling away from a standing start. A severe test is to start the engine, apply the brakes, shift into high gear and SLOWLY release the clutch pedal. A healthy clutch will stall the engine. If it slips it may be due to: · A worn pressure plate or clutch plate · Oil soaked clutch plate · Insufficient pedal free-play
Clutch drags or fails to release	The clutch disc and some transmission gears spin briefly after clutch disengagement. Under normal conditions in average temperatures, 3 seconds is maximum spin-time. Failure to release properly can be caused by: · Too light transmission lubricant or low lubricant level · Improperly adjusted clutch linkage
Low clutch life	Low clutch life is usually a result of poor driving habits or heavy duty use. Riding the clutch, pulling heavy loads, holding the car on a grade with the clutch instead of the brakes and rapid clutch engagement all contribute to low clutch life.

TORQUE SPECIFICATIONS

Component	U.S.	Metric
Justy 5 Speed Transaxle:		
Crossmember retaining bolts (right side)	72-87 ft. lbs.	98-118 Nm
Crossmember retaining bolts (left side)	27-49 ft. lbs.	37-67 Nm
Oil drain plug	22-28 ft. lbs.	30-38 Nm
Speedometer gear retaining bolt	10-13 ft. lbs.	14-18 Nm
Bearing retainer plate-to-main case	17-20 ft. lbs.	23-26 Nm
5th gear locknut	54-62 ft. lbs.	73-84 Nm
Side cover retaining bolts	17-20 ft. lbs.	23-26 Nm
4WD switch assembly	12-14 ft. lbs.	16-20 Nm
Shifter arm-to-clutch housing	6.7-7.8 ft. lbs.	9.1-10.6 Nm
Main case retaining bolts	17-20 ft. lbs.	23-26 Nm
Shifter rail spring plug	13.4-15.6 ft. lbs.	18.1-21.1 Nm
Clutch release fork pivot	11-18 ft. lbs.	15-25 Nm
Final gear retaining bolts	42-49 ft. lbs.	57-67 Nm
Backlash inspection plug	30-35 ft. lbs.	41-47 Nm
Front Wheel Drive 5 Speed Transaxle:		
Case retaining bolts (8mm)	17-20 ft. lbs.	23-26 Nm
Case retaining bolts (10mm)	27-31 ft. lbs.	36-42 Nm
Drain plug	30-35 ft. lbs.	41-47 Nm
Rear crossmember bolts	65-87 ft. lbs.	88-118 Nm
Engine-to-transaxle bolts	34-40 ft. lbs.	46-54 Nm
Transverse link--crossmember	43-51 ft. lbs.	59-69 Nm
Transverse link--stabilizer	14-22 ft. lbs.	20-29 Nm
Shift rod retaining bolts	7-11 ft. lbs.	10-16 Nm
Shifter stay bolts	10-16 ft. lbs.	14-22 Nm
Front crossmember bolts	36-64 ft. lbs.	51-86 Nm
Drive pinion shaft bolt		
turbocharged engine	82-91 ft. lbs.	112-124 Nm
non-turbocharged engine	54-62 ft. lbs.	73-84 Nm
Crown gear retaining bolts	42-49 ft. lbs.	57-67 Nm
Retaining plugs	14 ft. lbs.	20 Nm
Mainshaft bolt		
turbocharged engine	82-91 ft. lbs.	112-124 Nm
non-turbocharged engine	54-62 ft. lbs.	73-84 Nm
Selective 5 Speed Transaxle:		
Case retaining bolts (8mm)	17-20 ft. lbs.	23-26 Nm
Case retaining bolts (10mm)	27-31 ft. lbs.	36-42 Nm
Drain plug	30-35 ft. lbs.	41-47 Nm
Transfer case bolts	14 ft. lbs.	20 Nm
Rear crossmember bolts	65-87 ft. lbs.	88-118 Nm
Engine-to-transaxle bolts	34-40 ft. lbs.	46-54 Nm
Transverse link--crossmember	43-51 ft. lbs.	59-69 Nm
Transverse link--stabilizer	14-22 ft. lbs.	20-29 Nm
Shift rod retaining bolts	7-11 ft. lbs.	10-16 Nm
Shifter stay bolts	10-16 ft. lbs.	14-22 Nm
Driveshaft retaining bolts	13-20 ft. lbs.	18-27 Nm
Center bearing bolts	25-33 ft. lbs.	34-44 Nm
Front crossmember bolts	36-64 ft. lbs.	51-86 Nm
4WD switch retaining bolts	13 ft. lbs.	18 Nm
Drive pinion shaft bolt	82-91 ft. lbs.	112-124 Nm
Crown gear retaining bolts	42-49 ft. lbs.	57-67 Nm
Retaining plugs	14 ft. lbs.	20 Nm
Input shaft holder retaining bolts	13-16 ft. lbs.	18-21 Nm

TORQUE SPECIFICATIONS

Component	U.S.	Metric
Full-time 4WD transaxle:		
Case retaining bolts (8mm)	17-20 ft. lbs.	23-26 Nm
Case retaining bolts (10mm)	27-31 ft. lbs.	36-42 Nm
Drain plug	30-35 ft. lbs.	41-47 Nm
Transfer case bolts	14 ft. lbs.	20 Nm
Rear crossmember bolts	65-87 ft. lbs.	88-118 Nm
Engine-to-transaxle bolts	34-40 ft. lbs.	46-54 Nm
Transverse link--crossmember	43-51 ft. lbs.	59-69 Nm
Transverse link--stabilizer	14-22 ft. lbs.	20-29 Nm
Shift rod retaining bolts	7-11 ft. lbs.	10-16 Nm
Shifter stay bolts	10-16 ft. lbs.	14-22 Nm
Driveshaft retaining bolts	13-20 ft. lbs.	18-27 Nm
Center bearing bolts	25-33 ft. lbs.	34-44 Nm
Front crossmember bolts	36-64 ft. lbs.	51-86 Nm
4WD switch retaining bolts	13 ft. lbs.	18 Nm
Drive pinion shaft bolt	82-91 ft. lbs.	112-124 Nm
Crown gear retaining bolts	42-49 ft. lbs.	57-67 Nm
Retaining plugs	14 ft. lbs.	20 Nm
Input shaft holder retaining bolts	13-16 ft. lbs.	18-21 Nm
Clutch:		
Pressure plate bolts	12.7 ft. lbs.	17.2 Nm
Master cylinder mounting bolts	15 ft. lbs.	21 Nm
Slave cylinder and Damper	30 ft. lbs.	41 Nm
Clutch fluid lines	13 ft. lbs.	18 Nm
Automatic transaxle:		
Brake band adjusting bolt	18 ft. lbs.	25 Nm
XT:		
rear crossmember cushion bolts	20-35 ft. lbs.	27-37 Nm
rear crossmember front bolts	65-87 ft. lbs.	88-118 Nm
rear crossmember rear bolts	27-49 ft. lbs.	37-67 Nm
engine-to-transaxle bolts	34-40 ft. lbs.	46-54 Nm
transverse link bolt	43-51 ft. lbs.	59-69 Nm
stabilizer bolts	14-22 ft. lbs.	20-29 Nm
converter-to-driveplate	17-20 ft. lbs.	23-26 Nm
STD., Loyale and XT with 3 speed electronic transaxle:		
rear crossmember bolts	39-49 ft. lbs.	52-67 Nm
engine-to-transaxle bolts	34-40 ft. lbs.	46-54 Nm
driveshaft-to-pinion flange	13-20 ft. lbs	18-26 Nm
center bearing retaining bolts	25-33 ft. lbs.	34-44 Nm
transverse link bolt	43-51 ft. lbs.	59-69 Nm
stabilizer bolts	14-22 ft. lbs.	20-29 Nm
converter-to-driveplate	17-20 ft. lbs.	23-26 Nm
XT, Legacy and SVX with 4 speed electronic transaxle:		
rear crossmember bolts	39-49 ft. lbs.	52-67 Nm
engine-to-transaxle bolts	34-40 ft. lbs.	46-54 Nm
driveshaft-to-pinion flange	13-20 ft. lbs.	18-26 Nm
center bearing retaining bolts	25-33 ft. lbs.	34-44 Nm
transverse link bolt	43-51 ft. lbs.	59-69 Nm
stabilizer bolts	14-22 ft. lbs.	20-29 Nm
converter-to-driveplate	17-20 ft. lbs.	23-26 Nm
Driveshaft:		
Pinion flange bolts	17-24 ft. lbs.	24-32 Nm
Center bearing attaching bolts	25-33 ft. lbs.	34-44 Nm
Rear Axle:		
Pinion nut	123-145 ft. lbs.	167-196 Nm
Differential carrier:		
Rear mounting nuts	53 ft. lbs.	72 Nm
Front mounting bolts	53 ft. lbs.	72 Nm

8

SUSPENSION AND STEERING

WHEELS

Wheel and Tire

REMOVAL & INSTALLATION

➡ **Before removing the wheel and tire assembly, make sure that the vehicle is properly supported. Use the recommended jacking points and always block the wheel** opposite the point you are jacking. **When possible, use jackstands as an added safety precaution.**

1. If using a scissors jack or similar floor jack, block the wheel diagonally opposite the side being lifted.

2. Remove the hub cap or center cap, note that on some models this can not be done until the lug nuts are removed.

3. Loosen the lug nuts slightly, using the appropriate sized wrench.

4. Lift the vehicle with the jack and remove the lug nuts. Remove the tire.

5. Install the tire in position and install the lug nuts, do not completely tighten the lug nuts until the vehicle is lowered.

6. Lower the vehicle and tighten the lug nuts. The nuts should be tightened in a "X" pattern to 58–72 ft. lbs. (78–98 Nm) on all models except the SVX. On the SVX tighten the lug nuts to 72–87 ft. lbs. (98–118 Nm).

FRONT SUSPENSION

General Information

➡ **All of the suspension mounting fasteners used in these vehicles, use self-locking nuts. These nuts can not be reused after being removed, new nuts must be used. Failure to use new self-locking nuts may result in the bolt working loose, causing loss of vehicle control.**

STRUT TYPE SUSPENSION

◆ SEE FIGS. 1–2

All of the Subaru models covered in this manual use a strut type independent front suspension. The strut is surrounded by a coil spring. The top of the strut is mounted to the body through a rubber cushion to damp vibration and the lower end if mounted to the steering knuckle.

The transverse link has a permanently lubricated ball joint installed by nut at the outer end and is fitted to the front crossmember through a rubber cushion. The leading rod is bolted at the outer end to the transverse link and the inner end of the leading rod is connected to the leading rod bracket. The front crossmember is bolted to the body through rubber cushions.

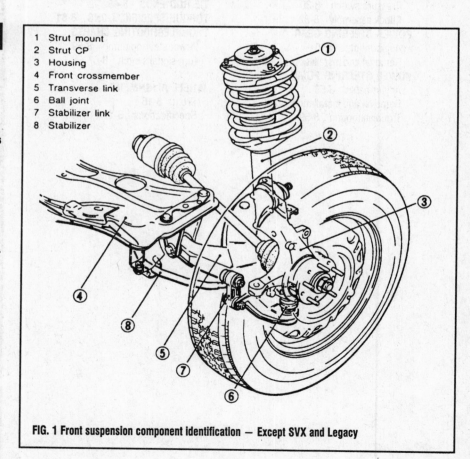

1 Strut mount
2 Strut CP
3 Housing
4 Front crossmember
5 Transverse link
6 Ball joint
7 Stabilizer link
8 Stabilizer

FIG. 1 Front suspension component identification — Except SVX and Legacy

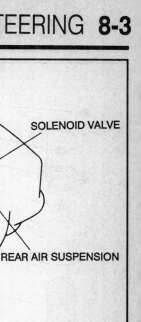

SOLENOID VALVE

FRONT AIR SUSPENSION

SOLENOID VALVE

REAR AIR SUSPENSION

AIR PIPE

CONTROL UNIT (LOCATED UNDER THE FRONT SEAT

DRIER

COMPRESSOR

AIR TANK

FIG. 2 Air suspension component view

The stabilizer bar is connected to the front crossmember and its end are connected to the transverse links.

The overall design of the suspension reduces road vibration that is transmitted to the passenger compartment.

PNEUMATIC SUSPENSION SYSTEM

This suspension system is used on 4WD models except the Justy. The air suspension system is virtually identical to the standard strut type suspension except that the coil springs are replaced by air springs.

The addition of the air springs allows the vehicle ride to be changed by the operator and it allows the suspension height to be maintained when the vehicle is loaded. Each of the air springs has a ride height sensor attached that allows the height to monitored individually at each wheel. A compressor distributes air to each of the air springs as it is needed.

➡ **A further description of the operation of and the repair of the pneumatic suspension can be found later in this section under "Pneumatic Suspension System".**

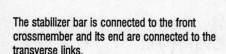

Strut Assembly

REMOVAL & INSTALLATION

◆ SEE FIGS. 3–4

Justy

1. Disconnect the negative battery cable. Remove the bolts that retain the strut assembly to the body.

2. Raise and support the vehicle safely. Remove the tire and wheel assembly.

3. Remove the brake hose from the brake hose bracket on the strut assembly. Remove the retaining bolt that retains the brake hose bracket to the strut.

4. Properly support the hub and disc assembly. Remove the retaining bolt from the strut to the housing.

5. Fit the proper tool into the housing slit and pull the strut assembly from the housing.

6. Remove the strut from the vehicle.

To Install:

7. Install the strut and tighten the upper attaching nuts to 29–43 ft. lbs. (39–59 Nm); lower attaching bolts to 25–40 ft. lbs. (34–54 Nm).

8. Install the brake hose and bracket assembly. Install the wheel and lower the vehicle.

Except Justy

1. Disconnect the negative battery cable. If equipped with air suspension, remove the cover and the air line assembly.

2. Remove the bolts that retain the strut assembly to the body.

3. Raise and support the vehicle safely. Remove the tire and wheel assembly.

4. Disconnect the brake hose from the caliper body. Pull the brake hose retaining clip and remove the brake hose from the damper strut bracket. If equipped with ABS, remove the wire bracket from the strut housing.

5. Remove the bolt that retains the damper strut to the housing. Remove the bolt that retains the damper strut bracket to the housing. On models equipped with air suspension, disconnect the electrical lead and the air hose from the strut.

6. Pull the strut assembly from the housing gradually and carefully, with the housing assembly in the downward position. On models equipped with air suspension, use care not to tear the air diaphragm.

7. Remove the strut assembly from the vehicle.

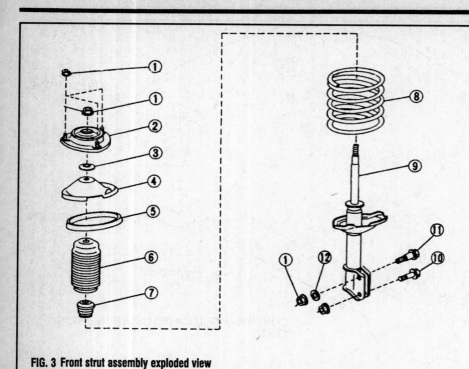

1 Self lock nut
2 Strut mount
3 Spacer
4 Upper spring seat
5 Rubber seat
6 Dust cover
7 Helper
8 Coil spring
9 Strut CP
10 Flange bolt
11 Adjusting bolt
12 Washer

*: Parts unsuitable for re-use

FIG. 3 Front strut assembly exploded view

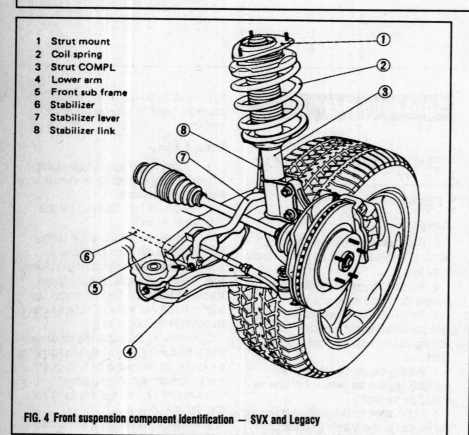

1 Strut mount
2 Coil spring
3 Strut COMPL
4 Lower arm
5 Front sub frame
6 Stabilizer
7 Stabilizer lever
8 Stabilizer link

FIG. 4 Front suspension component identification — SVX and Legacy

10. Install the wheel and tire. Lower the vehicle, connect the negative battery cable and test drive the vehicle.

OVERHAUL

◆ SEE FIGS. 5–6

1. Remove the damper from the vehicle. Install a spring compressor on the spring and remove the self-locking nut from the damper.

2. Remove the rubber cover and the center retaining nut.

3. Slowly release the compressor and remove the spring.

4. Remove the upper mounting cap, washers, thrust plates, bushing and dust cover.

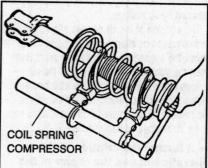

COIL SPRING COMPRESSOR

FIG. 5 Coil spring compressor installed on strut assembly for spring removal

To Install:

8. Install the strut assembly on the vehicle. Tighten the strut attaching bolts to 28–37 ft. lbs. (38–50 Nm).

9. Install the brake hose on the caliper and bleed the brake system. If equipped with air suspension, install the air line assembly.

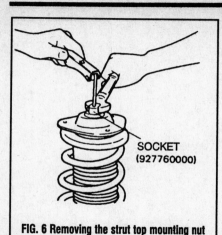

FIG. 6 Removing the strut top mounting nut

SOCKET
(927760000)

➡ **Before discarding any parts, check a parts list to determine which parts are available as replacements.**

5. To reassemble, 1st: pull the strut shaft all the way out, hold it in this position and slide the rubber bumper down the shaft to the strut body. This should hold the shaft in the extended position.

6. Install the spring and its top plate. Make sure the spring seats properly.

7. Install the partially assembled strut in the compressor. Compress the strut until the shaft protrudes through the top plate about 25mm.

8. Now install the bushings, thrust plates, top mounting cap washers and retaining nuts in the reverse order of removal. Tighten the retaining nut to 22 ft. lbs. (31 Nm).

9. Once the retaining nut is installed, release the tension on the compressor and loosen the thumbscrew on the bottom plate. Separate the bottom plates and remove the compressor.

INSPECTION

1. Check for wear or damage to bushings and needle bearings.

2. Check for oil leaks from the struts.

3. Check all rubber parts for wear or damage.

4. Bounce the vehicle to check shock absorbing effectiveness. The vehicle should continue to bounce for no more than two cycles.

1. Upper washer
2. Strut mount
3. Upper washer
4. Oil seal
5. Upper bearing spacer
6. Thrust bearing
7. Lower bearing spacer
8. Bushing
9. Upper spring seat
10. Dust cover
11. Coil spring
12. Helper
13. Strut
14. Tension rod
15. Bushing
16. Plate
17. Bushing
18. Collar
19. Bracket
20. Bushing
21. Clamp
22. Bracket
23. Bushing
24. Crossmember
25. Stabilizer
26. Clamp
27. Bushing
28. Ball joint
29. Rubber bushing
30. Transverse link
31. Castle nut
32. Cotter pin

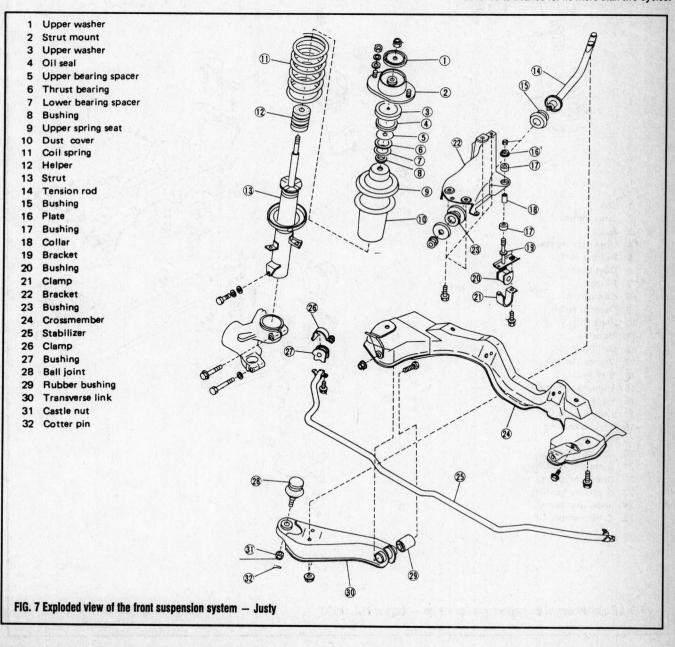

FIG. 7 Exploded view of the front suspension system — Justy

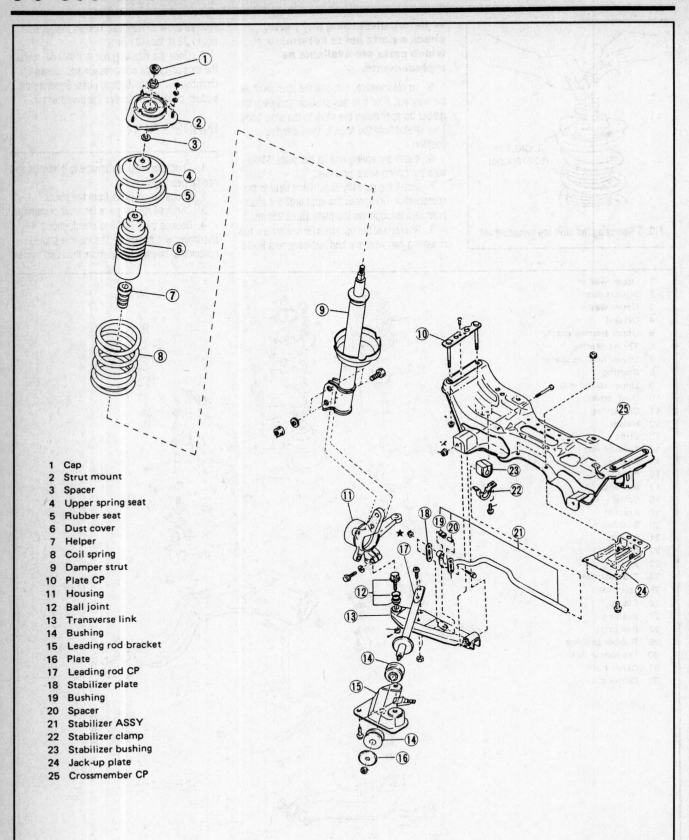

1   Cap
2   Strut mount
3   Spacer
4   Upper spring seat
5   Rubber seat
6   Dust cover
7   Helper
8   Coil spring
9   Damper strut
10 Plate CP
11 Housing
12 Ball joint
13 Transverse link
14 Bushing
15 Leading rod bracket
16 Plate
17 Leading rod CP
18 Stabilizer plate
19 Bushing
20 Spacer
21 Stabilizer ASSY
22 Stabilizer clamp
23 Stabilizer bushing
24 Jack-up plate
25 Crossmember CP

FIG. 8 Exploded view of the front suspension system — Loyale, STD. and XT

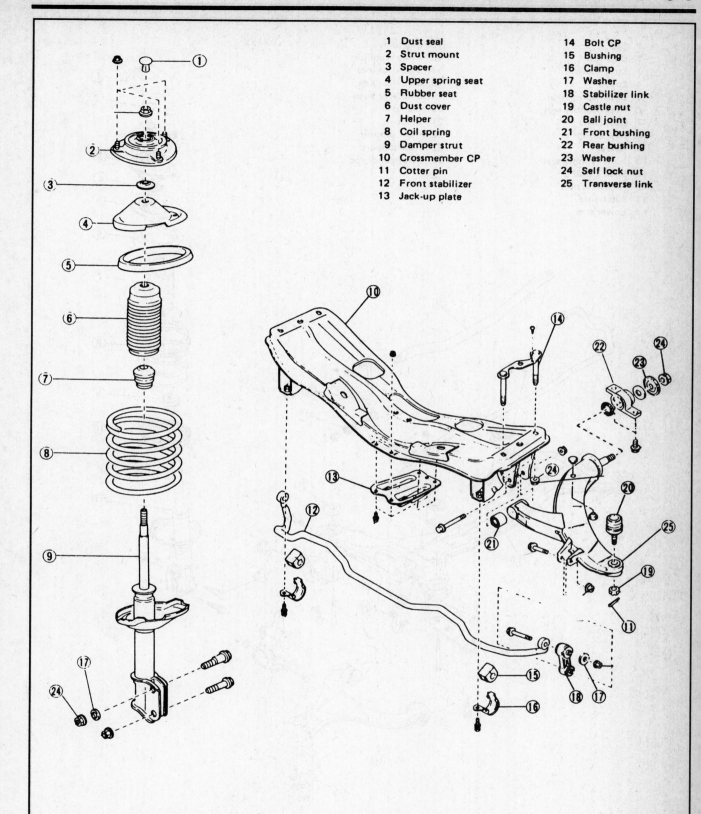

1 Dust seal
2 Strut mount
3 Spacer
4 Upper spring seat
5 Rubber seat
6 Dust cover
7 Helper
8 Coil spring
9 Damper strut
10 Crossmember CP
11 Cotter pin
12 Front stabilizer
13 Jack-up plate

14 Bolt CP
15 Bushing
16 Clamp
17 Washer
18 Stabilizer link
19 Castle nut
20 Ball joint
21 Front bushing
22 Rear bushing
23 Washer
24 Self lock nut
25 Transverse link

FIG. 9 Exploded view of the front suspension system — Legacy

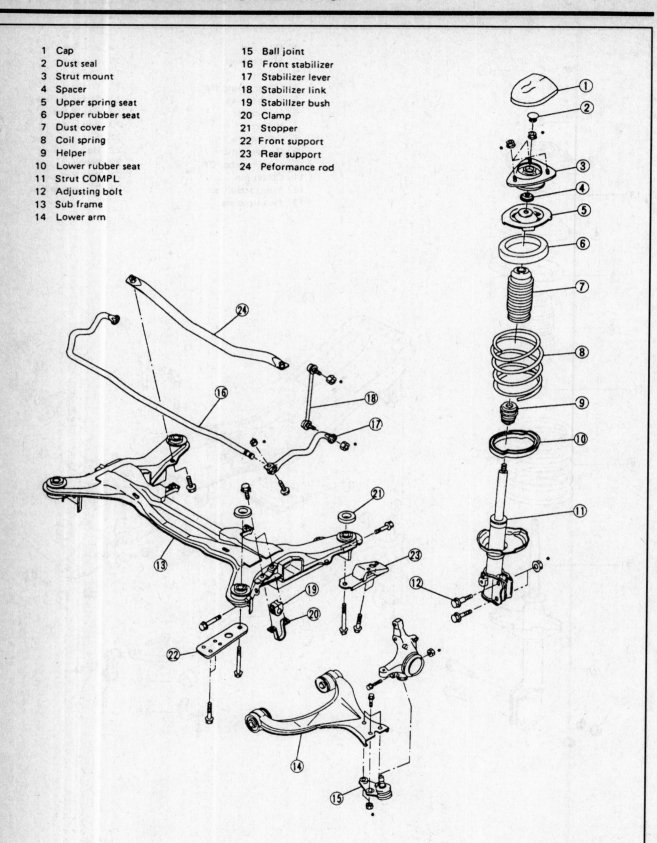

1 Cap
2 Dust seal
3 Strut mount
4 Spacer
5 Upper spring seat
6 Upper rubber seat
7 Dust cover
8 Coil spring
9 Helper
10 Lower rubber seat
11 Strut COMPL
12 Adjusting bolt
13 Sub frame
14 Lower arm
15 Ball joint
16 Front stabilizer
17 Stabilizer lever
18 Stabilizer link
19 Stabilizer bush
20 Clamp
21 Stopper
22 Front support
23 Rear support
24 Peformance rod

FIG. 10 Exploded view of the front suspension system — SVX

Ball Joints

INSPECTION

1. Raise and support the vehicle safely.
2. Using a prybar, position it under the wheel, then pry upward on the wheel several times. If more than 0.012 in. (3mm) of movement is noticed at the ball joint it should be replaced.
3. Inspect the dust seal, if damaged it should be replaced.

REMOVAL & INSTALLATION

♦ SEE FIGS. 11–13

Except SVX

1. Raise and support the vehicle safely. Remove the tire and wheel assembly.
2. Properly support the lower control arm assembly. Remove the cotter pin and castle nut from the ball joint.
3. Disconnect the ball joint from the lower control arm assembly.
4. Remove the bolt retaining the ball joint to the housing. Remove the ball joint from the housing.

To Install:

5. Install the ball joint into the housing and tighten the nut to 28–37 ft. lbs. (38–50 Nm).
6. Connect ball joint to the transverse link and tighten the castle nut to 29 ft. lbs. (39 Nm). Install the cotter pin in the castle nut.
7. Install the front wheels and lower the vehicle.

SVX

1. Raise and safely support the front of the vehicle.
2. Remove the front wheel.
3. Remove the ball joint pinch bolt.

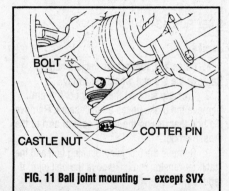

FIG. 11 Ball joint mounting — except SVX

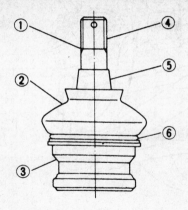

1	Stud
2	Boot cracks and damage
3	Socket deformation
4	Threads damage and deformation
5	Flaws on tapered portion
6	Clip

FIG. 12 Ball joint inspection points

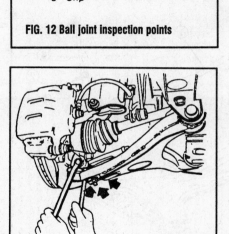

FIG. 13 Removing the ball joint assembly — SVX

4. Remove the 3 ball joint retaining bolts from the lower control arm.
5. Remove the ball joint.

To Install:

6. Install the new ball joint into position.

➡ **The ball joint retaining bolt nuts must be replaced. The pinch bolt nut must also be replaced. Failure to replace the nuts could result in the nuts working loose causing loss of vehicle control.**

7. Install the lower control arm-to-ball joint retaining bolts and using new nuts torque them to 79.7–101.8 ft. lbs. (108–138 Nm).
8. Install the ball joint end into the housing and install the pinch bolt using a new nut. Tighten the pinch bolt to 33.2–43.5 ft. lbs. (45–59 Nm).
9. Install the front wheel and lower the vehicle.

Front Stabilizer

REMOVAL & INSTALLATION

♦ SEE FIGS. 14–17

1. Raise and safely support the front of the vehicle.
2. Remove the wheels.
3. Mark the location and direction of the stabilizer mountings. This will ensure proper installation. Remove the right side ABS sensor clamp, if equipped.
4. Remove the stabilizer-to-crossmember bolts. On the SVX, remove the 2 stabilizer link bolts and remove the stabilizer link.
5. Remove the bolts that secure the stabilizer to the front transverse link.

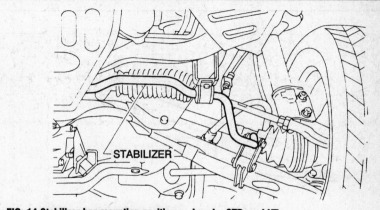

FIG. 14 Stabilizer bar mounting position — Loyale, STD. and XT

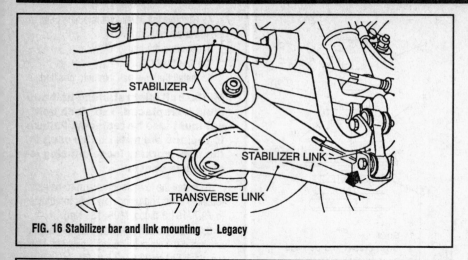

FIG. 16 Stabilizer bar and link mounting — Legacy

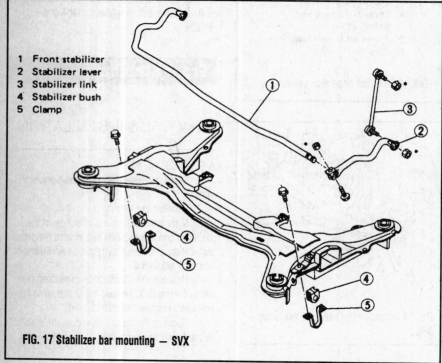

1 Front stabilizer
2 Stabilizer lever
3 Stabilizer link
4 Stabilizer bush
5 Clamp

FIG. 17 Stabilizer bar mounting — SVX

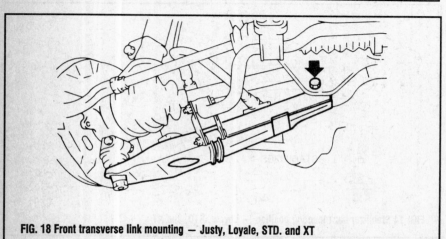

FIG. 18 Front transverse link mounting — Justy, Loyale, STD. and XT

6. Remove the jack-up plate from the crossmember and remove the stabilizer from the vehicle. On the SVX it will have to be removed from the right side.

To Install:

7. Check all of the bushings for deformity or tears. Replace any bushing that shows signs of deterioration.

8. Install the bushings and housings on the stabilizer, aligning any marks before removal.

9. Install the stabilizer into position and install the retaining bolts. Tighten bolts to the following torque:

a. Except SVX: Jack-up plate-to-crossmember — 17–31 ft. lbs. (23–42 Nm). Stabilizer link-to-transverse link — 18–25 ft. lbs. (25–34 Nm). Stabilizer-to-crossmember — 15–21 ft. lbs. (21–28 Nm).

b. SVX: Stabilizer link-to-stabilizer lever — 23–31 ft. lbs. (32–42 Nm). Stabilizer bar-to-stabilizer lever — 33–43 ft. lbs. (45–59 Nm). Stabilizer bar-to-crossmember — 15–21 ft. lbs. (21–28 Nm).

10. Install the right side ABS sensor clamp, if removed.

11. Install the wheels and lower the vehicle.

Lower Control Arm (Transverse Link)

The Justy, Loyale, STD. and XT all use the same type of lower control arm (Subaru refers to it as the transverse link), the design is the same for these models with the Justy having a slightly different removal procedure. The Legacy uses a different style of transverse link than the other models and the SVX is the only Subaru model that actually uses a what is commonly called a lower control arm.

REMOVAL & INSTALLATION

♦ SEE FIGS. 18–20

Justy

1. Raise and support the vehicle safely. Remove the tire and wheel assembly.

2. Properly support the lower control arm. Remove the brake hoses as necessary. Remove the bolt that retains the lower control arm to the crossmember.

3. Remove the ball joint retaining bolt and the stabilizer tension rods. Remove the ball joint, if required.

4. Remove the lower control arm from the vehicle.

To Install:

5. Install the ball joint, if removed. Install the lower control arm. Tighten the crossmember-to-control arm bolt to 43–58 ft. lbs. (59–78 Nm) only after the vehicle is on the ground with the chassis loaded.

6. Install the castle nut on the ball joint and tighten to 29 ft. lbs. (39 Nm).

7. Temporarily install the tension rod-to-control arm bolt. Then, install the tension rod-to-bracket bolt and tighten to 40–54 ft. lbs. (54–74 Nm). Now, tighten the tension rod-to-control arm bolt to 54–69 ft. lbs. (74–93 Nm).

➡ It is very important that the tension rod bolts be tightened in the order given in the text. If the tightening sequence is reversed, the tension rod will interfere with the bracket causing unusual noise.

8. Install the wheels. If components were replaced, have the alignment checked.

Loyale, STD. and XT

1. Raise and support the vehicle safely. Remove the tire and wheel assembly.

2. As required, remove the parking brake cable from the lower control arm assembly.

3. Remove the bolt that retains the stabilizer assembly to the lower control arm.

4. Remove the front exhaust pipe, as necessary to gain working clearance.

5. Properly support the lower control arm assembly. Remove the ball joint from its mounting.

6. Remove the lower control arm to crossmember retaining bolt. Remove the lower control arm from the vehicle.

To Install:

7. Install the lower control arm. Tighten the retaining bolt to 43–51 ft. lbs. (59–69 Nm) only after the vehicle is on the ground with the chassis loaded.

8. Install the ball joint and tighten the castle nut to 18–22 ft. lbs. (25–29 Nm). Install any exhaust system components previously removed.

9. Install the stabilizer assembly and tighten the bolts to 14–22 ft. lbs. (20–29 Nm). Install the parking brake cable bracket.

10. Install the wheels, lower the vehicle and check the alignment.

Legacy

1. Raise and safely support the front of vehicle.

2. Remove the wheel and tire assembly.

3. Disconnect the stabilizer link and the transverse link.

4. Remove the ball joint-to-housing retaining bolt and remove the ball joint end from the housing.

5. Remove the nuts (not the bolts) that retain the transverse link to the crossmember.

6. Remove the 2 bolts securing the rear of the transverse link to the chassis.

7. Remove the bolts from the transverse link and lower it from the vehicle.

To Install:

8. Install the transverse link into position and loosely install the 2 bolts that retain the link to the chassis.

> **⁕⁕⁕ CAUTION**
>
> **All of the retaining nuts used are of the self-locking type and must be replaced when they are removed. Failure to replace the bolts may cause the retaining bolts to work loose and cause loss of vehicle control and personal injury**

9. Install the bolts used to retain the transverse link to the crossmember and loosely install the nuts.

10. Install the ball joint into the housing. Tighten the ball joint pinch bolt to 29–43 ft. lbs. (39–59 Nm).

11. Connect the stabilizer link to the transverse link and loosely install the bolts.

12. The suspension bolts must be tightened in the following order:

    a. Transverse link-to-stabilizer: 14–22 ft. lbs. (20–29 Nm).

    b. Transverse link-to-crossmember: 61–83 ft. lbs. (83–113 Nm).

    c. Transverse link rear bushing-to-chassis: 145–217 ft. lbs. (196–294 Nm).

13. Move the transverse link back and forth until the clearance between the link and bushing is 1–1.5mm. The torque for the transverse link end bushing is 152–195 ft. lbs. (206–265 Nm).

14. Install the wheel and lower the vehicle.

SVX

1. Raise and safely support the front of the vehicle.

2. Remove the front wheel.

3. Separate the ball joint from the housing.

4. Remove the rear control arm support bolts.

5. Remove the left and right retaining bolts and lower the arm from the vehicle.

To Install:

> **⁕⁕⁕ CAUTION**
>
> **All of the retaining nuts used are of the self-locking type and must be replaced when they are removed. Failure to replace the bolts may cause the retaining bolts to work loose and cause loss of vehicle control and personal injury**

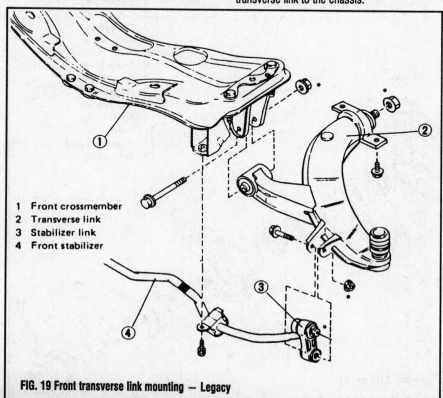

1 Front crossmember
2 Transverse link
3 Stabilizer link
4 Front stabilizer

FIG. 19 Front transverse link mounting — Legacy

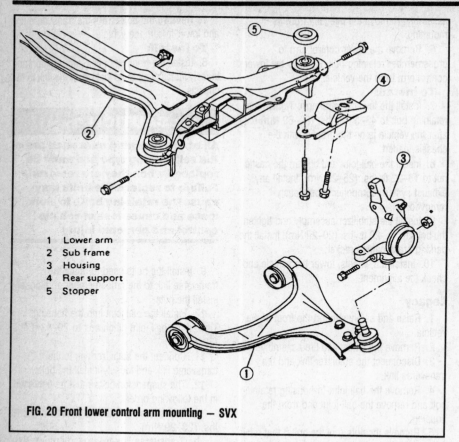

1 Lower arm
2 Sub frame
3 Housing
4 Rear support
5 Stopper

FIG. 20 Front lower control arm mounting — SVX

6. Install the lower control arm assembly and the rear support bolts. Keep all of the bolts loose.

7. Install the ball joint to the housing and loosely install the retaining bolt.

➡ **The suspension bolts must be tightened with the vehicle on the ground and the weight of the vehicle on the suspension.**

8. Install the wheel and lower the vehicle to the ground.

9. Tighten the ball joint retaining bolt to 33–43 ft. lbs. (45–59 Nm). Tighten the rear support-to-sub frame bolts to 93–123 ft. lbs. (127–167 Nm). Tighten the lower arm rear retaining bolts to 56–73 ft. lbs. (76–100 Nm).

Knuckle and Spindle

REMOVAL & INSTALLATION

◆ SEE FIGS. 21–25

1. Disconnect the ground cable from the battery.

2. Apply the parking brake.

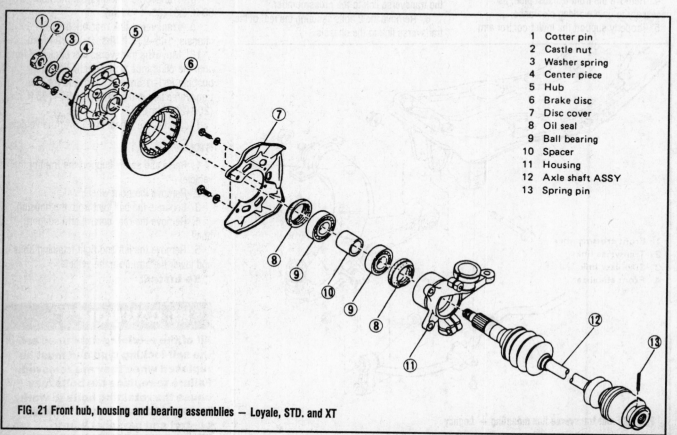

1 Cotter pin
2 Castle nut
3 Washer spring
4 Center piece
5 Hub
6 Brake disc
7 Disc cover
8 Oil seal
9 Ball bearing
10 Spacer
11 Housing
12 Axle shaft ASSY
13 Spring pin

FIG. 21 Front hub, housing and bearing assemblies — Loyale, STD. and XT

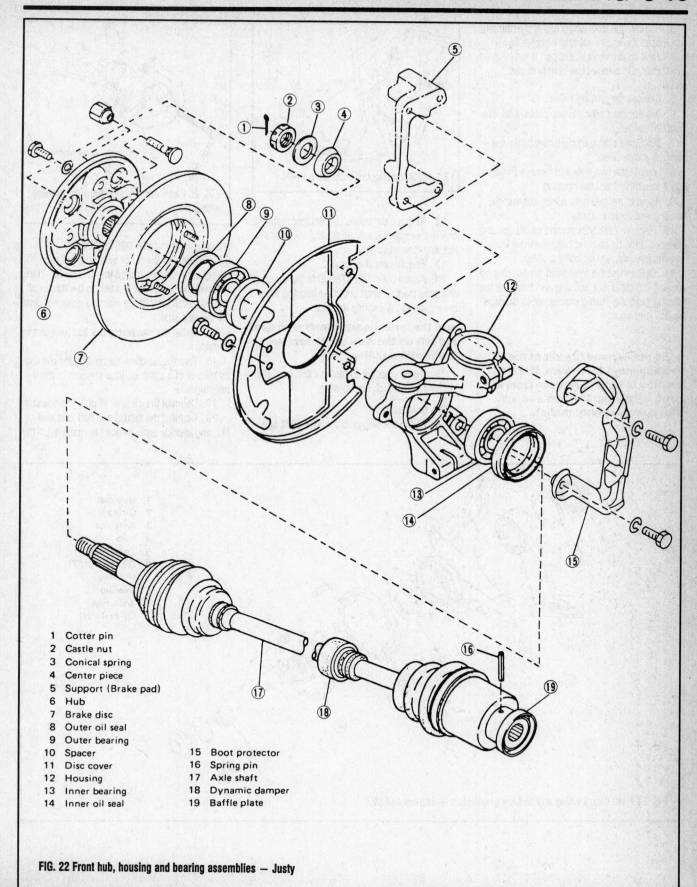

1 Cotter pin
2 Castle nut
3 Conical spring
4 Center piece
5 Support (Brake pad)
6 Hub
7 Brake disc
8 Outer oil seal
9 Outer bearing

10 Spacer	15 Boot protector
11 Disc cover	16 Spring pin
12 Housing	17 Axle shaft
13 Inner bearing	18 Dynamic damper
14 Inner oil seal	19 Baffle plate

FIG. 22 Front hub, housing and bearing assemblies — Justy

3. Remove the front wheel cap and cotter pin, and loosen the castle nut and wheel nuts.

4. Jack up the vehicle, support it with jackstands and remove the front tires and wheels.

5. Release the parking brake.

6. Pull out the parking brake cable outer clip from the caliper.

7. Disconnect the parking brake cable end from the caliper lever.

8. Loosen the two nuts and remove the disc brake assembly from the housing.

9. Remove the two nuts which connect the housing and damper strut.

10. Remove the cotter pin and castle nut, and disconnect the tie rod end ball joint from the housing knuckle arm by using a puller.

11. Disconnect the strut from the housing by opening the slit of the housing and lowering the housing gradually, being careful not to damage the ball joint boot.

➡ **Do not expand the slit of the housing more than 4mm. If the housing is hard to remove from the strut, lightly tap the hub and disc with a large rubber mallet.**

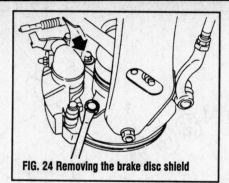

FIG. 24 Removing the brake disc shield

12. Remove the castle nut, washer spring center piece on the axle shaft, and take out the hub and disc assembly.

13. Remove the disc cover.

14. Attach puller 926470000 to the housing and drive the axle shaft out of the housing toward the engine at the bearing location.

➡ **If the inner bearing and/or oil seal are left on the axle shaft, remove them with a puller.**

15. Disconnect the transverse link from the housing, and detach the housing.

To Install:

16. Fit the housing onto the axle shaft and

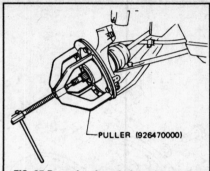

PULLER (926470000)

FIG. 25 Removing the axle from the housing with a puller

attach spacer installer 925130000 or 922430000, on the outer bearing inner race taking care not to damage the oil seal lip. Then, connect the rod of the installer to the thread of the axle shaft so that the housing does not drop off the axle shaft.

17. Install the transverse link ball joint to the housing.

18. Turn the handle while holding the rod end, by means of a spanner, thus pushing in the housing.

19. Connect the damper strut to the housing.

20. Connect the tie rod end ball joint and housing knuckle arm. Torque the castle nut. After

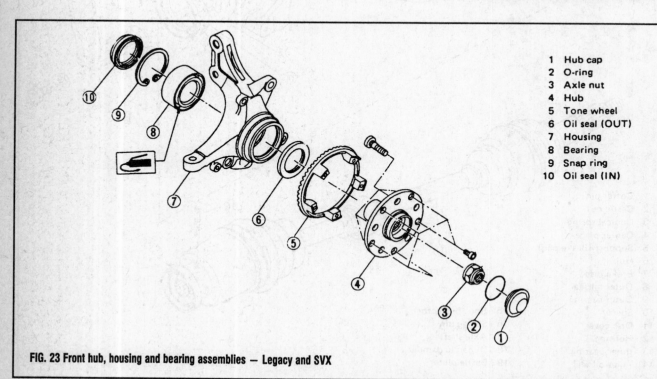

1 Hub cap
2 O-ring
3 Axle nut
4 Hub
5 Tone wheel
6 Oil seal (OUT)
7 Housing
8 Bearing
9 Snap ring
10 Oil seal (IN)

FIG. 23 Front hub, housing and bearing assemblies — Legacy and SVX

tightening the nut to the specified torque, further torque the nut just enough to align the holes of the nut and ball stud. Then insert a cotter pin into the ball stud and bend it around the castle nut.

21. Install the disc cover to the housing.

22. Install the hub and disc assembly onto the axle shaft.

➡ **Be sure to press the hub and disc assembly onto the axle shaft until the end surface of the hub contacts the ball bearing. If the assembly is hard to press, rotate it to locate the point where it is easily pressed.**

23. Install the brake caliper to the housing assembly.

24. Connect the parking brake cable to the brake assembly.

25. Apply the parking brake.

26. Position the center piece, washer spring and castle nut in this order onto the axle shaft and tighten the castle nut to 145 ft. lbs. (196 Nm) on all models except the SVX and Legacy, on the SVX and Legacy tighten the castle nut to 123–152 ft. lbs. (167–206 Nm) then insert a new cotter pin and bend it around the nut.

➡ **After tightening the nut to the specified torque, retighten it further until a slot of the castle nut is aligned to the hole in the axle shaft.**

27. Install the wheel and hub cap.

28. Remove the jack stands, lower the vehicle and reconnect the negative battery cable.

Front Hub and Bearing

REMOVAL, PACKING AND INSTALLATION

♦ SEE FIGS. 26–32

Except Justy

1. Refer to the "Front Halfshaft, Removal and Installation" procedures in this section and remove the halfshaft from the vehicle; be sure to remove the steering knuckle from the vehicle.

2. Using your finger, move the spacer (inside the steering knuckle) in the radial direction.

3. Using a brass bar, insert it through the inner race of the outer bearing, then tap the bar with a hammer to drive out the bearing (with the oil seal); discard the bearing and the oil seal.

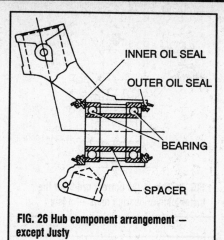

FIG. 26 Hub component arrangement — except Justy

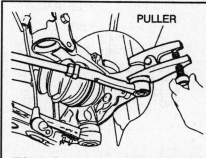

FIG. 26a Separating the ball joint with a ball joint puller

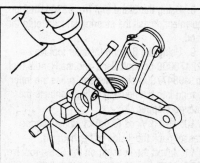

FIG. 27 Remove the bearing race by tapping it out, using a bar and a hammer — except Justy

4. Remove the spacer and the inner bearing.

5. Position the brass bar through the outer race of the inner bearing, then using a hammer, drive the out the bearing (with the oil seal); discard the bearing and the oil seal.

To Install:

6. Clean and inspect the parts for wear, cracks and/or damage; if necessary, replace the damaged parts.

7. Using new bearings, pack them with wheel bearing grease.

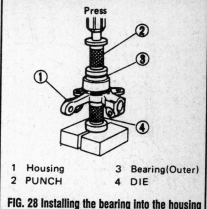

FIG. 28 Installing the bearing into the housing using a die and press — Except Justy

8. Using the Die tool No. 926490000 or equivalent, install the steering knuckle onto the die.

9. Using a press and the Punch tool No. 926490000 or equivalent, press the outer bearing into the housing until it contacts the housing stopper.

10. Using 1/2 oz (14g) of wheel bearing grease, pack the inside of the housing.

11. Invert the housing on the Die tool No. 926490000 or equivalent, and install the spacer.

12. Using a press and the Punch tool No. 926490000 or equivalent, press the inner bearing into the housing until it contacts the housing stopper.

13. Using a press and the Punch tool No. 926490000 or equivalent, position the new outer oil seal in the punch tool so that the lip faces the groove, then press it into the steering knuckle housing, until it comes in contact with the bearing end face.

14. Invert the steering knuckle housing onto the Punch tool No. 926490000 or equivalent, so that the seal lip faces the groove.

15. Using a press and the Die tool No. 926490000 or equivalent, press the new inner oil seal into the steering knuckle housing, until it comes in contact with the bearing end face.

16. To install the steering knuckle, fit the housing onto the axle shaft and attach a spacer of the installation tool No. 922430000 or equivalent, on the outer bearing inner race; be careful not to damage the oil seal. Thread the axle shaft onto the installation tool, then turn the handle to draw the axle into the housing, until it is seated.

17. Install the remaining components in reverse order.

Justy

1. Refer to the "Front Halfshaft, Removal and Installation" procedures in this section and

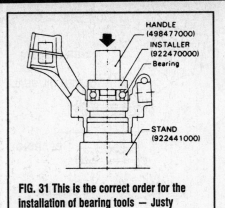

FIG. 31 This is the correct order for the installation of bearing tools — Justy

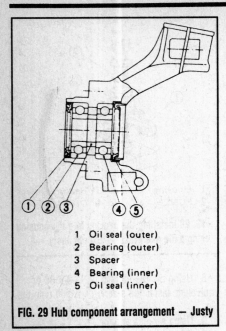

1 Oil seal (outer)
2 Bearing (outer)
3 Spacer
4 Bearing (inner)
5 Oil seal (inner)

FIG. 29 Hub component arrangement — Justy

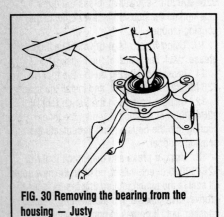

FIG. 30 Removing the bearing from the housing — Justy

remove the halfshaft from the vehicle; be sure to remove the steering knuckle from the vehicle.

2. Using your finger, move the spacer (inside the steering knuckle) in the radial direction.

3. Using a brass bar, insert it through the inner race of the outer bearing, then tap the bar with a hammer to drive out the bearing (with the oil seal); discard the bearing and the oil seal.

4. Remove the spacer and the inner bearing.

5. Position the brass bar through the outer race of the inner bearing, then using a hammer, drive the out the bearing (with the oil seal); discard the bearing and the oil seal.

To Install:

6. Clean and inspect the parts for wear, cracks and/or damage; if necessary, replace the damaged parts.

7. Using new bearings, pack them with grease.

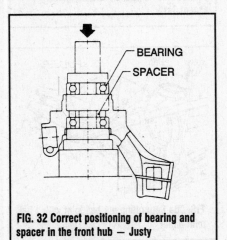

FIG. 32 Correct positioning of bearing and spacer in the front hub — Justy

8. Using the Stand tool No. 922441000 or equivalent, install the steering knuckle onto the stand.

9. Using the Bearing Installer tool No. 922470000 or equivalent, and the Handle tool No. 498477000 or equivalent, press the inner bearing into the housing until it contacts the housing stopper.

10. Using ¼ oz (6.8g) of wheel bearing grease, pack the inside of the housing.

11. Invert the housing on the Stand tool No. 922441000 or equivalent, and install the spacer.

12. Using the Bearing Installer tool No. 922470000 or equivalent, and the Handle tool No. 498477000 or equivalent, press the outer bearing into the housing until it contacts the housing stopper.

13. Using a press and the Oil Seal Installer tool No. 922450000 or equivalent, press the new outer oil seal into the steering knuckle housing, until it comes in contact with the bearing end face.

14. Invert the steering knuckle housing.

15. Using a press and the Oil Seal Installer tool No. 922460000 or equivalent, press the new inner oil seal into the steering knuckle housing, until it comes in contact with the bearing end face.

16. To complete the installation, reverse the remaining removal procedures.

Front End Alignment

Front wheel alignment (also known as front end geometry) is the position of the front wheels relative to each other and to the vehicle. Correct alignment must be maintained to provide safe, accurate steering, vehicle stability and minimum tire wear. The factors which determine wheel alignment are interdependent. Therefore, when one of the factors is adjusted, the others must be adjusted to compensate.

CASTER

Caster angle is the number of degrees that a line, drawn through the center of the upper and lower ball joints and viewed from the side, can be tilted forward or backward. Positive caster means that the top of the upper ball joint is tilted toward the rear of the vehicle and negative caster means that it is tilted toward the front. A vehicle with a slightly positive caster setting will have its lower ball joint pivot slightly ahead of the tire's center. This will assist the directional stability of the vehicle by causing a drag at the bottom center of the wheel when it turns, thereby, resisting the turn and tending to hold the wheel steady in whatever direction the vehicle is pointed. Therefore, the vehicle is less susceptible to cross winds and road surface deviations. A vehicle with too much (positive) caster will be hard to steer and shimmy at low speeds. A vehicle with insufficient (negative) caster may tend to be unstable at high speeds and may respond erratically when the brakes are applied.

CAMBER

Camber angle is the number of degrees that the wheel itself is tilted from a vertical line when viewed from the front. Positive camber means that the top of the wheel is slanted away from the vehicle, while negative camber means that it is tilted toward the vehicle. Ordinarily, a vehicle will have a slight positive camber when unloaded. Then, when the vehicle is loaded and rolling down the road, the wheels will just about be vertical. If you started with no camber at all, then loading the vehicle would produce a negative camber. Excessive camber (either positive or negative) will produce rapid tire wear, since one side of the tire will be more heavily loaded than the other side.

STEERING AXIS INCLINATION

Steering axis inclination is the number of degrees that a line drawn through the upper and lower ball joints and viewed from the front, is tilted to the left or right. This, in combination with caster, is responsible for the directional stability and self-centering of the steering. As the steering knuckle swings from lock-to-lock, the spindle generates an arc, causing the vehicle to be raised when its turned from the straight-ahead position. The reason the vehicle body must rise is straight-forward: since the wheel is in contact with the ground, it cannot move down. However, when it is swung away from the straight-ahead position, it must move either up or down (due to the arc generated by the steering knuckle). Not being able to move down, it must move up. Then, the weight of the vehicle acts against this lift and attempts to return the spindle to the straight-ahead position when the steering wheel is released.

TOE-IN

Toe-in is the difference (in inches) between the front and the rear of the front tires. On a vehicle with toe-in, the distance between the front wheels is less at the front than at the rear. Toe-in is normally only a few fractions of an inch, it is necessary to ensure parallel rolling of the front wheels and to prevent excessive tire wear. As the vehicle is driven at increasingly faster speeds, the steering linkage has a tendency to expand slightly, thereby, allowing the front wheels to turn out and away from each other. Therefore, initially setting the front wheels so that they are pointing slightly inward (toe-in), allows them to turn straight ahead when the vehicle is underway.

WHEEL ALIGNMENT

Year	Model	Caster Range (deg.)	Caster Preferred Setting (deg.)	Camber Range (deg.)	Camber Preferred Setting (deg.)	Toe-in (in.)	Steering Axis Inclination (deg.)
1985	2WD XT Coupe	$3^5/_{16}$P–$4^{13}/_{16}$P	$4^1/_{16}$P	$^3/_4$N–$^3/_4$P	0	$^1/_8$–$^1/_8$	NA
	4WD XT Coupe	$2^5/_8$P–$4^1/_8$P	$3^3/_8$P	$^1/_{16}$N–$1^3/_8$P	$^5/_8$P	$^3/_{64}$–$^1/_8$	NA
	2WD Sedan	$1^3/_4$P–$3^1/_4$P	$2^1/_2$P	0–$1^1/_2$P	$^3/_4$P	$^{13}/_{64}$–$^3/_{64}$	NA
	4WD Sedan with Air Sup.	$1^7/_{16}$P–$2^{15}/_{16}$P	$2^3/_{16}$P	$^7/_{16}$P–$1^{15}/_{16}$P	$1^{13}/_{16}$P	$^{13}/_{64}$–$^3/_{64}$A	NA
	4WD Sedan without Air Sup.	$1^1/_{16}$P–$2^9/_{16}$P	$1^{13}/_{16}$P	$^{15}/_{16}$P–$2^7/_{16}$P	$1^{11}/_{16}$P	$^{13}/_{64}$–$^3/_{64}$ ①	NA
	2WD SW	$1^5/_{16}$P–$2^{13}/_{16}$P	$2^1/_{16}$P	$^1/_4$P–$1^3/_4$P	1P	$^{13}/_{64}$–$^3/_{64}$ ①	NA
	4WD SW with Air Sup.	$1^7/_{16}$P–$2^{15}/_{16}$P	$2^3/_{16}$P	$^7/_{16}$P–$1^{15}/_{16}$P	$1^{13}/_{16}$P	$^{13}/_{64}$–$^3/_{64}$ ①	NA
	4WD SW without Air Sup.	$^{13}/_{16}$P–$2^5/_{16}$P	$1^9/_{16}$P	$^{15}/_{16}$P–$2^7/_{16}$P	$1^3/_4$P	$^{13}/_{64}$–$^3/_{64}$ ①	NA
	2WD Hatchback	$1^1/_4$N–$^1/_4$P	$^1/_2$N	$1^7/_{16}$P–$2^{15}/_{16}$P	$2^3/_{16}$P	$^1/_4$–$^5/_{32}$	NA
1986	2WD XT Coupe	$3^5/_{16}$P–$4^{13}/_{16}$P	$4^1/_{16}$P	$^3/_4$N–$^3/_4$P	0	$^1/_8$–$^1/_8$	NA
	4WD XT Coupe	$2^5/_8$P–$4^1/_8$P	$3^3/_8$P	$^1/_{16}$N–$1^3/_8$P	$^5/_8$P	$^3/_{64}$–$^1/_8$	NA
	2WD Sedan	$1^3/_4$P–$3^1/_4$P	$2^1/_2$P	0–$1^1/_2$P	$^3/_4$P	$^{13}/_{64}$–$^3/_{64}$ ①	NA
	4WD Sedan with Air Sup.	$1^7/_{16}$P–$2^{15}/_{16}$P	$2^3/_{16}$P	$^7/_{16}$P–$1^{15}/_{16}$P	$1^{13}/_{16}$P	$^{13}/_{64}$–$^3/_{64}$ ①	NA
	4WD Sedan without Air Sup.	$1^1/_{16}$P–$2^9/_{16}$P	$1^{13}/_{16}$P	$^{15}/_{16}$P–$2^7/_{16}$P	$1^{11}/_{16}$P	$^{13}/_{64}$–$^3/_{64}$ ①	NA
	2WD SW	$1^5/_{16}$P–$2^{13}/_{16}$P	$2^1/_{16}$P	$^1/_4$P–$1^3/_4$P	1P	$^{13}/_{64}$–$^3/_{64}$ ①	NA
	4WD SW with Air Sup.	$1^7/_{16}$P–$2^{15}/_{16}$P	$2^3/_{16}$P	$^7/_{16}$P–$1^{15}/_{16}$P	$1^{13}/_{16}$P	$^{13}/_{64}$–$^3/_{64}$ ①	NA
	4WD SW without Air Sup.	$^{13}/_{16}$P–$2^5/_{16}$P	$1^9/_{16}$P	$^{15}/_{16}$P–$2^7/_{16}$P	$1^3/_4$P	$^{13}/_{64}$–$^3/_{64}$ ①	NA
	2WD Hatchback	$1^1/_4$N–$^1/_4$P	$^1/_2$N	$1^7/_{16}$P–$2^{15}/_{16}$P	$2^3/_{16}$P	$^1/_4$–$^5/_{32}$	NA

WHEEL ALIGNMENT

Year	Model	Caster Range (deg.)	Caster Preferred Setting (deg.)	Camber Range (deg.)	Camber Preferred Setting (deg.)	Toe-in (in.)	Steering Axis Inclination (deg.)
1987	2WD XT Coupe	3⁵/₁₆P–4¹³/₁₆P	4¹/₁₆P	¾N–¾P	0	⅛–⅛	NA
	4WD XT Coupe	2⅝P–4⅛P	3⅜P	1/16N–1 3/8P	⅝P	3/64–⅛	NA
	2WD Sedan	1¾P–3¼P	2½P	0–1½P	¾P	13/64–3/64 ①	NA
	4WD Sedan with Air Sup.	1 7/16P–2 15/16P	2 3/16P	7/16P–1 15/16P	1 13/16P	5/64–5/16 ①	NA
	4WD Sedan without Air Sup.	1 1/16P–2 9/16P	1 13/16P	15/16P–2 7/16P	1 11/16P	5/64–5/16 ①	NA
	2WD SW	1 5/16P–2 13/16P	2 1/16P	¼P–1¾P	1 ⑯	13/64–3/64 ①	NA
	4WD SW with Air Sup.	1 7/16P–2 15/16P	2 3/16P	7/16P–1 15/16P	1 13/16P	5/64–5/15 ①	NA
	4WD SW without Air Sup.	13/16P–2 5/16P	1 9/16P	15/16P–2 7/16P	1¾P	5/64–5/16 ①	NA
	Justy	1½P–3½P	2½P	5/16N–1 11/16P	11/16P	3/32–½ ①	NA
1988	2WD XT Coupe	3 15/16P–4 13/16P	4 1/16P	¾N–¾P	0	⅛–⅛	NA
	4WD XT Coupe (4 cylinder)	2⅝P–4⅛P	3⅜P	1/16N–1 3/8P	⅝P	3/64–⅛	NA
	4WD XT Coupe (6 cylinder)	2¾P–4¼P	3½P	1/16P–1 9/16P	13/16P	3/64–13/64	NA
	2WD Sedan	1¾P–3¼P	2½P	0–1½P	¾P	13/64–3/64 ①	NA
	4WD Sedan with Air Susp.	1 7/16P–2 15/16P	2 3/16P	7/16P–1 15/16P	1 13/16P	5/64–5/16 ①	NA
	4WD Sedan without Air Susp.	1 1/16P–2 9/16P	1 13/16P	15/16P–2 7/16P	1 11/16P	5/64–5/16 ①	NA
	2WD SW	1 5/16P–2 13/16P	2 1/16P	¼P–1¾P	1P	13/64–3/64	NA
	4WD SW with Air Susp.	1 7/16P–2 15/16P	2 3/16P	7/16P–1 15/16P	1 13/16P	5/64–5/15 ①	NA
	4WD SW	13/16P–2 5/16P	1 9/16P	15/16P–2 7/16P	1¾P	5/64–5/16 ①	NA
	Justy	1½P–3½P	2½P	5/16N–1 11/16P	11/16P	3/32–½ ①	NA
1989	2WD XT Coupe	3 15/16P–4 13/16P	4 1/16P	¾N–¾P	0	⅛–⅛ ①	NA
	4WD XT Coupe (4 cylinder)	2⅝P–4⅛P	3⅜P	1/16N–1 3/8P	⅝P	⅜ ① –⅛ ①	NA
	4WD XT Coupe (6 cylinder)	2¾P–4¼P	3½P	1/16P–1 9/16P	13/16P	⅜ ① –⅛ ①	NA
	2WD Sedan	1¾P–3¼P	2½P	0–1½P	¾P	¼–1/16 ①	NA
	4WD Sedan with Air Susp.	1 7/16P–2 15/16P	2 3/16P	7/16P–1 15/16P	1 13/16P	1/16 ① –3/16 ①	NA
	4WD Sedan without Air Susp.	1 1/16P–2 9/16P	1 13/16P	15/16P–2 7/16P	1 11/16P	1/16 ① –3/16 ①	NA
	2WD SW	1 5/16P–2 13/16P	2 1/16P	¼P–1¾P	1P	1/16 ① –3/16 ①	NA
	4WD SW with Air Susp.	1 7/16P–2 15/16P	2 3/16P	7/16P–1 15/16P	1 13/16P	1/16 ① –3/16 ①	NA
	4WD SW	13/16P–2 5/16P	1 9/16P	15/16P–2 7/16P	1¾P	1/16 ① –3/16 ①	NA
	Justy	1½P–3½P	2½P	5/16N–1 11/16P	11/16P	5/16–1/16 ①	NA
	Legacy FWD Sedan	2 1/16P–4 1/16P ③	3 1/16P ④	¾N–¼P	¼N	1/16–1/16 ①	NA
	Legacy 4WD Sedan ②	2P–4P	3P	½N–½P	0	1/16–1/16 ①	NA

WHEEL ALIGNMENT

Year	Model	Caster Range (deg.)	Caster Preferred Setting (deg.)	Camber Range (deg.)	Camber Preferred Setting (deg.)	Toe-in (in.)	Steering Axis Inclination (deg.)
1990	2WD XT Coupe	3 15/16P–4 13/16P	4 1/16P	3/4N–3/4P	0	1/8–1/8 ①	NA
	4WD XT Coupe (4 cylinder)	2 5/8P–4 1/8P	3 3/8P	1/16N–1 3/8P	5/8P	3/8 ① –1/8 ①	NA
	4WD XT Coupe (6 cylinder)	2 3/4P–4 1/4P	3 1/2P	1/16P–1 9/16P	13/16P	3/8 ① –1/8 ①	NA
	2WD Loyale Sedan	1 3/4P–3 1/4P	2 1/2P	0–1 1/2P	3/4P	1/4–1/16 ①	NA
	4WD Loyale Sedan without Air Susp.	1 1/16P–2 9/16P	1 13/16P	15/16P–2 7/16P	1 11/16P	1/16 ① –3/16 ①	NA
	2WD Loyale SW	15/16P–2 13/16P	2 1/16P	1/4P–1 3/4P	1P	1/16 ① –3/16 ①	NA
	4WD Loyale SW	13/16P–2 5/16P	1 9/16P	15/16P–2 7/16P	1 3/4P	1/16 ① –3/16 ①	NA
	Justy	1 1/2P–3 1/2P	2 1/2P	5/16N–1 11/16P	11/16P	5/16–1/16 ①	NA
	Legacy FWD Sedan	2 1/16P–4 1/16P ③	3 1/16P ④	3/4N–1/4P	1/4N	1/16–1/16 ①	NA
	Legacy 4WD Sedan ②	2P–4P	3P	1/2N–1/2P	0	1/16–1/16 ①	NA
	Legacy 4WD Wagon	1 3/4P–3 3/4P	2 3/4P	1/2N–1/2P	0	1/16–1/16 ①	NA
1991	2WD XT Coupe	3 15/16P–4 13/16P	4 1/16P	3/4N–3/4P	0	1/8–1/8 ①	NA
	4WD XT Coupe (4 cylinder)	2 5/8P–4 1/8P	3 3/8P	1/16N–1 3/8P	5/8P	3/8 ① –1/8 ①	NA
	4WD XT Coupe (6 cylinder)	2 3/4P–4 1/4P	3 1/2P	1/16P–1 9/16P	13/16P	3/8 ① –1/8 ①	NA
	2WD Loyale Sedan	1 3/4P–3 1/4P	2 1/2P	0–1 1/2P	3/4P	1/4–1/16 ①	NA
	4WD Loyale Sedan without Air Susp.	1 1/16P–2 9/16P	1 13/16P	15/16P–2 7/16P	1 11/16P	1/16 ① –3/16 ①	NA
	2WD Loyale SW	15/16P–2 13/16P	2 1/16P	1/4P–1 3/4P	1P	1/16 ① –3/16 ①	NA
	4WD Loyale SW	13/16P–2 5/16P	1 9/16P	15/16P–2 7/16P	1 3/4P	1/16 ① –3/16 ①	NA
	Justy	1 1/2P–3 1/2P	2 1/2P	5/16N–1 11/16P	11/16P	5/16–1/16 ①	NA
	Legacy FWD Sedan	2 1/16P–4 1/16P ③	3 1/16P ④	3/4N–1/4P	1/4N	1/16–1/16 ①	NA
	Legacy 4WD Sedan ②	2P–4P	3P	1/2N–1/2P	0	1/16–1/16 ①	NA
	Legacy 4WD Wagon	1 3/4P–3 3/4P	2 3/4P	1/2N–1/2P	0	1/16–1/16 ①	NA
1992	2WD XT Coupe	3 15/16P–4 13/16P	4 1/16P	3/4N–3/4P	0	1/8–1/8 ①	NA
	4WD XT Coupe (4 cylinder)	2 5/8P–4 1/8P	3 3/8P	1/16N–1 3/8P	5/8P	3/8 ① –1/8 ①	NA
	4WD XT Coupe (6 cylinder)	2 3/4P–4 1/4P	3 1/2P	1/16P–1 9/16P	13/16P	3/8 ① –1/8 ①	NA
	2WD Loyale Sedan	1 3/4P–3 1/4P	2 1/2P	0–1 1/2P	3/4P	1/4–1/16 ①	NA
	4WD Loyale Sedan without Air Susp.	1 1/16P–2 9/16P	1 13/16P	15/16P–2 7/16P	1 11/16P	1/16 ① –3/16 ①	NA
	2WD Loyale SW	15/16P–2 13/16P	2 1/16P	1/4P–1 3/4P	1P	1/16 ① –3/16 ①	NA
	4WD Loyale SW	13/16P–2 5/16P	1 9/16P	15/16P–2 7/16P	1 3/4P	1/16 ① –3/16 ①	NA
	Justy	1 1/2P–3 1/2P	2 1/2P	5/16N–1 11/16P	11/16P	5/16–1/16 ①	NA
	Legacy FWD Sedan	2 1/16P–4 1/16P ③	3 1/16P ④	3/4N–1/4P	1/4N	1/16–1/16 ①	NA

WHEEL ALIGNMENT

Year	Model	Caster Range (deg.)	Caster Preferred Setting (deg.)	Camber Range (deg.)	Camber Preferred Setting (deg.)	Toe-in (in.)	Steering Axis Inclination (deg.)
1992	Legacy 4WD Sedan ②	2P–4P	3P	½N–½P	0	1/16–1/16 ①	NA
	Legacy 4WD Wagon	1¾P–3¾P	2¾P	½N–½P	0	1/16–1/16 ①	NA
	SVX	1¾P–3¾P	2¾P	½N–½P	0	1/16–1/16 ①	NA

Air Susp.—Air suspension
SW—Station Wagon
N—Negative
P—Positive
① Toe out
② Same with air suspension
③ Legacy FWD Wagon—1¹³/₁₆P–3¹³/₁₆P
④ Legacy FWD Wagon—2¹³/₁₆P

PNEUMATIC (AIR) SUSPENSION SYSTEM

➡ **The basic mechanical components of the air suspension system are identical to those of the standard strut type suspension. The only differences in the two systems are those directly related to the operation of the air suspension system itself. The servicing of the air suspension system components will be covered here, the rest of the components can be serviced by following the strut type suspension service procedures found earlier in this section.**

GENERAL DESCRIPTION

◆ SEE FIGS. 33–34

The 4WD models are equipped with an air suspension and height control system to compensate for off-road conditions and vehicle load. The system has 2 height control settings (NORMAL AND HIGH), which range from 30–40mm depending on the vehicle. To achieve this, the air volume in each air spring is adjusted according to a vehicle height sensor located within the shock.

SYSTEM COMPONENTS

The system uses a selector switch which changes the vehicle height to NORMAL or HIGH, a warning indicator which indicates the vehicle height and also illuminates in case of system malfunction, vehicle height sensors built into each air spring which detect proper vehicle height at each wheel, 6 solenoid valves, a control unit which opens and closes the solenoid in the proper order by measuring the signals from the height sensor, an air tank and compressor which are operated by a pressure switch, a drier and air lines.

Diagnosis and Testing

◆ SEE FIGS. 35–40

SELF DIAGNOSTICS

The Air Suspension systems incorporates a function which will display any malfunctions in the system by illuminating and blinking the height indicator. If there is any abnormality in the system the height indicator will begin to blink and the system should then be put into self-diagnostics to determine the problem. To start the self-diagnostics function proceed as follows:

STD. and XT

1. Turn the ignition switch OFF and the height selector switch to ON (HIGH).
2. Turn the ignition switch ON, then turn the ignition switch OFF.
3. Set the height selector switch to the OFF (NORMAL) position.
4. Turn the ignition switch ON, then turn the ignition switch OFF.
5. Set the height selector switch to the ON (HIGH) position and turn the ignition switch ON.
6. The system is now set in the self-diagnosis mode.
7. Determine the system malfunction code by observing the number of blinks of the vehicle height sensor.
8. Check and correct any malfunctions.
9. To clear memory and reset the system, turn the ignition switch OFF and disconnect the negative battery terminal for 10 seconds.

Legacy

1. Turn the ignition switch OFF.
2. Connect a jumper from terminal 1 to the ground terminal of the diagnosis connector located below the instrument panel lower cover.
3. Turn the ignition switch ON.
4. The trouble codes will then be indicated by blinking of the height indicator lamp.
5. Check and correct any malfunctions.
6. To clear memory and reset the system, turn the ignition switch OFF and disconnect the negative battery terminal for 10 seconds.

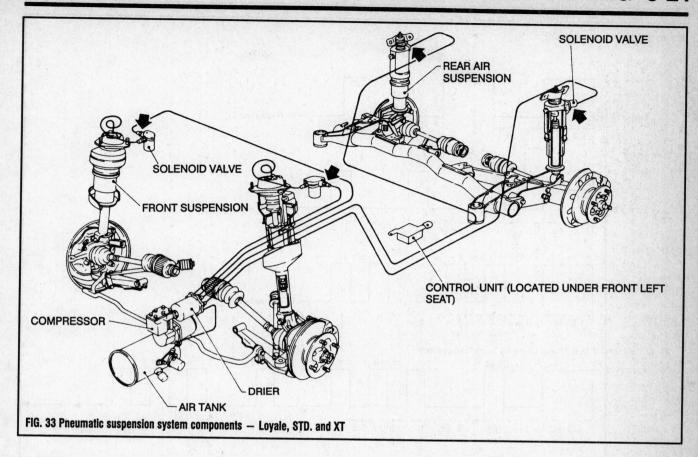

FIG. 33 Pneumatic suspension system components — Loyale, STD. and XT

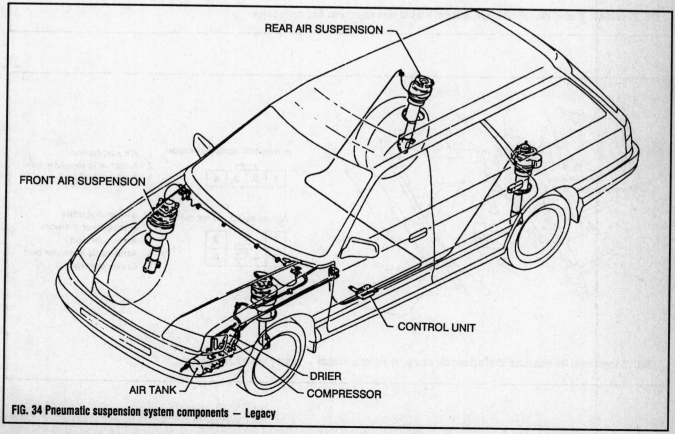

FIG. 34 Pneumatic suspension system components — Legacy

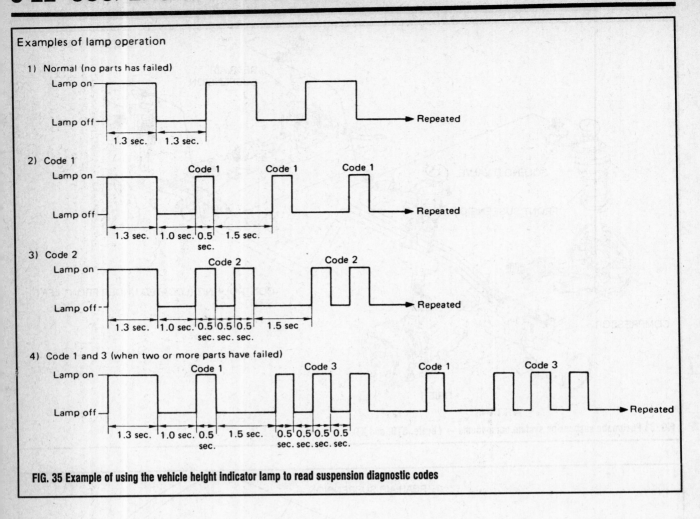

FIG. 35 Example of using the vehicle height indicator lamp to read suspension diagnostic codes

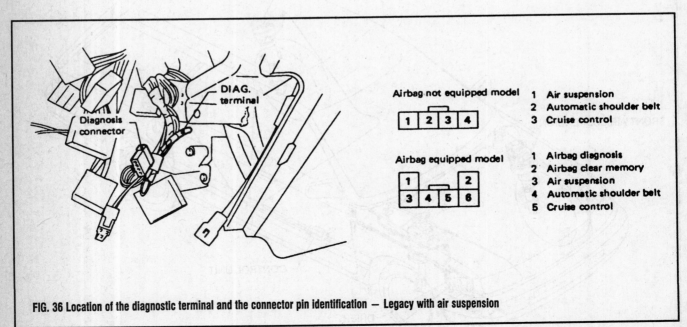

FIG. 36 Location of the diagnostic terminal and the connector pin identification — Legacy with air suspension

AIR SUSPENSION SYSTEM TROUBLE CODES

Code No.	Item to diagnose	Trouble	Cause
1	Height sensor Front Right	High and Low signals for vehicle height were entered simultaneously.	Faulty vehicle height sensor. Short harness.
2	Height sensor Front Left		
3	Height sensor Rear Right		
4	Height sensor Rear Left		
5	Solenoid valve Front Right	Output continued for 10 minutes.	Faulty solenoid valve. Air line leaks air or is clogged. Faulty control unit. Short harness of faulty wiring.
6	Solenoid valve Front Left		
7	Solenoid valve Rear Right		
8	Solenoid valve Rear Left		
9	Compressor relay		Faulty pressure switch. Faulty compressor relay. Leakage from air tank. Defective charge solenoid valve Short harness or faulty wiring. Faulty control unit.
10	Exhaust solenoid valve	Output was emitting while diagnosis code 5, 6, 7 or 8 was indicated.	Clogged air line. Faulty solenoid valve. Short harness or faulty wiring. Faulty control unit.

AIR SUSPENSION SYSTEM TROUBLESHOOTING

Symptom	Trouble	Cause
Car height does not change.	Car height does not change height control switch is pushed with ignition switch ON. However, the following are not indications of trouble (The height indicator light does not blink): ① Non-operation mode • While making a turn • When one wheel is stuck in a ditch or rides on an obstacle — — This can be corrected after the car is removed from the ditch or obstacle. ② While car is being driven at a speed greater than 90 km/h (56 MPH). ③ Frequent shifting of car height (more than 6 times in 10 minutes) — — This can be reset by turning ignition switch OFF. The car height up speed will be reduced 2 to 5 mm (0.08 to 0.20 in) per 10 sec if five or more occupants [5 persons + 100 kg (221 lb) load] are in the car. This reduction of up speed is not faulty. It will be corrected when the load is reduced and the ignition switch is turned OFF for resetting.	Faulty height control switch
		Faulty vehicle height sensor
		Faulty control unit
		Solenoid valve coil broken
		Faulty electrical circuit
		Solenoid valve sticking
		Clogged air line
		Faulty compressor or pressure switch
		Air discharge solenoid valve sticking
	Car does not return to NORMAL from the HIGH position while driving at a speed greater than 90 km/h (56 MPH).	Vehicle speed sensor malfunctioning
		Faulty control unit
		Faulty electrical circuit

AIR SUSPENSION SYSTEM TROUBLESHOOTING CONTINUED

Symptom		Trouble	Cause
Car height changes repeatedly during operation.		Car height changes repeatedly during operation without using height control switch.	Faulty control unit
			Faulty height control switch circuit
			Faulty control unit power circuit
			Air leakage from air suspension ASSY
			Faulty vehicle height sensor (monitors the NORMAL position only)
Car height increases.	Ignition switch OFF	Front or rear of car rises if car is left as it is.	Improper sealing of affected air suspension solenoid valves or charge solenoid valve
	Ignition switch ON	Front or rear of car rises abnormally.	Faulty vehicle height sensor
			Faulty control unit
			Broken solenoid valve coil/affected air suspension solenoid valve or discharge solenoid
			Faulty electrical circuit
			Sticking solenoid valve/affected air suspension solenoid valve or discharge solenoid valve
			Clogged air line
		Car height is set to HIGH without pushing height control switch. However, during high-speed operation [90 km/h (56 MPH), min.], car height is automatically set to NORMAL and, during deceleration [60 km/h (37 MPH), max.] car height is again set to HIGH. This is not an indication of trouble.	Faulty control unit
			Faulty height control switch circuit
			Faulty control unit power circuit
		When ignition switch is turned ON, car height is always set to HIGH.	"B" power supply connector (for clock) disconnected
			Breaks in "B" power supply circuit
			Faulty control unit
Car height decreases.	Ignition switch OFF	Front of car height decreases when car is left as it is.	Air leakage from air pipe or joint on top of strut mount
			Air leakage from front solenoid valve or faulty seal
			Air leakage from front air suspension ASSY

AIR SUSPENSION SYSTEM TROUBLESHOOTING CONTINUED

Symptom		Trouble		Cause	
Car height decreases. (Cont'd)	Ignition switch ON	Rear of car height decreases when car is left as it is.		Air leakage from rear solenoid valve or faulty seal	
				Air leakage from rear air suspension ASSY	
		Front or rear of car is abnormally low.	Compressor does not operate.		
			Compressor operates.	Car is set to the NORMAL position when left unattended with ignition switch ON for 5 minutes.	Air leakage from tank ASSY
					Air leakage from air line
				Car is not set to the HIGH position when left unattended with ignition switch ON for 5 minutes.	Faulty vehicle height sensor
					Faulty control unit
					Broken solenoid valve coil
					Faulty electrical circuit
					Sticking solenoid valve
					Clogged air line
					Air leakage from air line
		Car height decreases to NORMAL without pushing height control switch. During high-speed operation, [90 km/h (56 MPH), min.], car height automatically decreases to NORMAL. During deceleration, [60 km/h (37 MPH), max.] car height automatically returns to HIGH. This is not an indication of trouble.		Faulty control unit	
				Faulty height control switch circuit	
				Faulty control unit power circuit	
		Car is set to the NORMAL position as soon as ignition switch is turned ON.		"B" power supply connector (for clock) disconnected	
				Breaks in "B" power supply circuit	
				Faulty control unit	

AIR SUSPENSION SYSTEM TROUBLESHOOTING CONTINUED

Symptom	Trouble	Cause	
Compressor mal-functions.	Compressor keeps on running. (When engine is in operation, compressor keeps running over 8 minutes if left alone without getting in and out of vehicle.)	Vehicle height lowers if left alone with ignition switch off for over 15 minutes.	
		Vehicle height does not lower even if left alone with ignition switch off for over 15 minutes.	Faulty pressure switch
			Faulty control unit
			Defective compressor relay
			Defective electric circuit
			Faulty compressor
			Tank solenoid valve broken or sticking
			Air leaks from tank ASSY
			Air line leaks air or clogs
	Compressor operates frequently. (When engine is in operation, compressor operates frequently if left alone without getting in and out of vehicle for over 5 minutes.)	When ignition switch is off, vehicle height lowers if left alone for over 15 minutes.	
		When ignition switch is off, vehicle height does not lower even if left alone for over 15 minutes.	Faulty pressure switch
			Faulty control unit
			Defective electric circuit
			Air leakage from tank ASSY
	Compressor will not operate. (If compressor operates frequently and its temperature rises, circuit breaker will operate to stop compressor; if left as it is for some time and its temperature drops, it will restart.)	Compressor malfunctioning	
		Faulty pressure switch	
		Faulty control unit	
		Defective electric circuit	

AIR SUSPENSION SYSTEM TROUBLESHOOTING CONTINUED

Symptom	Trouble	Cause
Vehicle height indicator light blinks. (Warning of system failure.)	Vehicle height indicator light blinks when ignition switch is turned on.	Vehicle height sensor malfunctioning
		Faulty control unit
		Defective vehicle height sensor circuit
	Vehicle height indicator light blinks after more than 10 minutes passed with ignition switch turned on.	Compressor malfunctioning
		Faulty solenoid valve
		Faulty control unit
		Air leaks from tank ASSY
		Air line leaks air or clogs
		Air leaks from air suspension ASSY
Vehicle height indicator light blinks (Warning of system failure).	Vehicle height indicator light blinks when ignition switch is turned on.	Vehicle height sensor malfunctioning.
		Faulty control unit.
		Faulty vehicle height sensor circuit.
	After vehicle height indicator blinks as a warning, it goes off.	Vehicle height sensor malfunctioning.
		Faulty control unit.
		Faulty vehicle height sensor circuit.
	Vehicle height indicator light blinks after more than ten minutes has passed with ignition switch turned on.	Defective compressor or compressor relay.
		Faulty solenoid valve.
		Control unit malfunctioning.
		Air leakage from air tank ASSY.
		Air leakage from air suspension ASSY.
		Air line leaks air or is clogged.

Height Sensor

TESTING

STD. and XT

1. Disconnect the height sensor wire connector at the air shock.
2. Disconnect air shock line and bleed air from the shock.
3. Using an ohmmeter, check for continuity between the terminals of the height sensor side wire connector.

4. While using the ohmmeter, compress and extend each shock and observe when there is continuity.
5. If not as specified, replace or repair the height sensor.

Legacy

1. Remove the solenoid valve and air line.
2. Disconnect the height control wire connector.
3. With shock compressed, check the resistance between terminal 2 and 4 is a minimum of 1 megaohm.
4. With the shock expanded, check the resistance between terminal 2 and 4 is 0 ohms.
5. With shock compressed, check the resistance between terminal 2 and 3 is 0 ohms.
6. With the shock expanded, check the resistance between terminal 2 and 3 is a minimum of 1 megaohm.
7. If not as specified, repair or replace the height sensor.

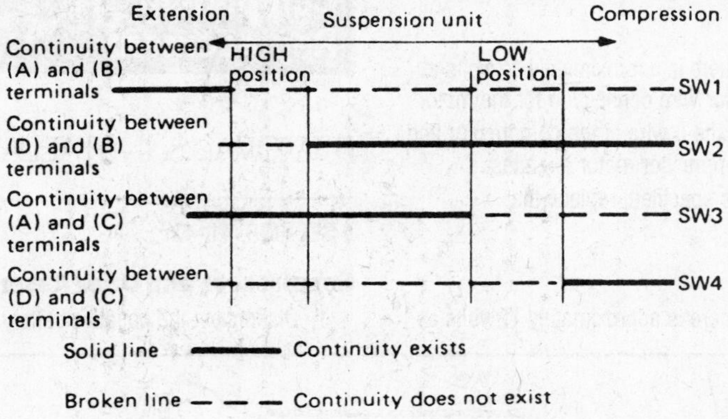

Control Unit

TESTING

Legacy

1. Measure the voltage between the control unit connector and ground.
2. Verify the voltage between terminal 2 and ground at connector P34 is approximately 10-12 volts.
3. Turn the ignition switch ON, verify the voltage between terminal 3 and ground at connector P34 is approximately 10-12 volts.
4. Verify the resistance between terminal 9 and ground at connector P34 is 0 ohms.

Solenoid Valve

TESTING

1. Disconnect solenoid wire connector at each shock.
2. Apply 12 volts across each terminal of the shock solenoid valve.
3. Listen for sound of solenoid functioning.
4. If no sound is heard, replace the solenoid valve.
5. Next, check for approximately 30 ohms of resistance between the terminals of the valve.
6. If not as specified, replace the solenoid valve.

Compressor Relay

TESTING

1. Remove the compressor relay.
2. Verify that there is no continuity between terminals C and D using an ohmmeter.

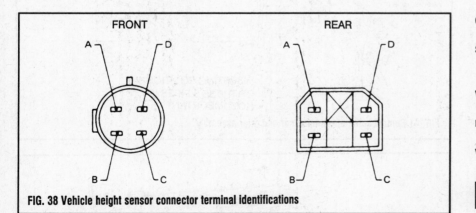

FIG. 37 Vehicle height sensor testing, check for continuity in these positions

FIG. 38 Vehicle height sensor connector terminal identifications

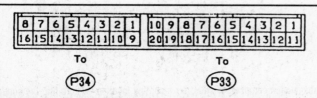

FIG. 39 Control unit connector pin identification — Legacy with air suspension

Terminal arrangement

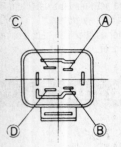

Circuit diagram

FIG. 40 Air suspension compressor relay — terminal identification

3. Apply 12 volts across terminal B and ground terminal A, there should now be continuity between terminals C and D.

4. If not as specified, replace the relay.

Pressure Switch

TESTING

STD. and XT

1. Disconnect the pressure switch wire connector.

2. Connect an ohmmeter between the terminals of the pressure switch.

3. Verify the pressure switch resistance is 1 megaohm minimum when the compressor tank pressure is approximately 132–147 psi (910–1014 kpa).

4. Release the compressor tank pressure slowly and verify there is no resistance at pressure switch terminals when tank pressure reaches approximately 125 psi (862 kpa).

5. If not as specified, replace the pressure switch.

Legacy

1. Disconnect the pressure switch wire connector.

2. Connect an ohmmeter between the terminals of the pressure switch.

3. Verify the pressure switch resistance is 1 megaohm minimum when the compressor tank pressure is approximately 137 psi (945 kpa).

4. Release the compressor tank pressure slowly and verify there is no resistance at pressure switch terminals when tank pressure reaches approximately 111 psi (765 kpa).

5. If not as specified, replace the pressure switch.

Compressor

TESTING

STD.

1. Verify there is approximately 12 volts at the compressor wire connection for the motor.

2. Ground the L wire at the compressor and verify that compressor motor operates.

3. If not as specified, replace the compressor.

XT

1. Verify there is approximately 12 volts at the compressor wire connection for the motor.

2. Ground the L/W wire at the compressor and verify that compressor motor operates.

3. If not as specified, replace the compressor.

Legacy

1. Disconnect the wire connector from the compressor.

2. Using an ohmmeter, verify the resistance between terminals 1 and 3 is 2.5–3.5 ohms.

3. Apply 12 volts to terminals 1 and 3 and verify the compressor operates.

4. If not as specified, replace the compressor.

Component Replacement

REMOVAL & INSTALLATION

◆ SEE FIGS. 41–42

Compressor and Drier Assembly

1. Disconnect the negative battery cable.

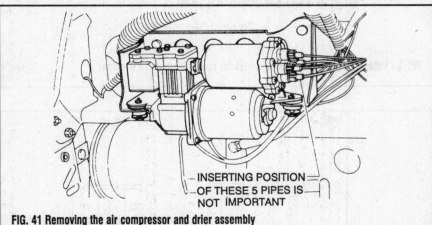

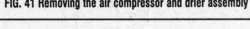

INSERTING POSITION OF THESE 5 PIPES IS NOT IMPORTANT

FIG. 41 Removing the air compressor and drier assembly

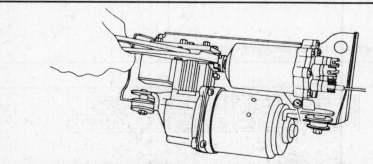

FIG. 42 Air suspension compressor and drier mounting location — note that the connections of the air pipes to the compressor can be in any order

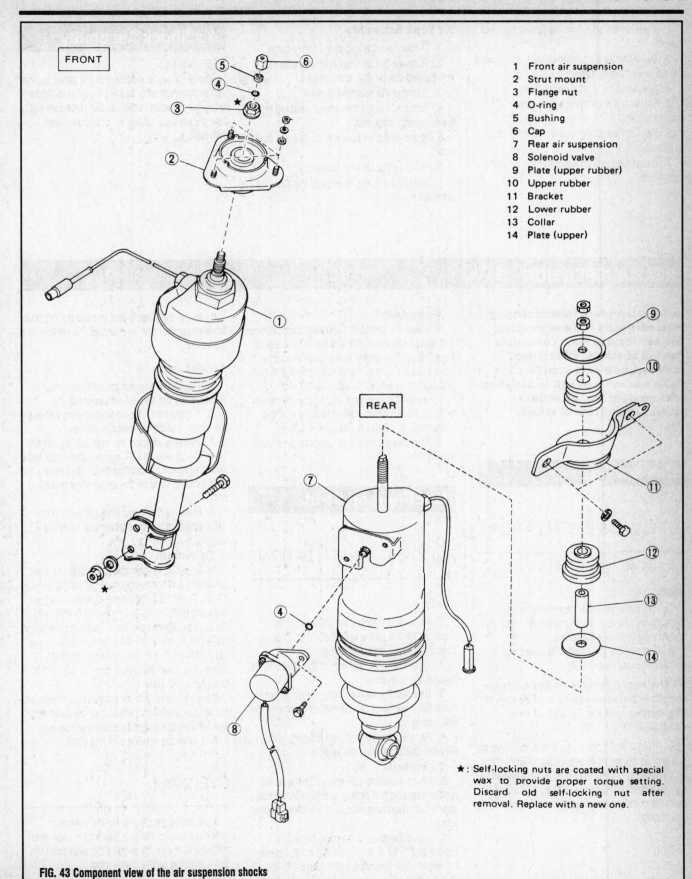

FRONT

1 Front air suspension
2 Strut mount
3 Flange nut
4 O-ring
5 Bushing
6 Cap
7 Rear air suspension
8 Solenoid valve
9 Plate (upper rubber)
10 Upper rubber
11 Bracket
12 Lower rubber
13 Collar
14 Plate (upper)

REAR

★: Self-locking nuts are coated with special wax to provide proper torque setting. Discard old self-locking nut after removal. Replace with a new one.

FIG. 43 Component view of the air suspension shocks

2. Remove the front half portion of the mud guard.

3. Using the air pipe removal tool, disconnect the air lines from the drier.

4. Disconnect the wire connectors.

5. Remove the compressor and drier mounting nuts.

6. Remove the compressor and drier as an assembly.

7. Installation is the reverse of the removal procedure.

Air Tank Assembly

1. Disconnect the negative battery cable.

2. Remove the air lines from the solenoid valve using the air line removal tool.

3. Remove the solenoid coupler.

4. Remove the left turn signal housing from the bumper, if required.

5. Remove the air tank attaching bolts and nuts.

6. Remove the air tank assembly.

7. Installation is the reverse of the removal procedure.

Air Shock Assembly

♦ SEE FIG. 43

The air shock is removed in the same manner as the standard strut assembly, refer to those procedures earlier in this section. Use care not to tear the shock's rubber air chamber when removing it.

REAR SUSPENSION

➡ **All of the suspension mounting fasteners used in these vehicles, use self-locking nuts. These nuts can not be reused after being removed, new nuts must be used. Failure to use new self-locking nuts may result in the bolt working loose, causing loss of vehicle control.**

Coil Springs

REMOVAL & INSTALLATION

♦ SEE FIG. 44

Justy

1. Raise and support the vehicle safely. Remove the tire and wheel assembly. Properly support the rear axle assembly.

2. Remove the strut bolt trim cover and remove the strut upper bolts.

➡ **The rear spring is under extreme tension. Serious injury can result if the spring should fly out of the vehicle.**

3. Place a floor jack under the control arm to prevent the spring from expanding. Remove the rear spindle to control arm bolt. Slowly lower the control arm until all spring pressure is released. Push the control arm downward, and remove the coil spring.

To install:

4. Place the spring in the holder cups. Ensure that the spring insulators are installed. Using a floor jack, lift up on the lower control arm to compress the spring. Install the control arm bolts and tighten to 54–69 ft. lbs. (74–93 Nm).

5. Install the rear strut and tighten the lower bolts to 72–87 ft. lbs. (98–118 Nm) and the upper nuts to 40–54 ft. lbs. (54–74 Nm).

6. Remove the rear axle supports and lower the vehicle.

MacPherson Strut

REMOVAL & INSTALLATION

Justy

1. Raise and support the vehicle safely. Remove the tire and wheel assembly. Properly support the rear axle assembly.

2. From the upper portion of the strut mount, remove the trim cover.

3. Remove the strut to body retaining nut. Push the lower arm downward, and remove the coil spring.

4. Remove the strut to axle housing bolts. Remove the strut from the vehicle.

To install:

5. When installing coil spring, fit the lower rubber seat and coil spring end face in the coil spring seat mounting recess of the lower control arm.

6. Install the strut-to-housing bolts and tighten to 72–87 ft. lbs. (98–118 Nm). Tighten the upper strut mounting nut to 43–51 ft. lbs. (59–69 Nm).

6. Install the wheels and remove the supports from under the rear axle. Lower the vehicle and test drive.

Except Justy

1. Raise and support the vehicle safely. Remove the tire and wheel assembly.

2. If equipped with air suspension, remove the cover and disconnect the air line.

3. Properly support the rear axle assembly. On STD., Loyale and XT remove the upper strut retaining bracket mounting bolts. On Legacy and SVX models, remove the upper strut mounting nut.

4. Remove the lower strut retaining bolts.

5. Remove the strut assembly from the vehicle.

To install:

6. On STD., Loyale and XT, install the strut assembly and tighten the lower attaching bolts to 51–87 ft. lbs. (69–118 Nm), tighten the upper retaining bolts to 65–94 ft. lbs. (88–127 Nm). On Legacy, tighten the lower mounting bolts to 137–174 ft. lbs. (186–235 Nm) and the upper nut to 36–51 ft. lbs. (49–69 Nm). On SVX, tighten the lower mounting bolts to 98–127 ft. lbs. (132–172 Nm).

7. If equipped with air suspension, reconnect the air line. Install the wheel and tire assembly and remove the supports under the rear axle.

8. Lower the vehicle and test drive.

OVERHAUL

1. Remove the strut from the vehicle as described above. Place a piece of rubber over the jaws of a vise, to protect the strut cylinder, and clamp the strut into the vise.

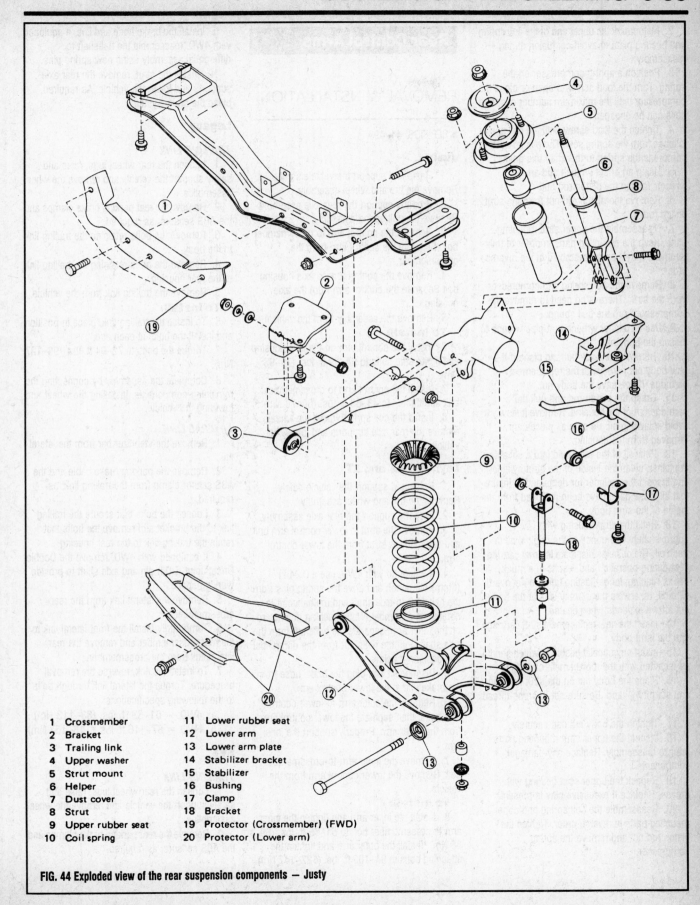

1	Crossmember	11	Lower rubber seat
2	Bracket	12	Lower arm
3	Trailing link	13	Lower arm plate
4	Upper washer	14	Stabilizer bracket
5	Strut mount	15	Stabilizer
6	Helper	16	Bushing
7	Dust cover	17	Clamp
8	Strut	18	Bracket
9	Upper rubber seat	19	Protector (Crossmember) (FWD)
10	Coil spring	20	Protector (Lower arm)

FIG. 44 Exploded view of the rear suspension components — Justy

2. Matchmark the upper end of the coil spring and bearing plate to avoid confusion during reassembly.

3. Position a spring compressor on the spring. Turn the load screw to open or close the compressor until the maximum number of spring coils can be engaged.

4. Tighten the load screw until the coil spring is loose from the spring seat. There is no need to compress the spring further than this point.

5. Using an offset wrench and an Allen wrench, loosen the piston rod nut.

6. Remove the piston rod nut from the strut piston rod.

7. Disassemble the upper strut mounting parts. Keep the mounting parts in order of their removal. They'll be reassembled in the reverse order.

8. Remove the coil spring and compressor from the strut. There is no need to remove the compressor from the coil spring.

9. Use a spanner wrench or a pipe wrench to loosen the body nut.

10. Remove the body nut and discard if a new body nut came with the replacement cartridge. If not, save the body nut.

11. Grasp the piston rod and pull the cartridge out of the housing. Remove it slowly to avoid splashing oil. Be sure all pieces are removed from the housing.

12. Pour all of the strut fluid into a suitable container, clean the inside of the strut cylinder, and inspect the cylinder for dents and to insure that all loose parts have been removed from the inside of the strut body.

13. Refill the strut housing with approximately one ounce of the original oil or fresh oil. The oil helps dissipate internal cartridge heat during operation and results in a much cooler running, longer lasting unit. Do not overfill with oil; otherwise the oil may leak at the body nut after it expands when heated.

14. Insert the new replacement strut cartridge into the strut body.

15. Insert any special bushings which should be included with the replacement cartridge.

16. Place the body nut on the strut housing and start it by hand. Be sure not to cross-thread it.

17. Tighten the body nut cap securely.

18. Inspect the upper strut mounting parts prior to reassembly. Replace any damaged components.

19. Repack the upper strut bearing with grease. Replace if excessive play is present.

20. Reassemble the coil spring and upper mounting parts in reverse order. Tighten the piston rod nut and remove the spring compressor.

Rear Control Arms

REMOVAL & INSTALLATION

◆ SEE FIGS. 44–49

Justy

1. Raise and support the vehicle safely. Remove the tire and wheel assembly.

2. Properly support the rear axle assembly. Remove the coil spring assembly.

3. Remove the control arm to crossmember bolt. Separate the control arm from the crossmember.

4. Remove the control arm to axle housing bolt Separate the control arm from the axle housing.

5. Remove the assembly from the vehicle.

To Install:

6. Install the control arm on the axle housing and tighten the bolts to 54–69 ft. lbs. (74–93 Nm).

7. Install the control arm to crossmember bolt and tighten to 43–58 ft. lbs. (59–78 Nm).

8. Install the coil spring. Install the wheels, remove the rear axle supports and lower the vehicle.

Loyale, STD. and XT

1. Raise and support the vehicle safely. Remove the tire and wheel assembly.

2. Properly support the rear axle assembly.

3. Remove the strut to lower control arm bolt and separate the strut from the lower control arm.

4. If equipped with 4WD, use a 0.24 in. (6mm) pin punch and drive the spring pins from the halfshaft-to-axle shaft and the halfshaft to differential assembly. While pushing downward on the inner arm, separate the halfshaft from the axle shaft. Pull the halfshaft from the differential and position it aside.

5. Disconnect and plug the brake hose from the brake line at the lower control arm.

6. Remove the outer arm-to-lower control arm bolts, then separate the lower control arm from the outer arm. Properly support the inner arm.

7. Remove the inner arm-to-crossmember bolt. Remove the lower control arm from the vehicle.

To Install:

8. Install the inner arm and tighten the inner arm to crossmember bolt to 51–65 ft. lbs. (69–88 Nm). Install the outer arm and tighten the attaching bolts to 94–108 ft. lbs. (127–147 Nm).

9. Install the brake hose and line. If equipped with 4WD, reassemble the halfshaft to differential assembly using new spring pins.

10. Install the strut, remove the rear axle supports and lower the vehicle. As required, bleed the brake system.

Legacy

TRAILING LINK

1. Loosen the rear wheel lugs, raise and safely support the vehicle and remove the wheel assemblies.

2. Remove the rear parking brake clamps and the ABS sensors, as required.

3. Remove the bolts retaining the trailing link to the body.

4. Remove the bolts retaining the trailing link to the rear housing.

5. Remove the trailing link from the vehicle.

To install:

6. To install the trailing link, place in position and install the bolts at each end.

7. Torque the bolts to 72–94 ft. lbs. (98–127 Nm).

8. Complete the assembly by connecting the remaining components, installing the wheel and lowering the vehicle.

LATERAL LINK

1. Remove the stabilizer bar from the lateral link.

2. Remove the parking brake cable and the ABS sensor clamp from the trailing link, as required.

3. Loosen the bolts that secure the trailing link to the bracket and remove the bolts that retain the trailing link to the rear housing.

4. If equipped with 4WD, remove the Double Offset Joint (DOJ) pin and axle shaft to provide working space.

5. Remove the lateral link from the rear crossmember.

6. Temporarily install the front lateral link to the rear crossmember and remove the rear lateral link from the crossmember.

7. To install the link, reverse the removal procedure. Torque the lateral link through bolts to the following specifications:
   a. 4WD — 61–83 ft. lbs. (83–113 Nm)
   b. FWD — 87–116 ft. lbs. (118–157 Nm)

SVX

TRAILING LINK

1. Loosen the rear wheel lugs, raise and safely support the vehicle and remove the wheel assemblies.

2. Remove the rear parking brake clamps and the ABS sensors, as required.

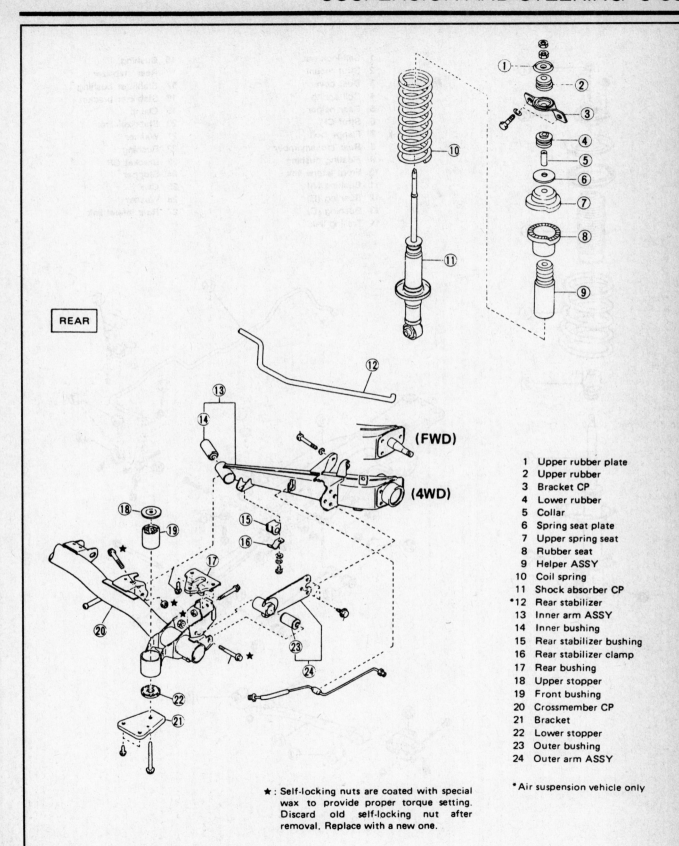

REAR

(FWD)

(4WD)

1 Upper rubber plate
2 Upper rubber
3 Bracket CP
4 Lower rubber
5 Collar
6 Spring seat plate
7 Upper spring seat
8 Rubber seat
9 Helper ASSY
10 Coil spring
11 Shock absorber CP
*12 Rear stabilizer
13 Inner arm ASSY
14 Inner bushing
15 Rear stabilizer bushing
16 Rear stabilizer clamp
17 Rear bushing
18 Upper stopper
19 Front bushing
20 Crossmember CP
21 Bracket
22 Lower stopper
23 Outer bushing
24 Outer arm ASSY

* Air suspension vehicle only

★ : Self-locking nuts are coated with special wax to provide proper torque setting. Discard old self-locking nut after removal. Replace with a new one.

FIG. 45 Exploded view of the rear suspension system — Loyale, STD. and XT

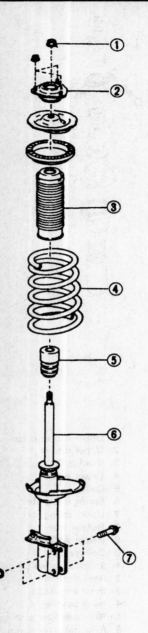

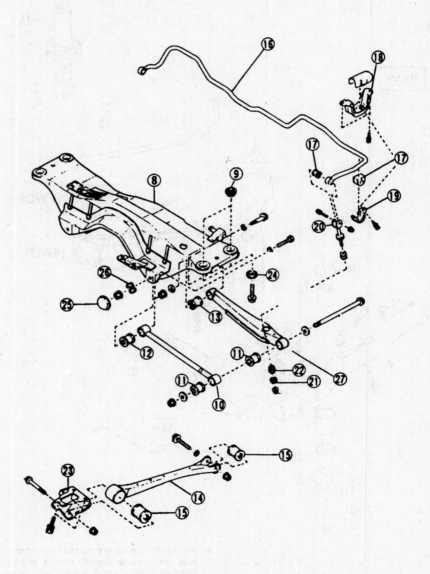

1 Self-lock nut
2 Strut mount
3 Dust cover
4 Coil spring
5 Rear helper
6 Strut CP
7 Flange bolt
8 Rear crossmember
9 Floating bushing
10 Front lateral link
11 Bushing (A)
12 Bushing (B)
13 Bushing (C)
14 Trailing link
15 Bushing
16 Rear stabilizer
17 Stabilizer bushing
18 Stabilizer bracket
19 Clamp
20 Stabilizer link
21 Washer
22 Bushing
23 Bracket CP
24 Stopper
25 Cap
26 Washer
27 Rear lateral link

FIG. 46 Exploded view of the rear suspension system — Legacy with All Wheel Drive

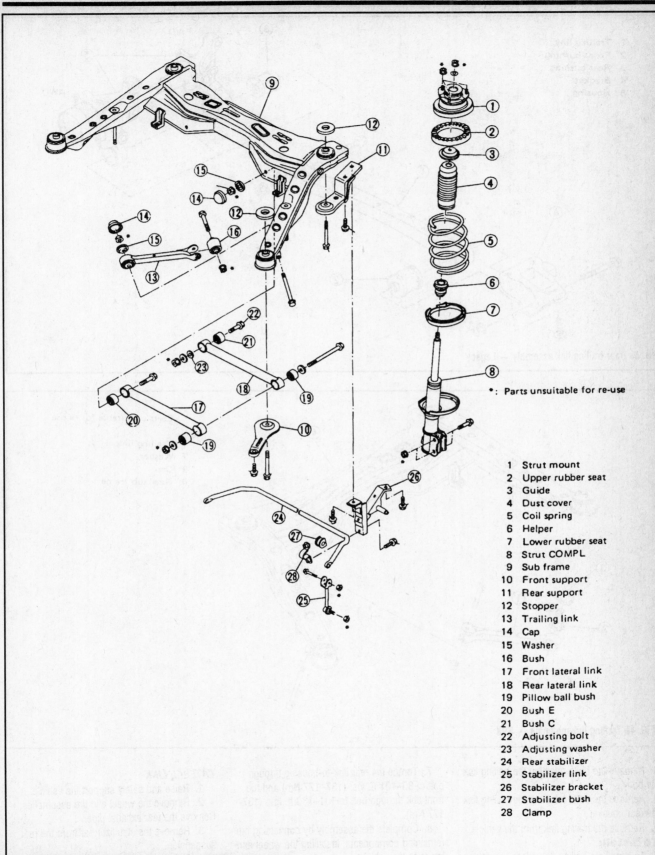

•: Parts unsuitable for re-use

1 Strut mount
2 Upper rubber seat
3 Guide
4 Dust cover
5 Coil spring
6 Helper
7 Lower rubber seat
8 Strut COMPL
9 Sub frame
10 Front support
11 Rear support
12 Stopper
13 Trailing link
14 Cap
15 Washer
16 Bush
17 Front lateral link
18 Rear lateral link
19 Pillow ball bush
20 Bush E
21 Bush C
22 Adjusting bolt
23 Adjusting washer
24 Rear stabilizer
25 Stabilizer link
26 Stabilizer bracket
27 Stabilizer bush
28 Clamp

FIG. 47 Exploded view of the rear suspension system — SVX

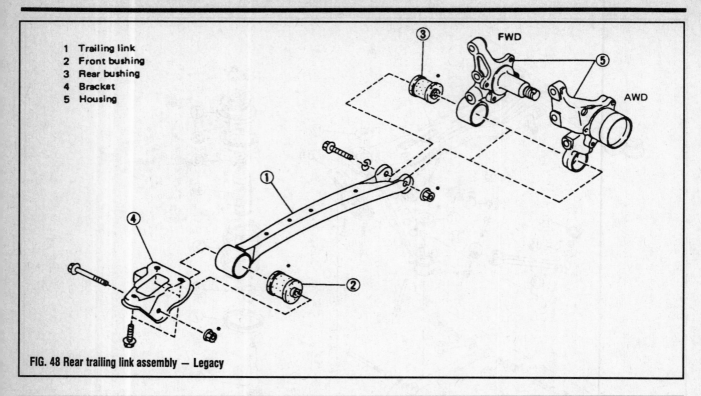

1 Trailing link
2 Front bushing
3 Rear bushing
4 Bracket
5 Housing

FIG. 48 Rear trailing link assembly — Legacy

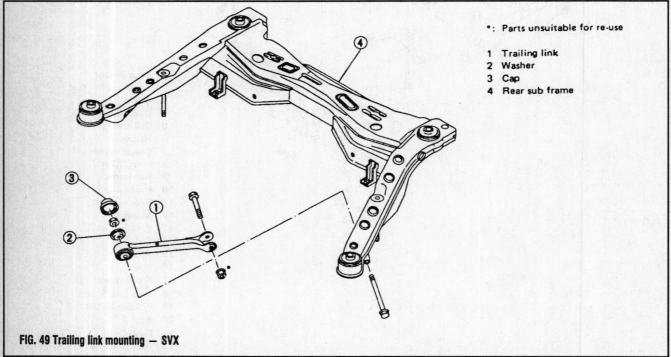

*: Parts unsuitable for re-use

1 Trailing link
2 Washer
3 Cap
4 Rear sub frame

FIG. 49 Trailing link mounting — SVX

3. Remove the bolts retaining the trailing link to the body.

4. Remove the bolts retaining the trailing link to the rear housing.

5. Remove the trailing link from the vehicle.

To Install:

6. To install the trailing link, place in position and install the bolts at each end.

7. Torque the rear link-to-housing through bolt to 80–101 ft. lbs. (137–177 Nm) and the front link through bolt to 101–130 ft. lbs. (137–177 Nm).

8. Complete the assembly by connecting the remaining components, installing the wheel and lowering the vehicle.

LATERAL LINK

1. Raise and safely support the vehicle.

2. Remove the wheel and tire assemblies. Remove the rear exhaust pipe.

3. Remove the stabilizer bar from the rear suspension.

4. Remove the parking brake cable and ABS sensor harness brackets.

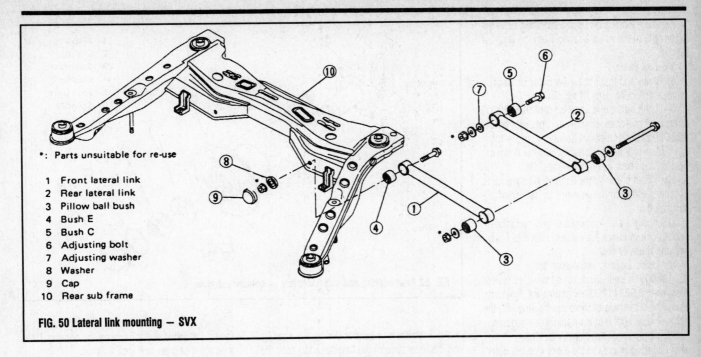

*: Parts unsuitable for re-use

1   Front lateral link
2   Rear lateral link
3   Pillow ball bush
4   Bush E
5   Bush C
6   Adjusting bolt
7   Adjusting washer
8   Washer
9   Cap
10 Rear sub frame

FIG. 50 Lateral link mounting — SVX

5. Disconnect the parking brake cable clamp.
6. Disconnect the trailing link at the housing.
7. Disconnect the lateral links at the housing assembly.
8. Using a suitable halfshaft removing tool, carefully pry the halfshaft from the rear differential and support it with a wire from the body.
9. Place an alignment mark on the lateral link-to-crossmember bolt. This bolt must be installed in the same position or rear wheel alignment will be incorrect.
10. Remove the later link-to-rear crossmember bolts and remove the link.

To Install:
11. Install the lateral link to the crossmember and loosely install the bolts.

➡ **All of the fasteners must be tightened with the weight of the vehicle on the suspension. Be sure to align the marks made during removal on the rear lateral link bolts.**

12. Connect the lateral link at the housing assembly. Loosely install the bolts.
13. Connect The trailing link at the housing and loosely install the bolts.
14. Reposition the ABS harness and the parking brake cable clips.
15. Install the rear exhaust pipe and the rear tire assemblies.
16. Lower the vehicle to the ground and tighten all fasteners to the following torques:
   a. Front lateral link-to-sub frame through bolt (bolt without cap for the end) — 72–101 ft. lbs. (98–137 Nm).

   b. Rear lateral link-to-sub frame through bolt (bolt with cap, closest to the differential) — 61–83 ft. lbs. (83–113 Nm).
   c. Trailing link-to-housing bolt — 80–101 ft. lbs. (108–137 Nm).
   d. Stabilizer link nut — 12–17 ft. lbs. (16–14 Nm).

Rear Wheel Bearings

➡ SEE FIGS. 51–52

ADJUSTMENT

2WD

1. Raise and support the vehicle safely. Remove the rear wheel assembly.
2. Temporarily tighten the axle nut to 36 ft. lbs. on all vehicles except Justy or to 29 ft. lbs. for Justy.
3. Turn the drum or disc back and forth several times to ensure that bearings are properly seated.
4. Turn the nut backwards $1/8–1/4$ turn in order to obtain the correct starting force.
5. Using a spring gauge at 90 degrees to the wheel lug, check the rotating force. Specifications should be 1.9–3.2 lbs. for all vehicles except Justy. For Justy the specification is 3.1–4.4 lbs.
6. After the adjustment is completed, bend the lock washer. After installing a new O-ring to the grease cap, install the cap.

REMOVAL & INSTALLATION

1. Raise and support the vehicle safely. Remove the rear tire and wheel assembly.
2. If equipped with rear disc brakes, remove the caliper and properly support it.
3. Using a small prybar, remove the rear wheel grease cap.
4. Using a hammer and a punch, flatten the lock washer and loosen the axle nut. Remove the lock washer and the thrust plate. When removing the drum or disc, be careful not to drop the inner race from the outer bearing.

➡ **If the brake drum on the Justy is difficult to remove, use wheel puller tool 9224930000 or equivalent, to remove the brake drum.**

5. Using a gear puller, remove the spacer and the inner race of the inner bearing.
6. Using a brass drift and a hammer, drive the outer race of the inner bearing from the drum or disc.

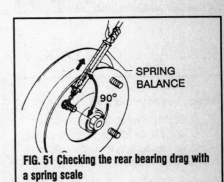

SPRING BALANCE

90°

FIG. 51 Checking the rear bearing drag with a spring scale

7. Using a brass drift and a hammer, drive the outer race of the outer bearing from the drum or disc.

To Install:

8. Clean and inspect the parts for damage, replace defective parts, if necessary.

9. Using bearing installation tool 925220000 or equivalent, for all vehicles except Justy or tool 922111000 or equivalent, for Justy, press the outer race of the inner bearing into the drum or disc until it seats against the shoulder.

10. When pressing the bearing, be sure not to exceed the load to the bearing, so as not to damage it.

11. Apply a small amount of grease to the oil seal lips, then install the oil seal until it is flush with the drum or disc.

12. Using bearing installation tool 921130000 or equivalent, for all vehicles except Justy or tool 922111000 or equivalent, for Justy, press the outer race of the outer bearing into the drum or disc until it seats against the shoulder.

13. Apply approximately 1/8 oz (3.5g) of wheel bearing grease to the inner and the outer bearings. Fill the disc or drum hub with 1 oz (28g) of wheel bearing grease.

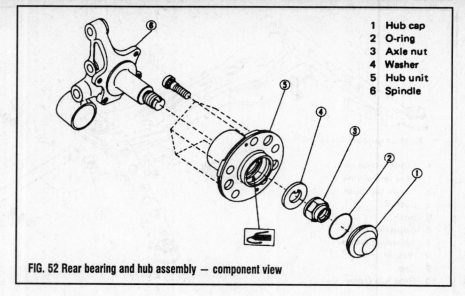

1	Hub cap
2	O-ring
3	Axle nut
4	Washer
5	Hub unit
6	Spindle

FIG. 52 Rear bearing and hub assembly — component view

14. Install a new spacer O-ring, the spacer and the inner race of the inner bearing onto the trailing arm spindle.

15. When installing the spacer, be sure to face the stepped surface toward the bearing. Use a new thrust plate and lock washer.

16. To complete the installation, reverse the removal procedure. Adjust the wheel bearing.

STEERING

♦ SEE FIGS. 53–56

> ### ❋❋ CAUTION
>
> **Properly disarm the air bag on vehicles equipped with the SRS system. Failure to do so can cause serious injury. The procedure can be found in Section 6 of this manual under the heading "Supplemental Restraint System".**

Steering Wheel

REMOVAL & INSTALLATION

Except Legacy and SVX

1. Disconnect the negative battery cable.
2. Disconnect the horn lead from the wiring harness, located beneath the instrument panel. On the XT Coupe, remove the horn pad.

➡ **If equipped with telescopic steering wheel, remove the telescopic lever assembly.**

3. Working behind the steering wheel, remove the steering wheel cover to steering wheel screws. It may be necessary to lower the column from the dash by removing the screws.

4. Lift the crash pad assembly from the front of the wheel.

5. Matchmark the steering wheel and the column for installation.

6. Remove the steering wheel retaining nut. Using a steering wheel puller tool, remove the steering wheel from the column.

To install:

7. Install the steering wheel on the column in the same position as removed. Tighten the center nut to 36–43 ft. lbs. (49–59 Nm) on Justy and 22–29 ft. lbs. (29–39 Nm) on STD., Loyale and XT.

➡ **Do not hammer on the steering wheel or the steering column, as damage to the collapsible column could result.**

8. Install the crash pad assembly and wheel cover.

9. If the column was lowered, tighten steering column-to-dash screws.

10. Install the telescopic lever, if removed. Connect the horn lead and install the horn pad, if removed.

Legacy and SVX

> ### ❋❋ CAUTION
>
> **Properly disarm the air bag on vehicles equipped with the SRS system. Failure to do so can cause serious injury. The procedure can be found in Section 6 of this manual under the heading "Supplemental Restraint System".**

1. Properly disarm the air bag system, on models equipped. Disconnect the negative battery cable.

> ### ❋❋ CAUTION
>
> **Wait at least 10 minutes after disarming the air bag to avoid accidental deployment.**

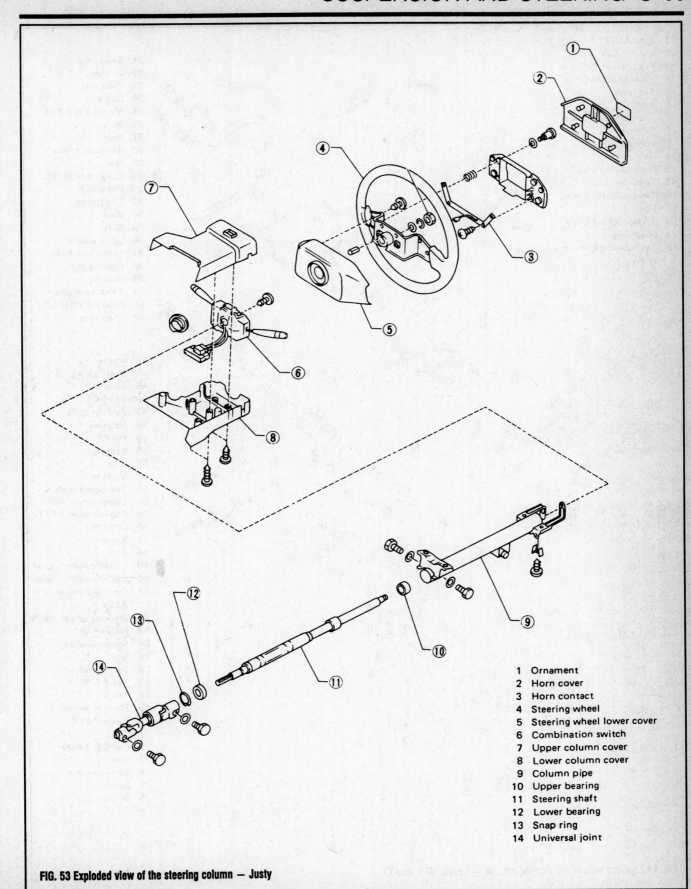

1 Ornament
2 Horn cover
3 Horn contact
4 Steering wheel
5 Steering wheel lower cover
6 Combination switch
7 Upper column cover
8 Lower column cover
9 Column pipe
10 Upper bearing
11 Steering shaft
12 Lower bearing
13 Snap ring
14 Universal joint

FIG. 53 Exploded view of the steering column — Justy

1 Pipe ASSY
2 Shaft ASSY
3 Fix bracket CP
4 Inner bracket CP
5 Tilt lever
6 Bolt
7 Tilt adjusting screw
8 Bearing
9 Washer
10 Bolt
12 Wing bracket ASSY
13 Telescopic shaft
14 Telescopic lock shaft
15 Rod
16 Telescopic lock key
17 Snap ring
19 Telescopic adjusting
    screw
20 Nut

21 Snap ring
22 Washer
23 Dust seal
24 Spacer
25 Memory pin ASSY
26 Bolt
27 Bolt
28 Telescopic lever
29 Nut
30 Column pipe CP
31 Pin ASSY
33 Tilt spring
34 Boss
35 Bolt
36 Lock washer
37 Telescopic bush
38 Bearing bush
39 Bearing
40 Telescopic guide
41 Steering shaft CP
42 Snap ring

43 Washer
44 Shaft spring
45 Washer
46 Bearing
47 Bearing bush
48 Housing
49 Pin CP
50 Bearing
51 Clip
52 Stopper
53 Toe board bush
54 Lower cover ASSY
55 Pop-up cable ASSY
56 Dress nut
57 Knob
58 Cap
59 Lower column cover
60 Upper column cover
61 Combination switch
    ASSY
62 Steering wheel ASSY
63 Washer
64 Spring washer
65 Nut
66 Spring washer
67 Pad ASSY
68 Pad
69 Steering sensor
70 Screw ASSY
71 Clip
72 Pad CP (Knee)
73 Washer
74 Spring washer
75 Screw
76 Screw

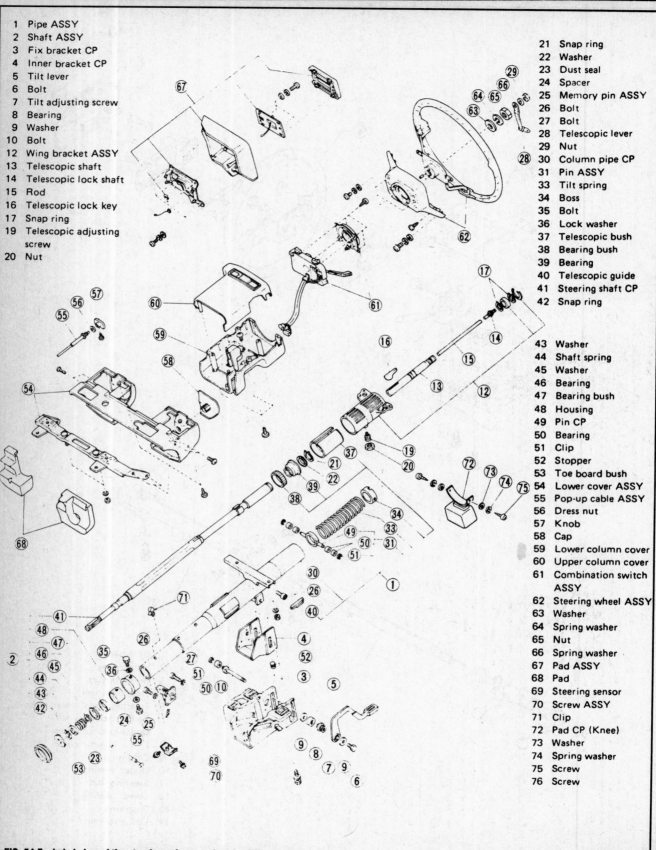

FIG. 54 Exploded view of the steering column — Loyale, STD. and XT

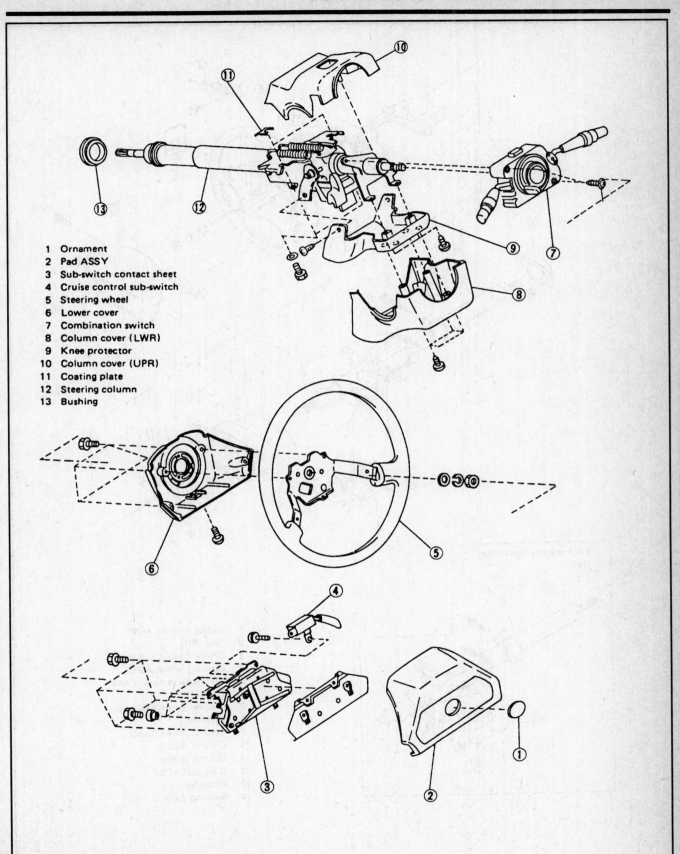

1   Ornament
2   Pad ASSY
3   Sub-switch contact sheet
4   Cruise control sub-switch
5   Steering wheel
6   Lower cover
7   Combination switch
8   Column cover (LWR)
9   Knee protector
10 Column cover (UPR)
11 Coating plate
12 Steering column
13 Bushing

FIG. 55 Steering wheel and column assembly — Legacy

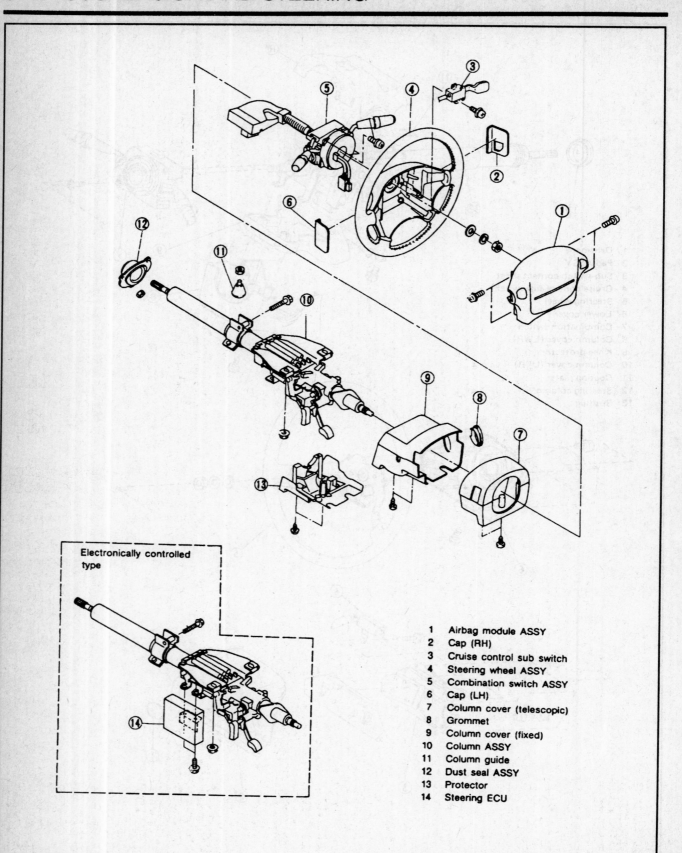

Electronically controlled type

1 Airbag module ASSY
2 Cap (RH)
3 Cruise control sub switch
4 Steering wheel ASSY
5 Combination switch ASSY
6 Cap (LH)
7 Column cover (telescopic)
8 Grommet
9 Column cover (fixed)
10 Column ASSY
11 Column guide
12 Dust seal ASSY
13 Protector
14 Steering ECU

FIG. 56 Steering wheel and column assembly — SVX

2. Disconnect the horn lead from the wiring harness, located beneath the instrument panel. On models without air bag, remove the horn pad by pulling it off.

➡ If equipped with telescopic steering wheel, remove the telescopic lever assembly.

3. On models with an air bag, working behind the steering wheel, remove the steering column covers. Use a No. 30 Torx® bit and remove the air bag module retaining bolts.

4. Disconnect the air bag module connector and remove the module from the steering wheel. Place the module face up on a flat surface.

5. Matchmark the steering wheel and the column for installation.

6. Remove the steering wheel retaining nut. Using a steering wheel puller tool, remove the steering wheel from the column.

To Install:

7. Install the steering wheel on the column in the same position as removed. Tighten the center nut to 22–29 ft. lbs. (29–39 Nm).

➡ Do not hammer on the steering wheel or the steering column, as damage to the collapsible column could result.

8. Install the crash pad or air bag assembly and the column covers.

9. Install the telescopic lever, if removed. Connect all of the electrical leads. Re-arm the air bag as explained in Section 6 of this manual.

Turn Signal (Combination) Switch

REMOVAL & INSTALLATION

The turn signal switch is part of the combination switch assembly, removal and installation of these components can be found in Section 6 of this manual.

Ignition Switch

REMOVAL & INSTALLATION

➡ The ignition switch is mounted to

the steering column using shear bolts. These bolts are constructed so the heads shear off when the bolt is torqued.

1. Disconnect the negative battery cable. Remove the steering wheel.

2. Remove the upper and lower steering column covers from the steering column.

3. Remove the hazard knob.

4. Drill a pilot hole into the shear bolts, then using a screw extractor, remove the screws from the steering column.

5. Remove the ignition switch from the steering column.

To Install:

6. Install the ignition switch using new shear bolts.

7. Install the hazard knob, steering column covers and the steering wheel.

8. Connect the negative battery cable and check the switch for proper operation.

Steering Column

REMOVAL & INSTALLATION

Except XT Coupe

❈❈❈ CAUTION

Properly disarm the air bag on vehicles equipped with the SRS system. Failure to do so can cause serious injury. The procedure can be found in Section 6 of this manual under the heading "Supplemental Restraint System".

1. Properly disarm the air bag on models so equipped. Disconnect the negative battery cable.

❈❈❈ CAUTION

Wait at least 10 minutes after disarming the air bag to avoid accidental deployment.

2. Remove the universal joint connecting bolts and then remove the universal joint.

3. Disconnect the ignition and combination switch electrical connectors under the dash. Disconnect any other electrical connector attached to the steering column.

4. Remove any other component which impedes the removal of the steering column. On XT Coupe, remove the speedometer cable.

5. Remove the steering shaft attaching bolts under the dash. Remove the steering column from inside the interior.

6. If equipped with telescopic column, set the steering column to its lowest position and install a tilt lock bolt from below the column bracket.

To Install:

7. Install the steering column from the interior side and tighten attaching bolts to 14–22 ft. lbs. (20–29 Nm). Remove the telescopic lock bolt.

8. Install all under dash components previously removed and reconnect all electrical connectors.

9. Install the universal joint and tighten to 15–20 ft. lbs. (21–26 Nm). Connect the negative battery cable.

10. Check all operations of the steering column before driving vehicle.

XT Coupe

1. Disconnect the negative battery terminal.

2. Remove the universal joint connecting bolts and remove the universal.

❈❈❈ WARNING

Not only when removing steering shaft/column but when removing steering column for servicing of other parts, be sure to remove the universal joint. The steering column must not be lowered with only the column mounting bolts loosened.

3. Remove the lower cover under the instrument panel.

4. Remove the ventilation duct under the steering column.

5. Disconnect the wiring harness connectors for the ignition switch, combination switch, control wing switch, and combination meter. Then, remove the screws securing the harness under the column bracket.

6. Remove the meter cable.

7. Pull the knob to pop up the steering wheel, remove the cable and push down the steering wheel to relock it.

8. After setting the steering wheel to its lowest position, fasten the tilt lock bolt from below the column bracket. Then temporarily tighten the bolt until its bearing surface touches.

➡ **This step may be omitted when the entire steering column assembly is to be disassembled.**

9. Remove the steering column mounting bolts under the instrument panel.

10. Pull out the steering shaft assembly from the toe board toward the inside of the passenger compartment.

❋❋❋ CAUTION

Because the combination meter is removed with the shaft assembly, be careful not to damage the meter and instrument panel surface.

To Install:

11. Insert the steering shaft assembly into the toe board bushing and temporarily tighten the three bolts.

12. Remove the lock bolt fastening column pipe and bracket. Loosen the tilt lever, move the shaft up and down several times, and tighten the tilt lever.

13. Tighten the mounting bolts to 14–22 ft. lbs. (20–29 Nm). Make sure that the tilt and lock mechanism works properly.

14. Connect the meter cable, harness and pop up cable.

15. Install the steering wheel and torque the retaining bolt to 22–29 ft. lbs. (29–39 Nm).

16. Clearance between the column cover and the steering wheel is 2–4mm.

17. Install the telescopic lever so that its knob is parallel with the steering wheel spoke. Tighten the nut temporarily.

18. Confirm that the telescoping is performed smoothly when the telescope lever is released and that the lock mechanism works properly.

19. While holding the telescopic lever stationary, tighten the retaining nut 9–12 ft. lbs.

20. Connect the harness to the pad assembly and install the pad assembly to the steering wheel.

21. Install the universal joint, long yoke side to steering gear and short yoke side to pinion, and torque the retaining bolts to 15–20 ft. lbs. (22–32 Nm).

➡ **Make sure that each coupling bolt passes through the cutout at the serrated section of the steering shaft or the one on the gear box pinion.**

Tie Rod Ends

REMOVAL & INSTALLATION

1. Raise and support the vehicle safely.
2. Remove the front tire and wheel assemblies.
3. Remove the cotter pin and castle nut from the tie rod end stud.
4. Using a ball joint puller, separate the tie rod end from the steering knuckle.

To Install:

5. Install the tie rod and tighten the castle nut to 18–22 ft. lbs. Install a new cotter pin.
6. Install the front tire and lower the vehicle.

Manual Steering Gear

◆ SEE FIGS. 57–60

REMOVAL & INSTALLATION

Justy

1. Disconnect the negative battery cable. Raise and support the vehicle safely. Remove the front tire and wheel assemblies.
2. Disconnect the universal joint coupling bolts. Remove the dust seal.
3. Using the proper tools, disconnect the tie rod ends from the knuckle arms.
4. Remove the steering gear retaining bolts. Lower the assembly and pull the pinion from the dust seal toward the engine compartment.
5. Remove the steering gear from the vehicle.

To Install:

6. Installation is the reverse of the removal

procedure. Tighten the rack mounting bolts to 33–43 ft. lbs. (44–59 Nm).

7. Adjust the toe-in and the turning angles to specifications.

8. Tighten the tie rod end to 18–22 ft. lbs. (25–29 Nm).

XT Coupe

1. Be sure the parking brake lever is in the released position. Disconnect the negative battery cable.
2. Raise and support the vehicle safely. Remove the front tire and wheel assemblies.
3. Remove the outer tie rod end cotter pin. Remove the castle nut. Using the proper tool, remove the tie rod end from the steering knuckle.
4. Remove the pinch bolt from the torque rod universal joint.

➡ **Do not attempt to remove the steering gear assembly or crossmember with the pinch bolt installed to the torque rod universal joint.**

5. Loosen the exhaust manifold retaining bolts. Lower the exhaust pipe.
6. Remove the steering gear retaining bolts.
7. Move the assembly toward the pinion. As the pinion shafts comes off the torque rod, rotate the steering gear rearward and remove it from the vehicle, toward the pinion.

To Install:

8. Installation is the reverse of the removal procedure. Tighten the rack retaining bolts to 33–43 ft. lbs. (44–59 Nm).
9. Adjust the toe-in and the turning angles to specifications.
10. Tighten the tie rod end to steering knuckle nuts to 18–22 ft. lbs. (25–29 Nm).

Except Justy and XT Coupe

1. Disconnect the negative battery cable.
2. Raise and support the vehicle safely. Remove the front tire and wheel assemblies.

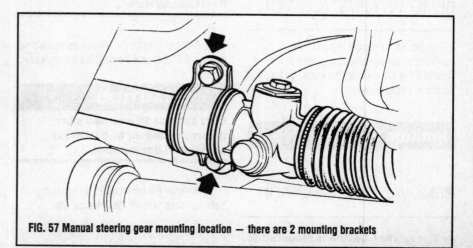

FIG. 57 Manual steering gear mounting location — there are 2 mounting brackets

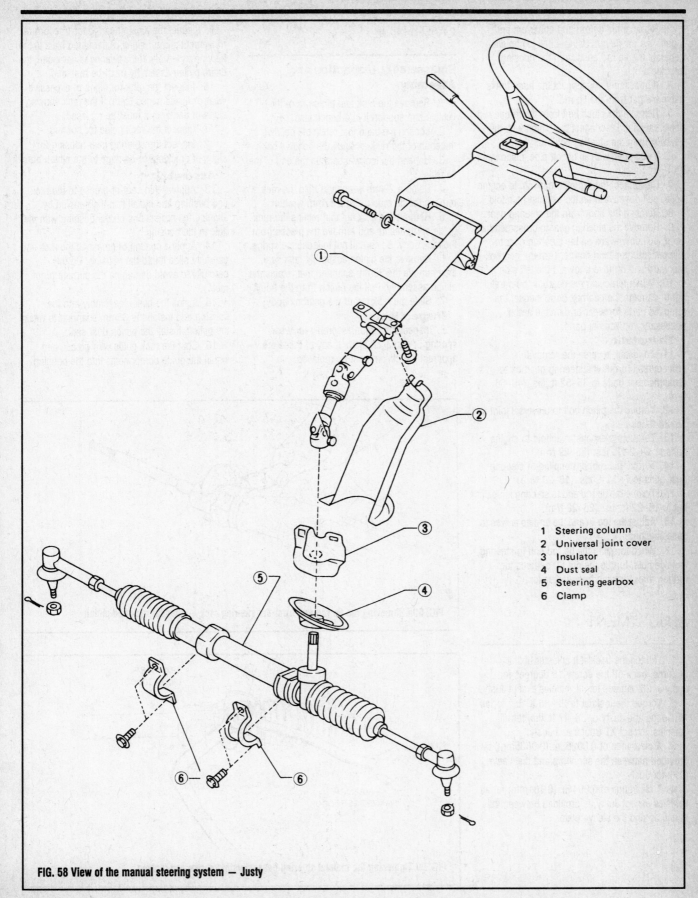

1 Steering column
2 Universal joint cover
3 Insulator
4 Dust seal
5 Steering gearbox
6 Clamp

FIG. 58 View of the manual steering system — Justy

3. Remove the tie rod end cotter pin and loosen the castle nut. Using a ball joint puller, separate the tie rod ends from the housing knuckle arm.

4. If necessary, disconnect the hand brake cable hanger from the tie rod.

5. Remove the pinch bolt from the torque rod universal joint. Disconnect the pinion with the gearbox from the steering column.

6. If equipped with an hot air pipe, disconnect it.

7. Disconnect the exhaust manifold to engine bolts, pull downward on the exhaust manifold.

8. Remove the boot from the steering gear.

9. Remove the steering gear to crossmember bolts, pull downward on the steering gear to disconnect the pinion flange. Turn the gearbox rearward and remove it toward the left side.

10. When removing the gearbox, be careful not to damage the gearbox boot. Inspect the removed parts for wear or damage and if necessary, replace the parts.

To install:

11. To install, reverse the removal procedures. Torque the steering gearbox to crossmember bolts to 35–52 ft. lbs. (48–66 Nm).

12. Torque the pinch bolt to universal joint to 15–20 ft. lbs.

13. Torque the exhaust manifold to engine bolts to 19–22 ft. lbs. (25–29 Nm).

14. Torque the rubber coupling to steering gear bolts to 7–14 ft. lbs. (10–20 Nm).

15. Torque the tie rod end to steering knuckle nut to 18–22 ft. lbs. (26–29 Nm).

16. Adjust the toe-in and the turning angles to specifications.

17. When torquing the tie rod end to steering knuckle nuts, torque the nut 60 degrees turn further, after torquing to specification.

ADJUSTMENT

1. Tighten the backlash adjuster until it bottoms, back off the screw 15 degrees for Justy or 25 degrees for all vehicles except Justy.

2. Torque the locknut to 22–36 ft. lbs. for all XT Coupe and Justy or 36–47 ft. lbs. for all vehicles, except XT Coupe and Justy.

3. A clearance of 0.0025 in. (0.0635mm) is provided between the screw tip and the sleeve plate for Justy.

4. A clearance of 0.004 in. (0.101mm) for all vehicles except Justy, is provided between the screw tip and the sleeve plate.

OVERHAUL

Disassembly, Inspection and Assembly

1. Remove the rack and pinion from the vehicle and support it in a bench vise.

2. Loosen the band that retain the bellows on the ends of the rack and pull the bellows back.

3. Unbend the lockwashers on the end of the tie rods.

4. Using a 22mm wrench to hold the rack, remove the tie rods using a 17mm wrench.

5. Remove the lock nut that retains the rack guide components and remove the pieces from the rack body. Be careful not to loose the spring.

6. Remove the pinion assembly dust seal, then remove the 35mm snapring that retains the pinion assembly. Pull the pinion from the body.

7. Slide the rack out of the gearbox body.

Inspection:

8. Inspect the pinion assembly for wear, scoring or damaged teeth. If any of these are apparent the pinion must be replaced.

9. Inspect the pinion bearing for freedom of movement and for signs of damaged balls in the bearing assembly. If the bearing is damaged, the entire pinion assembly must be replaced.

10. Inspect the rack for signs of excessive wear or for damaged teeth. If the rack shows signs of damage, it must be replaced.

11. Inspect the rack guide for scoring.

12. Inspect the steering gear housing for signs of cracking, or damage to the pinion bore.

Assembly:

13. Apply a thin coat of grease to the rack end bushing and install it in the housing by aligning the projections on the bushing with the hole in the housing.

14. Apply a coating of grease to the rack and carefully slide it into the housing. Do this carefully to avoid damaging the surface of the rack.

15. Install the pinion assembly into the housing and install the 35mm snapring to retain the pinion. Install the pinion dust seal.

16. Coat the rack guide with grease and install the guide components into the housing.

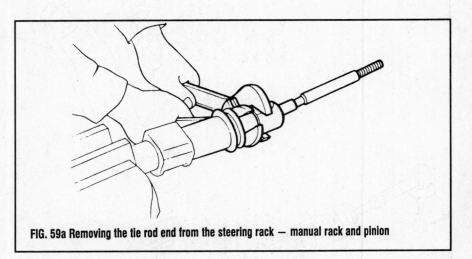

FIG. 59a Removing the tie rod end from the steering rack — manual rack and pinion

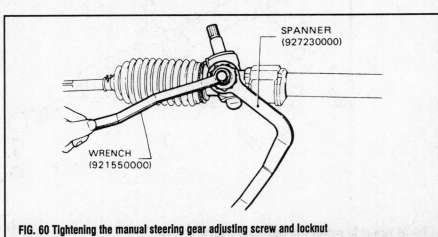

FIG. 60 Tightening the manual steering gear adjusting screw and locknut

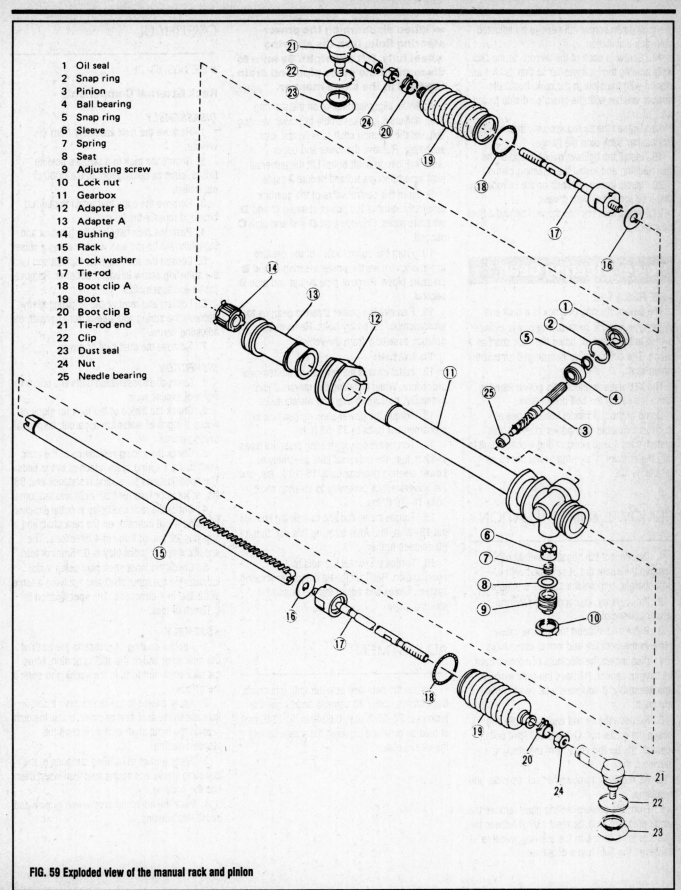

1 Oil seal
2 Snap ring
3 Pinion
4 Ball bearing
5 Snap ring
6 Sleeve
7 Spring
8 Seat
9 Adjusting screw
10 Lock nut
11 Gearbox
12 Adapter B
13 Adapter A
14 Bushing
15 Rack
16 Lock washer
17 Tie-rod
18 Boot clip A
19 Boot
20 Boot clip B
21 Tie-rod end
22 Clip
23 Dust seal
24 Nut
25 Needle bearing

FIG. 59 Exploded view of the manual rack and pinion

The rack guide screw will need to be adjusted after rack installation.

17. Screw in each of the tie rods to the rack, while holding the lock washer so that its tabs are aligned with the slots in the rack. Install the stopper washer with the chamfered side facing out.

18. Tighten the tie rod securely then bend the lockwasher back onto the flange.

19. Install the bellows over the end of the rack housing and install the retaining clamp.

20. Install the tie rod ends on the tie rods and fill the tie rod boots with grease.

21. Install the rack into the vehicle and adjust the rack.

Power Steering Gear

♦ SEE FIGS. 61–62

The power steering gearbox is a rack and pinion type integral system. The power cylinder is built in the gearbox, using the rack shaft as a piston. The control valve is arranged around the pinion shaft.

The XT6 uses an electronic power steering pump instead of the belt driven type.

Some of the late model vehicles use an electronic variable type power steering, this system uses speed sensors and a control unit to vary the amount of steering assist based on vehicle needs.

REMOVAL & INSTALLATION

1. Disconnect the negative battery cable. Remove the spare tire. If equipped with a turbocharger, remove the spare tire support.

2. If necessary, disconnect the thermo-sensor connector.

3. Raise and support the vehicle safely. Remove the front tire and wheel assemblies.

4. Disconnect the electrical connector from the oxygen sensor. Remove the front exhaust pipe assembly. If equipped with an air stove, remove it.

5. Remove the tie rod end cotter pin and loosen the castle nut. Using a ball joint puller, separate the tie rod ends from the steering knuckle arm.

6. As required, remove the jack up plate and the clamp.

7. From the power steering gear, remove the center pressure pipe, connect a vinyl hose to the pipe and joint, then turn the steering wheel to discharge the fluid into a container.

➡ **When discharging the power steering fluid, turn the steering wheel fully, left and right. Be sure to disconnect the other pipe and drain the fluid in the same manner.**

8. Make alignment marks on the steering shaft universal joint assembly to power steering unit and the steering shaft to universal joint assembly. Remove the lower and upper universal joint to shaft bolts. Lift the universal joint assembly upward and secure it aside.

9. From the control valve of the gearbox assembly, remove the power steering **C** and **D** pressure pipes. Remove pipe **D** first and pipe **C** second.

10. From the control valve of the gearbox assembly, remove the power steering **A** and **B** pressure pipes. Remove pipe **A** first and pipe **B** second.

11. Remove the power steering gearbox to crossmember assembly bolts. Remove the gearbox assembly from the vehicle.

To Install:

12. Installation is the reverse of the removal procedure. When installing the universal joint assembly, be sure to align the matchmarks.

13. Torque the power steering gearbox to crossmember bolts to 35–52 ft. lbs.

14. Torque the power steering pressure pipes 7–12 ft. lbs., the universal joint assembly to power steering gearbox bolts 16–19 ft. lbs. and the universal joint assembly to steering shaft bolts 16–19 ft. lbs.

15. Torque the tie rod end to steering knuckle nut 18–22 ft. lbs. After torquing this nut, turn it 60 degrees further.

16. Torque the wheel lug nuts to specification. Refill and bleed the power steering system. Check and adjust the toe-in and the steering angle.

ADJUSTMENT

Tighten the backlash adjuster until it bottoms, back off the screw 30 degrees and torque the locknut to 22–36 ft. lbs., 0.0049 in. (0.1245mm) should be provided between the screw tip and the sleeve plate.

OVERHAUL

♦ SEE FIGS. 63–71

Rack External Components

DISASSEMBLY

1. Remove the rack assembly from the vehicle.

2. Secure the rack in a suitable holding fixture, such as holding tool 926200000 or equivalent.

3. Remove the clips that retain the tie rod boot and remove the boot.

4. Push the rack fully into the gearbox and straighten the tie rod lock washer using a chisel.

5. Loosen the rack adjuster locknut and turn the adjusting screw in until it bottoms. Remove the tie rod assemblies.

6. Loosen and remove the adjusting screw. Remove the spring and sleeve from beneath the adjusting screw.

7. Remove the dust seal or cover.

INSPECTION

1. Clean all disassembled parts and check for signs of excess wear.

2. Check the inside of the rack for signs of water. If signs of water are apparent, inspect all sealing points.

3. Check the sliding resistance of the rack shaft using a spring scale attached to the ends. The specifications for sliding resistance are: 68 lbs. of force or less for both right and left turns.

4. Check the rack shaft play in radial direction by using a dial indicator on the rack shaft and applying 22 lbs. of force in 4 directions. The specification for radial play is 0.15mm or less.

5. Check the input shaft play using a dial indicator on the input shaft and applying a force of 22 lbs. in 4 directions. The specification is 0.18mm or less.

ASSEMBLY

1. Apply a coating of grease to the teeth of the rack shaft and to the sliding portion. Move the rack back and forth in the housing to spread the grease.

2. Apply grease to the dust sleeve insertion hole and to the dust seal or cover. Install the dust seal on the input shaft until it reaches the stepped portion.

3. Apply grease the sliding surfaces of the adjusting sleeve and spring seat then insert them into the housing.

4. Pack the adjusting screw with grease and install into housing.

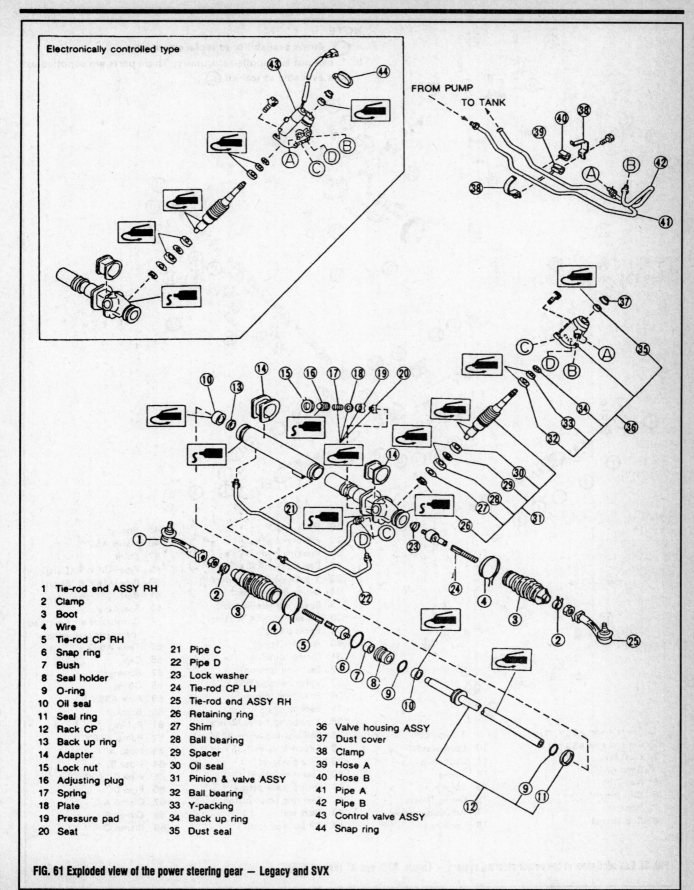

Electronically controlled type

FROM PUMP
TO TANK

1 Tie-rod end ASSY RH
2 Clamp
3 Boot
4 Wire
5 Tie-rod CP RH
6 Snap ring
7 Bush
8 Seal holder
9 O-ring
10 Oil seal
11 Seal ring
12 Rack CP
13 Back up ring
14 Adapter
15 Lock nut
16 Adjusting plug
17 Spring
18 Plate
19 Pressure pad
20 Seat

21 Pipe C
22 Pipe D
23 Lock washer
24 Tie-rod CP LH
25 Tie-rod end ASSY RH
26 Retaining ring
27 Shim
28 Ball bearing
29 Spacer
30 Oil seal
31 Pinion & valve ASSY
32 Ball bearing
33 Y-packing
34 Back up ring
35 Dust seal

36 Valve housing ASSY
37 Dust cover
38 Clamp
39 Hose A
40 Hose B
41 Pipe A
42 Pipe B
43 Control valve ASSY
44 Snap ring

FIG. 61 Exploded view of the power steering gear — Legacy and SVX

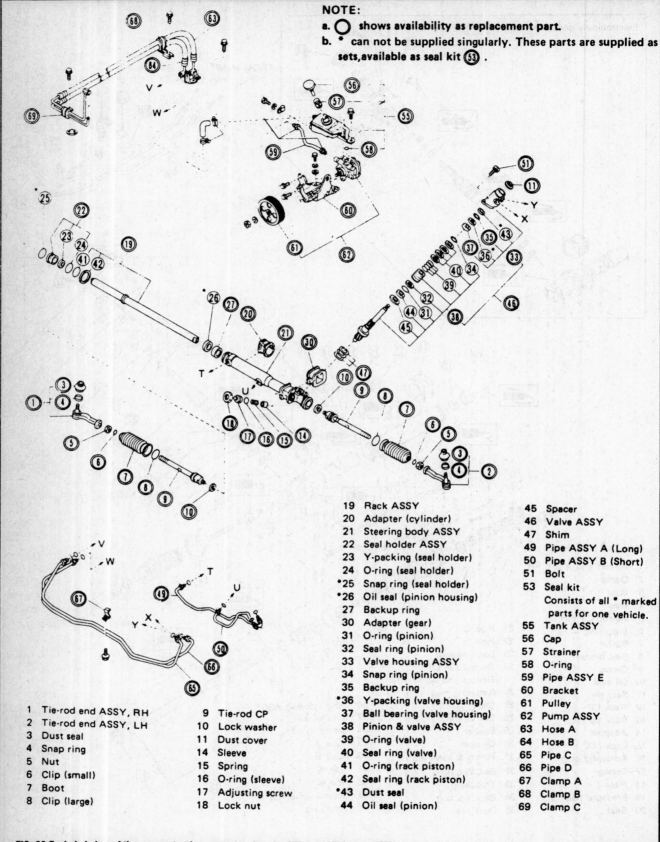

NOTE:
a. ◯ shows availability as replacement part.
b. * can not be supplied singularly. These parts are supplied as sets, available as seal kit ⑤③ .

19	Rack ASSY	45	Spacer
20	Adapter (cylinder)	46	Valve ASSY
21	Steering body ASSY	47	Shim
22	Seal holder ASSY	49	Pipe ASSY A (Long)
23	Y-packing (seal holder)	50	Pipe ASSY B (Short)
24	O-ring (seal holder)	51	Bolt
*25	Snap ring (seal holder)	53	Seal kit
*26	Oil seal (pinion housing)		Consists of all * marked
27	Backup ring		parts for one vehicle.
30	Adapter (gear)	55	Tank ASSY
31	O-ring (pinion)	56	Cap
32	Seal ring (pinion)	57	Strainer
33	Valve housing ASSY	58	O-ring
34	Snap ring (pinion)	59	Pipe ASSY E
35	Backup ring	60	Bracket
*36	Y-packing (valve housing)	61	Pulley
37	Ball bearing (valve housing)	62	Pump ASSY
38	Pinion & valve ASSY	63	Hose A
39	O-ring (valve)	64	Hose B
40	Seal ring (valve)	65	Pipe C
41	O-ring (rack piston)	66	Pipe D
42	Seal ring (rack piston)	67	Clamp A
*43	Dust seal	68	Clamp B
44	Oil seal (pinion)	69	Clamp C

1	Tie-rod end ASSY, RH	9	Tie-rod CP
2	Tie-rod end ASSY, LH	10	Lock washer
3	Dust seal	11	Dust cover
4	Snap ring	14	Sleeve
5	Nut	15	Spring
6	Clip (small)	16	O-ring (sleeve)
7	Boot	17	Adjusting screw
8	Clip (large)	18	Lock nut

FIG. 62 Exploded view of the power steering system — Loyale, STD. and XT (except XT6)

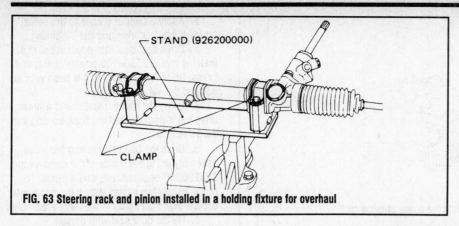

FIG. 63 Steering rack and pinion installed in a holding fixture for overhaul

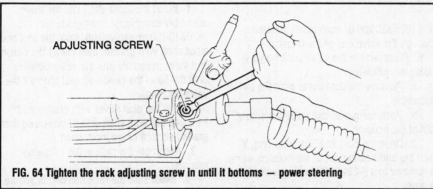

FIG. 64 Tighten the rack adjusting screw in until it bottoms — power steering

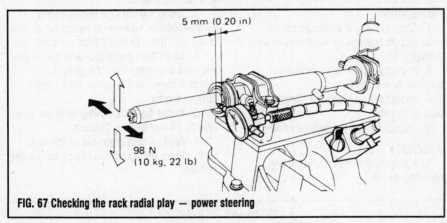

FIG. 67 Checking the rack radial play — power steering

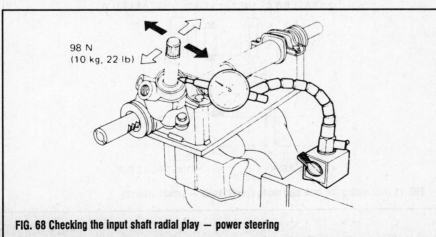

FIG. 68 Checking the input shaft radial play — power steering

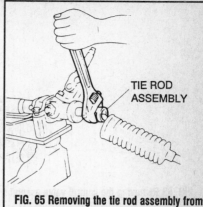

FIG. 65 Removing the tie rod assembly from the rack — power steering

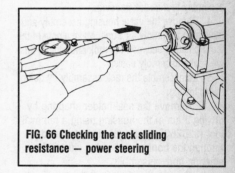

FIG. 66 Checking the rack sliding resistance — power steering

5. Install the tie rod assemblies by first sliding the rack out beyond the side of the housing by about 40mm. Tighten the adjusting screw fully to hold the rack in position.

6. Adjust the rack and pinion backlash in the following manner:

   a. Make sure the rack adjusting screw is completely tight by tightening it to 3.6 ft. lbs. (5 Nm) and backing it off about 1/2 a turn.

   b. Turn the adjusting screw until the rack turning torque increases steeply then back it off about 1/12 of a turn (30 degrees). Tighten the locknut to 22–36 ft. lbs. (29–49 Nm).

7. Bend the lockwashers on the tie rod ends using a chisel or equivalent tool.

8. Install the rack boots and install the retaining clips. Tighten the tie rod locknuts, if tie rod was removed.

9. Install the rack into the vehicle.

Control Valve

The control valve is the portion of the rack and pinion that distributes the fluid pressure.

DISASSEMBLY

1. Remove the rack assembly from the vehicle.

2. Secure the rack in a suitable holding fixture, such as holding tool 926200000 or equivalent.

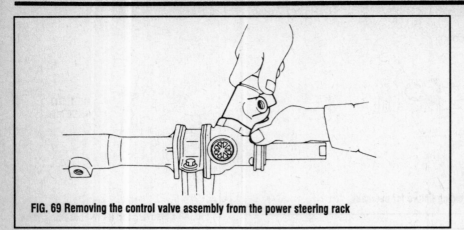

FIG. 69 Removing the control valve assembly from the power steering rack

3. Remove the 2 bolts that attach the valve assembly to the rack housing.

4. Remove the valve housing assembly and the pinion assembly as a unit. Make a note of the tooth position between the rack and pinion, this will make assembly easier.

5. Disassemble the rack assembly by doing the following:

a. Remove the seal holder snapring by driving it out of the housing using a removal tool (926260000 or equivalent) inserted through the boot groove in the side of the steering body assembly.

b. Remove the rack from the housing by pushing it from the valve side and extracting it at the opposite side. Use care when sliding the rack out of the housing to avoid damaging the housing.

c. Remove the high pressure seal by pushing it out of the housing using a removal tool (926330000 or equivalent) inserted through the valve end of the housing.

6. Disassemble the valve assembly by doing the following:

a. Remove the dust cover from the pinion assembly.

b. Push the pinion and valve assembly out of the housing.

c. Drive the dust seal, back-up ring, Y-packing and bearing out of the housing using a remover tool (926290000 or equivalent) and a press.

INSPECTION

1. Clean all parts in a suitable solvent.
2. Inspect bearings for roughness or signs of damage.
3. Inspect pinion gear for broken or excessively worn teeth.
4. Inspect the rack teeth for signs of excess wear or damage.
5. Inspect the seal for damage or wear.

ASSEMBLY

1. Assemble the valve assembly in the following manner:

a. Apply a coat of grease to the valve housing, back-up ring and the Y-packing.

b. Drive dust seal into position using an installer tool (926300000 or equivalent) and press. Drive the seal in until it is flush with the edge of the valve assembly.

c. Using the same installer and a press, drive the Y-packing and the back-up ring into the valve housing.

d. Drive the ball bearing into the valve assembly using the B side of the remover tool 926290000 or equivalent, and a press. To make installation easier, attach the bearing to the tool first than install in the valve assembly.

e. Fill the dust seal with grease.

f. Insert the input shaft into the valve assembly using input shaft guide tool (926310000 or equivalent). Coat the tool and input shaft with grease, then install the pinion and valve assembly into the valve housing until the lip of the pinion oil seal touches the valve housing.

g. Fill the dust cover with grease and install on the input shaft until it butts up against graded section of the input shaft.

2. Assemble the rack in the following manner:

a. Make sure the rack housing is secure in a holding fixture.

b. Using special seal installer tools (926240000 or equivalent) attach the oil seal to the tool (refer to FIG. 71 for position).

c. Insert the special tool with the oil seal into rack assembly from the gear side. Remove the oil seal near the piston then remove the tool.

d. Install the back-up ring from the gear side by sliding it down the rack.

e. Apply a coat of grease to the rack teeth, sleeve sliding portion and piston sealing surface.

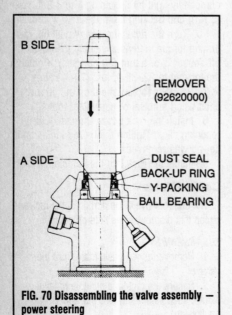

FIG. 70 Disassembling the valve assembly — power steering

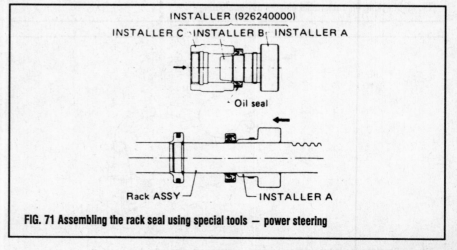

FIG. 71 Assembling the rack seal using special tools — power steering

f. Insert the rack assembly into the housing on the cylinder side.

g. Apply a thin coat of grease to the holder assembly and slide it onto the rack end on the cylinder side. Apply a coat of grease to the holder snapring and install it into the holder.

h. Using an installer tool (926320000 or equivalent) drive the back-up ring and oil seal into position in the housing.

3. Be sure that the valve assembly is clean. Attach shims to the stepped lip of the rack housing and apply a bead of sealer (Fuji Bond C: 004403004 or equivalent) to the lip of the pinion housing.

4. Pull the rack assembly out 77mm beyond the housing on the pinion side.

5. Apply grease to the pinion gear teeth and ball bearings.

6. Position the input shaft gear so that the cutout faces toward the sleeve boss. Push the valve assembly housing into position.

7. Move the rack assembly back and forth and tighten the retaining bolts on the valve assembly alternately to a final torque of 14–22 ft. lbs. (20–29 Nm).

8. Check the movement of the rack for binding, correct if needed.

Power Steering Pump

REMOVAL & INSTALLATION

♦ SEE FIGS. 72–75

Except XT6

1. Disconnect the negative battery cable.

2. Using a siphon, drain the power steering fluid from the reservoir.

3. Loosen, but do not remove the power steering pump pulley nut. Loosen the pulley drive belts.

4. Remove the power steering pump pulley nut and the pulley.

5. Disconnect and plug the **A** pressure hose from the **E** pipe. Disconnect the **B** pressure hose from the oil tank.

6. When disconnecting the **A** hose, use wrenches to prevent the **E** pipe from twisting.

7. Remove the **E** hose to reservoir clamp.

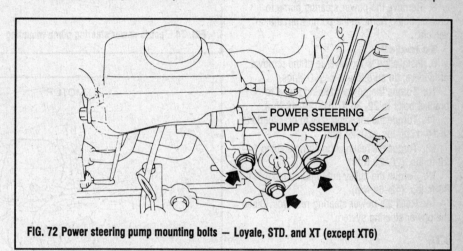

FIG. 72 Power steering pump mounting bolts — Loyale, STD. and XT (except XT6)

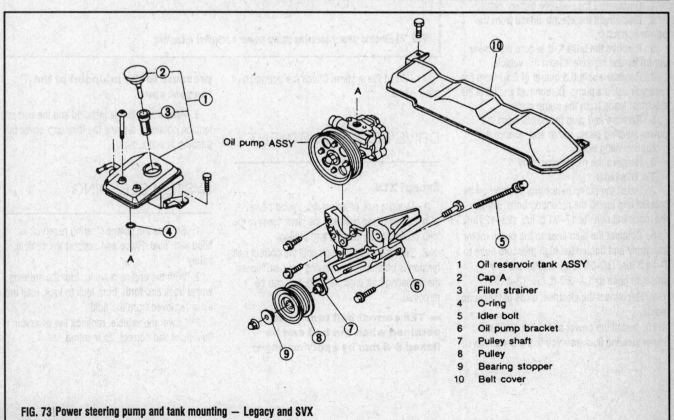

1	Oil reservoir tank ASSY
2	Cap A
3	Filler strainer
4	O-ring
5	Idler bolt
6	Oil pump bracket
7	Pulley shaft
8	Pulley
9	Bearing stopper
10	Belt cover

Oil pump ASSY

FIG. 73 Power steering pump and tank mounting — Legacy and SVX

Loosen the reservoir to bracket bolt, then remove the **A** and **B** bolts on the upper part of the reservoir, this will allow the fluid to run out.

➡ **To minimize the fluid loss from the reservoir, remove both bolts while the reservoir is pressed against the oil pump, then quickly remove the reservoir. It is a good idea to remove the pump and the reservoir as a unit, then separate the reservoir from the pump on a bench.**

8. Remove the power steering pump to bracket bolts. Remove the pump from the vehicle.

To Install:

9. Installation is the reverse of the removal procedure; be sure to use new O-rings.

10. Torque the power steering pump to bracket bolts to 22–36 ft. lbs. (29–49 Nm).

11. Torque the reservoir stay to bracket bolts to 14–17 ft. lbs. (20–24 Nm).

12. Torque the reservoir to pump bolts to 14–22 ft. lbs. (20–29 Nm).

13. Torque the pulley nut to pump nut to 31–46 ft. lbs. (42–62 Nm).

14. Refill the power steering reservoir. Bleed the power steering system.

XT6

1. Disconnect the negative battery cable.

2. Disconnect the electrical lead from the power controller.

3. Remove the bolts that secure the power controller and remove it from the vehicle.

4. Remove about 0.3 quarts of fluid from the reservoir using a pump. Disconnect and label the electrical leads from the pump motor.

5. Remove and plug the hoses from the power steering pump motor and remove the motor mounting bolts.

6. Remove the motor assembly.

To Install:

7. Install the pump motor into position on the bracket and install the mounting bolts. Tighten the mounting bolts to 17–31 ft. lbs. (23–42 Nm).

8. Connect the fluid lines to the pump motor assembly and tighten the high pressure hose to 7–14 ft lbs. (10–20 Nm). Tighten the low pressure hose to 1.4–2.2 ft. lbs. (2–3 Nm).

9. Reconnect the electrical leads to the pump motor.

10. Install the power controller. Refill the power steering fluid reservoir to the correct level.

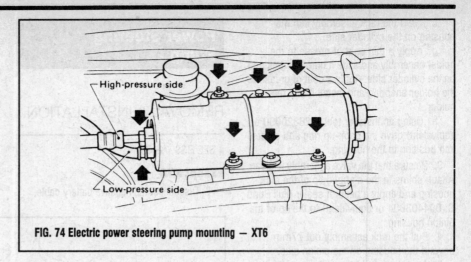

FIG. 74 Electric power steering pump mounting — XT6

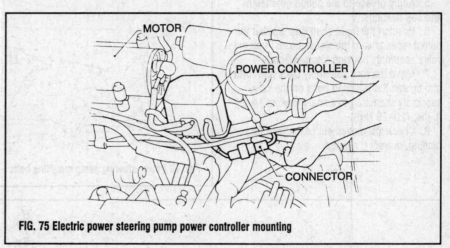

FIG. 75 Electric power steering pump power controller mounting

11. Bleed the system. Check the operation of the system.

DRIVE BELT ADJUSTMENT

Except XT6

1. Using a pair of adjustable jawed pliers, with a piece of rag between the jaws, remove the idler cover cap by turning and pulling.

2. Turn the adjusting bolt until the correct belt tension is obtained. If removing the belt, loosen the adjusting bolt until the drive belt can be removed.

➡ **The correct belt tension is obtained when the belt can be flexed 6–8 mm by applying finger pressure to the midpoint of the longest span.**

3. After a new belt is installed and the correct tension obtained, replace the idler cap cover by pushing in and turning.

SYSTEM BLEEDING

1. Be sure the power steering reservoir is filled with fluid. Raise and support the vehicle safely.

2. With the engine running, turn the steering wheel back and forth, from lock to lock, until the air is removed from the fluid.

3. Lower the vehicle, recheck the reservoir fluid level and correct, as required.

Troubleshooting the Turn Signal Switch

Problem	Cause	Solution
Turn signal will not cancel	• Loose switch mounting screws • Switch or anchor bosses broken • Broken, missing or out of position detent, or cancelling spring	• Tighten screws • Replace switch • Reposition springs or replace switch as required
Turn signal difficult to operate	• Turn signal lever loose • Switch yoke broken or distorted • Loose or misplaced springs • Foreign parts and/or materials in switch • Switch mounted loosely	• Tighten mounting screws • Replace switch • Reposition springs or replace switch • Remove foreign parts and/or material • Tighten mounting screws
Turn signal will not indicate lane change	• Broken lane change pressure pad or spring hanger • Broken, missing or misplaced lane change spring • Jammed wires	• Replace switch • Replace or reposition as required • Loosen mounting screws, reposition wires and retighten screws
Turn signal will not stay in turn position	• Foreign material or loose parts impeding movement of switch yoke • Defective switch	• Remove material and/or parts • Replace switch
Hazard switch cannot be pulled out	• Foreign material between hazard support cancelling leg and yoke	• Remove foreign material. No foreign material impeding function of hazard switch—replace turn signal switch.
No turn signal lights	• Inoperative turn signal flasher • Defective or blown fuse • Loose chassis to column harness connector • Disconnect column to chassis connector. Connect new switch to chassis and operate switch by hand. If vehicle lights now operate normally, signal switch is inoperative • If vehicle lights do not operate, check chassis wiring for opens, grounds, etc.	• Replace turn signal flasher • Replace fuse • Connect securely • Replace signal switch • Repair chassis wiring as required

Troubleshooting the Turn Signal Switch (cont.)

Problem	Cause	Solution
Instrument panel turn indicator lights on but not flashing	• Burned out or damaged front or rear turn signal bulb • If vehicle lights do not operate, check light sockets for high resistance connections, the chassis wiring for opens, grounds, etc. • Inoperative flasher • Loose chassis to column harness connection • Inoperative turn signal switch • To determine if turn signal switch is defective, substitute new switch into circuit and operate switch by hand. If the vehicle's lights operate normally, signal switch is inoperative.	• Replace bulb • Repair chassis wiring as required • Replace flasher • Connect securely • Replace turn signal switch • Replace turn signal switch
Stop light not on when turn indicated	• Loose column to chassis connection • Disconnect column to chassis connector. Connect new switch into system without removing old.	• Connect securely • Replace signal switch
Stop light not on when turn indicated (cont.)	Operate switch by hand. If brake lights work with switch in the turn position, signal switch is defective. • If brake lights do not work, check connector to stop light sockets for grounds, opens, etc.	 • Repair connector to stop light circuits using service manual as guide
Turn indicator panel lights not flashing	• Burned out bulbs • High resistance to ground at bulb socket • Opens, ground in wiring harness from front turn signal bulb socket to indicator lights	• Replace bulbs • Replace socket • Locate and repair as required
Turn signal lights flash very slowly	• High resistance ground at light sockets • Incorrect capacity turn signal flasher or bulb • If flashing rate is still extremely slow, check chassis wiring harness from the connector to light sockets for high resistance • Loose chassis to column harness connection • Disconnect column to chassis connector. Connect new switch into system without removing old. Operate switch by hand. If flashing occurs at normal rate, the signal switch is defective.	• Repair high resistance grounds at light sockets • Replace turn signal flasher or bulb • Locate and repair as required • Connect securely • Replace turn signal switch

Troubleshooting the Turn Signal Switch (cont.)

Problem	Cause	Solution
Hazard signal lights will not flash— turn signal functions normally	• Blow fuse • Inoperative hazard warning flasher • Loose chassis-to-column harness connection • Disconnect column to chassis connector. Connect new switch into system without removing old. Depress the hazard warning lights. If they now work normally, turn signal switch is defective. • If lights do not flash, check wiring harness "K" lead for open between hazard flasher and connector. If open, fuse block is defective	• Replace fuse • Replace hazard warning flasher in fuse panel • Conect securely • Replace turn signal switch • Repair or replace brown wire or connector as required

Troubleshooting the Power Steering Pump

Problem	Cause	Solution
Chirp noise in steering pump	• Loose belt	• Adjust belt tension to specification
Belt squeal (particularly noticeable at full wheel travel and stand still parking)	• Loose belt	• Adjust belt tension to specification
Growl noise in steering pump	• Excessive back pressure in hoses or steering gear caused by restriction	• Locate restriction and correct. Replace part if necessary.
Growl noise in steering pump (particularly noticeable at stand still parking)	• Scored pressure plates, thrust plate or rotor • Extreme wear of cam ring	• Replace parts and flush system • Replace parts
Groan noise in steering pump	• Low oil level • Air in the oil. Poor pressure hose connection.	• Fill reservoir to proper level • Tighten connector to specified torque. Bleed system by operating steering from right to left— full turn.
Rattle noise in steering pump	• Vanes not installed properly • Vanes sticking in rotor slots	• Install properly • Free up by removing burrs, varnish, or dirt
Swish noise in steering pump	• Defective flow control valve	• Replace part
Whine noise in steering pump	• Pump shaft bearing scored	• Replace housing and shaft. Flush system.

Troubleshooting the Power Steering Pump (cont.)

Problem	Cause	Solution
Hard steering or lack of assist	· Loose pump belt · Low oil level in reservoir **NOTE:** Low oil level will also result in excessive pump noise · Steering gear to column misalignment · Lower coupling flange rubbing against steering gear adjuster plug · Tires not properly inflated	· Adjust belt tension to specification · Fill to proper level. If excessively low, check all lines and joints for evidence of external leakage. Tighten loose connectors. · Align steering column · Loosen pinch bolt and assemble properly · Inflate to recommended pressure
Foaming milky power steering fluid, low fluid level and possible low pressure	· Air in the fluid, and loss of fluid due to internal pump leakage causing overflow	· Check for leaks and correct. Bleed system. Extremely cold temperatures will cause system aeriation should the oil level be low. If oil level is correct and pump still foams, remove pump from vehicle and separate reservoir from body. Check welsh plug and body for cracks. If plug is loose or body is cracked, replace body.
Low pump pressure	· Flow control valve stuck or inoperative · Pressure plate not flat against cam ring	· Remove burrs or dirt or replace. Flush system. · Correct
Momentary increase in effort when turning wheel fast to right or left	· Low oil level in pump · Pump belt slipping · High internal leakage	· Add power steering fluid as required · Tighten or replace belt · Check pump pressure. (See pressure test)
Steering wheel surges or jerks when turning with engine running especially during parking	· Low oil level · Loose pump belt · Steering linkage hitting engine oil pan at full turn · Insufficient pump pressure	· Fill as required · Adjust tension to specification · Correct clearance · Check pump pressure. (See pressure test). Replace flow control valve if defective.
Steering wheel surges or jerks when turning with engine running especially during parking (cont.)	· Sticking flow control valve	· Inspect for varnish or damage, replace if necessary
Excessive wheel kickback or loose steering	· Air in system	· Add oil to pump reservoir and bleed by operating steering. Check hose connectors for proper torque and adjust as required.

Troubleshooting the Power Steering Pump (cont.)

Problem	Cause	Solution
Low pump pressure	• Extreme wear of cam ring • Scored pressure plate, thrust plate, or rotor • Vanes not installed properly • Vanes sticking in rotor slots • Cracked or broken thrust or pressure plate	• Replace parts. Flush system. • Replace parts. Flush system. • Install properly • Freeup by removing burrs, varnish, or dirt • Replace part

TORQUE SPECIFICATIONS

Component	English	Metric
Lug nuts except SVX	58–72 ft. lbs.	78–98 Nm
Lug nuts SVX	72–87 ft. lbs.	98–118 Nm
Front Strut Assembly:		
Justy		
lower attaching bolts	25–40 ft. lbs.	34–54 Nm
upper attaching nuts	29–43 ft. lbs.	39–59 Nm
Except Justy		
attaching bolts	28–37 ft. lbs.	38–50 Nm
Strut upper plate retaining nut	22 ft. lbs	31 Nm
Ball Joint:		
Except SVX		
ball joint-to-housing bolt	28–37 ft. lbs.	38–50 Nm
ball joint-to-transverse link nut	29 ft. lbs.	39 Nm
SVX		
ball joint-to-control arm bolts	79.7–101.8 ft. lbs.	108–138 Nm
ball joint-to housing pinch bolt	33.2–43.5 ft. lbs.	45–59 Nm
Front Stabilizer:		
Except SVX		
jack-up plate-to-crossmember	17–31 ft. lbs.	2–42 Nm
stabilizer link-to-transverse link	18–25 ft. lbs.	25–34 Nm
stabilizer-to-crossmember	15–21 ft. lbs.	21–28 Nm
SVX		
stabilizer link-to-stabilizer lever	23–31 ft. lbs.	32–42 Nm
stabilizer bar-to-stabilizer lever	33–43 ft. lbs.	45–59 Nm
stabilizer bar-to-crossmember	15–21 ft. lbs.	21–28 Nm
Transverse Link:		
Justy		
transverse link-to-crossmember	43–58 ft. lbs.	59–78 Nm
tension rod-to-bracket bolt	40–54 ft. lbs.	54–74 Nm
tension rod-to-transverse link bolt	54–69 ft. lbs.	74–93 Nm
Loyale, STD. and XT		
transverse link bolt	43–51 ft. lbs.	59–69 Nm
stabilizer assembly bolts	14–22 ft. lbs.	20–29 Nm
Legacy		
transverse link-to-stabilizer	14–22 ft. lbs.	20–29 Nm
transverse link-to-crossmember	61–83 ft. lbs.	83–113 Nm
transverse link rear bushing-to-chassis	145–217 ft. lbs.	196–294 Nm
transverse link end bushing nut	152–195 ft. lbs.	206–265 Nm
SVX		
rear support-to-sub frame bolts	93–123 ft. lbs.	126–167 Nm
lower control arm retaining bolts	56–73 ft. lbs.	76–100 Nm

TORQUE SPECIFICATIONS

Component	English	Metric
Rear Strut Assembly:		
Justy		
lower strut-to-housing bolts	72–87 ft. lbs.	98–118 Nm
upper strut mounting nuts	43–51 ft. lbs.	59–69 Nm
Loyale, STD. and XT		
lower strut attaching bolts	51–87 ft. lbs.	69–118 Nm
upper strut retaining bolts	65–94 ft. lbs.	88–127 Nm
Legacy		
lower strut mounting bolts	137–174 ft. lbs.	186–235 Nm
upper strut mounting nuts	36–51 ft. lbs.	49–69 Nm
SVX		
lower strut mounting bolts	98–127 ft. lbs.	132–172 Nm
upper strut mounting nuts	36–51 ft. lbs.	49–69 Nm
Rear Control Arms:		
Justy		
control arm-to-axle housing bolts	54–69 ft. lbs.	74–93 Nm
control arm-to-crossmember bolts	43–58 ft. lbs.	59–78 Nm
Loyale, STD. and XT		
inner arm-to-crossmember bolts	51–65 ft. lbs.	69–88 Nm
outer arm attaching bolts	94–108 ft. lbs.	127–147 Nm
Legacy		
trailing link mounting bolts	72–94 ft. lbs.	98–127 Nm
lateral link through bolts—		
FWD models	61–83 ft. lbs.	83–113 Nm
4WD models	87–116 ft. lbs.	118–157 Nm
SVX		
rear trailing link-to-housing bolt	80–101 ft. lbs.	137–177 Nm
front trailing link through bolt	101–130 ft. lbs.	137–177 Nm
front lateral link-to-sub frame through bolt		
(bolt without cap for the end)	72–101 ft. lbs.	98–137 Nm
rear lateral link-to-sub frame through bolt		
(bolt with cap, closest to the differential)	61–83 ft. lbs.	83–113 Nm
stabilizer link nut	12–17 ft. lbs.	16–14 Nm
Steering Wheel:		
retaining nut		
Justy	36–43 ft. lbs.	49–59 Nm
Loyale, STD. and XT	22–29 ft. lbs.	29–39 Nm
Legacy and SVX	22–29 ft. lbs.	29–39 Nm
Manual Steering Gear:		
Rack and pinion mounting bolts		
Justy and XT	33–43 ft. lbs.	44–59 Nm
Except Justy and XT	35–52 ft. lbs.	48–66 Nm

9

BRAKES

BRAKE OPERATING SYSTEM

Understanding the Brakes

HYDRAULIC SYSTEM

The brake pedal operates a hydraulic system that is used for 2 reasons. First, fluid under pressure can be carried to all parts of the vehicle by small hoses or metal lines without taking up a lot of room or causing routing problems. Second, the hydraulic fluid offers a great mechanical advantage — little foot pressure is required on the pedal, but a great deal of pressure is generated at the wheels.

The brake pedal is linked to a piston in the brake master cylinder, which is filled with hydraulic brake fluid. The master cylinder consists of a cylinder, containing a small piston and a fluid reservoir.

Modern master cylinders are actually 2 separate cylinders. The 2 cylinders are actually separated, allowing for emergency stopping power should one part of the system fail. The braking force is applied to one rear wheel and one front wheel in diagonal pattern. This system is known as the dual diagonal system.

The entire hydraulic system from the master cylinder to the wheels is full of hydraulic brake fluid. When the brake pedal is depressed, the pistons in the master cylinder are forced to move, exerting tremendous force on the fluid in the lines. The fluid has nowhere to go and forces the wheel cylinder piston (drum brakes) or caliper pistons (disc brakes) to exert pressure on the brake shoes or pads. The resulting friction between the brake shoe and wheel drum or the brake pad and disc slows the vehicle and eventually stops it.

Also attached to the brake pedal is a switch which lights the brake lights as the pedal is depressed. The lights stay **ON** until the brake pedal is released and returns to its normal position.

Each wheel cylinder in a drum brake system contains 2 pistons, one at either end, which push outward in opposite directions. In disc brake systems, the wheel cylinders are part of the caliper; there can be as many as 4 or as few as 1. Whether disc or drum type, all pistons use some type of rubber seal to prevent leakage around the piston and a rubber dust boot seals the outer ends of the wheel cylinders against dirt and moisture.

When the brake pedal is released, a spring pushes the master cylinder pistons back to their normal position. Check valves in the master cylinder piston allow fluid to flow toward the wheel cylinders or calipers as the piston returns. As the brake shoe return springs pull the brake shoes back to the released position, excess fluid returns to the master cylinder through compensating ports, which have been uncovered as the pistons move back. Any fluid that has leaked from the system will also be replaced through the compensating ports.

All brake systems use a switch to activate a light, warning of brake failure. The switch is located in a valve mounted near the master cylinder. A piston in the valve receives pressure on each end from the front and rear brake circuits. When the pressures are balanced, the piston remains stationary but when one circuit has a leak, greater pressure during the application of the brakes will force the piston to one side or the other, closing the switch and activating the warning light.

Disc brake systems also have a metering valve to prevent the front disc brakes from engaging before the rear brakes have contacted the drums. This ensures that the front brakes will not normally be used alone to stop the vehicle. A proportioning valve is also used to limit pressure to the rear brakes to prevent rear wheel lock-up during hard braking.

DRUM BRAKES

Drum brakes use two brake shoes mounted on a stationary backing plate. These shoes are positioned inside a circular cast iron drum which rotates with the wheel assembly. The shoes are held in place by springs; this allows them to slide toward the drums (when they are applied) while keeping the linings and drums in alignment. The shoes are actuated by a wheel cylinder which is usually mounted at the top of the backing plate. When the brakes are applied, hydraulic pressure forces the wheel cylinder's two actuating links outward. Since these links bear directly against the top of the brake shoes, the tops of the shoes are forced outward against the inner side of the drum. This action forces the bottoms of the two shoes to contact the brake drum by rotating the entire assembly slightly (known as servo action). When pressure within the wheel cylinder is relieved, return springs pull the shoes back away from the drum.

Most modern drum brakes are designed to self-adjust during application when the vehicle is moving in reverse. This motion causes both shoes to rotate very slightly with the drum, rocking an adjusting lever. The self-adjusters are only intended to compensate for normal wear. Although the adjustment is "automatic", there is a definite method to actuate the self-adjuster, which is done during normal driving. Driving the vehicle in reverse and applying the brakes usually activates the automatic adjusters. If the brake pedal was low, you should be able to feel an increase in the height of the brake pedal.

DISC BRAKES

Instead of the traditional expanding brakes that press outward against a circular drum, disc brake systems utilize a cast iron disc with brake pads positioned on either side of it. Braking effect is achieved in a manner similar to the way you would squeeze a spinning disc between your fingers. The disc (rotor) is a one-piece casting with cooling fins between the two braking surfaces. This enables air to circulate between the braking surfaces making them less sensitive to heat buildup and more resistant to fade. Dirt and water do not affect braking action since contaminants are thrown off by the centrifugal action of the rotor or scraped off by the pads. Also, the equal clamping action of the two brake pads tends to ensure uniform, straight-line stops. All disc brakes are inherently self-adjusting.

There are three general types of disc brake:
1. A fixed caliper, 4-piston type.
2. A floating caliper, single piston type.
3. A sliding caliper, single piston type.

The fixed caliper design uses two pistons mounted on either side of the rotor (in each side of the caliper). The caliper is mounted rigidly and does not move.

The sliding and floating designs are quite similar and often considered as one. The pad on the inside of the rotor is moved into contact with the rotor by hydraulic force. The caliper, which is not held in a fixed position, moves slightly, bringing the outside pad into contact with the rotor. There are various methods of attaching floating calipers; some pivot at the bottom or top and some slide on mounting bolts.

POWER BRAKE BOOSTERS

A vacuum diaphragm is located behind the master cylinder and assists the driver in applying the brakes, reducing both the effort and travel he must put into moving the brake pedal.

The vacuum diaphragm housing is connected to the intake manifold by a vacuum hose. A check valve at the point where the hose enters the diaphragm housing ensures that during periods of low manifold vacuum brake assist vacuum will not be lost.

Depressing the brake pedal closes off the vacuum source and allows atmospheric pressure to enter on one side of the diaphragm. This causes the master cylinder pistons to move and apply the brakes. When the brake pedal is released, vacuum is applied to both sides of the diaphragm and return springs return the diaphragm and master cylinder pistons to the released position. If the vacuum fails, the brake pedal rod will butt against the end of the master cylinder actuating rod and direct mechanical application will occur as the pedal is depressed.

Subaru uses a dual hydraulic system, with the brakes connected diagonally. In other words, the right front and left rear brakes are on the same hydraulic line and the left front and right rear are on the other line. This has the added advantage of front disc emergency braking, should either of the hydraulic systems fail. The diagonal rear brake serves to counteract the sway from single front disc braking.

A leading/trailing drum brake is used for the rear brakes, with disc brakes for the front. All Subaru's are equipped with a brake warning light, which is activated when a defect in the brake system occurs.

HYDRAULIC SYSTEM

The hydraulic system is composed of the master cylinder and brake booster, the brake lines, the brake pressure differential valve(s), the wheel cylinders (drum brakes) and calipers (disc brakes).

The master cylinder serves as a brake fluid reservoir and (along with the booster) as a hydraulic pump. Brake fluid is stored in the two sections of the master cylinder. Each section corresponds to each part of the dual braking system. This tandem master cylinder is required by Federal law as a safety device.

When the brake pedal is depressed, it moves a piston mounted in the bottom of the master cylinder. The movement of this piston creates hydraulic pressure in the master cylinder. This pressure is carried to the wheel cylinders or the calipers by brake lines, passing through the pressure differential or proportioning valve.

When the hydraulic pressure reaches the wheels, after the pedal has been depressed, it enters the wheel cylinders or calipers. Here it comes into contact with a piston(s). The hydraulic pressure causes the piston(s) to move,

which moves the brake shoes or pads (disc brakes), causing them to contact the drums or rotors (disc brakes). Friction between the brake shoes and the drums causes the vehicle to slow. There is a relationship between the amount of pressure that is applied to the brake pedal and the amount of force which moves the brake shoes against the drums. Therefore, the harder the brake pedal is depressed, the quicker the vehicle will stop.

Since the hydraulic system is one which operates on fluids, air is a natural enemy of the brake system. Air in the hydraulic system retards the passage of hydraulic pressure from the master cylinder to the wheels. Anytime a hydraulic component below the master cylinder is opened or removed, the system must be bled of air to ensure proper operation. Air trapped in the hydraulic system can also cause the brake warning light to turn **ON**, even though the system has not failed. This is especially true after repairs have been performed on the system.

HILL HOLDER SYSTEM

▶ SEE FIGS. 1–2

A feature unique to Subaru, the hill holder is a system designed to engage a single brake channel when a manual transaxle vehicle is stopped on an uphill. The system in effect holds the vehicle, to enable ease of starting on an uphill.

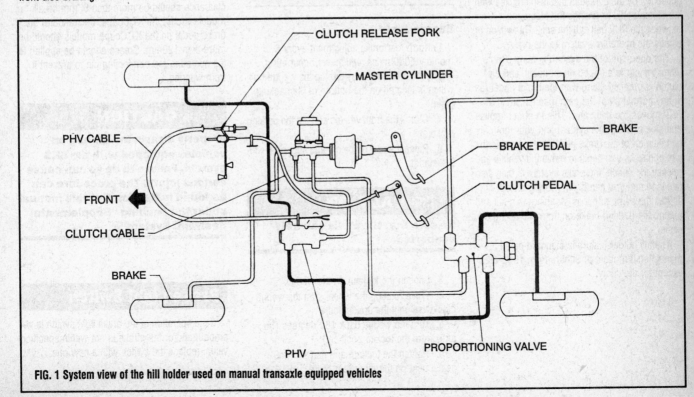

FIG. 1 System view of the hill holder used on manual transaxle equipped vehicles

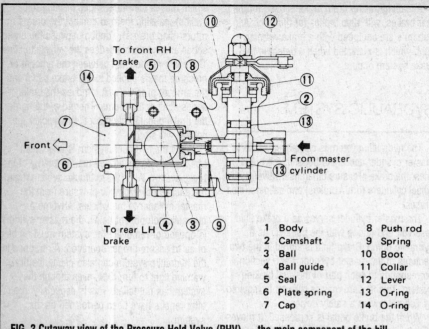

FIG. 2 Cutaway view of the Pressure Hold Valve (PHV) — the main component of the hill holder system

To front RH brake
To rear LH brake
Front
From master cylinder

1	Body	8	Push rod
2	Camshaft	9	Spring
3	Ball	10	Boot
4	Ball guide	11	Collar
5	Seal	12	Lever
6	Plate spring	13	O-ring
7	Cap	14	O-ring

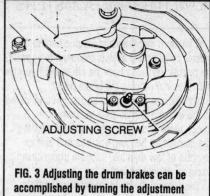

FIG. 3 Adjusting the drum brakes can be accomplished by turning the adjustment screw

ADJUSTING SCREW

The system consists of the basic brake system components and the addition of the Pressure Hold Valve (PHV). The pressure hold valve is connected to one of the service brake pipes. When the clutch pedal is depressed on an uphill the pushrod in the PHV is pushed in and/or pulled out by the camshaft that is interlinked with the clutch pedal to change the clearance between the PHV ball and the seal. This opens or closes the hydraulic system to the brakes.

The operation of the system is fairly simple; when the car is stopped on an uphill, and the clutch is pressed along with the brake pedal (as in any normal stop) the cam mechanism in the PHV moves the ball valve. This in effect applies one side of the brake system and your foot can be taken off of the brake pedal and moved to the gas pedal. As you begin to move the vehicle and release the clutch, the brake system is then also released and you can begin moving ahead. This all has the same effect as stopping on a hill and putting the parking brake on, to make taking off easier.

The hill holder feature is standard on all manual shift models of Subaru from 1985-92, except for the Justy.

Adjustments

REAR DRUM BRAKES

Except Justy

Perform rear brake adjustment every 6 months/6,000 miles, whichever occurs first. Adjust the rear brakes by turning the wedge bolt, which is located on the bottom of the backing plate.

1. Chock the front wheels and set the parking brake.

2. Raise the rear of the car and support it with jackstands.

✳✳ CAUTION

Be sure that the car is securely supported.

3. Loosen the locknut on the wedge.

4. While rotating the wheel, turn the wedge clockwise until the brakes lock.

5. Turn the wedge back 180 degrees ($\frac{1}{2}$ turn) from the locked position.)

6. Tighten the locknut and perform the adjustment on the other rear drum.

Justy

The Justy rear drum brakes use a conventional style star wheel adjuster mechanism. To adjust the brakes, remove the rubber adjuster hole cover and using a slightly curved small prybar inserted through the hole, turn the star wheel until the brake shoes begin to drag on the brake drum. The wheel should be hard to turn, then back off the adjuster slightly, until the wheel frees up.

BRAKE PEDAL

Adjust the brake pedal by adjusting the brake booster operating rod length. Brake pedal clearance should be more than 67mm on all models except the XT Coupe. Clearance of the brake pedal on the XT Coupe models should be more than 120mm. Grease should be applied to the operating rod connecting pin to prevent it from wearing.

✳✳ CAUTION

Properly disarm the air bag on vehicles equipped with the SRS system. Failure to do so can cause serious injury. The procedure can be found in Section 6 of this manual under the heading "Supplemental Restraint System".

Brake Light Switch

If the operation of the brake light switch is not smooth and/or the stroke is not within specified value, replace the switch with a new one.

REMOVAL & INSTALLATION

Disconnect the electrical connector from the brake light switch and remove the switch from the brake pedal bracket. Install the switch in the reverse order, reconnect the electrical connector. Then check to make sure that switch specifications are 1.8–3.3mm.

Master Cylinder

REMOVAL & INSTALLATION

♦ SEE FIGS. 4–5

1. Disconnect the negative battery cable. Disconnect and plug the brake lines at the master cylinder.

2. It is advised to thoroughly drain the fluid from the master cylinder before performing any removal procedures.

3. If equipped with fluid level indicator, disconnect the electrical harness connector from the master cylinder.

4. Remove the master cylinder to power brake booster retaining nuts. Remove the master cylinder from its mounting.

To Install:

5. Bench bleed the master cylinder prior to installation.

6. Install the master cylinder on the power booster and tighten the nuts to 7–13 ft. lbs. (10–18 Nm).

7. Connect the fluid level indicator. Connect the brake lines and tighten the flare nut to 9–13 ft. lbs. (13–18 Nm).

8. Bleed the brake system as required.

OVERHAUL

1. Remove the master cylinder from the vehicle and mount it securely on a bench.

2. Remove the reservoir cap, fluid level sensor, filter and seal.

3. Remove the outer snapring from the secondary piston assembly. Remove the washer secondary cup and secondary piston bushing.

4. Remove the stop bolt, and remove the inner snapring while pushing on the secondary piston assembly.

5. Remove the primary piston assembly from the bore.

6. Remove the screw from the secondary piston and remove the spring.

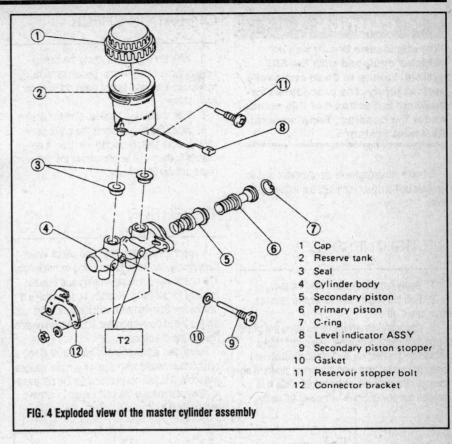

1	Cap
2	Reserve tank
3	Seal
4	Cylinder body
5	Secondary piston
6	Primary piston
7	C-ring
8	Level indicator ASSY
9	Secondary piston stopper
10	Gasket
11	Reservoir stopper bolt
12	Connector bracket

FIG. 4 Exploded view of the master cylinder assembly

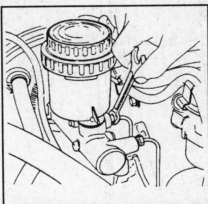

FIG. 5 Disconnecting the brake lines from the master cylinder

7. Clean all parts thoroughly, with clean brake fluid.

➡ **Only use clean brake fluid to clean master cylinder components. Other solvents may damage the components.**

8. Lubricate new piston assemblies with brake fluid then install them in the master cylinder body.

9. Press down on the piston assembly and install the stop bolt in the master cylinder body. Tighten the stop bolt to 7 ft. lbs. (10 Nm).

10. Again press down on the piston assembly and install the inner snapring.

11. Install the secondary cups, bushing and outer snapring.

12. Insert a new seal on the master cylinder mounting flange and install the master cylinder in the vehicle. Bleed the brake system when finished.

Power Brake Booster

♦ SEE FIGS. 6–8

The power brake booster uses engine manifold vacuum against a diaphragm to assist in the application of the brakes. The vacuum is regulated to be proportional to the pressure placed on the pedal.

✳✳ CAUTION

Properly disarm the air bag on vehicles equipped with the SRS system. Failure to do so can cause serious injury. The procedure can be found in Section 6 of this manual under the heading "Supplemental Restraint System".

If brake performance is questionable and the booster unit suspect, conduct the following tests.

AIR TIGHTNESS TEST

1. Apply hand brake and start engine.
2. Run the engine for one or two minutes, then turn it off.
3. Apply brakes several times using the same force as in normal braking. The pedal stroke should be greatest on the first application and become smaller with each additional stroke. If no change occurs in the pedal height while it is applied the power brake unit could be faulty.

OPERATION CHECK

1. With the engine off. Apply the brakes several times using normal pedal pressure, make sure the pedal height does not vary on each stroke.
2. With the brakes applied, start the engine.
3. When the engine starts the brake pedal should move slightly toward the floor. If no change in the pedal height occurs the power brake unit could be faulty.

INSPECTION

Inspect the vacuum hose and check valve periodically, the hose for cracking or brittleness. The check valve (engine running and brakes applied) for air leaks. Replace hose or valve if necessary. Sometimes a stuck check valve can act like a bad power booster. If this is suspected, replace the check valve.

Rebuilding a power brake booster or doing a complete pressure test requires special gauges and tools. It is just not practical for the car owner to attempt servicing the unit except to remove and replace it.

REMOVAL & INSTALLATION

Except SVX

1. Remove the master cylinder.
2. Disconnect the vacuum hose.
3. Disconnect the brake pedal from the power booster push rod by removing the clevis pin.
4. Remove the four nuts that mount the booster to the firewall.
5. Remove the booster.
6. Reverse steps 1 through 5 to install the unit. Tighten the mounting bolts to 7–13 ft. lbs. (13–18 Nm).

SVX

1. Disconnect the negative battery cable. Properly discharge the air conditioning system.
2. Raise and safely support the vehicle. Remove the performance rod from beneath the transaxle. It is bolted to the sub frame assembly.
3. Drain about 1 quart of transaxle fluid from the transaxle.
4. Remove the upper transaxle dipstick housing bolt and remove the lower bolt.
5. Lower the vehicle slightly and remove the cruise control actuator from the firewall.
6. Disconnect the positive battery wire from the starter.
7. Disconnect and plug the low pressure air conditioning line (refer to Section 6 for the procedure).
8. Disconnect the vacuum hose from the brake booster.
9. Remove the master cylinder from the booster. Inside of the vehicle, remove the snap pin and the clevis from the actuator rod.
10. Inside of the vehicle, remove the 4 nuts that secure the booster. Remove the brake booster from the engine compartment.

To install:

11. Install the brake booster in position and install the mounting nuts. Tighten the mounting bolts to 7–13 ft. lbs. (13–18 Nm).
12. Reconnect the actuator rod at the pedal assembly. Install the master cylinder onto the booster.
13. Connect the vacuum hose at the booster. Connect the refrigerant low pressure line.
14. Connect the positive battery cable at the starter. Install the cruise control actuator.
15. Raise and safely support the vehicle. Install the transaxle dipstick housing. Install the performance rod.
16. Lower the vehicle. Properly recharge the air conditioning system.
17. Fill the transaxle to the proper level. COnnect the negative battery cable.

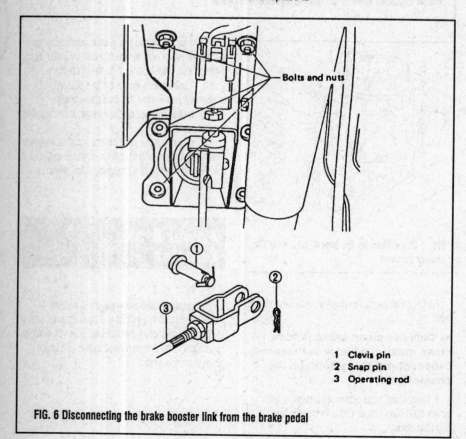

Bolts and nuts

1 Clevis pin
2 Snap pin
3 Operating rod

FIG. 6 Disconnecting the brake booster link from the brake pedal

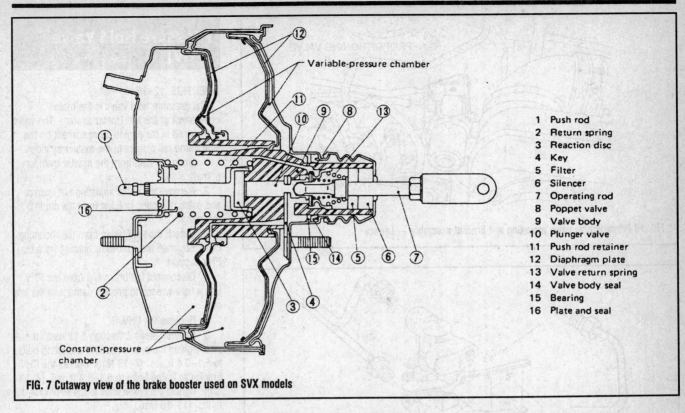

Variable-pressure chamber

Constant-pressure chamber

1 Push rod
2 Return spring
3 Reaction disc
4 Key
5 Filter
6 Silencer
7 Operating rod
8 Poppet valve
9 Valve body
10 Plunger valve
11 Push rod retainer
12 Diaphragm plate
13 Valve return spring
14 Valve body seal
15 Bearing
16 Plate and seal

FIG. 7 Cutaway view of the brake booster used on SVX models

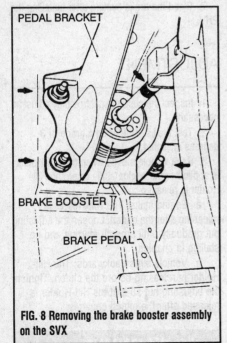

PEDAL BRACKET

BRAKE BOOSTER

BRAKE PEDAL

FIG. 8 Removing the brake booster assembly on the SVX

Brake Fluid Level Warning Indicator

The low brake fluid warning device (cars equipped) is contained in the reservoir of the master cylinder. If the brake fluid level falls about 18mm below the MAX line, a float closes an electrical circuit which causes the warning lamp on the dash panel to light.

Refilling the master cylinder will cause the warning lamp to go out. However, the entire brake system should be inspected for signs of leakage so the loss of brake fluid can be accounted for.

Proportioning Valve

▶ SEE FIGS. 9–11

The proportioning valve is attached to a bracket and is located directly under the master cylinder. It's purpose is to provide even braking pressure to all of the wheels.

REMOVAL & INSTALLATION

Except Justy

1. Disconnect the negative battery cable. On SVX, remove the windshield washer fluid reservoir.

2. Disconnect and plug the brake tubes from the proportioning valve. If equipped with an electrical connector, disconnect it.

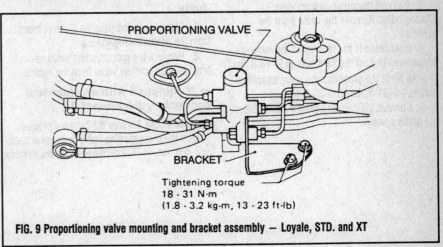

PROPORTIONING VALVE

BRACKET

Tightening torque
18 - 31 N·m
(1.8 - 3.2 kg-m, 13 - 23 ft-lb)

FIG. 9 Proportioning valve mounting and bracket assembly — Loyale, STD. and XT

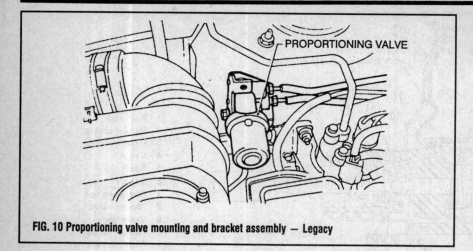

FIG. 10 Proportioning valve mounting and bracket assembly — Legacy

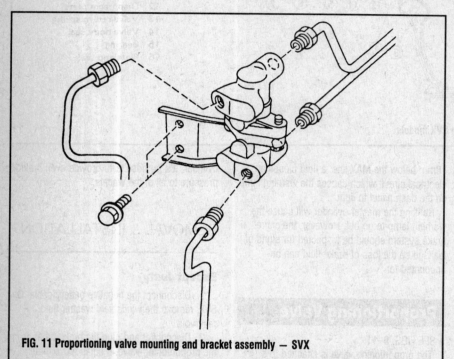

FIG. 11 Proportioning valve mounting and bracket assembly — SVX

3. Remove the proportioning valve-to-bracket bolts. Remove the valve from the vehicle.

4. Installation is the reverse of the removal procedure. Tighten the flare nuts to 9–13 ft. lbs. (13–18 Nm); the proportioning valve attaching nuts to 15–21 ft. lbs. (20–29 Nm).

5. Connect the negative battery cable. Bleed the brake system.

Justy

1. Disconnect and plug the 6 brake tubes from the proportioning valve.

2. Remove the proportioning valve-to-bracket bolts and the valve from the vehicle.

➡ **If equipped with an electrical connector, disconnect it.**

3. To install, reverse the removal process. Torque the proportioning valve-to-bracket bolts to 3–5 ft. lbs. (4–7 Nm). Bleed the brake system.

Pressure Hold Valve (PHV)

◆ SEE FIGS. 12–15

The pressure hold valve is the main component of the Hill-Holder system. The valve is mounted in the engine compartment on the side frame rail closest to the master cylinder.

1. Drain the fluid from the master cylinder primary side.

2. Remove the cable adjusting nut, clamp and cable mounting bracket from the engine mounting.

3. Detach the PHV cable from the mounting clips. Separate the connector bracket from the PHV support.

4. Disconnect the brake line from the PHV. Use a flare wrench to prevent damage to the line nut.

5. Remove the PHV.

6. Reverse steps 1 through 5 to install the unit. Tighten the bracket to PHV mounting bolts to 5.1–9.4 ft. lbs. (7–13 Nm). Tighten the PHV bracket to frame bolts to 5.1–9.4 ft. lbs. (7–13 Nm). Tighten the brake lines to the PHV to 9–13 ft. lbs. (13–18 Nm).

7. Bleed the brake system after installing the PHV.

ADJUSTMENT

1. Inspect the clutch pedal free play adjust as necessary.

2. Test the Hill-Holder on a grade of 3 degrees or higher.

3. If the vehicle moves when the Hill-Holder is applied or the engine stalls when the Hill-Holder is released:

a. Engine stalls: The Hill-Holder is releasing after the clutch. Loosen the adjusting nut gradually until smooth starting and no stalling is enabled.

b. Vehicle slips backwards: The Hill-Holder is releasing before the clutch. Tighten the adjusting nut so that the Hill-Holder is released after the clutch engages.

✳✳ WARNING

When adjusting the control cable nut be sure to prevent the cable from turning.

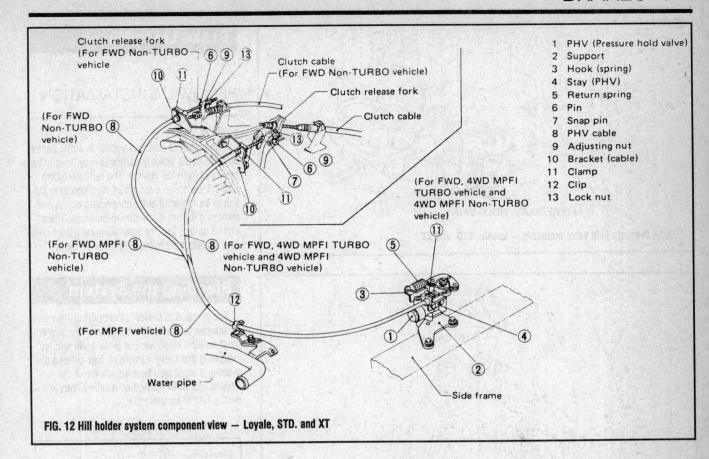

1. PHV (Pressure hold valve)
2. Support
3. Hook (spring)
4. Stay (PHV)
5. Return spring
6. Pin
7. Snap pin
8. PHV cable
9. Adjusting nut
10. Bracket (cable)
11. Clamp
12. Clip
13. Lock nut

FIG. 12 Hill holder system component view — Loyale, STD. and XT

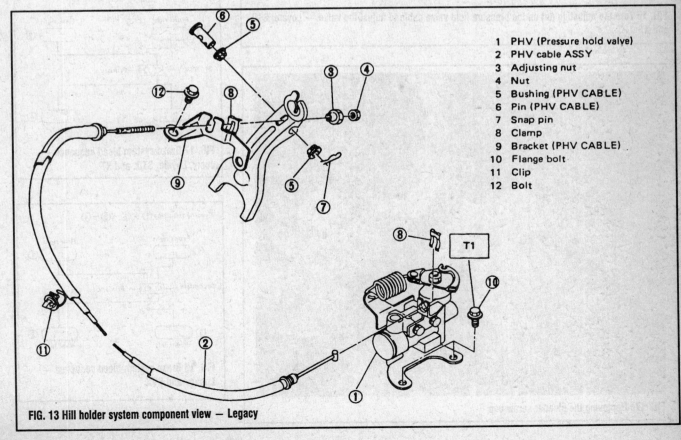

1. PHV (Pressure hold valve)
2. PHV cable ASSY
3. Adjusting nut
4. Nut
5. Bushing (PHV CABLE)
6. Pin (PHV CABLE)
7. Snap pin
8. Clamp
9. Bracket (PHV CABLE)
10. Flange bolt
11. Clip
12. Bolt

FIG. 13 Hill holder system component view — Legacy

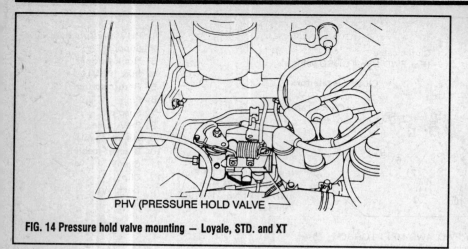

FIG. 14 Pressure hold valve mounting — Loyale, STD. and XT

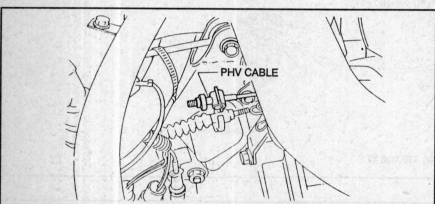

FIG. 15 Turn the adjusting nut on the pressure hold valve cable to adjust the valve — Loyale, STD. and XT

FIG. 17a Removing the bleeder screw cap

Brake Lines/Hoses

REMOVAL & INSTALLATION

♦ SEE FIG. 16

Although it is seldom needed, in some cases any one of the brake lines/hoses may need to be removed from the vehicle. The removal of the brake lines/hoses consists of disconnecting the lien to be replaced at its connecting points and removing it from its mounting brackets. There can be quite a few brackets supporting the brake line, so take care to trace its path correctly.

Bleeding the System

The purpose of bleeding the brakes is to expel air trapped in the hydraulic system. The system must be bled whenever the pedal feels spongy, indicating that compressible air has entered the system. It must also be bled whenever the system has been opened or repaired. You will need a helper for this job.

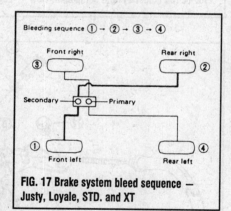

FIG. 17 Brake system bleed sequence — Justy, Loyale, STD. and XT

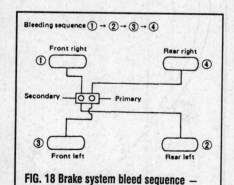

FIG. 18 Brake system bleed sequence — Legacy and SVX

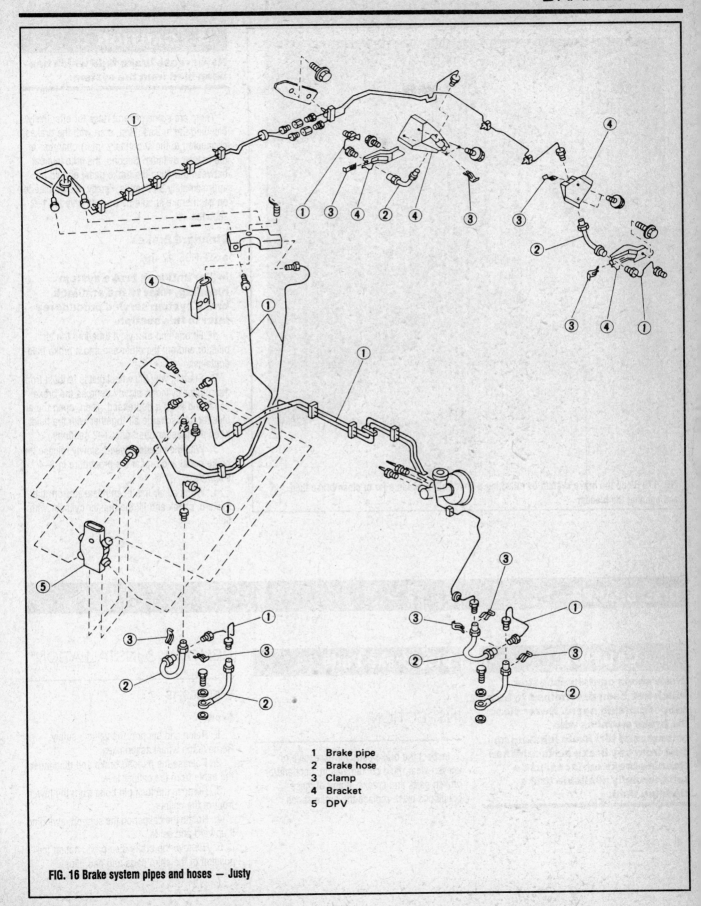

1 Brake pipe
2 Brake hose
3 Clamp
4 Bracket
5 DPV

FIG. 16 Brake system pipes and hoses — Justy

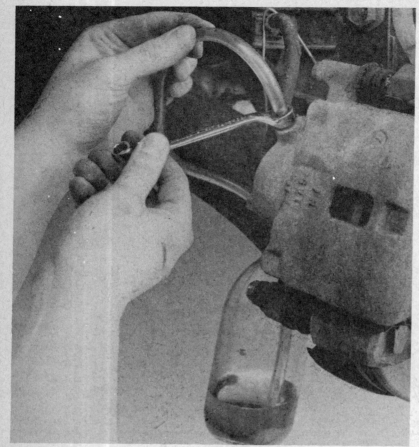

FIG. 17b Bleed the brake system by attaching a hose subnerged in a jar of clean brake fluid and opening the bleeder

There are some general rules for effectively bleeding the brakes. First, start with the brakes connected to the secondary (rear) chamber of the master cylinder. Second, the time interval between pumping the brake pedal should be approximately 3 seconds. Finally, the air bleeder on each brake should be opened only for 1–2 seconds.

Standard Brakes

▸ SEE FIGS. 17–18

➡ **For anti-lock brake system bleeding, refer to the anti-lock brake system service procedures later in this section.**

1. Fit one end of a vinyl tube into the air bleeder and put the other end into a brake fluid container.
2. Starting with the wheel that is farthest from the master cylinder, slowly depress the brake pedal and keep it depressed. Then, open the air bleeder to discharge air together with the fluid. Keep the bleeder open only 1–2 seconds.
3. With the bleeder closed, slowly release the brake pedal and repeat the procedure in 3–4 seconds.
4. When all air has been released from the system, check and fill the master cylinder with fluid.

DISC BRAKES

Disc Brake Pads

INSPECTION

Inspect the brake pads for excessive or uneven wear, fluid contamination, bent and/or broken parts and cracks. If any of these conditions exist, replace the brake shoes.

REMOVAL & INSTALLATION

▸ SEE FIGS. 19–27

Front

1. Raise and support the vehicle safely. Remove the wheel assemblies.
2. Release the parking brake and disconnect the cable from the caliper lever.
3. Remove the lock pin bolts from the lower front of the caliper.
4. Rotate the caliper on the support, swinging it upward and aside.
5. Remove the brake disc pads, noting the position of the shim pads and pad clips.

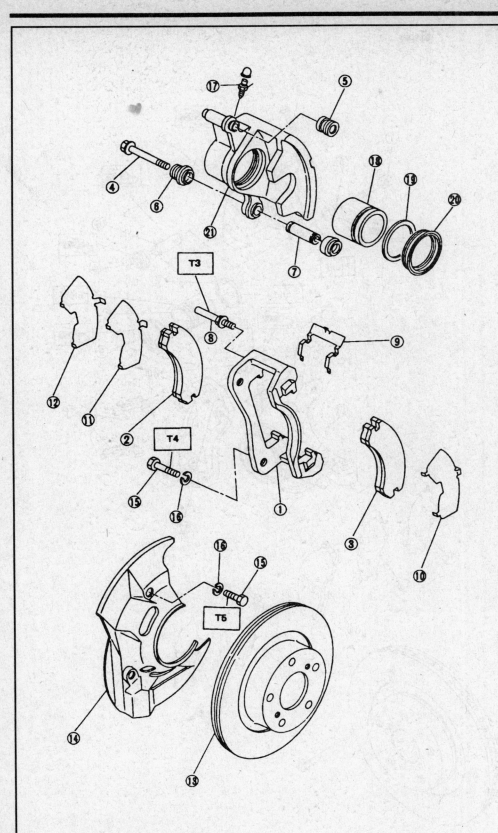

1 Support
2 Pad COMPL (Inside)
3 Pad COMPL (Outside)
4 Lock pin
5 Guide pin boot
6 Lock pin boot
7 Lock pin sleeve
8 Guide pin
9 Pad clip
10 Outer shim
11 Inner shim
12 Shim
13 Front brake disc
14 Front disc cover
15 Bolt
16 Washer
17 Air bleeder screw
18 Piston
19 Piston seal
20 Piston boot
21 Caliper body

FIG. 19 Front disc brake components — Legacy (non-turbo), Loyale, STD. and XT

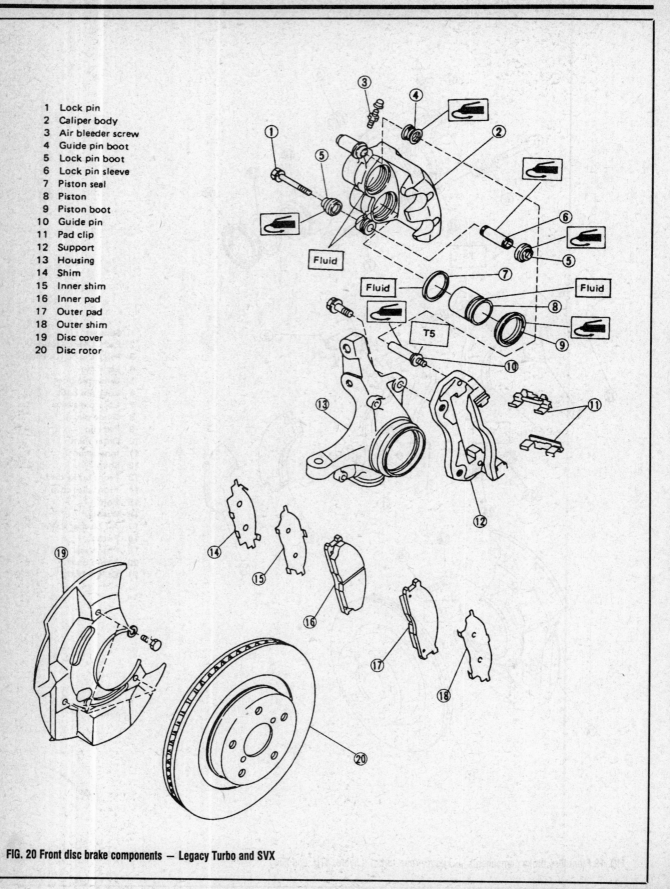

1 Lock pin
2 Caliper body
3 Air bleeder screw
4 Guide pin boot
5 Lock pin boot
6 Lock pin sleeve
7 Piston seal
8 Piston
9 Piston boot
10 Guide pin
11 Pad clip
12 Support
13 Housing
14 Shim
15 Inner shim
16 Inner pad
17 Outer pad
18 Outer shim
19 Disc cover
20 Disc rotor

FIG. 20 Front disc brake components — Legacy Turbo and SVX

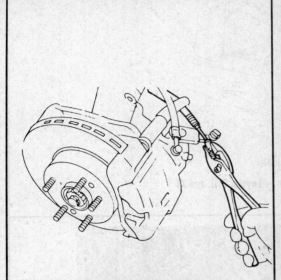

FIG. 21 Disconnecting the parking brake cable from the brake caliper — Loyale, STD. and XT

FIG. 21a Inspect the brake pads for wear by looking through the end of the caliper

FIG. 21b Clean the brakes before disassembly, use a suitable brake cleaning agent

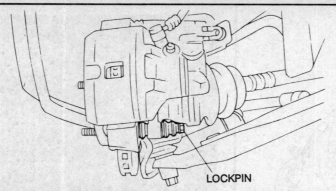

FIG. 22 Remove the lower lock pin to pivot the caliper — Loyale, STD. and XT

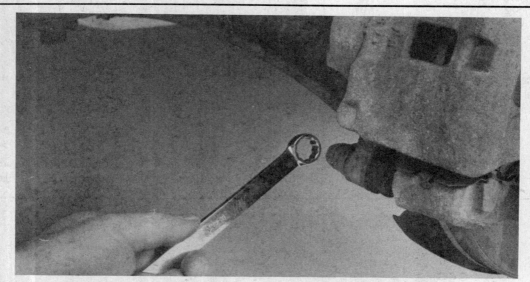

FIG. 22a Remove the lower lockpin using an appropriate wrench

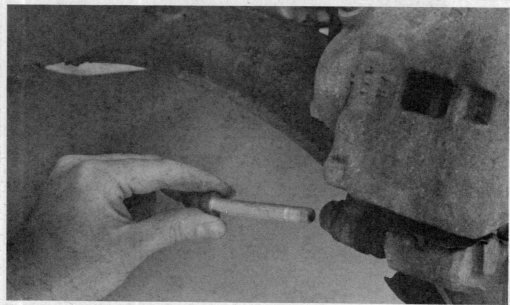

FIG. 22b Removing the lower lockpin from the caliper—Legacy

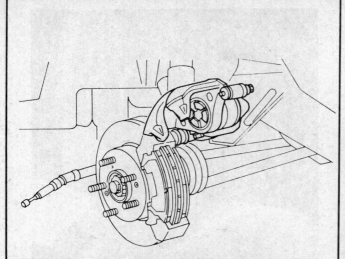

FIG. 23 Pivot the caliper upward to remove the brake pads — Loyale, STD. and XT

FIG. 23a Pivot the caliper upwards—Legacy

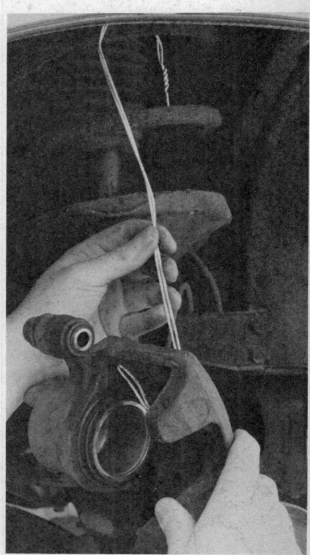

FIG. 23b Support the caliper from the strut spring using a piece of wire

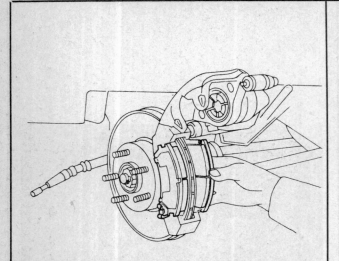

FIG. 24 Removing the brake pads from the support — Loyale, STD. and XT

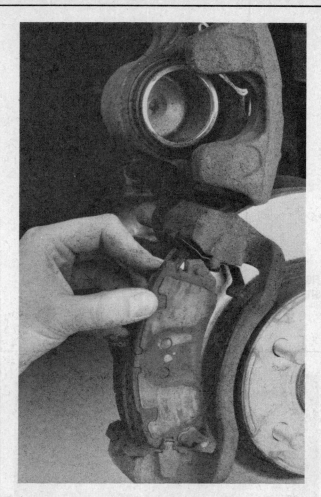

FIG. 24a Remove the brake pads frpm the support — Legacy

FIG. 24b Removing the pad retainer clips

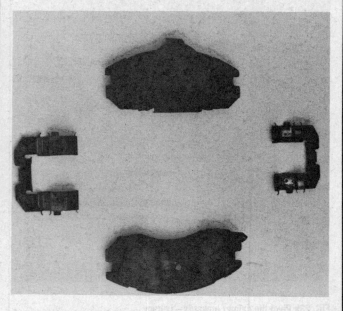

FIG. 24c Brake pads and clips

To install:

6. Inspect the brake rotor, calipers and retaining components. Correct as necessary.

7. Remove a small portion of brake fluid from the master cylinder reservoir. With an appropriate tool, turn the caliper piston clockwise into the cylinder bore and align the notches. Be sure the boot is not twisted or pinched.

➡ **Do not force the piston straight into the caliper bore. The piston is mounted on a threaded spindle which will bend under pressure.**

8. Install the new pads into the calipers, being sure all shims and clips are in their original positions.

9. Swing the calipers down into position and install the lock pin bolts. Tighten the lock pin bolt to the following specifications:

    a. Justy — 16–23 ft. lbs. (22–31 Nm).

    b. Loyale, STD. and XT — 33–40 ft. lbs. (44–54 Nm).

    c. Legacy — 25–33 ft. lbs. (34–44 Nm).

    d. SVX — 25–33 ft. lbs. (34–44 Nm).

10. Reconnect the parking brake cable and fill the master cylinder reservoir.

11. Install the wheel assembly. Bleed the brakes as required and lower the vehicle. Road test the vehicle.

Rear

1. Raise and safely support the vehicle. Remove the wheel assemblies.

2. Disconnect the brake pad lining wear indicator, if equipped. Remove any anti-rattle springs or clips, if equipped.

3. Pull the caliper away from the center of the vehicle to push piston into caliper bore. Remove the caliper guide pins and remove the caliper from the rotor. Hang the caliper from the body with a support wire.

4. Slide the disc pads from the caliper, noting any shims or shields behind the pad.

FIG. 24d Using a C-clamp to set the caliper piston before installing the brake pads

FIG. 25a View of the rear brake caliper mounting—Legacy

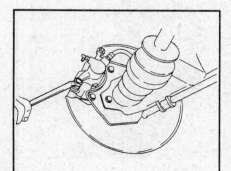

FIG. 25 Remove the lower mounting bolt on rear disc brakes, to pivot the caliper — Loyale, STD. and XT

FIG. 25b Clean the brakes before disassembly, use a suitable brake cleaning agent

FIG. 25c Remove the lower lockpin using an appropriate wrench

FIG. 25d Removing the lower lockpin from the caliper—Legacy

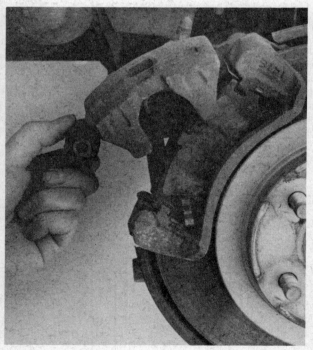

FIG. 25e Pivot the caliper upwards—Legacy

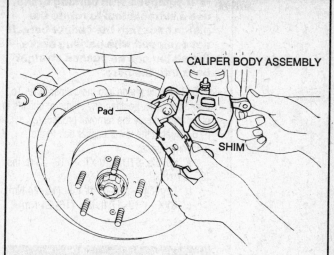

FIG. 26 Pivot the caliper body upward and remove the rear disc brake pads — Loyale, STD. and XT

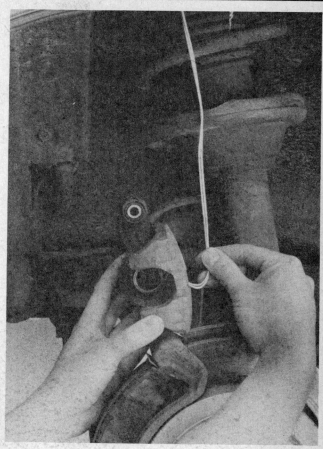

FIG. 26a Support the caliper from the strut spring using a piece of wire

FIG. 26b Remove the brake pads frpm the support — Legacy

FIG. 26c Removing the pad retainer clips

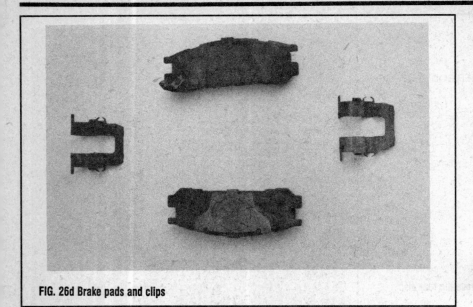

FIG. 26d Brake pads and clips

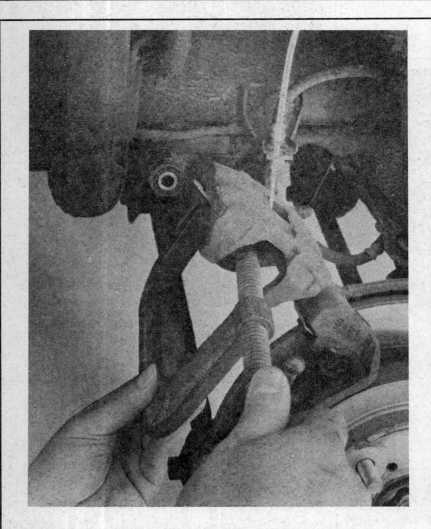

FIG. 26e Using a C-clamp to set the caliper piston before installing the brake pads

➡ If equipped with parking brake, use a suitable tool to rotate the piston back into the caliper bore. If not equipped with parking brake, the piston can be pushed straight back into the bore.

5. Push the piston into the caliper bore. To install the pads, position any shims or shields in place and reverse the removal procedure.

6. Tighten the lower caliper bolt to the following torque:

    a. Loyale, STD. and XT — 16–23 ft. lbs. (22–31 Nm).

    b. Legacy — 12–17 ft. lbs. (16–24 Nm).

    c. SVX — 12–17 ft. lbs. (16–24 Nm).

Disc Brake Calipers

REMOVAL & INSTALLATION

◆ SEE FIGS. 28–30

Front

1. Raise and support the vehicle safely. Remove the front wheels.

2. Remove the brake hose from the caliper body and plug the hose to prevent the entrance of dirt or moisture.

3. Remove the hand brake cable and brake pads. Remove the caliper assembly by pulling it out of the support. Do not remove the guide pin unless it damaged.

To Install:

4. Rotate the piston until the notch at the head of the piston is vertical.

5. Install the hand brake cable and brake pads. Install the caliper assembly on the support and tighten the support bolt to 36–51 ft. lbs. (49–69 Nm).

6. Connect the brake hose and tighten the fitting to 11–15 ft. lbs. (15–21 Nm).

7. Bleed the brake system. Install the wheels and lower the vehicle. Check the fluid level in the master cylinder.

Rear

1. Raise and support the vehicle safely. Remove the rear wheels.

2. Disconnect and plug the brake hose from the caliper body.

3. Remove the bolts securing the caliper to the support and remove the caliper.

To Install:

4. Install the caliper and tighten the attaching bolts to 34–43 ft. lbs. (46–58 Nm).

5. Connect the brake hose and tighten the fitting to 12–14 ft. lbs. (16–20 Nm).

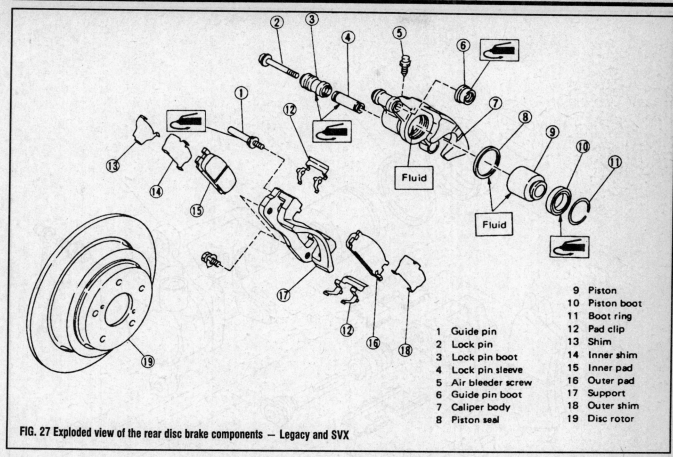

1 Guide pin
2 Lock pin
3 Lock pin boot
4 Lock pin sleeve
5 Air bleeder screw
6 Guide pin boot
7 Caliper body
8 Piston seal
9 Piston
10 Piston boot
11 Boot ring
12 Pad clip
13 Shim
14 Inner shim
15 Inner pad
16 Outer pad
17 Support
18 Outer shim
19 Disc rotor

FIG. 27 Exploded view of the rear disc brake components — Legacy and SVX

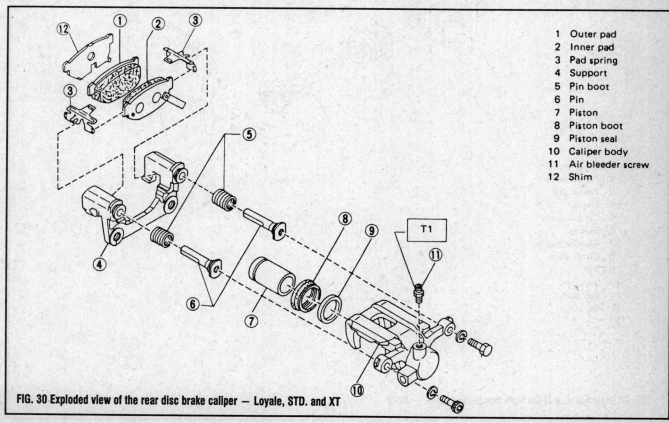

1 Outer pad
2 Inner pad
3 Pad spring
4 Support
5 Pin boot
6 Pin
7 Piston
8 Piston boot
9 Piston seal
10 Caliper body
11 Air bleeder screw
12 Shim

FIG. 30 Exploded view of the rear disc brake caliper — Loyale, STD. and XT

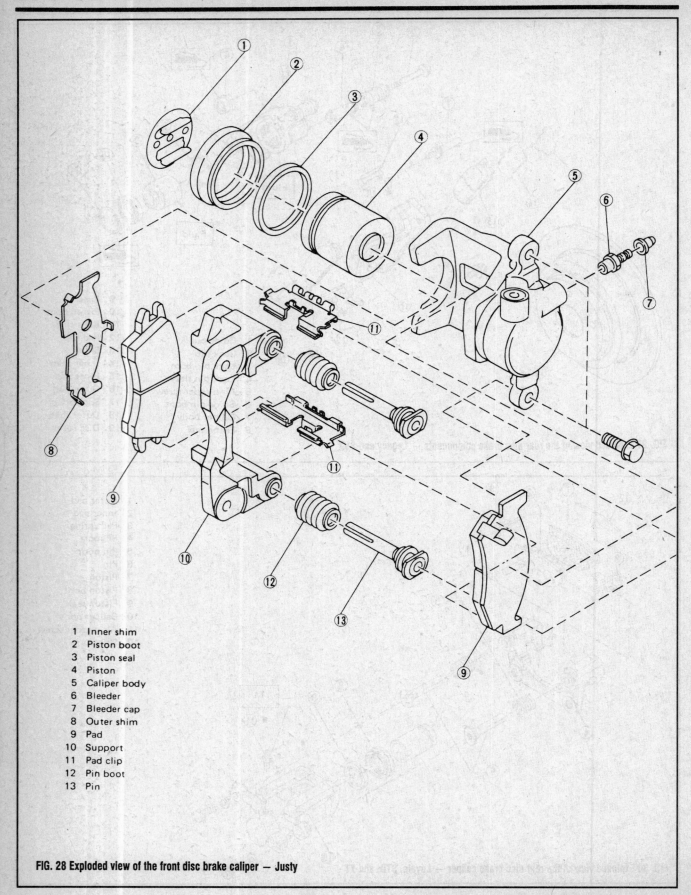

1   Inner shim
2   Piston boot
3   Piston seal
4   Piston
5   Caliper body
6   Bleeder
7   Bleeder cap
8   Outer shim
9   Pad
10 Support
11 Pad clip
12 Pin boot
13 Pin

FIG. 28 Exploded view of the front disc brake caliper — Justy

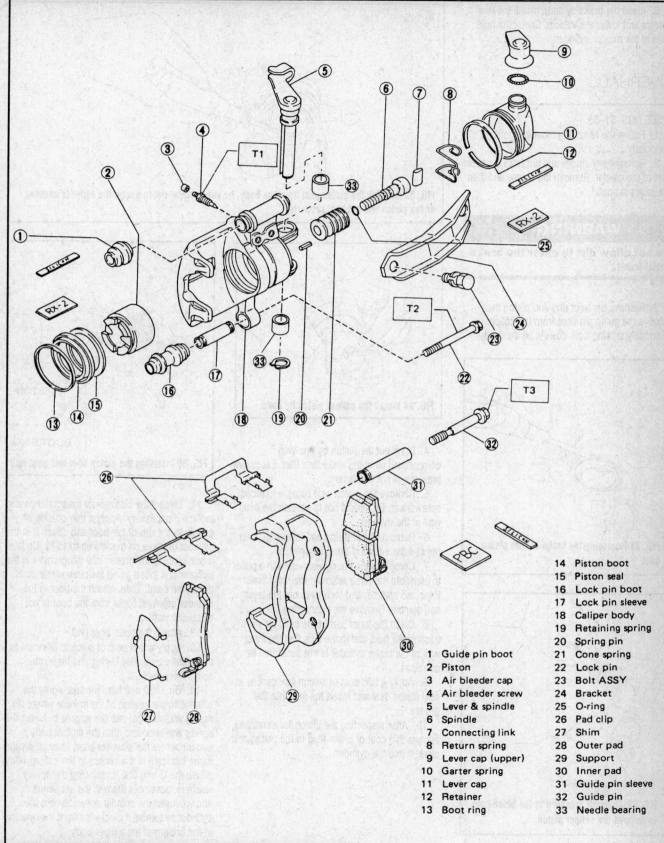

14	Piston boot
15	Piston seal
16	Lock pin boot
17	Lock pin sleeve
18	Caliper body
19	Retaining spring
20	Spring pin
21	Cone spring
22	Lock pin
23	Bolt ASSY
24	Bracket
25	O-ring
26	Pad clip
27	Shim
28	Outer pad
29	Support
30	Inner pad
31	Guide pin sleeve
32	Guide pin
33	Needle bearing

1	Guide pin boot
2	Piston
3	Air bleeder cap
4	Air bleeder screw
5	Lever & spindle
6	Spindle
7	Connecting link
8	Return spring
9	Lever cap (upper)
10	Garter spring
11	Lever cap
12	Retainer
13	Boot ring

FIG. 29 Exploded view of the front disc brake caliper — Loyale, STD. and XT

6. Bleed the brake system. Install the rear wheels and lower the vehicle. Check the fluid level in the master cylinder.

OVERHAUL

♦ SEE FIGS. 31–35

1. Follow the removal procedure outlined previously.

2. Remove any sludge and dirt from the outer part of the caliper. Remove the sleeve and then the lock pin boot.

❊❊❊ WARNING

Do not allow dirt to enter the brake fluid inlet.

3. Remove the boot ring and piston then remove the guide pin boot from the caliper by alternately tapping both dowels on the boot.

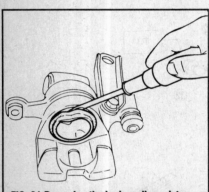

FIG. 31 Removing the brake caliper piston boot

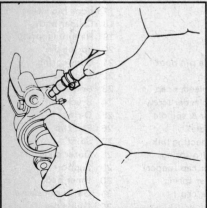

FIG. 32 Apply air pressure to the bleed hole to remove the caliper piston

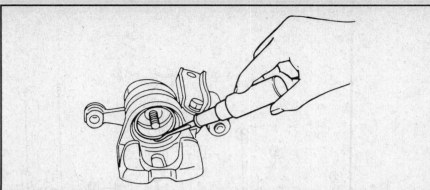

FIG. 33 Remove the piston seal from the body, be very careful not to gouge the cylinder housing or the piston will not seal properly

FIG. 34 Install the caliper piston by hand

4. Draw out the piston by applying compressed air at the brake fluid inlet. Excessive pressure is not necessary.

5. Remove the piston seal using a rounded screwdriver. Be careful not to scratch the inner wall of the cylinder.

6. Remove the cap ring and lever cap, then remove the snapring from the spindle.

7. Compress the spring washers with a puller to eliminate the force retaining the hand brake lever and spindle, and then slide out the lever and spindle. Remove the connecting link.

8. Clean the inner part of the cylinder with fresh brake fluid and make sure that the inner wall of the brake cylinder is not scratched or corroded.

9. Apply a thin coat of silicon lubricant to a new piston seal and insert the seal into the groove.

10. After inspecting the piston for scratches, apply a thin coat of brake fluid to the piston and insert it into the cylinder.

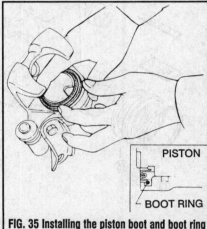

PISTON

BOOT RING

FIG. 35 Installing the piston boot and boot ring

11. Inspect the piston boot for scratches and replace if necessary. Apply a thin coating of grease to the rim of the boot and attach it in the cylinder grooves on models up to 1979. On later models, apply the grease into the grooves in the cylinder and those along the circumference of the piston head. Then, attach the boot in the cylinder grooves. Make sure the boot is not twisted anywhere.

12. Attach the outer boot ring.

13. Apply a thin coat of silicone lubricant to the spindle assembly O-ring and insert the spindle assembly.

14. On 1980 and later models, apply the silicone to the section of the spindle where the spring washers go, into the spaces between the spring washers, and onto the caliper body surface where the washers bear. Then, apply the same lubricant to the recess in the caliper body where the O-ring fits. If replacing the spring washers, assemble them in the sequence shown. Insert the spindle assembly into the cylinder by turning it clockwise from the opening at the bottom of the caliper body.

15. Coat the O-ring with silicone compound and install it into the recess carefully. Then, apply a grease designed for this type of service (example: NIGLUBE RX-2) to the head of the spindle assembly and onto the inner wall of the caliper body. Install the connecting link and return spring.

16. Now, press in a set of spring washers and hold them there with a puller. Apply the grease to the grooves in the lever and spindle in which the lever cap and connecting link are to be fitted. Make sure the caliper bore is clean. Then, fit the connecting link into the groove at the head of the spindle. Insert the lever and spindle complete with the lever cap and garter spring. Make sure the inner tip of the return spring hooks and that it fits into the groove in the lever and spindle. Then remove the puller.

17. Insert the hand brake lever and spindle shaft assembly at the rear of the caliper. Be careful not to knock the connecting link out of place. Apply silicone grease to the groove of the caliper body where the lever cap will go. Apply it also to the snapring.

18. Install the snapring at the end of the lever and spindle shaft. Then apply sufficient silicone grease to the space around the connecting link and lever and spindle to fill the inside of the lever cap after it is installed.

19. Fit the lever cap into the slot at the rear of the caliper body and anchor it in place with the cap ring. Make sure you don't damage the lever cap with the sharp edge of the cap ring.

20. On late model calipers with guide pins, make sure the hole the guide pin slides into is clean. Install a new guide pin boot by evenly tapping all around the metal periphery.

21. See the last portion of the appropriate brake pad removal and installation procedure above for caliper installation. Make sure to rotate the caliper piston to the proper position. Coat the entire guide pin, and all but the outer end of the lockpin, with silicone grease. Make sure both boots fit properly in the guide pin and lock pin grooves. If the boots get full of air during installation, simply squeeze them gently to release excess air.

22. Install new brake line connection gaskets. Bleed the system when complete.

Brake Disc (Rotor)

REMOVAL & INSTALLATION

1. Raise and support the vehicle safely. Remove the front wheels.

2. Remove the brake caliper assembly and suspend out of the way.

3. Remove the castle nut, conical spring and center piece. Remove the center piece by inserting a screwdriver into the center slit and lightly tapping.

4. Pull the hub and disc assembly from the half shaft by hand.

To install:

5. Install the hub and disc assembly on the axle shaft. Install the conical spring and castle nut and temporarily tighten. Ensure that the conical spring is installed in the correct direction.

6. Install the caliper assembly and tighten the bolts to specification.

7. Install the castle nut and tighten to specification. Install the wheels and lower the vehicle.

REAR DRUM BRAKES

❈ CAUTION

Brake shoes contain asbestos, which has been determined to be a cancer causing agent. Never clean the brake surfaces with compressed air! Avoid inhaling any dust from any brake surface! When cleaning brake surfaces, use a commercially available brake cleaning fluid.

Brake Drums

REMOVAL & INSTALLATION

♦ SEE FIGS. 36–37
1. Raise and support the vehicle safely. Remove the wheels.

2. Pry off the center cap using an appropriate tool. Remove the castle nut, conical spring and center piece. Remove the center piece by inserting a screwdriver into the center slit and lightly tapping.

3. Pull brake drum off by hand.

To install:

4. Install the brake drum on the axle. Install the center piece, conical spring and castle nut. Ensure that the conical spring is installed in the correct direction. The word **OUT** should be facing you. Tighten the castle nut to 108 ft. lbs. (147 Nm).

5. Install the center cap and wheels. Lower the vehicle.

INSPECTION

All Models

After removing the brake drum, inspect the inner braking surface for excessive wear or damage. If it is unevenly worn, streaked, or cracked, have it resurfaced or replaced. The standard inside diameter of the brake drum is 180mm. The maximum allowed diameter is 182mm.

BEARING PRELOAD ADJUSTMENT

1. Torque the castle nut to 36 ft. lbs. while rotating the drum back and forth to seat the bearing. Loosen the nut about 3mm.

2. Then, attach a spring scale to one of the wheel studs. Pull on the spring scale at a 90 degree angle to the diameter of the brake drum and measure the force required to start the drum turning. It should be 2.6–4.0 lbs. Loosen or tighten the nut slightly to get the right rolling resistance.

3. When the rolling resistance is right, bend the lockwasher over to hold the nut in place.

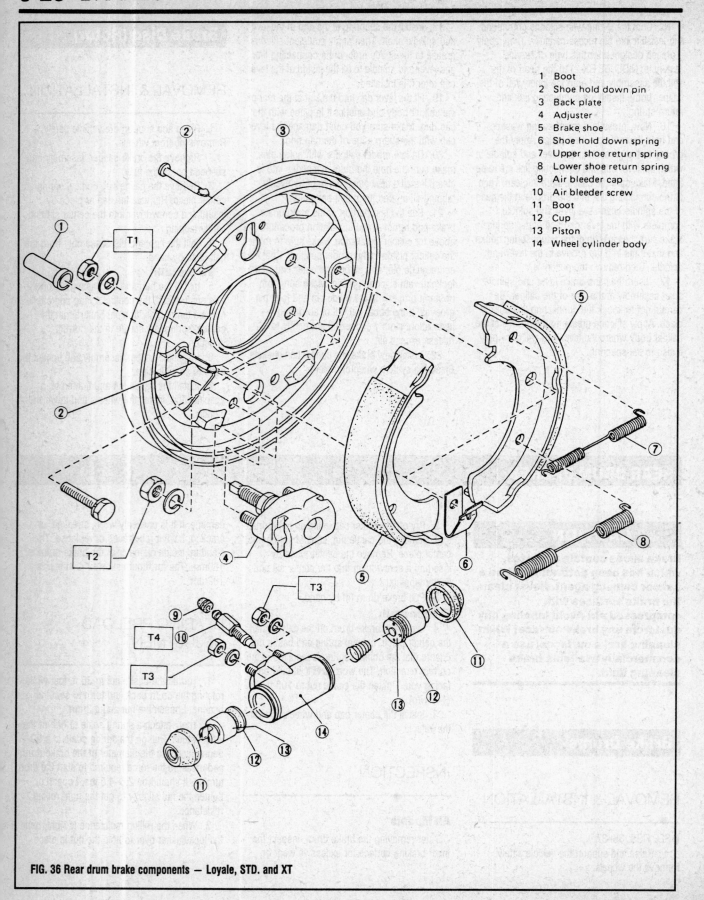

1 Boot
2 Shoe hold down pin
3 Back plate
4 Adjuster
5 Brake shoe
6 Shoe hold down spring
7 Upper shoe return spring
8 Lower shoe return spring
9 Air bleeder cap
10 Air bleeder screw
11 Boot
12 Cup
13 Piston
14 Wheel cylinder body

FIG. 36 Rear drum brake components — Loyale, STD. and XT

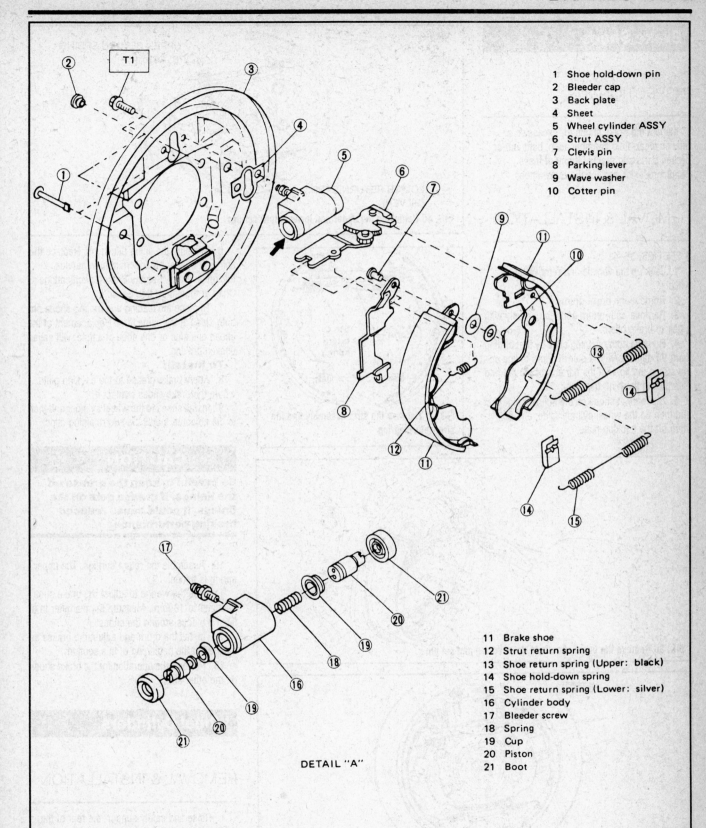

1	Shoe hold-down pin
2	Bleeder cap
3	Back plate
4	Sheet
5	Wheel cylinder ASSY
6	Strut ASSY
7	Clevis pin
8	Parking lever
9	Wave washer
10	Cotter pin

11	Brake shoe
12	Strut return spring
13	Shoe return spring (Upper: black)
14	Shoe hold-down spring
15	Shoe return spring (Lower: silver)
16	Cylinder body
17	Bleeder screw
18	Spring
19	Cup
20	Piston
21	Boot

DETAIL "A"

FIG. 37 Rear drum brake components — Justy

Brake Shoes

INSPECTION

Inspect the brake shoes for excessive or uneven wear, fluid contamination, bent and/or broken parts and cracks. If any of these conditions exist, replace the brake shoes.

REMOVAL & INSTALLATION

♦ SEE FIGS. 38–41

1. Jack up the vehicle and remove the wheels.
2. Remove the brake drums.
3. Remove both return springs carefully with a pair of brake pliers.
4. Remove both retaining clips by first turning them 90 degrees with a pair of pliers to line up the slot in the lip with the flat end of the pin and then pulling them off the pins.
5. Disconnect shoes on the adjuster side first and then on the wheel cylinder side, and pull them off the backing plate.

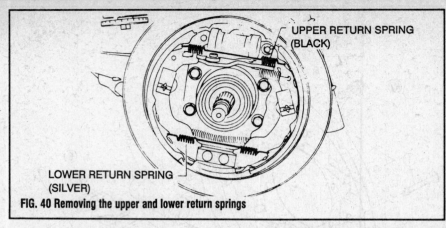

FIG. 40 Removing the upper and lower return springs

UPPER RETURN SPRING (BLACK)

LOWER RETURN SPRING (SILVER)

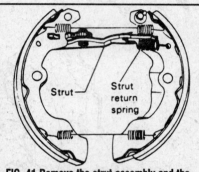

FIG. 41 Remove the strut assembly and the strut return spring

Strut   Strut return spring

6. Measure the lining thickness. Replace the linings if they are below minimum service thickness limits. See the Brake Specifications Chart at the end of this Section.
7. Replace the leading and trailing shoes on both sides at the same time. Replacement of the shoes one side or one shoe at a time, will cause uneven braking.

To Install:

8. Apply brake grease to the backing plate where the brake shoes contact it.
9. Install shoes to the wheel cylinder and then to the adjuster. Install the two retaining clips.

❊❊ CAUTION

Be careful to keep the grease off the linings. If grease gets on the linings, it could cause reduced braking performance.

10. Assemble the return springs. The upper spring is thinner.
11. Use the wedge to adjust the brake shoe diameter to 180mm. Measure the diameter in at least 3 places around the shoes.
12. Install the drum and adjust the brakes as outlined at the beginning of this section.
13. Perform the operation for the brake shoes on the other side.

Wheel Cylinders

REMOVAL & INSTALLATION

1. Raise and safely support the rear of the vehicle.
2. Remove the wheel and tire assembly.

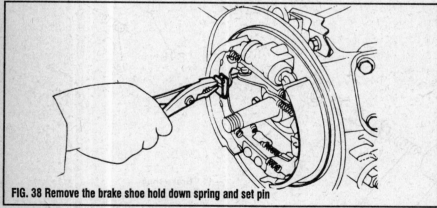

FIG. 38 Remove the brake shoe hold down spring and set pin

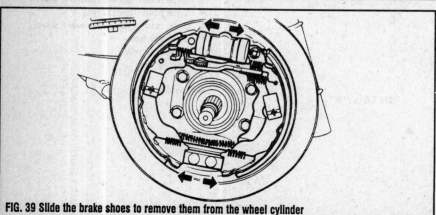

FIG. 39 Slide the brake shoes to remove them from the wheel cylinder

3. Remove the brake shoes, as described earlier in this section.

4. Disconnect and plug the fluid line for the wheel cylinder at the backing plate.

5. Remove the wheel cylinder mounting bolt and remove the wheel cylinder from the backing plate. Be careful not to loose the sheet shim that is behind the backing plate.

To Install:

6. Install the wheel cylinder into position on the backing plate, be sure to place the sheet shim behind it. See FIGS. 36 and 37 for wheel cylinder mounting.

7. Tighten the wheel cylinder mounting bolt to 8 ft. lbs. (11 Nm) on Justy and 5–7 ft. lbs. (8–10 Nm) on Loyale, STD. and XT.

8. Reconnect the fluid line to the wheel cylinder.

9. Install the brake system components. Install the wheel and tire assembly.

10. Lower the vehicle. Fill and bleed the brake system.

PARKING BRAKE

Cable

◆ SEE FIGS. 42–46

ADJUSTMENT

1. Pull the parking brake lever up forcefully. Release it and repeat several times.

2. It should take the specified number of notches to apply the parking brake.
- Except Justy — 3–5 notches
- Justy — 6 notches

3. Loosen the locknut on the turn buckle and adjust the length of the cable, so the parking brake is applied within specification.

4. Tighten the locknut and recheck operation of the parking brake lever.

REMOVAL & INSTALLATION

➡ **The procedures outlined here are to be used as an outline. The position and number of clamps used to retain the parking brake cables may vary depending on vehicle year and time of production. Follow each of the cables from end to end, to be sure of routing and mounting.**

Justy

1. Set the parking brake lever.

2. Remove the hub cap, the cotter pin, the castle nut and the wheel lug nuts.

3. Raise and support the vehicle safely. Release the brake lever.

4. Remove the wheel assemblies and the brake drums.

5. Disassemble the equalizer joint to separate the parking brake cable from the rod.

6. Remove the exhaust cover to vehicle bolts and the cover.

7. Remove the cable clamps and the hangers.

8. Disconnect the parking brake cable from the parking brake lever.

9. Disconnect the parking brake cable from the backing plate of the rear brake assemblies.

To Install:

10. Install the parking brake cable on the backing plate of the rear brakes and on the parking brake lever.

11. Install all cable clamps. Torque the mounting clamps and hanger bolts to 9–17 ft. lbs. (13–23 Nm). Ensure that the cable is not binding.

12. Install the exhaust cover, equalizer joint, wheel assemblies and brake drums. Torque the exhaust cover to body bolts to 4–7 ft. lbs.

13. Ensure that the brake cable is not binding by applying and releasing the handle several times. Adjust the parking brakes.

Except Justy

1. Raise and support the vehicle safely. Remove the front wheels.

2. Remove the parking brake cover and loosen the locknut. Loosen the parking brake adjuster until the tension is almost released, then, disconnect the inner cable ends from the equalizer.

3. Remove the clips that fasten the cable grommets in place where the cable passes through the body.

4. Pull the parking brake cable clamp from the caliper or brake shoe and disconnect the end of the cable.

5. Remove the cable to transverse link bracket bolts and the bracket.

6. Remove the cable to crossmember bracket bolt and the bracket.

7. Detach the cable rear crossmember guide and pull the cable from the passenger compartment.

To Install:

8. Install the cable through all guides and brackets. Make sure the cable passes through the guide inside the driveshaft tunnel. Install the cable on the caliper end.

9. Install the cable to the parking brake lever. Adjust the cable to specification.

10. Ensure that the cable is not binding by applying and releasing the cable several times. Adjust the parking brakes.

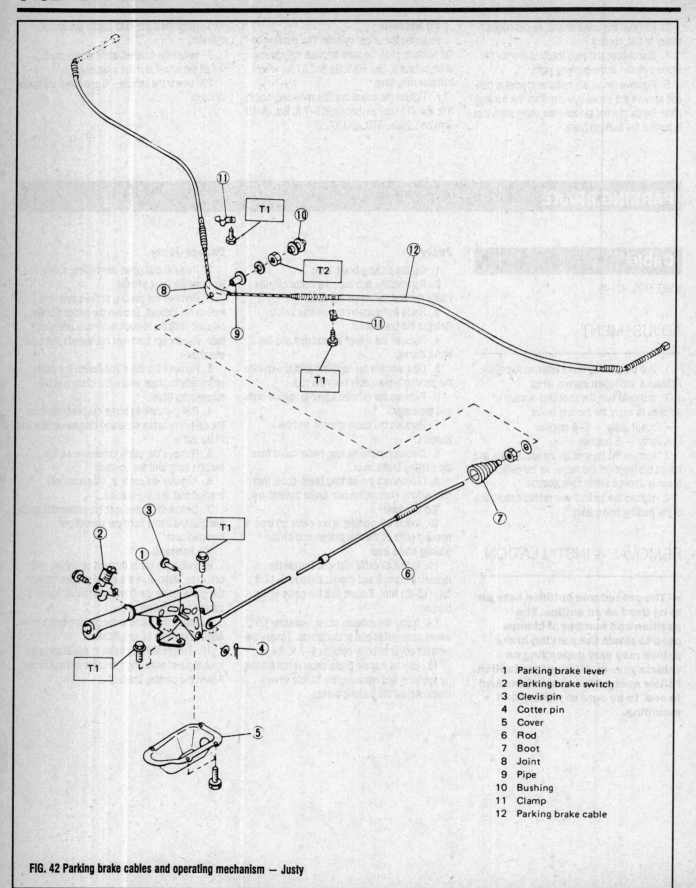

1 Parking brake lever
2 Parking brake switch
3 Clevis pin
4 Cotter pin
5 Cover
6 Rod
7 Boot
8 Joint
9 Pipe
10 Bushing
11 Clamp
12 Parking brake cable

FIG. 42 Parking brake cables and operating mechanism — Justy

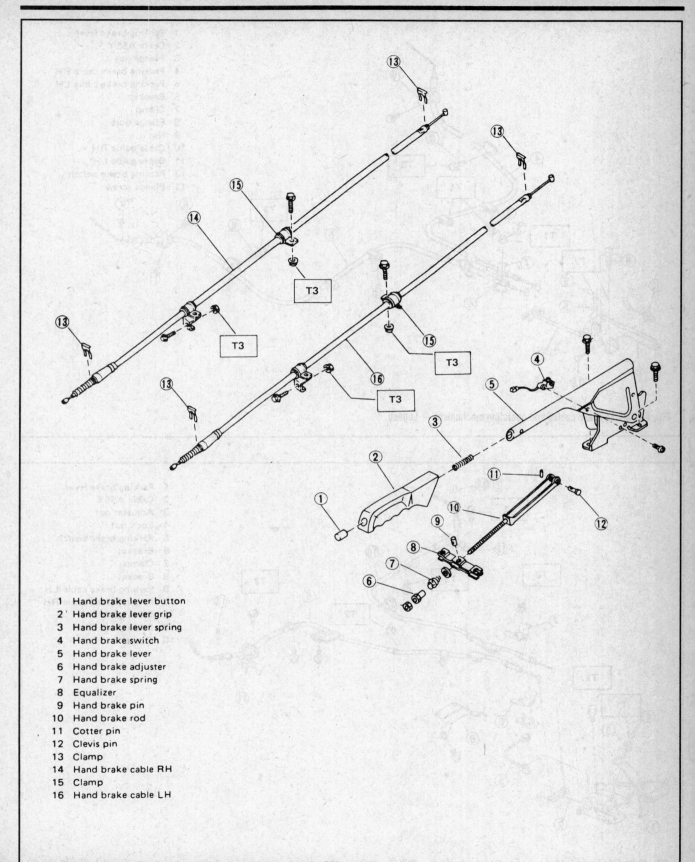

1 Hand brake lever button
2 Hand brake lever grip
3 Hand brake lever spring
4 Hand brake switch
5 Hand brake lever
6 Hand brake adjuster
7 Hand brake spring
8 Equalizer
9 Hand brake pin
10 Hand brake rod
11 Cotter pin
12 Clevis pin
13 Clamp
14 Hand brake cable RH
15 Clamp
16 Hand brake cable LH

FIG. 43 Parking brake cables and operating mechanism — Loyale, STD. and XT

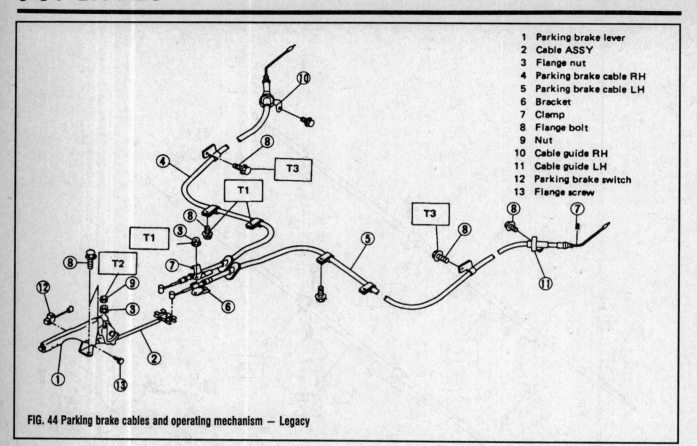

1 Parking brake lever
2 Cable ASSY
3 Flange nut
4 Parking brake cable RH
5 Parking brake cable LH
6 Bracket
7 Clamp
8 Flange bolt
9 Nut
10 Cable guide RH
11 Cable guide LH
12 Parking brake switch
13 Flange screw

FIG. 44 Parking brake cables and operating mechanism — Legacy

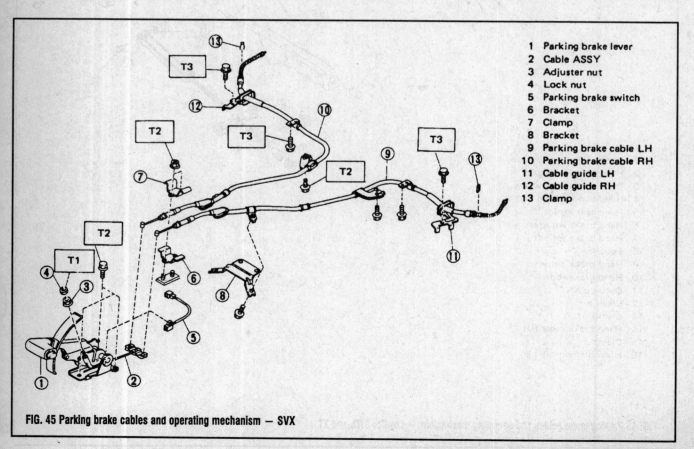

1 Parking brake lever
2 Cable ASSY
3 Adjuster nut
4 Lock nut
5 Parking brake switch
6 Bracket
7 Clamp
8 Bracket
9 Parking brake cable LH
10 Parking brake cable RH
11 Cable guide LH
12 Cable guide RH
13 Clamp

FIG. 45 Parking brake cables and operating mechanism — SVX

Parking Brake Shoes

REMOVAL & INSTALLATION

Legacy and SVX models equipped with rear disc brakes, incorporate a parking brake shoe assembly. This system uses the inside of the rear brake rotor as a brake drum and a set of brake shoes that act on the inner surface of the rotor to hold the vehicle. The mechanism that operates the parking brake shoes is the same as if it were a standard drum brake.

1. Raise and safely support the vehicle. Remove the tire and wheel assemblies.

2. Remove the brake caliper and pad assemblies, as outlined earlier in this section. Do not disconnect the brake hose from the caliper.

Support the caliper from the chassis with a piece of wire.

3. Remove the brake disc assembly.

4. Remove the primary and secondary return springs from the brake shoes.

5. Remove the front hold-down spring and pin. Remove the brake shoe strut and strut spring.

6. Remove the adjuster assembly. Remove the brake shoes.

7. Remove the parking brake cable from the parking brake lever. Remove the parking brake lever from the brake shoe.

To Install:

8. Apply a light coating of grease to the points shown in FIG. 46. Install the parking brake lever on the shoe.

9. Connect the parking brake cable to the

lever. Install the adjusting screws spring to the trailing brake shoe.

10. Install the rear shoe hold-down spring and pin. Install the adjusting screw spring to the front brake shoe.

11. Install the adjuster assembly in between the front and rear shoes. Install the strut assembly and the spring.

12. Install the shoe guide plate to the anchor pin and install the return springs.

13. Install the brake rotor, caliper and pad assemblies. Install the wheel and tire assembly.

14. Adjust the parking brake through the opening in the backing plate (covered with a small rubber plug) by inserting a brake adjuster tool or equivalent and turning the star wheel. Turn the adjuster until the brake shoes are touching the inside of the rotor, then turn it back 2 or 3 times. Check the operation of the parking brake.

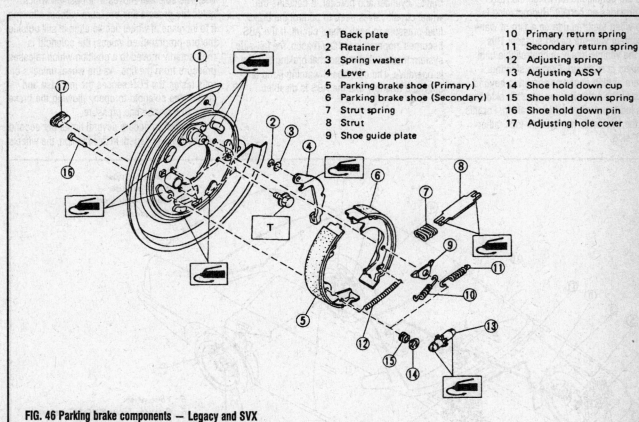

1	Back plate	10	Primary return spring
2	Retainer	11	Secondary return spring
3	Spring washer	12	Adjusting spring
4	Lever	13	Adjusting ASSY
5	Parking brake shoe (Primary)	14	Shoe hold down cup
6	Parking brake shoe (Secondary)	15	Shoe hold down spring
7	Strut spring	16	Shoe hold down pin
8	Strut	17	Adjusting hole cover
9	Shoe guide plate		

FIG. 46 Parking brake components — Legacy and SVX

FOUR WHEEL ANTI-LOCK BRAKE SYSTEM

General Description

Anti-lock braking systems (ABS) are designed to prevent locked-wheel skidding during hard braking or during braking on slippery surfaces. The front wheels of a vehicle cannot apply steering force if they are locked and sliding; the vehicle will continue in its previous direction of travel. The four wheel anti-lock brake systems found on Subaru vehicles hold the wheels just below the point of locking, thereby allowing some steering response and preventing the rear of the vehicle from sliding sideways under braking.

There are conditions for which the ABS system provides no benefit. Hydroplaning is possible when the tires ride on a film of water, losing contact with the paved surface. This renders the vehicle totally uncontrollable until road contact is regained. Extreme steering maneuvers at high speed or cornering beyond the limits of tire adhesion can result in skidding which is independent of vehicle braking. For this reason, the system is named anti–lock rather than anti–skid.

Under normal braking conditions, the ABS system functions in the same manner as a standard brake system. The system is a combination of electrical and hydraulic components, working together to control the flow of brake fluid to the wheels when necessary.

The anti-lock brake system electronic control unit (ECU) is the electronic brain of the system, receiving and interpreting speed signals from the speed sensors. The ECU will enter anti-lock mode when it senses impending wheel lock at any wheel and immediately control the brake line pressure(s) to the affected wheel(s). The hydraulic actuator assembly is separate from the master cylinder and booster. It contains the wheel circuit valves used to control the brake fluid pressure to each wheel circuit. If the ABS becomes inoperative for any reason, the fail-safe system insures that the normal braking system is operative. The dashboard warning lamp is activated to show that the ABS is disabled.

SYSTEM OPERATION

The Subaru Legacy anti-lock brake system uses a 4-sensor, 4-channel system. A speed signal for each wheel is generated by a speed sensor at the wheel. The hydraulic actuator contains 4 control solenoids, one for each wheel brake line. The system is capable of controlling brake line fluid pressure to any or all of the wheels as the situation demands.

When the ECU receives signals showing one or more wheels about to lock, it sends an electrical signal to the solenoid valve(s) within the actuator to release the brake pressure in the line. The solenoid moves to a position which holds the present line pressure without allowing it to increase. If wheel deceleration is still outside the pre-programmed values, the solenoid is momentarily moved to a position which releases pressure from the line. As the wheel unlocks or rolls faster, the ECU senses the increase and signals the solenoid to open, allowing the brake pedal to increase line pressure.

This cycling occurs several times per second when ABS is engaged. In this fashion, the wheels

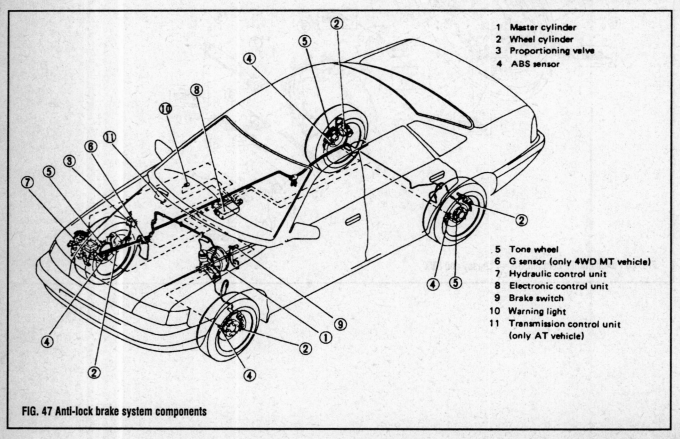

1 Master cylinder
2 Wheel cylinder
3 Proportioning valve
4 ABS sensor

5 Tone wheel
6 G sensor (only 4WD MT vehicle)
7 Hydraulic control unit
8 Electronic control unit
9 Brake switch
10 Warning light
11 Transmission control unit (only AT vehicle)

FIG. 47 Anti-lock brake system components

are kept just below the point of lock–up and control is maintained. When the hard braking ends, the ECU resets the solenoids to its normal or build mode. Brake line fluid pressures are then increased or modulated directly by pressure on the brake pedal. Fluid released to the ABS reservoirs is returned to the master cylinder by the pump and motor within the actuator.

The front and rear wheels are controlled individually, although the logic system in the ECU reacts only to the lowest rear wheel speed signal. This method is called Select Low and serves to prevent the rear wheels from getting greatly dissimilar signals which could upset directional stability.

The operator may hear a popping or clicking sound as the pump and/or control valves cycle on and off during normal operation. The sounds are due to normal operation and are not indicative of a system problem. Under most conditions, the sounds are only faintly audible. If ABS is engaged, the operator may notice some pulsation in the body of the vehicle during a hard stop; this is generally due to suspension shudder as the brake pressures are altered rapidly and the forces transfer to the vehicle.

Although the ABS system prevents wheel lock–up under hard braking, as brake pressure increases wheel slip is allowed to increase as well. This slip will result in some tire chirp during ABS operation. The sound should not be interpreted as lock–up but rather than as indication of the system holding the wheel(s) just outside the point of lock–up. Additionally, the final few feet of an ABS–engaged stop may be completed with the wheels locked; the electronic controls do not operate below about 3 mph.

SYSTEM COMPONENTS

Wheel Speed Sensors

The speed of the front and rear wheels is monitored by the sensor. A toothed tone wheel rotates in front of the sensor, generating a small AC voltage which is transmitted to the ECU. The controller compares the signals and reacts to rapid loss of wheel speed at a particular wheel by engaging the ABS system. Each speed sensor is individually removable. In most cases, the toothed wheels may be replaced if damaged, but disassembly of other components such as hub and knuckle, constant velocity joints, or axles may be required.

ABS Electronic Control Unit (ECU)

The solid-state control unit computes the rotating speed of the wheels by the signal current

sent from each sensor. When impending lock-up is detected, the ECU signals the actuator solenoids to move to predetermined positions to control brake fluid pressure to the wheels. The control unit also controls the on-off operation of the solenoid valve relay and the pump relay.

The ECU constantly monitors the function of components within the system. If any electrically detectable fault occurs, the control unit will illuminate the dashboard warning light to alert the operator. When the dash warning lamp is lit, the ABS system is disabled. The vehicle retains its normal braking capabilities without the benefit of anti-lock.

The ECU will assign and store a diagnostic or fault code. The code may be read and used for system diagnosis. If more than one fault occurs, the system will only display the first code noted. Repairs must be made based on the first code, after which the vehicle must be road tested to expose any subsequent faults.

The ECU is located under the right front seat.

ABS Hydraulic Unit

The actuator contains the solenoid control valves, pump and motor, reservoirs for temporary collection of brake fluid released from the lines as well as check and relief valves. The actuator is located at the right front of the engine compartment.

The relays and solenoids are controlled by the ECU. Under normal braking conditions, the solenoids are in the open or pressure-build position, allowing brake fluid to pass proportional to pedal pressure. During anti-lock function, the solenoids are commanded into positions to either hold or release brake fluid line pressures as required. When anti-lock function is no longer needed, the solenoids reset to the normal position. Additionally, if the ECU detects a system fault, the solenoids are immediately set to the normal or default position.

The control relays for the pump motor and solenoid valves are located externally on the actuator case. These relays are the only components on or in the actuator which may be replaced. Any failure within the actuator requires the unit to be replaced.

ABS Warning Lamp

The ABS dashboard warning lamp is controlled by the ABS controller. The lamp will illuminate briefly when the ignition switch is turned **ON** as a bulb check. The lamp should then extinguish and remain out during vehicle operation. If only the ABS warning lamp illuminates while driving, the controller has noted a fault within the ABS system. ABS function is halted, but normal braking is maintained.

BRAKE Warning Lamp

The red BRAKE warning lamp on the dashboard functions in the usual manner, warning of a fault within the hydraulic system. It is possible that a hydraulic fault within the ABS system will also trigger the BRAKE lamp. If both the ANTI-LOCK and BRAKE warning lamps are illuminated, great care must be taken in operating the vehicle; the function of the conventional brake system may be impaired.

During diagnosis of apparent ABS problems, make certain that the problem is not rooted in the normal brake system.

G-Sensor

Found only on 4WD vehicles with manual transmissions, the G-sensor transmits a deceleration signal to the ECU. It is located on the right front wheel well.

Diagnosis and Testing

SERVICE PRECAUTIONS

- If the vehicle is equipped with air bag or Supplemental Restraint Systems (SRS), always properly disable the system before working on or around system components.
- Always use a digital, high-impedance volt-ohmmeter (DVOM) for testing unless specified otherwise. Minimum impedance should be 10 kilo-ohms per volt.
- Certain components within the ABS system are not intended to be serviced or repaired individually. Only those components with removal and installation procedures should be serviced.
- Do not use rubber hoses or other parts not specifically specified for the ABS system. When using repair kits, replace all parts included in the kit. Partial or incorrect repair may lead to functional problems and require the replacement of components.
- Lubricate rubber parts with clean, fresh brake fluid to ease assembly. Do not use lubricated shop air to clean parts; damage to rubber components may result.
- Use only DOT 3 brake fluid from an unopened container.
- If any hydraulic component or line is removed or replaced, it may be necessary to bleed the entire system.

• A clean repair area is essential. Always clean the reservoir and cap thoroughly before removing the cap. The slightest amount of dirt in the fluid may plug an orifice and impair the system function. Perform repairs after components have been thoroughly cleaned. Do not allow ABS components to come into contact with any substance containing mineral oil; this includes used shop rags.

• The anti-lock brake control unit is a microprocessor similar to other computer units in the vehicle. Insure that the ignition switch is **OFF** and the negative battery cable disconnected before removing or installing controller harnesses. Avoid static electricity discharge at or near the controller.

• If any arc welding is to be done on the vehicle, the ABS electronic controller should be disconnected before welding operations begin.

• If the vehicle is to be baked after paint repairs, disconnect and remove the ECU from the vehicle.

• Never disconnect any electrical connection with the ignition switch **ON** unless instructed to do so in a test.

• Avoid touching module connector pins.

• Leave new components and modules in the shipping package until ready to install them.

• Always touch a vehicle ground after sliding across a vehicle seat or walking across vinyl or carpeted floors to avoid static charge damage.

• Never allow welding cables to lie on, near or across any vehicle electrical wiring.

VISUAL INSPECTION

Before diagnosing an apparent ABS problem, make absolutely certain that the normal braking system is in correct working order. Many common brake problems (dragging parking brake, seepage, etc.) will affect the ABS system. A visual check of specific system components may reveal problems creating an apparent ABS malfunction. Performing this inspection may reveal a simple failure, thus eliminating extended diagnostic time.

1. Inspect the tire pressures; they must be approximately equal for the system to operate correctly.

2. Inspect the brake fluid level in the reservoir.

3. Inspect brake lines, hoses, master cylinder assembly and brake calipers or wheel cylinders for leakage.

4. Visually check brake lines and hoses for excessive wear, heat damage, punctures, contact with other parts, missing clips or holders, blockage or crimping.

5. Check the calipers and wheel cylinders for rust or corrosion. Check for proper sliding action if applicable.

6. Check the caliper and wheel cylinder pistons for freedom of motion during application and release.

7. Inspect the wheel speed sensors for proper mounting and connections.

8. Inspect the sensor wheels for broken teeth or poor mounting.

9. Inspect the wheels and tires on the vehicle. They must be of the same size and type to generate accurate speed signals.

10. Confirm the fault occurrence with the operator. Certain driver induced faults, such as not releasing the parking brake fully, will set a fault code and/or trigger the dash warning light. Excessive wheel spin on low-traction surfaces may be read as a fault by the ECU. High speed acceleration or riding the brake pedal may also set fault codes and/or trigger a warning lamp. These induced faults are not system failures but examples of vehicle performance outside the parameters of the control unit.

11. Many system shut–downs are due to loss of sensor signals to or from the controller. The most common cause is not a failed sensor but a loose, corroded or dirty connector. Incorrect adjustment of the wheel speed sensor will cause a loss of wheel speed signal. Check harness and component connectors carefully.

TROUBLESHOOTING

Always begin with the visual inspection; many apparent ABS faults may be traced to the conventional brake system. After the visual inspection, put the vehicle into self-diagnostics and record any fault code displayed. Refer the appropriate diagnostic chart for the code transmitted.

After repairs have been made based on the diagnostic code, again use self-diagnostics to check for additional codes.

If the ABS dash warning lamp is lit but no fault codes are present, refer to the General Troubleshooting charts for further guidance.

GENERAL ABS TROUBLESHOOTING CHART A

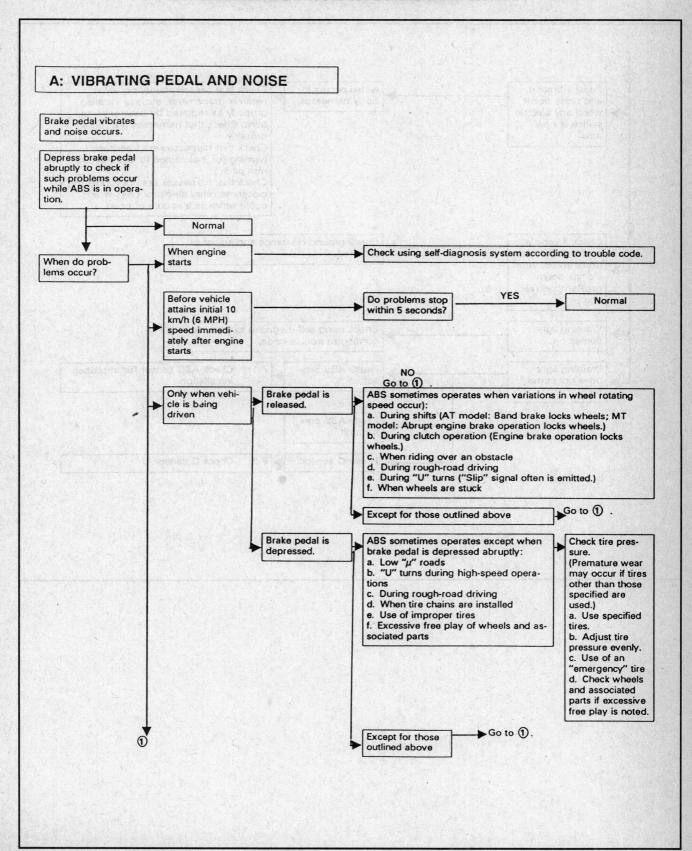

GENERAL ABS TROUBLESHOOTING CHART A CONTINUED

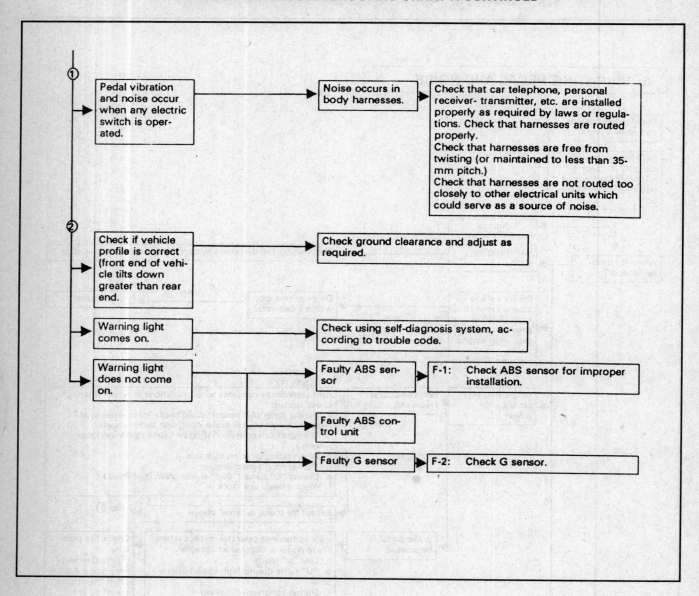

GENERAL ABS TROUBLESHOOTING CHARTS B AND C

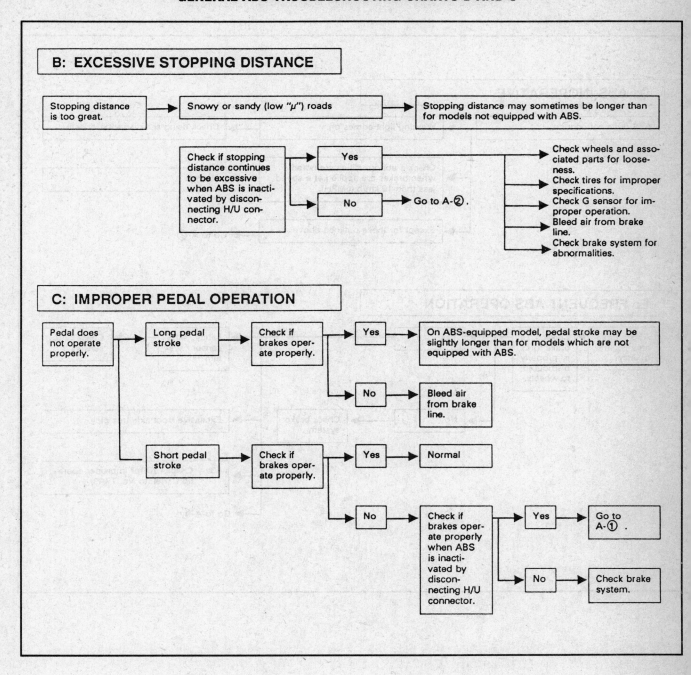

B: EXCESSIVE STOPPING DISTANCE

Stopping distance is too great. → Snowy or sandy (low "μ") roads → Stopping distance may sometimes be longer than for models not equipped with ABS.

Check if stopping distance continues to be excessive when ABS is inactivated by disconnecting H/U connector.

- Yes → Check wheels and associated parts for looseness.
  - Check tires for improper specifications.
  - Check G sensor for improper operation.
  - Bleed air from brake line.
  - Check brake system for abnormalities.
- No → Go to A-②.

C: IMPROPER PEDAL OPERATION

Pedal does not operate properly.

Long pedal stroke → Check if brakes operate properly.
- Yes → On ABS-equipped model, pedal stroke may be slightly longer than for models which are not equipped with ABS.
- No → Bleed air from brake line.

Short pedal stroke → Check if brakes operate properly.
- Yes → Normal
- No → Check if brakes operate properly when ABS is inactivated by disconnecting H/U connector.
  - Yes → Go to A-①.
  - No → Check brake system.

GENERAL ABS TROUBLESHOOTING CHARTS D AND E

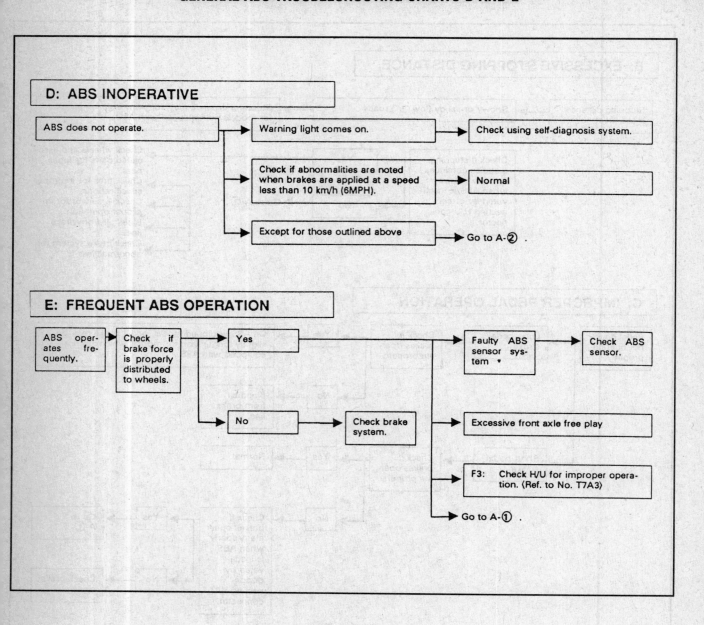

D: ABS INOPERATIVE

ABS does not operate.

→ Warning light comes on. → Check using self-diagnosis system.

→ Check if abnormalities are noted when brakes are applied at a speed less than 10 km/h (6MPH). → Normal

→ Except for those outlined above → Go to A-②.

E: FREQUENT ABS OPERATION

ABS operates frequently. → Check if brake force is properly distributed to wheels.

→ Yes → Faulty ABS sensor system • → Check ABS sensor.

→ No → Check brake system.

→ Excessive front axle free play

→ F3: Check H/U for improper operation. (Ref. to No. T7A3)

→ Go to A-①.

BASIC ABS TROUBLESHOOTING PROCEDURE

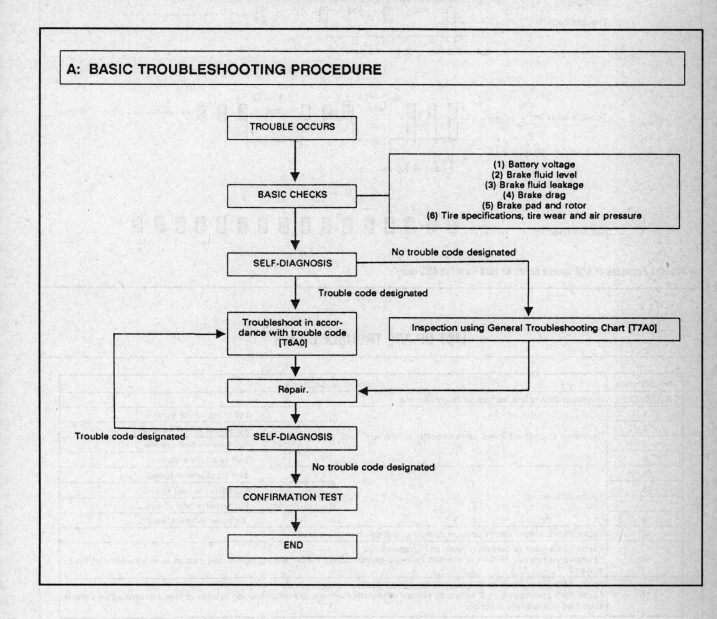

A: BASIC TROUBLESHOOTING PROCEDURE

TROUBLE OCCURS

↓

BASIC CHECKS

(1) Battery voltage
(2) Brake fluid level
(3) Brake fluid leakage
(4) Brake drag
(5) Brake pad and rotor
(6) Tire specifications, tire wear and air pressure

↓

SELF-DIAGNOSIS

→ No trouble code designated → Inspection using General Troubleshooting Chart [T7A0]

Trouble code designated

↓

Troubleshoot in accordance with trouble code [T6A0]

↓

Repair.

↓

SELF-DIAGNOSIS

Trouble code designated ←

No trouble code designated

↓

CONFIRMATION TEST

↓

END

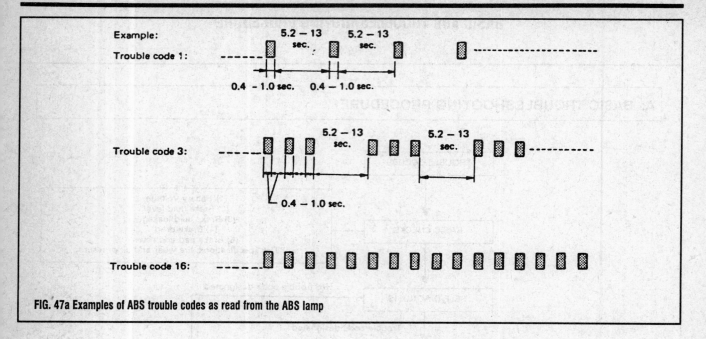

FIG. 47a Examples of ABS trouble codes as read from the ABS lamp

LIST OF ABS TROUBLE CODES

Trouble code	Contents of diagnosis	
0 [LED OFF]	Improper power line voltage or faulty harness	
1	Broken or shorted solenoid valve circuit(s) in hydraulic unit	Left front wheel control
2		Right front wheel control
3		Right rear wheel control
4		Left rear wheel control
5	Faulty ABS sensor	Left front wheel speed
6		Right front wheel speed
7		Right rear wheel speed
8		Left rear wheel speed
9	Faulty motor and/or motor relay or broken or shorted harness circuit	
10	Faulty valve relay or broken or shorted harness circuit Faulty valve relay or broken or shorted harness, or interrupted ABS (causing brakes to function as a conventional brake system)	
16	Faulty ABS control unit or G sensor or broken or shorted harness circuit Faulty ABS control unit or G sensor or broken or shorted harness, or malfunctioning system or line unidentified by vehicle speed sensor fail-safe function.	

Self-Diagnostic and Reading Codes

Drive the vehicle over 20 mph for at least one minute. Stop the vehicle in a safe location with the engine running. If the self-diagnostic circuit detects a fault, the dash warning lamp will come on.

1. The fault code will be transmitted by the flashing of the LED display on the electronic control unit under the right passenger's seat.

2. The code will be transmitted automatically about 10–12 seconds after the ABS dashboard warning lamp comes on.

3. Read the number of short flashes as the number of the code, i.e., 16 flashes represents Code 16. The flash pattern will repeat after a 5–13 second pause. Viewing the output several times is recommended for accuracy.

4. Both the LED and the dash warning lamp remain activated until the ignition key is switched **OFF**. When the ignition is switched **OFF**, the memory is erased and the code is lost. The vehicle must be re-driven and placed into self-diagnostics.

5. If the LED does not activate when the dash warning lamp is lit, the power supply may be inoperative.

ABS CONTROL UNIT I/O SIGNAL VOLTAGE

A: I/O SIGNAL VOLTAGE

```
18 17 16 15 14 13 12 11 10 9 8 7 6 5 4 3 2 1
35 34 33 32 31 30 29 28 27 26 25 24 23 22 21 20 19
```

TO (P12)

Contents		Terminal No.	With engine idling	Input/output signals	
				Measured value	Measuring conditions
ABS sensor	Left front wheel	22, 5*	0V	200 — 300 mV (AC range)	• No. 22 or No. 5* — No. 4 • Vehicle speed 2.75 km/h (1.7 MPH)
	GND	4			
	Right front wheel	11	0V	200 — 300 mV (AC range)	• No. 11 — No. 21 • Vehicle speed 2.75 km/h (1.7 MPH)
	GND	21			
	Left rear wheel	7	0V	200 — 300 mV (AC range)	• No. 7 — No. 9 • Vehicle speed 2.75 km/h (1.7 MPH)
	GND	9			
	Right rear wheel	24	0V	200 — 300 mV (AC range)	• No. 24 — No. 26 • Vehicle speed 2.75 km/h (1.7 MPH)
	GND	26			
G sensor		16	13 — 14V	0V	
Stop light switch		25	0V	13 — 14V	When brake pedal is depressed.
Motor monitoring		14	0V	13 — 14V	When motor operates.
Valve power-supply monitoring		32	13 — 14V	13 — 14V	—
Hydraulic unit	Solenoid Left front wheel	2	13 — 14V	0V	When solenoid is energized to produce output.
	Solenoid Right front wheel	35	13 — 14V	0V	
	Solenoid Left rear wheel	18	13 — 14V	0V	
	Solenoid Right rear wheel	19	13 — 14V	0V	
	Valve relay coil	27	0V	0V	—
	Motor relay coil	28	13 — 14V	0V	When motor operates to produce output
Warning light		29	0V	13 — 14V	Ignition switch ON (Engine OFF)
Power supply	Alternator	15	13 — 14V	1.7V	Ignition switch ON (Engine OFF)
	Battery	1	13 — 14V	13 — 14V	—
	Relay coil (valve, motor, etc.)	17	13 — 14V	13 — 14V	—
Grounding line		10	0V	0V	—
		20	0V	0V	—
		34	0V	0V	—

*: FWD model

ABS CONTROL UNIT I/O SIGNAL DIAGRAM

B: I/O SIGNAL DIAGRAM

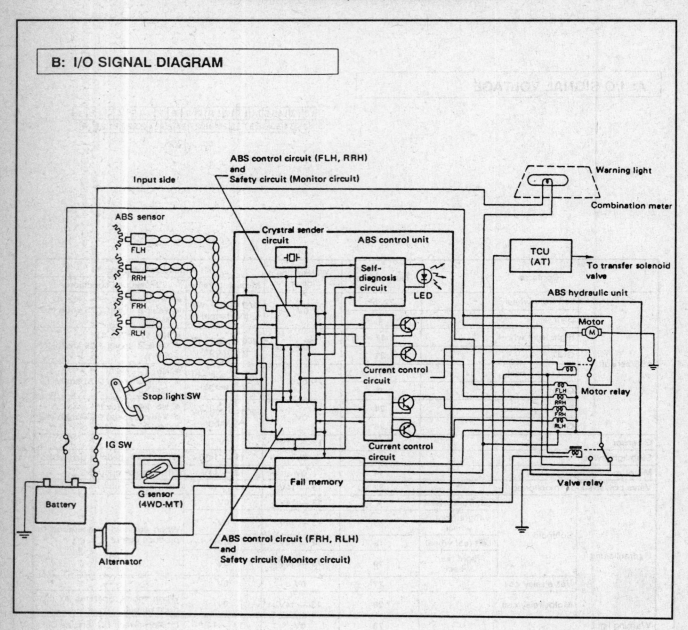

TROUBLE CODE 0 — IMPROPER LINE VOLTAGE OR FAULTY HARNESS

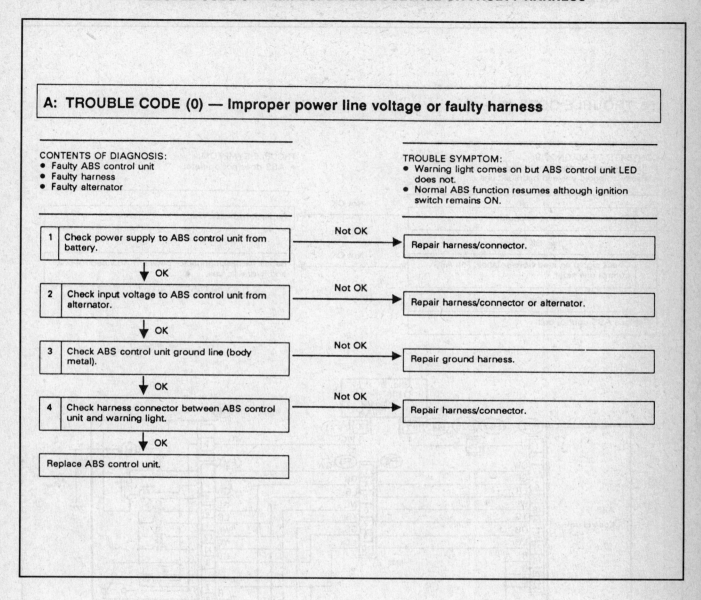

A: TROUBLE CODE (0) — Improper power line voltage or faulty harness

CONTENTS OF DIAGNOSIS:
- Faulty ABS control unit
- Faulty harness
- Faulty alternator

TROUBLE SYMPTOM:
- Warning light comes on but ABS control unit LED does not.
- Normal ABS function resumes although ignition switch remains ON.

1 | Check power supply to ABS control unit from battery. — Not OK → Repair harness/connector.

↓ OK

2 | Check input voltage to ABS control unit from alternator. — Not OK → Repair harness/connector or alternator.

↓ OK

3 | Check ABS control unit ground line (body metal). — Not OK → Repair ground harness.

↓ OK

4 | Check harness connector between ABS control unit and warning light. — Not OK → Repair harness/connector.

↓ OK

Replace ABS control unit.

TROUBLE CODES 1–4 — FAULTY SOLENOID VALVE CIRCUIT IN HYDRAULIC UNIT

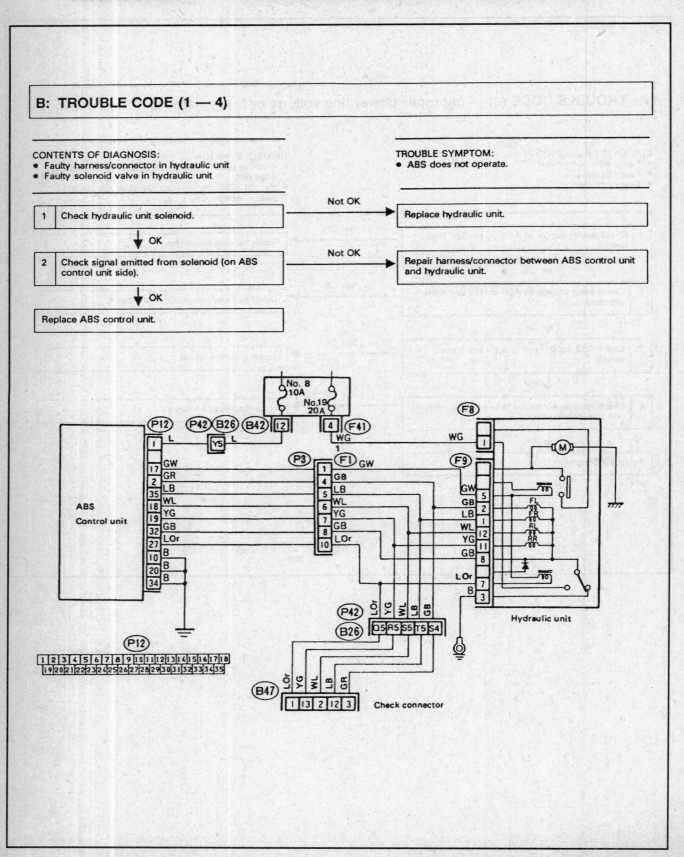

B: TROUBLE CODE (1 — 4)

CONTENTS OF DIAGNOSIS:
- Faulty harness/connector in hydraulic unit
- Faulty solenoid valve in hydraulic unit

TROUBLE SYMPTOM:
- ABS does not operate.

1. Check hydraulic unit solenoid. — Not OK → Replace hydraulic unit.

↓ OK

2. Check signal emitted from solenoid (on ABS control unit side). — Not OK → Repair harness/connector between ABS control unit and hydraulic unit.

↓ OK

Replace ABS control unit.

Hydraulic unit

ABS Control unit

Check connector

TROUBLE CODE 5–6 — FAULTY FRONT ABS SENSOR

C: TROUBLE CODE (5 and 6)

CONTENTS OF DIAGNOSIS:
- Faulty front ABS sensor or harness
- Faulty ABS control unit

TROUBLE SYMPTOM:
- ABS does not operate.

| 1 | Check signal emitted from sensor (on ABS control unit side). | OK → | Replace ABS control unit. |

↓ Not OK

| 2 | Check sensor. | OK → | Repair harness/connector. |

↓ Not OK

| Replace sensor. |

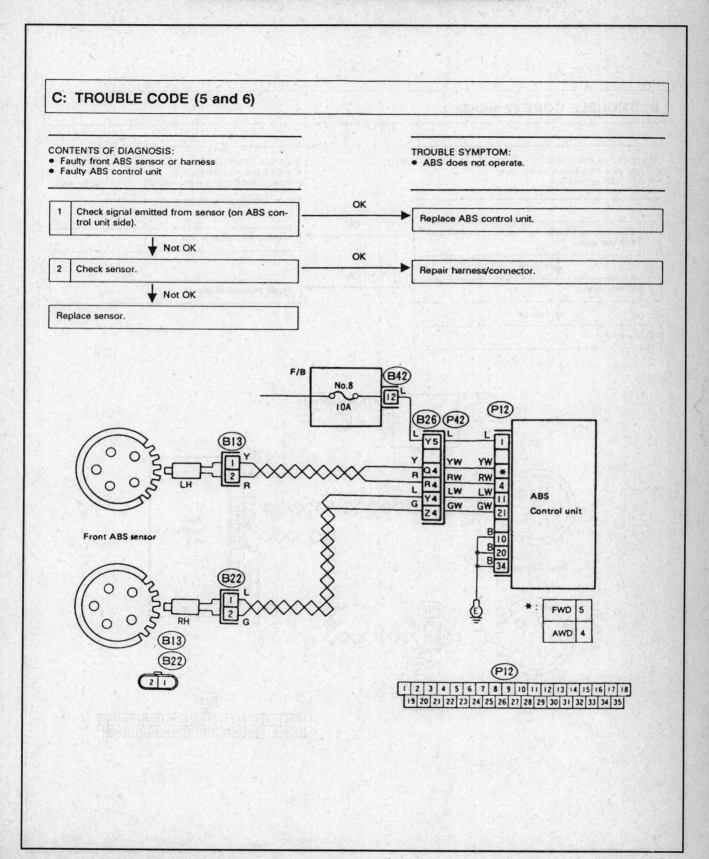

Front ABS sensor

TROUBLE CODES 7–8 — FAULTY REAR ABS SENSOR

D: TROUBLE CODE (7 and 8)

CONTENTS OF DIAGNOSIS:
- Faulty rear ABS sensor or harness
- Faulty ABS control unit

TROUBLE SYMPTOMS:
- ABS does not operate.
- Rear wheels only are occasionally controlled by ABS.

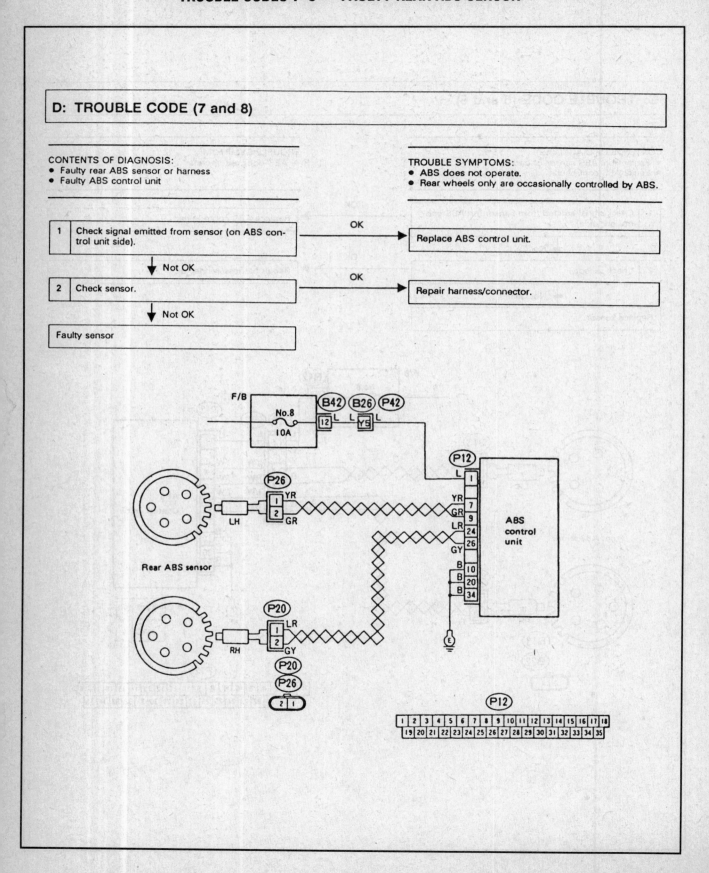

| 1 | Check signal emitted from sensor (on ABS control unit side). | → OK → | Replace ABS control unit. |

↓ Not OK

| 2 | Check sensor. | → OK → | Repair harness/connector. |

↓ Not OK

Faulty sensor

TROUBLE CODE 9 — FAULTY HYDRAULIC MOTOR OR MOTOR RELAY

E: TROUBLE CODE (9)

CONTENTS OF DIAGNOSIS:
- Faulty main power supply
- Faulty hydraulic motor or motor relay built into hydraulic unit

TROUBLE SYMPTOM:
- ABS does not operate.

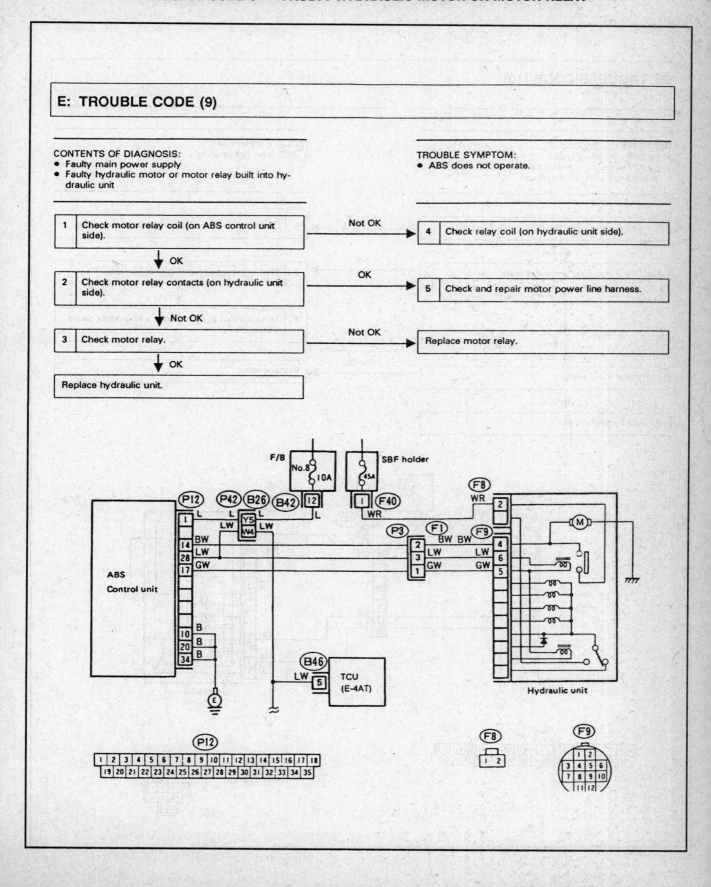

1	Check motor relay coil (on ABS control unit side).

Not OK →

4	Check relay coil (on hydraulic unit side).

↓ OK

2	Check motor relay contacts (on hydraulic unit side).

OK →

5	Check and repair motor power line harness.

↓ Not OK

3	Check motor relay.

Not OK →

Replace motor relay.

↓ OK

Replace hydraulic unit.

F/B No.8 10A   SBF holder 45A

P12 P42 B26 B42 I2 I F40 F8 WR 2

ABS Control unit

Hydraulic unit

TCU (E-4AT)

P12

F8

F9

TROUBLE CODE 10 — FAULTY VALVE RELAY OR INTERRUPTED SYSTEM OPERATION

F: TROUBLE CODE (10)

CONTENTS OF DIAGNOSIS:
- Faulty main power supply
- Faulty hydraulic unit valve relay
- Interference with other system

TROUBLE SYMPTOM:
- ABS does not operate.

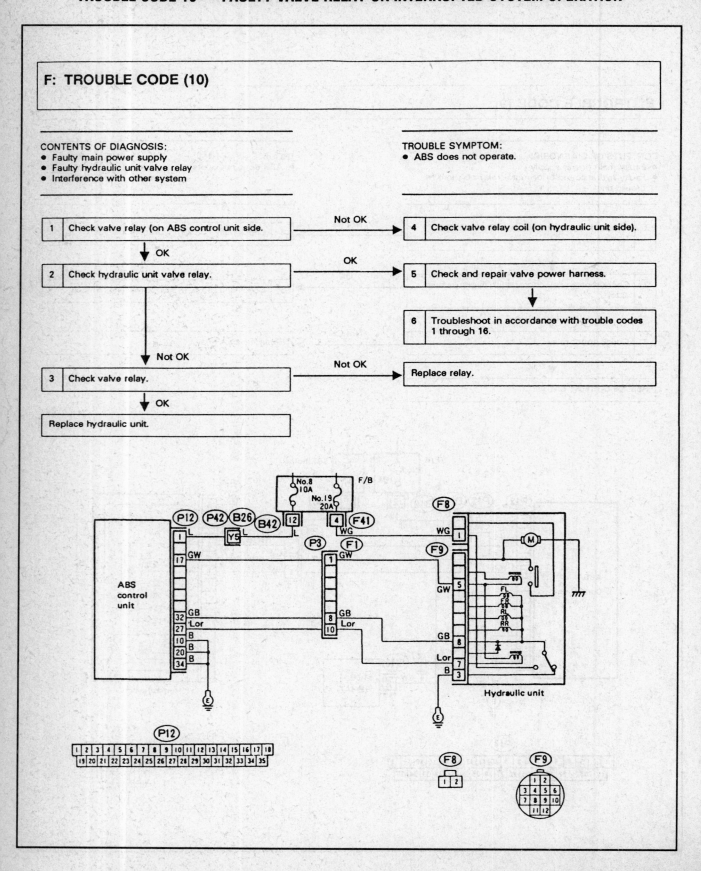

TROUBLE CODE 16 — FAULTY ABS CONTROL UNIT OR G-SENSOR

G: TROUBLE CODE (16)

CONTENTS OF DIAGNOSIS:
- Faulty ABS control unit
- Faulty power supply to ABS control unit or faulty ground system
- Faulty G sensor
- Faulty G-sensor harness and connector

TROUBLE SYMPTOMS:
- ABS control unit does not operate.
- ABS activates faster than specifications when braking on high "μ" (dry asphalt) road.
- Warning light comes on and trouble code "16" is displayed approximately 20 seconds after vehicle starts.

| 1 | Check continuity in G-sensor circuit (on ABS control unit side. | → OK → | Faulty ABS control unit. (Replace after inspection of power supply.) |

↓ Not OK

| 2 | Check G sensor. | → OK → | 3 | Check harness between ABS control unit and G sensor. |

↓ Not OK

Replace G sensor.

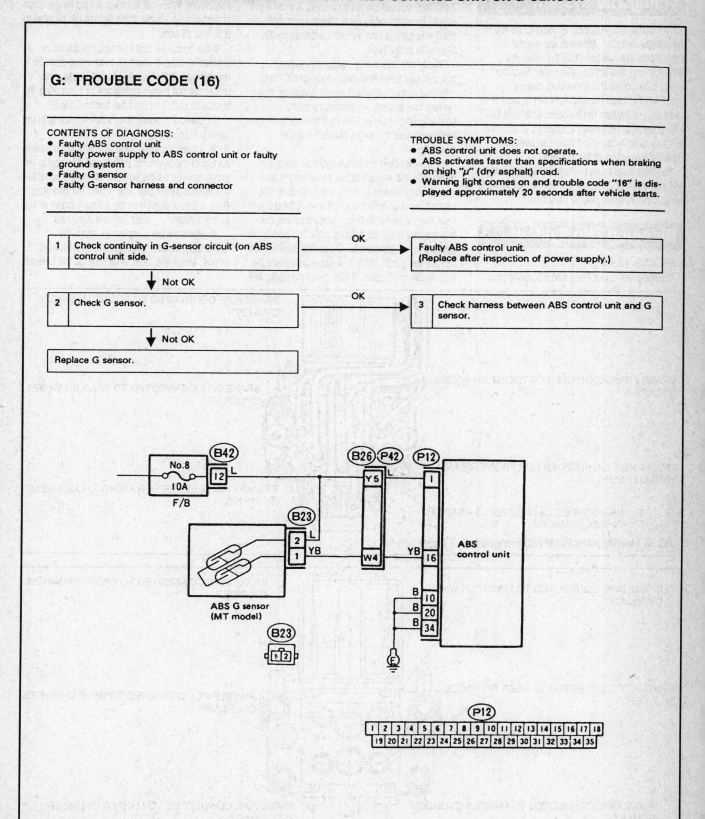

ABS G sensor
(MT model)

ABS control unit

Filling The System

The brake fluid reservoir is located on top of the master cylinder. Although no special procedures are needed to fill the fluid, the reservoir cap and surrounding area must be wiped clean of all dirt and debris before removing the cap. The slightest dirt in the fluid can cause a system malfunction. Use only DOT 3 fluid from an unopened container. Use of old, polluted or non-approved fluid can seriously impair the function of the system.

The fluid level must be kept between the MAX and MIN lines at all times. Do not overfill beyond the MAX line; fluid spillage may result.

Bleeding The System

◆ SEE FIGS. 48–49

Bleeding the brake lines and components in the ABS system is performed using the common 2-person, manual bleeding method. A vinyl hose should be attached to each bleeder port with the other end placed into a clear container partially filled with brake fluid.

If only one brake line , caliper or wheel cylinder has been loosened or replaced, then only that individual wheel needs bleeding. If any system component — master cylinder, proportioning valve or ABS hydraulic unit — has been replaced, the entire system requires bleeding.

When bleeding the entire system, always begin with the wheels in the secondary brake circuit, the proceed to the primary circuit. The correct order is right front, left rear, left front and right rear. When bleeding, slowly depress the brake pedal and hold it down while the bleeder is opened for 1–2 seconds. Close the bleeder and release the pedal. Wait 3–4 seconds before the next pedal application. Rapid pedal pumping will actually complicate the bleeding and extend the procedure. When air bubbles are no longer seen in the escaping brake fluid, tighten the bleeder to 6 ft. lbs. (8 Nm).

If the hydraulic unit has been replaced or drained of fluid, it must be bled using specific procedures. This bleeding is not necessary under normal repair conditions not involving the hydraulic unit. To bleed the hydraulic unit:

1. Bleed the brake lines at all 4 wheels in the normal fashion.

2. Attach the vinyl hose to one of the bleeders on top of the hydraulic unit. Bleed this port in the same fashion as the wheels. Move the hose to the other bleeder port and repeat the bleeding. Both of these port bleed the primary brake circuit in the actuator — front left and right rear.

3. Remove the cone screw from the secondary bleeder port and install a bleeder screw. Install the clear vinyl tube on the bleeder.

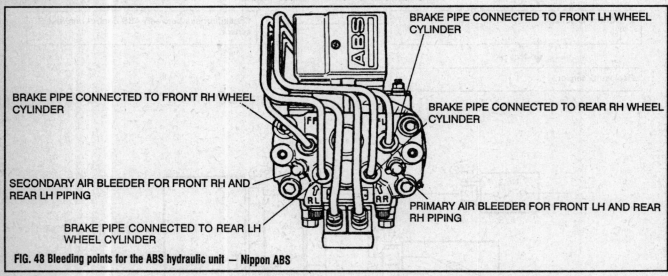

FIG. 48 Bleeding points for the ABS hydraulic unit — Nippon ABS

BRAKE PIPE CONNECTED TO FRONT LH WHEEL CYLINDER

BRAKE PIPE CONNECTED TO FRONT RH WHEEL CYLINDER

BRAKE PIPE CONNECTED TO REAR RH WHEEL CYLINDER

SECONDARY AIR BLEEDER FOR FRONT RH AND REAR LH PIPING

BRAKE PIPE CONNECTED TO REAR LH WHEEL CYLINDER

PRIMARY AIR BLEEDER FOR FRONT LH AND REAR RH PIPING

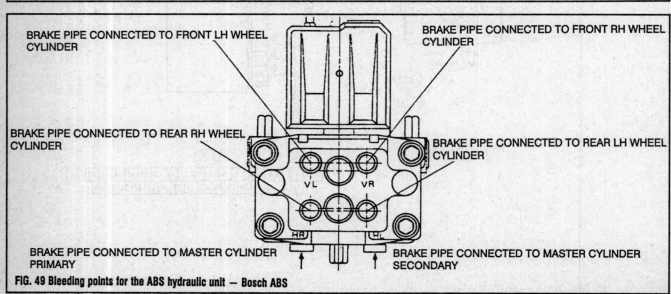

FIG. 49 Bleeding points for the ABS hydraulic unit — Bosch ABS

BRAKE PIPE CONNECTED TO FRONT LH WHEEL CYLINDER

BRAKE PIPE CONNECTED TO FRONT RH WHEEL CYLINDER

BRAKE PIPE CONNECTED TO REAR RH WHEEL CYLINDER

BRAKE PIPE CONNECTED TO REAR LH WHEEL CYLINDER

BRAKE PIPE CONNECTED TO MASTER CYLINDER PRIMARY

BRAKE PIPE CONNECTED TO MASTER CYLINDER SECONDARY

4. Open the bleeder and depress the brake pedal slowly; hold the pedal depressed.

5. With the pedal depressed, intermittently apply the AV electrical signal to the solenoid valve. To apply the AV signal:

a. Disconnect both battery terminals.

b. Disconnect the 2-pin and 12-pin connectors at the hydraulic assembly.

c. At the 12-pin connector, connect terminals 1 and 3 to battery ground. Connect terminals 5 and 7 to the positive terminal of the battery. Take great care not to short terminals 5 and 7 to the grounded terminals nearby.

d. When the last connection is made, the AV signal is transmitted to the solenoids. Do not send this signal for more than 5 seconds. Break the connection at the positive terminal after 2–3 seconds.

6. When the brake pedal moves to the end of its stroke, close the bleeder and allow the pedal to return. If the AV signal is not transmitted for any reason, the bleeder need not be closed before returning the pedal.

7. Repeat Steps 4, 5 and 6 until the fluid in the tube contains no air.

8. With the AV signal disconnected and the brake pedal released, remove the bleeder fitting and re-install the cone screw. Tighten the cone screw to 6 ft. lbs. (8 Nm).

9. Repeat the procedure from Step 3 for the other secondary bleeder port. Both secondary ports must be bled.

10. Carefully remove the jumper wires from the 12-pin connector. Do not allow the terminals to short to each other or to ground.

11. Connect the 2- and 12-pin connectors at the hydraulic unit. Connect the battery cables with the ignition **OFF**.

Electronic Control Unit (ECU)

REMOVAL & INSTALLATION

♦ SEE FIG. 50

➡ **The control unit is located under the right front seat. On all models except the Legacy, the seat must be removed to gain access to the control unit. On the Legacy, the control unit can be reached by removing the door sill molding and pulling the carpet back.**

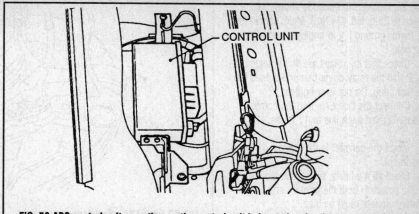

FIG. 50 ABS control unit mounting — the control unit is located under the passengers seat

1. Disconnect the negative battery cable. On all models except the Legacy, remove the right front seat. On the Legacy, remove the door sill molding and pull the carpet back.

2. Lift the carpet out of the way. Remove the 2 bolts holding the ECU to the body.

3. Lift the ECU away from the floor. Remove the small screws securing the connector to the control unit.

4. Carefully disconnect the multi-pin harness connector from the ECU.

5. Reassemble in reverse order. Make certain the connector is firmly seated and not crooked. Always install the small connector retaining screws.

Hydraulic Actuator

REMOVAL & INSTALLATION

♦ SEE FIG. 51

1. Disconnect the harness connectors at the hydraulic unit.

2. Remove the emission canister from the engine compartment to allow access.

3. Disconnect the inlet and outlet lines from the top of the actuator. Label the lines before removal; exact reinstallation is required.

5. Immediately plug the lines and ports to prevent entry of dirt and debris into the system.

6. Remove the screw holding the ABS relay cover and remove the cover.

7. Remove the bolts holding the hydraulic unit bracket to the body. Note that one of these bolts has the pump motor ground lug attached.

8. Lift the actuator and bracket clear of the vehicle. Keep the unit upright at all times; do not drop or bump it.

9. The brackets and relays may be removed for transfer to a replacement unit.

10. Except for the 2 relays, the hydraulic unit contains no replaceable components. Never attempt to disassemble the unit or repair it.

To Install:

11. Install or transfer the relays and brackets. The nuts on the bushing bolts holding the hydraulic unit to the brackets should be tightened to 6 ft. lbs. (8 Nm).

12. Install the hydraulic unit and brackets into the engine compartment. The nuts and bolts

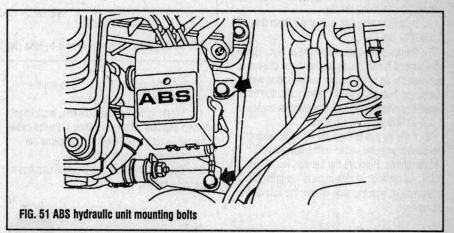

FIG. 51 ABS hydraulic unit mounting bolts

holding the brackets to the body should be tightened to 25 ft. lbs. (34 Nm). Make certain the pump motor ground lug in engaged beneath the proper bolt.

13. Check that the relays are firmly seated in place. Install the relay cover box and tighten the screw just snug. Do not over tighten.

14. Connect the brake lines to the correct positions. Tighten each line to 11 ft. lbs. (15 Nm).

15. Install the canister in the engine compartment.

16. Bleed all 4 wheels, then bleed the hydraulic actuator. Both the primary and secondary circuits must be bled.

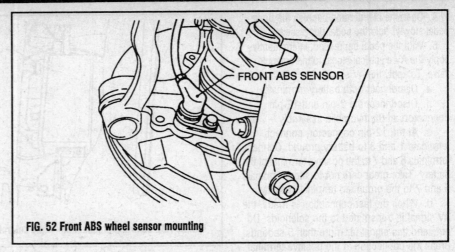

FIG. 52 Front ABS wheel sensor mounting

Wheel Speed Sensor

REMOVAL & INSTALLATION

◆ SEE FIGS. 52, 53

Front

1. Disconnect the speed sensor harness connector in the engine compartment.

2. Remove the bolts holding the sensor harness brackets and clips. Take careful note of placement and location of harness retainers; exact reassembly is required.

3. Remove the sensor retaining bolt at the front hub.

4. Remove the front wheel speed sensor by lifting it straight out of the housing. Do not damage the tip of the sensor by hitting it against surrounding components. Protect the tip from damage after it is removed. Inspect the sensor tip for any damage or accumulated debris. Clean or replace as necessary.

To Install:

5. Place the sensor into the mount without damaging or striking the tip.

6. Install the retaining bolt and tighten it to 10 ft. lbs. (14 Nm.)

7. Remove the caliper and brake disc. Use a non-ferrous feeler gauge to check the clearance between the tip of the sensor and the tone wheel. Rotate the hub and check clearance to the tone wheel at several locations. Standard clearance is 0.039–0.059 in. (1.0–1.5 mm).

8. If the air gap to the tone wheel is too small, the sensor may be raised using special ABS sensor shims. Remove the sensor, install the shim and recheck. If clearance is too great, there is a problem with the tone wheel, the hub and/or the sensor.

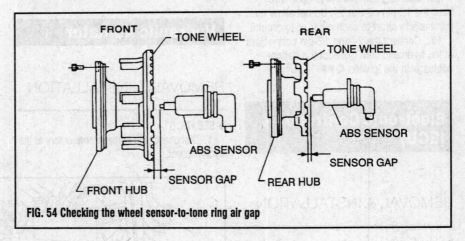

FIG. 53 Rear ABS wheel sensor mounting

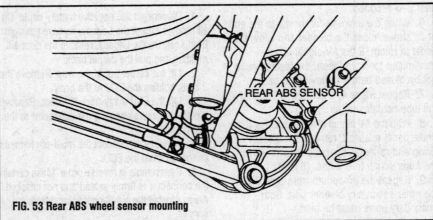

FIG. 54 Checking the wheel sensor-to-tone ring air gap

9. Once the air gap is correct, re-set the retaining bolt to the correct torque.

10. Working from the sensor end, install each harness clip and retainer, making sure the cable is routed exactly as before. Do not allow the cable to become twisted or kinked.

11. Connect the sensor to the ABS harness in the engine compartment.

Rear

1. Remove the rear seat. Disconnect the ABS harness connector.

2. Remove the rear sensor harness retaining bracket from the rear trailing link. Remove any other retainers or clips holding the harness. Take note of the cable routing and retainer placement; exact reassembly is required.

3. Remove the retaining bolt holding the sensor to the hub.

4. Remove the rear wheel speed sensor by lifting it straight out of the housing. Do not damage the tip of the sensor by hitting it against surrounding components. Protect the tip from damage after it is removed. Inspect the sensor tip for any damage or accumulated debris. Clean or replace as necessary.

To Install:

5. Place the sensor into the mount without damaging or striking the tip.

6. Install the retaining bolt and tighten it to 10 ft. lbs. (14 Nm.)

7. Remove the caliper and brake disc. Use a non-ferrous feeler gauge to check the clearance between the tip of the sensor and the tone wheel. Rotate the hub and check clearance to the tone wheel at several locations. Standard clearance is 0.031–0.051 in. (0.8–1.3 mm).

8. If the air gap to the tone wheel is too small, the sensor may be raised using special ABS sensor shims. Remove the sensor, install the shim and recheck. If clearance is too great, there is a problem with the tone wheel, the hub and/or the sensor.

9. Once the air gap is correct, again set the retaining bolt to the correct torque.

10. Working from the sensor end, install each harness clip and retainer, making sure the cable is routed exactly as before. Do not allow the cable to become twisted or kinked.

11. Connect the sensor to the ABS harness under the rear seat. Install the rear seat.

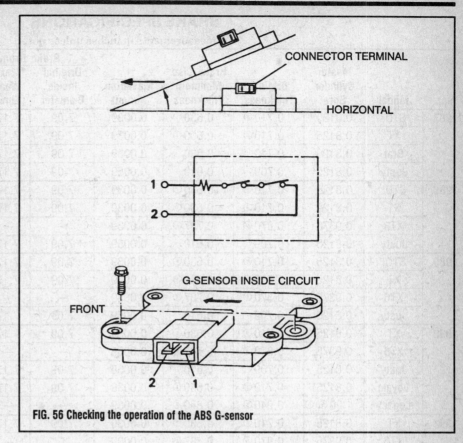

FIG. 56 Checking the operation of the ABS G-sensor

G-SENSOR

REMOVAL & INSTALLATION

The G-sensor may be removed by unbolting it from the fender apron. Disconnect the wire harness and remove the unit. The G-sensor may be tested with an ohmmeter.

Resting flat on a level surface, the sensor should have approximately 610 ohms resistance. Acceptable variance is ± 60 ohms. When tilted in the direction of travel, the resistance should become at least 100 kilo-ohms when the unit is held at an angle of 14–21 degrees. The G-sensor only operates in the direction of travel; no effect will be seen from tilting in any other direction.

When reinstalling the sensor, make absolutely certain it is placed in the correct position. If installed backwards, it will not allow the system to work.

Connect the wiring harness and secure the retaining bolts.

BRAKE SPECIFICATIONS
All measurements in inches unless noted

| Year | Model | Master Cylinder Bore | Brake Disc | | | Brake Drum Diameter | | | Minimum Lining Thickness | |
			Original Thickness	Minimum Thickness	Maximum Runout	Original Inside Diameter	Max. Wear Limit	Maximum Machine Diameter	Front	Rear
1985	STD.	0.8125	0.710 ⑧	0.630 ①	0.0039	7.09	7.17	7.17	0.295	0.256 ②
	XT	0.8125	0.710 ⑧	0.630 ①	0.0039	7.09	7.17	7.17	0.295	0.256 ②
	Brat	0.8125	0.710	0.630	0.0039	7.09	7.17	7.17	0.295	0.059
1986	STD.	0.8125	0.710 ⑧	0.630 ①	0.0039	7.09	7.17	7.17	0.295	0.256 ②
	XT	0.8125	0.710 ⑧	0.630 ①	0.0039	7.09	7.17	7.17	0.295	0.256 ②
	Brat	0.8125	0.710	0.630	0.0039	7.09	7.17	7.17	0.295	0.059

BRAKE SPECIFICATIONS

All measurements in inches unless noted

Year	Model	Master Cylinder Bore	Brake Disc Original Thickness	Brake Disc Minimum Thickness	Brake Disc Maximum Runout	Brake Drum Diameter Original Inside Diameter	Brake Drum Diameter Max. Wear Limit	Brake Drum Diameter Maximum Machine Diameter	Minimum Lining Thickness Front	Minimum Lining Thickness Rear
1987	STD.	0.8125	0.710⑧	0.630①	0.0039	7.09	7.17	7.17	0.295	0.256②
	XT	0.8125	0.710⑧	0.630①	0.0039	7.09	7.17	7.17	0.295	0.256②
	Brat	0.8125	0.710	0.630	0.0039	7.09	7.17	7.17	0.295	0.059
	Justy	0.8125	0.709	0.610	0.0059	7.09	7.17	7.17	0.295③	0.067
1988	STD.	0.8125	0.710⑧	0.630①	0.0039	7.09	7.17	7.17	0.295	0.256②
	XT	0.8125	0.710⑧	0.630①	0.0039	7.09	7.17	7.17	0.295	0.256②
	XT6	0.9375	0.870⑧	0.787④	0.0039	—	—	—	0.295	0.315
	Justy	0.8125	0.709	0.610	0.0059	7.09	7.17	7.17	0.295③	0.067
1989	STD.	0.8125	0.710⑧	0.630①	0.0039	7.09	7.17	7.17	0.295	0.256②
	XT	0.8125	0.710⑧	0.630①	0.0039	7.09	7.17	7.17	0.295	0.256②
	XT6	0.9375	0.870⑧	0.787④	0.0039	—	—	—	0.295	0.315
	Justy	0.8125	0.709	0.610	0.0059	7.09	7.17	7.17	0.295③	0.067
1990	XT	0.8125	0.710⑧	0.630①	0.0039	7.09	7.17	7.17	0.295	0.256②
	XT6	0.9375	0.870⑧	0.787④	0.0039	—	—	—	0.295	0.315
	Justy	0.8125	0.709	0.610	0.0059	7.09	7.17	7.17	0.295③	0.067
	Loyale	0.8125	0.710⑧	0.630①	0.0039	7.09	7.17	7.17	0.295	0.256②
	Legacy	1.00⑤⑥	0.940⑧	0.870⑦	0.0039	—	—	—	0.295	0.256
1991	XT	0.8125	0.710⑧	0.630①	0.0039	7.09	7.17	7.17	0.295	0.256②
	XT6	0.9375	0.870⑧	0.787④	0.0039	—	—	—	0.295	0.315
	Justy	0.8125	0.709	0.610	0.0059	7.09	7.17	7.17	0.295③	0.067
	Loyale	0.8125	0.710⑧	0.630①	0.0039	7.09	7.17	7.17	0.295	0.256②
	Legacy	1.00⑤⑥	0.940⑧	0.870⑦	0.0039	—	—	—	0.295	0.256
1992	Justy	0.8125	0.709	0.610	0.0059	7.09	7.17	7.17	0.295③	0.067
	Loyale	0.8125	0.710⑧	0.630①	0.0039	7.09	7.17	7.17	0.295	0.256②
	Legacy	1.00⑤⑥	0.940⑧	0.870⑦	0.0039	—	—	—	0.295	0.256
	SVX	1.0625	1.100⑧	1.020①	0.0039	—	—	—	0.295	0.256

NOTE: STD. Includes 2 door, 3 door, 4 door and Wagon models
① Rear disc: 0.335 in.
② With drum brakes: 0.059 in.
③ GL Models: 0.315 in.
④ Rear disc: 0.335 in.
⑤ LX model with 4WD: 1.0625 in.
⑥ With ABS: 1.0625 in.
⑦ Rear disc: 0.335 in.
⑧ Rear disc thickness: 0.390 in.

Troubleshooting the Brake System

Problem	Cause	Solution
Low brake pedal (excessive pedal travel required for braking action.)	• Excessive clearance between rear linings and drums caused by inoperative automatic adjusters	• Make 10 to 15 alternate forward and reverse brake stops to adjust brakes. If brake pedal does not come up, repair or replace adjuster parts as necessary.
	• Worn rear brakelining	• Inspect and replace lining if worn beyond minimum thickness specification
	• Bent, distorted brakeshoes, front or rear	• Replace brakeshoes in axle sets
	• Air in hydraulic system	• Remove air from system. Refer to Brake Bleeding.
Low brake pedal (pedal may go to floor with steady pressure applied.)	• Fluid leak in hydraulic system	• Fill master cylinder to fill line; have helper apply brakes and check calipers, wheel cylinders, differential valve tubes, hoses and fittings for leaks. Repair or replace as necessary.
	• Air in hydraulic system	• Remove air from system. Refer to Brake Bleeding.
	• Incorrect or non-recommended brake fluid (fluid evaporates at below normal temp).	• Flush hydraulic system with clean brake fluid. Refill with correct-type fluid.
	• Master cylinder piston seals worn, or master cylinder bore is scored, worn or corroded	• Repair or replace master cylinder
Low brake pedal (pedal goes to floor on first application—o.k. on subsequent applications.)	• Disc brake pads sticking on abutment surfaces of anchor plate. Caused by a build-up of dirt, rust, or corrosion on abutment surfaces	• Clean abutment surfaces
Fading brake pedal (pedal height decreases with steady pressure applied.)	• Fluid leak in hydraulic system	• Fill master cylinder reservoirs to fill mark, have helper apply brakes, check calipers, wheel cylinders, differential valve, tubes, hoses, and fittings for fluid leaks. Repair or replace parts as necessary.
	• Master cylinder piston seals worn, or master cylinder bore is scored, worn or corroded	• Repair or replace master cylinder
Spongy brake pedal (pedal has abnormally soft, springy, spongy feel when depressed.)	• Air in hydraulic system	• Remove air from system. Refer to Brake Bleeding.
	• Brakeshoes bent or distorted	• Replace brakeshoes
	• Brakelining not yet seated with drums and rotors	• Burnish brakes
	• Rear drum brakes not properly adjusted	• Adjust brakes

Troubleshooting the Brake System (cont.)

Problem	Cause	Solution
Decreasing brake pedal travel (pedal travel required for braking action decreases and may be accompanied by a hard pedal.)	• Caliper or wheel cylinder pistons sticking or seized • Master cylinder compensator ports blocked (preventing fluid return to reservoirs) or pistons sticking or seized in master cylinder bore • Power brake unit binding internally	• Repair or replace the calipers, or wheel cylinders • Repair or replace the master cylinder • Test unit according to the following procedure: (a) Shift transmission into neutral and start engine (b) Increase engine speed to 1500 rpm, close throttle and fully depress brake pedal (c) Slow release brake pedal and stop engine (d) Have helper remove vacuum check valve and hose from power unit. Observe for backward movement of brake pedal. (e) If the pedal moves backward, the power unit has an internal bind—replace power unit
Grabbing brakes (severe reaction to brake pedal pressure.)	• Brakelining(s) contaminated by grease or brake fluid • Parking brake cables incorrectly adjusted or seized • Incorrect brakelining or lining loose on brakeshoes • Caliper anchor plate bolts loose • Rear brakeshoes binding on support plate ledges • Incorrect or missing power brake reaction disc • Rear brake support plates loose	• Determine and correct cause of contamination and replace brakeshoes in axle sets • Adjust cables. Replace seized cables. • Replace brakeshoes in axle sets • Tighten bolts • Clean and lubricate ledges. Replace support plate(s) if ledges are deeply grooved. Do not attempt to smooth ledges by grinding. • Install correct disc • Tighten mounting bolts
Chatter or shudder when brakes are applied (pedal pulsation and roughness may also occur.)	• Brakeshoes distorted, bent, contaminated, or worn • Caliper anchor plate or support plate loose • Excessive thickness variation of rotor(s)	• Replace brakeshoes in axle sets • Tighten mounting bolts • Refinish or replace rotors in axle sets
Noisy brakes (squealing, clicking, scraping sound when brakes are applied.)	• Bent, broken, distorted brakeshoes • Excessive rust on outer edge of rotor braking surface	• Replace brakeshoes in axle sets • Remove rust

Troubleshooting the Brake System (cont.)

Problem	Cause	Solution
Hard brake pedal (excessive pedal pressure required to stop vehicle. May be accompanied by brake fade.)	• Loose or leaking power brake unit vacuum hose • Incorrect or poor quality brake-lining • Bent, broken, distorted brakeshoes • Calipers binding or dragging on mounting pins. Rear brakeshoes dragging on support plate.	• Tighten connections or replace leaking hose • Replace with lining in axle sets • Replace brakeshoes • Replace mounting pins and bushings. Clean rust or burrs from rear brake support plate ledges and lubricate ledges with molydisulfide grease. **NOTE:** If ledges are deeply grooved or scored, do not attempt to sand or grind them smooth—replace support plate.
	• Caliper, wheel cylinder, or master cylinder pistons sticking or seized • Power brake unit vacuum check valve malfunction	• Repair or replace parts as necessary • Test valve according to the following procedure: (a) Start engine, increase engine speed to 1500 rpm, close throttle and immediately stop engine (b) Wait at least 90 seconds then depress brake pedal (c) If brakes are not vacuum assisted for 2 or more applications, check valve is faulty
	• Power brake unit has internal bind	• Test unit according to the following procedure: (a) With engine stopped, apply brakes several times to exhaust all vacuum in system (b) Shift transmission into neutral, depress brake pedal and start engine (c) If pedal height decreases with foot pressure and less pressure is required to hold pedal in applied position, power unit vacuum system is operating normally. Test power unit. If power unit exhibits a bind condition, replace the power unit.

Troubleshooting the Brake System (cont.)

Problem	Cause	Solution
Hard brake pedal (excessive pedal pressure required to stop vehicle. May be accompanied by brake fade.)	• Master cylinder compensator ports (at bottom of reservoirs) blocked by dirt, scale, rust, or have small burrs (blocked ports prevent fluid return to reservoirs). • Brake hoses, tubes, fittings clogged or restricted • Brake fluid contaminated with improper fluids (motor oil, transmission fluid, causing rubber components to swell and stick in bores • Low engine vacuum	• Repair or replace master cylinder **CAUTION:** Do not attempt to clean blocked ports with wire, pencils, or similar implements. Use compressed air only. • Use compressed air to check or unclog parts. Replace any damaged parts. • Replace all rubber components, combination valve and hoses. Flush entire brake system with DOT 3 brake fluid or equivalent. • Adjust or repair engine
Dragging brakes (slow or incomplete release of brakes)	• Brake pedal binding at pivot • Power brake unit has internal bind • Parking brake cables incorrrectly adjusted or seized • Rear brakeshoe return springs weak or broken • Automatic adjusters malfunctioning • Caliper, wheel cylinder or master cylinder pistons sticking or seized • Master cylinder compensating ports blocked (fluid does not return to reservoirs).	• Loosen and lubricate • Inspect for internal bind. Replace unit if internal bind exists. • Adjust cables. Replace seized cables. • Replace return springs. Replace brakeshoe if necessary in axle sets. • Repair or replace adjuster parts as required • Repair or replace parts as necessary • Use compressed air to clear ports. Do not use wire, pencils, or similar objects to open blocked ports.
Vehicle moves to one side when brakes are applied	• Incorrect front tire pressure • Worn or damaged wheel bearings • Brakelining on one side contaminated • Brakeshoes on one side bent, distorted, or lining loose on shoe • Support plate bent or loose on one side • Brakelining not yet seated with drums or rotors • Caliper anchor plate loose on one side • Caliper piston sticking or seized • Brakelinings water soaked • Loose suspension component attaching or mounting bolts • Brake combination valve failure	• Inflate to recommended cold (reduced load) inflation pressure • Replace worn or damaged bearings • Determine and correct cause of contamination and replace brakelining in axle sets • Replace brakeshoes in axle sets • Tighten or replace support plate • Burnish brakelining • Tighten anchor plate bolts • Repair or replace caliper • Drive vehicle with brakes lightly applied to dry linings • Tighten suspension bolts. Replace worn suspension components. • Replace combination valve

Troubleshooting the Brake System (cont.)

Problem	Cause	Solution
Noisy brakes (squealing, clicking, scraping sound when brakes are applied.) (cont.)	• Brakelining worn out—shoes contacting drum of rotor	• Replace brakeshoes and lining in axle sets. Refinish or replace drums or rotors.
	• Broken or loose holdown or return springs	• Replace parts as necessary
	• Rough or dry drum brake support plate ledges	• Lubricate support plate ledges
	• Cracked, grooved, or scored rotor(s) or drum(s)	• Replace rotor(s) or drum(s). Replace brakeshoes and lining in axle sets if necessary.
	• Incorrect brakelining and/or shoes (front or rear).	• Install specified shoe and lining assemblies
Pulsating brake pedal	• Out of round drums or excessive lateral runout in disc brake rotor(s)	• Refinish or replace drums, re-index rotors or replace

TORQUE SPECIFICATIONS

Component	English	Metric
Blower motor bolts	7 ft. lbs.	10 Nm
Heater unit mounting bolts	6.9 ft. lbs.	9.3 Nm
Air conditioning compressor mounting bolts		
STD. and Loyale	22 ft. lbs.	30 Nm
XT	33 ft. lbs.	44 Nm
Legacy	31 ft. lbs.	42 Nm
SVX	29 ft. lbs.	39 Nm
Refrigerant lines-to-compressor	14 ft. lbs.	20 Nm
Condenser retaining bolts	7 ft. lbs.	10 Nm
Refrigerant lines to condenser	14 ft. lbs.	20 Nm
Discharge pipe-to-evaporator		
Except Legacy and SVX	14 ft. lbs.	20 Nm
Legacy and SVX	18 ft. lbs.	25 Nm
Suction pipe nut-to-evaporator		
Except Legacy and SVX	22 ft. lbs.	29 Nm
Legacy and SVX	7 ft. lbs.	10 Nm
Receiver/Drier		
Mounting bolts	7 ft. lbs.	10 Nm
Refrigerant pipes		
Except SVX and Legacy	12 ft. lbs.	17 Nm
SVX and Legacy	7 ft. lbs.	10 Nm
Cruise control		
Vacuum pump and valve mounting bolts	65 inch lbs.	7.4 Nm
Actuator assembly mounting nuts	65 inch lbs.	7.4 Nm
Windshield wiper arm nut		
Except XT, Loyale and STD.	13 ft. lbs.	18 Nm
XT, Loyale and STD.	65 inch lbs.	7.4 Nm
Windshield wiper motor mounting nuts	65 inch lbs.	7.4 Nm
Headlamp assembly mounting nuts		
except XT	61 inch lbs.	6.9 Nm
XT-headlamp assembly bolts	17 ft. lbs.	23 Nm

10

BODY

EXTERIOR

Doors

REMOVAL & INSTALLATION

◆ SEE FIGS. 1–9

The removal procedure for the front and rear doors (on models equipped) is basically the same. The door hinge bolt torque and the alignment procedures are the same.

➡ **If the door being removed is to be reinstalled, matchmark the hinge position.**

1. Disconnect the negative battery cable. Remove the door check spring pin. On models with power windows and/or locks, remove the lower A-pillar trim and disconnect the electrical leads.

2. Support the bottom of the door using a floor jack, with a block of wood on it to protect the door.

3. On Justy, Legacy and SVX remove the hinge-to-door attaching bolts and remove the

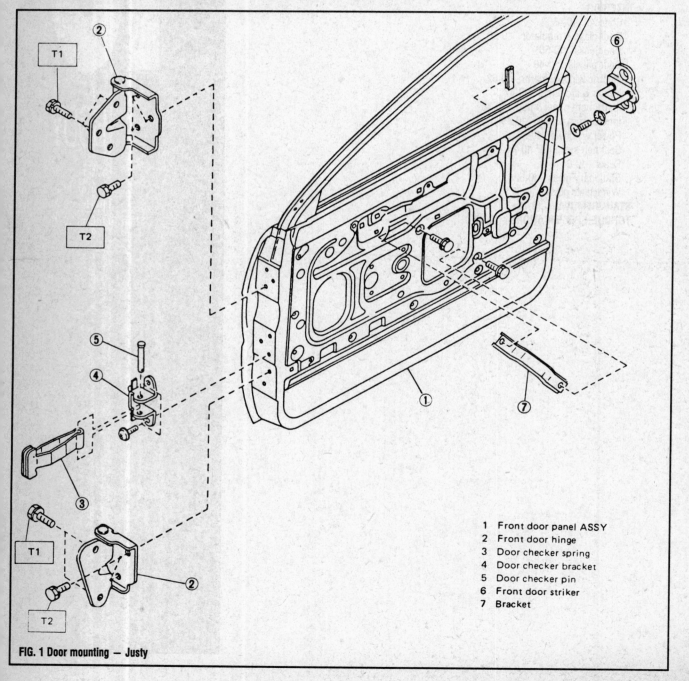

1 Front door panel ASSY
2 Front door hinge
3 Door checker spring
4 Door checker bracket
5 Door checker pin
6 Front door striker
7 Bracket

FIG. 1 Door mounting — Justy

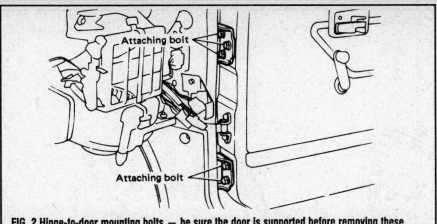

FIG. 2 Hinge-to-door mounting bolts — be sure the door is supported before removing these

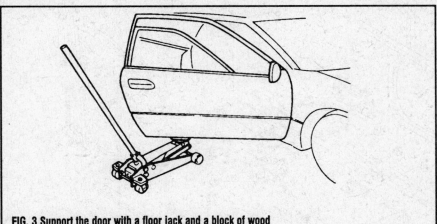

FIG. 3 Support the door with a floor jack and a block of wood

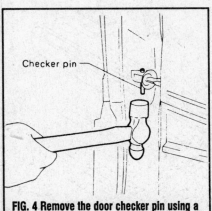

FIG. 4 Remove the door checker pin using a hammer

door from the vehicle. On Loyale, STD. and XT, remove the hinge-to-body bolts and remove the door.

4. Remove any needed trim components from the door.

To Install:

5. Install the door on the floor jack and position it to the door hinges.

6. Install the door hinge bolts, making sure the alignment marks made during removal line up. Tighten the hinge bolts on Justy models to 14–19 ft. lbs. (20–25 Nm), on Loyale, STD. and XT to 18–25 ft. lbs. (25–34 Nm) and on Legacy and SVX to 14–22 ft. lbs. (20–29 Nm).

7. Remove the jack and check the door alignment around its perimeter, adjust it as needed by loosening the hinge bolts and moving it slightly.

ALIGNMENT

➡ **The holes for the hinges are oversized to provide for latitude in alignment. Align the door hinges first, then the striker.**

Hinges

1. If a door is being installed, first mount the door and tighten the hinge bolts lightly. If the door has not been removed, determine which hinge bolts must be loosed to effect alignment.

2. Loosen the necessary bolts just enough to allow the door to be moved with a padded prybar.

3. Move the door in small movements and check the fit after each movement. Be sure that there is no binding or interference with adjacent panels. Keep repeating this procedure until the door is properly aligned. Tighten all the bolts. Shims may be either fabricated or purchased to install behind the hinges as an aid in alignment.

Striker Plate

➡ **The striker is attached to the pillar using oversized holes, providing latitude in movement.**

Striker adjustment is made by loosening the bolts and moving the striker plate in the desired direction or adding or deleting shims behind the plate, or both. The striker is properly adjusted when the locking latch enters the striker without rubbing and the door closes fully and solidly, with no play when closed.

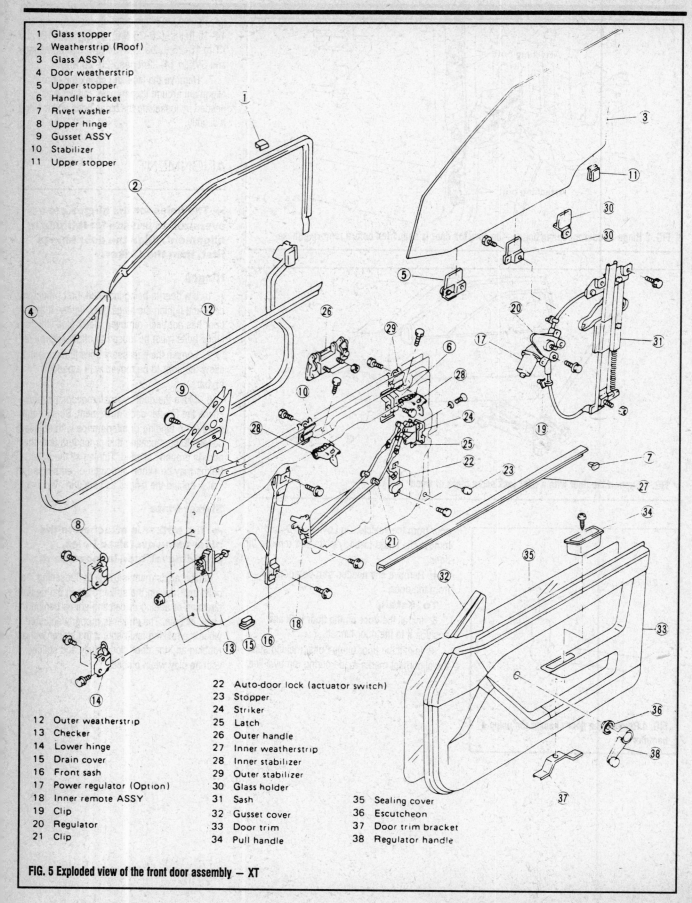

1 Glass stopper
2 Weatherstrip (Roof)
3 Glass ASSY
4 Door weatherstrip
5 Upper stopper
6 Handle bracket
7 Rivet washer
8 Upper hinge
9 Gusset ASSY
10 Stabilizer
11 Upper stopper

12 Outer weatherstrip
13 Checker
14 Lower hinge
15 Drain cover
16 Front sash
17 Power regulator (Option)
18 Inner remote ASSY
19 Clip
20 Regulator
21 Clip

22 Auto-door lock (actuator switch)
23 Stopper
24 Striker
25 Latch
26 Outer handle
27 Inner weatherstrip
28 Inner stabilizer
29 Outer stabilizer
30 Glass holder
31 Sash
32 Gusset cover
33 Door trim
34 Pull handle

35 Sealing cover
36 Escutcheon
37 Door trim bracket
38 Regulator handle

FIG. 5 Exploded view of the front door assembly — XT

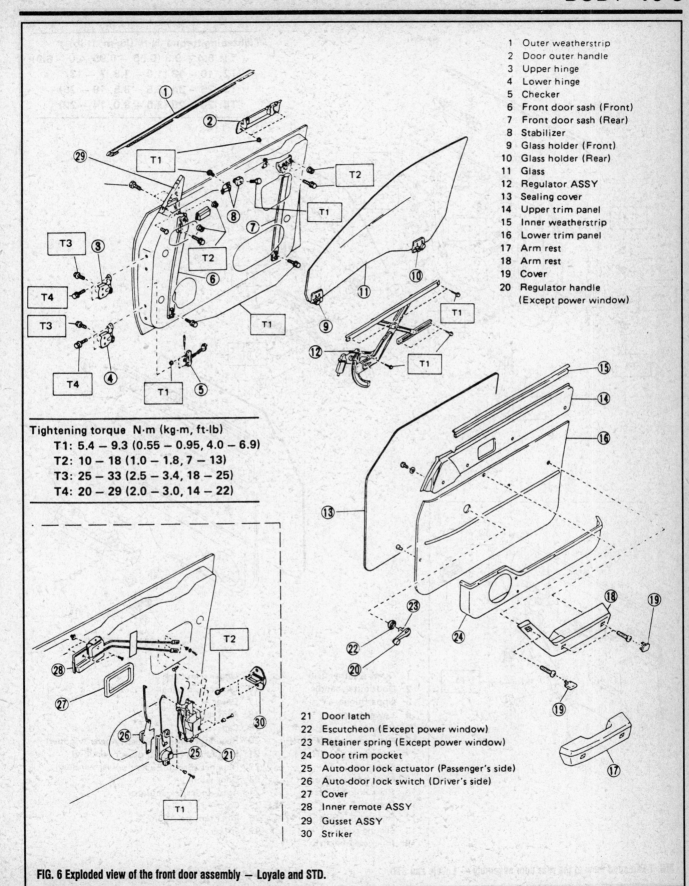

1 Outer weatherstrip
2 Door outer handle
3 Upper hinge
4 Lower hinge
5 Checker
6 Front door sash (Front)
7 Front door sash (Rear)
8 Stabilizer
9 Glass holder (Front)
10 Glass holder (Rear)
11 Glass
12 Regulator ASSY
13 Sealing cover
14 Upper trim panel
15 Inner weatherstrip
16 Lower trim panel
17 Arm rest
18 Arm rest
19 Cover
20 Regulator handle
    (Except power window)

Tightening torque N·m (kg-m, ft-lb)
T1: 5.4 — 9.3 (0.55 — 0.95, 4.0 — 6.9)
T2: 10 — 18 (1.0 — 1.8, 7 — 13)
T3: 25 — 33 (2.5 — 3.4, 18 — 25)
T4: 20 — 29 (2.0 — 3.0, 14 — 22)

21 Door latch
22 Escutcheon (Except power window)
23 Retainer spring (Except power window)
24 Door trim pocket
25 Auto-door lock actuator (Passenger's side)
26 Auto-door lock switch (Driver's side)
27 Cover
28 Inner remote ASSY
29 Gusset ASSY
30 Striker

FIG. 6 Exploded view of the front door assembly — Loyale and STD.

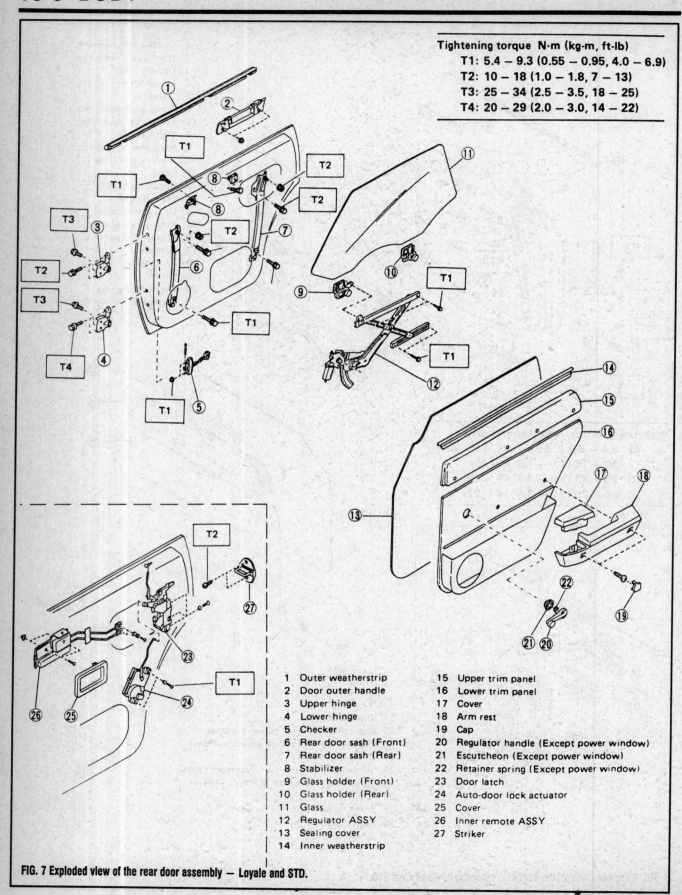

Tightening torque N·m (kg-m, ft-lb)
T1: 5.4 — 9.3 (0.55 — 0.95, 4.0 — 6.9)
T2: 10 — 18 (1.0 — 1.8, 7 — 13)
T3: 25 — 34 (2.5 — 3.5, 18 — 25)
T4: 20 — 29 (2.0 — 3.0, 14 — 22)

1	Outer weatherstrip	15	Upper trim panel
2	Door outer handle	16	Lower trim panel
3	Upper hinge	17	Cover
4	Lower hinge	18	Arm rest
5	Checker	19	Cap
6	Rear door sash (Front)	20	Regulator handle (Except power window)
7	Rear door sash (Rear)	21	Escutcheon (Except power window)
8	Stabilizer	22	Retainer spring (Except power window)
9	Glass holder (Front)	23	Door latch
10	Glass holder (Rear)	24	Auto-door lock actuator
11	Glass	25	Cover
12	Regulator ASSY	26	Inner remote ASSY
13	Sealing cover	27	Striker
14	Inner weatherstrip		

FIG. 7 Exploded view of the rear door assembly — Loyale and STD.

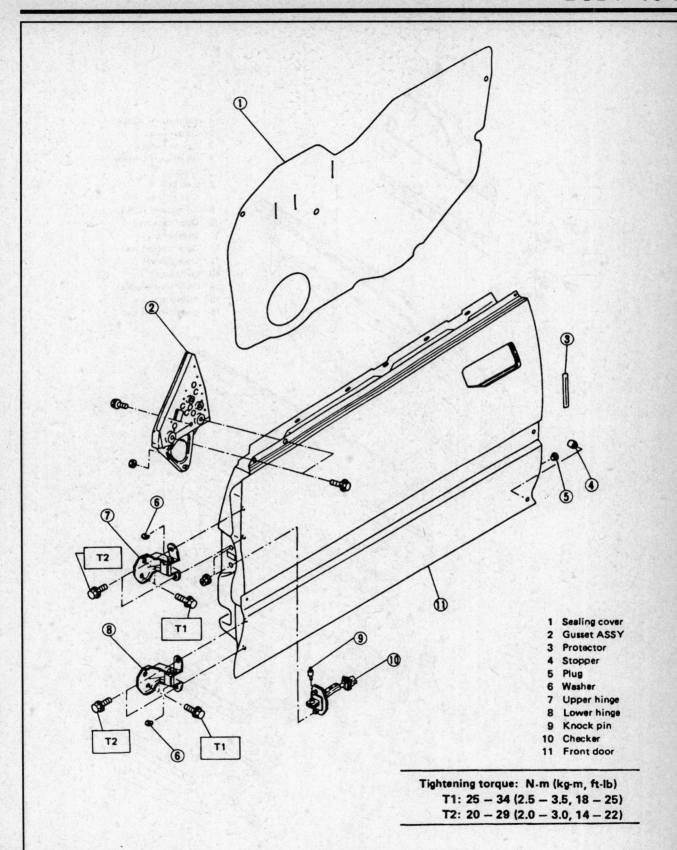

1 Sealing cover
2 Gusset ASSY
3 Protector
4 Stopper
5 Plug
6 Washer
7 Upper hinge
8 Lower hinge
9 Knock pin
10 Checker
11 Front door

Tightening torque: N·m (kg-m, ft-lb)
T1: 25 — 34 (2.5 — 3.5, 18 — 25)
T2: 20 — 29 (2.0 — 3.0, 14 — 22)

FIG. 8 Front door assembly mounting components — Legacy

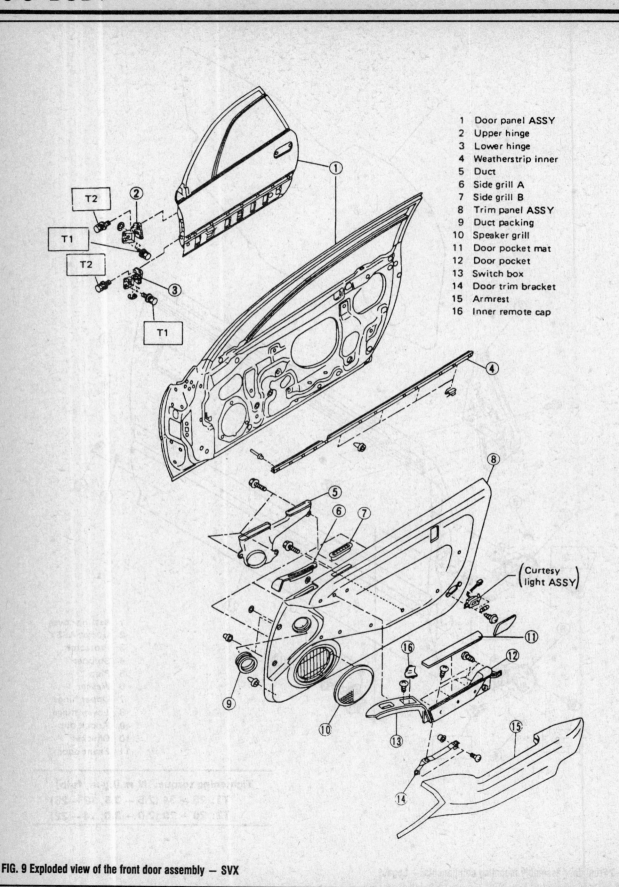

1   Door panel ASSY
2   Upper hinge
3   Lower hinge
4   Weatherstrip inner
5   Duct
6   Side grill A
7   Side grill B
8   Trim panel ASSY
9   Duct packing
10 Speaker grill
11 Door pocket mat
12 Door pocket
13 Switch box
14 Door trim bracket
15 Armrest
16 Inner remote cap

(Curtesy light ASSY)

FIG. 9 Exploded view of the front door assembly — SVX

Hood

REMOVAL & INSTALLATION

▶ SEE FIGS. 10–13

➡ **You are going to need an assistant for this job.**

1. Open the hood and trace the outline of the hinges on the body.

➡ **On some models, the hood also has 2 struts that hold it open, these must be disconnected at the hood before it can be removed.**

2. While an assistant holds the hood, remove the hinge-to-body bolts and lift the hood off.

3. Reverse the above process to install the hood. Align the outlines previously made. Tighten the hood retaining bolts to 9–17 ft. lbs. (13–23 Nm).

4. Check that the hood closes properly. Adjust hood alignment, if necessary.

ALIGNMENT

Hood alignment can be adjusted front-to-rear or side-to-side by loosening the hood-to-hinge or hinge-to-body bolts. The front edge of the hood can be adjusted for closing height by adding or deleting shims under the hinges. The rear edge of the hood can be adjusted for closing height by raising or lowering the hood bumpers.

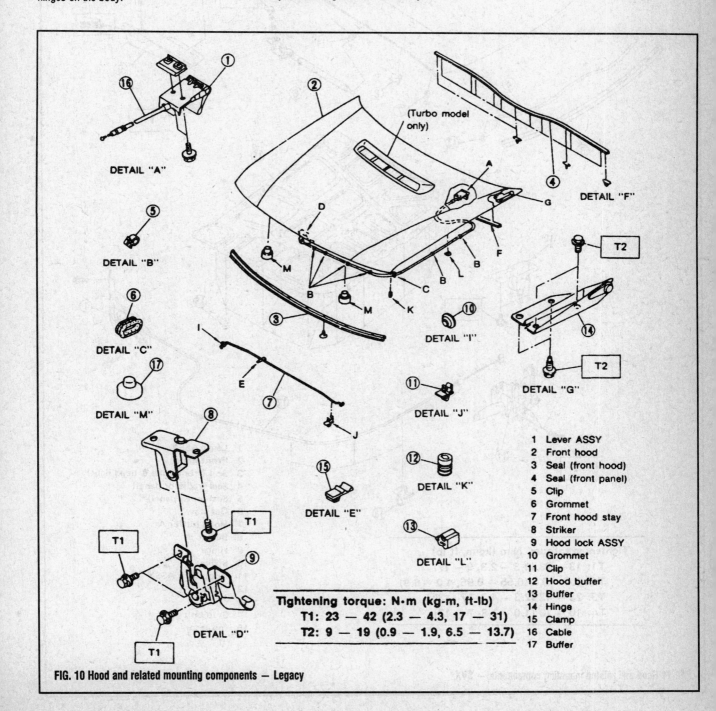

1 Lever ASSY
2 Front hood
3 Seal (front hood)
4 Seal (front panel)
5 Clip
6 Grommet
7 Front hood stay
8 Striker
9 Hood lock ASSY
10 Grommet
11 Clip
12 Hood buffer
13 Buffer
14 Hinge
15 Clamp
16 Cable
17 Buffer

Tightening torque: N·m (kg-m, ft-lb)
T1: 23 — 42 (2.3 — 4.3, 17 — 31)
T2: 9 — 19 (0.9 — 1.9, 6.5 — 13.7)

FIG. 10 Hood and related mounting components — Legacy

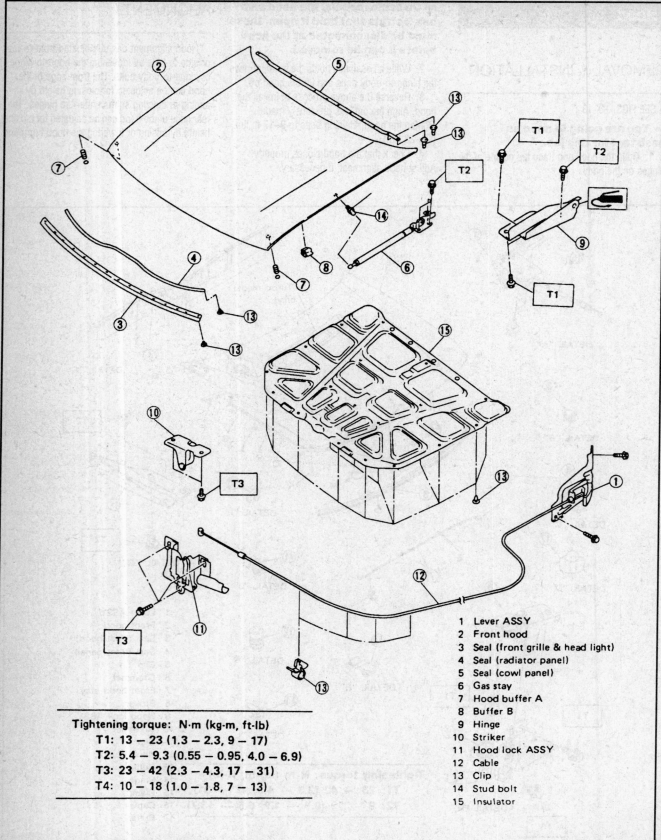

Tightening torque: N·m (kg-m, ft-lb)
T1: 13 — 23 (1.3 — 2.3, 9 — 17)
T2: 5.4 — 9.3 (0.55 — 0.95, 4.0 — 6.9)
T3: 23 — 42 (2.3 — 4.3, 17 — 31)
T4: 10 — 18 (1.0 — 1.8, 7 — 13)

1 Lever ASSY
2 Front hood
3 Seal (front grille & head light)
4 Seal (radiator panel)
5 Seal (cowl panel)
6 Gas stay
7 Hood buffer A
8 Buffer B
9 Hinge
10 Striker
11 Hood lock ASSY
12 Cable
13 Clip
14 Stud bolt
15 Insulator

FIG. 11 Hood and related mounting components — SVX

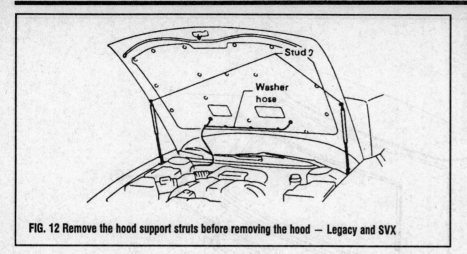

FIG. 12 Remove the hood support struts before removing the hood — Legacy and SVX

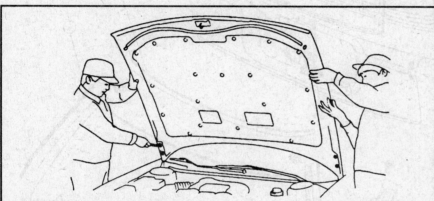

FIG. 13 Remove the hood with the air of an assistant — be careful not to damage the hood or the vehicle

Hood Opener and Latch

REMOVAL & INSTALLATION

1. In the interior of the car, remove the bolts that retain the hood latch handle assembly and disconnect the opener cable.
2. Remove the front bumper assembly.
3. Remove the hood latch mounting bolts and disconnect the cable.
4. Remove the drivers side inner fender shield and pull the cable through the wheel well.

➡ **Tie a rope to the end of the cable before pulling it through, this will allow you to pull the new cable into position.**

5. Install the new cable in position. Install the inner fender shield.

6. Install the cable at the hood latch and install the latch retaining bolts. Tighten the bolts to 7 ft. lbs. (10 Nm).
7. Connect the cable at the release assembly inside the vehicle and install the release assembly retaining bolts. Adjust the hood latch as needed.

Tailgate, Hatch or Trunk Lid

REMOVAL & INSTALLATION

◆ SEE FIGS. 14–20a

Legacy Wagon, Loyale Wagon, STD. Wagon and Justy

❄ WARNING

You will need an assistant during this procedure. Be careful not to scratch coated surfaces of the body and window glass during removal. Place a cloth over the affected area. Be careful not to damage the trim panels. Have an assistant help you when handling heavy parts. Be careful not to damage or lose small parts.

1. Remove the clips from the trim panel using a trim panel clip puller and detach the trim panel. Be careful not to damage the clips or their holes.
2. Disconnect the connector from the rear gate defogger terminal. Do not pull the lead wire, but unlock the connector and disconnect.
3. Disconnect the wiper connector and rear washer hose.
4. Unlock connector and disconnect from rear gate door switch. Do not pull the lead wire.
5. Disconnect the license lamp connector and high mount stop lamp connector.
6. Disconnect the auto door lock actuator connector.
7. If the disconnected harness is re-used, tie connector with a string and place on the upper side of the rear gate for ready use.

❄ WARNING

Do not forcefully pull cords, lead wires, etc. since damage may result. Carefully extract them in a wavy motion while holding the connectors.

8. Remove the rear wiper arm, the cap and special nut. Then detach the trim panel, remove the bolt from the rear wiper and remove the wiper.
9. Completely open the rear gate. Then remove the bolts which hold the gas stay to the rear gate.

❄ WARNING

Remove the bolts one at a time. Have a helper hold the rear gate while removing the bolts to prevent it from dropping. Be sure to place a folded cloth between the rear gate and body to prevent scratches.

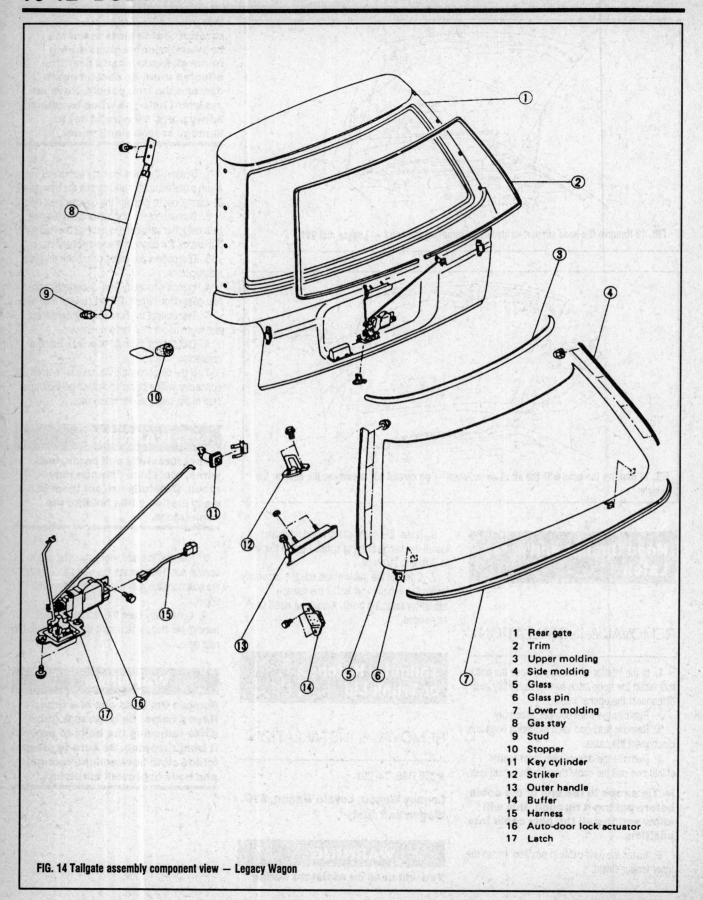

1. Rear gate
2. Trim
3. Upper molding
4. Side molding
5. Glass
6. Glass pin
7. Lower molding
8. Gas stay
9. Stud
10. Stopper
11. Key cylinder
12. Striker
13. Outer handle
14. Buffer
15. Harness
16. Auto-door lock actuator
17. Latch

FIG. 14 Tailgate assembly component view — Legacy Wagon

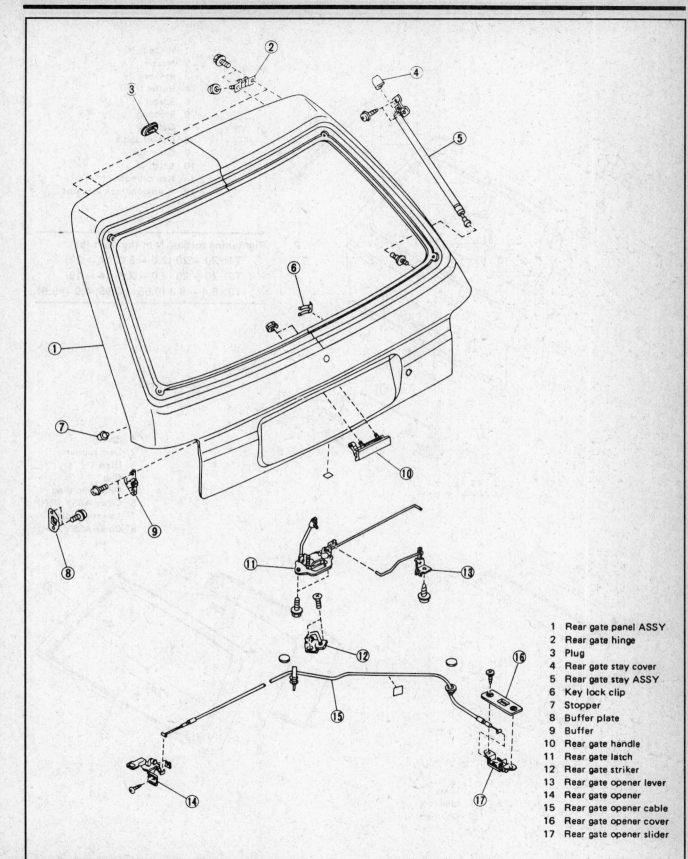

1   Rear gate panel ASSY
2   Rear gate hinge
3   Plug
4   Rear gate stay cover
5   Rear gate stay ASSY
6   Key lock clip
7   Stopper
8   Buffer plate
9   Buffer
10 Rear gate handle
11 Rear gate latch
12 Rear gate striker
13 Rear gate opener lever
14 Rear gate opener
15 Rear gate opener cable
16 Rear gate opener cover
17 Rear gate opener slider

FIG. 15 Tailgate assembly component view — Justy

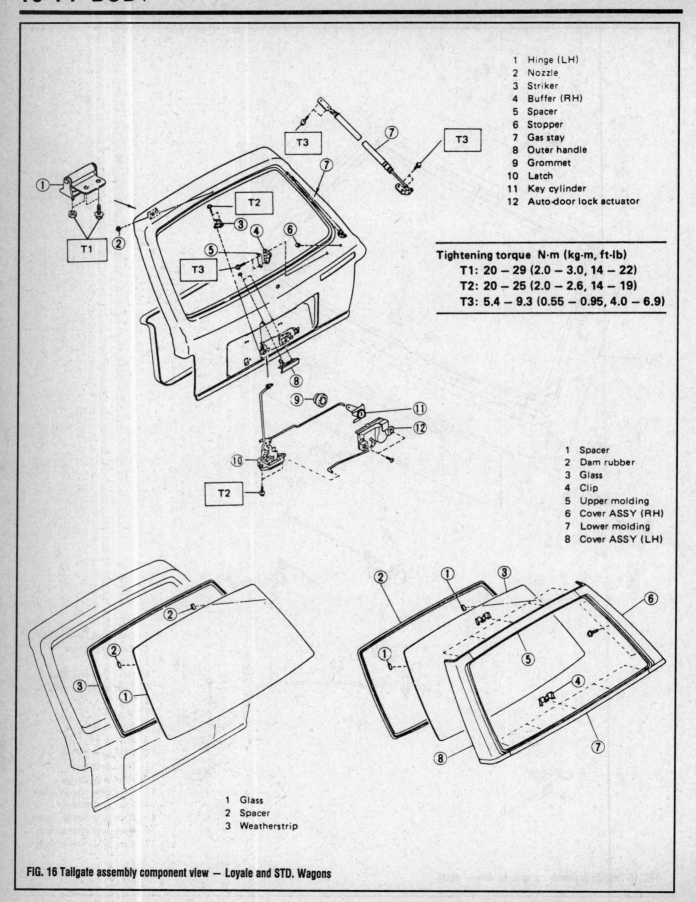

1 Hinge (LH)
2 Nozzle
3 Striker
4 Buffer (RH)
5 Spacer
6 Stopper
7 Gas stay
8 Outer handle
9 Grommet
10 Latch
11 Key cylinder
12 Auto-door lock actuator

Tightening torque N·m (kg-m, ft-lb)
T1: 20 — 29 (2.0 — 3.0, 14 — 22)
T2: 20 — 25 (2.0 — 2.6, 14 — 19)
T3: 5.4 — 9.3 (0.55 — 0.95, 4.0 — 6.9)

1 Spacer
2 Dam rubber
3 Glass
4 Clip
5 Upper molding
6 Cover ASSY (RH)
7 Lower molding
8 Cover ASSY (LH)

1 Glass
2 Spacer
3 Weatherstrip

FIG. 16 Tailgate assembly component view — Loyale and STD. Wagons

10. Remove trim side rail, and remove roof trim clips as far as the center pillar.

11. Hang roof trim down to prevent it from bending. Then remove the nuts which hold the hinge with a ratchet wrench placed between the roof trim and the car body, and detach the hinge.

12. Remove the rear gate.

To Install:

13. Position the rear gate onto the roof hinge.

14. Install the rear gate retaining nuts and tighten securely. Tighten the hinge mounting bolt-to-gate bolts to 14–22 ft. lbs. (20–29 Nm). Tighten the hinge mounting bolts-to-body to 14–22 ft. lbs. (20–29 Nm).

15. Position the roof trim and secure it using the retaining clips. Then install the trim side rails.

16. Install the gas stays to the rear gate and tighten the retaining bolt to 4–6 ft. lbs. (5–9 Nm) and the stud bolt to 7–13 ft. lbs. (10–18 Nm).

17. Close the rear gate and install the rear wiper, trim panel and wiper arm.

18. Connect the wiring harness to the rear wiper system.

19. Connect the auto door lock actuator connector.

20. Connect the license lamp connector and high mount stop lamp connector.

21. Connect the rear gate door switch.

22. Connect the wiper connector and rear washer hose.

23. Connect the connector to the rear gate defogger terminal.

24. Position the rear gate trim panel and install the retaining clips. Adjust the rear gate as needed.

Loyale and STD. 3-Door Models

1. Fold left and right rear backrest forward.

2. Remove the shoulder anchors of the left and right front seat belts.

3. Remove the left and right tonneau cover levers.

4. Remove the left and right rear quarter upper trim.

5. Remove the rear skirt trim.

6. Remove the rear quarter rear trim panel.

7. Using a trim clip puller, remove the clips which secure the rear gate trim panel. Remove the trim panel.

❊❊ WARNING

Be careful not to damage clip and clip holes.

---

8. Disconnect the gas stay harness connector from the rear gate.

9. Remove the stud bolts which secure gas stay to rear gate.

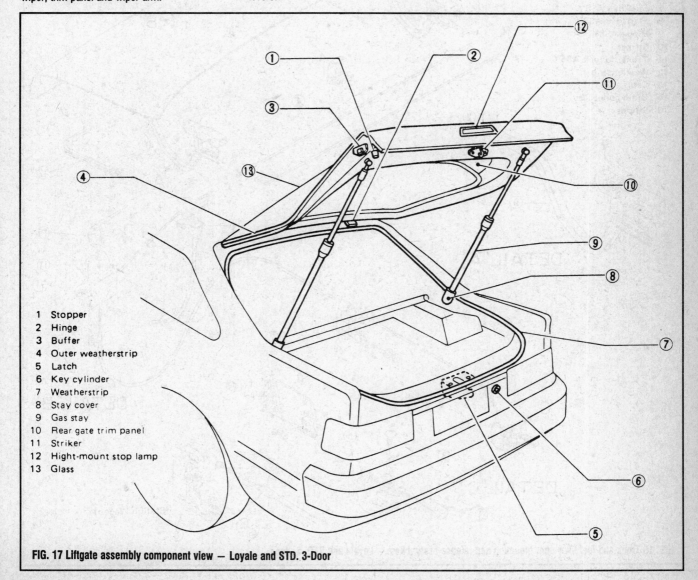

1	Stopper
2	Hinge
3	Buffer
4	Outer weatherstrip
5	Latch
6	Key cylinder
7	Weatherstrip
8	Stay cover
9	Gas stay
10	Rear gate trim panel
11	Striker
12	Hight-mount stop lamp
13	Glass

FIG. 17 Liftgate assembly component view — Loyale and STD. 3-Door

✺ WARNING

Remove the bolts one at a time. Have a helper hold the rear gate while removing the bolts to prevent it from dropping. Be sure to place a folded cloth between the rear gate and body to prevent scratches.

10. Remove the rear rail trim panel.

11. With a wrench inserted into the access hole, loosen the nuts which secure the hinge and remove the rear gate from the roof panel.

To install:

12. Position the rear gate onto the hinges and tighten the retaining nuts to 14–21 ft. lbs. (20–30 Nm).

13. Install the rear trim panel.

14. Install the gas stays to the rear gate and tighten the stud bolts to 7–13 ft. lbs. (10–18 Nm).

15. Connect the gas stay harness to the rear gate.

16. Position the rear gate trim panel onto the rear gate and install the retainer clips.

17. Install the rear quarter, left and right upper and skirt trim.

18. Install the left and right tonneau cover levers.

19. Install the shoulder anchors of the left and right front seat belts.

20. Raise the left and right rear backrest.

Legacy Sedan, Loyale Sedan, STD. Sedan, XT and SVX

1. Open the trunk lid and mark the hinge to trunk lid position.

2. Remove the trunk lid mounting bolts and remove the trunk lid from the hinges.

3. Install the trunk lid into position, making

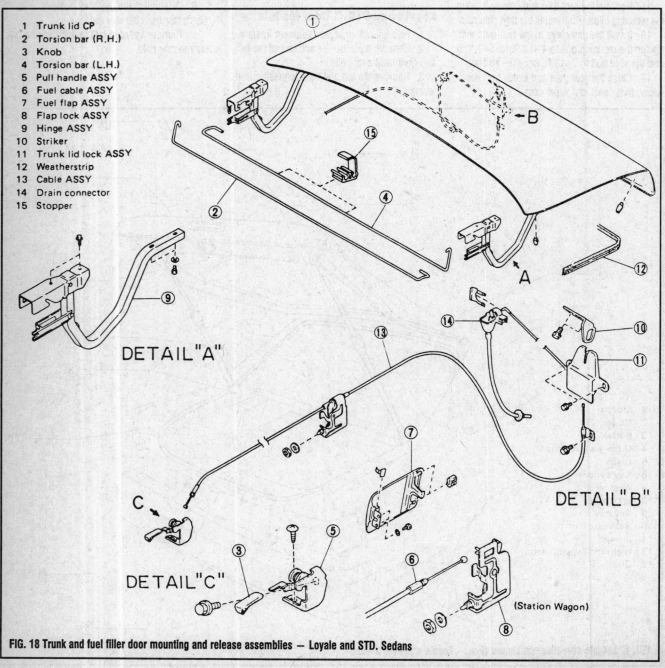

1 Trunk lid CP
2 Torsion bar (R.H.)
3 Knob
4 Torsion bar (L.H.)
5 Pull handle ASSY
6 Fuel cable ASSY
7 Fuel flap ASSY
8 Flap lock ASSY
9 Hinge ASSY
10 Striker
11 Trunk lid lock ASSY
12 Weatherstrip
13 Cable ASSY
14 Drain connector
15 Stopper

DETAIL "A"

DETAIL "B"

DETAIL "C"

(Station Wagon)

FIG. 18 Trunk and fuel filler door mounting and release assemblies — Loyale and STD. Sedans

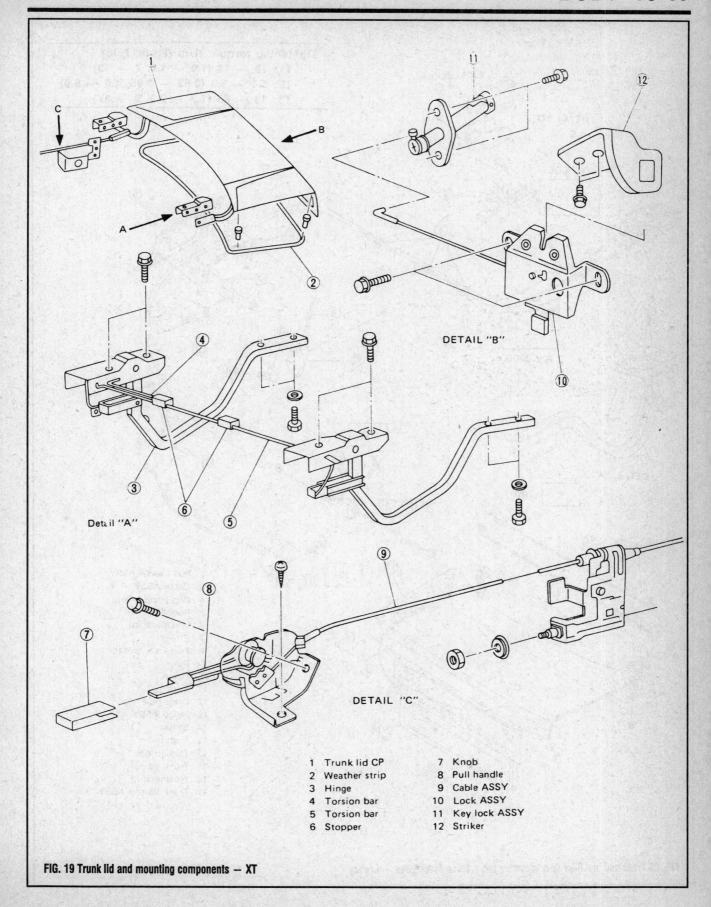

1	Trunk lid CP	7	Knob
2	Weather strip	8	Pull handle
3	Hinge	9	Cable ASSY
4	Torsion bar	10	Lock ASSY
5	Torsion bar	11	Key lock ASSY
6	Stopper	12	Striker

FIG. 19 Trunk lid and mounting components — XT

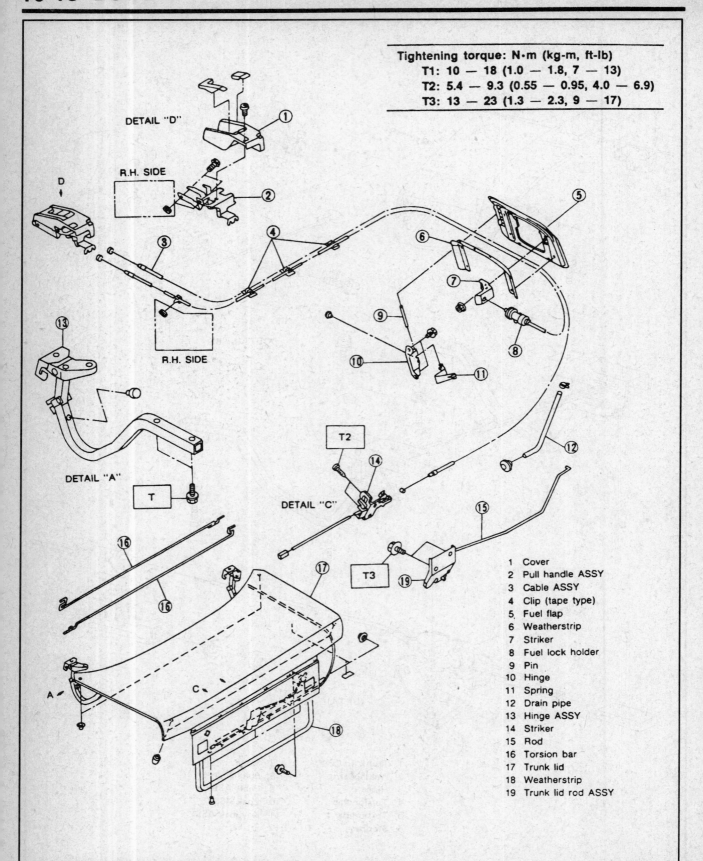

Tightening torque: N·m (kg-m, ft-lb)
T1: 10 — 18 (1.0 — 1.8, 7 — 13)
T2: 5.4 — 9.3 (0.55 — 0.95, 4.0 — 6.9)
T3: 13 — 23 (1.3 — 2.3, 9 — 17)

DETAIL "D"

R.H. SIDE

D

R.H. SIDE

DETAIL "A"

T

DETAIL "C"

T2

T3

1   Cover
2   Pull handle ASSY
3   Cable ASSY
4   Clip (tape type)
5   Fuel flap
6   Weatherstrip
7   Striker
8   Fuel lock holder
9   Pin
10 Hinge
11 Spring
12 Drain pipe
13 Hinge ASSY
14 Striker
15 Rod
16 Torsion bar
17 Trunk lid
18 Weatherstrip
19 Trunk lid rod ASSY

FIG. 20 Trunk and fuel filler door mounting and release assemblies — Legacy

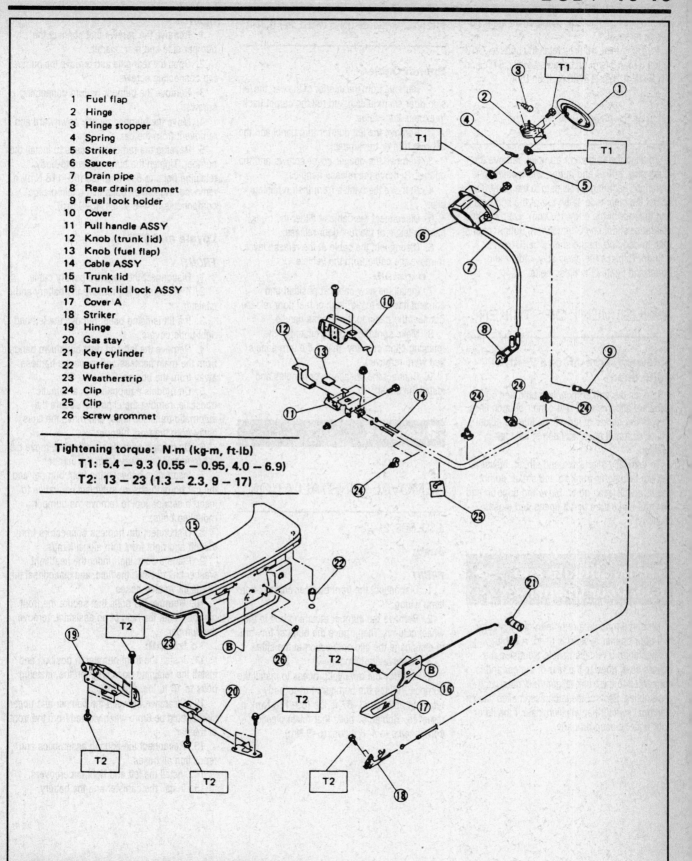

1 Fuel flap
2 Hinge
3 Hinge stopper
4 Spring
5 Striker
6 Saucer
7 Drain pipe
8 Rear drain grommet
9 Fuel look holder
10 Cover
11 Pull handle ASSY
12 Knob (trunk lid)
13 Knob (fuel flap)
14 Cable ASSY
15 Trunk lid
16 Trunk lid lock ASSY
17 Cover A
18 Striker
19 Hinge
20 Gas stay
21 Key cylinder
22 Buffer
23 Weatherstrip
24 Clip
25 Clip
26 Screw grommet

Tightening torque: N·m (kg-m, ft-lb)
T1: 5.4 — 9.3 (0.55 — 0.95, 4.0 — 6.9)
T2: 13 — 23 (1.3 — 2.3, 9 — 17)

FIG. 20a Trunk and fuel filler door mounting and release assemblies — SVX

sure to line up the marks made on the trunk lid during removal.

4. Tighten the trunk lid retaining bolts to 7–13 ft. lbs. (10–18 Nm) on Legacy, Loyale, STD. and XT, 9–17 ft. lbs. (13–23 Nm) on SVX.

ALIGNMENT

To align the tailgate or trunk lid, remove the glass stay, striker and buffer, and loosen bolts on hinges securing the tailgate to the body. Then adjust the clearance at the top of the end gate and the roof of the body 10.0mm ± 2mm. Side clearance should be 0 ± 1.5mm. Bottom of end gate to body clearance should be 5.4mm ± 1.5mm. Replace the glass stay, striker and buffer and tighten the hinge bolts.

ADJUSTMENT OF STRIKER

Sideward, Fore-Aft and Vertical Adjustment

Loosen the striker mounting bolt, and adjust sideward alignment so that center of latch lines up with the center of striker. Be sure to adjust striker so that it engages latch in full lock position.

To vertically align latch and striker, adjust so that the tailgate or trunk lid and striker do not interfere with each other. Move the door up and down to make sure that it opens and closes properly.

Trunk, Liftgate and Fuel Door Opener

On some models a remote trunk, liftgate or fuel door opener system is used. A cable connected to a release handle alongside the drivers seat, goes to the rear of the car and is connected to the trunk/tailgate/fuel door latch assemblies. Each of the latch assemblies has an electrical switch that will illuminate if the lid or door is not closed properly.

REMOVAL & INSTALLATION

Opener Cables

1. Remove from the interior of the car, the left side door sill moulding and roll the carpet back to expose the cables.
2. Remove the left quarter trim panel and the left rear trim or trunk panel.
3. Remove the opener cover screws and the opener. Remove the release handles.
4. Remove the cables from their retaining clip.
5. Disconnect the cable at either the trunk/hatch release or the fuel door release.
6. Disconnect the cable at the release lever. Remove the cable from the vehicle.

To Install:

7. Install the new cable in position and connect it to the trunk/hatch or fuel door release. Connect the cable to the release handle.
8. Make sure the cable is seated in the retaining clips properly. Install the trim panels that were removed.
9. Connect the release lever handles and install the cover.

Bumpers

REMOVAL & INSTALLATION

▶ SEE FIGS. 21–22

Justy

FRONT

1. Disconnect the front bumper combination lamp wiring.
2. Remove the bumper attaching bolt in the wheel column. Then, move the bumper forward to disengage the clip connection at the side.
3. Remove the bumper.
4. Reverse the removal process to install the bumper. Tighten the bumper strut-to-body retaining bolts to 51–87 ft. lbs (69–118 Nm), if removed. Tighten all bolts that retain plastic components to 4–6 ft. lbs. (5–9 Nm).

REAR

1. Remove the screws that connect the bumper side and rear quarter.
2. Open the rear gate and remove the bumper top connecting screws.
3. Remove the bumper bottom connecting screws.
4. Move the bumper slightly downward and remove it from the car.
5. Reverse the removal process to install the bumper. Tighten the bumper strut-to-body retaining bolts to 51–87 ft. lbs (69–118 Nm), if removed. Tighten all bolts that retain plastic components to 4–6 ft. lbs. (5–9 Nm).

Loyale and STD.

FRONT

1. Disconnect the negative battery cable.
2. If not using a lift, remove the battery and canister.
3. If a lift is being used, remove the left and right undercovers.
4. Remove the left and right holddown bands from the main harness and move the harness away from the bumper.
5. On models equipped with automatic transaxle, remove the clips that secure the automatic transaxle lines, and move the lines away from the front bumper.
6. On models with air conditioning, move the left transaxle line away from the bumper.
7. Insert rags between the front bumper and the car body to ensure sufficient clearance to insert a service tool to remove the bumper mounting bolts.
8. Disconnect the harness connectors from the left and right front turn signal lamps.
9. Place a container under the headlight washer unit to catch the fluid, and disconnect the headlight washer hoses.
10. Remove the bolts that secure the front bumper. With the help of an assistant, remove the bumper.

To Install:

11. Install the front bumper in position and install the retaining bolts. Tighten the retaining bolts to 16 ft. lbs. (22 Nm).
12. Clearance between the bumper and upper skirt should be 6mm when viewed from the front of the car.
13. Reconnect the lighting assemblies and reposition all hoses.
14. Install the left and right undercovers.
15. Install the canister and the battery.

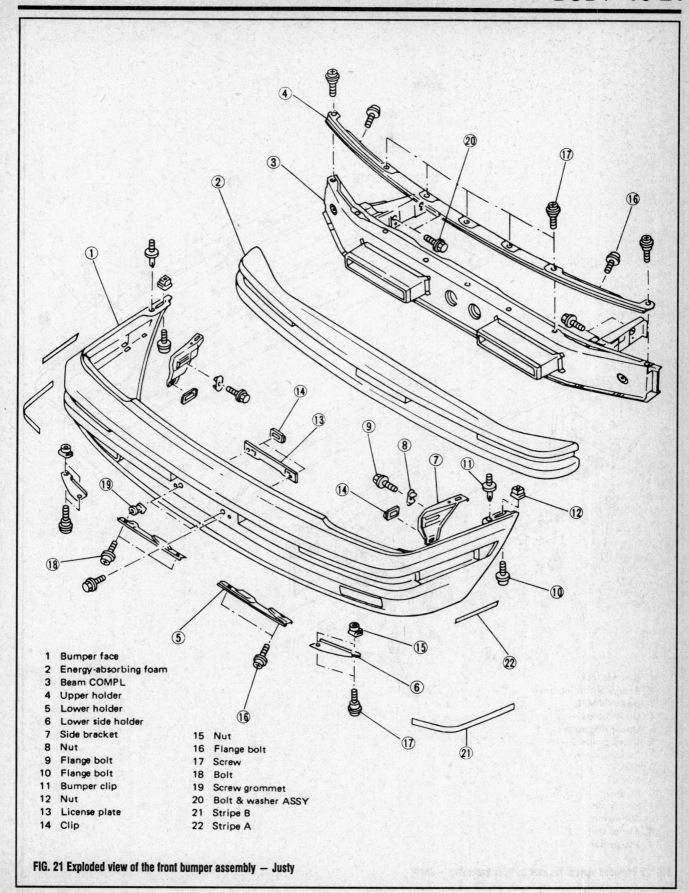

1 Bumper face
2 Energy-absorbing foam
3 Beam COMPL
4 Upper holder
5 Lower holder
6 Lower side holder
7 Side bracket
8 Nut
9 Flange bolt
10 Flange bolt
11 Bumper clip
12 Nut
13 License plate
14 Clip
15 Nut
16 Flange bolt
17 Screw
18 Bolt
19 Screw grommet
20 Bolt & washer ASSY
21 Stripe B
22 Stripe A

FIG. 21 Exploded view of the front bumper assembly — Justy

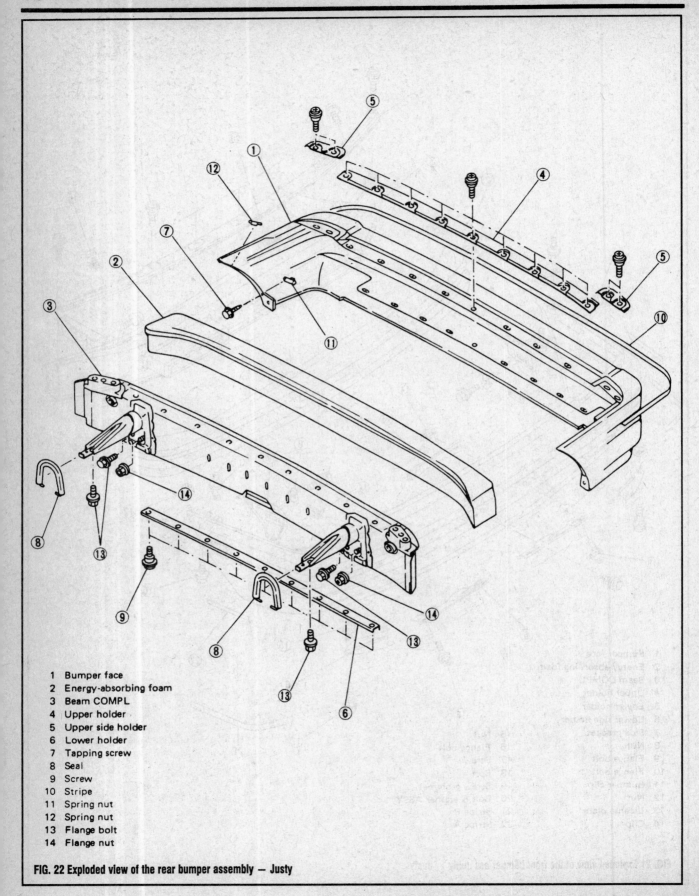

1 Bumper face
2 Energy-absorbing foam
3 Beam COMPL
4 Upper holder
5 Upper side holder
6 Lower holder
7 Tapping screw
8 Seal
9 Screw
10 Stripe
11 Spring nut
12 Spring nut
13 Flange bolt
14 Flange nut

FIG. 22 Exploded view of the rear bumper assembly — Justy

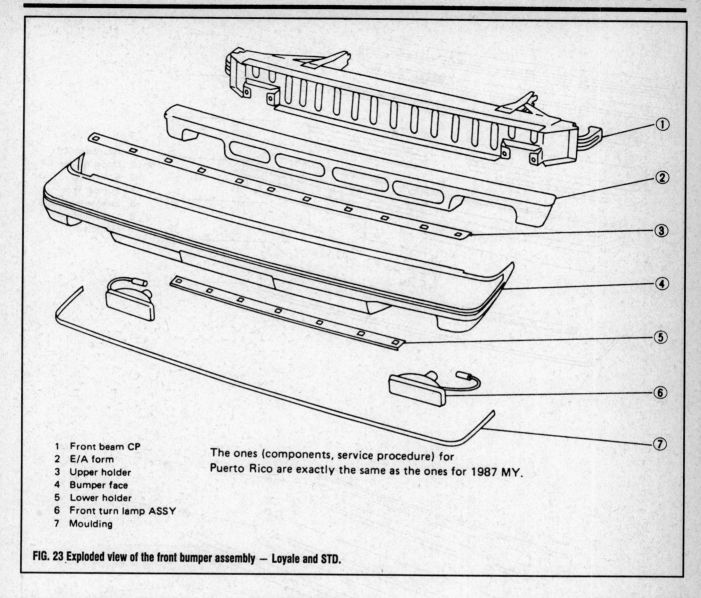

1 Front beam CP
2 E/A form
3 Upper holder
4 Bumper face
5 Lower holder
6 Front turn lamp ASSY
7 Moulding

The ones (components, service procedure) for
Puerto Rico are exactly the same as the ones for 1987 MY.

FIG. 23 Exploded view of the front bumper assembly — Loyale and STD.

REAR 4-DOOR SEDAN AND 3-DOOR MODELS

1. Open the trunk lid. Remove the trunk trim panel clips and detach the trim.

2. Remove both the side and center trunk covers.

3. Disconnect the rear light harness connector.

4. Remove the 2 flange nuts.

5. Extract the rear bumper half way. Remove the grommet from the license plate harness, and remove the connector through the hole in the skirt section.

6. Remove the rear bumper horizontally.

7. Install the bumper in position and install all trim pieces removed.

8. Tighten the flange nuts to 22–31 ft. lbs. (29–42 Nm).

REAR STATION WAGON

1. Remove the 2 bolts that secure each lower end of the bumper to the body.

2. Remove the plug from the wall on each side of the center sub-trunk and remove the rear bumper retaining bolts.

3. Remove the bumper assembly from the vehicle.

4. Install the bumper assembly in position and tighten the retaining bolts to 52–73 ft. lbs. (66–100 Nm).

XT Coupe

FRONT

1. Position the vehicle on a lift.
2. Set the head lights to upper beam.
3. Remove the battery.
4. Raise the vehicle.

5. Remove the mud guards (inner plastic fender shields).

6. Remove the under cover and air dam skirts.

7. Remove the bolts that secure the lower ducts.

8. Remove the bolts that secure the side bumpers.

9. Remove the bolts that secure the lower side of the side ducts.

10. Remove the bolts from the back of the bumper stay.

11. Lower the vehicle.

12. Remove the washer tank:

a. Disconnect the hose from the check valve on the back of the front bumper.

b. Remove the bolts and washers that hold the air cleaner.

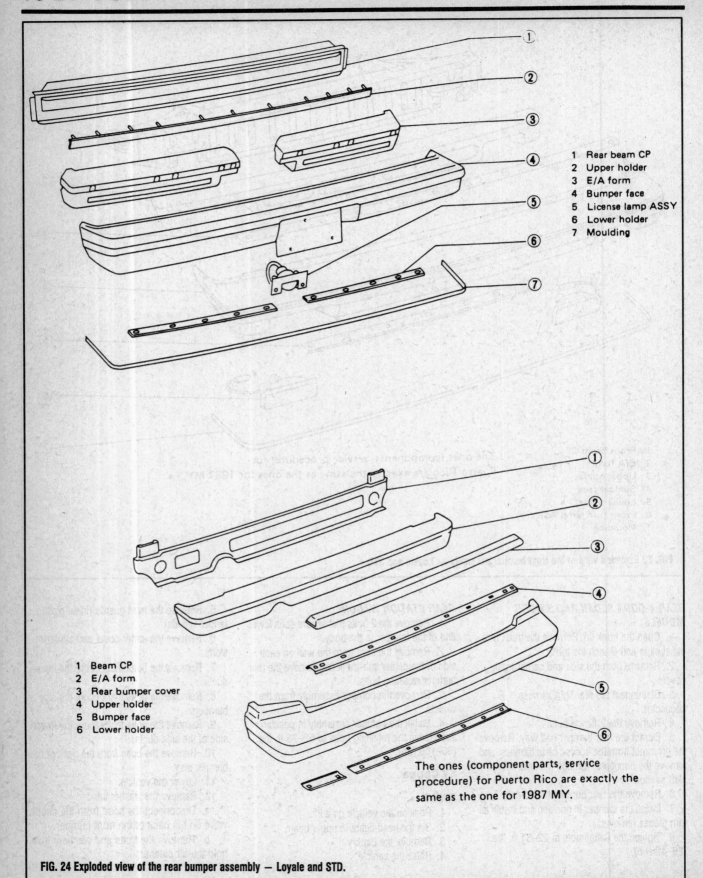

1 Rear beam CP
2 Upper holder
3 E/A form
4 Bumper face
5 License lamp ASSY
6 Lower holder
7 Moulding

1 Beam CP
2 E/A form
3 Rear bumper cover
4 Upper holder
5 Bumper face
6 Lower holder

The ones (component parts, service procedure) for Puerto Rico are exactly the same as the one for 1987 MY.

FIG. 24 Exploded view of the rear bumper assembly — Loyale and STD.

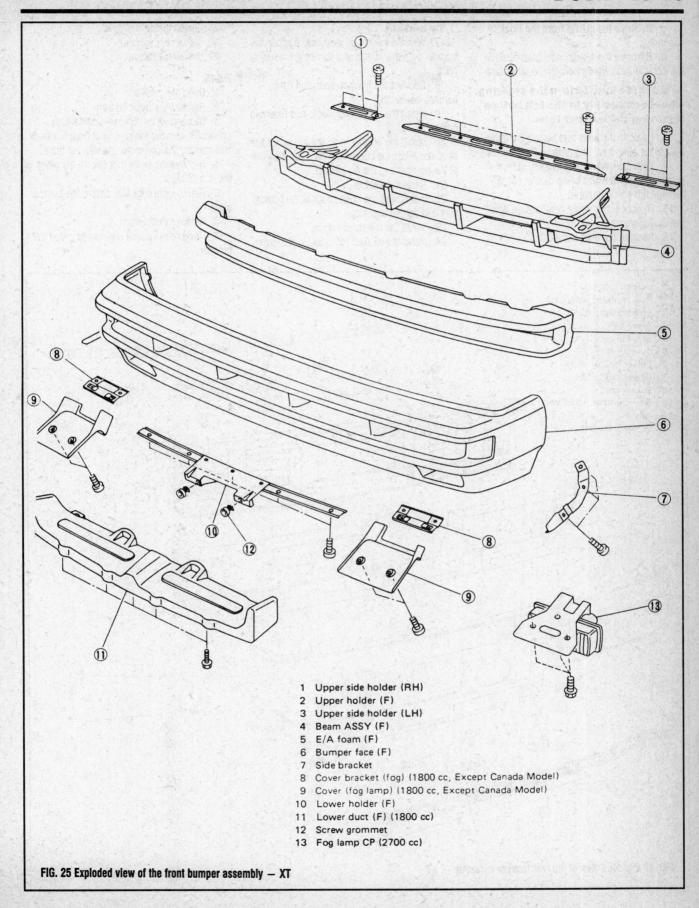

1   Upper side holder (RH)
2   Upper holder (F)
3   Upper side holder (LH)
4   Beam ASSY (F)
5   E/A foam (F)
6   Bumper face (F)
7   Side bracket
8   Cover bracket (fog) (1800 cc, Except Canada Model)
9   Cover (fog lamp) (1800 cc, Except Canada Model)
10 Lower holder (F)
11 Lower duct (F) (1800 cc)
12 Screw grommet
13 Fog lamp CP (2700 cc)

FIG. 25 Exploded view of the front bumper assembly — XT

c. Remove the clamp from the boot assembly.

d. Remove the air cleaner, then remove the conical nuts which hold the washer tank.

➡ **NOTE:Be sure to turn the steering wheel completely to the left before removing the washer tank.**

13. Remove the bolts that secure the upper side of the side duct, and remove the side duct.

14. With the help of an assistant, slide the bumper slightly forward being careful not to damage the wiring harness.

15. Disconnect the front combination light harness connector.

16. Remove the front bumper.

To Install:

17. With the help of an assistant, position the bumper onto the vehicle and tighten the retaining bolts.

18. Connect the front combination light harness connector.

19. Install the upper side ducts and retaining bolts.

20. Install the washer tank, the clamp for the boot assembly, the check valve hose on the back of the bumper and the air cleaner.

21. Raise the vehicle.

22. Install the bolts on the back of the bumper stay and tighten securely.

23. Install the lower side ducts.

24. Install the air dam skirts and under cover.

25. Install the mud guards.

26. Lower the vehicle.

27. Install the battery.

REAR

1. Open the trunk lid.

2. Remove the trunk lid trim.

3. Disconnect the license light harness connector, remove the grommet from the body and transfer the connector outside the trunk.

4. Remove the bolts that secure the sides of the rear bumper.

5. Remove the nuts that secure the bumper stays.

6. Remove the bumper.

7. Reverse the above process to install the bumper.

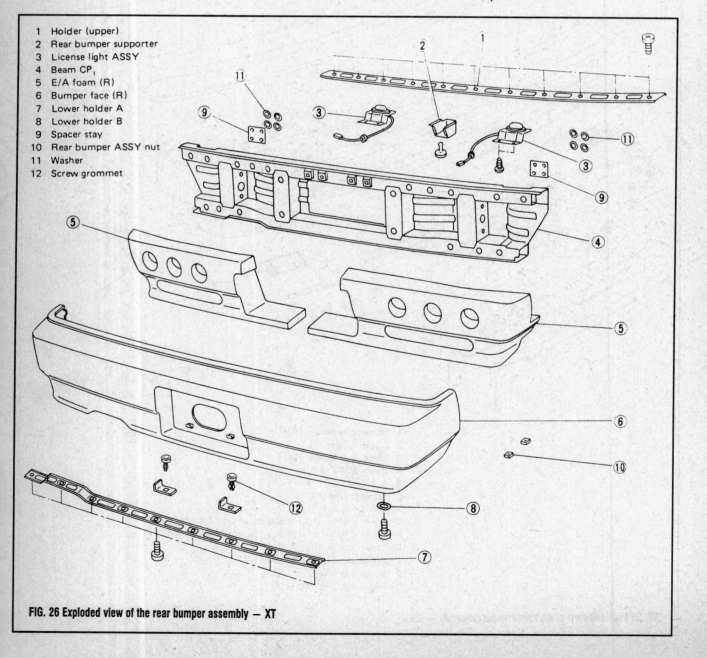

1 Holder (upper)
2 Rear bumper supporter
3 License light ASSY
4 Beam CP₁
5 E/A foam (R)
6 Bumper face (R)
7 Lower holder A
8 Lower holder B
9 Spacer stay
10 Rear bumper ASSY nut
11 Washer
12 Screw grommet

FIG. 26 Exploded view of the rear bumper assembly — XT

8. Adjust the clearance between the bumper and the rear combination light and between the bumper and the tail light to 8mm.

Legacy

When removing the front bumper on these models, use care to avoid damaging the air bag system wirings and components, which are routed near the front bumper. All air bag wiring is wrapped in yellow.

FRONT

> ❄ **CAUTION**
>
> **Properly disarm the air bag on vehicles equipped with the SRS system. Failure to do so can cause serious injury. The procedure can be found in Section 6 of this manual under the heading "Supplemental Restraint System".**

1. Properly disarm the air bag system, on models equipped. Disconnect the negative battery cable.
2. Remove the vapor canister.
3. Remove the inner fender shield.
4. Remove the bolts and nuts that retain the bumper at the side.
5. Remove the lower part of the bumper by releasing the clips.

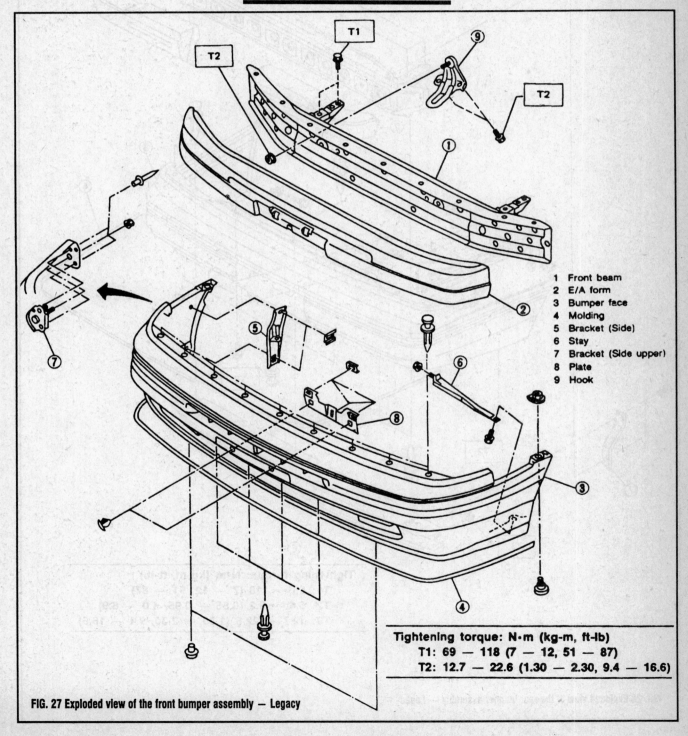

1 Front beam
2 E/A form
3 Bumper face
4 Molding
5 Bracket (Side)
6 Stay
7 Bracket (Side upper)
8 Plate
9 Hook

Tightening torque: N·m (kg-m, ft-lb)
T1: 69 — 118 (7 — 12, 51 — 87)
T2: 12.7 — 22.6 (1.30 — 2.30, 9.4 — 16.6)

FIG. 27 Exploded view of the front bumper assembly — Legacy

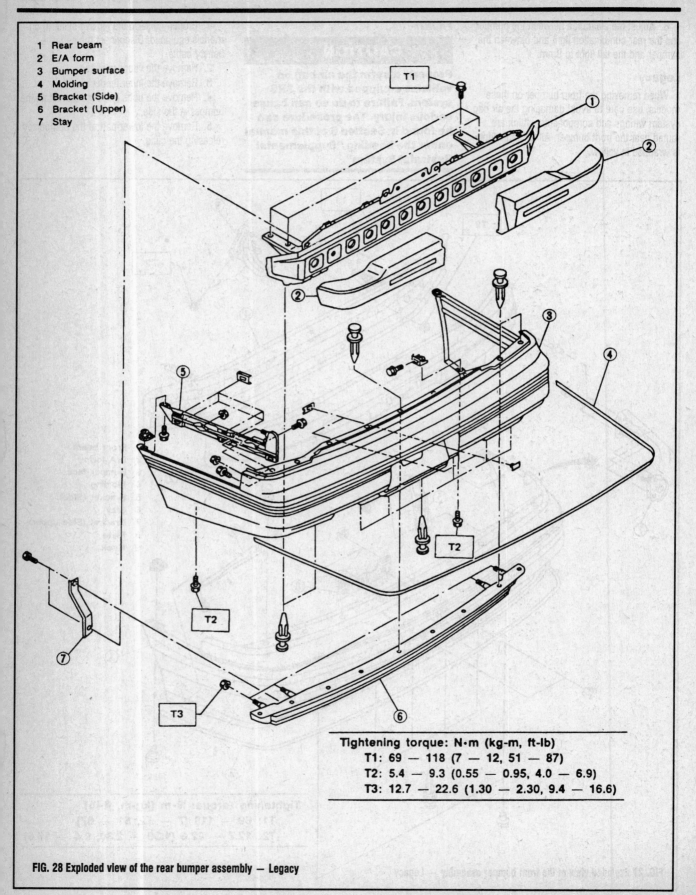

1 Rear beam
2 E/A form
3 Bumper surface
4 Molding
5 Bracket (Side)
6 Bracket (Upper)
7 Stay

Tightening torque: N·m (kg-m, ft-lb)
T1: 69 — 118 (7 — 12, 51 — 87)
T2: 5.4 — 9.3 (0.55 — 0.95, 4.0 — 6.9)
T3: 12.7 — 22.6 (1.30 — 2.30, 9.4 — 16.6)

FIG. 28 Exploded view of the rear bumper assembly — Legacy

6. From the engine compartment, remove the bumper stay retaining bolts.

7. With the help of an assistant, remove the bumper assembly from the vehicle.

To Install:

8. Install the bumper into position and tighten the stay bolts to 51–87 ft. lbs (69–118 Nm).

9. Install the lower part of the bumper by pushing it firmly into place and engaging the clips.

10. Install the side bumper retaining nuts and bolts. Install the inner fender shield.

11. Install the vapor canister and connect the negative battery cable.

REAR

1. Open the trunk lid or tailgate and remove the rear trim panel and clips.

2. Remove the bolts and nuts from the side of the bumper.

3. Remove the bumper stay retaining bolts.

4. With the help of an assistant, remove the bumper assembly from the vehicle.

5. Install the bumper into position and install the stay retaining bolts. Tighten the bolts to 51–87 ft. lbs. (69–118 Nm).

6. Install the side bumper retaining bolts. Install the rear trim panel.

SVX

When removing the front bumper on these models, use care to avoid damaging the air bag system wirings and components, which are routed near the front bumper. All air bag wiring is wrapped in yellow.

FRONT

❄ CAUTION

Properly disarm the air bag on vehicles equipped with the SRS system. Failure to do so can cause serious injury. The procedure can be found in Section 6 of this manual under the heading "Supplemental Restraint System".

---

1. Properly disarm the air bag system and disconnect the negative battery cable.

2. Raise and safely support the vehicle. Remove the engine under cover.

3. Detach the front side of the inner fender guards and remove the side bumper bolts.

4. Remove the bumper side stay from the bumper.

5. Remove the bolts securing the lower side of the bumper to the body.

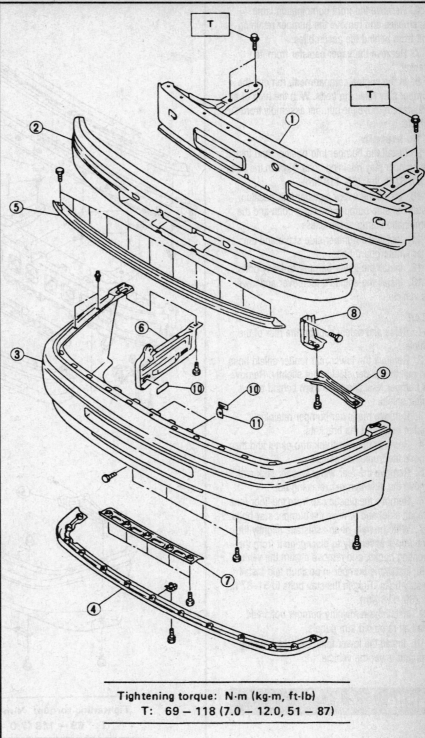

Tightening torque: N·m (kg·m, ft-lb)
T: 69 – 118 (7.0 – 12.0, 51 – 87)

1	Front beam	7	Holder (LWR)
2	Energy absorbing foam	8	Side stay bracket
3	Bumper face	9	Side stay
4	Front skirt (LWR)	10	Clip
5	Holder (UPR)	11	Net plate
6	Side bracket		

FIG. 29 Exploded view of the front bumper assembly — SVX

6. Remove the front combination lamp assemblies and remove the bumper retaining bolt from behind the assemblies.

7. Remove the vapor canister from its bracket.

8. In the engine compartment, remove the bumper stay retaining bolts. With the help of an assistant, remove the bumper assembly from the vehicle.

To Install:

9. Install the bumper into position and install the bumper stay retaining bolts. Tighten the bolts to 51–87 ft. lbs. (69–118 Nm).

10. Install the vapor canister into position. Install the side bumper retaining bolts and the combination lamp assemblies.

11. Install the bumper side stays and the inner fender guard bolts.

12. Install the lower bumper-to-body bolts.

13. Install the engine undercover and lower the vehicle.

REAR

1. Raise and safely support the rear of the vehicle.

2. Remove the lower rear fender shield bolts and pull the fender shields out slightly. Remove the bumper retaining bolts from behind the fender shield.

3. Remove the lower bumper retaining bracket bolts and the brackets.

4. Remove the rear trunk trim panel and then remove the trunk side panels.

5. Remove the rear wiper washer tank and remove the side bumper retaining nut.

6. Remove the plastic cap from the floor (one on each side) and remove the bumper stay bolts.

7. With the help of an assistant, slightly lift the bumper assembly to disengage it from the mounting hooks, and remove it from the vehicle.

8. Install the bumper in position and install the stay bolts. Tighten the stay bolts to 51–87 ft. lbs. (69–118 Nm).

9. Install the remaining bumper bolts and install all removed trim panels.

10. Install the lower fender shield retaining bolts and lower the vehicle.

Grille

REMOVAL & INSTALLATION

To remove the grille on all Subaru models, requires only that the grille retaining screws and clips be removed and the grill removed from the vehicle. Use care not to break the grille when pulling it away from the vehicle body.

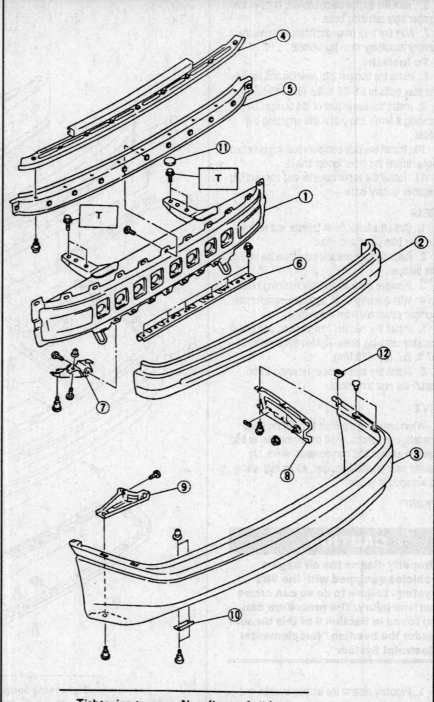

Tightening torque: N·m (kg-m, ft-lb)
T: 69 – 118 (7.0 – 12.0, 51 – 87)

1	Rear beam	7	Bracket (LWR)
2	Energy absorbing foam	8	Side bracket
3	Bumper face	9	Bracket (side LWR)
4	Holder (UPR)	10	Retainer (LWR)
5	Joint (holder UPR)	11	Cap
6	Holder (LWR)	12	J-net

FIG. 30 Exploded view of the rear bumper assembly — SVX

FIG. 31 Removing the power outside mirror from the door

Manual Outside Mirrors

REMOVAL & INSTALLATION

▶ SEE FIG. 31

1. Remove control knob handle.
2. Remove door corner finisher panel.
3. Remove mirror body attaching screws, and then remove mirror body
4. Installation is in the reverse order of removal.

➡ **Apply sealer to the rear surface of door corner finisher panel during installation to prevent water leak.**

Power Outside Mirror

The mirrors are controlled by a single switch assembly, located on the instrument panel or the door panel. The motors that operate the mirrors are part of the mirror assembly and cannot be replaced separately.

The mirror switch consists of a left-right change over select knob and control knobs. The switch is ready to function only when the ignition switch is in the **ACC** or **ON** position. Movement of the mirror is accomplished by the motor, located in the mirror housing.

REMOVAL & INSTALLATION

Mirror Assembly

1. Remove door corner finisher panel.

2. Remove mirror body attaching screws, and then remove mirror body
3. Disconnect the electrical connection.

➡ **On SVX and Legacy models, it will be necessary to remove the door trim panel to gain access to the electrical connection.**

4. Installation is in the reverse order of removal.

Mirror Control Switch

1. Disconnect the negative battery cable.
2. Use a small standard screwdriver and carefully pry the switch from its mounting (either in the dash board or the drivers door armrest).
3. Disconnect the electrical lead and remove the switch.
4. Install the switch in the reverse order of removal.

TESTING

Switch

Disconnect the harness from the switch. Check for continuity between the terminals in each switch position.

Mirror

1. Remove the mirror trim panel and disconnect the electrical lead to the mirror.
2. Test the mirror operation using the following procedures:

a. Tilt up—connect a 12 volt power source to terminal 1 and ground terminal 3.

b. Tilt down—connect a 12 volt power source to 3 terminal 3 and ground terminal 1.

c. Swing right—connect a 12 volt power source to terminal 3 and ground terminal 2.

d. Swing left—connect a 12 volt power source to terminal 2 and ground terminal 3.

3. If the mirror does not operate properly in any of these tests, replace the assembly.

Mast Antenna

REMOVAL & INSTALLATION

1. Disconnect the negative battery cable.
2. Disconnect the antenna wire from the radio.

Operation	Terminal connection	
	(+)	(−)
UP	1	3
DOWN	3	1
RIGHT	3	2
LEFT	2	3

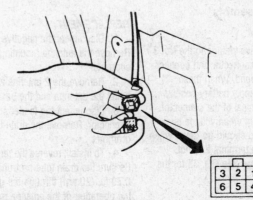

FIG. 32 Testing the rear view mirror motor

3. Push the antenna wire through the access hole under the instrument panel.

➡ **To make installation easier, tie a string to the end of the antenna wire before removing it from the vehicle. Pull the string up with the antenna wire and allow one end to stay visible at the inside of the vehicle. When installing the antenna, tie the wire to the other end of the string and pull it through.**

4. On models with the antenna on the side of the windshield:
   a. Remove the A pillar trim.
   b. Loosen the antenna mounting nut located beneath the trim panel.
   c. Move the antenna upward slightly then pull it out of the pillar with the antenna lead.

5. On models with roof mounted antenna, remove the antenna base mounting screw and pull the antenna off of the roof, drawing the wire out of the opening.

6. Install the antenna in position, guiding the wire into position. Install the antenna base plate, making sure it is flush with the body.

7. Connect the wire to the radio and check the operation.

8. Install any removed trim.

Power Antenna

The power antenna automatically raises the antenna mast to its full height whenever the radio and ignition are turned **ON**. The antenna retracts into the fender when either the ignition or the radio is turned **OFF**.

COMPONENT REPLACEMENT

◆ SEE FIGS. 33–35

Antenna Motor Assembly

TESTING

Connect battery positive voltage to the No. 3 terminal of the antenna connector and connect the No. 1 terminal to ground. When these connections are made, apply battery positive voltage to the No. 2 terminal of the connector. The antenna should go up when voltage is applied to terminal 2 and should go down when voltage is removed from terminal 2. If not, replace the antenna motor. See FIG. 35 for the connector identification.

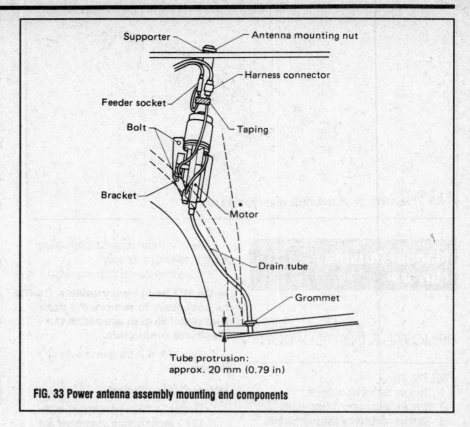

FIG. 33 Power antenna assembly mounting and components

(Labels: Supporter, Antenna mounting nut, Harness connector, Feeder socket, Taping, Bolt, Bracket, Motor, Drain tube, Grommet, Tube protrusion: approx. 20 mm (0.79 in))

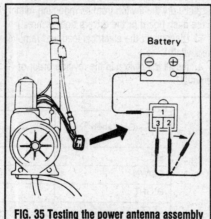

FIG. 35 Testing the power antenna assembly

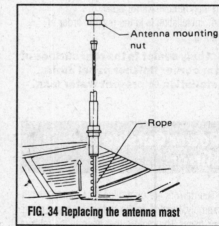

FIG. 34 Replacing the antenna mast

REPLACEMENT

1. Disconnect the negative battery cable. Remove the antenna mounting nut and supporter.

2. Remove the 2 antenna assembly-to-trunk bolts, the antenna and the band clip.

3. Disconnect the feeder socket and harness connector. Remove the drain tube from the grommet.

4. To install, reverse the removal procedures. Be sure the drain tube protrudes approximately 0.79 in. (20mm) through the grommet. Check the operation of the antenna mast.

Antenna Mast

1. Loosen the antenna mounting nut enough so it can be easily removed. Turn the radio and ignition switch **ON** and extend the antenna. Remove the antenna mounting nut.

2. Grasp the lower section of the antenna mast and lift it vertically. Extract the inner pipe and rope from the antenna housing.

To Install:

3. Insert the center pipe (supplied with the new antenna mast) into the antenna assembly tube until it bottoms.

4. Insert the antenna rod rope into the antenna housing through the centering pipe with the rack facing outward; at the same time, turn the radio switch **OFF**.

5. Be sure the antenna mast is vertical to the antenna housing. This prevents the rack from sustaining damage and making it easier to insert the rope. Remove the centering pipe from the antenna housing and detach it from the rope.

6. Face the inner pipe spring toward the center of the vehicle and insert the inner pipe into the antenna housing. Temporarily tighten the antenna mounting nut.

7. Turn the radio switch **ON** and **OFF** to ensure the antenna rod extends and retracts properly. Tighten the antenna mounting nut.

Fender

REMOVAL & INSTALLATION

◆ SEE FIGS. 36–40

❊❊ CAUTION

Properly disarm the air bag on vehicles equipped with the SRS system. Failure to do so can cause serious injury. The procedure can be found in Section 6 of this manual under the heading "Supplemental Restraint System".

1. On models equipped with an air bag, use caution when working on the front fenders, the air bag wiring and sensors are in this area. Raise and support the front of the vehicle so that it is just off of the ground.

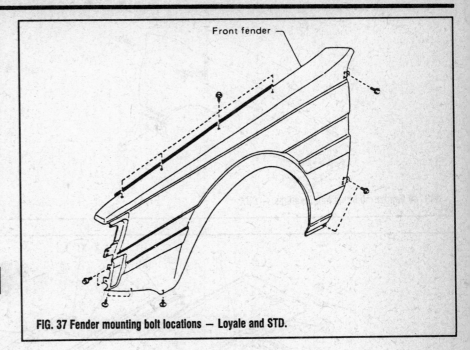
FIG. 37 Fender mounting bolt locations — Loyale and STD.

2. Remove the tire and wheel assembly.

3. Remove the inner fender cover assembly bolts and remove it.

4. Remove the fender mounting bolts. On some models it will be necessary to remove the front combination lamp assemblies, before removing the fender.

➡ **The fender is joined to the body with sealer at some points. When removing the fender, a small putty knife will help to break the seal in these areas.**

5. Remove the fender from the vehicle. Be careful of the painted surfaces.

To Install:

6. Apply body sealer (available from Honda) to the correct location. Install the fender in position, do not tighten the bolts. Check the fender-to-hood-to-door clearance. Once the clearance is correct and even, tighten all of the mounting bolts.

7. Install the inner fender assembly and its mounting bolts.

8. Install the wheel and tire assembly. Lower the vehicle.

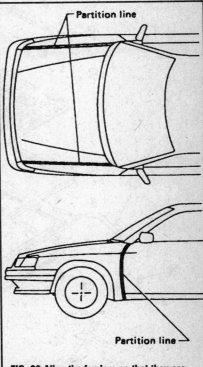
FIG. 39 Align the fenders so that they are even at these points

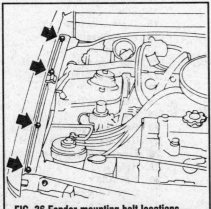
FIG. 36 Fender mounting bolt locations — Justy

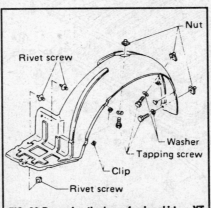
FIG. 38 Removing the inner fender skirt — XT

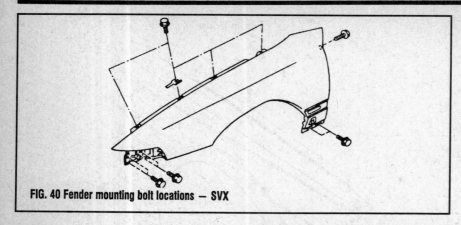

FIG. 40 Fender mounting bolt locations — SVX

Power Sunroof

♦ SEE FIGS. 41–43

The sunroof is operated by a switch, which is usually located in the headliner. The system is consists of the sunroof switch, motor drive cables and circuit breaker and a relay. The sunroof can be closed manually, (should it be necessary) by removing the headliner plug, insert the handle and turn the gear to close the sunroof.

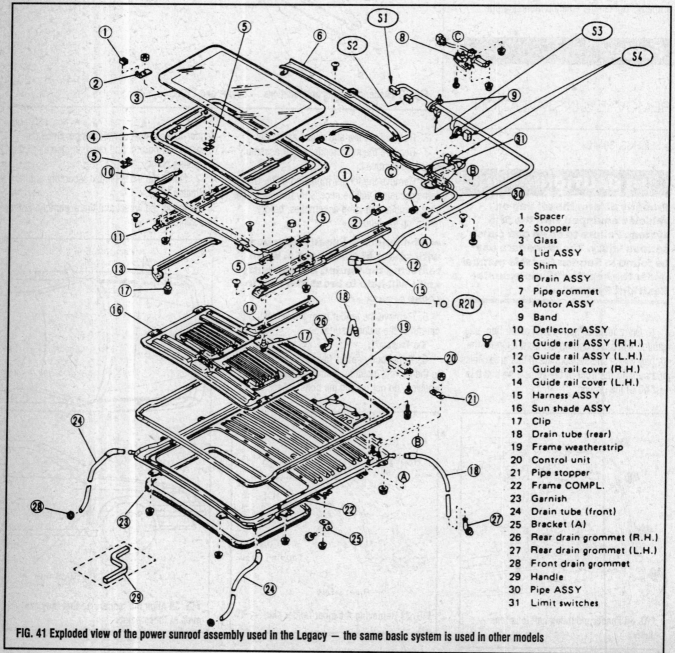

1 Spacer
2 Stopper
3 Glass
4 Lid ASSY
5 Shim
6 Drain ASSY
7 Pipe grommet
8 Motor ASSY
9 Band
10 Deflector ASSY
11 Guide rail ASSY (R.H.)
12 Guide rail ASSY (L.H.)
13 Guide rail cover (R.H.)
14 Guide rail cover (L.H.)
15 Harness ASSY
16 Sun shade ASSY
17 Clip
18 Drain tube (rear)
19 Frame weatherstrip
20 Control unit
21 Pipe stopper
22 Frame COMPL.
23 Garnish
24 Drain tube (front)
25 Bracket (A)
26 Rear drain grommet (R.H.)
27 Rear drain grommet (L.H.)
28 Front drain grommet
29 Handle
30 Pipe ASSY
31 Limit switches

FIG. 41 Exploded view of the power sunroof assembly used in the Legacy — the same basic system is used in other models

➡ **The sunroof assembly is equipped with water drain tubes. It is important to keep these drain tubes open. So it is recommended to blow compressed air through the drain tubes at regular intervals, in order to keep the drain tubes clear.**

DIAGNOSIS AND TESTING

SUNROOF CLOSING FORCE CHECK

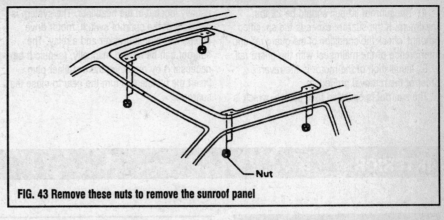

FIG. 43 Remove these nuts to remove the sunroof panel

Motor Installed

1. After installing all removed parts, using a second person, have them hold the switch to close the sunroof while measuring the force required to stop the sunroof with a suitable spring scale.

2. Read the force on the scale as soon as the glass stops moving, then immediately release the switch and spring scale. The closing force should be 44–55 lbs. (20–25 kg).

3. If the force required to stop the sunroof is not within specifications, adjust it, by turning the sunroof motor clutch adjusting nut (using the handle furnished by the manufacturer). Turn the nut clockwise to increase the force and counterclockwise to decrease the force.

4. After the proper adjustment has been made, install a new lockwasher and bend it against the flat of the adjusting nut.

COMPONENT REPLACEMENT

Sunroof Assembly

This is a general procedure may be altered for the vehicle being serviced.

1. Remove the roof trim. Disconnect the drain tubes and disconnect the motor harness connector.

2. Remove the 6 bolts from the sunroof frame bracket, starting from the front and moving to the rear.

3. Hold the front and rear side of the sunroof (a second person will be needed) and slide the sunroof assembly off by moving it to the rear.

4. Installation is the reverse order of the removal procedure.

HEIGHT ADJUSTMENT

1. Place shim(s) between the link bracket and the lid assembly to align the sunroof with the roof panel.

2. The difference in the height between the roof and the main seal should be adjusted to within the 0.051 in. ± 0.039 in. (1.3mm ± 1mm) range.

HORIZONTAL ADJUSTMENT

1. Loosen the 8 nuts which hold the sunroof lid assembly.

2. Move the sunroof lid assembly to either side, along the oblong hole at the stay location, until proper adjustment is reached. Then tighten the nuts.

3. Check to see if the deflector is positioned at a proper height. The height of the deflector cannot be adjusted. Repair or replace the deflector if it is deformed or damaged.

Sunroof Lid Assembly

1. Completely close the sunroof glass. Completely open the sunshade. Remove the bracket cap and screws and detach the bracket cover.

2. Completely close the sunroof lid assembly and lift it up. Remove the 8 nuts from the left and right ring bracket.

3. Working from inside the vehicle, slightly raise the sunroof lid assembly until it is disengaged from the link bracket. Hold both ends of the lid assembly and remove it at an angle.

Sunshade

1. Unhook the sunshade hooks. Move the sunroof lid assembly rearward.

2. Set the sunshade to the **FORWARD** position and remove the retaining nuts from both sides of the sunshade.

3. Installation is the reverse order of the removal procedure.

Sunroof Frame

1. Remove the sunroof trim. Disconnect the front and rear drain tubes.

2. Remove the bolts which hold the sunroof frame and detach the sunroof frame.

3. Installation is the reverse order of the removal procedure.

Sunroof Motor

1. Disconnect the negative battery cable. Remove the roof trim.

2. Remove the sunroof motor nut and harness coupler and remove the sunroof motor.

3. Before installing the motor, wrap a shop towel around the main seal of the sunroof lid. Then connect a suitable spring scale, pull the sunroof lid out using the spring scale.

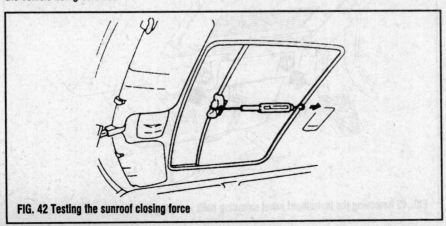

FIG. 42 Testing the sunroof closing force

4. The sunroof lid pull should be 22 lbs. maximum. If the sunroof exceeds the specified amount, check the condition of the guard rail and interference of the main seal with the guard rail.

5. Installation of the motor is the reverse order of the removal procedure.

The sunroof is operated by a switch, which is usually located in the headliner. The system is consists of the sunroof switch, motor drive cables and circuit breaker and a relay. The sunroof can be closed manually, (should it be necessary) by removing the headliner plug, insert the handle and turn the gear to close the sunroof.

➡ **The sunroof assembly is equipped with water drain tubes. It is important to keep these drain tubes open. So it is recommended to blow compressed air through the drain tubes at regular intervals, in order to keep the drain tubes clear.**

INTERIOR

Instrument Panel

❄❄ CAUTION

Properly disarm the air bag on vehicles equipped with the SRS system. Failure to do so can cause serious injury. The procedure can be found in Section 6 of this manual under the heading "Supplemental Restraint System".

REMOVAL & INSTALLATION

◆ SEE FIGS. 44–50

➡ While the instrument panel removal procedures here are specific for each vehicle, they should be used only as an outline. Manufacturers production changes and year-to-year trim level changes are not covered in these procedures.

Justy

1. Disconnect the negative battery cable.
2. Matchmark and remove the steering wheel.
3. Remove the glove box assembly and disconnect the defroster ducts.
4. Disconnect the heater control cables from the heater unit.
5. Remove the plastic bolt covers from the around the instrument panel.
6. Remove the instrument cluster, disconnecting the speedometer cable.

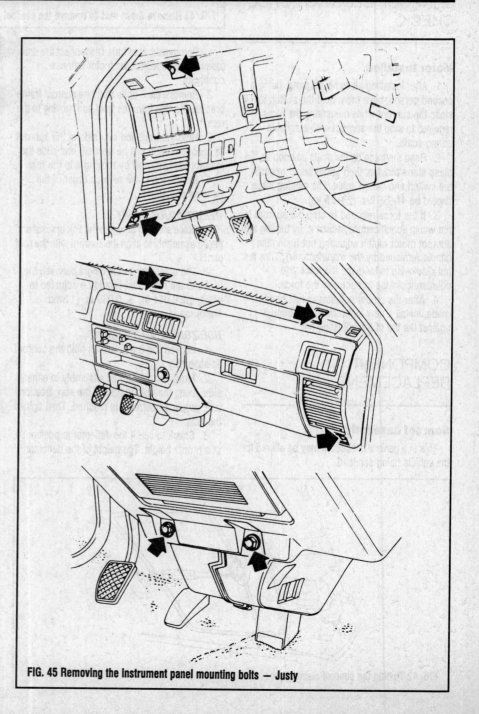

FIG. 45 Removing the Instrument panel mounting bolts — Justy

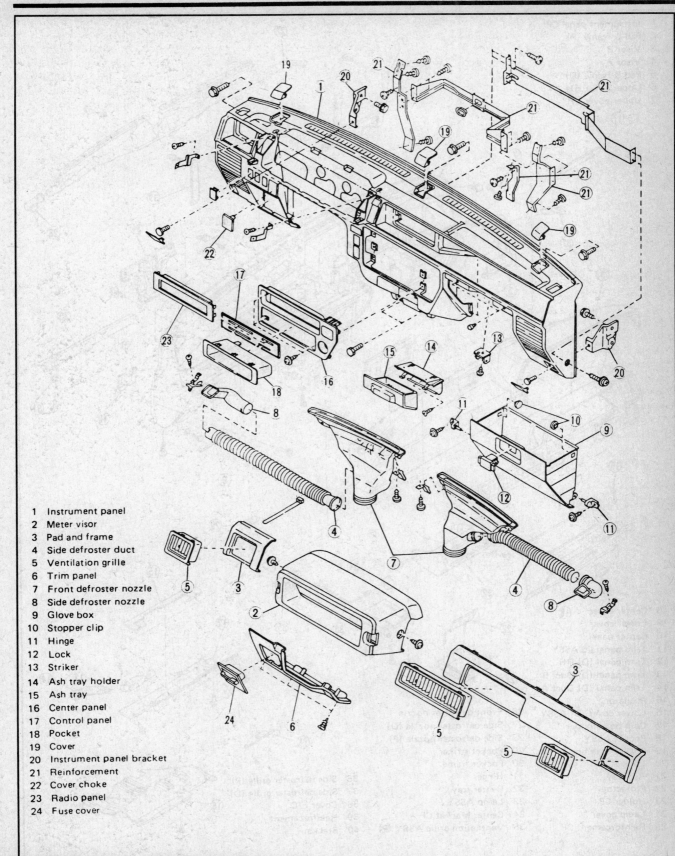

1   Instrument panel
2   Meter visor
3   Pad and frame
4   Side defroster duct
5   Ventilation grille
6   Trim panel
7   Front defroster nozzle
8   Side defroster nozzle
9   Glove box
10 Stopper clip
11 Hinge
12 Lock
13 Striker
14 Ash tray holder
15 Ash tray
16 Center panel
17 Control panel
18 Pocket
19 Cover
20 Instrument panel bracket
21 Reinforcement
22 Cover choke
23 Radio panel
24 Fuse cover

FIG. 44 Exploded view of the instrument panel assembly — Justy

1. Instrument panel CP
2. Pad & frame (P)
3. Visor B
4. Visor A
5. Pad & frame (D)
6. Upper cover RH
7. Upper cover LH

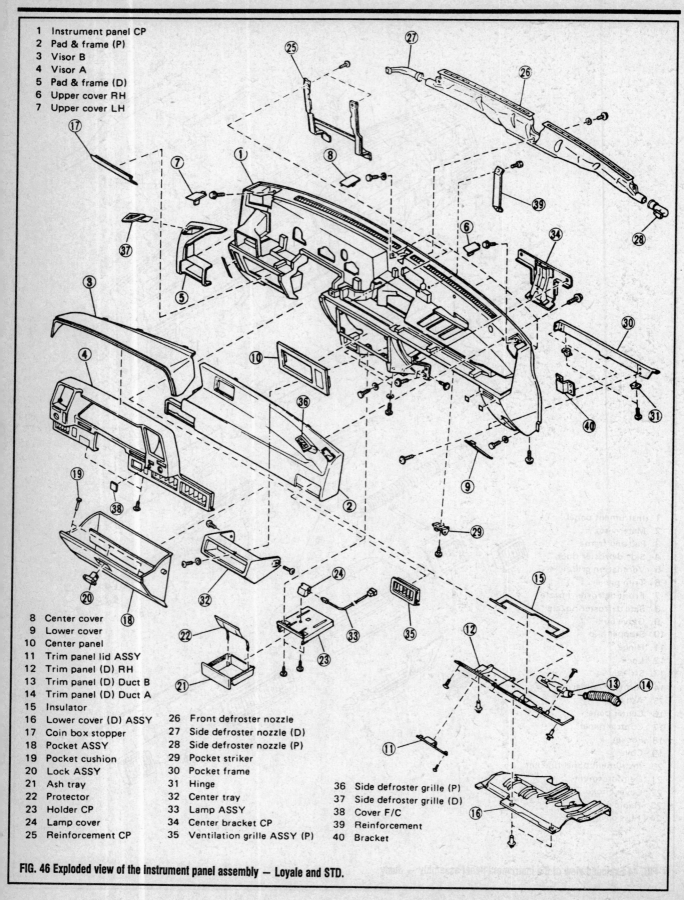

8. Center cover
9. Lower cover
10. Center panel
11. Trim panel lid ASSY
12. Trim panel (D) RH
13. Trim panel (D) Duct B
14. Trim panel (D) Duct A
15. Insulator
16. Lower cover (D) ASSY
17. Coin box stopper
18. Pocket ASSY
19. Pocket cushion
20. Lock ASSY
21. Ash tray
22. Protector
23. Holder CP
24. Lamp cover
25. Reinforcement CP

26. Front defroster nozzle
27. Side defroster nozzle (D)
28. Side defroster nozzle (P)
29. Pocket striker
30. Pocket frame
31. Hinge
32. Center tray
33. Lamp ASSY
34. Center bracket CP
35. Ventilation grille ASSY (P)

36. Side defroster grille (P)
37. Side defroster grille (D)
38. Cover F/C
39. Reinforcement
40. Bracket

FIG. 46 Exploded view of the instrument panel assembly — Loyale and STD.

7. Remove the bolts that retain the instrument panel to the firewall and with the help of an assistant, lift the instrument panel away from the firewall. Disconnect any electrical leads at this point.

8. Remove the instrument panel from the vehicle through the passengers side door.

➡ **Use care not to damage the instrument panel trim or the vehicle interior trim when removing the instrument panel.**

9. Remove any components from the instrument panel that are going to be replaced.

To Install:

10. Install the instrument panel in position with the help of an assistant. Connect all electrical leads.

11. Install the instrument panel retaining bolts.

12. Install the removed components on the instrument panel.

13. Install the heater duct and the glove box assembly.

14. Install the instrument cluster, connecting the speedometer cable and electrical leads.

15. Install any remaining components. Install the steering wheel on the column in the same position as removed. Tighten the center nut to 36–43 ft. lbs. (49–59 Nm).

16. Connect the negative battery cable. Check the operation of all accessories.

STD. and Loyale

1. Disconnect the negative battery cable.

2. Remove the lower trim panel on the drivers side (underneath steering column). The panel is held in place by 3 screws and trim clips.

3. Remove the bolts retaining the main fuse box assembly, allow the assembly to hang by the wires.

4. Remove the lower steering column cover and disconnect the ventilation duct from under the instrument panel.

5. Disconnect the cable from the air vent in the drivers side kick panel where it attaches to the control lever in the instrument panel.

6. Disconnect the temperature control cables at the heater unit.

7. Disconnect the vacuum lines at the heater case.

8. Disconnect the wiring harnesses on the drivers side.

9. Remove the instrument cluster an disconnect the speedometer cable.

10. Remove the steering wheel assembly.

11. Remove the center tray and console from between the seats.

12. Remove the lower trim panel from the passengers side. Remove the glove box assembly.

13. Disconnect the wiring harness connectors on the passengers side.

14. Remove the instrument panel retaining bolt covers from the panel. They can be pryed gently upward.

15. Remove the instrument panel bolts in the following places; 2 bolts at the lower ends of the instrument panel, 2 bolts at the lower center of the panel, 2 bolts at the upper ends of the panel and 2 bolts at the upper center of the panel.

➡ **When removing the instrument panel, check that all wiring and cables are disconnected before pulling it completely away from the firewall.**

16. With the help of an assistant, lift the panel and remove it from the vehicle. Use care not to damage the panel or the interior trim when removing it.

To Install:

17. With the help of an assistant, install the instrument panel into position at the firewall.

➡ **Be sure that no wires are caught between the panel and its mounting. Make sure that the panel is on top of the weatherstrip along the windshield and the strip is not folded along the windshield.**

18. Install the instrument panel retaining bolts. Install the bolt covers after tightening the bolts.

19. Connect the wiring at the passengers side of the instrument panel. Install the glove box assembly.

20. Install the lower cover on the passengers side. Install the center console and tray between the seats.

21. Install the steering wheel assembly. Tighten the steering wheel nut to 22–29 ft. lbs. (29–39 Nm).

22. Install the instrument cluster and connect the electrical wiring at the drivers side.

23. Connect the temperature control cables and the vacuum lines at the heater unit.

24. Connect the air vent cable at the drivers side air vent. Install the main fuse box in position.

25. Install the steering column lower trim and the lower instrument panel trim.

26. Install any remaining trim pieces and check the operation of all components.

27. Connect the negative battery cable and check the operation of all electrical components.

➡ **When checking electrical components, if any of the fuses should blow, check that there are no wires pinched by the instrument panel and correct it if there are.**

XT

➡ **When removing the instrument panel on the XT models, the steering shaft and column assembly are removed with the control wings as an assembly.**

1. Disconnect the negative battery cable.

2. Remove the steering wheel.

3. Remove the lower trim panel from the drivers side.

4. Remove the ventilation duct from the drivers side, it can be pulled out by hand.

5. Open the fuse box lid and remove the screws that retain the fuse box. Push the fuse box back and allow it to hang by the wires.

6. Remove the lower cover on the passengers side. Remove the glove box door assembly.

7. Remove the trim panel from the top of the instrument panel by prying it gently at both ends and in the middle. You will have to pull it upward with your hands to release the clips, be careful not to bend or break it.

8. Remove the center console assembly. Be sure to remove the control knobs for the ventilation controls.

9. Remove the radio assembly.

10. Disconnect the steering shaft coupler at the floor. Remove the steering column covers. Remove the column-to-instrument panel support bolts and remove the column, control wings and shaft as an assembly.

11. Disconnect the wiring harnesses on the drivers and passengers side.

12. Remove the 8 bolts that retain the instrument panel. With the help of an assistant, lift and remove the instrument panel.

➡ **When removing the instrument panel, check that all wiring and cables are disconnected before pulling it completely away from the firewall.**

13. With the help of an assistant, install the panel into position.

➡ **Be sure that no wires are caught between the panel and its mounting. Make sure that the panel is on top of the weatherstrip along the windshield and the strip is not folded along the windshield.**

14. Reconnect all electrical harnesses on the drivers and passengers side of the vehicle.

15. Install the steering column assembly. See Section 8 of this manual for torque specifications and installation instructions.

16. Install the center console assembly. Install the glove box assembly.

17. Install the upper instrument panel trim.

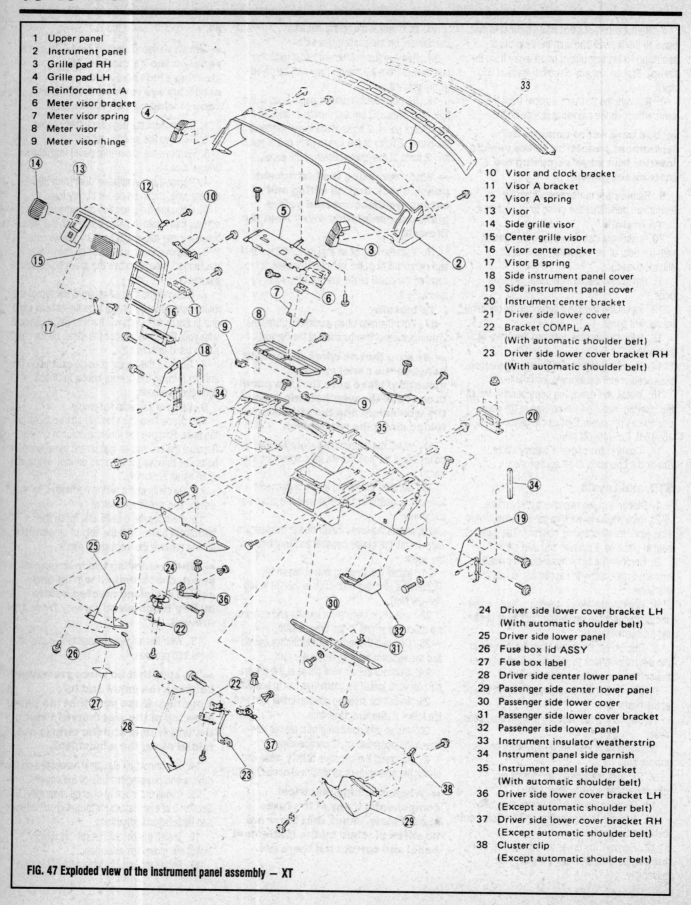

1 Upper panel
2 Instrument panel
3 Grille pad RH
4 Grille pad LH
5 Reinforcement A
6 Meter visor bracket
7 Meter visor spring
8 Meter visor
9 Meter visor hinge

10 Visor and clock bracket
11 Visor A bracket
12 Visor A spring
13 Visor
14 Side grille visor
15 Center grille visor
16 Visor center pocket
17 Visor B spring
18 Side instrument panel cover
19 Side instrument panel cover
20 Instrument center bracket
21 Driver side lower cover
22 Bracket COMPL A
(With automatic shoulder belt)
23 Driver side lower cover bracket RH
(With automatic shoulder belt)

24 Driver side lower cover bracket LH
(With automatic shoulder belt)
25 Driver side lower panel
26 Fuse box lid ASSY
27 Fuse box label
28 Driver side center lower panel
29 Passenger side center lower panel
30 Passenger side lower cover
31 Passenger side lower cover bracket
32 Passenger side lower panel
33 Instrument insulator weatherstrip
34 Instrument panel side garnish
35 Instrument panel side bracket
(With automatic shoulder belt)
36 Driver side lower cover bracket LH
(Except automatic shoulder belt)
37 Driver side lower cover bracket RH
(Except automatic shoulder belt)
38 Cluster clip
(Except automatic shoulder belt)

FIG. 47 Exploded view of the instrument panel assembly — XT

18. Install the ventilation tube on the drivers side. Install the fuse box in position and install the lower drivers side trim panel.

19. Install the passengers side lower trim panel. Install the radio and any other components removed.

20. Check the operation of all control levers and cables.

21. Connect the negative battery cable and check the operation of all electrical accessories.

➡ **When checking electrical components, if any of the fuses should blow, check that there are no wires pinched by the instrument panel and correct it if there are.**

Legacy

⁂ CAUTION

Properly disarm the air bag on vehicles equipped with the SRS system. Failure to do so can cause serious injury. The procedure can be found in Section 6 of this manual under the heading "Supplemental Restraint System".

---

1. Properly disarm the air bag system. Disconnect the negative battery cable.

2. Remove the center console retaining screws and remove the center console assembly.

3. Remove the instrument panel retaining bolt covers by prying them from the panel.

4. Remove the lower part of the front A pillar trim. Remove the instrument panel under covers from the drivers and passengers sides.

5. Remove the hood release cable from the hood release lever.

6. Disconnect the wiring harness connectors under the instrument panel.

7. Remove the instrument cluster assembly. Remove the glove box assembly

8. Disconnect the ventilation control cables and electrical connectors at the heater unit. Disconnect the vacuum line at the blower housing.

9. Disconnect the radio antenna feeder wire. Disconnect the main harness connector at the fuse box.

10. Remove the lower steering column covers. Remove the steering column retaining bolts and allow the column to hang down.

11. Remove the instrument panel retaining bolts.

➡ **When removing the instrument panel, check that all wiring and cables are disconnected before pulling it completely away from the firewall.**

12. With the help of an assistant, lift and remove the instrument panel from the vehicle.

To install:

13. With the help of an assistant, install the instrument panel in position in the vehicle.

➡ **Be sure that no wires are caught between the panel and its mounting. Make sure that the panel is on top of the weatherstrip along the windshield and the strip is not folded along the windshield.**

14. Install the panel retaining bolts. Install the retaining bolt covers.

15. Raise the steering column into position. Install the steering column covers.

16. Connect all electrical connectors under the instrument panel. Connect the ventilation control cables and electrical leads.

17. Install the instrument cluster assembly. Install the glove box assembly.

18. Install the center console assembly.

19. Install and connect any remaining components. Install the undercovers.

20. Check the operation of all control cables and switches.

21. Connect the negative battery cable and check the operation of all electrical accessories.

➡ **When checking electrical components, if any of the fuses should blow, check that there are no wires pinched by the instrument panel and correct it if there are.**

SVX

⁂ CAUTION

Properly disarm the air bag on vehicles equipped with the SRS system. Failure to do so can cause serious injury. The procedure can be found in Section 6 of this manual under the heading "Supplemental Restraint System".

---

1. Properly disarm the air bag system. Disconnect the negative battery cable.

2. Remove the center console assembly retaining screws and remove the center console.

3. Remove the front A pillar upper trim pieces.

4. Remove the radio grounding wire, which is screwed to the floor just behind the shifter assembly.

5. Remove the power mirror switch and remove the bolt located behind it.

6. Remove the lower drivers side instrument panel cover by removing the 6 clips and disconnecting the 3 connectors.

7. Remove the instrument cluster lower cover by removing the retaining bolts.

8. Disconnect the air bag assembly connector (YELLOW coated wires) at the bottom of the steering column.

9. Remove the lower steering column cover. Remove the steering column-to-bracket bolts and lower the column.

10. Remove the small bolt caps from both ends of the instrument panel and remove the bolts.

11. Remove the 2 sets of instrument panel switches by pulling them from their mountings. Disconnect the electrical leads from the switches.

12. Remove the instrument cluster visor assembly and remove the instrument cluster.

13. Remove the 4 bolts from behind where the instrument cluster was. Remove the 5 bolts from inside the glove box.

14. Disconnect the main harness connectors under the drivers side (6 connectors). Disconnect the 2 radio antenna leads.

➡ **When removing the instrument panel, check that all wiring and cables are disconnected before pulling it completely away from the firewall.**

15. With the help of an assistant, remove the instrument panel by pulling it sharply forward, this will release the retaining pins from the top of the panel. Remove the panel from the vehicle.

To install:

16. With the help of an assistant, install the panel into position in the vehicle. Align the pins at the top of the panel, with the grommets in the firewall and push the panel into position. Install the 4 screws in the instrument cluster opening and the 5 screws in the glove box opening.

➡ **Be sure that no wires are caught between the panel and its mounting. Make sure that the panel is on top of the weatherstrip along the windshield and the strip is not folded along the windshield.**

17. Connect the main wiring harness connectors. Connect the antenna leads.

18. Install the instrument cluster assembly. Install the instrument panel switch assemblies.

19. Install the retaining bolts at the ends of the instrument panel and install the bolt caps.

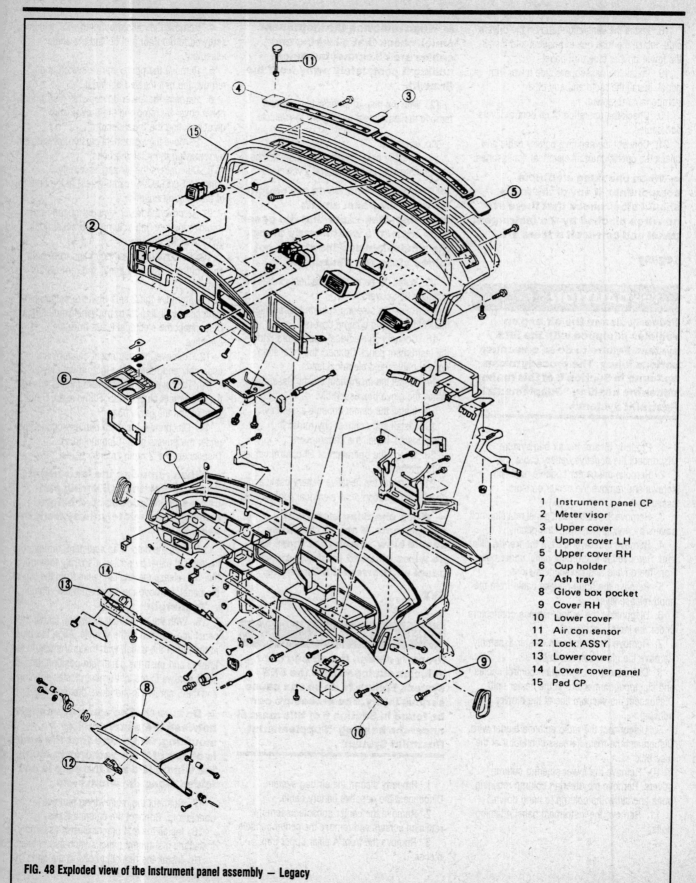

1 Instrument panel CP
2 Meter visor
3 Upper cover
4 Upper cover LH
5 Upper cover RH
6 Cup holder
7 Ash tray
8 Glove box pocket
9 Cover RH
10 Lower cover
11 Air con sensor
12 Lock ASSY
13 Lower cover
14 Lower cover panel
15 Pad CP

FIG. 48 Exploded view of the instrument panel assembly — Legacy

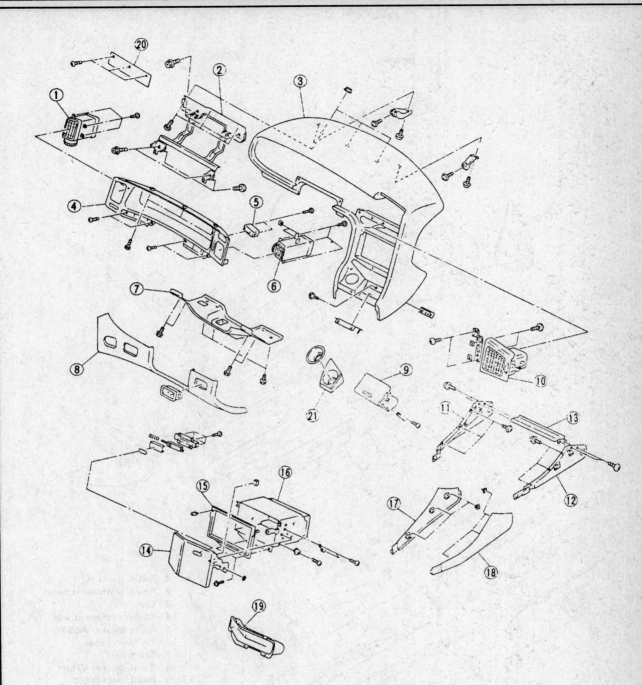

1	Grille vent (D SD L)	12	Base (P)
2	Bracket console compl.	13	Base (CTR)
3	Pad & frame B	14	Cover audio
4	Visor	15	Panel radio
5	Clock	16	Audio holder
6	Grille vent (D CTR)	17	Console panel (LH)
7	Panel lower cover	18	Console panel (RH)
8	Cover lower	19	Cover audio lid
9	Ashtray ASSY	20	Cover column
10	Grille vent (P CTR)	21	Panel cigar lighter
11	Base (D)		

FIG. 49 Exploded view of the instrument panel accessories — SVX

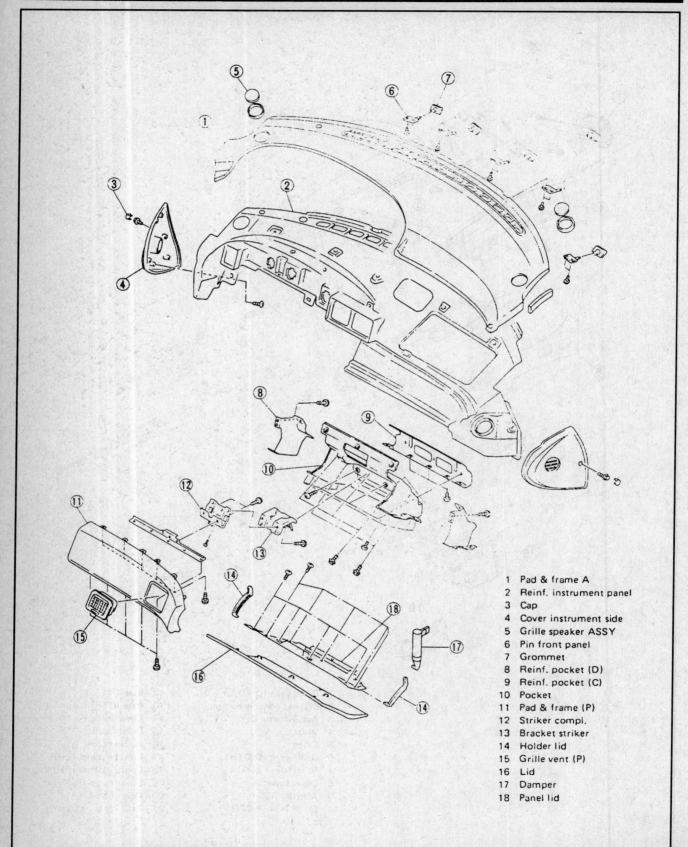

1 Pad & frame A
2 Reinf. instrument panel
3 Cap
4 Cover instrument side
5 Grille speaker ASSY
6 Pin front panel
7 Grommet
8 Reinf. pocket (D)
9 Reinf. pocket (C)
10 Pocket
11 Pad & frame (P)
12 Striker compl.
13 Bracket striker
14 Holder lid
15 Grille vent (P)
16 Lid
17 Damper
18 Panel lid

FIG. 50 Exploded view of the instrument panel assembly — SVX

20. Raise the steering column into position and install the retaining bolts.

21. Connect the air bag connectors. Install the instrument cluster lower cover.

22. Screw down the radio ground wire. Install the center console assembly. Install the lower instrument panel trim.

23. Install the bolt behind power mirror switch and install the switch.

24. Install any remaining components and trim pieces.

25. Check the operation of all cables and switches.

26. Connect the negative battery cable and check the operation of all electrical accessories.

➡ **When checking electrical components, if any of the fuses should blow, check that there are no wires pinched by the instrument panel and correct it if there are.**

Center Console

REMOVAL & INSTALLATION

◆ SEE FIGS. 51–55

❊ CAUTION

Properly disarm the air bag on vehicles equipped with the SRS system. Failure to do so can cause serious injury. The procedure can be found in Section 6 of this manual under the heading "Supplemental Restraint System".

1. Discharge the air bag system, on models equipped. Disconnect the negative battery cable.

2. On Loyale and STD. Remove the tray from under the parking brake lever by prying it up.

3. Pull the parking brake up and remove the shifter knob (with manual transaxle).

4. Remove the console cover on XT models and disconnect the cigarette lighter. Remove the ventilation control lever knobs. On XT models, remove the front seats.

5. On the SVX remove the side console panels by pulling them off (they are held in place by clips).

6. Remove any remaining console trays and covers.

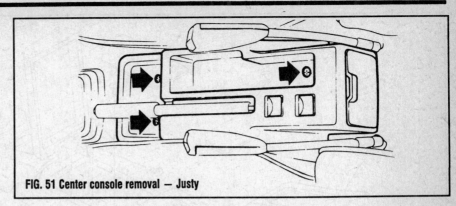

FIG. 51 Center console removal — Justy

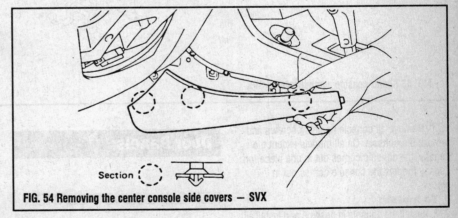

FIG. 52 Removing the center console — XT

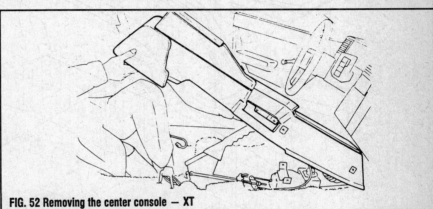

Section

FIG. 54 Removing the center console side covers — SVX

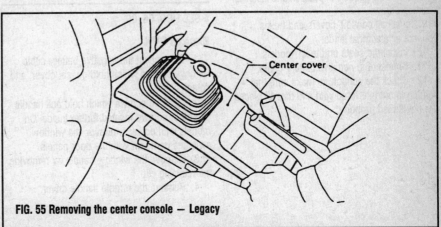

Center cover

FIG. 55 Removing the center console — Legacy

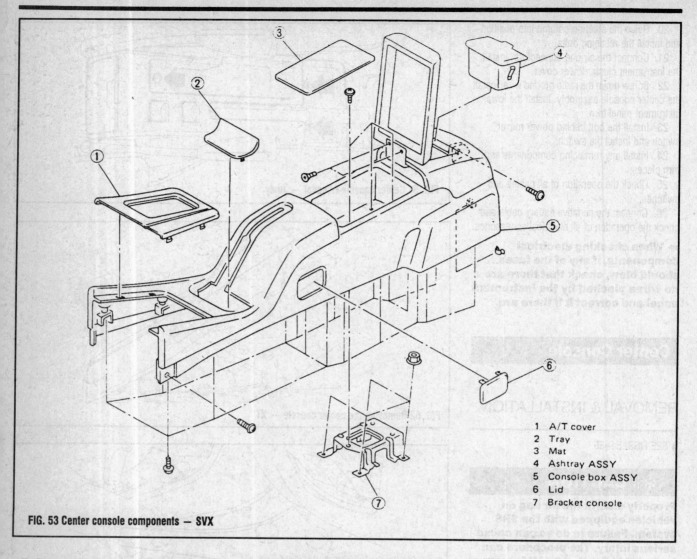

1	A/T cover
2	Tray
3	Mat
4	Ashtray ASSY
5	Console box ASSY
6	Lid
7	Bracket console

FIG. 53 Center console components — SVX

7. Remove all console retaining screws and remove the console. On all models except the Legacy, the console comes out in one piece, on Legacy models the console comes out in 2 pieces.

To Install:

8. Install the console in position and install all retaining screws.

9. Install all console covers and boxes. Connect all electrical leads.

10. Install the seats on the XT models.

11. Connect the negative battery cable.

12. Check the console to make sure that shifting is not interfered with and that all pieces are positioned properly.

Door Panels

REMOVAL & INSTALLATION

▶ SEE FIGS. 56–60

Except SVX

1. Disconnect the negative battery cable. Remove screws which hold gusset cover, and detach cover.

2. Remove screws which hold pull handle and other screws located further inside. On models with power windows, the window switches come off with the door panels.

3. Remove the window handle by removing the retaining clip.

4. Remove the remote handle cover.

5. Remove the clip attached to trim panel using a trim clip puller. Then remove the trim panel. The plastic sealing cover can be removed from the door at this time, if needed.

➡ **When removing the trim panel, use care not to damage the panel or to tear it with the tools.**

6. Install the trim panel in the reverse order of removal. Be sure that the panel is fully seated at all clips.

SVX

1. Disconnect the negative battery cable.

2. Remove the inner door handle cap.

3. Remove the screws that retain the trim panel to the door. You will have to lift the door pocket mat to get at 2 of the screws.

4. Carefully pry around the perimeter of the door and loosen the panel clips from the door.

5. As the door panel is coming off, disconnect the electrical leads from the panel.

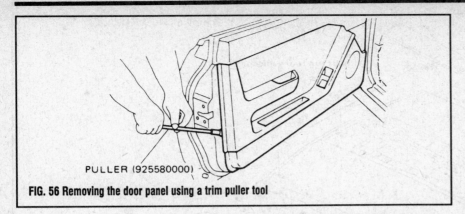

FIG. 56 Removing the door panel using a trim puller tool

PULLER (925580000)

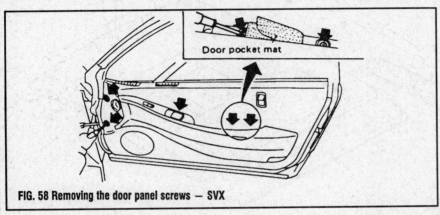

Door pocket mat

FIG. 58 Removing the door panel screws — SVX

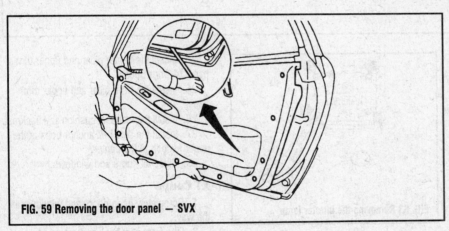

FIG. 59 Removing the door panel — SVX

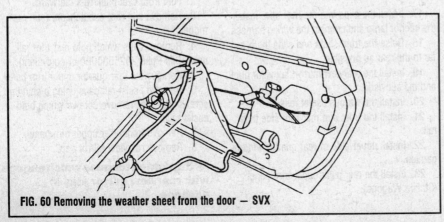

FIG. 60 Removing the weather sheet from the door — SVX

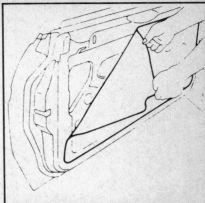

FIG. 57 Removing the weather sheet from the door assembly

➡ **When removing the trim panel, use care not to damage the panel or to tear it with the tools.**

  6. Remove the panel from the door.

  7. Install the panel in the reverse order of the removal procedure.

  8. Be sure to check the operation of all controls after installing the panel.

Headliner

REMOVAL & INSTALLATION

◆ SEE FIGS. 61–66

Except XT Coupe

  1. Completely open front and rear doors and lower windows all the way.

  2. Remove the seat belt anchor bolts at the upper section of the center pillar.

  3. Remove the rear seat cushion and backrest.

  4. Remove the front pillar and upper trim panel.

  5. Remove the center pillar and upper trim panel (4-Door Sedan).

  6. Remove the rear pillar upper trim panel (Station Wagons).

  7. Remove upper side of rear quarter window garnish.

  8. Remove roof side rear trim rail.

  9. Remove front roof side trim rail.

  10. Remove various assist rails.

  11. Remove sunvisor, sunvisor hook and rearview mirror.

  12. Move front seats all the way forward and fully fold left and right backrests.

  13. Remove interior lamp and disconnect harness.

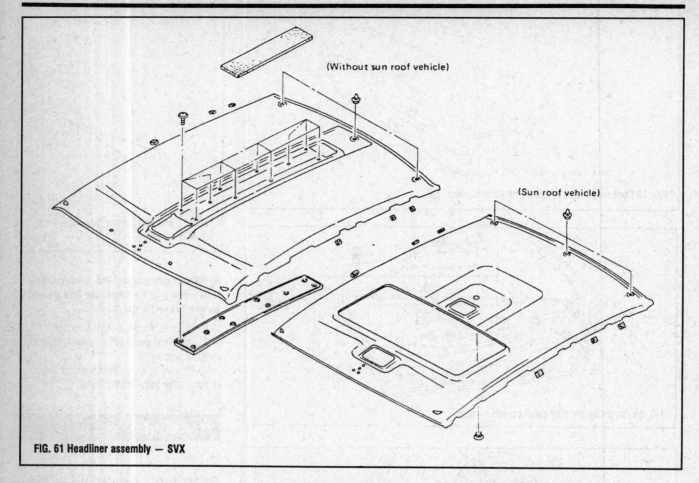

FIG. 61 Headliner assembly — SVX

(Without sun roof vehicle)

(Sun roof vehicle)

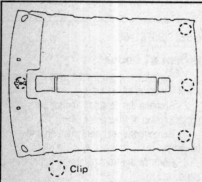

Clip

FIG. 62 Removing the headliner, it is retained by these clips

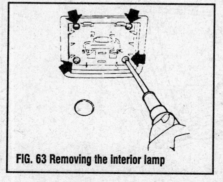

FIG. 63 Removing the interior lamp

14. Remove clips that hold the roof trim, being careful not to scratch the trim. It is advisable to position Clip Puller (925580000 or equivalent) on roof trim's surface so that roof trim will not be scratched.

15. Remove the roof trim, being careful not to break the edges during removal.

To Install:

16. Position the roof trim in the vehicle being careful not to break the edges.

17. Install the clips into the roof trim. Install the interior lamp and connect the wiring harness.

18. Raise the front seats and slide them as far to the rear as possible.

19. Install the rearview mirror, sunvisor hook and the sunvisor.

20. Install the various assist rails.

21. Install the front and rear roof side trim rail.

22. Install upper side of rear quarter window garnish.

23. Install the rear pillar upper trim panel (Station Wagons).

24. Install the center pillar and upper trim panel (4-Door Sedan).

25. Install the front pillar and upper trim panel.

26. Install the rear seat cushion and backrest.

27. Install the seat belt anchor bolts at the upper section of the center.

28. Close all doors and windows.

XT Coupe

1. Completely open doors and windows all the way.

2. Fold front seat back rest rearward.

3. Remove sun roof escutcheon, (sun roof models).

4. Remove clips which hold rear trim rail, using Clip Puller (925580000 or equivalent).

5. Remove the rear quarter upper trim panel.

6. Remove assist rail caps using a standard screwdriver, and remove screws which hold assist rails.

7. Remove front pillar upper trim panel.

8. Remove rearview mirror cap.

➡ **Straighten tongues which engage with rearview mirror stay in advance.**

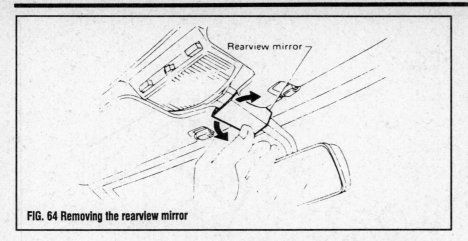

FIG. 64 Removing the rearview mirror

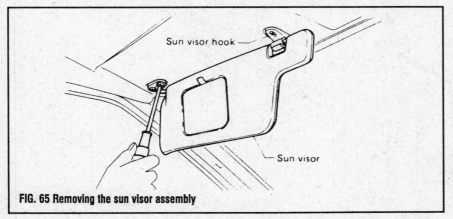

FIG. 65 Removing the sun visor assembly

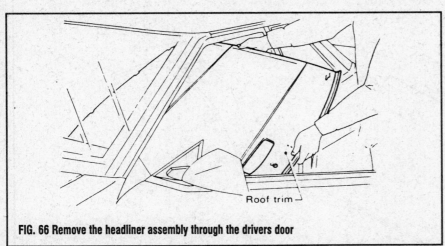

FIG. 66 Remove the headliner assembly through the drivers door

9. Remove spot and room lamp, and disconnect the harness connector.

10. Remove rearview mirror.

11. Turn roof clip on passengers side counterclockwise and remove.

12. Remove coat hanger on drivers side.

13. Remove sun visor and hook.

14. Remove clips which hold trim to roof, using Clip Puller (925580000 or equivalent).

15. Remove roof trim from car body, being careful not to fold edge section of roof trim.

To Install:

16. Work the panel into the vehicle through the door.

17. Install Remove roof trim to the car body, being careful not to fold edge section of roof trim.

18. Install the clips which hold trim to roof.

19. Install hook and sun visor .

20. Install coat hanger on drivers side.

21. Install roof clip on passengers side and turn clockwise to install.

22. Install rearview mirror.

23. Install spot and room lamp, and connect the harness connector.

24. Install rearview mirror cap.

25. Install front pillar upper trim panel.

26. Install assist rail caps and screws which hold assist rails.

27. Install the rear quarter upper trim panel.

28. Install clips which hold rear trim rail.

29. Install sun roof escutcheon, (sun roof models).

30. Raise the front seats and close the doors and windows.

Interior Trim

REMOVAL & INSTALLATION

⬧ SEE FIGS. 67–73

Removal of the interior trim panels is very simple if the time is taken to do it carefully. To remove any of the panels all that is needed is a screwdriver and a trim removal tool.

Select the panel that you are going to remove and located all of the retaining screws. Many of the screws are hidden behind plastic covers, so keep this in mind when looking. Once all of the screws are located, remove any interfering pieces, such as the removable panels in the XT or the Justy models. After removing the mounting screws, carefully pry the panel away from the body, releasing any retaining clips as needed. Be careful not to scratch or gouge the panels.

When installing the panels make sure that they are aligned properly on all sides before tightening the screws. When tightening the screws use an alternating pattern to tighten the panel evenly and prevent warpage.

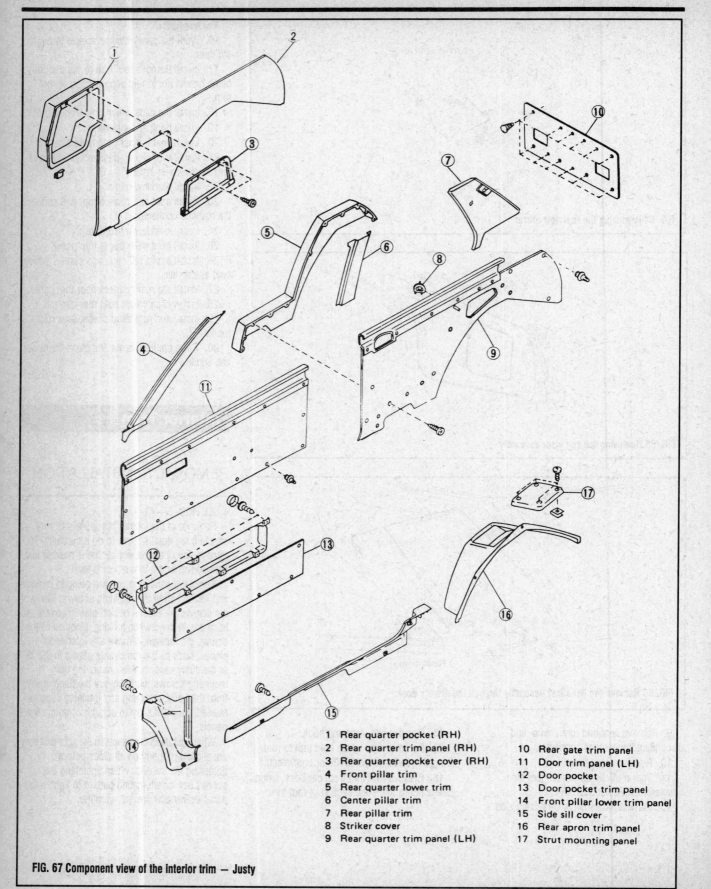

FIG. 67 Component view of the interior trim — Justy

1 Rear quarter pocket (RH)
2 Rear quarter trim panel (RH)
3 Rear quarter pocket cover (RH)
4 Front pillar trim
5 Rear quarter lower trim
6 Center pillar trim
7 Rear pillar trim
8 Striker cover
9 Rear quarter trim panel (LH)
10 Rear gate trim panel
11 Door trim panel (LH)
12 Door pocket
13 Door pocket trim panel
14 Front pillar lower trim panel
15 Side sill cover
16 Rear apron trim panel
17 Strut mounting panel

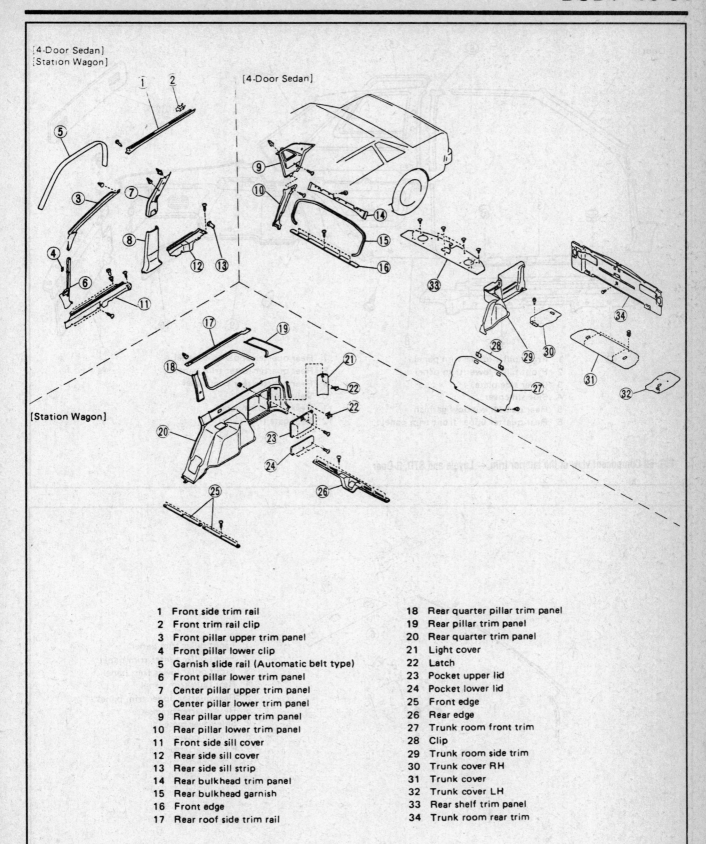

[4-Door Sedan]
[Station Wagon]

[4-Door Sedan]

[Station Wagon]

1	Front side trim rail	18	Rear quarter pillar trim panel
2	Front trim rail clip	19	Rear pillar trim panel
3	Front pillar upper trim panel	20	Rear quarter trim panel
4	Front pillar lower clip	21	Light cover
5	Garnish slide rail (Automatic belt type)	22	Latch
6	Front pillar lower trim panel	23	Pocket upper lid
7	Center pillar upper trim panel	24	Pocket lower lid
8	Center pillar lower trim panel	25	Front edge
9	Rear pillar upper trim panel	26	Rear edge
10	Rear pillar lower trim panel	27	Trunk room front trim
11	Front side sill cover	28	Clip
12	Rear side sill cover	29	Trunk room side trim
13	Rear side sill strip	30	Trunk cover RH
14	Rear bulkhead trim panel	31	Trunk cover
15	Rear bulkhead garnish	32	Trunk cover LH
16	Front edge	33	Rear shelf trim panel
17	Rear roof side trim rail	34	Trunk room rear trim

FIG. 68 Component view of the interior trim — Loyale and STD. Sedan and Wagon

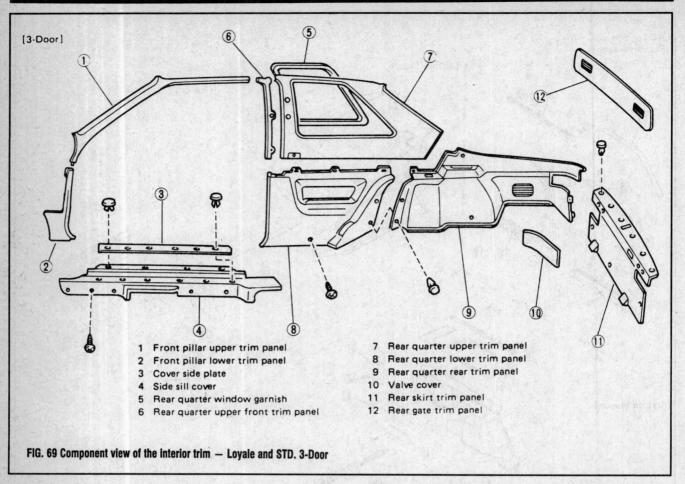

[3-Door]

1 Front pillar upper trim panel
2 Front pillar lower trim panel
3 Cover side plate
4 Side sill cover
5 Rear quarter window garnish
6 Rear quarter upper front trim panel
7 Rear quarter upper trim panel
8 Rear quarter lower trim panel
9 Rear quarter rear trim panel
10 Valve cover
11 Rear skirt trim panel
12 Rear gate trim panel

FIG. 69 Component view of the interior trim — Loyale and STD. 3-Door

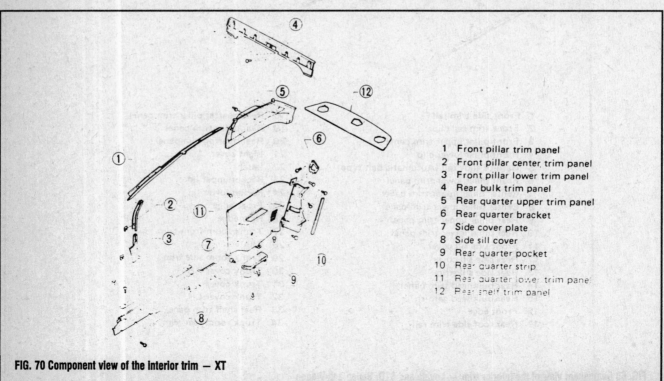

1 Front pillar trim panel
2 Front pillar center trim panel
3 Front pillar lower trim panel
4 Rear bulk trim panel
5 Rear quarter upper trim panel
6 Rear quarter bracket
7 Side cover plate
8 Side sill cover
9 Rear quarter pocket
10 Rear quarter strip
11 Rear quarter lower trim panel
12 Rear shelf trim panel

FIG. 70 Component view of the interior trim — XT

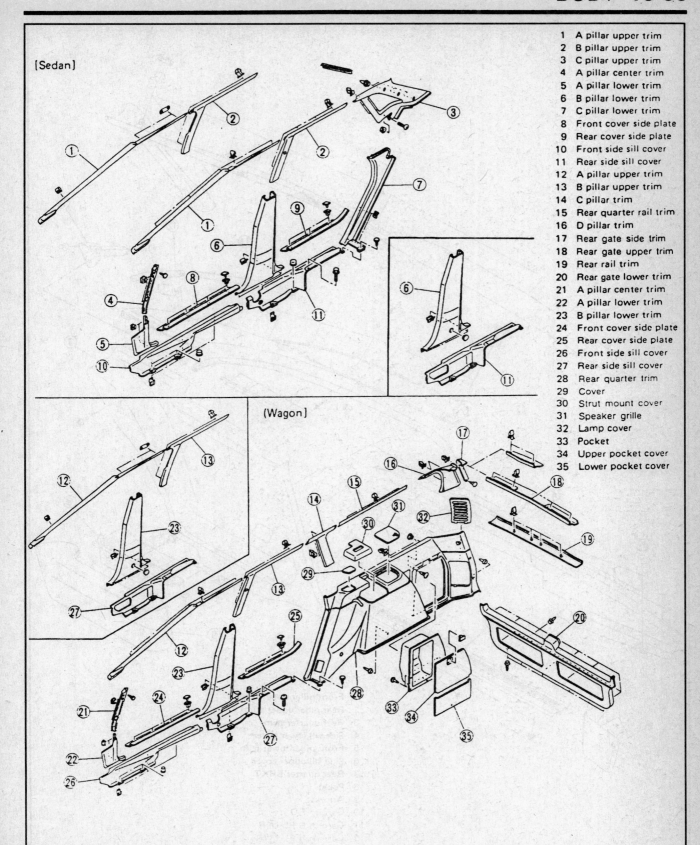

1   A pillar upper trim
2   B pillar upper trim
3   C pillar upper trim
4   A pillar center trim
5   A pillar lower trim
6   B pillar lower trim
7   C pillar lower trim
8   Front cover side plate
9   Rear cover side plate
10 Front side sill cover
11 Rear side sill cover
12 A pillar upper trim
13 B pillar upper trim
14 C pillar trim
15 Rear quarter rail trim
16 D pillar trim
17 Rear gate side trim
18 Rear gate upper trim
19 Rear rail trim
20 Rear gate lower trim
21 A pillar center trim
22 A pillar lower trim
23 B pillar lower trim
24 Front cover side plate
25 Rear cover side plate
26 Front side sill cover
27 Rear side sill cover
28 Rear quarter trim
29 Cover
30 Strut mount cover
31 Speaker grille
32 Lamp cover
33 Pocket
34 Upper pocket cover
35 Lower pocket cover

FIG. 71 Component view of the interior trim — Legacy

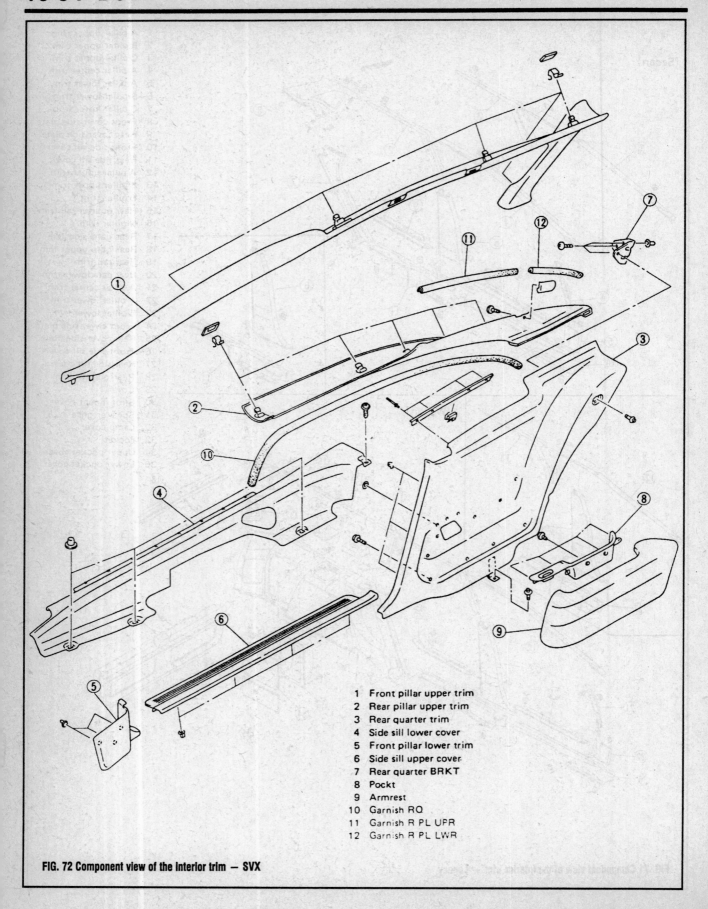

1 Front pillar upper trim
2 Rear pillar upper trim
3 Rear quarter trim
4 Side sill lower cover
5 Front pillar lower trim
6 Side sill upper cover
7 Rear quarter BRKT
8 Pockt
9 Armrest
10 Garnish RQ
11 Garnish R PL UPR
12 Garnish R PL LWR

FIG. 72 Component view of the interior trim — SVX

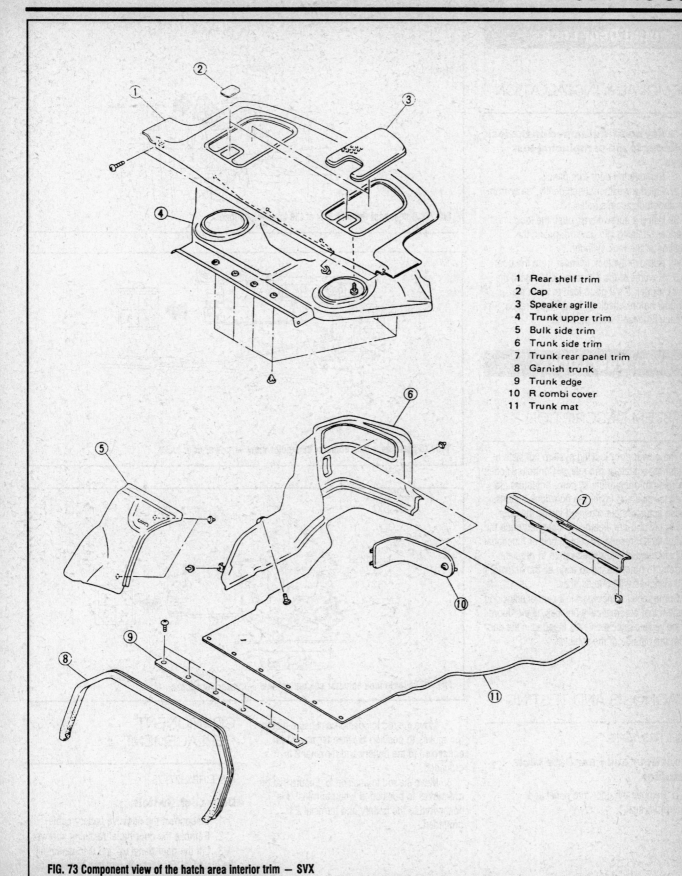

1 Rear shelf trim
2 Cap
3 Speaker agrille
4 Trunk upper trim
5 Bulk side trim
6 Trunk side trim
7 Trunk rear panel trim
8 Garnish trunk
9 Trunk edge
10 R combi cover
11 Trunk mat

FIG. 73 Component view of the hatch area interior trim — SVX

Manual Door Locks

REMOVAL & INSTALLATION

➡ **A key code is stamped on the lock cylinder to aid in replacing lost keys.**

1. Remove the door trim panel.

2. Pull the weather sheet, gently, away from the door lock access holes.

3. Using a screwdriver, push the lock cylinder retaining clip upward, noting the position of the lock cylinder.

4. Remove the lock cylinder from the door.

5. Reverse steps 1 through 4 to install the lock cylinder. It's a good idea to open the window before checking the lock operation, just in case it doesn't work properly.

Power Door Locks

SYSTEM DESCRIPTION

The power door locking system consists of switches, actuators and relays. Control switches are used to operate the system. Actuators are used to raise and lower the door lock buttons. These actuators are mounted inside the door assembly and are electrically operated once the switch is depressed. A control unit or functional relay is used to allow the system to regulate current, to function and to align all the actuators and switches with one another.

Some vehicles incorporate a central unlocking system that automatically unlocks all the doors of the vehicle once the key is inserted in the door from the outside of the vehicle.

DIAGNOSIS AND TESTING

◆ SEE FIGS. 75–76

Front Door and Rear Gate Lock Actuator

1. Remove the door trim panel and waterproof seal.

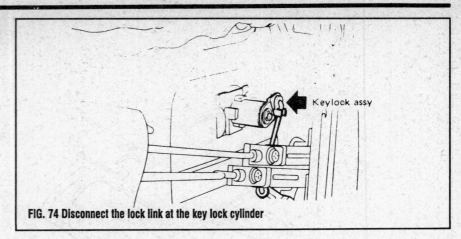

FIG. 74 Disconnect the lock link at the key lock cylinder

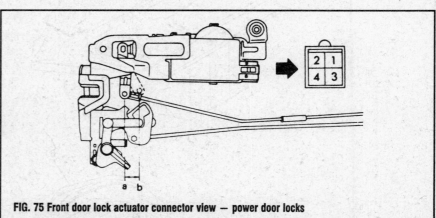

FIG. 75 Front door lock actuator connector view — power door locks

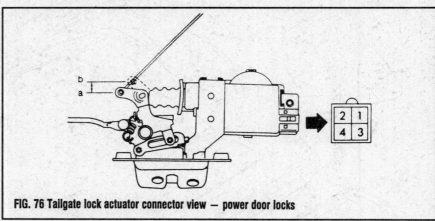

FIG. 76 Tailgate lock actuator connector view — power door locks

2. Move the rod to position **a**. Ensure that the rod moves to position **b** when terminal 4 is connected to the battery and terminal 2 is grounded.

3. Move the rod to position **b**. Ensure that the rod moves to position **a** when terminal 3 is connected to the battery and terminal 2 is grounded.

COMPONENT REPLACEMENT

◆ SEE FIGS. 77–78

Door Lock Switch

1. Disconnect the negative battery cable.

2. Remove the door panel retaining screws.

3. Lift the door panel up and disconnect all the electrical connections required to separate the door panel from the door.

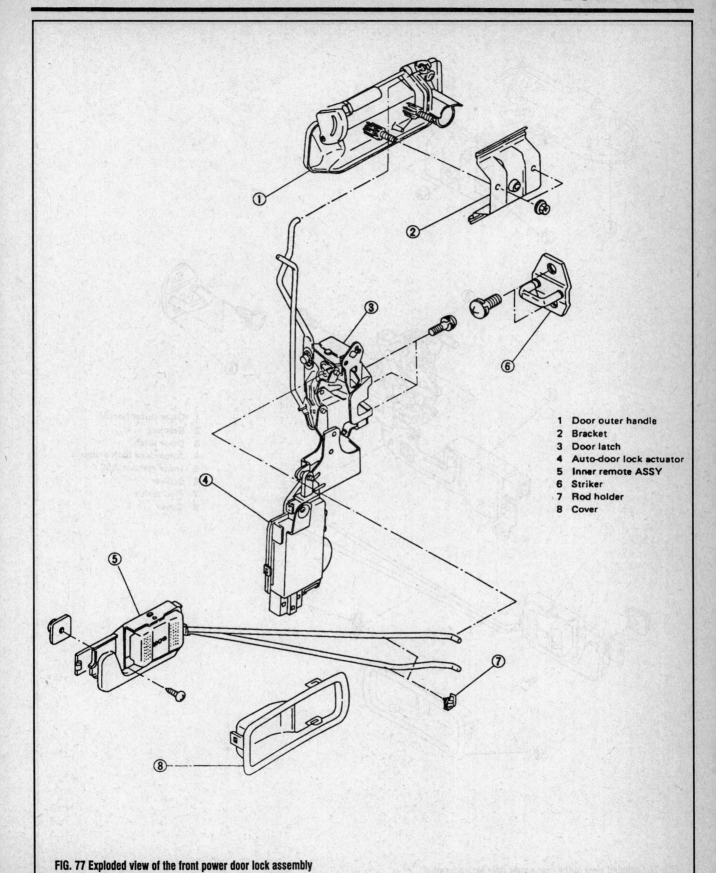

1 Door outer handle
2 Bracket
3 Door latch
4 Auto-door lock actuator
5 Inner remote ASSY
6 Striker
7 Rod holder
8 Cover

FIG. 77 Exploded view of the front power door lock assembly

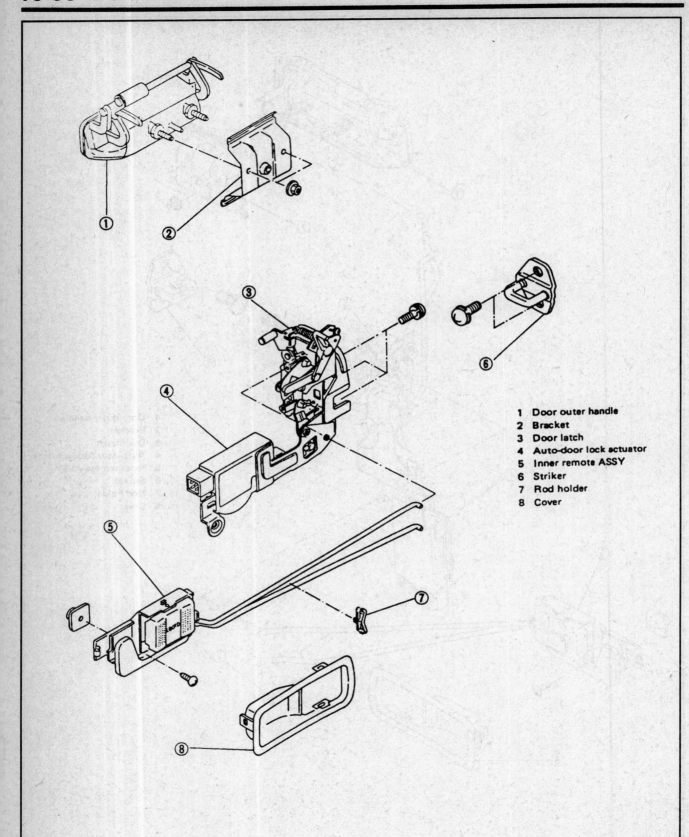

1 Door outer handle
2 Bracket
3 Door latch
4 Auto-door lock actuator
5 Inner remote ASSY
6 Striker
7 Rod holder
8 Cover

FIG. 78 Exploded view of the rear power door lock assembly

4. Remove the door panel from the vehicle. Remove the switch assembly from its mounting.

5. Installation is the reverse of the removal procedure.

Door Lock Actuator

1. Disconnect the negative battery cable.
2. Remove the door panel.
3. Disconnect the actuator electrical connector. Disconnect the required linkage rods.
4. Remove the actuator assembly retaining screws. Remove the actuator assembly from the vehicle.
5. Installation is the reverse of the removal procedure.

Door Glass and Manual Window Regulator

REMOVAL & INSTALLATION

⮞ SEE FIGS. 79–86
1. Remove the trim panel.
2. Remove the door handle assembly.
3. Remove the door panel sealing cover.

4. Remove the rear view mirror from the door.
5. Remove the outer weatherstrip.
6. Remove the inner stabilizer.
7. Loosen the upper stopper bolt from the front of door and glass stoppers, and move the door glass. Then, remove the upper stopper from the rear of the door. Remove the two bolts which hold the glass holder to the regulator slider.

⮞ **When removing bolts on the regulator slider, move the glass to a position where the bolts can be seen through the service hole. Mark the position and tightening**

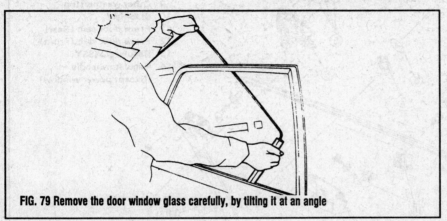

FIG. 79 Remove the door window glass carefully, by tilting it at an angle

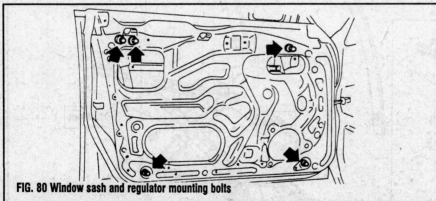

FIG. 80 Window sash and regulator mounting bolts

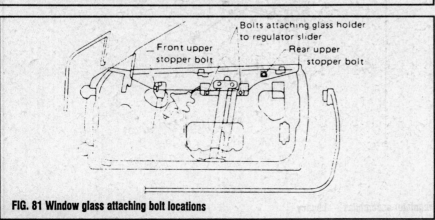

FIG. 81 Window glass attaching bolt locations

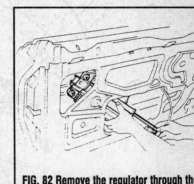

FIG. 82 Remove the regulator through the opening in the door

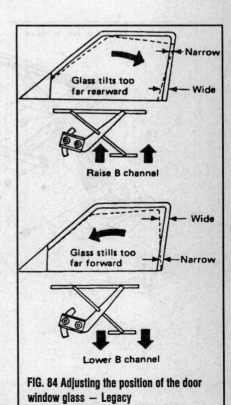

FIG. 84 Adjusting the position of the door window glass — Legacy

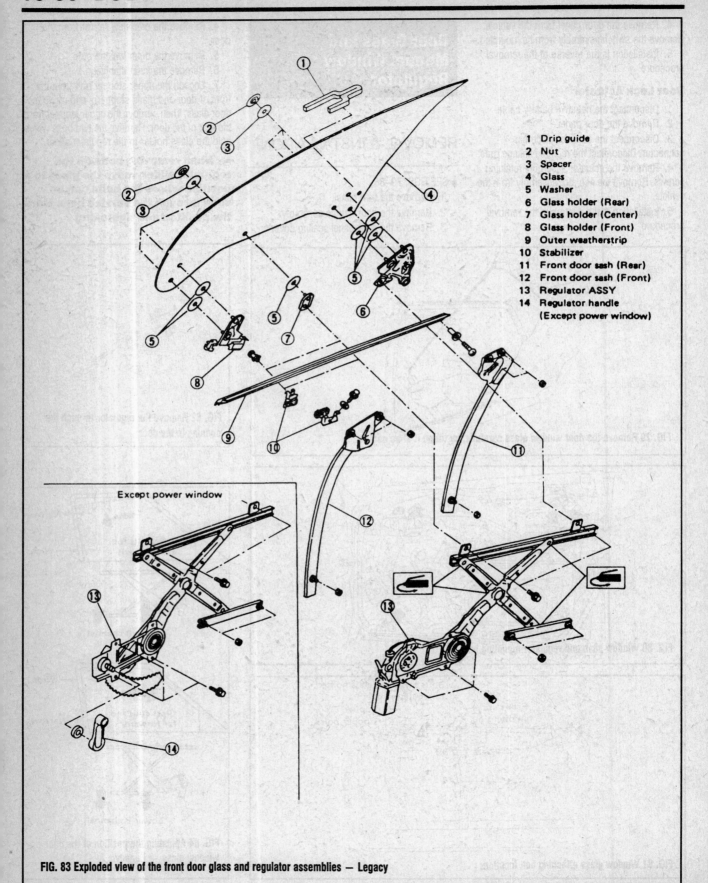

1 Drip guide
2 Nut
3 Spacer
4 Glass
5 Washer
6 Glass holder (Rear)
7 Glass holder (Center)
8 Glass holder (Front)
9 Outer weatherstrip
10 Stabilizer
11 Front door sash (Rear)
12 Front door sash (Front)
13 Regulator ASSY
14 Regulator handle
    (Except power window)

Except power window

FIG. 83 Exploded view of the front door glass and regulator assemblies — Legacy

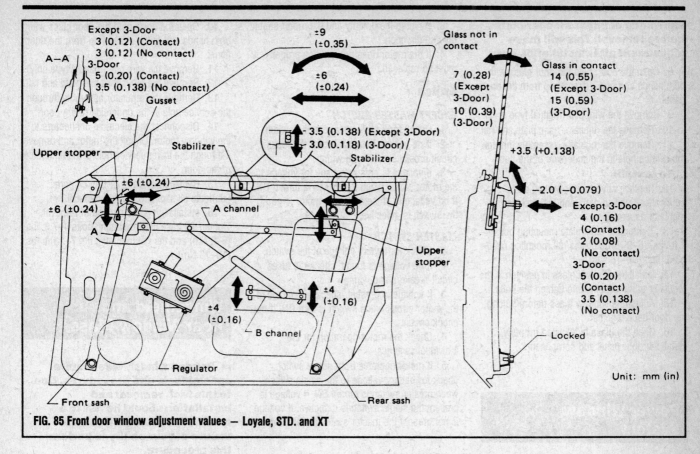

FIG. 85 Front door window adjustment values — Loyale, STD. and XT

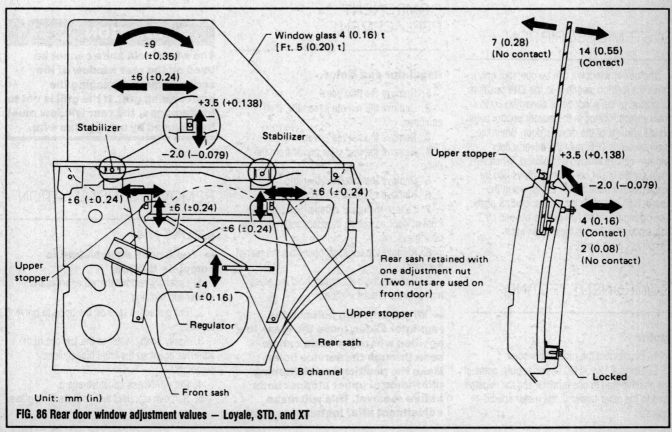

FIG. 86 Rear door window adjustment values — Loyale, STD. and XT

allowance of upper stopper bolts before removal. This will make adjustment after installation easy.

8. Open the door, hold the door glass with both hands and pull it straight up from the door panel.

9. Remove the wire clip (manual type only).

10. Remove the regulator base plate and rail.

11. Remove the regulator assembly through the service hole in the underside of the door.

To Install:

12. Replace any worn or broken parts. Lubricate all sliding parts and reinstall the regulator assembly.

13. Tighten the base plate mounting bolts 4–7 ft. lbs. (5–9 Nm) and the rail mounting nut 7–13 ft. lbs. (10–18 Nm).

14. Install the window glass in position in the regulator guide channel and tighten the bolts.

15. Adjust the window glass before putting the door back together.

16. Once the glass is adjusted properly, install the door panel and components.

Power Window System

SYSTEM DESCRIPTION

The power windows can be operated only when the ignition switch is in the **ON** position. Operation of the windows is controlled by the main switch located in the master control panel, on the armrest of the driver's door. When the main switch is OFF, only the driver's door window can be opened and closed. When the main switch is ON, all door windows can be opened and closed by the driver, using the appropriate switch in the master control panel. The passenger windows can be opened by depressing the switch located on each passenger door panel.

COMPONENT TESTING

Motor

1. Disconnect the motor connector.

2. Using a 12 volt DC power supply, connect the positive lead to one terminal and the negative lead to the other terminal; the motor should operate.

3. Reverse the polarity and the motor should reverse direction.

4. If the motor does not function properly, it must be replaced.

Switch

EXCEPT MASTER SWITCH

1. Check for battery voltage at the switch.

2. If no voltage is found, check the fuses, circuit breakers, relay and wiring.

3. If voltage is present, check for voltage to the motor circuit when the switch is turned ON. If no voltage is present and the motor is good, the switch is defective.

MASTER SWITCH

1. Check for battery voltage at the switch.

2. If no voltage is found, check the fuses, circuit breakers and wiring.

3. If voltage is present, check for voltage to the motor circuit when switch is turn ON. If not, check circuit.

4. Check the motor operation for the individual switches.

5. If motor operates from single switch, check for battery voltage to the single switch when master switch is turned ON. If voltage is present the single switch is defective, if voltage is not present the master switch is defective.

COMPONENT REPLACEMENT

Regulator and Motor

1. Remove the trim panel.

2. Remove the remote assembly, if so equipped.

3. Remove the sealing cover.

4. Remove the rear view mirror from the door.

5. Remove the outer weatherstrip.

6. Remove the inner stabilizer.

7. Loosen the upper stopper bolt from the front of door and glass stoppers and move the door glass.

8. Remove the upper stopper from the rear of the door.

9. Remove the bolts which hold the glass holder to the regulator slider.

➡ **When removing bolts on the regulator slider, move the glass to a position where the bolts can be seen through the service hole. Make the position and tightening allowance of upper stopper bolts before removal. This will make adjustment after installation easy.**

10. Open the door, hold the door glass with both hands and pull it straight up from the door panel.

11. Remove the wire clip (manual type only).

12. Remove the regulator base plate and rail.

13. Remove the regulator assembly through the service hole in the underside of the door.

14. Disconnect the electrical connectors to the window motor. Unbolt the motor and remove it through the lower service hole in the underside of the door.

15. Replace any worn or broken parts. Lubricate all sliding parts and reinstall.

16. Installation is the reverse of removal. Tighten the base plate mounting bolts 4–7 ft. lbs. (5–9 Nm) and the rail mounting nut 7–13 ft. lbs. (10–18 Nm).

Windshield and Rear Window Glass

➡ **Bonded windshields require special tools and procedures. Due to this fact, removal and installation should be left to a qualified technician if you are unsure of your ability to perform this procedure.**

❄ CAUTION

The windshield knife cannot be used on the rear window of the sedan without damaging the surrounding grill. If the grill is not to be damaged, the rear window must be removed by using piano wire.

REMOVAL & INSTALLATION

◆ SEE FIGS. 87–94

➡ **You'll need an assistant to complete this job.**

1. Carefully remove the wiper arms and windshield molding.

2. Put protective tape on the body to prevent damage.

3. Apply soapy water to the surface of the adhesive agent so the knife blade slides smoothly.

4. Cut off excess adhesive agent.

5. Remove stoppers and spacers from glass.

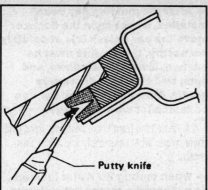

FIG. 87 Insert the windshield knife into the adhesive

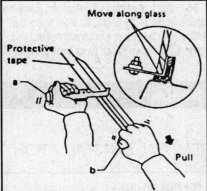

FIG. 88 Cut the adhesive by pulling the knife down with the extension handle

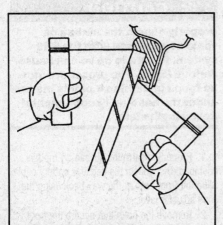

FIG. 89 The adhesive can also be cut by using a length of piano wire

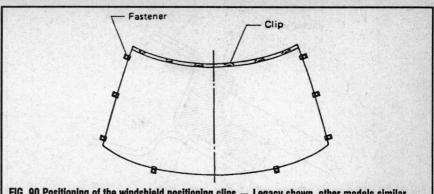

FIG. 90 Positioning of the windshield positioning clips — Legacy shown, other models similar

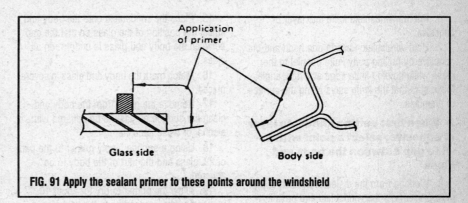

FIG. 91 Apply the sealant primer to these points around the windshield

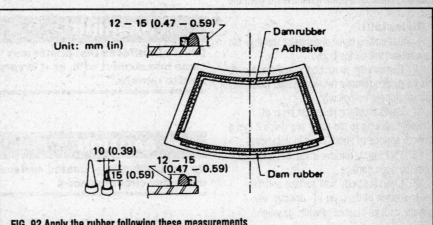

FIG. 92 Apply the rubber following these measurements

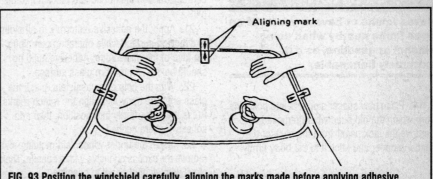

FIG. 93 Position the windshield carefully, aligning the marks made before applying adhesive

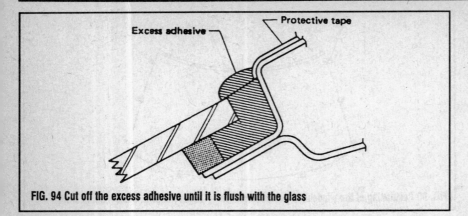

FIG. 94 Cut off the excess adhesive until it is flush with the glass

6. Put the windshield knife into layer of adhesive.

7. Hold windshield knife in one hand and cut adhesive by pulling putty knife parallel to the glass while holding knife edge at a right angle. Make sure that the knife stays along the surface of the glass.

➡ **When first putting knife into layer of adhesive, select a point with a wide gap between the body and glass.**

8. Working from the inside of the car, apply even pressure to the windshield and push it outward, while an assistant removes it from the car.

To Install:

9. After cutting layer of adhesive, remove the dam rubber left on the body.

10. Remove the remaining space stopper. At this time, also remove two-sided tape from spacer stopper completely.

11. Using a cutting knife, cut layer of adhesive sticking to the body and finish it into a smooth surface of about 2mm in thickness.

12. Thoroughly remove chips dirt and dust from the body surface.

13. Clean the body wall surface and the upper surface of the layer of adhesive with a solvent such as alcohol or white gasoline.

❊❊ CAUTION

Never smoke or have any form of an open flame nearby when using alcohol or gasoline, as it is extremely flammable.

14. Place new spacer stoppers into positions from which the old ones where removed. Remove the tack paper from the back of the spacer stopper and stick it to the body firmly.

15. Place the windshield onto the body and adjust the position of the glass so that the gap between the body and glass is uniform on all sides.

16. Match mark the body and glass in several places.

17. Remove the glass from the body and clean the surface of glass to be adhered with alcohol or white gasoline.

18. Using a sponge, apply primer to the part of the glass and the part of the body to be adhered.

19. Allow the primer to dry for about 10 minutes before proceeding to the next step.

❊❊ WARNING

Cover all surfaces that primer may come into contact with, as it is very hard to remove.

❊❊ CAUTION

Do not touch primer coated surface under any circumstances.

20. Cut the nozzle tip of the adhesive cartridge to a 45 degree angle, open the cartridge, attach the nozzle and place it into the gun.

21. Apply the adhesive uniformly to all sides of adhesion surface while operating gun along the face of the glass edge. Adhesive build up should be 12-15mm from glass surface.

22. With the help of an assistant, place the glass onto the body and align the match marks. Press the glass firmly into position, then add adhesive where needed.

23. Install the upper windshield molding and remove the excess adhesive with a spatula. Then clean with alcohol or white gasoline.

➡ **After the molding has been installed, do not open the doors or move the car unless it is absolutely necessary. If the doors must be opened, lower the windows, and open and close the doors very gently. After one hour the car can be tested for water leakage.**

24. Install the front lower molding, front pillar cover, wiper wheel assembly and wiper arm assembly.

➡ **When testing for water leakage, do not squirt a strong hose stream on the vehicle. If the vehicle must be moved, do so gently, sudden shock could cause the windshield to shift.**

25. After completing all operations, leave the vehicle alone for 24 hours. After 24 hours the vehicle may be driven, but should not be subjected to heavy shock for at least three days.

Seats

REMOVAL & INSTALLATION

◆ SEE FIGS. 95–102

Front Seat

❊❊ CAUTION

Properly disarm the air bag on vehicles equipped with the SRS system. Failure to do so can cause serious injury. The procedure can be found in Section 6 of this manual under the heading "Supplemental Restraint System".

1. Properly disarm the air bag on models equipped. Disconnect the negative battery cable. Slide the front seat all the way back using the slide adjuster lever.

2. Remove the bolts that secure the front section of the seat.

3. Move the seat all the way forward.

4. Remove the bolt cover on the rear end of the slide rail on the door side. On the XT Coupe, remove the seat anchor cover from the rear end of the slide rail on the tunnel side.

5. Remove the bolts that secure the rear section of the front seat.

6. Remove the front seat from the vehicle.

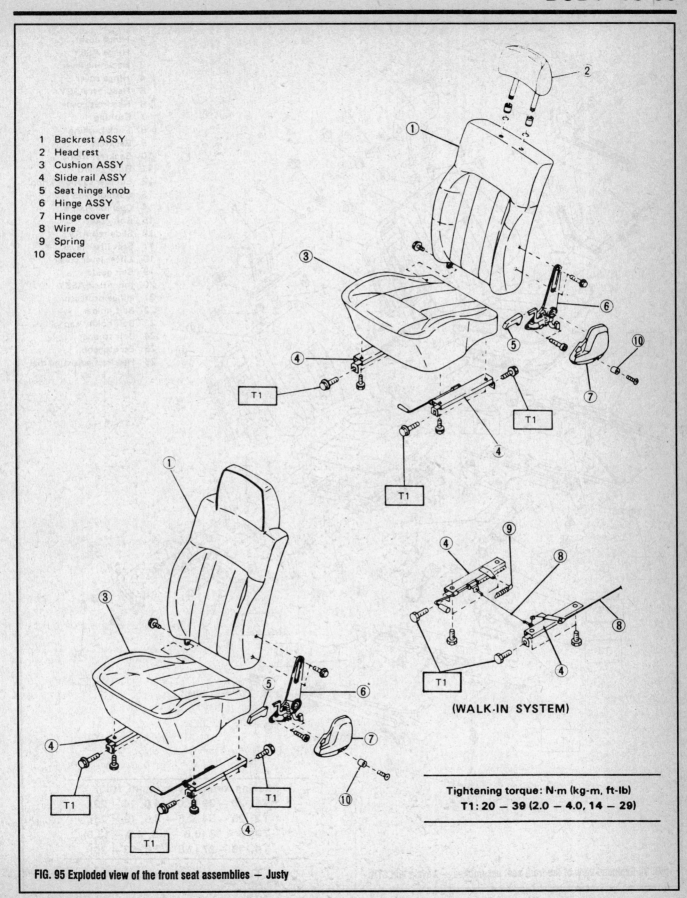

1   Backrest ASSY
2   Head rest
3   Cushion ASSY
4   Slide rail ASSY
5   Seat hinge knob
6   Hinge ASSY
7   Hinge cover
8   Wire
9   Spring
10 Spacer

(WALK-IN SYSTEM)

Tightening torque: N·m (kg-m, ft-lb)
T1: 20 — 39 (2.0 — 4.0, 14 — 29)

FIG. 95 Exploded view of the front seat assemblies — Justy

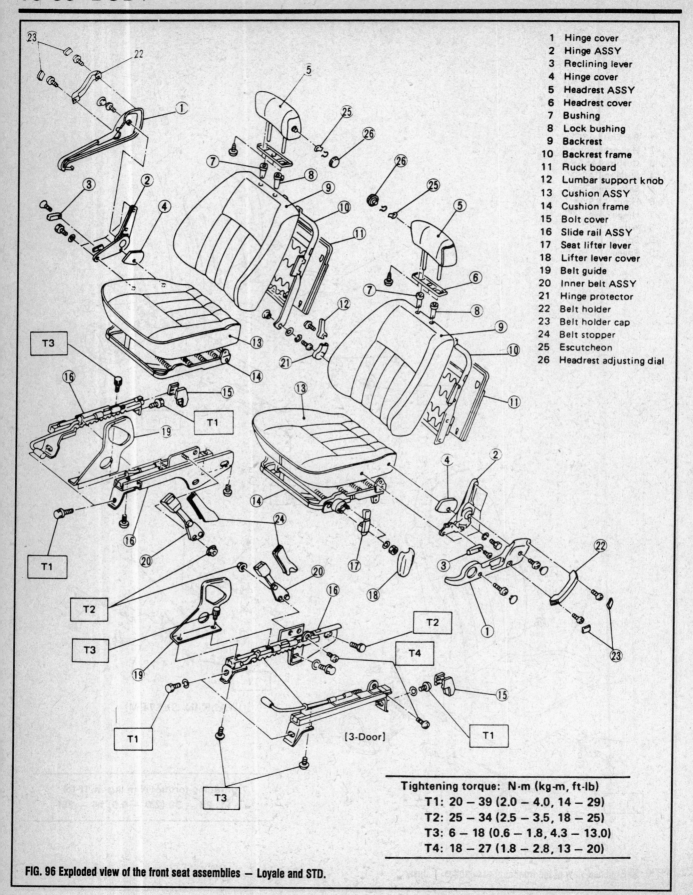

1	Hinge cover
2	Hinge ASSY
3	Reclining lever
4	Hinge cover
5	Headrest ASSY
6	Headrest cover
7	Bushing
8	Lock bushing
9	Backrest
10	Backrest frame
11	Ruck board
12	Lumbar support knob
13	Cushion ASSY
14	Cushion frame
15	Bolt cover
16	Slide rail ASSY
17	Seat lifter lever
18	Lifter lever cover
19	Belt guide
20	Inner belt ASSY
21	Hinge protector
22	Belt holder
23	Belt holder cap
24	Belt stopper
25	Escutcheon
26	Headrest adjusting dial

[3-Door]

Tightening torque: N·m (kg-m, ft-lb)
T1: 20 — 39 (2.0 — 4.0, 14 — 29)
T2: 25 — 34 (2.5 — 3.5, 18 — 25)
T3: 6 — 18 (0.6 — 1.8, 4.3 — 13.0)
T4: 18 — 27 (1.8 — 2.8, 13 — 20)

FIG. 96 Exploded view of the front seat assemblies — Loyale and STD.

Front Seat

1 Headrest
2 Backrest
3 Lumbar support knob
4 Reclining lever
5 Hinge cover
6 Slide rail ASSY
7 Bolt cover
8 Rail cap
9 Hinge ASSY
10 Cushion
11 Seat lifter lever
12 Lifter lever cover
13 Belt guide
14 Inner belt ASSY
15 Hinge protector
16 Belt holder
17 Belt holder cap
18 Belt stopper
19 Seat anchor cover

Rear Seat

1 Striker
2 Backrest
3 Hinge
4 Center bracket
5 Cushion

[Seat lifter equipped model]

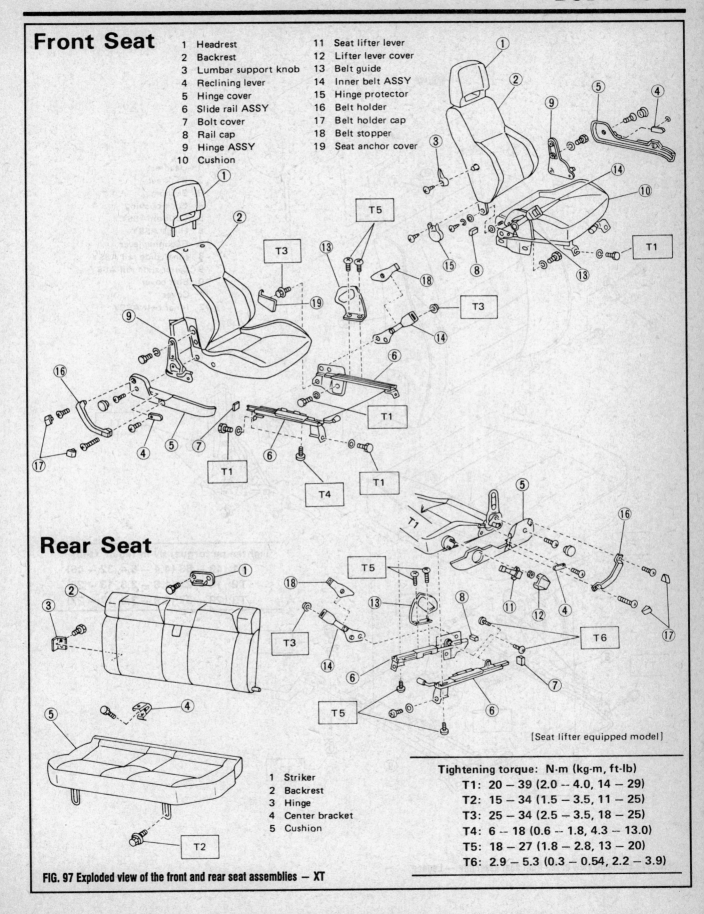

Tightening torque: N·m (kg-m, ft-lb)		
T1:	20 — 39	(2.0 -- 4.0, 14 — 29)
T2:	15 — 34	(1.5 — 3.5, 11 — 25)
T3:	25 — 34	(2.5 — 3.5, 18 — 25)
T4:	6 -- 18	(0.6 -- 1.8, 4.3 -- 13.0)
T5:	18 — 27	(1.8 — 2.8, 13 — 20)
T6:	2.9 — 5.3	(0.3 — 0.54, 2.2 — 3.9)

FIG. 97 Exploded view of the front and rear seat assemblies — XT

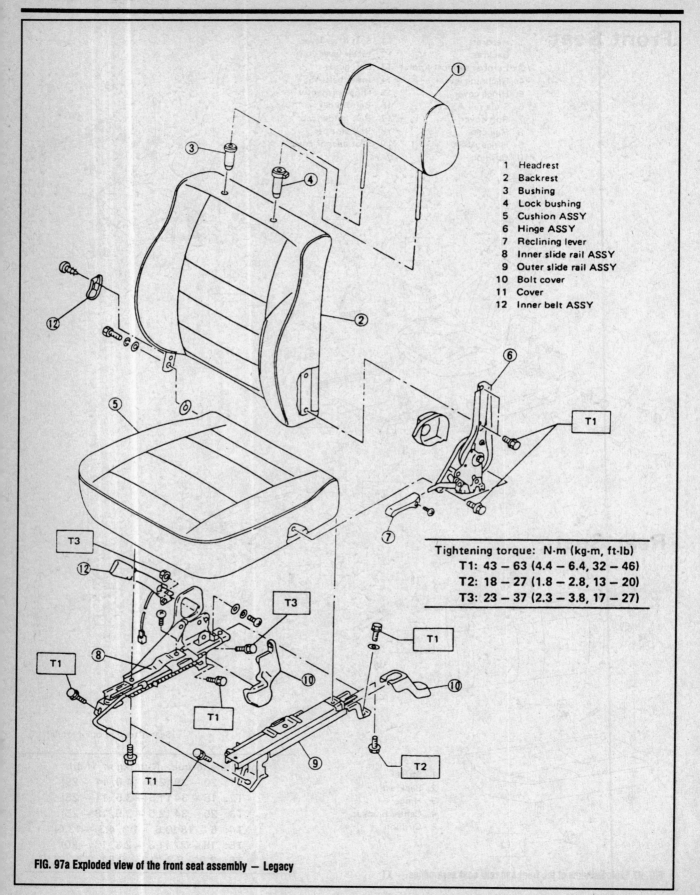

1   Headrest
2   Backrest
3   Bushing
4   Lock bushing
5   Cushion ASSY
6   Hinge ASSY
7   Reclining lever
8   Inner slide rail ASSY
9   Outer slide rail ASSY
10 Bolt cover
11 Cover
12 Inner belt ASSY

Tightening torque: N·m (kg-m, ft-lb)
T1: 43 — 63 (4.4 — 6.4, 32 — 46)
T2: 18 — 27 (1.8 — 2.8, 13 — 20)
T3: 23 — 37 (2.3 — 3.8, 17 — 27)

FIG. 97a Exploded view of the front seat assembly — Legacy

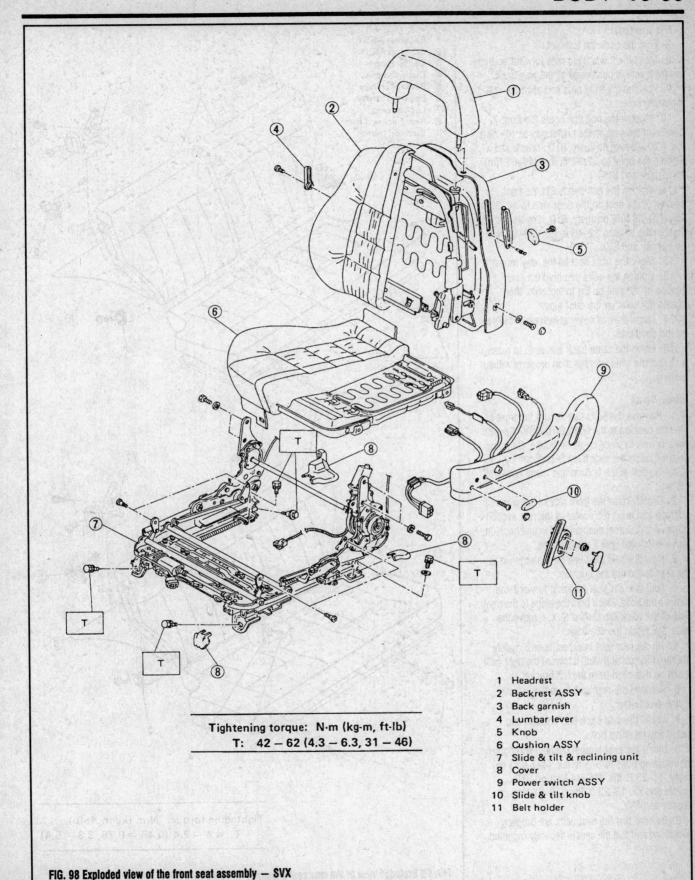

Tightening torque: N·m (kg-m, ft-lb)
T: 42 – 62 (4.3 – 6.3, 31 – 46)

1 Headrest
2 Backrest ASSY
3 Back garnish
4 Lumbar lever
5 Knob
6 Cushion ASSY
7 Slide & tilt & reclining unit
8 Cover
9 Power switch ASSY
10 Slide & tilt knob
11 Belt holder

FIG. 98 Exploded view of the front seat assembly — SVX

To Install:

7. Fold the backrest forward.

8. Move the lower slide rails forward so that the front seat is positioned all the way back.

9. Position the front seat and align the mounting holes.

10. Tighten the bolt that holds the front section of the seat on the tunnel side to 14–29 ft. lbs. ((20–39 Nm) on Justy, STD., Loyale and XT. Tighten the bolts to 32–46 ft. lbs. (43–63 Nm) on Legacy and SVX.

11. Tighten the bolt that holds the front section of the seat on the door side to 14–29 ft. lbs. ((20–39 Nm) on Justy, STD., Loyale and XT. Tighten the bolts to 32–46 ft. lbs. (43–63 Nm) on Legacy and SVX.

12. Move the front seat all the way forward.

13. Tighten the bolts that hold the rear section of the seat on the tunnel side, then tighten the bolts on the door side.

14. Install the bolt cover at the rear of the seat on the door side.

15. Move the seats back and forth to make sure that the slide rails function properly without binding.

Rear Seat

1. Remove the bolts that secure the front of the rear cushion to the floor. On the SVX the seat base is held in place by metal hooks. On some sedan models the seat back is fastened by an attaching bolt at the bottom and metal hooks at the top.

2. Slightly raise the front side of the rear seat cushion and push the center of the rear section down. With the seat cushion held in that position, move it forward until it is unhooked.

3. Pass the rear seat belt through the slit in the rear section of the cushion.

4. Fold the rear seat backrest forward and remove the bolts which hold the hinge to the right side of the backrest. On the SVX, remove the bolts that retain the seatback.

5. Tilt the rear seat backrest approximately 400mm forward and slide it toward the right until it can be detached from the left bracket.

6. Remove the rear seat from the vehicle.

To Install:

7. Install the seat back into position and install any retaining bolts.

8. Install the seat bottom cushion and tighten the retaining bolts to 3–5 ft. lbs. (4–7 Nm) on Justy, 11–25 ft. lbs. (15–34 Nm) on STD., Loyale and XT, 13–23 ft. lbs. (18–31 Nm) on Legacy and SVX.

9. Be sure that the seat belts are properly positioned and that the seat is securely mounted.

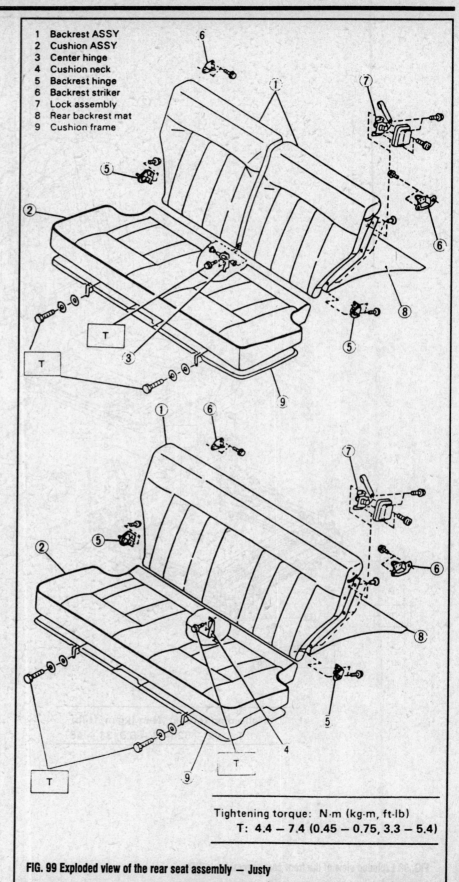

1 Backrest ASSY
2 Cushion ASSY
3 Center hinge
4 Cushion neck
5 Backrest hinge
6 Backrest striker
7 Lock assembly
8 Rear backrest mat
9 Cushion frame

Tightening torque: N·m (kg-m, ft-lb)
T: 4.4 – 7.4 (0.45 – 0.75, 3.3 – 5.4)

FIG. 99 Exploded view of the rear seat assembly — Justy

1 Backrest (Except fold-down type)
2 Inter lock ASSY (Key lock type)
3 Center striker (Key lock type)
4 Key cylinder (Key lock type)
5 Belt finisher
6 Cushion
7 Backrest
8 Lock cover RH
9 Lock cover LH
10 Main strap
11 Backrest RH
12 Backrest LH
13 Clip
14 Main outer hinge
15 Center bracket cover
16 Center lever cap
17 Center lever
18 Front center cover
19 Center lock
20 Center spring
21 Center panel
22 Rear center cover
23 Armrest hinge cover
24 Armrest
25 Armrest band

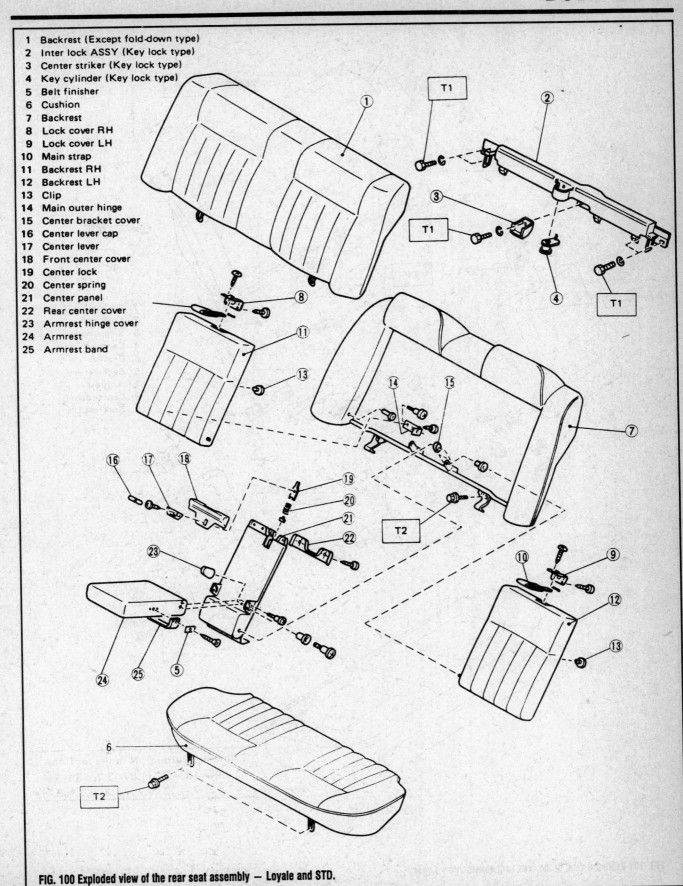

FIG. 100 Exploded view of the rear seat assembly — Loyale and STD.

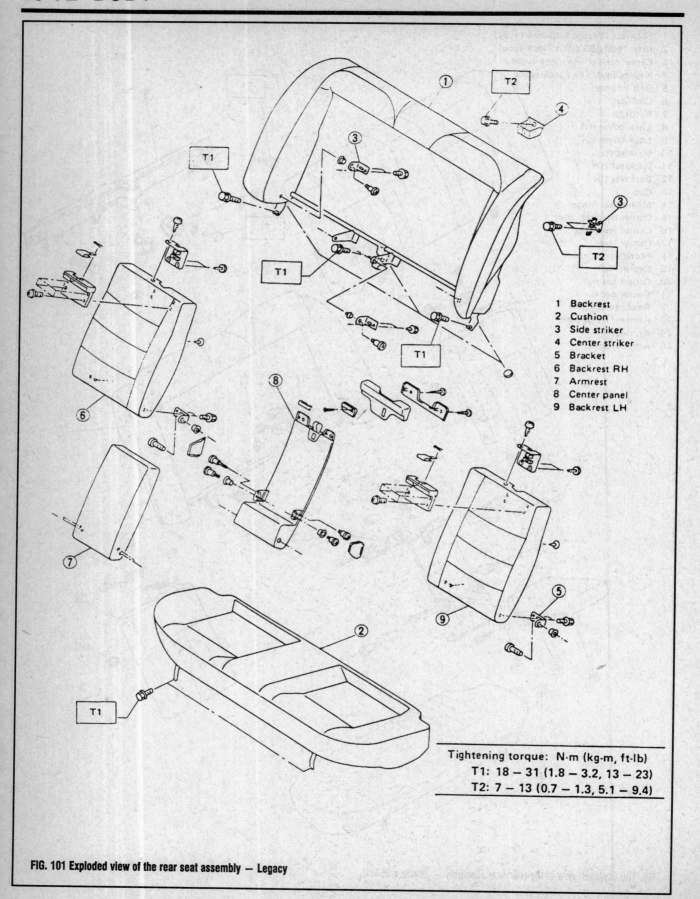

1 Backrest
2 Cushion
3 Side striker
4 Center striker
5 Bracket
6 Backrest RH
7 Armrest
8 Center panel
9 Backrest LH

Tightening torque: N·m (kg-m, ft-lb)
T1: 18 — 31 (1.8 — 3.2, 13 — 23)
T2: 7 — 13 (0.7 — 1.3, 5.1 — 9.4)

FIG. 101 Exploded view of the rear seat assembly — Legacy

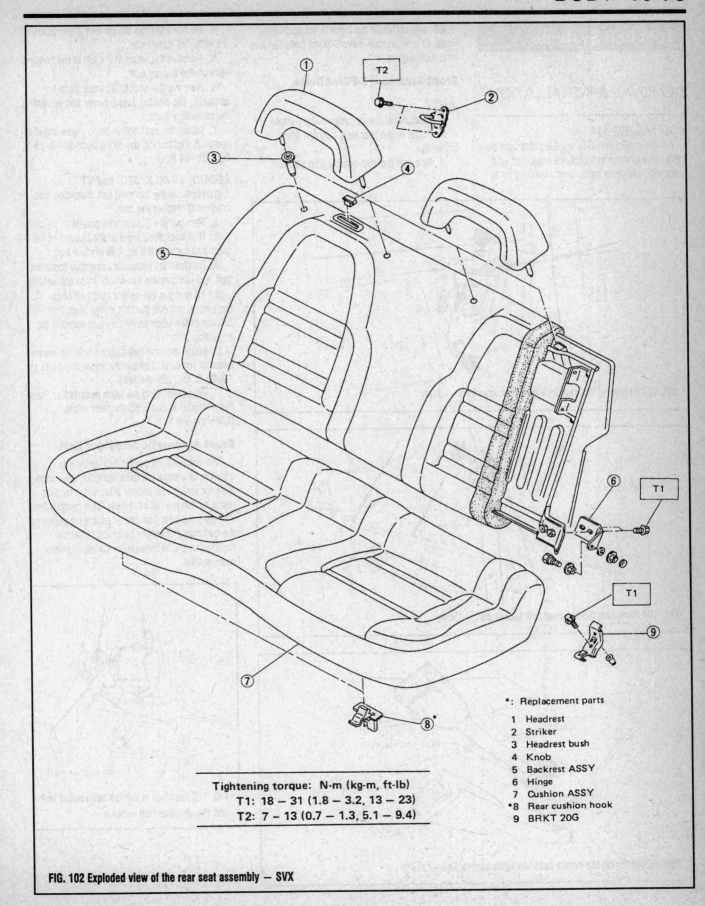

Tightening torque: N·m (kg-m, ft-lb)
T1: 18 — 31 (1.8 — 3.2, 13 — 23)
T2: 7 — 13 (0.7 — 1.3, 5.1 — 9.4)

*: Replacement parts

1 Headrest
2 Striker
3 Headrest bush
4 Knob
5 Backrest ASSY
6 Hinge
7 Cushion ASSY
*8 Rear cushion hook
9 BRKT 20G

FIG. 102 Exploded view of the rear seat assembly — SVX

Seat Belt Systems

REMOVAL & INSTALLATION

◆ SEE FIGS. 103–114

All late model vehicles have 3 point front seat belts, some of the vehicles are equipped with automatic shoulder belts. Some models up to 1989 have standard lap belts in the back seat, while all later models have 3 point belts for rear seat passengers.

Front Standard 3-Point Belts

JUSTY

1. Disconnect the negative battery cable.
2. Remove the rear seat cushion and backrest.
3. Remove the rear quarter trim panel.

4. Remove the top screw and lower bolt on the retractor assembly.
5. Remove the cover at the top of the belt and remove the anchor bolt.
6. Remove the seat belt center latch by removing the parking brake cover and removing the mounting bolts.
7. Install the seat belt in the reverse order of removal. Tighten the mounting bolts to 18–25 ft. lbs. (25–34 Nm).

LEGACY, LOYALE, STD. and XT

1. Remove the top seat belt mounting bolt cover and remove the bolt.
2. Remove the B pillar trim panels (2 pieces).
3. Roll back the carpet at the bottom of the B pillar and remove the lap belt anchor bolt.
4. Remove the retractor assembly mounting bolt and remove the assembly from the vehicle.
5. To remove the center seat belt latch assembly, remove the bolt cover from the bottom of the latch assembly and remove the mounting bolt.
6. Install the seat belt assembly in the reverse order of removal. Tighten the mounting bolts to 18–25 ft. lbs. (25–34 Nm).
7. When installing the latch assemblies, keep them angled at about 55 degrees while tightening the bolt.

Front Automatic Shoulder Belt

The automatic shoulder belt assembly consists of a track hat runs along the door frame, a motor and a belt anchor attached a moving metal tape in the rail assembly. This system uses a manual lap belt. The center mounting points for the automatic shoulder belts are retractor mechanisms that lock under sudden vehicle deceleration.

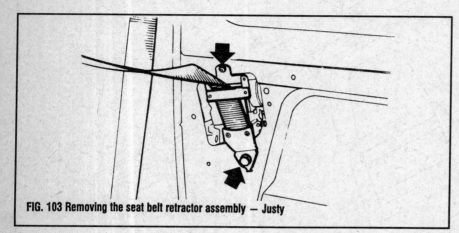

FIG. 103 Removing the seat belt retractor assembly — Justy

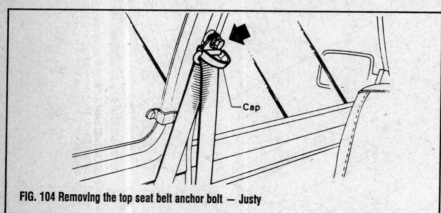

FIG. 104 Removing the top seat belt anchor bolt — Justy

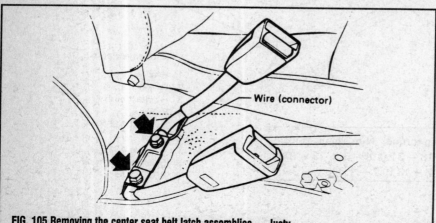

FIG. 105 Removing the center seat belt latch assemblies — Justy

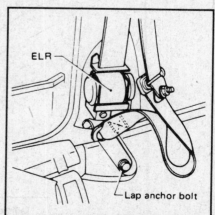

FIG. 106 Location of the lap belt anchor bolt and the shoulder belt retractor

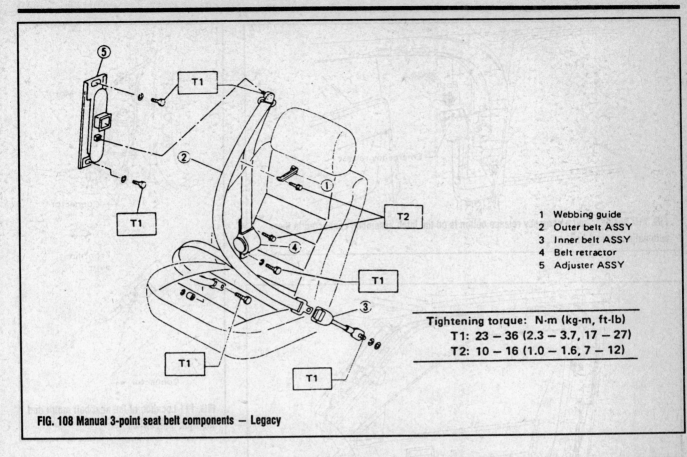

1	Webbing guide
2	Outer belt ASSY
3	Inner belt ASSY
4	Belt retractor
5	Adjuster ASSY

Tightening torque: N·m (kg-m, ft-lb)
T1: 23 — 36 (2.3 — 3.7, 17 — 27)
T2: 10 — 16 (1.0 — 1.6, 7 — 12)

FIG. 108 Manual 3-point seat belt components — Legacy

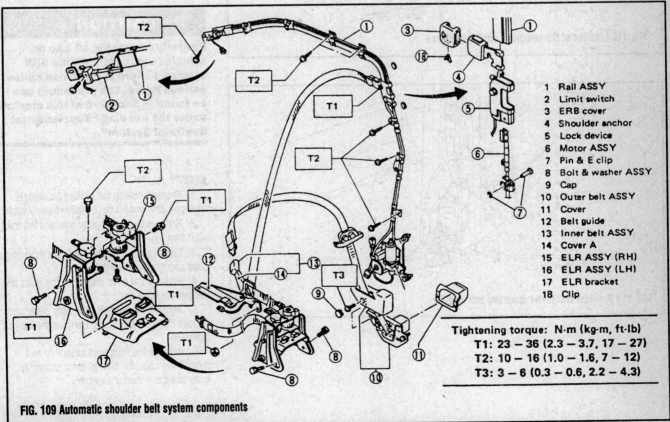

1	Rail ASSY
2	Limit switch
3	ERB cover
4	Shoulder anchor
5	Lock device
6	Motor ASSY
7	Pin & E clip
8	Bolt & washer ASSY
9	Cap
10	Outer belt ASSY
11	Cover
12	Belt guide
13	Inner belt ASSY
14	Cover A
15	ELR ASSY (RH)
16	ELR ASSY (LH)
17	ELR bracket
18	Clip

Tightening torque: N·m (kg-m, ft-lb)
T1: 23 — 36 (2.3 — 3.7, 17 — 27)
T2: 10 — 16 (1.0 — 1.6, 7 — 12)
T3: 3 — 6 (0.3 — 0.6, 2.2 — 4.3)

FIG. 109 Automatic shoulder belt system components

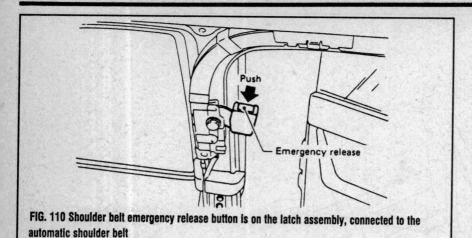

FIG. 110 Shoulder belt emergency release button is on the latch assembly, connected to the automatic shoulder belt

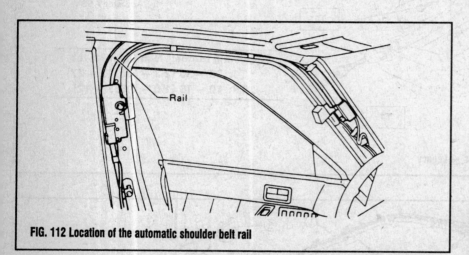

FIG. 112 Location of the automatic shoulder belt rail

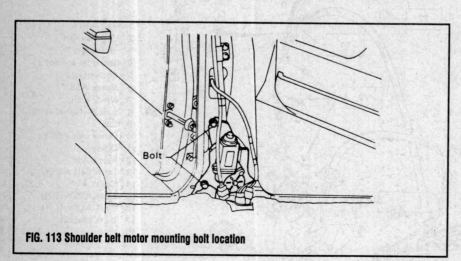

FIG. 113 Shoulder belt motor mounting bolt location

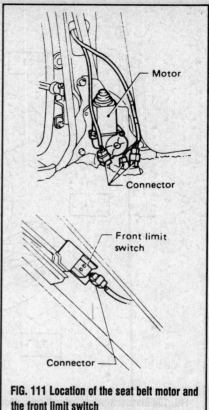

FIG. 111 Location of the seat belt motor and the front limit switch

❄ CAUTION

Properly disarm the air bag on vehicles equipped with the SRS system. Failure to do so can cause serious injury. The procedure can be found in Section 6 of this manual under the heading "Supplemental Restraint System".

EXCEPT JUSTY

1. Properly disarm the air bag on models equipped. Disconnect the negative battery cable.

2. Remove the center pillar trim and the front pillar trim.

3. Remove the shoulder belt track mounting bolts and remove the track.

4. Remove the drive unit mounting bolts and remove the drive unit.

5. Remove the lap belt assembly cover and remove the mounting bolts. Remove the lap belt assembly.

6. Remove the front seat assembly and remove the shoulder belt retractor assembly bolts and the retractor assembly.

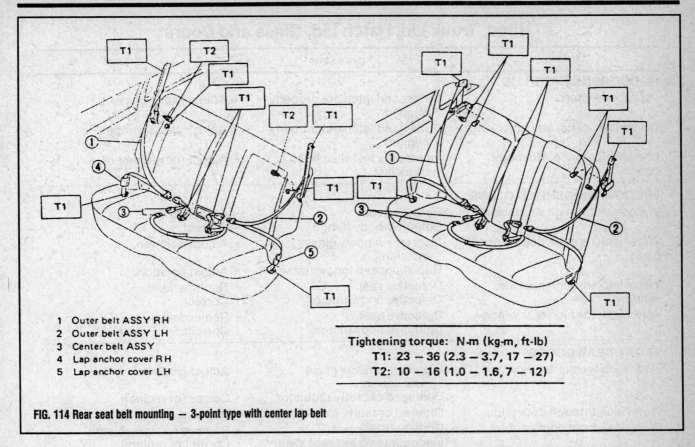

1 Outer belt ASSY RH
2 Outer belt ASSY LH
3 Center belt ASSY
4 Lap anchor cover RH
5 Lap anchor cover LH

Tightening torque: N·m (kg-m, ft-lb)
   T1: 23 — 36 (2.3 — 3.7, 17 — 27)
   T2: 10 — 16 (1.0 — 1.6, 7 — 12)

FIG. 114 Rear seat belt mounting — 3-point type with center lap belt

To Install:

7. Install the components in reverse order. Tighten the shoulder belt track bolts to 7–12 ft. lbs. (10–16 Nm). Tighten the drive unit bolts to 7–12 ft. lbs. (10–16 Nm).

8. Install the lap belt assembly and tighten the bolts to 17–36 ft. lbs. (23–49 Nm). Install the retractor assembly and tighten the mounting bolts to 17–36 ft. lbs. (23–49 Nm).

9. Install the seat and the interior trim panels. Connect the negative battery cable. Check the operation of the shoulder belt assembly.

Rear Seat Belts

LAP BELT

The rear lap belt is removed by simply removing the mounting bolts and pulling the belts out. Torque the belt mounting bolts to 17–27 ft. lbs. (23–36 Nm).

3-POINT BELT

The rear 3-point belt are removed in the same manner as the standard front belts, except for the removal of the rear quarter trim panel or C pillar panel.

Hood, Trunk Lid, Hatch Lid, Glass and Doors

Problem	Possible Cause	Correction
HOOD/TRUNK/HATCH LID		
Improper closure.	• Striker and latch not properly aligned.	• Adjust the alignment.
Difficulty locking and unlocking.	• Striker and latch not properly aligned.	• Adjust the alignment.
Uneven clearance with body panels.	• Incorrectly installed hood or trunk lid.	• Adjust the alignment.
WINDOW/WINDSHIELD GLASS		
Water leak through windshield	• Defective seal.	• Fill sealant
	• Defective body flange.	• Correct.
Water leak through door window glass.	• Incorrect window glass installation.	• Adjust position.
	• Gap at upper window frame.	• Adjust position.
Water leak through quarter window.	• Defective seal.	• Replace seal.
	• Defective body flange.	• Correct.
Water leak through rear window.	• Defective seal.	• Replace seal.
	• Defective body flange.	• Correct.
FRONT/REAR DOORS		
Door window malfunction.	• Incorrect window glass installation.	• Adjust position.
	• Damaged or faulty regulator.	• Correct or replace.
Water leak through door edge.	• Cracked or faulty weatherstrip.	• Replace.
Water leak from door center.	• Drain hole clogged.	• Remove foreign objects.
	• Inadequate waterproof skeet contact or damage.	• Correct or replace.
Door hard to open.	• Incorrect latch or striker adjustment.	• Adjust.
Door does not open or close completely.	• Incorrect door installation.	• Adjust position.
	• Defective door check strap.	• Correct or replace.
	• Door check strap and hinge require grease.	• Apply grease.
Uneven gap between door and body.	• Incorrect door installation.	• Adjust position.
Wind noise around door.	• Improperly installed weatherstrip.	• Repair or replace.
	• Improper clearance between door glass and door weatherstrip.	• Adjust.
	• Deformed door.	• Repair or replace.

How to Remove Stains from Fabric Interior

For best results, spots and stains should be removed as soon as possible. Never use gasoline, lacquer thinner, acetone, nail polish remover or bleach. Use a 3′ x 3″ piece of cheesecloth. Squeeze most of the liquid from the fabric and wipe the stained fabric from the outside of the stain toward the center with a lifting motion. Turn the cheesecloth as soon as one side becomes soiled. When using water to remove a stain, be sure to wash the entire section after the spot has been removed to avoid water stains. Encrusted spots can be broken up with a dull knife and vacuumed before removing the stain.

Type of Stain	How to Remove It
Surface spots	Brush the spots out with a small hand brush or use a commercial preparation such as K2R to lift the stain.
Mildew	Clean around the mildew with warm suds. Rinse in cold water and soak the mildew area in a solution of 1 part table salt and 2 parts water. Wash with upholstery cleaner.
Water stains	Water stains in fabric materials can be removed with a solution made from 1 cup of table salt dissolved in 1 quart of water. Vigorously scrub the solution into the stain and rinse with clear water. Water stains in nylon or other synthetic fabrics should be removed with a commercial type spot remover.
Chewing gum, tar, crayons, shoe polish (greasy stains)	Do not use a cleaner that will soften gum or tar. Harden the deposit with an ice cube and scrape away as much as possible with a dull knife. Moisten the remainder with cleaning fluid and scrub clean.
Ice cream, candy	Most candy has a sugar base and can be removed with a cloth wrung out in warm water. Oily candy, after cleaning with warm water, should be cleaned with upholstery cleaner. Rinse with warm water and clean the remainder with cleaning fluid.
Wine, alcohol, egg, milk, soft drink (non-greasy stains)	Do not use soap. Scrub the stain with a cloth wrung out in warm water. Remove the remainder with cleaning fluid.
Grease, oil, lipstick, butter and related stains	Use a spot remover to avoid leaving a ring. Work from the outisde of the stain to the center and dry with a clean cloth when the spot is gone.
Headliners (cloth)	Mix a solution of warm water and foam upholstery cleaner to give thick suds. Use only foam—liquid may streak or spot. Clean the entire headliner in one operation using a circular motion with a natural sponge.
Headliner (vinyl)	Use a vinyl cleaner with a sponge and wipe clean with a dry cloth.
Seats and door panels	Mix 1 pint upholstery cleaner in 1 gallon of water. Do not soak the fabric around the buttons.
Leather or vinyl fabric	Use a multi-purpose cleaner full strength and a stiff brush. Let stand 2 minutes and scrub thoroughly. Wipe with a clean, soft rag.
Nylon or synthetic fabrics	For normal stains, use the same procedures you would for washing cloth upholstery. If the fabric is extremely dirty, use a multi-purpose cleaner full strength with a stiff scrub brush. Scrub thoroughly in all directions and wipe with a cotton towel or soft rag.

TORQUE SPECIFICATIONS

Component	U.S.	Metric
Bumper mounting bolts:		
Justy-front bumper support-to-body	51-87 ft. lbs.	69-118 Nm
Justy-rear bumper support-to-body	51-87 ft. lbs.	69-118 Nm
Loyale and STD.-front bumper bolts	16 ft. lbs.	22 Nm
Loyale and STD.-rear bumper (except wagon)	22-31 ft. lbs.	29-42 Nm
Loyale and STD. Wagon-rear bumper	52-73 ft. lbs.	66-100 Nm
Legacy and SVX-front bumper	51-87 ft. lbs.	69-118 Nm
Legacy and SVX-rear bumper	51-87 ft. lbs.	69-118 Nm
Door Hinge bolts:		
Justy	14-19 ft. lbs.	20-25 Nm
Loyale, STD and XT	18-25 ft. lbs.	25-34 Nm
Legacy and SVX	14-22 ft. lbs.	20-29 Nm
Door side mounting bolts		
Justy, STD., Loyal and XT	14-29 ft. lbs.	20-39 Nm
Legacy and SVX	32-46 ft. lbs.	43-63 Nm
Front seat mounting bolts:		
Tunnel side mounting bolts		
Justy, STD., Loyal and XT	14-29 ft. lbs.	20-39 Nm
Legacy and SVX	32-46 ft. lbs.	43-63 Nm
Hood hinge bolts	9-17 ft. lbs.	13-23 Nm
Hood latch retaining bolts	7 ft. lbs.	10 Nm
Rear seat retaining bolts:		
Justy	3-5 ft. lbs.	4-7 Nm
Loyale, STD. and XT	11-25 ft. lbs.	15-34 Nm
Legacy and SVX	11-25 ft. lbs.	15-34 Nm
Seat belt assembly mounting bolts:		
Standard 3-point belt		
Justy	18-25 ft. lbs.	25-34 Nm
Legacy, Loyale, STD. and XT	18-25 ft. lbs.	25-34 Nm
Power shoulder belt system		
Shoulder belt track bolts	7-12 ft. lbs.	10-16 Nm
Drive unit bolts	7-12 ft. lbs.	10-16 Nm
Lap belt assembly	17-36 ft. lbs.	23-49 Nm
Retractor assembly	17-36 ft. lbs.	23-49 Nm
Tailgate mounting bolts:		
Hinge-to-tailgate bolts	14-22 ft. lbs.	20-29 Nm
Hinge-to-body bolts	14-22 ft. lbs.	20-29 Nm
Gas strut-to-tailgate	4-6 ft. lbs.	5-9 Nm
Trunk lid bolts	9-17 ft. lbs.	13-23 Nm
Window track assembly:		
Base plate	4-7 ft. lbs.	5-9 Nm
Rail mounting nut	7-13 ft. lbs.	10-18 Nm

GLOSSARY

AIR/FUEL RATIO: The ratio of air to gasoline by weight in the fuel mixture drawn into the engine.

AIR INJECTION: One method of reducing harmful exhaust emissions by injecting air into each of the exhaust ports of an engine. The fresh air entering the hot exhaust manifold causes any remaining fuel to be burned before it can exit the tailpipe.

ALTERNATOR: A device used for converting mechanical energy into electrical energy.

AMMETER: An instrument, calibrated in amperes, used to measure the flow of an electrical current in a circuit. Ammeters are always connected in series with the circuit being tested.

AMPERE: The rate of flow of electrical current present when one volt of electrical pressure is applied against one ohm of electrical resistance.

ANALOG COMPUTER: Any microprocessor that uses similar (analogous) electrical signals to make its calculations.

ARMATURE: A laminated, soft iron core wrapped by a wire that converts electrical energy to mechanical energy as in a motor or relay. When rotated in a magnetic field, it changes mechanical energy into electrical energy as in a generator.

ATMOSPHERIC PRESSURE: The pressure on the Earth's surface caused by the weight of the air in the atmosphere. At sea level, this pressure is 14.7 psi at 32°F (101 kPa at 0°C).

ATOMIZATION: The breaking down of a liquid into a fine mist that can be suspended in air.

AXIAL PLAY: Movement parallel to a shaft or bearing bore.

BACKFIRE: The sudden combustion of gases in the intake or exhaust system that results in a loud explosion.

BACKLASH: The clearance or play between two parts, such as meshed gears.

BACKPRESSURE: Restrictions in the exhaust system that slow the exit of exhaust gases from the combustion chamber.

BAKELITE: A heat resistant, plastic insulator material commonly used in printed circuit boards and transistorized components.

BALL BEARING: A bearing made up of hardened inner and outer races between which hardened steel balls roll.

BALLAST RESISTOR: A resistor in the primary ignition circuit that lowers voltage after the engine is started to reduce wear on ignition components.

BEARING: A friction reducing, supportive device usually located between a stationary part and a moving part.

BIMETAL TEMPERATURE SENSOR: Any sensor or switch made of two dissimilar types of metal that bend when heated or cooled due to the different expansion rates of the alloys. These types of sensors usually function as an on/off switch.

BLOWBY: Combustion gases, composed of water vapor and unburned fuel, that leak past the piston rings into the crankcase during normal engine operation. These gases are removed by the PCV system to prevent the buildup of harmful acids in the crankcase.

BRAKE PAD: A brake shoe and lining assembly used with disc brakes.

BRAKE SHOE: The backing for the brake lining. The term is, however, usually applied to the assembly of the brake backing and lining.

BUSHING: A liner, usually removable, for a bearing; an anti-friction liner used in place of a bearing.

BYPASS: System used to bypass ballast resistor during engine cranking to increase voltage supplied to the coil.

CALIPER: A hydraulically activated device in a disc brake system, which is mounted straddling the brake rotor (disc). The caliper contains at least one piston and two brake pads. Hydraulic pressure on the piston(s) forces the pads against the rotor.

CAMSHAFT: A shaft in the engine on which are the lobes (cams) which operate the valves. The camshaft is driven by the crankshaft, via a belt, chain or gears, at one half the crankshaft speed.

CAPACITOR: A device which stores an electrical charge.

CARBON MONOXIDE (CO): A colorless, odorless gas given off as a normal byproduct of combustion. It is poisonous and extremely dangerous in confined areas, building up slowly to toxic levels without warning if adequate ventilation is not available.

CARBURETOR: A device, usually mounted on the intake manifold of an engine, which mixes the air and fuel in the proper proportion to allow even combustion.

CATALYTIC CONVERTER: A device installed in the exhaust system, like a muffler, that converts harmful byproducts of combustion into carbon dioxide and water vapor by means of a heat-producing chemical reaction.

CENTRIFUGAL ADVANCE: A mechanical method of advancing the spark timing by using fly weights in the distributor that react to centrifugal force generated by the distributor shaft rotation.

CHECK VALVE: Any one-way valve installed to permit the flow of air, fuel or vacuum in one direction only.

CHOKE: A device, usually a movable valve, placed in the intake path of a carburetor to restrict the flow of air.

CIRCUIT: Any unbroken path through which an electrical current can flow. Also used to describe fuel flow in some instances.

CIRCUIT BREAKER: A switch which protects an electrical circuit from overload by opening the circuit when the current flow exceeds a predetermined level. Some circuit breakers must be reset manually, while most reset automatically

COIL (IGNITION): A transformer in the ignition circuit which steps up the voltage provided to the spark plugs.

COMBINATION MANIFOLD: An assembly which includes both the intake and exhaust manifolds in one casting.

COMBINATION VALVE: A device used in some fuel systems that routes fuel vapors to a charcoal storage canister instead of venting them into the atmosphere. The valve relieves fuel tank pressure and allows fresh air into the tank as the fuel level drops to prevent a vapor lock situation.

COMPRESSION RATIO: The comparison of the total volume of the cylinder and combustion chamber with the piston at BDC and the piston at TDC.

CONDENSER: 1. An electrical device which acts to store an electrical charge, preventing voltage surges.
2. A radiator-like device in the air conditioning system in which refrigerant gas condenses into a liquid, giving off heat.

CONDUCTOR: Any material through which an electrical current can be transmitted easily.

CONTINUITY: Continuous or complete circuit. Can be checked with an ohmmeter.

COUNTERSHAFT: An intermediate shaft which is rotated by a mainshaft and transmits, in turn, that rotation to a working part.

CRANKCASE: The lower part of an engine in which the crankshaft and related parts operate.

CRANKSHAFT: The main driving shaft of an engine which receives reciprocating motion from the pistons and converts it to rotary motion.

CYLINDER: In an engine, the round hole in the engine block in which the piston(s) ride.

CYLINDER BLOCK: The main structural member of an engine in which is found the cylinders, crankshaft and other principal parts.

CYLINDER HEAD: The detachable portion of the engine, fastened, usually, to the top of the cylinder block, containing all or most of the combustion chambers. On overhead valve engines, it contains the valves and their operating parts. On overhead cam engines, it contains the camshaft as well.

DEAD CENTER: The extreme top or bottom of the piston stroke.

DETONATION: An unwanted explosion of the air/fuel mixture in the combustion chamber caused by excess heat and compression, advanced timing, or an overly lean mixture. Also referred to as "ping".

DIAPHRAGM: A thin, flexible wall separating two cavities, such as in a vacuum advance unit.

DIESELING: A condition in which hot spots in the combustion chamber cause the engine to run on after the key is turned off.

DIFFERENTIAL: A geared assembly which allows the transmission of motion between drive axles, giving one axle the ability to turn faster than the other.

DIODE: An electrical device that will allow current to flow in one direction only.

DISC BRAKE: A hydraulic braking assembly consisting of a brake disc, or rotor, mounted on an axle, and a caliper assembly containing, usually two brake pads which are activated by hydraulic pressure. The pads are forced against the sides of the disc, creating friction which slows the vehicle.

DISTRIBUTOR: A mechanically driven device on an engine which is responsible for electrically firing the spark plug at a predetermined point of the piston stroke.

DOWEL PIN: A pin, inserted in mating holes in two different parts allowing those parts to maintain a fixed relationship.

DRUM BRAKE: A braking system which consists of two brake shoes and one or two wheel cylinders, mounted on a fixed backing plate, and a brake drum, mounted on an axle, which revolves around the assembly. Hydraulic action applied to the wheel cylinders forces the shoes outward against the drum, creating friction, slowing the vehicle.

DWELL: The rate, measured in degrees of shaft rotation, at which an electrical circuit cycles on and off.

ELECTRONIC CONTROL UNIT (ECU): Ignition module, amplifier or igniter. See Module for definition.

ELECTRONIC IGNITION: A system in which the timing and firing of the spark plugs is controlled by an electronic control unit, usually called a module. These systems have no points or condenser.

ENDPLAY: The measured amount of axial movement in a shaft.

ENGINE: A device that converts heat into mechanical energy.

EXHAUST MANIFOLD: A set of cast passages or pipes which conduct exhaust gases from the engine.

FEELER GAUGE: A blade, usually metal, of precisely predetermined thickness, used to measure the clearance between two parts. These blades usually are available in sets of assorted thicknesses.

F-HEAD: An engine configuration in which the intake valves are in the cylinder head, while the camshaft and exhaust valves are located in the cylinder block. The camshaft operates the intake valves via lifters and pushrods, while it operates the exhaust valves directly.

FIRING ORDER: The order in which combustion occurs in the cylinders of an engine. Also the order in which spark is distributed to the plugs by the distributor.

FLATHEAD: An engine configuration in which the camshaft and all the valves are located in the cylinder block.

FLOODING: The presence of too much fuel in the intake manifold and combustion chamber which prevents the air/fuel mixture from firing, thereby causing a no-start situation.

FLYWHEEL: A disc shaped part bolted to the rear end of the crankshaft. Around the outer perimeter is affixed the ring gear. The starter drive engages the ring gear, turning the flywheel, which rotates the crankshaft, imparting the initial starting motion to the engine.

FOOT POUND (ft.lb. or sometimes, ft. lbs.): The amount of energy or work needed to raise an item weighing one pound, a distance of one foot.

FUSE: A protective device in a circuit which prevents circuit overload by breaking the circuit when a specific amperage is present. The device is constructed around a strip or wire of a lower amperage rating than the circuit it is designed to protect. When an amperage higher than that stamped on the fuse is present in the circuit, the strip or wire melts, opening the circuit.

GEAR RATIO: The ratio between the number of teeth on meshing gears.

GENERATOR: A device which converts mechanical energy into electrical energy.

HEAT RANGE: The measure of a spark plug's ability to dissipate heat from its firing end. The higher the heat range, the hotter the plug fires.
HUB: The center part of a wheel or gear.

HYDROCARBON (HC): Any chemical compound made up of hydrogen and carbon. A major pollutant formed by the engine as a byproduct of combustion.

HYDROMETER: An instrument used to measure the specific gravity of a solution.

INCH POUND (In.lb. or sometimes, in. lbs.): One twelfth of a foot pound.

INDUCTION: A means of transferring electrical energy in the form of a magnetic field. Principle used in the ignition coil to increase voltage.

INJECTION PUMP: A device, usually mechanically operated, which meters and delivers fuel under pressure to the fuel injector.

INJECTOR: A device which receives metered fuel under relatively low pressure and is activated to inject the fuel into the engine under relatively high pressure at a predetermined time.

INPUT SHAFT: The shaft to which torque is applied, usually carrying the driving gear or gears.

INTAKE MANIFOLD: A casting of passages or pipes used to conduct air or a fuel/air mixture to the cylinders.

JOURNAL: The bearing surface within which a shaft operates.

KEY: A small block usually fitted in a notch between a shaft and a hub to prevent slippage of the two parts.

MANIFOLD: A casting of passages or set of pipes which connect the cylinders to an inlet or outlet source.

MANIFOLD VACUUM: Low pressure in an engine intake manifold formed just below the throttle plates. Manifold vacuum is highest at idle and drops under acceleration.

MASTER CYLINDER: The primary fluid pressurizing device in a hydraulic system. In automotive use, it is found in brake and hydraulic clutch systems and is pedal activated, either directly or, in a power brake system, through the power booster.

MODULE: Electronic control unit, amplifier or igniter of solid state or integrated design which controls the current flow in the ignition primary circuit based on input from the pick-up coil. When the module opens the primary circuit, the high secondary voltage is induced in the coil.

NEEDLE BEARING: A bearing which consists of a number (usually a large number) of long, thin rollers.

OHM:(Ω) The unit used to measure the resistance of conductor to electrical flow. One ohm is the amount of resistance that limits current flow to one ampere in a circuit with one volt of pressure.

OHMMETER: An instrument used for measuring the resistance, in ohms, in an electrical circuit.

OUTPUT SHAFT: The shaft which transmits torque from a device, such as a transmission.

OVERDRIVE: A gear assembly which produces more shaft revolutions than that transmitted to it.

OVERHEAD CAMSHAFT (OHC): An engine configuration in which the camshaft is mounted on top of the cylinder head and operates the valves either directly or by means of rocker arms.

OVERHEAD VALVE (OHV): An engine configuration in which all of the valves are located in the cylinder head and the camshaft is located in the cylinder block. The camshaft operates the valves via lifters and pushrods.

OXIDES OF NITROGEN (NOx): Chemical compounds of nitrogen produced as a byproduct of combustion. They combine with hydrocarbons to produce smog.

OXYGEN SENSOR: Used with the feedback system to sense the presence of oxygen in the exhaust gas and signal the computer which can reference the voltage signal to an air/fuel ratio.

PINION: The smaller of two meshing gears.

PISTON RING: An open ended ring which fits into a groove on the outer diameter of the piston. Its chief function is to form a seal between the piston and cylinder wall. Most automotive pistons have three rings: two for compression sealing; one for oil sealing.

PRELOAD: A predetermined load placed on a bearing during assembly or by adjustment.

PRIMARY CIRCUIT: Is the low voltage side of the ignition system which consists of the ignition switch, ballast resistor or resistance wire, bypass, coil, electronic control unit and pick-up coil as well as the connecting wires and harnesses.

PRESS FIT: The mating of two parts under pressure, due to the inner diameter of one being smaller than the outer diameter of the other, or vice versa; an interference fit.

RACE: The surface on the inner or outer ring of a bearing on which the balls, needles or rollers move.

REGULATOR: A device which maintains the amperage and/or voltage levels of a circuit at predetermined values.

RELAY: A switch which automatically opens and/or closes a circuit.

RESISTANCE: The opposition to the flow of current through a circuit or electrical device, and is measured in ohms. Resistance is equal to the voltage divided by the amperage.

RESISTOR: A device, usually made of wire, which offers a preset amount of resistance in an electrical circuit.

RING GEAR: The name given to a ring-shaped gear attached to a differential case,or affixed to a flywheel or as part a planetary gear set.

ROLLER BEARING: A bearing made up of hardened inner and outer races between which hardened steel rollers move.

ROTOR: 1. The disc-shaped part of a disc brake assembly, upon which the brake pads bear; also called, brake disc.
2. The device mounted atop the distributor shaft, which passes current to the distributor cap tower contacts.

SECONDARY CIRCUIT: The high voltage side of the ignition system, usually above 20,000 volts. The secondary includes the ignition coil, coil wire, distributor cap and rotor, spark plug wires and spark plugs.

SENDING UNIT: A mechanical, electrical, hydraulic or electromagnetic device which transmits information to a gauge.

SENSOR: Any device designed to measure engine operating conditions or ambient pressures and temperatures. Usually electronic in nature and designed to send a voltage signal to an on-board computer, some sensors may operate as a simple on/off switch or they may provide a variable voltage signal (like a potentiometer) as conditions or measured parameters change.

SHIM: Spacers of precise, predetermined thickness used between parts to establish a proper working relationship.

SLAVE CYLINDER: In automotive use, a device in the hydraulic clutch system which is activated by hydraulic force, disengaging the clutch.

SOLENOID: A coil used to produce a magnetic field, the effect of which is to produce work.

SPARK PLUG: A device screwed into the combustion chamber of a spark ignition engine. The basic construction is a conductive core inside of a ceramic insulator, mounted in an outer conductive base. An electrical charge from the spark plug wire travels along the conductive core and jumps a preset air gap to a grounding point or points at the end of the conductive base. The resultant spark ignites the fuel/air mixture in the combustion chamber.

SPLINES: Ridges machined or cast onto the outer diameter of a shaft or inner diameter of a bore to enable parts to mate without rotation.

TACHOMETER: A device used to measure the rotary speed of an engine, shaft, gear, etc., usually in rotations per minute.

THERMOSTAT: A valve, located in the cooling system of an engine, which is closed when cold and opens gradually in response to engine heating, controlling the temperature of the coolant and rate of coolant flow.

TOP DEAD CENTER (TDC): The point at which the piston reaches the top of its travel on the compression stroke.

TORQUE: The twisting force applied to an object.

TORQUE CONVERTER: A turbine used to transmit power from a driving member to a driven member via hydraulic action, providing changes in drive ratio and torque. In automotive use, it links the driveplate at the rear of the engine to the automatic transmission.

TRANSDUCER: A device used to change a force into an electrical signal.

TRANSISTOR: A semi-conductor component which can be actuated by a small voltage to perform an electrical switching function.

TUNE-UP: A regular maintenance function, usually associated with the replacement and adjustment of parts and components in the electrical and fuel systems of a vehicle for the purpose of attaining optimum performance.

TURBOCHARGER: An exhaust driven pump which compresses intake air and forces it into the combustion chambers at higher than atmospheric pressures. The increased air pressure allows more fuel to be burned and results in increased horsepower being produced.

VACUUM ADVANCE: A device which advances the ignition timing in response to increased engine vacuum.

VACUUM GAUGE: An instrument used to measure the presence of vacuum in a chamber.

VALVE: A device which control the pressure, direction of flow or rate of flow of a liquid or gas.

VALVE CLEARANCE: The measured gap between the end of the valve stem and the rocker arm, cam lobe or follower that activates the valve.

VISCOSITY: The rating of a liquid's internal resistance to flow.

VOLTMETER: An instrument used for measuring electrical force in units called volts. Voltmeters are always connected parallel with the circuit being tested.

WHEEL CYLINDER: Found in the automotive drum brake assembly, it is a device, actuated by hydraulic pressure, which, through internal pistons, pushes the brake shoes outward against the drums.

MASTER

INDEX